Contents

A MAN WORKING IN A RICE FIELD, UBUD (P247), BALI

SPECIAL FEATURES

ON THE ROAD

TOONMAN/GETTY IMAGES ©

Indonesia

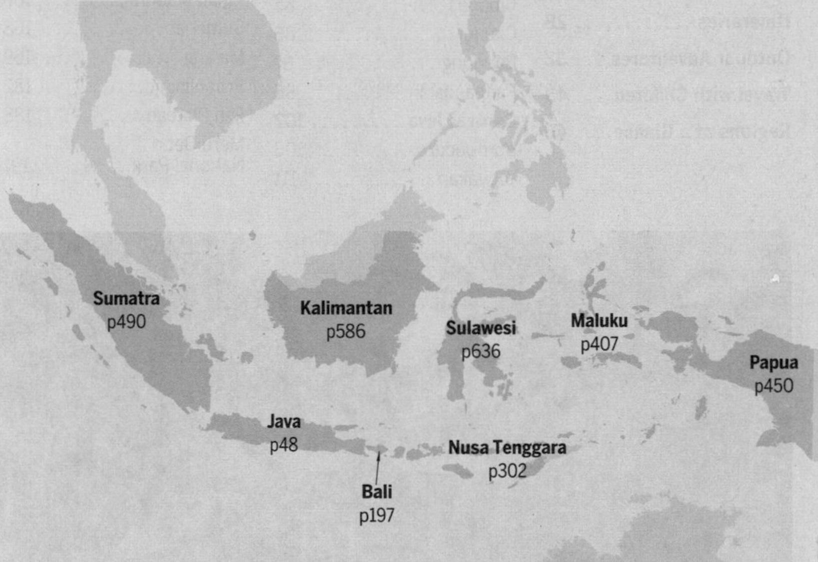

THIS EDITION WRITTEN AND RESEARCHED BY

Loren Bell, Stuart Butler, Trent Holden, Anna Kaminski, Hugh McNaughtan, Adam Skolnick, Iain Stewart, Ryan Ver Berkmoes

PLAN YOUR TRIP

ON THE ROAD

PETE SEAWARD/GETTY IMAGES ©

Contents

PURA ULUN DANU BRATAN (P287), BALI

Welcome to Indonesia

Indonesia's numbers astound: more than 17,000 islands, of which 8000 are inhabited, and across which over 300 languages are spoken. It's a beguiling country offering myriad adventures.

Rich Diversity

The world's fourth most populous country – 255 million and counting – is a sultry kaleidoscope that runs along the equator for 5000km. From the western tip of Sumatra to the eastern edge of Papua, this nation defies homogenisation. It is a land of so many cultures, peoples, animals, customs, plants, sights, artworks and foods that it is like 100 countries melded into one.

The people are as radically different from each other as if they came from different continents, with every island a unique blend of the men, women and children who live upon it. Over time deep and rich cultures have evolved, from the mysteries of the spiritual Balinese to the utterly non-Western belief system of the Asmat people of Papua.

Beaches & Volcanoes

Venturing across Indonesia you'll see a dramatic landscape, as diverse as those living upon it. Sulawesi's wildly multi-limbed coastline embraces white-sand beaches and diving haunts, while Sumatra is contoured by a legion of nearly 100 volcanoes marching off into the distance, several capable of erupting at any time.

Amazing Spectacle

Dramatic sights are the norm. There's the sublime: an orangutan lounging in a tree. The artful: a Balinese dancer executing precise moves that would make a robot seem loose-limbed. The idyllic: a deserted stretch of blinding white sand on Sumbawa set off by azure surf breaks. The astonishing: the mobs in a cool, glitzy Jakarta mall on a Sunday. The intriguing: the too-amazing-for-fiction tales of the twisted history of the beautiful Banda Islands. The heart-stopping: the ominous menace of a Komodo dragon. The humbling: a woman bent double with a load of firewood on Sumatra. The delicious: a south Bali restaurant. The shocking: the funeral ceremonies of Tana Toraja. The solemn: the serene magnificence of Borobudur.

Great Adventure

This ever-intriguing, ever-intoxicating land offers some of the last great adventures on earth. Sitting in the open door of a train whizzing across Java, idling away time on a ferry bound for Kalimantan, hanging on to the back of a scooter on Flores, rounding the mystifying corner of an ancient West Timor village or simply trekking through wilderness you're sure no one has seen before – you'll enjoy endless exploration of the infinite diversity of Indonesia's 17,000-odd islands.

Why I Love Indonesia

By Ryan Ver Berkmoes, Writer

I was driving across beautiful Flores and rounding a corner somewhere east of the steamy port town of Ende, when the most brilliant view of a volcano filled my windscreen. Conical, with obvious recent lava flows down the side and a little ominous wisp of steam rising from the top. And I thought: 'That's the third one today!' And so it goes in Indonesia – where the natural beauty is as diverse as the people who live among it. You can have world-class fun on Bali and the next day be way off the grid in the incredible Bandas.

For more about our writers, see page 820

Above: Gunung Bromo (p183), Java

Indonesia

ANDAMAN SEA
THAILAND
LAOS
MYANMAR (BURMA)
BANGKOK
CAMBODIA
PHNOM PENH
VIETNAM
HO CHI MINH CITY (Saigon)
SOUTH CHINA SEA
Gulf of Thailand
110°E
115°E
95°E
Gunung Leuser National Park
Steamy, wildlife-rich jungle (p534)
Kerinci Valley
Lush lakes, waterfalls and rice paddies (p560)
Kapuas Hulu
Plunge deep into the heart of Borneo (p596)
Tanjung Puting
Get close to some orangutans (p600)
Banda Aceh
PENINSULAR MALAYSIA
Bukit Lawang
Medan
Selat Malaka
Kota Kinabalu
BRUNEI
BANDAR SERI BEGAWAN
SARAWAK
Pulau Simeulue
Danau Toba
KUALA LUMPUR
Pulau Nias
Equator
SINGAPORE
Kuching
EAST MALAYSIA
Pekanbaru
Kerinci Valley
Riau Islands
Pontianak
Sintang
KALIMANTAN
Padang
SUMATRA
Pulau Siberut
Pulau Bangka
Jambi
Samarinda
Balikpapan
Pangkal Pinang
Mentawai Islands
Palangkaraya
Pangkalanbun
Palembang
Loksado
Tanjung Puting National Park
Bengkulu
Pulau Belitung
Banjarmasin
Selat Makassar
Bandarlampung
JAVA SEA
Pulau Enggano
Serang
JAKARTA
Bandung
JAVA
Bogor
Semarang
Pulau Madura
Borobudur
Solo
Surabaya
Cilacap
Yogyakarta
Malang
BALI
Kerobokan
Ubud
Denpasar
Mataram
Pulau Sumbawa
Jakarta
The capital parties 24/7 (p52)
Borobudur
One of the wonders of the world (p106)
Christmas Is (Australia)
Ubud
Bali's cultural heart (p247)
Gili Islands
Three fun-filled idylls (p324)
INDIAN OCEAN

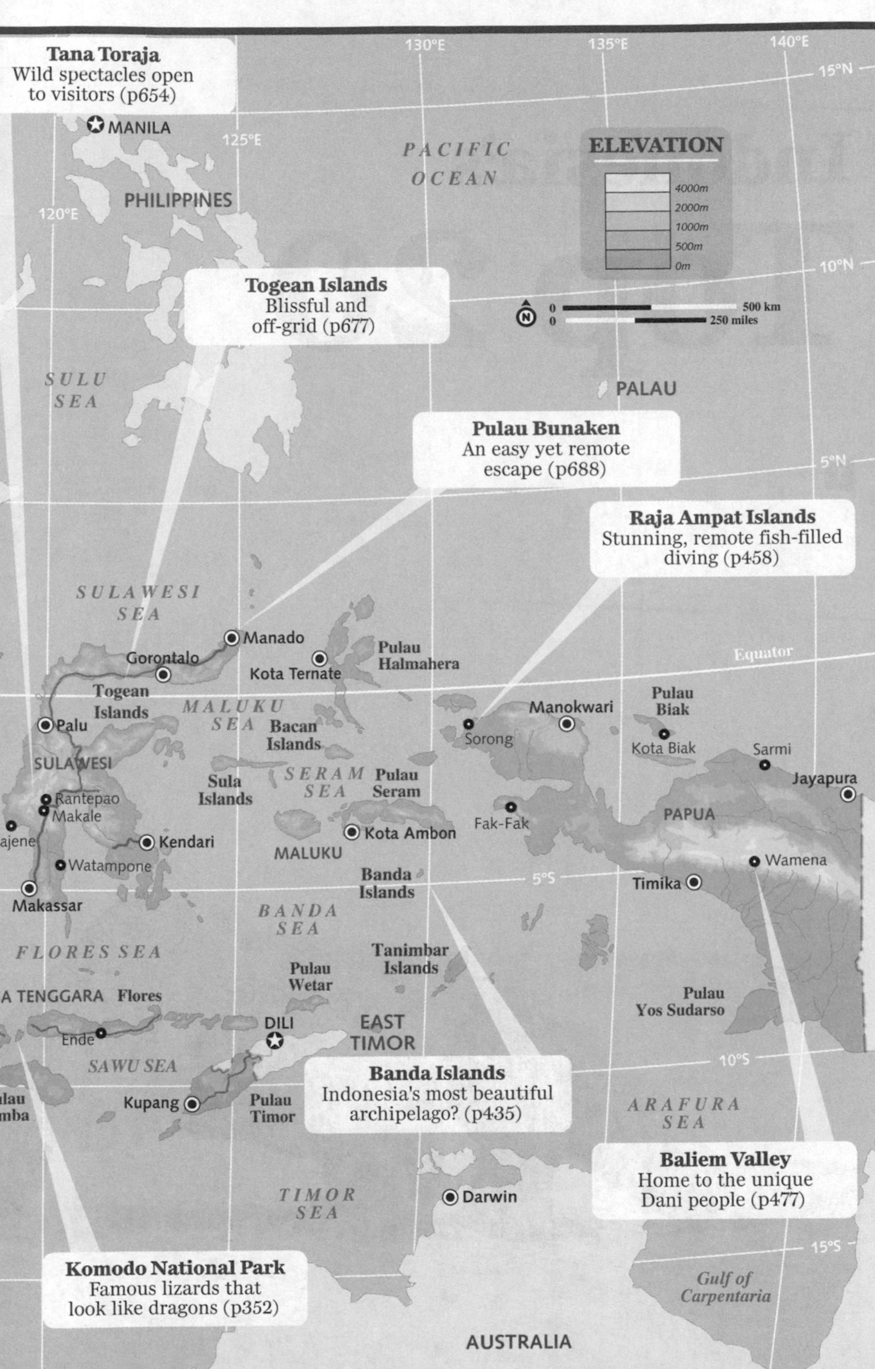

Tana Toraja
Wild spectacles open to visitors (p654)
Togean Islands
Blissful and off-grid (p677)
Pulau Bunaken
An easy yet remote escape (p688)
Raja Ampat Islands
Stunning, remote fish-filled diving (p458)
Banda Islands
Indonesia's most beautiful archipelago? (p435)
Baliem Valley
Home to the unique Dani people (p477)
Komodo National Park
Famous lizards that look like dragons (p352)
ELEVATION
4000m
2000m
1000m
500m
0m
500 km
250 miles
MANILA
PHILIPPINES
PACIFIC OCEAN
SULU SEA
PALAU
SULAWESI SEA
Manado
Gorontalo
Kota Ternate
Pulau Halmahera
Togean Islands
MALUKU SEA
Palu
Bacan Islands
SULAWESI
Sula Islands
SERAM SEA
Pulau Seram
Rantepao
Makale
Majene
Kendari
Watampone
Makassar
Kota Ambon
MALUKU
Banda Islands
BANDA SEA
FLORES SEA
Pulau Wetar
Tanimbar Islands
Flores
Ende
DILI
EAST TIMOR
SAWU SEA
Kupang
Pulau Timor
TIMOR SEA
Darwin
Sorong
Manokwari
Pulau Biak
Kota Biak
Sarmi
Jayapura
Fak-Fak
PAPUA
Wamena
Timika
Pulau Yos Sudarso
ARAFURA SEA
Gulf of Carpentaria
AUSTRALIA
Equator

Indonesia's Top 20

1

Komodo National Park

1 Indonesia's best-known national park (p352) comprises several islands and some of the country's richest waters within its 1817 sq km. Expect hulking mountainous islands blanketed in savannah, laced with trails and patrolled by the world's largest lizard: the Komodo dragon. That's the big draw here, and it's easy to spot them, but there's also big nature beneath the water's surface where kaleidoscopic bait draws big pelagics like sharks and manta rays in great numbers. Nearby Labuanbajo, on the island of Flores, is the perfect traveller base. Komodo dragon (p353)

Balinese Dance

2 Enjoying a Balinese dance performance is a highlight of a visit to Indonesia's most famous holiday island. The haunting sounds, elaborate costumes, careful choreography and even lighthearted comic routines add up to great entertainment. Swept up in the spectacle, you'll soon understand why Balinese culture is among the world's most developed. The music that often accompanies traditional dance is based around an ensemble known as a gamelan. The melodic, sometimes upbeat and sometimes haunting percussion is a night-time staple of life in Ubud (p247), Bali's cultural centre.

BARRY KUSUMA/GETTY IMAGES ©

2

TROPICAL STUDIO/SHUTTERSTOCK ©

PHILIP LEE HARVEY/LONELY PLANET ©

Borobudur

3 The breathtaking Borobudur temple complex (p106) is a stunning and poignant epitaph to Java's Buddhist heyday in the 9th century AD and is a highlight of a visit to Indonesia. One of the most important Buddhist sites in the world and one of the finest temple complexes in Southeast Asia, the temple consists of six square bases topped by three circular ones. Nearly 1500 narrative relief panels on the terraces illustrate Buddhist teachings and tales, while 432 Buddha images sit in chambers on the terraces.

Stupas at the top of Borobudur

Jakarta Nightlife

4 If you have the stamina, Jakarta (p67) has the action, for this is Southeast Asia's best-kept party secret. Sure, Indonesia is a predominantly Muslim nation where traditions run deep, but in Jakarta, almost anything goes – the scene can get very underground in the north of town. The city has it all: superstylin' lounges frequented by the oh-so-beautiful crowd, low-key bars where the soundtrack is vintage 1970s funk, alt-rock music venues and electro clubs where DJs attain messiah-like status.

Tanjung Puting National Park

5 *African Queen* meets jungle safari in this ever-popular national park (p600) in southern Kalimantan, where you can not only get up close and personal with Asia's largest ape, the orangutan, but also cruise the jungle in high style aboard your own private houseboat. The typically three-day journey takes you on a round trip up the Sungai Sekonyer to Camp Leakey, with stops at several orangutan feeding stations and plenty of impromptu wildlife spotting. Despite its creature comforts, the experience still manages to be authentic adventure travel, and is open to anyone.

Mother and baby orangutans

Raja Ampat Islands

6 The remote, still-being-discovered Raja Ampat Islands (p458) off Papua's northwest tip are a diver's dream. Raja Ampat is home to the greatest diversity of marine life on the planet, from giant manta rays and epaulette sharks that use their fins to 'walk' on the sea floor to myriad multicoloured nudibranchs ('sea slugs'), fantastic pristine coral, and every size, shape and hue of fish you can imagine. The snorkelling is great too, and the above-water scenery is just as unique and sublime.

Banda Islands

7 Here is a rich and intoxicating cocktail of history, culture and raw natural beauty. The Banda Islands (p435) – a remote archipelago draped in jungle and spice trees, fringed with white sand, surrounded by clear blue seas and pristine reefs – kickstarted colonisation and helped shape the modern world. Fly to the capital – Bandaneira – from Ambon, stroll the wide avenues, admire late-colonial relics, then charter a boat to the outer islands, where village life is warm and easy, and stress peels from your soul by the second.

6

7

Karimunjawa

8 Set 90km off the north coast of Central Java is an archipelago as remote and wild as any in east Indonesia, yet still accessible by ferry and flights from Semarang and Surabaya. The Karimunjawa Islands are a group of 27 coral-fringed beauties, some are uninhabited and off limits to visitors, but most are accessible on day tours from the main island of Karimunjawa (p154), jungled and mountainous, fringed with white-sand beaches and swaying with coconut palms. Magic.

Kapuas Hulu

9 At the headwaters of the Sungai Kapuas (p596), Indonesia's longest river, awaits everything you need for a primal jungle adventure. Step into the past at Kalimantan's oldest longhouse perched high on its gnarled ironwood pillars. Snake through Danau Sentarum's photogenic mudflats on narrow fish-packed waterways that are seasonally submerged. Soak up the port town of Putussibau. Tackle roiling rapids and leech-infested forests on the epic Cross-Borneo Trek. Or, strike off into the darkest corner of the island in search of new rainforest species in Betung Kerihun National Park.

8

KIMBERLEY COOLE/GETTY IMAGES ©

9

Gili Islands

10 One of Indonesia's greatest joys is hopping on a fast boat from busy Bali and arriving on one of the irresistible Gili Islands (p324). Think sugar-white sand, bathtub-warm, turquoise waters and wonderful beach resorts and bungalows just begging you to extend your stay. Not to mention the coral reefs that are teeming with sharks, rays and turtles. Savour the dining and nightlife on Gili Trawangan, the perfect balance of Gili Air and the pint-sized charms of Gili Meno. Or simply do nothing at all.

Gili Trawangan (p326)

Ubud

11 Famous in books and movies, the artistic heart of Bali (p247) exudes a compelling spiritual appeal. The streets are lined with galleries where artists, both humble and great, create. Beautiful dance performances showcasing the island's rich culture grace a dozen stages nightly. Museums honour the works of those inspired here over the years, while people walk the rice fields to find the perfect spot to sit in lotus position and ponder life's endless possibilities. Ubud is a state of mind and a beautiful state of being.

Balinese women carrying ceremonial offerings

Baliem Valley

12 Trekking in Papua's Baliem Valley (p477) takes you into the world of the Dani, a mountain people whose traditional culture still stands proud despite changes wrought by Indonesian government and Christian missionaries. You'll sleep in their villages of grass-roofed huts, climb narrow jungle trails, traverse panoramic open hillsides, cross raging rivers by wobbly hanging footbridges, and be charmed by the locals' smiles. A tip for those bridges: don't look at the water, but do look where you're putting your feet!

Dani man, Obia (p482)

Pulau Bunaken

13 You know those gardens that seem to have hundreds of plant species artistically thriving together in small decorative plots? Now imagine that done with coral in every colour from stark black and white to intense purples. Next cover it all in clear water teeming with iridescent fish, some in thick schools. The water around Pulau Bunaken (p688) is more beautiful than you could imagine and yet it gets better: turtles the size of armchairs, reef sharks and, if you're lucky, dolphins and dugongs that swim casually through the scene.

Sea anemone on a coral reef

12

13

FABIO LAMANNA/GETTY IMAGES ©

WANTET/GETTY IMAGES ©

Tana Toraja

14 Life revolves around death in this countryside of rice terraces, boat-shaped roofs and doe-eyed buffalo in Sulawesi. Tana Torajan (p654) funeral ceremonies last days, and involve countless animal sacrifices for the upper classes. The festivities start with bet-heavy bullfights then lead into days of prayer, feasting and dances. At the end, the deceased is brought to their resting place. This could be carved into a cliff face and fronted by their own wooden effigy, in a cave where relatives can visit the bones, or in hanging graves suspended from cave edges.

Woman wearing traditional finery at a funeral ceremony

Togean Islands

15 Almost smack on the equator, the blissful, off-grid Togean Islands (p677) are an unadulterated vision of the tropics, with blinding white-sand beaches fringed by coconut palms, a smattering of fishing villages, homestay digs, and world-class snorkelling and diving on majestic coral reefs. Things are so mellow here that there's even a jellyfish lake where the jellies don't sting. You can forget all about news headlines and Facebook updates – internet access and cellular coverage is near zero.

Volcanoes

16 Indonesia's countless volcanoes don't get much smaller and more perfectly formed than Gunung Api (p441), a miniature Mt Fuji, which shelters the natural harbour of the Banda Islands. Topping out at a rather diminutive 666m, it erupted as recently as 1988, and can be climbed in an arduous three hours. Among the many others worth exploring are Bali's Agung (p271), Lombok's Rinjani (p315), Java's Bromo (p183), and the infamous Krakatau (p77). Explorations can take several hours or days and guides are almost always recommended. One reward: stunning summit sunrises.

17

18

Gunung Leuser National Park

17 This vast slab of steamy tropical jungle draped across the mountains and valleys of northern Sumatra (p534) is filled with cheeping, squeaking, growling animal life. It's a naturalist's and adventure traveller's fantasy. Sitting pretty beside a chocolate-coloured river, the village of Ketambe is a relaxing place to rest up for a few days. More importantly, it makes a great base camp for multiday hiking expeditions in search of howling gibbons, lethargic orangutans and maybe even a tiger or two.

Lar (white-handed) gibbon

Indonesian Food

18 When you eat in Indonesia, you savour the essence of the country. The abundance of rice reflects Indonesia's fertile landscape, the spices are reminiscent of a time of trade and invasion, and the fiery chilli echoes the passion of the people. Chinese, Portuguese, colonists and traders have all influenced the flavours (p742), which include coriander, lemongrass, coconut, and palm sugar. *Sate* (skewered meat), nasi goreng (fried rice) and gado gado (vegetables with peanut sauce) are justly famous; regional variations are endless.

Kerinci Valley

19 Detour from bustling Bukittinggi to West Sumatra's Kerinci Valley (p560), whose appeal lies in its many lakes and waterfalls, its lush, photogenic rice paddies and low-key, traditional villages. After something more strenuous? Then take up the challenge of the Kerinci volcano that looms above the valley and tackle it in a tough overnight climb. If wildlife is your passion, go in search of monkeys, civets, hundreds of bird species and the elusive Sumatran tiger in the Kerinci Seblat National Park (p563).

Kerobokan

20 South Bali's Kerobokan (p216), and its neighbours Seminyak and Canggu, may be just north of notorious Kuta, but in many respects the trio feels like another island. They're flash, brash and filled with hipsters and expats. It's beguiling, rarefied and just this side of too-cool. The beach is part of a stunning swathe of sand stretching to the horizon in both directions. Countless boutiques, many run by top local designers, vie for your daytime attention. At night have a fabulous meal, then hit a club.

Potato Head (p223) beach club

JOHN HARPER/GETTY IMAGES ©

Need to Know

For more information, see Survival Guide (p762)

Currency
Rupiah (Rp)

Language
Bahasa Indonesia

Visas
The visa situation (p774) is complex and fast-changing.

Money
ATMs available and credit cards accepted in cities and popular tourist areas such as Bali. US dollars best for exchange elsewhere.

Mobile Phones
Cheap local SIM cards sold everywhere. Widespread 3G data.

Time
Western Indonesian Time (GMT/UTC plus seven hours); Central Indonesian Time (GMT/UTC plus eight hours); Eastern Indonesian Time (GMT/UTC plus nine hours).

When To Go

High Season
(Jul & Aug)

- Tourist numbers surge across Indonesia, from Bali to Sulawesi and beyond.
- Room rates can spike by 50%.
- Dry season except in Maluku and Papua, which are rainy.

Shoulder
(May, Jun & Sep)

- Dry season outside Maluku and Papua.
- Best weather in Java, Bali and Lombok (dry, not so humid).
- You can travel more spontaneously.

Low Season
(Oct–Apr)

- Wet season in Java, Bali and Lombok (and Kalimantan flowers).
- Dry season (best for diving) in Maluku and Papua.
- Easy to find deals and you can travel with little advance booking (except at Christmas and New Year).

Useful Websites

Inside Indonesia (www.insideindonesia.org) News and thoughtful features.

Jakarta Globe (www.thejakartaglobe.com) Top-notch national English-language newspaper.

Jakarta Post (www.thejakartapost.com) Indonesia's original English-language daily.

tiket.com A convenient way for foreigners to purchase flights with their credit cards.

LonelyPlanet.com (www.lonelyplanet.com/indonesia) Share knowledge and experiences with other travellers.

Important Numbers

Mobile phones are common across Indonesia; numbers usually start with 08 and don't require an area code.

Indonesia country code	☎62
International call prefix	☎001/017
International operator	☎102
Directory assistance	☎108

Exchange Rates

Australia	A$1	9880Rp
Canada	C$1	10,225Rp
Euro	€1	14,530Rp
Japan	¥100	11,115Rp
New Zealand	NZ$1	8960Rp
UK	UK£1	20,735Rp
US	US$1	13,650Rp

For current exchange rates see www.xe.com.

Daily Costs

Budget: Less than 500,000Rp

- Simple rooms less than 200,000Rp
- Cheap street meals under 20,000Rp
- Travel like a local through much of Indonesia outside of major cities and tourist areas

Midrange: 500,000–2,000,000Rp

- Double rooms with air-con and wi-fi US$30–$80
- Cheap flights to shorten distances
- Guides plus meals in restaurants (where they exist)

Top End: More than 2,000,000Rp

- Stay at resorts, often noted boutique properties in remote places
- Use flights and cars with drivers to get around
- Book special tours for activities like diving and visit top restaurants on Bali

Opening Hours

Banks 8am–2pm Monday to Thursday, 8am–noon Friday, 8am–11am Saturday

Government offices 8am–3pm Monday to Thursday, 8am–noon Friday.

Restaurants 8am–10pm

Shops 9am or 10am–5pm, larger shops and tourist areas to 8pm; many closed Sunday

Arriving in Indonesia

Soekarno-Hatta International Airport (Jakarta, CGK; p776) Jakarta is the primary entry point to Indonesia but most people merely change planes here before continuing on to their final destination. If staying in Jakarta, you can reach your hotel by taxi, pre-arranged ride or bus.

Ngurah Rai International Airport (Bali, DPS; p776) Bali is the only airport with significant international service apart from Jakarta. Prepaid 24-hour taxis are available to all parts of Bali. It's 60,000Rp for Kuta, 90,000Rp to Seminyak and 250,000Rp for Ubud.

Getting Around

Transport in Indonesia takes many forms.

Boat Slow and fast boats link the many islands but beware of rogue operators with dodgy safety standards.

Bus Travel almost everywhere cheaply and slowly on buses of all sizes.

Car Rent a small 4WD for US$30 a day, get a car and driver from US$60 a day.

Motorbike Rent one for as little as 60,000Rp a day.

Ojek Get a cheap ride on the back of a motorbike. Used everywhere.

Taxi In cities and tourist areas; fairly cheap but only use Blue Bird taxis to avoid scams.

For much more on **getting around**, see p778

What's New

Jakarta's New Restaurant Row
Just south of the city centre, Jakarta's Jl Senopati has become an emerging dining district with restaurants and cafes of all flavours and price ranges, lined up shoulder to shoulder. (p66)

Breve Azurine, Java
One of our favourite new hotels is an island lodge on Karimunjawa, set on its own private cove with views of jungled mountains, virgin beaches and an endless blue sea. (p157)

Canggu, Bali
Taking over from Seminyak as Bali's new cool hang-out, the hip expat enclave of Canggu flourishes with beach bars, third-wave coffee, creative menus and boutiques. (p225)

Labuanbajo's New Airport, Nusa Tenggara
Flores is hot, thanks to Komodo National Park, beautiful beaches and great drives. It's easier than ever to visit, thanks to this new facility at the tourist hub of Labuanbajo. (p362)

West Sumba, Nusa Tenggara
The unique animist cultures and untouched beaches can now be enjoyed in comfort thanks to new hotels and restaurants, especially in Tambolaka. (p401)

Kerinci Valley, Sumatra
Travellers are now discovering and taking part in multiday jungle treks to remote villages and lakes while reveling in the Kerinci Valley's other attractions. (p560)

Bengkulu, Sumatra
The Bengkulu region's remote waterfalls, low-key villages and rock-climbing sites are now becoming a destination in their own right. (p565)

New Roads in Kalimantan
Road improvements make it possible to circumnavigate Kalimantan (almost) entirely on asphalt, slashing travel times and costs. (p586)

Derawan Archipelago, Kalimantan
Maratua Guesthouse provides a more affordable option for exploring the Derawan Archipelago, while the almost-long-enough runway puts Maratua island entirely within reach. (p633)

Ampana, Sulawesi
Ampana, a coastal town in Central Sulawesi, is fast becoming a travel hub, with a new airport, improved road connections and a slew of excellent new places to stay. (p676)

Tomohon, Sulawesi
Tomohon in Sulawesi's north now has an excellent new lodge, the Highland Resort, from where fascinating hiking trips and tours can be arranged. (p692)

Banda Islands, Maluku
The fast boat to Banda has really opened up these hitherto-hidden isles. Just six hours from Ambon and you're in one of Indonesia's most stunning destinations. (p435)

For more recommendations and reviews, see **lonelyplanet.com/Indonesia**

If You Like…

Island Hopping

With 17,000-odd islands to choose from, your opportunities to bounce from one idyllic little discovery to the next are endless.

Derawan Archipelago This archipelago has several versions of tropical paradise, from backpacker hang-outs to an uncrowded atoll. (p633)

Raja Ampat Islands Jungle-covered hills, pristine beaches and waters teeming with the world's greatest diversity of marine life. (p458)

Karimunjawa Islands Often overlooked, these idyllic coral-fringed islets are enjoying better transport connections and facilities. (p154)

Banyak Islands Spend just one day on each and soon you'll be lost in a perfect island cliché. (p531)

Riung Seventeen Islands Marine Park actually has 23 islands good for lazy days snorkelling and swimming. (p368)

Diving & Snorkelling

Indonesia has some of the world's best diving, from the plethora of operators and schools in Bali to remote spots that will challenge – and thrill – experts.

Komodo National Park Warm and cold currents keep reefs nourished and attract large groups of sharks, mantas and dolphins. (p352)

Pulau Weh Hover above a clownfish and look up to see a giant whale shark. (p526)

Pulau Lembeh Arguably the world's greatest muck diving, with a bevy of macro exotica to encounter. (p694)

Derawan Archipelago Dive off Pulau Maratua, where big pelagic fish and schools of barracuda are common. (p633)

Pulau Bunaken Combine a tropical idyll with excellent snorkelling and diving atop pristine coral reefs and critter-filled muck. (p688)

Bali The wreck of the *Liberty*, just metres from the shore in Tulamben, offers better diving year on year as its colourful soft corals grow, attracting more critters. (p197)

Raja Ampat Islands Save up for that liveaboard trip to this remote West Papua diver's paradise: you won't regret it. (p458)

Hiking

Many parts of Indonesia are still wild and remote. Hikes (from part of a day to weeks) through these lands and cultures are the reason many visit the country.

Kerinci Seblat National Park Challenging volcanoes (such as the mighty Gunung Kerinci) and remote jungle trails leading to hidden lakes and waterfalls draw hikers. (p563)

Gunung Semeru Java's highest peak is a tough challenge with breathtaking volcano vistas of a cone-studded horizon. (p187)

Gunung Rinjani Indonesia's second-highest volcano, sacred to Balinese Hindus and Sasak Muslims, promises a magical summit sunrise. (p315)

Tomohon Suspended between volcanic peaks, the Tomohon region offers grand vistas of volcanic peaks. (p692)

Mamasa to Tana Toraja Walk past terraced rice fields and jungle, stay in villages where the welcome is plentiful. (p667)

Beaches

The problem isn't finding a beach, the problem is choosing one from the myriad options.

Gili Islands Near Bali and Lombok, these three testaments to hedonism are ringed by pure white sand. (p324)

Pantai Trikora Chill out in beachfront homestays along

Pantai Trikora, the more rustic flipside to Pulau Bintan's luxury array of manicured resorts. (p573)

Rote Alongside its epic surf, we love Rote for its miles of empty beaches and sweet solitude. (p391)

Banyak Islands This chain of largely uninhabited sandy dots fringed by pristine coral reefs has Sumatra's best beaches. (p531)

Pulau Tabuhan A white-sand jewel floating just offshore of Banyuwangi. (p194)

Kei Kecil Watch canoes carved in the shadow of a perfect beach. (p447)

Surfing

Surf breaks are found all across Indonesia. Each year new ones are named by surfers in search of the perfect wave.

Bali Legendary surf breaks are found around the island; Ulu Watu is world-famous. (p197)

Mentawai Islands Make a waverider's pilgrimage to some of the planet's most iconic and challenging breaks. (p544)

G-Land This legendary big wave, off Java's extreme southeast corner, just barrels on and on. (p193)

Watu Karung Southwest of Pacitan, East Java's newest surf hotspot has perfect barrels. (p181)

West Sumbawa Of the many Nusa Tenggara waves, only one, Supersuck, attracts surfers from Oahu's North Shore. (p342)

Pulau Nias The long, hollow right of Lagundri has long been considered one of the world's best waves. (p515)

Top: Pura Taman Ayun (p301), Bali
Bottom: Surfing in West Sumbawa (p342)

Wildlife

Orangutans are the stars of a world of wildlife that includes elephants, 'dragons' and all manner of birds.

Palangka Raya The Sungai Kahayan offers plenty of orangutans, crocodiles and more. (p605)

Meru Betiri National Park A rainforest home to exotica including rhinoceros, hornbills, sea turtles and the world's longest snake. (p191)

Papua Birds of paradise – these birds of legendary colour and plumage, and exhibitionist mating dances – hide deep in the Papuan forests. (p450)

Way Kambas National Park Spy elephants and rare birds; learn about efforts to save the endangered Sumatran rhino. (p583)

Alas Purwo National Park Join a nocturnal safari to watch turtles nest and wild leopards roam the jungled, limestone peninsula. (p192)

Komodo National Park The world's largest lizard roams Komodo and Rinca islands while a plethora of marine life awaits underwater. (p352)

Temples

Indonesia might not be as well known for temples as its neighbours, yet between Java and Bali you'll find some of the region's most ancient and beautiful.

Borobudur Indonesia's most famous temple lives up to the hype: come at dawn to experience the ethereal beauty of this stacked Buddhist complex. (p106)

Prambanan Just 50-odd kilometres from Borobudur, this enormous 9th-century wonder near Yogyakarta is the largest Hindu temple in ancient Java. (p130)

Pura Luhur Batukau One of Bali's most important temples is a misty, remote place that's steeped in ancient spirituality. (p289)

Pura Taman Ayun A beautiful moated temple with a royal past; part of Unesco's recognition of Bali's rice traditions. (p301)

Month by Month

TOP EVENTS

Bali's Galungan & Kuningan, dates vary

Pasola, February

Idul Fitri, July

Tana Toraja Funeral Festivals, July & August

January

The first part of the month is busy in Bali as a fair bit of Australia arrives for Christmas and New Year holidays. Europeans searching for warmth also arrive in large numbers.

Gerebeg

Java's three most colourful festivals are held annually in Yogyakarta at the end of January and April and the beginning of November. Huge numbers of people in traditional dress march in processions with garish floats all to the tune of gamelan music. (p116)

February

It's dry season in the east. This is a good time to hit dive and snorkel sites in Maluku and Papua, where the waters will be especially clear.

Pasola

Nusa Tenggara's biggest festival (p405): vividly dressed teams of horsemen engage in mock, though sometimes bloody, battles in West Sumba. Often coincides with Nyale (p320) in Lombok, a huge fishing festival celebrated by the Sasaks.

Cap Goh Meh

Dragons and lions dance on Chinese Lunar New Year in ethnic communities across Indonesia. Some of the most colourful are in Singkawang, where these creatures dance alongside possessed Chinese and Dayak holy men during Kalimantan's biggest Chinese Lunar New Year celebration. (p594)

March

A good time to visit Indonesia as crowds are few and options are many. The rainy season is tailing off in Java, Bali and western Nusa Tenggara.

Java Jazz Festival

Held in early March at the Jakarta Convention Center, this huge festival attracts acclaimed international artists (including Natalie Cole in 2015). This is a major event on the cultural calendar and each year the list of luminaries on the performance list grows. (p61)

Nyepi

Bali's major Hindu festival, Nyepi celebrates a new year on the religious calendar. It's marked by inactivity – to convince evil spirits that Bali is uninhabited. The night before sees community celebrations with *ogoh-ogoh,* huge papier-mâché monsters that go up in flames. Held in March or early April. (p202)

June

A relaxed time in Indonesia sees few crowds anywhere.

Danau Sentani

Festival Danau Sentani features spectacular traditional dances and chanting as well as boat events, music, crafts and more. A highlight of Papua's north, it centres on lakeside Kalkhote, near Sentani town. (p471)

GALUNGAN & KUNINGAN

Galungan, which celebrates the death of a legendary tyrant called Mayadenawa, is one of Bali's major festivals. During this 10-day period, all the gods come down to earth for the festivities. *Barong* (mythical lion-dog creatures) prance from temple to temple and village to village, and locals rejoice with feasts and visits to families. The celebrations culminate with the Kuningan festival, when the Balinese say thanks and goodbye to the gods.

Every village in Bali will celebrate Galungan and Kuningan in grand style and visitors are welcome to join in. This is an excellent time to visit Bali. (The *wuku* calendar is used to determine festival dates, which are typically every 210 days.)

YEAR	GALUNGAN	KUNINGAN
2016	7 Sep	17 Sep
2017	5 Apr & 1 Nov	15 Apr & 11 Nov
2018	30 May & 26 Dec	9 Jun & 5 Jan 2019

July

Although visitor numbers are high in Bali and other areas popular with tourists, July is often the coolest and driest time of the year outside Maluku and Papua.

Idul Fitri

Idul Fitri is the traditional end of Ramadan, the Muslim month of fasting, and this huge holiday sees tens of millions of people travelling to their home villages or going on holiday to places like Bali. The date is slightly earlier each year.

Tana Toraja Funeral Festivals

A Sulawesi highlight and an excellent reason to visit the island. Held during July and August, the ceremonies often shock first-time visitors. Toraja working throughout the country return home for celebrations and funeral rituals. (p661)

August

Independence Day on 17 August sees a spectacle of parades and celebrations in Jakarta and across the country. You'll see school kids out practising their marching in the prior weeks. Note that Bali gets busy with Australians escaping the southern hemisphere winter.

Bidar Races

Spectacular *bidar* (canoe) races are held on South Sumatra's Sungai Musi in Palembang every 17 August and 16 June (the city's birthday). There is also a dragon-boat festival in Padang in July or August. Up to 60 rowers power these boats.

Baliem Valley Festival

A celebration of indigenous culture in Papua's Baliem Valley, with mock 'tribal fighting', full traditional regalia, dance and music. The festivities take place over two days during the second week of August. (p478)

Erau International Folk & Art Festival

Every August thousands of Dayaks from across Kalimantan attend the Erau festival in Tenggarong, a vast intertribal party punctuated by traditional dances, ritual ceremonies and other events. It draws folk dancers worldwide; plan ahead to reserve space. (p624)

October

A good month for travel with few crowds and many good deals. It's the start of the rainy season in Java and Bali but in recent years there has been less rain.

Ubud Writers & Readers Festival

This Ubud festival brings together scores of writers and readers from around the world in a celebration of writing – especially that which touches on Bali. Its reputation grows each year. (p255)

Madura Bull Races

Bull racing is the major sport on Pulau Madura, the island off Java. Teams compete throughout the year to see who will go to the finals held every October in Pamekasan. These competitions feature over 100 racing bulls and legions of fervent fans. Note that the festival is associated with animal welfare issues. (p170)

Itineraries

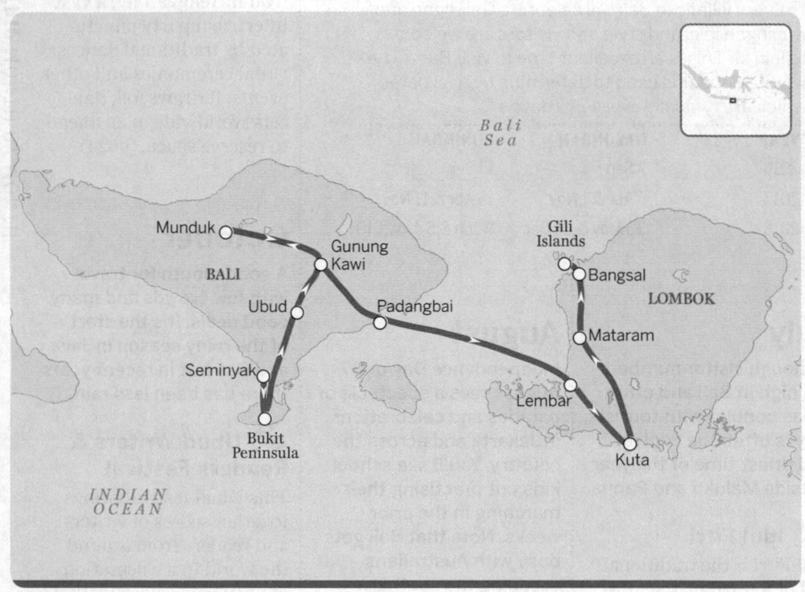

Bali & Lombok

Mix the offbeat with the sublime in Indonesia's heart of tourism.

Start in Bali, acclimatising in the resorts, clubs and shops of **Seminyak**. Dose up on sun at the beach, then explore the little beaches and surf breaks of the **Bukit Peninsula**.

Head north to immerse yourself in the 'other' Bali – the culture, temples and rich history of **Ubud**. Visit **Gunung Kawi**, an ancient site worthy of *Indiana Jones*, and the nearby craft villages. Take a cooking course, learn woodcarving and revel in Bali's famous traditional dance. Then escape to the misty mountains for treks to waterfalls amid coffee plantations in and around **Munduk**.

Next is Lombok. Ferry from Bali's beachy port town of **Padangbai** to **Lembar**, Lombok's launching pad. Head to **Kuta** for mellow vibes amidst the wonderful beaches of south Lombok. Then potter through the rice fields and Hindu temples around **Mataram**.

Ferry from **Bangsal** to the deservedly celebrated **Gili Islands**, where seamless beaches, translucent water and vivid reefs beg for snorkel-clad swimmers. Or if time's short, catch a fast boat direct to the Gilis from Bali.

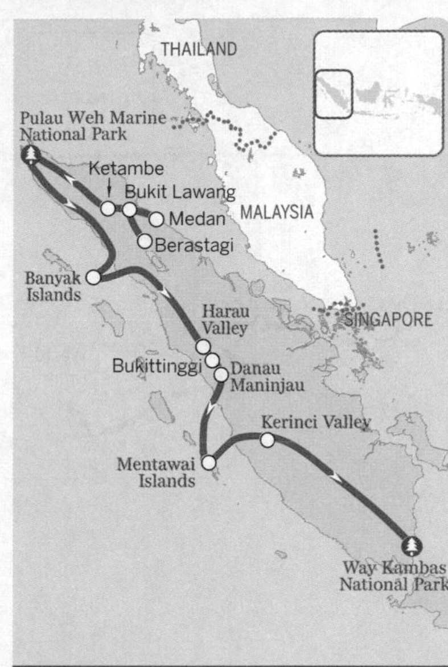

Java Jaunt

Indonesia's most populous island mixes the nation's future, past and natural beauty.

Begin in **Jakarta** and wrap your senses around the dizzying smells, sounds, sights and people of Indonesia's teeming capital. Linger long enough to binge on Bintang beer and shopping, then head to **Batu Karas** for classic laid-back beach vibes or go for the resorts of nearby **Pangandaran**.

After you've worshipped the sun for a week or so, catch the train to **Yogyakarta**, Java's cultural capital. Dabble in batik, amble through the *kraton* (walled city palace) and part with your rupiah at the vibrant markets. A day trip to majestic **Borobudur** is a must.

From Yogyakarta, journey to the laid-back city of **Solo**, via the enigmatic temples of **Prambanan**. Head into the clouds at awesome **Bromo-Tengger-Semeru National Park**, spending a night on the lip of Tengger crater. From here head to the southeast coast and **Meru Betiri National Park**. You just might see the amazing giant squirrel. Finally, follow the coast to **Alas Purwo National Park**, where there's leopards and amazing surfing at G-Land.

Sumatra

Sumatra is quite huge and you'll have to hustle to fully appreciate its myriad natural charms within visa constraints.

Start your explorations in **Medan**, which has great transport connections. Then get right out of town and head to **Bukit Lawang**, where you can see the island's most famous residents, the orangutans. It's a short jaunt from here to **Berastagi**, a laid-back hill town set amid volcanoes.

Head northwest to **Ketambe** for some jungle trekking in Gunung Leuser National Park, then on to the large sea creatures at **Pulau Weh Marine National Park** off the coast. Head back south and travel off the west coast to the **Banyak Islands**, a surfing and beach paradise. Back ashore, follow the Trans-Sumatran Hwy south to **Bukittinggi**, a good base for exploring the cultures and beauty of the **Harau Valley** and **Danau Maninjau**.

More surf and sand awaits at the **Mentawai Islands**. Next, head inland to the volcanic **Kerinci Valley** and Kerinci National Park for remote jungle villages. Finally, head far south to **Way Kambas National Park**, where the highlights include elephants.

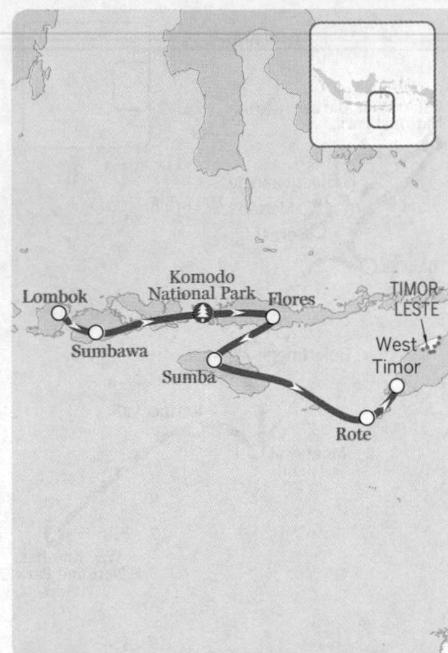

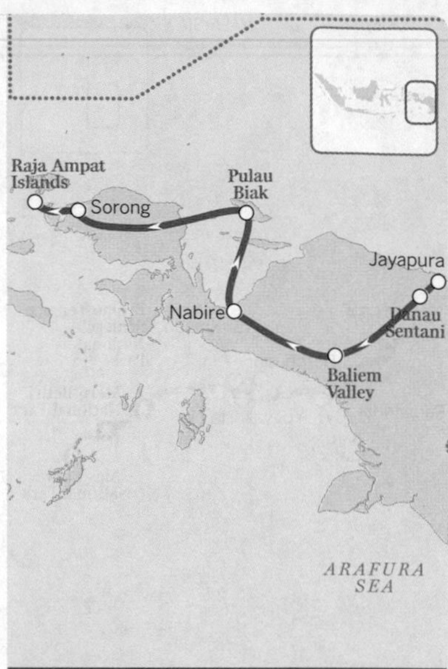

Nusa Tenggara

Lombok is well known to visitors and Flores is the new darling, but the island province of Nusa Tenggara holds many more surprises.

Head east from **Lombok**. Admire the beautiful coastline and surf breaks that dot **Sumbawa** such as Maluk and Pantai Lakey. Catch the ferry to Labuanbajo on **Flores**, the fast-growing hub for exploring nearby **Komodo National Park**. Enjoy dragons and beautiful little island beaches. Note that you can also journey from Lombok to Flores by liveaboard boat.

Flores is a rugged volcanic island with thriving ancient cultures and dramatic terrain. Stop in Bajawa to explore volcanoes and villages, then use mountainside Moni as a base for visiting the vivid waters at Kelimutu. Stop off at the lovely beaches near Paga.

Now take ferries south to isolated and timeless **Sumba**, where some superb beaches are just starting to attract visitors. After indulging in sun and isolation, fly to Kupang in **West Timor**. Visit entrancing ancient villages like None, Boti and Temkessi in the surrounding areas to the east, then jump over to **Rote** for relaxed beach vibes.

Papua

Papua is the launching pad for this route through some of Indonesia's most exotic and beautiful territory. You can do it in 30 days with judicious use of flights, otherwise take your time for the full land and sea adventure.

Start at the transport hub of **Jayapura**. But you'll only be there long enough to charter a boat to visit the magnificent **Danau Sentani**, a 96.5-sq-km lake with 19 islands perfect for inland island-hopping.

Back on dry land, take to the air to get to the beautiful **Baliem Valley**, rich in culture and trek-worthy mountain scenery, and home to the Dani people, an ethnic group whose members have eschewed most modern things and live a traditional life. Enjoy mountain views from a thatched hut.

Fly to **Nabire** and spot whale sharks off the coast – you can even swim with them. Now fly up for some idle island time on **Pulau Biak**. Next it's a flight to **Sorong**, a base for trips out to the **Raja Ampat Islands** – a paradise for divers and snorkellers with Indonesia's most abundant and varied marine life. It's also good for birdwatching and sublime tropical-island scenery.

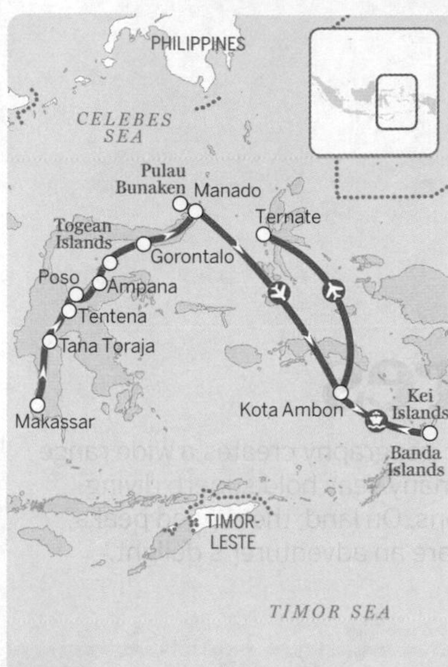

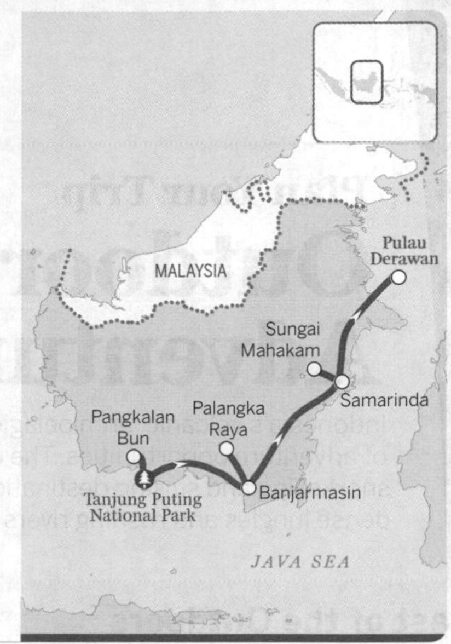

8 WEEKS Sulawesi & Maluku

Explore two of Indonesia's greatest concentration of islands in these little-visited regions.

In **Makassar**, pause for excellent seafood. But don't overdo it, as you want to be fully alive for the elaborate funeral ceremonies in **Tana Toraja**, a nine-hour bus trip from Makassar. From here, another long bus ride (13 hours) takes you to the transport hub of **Poso**. Break your journey at the tidy lakeside town of **Tentena**. A five-hour bus ride from Poso gets you to **Ampana**, where you take a ferry to the amazing, beguiling **Togean Islands** for days of island- and hammock-hopping between iconic beaches.

Tearing yourself away, boat to **Gorontalo**, then bus it or fly to **Manado** and take a boat to laid-back **Pulau Bunaken**. Fly from Manado to **Kota Ambon** on Maluku's Pulau Ambon. Pause only briefly, then take the new fast ferry to the crystalline seas, multicoloured reefs and empty beaches of the historic **Banda Islands**. Make the jaunt southeast to the **Kei Islands**, for one perfect beach after another. Finally, make your way back to Ambon and fly to **Ternate**, which is a pretty tropical-island paradise.

6 WEEKS Kalimantan

Mysterious rivers of unfathomable length are the avenues to discover Kalimantan's incredible diversity of life, including orangutans.

Unassuming **Pangkalan Bun** is the entry point to this excursion – it's the launching pad for trips into glorious **Tanjung Puting National Park**, one of Indonesia's best orangutan haunts. Scan the canopy for their amber bodies as you amble down the beautiful Sungai Sekonyer.

Rejoin reality in colourful **Banjarmasin**. Dabble in Kalimantan's most beguiling city – brave a 5am call for the animated floating markets, then cruise the canals and meet the locals at dusk. Begin another classic river adventure by navigating up the Sungai Kahayan to **Palangka Raya**, a hub for yet more orangutan-watching.

From Banjarmasin, travel overland to **Samarinda** and make an expedition along the **Sungai Mahakam**. Several days upstream will land you in the river's western reaches, which are peppered with semitraditional Dayak villages and preserved forests. Travel back to the coast and head north to primitive **Pulau Derawan** and its offshore underwater wonders.

Plan Your Trip

Outdoor Adventures

Indonesia's volcanic, archipelagic geography creates a wide range of adventure opportunities. The many seas hold superb diving, snorkelling and surfing destinations. On land, the rugged peaks, dense jungles and rushing rivers are an adventurer's delight.

Best of the Outdoors

Best Beach

The beaches of south Lombok, especially those that line the bays around Kuta (Lombok, not Bali), are beautiful and worth a trip.

Best Diving

The Raja Ampat Islands are on many a diver's bucket list, and with good reason: the wealth and variety of marine life is nothing short of astonishing.

Best Surfing

Tough competition, but we say Sumatra for its pure perfection and consistency. The Mentawais and Nias are home to some of the world's most legendary waves.

Best Hiking & Trekking

The Baliem Valley draws acolytes from around the world for hikes among some of the world's most unique cultures.

Best Wildlife-Watching

Kalimantan's Tanjung Puting National Park: anchor along one of its iconic rivers and watch orangutans go about their business just metres away.

When to Go

There are vast variations in the weather across the huge swathe of islands that is Indonesia. Generally the dry season in Java, Bali and Lombok is from May to September, while Maluku and Papua have their best weather from October to April. But exceptions are the rule, and you'll want to carefully research any location you plan to visit if the weather will play a role in your enjoyment.

Beaches

With 17,000-plus islands, Indonesia has a lot of beaches. These range from the wildly popular beaches on south Bali to those for hard-core partiers on the Gili Islands, and to literally hundreds more where your footprints will be the first of the day.

Pantai is 'beach' in Bahasa Indonesia.

Note that sunscreen can be hard to find outside of major tourist areas.

Where to Go

Java

Beaches near cities in Java can be virtually overrun on weekends, but venture a little further and you'll find some great sand.

➡ **Batu Karas** (p101) A simple village with two great beaches and a classic laid-back vibe.

➡ **Southwest of Yogyakarta** (p126) Explore this beautiful coastline, a succession of alluring golden-sand coves divided by craggy headlands (but skip Parangritis, which is not in the same league).

➡ **Karimunjawa Islands** (p154) Some 27 islands comprise this offshore marine park, which gets very few visitors. It has among the finest beaches in Indonesia.

➡ **Pulau Tabuhan** (p194) A tiny rugged island hidden between Java and Bali, where you can camp on its white-sand beach.

Bali

Fabled for its beaches, Bali actually pales in comparison to scores of other islands in Indonesia. What the island does have is a thriving beach culture, with surfing and places to imbibe, ranging from the dead-simple to the hipster-luxe. Locals and visitors alike pause on west-facing beaches at sunset.

➡ **Kuta Beach** (p208) This is the original draw for tourists, with a golden-sand arc sweeping past Canggu to the northwest. Raw surf hits here, delighting surfers.

➡ **Bukit Peninsula** (p229) The west side has famous surf spots and beaches such as Bingen and Padang Padang that feature little pockets of bright sand below limestone cliffs. The east side has reef-protected strands, such as the one at Nusa Dua.

➡ **East Bali** (p266) A long series of open-water beaches begins north of reef-protected Sanur. Waves pound volcanic sand that ranges from a light grey to charcoal black.

Nusa Tenggara

Nusa Tenggara is probably the region of Indonesia with the most beaches awaiting discovery.

➡ **Gili Islands** (p324) The Gilis are easily reached from Bali and Lombok, and you can snorkel right off the blinding white sands. Gili Trawangan has one of the country's most vibrant party scenes.

➡ **Lombok** (p304) Head south for the pristine white-sand islands of Gili Asahan and the north coast of Gili Gede. Kuta is an immense series of one spectacular beach or bay after another. Get there, rent a motorbike and explore.

➡ **Sumbawa** (p342) In west Sumbawa the best beaches are south of Maluk in Rantung and north in Jelenga. In the east, head to the Lakey area.

➡ **Flores** (p354) Head to the islands off Labuanbajo and you'll find bliss, especially on Pulau Sebayur and Pulau Kanawa. Pantai Merah on Komodo Island (p351) is famous for its sublime pink-sand beaches. The Seventeen Islands Marine Park off the Riung coast also has a dozen remote islands with epic and empty white-sand beaches to laze upon.

➡ **Rote** (p391) The main beach in Nemberala town is beautiful enough, but the beaches just get wider and whiter the further south you travel. Ba'a is the most beautiful of the bunch. We also enjoy the empty sugary beaches on nearby islands Pulau Do'o and Pulau Ndao.

Maluku

The fine beaches here have barely been discovered.

➡ **Banda Islands** (p435) Maluku's best beaches are all in the Bandas. Charter a boat from Bandaneira and enjoy exquisite empty beaches on Pulau Hatta, Pulau Ai, and Pulau Run (Rhun). But the best of the Banda bunch is Pulau Neilaka, more a white sandbar than an island.

➡ **Kei Islands** (p444) Sugary Pasir Panjang is ground zero for beach lounging. The petroglyph-swathed cliffs and mind-bending scenery at Ohoidertawun are also worth consideration. Rent a bike and make the two-hour trek to the stunning, remote and drop-dead gorgeous beaches of Pantai Ohoidertutu.

Papua

Papua is not a beach destination per se, but there are some fine ones here.

➡ **Raja Ampat Islands** (p458) There are some divine and empty beaches here, but due to the high cost of reaching the area they tend to be enjoyed mainly as a secondary activity by people who are diving and/or snorkelling.

➡ **Pulau Biak** (p473) The Padaido Islands off Pulau Biak have some good beaches that are not too hard to reach.

Sumatra

The best beaches on this huge island are actually on tiny islands offshore, although many, such as the Mentawai Islands, are more worth the difficulty in and (expense of) accessing if you're also heading there for surfing.

➡ **Pulau Bintan** (p572) A gem in the Riau Islands, this island has some fine beaches where you can live the tropical fantasy in a hut.

➡ **Banyak Islands** (p531) Banyak means 'many', and it's true there are many fine beaches among the 99 islands in this remote and seldom-visited chain off Aceh.

Cycling

Cycling in Indonesia is booming in popularity as petrol prices skyrocket. Lowland towns such as Yogyakarta and Solo in Java teem with bikes, and bicycles are gaining popularity in Bali. Lombok has good roads for bikes.

Where to Go

Java

Yogyakarta is a big biking centre: pedal out to see the Prambanan temples (p130). Bikes are also for rent at Borobudur, while Solo is another good place to join a bike tour.

Bali

Bike tours are available across the island. Some are simple downhill jaunts through rice fields while others are much more adventurous. You can rent bikes for around 25,000Rp per day.

Nusa Tenggara

Bicycles are available for hire on the Gili Islands; Trawangan is best suited for exploration.

Sumatra

Cycling the languid streets of Danau Toba (p511) is a great way to explore the island. On Danau Maninjau (p558) you can peddle around the lake on a bicycle tour.

Diving

With so many islands and so much coral, Indonesia offers wonderful possibilities for diving.

Where to Go

Java

While the island isn't known for its diving, the Karimunjawa Islands (p154) have some spots, including a century-old Norwegian wreck dive.

Bali

Indonesia's tourist hub has a plethora of excellent dive shops, schools and operators.

➡ **Nusa Penida** (p246) Serious diving that includes schools of manta rays and 2.5m sunfish.

➡ **Pulau Menjangan** (p297) Spectacular 30m wall off a small island. Good for divers and snorkellers of all skills and ages.

➡ **Tulamben** (p282) A popular sunken WWII freighter lies right off the shore.

Nusa Tenggara

A vast range of diving opportunities awaits. Major destinations have land-based dive shops. For untapped dive sites, bring your own buoyancy control devices, regulators and computers (tanks are usually accessible) and explore Rote, Sumbawa and Sumba.

➡ **Gili Islands** (p336) Among the best places to get certified worldwide; accessible reefs are within a 10-minute boat ride.

➡ **Lombok** (p304) If you get lucky you can see schooling hammerheads at Blongas, usually in mid-September.

➡ **Flores** (p354) World-class sites within the Komodo National Park; in peak season up to 50 liveaboards ply these waters.

➡ **Alor Archipelago** (p379) Crystalline waters and arguably the most pristine reefs in Indonesia, and you'll have the sites almost all to yourself.

Maluku

Diving has great promise here but is mostly undeveloped.

➡ **Banda Islands** (p435) Seasonal dives can explore lava flow off Pulau Gunung Api, or the wonderful coral-crusted walls off Pulau Hatta, Pulau Ai and Pulau Run.

➡ **Pulau Ambon** (p430) Something of a dive mecca. There are reef dives outside the bay off the Ambon coast, but most divers come here for the excellent muck diving on the slopes within Teluk Ambon.

Papua

Bring your own equipment to ensure you get the most out of the journey.

➡ **Raja Ampat Islands** (p458) Among the best in the world for the diversity and quantity of marine life. It's a remote area and quite expensive. Most divers head out on liveaboard boats for one- to two-week cruises, or stay at the handful of dive resorts.

➡ **Pulau Biak** (p473) An excellent dive site that's overshadowed by Raja Ampat.

Sumatra

Diving on Mentawai is still a fledgling activity although certification courses are now available through a handful of resorts.

➡ **Pulau Weh** (p526) A small coral-ringed island with 20 dive sites that's growing in popularity. Whale sharks often visit.

Kalimantan

Kalimantan has a growing number of dive resorts with house reefs and fast boats to access islands.

➡ **Derawan Archipelago** (p633) Features a good diversity: Pulau Derawan has excellent macro diving; Pulau Sangalaki is famous for mantas; Pulau Maratua has sharks, rays and barracuda.

Sulawesi

New dive areas are opening up, but favourites such as Bunaken are popular for a reason.

➡ **Pulau Bunaken** (p688) Part of a large marine park, this island, which is easily reached from Manado, offers all sorts of diving.

➡ **Pantai Bira** (p649) Varied marine life, including groupers, rays and occasional whale sharks, and colourful corals.

➡ **Lembeh Strait** (p694) Muck diving at its finest; a weird and wonderful world of bizarre critters awaits discovery between Pulau Lembeh and Bintung.

Safe Diving

Before embarking on a scuba-diving or snorkelling trip, consider the following points to ensure a safe and enjoyable experience. See Responsible Travel (p763) for tips on responsible diving.

➡ Ensure you possess a current diving certification card from a recognised scuba diving instruction agency.

➡ Be sure you are healthy and feel comfortable diving.

➡ Obtain reliable information about physical and environmental conditions at the dive site. Ask your operator or guide detailed questions.

➡ Dive only at sites within your realm of experience and engage the services of a certified dive instructor.

➡ Check your equipment thoroughly beforehand. For much of Indonesia, the equipment (if it's available) may not be in top condition. Bali is your best bet for finding reliable equipment for hire.

Snorkelling

For many, there's bliss to be found in the simplicity of snorkelling beautiful waters right off the beaches. Most dive operators will let snorkellers hitch a ride on trips, but don't expect much in the way of decent masks and fins outside of the most popular sites. Bring your own if you're picky. There are also some wonderful free-diving outfits.

Where to Go

Java

Java has some healthy coral reefs that make for good low-key snorkelling spots.

➡ **Karimunjawa Islands** (p154) This archipelago has a number of islands fringed by colourful corals.

➡ **Baluran National Park** (p196) An offshore site features a drop with plenty of fish and corals.

Bali

Bali is ringed by good snorkelling sites that are easily reached.

➡ **Pulau Menjangan** (p297) A steady current takes you right along the edge of the beautiful 30m coral wall.

➡ **Tulamben** (p282) A popular sunken WWII freighter is easily reached right offshore.

➡ **Amed** (p280) This coastline along east Bali has plenty of colourful coral and fish directly off the beach.

Nusa Tenggara

Nusa Tenggara has the best selection of snorkelling sites in the country. You can snorkel all of the Moyo and Alor (p379) dive sites and share a boat with the divers.

➡ **Gili Islands** (p324) As well as masses of tropical fish, turtles are almost guaranteed from any of the many tour boats.

JODY WATT/DESIGN PICS/GETTY IMAGES ©

Top: Gunung Rinjani (p315) base camp, Nusa Tenggara

Bottom: Snorkelling near Pulau Misool (p460), Raja Ampat Islands

➡ Komodo Islands (p360) The best snorkel sites are around Pulau Kanawa, Pulau Sebayur and off Pantai Merah.

Maluku

There are plenty of accessible coral gardens on the many islands here.

➡ Banda Islands (p437) Can be snorkelled, though you'll need to free dive a bit to get the best views of the drop-offs. You might see turtles and sharks off Pulau Hatta.

➡ Lease Islands (p431) These rarely visited islands with wonderful clear waters offer great snorkelling, including off uninhabited Pulau Molana.

Papua

Divers aren't the only ones having fun here.

➡ Raja Ampat Islands (p460) Many superb snorkelling sites are reachable just by walking off a beach or taking a boat. Dive resorts and homestays all offer snorkelling.

➡ Nabire (p476) Snorkel with whale sharks.

Sumatra

The best snorkelling is around the little islands offshore. Rudimentary day trips are available, but travellers are advised to bring their own snorkelling gear.

➡ Pulau Bintan Pantai Trikora (p573) on the east coast and is good for snorkelling, especially at high tide.

➡ Pulau Weh (p526) This island off the tip of Sumatra has beautiful coral gardens full of marine life, including turtles.

Kalimantan

➡ Derawan Archipelago (p633) Features some of the country's best snorkelling; head to its outer islands, as reefs around Pulau Derawan are damaged.

Sulawesi

Sulawesi has a large number of great snorkelling sites.

➡ Pulau Bunaken (p689) Great for snorkelling for many of the same reasons that it's a good dive location.

➡ Togean Islands (p677) Given the challenges in reaching these idyllic little gems, it's nice that there's good underwater action once you get here.

Surfing

Indonesia lures surfers from around the globe, many with visions of empty palm-lined beaches, bamboo bungalows and perfect barrels peeling around a coral reef. The good news is that mostly the dreams come true, but just like anywhere else, Indonesia is subject to flat spells, onshore winds and crowding (particularly on Bali). A little research and preparation go a long way.

There are usually boards for rent (but don't expect great quality), and surf schools are located at the major surf sites.

Where to Go

Java

Java is still being explored by surfers, who find new breaks every year. Its popular breaks at G-Land, Cimaja, Batu Karas and Pacitan have surf schools and shops.

➡ G-Land (p193) One of the world's best left-handers, G-Land is a holy grail for expert surfers. With consistently perfect waves and long rides, it's worthy of all the hype.

➡ Cimaja (p83) A popular surf spot at Pelabuhan Ratu. The fabled Ombak Tujuh break is off a pebble beach.

➡ Pulau Panaitan (p78) Home to some of Indo's biggest waves including the fast and powerful Apocalypse, and long left barrels at One Palm Point.

➡ Batu Karas (p101) One of several good breaks around Pangandaran, a popular surf spot off the southern coast of Central Java.

➡ Pacitan (p181) This town on a beautiful little horseshoe bay rewards surfers who make the trek.

Bali

Despite the crowds, Bali remains a surfer's paradise, with some of the best tubes in the world. Breaks are found right around the south side of the island, and there's a large infrastructure of schools and board-rental places.

➡ Kuta Beach (p208) Where surfing came to Asia. Generally a good place for beginners (unless it's pumping) with long, steady breaks.

➡ Bukit Pensinsula (p229) From Bali's largest sets at Ulu Watu and Padang Padang, to world-class breaks at Balangan and Bingin, this is one of Indo's best surf spots.

SURF INFO ONLINE

Bali Waves (www.baliwaves.com) Surf reports, including webcams of top spots.

Magic Seaweed (www.magicseaweed.com) Popular and respected for reliable surf reports and forecasts.

SurfAid International (www.surfaidinternational.org) Surfer-run aid organisation.

Surf Travel Company (www.surftravel.com.au) Australian outfit with camps, yacht charters, destination information, surfer reviews and more.

WannaSurf (www.wannasurf.com) Surf reports, current conditions and a message board.

➡ **Keramas** (p267) Right-hand break that's fast, powerful and hollow. The world pro comp is held here, and it also has the novelty of night surfing under lights.

➡ **Medewi** (p301) Famous point break with a ride right into a river mouth.

➡ **Nusa Lembongan** (p242) The island is a mellow scene for surfers who come for the right-hand breaks known as Shipwrecks and Lacerations, and the less challenging leftie at Playgrounds.

Nusa Tenggara

You could spend years exploring – and discovering! – places to surf in Nusa Tenggara.

➡ **Lombok** South Lombok is a surf paradise. There are numerous breaks from Ekas to Gerupuk to Kuta, all of which can be accessed from Kuta (p319). Tanjung Desert (Desert Point; p308) is more of a surf camp and it's also legendary.

➡ **Sumbawa** Jelenga (Scar Reef: p343) and Maluk (p343) are among the greatest and most overlooked surf breaks in the world. Surfers regularly descend here to surf Supersuck, which offers one of the best barrels anywhere.

➡ **Rote** T-Land (p392) is the legendary left, but there are hollow waves in Bo'a (p393), as well.

➡ **Sumba** (p394) West Sumba has the best breaks, but it's not set up for tourists. You'll have to hire a car, drive into remote villages and paddle out on sight and feel.

Sumatra

Arguably Indonesia's hottest surf region; new areas such as Krui are attracting surfers in the know and further areas are opening up all the time.

➡ **Mentawai Islands** (p546) Surfing is huge business in the Mentawais, where you'll find some of the world's best waves. Everything's here, from local fixers arranging speedboat transport, to simple losmens (basic accommodation), or seven- to 10-day all-inclusive trips on surf boats. Primo breaks include Macaronis and Lance's Right.

➡ **Pulau Nias** (p515) A low-key place for low-key surfers. The one place on Sumatra where you can rent a decent board cheaply. Good schools for beginners.

➡ **Krui** (p578) A largely undiscovered surf spot that has yet to attract mobs, not unlike other Sumatra secret spots Banyaks and Simelue.

➡ **Bono** (p515) Hands down Indo's most bizarre wave, this freshwater tidal bore generates a perfect set rolling in along a brown river.

Kitesurfing

Surfing isn't the only way to catch a wave in Indo these days; kitesurfing is fast catching on as a popular water sport.

Where to Go

Java

➡ **Banyuwangi** (p194) For those with their own gear, Pulau Tabuhan gets some good winds for kitesurfing. It hosts the Tabuhan Island Pro in August.

Bali

➡ **Sanur** (p234) The best spot on Bali for kitesurfing. Rip Curl has set up shop, and offers kitesurfing lessons and equipment hire, as well as windsurfing and stand-up paddle boarding (SUP).

Nusa Tenggara

➡ **Pantai Lakey & Hu'u** (p347) One of the world's top 10 kitesurfing destinations; the season runs from July to November.

➡ **Kuta** (p319) Several operators offer lessons and rental.

Sumatra

➡ **Aceh** From May to September, Lampu'uk on Aceh's west coast is popular for kitesurfing. If you're a beginner, Aceh Kitecamp (p529) in Lhok Nga is the best place to head.

Rafting & Kayaking

Some of the rivers tumbling down Indonesia's volcanic slopes draw adventure operators and thrill-seeking tourists. For something more relaxing, jump in a sea kayak for a paddle around.

Where to Go

Java

Java probably has Indonesia's best white-water rafting.

➡ **Sungai Citarak** (p83) Churns out Class II to IV rapids.

➡ **Green Valley** (p101) Located near Pangandaran; you can skip a raft altogether and go 'body rafting' in a life jacket.

Bali

Two reputable operators are Bali Adventure Tours (p251) and Bio (p251), which offer rafting, river boarding and tubing.

➡ **Sungai Ayung** (p251) Features 33 Class II to III rapids, which are fun and suitable for all levels.

Nusa Tenggara

➡ **Komodo National Park** (p352) Glide through the park on a guided kayak tour from Labuanbajo.

➡ **Gili Air** (p338) Hire a kayak to look down upon reefs through gin-clear waters.

Kalimantan

➡ **Loksado** (p613) The bamboo rafting here is more of a relaxing paddle than an adrenaline rush.

Papua

➡ **Raja Ampat Islands** (p461) Rent a kayak with or without a guide to explore pristine waters.

Sumatra

➡ **Bukit Lawang** (p501) Finish off your sweaty jungle trek with an enjoyable wet 'n' wild river journey down fun rapids.

➡ **Banyak Islands** (p532) Jump in a sea kayak to explore dozens of tropical islands.

Sulawesi

➡ **Sungai Sa'dan** (p662) Lures adventure junkies to tackle its 20-odd rapids (some up to Class IV).

➡ **Tana Toraja** (p655) Rafting agents in Rantepao organise trips down its canyon.

➡ **Minahasa** (p692) Combine rafting rapids with wildlife-watching.

Hiking, Trekking & Climbing

Setting off on foot in Indonesia offers limitless opportunities for adventure and exploration, from volcanic peaks with jaw-dropping dawn views to remote jungle treks; you can leave civilisation behind. See Responsible Travel (p763) for tips on responsible trekking.

Where to Go

Java

Java has some great walks. Guides are always available at national park offices, or via guesthouses. Tents and sleeping bags can be rented at Semeru. Organised hikes can be set up in Kalibaru (to Merapi) and Malang (to Semeru).

➡ **Gunung Bromo** (p183) One of three volcanic cones (one active) that emerge from an otherworldly caldera. Highly recommended and popular.

➡ **Gede Pangrango National Park** (p85) Waterfalls and the nearly 3000m-high Gunung Gede, an active volcano, are the highlights.

➡ **Gunung Lawu** (p142) On the border of Central and East Java, this 3265m mountain is dotted with ancient Hindu temples.

➡ **Gunung Semeru** (p187) It's a tough three-day trek to the top of Java's tallest peak, which is nearly always volcanically active.

➡ **Ijen Plateau** (p188) Coffee plantations, misty jungle, volcanic cones and a spectacular crater lake are the allures here.

Bali

Bali is very walkable. No matter where you're staying, ask for recommendations, and set off for discoveries and adventures.

➡ **Gunung Agung** (p271) Sunrises and isolated temples on Bali's most sacred mountain.

➡ **Gunung Batur** (p284) This volcano's otherworldly scenery almost makes you forget about the hassles.

➡ **Munduk** (p288) Lush, spice-scented, waterfall-riven landscape high in the hills.

➡ **Sidemen Road** (p269) Rice terraces and lush hills; comfy lodgings for walkers.

➡ **Bali Barat National Park** (p296) A range of hikes through alternating habitats of jungle, savannah and mangroves.

➡ **Ubud** (p256) Beautiful walks between one hour and one day through rice, river-valley jungles and ancient monuments.

Nusa Tenggara

Lombok and Flores are both easily accessible and home to some top hikes.

➡ **Gunung Rinjani** (p315) Indonesia's second-tallest volcano is on Lombok. The standard trek is three to four days long; it begins near a sacred waterfall, skirts lakes and hot springs, and culminates with sunrise on one of two peaks.

➡ **Flores** Enjoy hikes to remote villages only accessible by trail, the most interesting of which is the trek to Wae Rebo (p364) in the Manggarai region. You can also climb Gunung Inerie (p368) in the Bajawa area, or hike to the remote Pauleni Village (p367) near Belaragi.

Maluku

➡ **Gunung Api** (p441) Head up this perfectly formed volcanic cone on a three-hour (quite arduous) self-guided trek.

Papua

For many people, trekking is the reason to visit Papua.

➡ **Baliem Valley** (p482) World-class trekking: great hiking in wonderful mountain scenery among friendly, traditional people. It's possible to sleep most nights in villages; some simpler routes don't require guides or porters.

➡ **Korowai region** (p489) Tough jungle trekking in an area populated by ex-headhunters who live in tree houses. You'll need a well-organised, expensive guided trip.

➡ **Carstensz Pyramid & Gunung Trikora** (p488) You'll need mountaineering skills to climb the two highest mountains in Oceania. Both involve high altitudes and camping in a cold climate. Organise through specialist agencies.

Sumatra

Unsurprisingly, this vast island offers a huge range of overland adventures.

➡ **Mentawai Islands** (p544) There is still dense, untouched jungle here that you can penetrate by longboat on river journeys. Local guides will take you to their isolated abodes.

➡ **Berastagi** (p505) A cool retreat from steamy Medan. Easy treks include volcanoes.

➡ **Bukittinggi** (p551) You can meander through tiny villages or head off into the jungle for the three-day trek to Danau Maninjau.

➡ **Kerinci Seblat National Park** (p563) Dense rainforest, high mountains and rare animals such as rhinos are the highlights of treks through Sumatra's largest park.

Kalimantan

The jungles of Borneo remain seemingly impenetrable in vast areas, and that's all the more reason for intrepid trekkers to set out on a trail.

➡ **Cross-Borneo Trek** (p591) This uber-choice of Kalimantan treks is best undertaken by contacting either De'gigant Tours (p620) in Samarinda or Kompakh (p598) in Putussibau and going from there. No one should try to organise it by themselves.

➡ **Loksado** (p613) A real-life adventure park with dozens of rope and bamboo bridges across streams amid thick jungle.

➡ **Gunung Besar** (p613) The highest peak in the Meratus mountain range, Besar (1901m) is accessed via a week-long hike from Loksado.

Sulawesi

The region around Tana Toraja could occupy months of trekking.

➡ **Tana Toraja** (p661) Beautiful valleys and fascinating Torajan architecture and culture are highlights. Good guides are readily available in Rantepao.

➡ **Mamasa** (p667) West of Tana Toraja, this 59km trek linking Tana Toraja and Mamasa is a three-day treat.

➡ **Tomohon** (p693) Hike up to Gunung Lokon's crater lake.

Safe Hiking

Before embarking on a trekking or hiking trip, consider the following points to ensure a safe and enjoyable experience.

➡ Pay any fees and obtain any permits required by local authorities.

➡ Be sure you are healthy and feel comfortable walking for a sustained period.

➡ Obtain reliable information about physical and environmental conditions along your intended route.

➡ Be aware of local laws, regulations and etiquette about wildlife and the environment.

➡ Walk only in regions and on trails/tracks within your realm of experience.

➡ Be aware that weather conditions and terrain vary significantly from one region, or even from one trail or track, to another. Seasonal changes and sudden weather shifts can significantly alter any trail or track. These differences influence what to wear and what equipment to carry.

➡ Ask before you set out about the environmental characteristics that can affect your walk, and how experienced local walkers deal with these considerations.

➡ Strongly consider hiring a guide. Indonesia has many good guides who have invaluable local knowledge.

Guides

A guide can make or break your trip. Some travellers report disappointing trips with cheap guides, but high fees alone don't guarantee satisfaction. Here are some tips for choosing a guide.

➡ Meet the guide before finalising any trip. (If you're dealing with a tour agency, insist on meeting the guide you'll travel with, not the head of the agency.)

➡ Quiz the guide about the itinerary. That can begin by email or telephone, and will also provide a sample of their ability in your language. (Be aware that guides using email may have a helper handling that correspondence.) Listen to their ideas, and see if they listen to yours.

➡ Guides usually offer package prices and should be able to roughly itemise trip costs. Be clear on what's included in the package, particularly regarding transport and food.

➡ Some guides offer the option of charging you only their fee (250,000Rp to 600,000Rp per day) while you pay other expenses directly.

➡ Find out what you'll need from the guide, such as water.

➡ For ambitious treks in places such as Papua, you may need to hire porters to help carry your food and water, in addition to a guide.

Climbing & Canyoning

While still an emerging scene, there are reputable operators offering climbing, canyoning, abseiling and spelunking. Gear is provided, but serious climbers will want to bring their own.

Where to Go

Bali

➡ **Ubud** Based in Mas, outside of Ubud, **Adventure & Spirit** (☎0853-3388 5598; www.adventureandspirit.com; from US$110) offers very popular canyoning day trips out to central Bali that combine abseiling, swimming, jumping, climbing and ziplining through scenic gorges and waterfalls.

Nusa Tenggara

➡ **Flores** Head to the Cunca Wulang Cascades (p359) around Labuanbajo for 7m jumps off waterfalls into swimming holes.

Sumatra

This is the most well-known place in Indonesia for rock-climbers.

➡ **Harau Valley** (p558) The area is popular for rock climbing, in addition to hikes. Guides can be arranged here.

➡ **Bengkulu region** Rock climbing at Bukit Kandis (p568) and Goa Kacamata (p568) is suitable for all levels.

Sulawesi

➡ **Minahasa** (p692) Outside Tomohon, this scenic area is gaining recognition for its adventure activities, including abseiling, canyoning and 60m drops from Tekaan Telu waterfall.

Wildlife-Watching

Indonesia's wildlife is as diverse as everything else about the archipelago. Great apes, tigers, elephants and monkeys – lots of monkeys – plus one mean lizard are just some of the more notable critters you may encounter.

Where to Go

Java

The national parks are home to a huge range of animals and birds – and usually guides ready to lead you.

➡ **Ujung Kulon National Park** (p77) Extremely rare one-horned Javan rhinoceros and panthers live among the Unesco-listed rainforest.

➡ **Alas Purwo National Park** (p192) You may spot various deer, peacocks and even a leopard or two.

➡ **Baluran National Park** (p195) 4WD safaris head out to spot wild oxen and other large animals amid natural grasslands.

➡ **Meru Betiri National Park** (p191) Home to a vast range of wildlife, including leopards and the intriguing giant squirrel.

Bali

Other than its prevalence of macaque monkeys and the occasional monitor lizard, Bali has limited wildlife encounters.

➡ **Bali Barat National Park** (p296) Excellent for birdwatching, and also has multiple species of deer, monkey, wild pig and buffalo.

Nusa Tenggara

This vast collection of islands has one real star.

➡ **Komodo National Park** (p352) First and foremost is the area's namesake endemic species: the Komodo dragon (p353). But there are also slow-screeching flocks of flying foxes roosting on mangrove islands in the park.

➡ **Seventeen Islands Marine Park** (p369) Near Riung you can find barking deer, wild water buffalo and rich birdlife.

Maluku

Maluku remains a relatively untapped birder paradise. It's worth the effort and cash to access the national parks of Seram and Halmahera.

➡ **Aketajawe-Lolobata National Park** (p422) You can stalk Wallace's standard-winged bird of paradise in this eastern Halmahera reserve.

Papua

Papua is fantastic birdwatching territory, including for birds of paradise. It's more difficult to find other Papuan wildlife, including exotic marsupials such as tree kangaroos, cuscus and sugar gliders, though some expert local guides can help.

➡ **Raja Ampat Islands** (p460) Birds of paradise and many other species cause birdwatchers to flock here.

➡ **Pegunungan Arfak** (p466) Thickly forested mountains hide all manner of birds.

➡ **Wasur National Park** (p487) It's fairly easy to spot wallabies and deer here.

➡ **Danau Habbema** (p484) Cuscus, birds of paradise and sometimes tree kangaroos are found near this isolated lake.

Sumatra

Large mammals such as elephants, orangutans and the Sumatran tiger have homes amid the still untrodden tracts of wilderness here.

➡ **Gunung Leuser National Park** (p534) Famous for orangutans but also home to monkeys, elephants and tigers.

➡ **Kerinci Seblat National Park** (p563) Birds abound, and in the seldom-visited Ladeh Panjang region there's even a form of bear, as well as tigers.

➡ **Way Kambas National Park** (p583) Elephant-watching and birdwatching trips.

Kalimantan

Kalimantan is mostly about jungle river trips to experience wildlife such as orangutans and discover the myriad local cultures.

➡ **Tanjung Puting National Park** (p600) The orangutan-spotting is superb and you'll also see all manner of birds and reptiles.

➡ **Sungai Kapuas** (p596) Voyage from Pontianak to Sukadana by longboat.

Sulawesi

Tarsiers, a bizarre-looking nocturnal monkey with enormous eyes, are all the rage among Sulawesi wildlife-spotters.

➡ **Tangkoko-Batuangas Dua Saudara Nature Reserve** (p695) Your best bet to see tarsiers is here with a guide.

➡ **Lore Lindu National Park** (p673) Tarsiers, birds of paradise, monkeys and more are found in this protected area.

Plan Your Trip

Travel with Children

Want a great way to improve your Indonesia trip? Bring the kids! Parents say that they see more because children are so quickly whisked into everyday life across this child-loving archipelago. Natural barriers break right down as locals open their arms – and lives – to children.

Best Regions for Kids

Bali

The island at the heart of Indonesian tourism is ideal for kids. There are beautiful beaches, many with gentle surf, plus great spots for first-time snorkellers and surfers. Cool temples of *Indiana Jones* ilk dot the island and there are dozens of child-friendly hotels and resorts.

Java

Batu Karas is a wonderful and safe beach. The easy hiking around Gunung Bromo is a good choice for families. More remote, the beaches and offshore islands in Karimunjawa delight families while kids lap up the mysteries of Borobudur and Prambanan.

Nusa Tengarra

Lombok is a slightly more adventurous version of Bali but is still easy for families and has gorgeous beaches in the south. Of the Gilis (where no one ever got lost), Air combines a relaxed vibe with activities, hotels and restaurants that are great for kids. Flores offers amazing wildlife at Komodo National Park.

Indonesia for Kids

Travel outside cities requires patience, hardiness and experience – for both parents and kids. Most Indonesians adore children, especially ones touring their country; however, children may find the constant attention overwhelming. As one expat mum who has travelled with her family across Indonesia told us: 'It's actually easier with kids. People are more helpful than when you're alone as an adult. They want to make things easier for you.'

You will need to learn your child's age and sex in Bahasa Indonesia – *bulau* (month), *tahun* (year), *laki-laki* (boy) and *perempuan* (girl). You should also make polite enquiries about the other person's children, present or absent.

Children's Highlights

Outdoor Activities

➡ **Bali** (p197) Good for surfing and snorkelling and has classes geared to kids.

➡ **Pulau Bunaken, Sulawesi** (p688) Offers fabulous snorkelling where you can see dolphins, flying fish and more.

➡ **Kerinci Seblat National Park, Sumatra** (p563) Gentle hikes are popular with families.

STAYING SAFE

➡ A major danger to kids – and adults for that matter – is traffic and bad pavement and footpaths in busy areas.

➡ Check conditions carefully for any activity. Just because that rafting company sells tickets to families doesn't mean it accommodates the safety needs of children.

➡ Consider the health (p784) situation carefully, especially with regards to malaria and dengue fever.

➡ Rabies (p786) is a major problem, especially on Bali. Keep children away from stray animals, including cats, dogs and monkeys.

➡ As with adults, contaminated food and water present the most risks; children are more at risk from sunstroke and dehydration.

➡ Pharmaceutical supplies can usually be purchased in larger cities.

Animal-Spotting

➡ **Sacred Monkey Forest Sanctuary, Ubud** (p251) The primates here never cease to delight.

➡ **Camp Leakey, Kalimantan** (p601) Board a river trip to the province's best venue for families and the place to spot orangutans.

➡ **Komodo National Park, Nusa Tenggara** (p352) It's easy to see the fearsome dragons safely at this popular park.

Cultural Exchange

➡ **Temkessi, West Timor** (p390) Children can make friends with their peers in the ancient villages of this area.

➡ **Putussibau, Kalimantan** (p597) The communal living in the longhouses of the Kapuas Hulu region helps kids quickly make friends with their Dayak counterparts.

➡ **Yogyakarta, Java** (p111) A classic destination for Indonesian schoolkids and yours will enjoy its myriad cultural attractions as well.

Planning & Practicalities

Kid-friendly facilities are generally limited to Bali, which caters well to holidaying families. Elsewhere you will find Indonesia very hit or miss in terms of specifically catering to children, even as it warmly welcomes them.

What you bring from home and what you source in Indonesia largely depends on where you're going and what you'll need. As always, you can get most things you might need on Bali (or to a certain extent Lombok, Jakarta and Yogyakarta) but there is the trade-off of tracking down what you need and simply adding it to your luggage.

For very young children, the dilemma is to bring either a backpack carrier or a pram/stroller. If you can, bring both. Prams are tough going on uneven or nonexistent footpaths, but are worthwhile in south Bali and other developed areas.

Other considerations:

➡ Children's seats for cars are rare, or where they exist, may be of low quality.

➡ Sunscreen and mosquito repellent are difficult to reliably find on Bali and nonexistent other places.

➡ Baby wipes, disposable nappies (diapers) and baby formula are all readily available in cities and big towns but seldom elsewhere.

➡ Bali has a ready supply of babysitters (and lots of nightlife to divert parents). Elsewhere you will be providing the childcare.

➡ Nappy-changing facilities usually consist of the nearest discreet, flat surface.

➡ Breastfeeding in public is acceptable in areas such as Bali, Papua and Sumatra away from Aceh but virtually unseen in Maluku, Sulawesi and Kalimantan. In parts of west Java and the conservative islands of Nusa Tengarra it's inappropriate. Take your cue from local mothers.

➡ Hotels and guesthouses often have triple and family rooms, plus extra beds can be supplied on demand. Baby beds and highchairs, however, are uncommon.

➡ Larger resorts often have special programs and facilities for kids that include lots of activities during the day and evening.

➡ With widespread 3G data and wi-fi, a smartphone or tablet is handy so children can tell those at home about everything they're missing and have an easy escape from the trip itself.

Regions at a Glance

Indonesia's 17,000-odd islands are dominated by a few large ones. Sumatra, Java and Sulawesi are diverse places that have swathes of untouched lands. Kalimantan and Papua are part of even larger islands and offer plenty of opportunity for serious adventure and exploration. Java remains the heart of the country historically, culturally and economically. Nusa Tenggara and Maluku comprise hundreds of islands, from ever-more-popular Lombok to the relative isolation of the Banda Islands. Although small in size, Bali figures large for visitors, drawing half of Indonesia's tourists. As always, your biggest consideration will be managing the time on your visa.

Java

Culture
Volcanoes
Temples

Javanese culture fuses animist, Buddhist and Hindu influences with both mystic traditions and orthodox Islamic practices. Monuments, mosques and temples that reflect this spiritual complexity exist alongside a spectacular tropical landscape spiked with smoking volcanoes.

p48

Bali

Culture
Nightlife
Surfing

The rich culture of Bali is matched by its myriad attractions for visitors: excellent dining and nightlife, hundreds of good places to stay, famous beaches, epic surfing, alluring shopping and a gracious welcome.

p197

Nusa Tenggara

Surfing
Diving
Culture

Whether you're here for waves, or to dive deep underwater or into ancient cultures, Nusa Tenggara offers gifts unmatched. From Lombok to Timor via Flores you will be tempted, blessed, satiated and leave hungry for more.

p302

Maluku

Diving
Culture
Beaches

Empires rose and fell to control the precious spices of these diverse, beautiful islands. Push past their present-day isolation to discover brilliant coral gardens, jungle-swaddled volcanoes, mouldering colonial mansions and a history as rich as it is troubled.

p407

Papua

Diving & Snorkelling
Hiking
Tribal Culture

Remote Papua is an adventurer's fantasy. From high mountain valleys and snaking jungle rivers to translucent coastal waters teeming with life, it offers superb trekking and world-class diving among proud indigenous peoples whose traditions stand strong.

p450

Sumatra

Wildlife
Hiking
Surfing

Sumatra is one big, steamy, jungle-covered adventure where you can go from surfing some of the world's best waves and snorkelling amid pristine reefs to trekking through dense rainforest in search of orangutans or ascending active volcanoes.

p490

Kalimantan

River Journeys
Diving
Wildlife

Cut by countless rivers, Borneo's legendary rainforest attracts wildlife enthusiasts and hardened trekkers. Dayak longhouses preserve the rich communal culture of a forgotten era, while the underwater paradise of the Derawan Archipelago draws in-the-know divers.

p586

Sulawesi

Culture
Diving
Hiking

Wind your way through this crazy-shaped island of elaborate funeral ceremonies, trails through terraced rice fields and tarsier-filled jungles to coasts of abundant corals, thriving underwater fauna and cultures that revolve around the sea.

p636

On the Road

Sumatra
p490
Kalimantan
p586
Sulawesi
p636
Maluku
p407
Papua
p450
Java
p48
Nusa Tenggara
p302
Bali
p197

Java

Includes ➡

Why Go?

The heart of the nation, Java is an island of megacities, mesmerising natural beauty, magical archaeological sites and profound traditions in art, music and dance.

Boasting a dazzling array of bewitching landscapes – iridescent rice paddies, smoking volcanoes, rainforest and savannah, not to mention virgin beaches – most journeys here are defined by scenic excesses. The island is at its most excessive in the cities: crowded, polluted, concrete labyrinths that buzz and roar. Dive into Jakarta's addictive mayhem, soak up Yogyakarta's soul and stroll though Solo's batik laneways en route to the island's all-natural wonders.

Home to 140 million people and the most populated island on earth, Java travel can be slow going, particularly in the west. However, the rail network is generally reliable and efficient, and flights are inexpensive. Your endurance will be rewarded with fascinating insights into Indonesia's most complex and culturally compelling island.

Best Places to Eat

- ➡ Lara Djonggrang (p66)
- ➡ Mediterranea (p121)
- ➡ Lodges Ekologika on Portibi Farms (p83)
- ➡ Pasar Ikan, Pangandaran (p99)
- ➡ Por Que No (p65)

Best Places to Stay

- ➡ Hotel Tugu Malang (p172)
- ➡ Breve Azurine (p157)
- ➡ The Phoenix (p119)
- ➡ Hotel Indonesia Kempinski (p62)
- ➡ Bangsring Breeze (p195)

When to Go

Jakarta

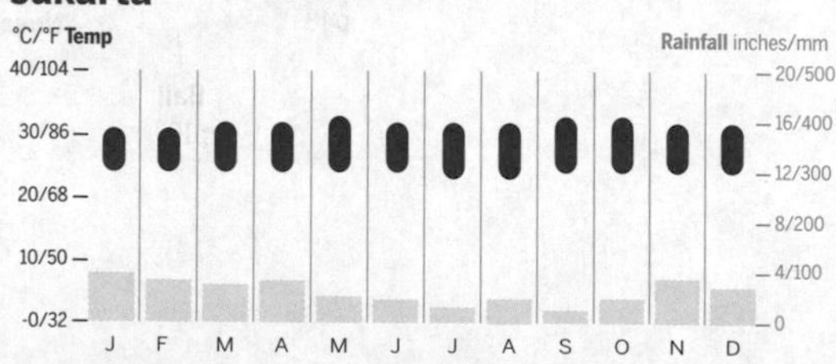

May Spectacular Waisak processions to mark the birth of Buddha in Borobudur.

Jun Perhaps the perfect month for travel, with clear skies and few crowds.

Oct The climax of the bull-racing season in Madura.

Java Highlights

1. Experiencing the ethereal beauty of **Borobudur temple** (p106) at sunrise.
2. Gazing over the horizon-filling moonscape scenery at **Gunung Bromo** (p183).
3. Hiking to the crater lake of **Kawah Ijen** (p188) with strong-armed sulphur miners.
4. Time travelling to Java's golden age in the cultural capital of **Yogyakarta** (p111).
5. Exploring magnificent national parks: **Ujung Kulon** (p77), **Meru Betiri** (p191), and **Alas Purwo** (p192).
6. Meeting the locals via a community tourism project in **Cianjur** (p86).
7. Getting off the road and experiencing the palm-fringed **Karimunjawa Islands** (p154).
8. Surfing Java's legendary waves at **Cimaja** (p83), **Batu Karas** (p101) or **G-Land** (p193).

History

Java has a history of epic proportions and a record of human habitation that extends back 1.7 million years to when 'Java Man' roamed the river banks. Waves of migrants followed, moving down through Southeast Asia.

Early Javanese Kingdoms

Blessed with exceptional fertility from its mineral-rich volcanic soil, Java has long played host to intensive *sawah* (wet rice) agriculture.

Small principalities emerged, including the Hindu Mataram dynasty, in the 8th century, with worship centred on the god Shiva. Hinduism coexisted with Buddhism for centuries, and the massive Hindu Prambanan complex was constructed within a century of Borobudur, the world's biggest Buddhist monument.

Mataram eventually fell, perhaps at the hands of the Sumatra-based Sriwijaya kingdom. The Javanese revival began in AD 1019 under King Airlangga, a semi-legendary figure who formed the first royal link with Bali.

Early in the 13th century the legendary Ken Angrok briefly succeeded in uniting much of Central and East Java, and Javanese culture flourished brightly.

With the emergence of the much-celebrated Majapahit kingdom, ruling from Trowulan, came the first Javanese commercial kingdom. The kingdom traded with China and most of Southeast Asia, and grew to claim sovereignty over the entire Indonesian archipelago.

Islamic Kingdoms

Islamic influence grew in Java in the 15th and 16th centuries, and Muslim military incursions into East Java forced many Hindu-Buddhists eastwards to Bali. By the 17th century, the Muslim kingdoms of Mataram and Banten were the only two powers in Java left to face the arrival of the Dutch.

Dutch Period

As the Dutch set up camp in Batavia (Jakarta), Banten remained a powerful force, but civil war within the royal house led to its eventual collapse.

The Mataram dynasty also became plagued by infighting, and following three Javanese Wars of Succession, the last in 1746, the Dutch split the kingdom, creating the royal houses of Solo and Yogyakarta.

Resistance to Dutch influence continued, erupting in the anti-Dutch Java War (1825–30), but the colonists defeated the revolts and subsequently Javanese courts became little more than ritual establishments, overseen by a Dutch *residen* (governor).

Java Today

Java still rules the roost when it comes to political and economic life in Indonesia. It has the bulk of the country's industry, is easily its most developed island, and has over the years received the lion's share of foreign investment.

The economic crisis of the late '90s hit hard, when huge numbers of urban workers lost their jobs and rioters targeted Chinese communities. But Java bounced back relatively quickly, and enjoyed a period of comparative stability and growing prosperity in the early 21st century. Glittering shopping malls and a boom in the tech business are the most obvious signs of Java's steady (if unspectacular) modernisation.

Bali apart, Java is the most outward-looking island in Indonesia, and its literate, educated population is the most closely connected to the rest of the world. Extraneous influences matter here, and Java is the most Westernised island in the country and also the corner of the nation most influenced by radical pan-Islamic ideology. While most Javanese are moderate Muslims, there's an increasingly vocal conservative population (as well as tiny numbers of fanatics prepared to cause death and destruction in the name of jihad). The Bali bombers all came from Java, and Java-based terrorists targeted foreign investments in Jakarta in 2003 and 2004, as well as several international hotels in 2009.

Today, Java can look to the future with some optimism. Thanks to an upsurge in foreign travel, its people are increasingly prosperous and cosmopolitan. But as the island develops at pace, pressing environmental issues (including pollution and the floods that threaten Jakarta most years) are an increasing threat. Infrastructure woes – inadequate highways and waste management, and a lack of investment in train and metro networks – also hamper growth. This makes the recent slide in the rupiah and economic struggles more predictable than surprising.

As of 2015, the latest trend in government has been conservative. One recent law banned the sale of beer in supermarkets and minimarts (later reversed), and another set a new national closing time for bars and clubs at midnight. However, the man running Jakarta, Governor Basuki 'Ahok' Tjahaja Purnama, is an anti-corruption progressive who

JAVA MAN

Charles Darwin's *On the Origin of Species* (1859) spawned a new generation of naturalists in the 19th century, and his theories sparked acrimonious debate across the world. Ernst Haeckel's *The History of Natural Creation* (1874) expounded Darwin's theory of evolution and surmised that primitive humans had evolved from a common ape-man ancestor, the famous 'missing link'.

One student of the new theories, Dutch physician Eugene Dubois, went to Java in 1889 after hearing of the uncovering of a skull at Wajak, near Tulung Agung in East Java. Dubois worked at the dig, uncovering other fossils closely related to modern humans. In 1891 at Trinil in East Java's Ngawi district, Dubois unearthed an older skullcap, along with a femur and three teeth he later classified as originating from *Pithecanthropus erectus*, a low-browed, prominent-jawed early human ancestor, dating from the Middle Pleistocene epoch. His published findings of 'Java Man' caused such a storm in Europe that Dubois buried his discovery for 30 years.

Since Dubois' findings, many older examples of *Homo erectus* (the name subsequently given to *Pithecanthropus erectus*) have been uncovered in Java. The most important and most numerous findings have been at Sangiran, where in the 1930s Ralph von Koenigswald found fossils dating back to around 1 million BC. In 1936, at Perning near Mojokerto, the skull of a child was discovered and was purported to be even older. Most findings have been along Sungai Bengawan Solo (Bengawan Solo River) in Central and East Java.

Geochronologists have now dated the bones of Java's oldest *Homo erectus* specimens at 1.7 million years, but also postulate that the youngest fossils may be less than 40,000 years old. This means that *Homo erectus* existed in Java at the same time as *Homo sapiens*, who arrived on the island some 60,000 years ago, and reignites the debate about whether humankind evolved in Africa and migrated from there, or whether humans evolved on several continents concurrently. Those interested in learning more should pick up a copy of Carl Swisher, Garniss Curtis and Roger Lewin's extremely readable book *Java Man*.

has become a folk hero for live streaming every meeting he has with government ministers and legislators. Corruption has long hindered fairness and growth in Java, and Ahok is hoping to buck that trend and establish a new mode of governance that can last.

Culture

Javanese culture is a rich mix of customs that date back to animist beliefs and Hindu times. Ancient practices are fused with endemic Muslim traditions, which retain mystical Sufi elements beneath a more obvious orthodox and conservative Islamic culture.

The Javanese cosmos is composed of different levels of belief stemming from older and more accommodating mysticism, the Hindu court culture and a very real belief in ghosts and numerous benevolent and malevolent spirits. Underneath the unifying code of Islam, magic power is concentrated in amulets and heirlooms (especially the Javanese dagger known as the kris); in parts of the human body, such as the nails and the hair; and in sacred musical instruments. The *dukun* (faith healer and herbal doctor or mystic) is still consulted when illness strikes. *Jamu* (herbal medicine) potions are widely taken to do everything from boost libido to cure asthma.

Refinement and politeness are highly regarded, and loud displays of emotion, coarseness, vulgarity and flamboyant behaviour are considered *kasar* (bad manners; coarse). *Halus* (refined) Javanese is part of the Hindu court tradition, which still exists in the heartland of Central Java. In contrast to Islam, the court tradition has a hierarchical world view, based on privilege and often guided by the gods or nature spirits.

Indirectness is a Javanese trait that stems from an unwillingness to make others feel uncomfortable. It is impolite to point out mistakes and sensitivities, or to directly criticise authority.

Java has three main ethnic groups, each speaking their own language: the Javanese of Central and East Java (where *halus* is taken very seriously); the Sundanese of West Java; and the Madurese from Pulau Madura (who have a reputation for blunt-speaking and informality). Small pockets of Hindus remain, including the Tenggerese of the Bromo area and the Badui of West Java, whose religion retains many animist beliefs. Even metropolitan Jakarta identifies its own polyglot tradition in the Betawi, the name for the original inhabitants of the city.

Getting There & Around

AIR

Jakarta has numerous international and domestic connections. Other useful international gateway Javanese cities are Surabaya, Solo, Bandung, Yogyakarta and Semarang. Domestic flights can be very convenient and affordable: Jakarta–Yogyakarta is a very popular route. If your time is short, it's worth booking a few internal flights to cut down on those hours on the road.

SEA

Very few travellers now use Pelni passenger ships, but there are connections between Jakarta and most ports in the nation. Ferries run round the clock between Banyuwangi/Ketapang harbour in East Java and Gilimanuk in Bali, and also between the Javanese port of Merak and Bakauheni in southern Sumatra.

BUS

Buses connect virtually anywhere and everywhere in Java, and also run to Sumatra, Bali and even Nusa Tenggara. Unfortunately Java's road network is woefully inadequate, so journeys tend to be very slow and tiring, particularly in the west of the island.

TRAIN

Java has a fairly punctual and efficient rail service running right across the island. Overall, train travel certainly beats long bus journeys, so try to take as many as you can. You can check timetables and make online bookings at www.kereta-api.co.id, though it's not very user-friendly.

Unfortunately, network capacity (many of the lines are single tracks) is very limited and demand often exceeds supply. During holiday periods trains are always booked weeks or months ahead.

JAKARTA

☎021 / POP 10.2 MILLION

One of the world's greatest megalopolises, Jakarta is a dynamic city of daunting extremes that's developing at a pace that throws up challenges and surreal juxtapositions on every street corner. An organism unto itself, this is a town in the midst of a very public metamorphosis, and despite the maddening traffic, life here is lived at an all-out pace, driven by an industriousness and optimism that's palpable. Dysfunction be damned.

Translation: it's no oil painting, yet beneath the unappealing facade of new build high-rises, relentless concrete and grid-locked streets, fringed with rickety slums and shrouded in a persistent blanket of smog, Jakarta has many faces and plenty of surprises. Its citizens – even the poorest among them – are remarkably good-natured and positive, and compared to many of the world's capitals, crime levels are low.

From the steamy, richly scented streets of Chinatown to North Jakarta's riotous, decadent nightlife, the city is filled with unexpected corners. Here it's possible to rub shoulders with Indonesia's future leaders, artists, thinkers, movers and shakers in a bohemian

TOP FIVE JAVA READS

- *A Shadow Falls: In the Heart of Java* by Andrew Beatty. Based on sustained research in a remote Javanese village, this study examines the cultural conflict between mystic Javanese traditionalists and orthodox Islam.
- *Jakarta Inside Out* by Daniel Ziv. A collection of humorous short stories tackling the vibrant underbelly of Indonesia's capital.
- *The Religion of Java* by Clifford Geertz. A classic book on Javanese religion, culture and values. It's slightly dated (it was based on research done in the 1950s) but is nonetheless fascinating reading.
- *Javanese Culture* by Koentjaraningrat. One of the most comprehensive studies of Javanese society, history, culture and beliefs. This excellent reference book covers everything from Javanese toilet training to kinship lines.
- *Raffles and the British Invasion of Java* by Tim Hannigan. An excellent, authoritative account of the brief period of British rule, and the role of Sir Thomas Stamford Raffles, in the early 19th century.

cafe or a sleek lounge bar and then go clubbing till dawn and beyond, the sober desires of current lawmakers notwithstanding.

History

Jakarta's earliest history centres on the port of Sunda Kelapa, in the north of the modern city. When the Portuguese arrived it was a bustling port in the last Hindu kingdom of West Java, but they were driven out in 1527 and the city was renamed Jayakarta, meaning 'victorious city'.

Dutch Rule

At the beginning of the 17th century the Dutch and English jostled for power in the region, with the Dutch prevailing. The city was renamed Batavia and made the capital of the Dutch East Indies, as Amsterdam-style houses and canals were constructed.

By 1740 ethnic unrest lead to the massacre of 5000 Chinese, and virtually the entire community was subsequently moved to Glodok, outside the city walls. Dutch colonial rule came to an end with the Japanese occupation in 1942 and the name Jakarta was restored.

Post Independence

Over the next four decades, the capital struggled under the weight of an ever-increasing population of poor migrants, but by the 1990s Jakarta's economic situation had turned around. This all changed, however, with the economic collapse of 1997. The capital quickly became a political battleground and the epicentre of protests demanding Suharto's resignation.

Jakarta erupted in rioting after the deaths of student protesters, as thousands took to the streets and looted malls. The Chinese were hardest hit, with shocking tales of rape and murder emerging after the riots.

The City Today

Jakarta has suffered on several fronts since the beginning of the 21st century. Severe floods (which strike every rainy season) frequently cause massive damage to homes and infrastructure, and in the early part of the millennium terrorists targeted Western interests, bombing US-owned hotels and the Australian embassy with terrifying frequency. But that all seemed to change around the time Barack Obama, today considered a favourite son of Indonesia, was elected US president, which coincided with Indonesia's abundance of natural resources translating into favourable trade deals and a gathering economy. That, along with Thailand's political turmoil, placed Indonesia on a shortlist of countries that managed to avoid the global recession.

But in the past several years, the currency has tanked and the economy has begun to grind to a halt along with countless development projects. Of late, there has also been a series of regressive regulations passed by federal lawmakers targeting the bar and nightlife industry. First there was the so-called beer ban, in which beer was no longer available in minimarts and liquor stores. That law was later reversed after popular outcry (though good luck finding it in most Javanese minimarts). More recently, the so-called no-fun initiative dictates all bars and clubs are to close at midnight. However, the law was not well enforced at press time, and time will tell if it lasts at all.

Through it all, Jakarta's public transport system has remained hopelessly inefficient compared with many Chinese cities, Bangkok and Kuala Lumpur, and there remains much to be done before Jakarta becomes a modern metropolis.

Sights

Kota

Despite its nooks of fun and culture, to the uninitiated Jakarta can feel overwhelming and its gifts inaccessible. Kota is where they're easy to find.

The old town of Batavia, now known as Kota, was the hub of Dutch colonial Indonesia. Today, it's a faded vision of a once-grand empire, replete with crumbling historic buildings and stinky canals where handicrafts and art are sold on the street. Some of the whitewashed Dutch colonial buildings have been turned into museums and cavernous cafes as elegant as they are lazy, often with good tunes on the stereo, but with so many fine old structures still vacant there remains loads of room for growth.

Taman Fatahillah, Kota's central cobblestone square, surrounded by imposing colonial buildings including the former town hall, is where you can get your bearings. A block west of the square is **Kali Besar**, the great canal along Sungai Ciliwung (Ciliwung River), lined with once-grand homes of the wealthy, most built in the early 18th century. Check out the red-tiled facade of **Toko Merah** (Map p56; Jl Kali Besar Barat, Red Shop), the former home of Governor General

Jakarta

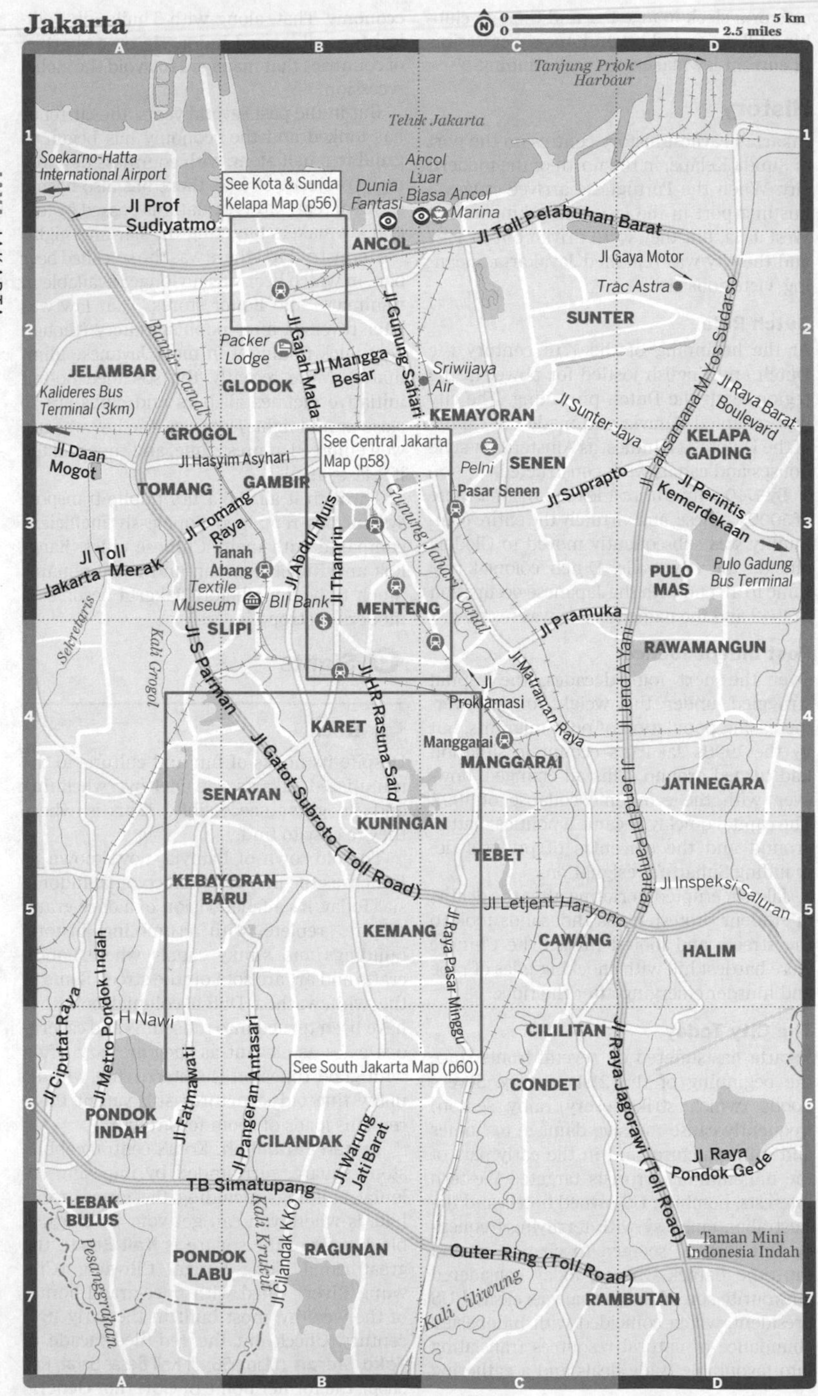

0 5 km
0 2.5 miles
Tanjung Priok Harbour
Teluk Jakarta
Soekarno-Hatta International Airport
Jl Prof Sudiyatmo
See Kota & Sunda Kelapa Map (p56)
Dunia Fantasi
Ancol Luar Biasa Ancol
Marina
Jl Toll Pelabuhan Barat
ANCOL
Jl Gaya Motor
Trac Astra
SUNTER
Jl Gajah Mada
Jl Gunung Sahari
Packer Lodge
Jl Mangga Besar
Sriwijaya Air
JELAMBAR
Kalideres Bus Terminal (3km)
GLODOK
Banjir Canal
KEMAYORAN
Jl Laksamana M Yos Sudarso
Jl Raya Barat Boulevard
Jl Sunter Jaya
KELAPA GADING
GROGOL
See Central Jakarta Map (p58)
Jl Daan Mogot
Jl Hasyim Asyhari
Pelni
SENEN
TOMANG
GAMBIR
Pasar Senen
Jl Suprapto
Jl Perintis Kemerdekaan
Jl Tomang Raya
Gunung Jahari Canal
Jl Abdul Muis
Jl Thamrin
Pulo Gadung Bus Terminal
Jl Toll Jakarta Merak
Tanah Abang
PULO MAS
Textile Museum
BII Bank
MENTENG
Sekretaris
SLIPI
Jl Pramuka
Kali Grogol
RAWAMANGUN
Jl S Parman
Jl HR Rasuna Said
Jl Proklamasi
Jl Matraman Raya
Jl Jend A Yani
KARET
Jl Gatot Subroto (Toll Road)
Manggarai
MANGGARAI
SENAYAN
Jl Jend DI Panjaitan
JATINEGARA
KUNINGAN
TEBET
KEBAYORAN BARU
Jl Inspeksi Saluran
Jl Letjent Haryono
KEMANG
Jl Raya Pasar Minggu
CAWANG
HALIM
Jl Metro Pondok Indah
Jl Ciputat Raya
H Nawi
CILILITAN
Jl Raya Jagorawi (Toll Road)
See South Jakarta Map (p60)
Jl Fatmawati
Jl Pangeran Antasari
CONDET
PONDOK INDAH
CILANDAK
Jl Warung Jati Barat
Jl Raya Pondok Gede
TB Simatupang
LEBAK BULUS
Kali Krukut
Jl Cilandak KKO
Pesanggrahan
PONDOK LABU
RAGUNAN
Outer Ring (Toll Road)
Taman Mini Indonesia Indah
Kali Ciliwung
RAMBUTAN

van Imhoff. At the northern end of Kali Besar is the last remaining Dutch drawbridge, the Chicken Market Bridge, which dates from the 17th century.

Walking along the canal to the restored drawbridge, you'll see real life unfold. Bemo (minibus) drivers getting massages, playing chess, and eating *bakso* (meatball soup) curbside before their shift. Laundry drying on the railings. Here are garbage dumps and florists, and all manner of cottage industries half-hidden behind courtyards of relics. This is Jakarta's subsistence poetry of struggle and will.

To reach Taman Fatahillah, take the busway Korridor I from Blok M or Jl Thamrin to Kota train station and walk. Trains from Gondangdia, near Jl Jaksa, also run here. A taxi will cost around 40,000Rp from Jl Thamrin.

Museum Bank Indonesia MUSEUM

(Map p56; Pintu Besar Utara III; audio guides 50,000Rp; ⌚8am-3.30pm Tue-Thu, 8-11.30am & 1-3.30pm Fri, 8am-4pm Sat & Sun) FREE One of the nation's best, this museum is dedicated to the history of Indonesia from a loosely financial perspective, in a grand, expertly restored, neoclassical former bank headquarters that dates from the early 20th century. All the displays (including lots of zany audiovisuals) are slickly presented on flatscreens and engaging, with exhibits about the spice trade and the financial meltdown of 1997 (and subsequent riots) as well as a gallery dedicated to currency, with notes from virtually every country in the world.

Museum Sejarah Jakarta MUSEUM

(Map p56; Taman Fatahillah; admission 5000Rp; ⌚9am-3pm Tue-Sun) Also known as Museum Kesejarahan Jakarta, the Jakarta History Museum is housed in the old town hall of Batavia, a stately Dutch colonial structure that was once the epicentre of an empire. This bell-towered building, built in 1627, served the administration of the city and was also used by the city law courts. Today, it's a poorly presented museum of peeling plasterwork and lots of heavy, carved ebony and teak furniture from the Dutch period.

But you will find the odd exquisite piece, such as the stunning black granite sculpture of Kali, a Hindu goddess associated with death and destruction. There are longstanding plans to renovate the museum, but work had been delayed at the time of research.

Museum Wayang MUSEUM

(Map p56; ☎021-692 9560; Taman Fatahillah; admission 5000Rp; ⌚9am-3pm Tue-Sun) This puppet museum has one of the best collections of *wayang* puppets in Java and its dusty cabinets are full of a multitude of characters from across Indonesia, as well as China, Vietnam, India, Cambodia and Europe. The building itself dates from 1912. There are free *wayang* performances here on Sunday at 10am. Be warned: we have received reports of a scam involving freelance guides who pressure people into making exorbitant purchases after a tour of the exhibits.

Museum Bank Mandiri MUSEUM

(Map p56; Jl Pintu Besar Utara; ⌚9am-3pm Tue-Sun) FREE In complete contrast to the polish and modernity at the Museum Bank Indonesia next door, this banking museum is all but empty, with echoing corridors and deserted tills. Nevertheless, it's fascinating to explore the interior of this fine art deco structure, marvelling at the marble counters and vintage counting machines, abacuses and colossal cast-iron safes.

Balai Seni Rupa MUSEUM

(Map p56; Taman Fatahillah; admission 5000Rp; ⌚9am-3pm Tue-Sun) Built between 1866 and 1870, the former Palace of Justice building is now a fine arts museum. It houses contemporary paintings with works by prominent artists, including Affandi, Raden Saleh and Ida Bagus Made. Part of the building is also a ceramics museum, with Chinese ceramics and Majapahit terracottas.

Gereja Sion CHURCH

(Map p56; Jl Pangeran Jayakarta) FREE Dating from 1695, this is the oldest remaining church in Jakarta. Also known as Gereja Portugis (Portuguese Church), it was built just outside the old city walls for slaves captured from Portuguese trading ports. The exterior of the church is very plain, but inside there are copper chandeliers, a baroque pulpit and the original organ.

Sunda Kelapa

A kilometre north of Taman Fatahillah, the old port of **Sunda Kelapa** (admission 2000Rp) is full of magnificent Makassar schooners (*pinisi*). The dock scene here has barely changed for centuries, with porters unloading cargo from sailing ships by hand and trolley, though it's far less busy today.

Kota & Sunda Kelapa

Kota & Sunda Kelapa

Sights

1 Balai Seni Rupa C3
2 Gereja Sion C3
3 Jin De Yuan B4
4 Museum Bahari A1
5 Museum Bank Indonesia B3
6 Museum Bank Mandiri B3
7 Museum Sejarah Jakarta B3
8 Museum Wayang B3
9 Petak Sembilan Street Market B4
10 Toko Merah B3
11 Watchtower A1

Eating

12 Café Batavia B3
13 Historia B3
14 Kedai Seni Djakarté B3
15 Santong Kuo Tieh 68 .... B4
Warung Kota Tua .... (see 14)

Drinking & Nightlife

Café Batavia .... (see 12)

Shopping

16 Mangga Dua Mall D3

Sadly, the atmospheric **Pasar Ikan** (Fish Market) – always a tourist favourite – was destroyed by fire and relocated, but if you make your way to the Museum Bahari you will likely make the acquaintance of **Pak Catur** (☎ 0852 1763 4281), who will offer a motorbike ride through the working harbour and into the nearby Muara Baru slum, as well as a buzz through Glodok that you won't soon forget. This is the real, manic, overpopulated Jakarta, bursting with humanity and pain. It's not for the fainthearted. As Pak Catur says, 'price depend on you'.

Museum Bahari MUSEUM

(Map p56; www.museumbahari.org; admission 5000Rp; ⌚9am-3pm Tue-Sun) Near the entrance to Sunda Kelapa, several old VOC warehouses (dating back to 1652) have been converted into the Museum Bahari. This is a good place to learn about the city's maritime history, and though the wonderful old buildings (some renovated) are echoingly empty, there are some good information panels (in English and Bahasa Indonesia).

Under the heavy wooden beams of the vast old storage premises are various random exhibits: a sextant (used for astronomical navigation), various traditional boats from around Indonesia, the shell of a giant clam, plenty of pickled fish and a lighthouse lamp or two. The sentry posts outside are part of the old city wall.

Watchtower HISTORIC BUILDING

(Map p56; admission 5000Rp) Just before the entrance to the Museum Bahari is a watchtower, built in 1839 to sight and direct traffic to the port. There are good views over the harbour, but opening hours are haphazard – ask for the caretaker if it is closed.

Glodok

The neighbourhood of Glodok, the traditional enclave of the Chinese community, is an archetypal downtown district full of bustling lanes, street markets, a shabby mall or two and some of the world's most decadent nightlife. It was also the site of the terrible riots of May and November 1998, which reduced huge swathes of the area to ash and rubble.

Most of the fun here is simply experiencing the (very) Chinese vibe of the place, eating some dumplings and browsing the myriad stalls and stores selling everything from traditional medicine to dodgy DVDs.

Jin De Yuan BUDDHIST TEMPLE

(Dharma Bhakti Temple; Map p56; www.jindeyuan.org; Jl Kemenangan III 13) FREE This large Chinese Buddhist temple compound dates from 1755 and is one of the most important in the city. The main structure has an unusual roof crowned by two dragons eating pearls, while the interior is richly atmospheric: dense incense and candle smoke waft over Buddhist statues, ancient bells and drums, and some wonderful calligraphy. Unfortunately recent Chinese New Year celebrations – including fireworks – set fire to half of the original structure. It was undergoing reconstruction when we visited.

Petak Sembilan Street Market MARKET

(Map p56) Be sure to wander down the impossibly narrow Petak Sembilan street market off Jl Pancoran, lined with crooked houses with red-tiled roofs. It's a total assault on the senses, with skinned frogs and live bugs for sale next to an open sewer.

Central Jakarta

If a centre for this sprawling city had to be chosen, then Merdeka Square (Lapangan Merdeka) would be it. This huge grassy expanse is home to Sukarno's monument to the nation, and is surrounded by a couple of museums and some fine colonial buildings.

★**Museum Nasional** MUSEUM

(Map p58; ☎021-381 1551; www.museumnasional.or.id; Jl Merdeka Barat 12; admission 10,000Rp; ⌚8am-4pm Tue-Fri, 8am-5pm Sat-Sun) The National Museum, built in 1862, is the best of its kind in Indonesia and an essential visit. The enormous collection begins around an open courtyard stacked with magnificent millennia old statuary including a colossal 4.5m stone image of a Bhairawa king from Rambahan in Sumatra, who is shown trampling on human skulls. The ethnology section is superb, with Dayak puppets and wooden statues from Nias sporting beards (a sign of wisdom) plus some fascinating textiles.

Over in the spacious new wing there are four floors with sections devoted to the origin of mankind in Indonesia, including a model of the Flores 'hobbit'. There's also a superb display of gold treasures from Candi Brahu in Central Java: glittering necklaces, armbands and a bowl depicting scenes from the *Ramayana*.

The Indonesian Heritage Society organises free English tours of the National Museum, at 10.30am on Tuesdays, and on Thursdays at 10.30am and 1.30pm. Tours are also available in French, Japanese and Korean and at other times; consult the website for the latest schedule.

Lapangan Banteng NEIGHBOURHOOD

(Banteng Sq; Map p58) Just east of Merdeka Sq, Lapangan Banteng has some of Jakarta's best colonial architecture. The **twin-spired Catholic cathedral** (Map p58; Jl Katedral 7B) was built in 1901. Directly opposite is Jakarta's principal place of Muslim worship. The striking, modernist **Mesjid Istiqlal** (Map p58; Jl Veteran I) FREE, highlighted by geometrically grated windows, was designed by Catholic architect Frederich Silaban and completed

Central Jakarta

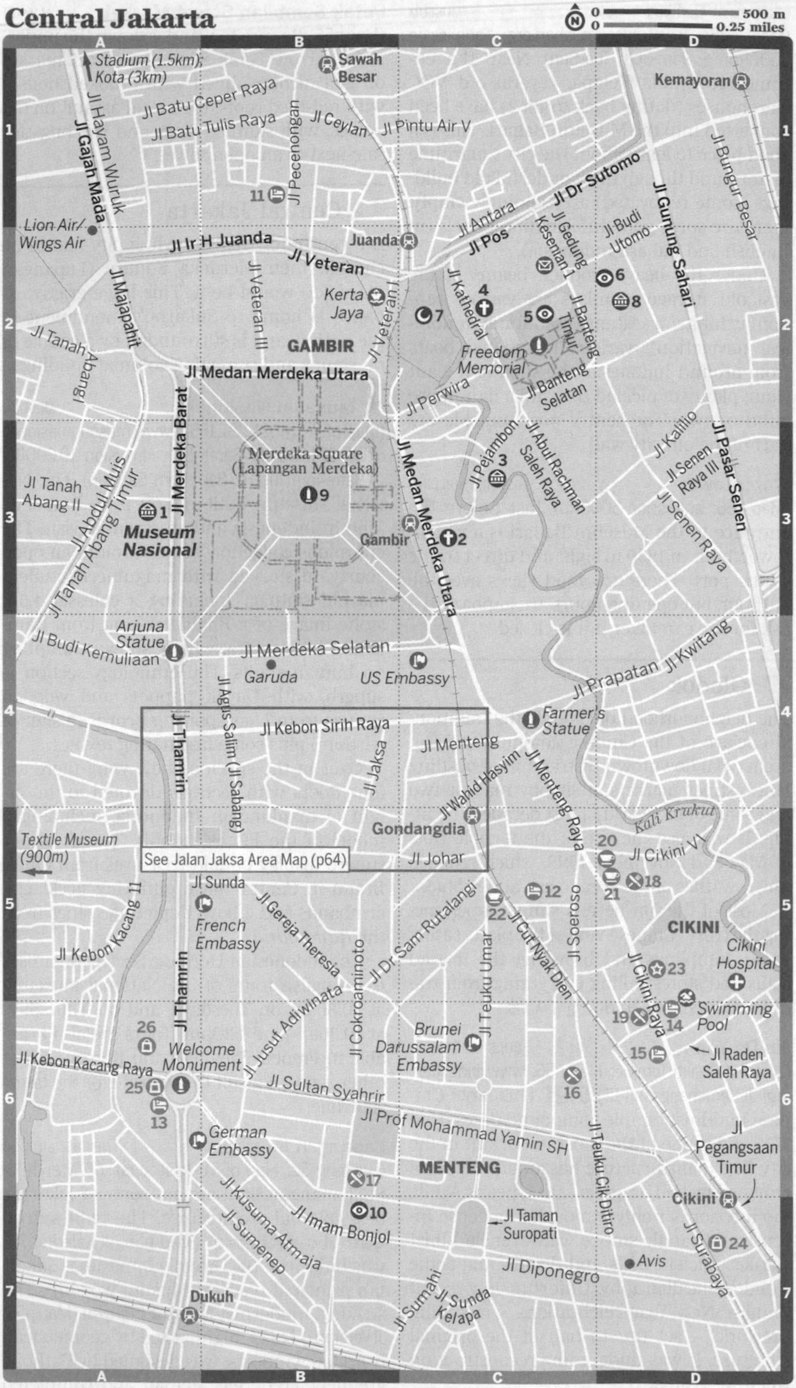

0 — 500 m
0 — 0.25 miles

Stadium (1.5km); Kota (3km)
Sawah Besar
Kemayoran
Jl Batu Ceper Raya
Jl Batu Tulis Raya
Jl Pecenongan
Jl Ceylan
Jl Pintu Air V
Jl Hayam Wuruk
Jl Gajah Mada
Jl Dr Sutomo
Jl Bungur Besar
Jl Gunung Sahari
11
Lion Air/Wings Air
Jl Ir H Juanda
Juanda
Jl Antara
Jl Pos
Jl Gedung Kesenian 1
Jl Budi Utomo
Jl Veteran
6
8
Jl Majapahit
Jl Veteran III
Kerta Jaya
Jl Veteran I
4
Jl Kathedral
7
5
Jl Banteng Timur
GAMBIR
Jl Tanah Abang I
Freedom Memorial
Jl Medan Merdeka Utara
Jl Banteng Selatan
Jl Perwira
Jl Merdeka Barat
Merdeka Square (Lapangan Merdeka)
Jl Medan Merdeka Utara
3
Jl Pejambon
Jl Abul Rachman Saleh Raya
Jl Kalilio
Jl Senen Raya III
Jl Pasar Senen
Jl Tanah Abang II
Jl Abdul Muis
Jl Tanah Abang Timur
1
Museum Nasional
9
Gambir
2
Jl Senen Raya
Arjuna Statue
Jl Budi Kemuliaan
Jl Merdeka Selatan
Garuda
US Embassy
Jl Prapatan
Jl Kwitang
Jl Agus Salim (Jl Sabang)
Jl Thamrin
Jl Kebon Sirih Raya
Jl Menteng
Farmer's Statue
Jl Jaksa
Jl Wahid Hasyim
Jl Menteng Raya
Gondangdia
Kali Krukut
Textile Museum (900m)
See Jalan Jaksa Area Map (p64)
Jl Johar
20
Jl Cikini V
21
18
Jl Sunda
12
Jl Soeroso
22
French Embassy
Jl Gereja Theresia
Jl Dr Sam Rutalangi
Jl Cut Nyak Dien
CIKINI
Jl Kebon Kacang II
Jl Cokroaminoto
Jl Teuku Umar
Jl Cikini Raya
23
Cikini Hospital
Jl Thamrin
Jl Jusuf Adiwinata
Brunei Darussalam Embassy
19
14
Swimming Pool
26
Welcome Monument
15
Jl Raden Saleh Raya
Jl Kebon Kacang Raya
25
Jl Sultan Syahrir
16
13
Jl Prof Mohammad Yamin SH
Jl Teuku Cik Ditiro
Jl Pegangsaan Timur
German Embassy
MENTENG
17
Cikini
Jl Kusuma Atmaja
10
Jl Taman Suropati
Jl Sumenep
Jl Imam Bonjol
Jl Surabaya
24
Jl Diponegro
Avis
Dukuh
Jl Sumahi
Jl Sunda Kelapa

Central Jakarta

Top Sights
1 Museum Nasional ... A3

Sights
2 Emanuel Church ... C3
3 Gedung Pancasila ... C3
4 Gereja Katerdral Jakarta ... C2
5 Lapangan Banteng ... C2
6 Mahkamah Agung ... D2
7 Mesjid Istiqlal ... C2
8 Ministry of Finance Building ... D2
9 Monas ... B3
10 SDN Menteng 1 School ... B7

Sleeping
11 Alila Jakarta ... B1
12 Gondia International Guesthouse ... C5
13 Hotel Indonesia Kempinski ... A6
14 Ibis Budget Hotel ... D6
15 Six Degrees ... D6

Eating
16 Lara Djonggrang ... C6
17 Por Que No ... B6
18 Vietopia ... D5
19 Warung Daun ... D6

Drinking & Nightlife
20 Bakoel Koffie ... D5
21 Dua Nyonya ... D5
22 Kunstkring Paleis ... C5

Entertainment
23 Taman Ismail Marzuki ... D5

Shopping
24 Flea Market ... D7
25 Grand Indonesia ... A6
26 Plaza Indonesia ... A6

in 1978. The mosque has five levels, representing the five pillars of Islam; its dome is 45m across and its minaret tops 90m.

During Ramadan more than 200,000 worshippers can be accommodated here. Non-Muslim visitors are welcome. You have to sign in first and then you'll be shown around by an English-speaking guide (who will expect a tip).

To the east of Lapangan Banteng is the **Mahkamah Agung** (Supreme Court; Map p58), built in 1848, and next door is the colonial **Ministry of Finance Building** (Map p58; off Jl Dr Wahidin), formerly the Witte Huis (White House), which dates from 1809 and was the administrative centre for the Dutch.

To the southwest is **Gedung Pancasila** (Map p58; Jl Pejambon), which is an imposing neoclassical building built in 1830 as the Dutch army commander's residence. It later became the meeting hall of the Volksraad (People's Council), but is best known as the place where Sukarno made his famous Pancasila speech in 1945, laying the foundation for Indonesia's constitution. Just west along Jl Pejambon from Gedung Pancasila is the **Emanuel Church** (Map p58; Jl Pejambon), another classic building dating from 1893.

Monas MONUMENT
(Monumen Nasional; Map p58; Merdeka Sq; museum entry 5,000Rp, to reach the top 10,000Rp; 8.30am-5pm, closed last Mon of month) Ingloriously dubbed 'Sukarno's final erection', this 132m-high National Monument, which rises into the shroud of smog and towers over Merdeka Sq, is both Jakarta's principal landmark and the most famous architectural extravagance of the former president. Begun in 1961, Monas was not completed until 1975, when it was officially opened by Suharto. The monument is constructed from Italian marble, and is topped with a sculpted flame, gilded with 35kg of gold leaf.

Entrance to the monument is via an underground tunnel behind it as you approach from the park entrance.

Textile Museum MUSEUM
(021-392 0331; www.museumtekstiljakarta.com; Jl Aipda KS Tubun 2-4; admission 10,000Rp; 9am-3pm Tue-Sun) Very much a worthwhile visit if you've any interest in weavings and fabrics, this museum houses a collection of around 2000 precious textiles, including hundreds of batik pieces, both antique and contemporary, lots of looms and a garden containing plants used for natural dyes. It's about 2km southwest of Merdeka Sq, and not easily reached by public transport.

Activities

Massage

Jakarta has massage establishments that range from ultra-luxe spas to dodgy set-ups that are fronts for brothels. The hygienic

South Jakarta

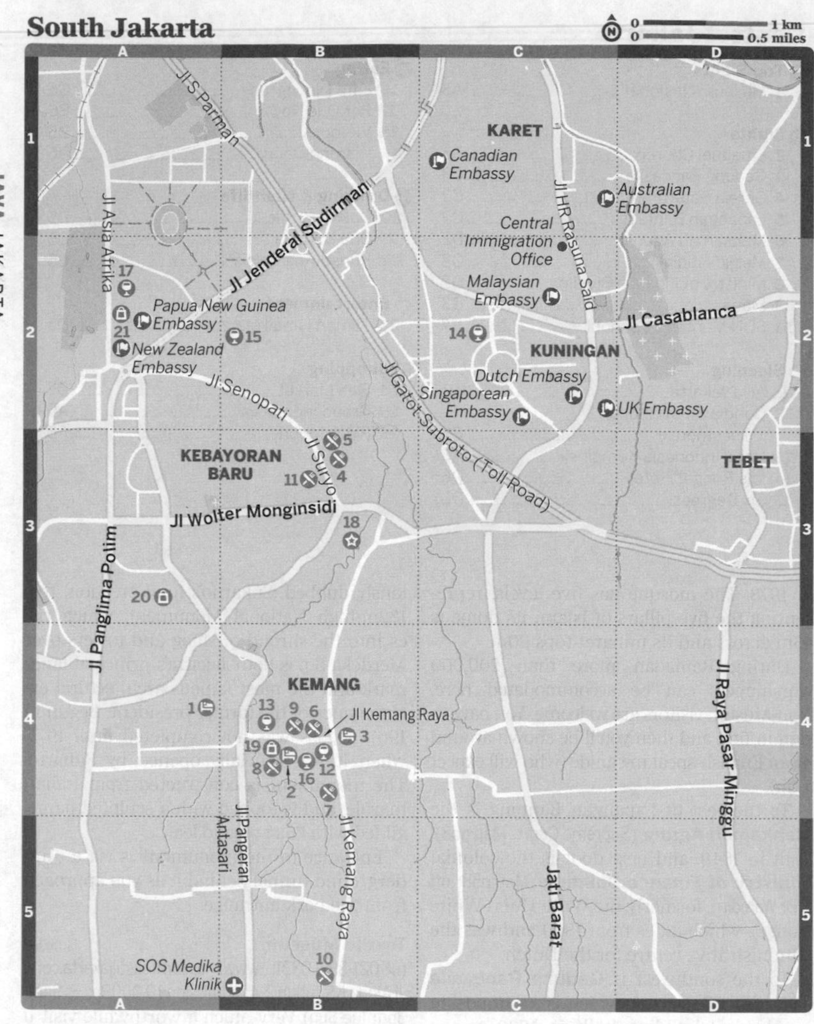

and affordable massage and sauna facilities at **Bersih Sehat** (Map p64; ☎021-390 0204; www.bersihsehat.com; Jl Wahid Hasyim 106; treatments from 70,000Rp; ⏲10am-9pm) are highly recommended.

For a really memorable experience, head to **Jamu Traditional Spa** (☎021-765 9691; www.jamutraditionalspa.com; Jl Cipete VIII/94B, Cipete; massage & treatments 95,000-1,000,000Rp; ⏲8am-9pm) in south Jakarta, which uses *jamu* (Indonesian herbs with medicinal and restorative properties) for its treatments.

Tours

Numerous travel agencies offer daily tours of Jakarta. Bookings can be made through the tourist office and major hotels.

Hidden Jakarta Tours GUIDED TOUR
(☎0812 803 5297; www.realjakarta.blogspot.com; US$50 per person) Want to see the other Jakarta, away from air-conditioned malls? This company offers tours of the city's traditional *kampung*, the urban villages of the poor. These tours take you along trash-choked riverways, into cottage industry factories and allow you to take tea in residents' homes.

South Jakarta

Sleeping

1 Dharmawangsa A4
2 Fave Hotel B4
3 Kemang Icon B4

Eating

4 Cantina 18 .... B3
5 Darling Rice Club B3
6 D'Fest B4
7 Kampung Kemang B4
8 Parc 19 .... B4
9 Payon B4
10 Toscana B5
11 Tredici B3
Warung Turki .... (see 7)

Drinking & Nightlife

12 365 Ecobar B4
13 Eastern Promise B4
14 Potato Head C2
15 Potato Head Garage B2
16 Tree House B4
17 X2 .... A2

Entertainment

18 Phoenix B3

Shopping

19 Colony B4
20 Pasaraya A3
Perimter .... (see 3)
Periplus .... (see 19)
21 Plaza Senayan A2

Festivals & Events

Independence Day CULTURAL
Indonesia's independence is celebrated on 17 August; the parades in Jakarta are the biggest in the country.

Java Jazz Festival MUSIC
(www.javajazzfestival.com) Held at the Jakarta Convention Center in early March in Senayan. Attracts acclaimed international artists, including jazz heavyweights like Ramsey Lewis and Brad Mehldau. Crossover pop stars such as Bobby McFerrin and Meshell Ndegeocello played in 2015.

Jakarta Anniversary FAIR
The 22nd of June marks the establishment of the city in 1527. Celebrated with fireworks and the Jakarta Fair.

Jalan Jaksa Street Fair CULTURAL
Features Betawi dance, theatre and music, art and photography. Held for one week in August.

Indonesian Dance Festival DANCE
(www.facebook.com/indonesiandancefestival) Features contemporary and traditional performances at the Taman Ismail Marzuki (p69) in November.

JiFFest FILM
(Jakarta International Film Festival; ☎021-3005 6090; www.muvila.com/jiffest) Internationally sponsored and lauded, Indonesia's premier film festival is held in November and December.

Sleeping

Backpackers be prepared: Jakarta lacks good budget options, so book ahead or consider a midrange option (which are plentiful). At the luxury end of the market, there are some excellent deals with four-star hotels available from as low as US$70 per night.

Jalan Jaksa Area

Once Jakarta's backpacking hub, though travellers are thin on the ground these days, probably because most hotels on Jl Jaksa are grungy if not sleazy. That said, you will find a selection of restaurants and bars, as well as some terrific midrange options on nearby Jl Wayid Hasim and Jl Sabang. The location, near Jl Thamrin (for the busway) and Gambir train station, remains excellent.

Hostel 35 GUESTHOUSE $
(Map p64; ☎021-392 0331; Jl Kebon Sirih Barat I 35; r with fan/air-con 150,000/250,000Rp; ❄📶) A good option for the price. The clean, if aged, tiled rooms have high ceilings and come with breakfast, and the lobby/lounge area with rattan sofas is inviting and decorated with fine textiles and tasteful photography.

★**Kosenda Hotel** BOUTIQUE HOTEL $$
(Map p64; ☎021-3193 6868; kosendahotel.com; Jl KH Wahid Hasyim 127; r from 750,000Rp; ❄📶) Hip but not overbearing, minimalist and modern but comfortable, rooms aren't huge but they are very clean and tastefully designed with wall-length built-in desks, floating beds and glass-box baths. Prices are a steal when offered on booking websites. It does a lovely

OBAMA IN JAKARTA

Barack Obama moved to Jakarta in 1967 following his mother's marriage to Lolo Soetoro, an Indonesian geographer; the couple met while studying at the University of Hawaii. Obama lived for four years in the Indonesian capital, including a period in the exclusive central suburb of Menteng, where he attended the **SDN Menteng 1** (Map p58) government-run school. The school is still going strong and there's a plaque at the front gate, as well as a Barry statue in the yard, commemorating its most famous alumnus.

A popular child, he was nicknamed 'Barry' by his fellow students. It's been reported that he declared an ambition to become president while at this school. Obama lived close by on Jl Taman Amir Hamzah, in a handsome terracotta-tiled Dutch villa with art deco–style windows.

When asked if he missed anything from his time in the country, Obama, who speaks Bahasa Indonesia, said he dreamed of '*bakso* (meatball soup), nasi goreng (fried rice) and *rambutan* (a red fruit similar to lychee)'.

On his return to the city as president in 2010, he confessed, 'I barely recognise it. When I first came here in 1967, everyone rode on becaks (bicycle rickshaws).'

breakfast buffet, makes excellent coffee, has a good 24-hour restaurant in the lobby and a superb rooftop bar.

Max One HOTEL **$$**
(Map p64; ☎021-316 6888; www.maxonehotels.com; Jl Agus Salim 24; r from 550,000Rp; ❄@📶) A moderately priced hip hotel. Rooms are smallish but nicely styled, with a pleasing pastel colour scheme. We love the steep weekend discounts, in-house minimart and excellent location.

Hotel Cipta HOTEL **$$**
(Map p64; ☎021-3193 0424; www.ciptahotel.com; Jl KH Wahid Hasyim 53; r 580,000Rp; ❄📶) Looking like a cross between an alpine mountain lodge and a pagoda, Cipta is not fabulous, but its clean, carpeted rooms with wood furnishings are comfortable and bright enough, and bathrooms sparkle. Weekend discounts plummet to 330,000Rp. If you can book at that price, you'll be thrilled.

Cikini & Menteng

Cikini (south) and Menteng (southeast) of Jaksa have a selection of decent midrange hotels, a guesthouse or two and some excellent restaurants and cafes.

Six Degrees HOSTEL **$**
(Map p58; ☎021-314 1657; www.jakarta-backpackers-hostel.com; Jl Cikini Raya 60B-C, Cikini; dm 125,000-160,000Rp, d 280,000Rp; ❄@📶) Set in a mini-mall, this hostel – run by a helpful and friendly Irish/English/Sumatran team – remains popular with travellers. There's a relaxed, sociable atmosphere, a pool table and TV room, a guests' kitchen and roof garden. Dorms are tight but clean; breakfast is included. It's tricky to find, but located right opposite the Ibis Budget Hotel.

Gondia International Guesthouse GUESTHOUSE **$**
(Map p58; ☎021-390 9221; gondiaguesthouse.com; Jl Gondangdia Kecil 22; r 400,000-500,000Rp; ❄) This modest-looking guesthouse, with hostel-esque signage, occupies a leafy garden plot on a quiet suburban street and has spacious tiled rooms. Breakfast included.

Ibis Budget Hotel HOTEL **$$**
(Map p58; ☎021-3190 8188; www.ibis.com; Jl Cikini Raya 75; r from 571,000Rp; ❄📶🏊) A modern 3-star hotel in a good location. It's institutional but clean, with flat-screen TVs and wi-fi. Downstairs there are several restaurants, a minimart, and you'll find a huge pool right behind the hotel.

★**Hotel Indonesia Kempinski** HOTEL **$$$**
(Map p58; ☎021-2358 3800; kempinski.com; Jl Thamrin 1; r from 2,500,000Rp; ❄@📶🏊) Formerly Hotel Indonesia, Jakarta's original luxury hotel, this renovated and re-imagined beauty still delivers the glamour. Upper-level rooms are huge with tasteful rugs and black wood floors, sumptuous marble baths, glass desks, ergonomic desk chairs, wood furnishings, quality linens and firm beds.

Factor in the rooftop pool, gym and spa, the decadent buffet breakfast, and its location on the traffic circle, and you have an ideal Jakarta launch pad. Best rates are online via booking websites or through local travel agents.

Other Areas

Packer Lodge HOSTEL $

(☎021-629 0162; www.thepackerlodge.com; Jl Kermunian IV 20-22; dm 145,000-155,000Rp, s 205,000-215,000Rp, d 310,000Rp;) The new cute hostel on the block, this self-annointed, owner-operated boutique hostel set in Glodok offers hip, Ikea-chic environs and plenty of amenities close to Kota. Choose among the four- or eight-bed dorms where the bunks are curtained pods with electrical outlets, lights and USB charger. Earplugs included.

The singles and doubles have less personality but more privacy. All share common Western baths and a spacious common kitchen. Activities and smiles abound.

Fave Hotel HOTEL $$

(Map p60; ☎021-718 1320; favehotels.com; Jl Kemang 16, Kemang; r from 421,200Rp) Modern and creative, this edition of the Indonesian, three-star micro-hotel offers small but liveable quarters with room service, pre-fab furnishings, plush linens and not much else. Still solid value.

★ **Kemang Icon** BOUTIQUE HOTEL $$$

(Map p60; ☎021-719 7989; www.alilahotels.com/kemangicon; Jl Kemang Raya I; r from 1,751,000Rp;) Terrific all-suite hip hotel with gorgeous rooms, kitted out with cutting-edge design and state-of-the-art bathrooms. It has a rooftop lap pool, a fine restaurant, and the staff go the extra mile to help out guests. The atrium lobby is fabulous, and so is the cool art gallery, Perimeter. It's located in the heart of the happening Kemang area.

Dharmawangsa HOTEL $$$

(Map p60; ☎021-725 8181; www.the-dharmawangsa.com; Jl Brawijaya Raya 26; r from US$253;) One of *the* city addresses, this luxurious hotel exudes style and class, with huge rooms and unmatched standards of service (each guest is assigned a private butler!). The restaurants and leisure facilities – including two pools, a fine spa, and squash and tennis courts – are also outstanding.

Alila Jakarta HOTEL $$$

(Map p58; ☎021-231 6008; www.alilahotels.com/jakarta; Jl Pecenongan 7-17; r from 1,090,000Rp;) An excellent modern hotel, in the north of the city not far from most of the sights. The attention to detail is impressive; the aromatherapy oil wafting across the stylish reception area sets a great initial impression. The outdoor pool, gym and restaurants are excellent.

Eating

Jakarta is a world-class eating destination. You'll find an amazing choice including oh-so refined Javanese imperial cuisine, hit-the-spot street grub and, if you're pining for something familiar, you can find Western food from gourmet French to fish and chips.

Two excellent street-food hotspots are Jl Pecenongan (about 500m north of Monas) for *sate babi* (pork satay) and fresh seafood, and Jl Sabang (just west of Jl Jaksa) for *sate ayam* (chicken satay) with *lontong* (sticky rice) and other delicacies.

Shopping malls are also good tucker terrain; many have inexpensive food courts.

JAKARTA FOR CHILDREN

Ancol Luar Biasa (☎021-6471 0497; www.ancol.com; basic admission incl entry to Pasar Seni 25,000Rp; ⏲24hr) On Jakarta's bayfront, the people's 'Dreamland' is a landscaped recreation complex popular with families. It has amusement rides and sporting and leisure facilities, including bowling, but gets extremely crowded on weekends. Prime attractions include the Pasar Seni (Art Market), which has sidewalk cafes, craft shops, cable-car rides, art exhibitions, and live jazz every Friday, and the **Atlantis Water Adventure** water-park complex, which costs an additional 150,000Rp to enjoy a wave pool, waterslides and a slide pool, plus artificial beaches.

The Gondola, a cable-car system, provides great views of the bay. The huge **Dunia Fantasi** (Fantasy Land; ☎021-6471 2000; Mon-Fri 190,000Rp, Sat & Sun 270,000Rp; ⏲10am-6pm Mon-Fri, 10am-8pm Sat & Sun) fun park includes the Halilintar twisted roller-coaster ride and Kora Kora (swinging ship). Marine mammal lovers, be warned: Sea World lives here, too.

Koridor 5 of the busway runs to Ancol. A taxi will cost around 70,000Rp from Jl Thamrin.

Jalan Jaksa Area

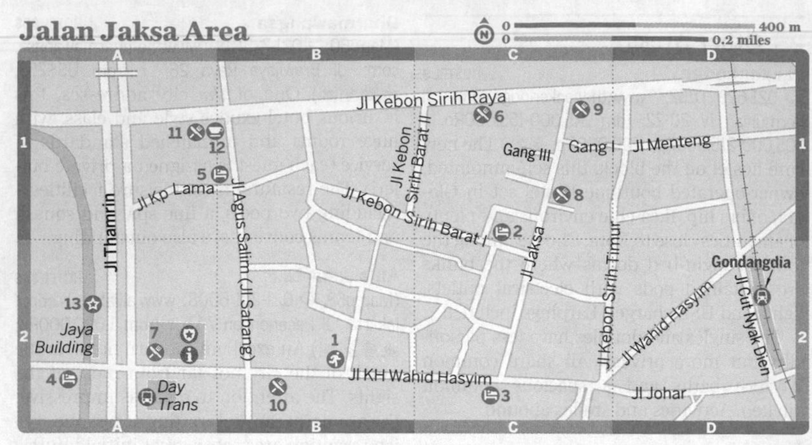

Jalan Jaksa Area

Activities, Courses & Tours
1 Bersih Sehat B2

Sleeping
2 Hostel 35 .... C1
3 Hotel Cipta C2
4 Kosenda Hotel A2
5 Max One B1

Eating
6 Daoen Sirih C1
7 Garuda A2
8 KL Village C1
9 Sate Khas Senayan C1
10 Saung Grenvil B2
11 Shanghai Blue 1920 .... A1

Drinking & Nightlife
Awan Lounge .... (see 4)
12 Kopi Oey Sabang B1

Entertainment
13 Jaya Pub A2

Jalan Jaksa Area

Jl Jaksa has a crop of backpacker-geared cafes and many authentic places on nearby streets.

Daoen Sirih INDONESIAN $
(Map p64; Jl Kebon Sirih 41-43; meals 12,000-25,000Rp; 11am-10pm) Non-touristy and a short stroll northwest of Jl Jaksa, this large, bamboo-roofed, open-sided food court has a wide selection of cook-shacks offering dishes such as *nasi goreng kambing* (spicy rice with goat) and *sate Madura* (skewered meat with sweet soy sauce), as well as noodles and espresso.

KL Village MALAY, INDONESIAN $
(Map p64; 021-3192 5219; Jl Jaksa 21-23; mains from 23,000Rp; 7am-11pm Sun-Wed, 24hr Thu-Sat;) Ever-popular Malaysian-style place that serves up inexpensive grub such as black-pepper chicken, *canai* (Malay-Indian bread) and *martabak* (stuffed pancake). If you're suffering after a long flight (or a long night), try one of the health-kick juices: 'heart and the brain' or 'sugar balance'.

Sate Khas Senayan INDONESIAN $
(Map p64; 021-3192 6238; Jl Kebon Sirih Raya 31A; mains 30,000-50,000Rp; 11.30am-10pm;) Upmarket air-conditioned restaurant at the northern end of Jl Jaksa. It is renowned for its superb *sate* – skewers of chicken, beef and lamb – plus Indonesian favourites such as *ayam goreng kremes* (fried chicken in batter) and *gurame bakar* (grilled fish).

★ Garuda INDONESIAN $$
(Map p64; 021-6262 9440; Jl Hayam Wuruk 100; meals from 100,000Rp; 24hr;) A smoky, fluorescent-lit, all-day, all-night depot of locally loved Padang food goodness, throbbing with Bollywood tunes and Indo-pop, and packed with locals. Little dishes of tempting flavours are piled on your table with lightning speed: jackfruit curry, chilli prawns, *tempe penyet* (fried tempe with spicy sauce),

rendang (beef coconut curry), potato and corn fritters. All of it made fresh.

If you touch one part, you buy it all, so prices add up. But it's so worth it.

Shanghai Blue 1920 CHINESE, INDONESIAN **$$**
(Map p64; ☎021-391 8690; www.tuguhotels.com/shblue; Jl Kebon Sirih Raya 77-79; mains 50,000-130,000Rp; ⏰12.30-11pm) Outstanding *masakan peranakan* (Chinese-influenced Indonesian cuisine) served in a room loaded with flamboyant furnishings, some rescued from an old Batavia teahouse. Standouts from the menu include drunken shrimp cooked with traditional Chinese wine, and crispy fish with mango and sweet chilli sauce.

Saung Grenvil SEAFOOD **$$**
(Map p64; ☎021-392 0333; www.saung-grenvil.com; Jl Wahid Hasyim 87; meals 100,000-180,000Rp) One of three locations in the city, and renowned for its outstanding seafood, particularly the Padang-style chilli crab, though there are plenty of other seafood options. Get an order of fried rolls to soak up that Padang sauce.

Kota, Sunda Kelapa & Glodok

Santong Kuo Tieh 68 CHINESE **$**
(Map p56; ☎021-692 4716; Jl Pancoran; 10 dumplings 20,000Rp; ⏰10am-9pm) You'll see cooks preparing fried and steamed Chinese pork dumplings out front of this humble but highly popular little place. The *bakso ikan isi* (fish balls) are also good.

Warung Kota Tua INDONESIAN **$**
(Map p56; Jl Pintu Besar Utara 11; meals 20,000-25,000Rp; ⏰8am-8pm) On the west side of Taman Fatahillah square, this semi-renovated old warehouse (an open-sided space with exposed brick walls and artwork) is a relaxed location for a reasonably priced meal, coffee, tea or juice. Try the *ayam bakar* (grilled chicken), *mie medan* (Sumatran noodles) or *nasi cap cai* (rice with mixed vegetables).

Kedai Seni Djakarté INDONESIAN **$**
(Map p56; Jl Pintu Besar Utara 17; mains 21,000-45,000Rp; ⏰9am-9pm Sun-Thu, to 10pm Fri & Sat) One of several similar places around Taman Fatahillah square, this is installed in the basement of an old Dutch building. You can eat inside under the ceiling fans or sweat it out on the outdoor tables. The cheap and tasty dishes are classic Indonesian comfort food (think nasi goreng).

★Historia INDONESIAN **$$**
(Map p56; ☎021-3176 0555; Jl Pintu Besar Utara 11; mains 35,000-73,000Rp; ⏰10am-10pm Sun-Thu, to 2am Fri & Sat) Historia's tasty dishes from around the archipelago include fried fish with a Sumatran sambal (*Ikan goreng sambal adaliman*), Javanese mixed rice (*nasi campur*), and all manner of oxtail – in soup, grilled, deep fried or braised with ground chilli. Served in hip, tiled, warehouse environs with soaring ceilings and an attached bar where DJs spin and bands rock.

Café Batavia INTERNATIONAL **$$**
(Map p56; ☎021-691 5531; cafebatavia.com; Jl Pintu Besar Utara 14; mains 75,000-190,000Rp; 📶) This historic restaurant overlooks Taman Fatahillah square in Kota, the old Dutch quarter. Its old parlour floors, marble tabletops, art deco furnishings and jazz on the hi-fi make it an essential stop for an atmospheric drink or a long lunch. It can be quiet in the evening.

Cikini & Menteng

Vietopia VIETNAMESE **$$**
(Map p58; ☎021-391 5893; Jl Cikini Raya 33; mains 35,000-60,000Rp; ⏰11.30am-10.30pm; 📶🌶) A stylish yet humble oasis on an otherwise relentlessly traffic-clogged drag, this authentic Vietnamese place offers delicious, moderately priced and delicately spiced cooking, including flavoursome *pho bo* (beef broth) and other classics from Vietnam. Vegetarian menu available.

Warung Daun INDONESIAN **$$**
(Map p58; ☎021-391 0909; www.warungdaun.com; Jl Cikini 26; 26,000-98,000Rp; ⏰11:30am-9pm) Eating Indonesian is frequently tasty, but often unhealthy thanks to MSG, low-quality oil and a dearth of organic ingredients. This re-imagined warung (food stall) attempts to right the path. Expect delectable Sundanese and Chinese Indonesian dishes, prepared using organic ingredients whenever possible, and presented tastefully.

★Por Que No TAPAS **$$$**
(Map p58; ☎021-390 1950; Jl Cokroaminoto 91; dishes 30,000-100,000Rp; ⏰5pm-midnight; 📶) A tucked-away, super-stylish rooftop tapas bar on the 5th floor of the De Ritz Building in Menteng, and popular with those who know. It grills and slices tenderloin, does a magnificent squid-ink paella, prawns sauteed with chilli and garlic, and eggplant fried with honey and truffle oil. And the churro ice-cream sandwiches? Best save room for dessert.

★Lara Djonggrang INDONESIAN $$$
(Map p58; ☎021-315 3252; www.tuguhotels.com/laradjonggrang; Jl Teuku Cik Ditiro 4; mains 48,000-108,000Rp; ⏲12.30-11pm; 📶) While many Jakartan restaurants lack atmosphere, that accusation could never be levelled at Lara Djonggrang – as you enter it's easy to think you've stumbled across some lost temple. One that serves perfectly executed and creatively presented imperial Indonesian cuisine from across the archipelago.

It offers Makassar-style squid and crab, Alor-style tamarind shrimp, and lobster cooked like they do in Aceh, with two kinds of chilli. There's a good wine list and staff are well informed and efficient. Prices are quite affordable considering the quality. Oh, and the bar is in fact created from an actual 200-year-old temple, which was set to be demolished until it was deconstructed and rebuilt here.

Kemang

Kemang is a good choice for a night on the town, with some great restaurants, bars and nightlife, including many exclusive places. For inexpensive grub check out D'Fest, which has 50 or so stalls.

D'Fest FOOD COURT $
(Map p60; Jl Kemang Raya 19C; mains 20,000-60,000Rp; ⏲5pm-midnight) Very sociable and popular open-air food court complete with stylish sofa seating and an array of international and local food stalls. It has Middle Eastern kebab joints, lots of Japanese options, *soto* (soup) places, *roti canai* (Malay-Indian flaky flatbread), plus a beerhouse. There's often live music here on weekend nights.

Kampung Kemang FOOD COURT $
(Map p60; Jl Kemang Raya 18; meals 50,000Rp; ⏲11am-11pm) A popular Kemang food court with permanent fried chicken and ramen kitchens and a handful of smaller stalls too, most specialising in Indonesian comfort food. It buzzes at night.

Payon INDONESIAN $$
(Map p60; ☎021-719 4826; www.facebook.com/payon.restaurant; Jl Kemang Raya 17; mains 23,000-130,000Rp; ⏲10.30am-10.30pm) Something of a secret garden where you dine under a delightful open pagoda surrounded by greenery. Chefs prepare authentic Javanese cuisine from an open kitchen, and many dishes are served on banana leaves, echoing the rural Indonesian flavour.

Warung Turki TURKISH $$
(Map p60; ☎021-2905 5898; Jl Kemang Raya 18A; mains 45,000-145,000Rp; ⏲noon-9.30pm Sun-Thu, to midnight Fri & Sat) Upscale Turkish fare prepared in a wood-fired clay oven and served in a high-design shell spanning three floors. They slow-roast lamb and chicken, stuff their homemade bread and layer sinful baklava. Enjoy yours on the enclosed rooftop patio, with its glass ceiling dangling with lanterns.

Parc 19 INDONESIAN, FUSION $$
(Map p60; ☎021-719 9988; www.parc19.com; Jl Taman Kemang 19; mains 70,000-240,000Rp; ⏲10am-midnight) The industrial design, complete with a brick-and-wood bar and reclaimed wood seating, outdoes the menu, which wanders from pizza to kebabs to Indonesian favourites including a Balinese duck. But it's still worth it for the ambience.

Toscana ITALIAN $$$
(Map p60; ☎021-718 1217; www.toscanajakarta.com; Jl Kemang Raya 120; mains 33,000-303,000Rp; ⏲5.30-11pm) Elegant Italian place renowned for its pizzas (baked in a wood-fired oven), pasta and risotto and great fish dishes (try the pan-fried grouper with potato and black olives). Also boasts a good selection of Tuscan wines.

Senopati

An upmarket restaurant row in south Jakarta, stretches from Jl Senopati to Jl Suryo and lacks the expat overwhelm of Kemang. The high-speed traffic makes a leisurely stroll next to impossible, however.

Darling Rice Club INDONESIAN $$
(Map p60; Jl Suryo 19; mains 30,000-70,000Rp; ⏲11am-10pm; 📶) Set above a showroom of cool vintage bikes, motorcycles and cars, this gourmet warung serves mixed rice dishes in upmarket environs.

Tredici ITALIAN $$$
(Map p60; ☎021-720 4567; www.facebook.com/trediciristorante; Jl Suryo 42; mains 72,000-265,000Rp; ⏲10.30am-10pm) A slice of authentic Italy in manic Jakarta, this Senopati mainstay is popular among expats for thin-crust pizzas, homemade pasta, outstanding risotto and perfectly prepared steaks. It even serves prosciutto and melon. This is an Italian kitchen to seek out and explore and the wine list proves it. Grab a table on the patio and stay a while.

Cantina 18 ITALIAN **$$$**

(Map p60; ☎021-2751 0539; www.cantina-18.com; Jl Suryo 25; mains 80,000-260,000Rp; ⏲11am-11pm) Three Italian pals from the motherland deliver upmarket Italian flavour with modern flare. They offer a terrific selection of antipasti and carpaccio, and a choice of pasta and risotto dishes, as well as grilled seafood and delectable pork ribs in red wine sauce. The terrific food outdoes the chintzy design. Don't hold it against them.

Drinking & Nightlife

If you're expecting the capital of the world's largest Muslim country to be a sober city with little in the way of drinking culture, think again. Bars are spread throughout the city, with casual places grouped around Jl Jaksa, fancy-pants rooftop lounge bars and beer gardens in central and south Jakarta, and many more places in between. Cafe culture has really taken off in the last few years. All the malls have a Starbucks (or an Indo clone) selling extortionately priced coffee, but there are some very interesting and quirky local cafes emerging, too.

The recent national crackdown on selling beer and alcohol has cost some restaurants their liquor licence and the ban on selling beer from minimarts was still in effect in Jakarta in 2015, even while the law was reversed in Bali. We'd heard of long-time expats having to purchase their home Bintang stash from the storage area of their favourite supermarket. On top of that, the so-called no-fun initiative capped closing time of all bars and clubs at midnight, although enforcement has been lax thus far.

Bars

★Awan Lounge BAR

(Map p64; www.awanlounge.com; Jl KH Wahid Hasyim 127; ⏲5pm-1am Sun-Thu, to 2am Sat & Sun) Set on the top floor of Kosenda Hotel, here is a lovely rooftop garden bar that manages to be both understated and dramatic. There's a vertical garden, ample tree cover, plenty of private nooks flickering with candlelight and a vertigo-inducing glass skylight that plummets nine floors down.

It has a tasty bar menu, electronica thumps at a perfect volume, and the crowd is mixed local and expat. Weekends can get overly crowded. Midweek it's an ideal date-night rendezvous.

CLUBBING IN JAKARTA

Jakarta has been one of Southeast Asia's biggest clubbing hotspots for decades, thanks to great venues (mostly dark and sleazy in the north of the city and polished and pricey in the south), internationally renowned DJs and bombastic sound systems.

Entrance is typically 50,000Rp to 100,000Rp, but includes a free drink. Clubs open around 9pm, and – up until recently – don't really get going until after midnight. However, at research time the new 'no-fun law' threatened to change all this, though nobody was quite sure what would happen. Clubs were functioning normally during write-up, though attendance had slipped.

Take heart, there is always the underground scene set in Glodok, where clubs get so deep down and dirty that they make the UK's acid house scene of the 1980s seem like a teddy bear's picnic.

Online listings, such as www.indoclubbing.com, www.jakarta100bars.com and especially www.whatsnewjakarta.com, can all be helpful in planning a night out.

Potato Head BAR

(Map p60; www.ptthead.com/jakarta; Pacific Place Mall, Jl Sudirman 52-53; 📶) Brilliant warehouse-style bar-bistro with remarkable artistic decor (including a vertical garden, lots of statement art and vintage seating) that also promotes music and cultural events. Great cocktails, great grub, great concept. Check the website for upcoming shows.

365 Ecobar BAR

(Map p60; www.ecobar.co.id; Jl Kemang Raya; ⏲5pm-2am Mon-Thu, to 4am Fri & Sat) Occupying a minimalist, corrugated-tin prefab structure with walls scrawled in evocative street art, an island bar huddled with colourful bar stools, and rotating DJs, this is the new cool spot in Kemang and it draws a regular, mixed Indo and expat crowd.

Tree House BAR

(Map p60; Jl Kemang 72; ⏲4pm-midnight Tue-Thu & Sun, to 3am Fri-Sat; 📶) A great neighbourhood bar, Tree House is an intimate hang-out on a Kemang backstreet with rotating art exhibitions and classic funk, soul and hip-hop on the sound system.

A CUP OF JAVA

Java is so synonymous with coffee, one of the world's favourite drugs – sorry, *drinks* – that in some countries the term *java* has become a catchphrase for a cup of the hot brown stuff.

Coffee was introduced to Indonesia by the Dutch, who initially founded plantations around Jakarta, Sukabumi and Bogor. Due to the country's excellent coffee-growing conditions, plantations began springing up across Java, and even in parts of Sulawesi and Sumatra. Early on, the prominent coffee was arabica; arabica coffees were traditionally named after the port they were exported from, hence the common worldwide terms of *java* and *mocha* (from Yemen) for coffee.

Commonly thought of as a bean, coffee is actually a fruit pit or berry. Around 2000 berries are needed to make one pound of coffee. The most expensive coffee in the world, fetching anywhere between US$100 and US$600 a pound, is *kopi luwak*, a fully flavoured coffee produced in Java (it is also exported from the Philippines, Vietnam and southern India). What makes *kopi luwak* – also known as civet coffee – so expensive is the process by which it gains its unusually rich flavour. The local palm civet, a cat-like animal, gorges itself on coffee berries and passes the inner pit through its digestive tract unharmed. Along the way the pits are affected by the animal's stomach enzymes and come out the other end smelling of roses (or rich coffee in this case). The coffee has been appetisingly nicknamed 'cat poop' or 'monkey poo' coffee.

Today, Indonesia is the fourth-largest producer of coffee in the world. Robusta has replaced arabica as the leading coffee of choice, currently making up some 75% of the country's exports. For further reading on Indonesia's love affair with coffee, pick up a copy of *A Cup of Java* by Gabriella Teggia and Mark Hanusz.

Eastern Promise PUB

(Map p60; ☎021-7179 0151; www.easternpromise-jakarta.com; Jl Kemang Raya 5;) A classic British-style pub in the heart of Kemang, with a pool table, welcoming atmosphere and filling international and Indian grub. Service is prompt and friendly, the beer's cold and there's live music on weekends. It's a key older expat hang-out.

Kunstkring Paleis CAFE, COCKTAIL BAR

(Map p58; ☎021-390 0899; tuguhotels.com; Jl Teuku Umar 1) High tea or cocktails? You can have both, plus a divine Indonesian dinner in between at this re-imagined Dutch colonial, once Batavia's fine arts centre (it showed works of Van Gogh, Picasso, Chagall and Gauguin in its day). It remains a room filled with art.

The main Pangeran Diponegoro Room, replete with wall-sized canvases, is where you'll have traditional tea service with an Indonesian twist. Or come a bit later and enjoy a drink in the red-lit Susie Wong lounge, named and inspired by the infamous Hong Kong madame.

Cafes

Café Batavia BAR

(Map p56; www.cafebatavia.com; Jl Pintu Besar Utara 14) This classy restaurant doubles as an evocative place for a cocktail, a cool Bintang or a coffee.

Kopi Oey Sabang CAFE

(Map p64; www.kopioey.com; Jl Agus Salim 16A; drinks from 15,000-27,000Rp; 9am-10pm;) Gorgeous little cafe modelled on an old Chinese teahouse, complete with antique tiles and vintage prints on the walls, marble tabletops and a great selection of drinks. It serves Vietnamese coffee, turmeric tea and snacks that reflect Indonesia's heritage, including Dutch croquettes and Padang-style *roti*.

Dua Nyonya CAFE

(Map p58; www.duanyonyacafe.com; Jl Cikini Raya 27; 11am-10pm) Primarily a cafe, Dua Nyonya is an intimate place on two levels that serves fine Indonesian coffee (from Bali, Toraja and Aceh) and traditional food including rice dishes such as *nasi bebek goreng keramat* (fried rice with duck). Classical music and art add to the ambience.

Bakoel Koffie CAFE

(Map p58; Jl Cikini Raya 25; 9am-11pm;) Occupying a fine old Dutch building, twirling with ceiling fans, this elegant (if pricey) cafe offers strong coffee using beans from across the archipelago. Snacks and cakes are also served, along with nasi goreng and *ayam bakar* (grilled chicken).

Clubs

Potato Head Garage CLUB
(Map p60; ☎021-5797 3330; www.pttgarage.com; Jl Sudirman 52-53; cover charge varies; ⏲11am-1am) Leave it to the Potato Heads to convert an abandoned stadium into a massive thumping dance club, swirling with style. It serves food, and the decor is typically tasteful with a lean toward vintage, but this is first and foremost a dance spot where you and 1000 friends can get loose and rejoice in the night.

X2 CLUB
(Map p60; www.x2club.net; Jl Asia Afrika 8, Plaza Senayan) Huge upmarket club with a capacity to hold more than 2000. Expect a young crowd, futuristic lighting and three dance zones, though the music can be quite commercial.

☆ Entertainment

Jakarta offers a range of traditional music, dance and theatre performances, as well as a solid live music scene: jazz combos, rock bands and singer-songwriters.

Cultural Performances

Museum Wayang (p55) holds *wayang kulit* and *golek* (puppet) performances on Sundays between 10am and 2pm.

Check the website of the Jakarta Arts Council (www.dkj.or.id) for event listings.

Taman Ismail Marzuki PERFORMING ARTS
(TIM; Map p58; ☎021-3193 7325; www.tamanismailmarzuki.com; Jl Cikini Raya 73) Jakarta's premier cultural centre has a great selection of cinemas, theatres and exhibition spaces. Performances (such as Sundanese dance and gamelan music events) are always high quality and the complex has a couple of good casual restaurants, too.

Live Music

Jazz lovers should check out www.jakartajazz.com for event listings.

Jaya Pub LIVE MUSIC
(Map p64; ☎021-3192 5633; Jl Thamrin 12; ⏲5pm-2am) Conveniently located in the heart of town, this pub caters to an older crowd and showcases live bluesy rock and jazz artists. Also serves food.

Phoenix LIVE MUSIC
(Map p60; ☎021-722 1188; www.phoenixjakarta.com; Jl Wijaya I 25) Formerly the Nine Muses Club, this upmarket European-style garden restaurant and lounge hosts acoustic performances on Wednesdays and Fridays, plus some jazz nights and DJs on Saturdays.

Shopping

Jakarta has real retail appeal. The capital has handicrafts from across the nation, gargantuan malls stuffed with big brand and luxury labels (though prices are rarely a bargain) and lots of galleries full of interesting contemporary art and design goods. Jl Kebon Sirih Timur, just east of Jl Jaksa, has a number of shops that sell antiques and curios.

Because of the traffic in Jakarta, it is best not to try to cover too much ground. You could end up seeing a lot of exhaust fumes and no shop windows.

Cikini & Menteng

The destination for glitzy malls, all manner of electronics and one hell of a flea market.

Flea Market MARKET
(Map p58; Jl Surabaya; ⏲8am-4pm) Jakarta's famous flea market is in Menteng. It has woodcarvings, furniture, textiles, jewellery, old vinyl records and many (dubious) antiques. Bargain like crazy.

Plaza Indonesia MALL
(Map p58; www.plazaindonesia.com; Jl Thamrin 28-30; 📶) This mall is centrally located and very classy, with a wide selection of stores that includes leading Indonesian design boutiques and the likes of Cartier and Lacroix. Check out Toko Ampuh for local medicines and remedies and Batik Karis for high-quality Indonesian batik. In the basement there's an excellent, inexpensive food mall.

Grand Indonesia MALL
(Map p58; www.grand-indonesia.com; Jl Thamrin) This luxury mall contains a tempting plethora of luxury fashion outlets, good local and international restaurants, and a cineplex.

Pasaraya DEPARTMENT STORE
(Map p60; www.pasaraya.co.id; Jl Iskandarsyah II/2) Opposite Blok M Mall, this department store has two huge floors that seem to go on forever and are devoted to batik and handicrafts from throughout the archipelago.

Mangga Dua Mall MALL
(Map p56; Jl Mangga Dua) *The* place for electronics, DVDs and CDs (and even Russian watches), with numerous other malls in the area.

Kemang Area

Edgy art and trendy design for the expatriate and upwardly mobile Jakartan.

DON'T MISS

SALE SEASON

The annual Jakarta Great Sale (JGS) festival caters to the capital's avid mall-goers, and plenty of tourists from Malaysia. Held at many shopping centres in Jakarta during June and July, it features slashed prices, midnight sales, competitions, and social and cultural activities.

Perimeter ART
(Map p60; www.perimeterspace.com; Jl Kemang Raya; ⏲10am-7pm) Set in the uber-hip Kemang Icon lobby, where rotating shows included an exhibition from artist Agus Suwage on our visit. If the weird and evocative hold much allure, poke your head in to see what's on.

Colony MALL
(Map p60; www.colony6kemang.com; Jl Kemang Raya 6; ⏲10am-10pm) In a city splashed with splashy malls, each one bigger and glitzier than the last, this understated but tasteful shopping centre stands out. It has a **Periplus** (Map p60; ☎021-718 7070; ground fl, No 5 ⏲9am-7pm) bookshop and a cool cafe called **Liberica** – attracting all the Indo and expat hipsters. There's also a *shabu shabu* Japanese restaurant, a Pilates gym and more.

Other Areas

Plaza Senayan MALL
(Map p60; www.plaza-senayan.com; Jl Asia Afrika; 📶) Huge plaza with a cinema and stores including Marks & Spencer, a roster of big-bucks brands and lots of cafes.

Information

DANGERS & ANNOYANCES

For such a huge city with obvious social problems, Jakarta is surprisingly safe. Violent crime is rare and tourists are seldom targeted. You should exercise more caution after dark, however, particularly late at night in Glodok and Kota, where there are some seedy clubs and bars. Robberies by taxi drivers have been known to take place, so always opt for reputable firms, such as the citywide Blue Bird group.

Jakarta's buses and trains can be hopelessly crowded, particularly during rush hours, and this is when pickpockets ply their trade.

Some foreign embassies warn against travel to Indonesia and especially Jakarta, though overall there's little risk for travellers. That said, attacks against foreign interests have occurred and protests, although often peaceful, may still become violent with little warning.

Occasionally, bars and clubs have been smashed up by the city's self-appointed morality police, the Jakarta-based Front Pembela Islam (FPI or Islamic Defenders Front), especially during Ramadan.

EMERGENCY

Tourist Police (Map p64; ☎021-566000; Jl KH Wahid Hasyim) On the 2nd floor of the Jakarta Theatre.

IMMIGRATION

Central Immigration Office (Direktorat Jenderal Imigrasi; Map p60; ☎021-522 4658; www.imigrasi.go.id; Jl HR Rasuna Said 8 & 9) Provides information on visa extensions and renewals.

INTERNET ACCESS

Free wi-fi is common in cafes, restaurants, hotels and malls. Internet cafes are not easily found in the central area.

MEDIA

Jakarta Globe (www.thejakartaglobe.com) Excellent newspaper with stylish layout, quality reporting and illuminating features. The Jakarta coverage is impressive.

Jakarta Post (www.thejakartapost.com) English-language daily with news, views and cultural content.

MEDICAL SERVICES

Cikini Hospital (Map p58; ☎emergency 021-3899 7744, urgent care 021-3899 7777; www.rscikini.com; Jl Raden Saleh Raya 40) Caters to foreigners and has English-speaking staff.

SOS Medika Klinik (Map p60; ☎021-750 6001; Jl Puri Sakti 10, Cipete; ⏲7am-10pm) Offers English-speaking GP appointments, dental care, and emergency and specialist healthcare services.

MONEY

You're never far from an ATM in Jakarta.

BII Bank (Plaza Indonesia, Jl Thamrin; ⏲8am-4pm Mon-Sat) In the basement level of Plaza Indonesia.

POST

Main Post Office (Map p58; Jl Gedung Kesenian I; ⏲8am-7pm Mon-Fri, to 1pm Sat) Occupying an octagonal building near Lapangan Banteng.

TOURIST INFORMATION

Jakarta Visitor Information Office (Map p64; ☎021-316 1293, 021-314 2067; www.jakarta-tourism.go.id; Jl KH Wahid Hasyim 9; ⏲9am-7pm Mon-Fri, to 4pm Sat) Inside the Jakarta Theatre building. A helpful office; the staff here can answer many queries and set you up with tours of West Java. Practical information can be lacking but it does have a good stock of leaflets and publications and a colour map. There's also a desk at the airport.

TRAVEL AGENCIES

Travel agencies in the Jl Jaksa area are convenient places to start looking for international flights and long-haul bus tickets. Domestic air tickets usually cost the same from a travel agency as from the airline, but discounts are sometimes available.

WEBSITES

Jakarta.go.id (www.jakarta-tourism.go.id) The Jakarta City Government Tourism Office's official site; offers plenty of listings including transport and events.

JakChat (www.jakchat.com) English-language forums where you can discuss everything from bars to politics.

Living in Indonesia (www.expat.or.id) Geared at longer-term visitors; boasts everything from restaurant reviews and visa information to chat rooms.

Lonely Planet (www.lonelyplanet.com/indonesia/jakarta) Planning advice, author recommendations, traveller reviews and insider tips.

Getting There & Away

Jakarta is the main international gateway to Indonesia. It's also a major centre for domestic travel, with extensive bus, train, air and boat connections.

AIR

All international flights and most domestic flights operate from Soekarno-Hatta International Airport. Consult www.jakartaairportonline.com for airport information and schedules.

AirAsia (☎ 021-5050 5088; www.airasia.com) Links Jakarta to Semarang, Yogyakarta and Bali. Also has cheap non-stop flights to Kuala Lumpur and Bangkok.

Citilink (☎ 080 4108 0808; www.citilink.co.id) Flies to cities including Denpasar, Bandung, Malang, Banjarmasin, Pekanbaru and Surabaya.

Garuda (Map p58; www.garuda-indonesia.com) Indonesia's most established domestic carrier connects Jakarta with dozens of Indonesian cities including Denpasar, Yogyakarta, Makassar and Kupang, and offers limited international flights as well.

Lion Air/Wings Air (Map p58; www.lionair.co.id) Links Jakarta with cities all over the archipelago.

Sriwijaya Air (☎ 080 4177 7777; www.sriwijayaair.co.id) Links Jakarta with many cities in Java, Sumatra, Kalimantan, Sulawesi, Nusa Tenggara and Papua.

BOAT

Pelni shipping services operate on regular schedules to ports all over the archipelago. The **Pelni ticketing office** (☎ 021-6385 0960, 021-439 3106; www.pelni.co.id; Jl Angkasa 18) is northeast of the city centre in Kemayoran. Tickets (plus commission) can also be bought from the agent **Kerta Jaya** (Map p58; ☎ 021-345 1518; Jl Veteran I 27), opposite Mesjid Istiqlal.

Pelni ships all arrive at and depart from Pelabuhan Satu (dock No 1) at Tanjung Priok, 13km northeast of the city centre. Busway Koridor 12 provides a direct bus link; a taxi from Jl Jaksa is around 120,000Rp.

BUS

Jakarta's four major bus terminals – Kalideres, Kampung Rambutan, Pulo Gadung and Lebak Bulus – are all a long way from the city centre. Take the TransJakarta busway to these terminals as the journey can take hours otherwise. Trains are generally a better alternative for travelling to/from Jakarta. Tickets (some including travel to the terminals) for the better buses can be bought from agencies.

Kalideres Serves points west of Jakarta. Buses run to Merak (35,000Rp, 2½ hours) and Labuan (50,000Rp, 3½ hours). A few buses go to Sumatra from Kalideres, but most depart from Pulo Gadung terminal. Take busway Koridor 3 to get there.

Kampung Rambutan Mainly handles buses to points south and southwest of Jakarta such as Bogor (normal/air-con 12,000/20,000Rp, 45 minutes); Cianjur (air-con 35,000Rp, 2½ hours); Bandung (normal/air-con 50,000/60,000Rp, three hours); Pangandaran (85,000Rp to 90,000Rp, eight to nine hours) and Pelabuan Ratu (55,000Rp, four hours). Take busway Koridor 7 to get there.

Pulo Gadung Buses to Bandung, Central and East Java, Sumatra, Bali and even Nusa Tenggara. Bandung buses travel the toll road (47,000Rp to 60,000Rp, three hours), as do the long-haul Yogyakarta coaches (200,000Rp to 260,000Rp, 12 hours). Sumatra is another long haul from Jakarta by bus, but destinations include Bengkulu (from 300,000Rp) and Palembang (from 350,000Rp). Take busway Koridor 2 or 4 to get the terminal.

Lebak Bulus Long-distance deluxe buses to Yogyakarta, Surabaya and Bali; take Koridor 8 to get here.

MINIBUS

Door-to-door *travel* minibuses are not a good option in Jakarta because it can take hours to pick up or drop off passengers in the traffic jams.

TRANSJAKARTA BUSWAY

TransJakarta is a network of clean, air-conditioned buses that run on busways (designated lanes that are closed to all other traffic). They are the quickest way to get around the city.

Most busways have been constructed in the centre of existing highways, and stations have been positioned at roughly 1km intervals. Access is via elevated walkways and each station has a shelter. Fifteen busway lines (called *koridor*) are up and running.

Tickets cost 3500Rp to 9000Rp payable before you board, which covers any destination in the network (regardless of how many *koridor* you use). Buses (running 5am to 10pm) are well maintained and usually not too crowded, though you may have to wait a while for a bus with seating space during peak hours.

The busway system has dozens of feeder routes from within and outside the city. It has been a great success, but as most middle- and upper-class Jakartans remain as addicted as ever to their cars, the city's famous traffic jams are set to continue.

Unless you've the patience of a saint, take a train, plane or bus.

Day Trans (Map p64; 021-2967 6767; www.daytrans.co.id; Jl Thamrin; hourly 6am-8pm) Hourly minibuses to Bandung (110,000Rp to 125,000Rp) from Jl Thamrin.

TRAIN

Jakarta's four main train stations are quite central, making trains the easiest way out of the city. The most convenient and important is Gambir station, on the eastern side of Merdeka Sq, a 15-minute walk from Jl Jaksa. Gambir handles express trains to Bogor, Bandung, Yogyakarta, Solo, Semarang and Surabaya. Pasar Senen train station is to the east and mostly has economy-class trains while Tanah Abang station has economy trains to the west.

Check timetables online at www.kereta-api.co.id, or consult the helpful staff at the station's **information office** (021-692 9194). There's a slightly pricey taxi booking desk inside Gambir station; the fare to Jl Jaksa is roughly 45,000Rp.

Popular destinations include the following:

Bogor Trains leave from Gambir and Jakarta Kota stations. Air-conditioned trains (one hour, 15,000Rp) leave roughly hourly; there are also much slower and dirtier *ekonomi* trains (two hours, 8000Rp). All trains are horribly crowded during rush hours.

Bandung There are frequent trains to Bandung along a scenic hilly track, but be sure to book in advance (especially on weekends and public holidays). Comfortable *Argo Parahyangan* services depart from Gambir train station six times daily (business 60,000Rp, executive 80,000Rp to 95,000Rp, 3¼ hours) between 5.55am and 8.25pm.

Yogyakarta and **Solo** From Gambir there are six daily exclusive-class trains (300,000Rp to 450,000Rp, 7¼ to nine hours) to Yogyakarta, leaving between 8am and 8.45pm; four of these continue to Solo, 45 minutes further on.

Surabaya There are four daily exclusive-class trains between Gambir station and Surabaya (395,000Rp to 520,000Rp, 10½ to 11 hours).

Getting Around

TO/FROM THE AIRPORT

Jakarta's Soekarno-Hatta International Airport is 35km west of the city centre. A toll road links the airport to the city and the journey takes about an hour (longer during rush hour).

Damri (021-550 1290, 021-460 3708; www.busbandara.com; 40,000Rp; every 15-30 min) airport buses run between 4am and 8pm between the airport and Gambir train station (near Jl Jaksa) and several other points in the city including Blok M, Tanjung Priok and Kampung Rambutan bus station. From Gambir train station to Jl Jaksa or Cikini, a taxi is around 45,000Rp, or you could walk (it's just under 1km). Damri buses also run regularly to Bogor (55,000Rp to 75,000Rp, every 15 to 30 minutes). Taxis from the airport to Jl Thamrin/Jl Jaksa cost about 170,000Rp to 200,000Rp including tolls. Be sure to book via the official taxi desks, rather than using the unlicensed drivers outside.

Halim Perdana Kusuma airport is 11km south of the Cikini district and not served by pubic transport. A taxi from central Jakarta costs around 100,000Rp.

BUS

Jakarta has a good TransJakarta busway system, which has really sped up city travel in recent years. One of the most useful routes is Koridor 1, which runs north to Kota, past Monas and along Jl Sudirman.

Other buses are not very useful for visitors as they are much slower, hotter (no air-con) and crowded (pickpockets can be a problem). The tourist office can provide a map that plots the busway routes.

CAR

Jakarta has branches of the major car-rental operators, including **Avis** (Map p58; ☎021-314 2900; www.avis.co.id; Jl Diponegoro 25) and **Trac Astra** (☎021-650 6565; www.trac.astra.co.id; Jl Gaya Motor 1/10). Alternatively, enquire in travel agencies, as a vehicle with driver may be the most economical option.

The big operators charge about 800,000Rp per day with a driver (650,000Rp without), while private operators are often cheaper.

A number of the 'transport' guys who hang around on Jl Jaksa can also offer good deals.

LOCAL TRANSPORT

Bajaj (pronounced 'ba-jai') are similar to Thai tuk-tuks. They are not that common these days and if you hire one it's worth remembering that they are not allowed on many major thoroughfares.

Ojek are motorbike taxis. Drivers wait on busy street corners and usually wear a fluorescent-coloured vest. Getting about Jakarta on two wheels is a lot quicker than in a car, though it's obviously less safe and you're directly exposed to the city's air pollution. Negotiate a price first; a short ride will be about 20,000Rp. A new city-wide *ojek* network called **Go-Jek** (☎021-725 1110; www.go-jek.com) has recently been introduced, using registered drivers and an app so you can book and pay directly from your smartphone, like Uber.

In Kota you'll find becak, pushbike rickshaws with an additional padded seat on the back. These contraptions are ideal for shuttling to and from Sunda Kelapa; expect to pay 10,000Rp to 20,000Rp for a short ride.

TAXI

Taxis are inexpensive in Jakarta. All are metered and cost 5000Rp to 8000Rp for the first kilometre and around 300Rp for each subsequent 100m. Tipping is expected, if not demanded. Many taxi drivers provide a good service, but Jakarta has enough rogues to give its taxis a variable reputation. Stick to reputable companies such as **Blue Bird taxis** (☎021-794 1234; www.bluebirdgroup.com); a minimum of 30,000Rp is charged for ordered taxis. Uber is also in Jakarta these days, and can frequently be the same price and more comfortable than a taxi. Any tolls and parking fees – there are lots of them – are extra and paid by the passenger.

THOUSAND ISLANDS

☎021

A string of palm-fringed islands in the Jakarta Bay, Thousand Islands (Pulau Seribu) are the perfect respite for those stuck in the capital too long. If you're travelling onward through the nation, you could easily skip them – they're expensive by Indonesian standards, and mainly geared towards weekending Jakartans. But they do have white-sand beaches and calm, clear seas (aside from the islands closest to the mainland, which are plagued by trash).

Several have been developed into resorts with bungalows and water sports. Pulau Pramuka is the group's district centre, but most people live on Pulau Kelapa. Pulau Panjang has the only airstrip on the islands. There are actually only 130 islands, not a thousand.

You can book island trips at the **Ancol Marina** (☎021-6471 1822; Taman Impian Jaya Ancol) or via the Jakarta Visitor Information Office.

Getting There & Around

The resorts have daily speedboats from Jakarta's Ancol Marina for guests and day trippers, usually leaving between 8am and 11am and returning between 2pm and 5pm, with additional services on weekends. Some are just a 20-minute ride away, but the furthest islands take around two hours to reach. Return day-trip rates to the resorts with lunch include Pulau Bidadari (400,000Rp) and Pulau Macan (750,000Rp).

Locals will ferry you from one island to the next (but this can be pricey). Most islands are small enough to easily explore on foot and some have bikes for hire.

Pulau Bidadari

This is the closest resort island and is popular with Jakarta residents for day trips. It is one of the least interesting resorts, but you can use it to visit other islands such as Pulau Kahyangan, Pulau Kelor (which has the ruins of an old Dutch fort) or Pulau Onrust (where the remains of an 18th-century shipyard can be explored). Boats can be hired for the short trip from Pulau Bidadari for 100,000Rp per hour.

The island's **resort** (☎021-6471 3173; www.pulaubidadariecoresort.com; s/d per person incl full board from 985,000/1,605,000Rp) has a variety of simple cottages and sports facilities, and can be booked at Ancol Marina.

Pulau Macan

A couple of tropical dots in the ocean now host a wonderful ecoresort, **Tiger Island Village and Eco Resort** (☎0878 8234 1314, 0812 9753 1395; www.pulaumacan.com; cabins per person incl full board from 1,585,000Rp) 🍃, which uses recycled rainwater, solar panels and nature-friendly products. This beachside retreat may not be cheap, but the experience and location are special and there is good snorkelling offshore.

WEST JAVA

Many tourists only experience the lush, volcanic panoramas of West Java (Jawa Barat) through the murky window of a lumbering bus or train, but this dramatic, diverse region has plenty to detain the inquisitive traveller. Historically it's known as Sunda and its people and language are Sundanese.

West Java stretches from the remote islands of the Ujung Kulon National Park (last Javan home of the one-horned rhino) in the west to the sweeping beaches of Pangandaran in the east. In between, you can visit the infamous offshore volcano of Krakatau, surf in the chilled coastal resorts of Cimaja and Batu Karas, experience local culture in Cianjur and stroll through Bogor's lush botanical gardens. It's also the most densely populated region in the entire country and travel can be slow going as a result.

Banten

Most visitors head straight from Jakarta to Merak on their way to (or from) Sumatra, simply because there's not a lot in this area to attract your attention. Banten, however, can be an interesting if not happy diversion if you have time to kill. Once set on the edge of a lush network of rice fields, the fishing town of Banten was a great maritime capital, where the Dutch and English first landed in Java to secure trade and struggle for economic supremacy.

Its regional influence peaked during the reign of Sultan Agung (1651–83), and in 1680 he declared war on the Dutch, but conflict within the royal house ultimately led to his downfall. Agung fled Banten and finally surrendered in 1683; his defeat marked the real beginning of Dutch territorial expansion in Java.

On the coast due north of Serang, the chief landmark here is the 16th-century mosque **Mesjid Agung**, which was once a good example of early Islamic architecture; its great white octagonal minaret was reputedly designed by a Chinese Muslim. The roof has since been repaired, however, and it no longer carries the same historical gravitas.

Banten has once again become a major port of multinational interest, whose fate seems tied to the hands of those who are not of this land. In other words, it is a perfect example of warp-speed, globalised development, as what's left of this breadbasket gets gobbled up, one shovelful at a time.

Getting There & Away

Take a bus from Jakarta's Kalideres bus terminal to Serang (30,000Rp, 1½ hours), 10km south of Banten, from where a minibus (12,000Rp, 20 minutes) will drop you near the Mesjid Agung, Banten's old mosque. Development is taking place in the surrounding county.

Merak

0254

Right on the northwestern tip of Java, 140km from Jakarta, Merak is an ugly port town, the terminus for ferries shuttling to south Sumatra. In a decade or so a new Selat Sunda bridge should connect Java and Sumatra here, but for now you'll be boarding a boat between these two great islands.

Getting There & Away

The bus terminal and train station are at the ferry dock.

Ferries to Bakauheni in Sumatra depart every 30 minutes, 24 hours a day. Foot passengers pay 15,000Rp, and the journey is about two hours. Fast boats (41,000Rp, 45 minutes) also make this crossing, but they don't run in heavy seas. The through-buses to Bandarlampung are the easiest option.

Frequent buses make the run between Merak and Jakarta (100,000Rp to 130,000Rp, 2½ hours). Most go to the capital's Kalideres bus terminal, but buses also run to/from Pulo Gadung and Kampung Rambutan. Other buses run all over Java, including Bogor (150,000Rp) and Bandung (160,000Rp to 200,000Rp). For Labuan (30,000Rp), a change at Cilegon is required.

There are also infrequent trains to Jakarta, but most are economy class.

Carita

0253

Close enough to the industrial blitz of Ciregon to be at least slightly confusing, Carita is a different world, with rising jade hills clumped with palms and laced with rivers. The sandy beach crashes with one small surf break, Karang Bolong, and the area is popular with

MANIC DEVELOPMENT IN BANTEN

This is what happens when a government and her people have justifiably thirsted for more for way too long, when the desires for better-paying jobs, bigger industry, sweeter comforts and a more robust economy collide with what used to be a hand-to-mouth agrarian history. There are few corners of the world that better exemplify this version of progress than the rapidly changing neo-industrial sector that is Ciregon and Setam. Here, in the Banten district (just north of the town of Banten), are countless massive scrap-metal yards and petrochemical, plastic and cement factories. Where once there was a breadbasket, there is now a skyline of belching smokestacks.

To make way for the mayhem, entire mountainsides have been levelled. Just inland lies a six-month-old road that is now a land bridge between eras. On one side is the emerging urbanised industrial landscape, with the newest factories and warehouses set between hills, still populated by working families in rickety houses, that are gradually being eaten away by backhoes. On the other side is a verdant valley, stitched with rice fields, pure and elegant, swaying with coconut palms. Or maybe, by the time you read this, that will be gone too. It's possible: after all, the entire region is slated for development and when it's completed and fully urbanised, Ciregon and Setam will form a new industrial suburb of Jakarta, home to more than a million people. It will be one more big West Java city where food will be imported and life more manic and consumptive than ever before. Is this progress? Or is it simply an inevitable byproduct of the global village? After all, the subsistence farm life may be quaint, but it certainly isn't easy. Perhaps that's why, in this corner of the world, its days are numbered.

weekenders from Jakarta. But unless you're headed to Krakatau, visible on the horizon from most of the resorts, or the Ujung Kulon National Park, it's not worth your time.

Sights & Activities

About 2km from Carita over the rice paddies you can see the village of Sindanglaut (End of the Sea), which is where the giant tsunami of 1883 ended its destructive run. Hutan Wisata Carita is a forest reserve with walks through the hills and jungle. Curug Gendang waterfall is a three-hour return hike through the reserve.

Tours

Virtually everyone in town is peddling a Krakatau tour. Travel agencies, including **Java Rhino** (☎0812 1275 2333; www.krakatoatour.com), and **Krakatau Tour** (☎0813 8666 8811; www.krakatau-tour.com), can organise trips. Check your tour boat first as waves can be rough, and make sure it has a radio and life jackets on board. Day trips to Krakatau start at 2,500,000Rp after bargaining. Trips to Ujung Kulon start at 6,250,000Rp for a three-day tour.

Sleeping & Eating

Rates increase on weekends by about 20% at most places.

Sunset View HOTEL **$**
(☎0253-801 075; www.augusta-ind.com; r with fan from 225,000Rp, with air-con 295,000Rp;) This centrally located hotel on the inland side of the coastal road offers large, clean rooms. The restaurant downstairs serves Indonesian grub.

Archipelago HOTEL **$$$**
(☎0253-880 888; www.archipelago-carita.com; Jl Raya Carita Km10; r 700,000Rp, cottages 1,750,000Rp;) Nest in a cool Torajan-style cottage or smaller, modern 'Jakarta rooms' right on the beach; this is the nicest choice in Carita. It has a nice pool and views of fishing platforms and Krakatau from its perch, but no restaurant.

Pondok Makan ABG INDONESIAN **$**
(Jl Raya Carita Km9; mains 18,000-36,000Rp) This traditional-style restaurant specialises in *ayam kalasan goreng* (fried chicken with special herbs). Wash it down with a cold Bintang or a fresh fruit juice (6000Rp). It's just behind the Hotel Rakata on the main beach road.

Getting There & Away

To get to Carita from Jakarta, take a bus to Labuan and then an *angkot* (minibus) to Carita (10,000Rp). On weekends allow extra time for the journey.

West Java

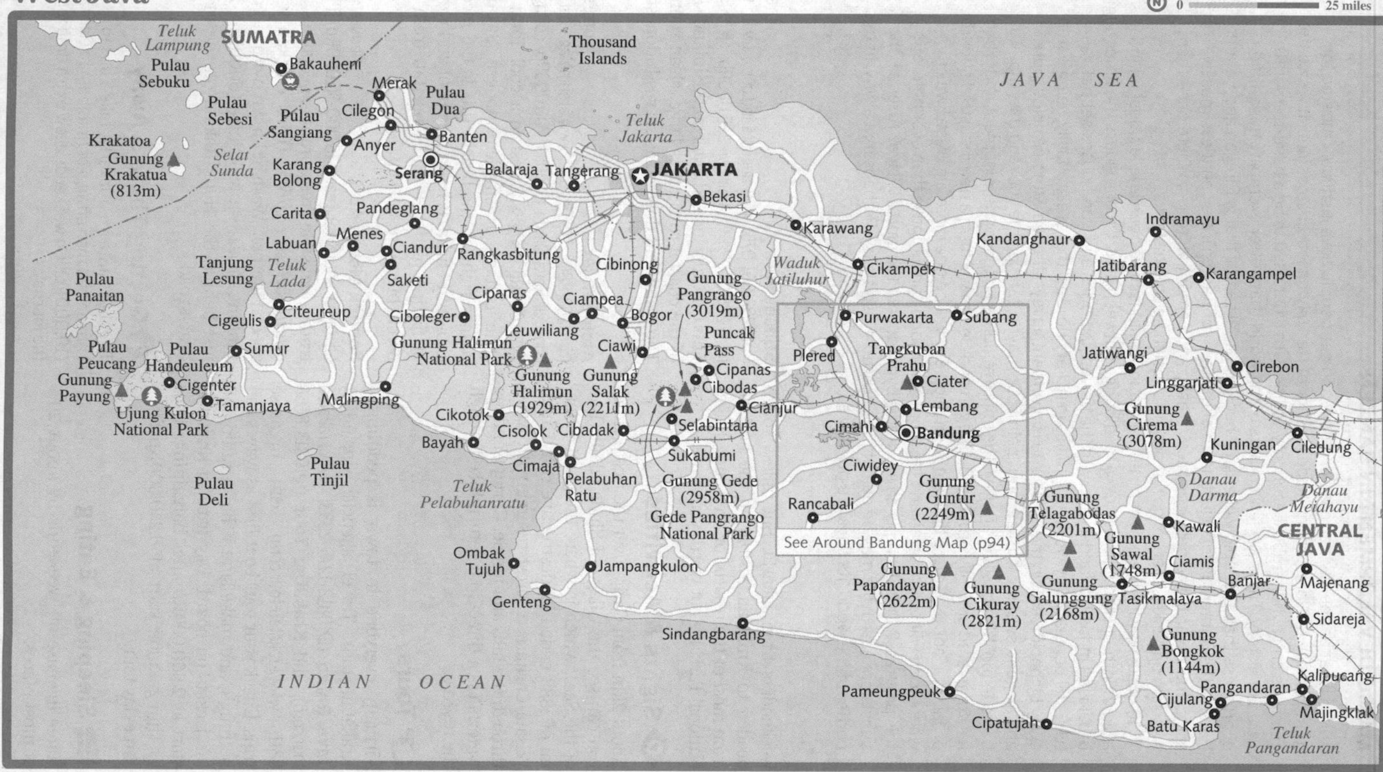
0 50 km
0 25 miles
N
SUMATRA
Teluk Lampung
Pulau Sebuku
Bakauheni
Pulau Sebesi
Krakatoa
Gunung Krakatua (813m)
Selat Sunda
Pulau Sangiang
Merak
Cilegon
Anyer
Pulau Dua
Banten
Serang
Karang Bolong
Carita
Pandeglang
Labuan
Menes
Ciandur
Saketi
Rangkasbitung
Tanjung Lesung
Teluk Lada
Pulau Panaitan
Citeureup
Cigeulis
Sumur
Pulau Peucang
Pulau Handeuleum
Gunung Payung
Cigenter
Tamanjaya
Ujung Kulon National Park
Pulau Deli
Pulau Tinjil
Malingping
Ciboleger
Cipanas
Gunung Halimun National Park
Gunung Halimun (1929m)
Leuwiliang
Ciampea
Cikotok
Bayah
Cisolok
Cimaja
Pelabuhan Ratu
Teluk Pelabuhanratu
Cibadak
Thousand Islands
Teluk Jakarta
Balaraja
Tangerang
JAKARTA
Bekasi
Cibinong
Bogor
Ciawi
Gunung Salak (2211m)
Gunung Pangrango (3019m)
Puncak Pass
Cipanas
Cibodas
Cianjur
Selabintana
Sukabumi
Gunung Gede (2958m)
Gede Pangrango National Park
Ombak Tujuh
Genteng
Jampangkulon
Sindangbarang
INDIAN OCEAN
JAVA SEA
Karawang
Waduk Jatiluhur
Cikampek
Purwakarta
Subang
Plered
Tangkuban Prahu
Ciater
Lembang
Cimahi
Bandung
Ciwidey
Rancabali
Gunung Guntur (2249m)
See Around Bandung Map (p94)
Gunung Papandayan (2622m)
Gunung Cikuray (2821m)
Pameungpeuk
Cipatujah
Kandanghaur
Indramayu
Jatibarang
Karangampel
Jatiwangi
Cirebon
Linggarjati
Gunung Cirema (3078m)
Kuningan
Ciledung
Danau Darma
Danau Meiahayu
Gunung Telagabodas (2201m)
Kawali
Gunung Sawal (1748m)
Ciamis
Gunung Galunggung (2168m)
Tasikmalaya
Banjar
CENTRAL JAVA
Majenang
Sidareja
Gunung Bongkok (1144m)
Kalipucang
Pangandaran
Majingklak
Cijulang
Batu Karas
Teluk Pangandaran

Labuan

0253 / POP 49,200

The dreary little port of Labuan is merely a jumping-off point for Carita or for Ujung Kulon National Park, but it is home to the helpful **Labuan PHKA office** (0253-801731; www.ujungkulon.org; 8am-4pm Mon-Fri), which manages the park. It's located 2km north of town towards Carita (look for the rhino statue).

Frequent buses depart from Kalideres bus terminal in Jakarta for Labuan (50,000Rp, 3½ hours). Regular buses also operate between Labuan and Bogor (50,000Rp, four hours). *Angkot* for Carita (5000Rp, 30 minutes) leave from the market, 100m from the Labuan bus terminal.

Gunung Krakatau

The legendary peak of Krakatau, the most famous of the world's famous volcanoes, is a name almost everyone knows – but few actually know of its location (take the film makers of *Krakatoa, East of Java*, for instance). Resting in relative peace some 50km from the West Java coast and 40km from Sumatra, the volcano is nowadays a shadow of its former self – a small group of disconnected islands centred on Anak Krakatau (Child of Krakatau), a volcanic mass that has been on the boil since 1928.

The highlight of any trip to Krakatau is rounding Pulau Rakata and first glimpsing the menacing peak of Krakatau's child.

Activities

Krakatau is only accessible by boat. At the time of research it was possible to land on the eastern side of Anak Krakatau and explore the lower parts of the cone, but this is very much dependent on volcanic activity. Walking to the edge of the caldera is never advisable – people have been killed by flying rocks. Always seek qualified advice before making any trip to the volcano.

After Krakatau, tours usually move on to hike and snorkel on neighbouring islands. Overnight tours set up camp on either Rakata or Verlaten islands.

Information

Labuan PHKA office has solid information on the volcano; otherwise consult tour agencies in Carita about Anak Krakatau's current activity.

Getting There & Away

Most visitors to Krakatau come from Carita. However, Krakatau officially lies in Sumatra's Lampung province, and it is slightly quicker and cheaper to reach Krakatau from the small port of Kalianda.

Chartering a boat is the only way to get to Krakatau; always charter the best vessel you can afford. During the rainy season (November to March) there are strong currents and rough seas, but even during the dry season strong southeast winds can make a crossing inadvisable. Krakatau is a 90-minute ride from Carita in a fast boat when weather conditions are fine. It's a long one-day trip, but it's definitely worth the effort – *if* you can hire a safe boat.

Small fishing boats may be cheap, but being pushed around in high oceanic swells won't feel like value for money. Reliable boats with radios and life jackets start at 2,000,000Rp to 2,500,000Rp for a small utility boat (maximum of six people) and go up to around 3,000,000Rp for faster boats (eight to 10 people). These can be organised through Carita tour agents.

Ujung Kulon National Park

On the remote southwestern tip of Java, this Unesco World Heritage–listed **national park** (www.ujungkulon.org; admission 150,000-225,000Rp) has remained an outpost of prime rainforest and untouched wilderness, virgin beaches and healthy coral reefs. It's relatively inaccessible; few people visit Indonesia's first national park, but it is one of the most rewarding in all Java.

Ujung Kulon is best known as the last refuge of the one-horned Javan rhinoceros, one of the globe's most critically endangered mammals – there are only thought to be between 50 to 60 remaining, all right here.

Numbers are thought to be stable and the rhinos are breeding, however they are an extremely rare sight and you are far more likely to come across *banteng* (wild cattle), wild pigs, otters, deer, squirrels, leaf monkeys, gibbons and big monitor lizards. Panthers also live in the forest and pythons and crocodiles in the river estuaries. Green turtles nest in some of the bays and the birdlife is excellent.

The national park also includes the nearby island of Panaitan (where Captain James Cook anchored HMS *Endeavour* in 1771) and the smaller offshore islands of Peucang and Handeuleum. Much of the peninsula is dense lowland rainforest and a mixture of scrub, grassy plains, swamps, pandanus palms and

DAY INTO NIGHT

Few volcanoes have as explosive a place in history as Krakatau, the island that blew itself apart in 1883. Turning day into night and hurling devastating tsunamis against the shores of Java and Sumatra, Krakatau quickly became vulcanology's A-list celebrity.

Few would have guessed that Krakatau would have snuffed itself out with such a devastating swansong. It had been dormant since 1680 and was regarded as little more than a familiar nautical landmark for maritime traffic passing through the narrow Selat Sunda. But from May through early August 1883, passing ships reported moderate activity, and by 26 August Krakatau was raging.

At 10am on 27 August 1883, Krakatau erupted so explosively that on the island of Rodriguez, more than 4600km to the southwest, a police chief reported hearing the booming of 'heavy guns from eastward'.

With its cataclysmic eruptions, Krakatau sent up a column of ash 80km high and threw into the air nearly 20 cubic kilometres of rock. Ash fell on Singapore 840km to the north and on ships as far as 6000km away; darkness covered Selat Sunda from 10am on 27 August until dawn the next day.

Far more destructive were the great ocean waves Krakatau triggered. A tsunami more than 40m high swept over the nearby shores of Java and Sumatra, and the wave's passage was recorded far from Krakatau, reaching Aden (on the Arabian Peninsula) in 12 hours over a distance 'travelled by a good steamer in 12 days'. Measurable wave effects were even said to have reached the English Channel. Coastal Java and Sumatra were devastated: 165 villages were destroyed and more than 36,000 people were killed.

The following day a telegram sent to Singapore from Batavia (160km east of Krakatau) reported odd details such as 'fish dizzy and caught with glee by natives', and for three years ash clouds circled the earth, creating spectacular sunsets.

The astonishing return of life to the devastated islands has been the subject of scientific study ever since. Not a single plant was found on Krakatau a few months after the event; 100 years later, it seems almost as though the vegetation was never disturbed – although the only fauna are snakes, insects, rats, bats and birds.

Krakatau may have blown itself to smithereens, but it is currently being replaced by Anak Krakatau, which has been on the ascendant ever since its first appearance in 1930. Today, 'Krakatau's child' is growing at the rate of 7m per year, and this anger-prone volcanic kid is certainly a chip off the old block, sending out showers of glowing rocks and belching smoke and ash.

long stretches of sandy beach on the west and south coasts.

Most people visit Ujung Kulon on a tour organised through an agency, but it's also possible to head to Tamanjaya village and access the park from there or to make arrangements directly through the park office, which will link you up with a boat operator.

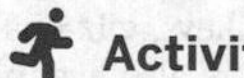

Activities

Tamanjaya village, the main gateway to the park, has budget accommodation and guides. One three-day hike across to the west coast via beaches and river crossings and on to Pulau Peucang is very popular, but there are decent alternatives, including a route that takes in good coastal scenery and the lighthouse at Tanjung Layar, the westernmost tip of mainland Java. Or, for wildlife-viewing, you can set up a series of day hikes in Tamanjaya.

Pulau Peucang is another entry point, but it can only be reached by chartered boat. There's good accommodation and a restaurant. Peucang also has beautiful white-sand beaches and coral reefs on its sheltered eastern coast (snorkelling gear is available). Hikers might be able to hitch a lift on a boat out of Peucang, but don't count on it.

There is also comfortable but simple accommodation at Pulau Handeuleum, which is ringed by mangroves. It has some Timor deer but doesn't have Peucang's attractions. Canoes can be hired (50,000Rp) for the short cruise up a jungle river where you might see pythons – they're often spotted hanging on branches above the water.

Large Pulau Panaitan is more expensive to reach but has some fine beaches and hiking. It's a day's walk between the PHKA posts at Legon Butun and Legon Haji, or you can walk to the top of Gunung Raksa, topped by a Hindu statue of Ganesha. Panaitan is a legendary surfing spot, with breaks including the infamous One Palm Point, a left-hand barrel that spins over a sharp reef.

Tours

Tours can be set up in Tamanjaya itself, with the park office in Labuan or via more expensive Carita tour agencies. Basically you can either walk or boat into the park; there are no roads. Either way you must have a guide.

Factor in food costs (around 50,000Rp per day, per person), your guide (150,000Rp per day) and tent rental (around 100,000Rp per trip). Bring along lightweight food, such as packaged noodles, and drinking water if you are hiking; otherwise food can be organised by tour operators or the park wardens. Supplies are available in Tamanjaya, but in Sumur and Labuan there is far more choice. Boat trips are much more expensive as the boat hire costs 3,500,000Rp (for up to 10 people).

If you'd rather get organised in advance, book through the park office in Labuan. A three-day/two-night all-inclusive tour costs about 7,500,000Rp (for two people). This includes return road and sea transport on a wooden boat, accommodation inside the national park, snorkelling, canoeing, hiking and meals. You'll pay double for a much more comfortable and faster speedboat.

Surf packages are also available to Panaitan; Bali-based **Surf Panaitan** (☎0361-850 0254; www.surfpanaitan.com) charges from US$900 for a seven-day trip.

Sleeping & Eating

Advance bookings are recommended for Pulau Peucang and Handeuleum, particularly at weekends; contact the Labuan PHKA office. Within the park you can camp or stay at the primitive huts for a small fee. Food and supplies are available in Tamanjaya.

Sunda Jaya Homestay GUESTHOUSE **$**
(☎0818 0618 1209; http://sundajaya.blogspot.com; Tamanjaya; r per person 150,000-200,000Rp, meals 30,000-50,000R) This Tamanjaya guesthouse was orginially built by the World Wildlife Fund and has four simple, clean rooms, each with two single beds and mosquito nets. Bathrooms are shared. Good meals are offered and there's free tea and coffee. The genial owner is an expert on the national park and can organise guides and supplies.

Pulau Handeuleum Lodge LODGE **$$**
(www.ujungkulon.org; r 250,000Rp) Set in a coconut grove, this lodge has been recently renovated and has six simple double rooms with fans. There's a kitchen, but you must bring your own food as the island has no other dining options, and you also must charter a boat from Tamanjaya (3,000,000Rp, one hour) to get here.

Pulau Peucang Lodge LODGE **$$$**
(d incl full board 1,300,000Rp; ❄) Choose among five different accommodation options, some of them surprisingly smart given the remote location. The attractive, air-conditioned Flora bungalows are the best of the bunch and offer hot-water bathrooms, reading lights, and a fridge. There's a good restaurant, and deer, monkeys and wild boar are often spotted around the grounds.

Information

The **Labuan PHKA office** (☎0253-801731; www.ujungkulon.org; ⏲8am-4pm Mon-Fri) is a useful source of information. You pay your entry fee when you enter the park, at the park office in Tamanjaya or on the islands. Hikers should try to pick up a copy of the excellent (but rarely available) *Visitor's Guidebook to the Trails of Ujung Kulon National Park* (50,000Rp) from the park office.

The best time to visit Ujung Kulon is in the dry season (April to October), when the sea is generally calm and the reserve less boggy. Malaria has been reported in Ujung Kulon.

Getting There & Away

From Labuan there's one direct bus to Tamanjaya (50,000Rp, 3½ hours) daily at noon. There are also hourly *angkot* as far as Sumur (35,000Rp, two hours) until around 4pm. From Sumur, an *ojek* to Tamanjaya is about 30,000Rp.

The road between Sumur and Tamanjaya is usually in very poor shape, particularly during rainy season.

You may also charter a boat to get here from Carita, Labuan or Sumur. Given the long stretch of open sea, fork out for a decent one. Speedboats are double the price of the wooden relics but worth it. Surf tours use their own transport.

Bogor

☎0251 / POP 1.02 MILLION

'A romantic little village' is how Sir Thomas Stamford Raffles described Bogor when he made it his country home during the British interregnum. As an oasis of unpredictable weather – it is credited with 322 thunderstorms a year – cool, quiet Bogor was the chosen retreat of colonials escaping the stifling, crowded capital.

Today, the long arm of Jakarta reaches the whole way to Bogor, infecting this second city with the overspill of the capital's perennial traffic and air-quality problems. The city itself isn't charmless, however. The local people are quite warm and friendly, the world-class botanical gardens are still beautiful and the two are certainly worthy of a sleepover.

Sights

Jl Suryakencana, steps from the garden gates, is a whirlwind of activity as shoppers spill en masse from within the byzantine concrete halls of **Pasar Baru** (cnr Jl Otto Iskandardinata & Suryakencana; 6am-1pm) onto the street. Inside, the morning market is awash with all manner of produce and flowers, meat and fish, second hand clothes and more. Hot, sweltering and loud, it's a hell of a browse. Dive into the barter and trade, and experience Bogor.

★Kebun Raya GARDENS

(Great Garden; www.bogor.indo.net.id/kri; admission 26,000Rp; 8am-5pm) At the heart of Bogor are the fabulous botanical gardens, known as the Kebun Raya, the city's green lung of around 87 hectares. Governor General Raffles first developed a garden here, but the spacious grounds of the Istana Bogor (Presidential Palace) were expanded by Dutch botanist Professor Reinwardt, with assistance from London's Kew Gardens, and officially opened in 1817. Colonial cash crops, such as tea, cassava, tobacco and cinchona, were first developed here by Dutch botanists.

Allow yourself at least half a day to enjoy Kebun Raya; keen gardeners could spend a week here and not be bored. It's tricky to pick out highlights in such a verdant wonderland – there are more than 15,000 species of trees and plants – but the gardens are said to contain 400 types of palms, including the footstool palm native to Indonesia, which tops 40m. There's a good stock of graceful pandan trees (look out for their unusual aerial roots) and some huge agave (used to make tequila) and cacti in the Mexican section. Drop by the Orchid House and take in the lovely, muddy ponds, which have dozens of giant water lilies over a metre across, and look out for monitor lizards, exotic birdlife and deer. The one nitpick is that signage isn't the garden's strong suit.

Near the main entrance of the gardens is a small memorial, erected in memory of Olivia Raffles, who died in 1814 and was buried in Batavia. There is also a cemetery near the palace with Dutch headstones including the tomb of DJ de Eerens, a former governor general.

Crowds flock here on Sunday, but the gardens are quiet at most other times. The southern gate is the main entrance; other gates are only open on Sunday and holidays. Don't miss the delightful Grand Garden Café (p82), the perfect spot for lunch.

Istana Bogor HISTORIC BUILDING

In the northwestern corner of the botanical gardens, the summer palace of the president was formerly the opulent official residence of the Dutch governors general from 1870 to 1942. Today, herds of white-spotted deer roam the immaculate lawns and the building contains Sukarno's huge art collection, which largely focuses on the female figure. The palace is only open to groups (minimum 10) by prior arrangement, and children are not allowed inside. Contact the tourist office for more information.

Batutulis SHRINE

(Jl Batutulis) The Batutulis is an inscribed stone dedicated to Sri Baduga Maharaja (1482–1521), a Pajajaran king credited with great mystical power. The stone is housed in a small shrine visited by pilgrims – remove your shoes and pay a small donation before entering. Batutulis is 2.5km south of the botanical gardens, almost opposite the former home of Sukarno. Sukarno's request to be buried here was ignored by Suharto, who wanted the former president's grave far from the capital.

Gong Workshop FACTORY

(0251-832 4132; Jl Pancasan 17) FREE Home industry at its finest: this is one of the few remaining gongsmiths in Java, where you can see gamelan instruments smelted over a charcoal fire by hand. A few pricey gongs and *wayang golek* puppets are on sale.

Tours

Tours of Bogor can be arranged through the tourist office (p82) for around 200,000/300,000Rp per half-day/day. The tours take in a working-class *kampung*, and various cottage industries including the gong

Bogor & Kebun Raya

Bogor & Kebun Raya

Top Sights

1 Kebun Raya B3

Sights

2 Gong Workshop A4
3 Istana Bogor B3
4 Pasar Baru B3

Sleeping

5 Abu Pensione A2
6 Savero Golden Flower C2
7 The 101 .... C4
8 Wisma Pakuan D4

Eating

9 De' Leuit D4
10 Grand Garden Café C3
11 Gumati Cafe A3
12 Kentjana C4

factory and tofu and *krupuk* (prawn cracker) kitchens. Speak to the office about hiking trips into Halimun National Park.

Sleeping

Bogor does not have a great choice of budget accommodation. Prices are a bit steep compared with the rest of Java.

Abu Pensione GUESTHOUSE $
(☎0251-832 2893; Jl Mayor Oking 15; r with fan/air-con from 175,000/275,000Rp; ❄) Safe, secure and set back from the road, rooms around the garden are spacious and well maintained, others facing the river at the rear are a bit dark. All are fine for a night or two. It's across the street from the train station and well located for ramblers.

Wisma Pakuan GUESTHOUSE $$
(0251-831 9430; wismapakuanbogor@yahoo.com; Jl Ciheuleut 12; r with fan 255,000Rp, with air-con 320,000Rp;) Twelve well-maintained rooms with high ceilings, flat-screen TVs and good beds. Those at the rear have views over a garden, where breakfast is served.

The 101 HOTEL $$
(0251-756 7101; www.the101hotels.com; Jl Suryakencana 179-181; r from 600,000Rp;) Relatively sleek, with a nice pool area, the hotel rises like a shark fin above the city, looming over the red roof tiles and domed mosques. It's set close to the gardens and the morning market. Rooms have tiled floors, flat-screen TVs and accent walls, which complete the tastefully modern, minimalist decor. Many have balconies.

Part of a small, nationwide chain and just six months old at research time, it's great value when booked through Agoda.com.

Savero Golden Flower HOTEL $$
(0251-835 8888; golden-flower.co.id/Bogor; Jl Raya Pajajaran 27; r from 678,000Rp;) Built in a colonial mansion style, this is the newest offering to Bogor's upmarket hotel division, blessed with a perfect location looming over the gardens. Despite the sumptuous appearance, however, the beige and white rooms aren't huge though they have class, with rain showers and plush linen. Just three months old when we stopped by; standard of service is high.

Eating & Drinking

For street food check out the night market along Jl Dewi Sartika and Jl Jenderal Sudirman. Or, if it's raining, the food court inside the Botani Square shopping mall is another good bet.

★**De' Leuit** INDONESIAN $$
(0251-839 0011; Jl Pakuan III; meals 10,000-99,000Rp; 11am-9pm;) The most happening eatery in Bogor. There's seating on three floors beneath a soaring, pyramid-shaped thatched roof, though the best tables are on the first two levels. It does *sate*, mixed rice dishes, fried *gurame fish*, and fried chicken, as well as a variety of local veggie dishes. Come with a group and eat Sundanese family-style.

Gumati Cafe INDONESIAN $$
(0251-832 4318; Jl Paledang 26 & 28; mains 17,000-64,000Rp; 10am-10pm;) This Sundanese restaurant offers arguably the best view in town with superlative vistas over Bogor's red-tiled rooftops towards the volcanic cone of Gunung Salak. There's an extensive menu, with tapas-style snacks and traditional dishes such as *sup ikan bambu* (soup with fish and bamboo).

Grand Garden Café INTERNATIONAL $$
(0251-835 0023; inside Kebun Raya; mains 30,000-80,000Rp; 10am-8pm Mon-Thu, 10am-10pm Fri-Sun) The cafe-restaurant in the botanical gardens is a wonderfully civilised place for a bite or a drink, with sweeping views down to the water lily ponds. It's a little pricey, but the tasty international and Indonesian food and sublime setting make it an essential stop.

Kentjana CHINESE $$
(0251-833 0698; Jl Suryakencana 143; dishes 35,000-120,000Rp; noon-10pm) A tasteful, soulful Chinese diner with a wonderful *mapo tofu* on the menu (the tofu was among the silkiest we've ever had), along with a number of ethnic Chinese Indonesian dishes. All served up in a gold and red room decked out with Chinese lanterns and artfully arranged black-and-white photos of yesteryear Bogor. The house sambal rocks.

Information

There's free wi-fi at the Botani Square mall, hotels and guesthouses.

BCA Bank (Jl Ir H Juanda 28; 8am-4pm Mon-Sat)

PHKA Headquarters (Jl Ir H Juanda 15; 7am-2.30pm Mon-Thu, to 11am Fri) The official body for the administration of all of Indonesia's wildlife reserves and national parks; located next to the main garden gates.

Post Office (Jl Ir H Juanda; 8am-2pm Mon-Sat)

Tourist Office (081 6195 3838; Jl Dewi Sartika 51; 8am-6pm) The friendly team here can help out with most queries about the region, provide a city map and also offer excellent, well-priced tours.

Getting There & Away

BUS

Every 15 minutes or so, buses depart from Jakarta's Kampung Rambutan bus terminal (10,000Rp to 15,000Rp, 45 minutes) for Bogor.

Buses depart frequently to Bandung (economy/air-con, 50,000/60,000Rp, 3½ hours), Pelabuhan Ratu (55,000Rp, three hours) and Labuan (55,000Rp, four hours). For Cianjur (30,000Rp, two hours), white minibuses (called *colt*) depart regularly from Jl Raya Pajajaran. Door-to-door *travel* minibuses go to Bandung for 100,000Rp.

Damri buses head direct to Jakarta's Soekarno-Hatta International Airport (55,000Rp, two to three hours) every 20 minutes from 4am to 11pm from Jl Raya Pajajaran.

CAR

The tourist office can recommend car drivers to explore the region around Bogor; rates start at 500,000Rp per day.

TRAIN

Express trains (15,000Rp, one hour) connect Bogor with the capital roughly every hour, though try to avoid travelling during rush hour. Economy trains are more frequent, but they are packed with people – some clinging to the roof.

Getting Around

Green *angkot* minibuses (3000Rp) shuttle around town, particularly between the bus terminal and train station. *Angkot* 03 does a counterclockwise loop of the botanical gardens on its way to Jl Kapten Muslihat, near the train station. *Angkot* 06 gets you to the bus terminal from the train station.

Becak are banned from the main road encircling the gardens. Taxis are extremely rare in Bogor.

Around Bogor

With lush forests, white-water rapids and an organic farm with a serious kitchen, Bogor's outskirts are worth a look.

Sights

Taman Nasional Gunung Halimun PARK

(www.halimunsalak.org; Jl Raya Cipanas; admission 250,000Rp) This mixed-use national park is home to small swatches of primary rainforest, but also includes plantations such as the Nirmala Tea Estate. The park's best feature is the rich montane forest in the highland regions around Gunung Halimun (1929m), its tallest peak. The big drawcard is white-water rafting. In Jakarta, **Pt Lintas Seram Nusantara** (☎021-835 5885; www.arusliar.co.id) organises white-water rafting on the Class II to IV (depending on season) Sungai Citarak on the southeastern edge of the park; a full-day excursion is 485,000Rp.

The usual access (you need your own transport) is through Cibadak on the Bogor–Pelabuhan Ratu road, from where you turn off to Cikadang and then on to the Nirmala Tea Estate. Rainfall in the park is between 4000mm and 6000mm per year. Most of this falls from October to May, when a visit is more or less out of the question.

Speak to the staff at the tourist office in Bogor about setting up a trip to Halimun.

Sleeping & Eating

★**Lodges Ekologika on Portibi Farms** FARMSTAY $$

(☎0813 8446 9096; www.portibi.com; huts US$10, bungalows US$35-65, r US$66; meals per day US$40) An organic farm and gourmet kitchen two hours from Jakarta, Portibi has developed a reputation around the city for imaginative meals cobbled together from ingredients grown on their 14 hectares. It's set on the terraced slopes of Gunung Salak (2200m), and most guests stay in charming rooms and bungalows built from reclaimed teak, glass and polished concrete, and blessed with magnificent views (with cheap and simple bamboo huts available for backpackers).

Whatever their budget, most guests spend their downtime in the Pacifist Cannibal Lounge. It is here, on the ground floor of the main house, where the owner, a recovering American academic, mixes original cocktails behind a curved reclaimed-timber bar, while the sound system thumps out classic punk anthems and neo-classic hip-hop beats.

But above all, the family-style meals are the thing. Think homemade ravioli, steamed barramundi, tempe tacos folded in housemade tortillas, and colourful salads, which are among the best we've ever had. Be warned, it's not just easy to overeat here. It's likely. Though it attracts mostly midrange customers, backpackers can take advantage of special midweek rates (all-inclusive US$30), though you'll be crashing in a hut.

Cimaja

☎0266

About 100km south of Bogor, Cimaja is an attractive, low-key surf resort with a good choice of accommodation and excellent waves. There's also a mystical quality to the place. After a long sunset session, as you wander back through the rice fields along the canals, you'll hear the ethereal calls to prayer filter through the palms. True, the line up can swell to over 20 guys in the high season, but you could get lucky and surf with three or four too. Plus, if you've been suffering in Java's teeming cities, the slow pace and oceanic air makes for an exhilarating change.

To get here you have to pass through the large, unlovely resort of Pelabuhan Ratu; Cimaja is 8km further west.

Sights & Activities

The main beach is a cobblestone affair, but scenic. It's often pounded by crashing surf, which sends the black and white cobbles rolling and rumbling. To some it sounds like God playing marbles. Thanks to the force, the stones and the rips, swimming can be treacherous, so take extreme care. You can stroll from the shore to the village via an idyllic patchwork of rice paddies. For a sandy beach you'll have to head west for a kilometre or so to Karang Hawu (Sunset Beach), a broad strip of dark sand with better swimming.

Cimaja is rightly renowned for its excellent surf. Some of the south coast's best waves include Cimaja Point, 200m from the Di Desa hotel. Indicator Point has a killer break which fires at high tide when there's a big swell, and Karang Hawu has a beach break that is good for beginners.

Diving, fishing, rafting and motorcycling trips can also be organised through your guesthouse, and so can surf lessons. They cost about 150,000Rp per day (excluding soft board rental). Most instructors and guides hang out at Café Loma.

Sleeping & Eating

Cimaja is very quiet during the week and fills up at weekends and during holidays, when prices rise by around 20% at many places.

Cimaja Homestay HOMESTAY $
(s/d 150,000/200,000Rp; ❄ 📶) Set in the rice fields just behind D Square is this sky-blue, concrete-block homestay, tended by lovely English-speaking staff who offer sparkling tiled rooms. Some have air-con.

Pondok Kencana LODGE $
(☎ 0266-431465; www.ombaktujuh.net; Jl Cisolok Km8; r with shared baths 135,000Rp, bungalows with shared/private baths 185,000/345,000Rp, meals from 35,000Rp; ❄ 📶) The first guesthouse in town, Australian-owned Pondok Kencana enjoys a hilltop location at the entrance to the village. There's a wide choice of attractive accommodation, many with viewing decks and shared kitchen access.

The owner can usually be found in the bar-restaurant, which serves filling international grub, including good breakfasts. He's a wealth of information.

★ **Nurda's** LODGE $$
(☎ 0813 1475 9937; www.cimajapoint.com; Jl Raya Cisolok; r with fan/air-con 250,000/300,000Rp; ❄ 📶) A surf lodge set around a gorgeous main house just off the beach. Rooms are tiled, modern and quite spacious, sharing a lovely bathroom. Sadly, some – though not all – have been tainted by smokers. Still, the restaurant is the most creative in town and serves fish and tempe burgers, chicken schnitzel, and grilled and fried seafood.

D Square BUNGALOW $$
(☎ 0266-644 0800; http://cimajasquare.com; Jl Raya Cisolok Km5; bungalows 150,000-300,000Rp; ❄ @ 📶) Expect brick, concrete and wood cottages, all good-sized and built over the rice paddies, and a decent restaurant wired with wi-fi, centrally located and walking distance from the waves. Unfortunately, window screens are torn and bathrooms can be mosquito sanctuaries.

Café Loma INDONESIAN $
(Jl Raya Cisolok; mains 12,000-30,000Rp) A very cheap little log-cabin–style warung where you can score a great breakfast for 20,000Rp, fresh juice for 5000Rp or a cup of Java coffee for just 3000Rp. Most mains, including *ikan mentega* (fish in butter sauce), are less than 30,000Rp. In the evening it's a low-key hang out for surfers, with cold Bintang.

Rumah Makan Joker SEAFOOD $$
(☎ 0813 8641 7378; Jl Raya Cisolok Km3; dishes 35,000-65,000Rp; ⏲ 10am-2am) Try to ignore that tired 'decorative' fish tank swirling with turtles in the entryway and don't sweat the fact that the veggies and fried *cumi cumi* (squid) are average at best. Because the *ikan bakar* (grilled fish) is reason enough to seek out the Joker among this long strand of seemingly identical seafood joints.

It will come rubbed with turmeric and charred to perfection. Bring your *bahasa* (or translator) to order appropriately.

Information

There are no banks in Cimaja, but you'll find several in Pelabuhan Ratu, 8km to the east, including **BCA Bank** (Jl Siliwangi; ⏲ 8am-4pm Mon-Sat) with an ATM. All the area's guesthouses have wi-fi.

Getting There & Around

To reach Cimaja, you first need to get to Pelabuhan Ratu. Buses run throughout the day from Bogor

(30,000Rp, three to four hours) to Pelabuhan Ratu. There is no direct access to or from Jakarta. You have to get to Bogor first.

Some buses continue on from Pelabuhan Ratu to Cimaja. These are supplemented by regular *angkot* (5000Rp, 30 minutes), which run about every 20 minutes. Some *angkot* then go on to Cisolok, past Sunset Beach.

Motorbikes can be hired for 60,000Rp per day from locals in Cimaja, and surfboard racks are available.

Around Cimaja

Although Cimaja's beach location is enviable, West Java has a way of making any town tremble with high-speed traffic terror. However, if you drive west, village life and those luscious rice paddies will soon come back into view and the traffic will die down. From here, it's all jade *sawah* (rice fields) set against the deep blue sea.

Sights & Activities

Pantai Karang Hawu VIEWPOINT

Pantai Karang Hawu, 4km west of Cimaja, is a towering cliff with caves, rocks and pools created by a large lava flow. According to legend, it was here where the goddess Nyai Loro Kidul leapt into the ocean to regain her lost beauty and never returned. Stairs lead up to a small *kramat* (shrine) at the top.

Cipanas HOT SPRINGS

About 3km west of Pantai Karang Hawu are the Cipanas hot springs. Boiling water sprays into the river, and you can soak downstream where the hot and cold waters mingle. It is a scenic area, with lush forest upstream and a waterfall, though it's crowded on weekends.

Cibodas

☎0263

Southwest of Bogor the highway steadily climbs in elevation, through a sprawling hill resort known as the Puncak that's popular with weekending Jakartans. This traffic-choked road winds up to 1490m before descending to Cibodas, famous for its stunning gardens, the **Kebun Raya Cibodas** (☎0263-512233; www.bogor.indo.net.id; per person 20,000Rp; ⊙8am-4pm). Spread over the steep lower slopes of Gunung Gede and Gunung Pangrango at an altitude of 1300m to 1440m, these lush gardens are among the dampest places in Java. The Dutch tried to cultivate quinine here (its bark is used in malaria medication), though the East Javan climate proved more suitable.

You'll find an outstanding collection of ferns and palms, 65 species of eucalyptus, Mexican mountain pines and glasshouses bursting with cacti and succulents. A road loops around the gardens, passing via the Japanese garden with its cherry trees, and there are also paths leading through forests of bamboo to the impressive Cismun waterfall.

Visitors must pay 2000Rp to enter Cibodas village.

Back on the main highway, you'll find that Cibodas, like most of West Java, is swelling beyond its original skin. Once a relatively prosperous yet simple tea and market town, with nice homes dotting the green hills, now there are gleaming malls, fashion outlets and upmarket lodging serving weekenders from Bogor and Jakarta.

Sleeping & Eating

Bali Ubud Guesthouse GUESTHOUSE $

(☎0263-512051; r from 150,000Rp) About 4km south of the entrance to the gardens, this wonderful Balinese-owned place has attractive rooms with balconies that enjoy spectacular valley views. The restaurant here also makes the most of the views, serving good Western and Indonesian food, and cold Bintang. However, they do keep caged pit bulls here.

Getting There & Away

The turn-off to Cibodas is on the Bogor–Bandung Hwy, a few kilometres west of Cipanas. The gardens are 5km from the main road. *Angkot* run from the roadside in Cipanas up to the gardens (5000Rp, 10 minutes).

Gede Pangrango National Park

The Cibodas gardens are right next to the main entrance to Gede Pangrango National Park, the highlight of which is the climb to the peak of the volcanically active **Gunung Gede** (2958m). From the top of Gede on a clear day you can see Jakarta and the south coast of Java.

Because it's close to Jakarta, this is an extremely popular mountain to climb. Numbers are restricted and during peak holiday season there may be a waiting list. At other times you can normally just rock up and trek the next day.

On arrival, register for the climb and obtain your permit (a steep 250,000Rp for foreigners) from the **PHKA office** (☎0263-512776) just outside the entrance to the gardens. The office has an information centre and pamphlets on the park, which is noted for its alpine forest and birdlife, including the rare Javan eagle. Officially, guides to the summit *have* to be hired here for 500,000Rp for a two-day round trip, though the main trail is easy to follow. Gunung Gede is closed to hikers during stormy weather, between January and March, and usually August too.

From Cibodas, the trail passes Telaga Biru (15 minutes), which is a blue-green lake. Cibeureum Falls (one hour away) lie just off the main trail. Most picnickers only go this far, though some continue on to the hot springs, 3½ hours from the gate. Treks to the falls alone are possible for just 150,000Rp plus the entry fee. The trail continues to climb another 1½ hours to Kandang Badak, where a hut has been built on the saddle between the peaks of Gunung Gede and Gunung Pangrango (3019m). Take the trail to the right for a hard three-hour climb to Pangrango. Most hikers turn left for the easier, but still steep, 1½-hour climb to Gede, which has more spectacular views. The Gede Crater lies below the summit, and you can continue on to the Suryakencana Meadow.

The 10km hike right to the top of Gunung Gede takes at least 12 hours there and back, so you should start as early as possible and take warm clothes (night temperatures can drop to 5°C), food, water and a torch (flashlight). Most hikers leave by 2am to reach the summit in the early morning before the mists roll in.

Cianjur

☎0263 / POP 159,000

East of Cibodas it's 19km to Cianjur, a market town that's famed throughout Java for the quality of its rice (there's also a brand-new Nike factory on the outskirts). Indeed, the town is enveloped by shimmering green paddy fields. Cianjur is no tourist town, and it isn't chock-full of sights, but if you wish to mix with locals and explore the area's fine trails and hillside villages, make your way here and book into the best homestay in West Java.

You'll find several banks on the main drag, Jl Cokroaminoto, and internet cafes are grouped together on Jl Siti Jenab.

Sights & Activities

The town (which is more an amalgamation of villages) has few attractions, but you can visit a huge plastic recycling plant to learn about waste management. Plastic is sent here from all over West Java to be separated by hand, then washed, chopped and dried before being sent on to plastic manufacturers. Do not be fooled, however: only a relative sliver of the plastic can be recycled and reused. Ninety per cent of single-use plastic is waste that either gets burned, which releases toxic fumes, or winds up in landfills or rivers, eventually washing out into the sea.

There are a couple of tea plantations close to town that are worth a visit; both are set in lush mountainside locations. **Gedeh tea plantation** (⏲8am-4pm Mon-Sat), 15km northwest of town via a potholed road, was established by the Dutch in 1916, and most of the original machinery is still in use. Between 400,000kg and 600,000kg of black tea is produced here monthly. Alternatively, **Sarongge** (⏲9am-2pm Mon-Thu & Sat) is a green-tea plantation and processing factory 20km north of town; it's open by appointment only. Tours to either plantation cost 150,000Rp per person.

Cianjur also makes a good base for trips to the Cibodas gardens. If you need to cool off head to **The John** (admission 30,000Rp; ⏲9am-5pm), a leisure complex with three swimming pools that's a decent picnic spot.

Sleeping & Eating

★**Chill Out Guest House** HOMESTAY **$$**
(☎0813 2172 9004; www.cianjuradventure.com; per person all-inclusive 200,000-250,000Rp) Set in the joyful and inviting middle-class family home of Yudhi Suryana, guests sleep in private or shared rooms with curtained-off beds and a shared bathroom. There's a large yard usually bustling with family, and three tasty meals included each day. Free laundry, too.

Best part: Yudhi arranges a handful of delightful tours in the region and all guests get a free visit to a floating village in a nearby lake, and to a local school. He also arranges bus and train tickets, and books private transport.

Lotek LP INDONESIAN **$**
(☎0263-264 554; Jl Irjuanda 28; meals 10,000-20,000Rp; ⏲6:30am-10pm) A scruffy storefront Sundanese diner run by a charming *ibu* (lady) who mixes the finest gado gado (12,000Rp) in West Java, plus authentically

LIVE WITH THE LOCALS

Author Yudhi Suryana (who for years lived in New Zealand) is building the tourism industry in Cianjur, one guest at a time. Through his wonderful **homestay**, and through his rare agenda of treks and driving tours, his goal is to offer independent travellers a slice of authentic Sundanese life. All guests at his homestay are offered a free tour to Cangling, a **floating village** on a nearby lake, with a fish-farming economy, and to a local school in town. The profusion of plastic around the floating village can be disappointing, but there is no doubt that you're seeing real Javanese life – with all its charms and challenges – up close.

Much more nourishing is the **Traditional Village Tour** (per person 175,000Rp, lunch included). Guests will take local *angkot* transport from the centre of Cianjur into the hills, where you'll follow a concrete *gang* (footpath) until it flakes away into earth. The 90-minute hike, past elegantly terraced rice fields and stands of clove, cardamom and guava trees, eventually leads to Kampung Gombong where you will have lunch at the wonderful braided bamboo home of your guide, Pak Ferdad. There's a lovely view, from high on a ridge above a deep river valley.

The whole village is filled with homes far from asphalt roads and served by small shops and tiny lanes that only the brave and knowledgeable can navigate with a motorbike. Lunch is prepared by Pak Ferdad's wife over an open flame in the kitchen. She also can make fresh palm sugar if you'd like to try it. Pak doesn't speak a lot of English, but he speaks enough, and Yudhi can arrange an English-speaking guide to join if that's important to you. After lunch you can have a massage and a nap before the lazy and beautiful wander back to the asphalt streets. This is the perfect antidote to those contagious urban blues so common in West Java.

Yudhi arranges airport pick-ups and drop-offs, as well as bus and train tickets to or from Jakarta, Bandung or Yogyakarta.

sweet and sticky *sate marangi* (beef satay; 5000Rp per stick).

Ikan Bakar Cianjur SEAFOOD $$
(☎0263-263 392; Jl Dr Muwardi 143; mains 30,000-60,000Rp; ⏲9am-10pm) A local institution with gurgling fountains, a koi pond entryway and a soaring tiled roof in the indoor-outdoor dining area. Choose your fish from the freshwater tanks – they have *gurame* or *nila*, which they butterfly and grill, pan-fry whole, or cook in tumeric soup.

ℹ Getting There & Away

From Jakarta the easiest way to Cianjur is via a daily minibus (125,000Rp, three hours, daily at 7am), which Yudhi from the Chill Out Guest House can book for you. This will pick you up from any Jakarta area hotel.

Otherwise, buses leave Jakarta's Kampung Rambutan every 30 minutes to Cipanas (35,000Rp, two hours) and Cianjur (35,000Rp, 2½ hours). On weekends (when traffic is terrible around Puncuk Pass) buses are routed via Jonggol (add an extra hour to your journey and an extra 10,000Rp to your tab). Buses to/from Bandung (normal/air-con 25,000/30,000Rp, two hours) run every half hour.

There are buses to Bogor from Cianjur (weekday/weekend 25,000/35,000Rp, 1½ to two hours) and the highway by Cipanas every 20 minutes.

Bandung

☎022 / POP 2.8 MILLION

A city of punks and prayer, serious religion and serious coffee – almost everything great and terrible about Indonesia can be found in Bandung. Here are teeming markets and good shopping, thriving cafes in reclaimed Dutch relics, palpable warmth and camaraderie on street corners and mind-numbing, air-trashing traffic almost everywhere you look. You may cringe at the systemic poverty and young teens smoking, and nod with respect at the city's thriving and growing middle class. Yes, Bandung has everything, except nature, and after the bottle-green hills of Cibodas, the sprawling bulk of Bandung is quite the urban reality check. But even if the local mountains are cloaked in smog, the city does make a good base for day trips to the surrounding countryside – high volcanic peaks, hot springs and tea plantations are all within reach.

Bandung

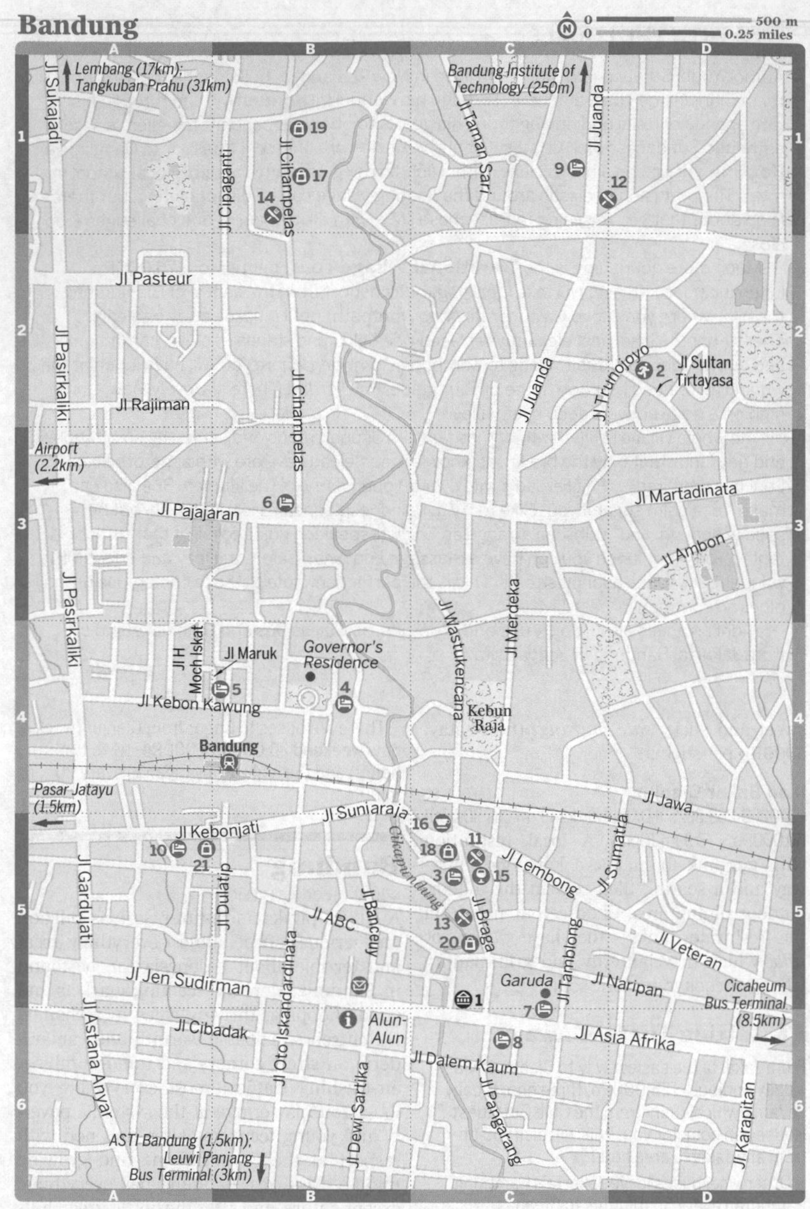

Bandung has three distinct districts that interest visitors. The Jl Braga area offers a strip of cafes and restaurants and is surrounded by markets and museums. The Jl Cihampelas district, or so-called Jeans Street area, offers discount retail and plenty of nibbles and hotels too, but the leafier north part of town is the most upmarket with the city's newest and trendiest restaurants dotting Jl Sultan Tirtayasa and Jl Trunojoyo.

Bandung

Sights
1 Museum Konperensi C5

Activities, Courses & Tours
2 Bersih Sehat D2

Sleeping
3 Chez Bon C5
4 Hotel Kenangan B4
5 Hotel Serena B4
6 Novotel B3
7 Prama Grand Preanger C6
8 Savoy Homann Hotel C6
9 The 101 .... C1
10 Yokotel A5

Eating
11 Braga Punya Carita C5
12 Capital 8 .... C1
13 Hangover C5
Kiosk .... (see 18)
14 Mangokok Manis B1

Drinking & Nightlife
North Sea Bar .... (see 11)
15 Roempoet C5
16 Wiki Koffee C5

Shopping
17 Bandung Jean Point B1
18 Braga City Walk C5
19 Cihampelas Walk B1
20 Kayu Solid C5
21 Pasar Baru A5

Sights

There are some fine Dutch art deco structures to admire on Jl Jenderal Sudirman and Jl Asia Afrika, two of the best being the Prama Grand Preanger (p90) and the Savoy Homann Hotel (p90), both of which have imposing facades. In the north of the city, Villa Isola is another wonderful Dutch art deco structure.

Villa Isola NOTABLE BUILDING
(Bumi Siliwangi; 0813 2245 3101, 022-201316; Jl Dr Setiabudhi 229; interior visits by appointment) FREE Around 7km north of the centre, Villa Isola is a landmark art deco building, a four-storey villa built by a Dutch media baron in the 1930s as a private residence. It's now the University of Education's administrative offices. This curvaceous architectural masterpiece is in excellent condition; from its balconies there's a fine perspective of Bandung. It's possible to enter the building if you call ahead.

Museum Konperensi MUSEUM
(Conference Museum; Jl Asia Afrika; 9am-3pm Mon-Fri) FREE The Museum Konperensi inside the Gedung Merdeka (Freedom Building) is dedicated to the Asia-Africa conference of 1955, which Bandung hosted and the echoes of which can still be seen in the city's branding today. There are a few interesting photos of Sukarno, Nehru, Ho Chi Minh, Nasser and other developing world leaders of the 1950s.

Bandung Institute of Technology UNIVERSITY
(ITB; www.itb.ac.id/en; Jl Ganeca; art gallery admission free; art gallery on request) Opened in 1920, the ITB was the first university open to Indonesians – Sukarno studied here, and it has a reputation for political activism. In 1998, in the lead-up to Suharto's downfall, up to 100,000 students rallied daily.

Set in spacious grounds, the complex contains some bizarre hybrid Indo-European architecture. Visit the art gallery, as its fine arts school is internationally famous. To reach the ITB, take a Lembang or Dago *angkot* from the train station and then walk down Jl Ganeca.

Activities

Adu domba, or 'ram fights', are held most Sundays between 9am and 1pm. While wildly popular in Bandung, animal welfare experts claim the spectacle is cruel; some travellers may find it distressing. For more information, contact the tourist information centre.

Bersih Sehat MASSAGE
(022-426 0765; www.bersihsehat.com; Jl Sultan Tirtayasa 31) This is an excellent massage and treatment salon. Rates are reasonable with a one-hour body massage costing 130,000Rp. A 90-minute treatment with a massage and *lulur* body scrub costs just 150,000Rp.

Tours

Freelance English-speaking **Enoss** (☎0852 2106 3788; enoss_travellers@yahoo.com) is a good-natured tour guide who runs one-day tours (400,000Rp per person) of the sights to the north and south of the city. The tours get you away from the more predictable touristy locations. He can also set up trips to Pangandaran (around 1,000,000Rp) via Garut.

Sleeping

Bandung is short on good budget places. Many of the luxury hotels offer online discounts, so shop around.

Chez Bon HOSTEL $

(☎022-426 0600; www.chez-bon.con; Jl Braga 45; per person 150,000Rp; ❄📶) A relatively new hostel set up a flight of scruffy marble stairs from Jl Braga. Bunks are set up in two-bed, six-bed and 16-bed arrangements. All are air-conditioned and come with lockers and wi-fi. Bathrooms are shared. It's a simple set up and a good deal with conscientious English-speaking management.

Hotel Kenangan HOTEL $$

(☎022-421 3244; www.kenanganhotel.com; Jl Kebon Sirih 4; r incl breakfast with fan/air-con from 265,000/395,000Rp; ❄📶) Towards the top end of the budget bracket, this breezy hotel is a great deal with comfortable rooms and free wi-fi. The location, close to the Governor's Residence, is central and quiet and staff are helpful. Prices rise a fraction on weekends. Economy rooms (with fans) can be dark, with tinted windows looking out into the interior halls.

Yokotel HOTEL $$

(☎022-421 9338; www.yokotel.com; Jl Kebonjati 17-19; r from 360,000Rp; ❄📶) A handsome new midranger with a welcoming, if cramped, tiled lobby, a homely facade and 19 rooms on three floors. Rooms aren't huge but have nice linens, wallpaper accents, wood floors, and are very clean, with coffee and tea, too.

Hotel Serena HOTEL $$

(☎022-420 4317; Jl Maruk 4-6; r/ste incl breakfast from 428,000/548,000Rp; ❄) This pleasant modern hotel has jacked up its prices, though the rooms have comfortable beds and are still fair value; the location is excellent. Prices rise 10% at weekends.

The 101 HOTEL $$

(☎022-426 0966; the101hotels.com; Jl Juanda 3; r from 750,000Rp; ❄📶🏊) Part of a national chain, The 101's reclaimed wood-panelled facade dripping with vines is cool, as are the Sino-Portuguese tiles in the lobby and groovy lounge spaces. Rooms are just as attractive with blonde-wood furnishings and chequerboard tile floors, though they aren't huge. It's set in the leafy north.

Novotel HOTEL $$$

(☎022-421 1001; www.novotel.com; Jl Cihampelas 23; r from 1,579,000Rp; ❄@📶🏊) A worthy splurge: rooms are stylish and service standards are very high. Although the pool is tiny, it has a great gym and a spa. Online discounts are easy to find.

★ **Savoy Homann Hotel** HISTORIC HOTEL $$$

(☎022-423 2244; www.savoyhomann-hotel.com; Jl Asia Afrika 112; r/ste from 1,660,000/1,840,000Rp; ❄@📶🏊) Dating back to 1921, this wonderful-looking hotel has a superb sweeping facade, and the rooms and communal areas retain real art deco class, with period lighting and stylish details galore. Promo deals are available on the website.

Prama Grand Preanger HISTORIC HOTEL $$$

(☎022-423 1631; www.preanger.aerowisata.com; Jl Asia Afrika 181; r/ste from 815,000/1,375,000Rp; ❄📶🏊) Dating back to 1929 and blessed with a photogenic lobby patisserie set beneath stained-glass skylights. The best rooms are those in the executive class, on the 1st floor. These are the originals, and though they have been recently renovated, art deco flourishes remain with reproduction furniture, marble floors and baths, and original lighting.

Rooms in the attached, modern wing are dark, with thin carpet, and are just OK.

Eating

In the centre, Jl Braga has a strip of cafes and restaurants. Many of Bandung's most exclusive places are concentrated in the north of town. For cheap eats check out the night warungs on Jl Cikapundung Barat, across from the *alun-alun* (main public square).

Kiosk INDONESIAN $

(Jl Braga, Braga City Walk; meals 15,000-45,000Rp; 🕙10am-10pm; 📶) This mini food court on the ground floor of the Braga City Walk is ideal for mixing with locals and sampling some unusual snacks from *kaki lima* (street vendor) style stalls. Order a *lotek* (Sundanese salad) or a noodle dish. Drinks include juices – try the *sirsak* (soursop) – cold beers and iced coffees.

Mangokok Manis ICE CREAM **$**
(Jl Cihampelas 101; sundaes 25,000-30,000Rp; noon-9pm) An uber-popular ice-cream joint on Jeans Street, where you build your own sundae from the foundation. First, choose a flavour: vanilla, chocolate, green tea, strawberry or rum raisin. Next add a favourite pudding: mango, egg, vanilla, coconut or black forest. Finish off with a topping, such as fresh fruit, Oreos or Kit Kats. Get it in a real bowl or a coconut shell.

Hangover PUB **$**
(Jl Braga 47; dishes 16,000-48,000Rp; 11am-midnight) A great new local pub, with classic rock and blues on the stereo and a comforting range of updated Western and Indo classics emerging from the kitchen. It does meatballs with fried rice, oxtail soup, chicken burgers and a delicious hot salty tofu. And it serves icy cold beer, of course.

Braga Punya Carita INDONESIAN **$$**
(Jl Braga; mains 27,000-75,000Rp; 11am-10pm) A new-school warung serving mixed rice dishes, oxtail and fish soup, and some forgettable Western options. For the rice dishes, you can choose between red or white rice then add the flavour from a menu of chicken Taliwang, grilled tempe, and salted fish, among others.

The decor beats the food, however, thanks to the cool front patio and an interior decorated with old Polaroids strung up on laundry lines.

Midori JAPANESE **$$**
(www.restoranmidori.com; Jl Sultan Tirtayasa 31; mains 34,000-88,000Rp; 10am-10pm) Nestled below the Bersih Sehat spa is this worthy Japanese restaurant. The sushi isn't special, so stick to the bento boxes which come with fried and grilled chicken, grilled cod or beef, tempura shrimp and squid, and many more choices. All affordable.

Capital 8 INTERNATIONAL **$$**
(022-253 4338; Jl Juanda 72; mains 40,000-125,000Rp; 9am-10pm;) A modern eatery set around a reflection pool, with terrific design and tasty bites. It has used reclaimed wood to build the tables and chairs, there's a bakery out front, and an adventurous menu artfully presented. In the morning, get a breakfast quesadilla or stuffed pancakes.

At lunch try the tandoori chicken and couscous salad, chicken avocado burrito or teriyaki lamb. It does do steaks and fish dishes, too.

Musamus Bistro & Bakery INTERNATIONAL **$$**
(022-426 6858; Musamusbistro@gmail.com; Jl Sultan Tirtayasa 35; mains 28,000-150,000Rp; 10am-11pm) Upscale eating in the trendy north, this split-level fine-dining haunt made from wood, concrete and glass, serves the closest Bandung comes to haute cuisine. It does a panko-crusted sea bass, a range of pasta dishes and a prodigious mixed grill including lamb chops with mint dressing and both local and imported beef.

Very popular with the local gentry, it also serves some Indonesian classics. Despite all appearances, prices are quite reasonable.

Drinking & Nightlife

After dark, Jl Braga has a typical downtown vibe, with small bars, pool halls, karaoke lounges and live music venues. Up in north Bandung, the well-heeled head to places along Jl Juanda, and students converge on Jeans Street (though there are few bars here).

★Wiki Koffee CAFE
(Jl Braga; 10am-midnight;) The coolest place on Jl Braga at research time, this smoky cafe is set in a restored old storefront and tastefully decorated with vintage furniture, art and fresh-cut flowers. This is where the hip, young and cute collide in intimate corners and at table and chair arrangements that feel like your living room.

It does a small food menu, with sweet snacks like waffles and salty ones like fried chicken wings. But it's mostly a hang spot with good coffee. Hence the long wait for a table.

Cups CAFE
(Jl Trunojoyo 25; 10am-10pm;) A polished-concrete atrium cafe with orchids hung on the wall, smoke in the air and mostly Western snacks and sandwiches on the menu. Fish and chips, Caesar salad, burgers and hot dogs are all here for the ordering, but coffee is Cups' thing. That's what draws Bandung's creative class for all-day work-and-sip sessions.

North Sea Bar BAR
(Jl Braga 82; noon-1am) The beer flows late at this pub-style expat and bar-girl hang-out, known locally as the 'naughty bar'. It's actually not that sleazy and there's a popular pool table.

Roempoet BAR
(Jl Braga 80) Intimate bar with live bands (mainly playing covers most nights) and a social vibe. Sizzling *sate* is also served.

Entertainment

Bandung is a good place to see Sundanese performing arts; however, performance times are haphazard – check with the tourist information centre for the latest schedules.

ASTI Bandung PERFORMING ARTS
(☎022-731 4982; Jl Buah Batu 212, Kampus STSI Bandung) In the southern part of the city about 3km from the centre, this is a school for traditional Sundanese arts – music, dancing and *pencak silat* (martial arts).

Saung Angklung PERFORMING ARTS
(☎022-727 1714; www.angklung-udjo.co.id; Jl Padasuka 118; adult/child under 12yr 75,000/50,000Rp; ⏲10.30am-5pm) Excellent *angklung* (bamboo musical instrument) performances, held daily in a Sundanese cultural centre that also hosts dance events and ceremonial processions. It's around 10km northeast of the city centre.

Shopping

With Bandung's glitzy malls and factory outlets, shopaholics come here from as far as Malaysia in search of labels and bargains. Bandung's celebrated Jeans Street, Jl Cihampelas, is at its best where the road narrows and cheap clothing stores are lined up shoulder to shoulder from Jl Pasteur at the southern end to Jl Hussen in the north. There is plenty of denim, though quality is iffy. You'll also find inexpensive T-shirts, leather jackets, backpacks and flip-flops. Jl Cibaduyut, in southwest Bandung, is to shoes what Jl Cihampelas is to jeans. Check out Jl Braga for antiques, art and curios. Jl Trunojoyo, in the leafy north end, offers the hippest, trendiest styles and shoppers.

Kayu Solid ARTS
(www.kayusolid.com; Jl Braga 29; ⏲11am-7pm) The coolest showroom on Jl Braga displays the artistry of nature. The medium here is huge slabs of tropical wood, minimally treated and displayed like fine art. Admire the wonders of teak, jackfruit, rosewood and many others. None of it is cheap, but it's still a better deal than in Jakarta.

If you're looking for that one-of-a-kind dining room or coffee table, it has the goods. It can arrange shipping.

Bandung Jean Point CLOTHING
(Jl Cihampelas 122; ⏲9.30am-9.30pm) Our favourite denim shop on Jeans Street, with its vaguely Old West branding; it offers export-quality jeans, jackets, pants and chambrays, too. Some creased and fresh from the factory, some faded and secondhand. Dig and ye might find.

Cihampelas Walk MALL
(www.cihampelaswalk.com; Jl Cihampelas 160; ⏲10am-10pm) A modern indoor-outdoor sweep of a shopping mall with a food court on the leafy ground floor and a blend of small businesses and international chains on two levels. There's also a kid-friendly arcade with rides and games here.

Bandung Supermal MALL
(Jl Gatot Subroto 289; 📶) More than 200 shops including Boss and Levi's, a huge Hero supermarket, a bowling alley and cinemas.

Braga City Walk MALL
(www.bragacitywalk.net; Jl Braga; 📶) Small upmarket shopping mall with boutiques, a food court, a cinema and supermarket.

Pasar Baru MARKET
(Jl Kebonjati) Somewhat grotty central market, but good for fresh fruit.

Pasar Jatayu MARKET
(Jl Arjuna) Search this flea market for collectables hidden amid the junk.

Information

Most of the upmarket shopping malls including the Bandung Supermal and Braga City Walk have free wi-fi, as do nearly all the hotels, cafes and restaurants. Banks are scattered across Bandung.

Adventist Hospital (☎022-203 4386; Jl Cihampelas 161; ⏲24hr) A missionary hospital with English-speaking staff.

Bandung Tourist Information Centre (☎022-727 1724; www.bandungtourism.com; Jl Ahmad Yani 277; ⏲9am-5pm Mon-Sat, to 2pm Sun)

TRAINS FROM BANDUNG

DESTINATION	COST (RP)	DURATION (HR)	FREQUENCY
Jakarta (Gambir)	105,000	3¼	11 daily
Surabaya	385,000-425,000	11-12	3 daily
Yogyakarta	200,000-325,000	7¼-8	6 daily

Managed by very helpful staff that offer lots of free information, and can help with bus and train tickets and also book tours of the Bandung region.

Main Post Office (cnr Jl Banceuy & Jl Asia Afrika; ⌚8am-2pm Mon-Sat)

Getting There & Away

AIR

Bandung airport is fast becoming an important international and domestic transport hub; a new terminal opened in 2012, boosting capacity. It's a key hub for **AirAsia** (☎022-5050 5088; www.airasia.com), with connections to Kuala Lumpur, Johor Bahru, Singapore and domestic cities including Denpasar. **Lion Air** (☎021-6379 8000; www.lionair.co.id) flies to Banjarmasin, Batam, Denpasar and Surabaya; **Garuda** (☎022-420 9468; Jl Asia Afrika 181, Grand Hotel Preanger) and **Citilink** (www.citilink.co.id) connect to Surabaya.

BUS

Five kilometres south of the city centre, **Leuwi Panjang bus terminal** (Jl Sukarno Hatta) has buses west to places such as Cianjur (normal/air-con 25,000/30,000Rp, two hours), Bogor (50,000/60,000Rp, 3½ hours), and to Jakarta's Kampung Rambutan bus terminal (37,000Rp to 47,000Rp, three hours). Buses to Bogor take at least an hour longer on weekends because of heavy traffic.

On the eastern outskirts, **Cicaheum bus terminal** serves Cirebon (normal/air-con 50,000/70,000Rp, four hours, hourly), Garut (normal/air-con 20,000/30,000Rp, two hours, every 40 minutes) and Pangandaran (normal/air-con 40,000/63,000Rp, six hours, hourly).

Cipaganti (☎022-612 6650; Jl Dr Djundjunan 143-149, Bandung Trade Center) runs minibuses every 30 minutes to many locations in Jakarta from its terminal in the Bandung Trade Center, 4km northwest of the centre. **Citi Flyer** (☎0804 1111 000; www.cititrans.co.id) offers luxury shuttle-bus service to the Jakarta airport (135,000Rp to 195,000Rp, three hours).

Getting Around

TO/FROM THE AIRPORT

Bandung's Husein Sastranegara airport is 4km northwest of town; it costs around 50,000Rp to get there by taxi from the centre.

BUS, ANGKOT & TAXI

Bandung is a fiendishly difficult city to negiotate on public transport, and few travellers bother as taxi rates are reasonable. Stick to the the ever-reliable **Blue Bird taxis** (☎022-756 1234).

Angkot run from Stasiun Hall (St Hall), on the southern side of the train station, to Dago, Ledeng and other destinations; fares cost from 3000Rp to 5000Rp. City buses (called Damri) run from west to east down Jl Asia Afrika to Cicaheum bus terminal, and from the train station to Leuwi Panjang bus terminal.

North of Bandung

Hot springs bubble from the earth and are piped into tubs at the soothing resorts north of Bandung.

Sights & Activities

Tangkuban Prahu VOLCANO

(admission weekday/weekend 200,000/300,000Rp; ⌚information centre 7am-5pm) This volcanic crater, 30km north of Bandung, has a flat, elongated summit that resembles an upturned boat (*prahu*). It's a huge tourist attraction and certainly a spectacular sight, but also something of a tourist trap. If you do decide to go, try to aim for early in the day as by noon the mist starts to roll in.

It's possible to circumnavigate most of the caldera on foot, but as wannabe guides can be aggressive and tourists have been robbed, there are better places for a highland walk.

Gracia Spa HOT SPRINGS

(☎0260-724 9997; www.graciaspa.com; admission 35,000Rp; ⌚7am-11pm) Eight kilometres northeast of Tangkuban Prahu in the village of Ciater, Gracia Spa is a hot spring set in gorgeous grounds on the lower slopes of the volcano. There are three large pools, a spa and a restaurant, and it's very quiet midweek.

Ciater is an attractive village surrounded by tea and clove plantations. The area has good walks, and a tea factory that offers tours.

Sari Ater Hot Spring Resort HOT SPRINGS

(☎0260-471700; www.sariater-hotel.com; admission 27,000Rp; ⌚24hr) This is Ciater's main attraction. Although they're quite commercialised, the pools are among the best of the hot springs around Bandung. Rooms (from 450,000Rp) and rustic bungalows are available here. The pools can get insanely busy on weekends.

South of Bandung

The mountains south of Bandung offer magnificent scenery, a rolling evergreen landscape of neatly cropped tea bushes, clumps of tropical forest and misty hilltops. Beyond the town of Ciwidey, every second house has a strawberry patch.

Around Bandung

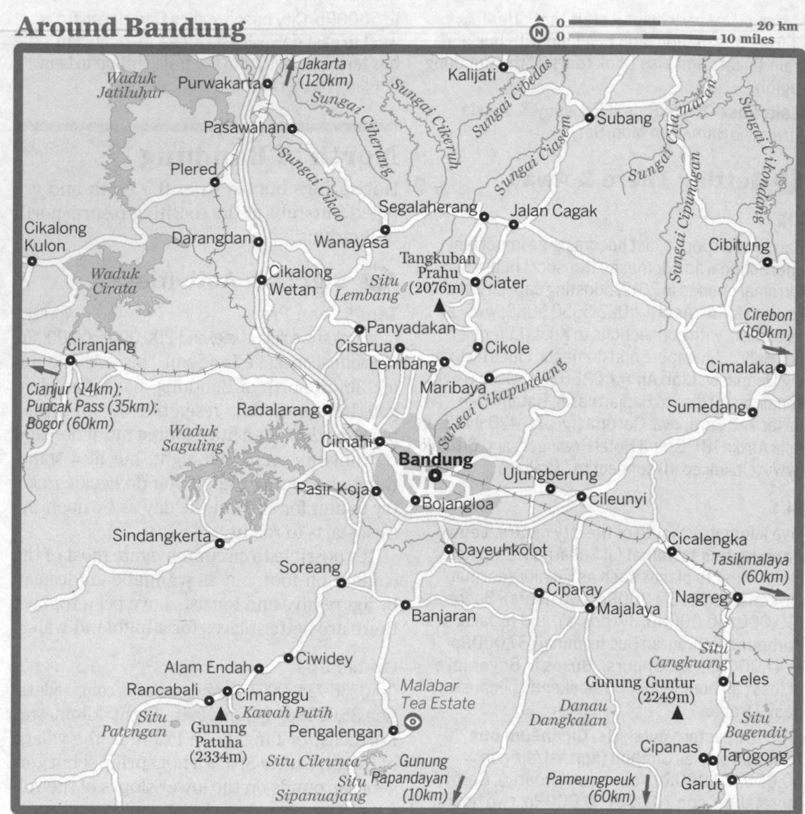

It's initially a struggle to get here through the endless Bandung suburbs and traffic, even on weekdays. On weekends, when Jakartans descend en masse – well, you've been warned.

Ciwidey itself has few attractions, but does have minimarts and hotels. About 3km south of town you can drop by **Kawi Wulung** (Jl Raya Pasir Jambu), a bamboo workshop where room dividers and chairs are made by hand. Next door, **Tahu Sumedang** (Jl Raya Pasir Jambu) is a traditional tofu factory where tofu is fried in coconut oil (and is for sale).

South of Ciwidey the road winds north through hills to the turn-off to **Kawah Putih** (admission 65,000Rp), an undeniably beautiful turquoise crater lake that's become something of an overdeveloped tourist attraction.

It's better to push on through the stunning scenery around **Rancabali**, 42km from Bandung, which is basically one big tea estate surrounded by lush green hills. Just south of Rancabali, Situ Patengan is a pretty lake with tearooms and boats catering to the Sunday crowds, while 3km south of here is lovely **Kawah Rengganis** (also known as Kawah Cibuni), a pretty, isolated river fed by hot springs and surrounded by billowing steam from volcanic vents. It's yet to be discovered by the tourist hordes and is wonderful for bathing. You have to park by the road and walk for a few minutes up to the pools; villagers here ask visitors for a 50,000Rp donation to visit their land.

If you want to visit a tea plantation, head for the **Malabar Tea Estate**, on the other side of Gunung Patuha, where you can tour the grounds and stay at the wonderful guesthouse, the Malabar Mess.

Sleeping & Eating

Hotel options are limited in this region, but there are a few places around Ciwidey as well as the Malabar Mess.

Malabar Mess HISTORIC HOTEL $$
(☎022-597 9401, bookings 022-203 8996; r from 350,000Rp) It's hard to beat this idyllically situated colonial guesthouse, located at an altitude of 1500m in a working tea plantation near the town of Pengalengan. The simple, clean rooms, each with a front porch and Dutch-era furnishings, make it a great place to kick back for a few days.

Saung Gawir INDONESIAN $$
(☎0812 2113 3664; Jl Raya Ciwidey; meals 30,000-70,000Rp) This restaurant and strawberry farm has startling valley views from its roadside perch in Alam Endah. Ignore the tour groups, pick a table and soak up the quintessential Javanese scenery as you feast on authentic local cusine. And, of course, it would be rude not to buy some berries while you're here.

Getting There & Away

Touring this region by public transport is possible but a pain. Most travellers explore the area on a tour from Bandung.

From Bandung's Leuwi Panjang terminal, frequent buses run to Ciwidey (15,000Rp, 1¼ hours). From Ciwidey *angkot* run to Situ Patengan (10,000Rp). Shared minibuses run from the highway to Kawah Putih (35,000Rp return). Buses run directly to Pengalengan (15,000Rp), where *ojek* hang out at the bus terminal.

Bandung to Pangandaran

Heading southeast from Bandung, the road passes through rolling hills and stunning volcanic peaks, skirting – at a safe distance – the particularly explosive Gunung Papandayan (2622m). This is the Bandung–Yogyakarta road as far as Banjar; the Bandung–Yogyakarta train line passes through Tasikmalaya and Banjar, but not Garut. After the choked streets of Jakarta and Bandung, these quieter back roads are a pleasure.

Garut & Cipanas

☎0262

Sixty-three kilometres southeast of Bandung, Garut is a once-lovely spa town that's now become featureless sprawl and a leatherware centre. But 6km north of here the pretty village of Cipanas makes a tranquil base for a day or two exploring volcanic scenery and soaking away any travelling tensions in a hot-spring bath or pool.

The region is famed for its *dodol* – a confectionery of coconut milk, palm sugar and sticky rice. The Picnic brand is the best quality, and it is possible to visit the **factory** (Jl Pasundan 102) in Garut.

Sleeping

Cipanas has a good choice of places to stay; all are strung along Jl Raya Cipanas, the resort's single road. Many of the flashier hotels have swimming pools heated by the springs; if you're staying at a cheaper option, it's possible to use the pools for a minimal fee (10,000/5000Rp per adult/child). Prices rise on weekends.

Tirtagangga Hotel HOTEL $$
(☎0262-232 549; Jl Raya Cipanas 130; r from 500,000Rp; ❄📶🏊) A large, well-run hotel offering good-value rooms with modern decor and generous bathrooms, many with tubs fed with hot-spring water. The huge pool is surrounded by palm trees and the restaurant serves authentic Indonesian food.

Sumber Alam RESORT $$
(☎0262-238 000; www.resort-kampungsumberalam.com; r 575,000-3,750,000Rp; @🏊) This upmarket resort has attractive thatch-and-timber bungalows built around and over ponds (complete with water lillies). The pool area is great. It's popular with Indonesian families, particularly at weekends, though note that the *azat* (call to prayer) from the nearby mosque is particularly enthusiastic.

Getting There & Away

Garut is connected with Bandung (fan/air-con 20,000/30,000Rp, two hours) and also Pangandaran (45,000Rp, four hours). *Angkot* connect Garut with Cipanas very regularly.

Around Garut

Twenty-eight kilometres southwest of Garut, twin-peaked **Gunung Papandayan** is one of the most active volcanoes in West Java. Papandayan exploded in 1772, a catastrophe that killed more than 3000. It erupted again in 2002 and thousands were forced to flee when pyroclastic flows devastated the area. Papandayan is periodically closed to visitors so check first with locals before setting out.

Craters to the west of Garut that can be visited are Kawah Darajat, 26km away, and Kawah Kamojang, 23km away, the site of a geothermal plant that has defused the once spectacular geyser activity and replaced it with huge pipes. Sigh, progress.

Sights

Kawah Papandayan VOLCANO

(admission 100,000Rp) The impressive bubbling yellow crater is just below the peak and clearly visible from the Garut valley on clear mornings. From the car-park it is an easy half-hour walk to the crater, which is riddled with bubbling mud pools, steam vents and crumbling sulphur deposits. Take care – keep well to the right when ascending through the crater.

Consider hiring a guide (around 350,000Rp per day, but many will allow bargaining) from the PHKA office, as the car park area is generally full of cowboys. For fine views, go early in the morning before the clouds roll in.

Gunung Papandayan's summit is a two-hour walk beyond the crater, and there are fields of Javan edelweiss near the top.

Getting There & Away

To get here, take a Cikajang minibus and get off at the turn-off on the outskirts of Cisurupan (10,000Rp), where you can catch a waiting *ojek* (40,000Rp one way, 13km).

Pangandaran

0265 / POP 52,163

Situated on a narrow isthmus, with a broad stretch of sand on either side and a thickly forested national park on the nearby headland, Pangandaran is West Java's premier beach resort. It's built-up, especially toward the south end where a jumble of concrete block towers stand shoulder to shoulder across the channel from the national park. Yet despite all that, for most of the year Pangandaran is a quiet, tranquil place to enjoy walks along the beach or through the forest. Of course, on weekends and during those peak holiday times, the town fills up to the point where you can hardly see empty sand for all the humanity.

Nevertheless, the beach is wide and long, and relentlessly pummelled by a heavy swell that doesn't make for great swimming, as dangerous rips swirl (listen to the lifeguards!). But it is a great place to get out on a board or learn how to ride (surf lessons can be easily arranged), as there's a sandbar bottom and it's a good learner break on small days. It also happens to be fun for serious surfers on bigger days.

Sadly, sections of the beach are littered with plastic and flotsam, especially during peak tourist time, and are in dire need of a clean up.

Sights & Activities

Pangandaran National Park NATIONAL PARK

(Taman Nasional Pangandaran; admission 210,000Rp; 7am-5pm) The Pangandaran National Park, which takes up the entire southern end of Pangandaran, is a wild expanse of dense forest. Within its boundaries live porcupines, *kijang* (barking deer), hornbills, monitor lizards and monkeys (including Javan gibbons). Small bays within the park enclose pretty tree-fringed beaches. The park is divided into two sections: the recreation park and the jungle.

Due to environmental degradation, the jungle is usually off limits. Well-maintained paths allow the recreation park to be explored, passing small caves (including Gua Jepang, which was used by the Japanese in WWII), the remains of a Hindu temple, Batu Kalde, and a nice beach on the eastern side. English-speaking guides hang around both entrances and charge around 100,000Rp (per group of four) for a two-hour walk or up to 200,000Rp for a five-hour trip.

Pangandaran's best swimming beach, white-sand Pasir Putih, lies on the western side of the national park. It's a thin stretch of soft sand fronted by a reef that's pretty well thrashed though plenty of fish still live, eat and love there. You can swim over here from the southern end of the main resort beach if the surf is not too rough, but take care of rip currents and the steady stream of boats that shuttle people back and forth (50,000Rp return). They will not be looking for you. The beach stretches to a point that gets a break when the swell is big. On calm days, the swim out to the point is peaceful and devoid of boat traffic. If you hop a boat from the main Pangandaran beach you won't have to pay the steep national park entry fee.

At sunset, huge fruit bats emerge from the forest. They fly down the length of Pangandaran's beach but have to evade local boys who patrol with barbed-wire kites. Few are trapped this way, but every now and then a bat's wing will get caught on a kite string and the creature will be brought crashing to the ground in a fit of squeals, before being dispatched to the cooking pot.

Surfing Lessons SURFING

(half-day lesson incl board hire 200,000-250,000Rp) Surfing lessons are offered at the northern end of the beach. Pangandaran is a good place to learn, and local instructors have 'soft' boards ideal for beginners. The friendly staff from **Pangandaran Surf** (www.pangandaransurf.com) are all lifesavers, speak English and understand local conditions. Board hire runs about 70,000Rp per day.

Tours

Popular Green Canyon and Green Valley tours (p101; 300,000Rp per person) depart from Pangandaran and usually combine 'home industry' visits that take in a sugar, *tahu* (tofu) or *krupuk* (prawn cracker) kitchen factory, as well as a *wayang golek* (three-dimensional wooden puppet) maker. If you rent a bike and drive yourself to the gates, you'll have to book your own boat (150,000Rp round trip) at Green Canyon. And your own guide (100,000Rp) and mandatory life jacket (20,000Rp), as well as the entry fee (15,000Rp) in Green Valley.

There are also tours to **Paradise Island**, an uninhabited nearby island with good beaches (including a 5km white-sand beach) and waves. Day trips cost around 400,000Rp per person (minimum six people). Before you leave, make an early-morning visit to Pangandaran's *pasar ikan* (fish market; p99) and fire up a fish barbecue when you get to the island for lunch. It's not a great trip for young children or those prone to sea sickness. The fit and hearty will love it.

Mas Rudin (0813 8005 6724; pangandaranguide.com) is a tremendous local guide who operates out of MM Books (p99) and offers fair prices on a range of tours. His website is a wealth of information. The guesthouses can organise guides for you as well.

Sleeping

Many places have flexible prices that are dependent on demand, so you might get a good deal on weekdays outside the main holiday periods. The main area for budget or independent travellers is off the northern section of the main beach, where guesthouses are dotted along a grid of quiet lanes just inland from the beach.

Pangandaran has a tightly controlled becak union, or mafia, depending on which side of the bike seat you're on. All hotels have to pay commission to the becak driver who takes you to your accommodation, so if you walk in on your own, you'll be in a better bargaining position.

Weekday prices are given; expect to pay 15% to 30% more at some places on weekends and holidays.

Rinjani Homestay GUESTHOUSE $
(0265-639757; r with fan/air-con 140,000/180,000Rp;) A welcoming family-run place with 10 pleasant, tiled rooms with wood furnishings and private porches. Sweet, quiet and good value. Holiday periods see price increases of up to 100,000Rp.

Mini Tiga Homestay GUESTHOUSE $
(0265-639436; www.minitigahomestay.weebly.com; s/d/tr incl breakfast 100,000/150,000/250,000Rp; @) Great brick and wood chalets with reasonable rates. The nine rooms are clean, spacious and have nice decorative touches – including bamboo walls and batik wall hangings. All have en-suite bathrooms and Western toilets. Good tours and transport tickets are also offered, including a popular tour of the nearby Green Canyon (250,000Rp).

Villa Angela GUESTHOUSE $
(0821 180 2400; Jl Pamugaran; r incl breakfast from 200,000Rp;) An attractive guesthouse with five spacious rooms (all with TV and bathroom, and a porch or balcony) in two villa-style houses with cold-water baths. Some smell musty, though a cross-breeze will do the trick. It's run by a welcoming family and has a nice garden.

★ **Adam's Homestay** HOTEL $$
(0265-639396; www.adamshomestay.com; Jl Pamugaran; r 250,000-550,000Rp;) Pangandaran's only real gem is a wonderfully relaxed, enjoyable place to stay with artistically presented rooms (many with balconies, beamed ceilings and outdoor bathrooms) spread around a verdant tropical garden bursting with exotic plants, lotus ponds and birdlife. There's good international and local food available, too.

Palu Vi HOTEL $$
(0265-630050; www.paluvihotel.com; Jl Bulak Laut 86; r from 420,000Rp; @) A newer, great-value modern hotel featuring floating beds, high ceilings and flat-screens in wood-panelled rooms. All the mod cons are at your fingertips.

Nyiur Beach Hotel BOUTIQUE HOTEL $$
(0265-639053; www.niyurbeachhotel.com; Jl Pamugaran 46; r from 648,000Rp) Set among the jumble of new, somewhat garish block towers is this original low-rise boutique hotel with Balinese style. It has an inviting pool area and sizeable rooms with high-end tile floors and linens, shuttered windows, wood furnishings,

Pangandaran

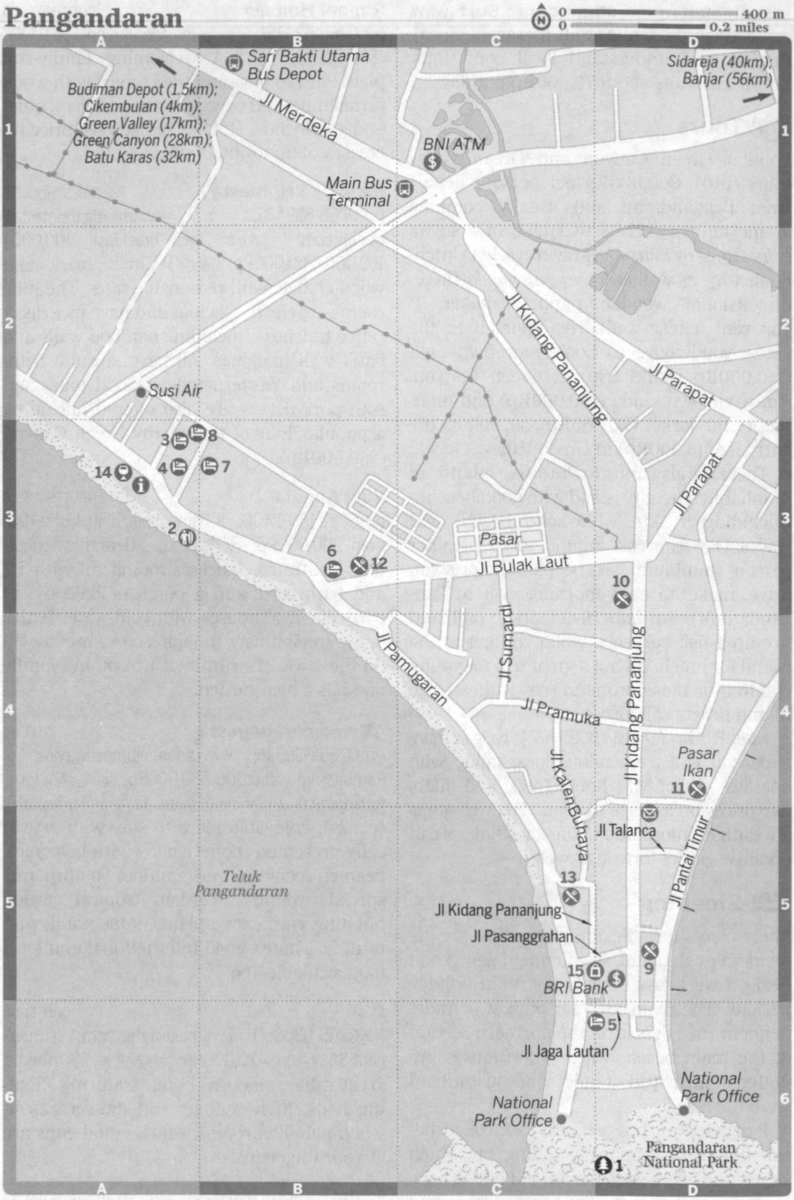

wall-mounted flat-screens, day beds, built-in desks and lovely bathrooms.

You can often get 20% to 30% discounts on Agoda.com. It has two locations in town. The other is forgettable. This one is wonderful.

Eating

Pangandaran is famous for its excellent seafood, and by far the best place to sample it is in the *pasar ikan* (fish market).

Pangandaran

Sights
1 Pangandaran National Park D6

Activities, Courses & Tours
2 Pangandaran Surf A3

Sleeping
3 Adam's Homestay A3
4 Mini Tiga Homestay A3
5 Nyiur Beach Hotel C6
6 Palu Vi B3
7 Rinjani Homestay B3
8 Villa Angela A3

Eating
9 Chez Mama Cilacap D5
10 Green Garden Cafe D3
11 Pasar Ikan D4
12 Relax Restaurant B3
13 Rumah Makan Christi C5

Drinking & Nightlife
14 Bamboo Beach Café A3

Shopping
15 MM Books D5

Green Garden Cafe INDONESIAN $
(Jl Kidang Pananjung 116; mains 12,000-25,000Rp; 8am-10pm;) There's not much of a garden in evidence, but you must try the delicious *batagor* (crispy tofu) here, which is fried in cassava flour and served with spicy peanut sauce. Down it with a fresh juice.

Rumah Makan Christi INDONESIAN $
(Jl Pamugaran; meals 15,000-40,000Rp; 7am-11pm) This clean, orderly *rumah makan* (restaurant), with a large interior and bench seating outside, is a good bet for local food. It fries, grills and stews tofu, chicken, and fish and offers a range of vegetarian dishes, too. All authentic Javanese. Pick and mix to your pleasure, then sit at the common table and dine with your new friends.

★ **Pasar Ikan** SEAFOOD $$
(Fish Market; Jl Raya Timor; large fish 40,000-70,000Rp; 11am-10pm) Pangandaran's terrific fish market consists of more than a dozen large, open-sided restaurants just off the east beach. **Karya Bahari** is considered the best – which is why it's so crowded – but all operate on exactly the same basis.

Select your fish or seafood (prawns, squid or mussels) from the glistening iced displays. Decide which sauce you fancy (usually garlic, oyster or sweet-and-sour) and it will arrive in minutes.

Relax Restaurant INTERNATIONAL, INDONESIAN $$
(0265-630377; Jl Bulak Laut 74; mains 28,000-72,000Rp; 8am-10:30pm) A dependable, slightly formal Swiss-owned restaurant with a restrained atmosphere thanks to the starched tablecloths and attentive service. The menu covers both Western and Indonesian fare; portions are generous. It's a great bet for breakfast with muesli, homemade yogurt and brown bread available.

Chez Mama Cilacap INDONESIAN $$
(0265-630098; Jl Kidang Pananjung 197; mains 30,000-75,000Rp; 8am-10:30pm Sun-Thu, to 11pm Fri & Sat) A large, airy thatched dining room, twirling with ceiling fans and offering a huge range of Indonesian specialities, but famous for fresh seafood, which you can choose from the cooler. Get the crab.

Drinking & Nightlife

★ **Bamboo Beach Café** BAR
(Jl Pamugaran; 9am-late) This fine beach bar lines up nicely with the waves, and is the perfect location to scout the swell with a cold Bintang in hand, particularly at sunset. Benches and tables with thatched umbrellas wander all the way to the beach and surround a dance floor that fronts a bandstand.

Shopping

MM Books BOOKS
(Jl Pasanggrahan; 9am-7pm) Sells a wide range of secondhand Western titles from a roadside shack. The proprietor, Mas Rudin, is one of the best and most trustworthy guides in town.

Information

A 3500Rp admission charge is officially levied at the gates on entering Pangandaran. Wi-fi is widely available in restaurants, hotels and guesthouses. There's an unofficial **tourist information office** (0852 9499 9906; beachside) by the waves.

BNI ATM (Jl Merdeka; 8am-4pm Mon-Sat) There's a second branch on Jl Bulak Laut.

BRI Bank (Jl Kidang Pananjung; 8am-4pm Mon-Sat) Changes cash dollars and major brands of travellers cheques.

National Park Office (Jl Pantai; 7am-5pm)

National Park Office (Jl Pangandaran; 7am-5pm)

WORTH A TRIP

CRUISING THE BACKWATER

It's still possible to do the once-popular backwater boat trip east of Pangandaran, via Majingklak harbour to Cilacap on the Citandui River, but there are no scheduled connections so you'll have to charter your own *compreng* (wooden boat). Boatmen in Majingklak will do the three-hour trip for 400,000Rp. Alternatively, you can call ahead through a tour agent in Pangandaran to Kalipucang harbour and organise a boat from there for the same price.

Wherever you begin, you will motor up a lazy green river, with low-rise jungled hills on both sides, passing through estuaries and meandering around islands thick with scrub. You will pass a series of riverside villages and wooden-boat harbours, slip through narrow channels into the mangroves where troops of monkeys maraud and solitary cranes meditate beneath a powder-blue sky. Toward the end you'll even pass Nusakambangan Prison Island where some of the so called 'Bali Nine' (p702) were executed by firing squad in the surrounding jungle. As you approach, the prison has the spooky isolated setting of a horror movie, then you round a bend and enter Cilacap's major industrial port, with fiery smokestacks coming from Indonesia's largest petrol refinery. Just like that, you're back in 'civilisation'.

From Cilacap there are direct buses to Yogyakarta (60,000Rp, five hours).

Post Office (Jl Kidang Pananjung; ⌚8am-2pm Sat)

ℹ Getting There & Away

Pangandaran can be a frustratingly slow and complicated place to get to. The nearest train station, Sidareja, is 41km away. Speak to Mas Rudin (p97) about organising train tickets.

AIR

Susi Air (☎0265-639120; www.susiair.com; Jl Merdeka 312) flies daily to Pangandaran airstrip (20km west of town) from Jakarta's Halim Perdana Kusuma airport (824,000Rp, one hour). Double-check your bookings before departure.

BUS

Many *patas* express buses to Jakarta and Bandung leave from the Sari Bakti Utama depot, just north of town, and Budiman bus depot, about 2km west of Pangandaran along Jl Merdeka. Other services also leave from the main terminal. Buses run to Bandung roughly every hour (40,000Rp to 63,000Rp, six hours) and to Jakarta's Kampung Rambutan terminal (85,000Rp to 90,000Rp, eight to nine hours). To Bandung, there are two daily **Sari Harum** (☎0265-607 7065) door-to-door *travel* minibuses (100,000Rp, six hours). To Yogyakarta, you'll find two daily **Estu Travel** (☎027-4668 4567, 0812 2284 4700) minibuses (110,000Rp to 160,000Rp, nine hours).

From the main bus terminal there are hourly buses to both Banjar (19,000Rp, two hours) and Sidareja (25,000Rp, 1½ hours) for train connections.

CAR

Travel agencies rent minibuses with drivers for about 900,000Rp per day including driver and petrol. The most popular trip is a three-day tour to Yogyakarta, usually via Wonosobo for the first night, Dieng for sunrise, then on to Borobudur. You'll reach Yogyakarta via Prambanan on the final day.

TRAIN

The nearest stations are Sidareja and Banjar. As the overland trip by bus to Yogyakarta takes a punishing eight or nine hours, train travel makes a lot of sense. From Sidareja there are two daily trains (3½ to four hours). Agents in Pangandaran organise combined minibus to Sidareja station and economy/business/exclusive-class train tickets for 140,000/230,000/350,000Rp. Or you could save some rupiah by catching a local bus to Sidareja and buying a train ticket there (avoiding commission), but this risks not getting a seat on the train once you arrive in Sidareja.

Banjar station, 65km away, is a better bet if you're heading for Jakarta.

Travel agents, hotels and the tourist information office can help with travel arrangements and tickets on all routes.

ℹ Getting Around

Pangandaran's brightly painted becak start at around 6000Rp and require heavy negotiation. Bicycles can be rented for 20,000Rp per day, and motorcycles cost around 50,000Rp per day.

Around Pangandaran

The scenic coastline around Pangandaran has some terrific surf beaches, forests, lagoons, fishing villages and a recreational park or two. It's a joy to explore by motorbike. Hotels and travel agencies can set up guided trips.

West of Pangandaran

Heading west of town, you travel along a pretty but busy coastal road lined with palm trees that runs through small villages and paddy fields.

At the tiny village of Ciokoto, 6km along this road, there's a large *wayang golek* workshop, with high-quality puppets for sale (400,000Rp to more than 1,000,000Rp). Next up is Karang Tirta, a lagoon set back from the beach with *bagang* (fishing platforms). It's 16km from Pangandaran and 2km south of the highway.

Inland from Parigi, near Cigugur, Gunung Tilu hilltop has fine views and is included in some tour itineraries.

Activities

Green Canyon BOAT TOUR, SWIMMING
(Cujang Taneuh; per boat 150,000Rp; ⏲7.30am-4pm Sat-Thu, 1-4pm Fri) The number one tour from Pangandaran is to Green Canyon. Boats buzz up the jungle-fringed, emerald river from a small marina to a waterfall and a beautiful canyon where there's fun swimming (though the current is often strong here). Locals take good care of the river and you won't see any plastic rubbish.

Boatmen work on a return-trip schedule of just 45 minutes, which only gives you about 15 minutes to swim and explore the narrowest and most beautiful part of the canyon. If you want to motor further upstream or stay longer you'll have to pay an extra 100,000Rp for 30 minutes. Many tour operators in Pangandaran run trips here for 300,000Rp and include 'countryside' excursions to make a full-day tour. To get there yourself, hire a boat from the Green Canyon river harbour on the highway, 1km before the turn-off to Batu Karas. The entrance is clearly signposted at several points along the highway.

Green Valley SWIMMING
(Sungai Citumang; entrance 15,000Rp, life vest for body rafting 20,000Rp, guide 100,000Rp; ⏲7am-5pm) Reached by a rough inland road from the village of Cipinda (8km from Pangandaran, look out for the sign Citumang), this attraction involves an easy riverside walk from a dam to a small but beautiful gorge called Green Valley. You can swim in the gorge and there are cliff jumps for the brave (or foolhardy).

Pay extra and you've the option of 'body rafting' the river back to the entrance instead of walking, which involves floating downstream using a life jacket for buoyancy – a surreal and delightful experience as you gaze up at the forest canopy. A guide is mandatory for body rafting.

Batu Karas

☎0265 / POP 3000

The idyllic fishing village and surfing hotspot of Batu Karas, 32km west of Pangandaran, is one of the most enjoyable places to kick back in West Java. It's as pretty as a picture – a tiny one-lane fishing settlement, with two beaches that are separated by a wooded promontory.

The main surfing beach is the smaller one, and it's a sweet bay tucked between two rocky headlands. The other is a long arcing black-sand number parked with pontoon fishing boats that shove off each night looking for fresh catch in the tides. There's good swimming, with sheltered sections that are calm enough for a dip, but many visitors are here for the breaks, and there's a lot of surf talk.

In recent years Batu Karas' popularity has started to take off as more (tasteful) guesthouses have opened, but the village still retains a low-key, relaxed charm. On weekends, however, it can become inundated with domestic tourists. The best time to surf and relax here is midweek.

Activities

This is one of the best places in Java to learn to **surf**. The Point (offshore from Java Cove) is perfect for beginners with paddle-in access from the beach, and slow, peeling waves over a sandy bottom. Other waves include The Reef, a deep-water reef break, and Bulak Bender, a challenging right-hander in the open ocean that's a 40-minute ride away by bike or boat.

The locally run surf co-op, just off the beach, charges 200,000Rp for a two-hour lesson including board hire. Longboards and shortboards (from 70,000Rp per day) are available from locals or the co-op. Although there are better nests these days, Jesfa homestay still rents motorbikes (per day 50,000Rp).

Sleeping & Eating

Nayla Homestay HOMESTAY $
(☎0852 1755 3017; d 150,000Rp) No wi-fi and no frills, just two small concrete rooms, clean and simple, on the main road and steps from the beach.

Wooden House GUESTHOUSE $
(☎0813 6919 4405; woodenhouse@yahoo.com; r 200,000Rp) Going for the log-cabin look, these three lovely rooms with high ceilings are kept tidy and access a shared balcony with sea views. Downstairs there's a good warung for local food, jaffles, salads and pancakes.

BK Homestay HOMESTAY $
(☎0822 6023 7802; incl breakfast r 200,000Rp;) Four terrific-value, fan-cooled rooms, all with floor-to-ceiling glass on one side, high ceilings, wood floors and wi-fi in the restaurant below. No hot water, but that won't matter much here. It's set off the main beach parking lot, right in the centre of things.

★ **Java Cove** BOUTIQUE HOTEL $$
(☎0265-708 2020; www.javacovebeachhotel.com; r 399,000-1,299,000Rp;) It's not gleaming new any longer, but this modernist beach hotel still delivers serenity. Tasteful (and damn near indestructible) rooms feature reclaimed wood floors, floating dressers, private terraces and wonderful service. The hip yet laid-back pool area is dotted with beanbags and blessed with ocean views.

The restaurant (mains 40,000Rp to 90,000Rp) serves tasty salads, pizzas, pasta and terrific fries – they call them potato wedges – not to mention buckets of icy Bintang.

Pondok Cowet GUESTHOUSE $$
(☎0815 7316 2286; www.facebook.com/pondokcowet; r 450,000-600,000Rp;) Tucked down a dirt road 50m from the main fishing beach, this new addition offers cool brick-house bunkers and rather creative modern rooms with a mosaic of floor-to-ceiling glass, exposed brick walls, pebbled bathroom floors and cow-print blankets.

L-Pari INTERNATIONAL $
(☎0822 6023 7802; 16,000-40,000Rp; 7am-10pm;) A tourist-driven kitchen serving international and local favourites. It does a tasty fish curry, pasta, fish and chips, and even mixes guacamole in season. All served in a stylish open-faced dining room dotted with sumptuous booths and decorated with photos printed on wood of the local groms (young surfers). Prices are reasonable.

Bayview Seafood SEAFOOD $$
(mains 15,000-70,000Rp; 11am-late Fri-Sun) On the main junction as you enter the village, and open only on weekends, this Indo-German *ikan bakar* (grilled fish) joint offers a range of seafood dishes. Choose your protein from the cooler, and they'll grill, sauté or fry it up. Pair yours with the *karedok* (cabbage salad with spicy peanut dressing).

Getting There & Away

You have to pay a toll of 3000Rp to enter the village. There's no public transport to Batu Karas but it can be reached from Pangandaran by taking a bus to Cijulang (10,000Rp) then an *ojek* for 30,000Rp. Or you can hire a motorbike in Pangandaran (per day 50,000Rp) and drive yourself, or book a pricey private car transfer (350,000Rp) – an outrageous rate given the distances involved, but that's the going rate in high season. Bargain for low-season discounts.

CENTRAL JAVA

Jakarta may be the nation's capital, but the Javan identity is at its strongest here, in the island's historic heartland. This is where Java's first major Indianised civilisation was born, and it was the stronghold of the great Islamic sultanates centred on the *kraton* (walled city palaces) of Yogyakarta and Solo as well. Even today, Central Java (Jawa Tengah) remains the province in which the island's cultural pulse beats loudest.

Though Central Java has a reputation for a short fuse when dealing with religious and political sentiments, it's a relaxed, easy-going province for tourists. Yogyakarta, at the centre of its own quasi-independent 'special region' stretching from the south coast to Gunung Merapi, and Solo, just 65km to the northeast, are Java's most interesting cities. But even Semarang, the province's busy, maritime capital, has some charm. Most visitors, though, will find the stupendous Borobudur and Prambanan temples the highlight of any trip to Java's centre. And well they should. No matter the crowds, it's at these two spectacular sites where history and spirit are palpable, infusing any morning or afternoon, sunrise or sunset with magic and mystery.

Central Java

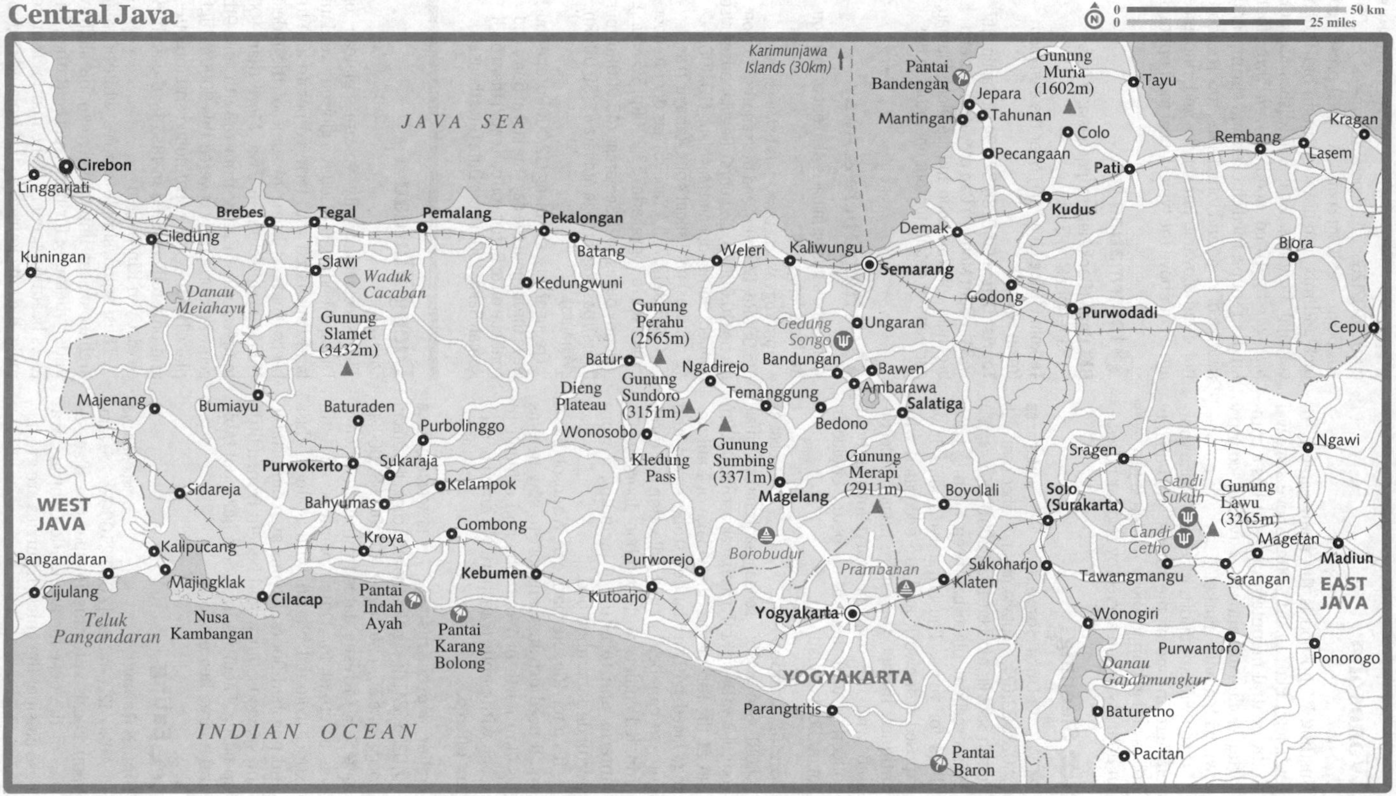

0 50 km
0 25 miles

JAVA SEA
INDIAN OCEAN
Karimunjawa Islands (30km)
WEST JAVA
EAST JAVA
YOGYAKARTA

Cirebon
Linggarjati
Kuningan
Ciledung
Danau Meiahayu
Brebes
Tegal
Slawi
Waduk Cacaban
Gunung Slamet (3432m)
Pemalang
Pekalongan
Batang
Kedungwuni
Majenang
Bumiayu
Baturaden
Purbolinggo
Purwokerto
Sukaraja
Kelampok
Bahyumas
Sidareja
Kroya
Gombong
Kebumen
Kalipucang
Pangandaran
Majingklak
Cijulang
Cilacap
Teluk Pangandaran
Nusa Kambangan
Pantai Indah Ayah
Pantai Karang Bolong
Kutoarjo
Purworejo
Gunung Perahu (2565m)
Batur
Dieng Plateau
Gunung Sundoro (3151m)
Wonosobo
Kledung Pass
Ngadirejo
Temanggung
Gunung Sumbing (3371m)
Magelang
Borobudur
Weleri
Kaliwungu
Semarang
Gedung Songo
Ungaran
Bandungan
Bawen
Ambarawa
Bedono
Salatiga
Gunung Merapi (2911m)
Prambanan
Yogyakarta
Parangtritis
Pantai Baron
Boyolali
Klaten
Sukoharjo
Solo (Surakarta)
Sragen
Candi Sukuh
Candi Cetho
Gunung Lawu (3265m)
Tawangmangu
Sarangan
Magetan
Madiun
Ngawi
Wonogiri
Purwantoro
Ponorogo
Danau Gajahmungkur
Baturetno
Pacitan
Pantai Bandengan
Jepara
Mantingan
Tahunan
Pecangaan
Gunung Muria (1602m)
Colo
Tayu
Kudus
Pati
Demak
Godong
Purwodadi
Rembang
Lasem
Kragan
Blora
Cepu

Wonosobo

☎0286 / POP 113,000

Bustling Wonosobo is the main gateway to the Dieng Plateau. At 900m above sea level in the central mountain range, it has a comfortable climate and is a typical country town with a busy market.

If you value comfort, it's easy to base yourself here in one of the town's good-quality hotels and get up to Dieng, which is just over an hour away and served by regular buses.

Sleeping

★Wisma Duta Homestay HOMESTAY **$$**
(☎0286-321674; dutahomestay@yahoo.com; Jl Rumah Sakit III; r incl breakfast 300,000Rp;) This excellent place has been hosting travellers for years. The attractive rooms have exposed stonework and are decorated with antiques. In fact, the entire house is decorated with the owner's marvellous antique collection, and there is no better choice in town. Book ahead.

Pondok Bamboo LODGE **$$**
(☎081 894 8495; sendangsaribamboo@gmail.com; Jl Raya Dieng Km7; r incl breakfast 350,000Rp) Set at the top of the tiny village of Kalikuning, laced with a slender stone street and cute as can be, is this collection of three shingled chalets with bamboo doors, walls, lanterns and furniture – including a wonderful dark bamboo bed.

It's a terrific alternative to Wonosobo, but you'll need private transport to stay here as it's 7km north of Wonosobo and difficult to reach with public transport. No lunch or dinner offered.

Gallery Hotel Kresna HISTORIC HOTEL **$$$**
(☎0286-324111; www.kresnahotel.com; Jl Pasukan Ronggolawe 30; r/ste from 840,000/1,580,000Rp;) Kresna dates from 1921, when it was a retreat for Dutch planters, and still exudes colonial charm with stained glass and polished floors. Rooms are comfortable and spacious, but would benefit from a little updating. Facilities include a bar, pool table and a large heated pool.

Eating

Shanti Rahayu INDONESIAN **$**
(Jl A Yani 122; meals 12,000-25,000Rp; 7am-9pm) Locals rate this inexpensive place as one of the best for authentic Central Javanese cuisine; the chicken curries are great.

Dieng INDONESIAN **$**
(☎0286-321266; Jl Sindoro 12; meals 25,000-40,000Rp; 10am-8pm) A well-presented pick-and-mix restaurant set in an old Dutch colonial building. Available dishes include *mie goreng* (fried noodles), *rendang*, four kinds of soups, fried chicken and shrimp, and a range of vegie and tofu dishes, too. It's good, not mind-blowing, but service and ambience are a cut above the typical local food option.

Information

BNI Bank (Bank Negara Indonesia; Jl A Yani; 8am-4pm Mon-Sat)

Telkom Office (Jl A Yani) Near the *alun-alun* (main square).

Tourist Office (☎0286-321194; Jl Kartini III; 8am-3pm Mon-Fri) Can provide maps and brochures of Wonosobo and the Dieng Plateau, and contact details for tour operators in the area.

Getting There & Away

Wonosobo's bus terminal is 4km out of town on the Magelang road.

From Yogyakarta take a bus to Magelang (25,000Rp, 1½ hours) and then another to Wonosobo (10,000Rp, 2½ hours). Regular buses also connect Borobudur and Magelang (10,000Rp, 40 minutes) until about 4pm. **Rahayu Travel** (☎0286-321217; Jl A Yani 95) has door-to-door minibuses to Yogyakarta (55,000Rp, 3½ hours).

Hourly buses go to Semarang (45,000Rp, four hours), passing through Ambarawa (30,000Rp, 2½ hours).

Frequent buses to Dieng (12,000Rp, one hour) leave throughout the day (the last at 5pm) and continue on to Batur; you can catch them on Jl Rumah Sakit, 100m from Duta Guesthouse.

Dieng Plateau

☎0286

The spectacular lofty volcanic plateau of Dieng (Abode of the Gods), a glorious, verdant landscape laced with terraced potato and tobacco fields, is home to some of the oldest Hindu architecture in Java. More than 400 temples, most dating from the 8th and 9th centuries, originally covered this 2000m-high plain, but they were abandoned and forgotten and only rediscovered in 1856 by the archaeologist Van Kinsbergen.

These squat, simple temples, while of great archaeological importance, can be slightly underwhelming for non-experts. Rather, Dieng's beautiful scenery is the main reason to make the long journey to this isolated region.

Any number of walks across the volcanically active plateau are possible – to mineral lakes, steaming craters or even the highest village in Java, Sembungan. Dieng is also base camp for the popular climb to Gunung Paru peak. Most start hiking in the wee hours to catch the sunrise on the summit.

You can either stay in Dieng village, or commute up from Wonosobo, which has better facilities. The route up to Dieng is stunning, snaking through vertiginous hillsides of terraced vegetable fields.

The temples and the main natural sights can be seen in one day on foot. Get a very early start if you can, before the afternoon mists roll in. It's a pleasant three- or four-hour loop south from Dieng village to Telaga Warna (Coloured Lake), Candi Bima (Bima Temple), Kawah Sikidang (Sikidang Crater) and then back to Candi Gatutkaca, the Arjuna Complex and the village.

Sights & Activities

Arjuna Complex HINDU TEMPLE

(admission incl Candi Gatutkaca & Kawah Sikidang 25,000Rp) The five main temples that form the Arjuna Complex are clustered together on the central plain. They are Shiva temples, but like the other Dieng temples they have been named after the heroes of the *wayang* stories of the Mahabharata epic: Arjuna, Puntadewa, Srikandi, Sembadra and Semar. All have mouth-shaped doorways and strange bell-shaped windows, and some locals leave offerings, burn incense and meditate here.

Raised walkways link the temples (as most of this land is waterlogged), and you can see the remains of ancient underground tunnels, which once drained the marshy flatlands.

Candi Gatutkaca is a small Shiva temple (a yoni was found inside) with a square base south of the main complex.

Telaga Warna LAKE

(admission weekdays/weekends 100,000/150,000Rp; 8am-4.30pm) Exquisitely beautiful and ringed by highland forest, the lake has turquoise and cobalt hues from the bubbling sulphur deposits around its shores. To lose the crowds, follow the trail counterclockwise to the adjoining lake, Telaga Pengilon, and past holy Gua Semar, a meditation cave. Then for a lovely perspective of the lakes return to the main road via a narrow trail that leads around Telaga Pengilon and up a terraced hillside.

Museum Kailasa Dieng MUSEUM

(admission 5000Rp; 8am-3pm) Southwest of the Arjuna Complex, this museum, set in two separate buildings, displays an array of Hindu statues and sculptures including Shiva's carrier, Nandi the bull (with the body of a man and the head of a bull); a headless image of Shiva himself depicted in the lotus position; and there's an animist gargoyle sporting an erection. There are also exhibits on local geology, farming, culture and the temple excavation process. All displays are in Bahasa Indonesia.

Candi Bima HINDU TEMPLE

FREE Candi Bima is unique in Java, with *kudu* (sculpted heads) looking like spectators peering out of windows.

Candi Dwarawati HINDU TEMPLE

FREE The restored Candi Dwarawati is on the northern outskirts of the village.

Gunung Sikunir VIEWPOINT

South of Dieng village, the main attractions are the sunrise overlook of Gunung Sikunir, 1km past Sembungan, and the shallow lake of **Telaga Cebong**. Views from Sikunir are spectacular, stretching across Dieng and east as far as Merapi and Merbabu volcanoes on a clear day. To reach the hill in time for sunrise, start at 4am from Dieng. It's a one-hour walk to Sembungan and another 30 minutes to the top of the hill. Most guides charge 100,000Rp to 150,000Rp per person.

Kawah Candradimuka LAKE

Nine kilometres from Dieng village is the pleasant 1.5km trail through the fields to Kawah Candradimuka. Another trail branches off to two lakes: Telaga Nila (a longer, two-hour walk) and Telaga Dringo. Just a few hundred metres past the turn-off to Kawah Candradimuka is Sumur Jalatunda. This well is in fact a deep hole some 100m across with vertical walls plunging to bright-green waters.

Kawah Sikidang LAKE

(admission incl with ticket to Arjuna Complex) Kawah Sikidang is a volcanic crater with steaming vents and frantically bubbling mud ponds. Exercise extreme caution here – there are no guard rails to keep you from slipping off the sometimes muddy trails into the scalding-hot waters. At research time, however, locals were building a brick path to make it easier to delineate the safe zone. Kawah Sibentang is a less spectacular crater nearby, and Telaga Lumut is another small lake.

Sembungan VILLAGE

South of the geothermal station, the paved road leads on to Sembungan, said to be the highest village in Java, at 2300m. Potato farming has made this large village relatively wealthy.

Kawah Sileri LAKE

Kawah Sileri, 2km off the main road and 6km from Dieng, is a smoking crater area with a hot lake.

Gunung Paru HIKING

A popular, steep, three-hour trek to Gunung Paru (2565m) begins in the village at 3am. The top isn't a defined peak but a rolling savannah with views of five volcanoes and eight mountains. Several outfitters offer the trek. Bu Djono does the deal for 250,000Rp. Bring extra water.

Sleeping & Eating

Dieng's dozen or more guesthouses are notoriously poor value. Spartan conditions, semi-clean rooms and cool or lukewarm water are the norm. There are decent sleeps, but you do get what you pay for here.

Food isn't Dieng's strong point either. Hotel and restaurant Bu Djono is your best bet and has beer, but be prepared to wait.

While in town you must try the local herb, *purwaceng*, often served as tea or with coffee, which warms the body in cold weather and is said to act like a kind of Dieng-style coca leaf.

The village is tiny and most accommodation is on the main road.

Bu Djono GUESTHOUSE $

(☎0852 2664 5669, 0286-642046; Jl Raya Dieng, Km26; r without bathroom 100,000Rp;) This simple, friendly place has been hosting backpackers for years and has a certain ramshackle charm with basic, clean, economy rooms. The pleasant, orderly restaurant downstairs (mains 15,000Rp to 25,000Rp) has tablecloths and lace curtains. Good tours to Gunung Paru are offered. It's close to the turn-off for Wonosobo.

Hotel Gunung Mas HOTEL $

(☎0286-334 2017; Jl Raya Dieng 42; d 180,000-275,000Rp) This solidly built hotel has a wide choice of reasonably clean rooms, with good light. Upstairs rooms have a little deck and keyhole views to the farmland. It's almost opposite the access road to the Arjuna Complex.

Homestay Flamboyan HOMESTAY $

(☎0852 2744 3029, 0813 2760 5040; www.flamboyandieng.com; Jl Raya Dieng; r 200,000Rp;) One of three homestays on this corner, and all are decent value. The carpets may be stained, but the cubist paintjobs are creative. All rooms have private bathrooms, high ceilings and good vibes.

Dahlia Homestay HOMESTAY $

(☎0852 2722 3433, 0852 2639 0053; Jl Raya Dieng; r 225,000Rp) This lovely family home offers quaint, simple rooms with wood furnishings and private bathrooms with hot water.

Homestay Arjuna HOMESTAY $

(☎0813 9232 9091; Jl Telaga Warna; r 200,000-250,000Rp) Rooms in this newly built, somewhat garish home are clean with hot-water bathrooms and detailed ceilings. Some access a lovely terrace overlooking verdant farmland. There's a koi pond in the lobby. It makes basic meals and offers free drinking water for reusable bottles. The call to prayer is crystal clear, though.

Information

The BRI Bank, near Hotel Gunung Mas, changes US dollars.

Getting There & Away

Dieng is 26km from Wonosobo (12,000Rp, one hour), which is the usual access point. It's possible to reach Dieng from Yogyakarta in one day (including a stop at Borobudur) by public bus, provided you leave early enough to make the connection; the route is Yogyakarta–Borobudur–Magelang–Wonosobo–Dieng.

Travel agents including Jogja Trans (p115) in Yogyakarta offer day trips that include sunset at Borobudur, but you'll spend a lot of your time on a bus and (unless you're fortunate) generally end up seeing Dieng clouded in mist.

Borobudur

☎0293

Along with Angkor Wat in Cambodia and Bagan in Myanmar, Java's Borobudur makes the rest of Southeast Asia's spectacular sites seem almost incidental. Looming out of a patchwork of bottle-green paddies and swaying palms, this colossal Buddhist monument has survived Gunung Merapi's eruptions, terrorist bombs and the 2006 earthquake to remain as enigmatic and as beautiful as it must have been 1200 years ago.

It's well worth planning to spend a few days in the Borobudur region, which is a supremely beautiful landscape of impossibly green rice fields and traditional rice-growing *kampung* (villages), all overlooked by soaring volcanic peaks. Locals call it the garden of Java.

This region is establishing itself as Indonesia's most important centre for Buddhism, and there are now three monasteries in the surrounding district. Visitors are welcome and you can even join the monks at prayer time for chanting.

History

Rulers of the Sailendra dynasty built Borobudur some time between AD 750 and 850. Little else is known about Borobudur's early history, but the Sailendras must have recruited a huge workforce, as some 60,000 cubic metres of stone had to be hewn, transported and carved during its construction. The name Borobudur is possibly derived from the Sanskrit words 'Vihara Buddha Uhr', which mean 'Buddhist Monastery on the Hill'.

With the decline of Buddhism and the shift of power to East Java, Borobudur was abandoned soon after completion and for centuries lay forgotten. It was only in 1815, when Sir Thomas Stamford Raffles governed Java, that the site was cleared and the sheer magnitude of the builders' imagination and technical skill was revealed. Early in the 20th century the Dutch began to tackle the restoration of Borobudur, but over the years the supporting hill had become waterlogged and the whole immense stone mass started to subside. A mammoth US$25-million Unesco-sponsored restoration project was undertaken between 1973 and 1983 to stabilise and restore the monument. This involved taking most of it apart stone by stone, adding new concrete foundations, inserting PVC and a lead drainage system, and then putting the whole shebang back together again.

In 1991 Borobudur was declared a World Heritage Site.

Sights

Borobudur Temple BUDDHIST TEMPLE

(admission 250,000Rp, sunrise and sunset 380,000Rp, 90min guided tour 1-5 people 100,000-150,000Rp; 6am-5.15pm) Indonesia's signature Buddhist monument, Borobudur is built from two million stone blocks in the form of a massive symmetrical stupa, literally wrapped around a small hill. Standing on a 118m by 118m base, its six square terraces are topped by three circular ones, with four stairways leading up through carved gateways to the top. Viewed from the air, the structure resembles a colossal three-dimensional tantric mandala (symbolic circular figure).

It has been suggested, in fact, that the people of the Buddhist community that once supported Borobudur were early Vajrayana or Tantric Buddhists who used it as a

BOROBUDUR UNDER ATTACK

In its 1200 years, Borobudur has repeatedly suffered attack from forces of nature and at the hands of humans.

During its period of abandonment, which lasted for as much as a millennia, earthquakes and volcanic eruptions destablised the monument further and the Javanese jungle reclaimed the site as giant roots penetrated the monument and prised apart stone blocks.

After rediscovery its fame grew and in 1896 King Chulalongkorn of Siam visited and removed dozens of sculptures and relief panels; some are now on display in the National Museum in Bangkok.

On 21 January 1985, bombs planted by opponents of Suharto exploded on the upper layers of the monument. Nine small stupas were damaged, but were later fully restored.

Periodically, the highly active Merapi volcano has also damaged the site – in 2010 eruptions covered the monument with a thick layer of dust and 55,000 stone blocks had to be removed so the blocked drainage system could be cleared.

Right now it's the sheer pressure of numbers that is most worrying. On holidays up to 90,000 people ascend the temple, and despite (deafening) warnings from PA systems, the selfish still clamber over the statues and deface the reliefs.

Many locals feel that a system to manage visitors must be introduced, with guides escorting groups around the monument.

MAKING THE MOST OF BOROBUDUR

Borobudur is Indonesia's most popular tourist attraction. It's crowded and noisy at all times, especially on weekends.

The golden rule is to arrive as early as you can – ideally be at the gate just before the site opens at 6am, or fork out extra for sunrise entry (4.30am). This way you'll arrive at the least crowded, coolest and most photogenic time of day. Most of the tour groups and school parties don't get in until 7.30am or later. Another choice would be to slip in late in the day, perhaps an hour before closing, when the sun dips low enough for the light to be right and the heat to subside. You can also pay that same extra fee to enter after closing for a sunset view. The view is magical from the top at either edge of the day, when you gaze from above the canopy, watch birds flutter and hear them sing as the light shifts and the mountains glow or fade into that hazy horizon.

Hawkers both outside and inside the archaeological park can be quite pushy, but will sometimes back off if you tell them in Bahasa Indonesia that you are a resident of Yogyakarta (*saya tinggal di Yogyakarta*).

Most visitors are groups from distant corners of Java. Many have never seen foreigners in the flesh before so expect plenty of requests for photos.

An MP3 player and some mystical tunes will help cut out the noise of the crowds. There's a small hill with some shade 100m or so directly south of the temple, where you can escape the hordes and contemplate the monument in peace.

Visitors who stay locally in Borobudur village hotels qualify for a 20,000Rp discount (ask for a voucher), another worthwhile reason to stay in the region for a few days and escape urban Java.

walk-through mandala. Though the paintwork is long gone, it's thought that the grey stone of Borobudur was once coloured to catch the sun.

The monument was conceived as a Buddhist vision of the cosmos in stone, starting in the everyday world and spiralling up to nirvana, or enlightenment. At the base of the monument is a series of reliefs representing a world dominated by passion and desire, where the good are rewarded by reincarnation as a higher form of life, while the evil are punished with a lower reincarnation. These carvings and their carnal scenes are covered by stone to hide them from view, but they are partly visible on the southern side.

Starting at the main eastern gateway, go clockwise (as one should around all Buddhist monuments) around the galleries of the stupa. Although Borobudur is impressive for its sheer bulk, the delicate sculptural work is exquisite when viewed up close. The pilgrim's walk is about 5km long and takes you along narrow corridors past nearly 1460 richly decorated narrative panels and 1212 decorative panels in which the sculptors have carved a virtual textbook of Buddhist doctrines as well as many aspects of Javanese life 1000 years ago – a continual procession of ships and elephants, musicians and dancing girls, warriors and kings.

On the third level there's a lengthy panel sequence about a dream of Queen Maya, which involved a vision of white elephants with six tusks. Monks and courtiers interpret this as a premonition that her son would become a Buddha, and the sequence continues until the birth of Prince Siddhartha and his journey to enlightenment. Many other panels are related to Buddhist concepts of cause and effect or karma.

Some 432 serene-faced Buddha images stare out from open chambers above the galleries, while 72 more Buddha images (many now headless) sit only partly visible in latticed stupas on the top three terraces – one is considered the lucky Buddha. The top platform is circular, signifying neverending nirvana.

Admission to the temple includes entrance to **Karmawibhangga archaeological museum**, which is just east of the monument and contains 4000 original stones and carvings from Borobudur and some interesting photographs. You might also see the Elephant House (more like an elephant prison), where two small elephants suffer, with their front feet chained together. This is the black eye of Borobudur, folks.

Museum Kapal Samurrarska MUSEUM

(inside Borobudur site; admission incl in Borobudur ticket) This museum, dedicated to the importance of the ocean and sea trade in Indonesia, houses an 18m wooden outrigger, a replica of a boat depicted on one of Borobudur's panels. This boat was sailed to Madagascar and on to Ghana in West Africa in 2003, to retrace 1000 ancient Javanese trading links and highlight the original spice trade with Africa.

Mendut Temple & Monastery BUDDHIST TEMPLE, MONASTERY

(admission incl Candi Pawon 3500Rp; ⌚8am-4pm) This exquisite temple, set within a cute neighbourhood around 3.5km east of Borobudur, may look insignificant compared with its mighty neighbour, but it houses the most outstanding statue in its original setting of any temple in Java. The magnificent 3m-high figure of Buddha is flanked by bodhisattvas: Lokesvara on the left and Vairapana on the right. The Buddha is also notable for his posture: he sits Western-style with both feet on the ground.

The statues are particularly evocative at night, when spotlit against the evening sky, and when you enter the soaring inner chamber it feels charged with an almost supernatural energy. Guards here will allow visitors to enter Mendut after dark if accompanied by a local guide (speak to Jaker).

Next to the temple is the Mendut Buddhist Monastery, leafy and prim, studded with palms and clumps of golden bamboo, shimmering with lotus palms and gleaming with Buddha nature. Guests are welcome to join the group meditations here at 7pm daily. You can also stay here for three-day, three-night meditation retreats.

Candi Pawon BUDDHIST TEMPLE

(admission 3500Rp; ⌚8am-4pm) Around 1.5km east of Borobudur, this small solitary temple is similar in design and decoration to the Mendut temple (one ticket covers both sites). It is not a stupa but resembles a Central Javanese temple, with its broad base, central body and pyramidal roof. Elaborately carved relief panels adorn its sides. Pot-bellied dwarfs pouring riches over the entrance to this temple suggest that it was dedicated to Kuvera, the Buddhist god of fortune.

Tours

Kaleidoscope of Java (p115) is an excellent Yogyakarta agency that operates fascinating tours of the Borobudur region.

Jaker TOUR

(☎0293-788845; jackpriyana@yahoo.com.sg; Jl Balaputradewa) Jaker is a group of guides and local activists based in the small settlement of Borobudur that surrounds the world's largest Buddhist monument. All Jaker members were born in the area, can provide expert local knowledge and speak fluent English.

Affordable rates are charged for trips to Selogriyo (towering rice terraces and a small Hindu temple), Tuksongo (a centre of glass-noodle production), tofu and pottery villages, a large batik workshop and to Setumbu hill for sunrise over the Borobudur monument.

Festivals & Events

Waisak RELIGIOUS

The Buddha's birth, his enlightenment and his reaching of nirvana are all celebrated on the full-moon day of Waisak when a great procession of saffron-robed monks travels from Mendut to Pawon then Borobudur, where candles are lit and flowers strewn about as offerings, followed by praying and chanting. This holiest of Buddhist events attracts thousands, and usually falls in May.

Festival of Borobudur CULTURAL

Around June, the Festival of Borobudur kicks off with a Ramayana-style dance, and goes on to feature folk-dancing competitions, handicrafts, white-water rafting and other activities.

Sleeping

There's a reasonable selection of hotels around Borobudur, though good budget places are limited. Visitors who stay in locally owned hotels get discounted entry to the monument; ask for your 15%-off voucher.

Rajasa Hotel & Restoran GUESTHOUSE $

(☎0293-788276; Jl Badrawati II; r incl breakfast with fan & cold water/air-con & hot water 200,000/400,000Rp, meals 20,000-25,000Rp; ❄📶) A deservedly popular, welcoming guesthouse with rooms that face rice fields (through railings) about 1.5km south of the bus terminal. The fan-cooled rooms are the best value, as you pay a lot more for air-conditioning and slightly smarter furniture. Meals are well priced.

Lotus II GUESTHOUSE $$

(☎0293-788845; jackpriyana@yahoo.com.sg; Jl Balaputradewa 54; r incl breakfast 250,000-275,000Rp; ❄@📶) This popular, friendly place is owned

WORTH A TRIP

VILLAGES AROUND BOROBUDUR

Away from the temples, the region around Borobudur is supremely beautiful: a verdant, fertile and classically Javanese landscape of villages and rice fields. Borobudur itself sits in a large bowl-shaped valley ringed by mountains and volcanoes that the locals call *mahagelan* – the giant bracelet.

Around 3km southwest of the monument, the small village of **Karang** is prime tofu-making terrain. There are several kitchens in the village, each producing around 50kg of *tahu* daily using traditional methods, cooking with coconut oil over a wood fire. The next settlement of **Nglipoh** is a ceramics centre, where locals say claypots have been made for more than 1000 years; everyone in the village is involved in production in some way. Today mostly *ibu* (cooking vessels) are made, though glazed ashtrays and other pots are for sale too. The potters are friendly and will let you try your hand on their wheels (just expect a giggle or two).

by one of the founders of Jaker (p109), so there's great local information and everyone speaks English. Rooms are clean and simple with wooden beds and high ceilings. The long rear balcony, overlooking rice fields, is perfect for your breakfast or an afternoon tea or beer. Book well ahead.

Rumah Dharma LODGE $$
(☎0813 9225 2557; www.rumah-dharma.com; r 650,000Rp) A popular new lodge recommended by travellers, with four small shingled cottages blessed with teak wood ceilings and set in the rice fields. Reserve ahead.

Rumah Boedi BOUTIQUE HOTEL $$$
(☎0293-559498; www.rumahboediborobudur.com; r from 990,000Rp; ❄📶) In a peaceful location about 3km east of the monument, this boutique spot offers gorgeous contemporary rooms (all feel very private) dotted around extensive, shady grounds. There's a (pricey) cafe-restaurant, too.

Manohara Hotel HOTEL $$$
(☎0293-788131; www.manoharaborobudur.com; r incl breakfast from 1,050,000Rp; ❄📶) With an unrivalled location in the grounds of the monument, and a cafe-restaurant that has views across to the main temple, this hotel's real trump card is that an unlimited, back-gate entry (and a discounted sunrise or sunset rate) to Borobudur is included in the room rate. Rooms are smallish and slightly dated, but they are comfortable and clean. If there are two of you it's a good deal. The restaurant, on the other hand, is not so magical. Dine out.

Amanjiwo HOTEL $$$
(☎0293-788333; www.amanresorts.com; ste from US$1,210; ❄@📶🏊) Perched on a hillside 4km south of Borobudur, with panoramic views towards the stupa, this five-star resort has it all. The incredibly commodious suites, many with private pools, are some of the finest in Indonesia. This is where the celebrities stay. Facilities include two tennis courts, a 40m pool and a spa.

Eating

For inexpensive local grub head to the Lotus Guesthouse (try the *soto*; soup) or you'll find warung outside the monument entrance.

Saung Makan Bu Empat SEAFOOD $$
(☎0293-914 0085; Jl Borobudor, Nyrajek; meals 45,000-65,000Rp; ⏲8am-10pm) Around 5km east of Borobudur village on the road to Yogyakarta, this traditional bamboo-and-timber restaurant is set around rice fields and gurgling streams. It's renowned for its fish and shrimp dishes. No alcohol is served but there are lots of delicious fresh fruit juices (10,000Rp) to choose from.

Patio INTERNATIONAL $$$
(☎0293-788888; www.plataranborobudur.com; mains from 60,000-300,000Rp; ⏲11am-10pm) For a special setting, this colonial-style hotel restaurant, 4km west of the monument, is hard to match – eat in the formal dining room or out on the terrace with views of Borobudur. Local mains are 60,000Rp to 100,000Rp while international dishes (try the rack of lamb) can cost up to 300,000Rp. There's a long wine list.

Information

For tourist information contact the **information office** (☎0293-788266; www.borobudurpark.com; ⏲6am-5.30pm) just beyond the temple's entrance. A **BNI Bank ATM** (Jl Medang Kamulan; ⏲8am-4pm Mon-Sat) is near the temple's entrance. Wi-fi connections are widely available in area guesthouses, hotels and restaurants.

Getting There & Away

From Yogyakarta, buses leave Jombor terminal (20,000Rp, 1¼ hours, every 30 minutes) to Borobudur. The last bus to/from Borobudur is at 4.30pm.

From Borobudur terminal buses go regularly to Magelang (10,000Rp) until 4pm. In Borobudur, becak cost 5000Rp to 10,000Rp anywhere in the village. Bicycles (30,000Rp) and motorbikes (60,000Rp to 70,000Rp) can be hired from hotels. Tours of Borobudur are easily arranged in Yogyakarta.

Yogyakarta

0274 / POP 636,660

If Jakarta is Java's financial and industrial powerhouse, Yogyakarta is its soul. Central to the island's artistic and intellectual heritage, Yogyakarta (pronounced 'Jogjakarta' and called Yogya or Jogja for short), is where the Javanese language is at its purest, Java's arts at their brightest and its traditions at their most visible.

Fiercely independent and protective of its customs, and still headed by its sultan, whose *kraton* remains the hub of traditional life, contemporary Yogya is nevertheless a huge urban centre (the entire metropolitan area is home to over 3.3 million) complete with cybercafes, malls and traffic jams, even as it remains a stronghold of batik, gamelan and ritual.

Put it all together and you have Indonesia's most liveable and lovable city, with countless hotels offering the best value in Java across all price ranges. Its restaurants are tasty and there are cultural attractions everywhere you look within the city and on the outskirts, where you'll find Indonesia's most important archaeological sites, Borobudur and Prambanan.

History

Yogyakarta owes its establishment to Prince Mangkubumi, who in 1755 returned to the former seat of Mataram and built the *kraton* of Yogyakarta. He took the title of sultan and created the most powerful Javanese state since the 17th century.

Yogya has always been a symbol of resistance to colonial rule; it was the heart of Prince Pangeran Diponegoro's Java War (1825–30) and became the capital of the republic from 1946 until independence in 1949.

When the Dutch occupied Yogya in 1948, the patriotic sultan locked himself in the *kraton* and let rebels use the palace as their headquarters. The Dutch did not dare move against the sultan for fear of arousing the anger of millions of Javanese who looked upon him almost as a god. As a result of the sultan's support of the rebels, Yogya was granted the status of a special region when independence finally came.

Sights

Most of Yogya's sights are in a small central area of the city centred on the *kraton* complex, and just to the north. But away from here and out in the eastern and southern suburbs are other attractions.

The Kraton & Around

The historic *kraton* area harbours most of Yogya's most important buildings and tourist attractions and is eminently walkable, which allows you to see contemporary life sprout from the ruins. This is no sleepy relic, but a unique urban neighbourhood.

Kraton PALACE

(Map p114; 0274-373321; admission 12,000Rp, camera 1000Rp, guided tour by donation; 8:30am-2pm Sat-Thu, to 1pm Fri) The cultural and political heart of this fascinating city is the huge palace of the sultans of Yogya, the *kraton*.

Effectively a walled city, this unique compound is home to around 25,000 people, and has its own market, shops, batik and silver cottage industries, schools and mosques. Around 1000 of its residents are employed by the sultan. Alas, the treasures here are poorly displayed, so don't expect much information to put the palace, its buildings or contents in context.

The innermost group of buildings, where the current sultan still resides, was built between 1755 and 1756. European-style touches to the interior were added in the 1920s. Structurally this is one of the finest examples of Javanese palace architecture, providing a series of luxurious halls and spacious courtyards and pavilions. An appreciation of history runs deep in Yogya, and the palace is attended by dignified elderly retainers who wear traditional Javanese dress.

The centre of the *kraton* is the reception hall, the Bangsal Kencana (Golden Pavilion), with its marble floor, intricately decorated

YOGYA IN...

Two Days

Start your day with a visit to the Kraton (p111) and a traditional performance of gamelan, *wayang* or dance, then spend the afternoon exploring the *kampung* surrounding the sultan's palace and nearby Taman Sari. In the evening stroll the narrow streets of the traditional Sosrowijayan area and its myriad restaurants.

Your second day could start with a wander down Jl Malioboro scouting for batik bargains, and a meander through Yogya's main market, Pasar Beringharjo (p113). A becak ride to Kota Gede (p113) to seek out silver could be finished off with a trip to Prawirotaman or to Mediterranea (p121) in neighbouring Jl Tirtodipuran for dinner.

Four Days

After exploring Yogya it's time to get out and see the wonders within striking distance of the city. Rise early and catch the sunrise at the incomparable Buddhist temple of Borobudur (p107), before exploring the verdant countryside and fascinating villages around the monument.

On day four, move on to Prambanan (p130), the Hindu masterpiece on the other side of the city; it's fun to make a whole day of it by cycling there via some of the minor outlying temples.

roof, Dutch-style stained-glass windows and great columns of carved teak.

A large part of the *kraton* is used as a museum and holds an extensive collection, including gifts from European monarchs, gilt copies of the sacred *pusaka* (heirlooms of the royal family) and gamelan instruments. One of the most interesting rooms contains the royal family tree, old photographs of grand mass weddings and portraits of the former sultans of Yogya.

A modern memorial building within the *kraton* is dedicated to the beloved Sultan Hamengkubuwono IX, with photographs and personal effects.

Other points of interest within the *kraton* include the male and female entrances, indicated by giant-sized 'he' and 'she' dragons (although the dragons look very similar).

Outside the *kraton*, in the centre of the northern square, there are two sacred *waringin* (banyan trees), where, in the days of feudal Java, white-robed petitioners would patiently sit hoping to catch the eye of the king. In the *alun-alun kidul* (southern square), two similar banyan trees are said to bring great fortune if you can walk between them without mishap blindfolded; on Friday and Saturday nights you can see the youth of Yogya attempting the feat to a chorus of laughter from friends.

There are performances in the *kraton*'s inner pavilion that are included in your entrance ticket. There's gamelan on Monday and Tuesday (10am to noon), *wayang golek* puppetry on Wednesday and Saturday (9am to noon), Javanese poetry readings on Friday (10am to 11:30am), and classical dance on Thursday (10am to noon) and Sunday (11am to noon).

The *kraton*'s entrance is on the northwestern side. It's closed on national holidays and for special ceremonies.

Be careful as there are scams practised by some batik sellers who hang around here.

Taman Sari PALACE

(Map p114; Jl Taman; admission 7000Rp; ⌚9am-3pm) Just southwest of the *kraton* is this complex, which once served as a splendid pleasure park of palaces, pools and waterways for the sultan and his entourage. It's said that the sultan had the Portuguese architect of this elaborate retreat executed, to keep his hidden pleasure rooms secret.

Built between 1758 and 1765, the complex was damaged first by Diponegoro's Java War, and an earthquake in 1865 helped finish the job. While much of what you see today lies in ruins, the bathing pools have been restored, and the tunnels and underground mosque are quite special.

Sono-Budoyo Museum MUSEUM

(Map p114; ☎0274-376775; admission 5000Rp; ⌚8am-1.30pm Tue-Thu & Sun, to noon Fri & Sat) This dusty, dimly lit treasure chest is the pick of Yogya's museums, with a first-class collection of Javanese art, including *wayang kulit* puppets, *topeng* (masks), kris and batik. It also has a courtyard packed with

Hindu statuary and artefacts from further afield, including superb Balinese carvings. *Wayang kulit* performances are held here.

Pasar Beringharjo MARKET

(Map p114; Jl A Yani; 8am-4pm) Yogya's main market, 800m north of the *kraton*, is a lively and fascinating place. The front section has a wide range of batik – mostly inexpensive *batik cap* (stamped batik). More interesting is the old section towards the back. Crammed with warungs and stalls selling a huge variety of fruit and vegetables, this is still very much a traditional market. The range of *rempah rempah* (spices) on the 1st floor is quite something. Come early in the morning for maximum atmosphere.

Museum Kareta Kraton MUSEUM

(Map p114; admission 5000Rp; 8am-4pm) Near the *kraton* entrance, Museum Kareta Kraton is a wonderful old carriage house with exhibits of the opulent chariots of the sultans. The leather-upholstered and intricately painted horse carts feature detailed craftsmanship. The biggest and most commanding are crowned with dragons and mouldings inlaid or coated with thick gold leaf.

Pakualaman Kraton MUSEUM

(Map p114; Jl Sultan Agung; 9.30am-1.30pm Tue, Thu & Sun) FREE This small museum includes a *pendopo* (large, open-sided pavilion) that can hold a full gamelan orchestra, and a curious colonial house. Outside opening times you can explore the grounds.

Eastern Yogyakarta

The east of the city has several more interesting sights, including the silver village of Kota Gede and several museums.

Kota Gede NEIGHBOURHOOD

(sacred tomb admission 5000Rp; sacred tomb around 9am-noon Sun, Mon & Thu, around 1-3pm Fri) Kota Gede, now an upmarket suburb of Yogyakarta, has been the hub of Yogya's silver industry since the 1930s, but it was once the first capital of the Mataram kingdom, founded by Panembahan Senopati in 1582. Senopati is buried in the small graveyard of an old mosque located to the south of the town's central market. You can visit the sacred tomb, but be sure to wear conservative dress when visiting.

Jl Kemasan, the main street leading into town from the north, is lined with busy silver workshops. Most of the shops have similar stock, including hand-beaten bowls, boxes, fine filigree and modern jewellery; they are closed on Sunday.

Kota Gede is about 5km southeast of Jl Malioboro. Catch bus 3A or 3B, take a becak (about 25,000Rp) or cycle there; it's flat most of the way.

Affandi Museum MUSEUM

(0274-562593; www.affandi.org; Jl Laksda Adisucipto 167; admission 25,000Rp, camera 25,000Rp, mobile phone with camera 15,000Rp; 9am-4pm except holidays) One of Indonesia's most celebrated artists, Affandi lived and worked in a wonderfully quirky riverside home studio, about 6km east of the town centre. Today it's the Affandi Museum, which has an extensive collection of his paintings, including some astonishing self-portraits and personal items. Check out his car, a real boy-racer's dream: a lime-green and yellow customised 1967 Galant with an oversized rear spoiler.

There's a great little cafe here, and Affandi's artistic touch even extends to the *mushullah* (prayer room), which occupies a converted horse carriage, painted in technicolour tones. It looks like a psychedelic gypsy cart. Catch bus 1A to reach this museum from Jl Malioboro.

Other Areas

Pasar Pasty MARKET

(Map p114; Ring Rd Selatan; 8am-4pm) Yogya's bird market has songbirds, owls, raptors and pigeons (for training), but occasionally also ravens (which, sadly, are still used in black magic). Note that some people might find it distressing to find endangered animals being sold here illegally. It's close to the Prawirotaman area south of the centre.

Museum Sasana Wiratama MUSEUM

(Monumen Diponegoro; admission by donation; 8am-noon Tue-Sun) In the northwest of the city, this museum honours the Indonesian hero Prince Pangeran Diponegoro, who was leader of the bloody but futile rebellion of 1825–30 against the Dutch. A motley collection of the prince's belongings and other exhibits are kept in the small museum at his former Yogya residence.

Courses

Yogya offers a variety of courses, with everything from cooking demonstrations to Bahasa Indonesia classes.

Yogyakarta

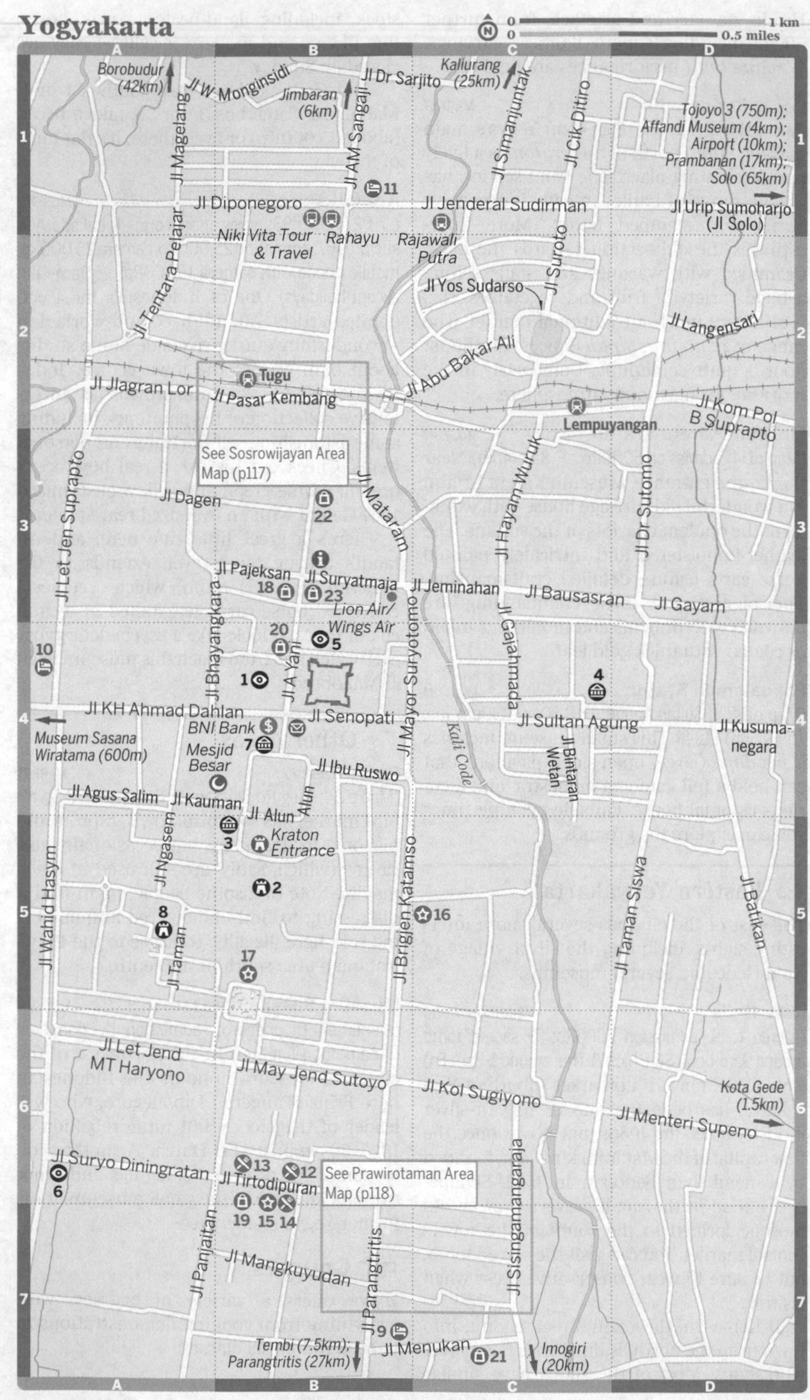

0 1 km
0 0.5 miles
Borobudur (42km)
Jl W Monginsidi
Jimbaran (6km)
Jl Dr Sarjito
Kaliurang (25km)
Jl Simanjuntak
Jl Cik Ditiro
Tojoyo 3 (750m); Affandi Museum (4km); Airport (10km); Prambanan (17km); Solo (65km)
Jl Magelang
Jl AM Sangaji
11
Jl Diponegoro
Jl Jenderal Sudirman
Jl Urip Sumoharjo (Jl Solo)
Jl Tentara Pelajar
Niki Vita Tour & Travel
Rahayu
Rajawali Putra
Jl Suroto
Jl Yos Sudarso
Jl Langensari
Jl Abu Bakar Ali
Tugu
Jl Jlagran Lor
Jl Pasar Kembang
Lempuyangan
Jl Kom Pol B Suprapto
See Sosrowijayan Area Map (p117)
Jl Let Jen Suprapto
Jl Dagen
22
Jl Mataram
Jl Hayam Wuruk
Jl Dr Sutomo
Jl Pajeksan
Jl Suryatmaja
18
23
Jl Jeminahan
Jl Bausasran
Jl Gayam
Lion Air/ Wings Air
20
5
10
Jl Bhayangkara
1
Jl A Yani
Jl Mayor Suryotomo
Jl Gajahmada
4
Jl KH Ahmad Dahlan
Jl Senopati
BNI Bank
Museum Sasana Wiratama (600m)
7
Mesjid Besar
Kali Code
Jl Sultan Agung
Jl Kusumanegara
Jl Bintaran Wetan
Jl Ibu Ruswo
Jl Agus Salim
Jl Kauman
Jl Alun
Alun
3
Kraton Entrance
Jl Ngasem
2
Jl Brigjen Katamso
Jl Wahid Hasym
8
16
Jl Taman Siswa
Jl Batikan
Jl Taman
17
Jl Let Jend MT Haryono
Jl May Jend Sutoyo
Jl Kol Sugiyono
Kota Gede (1.5km)
Jl Menteri Supeno
Jl Suryo Diningratan
6
13
12
Jl Tirtodipuran
See Prawirotaman Area Map (p118)
19
15
14
Jl Panjaitan
Jl Sisingamangaraja
Jl Mangkuyudan
Jl Parangtritis
9
Tembi (7.5km); Parangtritis (27km)
Jl Menukan
21
Imogiri (20km)

Yogyakarta

Sights
1 Gedung Negara (Governor's Building) ... B4
2 Kraton ... B5
3 Museum Kareta Kraton ... B5
4 Pakualaman Kraton ... C4
5 Pasar Beringharjo ... B4
6 Pasar Pasty ... A6
7 Sono-Budoyo Museum ... B4
8 Taman Sari ... A5

Sleeping
9 Dusun Jogja Village Inn ... B7
10 Edu Hostel ... A4
11 The Phoenix ... B1

Eating
12 Bu Ageng ... B6
13 Kedai Kebun ... B6
14 Mediterranea ... B6

Entertainment
15 Amsara ... B6
16 Purawisata ... C5
17 Sasono Hinggil ... B5
Sono-Budoyo Museum ... (see 7)

Shopping
18 Batik Keris ... B3
19 Batik Plentong ... B6
Batik Winotosastro ... (see 19)
20 Hamzah Batik ... B4
21 Lana Gallery ... C7
22 Mal Malioboro ... B3
23 Terang Bulan ... B3

Via Via COURSE
(Map p118; ☎0274-386557; www.viaviajogja.com; Jl Prawirotaman I 30) Well-structured language, cooking, batik and silver-jewellery-making courses for 80,000Rp to 200,000Rp, depending on the class size.

Alam Bahasa Indonesia LANGUAGE COURSE
(☎0274-589631; www.alambahasa.com; Kompleks Kolombo III, Jl Cendrawasih; per hour US$10) One-on-one and small-group Bahasa Indonesia language study from a professional school. Discounts for students.

Tours

Tour agents on Jl Prawirotaman and in the Sosrowijayan area offer a host of tour options at similar prices. Typical day tours and per-person rates (excluding entrance fees) are Borobudur (from 90,000Rp to 100,000Rp), Dieng (275,000Rp), Gedung Songo and Ambarawa (250,000Rp), Prambanan (75,000Rp), Borobudur and Parangtritis (250,000Rp), and Solo and Candi Sukuh (300,000Rp).

Longer tours, such as to Gunung Bromo and on to Bali (from 500,000Rp for two days and one night) and Bromo/Ijen (from 800,000Rp for three days and two nights) are also offered. Tours depend on the number of people (a minimum of four is often necessary).

Operators also arrange cars with driver, with rates starting at 500,000Rp per day.

Via Via Tours TOUR
(Map p118; www.viaviajogja.com; Jl Prawirotaman I 30) This famous cafe-restaurant offers a dozen different tours. There are numerous bike and motorbike tours, including a back road trip to Prambanan (190,000Rp to 210,000Rp), city walks (120,000Rp to 135,000Rp) and even a *jamu* (herbal medicine) and massage tour (235,000Rp to 265,000Rp) that takes in a visit to a specialist market. Tours to East Java are also offered.

Kaleidoscope of Java TOUR
(Map p118; ☎0812 2711 7439; www.kaleidoscopeofjavatour.com; Gang Sartono 823, Rumah Eyang) Fascinating tours of the Borobudur region. The day trip (300,000Rp) from Yogya involves sunrise from Menoreh hill; visits to Borobudur, Pawon and Mendut temples and a monastery, cottage industries and Javanese dance practices; and all meals.

Jogja Trans TOUR
(☎081 6426 0124, 0274-439 8495; www.jogjatrans.com; Gang 04/09, Madurejo, Prambanan) Good all-rounder for tours to places in Central Java and beyond, including Bromo and Ijen. It offers a fleet of cars with drivers (per day 500,000Rp), and also sells bus and minibus tickets and can make hotel bookings.

Great Tours TOUR
(Map p117; ☎0274-583221; www.greattoursjogja.com; Jl Sosrowijayan 29) It operates tours, sells bus and train tickets, and arranges chartered transport to destinations throughout Central Java.

Festivals & Events

Gerebeg CULTURAL
Three Gerebeg festivals – held at the end of January and April and the beginning of November – are Java's most colourful and grand processions. In traditional court dress, palace guards and retainers, not to mention large floats of decorated mountains of rice, all make their way to the mosque, west of the *kraton*, to the sound of prayer and gamelan music.

Contact the tourist information centre for an exact schedule.

Arts Festival ART
This annual festival, held for two weeks in June, features a wide range of shows and exhibitions. Most events are held at the Benteng Vredeburg.

Sleeping

Yogya has Java's best range of guesthouses and hotels, many offering excellent value for money. During the high season – July, August and Christmas and New Year – you should book ahead.

Sosrowijayan Area

This area is very popular with backpackers as most of Yogya's cheap hotels are in the souk-like maze of *gang* (alleys) within this traditional neighbourhood. But the best part about staying in what feels like a *bule* (foreigner) ghetto is that those little lanes spill out onto Jl Sosrowijayan and are within a short stroll of the more authentic Jl Malioboro.

Dewi Homestay HOMESTAY $
(Map p117; ☎0274-516014; dewihomestay@hotmail.com; Jl Sosrowijayan GT I 115; r 125,000Rp) An attractive, long-running place that has character, with a leafy, shady garden and spacious, charming rooms – many have four-poster beds draped with mosquito nets.

Losmen Lucy GUESTHOUSE $
(Map p117; ☎0274-513429; r with fan/air-con 125,000/200,000Rp; ❄) One of the best losmen in the area, this place is run by a house-proud lady and has 12 tidy, tiled rooms with good beds; all have en-suite *mandi* (Indonesian-style bathrooms).

Tiffa GUESTHOUSE $
(Map p117; ☎0274-512841; tiffaartshop@yahoo.com; Jl Sosrowijayan Wetan Gt II 12; s/d incl breakfast 125,000/150,000Rp) A tidy little losmen owned by a hospitable family, with a handful of smallish, quirky and charming rooms, each with private *mandi*. There's a communal balcony where you can tuck into your free breakfast and slurp tea or coffee. It's above an art shop.

105 Homestay GUESTHOUSE $
(Map p117; ☎0274-582896; homestay_105@yahoo.co.id; r with fan/aircon 120,000/200,000Rp; ❄📶) A lobby complete with Gaudi-esque tiles and a welcoming owner set a nice introduction at this guesthouse, which has seven classes of neat rooms in the heart of Sosrowijayan's souk-like backstreets.

Andrea Hotel GUESTHOUSE $
(Map p117; ☎0274-563502; www.andreahoteljogja.wordpress.com; Sosrowijayan I/140 Gang II; r incl breakfast 140,000-285,000Rp; ❄📶) They claim hotel, but it feels more losmen. Which means the rooms are fair value but lack soul. Still, it offers good-quality beds and linen and there's a slim street terrace where you can watch the Sosrowijayan world go by with a drink in your hand.

Bladok Losmen & Restaurant HOTEL $
(Map p117; ☎0274-560452; www.bladok.web.id; Jl Sosrowijayan 76; s with fan 100,000Rp, d with fan 150,000-240,000Rp, d with air-con 320,000Rp; ❄📶🏊) A dependable, well-run place that looks vaguely like an alpine Austrian chalet. Bladok's rooms won't disappoint, with lovely chunky wooden beds and furniture, high cleanliness standards and crisp, fresh linen; some have balconies. The (small) pool is a real bonus and the cafe-restaurant serves European food and homemade bread.

Sari Homestay HOMESTAY $
(Map p117; ☎0274-513428; Gang I 97; r 160,000Rp; ❄📶) The lobby is decked out in batik-wrapped columns, and the tiled rooms here come with pastel paint jobs, flat-screens and air-con. They can be dark, thanks to the tinted windows, but they're still a bargain.

Setia Kawan GUESTHOUSE $
(Map p117; ☎0274-512452, 081 2273 8963; www.bedhots.com; Jl Sosrowijayan GT 1/57; s/d with fan 175,000/190,000Rp, s/d with air-con 190,000-225,000Rp; ❄@) Inviting, well-run place that

Sosrowijayan Area

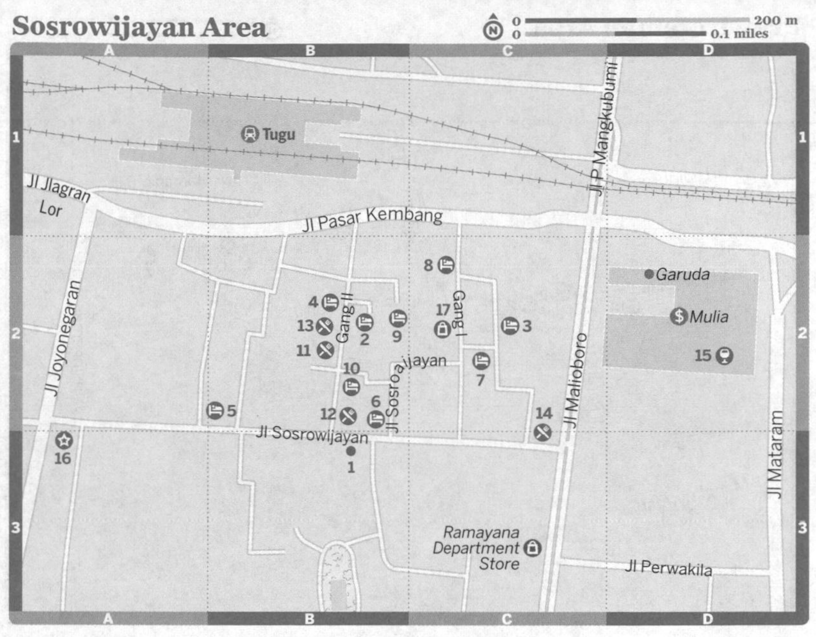

Sosrowijayan Area

Activities, Courses & Tours
1 Great Tours B3

Sleeping
2 1001 Malam B2
3 105 Homestay C2
4 Andrea Hotel B2
5 Bladok Losmen & Restaurant B2
6 Dewi Homestay B2
7 Losmen Lucy C2
8 Sari Homestay C2
9 Setia Kawan B2
10 Tiffa B2

Eating
11 Bedhot Resto B2
12 Hanis Restaurant & Bakery B2
13 Mi Casa es Tu Casa B2
14 Oxen Free C3

Drinking & Nightlife
Oxen Free .... (see 14)
15 Republic Positiva D2

Entertainment
16 Lucifer A3

Shopping
17 Boomerang Bookshop C2

occupies a fine, artistically decorated house. There are nice touches everywhere, with classic Vespa scooters in the lobby, a lounge area with TV/DVDs, computers for internet access and a good information board. Rooms are smallish but very attractive, though the swirling, hippie-ish murals and sloped ceiling could be a bit much after a heavy night.

1001 Malam HOTEL **$$**
(Map p117; www.1001malamhotel.com; Sosrowijayan Wetan Gt I/57; d from 550,000Rp;) A beautifully built Moroccan-style structure complete with hand-carved wooden doorways and a lovely Moorish courtyard decked out with craftsman tiles. It's certainly an inspirational setting, though arguably a bit overpriced given the competition.

Prawirotaman Area

This area has a few cheap places mixed in with lots of midrange choices. Plenty have pools and the choice of restaurants is excellent. But it does feel like a tourist ghetto within an Indonesian city.

Prawirotaman Area

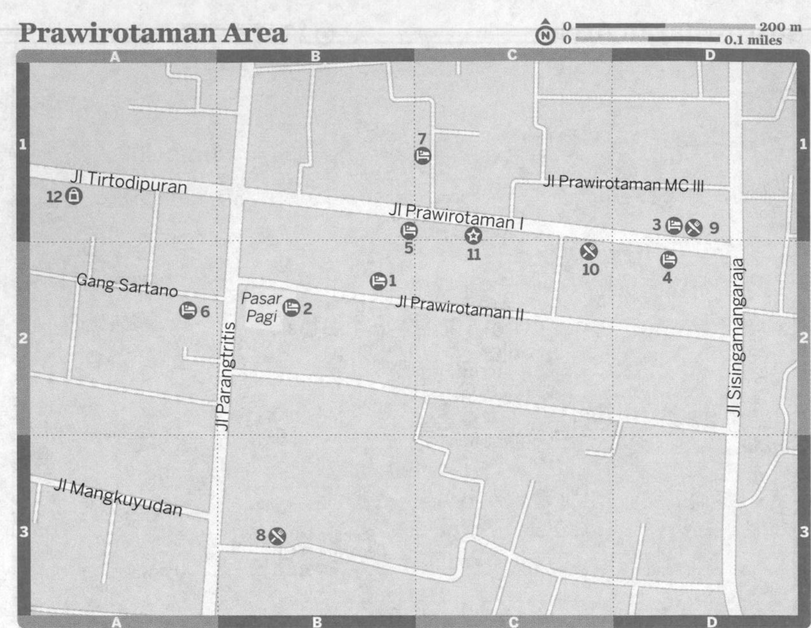

Prawirotaman Area

Activities, Courses & Tours
- Kaleidoscope of Java .... (see 6)
- Via Via .... (see 10)
- Via Via Tours .... (see 10)

Sleeping
1. Delta Homestay B2
2. Greenhost B2
3. Hotel Kirana D1
4. Kampoeng Djawa Hotel D2
5. Prambanan Guesthouse B1
6. Rumah Eyang A2
7. Via Via C1

Eating

8. Milas B3
9. Tempo del Gelato D1
10. Via Via C2

Entertainment

11. K Meals C1

Shopping

12. Gong A1

Kampoeng Djawa Hotel GUESTHOUSE $
(Map p118; ☎0274-378318; www.kampoengdjawahotel.com; Jl Prawirotaman I 40; r with fan 111,000-190,000Rp, with air-con 230,000Rp; ❄📶) Occupying a long, thin house, this place has character to spare. The rooms (in five price categories) have artistic touches including exposed brick walls, mosaic tiling and pebble-walled bathrooms. There's a peaceful rear garden for your complimentary tea or coffee (available all day) and afternoon snack. Staff are eager to help here.

Delta Homestay GUESTHOUSE $
(Map p118; ☎0274-327051; www.dutagardenhotel.com; Jl Prawirotaman II 597A; r with shared mandi 115,000-135,000Rp, r 230,000-250,000Rp; ❄📶🏊) A sunny backstreet guesthouse with a selection of small but perfectly formed rooms built from natural materials, each with a porch, grouped around a pool. It's peaceful here, staff are welcoming and breakfast is included.

Via Via GUESTHOUSE $
(Map p118; ☎0274-386557; www.viaviajogja.com; Prawirotaman 3/514A; r incl breakfast 150,000-200,000Rp; ❄📶) Part of the expanding Via Via empire, this fine guesthouse enjoys a quiet side-street location not far from the mothership cafe-restaurant (p121). It has seven stylish rooms with high ceilings,

good-quality beds and semi-open bathrooms. There's a garden at the rear for socialising.

Rumah Eyang GUESTHOUSE $
(Map p118; ☎0812 2711 7439; Jl Parangtritis, Gang Sartono 823; r incl breakfast from 220,000Rp;) A stylish suburban house that's been converted into an inviting guesthouse and art space. Rooms are simple and comfortable, but the real benefit here is that Atik, the Javanese writer-owner, is a font of knowledge about the region and offers great tours.

Prambanan Guesthouse HOTEL $$
(Map p118; ☎0274-376167; www.prambanangh.be; Jl Prawirotaman I 14; s/d with fan & cold shower 245,000/285,000Rp, with air-con & hot shower 380,000/400,000Rp ;) It's looking a bit tired these days, but it remains a peaceful place to stay with a small pool and attractive gardens. Cheaper rooms are quite plain, but the better options are plenty comfortable and have ikat-style textiles draped on good-quality beds.

Hotel Kirana HOTEL $$
(Map p118; ☎0274-376000; kirana.hotel@gmail.com; Jl Prawirotaman I 45; r incl breakfast from 370,000/395,000Rp;) A modest, well-kept hotel with clean tiled rooms with high ceilings and hot water. They are a little dark but well priced with frequent discounts offered. You'll find a nice lounge and garden area at the rear.

Greenhost BOUTIQUE HOTEL $$
(Map p118; ☎0274-389777; www.greenhosthotel.com; Jl Prawirotaman II; r from 520,000Rp;) This raw, natural wood and polished concrete structure dripping with vines is a terrific new boutique hotel. The lobby is the ground floor of a dramatic atrium, and though rooms aren't huge they offer polished concrete floors, raw-wood furnishings and floating beds. There's an indoor saltwater pool.

Dusun Jogja Village Inn HOTEL $$$
(Map p114; ☎0274-373031; www.jvidusun.co.id; Jl Menukan 5; r incl breakfast from 880,000Rp;) This fine hotel has a lovely Javanese feel thanks to its design and decor, and maintains high standards. Most of the luxurious rooms have ample balconies overlooking the stunning tropical garden and huge pool. It's a 10-minute walk from the restaurant action of Prawirotaman.

City Centre

Edu Hostel HOSTEL $
(Map p114; ☎0274-543295; www.eduhostels.com; Jl Suprapto 17; dm 80,000Rp;) The biggest hostel in Indonesia is set in a massive former condo complex, with a whopping 324 beds broken down into 60 separate dorm rooms, each with their own bathroom. There's a dipping pool and bar on the rooftop, and fat bikes for rent (four hours, 40,000Rp), though the location isn't great.

It's a kilometre from Jl Malioboro, 1.5km from the train station, and not that close to any of the real action.

★**The Phoenix** HISTORIC HOTEL $$$
(Map p114; ☎0274-566617; www.thephoenixyogya.com; Jl Jenderal Sudirman 9-11; r from 900,000Rp;) Right in the heart of the city, this historic hotel is easily the best in its class and is a Yogya landmark. Dating back to 1918, it's been sensitively converted to incorporate modern facilities. Rooms are gorgeous, and it's worth paying a little extra for those with balconies overlooking the pool area.

There's a spa and a great cafe, and the buffet breakfast spread is a sight for hungry bellies.

Outskirts

★**d'Omah** BOUTIQUE HOTEL $$$
(☎0274-368050; domahyogya.com; Jalan Parangtritis Km8.5, Tembi; r from 1,250,000Rp;) Tastefully built in traditional Javanese style with 23 gorgeous rooms, grouped in four villa-like compounds, each with a pool. It's a delight to explore the grounds, which are replete with art and sculpture and fringed by rice fields (illuminated by flickering torchlight at night). It's about 8km south of the centre.

Villa Hanis BOUTIQUE HOTEL $$$
(☎0274-867666; www.villahanis.com; Jl Palagan Km7.5; r from US$129;) This luxury B&B, owned by a Belgian-Indonesian couple, features rooms in a traditional Javanese teak house. It's in a rural location about 7km north of the centre, surrounded by rice fields, with views of Gunung Merapi.

Eating

Yogya is a great place to eat out with authentic street food and local places in the centre and some tasty restaurants geared to the Western palate concentrated in the Prawirotaman and adjacent Jl Tirtodipuran area to the south.

Sosrowijayan Area

There are loads of inexpensive noshing options in this area including a row of good warungs on Jl Pasar Kembang, beside the train line.

Bedhot Resto INTERNATIONAL $

(Map p117; Gang II; mains 18,000-42,000Rp; 8am-11pm;) Bedhot means 'creative' in old Javanese and this place is one of the more stylish eateries in Sosrowijayan. There's tasty Indonesian and international food – a cut above usual tourist fare – plus good juices and wi-fi.

Hanis Restaurant & Bakery INTERNATIONAL $

(Map p117; Jl Sosrowijayan, Gang II; mains 24,000-49,000Rp; 8am-11pm) If you are in dire need of international fare like, say, a breakfast of muesli and yogurt, some decent brown bread or chicken fajitas, this cute bakery and cafe could be your salvation. The cakes and pies look serious, too.

Oxen Free PUB $$

(Map p117; www.oxenfree.net; Jl Sosrowijayan 2; mains 30,000-60,000Rp; 11am-2am Sun-Thu, to 3am Fri & Sat;) The coolest new spot in the area is set in an old colonial building, dotted with reclaimed booths and lit by raw bulbs and old camping lanterns. Most descend on the beer garden out the back, for all-day Western breakfasts and roast chicken and lamb dinners. Attention veg-heads: it does a mean tempe steak, too. It also gets a fun bar crowd most nights.

Mi Casa es Tu Casa SPANISH, INDONESIAN $$

(Map p117; www.micasaestucasa.mye.name; Sosrowijayan Wetan GT I/141; mains 30,000-115,000Rp; 11am-10pm;) OK, the name is a cliche, but this stylish Basque-owned place is worth a try if you're in need of paella (115,000Rp for two, order well ahead) or crave tapas (mushroom risotto, *albóndigas* meatballs, gazpacho). It also serves Indonesian dishes and, um, cobra. If that's your thing.

Prawirotaman Area

Bu Ageng INDONESIAN $

(Map p114; 0274-387191; Jl Tirtodipuran 13; mains 14,000-30,000Rp; 11am-11pm Tue-Sun) Traditional Javanese dishes like *eyem penggeng*, chicken simmered in spiced coconut cream then grilled, are served in a tasteful interior space with wood columns and a bamboo-mat ceiling twirling with fans. The adventurous array of mixed rice platters includes dishes like beef tongue, smoked fish or beef stewed in coconut milk. There's even a durian bread pudding.

If you order the chicken, know that this is *kampung* chicken. It's truly free-range, lean, flavourful, slightly al dente and not that meaty. In other words, be a bone-sucker.

Milas INDONESIAN $

(Map p118; 0274-742 3399; Jl Prawirotaman IV 127; dishes 15,000-45,000Rp; 3-9pm Tue-Fri, noon-9pm Sat & Sun;) A great retreat from the streets, this secret garden restaurant is part of a project centre for street youth. It offers tasty vegetarian cooking including healthy snacks, sandwiches, salads and organic coffee.

Tempo del Gelato GELATERIA $

(Map p118; Jl Prawirotaman I; small/medium/large 20,000/40,000/65,000Rp; 11am-11pm) A stone-and-glass chapel to Italian ice cream. Flavours on rotation include ginger, guava, dragon fruit, chocolate, green tea, praline, lemongrass, rum raisin and coconut. Four months old at research time and already extremely popular.

YOGYA'S STREET FOOD

In the evening, street-food vendors line the northern end of Jl Malioboro; here you can try Yogya's famous *ayam goreng* (deep-fried chicken soaked in coconut milk) and dishes such as *sambal welut* (spicy eel) and *nasi langgi* (coconut rice with tempe). Many students head here in the evening to snack on *oseng oseng*, which is a kind of mini *nasi campur* (rice with a bit of everything) and only costs 5000Rp to 10,000Rp. It's a lot of fun with impromptu *lesahan* seating, mats spread on the ground and young Indonesians strumming their guitars into the wee small hours. Complemented by the clip-clop of the horse carts and the whirring clank of the becak mob, Jl Malioboro is that different world; that open doorway into an authentic Indonesian way of life.

During daylight hours look out for Yogya's famous *gudeg*, a jackfruit curry served with chicken, egg and rice, which is served from stalls all over town, particularly around markets.

★ Mediterranea MEDITERRANEAN $$
(Map p114; www.restobykamil.com; Jl Tirtodipuran 24A; mains 38,000-147,000Rp; ⌚11am-11pm Tue-Sun; 📶) This French-owned kitchen is a delight in every sense. Everything here is homemade, including the bread (which is baked twice daily). It also smokes its own salmon, slices a paper-thin beef carpaccio, offers a tasty tuna tataki, and grills kebabs, steaks and chops. The traditional range of wood-fired pizzas are marvellous, too.

Local expats consider chef Kamil Massard-Combe's spiced duck breast, served on a bed of risotto, to be the best dish in the city. Whatever you do, save room for dessert. It would be difficult to find a finer crème brûlée on this sweet earth. If it's a lively evening, dine indoors; if you crave romance, grab a candlelit table on the back patio.

Via Via INTERNATIONAL, INDONESIAN $$
(Map p118; ☎0274-386557; www.viaviajogja.com; Jl Prawirotaman I 30; mains 27,000-115,000Rp; 📶) Serving almost an exclusively Western crowd, Via Via does a variety of juices, lassis, felafel and curried chicken pitas, veggie burgers, pasta and some Indian dishes, too. The next-door shop offers backpacker essentials and a terrific tour desk beneath a yoga studio.

Kedai Kebun INDONESIAN $$
(Map p114; www.kedaikebun.com; Jl Tirtodipuran III; mains 30,000-109,000Rp; 📶✍) This fun bohemian cafe-gallery is a key hang-out for Yogya's artistic community. The menu is a blend of Indonesian and international comfort food, and vegans and vegetarians are well catered for. Still, the colourful setting is more exciting than the food. The attached gallery hosts regular events including art exhibitions where DJs spin.

Other Areas

★ Tojoyo 3 INDONESIAN $
(☎0274-419169; Jl Urip Sumoharjo 133; dishes 4000-12,500Rp; ⌚11am-11pm) A smoky, salty, tiled den of turmeric-rubbed, fried-chicken iniquity. Dishes are impossibly cheap and that lean-yet-juicy *kampung* chicken is improbably good. No wonder all the tables and benches are packed with locals, here to get their deep-fried fix. It's set on a commercial strip east of Jl Malioboro.

Omar Duwur Restaurant INDONESIAN, INTERNATIONAL $$$
(☎0274-374952; www.omahdhuwur.net; Jl Mondorakan 252; mains 39,000-175,000Rp; ⌚11am-10pm; 📶) Out in Kota Gede, this is one of Yogya's best restaurants, with a lavish setting in a 150-year-old colonial mansion, and a wide selection of Western (try the Australian tenderloin steak) and Eastern (the spiced, fried duck and oxtail soup are well executed) dishes.

Drinking & Nightlife

Cool cafes are opening across Yogya, particularly in the Prawirotaman area. If you want to sip a few beers, both Jl Sosrowijayan and Jl Parangtritis (in the Prawirotaman area) have a crop of bars; many have live music.

★ Oxen Free BEER GARDEN
(Map p117; www.oxenfree.net; Jl Sosrowijayan 2; ⌚11am-2am Sun-Thu, to 3am Fri & Sat) This reclaimed medical clinic from the old colonial days stood vacant for years before a local Indo-expat couple turned it into a mainstay on the nightlife scene. Most guests come to chill in the beer-garden booths where the Anker, Bintang, Bali Hai and San Miguel are perfectly chilled and can be served in beer towers.

It hosts a regular rotation of DJs and jazz bands, and throws theme parties, too. Student night is Thursday.

Republic Positiva CLUB
(Map p117; ☎0274-557525; Jl Malioboro 60; cover charge varies; ⌚7pm-3am) It calls itself a cafe and lounge, but this venue at the Garuda Hotel in the city centre is a nightclub all the way. There's a regular rotation of DJs, student nights on Wednesday, and ladies night every Friday.

Boshe CLUB
(☎0274-624041; www.boshevvipclub.com/jogja; Jl Magelang, Km6.5; ⌚10pm-2am) This venue boasts a large central dance floor and a pumping sound system, and draws a young student crowd with electronic DJs (unfortunately alternated with cheesy dance troupes). There's always a drink promo.

Entertainment

Yogya is one of the epicentres of traditional Javanese performing arts. Dance, *wayang* or gamelan is performed every morning at the *kraton*; check with the tourist office for current listings and any ongoing special

THE YOGYA SCENE

What makes Yogyakarta so easy to like is its accessibility. One can stroll the sights, sample the flavours and get a good night's sleep in an affordable, clean and comfortable room. The air is not full of smog and the sights nearby are magical. But that's not why so many international people have moved here. What makes them love their adopted city isn't the easily accessible qualities, but its shadow side.

Difficult to access but worth seeking out is Yogya's massive underground scene. Its art gallery openings and all-night dance parties by the riverside or on nearby beaches. DJs, live bands, MCs and ska punks are all here, but if you are on a quick blitz through Java you are likely to miss it. On the other hand, if you take a month-long *bahasa* intensive, sink in and stay awhile, you might just find the rhythm.

The following sites often post the latest happenings in and around Yogyakarta. Some are arts organisations, others are gallery or band pages. All post upcoming events when they have them.

Krack Studio (www.facebook.com/KrackStudio)

Kebun Binatang Film (www.facebook.com/kebunbinatangfilm)

IndoArtNow (www.facebook.com/indoartnow)

LifePatch (www.facebook.com/lifepatch)

HONF: The House of Natural Fiber (www.facebook.com/houseofnaturalfiber)

Kedai Kebun (www.facebook.com/kedai.kebun)

Yes No Klub (www.facebook.com/yesnoklubyk)

Lelagu Musik (www.facebook.com/Lelagu.musik)

Senyawa (www.facebook.com/senyawamusik)

Zoo (www.facebook.com/zooindonesia)

Jogja Noise Bombing (www.facebook.com/jogjanoisebombingpeople)

Dub Youth (www.facebook.com/DubyouthOfficial)

Sound Boutique (www.facebook.com/groups/64738459162)

D.I.G. Project (www.facebook.com/doingrouproject)

EnergyRoom (www.facebook.com/ENERGYROOM)

events (such as the spectacular Ramayana ballet held at Prambanan in the dry season).

Wayang Kulit

Leather-puppet performances can be seen at several places around Yogya every night of the week.

Sasono Hinggil PUPPETRY
(Map p114; South Main Sq) Most of the centres offer shortened versions for tourists, but here in the *alun-alun selatan* of the *kraton*, marathon all-night performances are held every second Saturday from 9pm to 5am (20,000Rp). Bring a pillow.

Sono-Budoyo Museum PUPPETRY
(Map p114; ☎0274-376775; admission 20,000Rp, camera 3000Rp; ⏲8pm-10pm Mon-Sat) Popular two-hour performances nightly from 8pm to 10pm (20,000Rp); the first half-hour involves the reading of the story in Javanese, so most travellers skip this and arrive later.

Dance

Most performances are based on the Ramayana or at least billed as 'Ramayana ballet' because of the famed performances at Prambanan.

Purawisata DANCE
(Map p114; ☎0274-375705; Jl Brigjen Katamso; 300,000Rp) This amusement park stages Ramayana performances daily at 8pm. You can dine here and watch the show.

Live Music

Jl Sosrowijayan is something of a live music hub with casual venues often rocking with local bands. At research time these were the most reliable choices.

Amsara LIVE MUSIC
(Map p114; Jl Tirtodipuran; ⌚noon-late) It calls itself an art and coffee shop, but this split-level joint feels like a restaurant and bar with frequent live acts. Regulars include a really good reggae band on Thursdays and a fun, mixed crowd every night. Locals call it 'Ascos'.

Lucifer LIVE MUSIC
(Map p117; Jl Sosrowijayan) An intimate bar and one of the city's key live music venues. There are bands most nights.

K Meals LIVE MUSIC
(Map p118; ☎0274-829 0097; www.kmealsrestaurant.com; Jl Prawirotaman I) A cool indoor-outdoor pub with live blues on Monday and reggae every Thursday.

Shopping

Yogyakarta is a shopper's paradise for crafts and antiques.

Jl Malioboro is one great, throbbing bazaar of souvenir shops and stalls selling cheap clothes, leatherwork, batik bags, *topeng* masks and *wayang golek* puppets. Look in some of the fixed-price shops on Jl Malioboro or nearby streets to get an idea of prices. **Hamzah Batik** (Map p114; ☎0274-588524; Jl A Yani 9; ⌚9am-9pm) is an excellent place to start looking, and when you're done shopping here try the traditional Javanese food on the roof terrace.

In the south of the city, Jl Prawirotaman and Jl Tirtodipuran (west of Jl Prawirotaman) have a selection of upmarket galleries, art shops and expensive batik factories. You'll find furniture, antiques, and a variety of crafts and curios from Java and further afield.

For regular shopping in the heart of town, head to **Mal Malioboro** (Map p114; Jl Malioboro; ⌚10am-9pm Mon-Sat, to 8pm Sun). **Ambarrukmo Plaza** (Jl Laksda Adisucipto; ⌚10am-9pm Mon-Sat, to 8pm Sun), 5km west of the centre, is more upmarket with boutiques, a good food court, cinema and supermarket; take bus 1B from the main post office.

Batik

Most of the batik workshops and several large showrooms are along Jl Tirtodipuran, south of the *kraton*. Many, such as **Batik Plentong** (Map p114; Jl Tirtodipuran 48) and **Batik Winotosastro** (Map p114; Jl Tirtodipuran 54), give free guided tours of the batik process from 9am to 3pm. These places cater to tour groups, so prices are very high – view the process here and shop elsewhere.

> **BUYING BATIK**
>
> If there's one Indonesian word that you'll remember from your trip to Yogya it's 'batik', which translates to something of a blessing and a curse. Batik is both one of Yogya's biggest draws (it's one of the city's purist art forms) and worst blights (due to the hard sell and scams directed at tourists).
>
> Plenty of tourists get suckered into buying overpriced batik. Perhaps the best strategy is to see as much stuff as you can before opening the purse strings – window-shop and start looking in the cheapest places, including the markets and mass-production galleries around Taman Sari. Small batik paintings start at around 50,000Rp (although the asking price may be 500,000Rp). You can then graduate to the upmarket galleries.

Batik is cheapest in the markets, especially Pasar Beringharjo, but quality is questionable. Jl Malioboro and Jl A Yani have good fixed-price places.

Batik Keris CLOTHING
(Map p114; www.batikkeris.co.id; Jl A Yani 71; ⌚9am-8pm) Excellent-quality batik at fixed prices. Best for traditional styles – men's shirts start at about 200,000Rp.

Terang Bulan CLOTHING
(Map p114; Jl A Yani 108; ⌚9am-8pm) Good fixed-price place for batik.

Antiques, Curios & Furniture

Although a few antiques can be found in the shops and markets, be aware that dealers spend an inordinate amount of time ageing puppets, masks and all manner of other goods in the pursuit of antiquity.

Jl Tirtodipuran and Jl Prawirotaman have stores selling artefacts and furniture from all over Indonesia. Prices are generally high – bargain furiously.

Gong HANDICRAFTS
(Map p118; ☎0274-385367; gong56jogja@yahoo.com; Jl Tirtodipuran 56; ⌚8am-10pm) A hole-in-the-wall storefront with an incredible collection of authentic antique wooden puppets and masks from across the archipelago, though most are from Java. Some are as much as 50 years old. To the discerning collector this is a treasure chest.

Bookstores

Gramedia BOOKS
(☎0274-433 1141; Jl Laksda Adisucipto, Ambarukmo Plaza; ⊙10am-8pm) Gramedia is 5km west of the centre and stocks a few new English-language titles.

Boomerang Bookshop BOOKS
(Map p117; ☎0878 4579 3942; Gang I 67; ⊙10am-8pm) Has used guidebooks and fiction, Periplus maps and books, plus souvenirs.

Silver

The village of Kota Gede specialises in silver, although it can be found all over town. Fine filigree work is a Yogya speciality. Kota Gede has some very attractive jewellery, boxes, bowls, cutlery and miniatures, and there are dozens of smaller silver shops on Jl Kemesan and Jl Mondorakan, where you can get some good buys if you bargain.

Guided tours of the process, with no obligation to buy, are available at the large factories. Most shops are closed on Sunday.

HS JEWELLERY
(www.hssilver.com; Jl Mondorakan I) Ask for a substantial discount off the marked prices.

MD JEWELLERY
(☎0274-375063; Jl Pesegah KG 8/44) Rings, bracelets, earrings and more. Down a small alley off the street; try for discounts.

Tom's Silver JEWELLERY
(☎0274-525416; Jl Ngeski Gondo 60) An extensive (and expensive) selection and some superb large pieces.

Art

Lana Gallery ART
(Map p114; ☎0818 0412 8277, 0877 3929 3119; rlhwildan@yahoo.com; Jl Menukan; ⊙Tue-Sun) A great range of contemporary art from new and emerging artists from across the archipelago, many of them graduates of Yogya's fine arts school. It's run by Wildan, one of the friendliest people you'll ever meet.

Information

The website www.yogyes.com is an excellent portal to the city and Central Java.

DANGERS & ANNOYANCES

Hassles from smooth-talking batik salesmen are a constant issue for every traveller in town. The tourist board gets hosts of complaints about these sharks, who may strike up conversations pretending to be guides. Inevitably you'll end up at a gallery where you'll get the hard sell and they'll rake in a big commission if you buy. A time-honoured scam is to pressure you to visit a 'fine-art student exhibition' or a 'government store' – there are no official shops or galleries in the city.

Some of these dodgy batik salesmen hang around the *kraton*, where they tell you that the *kraton* is closed or there are no performances, but they might offer to show you to the 'sultan's batik workshop' (which is actually just a very expensive commission-paying showroom).

Be aware too that due to a schism in the ruling family there are actually two separate entrances, and ticket offices, at the *kraton*. One entrance (with a 5000Rp charge) only allows you to view a small area, which contains some dioramas and horse carriages; it may be signposted 'Pagelaran'. Official-looking guys with IDs will try to shepherd you in here before inviting you to look at some of the 'sultan's batik'. This is *not* the main entrance to the *kraton*, which has a big clock by its ticket window (and an entrance fee of 12,000Rp).

Becak drivers are very pushy in Yogya; those offering 'special rates' of 1000Rp for one hour are also trying to get you into a batik gallery.

INTERNET ACCESS

Wi-fi is ubiquitous. Almost all guesthouses and restaurants have a decent connection.

MEDICAL SERVICES

Ludira Husada Tama Hospital (☎0274-620333; Jl Wiratama 4; ⊙24hr)

MONEY

There are numerous banks (and a few money changers) in the tourist areas. **BNI Bank** (Map p114; Jl Trikora I; ⊙8am-4pm Mon-Sat) is opposite the main post office. **Mulia** (Map p117; Jl Malioboro 60, Inna Garuda Hotel) has the best money-changing rates in Yogya, and changes euros, pounds, Australian, Canadian and US dollars, and Swiss francs.

POST

Main Post Office (Map p114; Jl Senopati; ⊙8am-2pm Mon-Sat)

TOURIST INFORMATION

Tourist Information Office (Map p114; ☎0274-562000; Jl Malioboro 16; ⊙8am-8pm Mon-Thu, to 7pm Fri & Sat; @) Perhaps the most well-organised office of its kind in the country. Here is delightful, helpful staff, free maps and good transport information. It produces a number of publications (including a calendar of events and a great map), and staff can book any and all transport, as well as local attractions and performances.

There are also counters at the airport and on the eastern side of the Tugu train station.

TRAVEL AGENCIES

Great Tours (p116) is best for sunrise tours, bus and minibus tickets, chartered transport and tours to Borobudur, Bromo and Ijen.

Getting There & Away

AIR

Yogyakarta has international connections to Singapore and Kuala Lumpur, plus many domestic links.

Solo airport, 60km away, also has international and domestic flights.

AirAsia (0274-5050 5088; www.airasia.com) Flies to Singapore, Kuala Lumpur, Jakarta and Denpasar.

Garuda (Map p117; www.garuda-indonesia.com) Links Yogya with Balikpapan, Denpasar and Jakarta.

Lion Air/Wings Air (Map p114; www.lionair.co.id) Flies to Balikpapan, Banjarmasin, Denpasar, Makassar, Jakarta and Surabaya.

Sriwijaya Air (www.sriwijayaair.co.id) To Balikpapan, Jakarta and Surabaya.

Wings Air (021-6379 8000; www.lionair.co.id) To Bandung and Surabaya.

BUS

Yogya's main bus terminal, Giwangan, is 5km southeast of the city centre; bus 3B connects it with Tugu train station and Jl Malioboro. Buses run from Giwangan to points all over Java, and also to Bali. For long trips make sure you take a luxury bus. It's cheaper to buy tickets at the bus terminal, but it's less hassle to simply check fares and departures with the ticket agents along Jl Mangkubumi, Jl Sosrowijayan or Jl Prawirotaman. These agents can also arrange pickup from your hotel.

To go to Prambanan (3600Rp) take a 1A city bus from Jl Malioboro. Buses to/from Borobudur use the Jombor terminal. To get there take a Transjogya bus 3A from Jl Malioboro to Jl Ahmad Dahlan, and change to a 2B for Jombor.

MINIBUS

Door-to-door *travel* minibuses run to all major cities from Yogya. Sosrowijayan and Prawirotaman agents sell tickets. Prices are similar to air-conditioned buses. Journeys of more than four hours can be cramped – trains and buses offer more comfort. Due to traffic patterns, it's much faster to get to Solo by train.

You can also buy direct from the minibus companies, which include **Rajawali Putra** (Map p114; 0274-583535; Jl Jenderal Sudirman 42), **Rahayu** (Map p114; 0274-561322; Jl Diponegoro 9A) and **Niki Vita Tour & Travel** (Map p114; 0274-561884; Jl Diponegoro 25). Destinations served include Semarang (80,000Rp, four hours), Surabaya (90,000Rp) and Malang (110,000Rp). For Pangandaran (110,000Rp, eight hours), **Estu Travel** (0274-668 4567; Jl Gampingan) has minibuses daily at 8am and 6.30pm.

TRAIN

Centrally located, Yogya's Tugu train station handles all business- and executive-class trains. Economy-class trains also depart from and arrive at Lempuyangan station, 1km to the east.

TRANSPORT FROM YOGYAKARTA

Bus

DESTINATION	FARE (RP)	DURATION (HR)	FREQUENCY
Bandung	air-con 120,000	10	3 daily
Borobudur	normal 20,000 (bring small bills)	1½	every 30min
Denpasar	air-con 325,000	19	3 daily
Jakarta	normal/air-con 200,000/260,000	12	10-12 daily between 3pm and 5pm

Train

DESTINATION	FARE (RP)	DURATION (HR)	FREQUENCY
Bandung	200,000–300,000	7-8¾	6 daily
Sidareja (for Pangandaran)	150,000	3½-4	2 daily
Jakarta	300,000–450,000	7-9	6 daily
Malang	250,000–300,000	7	3 daily
Solo	6000–20,000	1	14 daily

WORTH A TRIP

BEACHES SOUTHEAST OF YOGYAKARTA

Southeast of Yogyakarta, the coastline consists of a stunning series of sandy cove beaches divided by volcanic stone headlands and pounded by the full force of the Indian Ocean. It was once an isolated corner of Java with few facilities, but electricity was finally extended all the way to shore in the last few years, with a growing footprint to match. Still, few foreign travellers make it here, and it's largely the domain of a local weekender crowd. Midweek, however, you will have it to yourself.

The scenery is sublime, and exploring the coastal road as it winds through rolling hills, past fields of peanuts and cassava, and taking turn-offs down dirt roads to empty, exposed bays makes a wonderful excursion from Yogyakarta. However, as the open sea is rough, swimming is only advisable in selected, sheltered spots. Also, you'll need your own wheels as there's no public transport. Each of the following beaches require a separate 10,000Rp entry fee, payable at gates set just up the road from the beach.

It's 65km from Yogya to Indrayanti Beach (also known as Pulang Syawal), a lovely sandy cove with a steep profile, framed by giant boulders at the east end and views toward a series of spectacular golden sandy beaches to the west. The tiny ocean-facing **Indrayanti** (☎0878 3962 5215; huts incl breakfast 350,000Rp, mains 15,000-60,000Rp) huts are well overpriced but seafood at the restaurant, with tables sunk in the sand, is quite good. If you wish to stay the night – and considering the scenery, you should – find **Cemara Udang** (☎0823 2821 0384; Pantai Indriyanti; 400,000-500,000Rp; ❄) at the west end of the beach. The small office downstairs is literally built into the rock wall across the road from the beach. Rooms on the top floor have the best view on this stretch of coast, toward the rising offshore rocks of Drini beach and all the way to Kukup, from the common porch. Sunsets are dreamy here. There can be a massive shore break at low tide so take care if you wish to wade into the shallows. The wooden, cottage-like rooms have nice beds, air-con and cold-water showers.

Heading west it's a short hop to horseshoe-shaped Sundak Barat with some sheltered swimming and then on to Krakal, which has a few scruffy warungs near the main car park. If you nip over to the east side of Krakal bay there's a great stretch of deserted sand and you can grab a meal at the good, sea-facing **Rumah Makan Pantai Asmara** (meals 20,000-40,000Rp).

Around 5km west of Indrayanti, Drini forms a pretty double crescent of beaches, separated by a large offshore islet that you can reach via a walkway. Next up is Sepanjang, a long slim beach, and then Kukup, the most touristy beach on this stretch, with an excess of souvenir stalls and warungs. Still, you might want to try the *peyek* (seaweed crackers) for sale, and it does have three accommodation options, the best of which is **Penginapan Kukup Indah** (☎0878 3966 5441; r 75,000-200,000Rp; ❄).

To head back to Yogyakarta, it's best to push on to Parangtritis. This is a sprawling, unattractive resort with a rubbish problem, geared at day-tripping city dwellers, but it does have bus service.

Buses from Yogyakarta's Giwangan bus terminal, which pass down Jl Parangtritis at the end of Jl Prawirotaman, leave throughout the day for the one-hour journey (9000Rp). The last bus back from Parangtritis leaves at around 6pm.

ℹ Getting Around

TO/FROM THE AIRPORT

Yogya's Adi Sucipto airport, 10km east of the centre, is very well connected to the city by public transport. Bus 1A (3600Rp) runs there from Jl Malioboro. Pramek trains between Yogya and Solo stop at Maguwo station, which is right by the airport as well. Rates for taxis from the airport to the city centre are fixed at 70,000Rp.

BECAK

Yogyakarta has an oversupply of becak (cycle rickshaws); most drivers are quite pushy, but it can be a fun way to get around. Watch out for drivers who offer cheap hourly rates, unless you want to do the rounds of all the batik galleries that offer commission. A short trip is about 10,000Rp to 15,000Rp. To go from Jl Prawirotaman to Jl Malioboro costs around 25,000Rp.

BICYCLE

Bikes cost about 30,000Rp a day from hotels. Always lock your bike.

BUS

Yogya's reliable bus system, TransJogja consists of modern air-conditioned buses running from 6am to 10pm on six routes around the city to as far away as Prambanan. Tickets cost 3600Rp per journey. TransJogja buses only stop at the designated bus shelters. Bus 1A is a very useful service, running from Jl Malioboro past the airport to Prambanan. TransJogja route maps are available at the tourist information centre.

CAR & MOTORCYCLE

Travel agencies on Jl Sosrowijayan and Jl Prawirotaman rent out cars with drivers for trips in the Yogya region for 500,000Rp to 550,000Rp per day including petrol. Few drivers speak English, but it can still be an excellent way to explore the area. One reliable company is Jogja Trans (p115). Motorbikes cost around 50,000Rp to 90,000Rp per day.

TAXI

Metered taxis are cheap, costing 10,000Rp to 30,000Rp for short trips. If you call any of the cab companies for a ride around town, the minimum fee is 25,000Rp. **Citra Taxi** (☎0274-373737) is considered the most reliable. From Jl Prawirotaman to the airport, the fare is fixed at 70,000Rp.

Imogiri

A royal graveyard perched on a hilltop 20km south of Yogyakarta, Imogiri was first built by Sultan Agung in 1645 to serve as his own mausoleum. Since then it has become something of an A-list cemetery for royalty. There are three major courtyards – the central one contains the tombs of Sultan Agung and succeeding Mataram kings; the other two are dedicated to the sultans of Solo and Yogyakarta.

Pilgrims from across Central Java flock to the **tomb of Sultan Agung** (admission 1000Rp; ⏲10am-1pm Sun-Mon, 1.30-4pm Fri). You're welcome to join them but you must don full Javanese court dress, which can be hired for a small fee.

It's an impressive site, reached by a daunting flight of 345 steps. From the top of the stairway, a walkway circles the whole complex and leads to the summit, with a superb view over Yogyakarta to Gunung Merapi.

To get to Imogiri (10,000Rp, 40 minutes), take an *angkot* to Panggang and ask the conductor to let you off at the *makam* (graves). *Angkot* and buses from Yogyakarta (5000Rp) stop at the car park, from where it is about 500m to the base of the hill and the start of the steps. Note that the only compulsory entry charge is payable when you sign the visitors' book, inside the main compound.

Gunung Merapi

Few of Southeast Asia's volcanoes are as evocative, or as destructive, as Gunung Merapi (Fire Mountain). Towering 2930m over Yogyakarta, Borobudur and Prambanan, this immense Fujiesque peak is a threatening, disturbingly close presence for thousands. Merapi has erupted dozens of times over the past century; the massive 2010 eruption killed 353 and forced the evacuation of 360,000 more.

It's offically Indonesia's most active volcano – quite an accolade in a nation with 127 active cones – and some observers have theorised it was responsible for the mysterious evacuation of Borobudur and the collapse of the old Mataram kingdom during the 11th century.

Merapi is revered and feared in equal measure. Every year, offerings from Yogya's *kraton* are made to appease the mountain's foul temper. Eruptions, however, have not put a stop to people living on the mountain. With a population density of 700 people per sq kilometre, Merapi supports hundreds of small communities.

The hill resort of **Kaliurang**, 25km north of Yogyakarta, is the main access point for views of Merapi. Yogyakarta travel agencies sell night trips for views of the lava flows – there are several good viewpoints – but you can also do this yourself. Take a bus to Kaliurang (10,000Rp, one hour) from the Giwangan terminal, get off at the Kaliurang Hill Resort, then catch one of the waiting *ojek* (10,000Rp) to the viewpoint of **Kalu Aden**, from where there's a wonderful perspective of the lava action.

Activities

Merapi is frequently declared off limits to visitors. But if conditions permit, climbing the cone is possible in the dry season (April to September). Access is via the small village of Selo, on the northern side of the mountain. *Extreme caution* is advised.

During quiet periods, a 1am start from New Selo (1600m), a gathering of warungs and stalls at the trailhead, is necessary to reach the summit for dawn (a three- to four-hour trip). It is a tough, demanding walk, but usually manageable by anyone with a reasonable level of fitness. Some choose to leave at 5am for the trip to the summit and catch sunrise on the trail.

And about that trail: it's blessed with magnificent views of Gunung Merbabu across the valley and several other peaks, but the terrain isn't so pretty. In fact it alternates between dust and mud (depending upon the season), is quite steep, and can be slippery and rocky at all times of year, so be wise about your footwear. It eventually leads to a rocky, chilly campsite at 2500m on the third plateau (known as Pasar Bubrah) that some tours use as a last staging post. Depending on the state of the volcano's activity it may not be possible to continue further, and if you are hiking without a guide (certainly possible) this is where you must turn around as the rest of the walk is hard to figure and the footing treacherous. If conditions are favourable, the final ascent is very tough, past billowing vents and through loose volcanic scree and sand, which will consume all your remaining strength and takes about an hour.

From the summit, on clear days you'll be rewarded with amazing views deep into the 500m-wide crater from the rim, which is often enveloped by choking sulphurous gas. Be *ultra cautious* on the crater rim due to freezing winds and the instablity of the terrain. In 2015, one unlucky hiker made national news when he fell off the tallest rockpile on the edge while taking a selfie. No joke, #selfiescankill. His death prompted yet another trail closure as rescue teams worked to recover his remains.

Treks from Selo are not always well organised, but eaily arranged. Guides (250,000Rp) should warn against climbing if it looks dangerous. While they don't want to endanger lives, they may be prepared to take risks in order to get paid. Even during quieter periods, Merapi can suddenly explode into action. Entry into the national park costs 150,000Rp.

It has not been possible to climb the peak from Kaliurang since 1994 due to volcanic activity. However there is still excellent hiking around the lower reaches of Merapi, with superb views of lava flows. Christian Awuy, owner of Vogels Hostel, has organised climbs for years and is an excellent reference point. Six-hour sunrise hikes (US$25, minimum two people) from his hostel usually start at 4am and include a licensed guide equipped with two-way radios and food.

More pampered tours are offered by Elang Jiwa (p130). Its two-night Merapi package (per person 1,950,000Rp, minimum two people) includes a night at the lodge, a gourmet lunch on the trail, all the necessary trekking gear, a guide and translator, three meals and a foot spa afterward. And your feet will be disgusting, so that's a pleasant treat.

For up-to-date Merapi information and hiking accounts, consult www.gunungbagging.com.

Kaliurang & Kaliadem

☎0274

Kaliurang, 25km north of Yogyakarta, is the nearest hill resort to the city. At 900m, it has a cool, refreshing climate. During the rainy season, Kaliurang often sits in a thick cloud bank, but on clear days the views of Merapi are magical. The two museums are both worth a look and there is one great trek here too, making it a worthy sleepover.

Kaliadem is also a gateway to Merapi, and there are a number of off-road outfitters on the hill here, along with a compulsory 3000Rp entry fee payable at the gateway. On the way into Kaliadem you will pass the remains and foundations of homes destroyed in the 2010 eruption in which over 300 people died. Though the government has condemned the area, many lifelong residents have returned to reclaim their homes.

Sights & Activities

Ullen Sentalu MUSEUM
(☎0274-895161; www.ullensentalu.com; admission 50,000Rp; ⏲8.30am-4pm Tue-Fri, to 5pm Sat & Sun) The Ullen Sentalu museum is a surprise find on the slopes of Merapi. This large complex has a principal structure that resembles a Bavarian baron's mansion, which is surrounded by extensive gardens. Most of the rich collection of Javanese fine art, including oil paintings and sculpture, is housed in connecting underground chambers. There are wonderful artefacts to admire (including some priceless batik), but perhaps a little too much royal family glorification during the hour-long tour. Guests are admitted in groups, every 10 minutes.

Nirmolo Kaliurang Taman Nasional Gunung Merapi NATIONAL PARK

(Jl Kaliurang, Hutan Wisata Kaliurang; admission 151,000-155,000Rp; 8am-5pm) There are two entrances to this national park, set on the shoulders of Gunung Merapi. The more developed entrance on Jl Kaliurang costs an extra 4000Rp for some unknown reason and is surrounded by a dozen warungs, but it offers a more dramatic approach as the cliffs close in and loom over a ribbon road. Both gates access just a few kilometres of trails that lead to caves where Japanese soldiers hid during WWII, and two different hilltop views of Merapi.

Maps at the park entrance delineate the areas you are allowed to explore. Heed them and don't venture further; in a sudden eruption, lava can flow down the mountain at 300km/h. A 15-minute walk to the Promojiwo viewpoint offers vistas of Merapi and takes you past forest incinerated in the 2010 eruption. A 3km hike to Puncak Plawangan offers better views.

Vogels Hostel arranges mountain walks to see the lava flows. The six-hour return trek starts at 4am and climbs 1400m up the mountain to see the glowing lava at its best (US$25 per person, minimum two people). Overnight camping trips, village tours and birdwatching walks can also be arranged. Vogels' jeep tours (350,000Rp, four people) of Merapi mountain get you into old lava flows and close to the lookout if you'd rather not hoof it.

Merapi Museum MUSEUM

(Jl Kaliurang Km25.7; admission 5000Rp, film 5000Rp; 8am-3.30pm Tue-Sun) This impressive museum is located in a striking white angular structure that resembles a volcano. You'll find exhibits dedicated to Merapi, including a scale model that demonstrates previous eruptions from the 18th century until today, and how they altered the mountain's shape. There are vintage seismometers on display along with a motorbike torched and excavated from molten ash. Included with the film is an earthquake simulation that rumbles through the museum halls.

Belantara Adventure DRIVING TOUR

(0852 2736 6130; Jl Kaliadem; jeep tours 350,000Rp, 30min/2hr motorbike tours 50,000/150,000Rp) One of several outfitters on the main road above town, and like the others it offers off-road jeep tours (maximum four people) to a village that was decimated by the 2010 eruption. But these guys also offer off-road motorbike tours on 150cc bikes with knobby tires. Boots, helmets and gloves are provided. Thirty-minute tours are just a quick spin. Two-hour tours take you to that stricken village covered in ash.

Sleeping & Eating

Kaliurang is a sprawling hill resort with dozens of places to sleep, though most are often closed. For meals, head to Vogels. Kaliadem is home to one splashy resort.

Vogels Hostel HOSTEL $

(0274-895208; www.vogelshostel.blogspot.com; Jl Astamulya 76, Kaliurang; dm 25,000Rp, d with shared bathroom 100,000Rp, bungalows with bathroom & hot water 150,000Rp, mains 13,000-35,000Rp;) Vogels is a travellers' institution. The structure itself is a faded art deco villa constructed in 1926, one of just four left in town, and accommodation is pretty archaic too, with ageing furnishings. However, it's undoubtedly the best address for hikers.

The owner, Christian Awuy, is an authority on Merapi and its many moods; he can organise good guides and tours, and the whole place is stuffed with maps and information. The restaurant is decent and tour prices are quite fair.

Fuji Villa HOTEL $$

(0274-446 4144; www.fujivilla.com; Jl Pelajar 8, Kaliurang; r 330,000Rp;) Very cool Japanese-style chalets set in a leafy garden, with sliding windows and doors that recall the rice-paper windows of the motherland. The larger rooms have timber beds and daybeds, flat-screens and armchairs. Rooms come with breakfast. For lunch and dinner, head to Vogels.

The Cangkringan RESORT $$$

(0274-447 8653; www.cangkringan.com; Jl Raya Merapi Golf, Kaliadem; r from 919,000Rp, villas from 1,200,000Rp;) A modern spa and villa complex with a cool *joglo* lobby, a serene location in the foothills, a nice spa where you can book *lulur* scrubs, massages and more, and 19 sumptuous villas with marble-inlaid floors and private pools. The rooms are just OK for the price. There's a nice restaurant here, too.

Getting There & Away

Angkot from Yogyakarta's Jl Kaliurang cost 15,000Rp to 20,000Rp; the last leaves at 3pm. A taxi from Jl Malioboro will cost around 150,000Rp each way.

Selo

An exceptionally cute and authentic village, Selo is set on and between the slopes of two volcanoes, and stitched together with tobacco fields and vegetable plots, 50km west of Solo. There are a few homestays and one terrific lodge, though most tourists simply zip in after dark to climb Gunung Merapi or Merbabu for an epic sunrise view. Guides (250,000Rp return) can be easily arranged for the Merapi climb, but it's best to reserve ahead. Contact the local **guide association** (☎0878 3632 5955). Entry into Taman Nasional Gunung Merapi (p129) is around 150,000Rp.

From Selo, it is a very steep, three- to four-hour hike to the volcano's summit. Allow around 2½ hours for the descent. At the top the sulphurous fumes can be overpowering – take great care.

Sleeping & Eating

Elang Jiwa LODGE **$$**

(☎0821 7881 5657; www.elangjiwa.com; Rt 2, Rw 7, Dusun Ngaglik, Desa Samiran, Kecamatan Selo; per person 450,000Rp) In the saddle between Gunung Merbabu and Gunung Merapi, two homestays have been taken over by the French hoteliers behind the great Breve Azurine in Karimunjawa, and transformed into simple but elegant lodges, which are de facto base camps where trekkers can prepare to take on either peak.

Expect plenty of homely common spaces, cozy bedrooms with shared bathrooms, terrific espresso and mediocre food. Staff arrange trekking packages for the Merapi-bound, and five-star camping trips (2,700,000Rp two days/one night) on Gunung Merbabu. That experience includes porters, meals that are a steep step up from the lodge fare, and tents with mattresses.

Getting There & Away

Selo can be reached from Solo: take a bus to Magelang, stopping at Selo (16,000Rp, two hours) on the way. From Yogyakarta take a Magelang bus to Blabak (9000Rp, one hour) and an *angkot* or bus to Selo (6000Rp). **Arya Transport** (☎0813 2912 2122) offers two shared taxis per day (10am and 1pm) to and from Yogyakarta for 150,000Rp per person. A private car from Yogya is around 550,000Rp one way. However you get here, don't expect a pleasant drive. Over the past two years, the villages downhill from Selo have begun selling their sand to truckers who deliver it to the rapidly expanding cities of Central Java, wreaking havoc on the roads, which are often under repair as a result, filling the air with fine dust.

Prambanan

☎0274

Jaw-dropping and mystical, the spectacular temples of Prambanan, set in the plains, are the best remaining examples of Java's extended period of Hindu culture and are an absolute must.

All the temples in the Prambanan area were built between the 8th and 10th centuries AD, when Java was ruled by the Buddhist Sailendras in the south and the Hindu Sanjayas of Old Mataram in the north. Possibly by the second half of the 9th century, these two dynasties were united by the marriage of Rakai Pikatan of Hindu Mataram and the Buddhist Sailendra princess Pramodhavardhani. This may explain why a number of temples, including those of the Prambanan temple complex and the smaller Plaosan group, reveal both Shivaite and Buddhist elements in architecture and sculpture. But this is a Hindu site first and foremost, and the wealth of sculptural detail on the great Shiva temple here is the nation's most outstanding example of Hindu art.

Following this creative burst over a period of two centuries, the Prambanan Plain was abandoned when the Hindu-Javanese kings moved to East Java. In the middle of the 16th century there is said to have been a great earthquake that toppled many of the temples. Their destruction was accelerated by treasure hunters and locals searching for building materials. Most temples have now been restored to some extent, and, like Borobudur, Prambanan made the Unesco World Heritage list in 1991.

Prambanan suffered extensive damage in the 2006 earthquake. Though the temples survived, hundreds of stone blocks collapsed to the ground or were cracked (479 in the Shiva temple alone). Today, the main structures have been restored, though there remains a lot of work to be done, so expect some temples to be fenced off.

Sights

Prambanan Temples TEMPLE

(www.borobudurpark.co.id; admission 225,000Rp; ⏲6am-6pm) The huge Prambanan complex was erected in the middle of the 9th century – around 50 years later than Borobudur – but little is known about its early history. It's thought that it was built by Rakai Pikatan to commemorate the return of a Hindu dynasty to sole power in Java. Prambanan was in ruins for years, and while efforts were made in 1885 to clear the site, it was not until 1937 that reconstruction was first attempted.

Of the original group, the outer compound contains the remains of 244 temples. Eight minor and eight main temples stand in the highest central courtyard. **Candi Shiva Mahadeva**, dedicated to Shiva, is not only the largest of the temples but also the finest.

The main spire soars 47m and the temple is lavishly carved. The 'medallions' that decorate its base have a characteristic Prambanan motif – small lions in niches flanked by *kalpatura* (trees of heaven) and a menagerie of stylised half-human and half-bird *kinnara* (heavenly beings). The vibrant scenes carved onto the inner wall of the gallery encircling the temple are from the Ramayana – they tell how Lord Rama's wife, Sita, is abducted and how Hanuman the monkey god and Sugriwa the white-monkey general eventually find and release her.

Thankfully, after years of restoration, the temple's interior is accessible again. The main chamber at the top of the eastern stairway has a four-armed statue of Shiva the Destroyer and is notable for the fact that this mightiest of Hindu gods stands on a huge lotus pedestal, a symbol of Buddhism. In the southern cell is the pot-bellied and bearded Agastya, an incarnation of Shiva as divine teacher; in the western cell is a superb image of the elephant-headed Ganesha, Shiva's son, the god of knowledge. His right hand, usually holding his ivory tusk, was broken off in the earthquake. In the northern cell, Durga, Shiva's consort, can be seen killing the demon buffalo. Some people believe that the Durga image is actually an image of the Slender Virgin, who, legend has it, was turned to stone by a man she refused to marry. She is still an object of pilgrimage and her name is often used for the temple group.

Candi Vishnu touches 33m and sits just north of Candi Shiva Mahadeva. It's still possible to get up front and personal with this magnificent temple. Its impressive reliefs tell the story of Lord Krishna, a hero of the Mahabharata epic, and you can ascend its stone staircase to the inner chamber and see a four-armed image of Vishnu the Preserver.

Candi Brahma is Candi Vishnu's twin temple. It is south of Candi Shiva Mahadeva and carved with the final scenes of the Ramayana. It has a spectacular 'monster mouth' doorway. The interior was roped off for restoration at research time, but if you're able to gain access to its inner chamber it contains a four-headed statue of Brahma, the god of creation.

Candi Sewu, the 'Thousand Temples', dating from around AD 850, is magnificent with its dozens of outer shrines carved and restored with stupas. But it was once even more majestic with a large central Buddhist temple surrounded by four rings of 240 smaller 'guard' temples. Outside the compound stood four sanctuaries at the points of the compass, of which Candi Bubrah, now reduced to its stone foundation, is the most southern. The renovated main temple has finely carved niches around its inner gallery – these niches once held bronze statues.

Given its well-documented majesty, the complex can be crazy crowded at times, but if you come late in the day and wander the tracks behind the main temples, you can see them rise from the ruins of the outer temples in perfect silence and light.

Plaosan Temples TEMPLE

FREE Built around the same time as the Prambanan temple group, the Plaosan temples also combine both Hindu and Buddhist religious symbols and carvings. **Plaosan Lor** (Plaosan North) comprises two restored, identical main temples, surrounded by some 126 small shrines and solid stupas, most of which are now just a jumble of stone. Two giant *dwarapala* (temple guardian statues) stand at the front of each main temple, notable for their unusual three-part design.

These two-storey, three-room structures house impressive stone Bodhisattvas and are decorated with intricately carved *kala* (dragon) heads above the many windows.

Plaosan Kidul (Plaosan South) has more stupas and the remnants of a temple, but little renovation work has been done.

This northeastern group of temples is 3km from the Prambanan complex. It can be reached on foot by taking the road north from the main gate, going past Candi Sewu and then walking east for about 1km.

Southern Group TEMPLE

(admission 110,000Rp) **Kraton Ratu Boko** (Palace of King Boko) is a partly ruined Hindu palace complex dating from the 9th century. Perched on a hilltop overlooking Prambanan, it is believed to have been the central court of the mighty Mataram dynasty. You can see the large gateway and the platform of **Candi Pembakaran** (the Royal Crematorium), as well as a series of bathing places staggered on different levels leading down to the village. The sunset view over the Prambanan Plain is magnificent.

To reach Ratu Boko, travel 1.5km south on the road from Prambanan village to just southwest of where the river crosses the road. Near the 'Yogya 18km' signpost a steep rocky path leads up to the main site. Altogether it is about a one-hour walk. The site can be reached by car or motorcycle via a much longer route that goes around the back of the mountain.

The remains of the Buddhist temple, **Candi Sajiwan**, are not far from the village of Sajiwan, about 1.5km southeast of Prambanan village. Around the temple's base are carvings from the Jataka (episodes from the Buddha's various lives).

Western Group TEMPLE
(admission per temple 2000Rp) There are three temples in this group between Yogyakarta and Prambanan, two of them close to Kalasan village on the main Yogyakarta road. Kalasan and Prambanan villages are 3km apart, so it is easiest to take an *angkot* or bus to cover this stretch. **Candi Kalasan**, near Kalasan village, is one of the oldest Buddhist temples on the Prambanan Plain. A Sanskrit inscription of AD 778 refers to a temple dedicated to the female Bodhisattva Tara.

It has been partially restored and has some fine detailed carvings on its southern side, where a huge, ornate *kala* head glowers over the doorway. At one time it was completely covered in coloured, shining stucco, and traces of the hard, stonelike 'diamond plaster' that provided a base for paintwork can still be seen. The inner chamber of Kalasan once sheltered a huge bronze image of Buddha or Tara. It's set in a clump of coconut trees just off the main road; admission is adult/child 2000/1000Rp.

Candi Sari is about 200m north from Candi Kalasan, also in the middle of coconut and banana groves. This temple has the three-part design of the larger Plaosan temple but is probably slightly older. Some experts believe that its 2nd floor may have served as a dormitory for the Buddhist priests who took care of Candi Kalasan. The sculptured reliefs around the exterior are similar to those of Kalasan but are in much better condition.

Candi Sambisari is an isolated temple about 2.5km north of the main road, reached via a country lane. Sambisari is a Shiva temple and possibly the latest temple at Prambanan to be erected by the Mataram dynasty. It was discovered by a farmer in 1966. Excavated from under ancient layers of protective volcanic ash and dust, it lies almost 6m below the surface of the surrounding fields and is remarkable for its perfectly preserved state. The inner sanctum of the temple is dominated by a large lingam and yoni (stylised penis and vagina), typical of Shiva temples.

☆ Entertainment

Ramayana Ballet DANCE
(☎021-496408; www.borobudurpark.com) Held at the outdoor theatre just west of the main temple complex, the famous Ramayana Ballet is Java's most spectacular dance-drama. The story of Rama and Sita unfolds over four successive nights, two or three times each month from May to October (the dry season), leading up to the full moon.

With the magnificent floodlit Candi Shiva Mahadeva as a backdrop, nearly 200 dancers and gamelan musicians take part in a spectacle of monkey armies, giants on stilts, clashing battles and acrobatics.

Performances last from 7.30pm to 9.30pm. Tickets are sold in Yogyakarta through the tourist information office and travel agencies at the same price that you'll pay at the theatre box office (but they usually offer packages that include return transport from your hotel for 50,000Rp to 100,000Rp extra). Tickets cost from 10,000Rp to 250,000Rp, or 375,000Rp for VIP seats (padded chairs up front). All seats are on stone benches except the VIP.

ℹ Information

The Prambanan temples (p130) are usually visited from Yogyakarta (17km away), but they can also be visited from Solo (50km away). The main temple complex lies on the Yogyakarta–Solo highway. A 'minitrain' or tram (5000Rp) from the museum loops to Candi Sewu. The admission price includes camera fees and admission to the museum. Guides charge 75,000Rp to 100,000Rp for a one-hour tour for one to 20 people.

Most of the other (seldom-visited) outlying temples are within a 5km radius of Prambanan village. You'll need at least half a day to see them on foot, or they can be explored by bicycle or motorcycle if you ride to Prambanan. The best time to visit Prambanan is in the early morning or late in the day, when it's quiet, though you can never have Prambanan to yourself – expect plenty of attention from visiting school groups and requests for photos.

Getting There & Away

Prambanan is 17km northeast of Yogyakarta.

BICYCLE & MOTORCYCLE

You can visit all the temples by bicycle from Yogyakarta. The most pleasant route, though it's a longer ride, is to take Jl Senopati out past the zoo to the eastern ring road, where you turn left. Follow this right up to Jl Solo, turn right and then left at Jl Babarsari. Go past the Sahid Garden Hotel and follow the road counterclockwise around the school to the Selokan Mataram. This canal runs parallel to the Solo road, about 1.5km to the north, for around 6km to Kalasan, about 2km before Prambanan.

To view the western temples you need to return via the Solo road. The turn-off north to Candi Sambisari from the Solo road crosses the canal before leading another 1km to the temple. You can visit the temple, backtrack to the canal path and continue back to Yogyakarta.

If you are coming by motorcycle, you can combine the visit with a trip to Kaliurang. From Kaliurang, instead of going back to the main Yogyakarta–Solo road, take the 'Solo Alternatif' route signposted in the village of Pakem, about halfway between Yogyakarta and Kaliurang. From there the road passes through some beautiful countryside, before tipping you onto the highway just before Prambanan's main entrance.

BUS

From Yogyakarta, take TransYogya bus 1A (3600Rp, 40 minutes) from Jl Malioboro. From Solo, buses take 1½ hours and cost 15,000Rp.

Solo (Surakarta)

☎0271 / POP 520,000

Arguably the epicentre of Javanese identity and tradition, Solo is one of the least Westernised cities on the island. An eternal rival to Yogyakarta, this conservative town often plays second fiddle to its more conspicuous neighbour. But with backstreet *kampung* and elegant *kraton*, traditional markets and gleaming malls, Solo has more than enough to warrant at least an overnight visit. Two nights is better, and as there are some fascinating temples close by, it also makes a great base for forays into the hills of Central Java.

In many ways, Solo is also Java writ small, incorporating its vices and virtues and embodying much of its heritage. On the downside, the island's notoriously fickle temper tends to flare in Solo first – the city has been the backdrop for some of the worst riots in Java's recent history. On the upside, the city's long and distinguished past as a seat of the great Mataram empire means that it competes with Yogyakarta as the hub of Javanese culture.

Solo attracts students and scholars to its music and dance academies, and it's an excellent place to see traditional performing arts, as well as traditional crafts – especially batik, which is a local staple.

History

Following the sacking of the Mataram court at Kartosuro in 1742, the *susuhunan* (sultan), Pakubuwono II, decided to look for a more auspicious site. A location near the river Solo was chosen, and his imposing palace completed by 1745.

Pakubuwono II died after only four years in the city, and his heir, Pakubuwono III, managed to lose half of his kingdom to the court of Yogyakarta. Pakubuwono X (1893–1938), however, had more luck. He revived the prestige of the court through the promotion of culture and gave no time to fighting rival royals.

Following WWII, the royal court fumbled opportunities to play a positive role in the revolution, and lost out badly to Yogyakarta, which became the seat of the independent government. The palaces of the city soon became mere symbols of ancient Javanese feudalism and aristocracy.

With the overthrow of Suharto, Solo erupted following the riots in Jakarta in May 1998. For two days rioters went on a rampage, systematically looting and burning every shopping centre and department store and targeting Chinese-owned businesses.

Today, things have settled down again, and sleek new shopping malls and hotels have risen from the ashes of the old. Although Solo retains an earned reputation as a hotbed of radicalism, and its *madrassahs* (Islamic schools) have maintained links to extremist groups such as Jemaah Islamiah, *jilbab* (head coverings) aren't as ubiquitous here as they are in West Java, and it feels a lot less pious than many other Javanese cities.

Sights & Activities

Kraton Surakarta PALACE, MUSEUM

(Kraton Kasunanan; ☎0271-656432; admission 15,000Rp, guide 25,000-30,000Rp; ⏰9am-2pm) Once the hub of an empire, today the Kraton Surakarta is a faded memorial of a bygone era. It's worth a visit, but much of the *kraton* was destroyed by fire in 1985. Many of the inner buildings were rebuilt, but today the allure of this once-majestic palace has largely vanished and its structures are left bare and unloved. The main sight for visitors is the Sasono Sewoko museum.

The poor condition of today's *kraton* belies its illustrious history. In 1745 Pakubuwono II moved from Kartosuro to Solo in a day-long procession that transplanted everything belonging to the king, including the royal banyan trees – those remain magnificent – and the sacred Nyai Setomo cannon (the twin of Si Jagur in old Jakarta), which now sits in the northern palace pavilion.

Museum exhibits include an array of silver and bronze Hindu-Javanese figures, weapons, antiques and other royal heirlooms, plus the mother of all horse-carriage collections. Labelling is poor or non-existent and termites, woodworm and rot are serious issues.

A carved doorway leads to an inner courtyard, but most of the *kraton* is off limits and it's still the residence of the *susuhunan* (sultan). The upper storey of the Panggung Songgo Buwono, a 1782 tower that has endured the years intact, is said to be the *susuhunan*'s meditation sanctum where he communes with Nyai Loro Kidul (the Queen of the South Seas).

Dance practices are held on the grounds Sundays at 1pm.

Istana Mangkunegaran PALACE, MUSEUM

(admission 20,000Rp; ⏰8.30am-2pm Mon-Sat, 8.30am-1pm Sun) Dating to 1757, the Istana Mangkunegaran is in better condition than the *kraton* and is the home of the second house of Solo. The centre of the compound is the *pendopo*, a pavilion built in a mix of Javanese and European architectural styles. Its high, rounded ceiling was painted in 1937 and is intricately decorated with a central flame surrounded by figures of the Javanese zodiac, each painted in its own mystical colour.

In Javanese philosophy yellow guards against sleepiness, blue against disease, black against hunger, green against desire, white against lust, rose against fear, red against evil and purple against wicked thoughts.

Behind here is the *dalem* (residence), which forms the delightful palace museum. Most exhibits are from the personal collection of Mangkunegara VII. On display are gold-plated dresses for royal dances, a superb mask collection, jewellery and a few oddities, including huge Buddhist rings and gold genital covers.

A guide is mandatory (and worthwhile) for the museum. Most guides are very informative and speak English (a tip of 30,000Rp is appreciated).

At the pavilion, there's gamelan music, singing and dance-practice sessions on Wednesday, from 10am until noon.

House of Danar Hadi MUSEUM

(☎0271-714326; www.houseofdanarhadi.com; Jl Slamet Riyadi 261; admission 35,000Rp; ⏰9am-4pm, showroom to 9pm) Danar Hadi is one of the world's best batik museums, with a terrific collection of antique and royal textiles from Java, China and beyond. It occupies a stunning whitewashed colonial building. Entry includes an excellent guided tour (around 1½ hours, in English), which explains the history of the many pieces (10,000 in the collection). There's also a workshop where you can watch craftswomen at work creating new masterpieces, an upmarket storeroom and a souvenir shop.

Radya Pustaka Museum MUSEUM

(Jl Slamet Riyadi; admission 3000Rp; ⏰9am-4pm Tue-Sun) A small museum with good displays of gamelan instruments, jewelled kris, puppets and *wayang beber* (scrolls that depict *wayang* stories).

Mesjid Agung MOSQUE

FREE On the western side of the *alun-alun*, Mesjid Agung, featuring classical Javanese architecture, is the largest and most sacred mosque in Solo.

Taman Sriwedari AMUSEMENT PARK

(admission 12,000Rp, ride tickets per pack 60,000Rp; ⏰5-10:30pm Tue-Sat, 9am-10:30pm Sun) Solo's Sriwedari amusement park has fair rides and sideshow stalls, though an admission ticket doesn't get you on the rides. You'll need to buy a pack of ride tickets at the box office if you care to play. Nightly *wayang orang* performances (and other cultural shows) are held in the Sriwedari Theatre (p139).

TRADITION & DISASTER

Solo is a deeply superstitious city and many of its citizens are acutely observant of Javanese and Islamic ritual. So when the *kraton* (palace) ignited in flames on 1 January 1985, many locals saw it as a consequence of the incumbent sultan Pakubuwono XII's lack of observance of tradition. For years he'd been lax with his ceremonial duties, and his alleged womanising was the talk of the town. The sultan had also taken to living the high life in Jakarta rather than presiding over court life in Solo.

Firefighters responding quickly to the blaze found their engines could not fit through the main gateway (which was thought to be sacred), and initially refused to smash through it. Around 60% of the palace subsequently burned to the ground.

To appease deeply felt Javanese customs, a purification ceremony was performed. The head of a tiger, snake, buffalo and deer were buried, and tons of ashes were returned to the coast to quell the wrath of Nyai Loro Kidul, the Queen of the South Seas, whose influence over the tragic events was seen to be pivotal by many.

However, General Benny Murdani, who investigated the fire, was eager to counter locally held superstitions, stating 'reporters will *not* reach their own conclusions. The reason for the fire was an electrical short circuit'.

When Pakubuwono XII died in 2004, he left 37 children from six wives and mistresses, but no clear heir.

Jaladara Steam Train TRAIN
(☎0856 4200 3322; per person 150,000-360,000Rp; ⏰9am-11.30am) Trundling through the heart of the city, the Jaladara steam train (built in Germany in 1896) is a fun morning excursion in carriages with Victorian-style wood fittings. The trip (with English-speaking guide) starts at Purwosari train station (3km west of centre), and stops at Kampung Batik Kauman (for a visit to a batik worshop) before terminating at Sangkrah train station.

It's a great experience, but tour groups must charter the full train and prices vary depending upon the number of passengers on board.

Courses

Batik Mahkotalaweyan HANDICRAFTS
(☎0271-712276; www.batikmahkotalaweyan.com; Sayangan Kulon 9, Kampung Laweyan; 2hr course 50,000Rp) Offers batik courses ranging from a two-hour taster session to intensive programs lasting several days.

Tours

For some reason tours quoted from Solo can be pricey, so consider renting a car and a driver and doing it yourself for much less. Jogja Trans (p115) out of nearby Yogyakarta is a great option. Guesthouses and freelance guides offer city, regional and bike tours.

Ajib Bond GUIDE
(☎0818 0447 8488; ajib_efata@yahoo.com) Offers good city tours (400,000Rp, minimum two people). His bike trip (200,000Rp) to Mojolaban village via various cottage industries and the Bengawan Solo river is also recommended.

Miki Tours TOUR
(☎0271-29292; www.tiket24jam.com; Jl Yos Sudarso 17) This travel agent offers tours to the countryside around Solo, including Candi Sukuh (475,000Rp, minimum two people).

Festivals & Events

Kirab Pusaka CULTURAL
(Heirloom Procession) Since 1633, these colourful processions have been held on the first day of the Javanese month of Suro (between March and May). They start at Istana Mangkunegaran in the early evening and continue late into the night.

Sekaten RELIGIOUS
This festival marks the Prophet Muhammad's birthday and is held between May and July. It comprises two ceremonies with a week in between, culminating with a fair held on the *alun-alun* and the sharing of a rice mountain.

Solo Batik Carnival CULTURAL
Annual carnival in late June with processions, fashion shows and performances in the R Maladi stadium.

Solo (Surakarta)

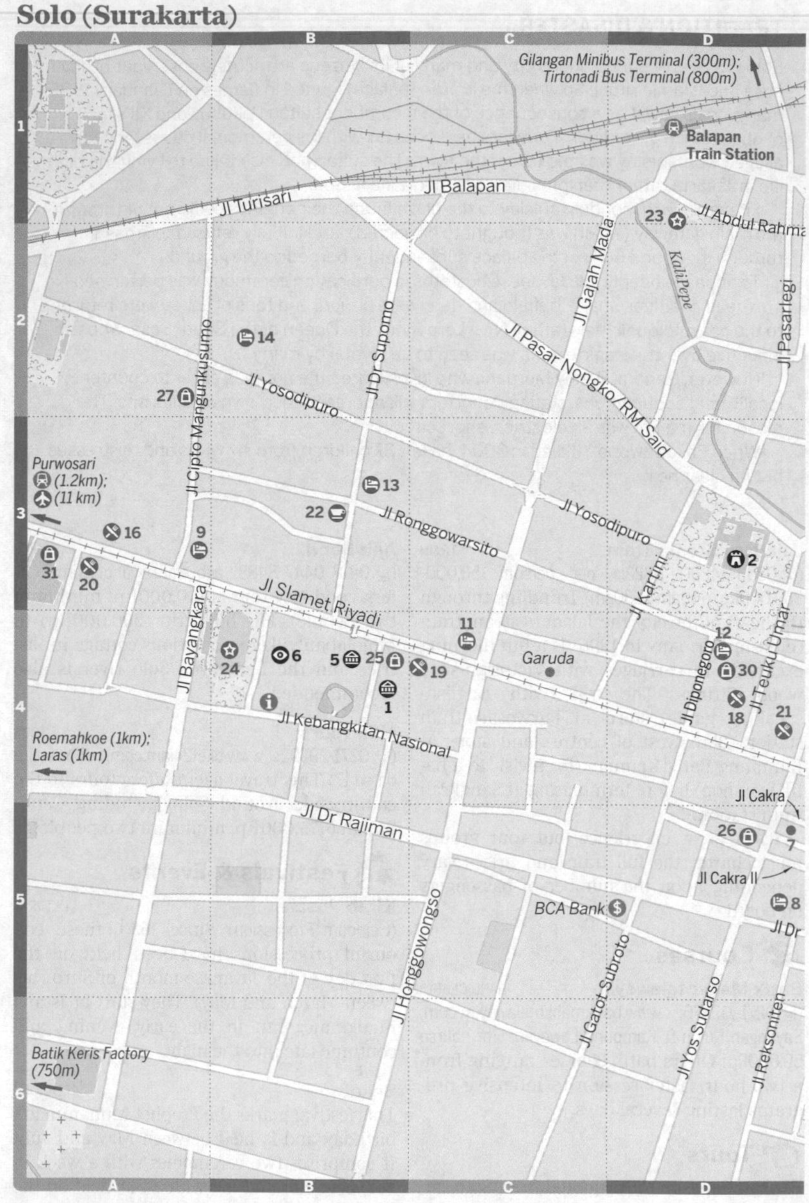

Sleeping

Solo has a few good budget hotels. Almost all offer travel information, tours, bus bookings, bicycles for rent, breakfast, and free tea/coffee. The midrange choices are excellent, too.

Warung Baru Homestay GUESTHOUSE $
(0271-656369; Jl Banda; r incl breakfast with fan/air-con from 100,000/150,000Rp;) This new guesthouse offers four great-value rooms set around a courtyard garden in a lovely home set down a small *gang* (alley). The more

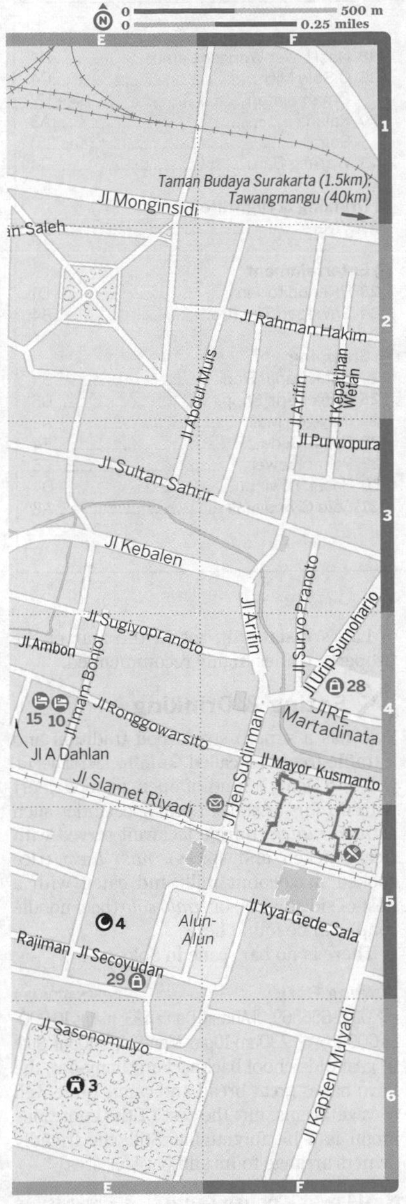

expensive rooms have hot water and bathtubs. Check in at its restaurant (p138).

Cakra Homestay HOMESTAY **$**
(☎0271-634743; Jl Cakra II 15; r with shared bath 150,000Rp, with private bath 200,000-250,000Rp; ❄📶🏊) This atmospheric place scores highly for those interested in Javanese culture (and the welcoming staff are keen to promote it). There's an amazing gamelan room with free performances on Tuesday and Thursday evenings. It also has a gorgeous pool area. However, the rooms are pretty simple. Breakfast is included. Shared bathrooms are Western and *mandi* style.

Red Planet HOTEL **$**
(☎0271-788 9333; www.redplanethotels.com; Jl Dr Supomo 49; r from 220,000Rp; ❄@📶) Another competitively priced, dressed-up three-star chain with branches in a handful of Indonesian cities. Rooms have wood floors, high ceilings, wall-mounted flat-screens, rain showers and security boxes, but they aren't huge and can feel slightly soulless despite the good value.

Istana Griya 2 GUESTHOUSE **$$**
(☎0271-661118; Jl Imam Bonjol 35; r incl breakfast 225,000-350,000Rp; ❄📶) In a good central location, this renovated place is a sister hotel to the original around the corner. It's more upmarket, with large modern rooms and hot-water showers.

Rumah Turi BOUTIQUE HOTEL **$$**
(☎0271-736606; www.rumahturi.com; Jl Srigading II 12, Turisari; r incl breakfast from 360,000Rp; ❄📶) A reclaimed and re-imagined old property draped with plants – there is no hotel quite like this deconstructed lodge where the restaurant is lit with bare bulbs and the garden is a work of art. Plants are stacked and set in metallic grids that climb along every wall. The rooftop also sprouts with life as does every ledge.

Standard rooms offer wood floors and furnishings, including unique designer desks, but are otherwise rather basic. Deluxe rooms (from 450,000Rp) have one glass wall, flat-screens and big beds, and are plenty comfortable.

De Solo HOTEL **$$**
(☎0271-714887; www.de-soloboutiquehotel.com; Jl Dr Supomo 8; r incl breakfast from 350,000Rp; ❄📶) An expanding modern hotel (boutique is pushing it) with a selection of uncluttered but smallish rooms in a quiet, convenient location. There's an attractive little garden cafe and a reasonably priced spa (massages from 150,000Rp per hour). Some rooms have been contaminated by smokers. Sniff before you sleep.

Solo (Surakarta)

Sights

1 House of Danar Hadi.......B4
2 Istana Mangkunegaran.......D3
3 Kraton Surakarta.......E6
4 Mesjid Agung.......E5
5 Radya Pustaka Museum.......B4
6 Taman Sriwedari.......B4

Activities, Courses & Tours

7 Miki Tours.......D5

Sleeping

8 Cakra Homestay.......D5
9 De Solo.......A3
10 Istana Griya 2.......E4
11 Novotel Solo.......C4
12 Omah Sinten Heritage Hotel.......D4
13 Red Planet.......B3
14 Rumah Turi.......B2
15 Warung Baru Homestay.......E4

Eating

16 Adem Ayem.......A3
17 Galabo.......F5
18 Nasi Liwet Wongso Lemu.......D4
19 O Solo Mio.......C4
Omah Sinten.......(see 12)
20 Ralana.......A3
Soga.......(see 25)
21 Warung Baru.......D4

Drinking & Nightlife

22 Vivere.......B3

Entertainment

23 RRI Auditorium.......D1
24 Sriwedari Theatre.......B4

Shopping

25 Batik Danar Hadi.......B4
26 Batik Keris Shop.......D5
27 Paragon Mall.......A2
28 Pasar Gede.......F4
29 Pasar Klewer.......E5
30 Pasar Triwindu.......D4
31 Solo Grand Mall.......A3

Novotel Solo HOTEL $$
(☎0271-724555; www.novotel.com; Jl Slamet Riyadi 272; r from 441,000Rp; ❄@📶🏊) In the heart of the city, with most attractions within walking distance, the Novotel has an enviable central location, and its 4-star amenities are a steal. Rooms are spacious and modern, staff are professional and helpful, and you'll find two pools, a spa and a fitness centre.

Omah Sinten Heritage Hotel BOUTIQUE HOTEL $$
(☎0271-641160; omahsinten.com; Jl Diponegoro 34/54; r 550,000Rp; ❄📶) Better known for its restaurant, however rooms are lovely in this three-floor, wood and brick walk-up. Think high ceilings, ceramic tiled floors, tasteful wood furniture and exposed brick in the bathrooms.

Roemahkoe HISTORIC HOTEL $$
(☎0271-714024; www.roemahkoe.info; Jl Dr Rajiman 501; standard/deluxe d incl breakfast from 650,000/970,000Rp; ❄📶) This remarkable art deco hotel is rich in history and loaded with atmosphere. Most of the 14 rooms feature wood panelling and stained-glass windows plus all the modern facilities you'd expect. Deluxe rooms have marble baths, raised platforms for the bed, wood floors and furnishings, and high ceilings with crown mouldings. Boutique in every way. Lara's restaurant, set in the rear of the property, comes highly recommended.

Eating & Drinking

Solo has a superb street-food tradition and a traffic-free area called **Galabo** (Jl Slamet Riyadi; ⏰5-11pm), a kind of open-air food court with dozens of stalls. Local specialities such as *nasi gudeg* (unripe jackfruit served with rice, chicken and spices), *nasi liwet* (rice cooked in coconut milk and eaten with a host of side dishes) or *timlo solo* (beef noodle soup) can be found here.

There is no bar scene in Solo.

Warung Baru INTERNATIONAL $
(☎0271-656369; Jl Ahmad Dahlan 23; mains 10,000-18,000Rp; ⏰7.30am-10pm Mon-Sat, 5-10pm Sun; 🥬) An old-school backpackers' hang-out, the Baru bakes great bread and caters quite well to vegetarians, but the rest of the enormous menu is a bit forgettable. Still, the friendly owners arrange tours and batik classes.

Nasi Liwet Wongso Lemu INDONESIAN $
(Jl Teuku Umar; meals 12,000-18,000Rp; ⏰4pm-1am) Solo street dining at its best, this evening-only stall, run by an *ibu* in traditional batik, specialises in *nasi liwet*: coconut-flavoured rice served on a banana leaf topped with shredded chicken, chicken liver (optional), egg, turmeric-cooked tofu and special

seasonings. Tables are set up with pickled vegetables, tofu fried in turmeric and chicken feet. This is cultural dining deluxe!

Adem Ayem INDONESIAN $
(☎0271-716992; Jl Slamet Riyadi 342; mains 14,000-60,000Rp; ⏰7am-10pm) Huge canteen-like place with swirling fans and photos of ye olde Surakarta. Grab one of the plastic-fantastic chairs and order the chicken – souped, fried or served up *gudeg*-style.

Omah Sinten INDONESIAN $$
(www.omahsinten.com; Jl Diponegoro 34-54; mains 25,000-55,000Rp; ⏰8am-10pm) At this restaurant you can dine on quality Javanese fare including lots of local Solonese specialities, like beef sliced and stewed in herbs and green chillies, or duck stewed in coconut milk. Why not enjoy both while listening to the tinkle of fountains and the calming waft of classical Javanese music? It's opposite the entrance to the Istana Mangkunegaran (p134).

Laras INDONESIAN, INTERNATIONAL $$
(☎0271-714024; www.roemahkoe.com; Roemahkoe Hotel, Dr Rajiman 501; mains 35,000-65,000Rp; ⏰7am-10pm; @📶) A classy hotel-restaurant where you can savour the unique surrounds of this historic building, which was once a batik factory. It's particularly evocative at night when candlelit, and on Saturdays when a gamelan orchestra plays. Specials include *selat Solo* (a local sliced-beef salad served with a boiled egg).

O Solo Mio ITALIAN $$
(☎0271-727264; Jl Slamet Riyadi 253; mains 29,000-139,000Rp) Homemade pasta, fresh-baked bread and wood-fired pizzas are served in a Dutch colonial building with original tiling in the front room and a lovely covered back patio.

Ralana INDONESIAN $$
(www.ralanaeatery.com; Jl Slamet Riyadi 301; mains 30,000-130,000Rp; ⏰10am-10pm) Most notable for the setting in a restored Dutch colonial compound (with some puzzling modern touches). The menu includes the usual Indonesian and international staples with some fun departures, like oxtail fried rice and an Asian fusion lasagne. It hosts live bands on weekends.

Soga INDONESIAN, INTERNATIONAL $$
(☎0271-727020; www.sogaresto.com; Jl Slamet Riyadi 261; mains 40,000-115,000Rp; ⏰11am-10pm; 📶) This upmarket Indonesian and fusion restaurant is part of the luxuriant Danar Hadi complex (p134), where you'll find the museum and showroom, too. Mains include short rib stewed in coconut milk, as well as a range of pasta dishes, steaks and chops at reasonable prices.

Vivere CAFE
(Jl Dr Supomo; ⏰8am-10pm) A cute new cafe serving coffee, pancakes, pasta and...coffee. OK, it's mostly a caffeine refuelling station for local hipsters, owned by a local hipster, but if you come by on Tuesday evening you can help members of the English club practise their budding language skills. They will love it!

☆ Entertainment

Solo is an excellent place to see traditional Javanese performing arts; Istana Mangkunegaran and Kraton Surakarta both have traditional Javanese dance practice.

Contact the tourist office for the latest schedules for all events.

Sriwedari Theatre THEATRE
(admission 3000Rp; ⏰performances 8-10pm Tue-Sat) At the back of Sriwedari amusement park (p134), Sriwedari Theatre has a long-running *wayang orang* troupe – it's well worth dropping by to experience this masked dance-drama; you can come and go as you please.

RRI Auditorium PERFORMING ARTS
(☎0271-641178; Jl Abdul Rahman Saleh 51) RRI holds an eclectic program of cultural performances, including *wayang orang* and *ketoprak* (folk theatre). There's a free *wayang orang* event on the second Tuesday of each month at 8pm.

Taman Budaya Surakarta PERFORMING ARTS
(TBS; ☎0271-635414; Jl Ir Sutami 57) This cultural centre hosts all-night *wayang kulit* performances; private dance lessons are also available.

Shopping

Solo is one of Indonesia's main textile centres, producing not only its own unique, traditional batik but also every kind of fabric.

For everyday shopping, check out the markets or the malls, including **Solo Grand Mall** (Jl Slamet Riyadi) and **Paragon Mall** (www.solo-paragon.com; Jl Cipto Mangunkusumo; 📶).

Batik

Solo has two urban batik villages, narrow streets full of family-run workshops that are a delight to explore. **Kampung Batik Kauman** is just south of Jl Slamet Riyadi, around Jl Cakra, in one of the main backpacker districts. Jl Cakra itself is a cute tiled lane lined with home-industry batik shops set in old mouldering Dutch-era relics. Even if you aren't into textiles, these narrow lanes and buildings dressed in faded pastels and shedding stucco make for some amazing photo ops.

Kampung Batik Laweyan (www.kampoenglaweyan.com) is centred in the lanes south of the Roemahkoe hotel (which was once a batik workshop). Residents in both areas are normally very welcoming to visitors and eager to sell a piece or two.

There are also some well-established manufacturers with showrooms displaying their range of sophisticated work.

Batik Keris Factory CLOTHING
(☎0271-714400; Jl Batik Keris; ⏰8am-5pm Mon-Sat) This factory, in Kampung Batik Laweyan, allows you to see the batik process up close. Its **shop** (Jl Yos Sudarso 62) has icy air-con and two full floors of fixed-price batik bags, skirts and shirts.

Batik Danar Hadi CLOTHING
(www.houseofdanarhadi.com; Jl Slamet Riyadi 261; ⏰9am-7pm) Danar Hadi is an important Solonese batik manufacturer and has a beautiful showroom.

Curios

Kris and other souvenirs can be purchased from street vendors found at the eastern side of the *alun-alun* near Kraton Surakarta. The gem sellers have a mind-boggling array of semi-precious stones. Jl Dr Rajiman (Secoyudan), which runs along the southern edge of the *alun-alun*, is the goldsmith street.

Markets

Pasar Triwindu MARKET
(Windujenar Market; Jl Diponegoro; ⏰9am-4pm) Solo's flea market is the place to search for antiques including *wayang* puppets, old batik and ceramics, as well as clocks, vinyl records, coins and vintage cameras.

Pasar Gede MARKET
(Jl Urip Sumoharjo; ⏰8am-6pm) This is the city's largest general market, selling all manner of produce, particularly fruit and vegetables.

Pasar Klewer MARKET
(Jl Secoyudan) This wonderfully rootsy textile market burned in a fire in 2015 and was being rebuilt when we stopped by. It's worth checking to see if it's back to grace.

ℹ Information

Many of Solo's hotels, guesthouses and restaurants have wi-fi.

BCA Bank (cnr Jl Dr Rajiman & Jl Gatot Subroto; ⏰8am-4pm Mon-Sat) Has currency-exchange facilities.

Main Post Office (Jl Jenderal Sudirman; ⏰8am-2pm Mon-Sat)

Tourist Office (☎0271-716501; Jl Slamet Riyadi 275; ⏰8am-4pm Mon-Sat) Staff are only moderately helpful here. They have maps, brochures and information on cultural events. They also peddle (slightly pricey) tours.

ℹ Getting There & Away

AIR

Solo's Adi Sumarmo airport offers regular flights to Jakarta with **Garuda** (☎0271-737500; www.garuda-indonesia.com; Hotel Riyadi Palace, Jl Slamet Riyadi 335), **Lion Air** (www.lionair.co.id) and **Citilink** (www.citilink.co.id).

BUS

The Tirtonadi bus terminal is 3km from the centre of the city. Only economy buses leave from here to destinations such as Prambanan (14,000Rp, 1½ hours) and Semarang (30,000Rp, 3¼ hours), plus Surabaya and Malang. Near the bus terminal, the Gilingan minibus terminal has express air-con *travel* minibuses to Semarang (55,000Rp), Surabaya and Malang (both 80,000Rp). It's easiest to reach Yogyakarta by train.

TRAIN

Solo is located on the main Jakarta–Yogyakarta–Surabaya train line and most trains stop at **Balapan** (☎0271-714039), the principal

TRAINS FROM SOLO

DESTINATION	FARE (RP)	DURATION (HR)	FREQUENCY
Jakarta	90,000–535,000	8¼-9	4 daily
Surabaya	115,000–285,000	3½-4	6 daily

WORTH A TRIP

SUHARTO'S MAUSOLEUM

In a commanding hilltop location 34km southeast of Solo, the **mausoleum** (Astana Giribangun; admission by donation; ⏲8am-5pm) of former president Suharto is a curious sight. Suharto planned this monument to himself well in advance of his death, securing the land and appointing an architect back in 1998. The resulting building is curiously low-key and lacking the gaudy excesses favoured by many ex-dictators – an unadorned mosque-like structure built on traditional Javanese *pendopo* (open-sided pavilion) lines.

Tombs of various less-favoured relatives are dotted around the edges of the building, while the inner sanctum, separated by carved wooden screens, contains five marble sarcophagi: Suharto himself, his mother, father, wife and one sister. Oddly enough, the whole place is eerily peaceful, and few visitors pay their respects these days – in stark contrast to the scenes in 2008 when tens of thousands lined the route of his funeral cortège from Solo airport. The Suharto cult of personality certainly has waned over the years.

While you're here you can stroll up to the burial place of Solo's royal Mangkunegara family, whose monuments pale by comparison. It's just 300m away on a neighbouring forested hilltop.

There's a cafe and a souvenir stall where you can purchase kitsch keyrings and the like. There is no public transport to the monument. Tour guides in Solo will include Giribangun on trips to Candi Sukuh and Candi Cetho. By road, head east of Solo to Karangpandan, and it's 7km south of the highway near the village of Mangadeg.

train station. Jebres train station, in the northeast of Solo, has a few very slow economy-class services to Surabaya and Jakarta. Trains to Yogyakarta cost 6000Rp to 20,000Rp.

ℹ Getting Around

Air-conditioned Batik Solo Trans buses connect Adi Sumarmo airport, 10km northwest of the centre, with Jl Slamet Riyadi. A taxi costs around 70,000Rp; **Kosti Solo taxis** (☎0271-856300) are reliable. Becak cost about 10,000Rp from the train station or bus terminal into the centre. Homestays can arrange bike hire for around 20,000Rp or a motorcycle for around 70,000Rp per day.

To set up car hire (per day 500,000Rp), call Jogja Trans (p115) in Yogyakarta. It can easily arrange pickup in Solo and shuttle you around the region.

Sangiran

Sangiran is an important archaeological excavation site (so important it gained World Heritage status in 1996), where some of the best examples of fossilised skulls of the prehistoric 'Java Man' (*Pithecanthropus erectus*) were unearthed by a Dutch professor in 1936.

The town's main (well, only) attraction is its small **museum** (admission 7500Rp; ⏲8am-4pm Tue-Sun), with a few skulls (one of *Homo erectus*), various pig and hippopotamus teeth, and fossil exhibits, including huge mammoth bones and tusks. Guides will also offer to take you to the area where shells and other fossils have been found in the crumbling slopes of the hill.

Take a Purwodadi-bound bus from Solo's bus terminal and ask to be dropped off at the Sangiran turn-off (5000Rp), 15km from Solo. It's then 4km to the museum (around 10,000Rp by *ojek*).

Gunung Lawu

Towering Gunung Lawu (3265m), lying on the border of Central and East Java, is one of the holiest mountains in Java. Mysterious Hindu temples dot its slopes, terraced with rice, tea and potato fields, and each year thousands of pilgrims seeking spiritual enlightenment climb its peak.

Although popular history has it that when Majapahit fell to Islam, the Hindu elite all fled east to Bali, Javanese lore relates that Brawijaya V, the last king of Majapahit, went west. Brawijaya's son, Raden Patah, was the leader of Demak and led the conquering forces of Islam against Majapahit, but rather than fight his own son, Brawijaya retreated to Gunung Lawu to seek spiritual enlightenment. There he achieved nirvana as Sunan Lawu, and today pilgrims come to the mountain to seek his spiritual guidance or to achieve magic powers.

WORTH A TRIP

CLIMBING GUNUNG LAWU

The village of Cemoro Sewu, 10km east of Tawangmangu, is the starting point for the hike to the summit of Gunung Lawu. Thousands of pilgrims flock to the summit on 1 Suro, the start of the Javanese New Year, but mystics and holidaying students make the night climb throughout the year, especially on Saturday night. Most start around 8pm, reaching the peak at around 2am for meditation.

For the best chance of witnessing a clear sunrise, start by 10.30pm at the latest. It is a long, steady six-hour hike, but one of the easiest mountains in Java to tackle. While the stony path has handrails in places, it is still best to bring a torch or headlamp. Alternatively, guides can make a night climb easier and lead you to the various pilgrimage sites along the way. Guides in Cemoro Sewu cost around 150,000Rp. Sign in at the PHKA post before starting the climb (admission to walk 20,000Rp).

The unique temples on the mountain – some of the last Hindu temples built in Java before the region converted to Islam – show the influence of the later *wayang* style of East Java, though they incorporate elements of fertility worship. The most famous temple is Candi Sukuh. Candi Cetho is another large complex that still attracts Hindu worshippers.

The small tea-farming village of Kemuning makes a pleasant gateway to both temples, with a few teahouses with tasty kitchens and one rather alluring guesthouse to consider, if you just can't bear to leave.

Sights

Candi Sukuh TEMPLE

(admission 10,000Rp; 8am-5pm) In a magnificent position 900m above the Solo plain, Candi Sukuh is one of Java's most enigmatic and striking temples. It's not a large site, but it has a large, truncated pyramid of roughhewn stone, and there are some fascinating reliefs and Barong statues. The pyramid was under renovation and surrounded by scaffolds when we last visited. Even so, on clear days the view of the terraced emerald valley and the volcano looming above are magical. The restoration is estimated to be completed in 2017.

It's clear that a fertility cult was practised here: several explicit carvings have led it to be dubbed the 'erotic' temple. It's a quiet, isolated place with a potent atmosphere.

Built in the 15th century during the declining years of the Majapahit kingdom, Candi Sukuh seems to have nothing whatsoever to do with other Javanese Hindu and Buddhist temples. The origins of its builders and strange sculptural style (with crude, squat and distorted figures carved in the *wayang* style found in East Java) remain a mystery and it seems to mark a reappearance of the pre-Hindu animism that existed 1500 years earlier.

At the gateway you'll find a large stone lingam and yoni. Flowers are still often scattered here, and locals believe these symbols were used to determine whether a wife had been faithful, or a wife-to-be was still a virgin. The woman had to wear a sarong and jump across the lingam – if the sarong fell off, her infidelity was proven. Other interesting cult objects include a monument depicting Bima, the Mahabharata warrior hero, with Narada, the messenger of the gods, both in a stylised womb. Another monument depicts Bima passing through the womb at his birth. In the top courtyard three enormous flat-backed turtles stand like sacrificial altars. A 2m lingam once topped the pyramid, but it was removed by Sir Thomas Stamford Raffles in 1815 and now resides in the National Museum in Jakarta.

If you're driving here note that there are almost no signposts to help direct you to the site and you have to pay a small fee to pass through Kemuning. Virtually all travellers get here on a tour from Solo or Yogyakarta. Public transport is very tricky: take a bus bound for Tawangmangu from Solo as far as Karangpandan (6000Rp), then a Kemuning minibus (2000Rp) to the turn-off to Candi Sukuh; from here it's a steep 2km walk uphill to the site or a 40,000Rp *ojek* ride. For around 70,000Rp, *ojek* will take you to both Sukuh and Cetho.

Candi Cetho TEMPLE

(admission 10,000Rp; 8am-4.30pm) Candi Cetho (pronounced Cheto) sits on the southern face of Gunung Lawu at around 1400m.

Thought to date from around 1350, this *candi* closely resembles a Balinese temple in appearance, though it combines elements of Shivaism and fertility worship. It's a larger temple than Sukuh and is spread over terraces rising up the misty hillside. The entrance is marked by temple guardians and you'll find a striking platform with a turtle head and a large lingam on the upper terrace.

There are six tiers altogether and it remains a focus of active worship. Balinese (and Javanese) Hindus visit Candi Cetho to pray and give offerings regularly. Indeed, the villagers who live just below the temple form one of Java's last remaining Hindu populations. The third tier is where you'll see the majority of the fruit, flowers, other offerings and burning incense – all from visiting pilgrims.

There are several homestays in the village, with simple rooms available for 75,000Rp to 100,000Rp per night. Cetho is usually included in the temple tours from Solo and Yogyakarta. By road, head to Kemuning then take the steep road through bucolic farmland, 9km past the Sukuh turn-off.

Sleeping

Sukuh Cottage HOTEL $$

(027-1702 4587; www.sukuh-cottage.com; r incl breakfast 400,000Rp;) Just before Sukuh temple – and enjoying the same exquisite views – this rural hotel has attractive rooms and villas built from natural materials dotted around a sublime grassy plot studded with mature trees. There's an elevated viewing platform and restaurant. Reserve ahead, as the lodge often gets booked out by tour groups in high season.

Eating & Drinking

Bale Branti TEAHOUSE

(Jalan Kaliondo No 1, Kemuning; snacks 10,000-22,000Rp; 9am-7pm) A new teahouse, set in an authentic *joglo* (traditional Javanese house) in Kemuning, with over a dozen wood tables shaded by parasols on the lip of the tea fields. It's a good place for local tea, and it does *nasi campur* (rice with side dishes), nasi goreng (fried rice) and *pisang goreng* (banana fritters), too.

Ndoro Donker TEAHOUSE

(Jl Afedling Kemuning 18; mains 10,000-60,000Rp; 9am-5pm) Named for the first tea mogul of Java and set in his 19th-century home on his old plantation. There is a more complete food menu here, and the setting, which abuts the tea fields, is just as lovely. The black and green tea is local; the rest is sourced from elsewhere on Java.

Tawangmangu

0271

Tawangmangu, a sprawling hill resort on the western side of Gunung Lawu, is a popular weekend retreat for Solonese. It's a pleasant enough place to escape the city heat and do a hike or two in the hills, but it's best done as a day trip.

Sights

Grojogan Sewu WATERFALL

(admission 110,000Rp; 6am-6pm) About 2km from town, Grojogan Sewu, a 100m-high waterfall, is a favourite playground for monkeys (as is the parking area). It is reached by a long flight of steps down a hillside, but you probably won't want to have a dip in the chilly, and filthy, swimming pool. From the bottom of the waterfall a trail leads to a good track to Candi Sukuh, a 2½-hour walk away. Some Solo guides offer treks.

This path is steep in parts but is also negotiable by motorbike. *Ojek* hang out at the beginning of the trail on weekends.

Sleeping & Eating

There are plenty of losmen on Jl Grojogan Sewu, a quieter street running between the waterfall and Jl Raya Lawu.

For cheaper eats, the road near the waterfall is inundated with warungs.

★ **Gria Tawang** INDONESIAN $

(0271-700 7413; mains 15,000-35,000Rp; 9am-5pm) An outstanding riverside warung, part of an outdoor activity centre, that offers traditional Javanese dishes cooked on log fires. You eat under wooden shelters overlooking a fast-flowing stream. The food takes time to prepare, so expect to wait. It's 2km west of Tawangmangu, on the road back to Solo.

Hotel Bintang HOTEL $

(0271-696269; www.bintangtw.hotelasiasolo.com; Jl Raya Lawu; r from 185,000-315,000Rp;) A modern hotel on the main drag with three floors of rooms of varying quality. Newer, sleeker rooms on the riverside have dark-wood furniture, LCD TV and stylish lighting. The others are simple, tiled numbers. Not much English is spoken but staff try to be helpful. There's a minimart, a cafe-restaurant and unfortunate karaoke on weekends.

Getting There & Away

Buses travel to Solo (12,000Rp to 15,000Rp) regularly. Minibuses (2000Rp) loop through town from the bus terminal up the main road, across to the waterfall and back.

North Coast

Central Java's north coast doesn't feature on most travellers' itineraries, but this steamy strip of land is not without charm.

The towns dotting the north coast are steeped in history. For many centuries the coast was the centre for trade with merchants from Arabia, India and China, who brought with them both goods and cultural values. In the 15th and 16th centuries the area was a springboard for Islam into Java, and the tombs of most of the country's great saints all lie along this coast.

Craft traditions are also impressive. Pekalongan is celebrated for its batik, while Jepara is a major centre for wooden furniture. If the sweet smell of *kretek* (clove cigarettes) is to your liking, then a trip to Kudus may appeal.

Central Java's capital is Semarang, a rapidly growing metropolis and major shipping centre. While it won't hold your interest for too long, it is a gateway to the splendid (and often forgotten) Karimunjawa Islands.

Semarang

☎024 / POP 1.6 MILLION

Steamy Semarang – bustling and strange, with bosomy hills, a somewhat restored historic core and rapidly developing, affluent outskirts – is home to a huge middle class, Chinese population and a massive north-coast port. Taken with a wide angle, this sprawling, schizophrenic city can feel charmless, but zoom in on its best pockets and there is life – especially in the old city, a gentrifying few blocks blooming with new cafes and restaurants and a wonderful art gallery, not to mention atmospheric colonial architecture. In contrast, the commercial area around Simpang Lima (Five Ways), with its malls, clogged freeways and business hotels, is emblematic of Java's sudden and dramatic shift into the 21st century. Like it or not, business is booming here.

Though Semarang is the provincial capital of Central Java, it lacks the magnetism of Solo and Yogyakarta. It does, however, have good transport connections (including international flights) so you may well pass through.

Sights

Old City NEIGHBOURHOOD

Semarang's richly atmospheric old city, often referred to as the Outstadt, its Dutch name, is well worth investigating. Sadly, most of the area's tremendous stock of colonial buildings are in an advanced state of decay, seemingly unloved and left to rot by the city authorities.

At the heart of this old quarter is the elegant church **Gereja Blenduk** (Jl Jenderal Suprapto) FREE, built in 1753, which has a huge cupola, a spectacular baroque-style organ and an unusual wooden pulpit. If the gates aren't locked tight, knock on the door and ask the caretaker to let you in. He just might! Towards the river from the church there are dozens of crumbling old Dutch warehouses, municipal buildings and townhouses with shuttered windows, flaking plaster and peeling paint. Be sure to drop by the Semarang Gallery (p144).

The old city is prone to flooding; if you visit during the rainy season it may not even be possible to explore some of the backstreets. Towards the centre of the city, Pasar Johar is one of Semarang's main markets. Facing the market is Semarang's **Mesjid Besar** (Grand Mosque; Jl Pemuda) FREE.

Semarang Gallery ART GALLERY

(☎024-355 2099; www.galerisemarang.com; Jl Taman Srigunting 5-6; admission 10,000Rp; ⏲10am-4:30pm) The shining star of the old city, this wonderful art gallery set in a stunning old Dutch warehouse feels like a museum and is dedicated to Indonesian contemporary art. Aan Arif of Yogyakarta had a solo show on when we came through. It featured, cool, blurred oil-on-canvas street scenes and portraits. Whatever is on, you can be sure it will be worth well more than the price of entry.

Chinatown NEIGHBOURHOOD

(south of Jl Jenderal Suprapto) Semarang's Chinatown is worth investigating, particularly around the riverside Gang Lombok. Rich with pagodas, shophouses, jade jewellers, pharmacists, fortune tellers and food stalls, Semarang is Indonesia's most Chinese city and the depth of culture here is compelling. The focus of the entire community is the **Tay Kak Sie temple** (Gang Lombok), dating back to 1746, with its huge drums and incense-clouded interior.

This temple overlooks the Sungai Semarang (Semarang River), where there's a model of one of the ships of legendary Chinese explorer Admiral Cheng Ho (he visited Java

WORTH A TRIP

JAMU (HERBAL MEDICINES)

Semarang is known for its *jamu* and has two large manufacturers; both have museums and offer tours. **Jamu Nyonya Meneer** (☎024-658 3088; www.njonjameneer.com; Jl Raya Kaligawe, Km4; ⏰museum 10am-3.30pm Sun-Fri) FREE is near the bus terminal, while **Jamu Jago** (☎024-747 2762; www.jago.co.id; Jl Setia Budi 273) FREE is 6km south of the city on the Ambarawa road.

several times). Next to the temple is Pujasera Tay Kak Sie, a Chinese food court and also a community hall used for martial arts. Sadly, the river is grossly polluted these days, and its odour is not easy on the nostrils.

Lawang Sewu HISTORIC BUILDING
(Jl Permuda; admission 10,000Rp; ⏰7am-9pm) Semarang's most famous landmark, Lawang Sewu ('Thousand Doors') is actually two colossal colonial buildings that were once one of the headquarters of the Indonesian railways during the Dutch era. Some renovation has recently been completed but most of the main L-shaped structure remains closed to visitors. Nevertheless, you can wander the empty corridors of the other huge building, where clerks and engineers once worked, and admire the features (including some magnificent stained glass and marble staircases).

The building is regarded as a haunted house by locals; during WWII the Japanese occupied the building and used the dungeons for interrogation. You can tour the flooded basement on a guided tour (not always available in English), see where many lost their lives and hear the gruesome tales of the atrocities that were committed here. It's a deeply moving experience, particularly at night.

Gedung Batu CHINESE TEMPLE
(Sam Po Kong Temple; admission free to worshippers, viewing compound 10,000Rp, temples 30,000Rp; ⏰24hr) This huge Chinese temple complex, 5km southwest of the city centre, has three main temple buildings and many smaller structures. Most are classically Indo-Chinese, with soaring pagoda-style roofs, massive drums and dangling Chinese lanterns. There's also an inner chamber in the form of a cave flanked by two great dragons, hence the temple's popular name, Gedung Batu (Stone Building). Inside the cave is a gilded statue of Sam Po, surrounded by fairy lights.

The complex was built in honour of Admiral Cheng Ho, the famous Muslim eunuch of the Ming dynasty, who led a Chinese fleet on seven expeditions to Java and other parts of Southeast and West Asia in the early 15th century. Cheng Ho has since become a saint known as Sam Po. He first arrived in Java in 1405 and is believed to have helped spread Islam.

Note that women are not allowed to enter the temples if they are menstruating, but they can visit the complex.

To get to Gedung Batu, take the Damri bus 2 from Jl Pemuda to Karang Ayu (a suburb west of central Semarang), and then an *angkot* to the temple. It takes about half an hour from central Semarang.

Ronggowarsito Museum MUSEUM
(Jl Abdulrachman; admission 10,000Rp; ⏰8am-2pm Tue-Sun) Ronggowarsito Museum is a large provincial museum with antiquities, crafts including batik and *wayang* puppets, and assorted fossils and curios collected from all over the state. The most interesting exhibit is a recycled stone panel from the Mantingan mosque – one side shows Islamic motifs, while the reverse shows the original Hindu-Buddhist scene. Javanese dance displays are held here on Friday morning. It's approximately 2km before the airport.

Semarang Harbour HARBOUR
Semarang harbour is worth a look to see *pinisi* (schooners) and other traditional ocean-going vessels that dock at Tambak Lorok.

Sleeping

Semarang lacks decent, cheap hotels. Midrange accommodation is good value, however. Backpackers should budget accordingly.

Hotel Raden Patah HOTEL $
(☎024-351 1328; Jl Jenderal Suprapto 48; r 150,000Rp; ❄) An old building with vintage beamed ceilings and light fixtures and clean basic rooms with queen beds and air-con on the cheap. Plus you are right in the old-town mix. For a night? Totally works.

Tjiang Residence GUESTHOUSE $
(☎024-354 0330; www.tjiangresidence.com; Jl Gang Pinggir 24; d incl breakfast 220,000Rp; ❄📶) In the heart of Chinatown, this budget hotel is steeped in old Chinese kitsch, a short stroll from the Tay Kak Sie temple. OK, the

Semarang

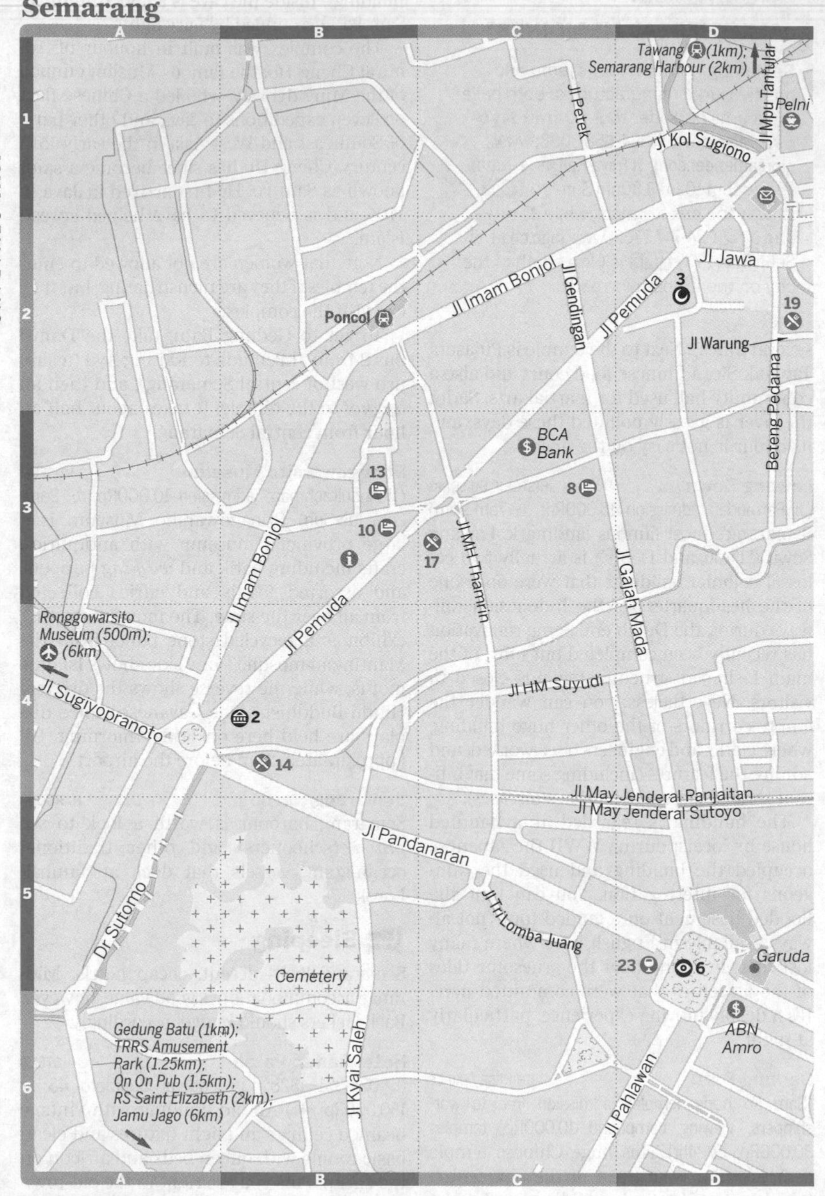

lobby smells of mildew, and so do the halls, but the rooms are fresh, if cramped, with wood floors, Ikea-chic desks and flat-screens.

Roemah Pantes HOTEL **$**
(024-358 0628; Jl Kalikuping 18; s/d incl breakfast 225,000/250,000Rp;) In a hard-to-find lane close to Gang Lombok in the heart of

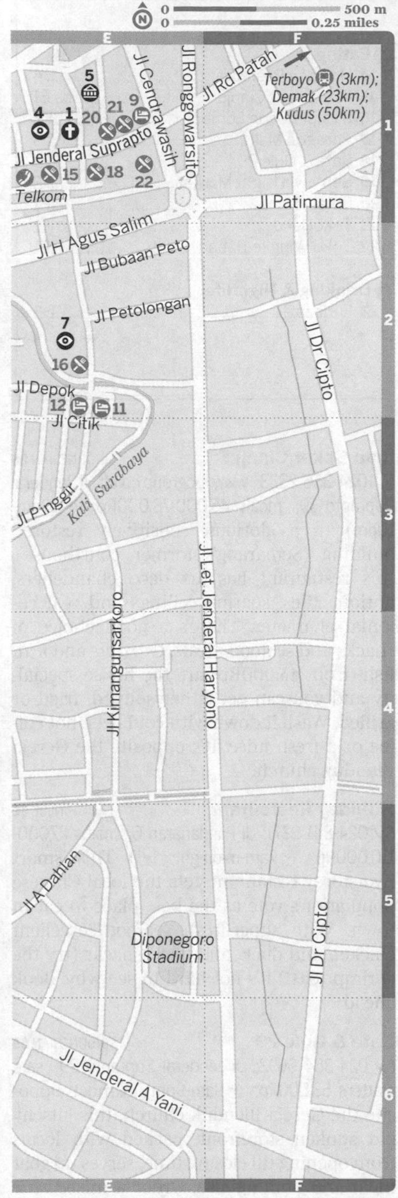

Chinatown, this small hotel has seven fairly spacious, reasonably clean, tiled rooms with duvets and hot-water bathrooms – though some are traced with soap scum. No English is spoken.

Whiz Hotel HOTEL **$$**

(☎024-356 6999; www.whizhotels.com/semarang; Jl Kapten Piere Tendean 9; s/d from 240,000/325,000Rp; ❄@🛜) Green-and-white no-frills hotel with competitive rates for its 148 sharp, inviting (though slightly cramped) rooms. It's fine if you're after a moderately priced place, but don't expect much in the way of service. Breakfast is basic.

Novotel Semarang HOTEL **$$**

(☎024-356 3000; www.novotel.com; Jl Pemuda 123; r from 520,000Rp; ❄@🛜🏊) Enjoys a good location between the old city and Simpang Lima, and its facilities are first-class, with an outdoor pool, a state-of-the-art gym and a spa with moderate prices. Rooms are contemporary, spacious and comfortable, many with city vistas. There are two cafe-restaurants and the breakfast buffet is solid. Best rates can be found on Agoda.com.

Gumaya Tower Hotel HOTEL **$$$**

(☎024-355 1999; www.gumayatowerhotel.com; Jl Gajah Mada 59-61; r from 690,000Rp; ❄@🛜🏊) Towering over the city, this luxury edifice has understated, well-designed rooms at surprisingly good value. Expect large LCD TVs, fast wi-fi and gorgeous bathrooms with tubs. There's an infinity pool, and panoramic city views from the top-deck bar. Popular with business travellers.

Eating

Semarang has a large Chinese population, and this is a good place to sample traditional dishes.

Simpang Lima is a good bet in the evenings with dozens of *kaki lima* (food carts) set up around the huge square, serving up snacks and offering traditional *lesahan* dining (on straw mats).

Paragon Mall (www.paragonsemarang.com; Jl Permuda) has Indonesian and Asian restaurants, cafes, and also a large supermarket in the basement for supplies. Plaza Simpang Lima also has an extensive food court on the 4th floor.

Semawis Night Market CHINESE **$**

(Jl Warung; meals 15,000-35,000Rp; ⏲5-11pm Fri-Sun) If you're here on a weekend head straight to the Semawis night market for fine Chinese-style noodles and *babi sate* (pork satay). There's always a sociable atmosphere here, with a bit of low-key karaoke crooning and fortune telling going on.

Semarang

Sights

1	Gereja Blenduk	E1
2	Lawang Sewu	B4
3	Mesjid Besar	D2
4	Old City	E1
5	Semarang Gallery	E1
6	Simpang Lima	D5
7	Tay Kak Sie Temple	E2

Sleeping

8	Gumaya Tower Hotel	C3
9	Hotel Raden Patah	E1
10	Novotel Semarang	B3
11	Roemah Pantes	E2
12	Tjiang Residence	E2
13	Whiz Hotel	B3

Eating

14	Holliday Restaurant	B4
15	Ikan Bakar Cianjur	E1
16	Lumpia Gang Lombok	E2
17	Paragon Mall	C3
18	Sate & Gule 29	E1
19	Semawis Night Market	D2
20	Spiegel	E1
21	TekoDeko	E1
22	Toko Wingko Babad	E1

Drinking & Nightlife

23	E Plaza	D5

Toko Wingko Babad BAKERY $

(☎024-354 2064; Jl Cendrawasih 14; cakes 3700-4500Rp; ⏰7am-6.30pm) A brilliant, anachronistic bakery and store where you can roll back the years and sample the delicious *wingko* (wonderful coconut cakes served warm), which are plain or flavoured with jackfruit, chocolate banana or durian. The jackfruit is especially addictive.

Lumpia Gang Lombok CHINESE $

(Gang Lombok II; lumpia 12,000Rp; ⏰8am-5pm) Riverside warung, next to the Tay Kak Sie temple, where you can feast on delicious prawn *lumpia* (spring rolls) that are served with pickled cucumber, lettuce and shredded vegetables. It's a tiny place where you chow down rubbing elbows with other diners.

TekoDeko CAFE $

(Jl Jenderal Suprapto 44; mains 21,000-45,000Rp) A fun tiled coffee house in another restored old relic. It does espresso drinks and pots of tea, sandwiches, pastas and nasi goreng, too. It also has a small shop and a great rooftop sun deck scattered with tables.

★ **Spiegel** FUSION $$

(Jl Jenderal Suprapto 34; mains 30,000-195,000Rp; ⏰10am-midnight; 📶) The coolest new spot in Semarang, Spiegel is set in a neglected old general store (circa 1895), once patronised by Dutch colonists. Here the island bar serves up tasty cocktails, and marble tables are the stage for vegetarian tapas like pan-roasted broccoli with lemon and parmesan, and more imaginative dishes including tasty chicken-tikka tacos and *moqueca*, a Brazilian seafood stew.

Ikan Bakar Cianjur INDONESIAN $$

(☎024-356 2333; www.ibcgroup.co.id; Jl Jenderal Suprapto 19; meals 45,000-78,000Rp; ⏰10am-10pm) In a glorious, sensitively restored building (Semarang's former courthouse), this restaurant has art deco chandeliers, antique tiles, soaring ceilings and real colonial character. There's a good choice of snacks and seafood meals. *Gurame* and *nila* fish (from 45,000Rp) are the house speciality and you can get either souped, fried or grilled. Wash it down with cold beer, hot coffee or a fresh juice. It's opposite the Gereja Blenduk church.

Holliday Restaurant CHINESE $$

(☎024-841 3371; Jl Pandanaran 6; mains 27,000-110,000Rp; ⏰7am-midnight; 🖉) This smart two-storey restaurant gets the local Chinese population's vote as the best place to eat in town. With super-fresh seafood, excellent chicken and duck, and good snacks (try the shrimp toast) it's not hard to see why. Book ahead.

Sate & Gule 29 INDONESIAN $$

(☎024-354 9692; Jl Jenderal Suprapto 29; sate platters 53,000Rp; ⏰9am-9pm) Almost opposite the Gereja Blenduk church, this kitschy old sunken storefront, packed with locals from opening till closing time, serves up goat meat and nothing else. Order a mixed *sate* and you'll get six skewers of grilled cuts including liver, served with pepper, slices of red onion and coconut-flavoured sauce. *Gule* is goat-meat soup. Get your local flavour here.

Drinking & Nightlife

On On Pub PUB

(☎024-831 3968; Jl Rinjani 21; ⏰5pm-1am Mon-Thu, to 2am Fri & Sat, 11am-1am Sun) A classic expat hang out in the hilly south of town, this pub sells ice-cold draught Bintang as well as decent international grub – try the German mixed grill. There's a pool table and a dart board.

E Plaza CLUB

(Jl Ruko Gajahmada Lantai II 29; club entrance 50,000Rp) Semarang can be lacking when it comes to nightlife but this complex, right by Simpang Lima, is highly popular and contains an upmarket club, cinema and lounge bar. It draws a young energetic crowd and is a good bet for a night out.

Entertainment

TBRS Amusement Park AMUSEMENT PARK

(☎024-831 1220; Jl Sriwijaya 29, Tegalwareng) For more traditional entertainment, this amusement park holds *wayang orang* performances every Saturday from 7pm to midnight, and *wayang kulit* most Thursdays. Check the latest schedule at the tourist office.

Information

ABN Amro (Jl Jenderal A Yani; ⏰8am-4pm Mon-Sat) Bank just off Simpang Lima.

BCA Bank (Jl Pemuda 90-92; ⏰8am-4pm Mon-Sat) Changes most currencies.

Central Java Tourist Office (☎024-351 5451; www.indonesia-tourism.com/central-java; Jl Pemuda 147; ⏰8am-3pm Mon-Fri) The Central Java Tourist Office has good booklets and information devoted to the city and the entire Central Java region. Transport and hotel information about the Karimunjawa Islands is reliable.

Main Post Office (Jl Pemuda; ⏰8am-2pm Mon-Sat) On a busy intersection near the Chinese market.

RS Saint Elizabeth (☎024-831 0076; www.rs-elisabeth.com; Jl Kawi) The best hospital in town. It's in the Candi Baru district.

Telkom (Jl Jenderal Suprapto 7)

Getting There & Away

AIR

Semarang airport is a vital hub with numerous international and domestic connections. **AirAsia** (☎024-5050 5088; www.airasia.com) flies to Kuala Lumpur and Jakarta. **Garuda** (☎024-845 4737; www.garuda-indonesia.com; Hotel Horison, Jl Ahmad Dahlan) and **Citilink** (www.citilink.co.id) connect Semarang with Jakarta. **Lion Air** (☎080 477 8899; www.lionair.co.id) connects Semarang with Jakarta, Bandung, Batam and Banjarmasim. **Sriwijaya Air** (☎021-640 5566; www.sriwijayaair.co.id) flies to Jakarta and Surabaya, and **Wings Air** (☎080 477 8899; www.lionair.co.id) flies to Surabaya.

BOAT

For ferry information, the **Pelni office** (☎024-354 0381, 024-354 6722; www.pelni.co.id; Jl Mpu Tantular 25; ⏰ticketing 8am-2pm Mon-Thu, to noon Fri & Sat) has timetables you can consult after its ticket sales windows shut (around 5pm). There are economy/1st-class boats to the following Kalimantan ports about every three or four days: Sampit (218,000/766,000Rp) and Pontianak (281,000Rp).

TRANSPORT FROM SEMARANG

Bus

DESTINATION	FARE (RP)	DURATION (HR)
Jepara	15,000	2½
Kudus	25,000	1¼
Pekalongan	50,000	3
Wonosobo	50,000	4
Yogyakarta	50,000	4

Train

DESTINATION	FARE (RP)	DURATION (HR)	FREQUENCY
Jakarta	65,000–365,000	6	5 daily
Pekalongan	45,000–65,000	1¼	8 daily

BUS

Semarang's **Terboyo bus terminal** is 4km east of town, just off the road to Kudus. Air-con minibuses also travel to destinations across the island, including Wonosobo (50,000Rp), Solo (30,000Rp), Yogyakarta (85,000Rp) and Surabaya (105,000Rp). Agents for luxury buses and air-conditioned minibuses include **Cipa Ganti** (☎ 024-9128 8588; Jl Sultan Agung 92), **Rahayu** (☎ 024-354 3935; Jl Let Jenderal Haryono 9) and **Nusantara Indah** (☎ 024-355 3984; Jl Let Jenderal Haryono 9B).

TRAIN

Semarang lies on the main north-coast Jakarta–Cirebon–Surabaya train route. **Tawang** (☎ 024-354 4544) is Semarang's main station for all exclusive- and business-class services. Economy-class trains depart from Semarang's Poncol train station.

Getting Around

TO/FROM THE AIRPORT

Ahmad Yani airport is 6km west of the centre. A taxi into town costs 55,000Rp (there's an official desk at arrivals), and around 40,000Rp when returning to the airport using the taxi meter.

PUBLIC TRANSPORT

City buses charge a fixed 3000Rp fare and terminate at the Terboyo bus terminal. Buses 1, 2 and 3 run south along Jl Pemuda to Candi Baru. Short becak rides cost around 5000Rp; a ride of more than 3km costs around 10,000Rp. Semarang has plenty of metered taxis; call **Blue Bird** (☎ 024-760 1234) or **Kosti Taxis** (☎ 024-761 3333).

Ambarawa

☎ 0298 / POP 58,000

The market town of Ambarawa, 28km south of Semarang, will be of interest to trainspotters as the site of the Ambarawa Train Station Museum. Historians will also note that it was once the site of a Japanese internment camp where up to 15,000 Europeans were held during WWII.

Ambarawa has hotels, but there's a much nicer place to stay in the nearby foothills.

Sights

Ambarawa Train Station Museum MUSEUM

(Museum Kereta Api Ambarawa; admission 10,000Rp; ⏲8am-4pm) If you are a fan of vintage railways, you will love these old tin-can, wood-panelled boxcars lingering on old tracks along with 22 wrought-iron, turn-of-the-century engines. Oiled, painted and maintained with loving care, it's no wonder they last. Visitors may climb aboard, pretend to work the brake or open the coal engine port. The museum is located in the premises of the old Koening Willem I station, which opened in 1873.

The beautifully tiled European passenger terminal at the far end of the museum is worth the long walk. With its ornate metalwork and old clocks, conductor offices filled with vintage typewriters and ticket windows stocked with telegraph machines, you feel the history here. The museum is a couple of kilometres outside town, just off the road to Magelang.

Sleeping

Mesa Stila Resort HOTEL $$$

(☎ 0298-596333; www.mesahotelsandresorts.com/mesastila; Pingit; villas from 1,621,000Rp; ❄ 📶 🏊) Nestled in a 22-hectare coffee plantation at an altitude of 900m, the Mesa Stila Resort (formerly the Losari Coffee Plantation) is one of Indonesia's most special (and expensive) hotels. The location, ringed by volcanoes, is sublime, and commodious villas make the most of the stunning views.

All sorts of themed spa packages are offered, there's an organic garden that provides for the resort's two restaurants, and you can sample the plantation's organic tea and coffee in the historic Club House. It's near Pingit village, some 12km southwest of Ambarawa. From Ambarawa, it's best to take a taxi (50,000Rp) to the resort.

Getting There & Away

Ambarawa can be reached by public bus from Semarang (15000Rp, one hour), and Yogyakarta (45,000Rp, three hours) via Magelang.

Demak

Demak, 25km east of Semarang, was the springboard from which Islam made its leap into Java. As the capital of the island's first Islamic state, it was from here that the Hindu Majapahit kingdom was conquered and much of Java's interior was converted.

The town's economic heyday has now passed and even the sea has retreated several kilometres, leaving this former port landlocked. But the role this small town once played has not been forgotten.

Buses from either Semarang or Kudus (both 10,000Rp) can drop you right outside the great mosque.

Sights

Mesjid Agung MOSQUE

FREE Demak's venerable Mesjid Agung (1466), notable for its triple-tiered roof, is Java's oldest mosque and one of the archipelago's foremost Muslim pilgrimage sites. Legend has it that it was built from wood by the *wali songo* (nine holy men) in a single night. Four main pillars in the central hall were originally made by four of the Muslim saints, and one pillar, erected by Sunan Kalijaga, is said to be made from scraps of timber magically fused together.

Today, the history of the mosque is outlined in the small museum to the side that is rarely open. If you do manage to gain access you will reportedly find some of the original woodwork, including magnificent carved doors.

The tombs of Demak's rulers are next to the mosque; the tomb of Raden Trenggono (leader of Demak's greatest military campaigns) attracts the most pilgrims.

Mesjid Agung is on the main road in the centre of town, beside the huge grassy *alun-alun*.

Kudus

0291 / POP 777,000

Kudus takes its name from the word *al-Quds* – the Arabic name for Jerusalem. Founded by the Muslim saint Sunan Kudus, it's an important pilgrimage site. Like much of Java, Kudus retains links with its Hindu past and the slaughter of cows is still forbidden here.

The town is moderately attractive, with an elongated main street that contains a huge tobacco factory. This is where the first *kretek* (clove cigarettes) were produced, and today Kudus is still a stronghold of *kretek* production – there are said to be 25 factories in the town. Sukun, a manufacturer outside of town, still produces *rokok klobot* (clove tobacco rolled in corn leaves).

Sights & Activities

Kudus is a hot town. If you want to cool off, **Omah Mode** (Jl Ahmed Yani 38; 8am-8pm) has a lovely pool area (30,000Rp, open 6am to 8pm) and there's a large water boom (25,000Rp) just behind the Kretek Museum, with slides and a channel that's ideal for kids.

KRETEK CIGARETTES

If Java has a smell, it is the sweet, spicy scent of the clove-flavoured *kretek*. The *kretek* has only been around since the early 20th century, but today the addiction is nationwide and accounts for 90% of the cigarette market, while sales of *rokok putih* (cigarettes without cloves) are languishing. So high is the consumption of cloves used in the *kretek* industry that Indonesia, traditionally a supplier of cloves in world markets, has become a substantial net importer from other world centres.

The invention of the *kretek* is attributed to a Kudus man, Jamahri, who claimed the cigarettes relieved his asthma. Later another local, Nitisemitol, who had a gift for business, started selling the cigarettes commercially. He mixed tobacco with crushed cloves rolled in *rokok klobot* (corn leaves); this was the prototype for his Bal Tiga brand, which he began selling in 1906.

Kudus became the centre for the *kretek* industry and at one stage the town had more than 200 factories, though today fewer than 50 cottage industries and a few large factories remain. Rationalisation in the industry has seen *kretek* production dominated by big producers, such as Sampoerna in Surabaya, Gudang Garam in Kediri and Djarum in Kudus.

Although filtered *kretek* are produced by modern machinery – Djarum churns out up to 140 million a day – nonfiltered *kretek* are still rolled by hand on simple wooden rolling machines. The best rollers can turn out around 4000 cigarettes in a day.

As to the claim that *kretek* are good for smoker's cough, cloves are a natural anaesthetic and do have a numbing effect on the throat. Any other claims to aiding health stop there – the tar and nicotine levels in the raw, slowly cured tobaccos are so high that some countries have banned or restricted their import.

Filtered *kretek* now dominate the market. There are 'mild' versions on offer, but for the *kretek* purist, the conical, crackling, nonfiltered *kretek* has no substitute – Sampoerna's Dji Sam Soe ('234') brand is regarded as the Rolls Royce of *kretek*. To see Sampoerna rollers in action visit the factory in Surabaya (p160).

Old Town NEIGHBOURHOOD

West of the river, Kauman, the oldest part of the city, has narrow streets and is reminiscent of a kasbah, with traders selling religious souvenirs, dates, prayer beads and caps. On Fridays, men dressed in white robes and women in *jilbab* (head coverings) of all hues make their way on foot to prayer. It's a serene, ethereal scene. They are headed to **Mesjid Al-Manar** (also known as Al-Aqsa and Menera).

The mosque was built in 1549 by Sunan Kudus and is famous for its red-brick *menara* (minaret). This minaret may have originally been the watchtower of the Hindu temple the mosque is said to be built on – its curiously squat form and flared sides certainly have more in common with Balinese temples than with traditional Islamic architecture. Inside the main temple, Muslim worshippers pray before a Hindu-style brick gateway, a fascinating juxtaposition of Javanese religious heritage.

From the courtyards behind the mosque, a palm-lined path leads to the imposing **Tomb of Sunan Kudus**, shrouded with a curtain of lace. The narrow doorway, draped with heavy gold-embroidered curtains, leads to an inner chamber and the grave.

Kretek Museum MUSEUM

(Jl Museum Kretek Jati Kulon; donations accepted; ⌚7.30am-4pm; ❄) This lonely, shabby old compound has some interesting exhibits of the history of *kretek* production, including some fascinating old photographs and machinery, though the fountain out front is as funky as the inside of a pair of charred lungs. Almost all explanations are in Bahasa Indonesia but there's a guide here who speaks English well. Next door, **Rumah Adat** is a traditional wooden Kudus house exhibiting the fabulous carving work the town is noted for.

Djarum Kretek Factory FACTORY

(Jl Ahmed Yani) FREE Djarum, opened in 1951, is the main employer in town and third-biggest *kretek* manufacturer in Indonesia. Ninety-minute tours of its modern factory are available between 8am and 11am.

Sleeping & Eating

Kudus has several good inexpensive hotels; all are on or just off the main drag, Jl Ahmed Yani.

You have to try *soto kudus* (a rich chicken soup), which the town is famous for. It's usually served up bright yellow (from turmeric) with lots of garlic, and the chicken is sometimes shredded. *Jenang kudus* is a sweet that's made of glutinous rice, brown sugar and coconut.

The best place for inexpensive food and such local specialities is **Taman Bojana**, a food-stall complex on the main roundabout in the centre of town.

Wisma Karima GUESTHOUSE $

(☎0291-431712; Jl Museum Kretek Jati Kulon III; r incl breakfast from 120,000Rp; ❄) Just off the highway on the south side of town, this guesthouse is orderly and good value. It's run by a welcoming family and has nine rooms, some quite spacious but all a little old-fashioned.

Hotel Kenari Asri HOTEL $$

(☎0291-446200; www.hotelkenari-central.com; Jl Kenari II; r incl breakfast 350,000-500,000Rp, ste 600,000Rp; ❄📶) Down a little lane off the main drag, this gaudy hotel looks like a fancy wedding cake, rising up in levels from the road. Its rooms are in good condition with flat-screens and modern furniture.

Sari Lembur Kuring INDONESIAN $

(Jl Agil Kusumadya 35; mains 18,000-50,000Rp) A large, pleasant restaurant complete with water features, where you can tuck into tasty Sundanese and Javanese food under a shady pagoda.

Information

The **BII Bank** (Jl Dr Lukmonohadi; ⌚8am-4pm Mon-Sat) has an ATM, and there are several more on Jl Ahmed Yani beside the Taman Bojana food complex (which also has public toilets).

Getting There & Away

Kudus is on the main Semarang–Surabaya road. The bus terminal is around 4km south of town. City minibuses run from behind the bus terminal to the town centre (3000Rp), or you can take a becak. Buses go from Kudus to Demak (5000Rp, 50 minutes) and Semarang (25,000Rp, 1½ hours), while minibuses go to Colo (9000Rp). Buses to Jepara (15,000Rp, 1¼ hours) leave from the Jetak subterminal, 4km west of town (3000Rp by minibus).

Jepara

☎0291 / POP 18,400

Famed as the best woodcarving centre in Java, Jepara's once booming furniture business brought it all the trappings of prosperity. The highwater days are done now, but as you enter town you'll still pass dozens of furniture showrooms offering contemporary, 'distressed' and 'antique' designs. Even the fields here are full of woodcarvings and half-finished wardrobes rather than rice and vegetables.

The laid-back town's broad avenues, neighbourhood lumber yards, small *gangs* lined with humble homes that open onto back-door canals, which lead to nearby beaches, make it a tranquil spot to take a break from the road. The area is home to a now dwindling population of expats and is still visited by buyers from all over the world, so it's more cosmopolitan than many small Indonesian towns.

Jepara is also a jumping-off point for the Karimunjawa Islands. Which is probably why you're here.

Sights

Museum RA Kartini MUSEUM

(admission 5000Rp; ⏲8am-2pm) On the north side of the *alun-alun,* this museum is dedicated to one of Indonesia's most celebrated women. One room is devoted to Kartini and contains portraits of her and her family, plus memorabilia. Other rooms contain assorted archaeological findings, including a yoni and lingam, and local art and artefacts, such as fine woodcarvings and ceramics. There's also a 16m skeleton of whale. It is sometimes possible to visit Kartini's old rooms, if you contact the tourist office.

Benteng VOC FORTRESS

Heading north from the Museum RA Kartini, cross the river and veer left up the hill to the old Dutch Benteng VOC. Over the last 50 years the fort's stonework has been pillaged, but the site has good views across town to the Java Sea. The cemetery nearby has some Dutch graves.

Pantai Kartini BEACH

The most popular beach is Pantai Kartini, 3km west of town – locals often call it Pemandian. From there you can rent a boat (around 150,000Rp return) to nearby Pulau Panjang, which has excellent white-sand beaches.

AN INDO ICON

Raden Ajeng Kartini, a writer, feminist and progressive thinker, was born in 1879, the daughter of the *bupati* (regent) of Jepara. She grew up in the *bupati*'s residence, on the eastern side of the *alun-alun*, excelled at school and learnt to speak fluent Dutch by the age of 12. It was in this residence that Kartini spent her *pingit* ('confinement' in Javanese), when girls from 12 to 16 are kept in virtual imprisonment and forbidden to venture outside the family home. She later used her education to campaign for women's rights and against colonialism, before dying at the age of 24 just after the birth of her first child. A national holiday is held on 21 April, known as Kartini Day, in recognition of her work.

Sleeping

Hotel Jepara Indah HOTEL $$

(☎0291-593548; Jl Cokeoaminoto 12; standard/deluxe from 350,000/395,000Rp; ❄📶) A four-storey concrete-tower hotel with modern, tiled rooms that are a bit dark due to tinted windows. Deluxe rooms are better updated. Walls are scuffed and tile is chipped here and there, but the digs are still reasonably clean.

Bayfront Villa INN $$

(☎0821 3634 6151; www.hoteljeparabayfront.com; standard/deluxe 750,000/850,000Rp) This laid-back inn on a clean, narrow stretch of beach offers a handful of homely, not fancy, rooms with creative paintjobs. All open onto a common terrace upstairs or pool deck downstairs. That pool is lovely, as is the little bar on the beach.

Ocean View Residence HOTEL, APARTMENTS $$

(☎0291-429 9022; www.oceanview-residence.com; standard/deluxe 770,000/875,000Rp; ❄📶🏊) Down a narrow lane that zigzags through rice fields, this beachside resort is a mash-up of modernist units with a party-people vibe. Standard rooms are quite simple and overpriced. Deluxe rooms are imaginatively desgined with full kitchens, ocean views and cool art on the wall.

Around the pool are ample lounges – and a thumping sound system – overlooking the scruffy beachfront.

Eating

Jepara is noted for its wonderful *soto ayam*. If you love chicken soup, you can find it in warung all around town.

Pondok Rasa INDONESIAN $
(☎0291-591025; Jl Pahlawan II; mains 15,000-65,000Rp; ✎) Inland, just across the river from the *alun-alun*, Rasa is a traditional Javanese restaurant with a pleasant garden setting and tasty Indonesian food served *lesahan* style. There's lots of choice for vegetarians.

★**Yam-Yam** INTERNATIONAL $$
(☎0291-598755; Jl Pantai Karang Kebagusan, Km5; mains from 25,000-78,000Rp; ⏲11am-10pm) There's no topping this stylish beachfront restaurant in Jepara, where candlelit wood tables are scattered around a pool that overlooks the bay. The thatched brick-house kitchen turns out solid Thai food, as well as grilled fish, steaks and chicken, big salads and a lot more.

Shopping

Intricately carved *jati* (teak) and mahogany furniture and relief panels are on display at shops and factories all around Jepara. However, the main carpentry centre is the village of Tahunan, 4km south of Jepara on the road to Kudus, where it's wall-to-wall furniture.

Brightly coloured, Sumba-style ikat weavings, using traditional motifs, are woven and sold in the village of Torso, situated 14km south of Jepara and 2km off the main road. Other original designs are also produced here. Unusual for Java, men predominantly do the weaving.

Pecangaan, 18km south of Jepara, produces rings, bracelets and other jewellery from *monel* (a stainless-steel alloy).

Information

Tourist Office (☎0291-591493; www.gojepara.com; Jl AR Hakim 51; ⏲8am-4pm Mon-Thu, 7-11am Fri) In the western part of town; has very helpful staff and runs a particularly informative website.

Getting There & Around

Frequent buses make the trip from Jepara to Kudus (15,000Rp, 1¼ hours) and Semarang (15,000Rp to 30,000Rp, 2½ hours). A few buses also go to Surabaya, but Kudus has more connections.

Becak are cheap and the best way to get around. From the terminal, about 1km west of the town centre, 10,000Rp will get you anywhere in town, including the Kartini harbour for boats to Karimunjawa.

Around Jepara

Sights

Mantingan MOSQUE
FREE The mosque and tomb of Ratu Kali Nyamat, the great warrior-queen, are in Mantingan, 4km south of Jepara. Kali Nyamat twice laid siege to Portugal's Melaka stronghold in the latter part of the 16th century. The mosque, dating back to 1549, was restored some years ago and the tomb lies to the side of it. It's noted for its Hindu-style embellishments and medallions.

Angkudes (minibuses) depart from the Jepara bus terminal, and can drop you outside the mosque for 3000Rp.

Pantai Bandengan BEACH
Jepara has some fine white-sand beaches. Pantai Bandengan (aka Tirta Samudra), 7km northeast of town, is one of the best beaches on the north coast – an arc of gently shelving white sand. The main public section can get littered, but just a short walk away the sand is clean, the water clear and the swimming safe. It's beautiful at sunset. To get here, take a bemo (minibus; 3000Rp) from Jl Pattimura in Jepara.

On weekdays you may have to charter a whole bemo (around 35,000Rp).

Karimunjawa Islands

☎0297 / POP 8700

The dazzling offshore archipelago of Karimunjawa, a marine national park, consists of 27 coral-fringed islands – only five of which are inhabited – that lie about 90km north of Jepara. The white-sand beaches are sublime, swimming is wonderful and the pace of life as relaxed as a destination defined by coconut palms and turquoise seas should be.

Holidaying Indonesians account for most of the visitors here, though Western travellers are starting to be seduced by the islands, too.

The main island, **Pulau Karimunjawa**, a lush mountainous beauty, is home to most of the archipelago's facilities and the majority of the islanders, most of whom are

THE PLASTIC PROBLEM

The idyllic island of Karimunjawa, 90km from Java and set in the middle of tempestuous seas, is blessed with spectacular, empty beaches and offshore islets that were once the absolute archetype of wild tropical beauty. They would be still if not for all the plastic refuse that washes up day and night from the open ocean. But Karimunjawa is by no means the only Java destination with a massive plastic garbage problem.

You can wander every street, *gang* and path in all of Java and rarely be far from a piece of plastic discarded thoughtlessly. Most of it is the single-use variety: water bottles (less recyclable than you think), plastic bags, thin plastic packaging and straws. But what makes Karimunjawa's plastic issue more troubling is that it isn't self-generated. Almost all of the litter is coming from Java's cities, directed here by the prevailing winds and tides. Thanks largely to inadequate waste management and lack of individual awareness, the plastic keeps coming and coming. Worse, the stuff that washes up onshore and ruins otherwise perfect beaches (and selfies) is actually a blessing. If it stays in the ocean, it accumulates an array of toxins and breaks down into microscopic, plankton-like bits, which get nibbled by fish, which get gobbled by other fish, which are eaten by people. That's how single-use plastic enters the food chain. The plastic that doesn't get digested will never disappear. It sinks to the bottom of the sea, or gets carried by depth currents around the world. This is why plastic has been found in deep sea sediment all over the world, including Arctic ice cores. In a world ensnared by a thousand and one ecological and social issues, single-use plastic is arguably our biggest plague.

So what to do? Kick the single-use plastic habit. Straws are for suckers. Don't use them, and pre-emptively refuse them in bars and restaurants. Avoid plastic bags. Better to bring your own reusable one and pay attention to what you buy. If it comes wrapped in single-use plastic, do without. Most of all, carry a stainless steel water bottle with you when you travel, in Indonesia or anywhere else. You don't want to drink water that has been sitting in warm plastic for days or weeks. Plus you'll find that every restaurant, warung, hotel and guesthouse will fill it up for free from their larger, reusable mineral water bottle. Because many Indonesians understand the problem very well. They live with it, and will be pleased that you are choosing to be part of the solution.

Javanese, though there are also some Bugis and Madurese families who live off fishing, tourism and seaweed cultivation. This island is also home to the archipelago's only real town, Karimunjawa, and despite widespread mangroves, a couple of good beaches.

So close to Java, yet so way out, Karimunjawa is the kind of place where a stray cow as big as a buffalo will wander onto a ragged soccer pitch to graze, where afternoon naps are sacrosanct, and where wind and weather can keep you delightfully stranded. And that is a wonderful thing.

The archipelago is divided into zones to protect the rich ecosystem. Zone One is completely out of bounds to all except national park rangers, with other areas set aside for sustainable tourism.

Access has improved recently, though during the rainy season boats don't always run. Flights tend to take off as scheduled, though they are also prone to cancellation in rough weather. An airstrip is located on adjacent Pulau Kemujan.

Sights & Activities

Pulau Karimunjawa is a delight to explore by bike. Most of the shoreline is fringed with mangroves. The best two stretches of sandy beach are **Batu Topeng** (2000Rp), and **Pantai Tanjung Gelam** (2000Rp entrance), both accessible from a concrete spit, 7km north of the main village. From that small road two tracks break off. The one closest to the main road leads to Batu Topeng. Pantai Tanjung Gelam has a more beautiful white-sand beach with a handful of warungs set up beneath tarps. Here, the turquoise bathwater stretches out to deeper blue. Even when the wind is blowing, it's often still on this side of the island as it's sheltered by Karimunjawa's mountainous spine. There's good snorkelling here, too. Both of these beaches are relatively devoid of plastic trash, which inundates the island's other beaches, thanks to the local villagers who keep it clean.

Park rangers can help you organise a hike up Pulau Karimunjawa's 600m peak,

Gunung Gendero. Ask about it at your guesthouse. In the far north of the island there's a network of walkways and platforms that allow you to explore the extensive mangroves that fringe Pulau Karimunjawa and neighbouring Pulau Kemujan.

Boat trips to other islands are an excellent day out; chartering a boat costs 400,000Rp to 500,000Rp per day, or hotel owners can often hook you up with tour groups to save costs. The uninhabited islands of Menjangan Besar and Menjangan Kecil both have sweeping white sands and decent snorkelling, and are within easy reach of Karimunjawa town.

Further out, Pulau Menyawakan is the site of Karimunjawa's only major resort. Pulau Nyamuk, Pulau Parang, Pulau Bengkoang and Pulau Genting are all home to small, traditional communities. The reefs around many of these islands offer decent snorkelling, and if the wind is still, the visibility clarifies and offers decent diving – though experienced divers will note that it's slightly pricier here than elsewhere in Indonesia. **Coconut Dive** (☎0813 9267 8888; www.satu-dunia.com; Jl Sutomo; two tanks 900,000Rp) is the best outfit in town. Its most popular dive site centres on a 100-year-old Norwegian wreck that plunges to 25m. You'll pay a surcharge if you are the only diver of the day.

As a marine park, many parts of Karimunjawa – including Pulau Burung and Pulau Geleang, home to nesting sea eagles – are officially off limits (though this protected status is unfortunately not always strictly enforced).

The islands can experience violent weather between December and February, and winds can kick up a fuss and the seas at anytime. If they do, flights and boat trips can be disrupted, though flights tend to function on schedule most of the time. Bottom line, if you are concerned about being stranded, it's better to fly.

Sleeping & Eating

The main village of Karimunjawa has a handful of simple homestays. There's very little difference among them, and most share set prices at 100,000 to 150,000Rp per person per night for a fan-cooled room and shared bathroom.

Book all accommodation well in advance, particularly if you're staying over on a Saturday night or during peak holiday times. Many hotels offer package deals that include transport from Jepara or Semarang.

The best choice for dinner is the **night market** (meals 50,000Rp; ⏲6-9pm) on the *alun-alun* in the centre of town. You'll find over a dozen stalls offering tasty *ikan bakar* (grilled fish), grilled corn, fried bananas, fresh juice and more. Place your order, then sit *lesahan* style on a mat on the grass field to tuck in.

Coconut House GUESTHOUSE **$**
(☎0297-414431, 0813 9267 8888; www.satu-dunia.com; Jl Sutomo; r 140,000-170,000Rp) The backpacker crash pad of choice when we visited, it's a village homestay with personality. Doors are made of reclaimed wood, there's a funky Ganesha mural, and rooms are clean and tiled with canopied beds, pastel paintjobs and wood furnishings. They all share bathrooms, as well as beanbags and a hammock swing on the common porch. There's an attached dive shop.

Puri Karimun HOMESTAY **$**
(☎0813 2645 9910; www.purikarimun.wordpress.com; r with fan/aircon 200,000/250,000Rp) A village homestay with modern, well-presented rooms with en-suite bathrooms. The red and lime paintjob stands out against the green mountain backdrop, and there's plenty of wood tables in the garden courtyard where you can chat with other guests and help yourself to complimentary tea and coffee.

Hotel Escape HOTEL **$$**
(☎0813 2574 8481; www.escapekarimun.com; Jl Danang Joyo; r from 300,000Rp; ❄📶) Rooms are clean, tiled numbers set in a roomy two-storey brick lodge close to town. There's no sandy beach here, rather the water washes up to a concrete ledge abutting a wide lawn shaded by coconut palms. Good Indonesian and Western food is available in the restaurant. It's a five-minute walk to the right of the main dock.

Karimunjannah GUESTHOUSE **$$**
(☎0822 2758 8961, 0877 1796 3238; www.karimunjannah.com; r 350,000Rp; 📶) A terrific choice for spacious, tiled rooms with mosaic bathrooms, high ceilings, flat-screens and wood furnishings. It has a small restaurant and plans for a beach bar, too. It's simple but very sweet.

Ayu Hotel BUNGALOW **$$**
(www.ayuhotel.com; r 444,000Rp; 📶) A nice German-Indo spot on the beach side of the main island road. Rooms are set in lovely hexagonal wooden cottages and a cozy stone lodge (the price is the same either way). Once

a week it does a massive Javanese feast (per person 75,000Rp to 100,000Rp) with curries, seafood, chicken and noodle dishes; seats are available for non-guests, too.

It also has basic rooms on offer at its village homestay (222,000Rp). Check in for both is located at the main property. No matter which class you choose, book well ahead via the website.

Coco Huts BUNGALOW **$$**
(☎0823 3719 7736; www.cocohuts-karimunjawa.com; r with fan 250,000Rp, bungalows 500,000-550,000Rp) Stilted up on a ridge and blessed with commanding views, these well-done rooms are more cottages than huts. It's owned by a well-known German footballer-turned-commentator who was born to missionary parents in Indonesia; profits from the inn fund his family's missionary activity.

★ **Breve Azurine** BOUTIQUE HOTEL **$$$**
(☎0821 7881 5657; www.breveazurine.com; r incl breakfast US$125-290; ⏱closed Jan-Mar) If you want to be reminded of Karimunjawa's considerable majesty every morning, afternoon and night, this is the spot for you. Set on the lip of a turquoise lagoon sheltered by a reef and blessed with a private beach and two more virgin beaches beyond, this boutique resort offers a choice of lodging – all of it tasteful.

You can grab a rustic cottage, outfitted with wonderfully weathered ceramic tile floors and wood furnishings, stone walls, and canopied beds. Or enjoy a split-level family cottage designed in much the same way. All offer panoramic views of mountain and sea that will chill you out quickly and keep you calm long after you leave.

Or you can book into the main lodge: a dark-wood jaw-dropper with an open common living room and pool table downstairs, and a wrap-around deck leading to a jetty that extends over the shallows. The massive suite upstairs overlooks 180 degrees of lagoon and open sea. The bar is kitschy-cute, and while the kitchen isn't fabulous, it's still good, the beer is cold and the cocktails are terrific. Management organises island-hopping, hiking and diving excursions and will gladly book all your transport too. There are free kayaks on offer, and the snorkelling out front is shallow yet sublime.

Kura Kura Resort RESORT **$$$**
(☎Semarang 024-7663 2510; www.kurakuraresort.com; Pulau Menyawakan; cottage/pool villa incl 2 meals US$210-510; ⏱closed Nov-Mar; ❄📶🏊) A luxury tropical-island escape situated on its own private island, with gorgeous seaview cottages and wonderful villas with private pools. There's about 800m of fine white sand, a restaurant (the menu includes lots of Italian dishes) and water-sports facilities. Most guests arrive by the resort's plane (US$150 each way from Semarang); supplements may be charged if planes are not full.

Cafe Amore INTERNATIONAL **$**
(meals 18,000-50,000Rp; @📶) A lovely spot set among reconstructed wooden *joglo* fronting the marina just outside village on road to main dock. Mains wander from pasta, chicken breast and steak dinners to Indo classics and seafood. It even grills lobster upon request. More importantly, it serves good coffee and cold beer.

ℹ Information

The small **tourist information booth** (☎085 325 0673, 0297-312253) at the harbour, by the dock, is usually open to greet boats. The Semarang tourist office (p149) can also help out with practicalities.

Karimunjawa has a post office, and there's wi-fi at Cafe Amore. There's a BRI ATM in the village that takes MasterCard, but it can run out of money, so bring ample cash. Electricity is spotty; many places use generators at night.

ℹ Getting There & Away

It is now possible to reach Karimunjawa by air from both Semarang (310,000Rp, 45 minutes) and Surabaya (420,000Rp, one hour) every Thursday and Friday with **Susi Air** (☎0800 122 7874; fly.susiair.com). Planes are tiny and seat just 12, so book ahead. The flight itself can be an adventure. But if winds are calm, it's a magical ride.

Karimunjawa's boat connections are improving every year, and there are links from both Semarang and Jepara. Check all schedules with the Semarang tourist office, which can also book tickets and make reservations.

At research time, from Jepara's Kartini harbour, the *Express Bahari* boat (executive class/VIP 150,000/175,000Rp, two hours) sailed to Karimunjawa on Mondays at 7am, Tuesdays and Fridays at 9am, and Saturdays at 10am, returning on Mondays at 1pm, Tuesdays at 10.30am, Saturdays at 8am and Sundays at 2pm. The *Siginjai* (economy/VIP 70,000/100,000Rp) sails from Jepara on Monday, Wednesday and Saturday at 7am, but takes four to six hours.

The *Kartini I* sails direct from Semarang at 9am on Mondays and Saturdays, returning on Wednesdays and Sundays at 1pm (business/executive class 140,000/160,000Rp, four hours). It also has departures on Thursdays and Fridays, when it sails via Jepara, which adds considerable time to the journey. From Jepara business/executive class is 70,000/85,000Rp.

Be warned, economy tickets will put you below deck in often choppy seas, where seasickness is more common than not, which is never pleasant.

As with lodging, it's vital to book transport well ahead of your trip, especially on weekends and during high season.

Getting Around

From Pulau Karimunjawa it costs 400,000Rp to 500,000Rp to charter a wooden boat for a day trip to the outer islands or 100,000Rp for the short hop to Pulau Menjangan Besar and Kecil. There are very infrequent *angkot* operating on the islands and *ojek* will do short trips for 20,000Rp. Hiring a moped (60,000Rp per day) is a superb way to get around the main island's 22km of rutted roads.

EAST JAVA

The least densely populated of Java's provinces, East Java (Jawa Timur) is a wild, rolling region with dizzying peaks, smoking volcanoes and unspoilt panoramas. While the regional capital, Surabaya, has all the accoutrements of a booming Indonesian city, including freeways, multiplexes and a trademark traffic problem, there are far more attractive bases. Malang is a civilised city with a temperate climate ringed by some fascinating Hindu temples. Blitar has more temples and a historic site or two to explore, and Banyuwangi, linked to Bali by a 24-hour ferry service, makes a decent launch pad to two exquisite national parks and one spectacular volcanic plateau.

For most visitors, East Java is all about the raw, rugged appeal of its volcano-studded scenery and awesome landscapes. Nowhere is more synonymous with this than the sublime Bromo-Tengger Massif region, incorporating the volcanic peaks of Gunung Bromo (2392m) and Gunung Semeru (3676m) – Java's highest mountain. The Bromo area and its puffing giants is an undisputed highlight, but the Ijen Plateau ranks very close, with a stunning crater lake, evocative coffee-plantation econcomy, good hiking and fewer travellers.

Baluran National Park is the most accessible of Java's wildlife reserves, but the southern route through East Java is the most scenic and has two great national parks: Meru Betiri, which protects a virgin beach where turtles nest; and Alas Purwo, which is hallowed among surfers for its gigantic reef breaks at G-Land. Just off the coast near Surabaya is the island of Madura, a place where traditions are particularly strong and famous bull races, known as *kerapan sapi*, are staged between August and October.

Surabaya

031 / POP 2.8 MILLION

Your initial impressions are not going to be great. A polluted, congested, business-driven city, Surabaya is not ideal for visitors. Just crossing the eight-lane highways that rampage through the centre is a challenge in itself. Attractions are slim on the ground, and against the calm of rural East Java, it is pandemonium writ large.

And yet if you've the patience to explore, Surabaya has quixotic little corners of interest. Its historic Arab quarter is fascinating: a labyrinthine warren of lanes leading to a historic mosque that's a place of pilgrimage. Surabaya also has one of Indonesia's biggest Chinatowns and a roster of impressive, though disintegrating, Dutch buildings.

For most foreign visitors, the city is merely a place to change planes, trains or buses. For locals, however, Surabaya is closely linked to the birth of the Indonesian nation, as it was here that the battle for independence began. To them, Surabaya is Kota Pahlawan (City of Heroes), and statues commemorating independence are scattered all over the city.

Sights

Old City

Even though much of Surabaya's historic centre is literally falling to pieces, the old city easily wins the Most Attractive Neighbourhood prize. With crumbling Dutch architecture – including the stunning old **governor's residence**, which was getting a major makeover when we came through – a souk-like Arab quarter and strong Chinese influences, it's by far the most atmospheric part of Surabaya to explore.

From the old city you can head north to the Kalimas harbour, where brightly painted *pinisi* (Makassar or Bugis schooners) from Sulawesi and Kalimantan unload their wares.

East Java

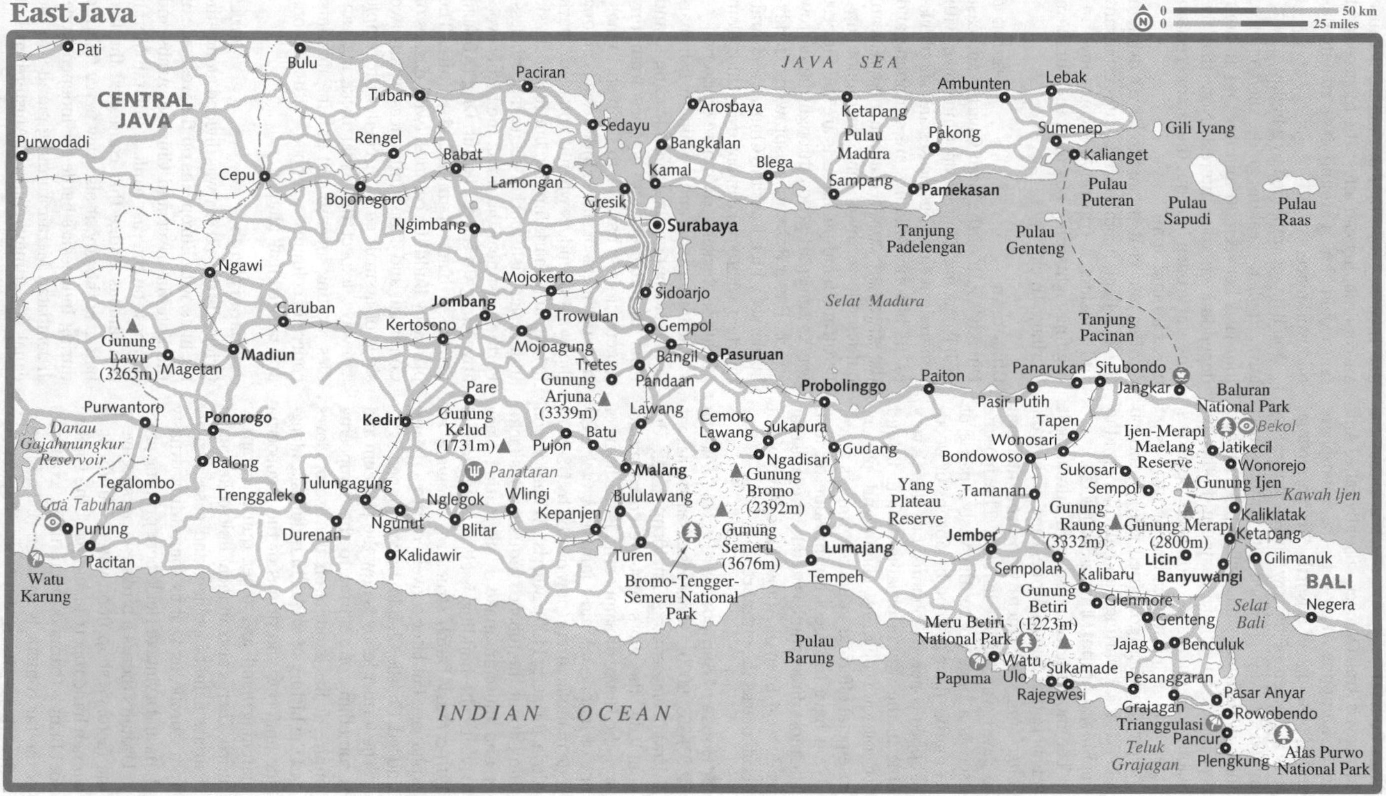

0 — 50 km
0 — 25 miles

JAVA SEA
Selat Madura
INDIAN OCEAN
Selat Bali
Teluk Grajagan

CENTRAL JAVA
BALI

Pati
Purwodadi
Bulu
Cepu
Tuban
Paciran
Rengel
Bojonegoro
Babat
Lamongan
Sedayu
Gresik
Ngimbang
Ngawi
Caruban
Madiun
Magetan
Gunung Lawu (3265m)
Kertosono
Jombang
Mojokerto
Mojoagung
Trowulan
Sidoarjo
Surabaya
Kamal
Bangkalan
Arosbaya
Blega
Sampang
Pulau Madura
Ketapang
Pakong
Pamekasan
Ambunten
Lebak
Sumenep
Kalianget
Gili Iyang
Pulau Sapudi
Pulau Raas
Pulau Puteran
Pulau Genteng
Tanjung Padelengan
Tanjung Pacinan
Gempol
Bangil
Pasuruan
Pandaan
Tretes
Gunung Arjuna (3339m)
Lawang
Cemoro Lawang
Sukapura
Ngadisari
Gunung Bromo (2392m)
Gunung Semeru (3676m)
Bromo-Tengger-Semeru National Park
Probolinggo
Gudang
Paiton
Pasir Putih
Panarukan
Situbondo
Jangkar
Baluran National Park
Bekol
Tapen
Wonosari
Bondowoso
Sukosari
Sempol
Ijen-Merapi Maelang Reserve
Jatikecil
Wonorejo
Gunung Ijen
Kawah Ijen
Gunung Merapi (2800m)
Gunung Raung (3332m)
Kaliklatak
Ketapang
Gilimanuk
Negera
Licin
Banyuwangi
Glenmore
Kalibaru
Genteng
Benculuk
Jajag
Pesanggaran
Grajagan
Pasar Anyar
Rowobendo
Trianggulasi
Pancur
Plengkung
Alas Purwo National Park
Sukamade
Rajegwesi
Gunung Betiri (1223m)
Meru Betiri National Park
Watu Ulo
Papuma
Sempolan
Jember
Tamanan
Yang Plateau Reserve
Lumajang
Tempeh
Pulau Barung
Turen
Bululawang
Malang
Batu
Pujon
Kepanjen
Panataran
Wlingi
Blitar
Nglegok
Gunung Kelud (1731m)
Pare
Kediri
Kalidawir
Ngunut
Tulungagung
Durenan
Trenggalek
Tegalombo
Ponorogo
Balong
Purwantoro
Danau Gajahmungkur Reservoir
Punung
Pacitan
Gua Tabuhan
Watu Karung

Arab Quarter NEIGHBOURHOOD

Surabaya's Arab Quarter – usually called Ampel or Kampung Arab – has the atmosphere and appearance of a North African medina. It is a warren of narrow lanes, marked by arched gateways crowned with Arabic script, and crowded with stalls selling prayer beads, *peci* (black Muslim felt hats) and other religious paraphernalia, alongside perfumes, dates and a plastic camel or two. *Nasi goreng kembing* (goat fried rice), is the top seller at local warungs, and all alleys lead to the **Mesjid Ampel** (Jl Ampel Suci) FREE.

The most sacred mosque in Surabaya, it was here that Sunan Ampel (one of the *wali songo* (nine holy men) who brought Islam to Java) was buried in 1481. The mosque itself is a huge space, the vast expanse of its marble floor divided by dozens of wood-wrapped concrete columns, but there's very little in the way of ornamentation. Behind the mosque pilgrims chant and present rose-petal offerings at Sunan Ampel's grave.

You have to access the mosque on foot. The most direct route is to take the lane that leads west from Jl Ampel Suci. A crowd of becak marks the entrance.

★**House of Sampoerna** MUSEUM

(☎031-353 9000; www.houseofsampoerna.com; Jl Taman Sampoerna; ⏲9am-10pm) FREE Undoubtedly the city's best-presented attraction, the House of Sampoerna is the home of one of Indonesia's most famous *kretek* cigarette manufacturers (now owned by US-giant Altria, formerly Philip Morris). Whatever you think about the tobacco industry, this factory and museum make a fascinating place to visit. The building itself is a wonderful 19th-century Dutch structure, originally an orphanage but later converted into a theatre (indeed, Charlie Chaplin once dropped by).

The former lobby is now the museum and is something of a shrine to the Sampoerna empire. It has exhibits on the use of cloves and the history of *kretek* in Indonesia, alongside uniforms and drums of the Sampoerna marching band and other quirky company curios. There's also an incredible collection of cigarette lighters, holders and cases, mainly from Europe, as well as some Ming dynasty china and a vintage Heidelberg printing press.

Upstairs there's a bird's-eye perspective of the factory's shop floor, where hundreds of women hand roll, trim and pack the Dji Sam Soe brand (banned from most countries as the tar content is so strong). The fastest rollers here churn out 4000 cigarettes a day, their fingers a blur of motion. Because air-conditioning can affect the tobacco (and fans would blow it around) it's a steamy, humid workplace.

You'll be accompanied by a highly informative, English-speaking guide; the complete tour lasts between 30 minutes and an hour depending on your interest. Note that the museum is open late, but the factory section closes around 3pm.

After your visit, be sure to have a drink in the excellent neighbouring cafe-restaurant and consider a trip on the company's intriguing sightseeing bus tour, the Surabaya Heritage Track.

Chinatown NEIGHBOURHOOD

Directly south of the Arab Quarter and east of Jl Panggung is Surabaya's Chinatown, with hundreds of small businesses and shophouses. Its historic buildings are crumbling and the streets are crowded and none-too-clean, but it's still worthy of some good photo ops. Becak and hand-pulled carts are still the best way to transport goods through the narrow streets. **Pasar Pabean** is a sprawling, darkly-lit market which links the Chinese and Arab quarters, where you can buy everything from Madurese chickens to Chinese crockery.

Each afternoon and evening a fish market breaks out on the streets leading to and from the market, with species from tiny fingernail-sized baitfish, to shellfish, to massive specimens of shark. Indonesia is among the worst offenders when it comes to shark fishing and shark finning, but it is a classic Indonesian fish market scene, nonetheless. Further east near the canal, the highly evocative **Kong Co Kong Tik Cun Ong** (Jl Dukuh) delivers a blast of unflitered culture. The primarily Buddhist complex (with dashes of Confucian and Taoist influences) spans two sides of a small *gang*, arched with temple gateways. Expect the usual flickering candles, wafting incense and praying pilgrims, concrete columns wrapped with dragons and latticed teak altars.

Jembatan Merah BRIDGE

Originally the old city was divided along ethnic lines, with Europeans on the west side of the Kali Mas river and Chinese, Arabs and Javanese on the east bank. Jembatan Merah is a famous bridge that connected the two halves of the city; it also saw fierce fighting during Indonesia's battle for independence. Jl Jembatan Merah, running parallel to the canal, is a grungy replica of Amsterdam, but worthy (although run-down) examples of Dutch architecture can be seen here.

Another impressive structure is the Indo-European–style **Gedung PTP XXII** (Jl Merak Cendrawasih) government office building.

Other Areas

Masjid al Akbar MOSQUE

(Jl Masjid Al Akbar Timur I) FREE Perhaps the most impressive modern mosque in Indonesia – you'll probably get a glimpse of Masjid al Akbar's magnificent array of bulbous turquoise-tiled domes as you exit the city. Staff are happy to show visitors around and will accompany you up the elevator to the top of the free-standing ottoman-style minaret, which offers spectacular views.

Take any bus heading for the main bus terminal, ask for the mosque and you'll be dropped off on Jl Ahmad Yani, a kilometre from the building. From here you can walk through quiet residential streets or take a becak. A taxi from central Surabaya is around 55,000Rp.

Monumen Kapal Selam SUBMARINE

(Jl Pemuda; admission 10,000Rp; 9am-9pm) Surabaya's foremost stretch of renovated waterside real estate centres on the iron hulk that is *Pasopati*, a Russian submarine commissioned into the Indonesian navy in 1962. You can poke around the interior, peek through the periscope and even climb into the torpedo tubes. It's in a small landscaped park among a couple of cafes popular with young smoochers.

Sleeping

Surabaya has a real dearth of good budget places: standards are low and poor-value rooms and disinterested staff tend to be the norm. This is another place in Java where you should consider blowing your budget and treating yourself.

Midrange accommodation options have improved greatly in recent years due to fierce competition. There are some excellent deals available in the luxury hotel sector, with rooms starting at US$50 for four-star hotels.

Sparkling Backpacker Hotel HOSTEL $

(031-532 1388; www.sparklingbackpacker.com; Jl Kayun 2A; r incl breakfast with shared/private bathrooms 125,000/235,000Rp;) 'Sparkling' is far too optimistic, but this hostel-style place is well located in the heart of the city, within a short walk of malls, restaurants and the river. Still, cleanliness could be better and the layout isn't great; many rooms lack a bathroom and the only shared one is located on the ground floor.

Hotel Paviljoen HOTEL $

(031-534 3449; Jl Genteng Besar 94-98; r with fan/air-con from 150,000/198,000-220,000Rp;) A respite from Surabaya's manic streets, this venerable colonial villa still has a twinkle of charm and grandeur. Rooms are basic and spartan but they are clean and have some lovely touches too, including Mediterranean-style shuttered windows. The location could not be better. Pay the extra rate for the bigger room.

Citihub HOTEL $$

(031-535 7066, 031-502 9292; www.citihubhotels.com; Jl Gub Suryo IJ; r 375,000Rp;) Right in the heart of the city, almost opposite the Tunjungan Plaza mall, this bright, inviting business hotel is a superb place to stay if you value your home comforts and don't mind compact living quarters. All rooms have luxury bedding, hip decor, a large LCD TV and wi-fi.

You have to leave a cash deposit of 200,000Rp and rent towels (5000Rp). There are five other Citihub hotels within the Surabaya city limits; check the website for details.

Ibis Rajawali HOTEL $$

(031-353 9994; www.ibishotel.com; Jl Rajawali 9-11; r from 392,000Rp;) Rajawali is a fine choice if you're looking to stay in the north of town. The entire place, from the reception to the rooms, is modern and businesslike, and there's a small gym and a spa. Some upper-floor rooms have views of the Suramadu Bridge.

Hotel 88 HOTEL $$

(031-534 9988; www.hotel88.co.id; Jl Kenongo 11; superior/deluxe 395,000/425,000Rp;) A modern new-build spot on a street getting transformed into a string of Indonesian style McMansions, with malls and monuments a short walk away. Rooms aren't magical but they are clean, with high ceilings, queen beds and flat-screens. Superior rooms don't have windows.

Mercure HOTEL $$

(031-562 3000; www.mercure.com; Jl Raya Darmo 68-78; r from 490,000Rp;) An excellent choice, this large hotel has first-class facilities, including an idyllic palm-fringed pool area.

Surabaya

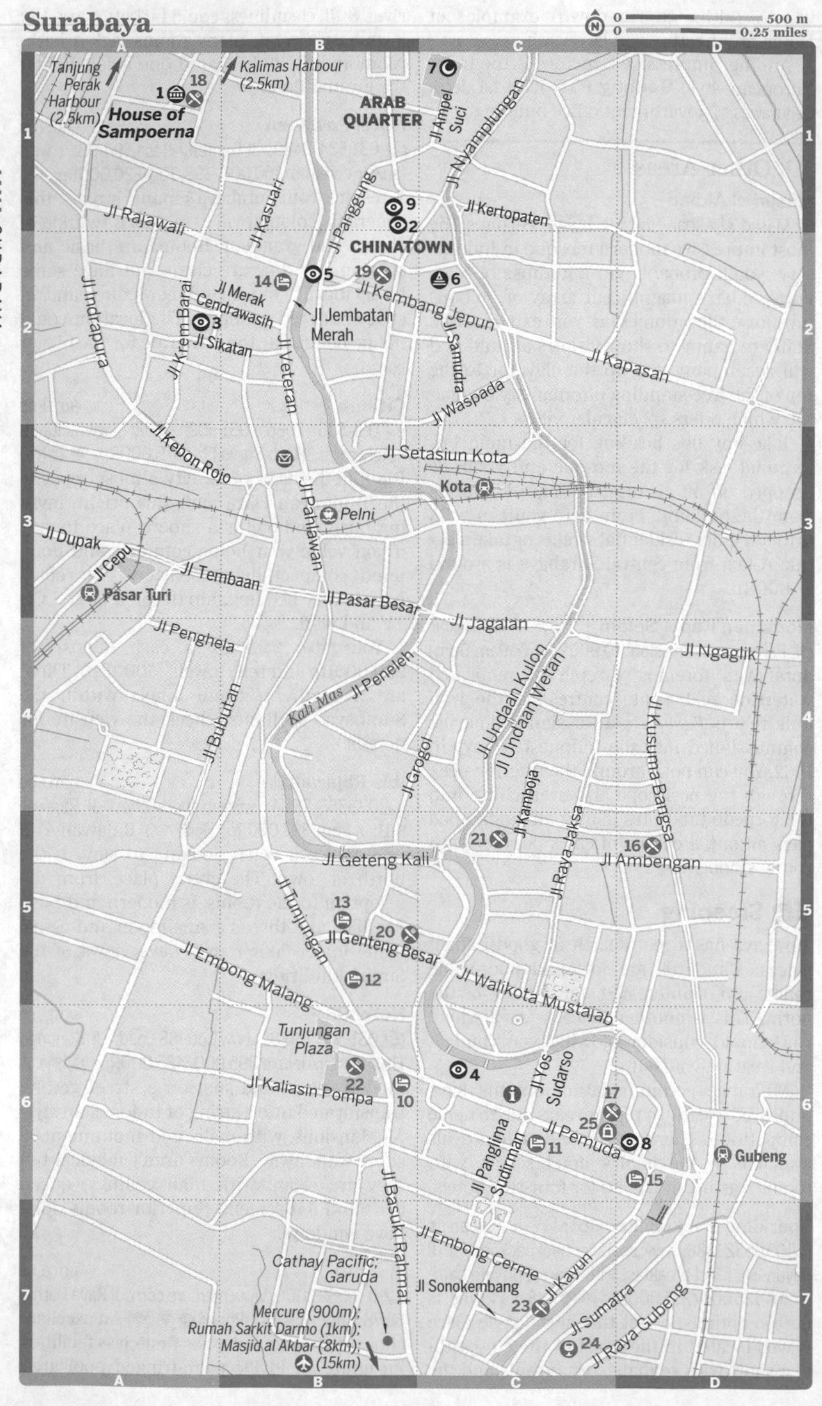
0 500 m
0 0.25 miles
Tanjung Perak Harbour (2.5km)
Kalimas Harbour (2.5km)
House of Sampoerna
ARAB QUARTER
CHINATOWN
Jl Ampel Suci
Jl Nyamplungan
Jl Panggung
Jl Kasuari
Jl Rajawali
Jl Kertopaten
Jl Indrapura
Jl Merak Cendrawasih
Jl Jembatan Merah
Jl Kembang Jepun
Jl Krem Barat
Jl Sikatan
Jl Veteran
Jl Samudra
Jl Kapasan
Jl Waspada
Jl Kebon Rojo
Jl Setasiun Kota
Kota
Pelni
Jl Pahlawan
Jl Dupak
Jl Cepu
Jl Tembaan
Pasar Turi
Jl Pasar Besar
Jl Jagalan
Jl Penghela
Jl Ngaglik
Kali Mas
Jl Peneleh
Jl Undaan Kulon
Jl Undaan Wetan
Jl Bubutan
Jl Kusuma Bangsa
Jl Grogol
Jl Kamboja
Jl Raya Jaksa
Jl Geteng Kali
Jl Ambengan
Jl Tunjungan
Jl Genteng Besar
Jl Embong Malang
Jl Walikota Mustajab
Tunjungan Plaza
Jl Kaliasin Pompa
Jl Yos Sudarso
Jl Pemuda
Jl Panglima Sudirman
Gubeng
Jl Basuki Rahmat
Jl Embong Cerme
Cathay Pacific; Garuda
Jl Sonokembang
Jl Kayun
Jl Sumatra
Jl Raya Gubeng
Mercure (900m); Rumah Sarkit Darmo (1km); Masjid al Akbar (8km); (15km)

Surabaya

Top Sights
1 House of Sampoerna A1

Sights
2 Chinatown B1
3 Gedung PTP XXII A2
4 Governor's Residence C6
5 Jembatan Merah B2
6 Kong Co Kong Tik Cun Ong Temple C2
7 Mesjid Ampel C1
8 Monumen Kapal Selam D6
9 Pasar Pabean B1

Sleeping
10 Citihub B6
11 Hotel 88 .... C6
12 Hotel Majapahit Surabaya B5
13 Hotel Paviljoen B5
14 Ibis Rajawali B2
15 Sparkling Backpacker Hotel D6

Eating
16 Ahimsa Vegan Lounge D5
17 Food Stalls C6
18 House of Sampoerna Café A1
19 Kya Kya B2
20 Pasar Genteng B5
21 Soto Ambengan Pak Sadi Asli C5
22 Tunjungan Plaza B6
23 Warungs C7

Drinking & Nightlife
24 Colors C7

Entertainment
Tunjungan 21 .... (see 22)

Shopping
25 Plaza Surabaya C6

There's also a decent gym and a reasonably priced spa. Rooms are modern, spacious and good value, though the cheaper options lack wow factor. Staff are efficient and helpful.

Artotel HOTEL **$$$**
(031-568 9000; www.artotelindonesia.com; Jl Dr Soetomo 79–81; r from 810,000Rp;) This aggressively artsy brand combines modern architecture and art into a somewhat loud but certainly original ambience that includes groovy public spaces and small but comfortable rooms with murals for headboards.

Hotel Majapahit Surabaya HISTORIC HOTEL **$$$**
(031-545 4333; www.hotel-majapahit.com; Jl Tunjungan 65; r from 1,480,000Rp;) A memorable place to stay, this landmark colonial hotel exudes class and heritage, with colonnaded courtyards, fountains, verdant greenery and a gorgeous pool area (though as it's located on a busy road, some background traffic noise bleeds into the scene). Rooms, some with private terraces overlooking the gardens, are beautifully presented and boast all modern facilities.

Staff are extremely helpful and capable, and the restaurant is one of the best in the city.

Bumi Surabaya HOTEL **$$$**
(031-531 1234; www.bumisurabaya.com; Jl Basuki Rahmat 106-128; r from 1,742,000Rp;) A self-styled 'city resort', this former Hyatt is one of Surabaya's best sleeps. Rooms are plush and spacious with all the modern convenience you'd expect in a four-star hotel. The breakfast buffet will sate you until dinner.

Eating

You won't be left hungry in Surabaya – the city has a huge array of eating options. Local dishes include *rawon*, a thick, black beef soup that tastes better than it sounds.

For cheap eats, **Pasar Genteng** (Jl Genteng Besar; mains 8000Rp; 9am-9pm) has good night warungs. Late-night munchies can also be had at the offshoot of Jl Pemuda, opposite the **Plaza Surabaya**, which buzzes with **food-stall** (mains 10,000-20,000Rp) activity around the clock, or among the strip of **warungs** (mains 10,000-20,000Rp) with their backs to the river along Jl Kayun.

In the old city, the once-throbbing Chinese night market, **Kya Kya** (Jl Kembang Jepun; mains 12,000-30,000Rp; 6-11pm), is now far less popular, though there are still a few food stalls here.

For an air-conditioned setting, **Tunjungan Plaza** (Jl Tunjungan; mains 35,000-60,000Rp) has a colossal selection of squeaky-clean Asian and Western restaurants and cafes; the food court is on the 5th floor.

Ahimsa Vegan Lounge VEGETARIAN **$**
(031-535 0466; Jl Kusuma Bangsa 80; dishes 10,000-25,000Rp; 8am-10pm;) An elegant, upmarket vegetarian restaurant owned by

a welcoming Indo-Chinese family, with delicious rice dishes (try *nasi hainan*, a mixed rice platter), salads and soups, including a vegetarian *bakso*. No MSG is used, which is nice. As for the muzak...

Soto Ambengan Pak Sadi Asli INDONESIAN $
(☎031-532 3998; Jl Ambengan 3A; soup 24,000Rp; ⏲8am-10pm) This dimly lit dive, filled with locals, is the original location of a chain of *soto ayam* warungs with several branches across Surabaya. Short on noodles, long on shredded chicken, the broth brims with oil and turmeric. Drop in a dollop and a half of the fine sambal and you'll feel nourished and satisfied.

House of Sampoerna Café INTERNATIONAL, INDONESIAN $$
(☎031-353 9000; Jl Taman Sampoerna; mains 30,000-82,000Rp; wi-fi) This cafe is adjacent to the House of Sampoerna museum and occupies a gorgeous colonial structure complete with stained-glass windows and classy seating – a memorable spot for a meal. The menu is divided into East and West, with classic Indonesian-style nasi goreng and Singapore *laksa*, along with New Zealand steaks and fish and chips.

There are great desserts, espresso and a full bar, including cocktails and cognac.

★**La Rucola** ITALIAN $$$
(☎031-567 8557; www.larucola.asia; Jl Soetomo 51; mains 70,000-220,000Rp; ⏲10.30am-11.30pm) A delightful Italian bistro serving upmarket Surabaya with authentic wood-fired pizzas and calzones topped and stuffed with bresaola, Italian sausage, oyster mushrooms, beef tenderloin, shrimp and more. It also does a range of perfectly grilled seafood and Australian steaks for an affordable price. The wine-by-the-glass selection is thin, but the bottle list is quite good.

Drinking & Nightlife

There are very few bars in Surabaya and the city does not have much of a drinking culture, though if you look hard enough you can find cold beer and live music.

Colors PUB
(☎031-503 0562; Jl Sumatra 81) Popular with expats, this large upmarket pub-club has live music and a DJ every night. There's a full bar and drinks are expensive. It doesn't get going until after 9pm.

Entertainment

Cinema complexes are found all around the city.

Tunjungan 21 CINEMA
(www.21cineplex.com; Jl Tunjungan, Tunjungan Plaza) This large cinema complex shows recent Hollywood releases in English and has good sound quality.

Information

Jl Pemuda has plenty of banks, as does Tunjungan Plaza. All hotels, most restaurants and each shopping mall, including Tunjungan Plaza, have wi-fi.

East Java Regional Tourist Office (☎031-853 1822; Jl Wisata Menanggal; ⏲7am-2pm Mon-Fri) About 3km south of the centre; has a few brochures on the province.

Main Post Office (Jl Kebon Rojo; ⏲8am-2pm Mon-Sat) Inconveniently located 4km north of the city centre.

Rumah Sakit Darmo (☎031-567 6253; www.rsdarmo.co.id; Jl Raya Darmo 90) Hospital with English- and Dutch-speaking doctors.

Tourist Information Centre (☎031-534 0444; Jl Pemuda; ⏲8am-8pm) Has helpful English-speaking staff, and can offer plenty of leaflets, a map of the city and also a file with good details about backpacker accommodation.

Getting There & Away

AIR

Surabaya Juanda airport is Indonesia's third busiest and is used by more than 20 airlines. There are international connections to cities in Asia and numerous domestic flights.

AirAsia (☎021-2927 0999; www.airasia.com) Flies to Bangkok and the Malaysian cities of Johor Bahru, Kuala Lumpur and Penang. Domestic routes include Bandung, Denpasar and Medan.

Cathay Pacific (☎080 4188 8888; www.cathaypacific.com; Jl Basuki Rachmat 122) Flies daily to/from Hong Kong.

Citilink (☎080 4108 0808; www.citilink.co.id) Flies to Balikpapan, Banjarmasin, Denpasar, Jakarta and Makassar, among other cities.

Garuda (☎031-546 8505; www.garuda-indonesia.com; Jl Basuki Rahmat 106-128) Connections to over a dozen Indonesian cities, including Bandung, Denpasar, Yogyakarta, Jakarta and Makassar.

Lion Air (☎031-503 6111; www.lionair.co.id; Jl Sulawesi 75) Lion and its sister airline, Wings, offer flights to Ambon, Balikpapan, Bandung, Banjarmasin, Batam, Denpasar, Jakarta, Kendari, Kupang, Makassar, Manado, Palangkaraya, Tarakan and Yogyakarta.

Sriwijaya Air (☎021-2927 9777; www.sriwijayaair.co.id) Flies to Balikpapan, Makassar, Manado, Semarang and Yogyakarta.

BOAT

Surabaya is an important port and a major transport hub for ships to the other islands. Boats depart from Tanjung Perak harbour; bus P1 from outside Tunjungan Plaza heads here. Pelni ships sail to Makassar in Sulawesi roughly twice a week (economy/1st class from 389,00/965,000Rp), Pontianak in Kalimantan (333,000/614,000Rp) about every 10 days, and Jakarta (243,000/1,500,000Rp) weekly. Head to the **Pelni ticket office** (☎031-352 1044; www.pelni.co.id; Jl Pahlawan 112) for more information.

BUS

Surabaya's main bus terminal, called **Purabaya** (or Bungurasih), is 13km south of the city centre. It's reasonably well organised and computer monitors display bus departure times; however, watch out for pickpockets. Crowded Damri city buses run between the bus terminal and the Jl Tunjungan/Jl Pemuda intersection in the city centre. A metered taxi costs around 70,000Rp.

Buses from Purabaya head to points all over Java, Madura and Bali. Most buses on long-distance routes, such as to Solo, Yogyakarta, Bandung and Denpasar, are night buses that leave in the late afternoon or evening. Bookings can be made at Purabaya bus terminal and travel agencies in the city centre (expect a mark-up). The most convenient bus agents are those on Jl Basuki Rahmat.

All buses heading south of Surabaya on the toll road get caught up in heavy traffic around the Gembol junction, thanks to the snarl-up around the mud volcano. During rush hour this can add an hour to your journey.

MINIBUS

Door-to-door *travel* minibuses are not normally a good way of travelling from Surabaya. The city is so big that you can spend two hours just collecting passengers from their hotels and homes before you even get started. Destinations and sample fares include Malang (85,000Rp), Solo (130,000Rp), Yogyakarta (140,000Rp) and Semarang (150,000Rp to 160,000Rp). **Cipa Ganti** (☎031-546 0302; www.cipaganti.co.id) is a recommended company, or you can try the agencies along Jl Basuki Rahmat.

TRAIN

From Jakarta, trains taking the fast northern route via Semarang arrive at the **Pasar Turi train station** (☎031-534 5014) southwest of Kota train station. Trains taking the southern route via Yogyakarta, and trains from Banyuwangi, arrive at **Gubeng train station** (☎031-503 3115) and most carry on through to Kota. Gubeng train station is much more central and sells tickets for all trains. There are only very infrequent, very slow economy-class trains to Malang.

TRANSPORT FROM SURABAYA

Bus

DESTINATION	FARE (RP; ECONOMY/AIR-CON)	DURATION (HR)	FREQUENCY
Banyuwangi	35,000/52,000	7	2 daily
Kudus	51,000/66,000	8	2 daily
Malang	9000/14,5000	2-3	6 daily
Probolinggo	10,000/16,100	2½	almost hourly
Semarang	57,000/95,000	9	3 daily
Solo	42,000/75,000	7½	3 daily
Sumenep	20,000/32,500	4½	2 daily

Train

DESTINATION	FARE (RP)	DURATION (HR)	FREQUENCY
Banyuwangi	130,000	7	2 daily
Probolinggo	70,000	2	2 daily
Semarang	155,000–340,000	4	5 daily
Solo	135,000–285,000	3½-4	6 daily
Yogyakarta	125,000–260,000	5	4 daily

Getting Around

TO/FROM THE AIRPORT

Taxis from Juanda airport (17km) operate on a coupon system and cost around 160,000Rp to/from the city centre including toll road fees. There are also regular Damri buses (20,000Rp) from the airport to Purabaya bus terminal, and then on to the city centre.

BUS

Surabaya has an extensive city bus network, with normal buses (2000Rp) and *patas* (express) buses (3000Rp per journey). Watch out for pickpockets, as buses can be crowded. One of the most useful services is the *patas* P1 bus, which runs from Purabaya bus terminal into the city along Jl Basuki Rahmat. In the reverse direction, catch it on Jl Tunjungan.

TAXI

Surabaya has air-conditioned metered taxis. Flag fall is 4000Rp to 6000Rp; reckon on around 25,000Rp for a trip of around 4km. **Blue Bird taxis** (☎031-372 1234) are the most reliable and can be called in advance. They will also make long-haul trips to Malang and beyond.

Trowulan

Trowulan was once the capital of the largest Hindu empire in Indonesian history. Founded by Singosari prince Wijaya in 1294, it reached the height of its power under Hayam Wuruk (1350–89), who was guided by his powerful prime minister, Gajah Mada. During this time Majapahit received tribute from most of the regions encompassing present-day Indonesia and even parts of the Malay Peninsula.

Its wealth was based on its control of the spice trade and the fertile rice-growing plains of Java. The religion was a hybrid of Hinduism – with worship of the deities Shiva, Vishnu and Brahma – and Buddhism, but Islam was tolerated, and Koranic burial inscriptions found on the site suggest that Javanese Muslims resided within the royal court. The empire came to a catastrophic end in 1478 when the city fell to the north-coast power of Demak, forcing the Majapahit elite to flee to Bali and opening Java up to the Muslim conquest.

Sir Thomas Stamford Raffles, the great British explorer and governor general of Java, rediscovered Trowulan in 1815, and though it was choked in forest, described the ruins as 'this pride of Java'.

The remains of the court are scattered over a large area around the village of Trowulan, 12km from Mojokerto. The Majapahit temples were mainly built from red-clay bricks that quickly crumbled. Many have been rebuilt and are relatively simple compared to the glories of structures such as Borobudur, but they do give a good idea of what was once a great city. As the temples are spread over a such a large area, it's best to either hire a becak or come in a car.

One kilometre from the main Surabaya–Solo road, the impressive **Trowulan Museum** (admission 10,000Rp; ⏲7am-3.30pm Tue-Sun) houses superb examples of Majapahit sculpture and pottery from East Java. Pride of place is held by the splendid statue of Kediri's King Airlangga as Vishnu astride a huge Garuda, taken from Belahan. The museum should be your first port of call for an understanding of Trowulan and Majapahit history, and it includes descriptions of the other ancient ruins in East Java.

Some of the most interesting ruins include the gateway of Bajang Ratu, with its strikingly sculpted *kala* heads; the Tikus Temple (Queen's Bath – used for ritual bathing and cleansing); and the 13.7m-high Wringinlawang Gate. The Pendopo Agung is an open-air pavilion built by the Indonesian army. Two kilometres south of the pavilion, the Troloyo cemetery is the site of some of the oldest Muslim graves found in Java, the earliest dating from AD 1376.

Trowulan is refreshingly hawker-free, though as there's a distinct lack of information on site you may want to hire a freelance guide (there's often one waiting at the museum). Expect to pay around 100,000Rp for a half-day.

Getting There & Away

Trowulan can be visited as a day trip from Surabaya, 60km to the northeast. From Surabaya's Purabaya bus terminal, take a Jombang bus (12,000Rp, 1½ hours), which can drop you at the turn-off to the museum; a becak tour of the sites will cost around 50,000Rp for a half-day excursion after bargaining.

Pulau Madura

POP 3.6 MILLION

The flat, rugged and deeply traditional island of Madura may now be connected to Java by Indonesia's longest bridge, but the character of the people and scenery feel like somewhere far away in time and geography.

Traditional culture is strong, the sarong and *peci* are the norm and the people are deeply Islamic – virtually all children attend *pesantren* (religious schools). Most famous for the colourful pageantry of their popular annual bull races, Madurese have a reputation throughout the nation for their quick tempers and brusqueness – perhaps an offshoot of their popular virility drink, *jamu madura*. While the Madurese can be disconcertingly blunt at times, they are more often extremely humble and hospitable.

Madura's southern side is lined with shallow beaches and cultivated lowland, while the northern coast alternates between rocky cliffs and great rolling sand-dune beaches, the best of which is at Lombang. At the extreme east is a tidal marsh and vast tracts of salt around Kalianget. The interior is riddled with limestone slopes, and is either rocky or sandy, so agriculture is limited. Sumenep is the only town, and unless the bull races are on, it attracts but a trickle of tourists.

History

In 1624 the island was conquered by Sultan Agung of Mataram and its government united under one Madurese princely line, the Cakraningrats. Until the middle of the 18th century the Cakraningrat family fiercely opposed Central Javanese rule and harassed Mataram, often conquering large parts of the kingdom.

By the beginning of the 1700s, however, the Dutch had secured control of the eastern half of Madura. The Cakraningrats then agreed to help the Dutch put down the 1740 rebellion in Central Java, but in the end they fared little better than their Javanese counterparts and ceded full sovereignty to the Dutch in 1743.

Under the Dutch, Madura was initially important as a major source of colonial troops, but later it became the main supplier of salt to the archipelago.

Overpopulation and poverty in Madura during the 1960s and 1970s lead to a policy of *transmigrasi* as millions of Madurese were resettled across the nation. Today, the diaspora is one of Indonesia's largest, and you'll find communities of (often staunchly traditional) Madurese in Kalimantan, Papua and Sumatra.

ℹ Getting There & Away

Buses go directly from Surabaya's Purabaya bus terminal via Bangkalan and Pamekasan through to Sumenep (normal/*patas* 20,000/32,000Rp, four hours) roughly every hour. Buses also run to Sumenep (passing through Surabaya) from Banyuwangi (via Probolinggo), Malang, Semarang and Jakarta.

From East Java there's a daily **ferry** (☎032-866 3054) from Jangkar harbour (near Asembagus) to Kalianget (60,000Rp, five to six hours) in Madura. At research time it departed at Jangkar at 1pm and from Kalianget at 8am. Schedules are weather-dependent and change regularly; contact the Sumenep tourist office (p168) to check times. Buses run from Situbondo to Jangkar. To get to Kalianget take minibus 'O' (3000Rp, 20 minutes) from Sumenep.

ℹ Getting Around

From Bangkalan, buses run along the main highway to Pamekasan (26,000Rp, 2½ hours) and Sumenep (30,000Rp, four hours). Minibuses also travel along the northern route to Arosbaya, Tanjung Bumi, Pasongsongan and Ambunten.

Madura's roads are almost all paved and in excellent condition, with relatively little traffic. As the island is mostly flat, Madura is a good cycling destination, although it does get very hot.

South Coast

The first port of call for most visitors is Kamal, a scruffy place of little interest. Many head directly to Bangkalan, the next town north of Kamal, to watch the bull races. If you've time to kill before a race, **Museum Cakraningrat** (10,000Rp; ⏲8am-2pm Mon-Sat) will entertain you for an hour or so with displays on Madurese history and culture. For a day trip you could do worse than head to the beach at Sambilangan, 7km south of town, where there's a lonely 90m lighthouse that gazes out over the Madura strait.

Sampang, 61km from Bangkalan, also stages bull races and is the centre of the regency of the same name. Further east is the important town of Pamekasan, the island's capital. Bull races are held in and around Pamekasan every Sunday from the end of July until early October; during October each year the city throbs with the festivities of the *kerapan sapi* grand final. About 35km east of Pamekasan, before Bluto, is Karduluk, a woodcarving centre.

Sumenep

☎0328 / POP 101,000

Compared with the rest of Madura, Sumenep, in the far east of the island, is a sleepy, refined town, with a Mediterranean air and quiet, lazy streets. By mid-afternoon the whole town seems to settle into a slow, collective siesta. With dozens of crumbling villas and a fine *kraton* and mosque, it is easily Madura's most interesting town.

Sights

Kraton PALACE

(6000Rp; ⏲7am-2pm Mon-Sat) Occupied by the present *bupati* (regent) of Sumenep, the grand *kraton* and its **Taman Sari** (Pleasure Garden; admission 2000Rp; ⏲7am-5pm) date back to 1750. The bathing pools once used by the royal women are still here, though they're no longer in use. There's also a small museum with an interesting collection of Madurese furniture, stone sculptures and *binggel* (heavy silver anklets worn by Madurese women). All were possessions of Madurese royals once upon a time.

The complex can only be visited on a guided tour arranged at the Royal Carriage-House Museum. On the first Sunday of the month, traditional dance or gamelan practice is held at the *kraton* (from 10am to 1pm; free).

Royal Carriage-House Museum MUSEUM

(admission 2000Rp included in Taman Sari entry; ⏲7am-5pm) Opposite the *kraton*, the Royal Carriage-House Museum contains the throne of Queen Tirtonegoro and a Chinese-style bed, which is reputedly 300 years old.

Asta Tinggi Cemetery CEMETERY

The tombs of the royal family are at the Asta Tinggi Cemetery, which looks out over the town from a peaceful hilltop 4km northwest of the centre. The main royal tombs are decorated with carved and painted panels; two depict dragons said to represent the colonial invasion of Sumenep.

Mesjid Jamik MOSQUE

FREE Sumenep's 18th-century Mesjid Jamik is notable for its three-tiered Meru-style roof, Chinese porcelain tiles and ceramics.

Festivals & Events

The Festival of Sumenep is usually celebrated biannually on 31 October and marks the founding of the town, with a program of cultural performances.

Sleeping & Eating

There are plenty of good, inexpensive eateries. Be sure to order the local speciality *sate kambing* (goat satay), which is often served with raw shallots and rice cakes. *Soto madura*, a spicy soup with nuts, lemongrass and beef, is another speciality. Good places to try these dishes include **Rumah Makan Kartini** (☎0328-662431; Jl Diponegoro 83; mains 12,000-20,000Rp) and **Rumah Makan 17 Agustus** (☎0328-662255; Jl Sudirman 34; mains from 10,000Rp).

Hotel C-1 HOTEL $

(☎0328-674368; www.hotelc1.net; Jl Sultan Abdurrahman; r 125,000-400,000Rp; ❄📶) The smartest place in town, this modern hotel has a good selection of simple rooms decorated with hand-carved wooden furniture. Cleanliness standards are good, mattresses are springy and the linen is fresh. It's about 2km southeast of the centre.

Entertainment

Bull Races BULL RACING

Sumenep is a centre for champion bull breeding, and on most Saturday mornings bull races can be seen at the Giling stadium. While the races are popular, it's worth looking into the animal welfare issues associated with this spectacle before opting in.

Shopping

The main businesses in town are antiques and batik, and many homes seem to have something for sale. In the market, **Rachma Batik** has good-quality gear and fair prices.

Information

Sumenep's **tourist office** (☎081 7933 0648, 0328-667148; kurniadi@consultant.com; Jl Sutomo 5; ⏲7am-3.30pm Mon-Fri) is run by enthusiastic and knowledegable staff, who can help out with most matters relating to both Sumenep and the island. **BCA** (⏲8am-4pm Mon-Sat) and **BNI banks** (⏲8am-4pm Mon-Sat) are on Jl Trunojoyo; both change cash. There's free wi-fi around the *alun-alun*.

Getting There & Away

Sumenep's main bus terminal is on the southern side of town, a 10,000Rp becak ride from the centre. Buses leave roughly hourly until 4pm for Surabaya's Purabaya bus terminal (normal/*patas* 20,000/32,000Rp, four hours) and big cities across Java, including Malang. Bus agents along Jl Trunojoyo sell tickets. The Giling bus

Sumenep

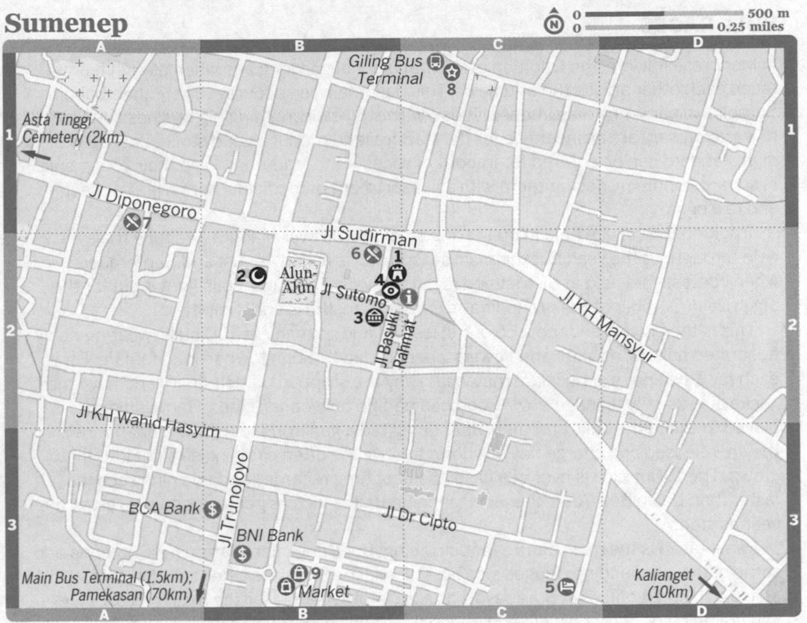

Sumenep

Sights

1 Kraton........B2
2 Mesjid Jamik........B2
3 Royal Carriage-House Museum........B2
4 Taman Sari........B2

Sleeping

5 Hotel C-1........C3

Eating

6 Rumah Makan 17 Agustus........B2
7 Rumah Makan Kartini........A1

Entertainment

8 Bull Races........C1

Shopping

9 Rachma Batik........B3

terminal for *angkot* heading north is right near the stadium, a short walk or becak ride from the centre. From Giling, minibuses go to Lombang, Slopeng, Ambunten and other north-coast destinations.

Around Sumenep

From Sumenep, the road to Kalianget, 10km southeast, passes many fine villas. About halfway between the two towns are the ruins of a Dutch fort dating from 1785, and a cemetery.

The Kalianget region is a centre for salt production – you'll see great mounds of the white powder piled up for export if you pass by in the dry season. Daily boats sail from here for Jangkar in East Java and to other islands in the Sumenep district.

You can go snorkelling at Pulau Talango, just offshore.

Malang

0341 / POP 820,000

With leafy, colonial-era boulevards and a breezy climate, Malang moves at a far more leisurely pace than the regional capital, Surabaya. It's a cultured city with several important universities, home to a large student population. The central area is not too large and quite walkable.

Established by the Dutch in the closing decades of the 18th century, Malang earned its first fortunes from coffee, which flourished on the surrounding hillsides. Today, the city's colonial grandeur is quickly

BULL RACES

In Madurese folklore, the tradition of *kerapan sapi* began long ago when plough teams raced each other across the arid fields. This pastime was encouraged by Panembahan Sumolo, an early king of Sumenep. Today, with stud-bull breeding big business on Madura, *kerapan sapi* are an incentive for the Madurese to produce good stock. Only bulls of a high standard can be entered for important races – the Madurese keep their young bulls in superb condition, dosing them with an assortment of medicinal herbs, honey, beer and raw eggs.

Traditional races are held in bull-racing stadiums all over Madura. Practice trials are held throughout the year, but the main season starts in late August and September, when contests are held at district and regency levels. The finest bulls fight it out for the big prize in October at the grand final in Pamekasan, the island's capital.

This is the biggest and most colourful festival and as many as 100 bulls, wearing richly decorated halters, ribbons and flowers, are paraded through town to loud fanfare. For each race, two pairs of bulls are matched. They are stripped of their finery and have their 'jockeys' – usually teenage boys – perched behind on wooden sleds. Gamelan music is played to excite the bulls and then, after being fed a generous tot of *arak* (palm wine), they're released and charge flat-out down the track – often plunging straight into the crowd. The 100m race is over in a flash: the best time recorded so far is nine seconds, faster than Usain Bolt. After the elimination heats the victors get to spend the rest of the year as studs.

Pamekasan is the main centre for bull racing, but Bangkalan, Sampang, Sumenep and some of the surrounding villages also host races. The East Java calendar of events, available from tourist offices in Surabaya, has a general schedule for the main races, but if you are on Madura over a weekend during the main season, you can be guaranteed that races or practices will be held somewhere on the island.

Do note that animal welfare, to put it mildly, is not among Indonesia's major public concerns, and despite their luxuriant diet, the bulls are often treated harshly if they lose, and during training sessions.

disappearing behind the homogenous facades of more modern developments, but there's still much to admire for now.

And with a number of Hindu temples and sights outside the city, Malang makes an ideal base to explore this intriguing corner of East Java.

Sights

The interior of the busy *alun-alun* in front of Hotel Tugu Malang is a lovely and lively park, with a monument at the centre of a pond floating with hundreds of lotus blossoms and surrounded by gorgeous spreading trees.

Across the main Surabaya road from the downtown area, the hazy, mystical and imposing silhouette of Mt Semeru looms over the wide avenue that is Jl Semeru. Gotta love symmetry.

If you have any compassion for animal welfare, Pasar Senggol, the bird and animal market, is best avoided.

Hotel Tugu Malang MUSEUM

(www.tuguhotels.com/malang; Jl Tugu III; wi-fi) Malang's most impressive museum isn't actually a museum at all, but a hotel: the boutique, four-star Hotel Tugu Malang (p172). A showcase for its owner, arguably Indonesia's foremost collector of Asian art and antiquities, the exhibit includes 10th-century ceramics, jade carvings from the 13th century, Ming dynasty porcelain, Qing dynasty woodcarvings and even the complete facade of a Chinese temple. Visitors are welcome to browse the collection, which is spread throughout the hotel premises (though you might consider it polite to buy a drink while you're here).

Jl Besar Ijen NEIGHBOURHOOD

Malang has some wonderful colonial architecture. Just northwest of the centre, Jl Besar Ijen is Malang's millionaires' row, a boulevard lined with elegant whitewashed mansions from the Dutch era. Many have been substantially renovated, but there's still much to admire. In late May, the area is closed to traffic and becomes the setting for the city's huge Malang Kembali festival.

Balai Kota NOTABLE BUILDING

(Town Hall; Jl Tugu) Close to the city centre, the Balai Kota is an immense Dutch administrative building, built in a hybrid of Dutch and Indonesian architectural styles with a tiered central roof that resembles a Javanese mosque.

Pasar Bunga MARKET

(7am-5pm) The flower market, Pasar Bunga, is pleasantly sited around a river valley and is the place to stroll in the morning.

Activities

Nuansa Fajar MASSAGE

(0341-324531; Jl Kahuripan 11A; massage per hour 50,000Rp, hotel visit per hour 60,000Rp; 5.30am-10pm) For a great massage (and to support the local community) head to Nuansa Fajar, a training centre that employs blind masseurs. Shiatsu, reflexology and traditional Javanese massages are offered.

Tours

Malang is a good place to set up a tour to Bromo; these are usually on the route via Tumpang. Costs very much depend on numbers and transport, but two/three/four people can expect to pay about 750,000/650,000/500,000Rp per person for a sunrise tour in a 4WD (they usually leave at 1.30am). Options to continue the trip on to Ijen and then Ketapang harbour (for Bali) are also popular.

Trips to southern beaches and temples around Malang are also possible. If you want to create your own itinerary, a day's car hire (with driver) starts at around 600,000Rp.

Helios Tours TOUR

(0341-362741; www.heliostour.net; Jl Pattimura 37) A well-organised operator with an incredible number of tour options, from standard day trips to Bromo to hard-core trekking expeditions to Gunung Semeru. Staff are switched-on and deal with lots of travellers.

Jona's Homestay TOUR

(0341-324678; Jl Sutomo 4) The owners of this homestay can organise tours to Bromo and around Malang; they also rent scooters to guests.

Festivals & Events

Malang Kembali CULTURAL

Held in late May, Malang Kembali celebrates *ludruk*, an old-time music hall tradition that was very popular in Java in the last century. Jl Besar Ijen, home to many wonderful old Dutch villas, is closed to traffic for five days and there's street theatre, live music, shows, and actors in period costumes. You can also taste traditional food and drinks.

Sleeping

Jona's Homestay HOMESTAY $

(0341-324678; Jl Sutomo 4; s/d with fan 115,000/130,000Rp, d with air-con from 230,000Rp;) This long-running homestay in a colossal colonial villa, with a digital ticker out front, is run by a sweet family that looks after guests well and offers tours. The location is convenient and quiet, though the rooms have aged somewhat. Some of the air-con options are huge and great value.

Kampong Tourist HOSTEL $

(0341-345797; www.kampongtourist.com; Hotel Helios, Jl Patimura 37; dm/r 120,000/160,000Rp;) The owners of this superb backpacking place have fashioned an excellent hostel on the rooftop of Hotel Helios. Most of the buildings have been beautifully constructed from bamboo and timber, and sprout like village huts from the concrete rooftop. Dorm beds are comfy, as are the gazebo-style private rooms, and there's a great shared shower block and a guest's kitchen, too.

You can tour the town and then socialise in the bar-cafe, with commanding city views, cold beer and snacks into the night. The hostel is solar powered.

Hotel Emma HOTEL $

(0341-363198; Jl Trunijoyo 21; r with fan and cold water 150,000-175,000Rp, with air-con and hot water 215,000-250,000Rp;) Almost opposite the train station, this is a friendly hotel. Cleanliness is taken seriously, rooms are spacious – the deluxe rooms are enormous – and good value. Many rooms have windows that open onto the interior of the building and these can feel claustrophobic. Breakfast included.

Hotel Helios HOTEL $$

(0341-362741; www.hotelhelios-malang.com; Jl Pattimura 37; r with fan/air-con 200,000Rp/312,000Rp;) Helios has steadily upgraded the quality and prices of its accommodation in recent years. Behind the flash reception you'll find a selection of bright, clean, comfortable rooms, most with flat-screen TVs, high ceilings, and modern bathrooms grouped around a rear garden (and cafe). The economy options are tiny and very spartan. Helios Tours is based here.

Malang

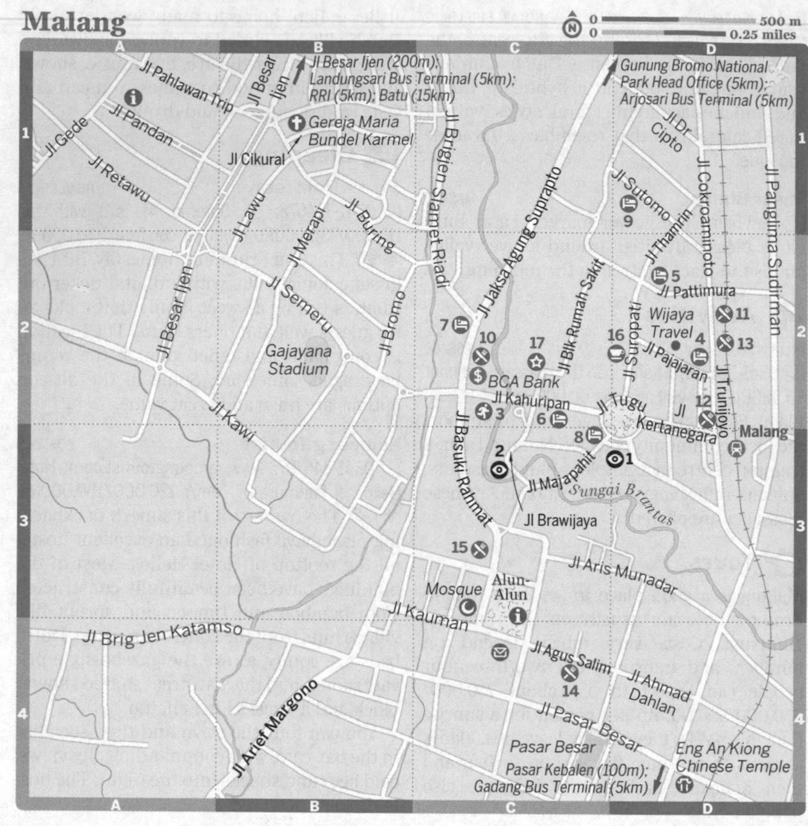

Hotel Sahid Montana HOTEL **$$**
(☎0341-362751; sahidmontana.com; Jl Kahuripan 9; r 320,000Rp) A tiled, three-star indoor-outdoor inn, serving mostly domestic tourists. Rooms are set on three floors around a garden gurgling with fountains. It's a decent choice, popular with tour groups.

Hotel Trio Indah II HOTEL **$$**
(☎0341-359083; www.hoteltrio2.com; Jl Brigjen Slamet Riadi 1-3; r 375,000-475,000Rp; ❄@☎) This hotel's great arched frontage resembles a Victorian railway terminal. It has 37 clean if unexceptional rooms, all with TV and air-con. There's room service and a cafe.

★**Hotel Tugu Malang** BOUTIQUE HOTEL **$$$**
(☎0341-363891; www.tuguhotels.com; Jl Tugu III; r from 900,000Rp; ❄@☎) For a real flavour of what Java has to offer, this remarkable luxury hotel, loaded with local character and genuine hospitality, sets the standard. It manages to be both laid-back and elegant. Owned by one of the foremost collectors of Indonesian and East Asian antiquities in the country, it doubles as a museum.

Room after room is filled with antiques and priceless artefacts, but that infusion of class and old-world history feels effortless rather than stodgy, mostly because the rooms are so inviting. With thick teak floors, platform king-sized beds, elegant bathrooms, high ceilings and wall-length desks, it's the type of nest that would make the perfect lovers' hideaway. The spa, wine bar and wonderful restaurant don't hurt. There's a reason global royalty have stayed here.

Eating & Drinking

For cheap eats head for Jl Agus Salim, which comes alive at night to the sights and smells of Malang's **night market** (mains 10,000-25,000Rp). Local specialities are *nasi rawon*

Malang

Sights

1 Balai Kota D3
Hotel Tugu Malang .... (see 8)
2 Pasar Bunga C3

Activities, Courses & Tours

Helios Tours .... (see 5)
Jona's Homestay .... (see 9)
3 Nuansa Fajar C2

Sleeping

4 Hotel Emma D2
5 Hotel Helios D2
6 Hotel Sahid Montana C2
7 Hotel Trio Indah II C2
8 Hotel Tugu Malang C3
9 Jona's Homestay D1
Kampong Tourist .... (see 5)

Eating

10 Agung C2
11 Goreng Kremes D2
12 Kertanegara D2
Melati .... (see 8)
13 Mie Tomcat D2
14 Night Food Market C4
15 Toko Oen C3

Drinking & Nightlife

16 Ben House D2

Entertainment

17 Taman Rekreasi Senaputra C2

(beef soup served with fried onion and rice) and *bakso malang* (meatball soup served with noodles and grilled fish), and are always worth a try.

Mie Tomcat NOODLES **$**
(Jl Trunijoyo; dishes 6000-9000Rp; 9am-11pm) A cool new designer warung popular with locals, with a Jenga-like exterior and cherry-wood furnishings inside and out. The staff speak no English but they do know how to make some tasty noodle soup, ramen and *mie goreng* (fried noodles). Use the helpful chalkboard spice-meter to stretch your personal heat index.

Goreng Kremes INDONESIAN **$**
(Jl Cokroaminoto 2d; dishes 5000-20,000Rp; 10am-10pm) A dressed-up warung dangling with lovely rattan lanterns and lined with bamboo wallpaper, serving fried chicken and duck meals to the Malang masses. Platters come with raw cabbage and long beans on the side. Rice costs extra.

Agung INDONESIAN **$**
(0341-357061; Jl Basuki Rahmat 80; mains 12,000-18,000Rp) This stylish spot has tasty, inexpensive local food including *martabak* (meat, egg and vegetable pancake-like dish), rice and fish dishes, plus great juices.

Toko Oen INTERNATIONAL **$**
(0341-364052; Jl Basuki Rahmat 5; mains 28,000-67,000Rp; 8am-9:30pm) Boasting an imposing art deco frontage that dates from 1930, Toko Oen is a throwback to ye olde days, with rattan furniture, waiters in starched whites, and Sinatra on the stereo. It serves middling Indonesian fare and cheap steaks, but it's the ice cream that, for some reason, is renowned among Indonesians. Don't expect much. It's all about the atmosphere here.

Kertanegara INDONESIAN **$$**
(0341-704 4141; www.kertanegararesto.com; Jl Kertanegara I; mains 20,000-80,000Rp; noon-11pm;) Occupying a large corner plot, this upmarket place has a great garden terrace, strung with oh-so-many Christmas lights. It serves flavoursome European, Indonesian and Chinese food with quite a good choice for vegetarians, and lots of seafood.

★ **Melati** INDONESIAN, INTERNATIONAL **$$**
(0341-363891; www.tuguhotels.com; Jl Tugu III; mains 40,000-120,000Rp;) The Tugu hotel's poolside restaurant is a romantic, atmospheric setting for a meal, with a relaxed air and attentive staff to guide you through the delicious Indonesian and Chinese Peranakan options. Several mixed rice dishes stand out. You can get a Malang version that comes with vegies stewed in coconut milk, marinated beef and died chicken. Or choose one with turmeric pickles and chicken in coconut cumin sauce. It also does a damn fine *rijstaffel* (selection of Indonesian dishes served with rice). Western mains include pasta and grilled meats, and are also excellent. The wine list rocks, and there's good whiskey behind the bar.

Ben House CAFE
(Jl Suropati 19; ⏲4pm-2am; 📶) A key nightspot for young hipsters, this brickhouse cafe has a great feel. The downstairs interior is decorated with low-rise wood tables and bench seating, funky vintage bicycles and musical instruments. The chalkboard menu offers cold beer, fresh juices, coffee and tea, and there's an inviting, alfresco upper deck.

☆ Entertainment

Taman Rekreasi Senaputra PERFORMING ARTS
(Jl Brawijaya; admission 7000Rp, children 13yr & under 6000Rp) Malang's cultural and recreational park has a swimming pool and children's playground and some quirky events. *Kuda lumping* (horse trance) dances (7000Rp) are performed every Sunday morning at 10am. The dancers ride rattan 'horses' then fall into a trance, writhing around on the ground with their eyes bulging. Still in a trance-like state they perform assorted masochistic acts without any apparent harm, such as eating glass. The bizarre spectacle will not be to everyone's taste.

On a more sober note, *wayang kulit* shows are regularly held here (usually on the fourth Sunday of the month); the tourist office has the latest schedule.

RRI PERFORMING ARTS
(☎0341-387500; Jl Candi Panggung) About 5km northwest of the city, this place has *wayang kulit* from 9pm on the first Saturday of the month.

ℹ Information

Malang has plenty of banks; most are congregated along Jl Basuki Rahmat, including **BCA** (⏲8am-4pm Mon-Sat). Wi-fi is available free at all area guesthouses and hotels, and most restaurants and cafes.

Gunung Bromo National Park Head Office (☎0341-490885; tn-bromo@malang.wasantara.net.id; Jl Raden Intan 6; ⏲8am-3pm Mon-Thu, to 11am Fri) For Bromo info.

Main Post Office (Jl Kauman Merdeka; ⏲8am-2pm Mon-Sat) Opposite the *alun-alun*.

Tourist Information Kiosk This small kiosk, on the *alun-alun*, is staffed by students.

Tourist Information Office (☎0341-558919; Jl Gede 6; ⏲8am-4pm Mon-Fri) Helpful, but 3km northwest of the *alun-alun*.

ℹ Getting There & Away

BUS & ANGKOT

Malang has three bus terminals. **Arjosari**, 5km north of town, is the main one with regular buses to Surabaya, Probolinggo and Banyuwangi. Long-distance buses to Solo, Yogyakarta, Denpasar and even Jakarta mostly leave in the early evening. Minibuses (called *angkot* or *mikrolet* locally) run from Arjosari to nearby villages such as Singosari and Tumpang. **Gadang** bus terminal is 5km south of the city centre, and sends buses along the southern routes to destinations such as Blitar (33,000Rp to 54,000Rp, two hours). Buses depart **Landungsari** bus terminal, 5km northwest of the city, to destinations west of the city, such as Batu (10,000Rp, 40 minutes).

MINIBUS

Plenty of door-to-door *travel* companies operate from Malang, and hotels and travel agencies can book them. Helios Tours (p171) and **Wijaya Travel** (☎0341-327072) are two reliable agencies. Minibuses travel to Solo (150,000Rp), Yogyakarta (150,000Rp) and Probolinggo (60,000Rp). Minibuses to Surabaya (50,000Rp) will drop you off at hotels in Surabaya (thus saving the long haul from Surabaya's bus terminal), but be warned that this can add up to a couple of hours to your trip.

TAXI

For a reliable taxi company, use **Citra** (☎0341-490555).

BUSES FROM MALANG

DESTINATION	FARE (RP)	DURATION (HR)	DEPARTURES
Banyuwangi	39,500–71,000	7	7am & 1pm
Denpasar	150,000	12	5pm
Jember	22,000–40,000	4½	every 90 minutes
Lovina (Bali)	180,000	12	5.30pm
Probolinggo	22,000–36,000	2½	hourly 5am-5pm
Solo	100,000	10	6.30pm
Surabaya	25,000	2½-3	hourly
Yogyakarta	105,000	11	7am, 1pm, 6.30pm

WORTH A TRIP

NORTH COAST

Fishing villages and their brightly painted *perahu* (boats) dot the north coast. The coast is lined with beaches; few are particularly wonderful, though turquoise shallows do make a stunning contrast with the white-stone shore.

Near Arosbaya, 27km north of Kamal, the tombs of the Cakraningrat royalty are at Air Mata (Tears) cemetery, superbly situated on the edge of a small ravine. The ornately carved headstone of Ratu Ibu, consort of Cakraningrat I, is the most impressive.

The village of Tanjung Bumi is situated on the northwest coast of Madura, about 60km from Kamal. Although primarily a fishing village, it is also a manufacturing centre for traditional Madurese batik and *perahu*.

Pasongsongan is a fishing settlement on the beach, where it may be possible to stay with villagers. Further east, Ambunten is the largest settlement on the north coast and has a bustling market. Just over the bridge, you can walk along the picturesque river, which is lined with *perahu*, and through the fishing village to the beach. East of Ambunten, Slopeng has a wide beach with sand dunes and coconut palms. The water is usually calm enough for swimming, but it is not always clean. Men fish the shallower water with large cantilevered hand nets. Slopeng is also known for its *topeng* (wooden-mask) making.

The stunning white sands of Pantai Lombang, 30km northeast of Sumenep, make it the best beach in Madura; there's no development here to spoil the idyllic scene. Locals harvest tree saplings for the bonsai market and sell coconuts to visitors.

TRAIN

Malang train station (☎0341-362208) is centrally located but not well connected to the main network. There are three daily trains to Yogyakarta (250,000Rp, eight hours) via Solo. Surabaya is only served by very slow and crowded economy trains. There is also a daily service to Banyuwangi (65,000Rp, 7½ hours), where you can hop on a ferry to Bali.

Getting Around

Mikrolet run all over town. Most buzz between the bus terminals via the town centre. These are marked A–G (Arjosari to Gadung and return), A–L (Arjosari to Landungsari) or G–L (Gadang to Landungsari). Trips cost 3000Rp.

Around Malang

The lush, palm-dappled rice and corn fields around Malang are scattered with evocative Hindu and Buddhist ruins, making for a fun half-day road trip.

Singosari Temples

The Singosari temples lie in a ring around Malang and are mostly funerary temples dedicated to the kings of the Singosari dynasty (AD 1222–92), the precursors of the Majapahit kingdom.

Tumpang is also home to the **Mangun Dhama Arts Centre** (☎034-178 7907), which has Javanese dance classes and performances, plus some gamelan, *wayang* and woodcarving courses. *Wayang kulit* and dance shows can be staged if pre-arranged, and books, dance DVDs, masks, puppets and batik are usually for sale.

If coming from Singosari, go to Blimbing where the road to Tumpang branches off the highway, and then catch a minibus. In Tumpang, the temple is only a short stroll from the main road.

Sights

Candi Singosari HINDU TEMPLE

(7am-5pm) FREE Situated right in the village of Singosari, 12km north of Malang, this temple stands 500m off the main Malang–Surabaya road. One of the last monuments erected to the Singosari dynasty, it was built in 1304 in honour of King Kertanegara, the fifth and last Singosari king, who died in 1292 in a palace uprising.

The main structure of the temple was completed, but for some reason the sculptors never finished their task. Only the top part has any ornamentation and the *kala* heads have been left strangely stark. Of the statues that once inhabited the temple's chambers, only the statue of Agastya (the Shivaite teacher

Around Malang

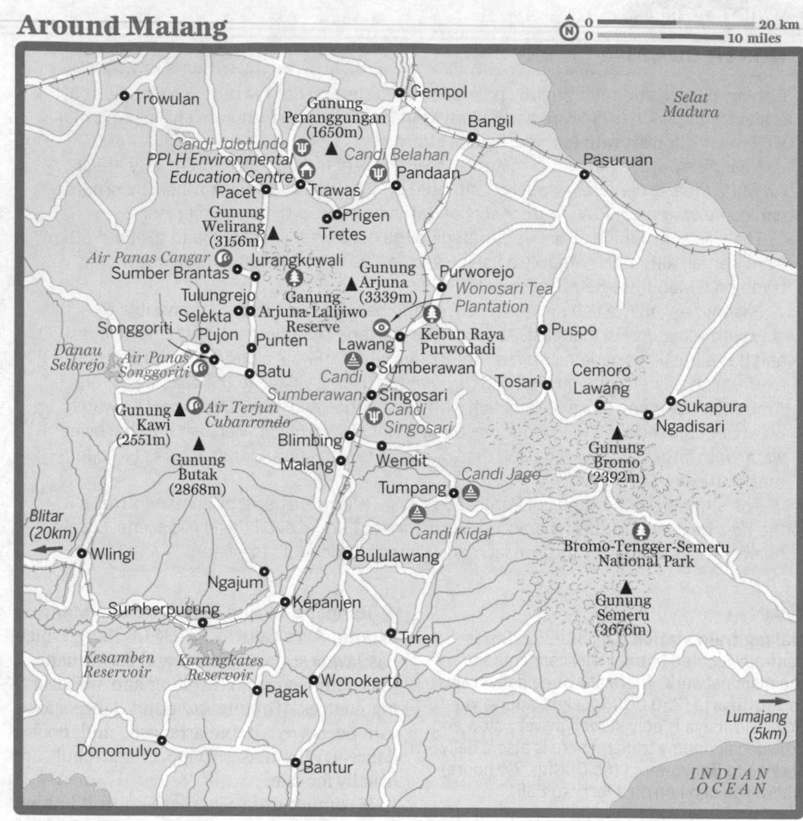

who, legend has it, walked across the water to Java) remains. The statues of Durga and Ganesha that were in the temple are now exhibited in the National Museum in Jakarta. As a result, it lacks the atmosphere of some of the other temples in the area, but locals do still visit to meditate and leave offerings, which is interesting to see.

About 200m beyond the temple are two enormous figures of *dwarapala* (guardians against evil spirits) wearing clusters of skulls and twisted serpents.

To reach Singosari, take a green *angkot* (5000Rp) from Malang's Arjosari bus terminal and get off at the Singosari market on the highway.

Candi Sumberawan BUDDHIST TEMPLE

(⌚7am-5pm) **FREE** This small, squat Buddhist stupa lies in the terraced, cultivated foothills of Gunung Arjuna, about 5km northwest of Singosari. It was built to commemorate the 1359 visit of Hayam Wuruk, the great Majapahit king. Within the temple grounds are a lingam stone and the crumbling origins of additional stupa along with the remains of recent offerings. But what makes it special is the approach.

You'll walk from the main village road – a checkerboard of tarps layered with drying corn – down a 400m dirt path, which parallels a canal, through the rice fields until you reach the ruins. Young men use the canal for bathing, so don't be surprised to see a naked body or two en route to the stupa. In Javanese culture it's polite to avert your eyes – the boys will duck down into the water in fits of giggles as you pass. Opposite the temple is a spring – the source of the gurgling canal – where locals go to cool off on sweltering weekends.

Take an *angkot* (3000Rp) from Singosari *pasar* (market) on the highway to Desa Sumberawan, then walk 500m down the road to the canal and the dirt path.

Candi Jago TEMPLE

(Jajaghu; admission 25,000Rp; ⏲7am-5pm) Along a small road near the market in Tumpang, 22km from Malang, Candi Jago was built between 1268 and 1280 and is thought to be a memorial to the fourth Singosari king, Vishnuvardhana. The temple has some interesting decorative carving from the Jataka and the Mahabharata, carved in the three-dimensional, *wayang kulit*–style typical of East Java.

This primarily Buddhist temple also has Javanese-Hindu statues, including a headless, six-armed, death-dealing goddess, a massive fanged Garuda, and a lingam, the symbol of Shiva's male potency. The best part is that you can scramble up the loosely restored temple to the top (watch your step) for exquisite views.

To reach Candi Jago take a white *angkot* from Malang's Arjosari bus terminal to Tumpang (4000Rp).

Candi Kidal HINDU TEMPLE

(admission 5000Rp; ⏲7am-4pm) Set in the village of Kidal, with houses rising all around – along with one conspicuously clucking chicken farm – this graceful temple was built around 1260 as the burial shrine of King Anusapati (the second Singosari king, who died in 1248). Now 12m high, it originally topped 17m and is an example of East Javanese architecture. Its slender form has pictures of the Garuda (mythical man-bird) on three sides, plus bold, glowering *kala* heads and medallions of the *haruna*.

Two *kala makara* (dragons) guard the steps – one is male and the other female. It remains a pilgrimage site and you will see the remains of offerings left within the shrine.

Hourly brown *angkot* (3000Rp) run from Tumpang market to Candi Kidal; the last one returns at 4pm.

Purwodadi

The **Kebun Raya Purwodadi** (admission 5000Rp, tours 15,000Rp; ⏲8am-4pm) are expansive dry-climate botanical gardens. The 85 hectares are beautifully landscaped and contain more than 3000 species, including 80 kinds of palm, a huge fern collection, a Mexican section, myriad orchids and many varieties of bamboo. The garden office to the south of the entrance has a map and leaflets. Air Terjun Cobanbaung is a high waterfall next to the gardens.

The gardens are easily reached; take any bus (10,000Rp) from Malang to Surabaya and ask to be dropped off at the entrance, which is 3km north of the town of Lawang.

Gunung Arjuna-Lalijiwo Reserve

This reserve includes the dormant volcano Gunung Arjuna (3339m), the semi-active Gunung Welirang (3156m) and the Lalijiwo Plateau on the northern slopes of Arjuna. Experienced and well-equipped hikers can walk from the resort town of Tretes to Selekta in two days, but you need a guide to go all the way. Alternatively, you can climb Welirang from Tretes or Lawang.

A well-used hiking path, popular with students on weekends and holidays, and also with soul-searchers who come to meditate on the mountain, begins in Tretes near the Kakak Bodo Recreation Reserve. Get information from the **PHKA post** (☎081 2178 8956; Jl Wilis 523) in the northern reaches of the town. Guides can be hired here for 300,000Rp to 400,000Rp per day; allow two days to climb one mountain and three days for both.

It's a hard, five-hour walk (17km) to the very basic huts used by the Gunung Welirang sulphur collectors. Hikers usually stay overnight here in order to reach the summit before the clouds roll in around mid-morning. Bring your own camping gear, food and drinking water (or hire it all at the PHKA post for around 200,000Rp per day), and be prepared for freezing conditions. From the huts it's a 4km climb to the summit. Allow at least six hours in total for the ascent, and 4½ hours for the descent.

The trail passes Lalijiwo Plateau, a superb alpine meadow, from where a trail leads to Gunung Arjuna, the more demanding peak. From Arjuna, a trail leads down the southern side to Junggo, near Selekta and Batu. It's a five-hour descent from Arjuna this way; a guide is essential.

ℹ Getting There & Away

To get to the start of the hike, take a bus to Pandaan (15,000Rp) from Malang or Surabaya and then a minibus to Tretes (10,000Rp).

Gunung Penanggungan

The remains of no fewer than 81 temples are scattered over the slopes of Gunung Penanggungan (1650m). This sacred Hindu mountain is said to be the peak of Mt Mahameru, which according to legend broke off and landed at its present site when Mt Mahameru was transported from India to Indonesia.

Historically this was a very important pilgrimage site for Hindus, and a few Javanese mystics, meditators and Hindus still visit the mountain today. Pilgrims make their way to the top of the mountain and stop to bathe in the holy springs adorned with Hindu statuary. The two main bathing places are **Candi Jolotundo** and **Candi Belahan**, the best examples of remaining Hindu art. Both are difficult to reach.

In a stunning setting on the evergreen western slopes of Penanggungan, the **PPLH Environmental Education Centre** (☎032-1722 1045; dm/bungalows 25,000/275,000Rp) is a supremely relaxing and interesting place. It's mainly set up to teach groups about the merits of organic agriculture, composting and garbage management. Expert guides can be hired for hikes (about 200,000Rp per day) and they'll gladly explain about plants used for herbal medicines. There's an organic restaurant and good, rustic accommodation is available in pretty bungalows with outdoor bathrooms, or in more basic dorms. School groups pass through from time to time, disturbing the tranquility somewhat, but most of the time it's very peaceful. To get there, take a Trawas-bound minibus (8000Rp) from Pandaan and an *ojek* (20,000Rp) from Trawas.

Batu

☎0341 / POP 88,000

Batu, 15km northwest of Malang, is a large hill resort on the lower reaches of Gunung Arjuna, surrounded by volcanic peaks. It's a popular weekend destination for locals, but makes a relaxed base during the week if you want to avoid staying in Malang.

There are several banks.

Sights & Activities

Songgoriti HOT SPRINGS

(admission 20,000Rp; ⏲7.30am-5pm) Songgoriti, 3km west of Batu, has well-known hot springs and a small, ancient Hindu temple on the grounds of the Hotel Air Panas Songgoriti. Nearby, Pasar Wisata is a tourist market selling mostly apples, bonsai plants and volcanic stone mortars and pestles. The waterfall **Air Terjun Cubanrondo** (admission 10,000Rp; ⏲7.30am-5pm) is 5km southwest of Songgoriti.

Sumber Brantas HOT SPRINGS

Higher up the mountain, the small village of Sumber Brantas, far above Selekta, is at the source of the Sungai Brantas (Brantas River). From here you can walk 2km to **Air Panas Cangar** (admission 10,000Rp; ⏲7.30am-5pm), hot springs high in the mountains surrounded by forest and mist.

Selekta SWIMMING

(admission 15,000Rp; ⏲7.30am-5pm) Selekta, a small resort 5km further up the mountain from Batu and 1km off the main road, is home to the Pemandian Selekta, a large swimming pool with a superb setting in landscaped gardens.

Sleeping & Eating

Accommodation is available in Batu, Songgoriti and all along the road to Selekta. Songgoriti and Selekta are small, quiet resorts; Batu has the best facilities but is more built-up. Add around 25% to prices for weekend rates.

Batu's Jl Panglima Sudirman is lined with restaurants and warungs.

Kampung Lumbung LODGE $$

(☎0341-540 6941; www.grahabunga.com; r/cottage from 500,000/1,300,000Rp;) A wonderful eco-hotel where the complex resembles a traditional village and all the buildings make good use of recycled wood and solar power. There's excellent local food in the restaurant, and the natural environment is sublime here; the climate is refreshing and the air is fresh. It's a kilometre south of central Batu.

Hotel Kartika Wijaya HISTORIC HOTEL $$

(☎0341-592600; www.kartikawijaya.com; Jl Panglima Sudirman 127; r incl breakfast from 550,000Rp;) An imposing colonial residence in sweeping grounds dotted with palms, lawns and tennis courts. The carpeted rooms are spacious and comfortable, though not that grand.

Pantara Cafe INDONESIAN $

(Jl Panglima Sudirman 123; dishes 12,000-37,000Rp) On the main drag in Batu, the Pantara serves up delicious Javanese food in atmospheric surrounds.

Getting There & Away

From Malang's Landungsari bus terminal take a Kediri bus or a *mikrolet* to Batu (5000Rp, 40 minutes). *Mikrolet* connect Batu's bus terminal with the centre via Panglima Sudirman.

From the bus terminal, *mikrolet* run to Selekta (3000Rp, 20 minutes) and Sumber Brantas (6000Rp, 45 minutes). *Mikrolet* turn off to Sumber Brantas at Jurangkuwali village. For Air Panas Cangar, walk 2km straight ahead from Jurangkuwali.

You'll find plenty of *ojek* around Batu to get you to all of these destinations.

South-Coast Beaches

The coast south of Malang has some good beaches, but facilities are limited. Sendangbiru is a picturesque fishing village separated by a narrow channel from Pulau Sempu. This island nature reserve has a couple of lakes, Telaga Lele and Telaga Sat, both ringed by jungle. Boats can be hired (around 200,000Rp return) to get you to Sempu. Take your own provisions.

A few kilometres before Sendangbiru, a rough track to the left leads 3km to Tambakrejo, a small fishing village with a sweeping sandy bay, which (despite the surf) is generally safe for swimming.

Balekambang is best known for its picturesque Hindu temple on the small island of Pulau Ismoyo, connected by a footbridge to the beach. Balekambang is one of the most popular beaches and is crowded on weekends. There are basic guesthouses in the village.

Getting There & Away

Minibuses from Malang's Gadang bus terminal travel to Sendangbiru (20,000Rp, two hours), past the turn-off to Tambakrejo. For Balekambang, buses run direct from Malang for 15,000Rp.

Blitar

0342 / POP 132,000

A low-key provincial city, Blitar makes a good base for visiting the Panataran temple complex and the spectacular active volcano of Gunung Kelud. It's also the home of Indonesia's first president, Sukarno; his memorial is worth checking out.

Sights

Makam Bung Karno MONUMENT

(admission 10,000Rp, includes entry into the museum; 7am-5pm) At Sentul, 2km north of the town centre, former president Sukarno's grave is marked by a massive black stone and an elaborate monument of columns and murals depicting his achievements. Sukarno (or Bung Karno) is widely regarded as the father of the Indonesian nation, although he was only reinstated as a national hero in 1978. Despite family requests that he be buried at his home in Bogor, Sukarno was buried in an unmarked grave next to his mother in Blitar.

His father's grave was also moved here from Jakarta. It was only in 1978 that the lavish million-dollar monument was built and the gravesite was opened to visitors. There's also a small museum devoted to the man, which has hundreds of historic photographs of Sukarno with heads of state including John F Kennedy and Ho Chi Minh.

The monument has an undeniable poignancy, and thousands of Indonesian pilgrims come here each year to pay their respects. Visitors peak around Independence Day (17 August) when men and women, dressed in their best batik and *jilbab*, gather and chant in his honour. Sadly, as you leave, things descend abruptly into tacky consumerism as you're directed through a seemingly never-ending maze of souvenir stalls.

A becak from Blitar town centre is around 10,000Rp. Panataran-bound *angkudes* (yellow minibuses; 3000Rp) pass by; ask for the *makam* (grave).

Museum Sukarno MUSEUM

(Jl Sultan Agung 59; admission by donation; 7am-5pm) For a more personal look into the life of Sukarno, head for the Museum Sukarno, located in the house where he lived as a boy. Photos, revolutionary posters and memorabilia (including a Bung Karno clock) line the front room, and you can see the great man's bedroom and check out his old Mercedes in the garage. The museum is about 1.5km from the centre of town.

Pasar Legi MARKET

Blitar's large public market, Pasar Legi is next to the bus terminal and worth a wander.

Sleeping & Eating

★**Tugu Sri Lestari** HISTORIC HOTEL $$

(0342-801766; www.tuguhotels.com; Jl Merdeka 173; incl breakfast r 375,000-1,000,000Rp;) One of East Java's best hotels. The rooms in the principal building are incredibly atmospheric, with high ceilings and grand teak beds; those in the modern extension at the rear are neat and functional. Service is warm and professional, and staff are full of tips about the city and region.

There's a real sense of history throughout the main structure, a Dutch colonial building from the 1850s. Be sure to ask staff to let you see the Sukarno room (he was a frequent visitor here) where you can sit at his old desk.

Puri Perdana MOTEL **$$**
(☎0342-801884; Jl Anjasmoro 78; r from 250,000Rp; ❄📶) Built like a motor inn, with rooms on two floors on either side of a landscaped driveway, digs are clean and tiled, low on frills but comfortable enough. Walk-in discounts can drop the price to 150,000Rp.

Bu Mamik INDONESIAN **$**
(Jl Kalimantan 11; mains 7500-32,000Rp; ⏰10am-11pm) Tasty *ayam bakar* (grilled chicken) is what brings droves of locals to this quaint, stilted indoor-outdoor restaurant with carved columns and twirling fans.

Waroeng Tugu Blitar INDONESIAN **$**
(www.tuguhotels.com/blitar; Jl Merdeka 173; mains 32,000-78,000Rp; ⏰8am-10pm; 🍷) After a hot day's sightseeing, drop by this fine hotel's 'waroeng' for local specialities, including *udang swarloka* (deep-fried shrimp balls), *tahu kembang jenar* (crispy tofu stuffed with mushrooms, bean sprouts and bamboo shoots) and *nasi kare ayam ny oei* (chicken cooked in yellow curry served with rice).

It offers a range of full salads and Western mains, too. Be sure to tour the hotel while you're here.

ℹ Information

There are several banks in town including **BCA Bank** (Jl Merdeka; ⏰8am-4pm Mon-Sat). Wi-fi is available in area hotels.

ℹ Getting There & Away

Regular buses run from Blitar to Malang (20,000Rp, 2½ hours) and Surabaya (45,000Rp, 4½ to five hours), as well as Solo (100,000Rp, six hours). The bus terminal is 4km south of town along Jl Veteran (3000Rp by *angkot* from the centre). *Angkudes* run from the western end of Jl Merdeka to Panataran temple for 6000Rp, passing close to Makam Bung Karno; you'll have to walk the last 300m or so.

Blitar has a few useful train connections, with three daily services heading to both Solo (160,000Rp to 465,000Rp, 4½ hours) and Yogyakarta (160,000Rp to 465,000Rp, five to 5½ hours).

Hiring a car and driver makes a lot of sense to see the sights; the Tugu hotel can organise this for 550,000Rp per day. Or hire an *ojek* for much less at around 100,000Rp.

Panataran

The **Hindu temples** (admission 3000Rp; ⏰7am-5pm) at Panataran (locally called 'Penataran') are the largest intact Majapahit temples, and the finest examples of ancient East Javanese architecture and sculpture. Construction began in 1197, during the Singosari dynasty, with building work continuing for another 250 years. Most of the important surviving structures date from the great years of the Majapahit kingdom during the 14th century.

Around the base of the first-level platform, the comic-strip carvings tell the story of a test between the fat, meat-eating Bubukshah and the thin, vegetarian Gagang Aking.

Further on is the small Dated Temple, so called because of the date '1291' (AD 1369) carved over the entrance. On the next level are colossal serpents snaking endlessly around the Naga Temple, which once housed valuable sacred objects.

At the rear stands the triple-tiered Mother Temple, its lowest panels depicting stories from the Ramayana. Behind is a small royal *mandi* (bathing tank) with a frieze depicting lizards, bulls and dragons around its walls.

Three hundred metres beyond the turn-off to the temples, the **Museum Panataran** (admission by donation; ⏰8am-2pm Tue-Thu, Sat & Sun, to 11am Fri) has an impressive collection of statuary from the complex, but labelling is poor.

The complex is set in a neighbourhood perched over rice fields and alive with domestic tourists, joyful children and meandering, pecking chickens. It's a lovely scene later in the day.

Panataran is 16km from Blitar (5000Rp by bus), and 3km north of the village of Nglegok.

Gunung Kelud

Around 30km directly north of Panataran, Gunung Kelud (1731m) is one of Java's most active, accessible and rewarding volcanoes to visit, with a plunging crater, steaming vents and a small crater lake. Kelud is in a near-permanent state of growl – an eruption in 1919 killed 5000 people and one in 2007 sent smoke 2.5km into the air and created a 250m-high cone within the caldera.

To get to the crater itself you have to walk through a 200m tunnel, built under the Japanese occupation. A torch (flashlight) isn't necessary but will reveal many bats. To get the best perspective of Kelud you need to hike a steep path up the side of the crater.

Entrance to Gunung Kelud is controlled at a **gateway** (admission 110,000Rp, car 20,000Rp; 6.30am-4pm Mon-Fri, 6am-5pm Sat & Sun) 10km before the summit because of the active nature of the beast.

There's no public transport to Kelud. The easiest way here is to hire a car or *ojek* from Blitar. After bargaining, the latter will do a half-day return trip via Panataran for around 100,000Rp.

Pacitan

0357

A long way from anywhere, the small south-coast town of Pacitan lies on a horseshoe bay ringed by rocky cliffs. It's a beach resort with limited accommodation and a few fresh seafood restaurants. Few foreigners make it here; those that do are here to surf.

The blonde beach at Pacitan is set in a rather dramatic bay shaped like a stemless wine glass. The natural harbour to the west is set against the towering jungled cliffs and there's a series of decent beach breaks as it meanders east toward a fine point break.

Pantai Ria Teleng, 4km or so from town, has golden sand and good surfing conditions for beginners as the waves break over a sandy bottom. Surf and bodyboards can be hired here, and there are lifeguards. Swimming is possible when the seas are calm – the safest area is towards the fishing boats at the southwestern end of the bay.

Pacitan has several banks. If you visit during the week, off-season, you've a good chance of having a virtually deserted beach to yourself.

Sleeping

Harry's Ocean House GUESTHOUSE $
(878 9514 5533; dm 35,000Rp, hut with shared bathroom 50,000Rp, r with fan/air-con 70,000/90,000Rp, cottages 150,000-250,000Rp;) There are four styles of rooms on offer here: dorms, a bamboo hut, concrete rooms and stilted wooden cottages with arced roofs. The property is on a back road inland from the beach. It actually has two branches in town and another in nearby Watu Karung. It's the choice spot among backpacking surfers.

Arya Homestay GUESTHOUSE $
(r 150,000Rp) Simple, fan-cooled titled rooms come with high slanted ceilings and friendly management on the inland road. If Harry's is booked, folks usually wind up here.

Surfer's Bay HOTEL $$
(0357-881474; r from 435,000Rp;) Across the street from the beach, this venerable place is under new, somewhat disinterested management. It offers old but clean tiled rooms, some with ocean views. All are a touch overpriced.

Getting There & Around

Buses run to Pacitan from Solo (60,000Rp, 4½ hours) and also from Ponorogo (20,000Rp, 2½ hours) via a scenic road. From Ponorogo, direct buses go to Blitar (32,000Rp, three hours).

Direct *travel* minibuses (50,000Rp, three hours) connect Yogyakarta with Pacitan; call **Aneka Jaya** (0357-304 4560) or **Purwo Widodo** (027-445 1690).

There's very little public transport around Pacitan. Motorbikes with surfboard racks can be rented from some Pacitan guesthouses (50,000Rp per day).

Around Pacitan

About 13km southwest of Pacitan via a rough hilly road, stunning **Watu Karung** is an evocative fishing village with an arc of fine white sand and turquoise water offshore. This is one of Java's best surf beaches, with rights and lefts and occasional barrels. As a result, more and more guesthouses have sprouted up in the area, and over 20 were in operation at research time. In many cases, fishermen have sold their boats to finance the homestays as the town tries to transition into a surfing hotspot. It remains to be seen if the economy can support such a shift or if the homestay bubble is about to burst. Case in point: Watu Karung is only busy during high season and still feels like a wonderfully sleepy tropical village most of the year.

This is also agate country, and hawkers sell reasonably priced polished stones and rings.

Watu Karung is not served by public transport; you'll need to hire a car in Pacitan or arrange transport with your guesthouse.

Sights & Activities

At Punung village, on the Solo road 30km northwest of Pacitan, is the turn-off to some magnificent limestone caves. **Goa Putri** is 2km from the highway, and the much more impressive **Gua Gong**, 8km away, is the largest and most dazzling cave system in the area.

The turn-off to the more famous **Gua Tabuhan** (Musical Cave) is 4km north on the highway beyond Punung, and then another 4km from there. This huge limestone cavern was a refuge for prehistoric humans 50,000 years ago. Pay the resident musicians here and they'll strike up an impressive 'orchestral' performance by striking rocks against stalactites, each in perfect pitch, and echoing pure gamelan melodies. You must hire a guide and lamp.

Sleeping

The homestays rent motorbikes and surfboards.

Pasir Putih HOMESTAY $
(☎0852 8102 3187; s/d 150,000/200,000Rp) Offers modern rooms with private patios overlooking the beach.

Watukarang Jungle Homestay HOMESTAY $
(☎0821 4370 7246; r incl breakfast 85,000Rp) Book a simple brick room with shared bathrooms. It also offers massages (one hour, 60,000Rp).

Istana Ombak RESORT $$$
(www.istanaombak.com; Jl Kerapu Milak 151; all-inclusive surf packages from US$240, walk-in room only from 800,000Rp; wi-fi) The only resort in the area is a stunner, with comfortable thatched cottages and villas, wired with wi-fi and satellite TV. It offers solid local surf intel and spectacular family-style dinners, not to mention a luscious stretch of beach. Owned by a former pro surfer from Australia who lived in a bamboo shack while he built the place, it is by far the best sleep in the area.

Guests can use mountain bikes and pick-up in Yogyakarta and Solo is offered.

Probolinggo

☎0335 / POP 217,000

For most travellers, Probolinggo is a bustling, featureless transit point in the fertile plains on the route to Gunung Bromo. You probably won't want to hang around here long, but the innovative tourist information people might try to change your mind. Better to keep moving.

Sleeping & Eating

Sinar Harapan HOTEL $
(☎0335-701 0335; Jl Bengawan Solo 100; r 120,000-200,000Rp; air-con, wi-fi) This new hotel has a contemporary feel, but its shine is fading. It rents out motorbikes for 60,000Rp per day.

Sumber Hidup CHINESE, INDONESIAN $
(Jl Dr Mosh Saleh II; mains 14,000-30,000Rp; ⏰11.30am-10pm) Large restaurant on the main strip that serves good Chinese food and Indonesian dishes. Doubles as an ice-cream parlour.

WORTH A TRIP

WHALE SHARK TOURS

Each year between January and March an annual migration causes quite a stir in Probolinggo. Twenty or more whale sharks, some measuring up to 8m, gather in the shallow seas off Pantai Benter, 8km east of the town. Boats take camera-toting local tourists on trips to see these marine giants, the world's largest fish (a harmless plankton feeder). In Javanese they're known as *geger lintang* ('stars on the back'), a reference to the star-like spots these sharks can be identified by. Boats only charge 10,000Rp or so per passenger. As the sea is usually very murky, snorkelling does not tend to be very rewarding.

Dangers & Annoyances

Probolinggo's bus terminal has a poor reputation with travellers. It's by no means dangerous, just not very honest and has more than its fair share of ticket touts eager to make a buck.

The main scam involves overcharging for bus tickets. Some reputable-looking ticket agents ask for double or more the standard price. You can check departure times and prices on the monitor in the waiting area, or head to Toto Travel. Unless it's a holiday (when you might want to book ahead) often the best thing to do is find the bus you need, and pay the fare onboard.

Also, when travelling to Probolinggo, make it clear to the ticket collector you want to be dropped off at the Bayuangga bus terminal; we've received emails from travellers complaining of being left at random travel agents and charged exorbitant fares for bus tickets.

Thieves are common on the buses in East Java, especially on buses departing from Probolinggo.

Information

The efficient **Tourist Information Centre** (☎0335-432420; www.dispobpar-kotaprobolinggo.com; Jl Suroyo; ⏰8am-3.30pm) by the train station is trying hard to change people's perceptions of Probolinggo. Staff organise city tours and can hook you up with local schools that are looking for English speakers to help students; you only need to spare an hour or two of your time.

The main post office and most of the banks are also on Jl Suroyo, which leads off the main drag Jl Panglima Sudirman.

Getting There & Away

BUS

Probolinggo's **Bayuangga bus terminal** is located about 5km from town on the road to Gunung Bromo. There are TV monitors here with bus departure information. Buses to Banyuwangi, Bondowoso and Surabaya depart frequently; most transport to Denpasar is between 7pm and 11pm. If want to make an advance reservation head to **Toto Travel** (0335-443 8267; Bayuangga bus terminal), where the owners speak English fluently.

Angkot run to/from the main street and the train station for 3000Rp.

MINIBUS

Gunung Bromo minibuses leave from a stop just outside Probolinggo's Bayuangga bus terminal, heading for Cemoro Lawang (35,000Rp, two hours) via Ngadisari (12,000Rp, 1½ hours) until around 4pm. Overcharging tourists is common on this route. Late-afternoon buses charge more to Cemoro Lawang when fewer passengers travel beyond Ngadisari. Make sure your bus goes all the way to Cemoro Lawang when you board.

TAXI

Taxis and freelance car drivers meet trains and wait for business at the bus station. A trip up to Cemoro Lawang costs around 350,000Rp to 400,000Rp after bargaining; more if it's late in the day.

TRAIN

About 2km north of town, the train station is 6km from the bus terminal. Probolinggo is on the Surabaya–Banyuwangi line. There are four daily exclusive- and business-class trains to Surabaya, both called *Mutiara Timur*. Two leave late at night, at 2:21am and 2:29am, and two leave at a more reasonable 1:24pm and 1:32pm (business/executive 90,000/125,000Rp, two hours). Trains travelling east to Banyuwangi leave at 10:59am and 11:07am, and at 11.52pm and 11:59pm (economy 60,000Rp to 100,000Rp, business/executive 105,000/140,000Rp, five hours). *Angkot* D (5000Rp) connects the train station with the bus terminal.

Gunung Bromo & Bromo-Tengger-Semeru National Park

0335

A lunarlike landscape of epic proportions and surreal beauty, the volcanic Bromo region is one of Indonesia's most breathtaking sights.

Rising from the guts of the ancient Tengger caldera, Gunung Bromo (2392m) is one of three volcanoes to have emerged from a vast crater, stretching 10km across. Flanked by the peaks of Kursi (2581m) and Batok (2440m), the smouldering cone of Bromo stands in a sea of ashen, volcanic sand, surrounded by the towering cliffs of the crater's edge. Just to the south, Gunung Semeru (3676m), Java's highest peak and one of its most active volcanoes, throws its shadow – and occasionally its ash – over the whole scene.

The vast majority of independent travellers get to Bromo via the town of Probolinggo and stay in Cemoro Lawang where facilities are good. There are other options in villages on the road up from Probolinggo.

Additional approaches via Wonokitri and Ngadas are also possible, but due to irregular public transport and poor road conditions they're only occasionally used by small tour groups.

Gunung Bromo

Gunung Bromo is unforgettable. It's not the mountain itself, but the sheer majesty of the

BUSES FROM PROBOLINGGO

DESTINATION	COST (RP; ECONOMY/AIR-CON)	DURATION (HR)
Banyuwangi	40,000/50,000	5
Bondowoso	20,000/30,000	2½
Denpasar	125,000/150,000	11
Jember	20,000/30,000	2½
Malang	20,000/30,000	2½
Surabaya	20,000/30,000	2½-3
Yogyakarta	90,000/150,000	10-11

TIPS FOR VISITING BROMO

➡ Bromo's popularity means that during high season (July, August, Indonesian holidays and the Christmas period) and weekends, the two main viewpoints can get very crowded between sunrise and the early morning. Organised tours all follow the same schedule, so consider visiting Gunung Penanjakan and the Bromo crater at other times of day.

➡ Walking from Cemoro Lawang to the Bromo crater only takes around 40 minutes, and enables you to take in the scenery and get your boots dusty in the grey volcanic sands of the Laotian Pasir (Sea of Sand).

➡ At any time of year it's cold in the early morning and temperatures can drop to single digits or near-freezing. Guesthouses rent out jackets for around 30,000Rp.

➡ The lip of the crater in Cemoro Lawang (between the Cemara Indah hotel and Lava View Lodge) has lots of viewing spots where you can savour Bromo's superb scenery away from the crowds.

➡ If you're unlucky and cloudy weather curtails your views of Bromo, drop by the gallery at the Java Banana hotel to see what you've missed. And then stay another day and hope that the skies clear.

experience: the immense size of the entire Tengger crater, the supernatural beauty of the scenery and the dramatic highland light that will saturate your brain with tranquility – for at least a little while.

Virtually all tours are planned to enable you to experience the mountain at sunrise. This is when the great crater is at its ethereal best and colours are most impressive. But visibility is usually good throughout the day in the dry season (June to September), even though the slopes below Cemoro Lawang may be covered in mist. Later in the day you'll also avoid the dawn crowds – things get especially busy during holiday periods. In the wet season it's often bright and clear at dawn but quickly clouds over.

It's a short, enjoyable hike to Bromo from Cemoro Lawang. The 3km (40-minute) 'trail' wanders down the crater wall and across the eerie Laotian Pasir (Sea of Sand) to the slopes of Bromo. White stone markers are easy to follow during the day but can be more elusive in the dark. Make sure you climb the right cone; Bromo has a stone staircase. Some hikers, disoriented in the dark, have attempted to climb neighbouring Batok. If you're lucky you will share the rim with groups of Balinese or Javanese Hindu pilgrims who have come to pray to one of the three most sacred mountains in Hindu lore and make offerings in the hopes of satisfying the volcano and the gods.

After ascending the 253 steps you'll come face to face with the steaming, sulphurous guts of the volcano. There are sweeping views back across the Laotian Pasir to the lip of the crater and over to Batok and the Hindu temple (open only on auspicious days in the pilgrim calendar) at its base.

Mercifully, there's little of the tacky commercialism (bar the odd souvenir seller) that besmirches many Indonesian scenic spots, though there is ample plastic litter on the rim (please pack your bottles and trash out). The local Tengger people may press you into accepting a horse ride across the crater bed but there's no serious hassle. No matter how many folks are gathered on the rim, it's still easy to connect spiritually with this sacred peak if you wander around the lip of the Bromo cone, away from the main viewing point.

History

Unsurprisingly, the eerie landscape of Bromo and its neighbouring volcanoes has spawned countless myths and legends. It is said that the Tengger crater was originally dug out with just half a coconut shell by an ogre smitten with love for a princess.

But Bromo is of particular religious significance to the Hindu Tengger people who still populate the massif. They first fled here to escape the wave of Islam that broke over the Majapahit kindgom in the 16th century. The Tengger believe that Bromo once fell within the realm of the childless King Joko Seger and Queen Roro Anteng, who asked the god of the volcano for assistance in producing an heir. The god obliged, giving them

25 children, but demanded that the youngest, a handsome boy named Dian Kusuma, be sacrificed to the flames in return. When the queen later refused to fulfil her promise, the young Dian sacrificed himself to save the kingdom from retribution.

Activities

The classic Bromo tour peddled by all hotels and guides in Cemoro Lawang (and other villages) involves a pick up around 3.30am and a 4WD journey up to the neighbouring peak of Gunung Penanjakan (2770m). This viewpoint offers the best vistas (and photographs) of the entire Bromo landscape, with Gunung Semeru puffing away on the horizon. After sunrise, 4WDs head back down the steep lip of the crater and then over the Laotian Pasir (Sea of Sand) to the base of Bromo. It's usually easy to hook up with others for this tour to share costs. Private jeeps cost 500,000Rp. If you pay for a single seat, expect to be crammed in with four or five others, though the price (150,000Rp) is right.

Alternatively, it's a two-hour hike to the top of Gunung Penanjakan, the so-called second viewpoint, from Cemoro Lawang. But King Kong Hill – perched just 20 minutes beyond the first viewpoint, and also on Penanjakan, set on a ledge jutting out from the main trail – has even better views than the top. From here looking toward the west you'll see Bromo bathed in that dawn light, along with Gunung Batok, with Gunung Semeru photobombing from behind. It can take up to an hour to reach it, but it's a stunning walk. Just up from the village, the slopes are planted with scallions, potatoes and cauliflower. You won't see them in the dark, but they make a lovely vista on the easy downhill stroll. Trekkers can also take an interesting walk across the Laotian Pasir to the village of Ngadas (8km), below the southern rim of the Tengger crater. From here, motorbikes and 4WDs descend to Tumpang, which is connected by regular buses to Malang.

Festivals & Events

In June, Jiwa Jawa lodge (p186) hosts a jazz festival, Gunung Jazz (www.jazzgunung.com) with performances from international and domestic artists held in the open-air hotel grounds.

Kasada RELIGIOUS

The wrath of Bromo is appeased during the annual Kasada festival, when Tenggerese Hindus come to Bromo to make peace with the mountain, and pray for health and good harvests. During this time, local daredevils descend into the crater and attempt to catch offerings in nets (money, food and even live chickens) thrown down by others above.

It's a risky business and is as dangerous as it sounds – every few years someone slips and the volcano claims another victim. The park's PHKA offices can tell you when Kasada occurs.

Sleeping & Eating

CEMORO LAWANG

On the lip of the Tengger crater overlooking Bromo, Cemoro Lawang is a tiny, charming highland village in a spectacular location. Its relaxed atmosphere and cool climate will come as quite a relief if you've been clocking up the kilometres in Java.

Unfortunately two hotels (both Lavas) have a near-duopoly here and charge prices that are heavily inflated from the norm in Indonesia. Both operate a triple-level pricing scheme, ramping up their rates from low (5 January through April) to high (May to mid-September) and up again in peak season (mid-September to 4 January). Rates increase further (by around 20%) on selected weekends, some days in August and over Christmas and New Year. Rates quoted here are for May to mid-September.

Tengger Indah HOMESTAY **$**

(Cemoro Lawang; r from 150,000Rp) An east-facing homestay in town, a stone's throw from the rim at the junction. Prim and painted with murals on the exterior, the interiors are simple, tiled and affordable. Nothing fancy.

Cafe Lava Hostel HOTEL **$$**

(☎0335-541 020; r without bathroom from 175,000Rp, with bathroom & breakfast from 425,000Rp; wi-fi) With a sociable vibe thanks to its streetside cafe and attractive layout (rooms are scattered down the side of a valley), this is first choice for most travellers, despite the steep prices. Economy rooms are very small but neat, and have access to a shared veranda and clean communual bathrooms (fitted with all-important hot showers).

More expensive rooms have little porches with great views and wood furniture. The restaurant serves up reasonable Indonesian and Western grub and cold Bintang.

Hotel Bromo Permai LODGE $$
(☎0335-541 049; d from 610,000Rp) With close to the same majestic vistas as Lava View (but not quite), the tiled rooms in the wooden building are clean and come with wood-panelled ceilings and flat-screens. The dark wood rooms are the newest of the bunch. The restaurant is decked out with more of the wood panelling and is washed in classical Indonesian music. All things considered, it's the best value on the hill.

Lava View Lodge HOTEL $$
(☎0335-541009; r/bungalows from 713,000/792,000Rp;) This is a well-run hotel located 500m along a side road on the eastern side of the village. As it's almost on the lip of the crater, you can stumble out your door to magnificent Bromo views. It's overpriced, but at least the wooden rooms and bungalows are comfortable enough (if dated) and staff are friendly and helpful.

There's a huge restaurant here with the usual mix of Indonesian and Western food, but beware the bad cover songs masquerading as live music some nights.

NGADISARI & WONOTORO

Yoschi's Hotel GUESTHOUSE $
(☎0335-541018; www.hotelyoschi.com; r without shower 240,000Rp, with shower from 540,000Rp, cottages from 900,000Rp; @) This rustic place has lots of character, with bungalows and small rooms dotted around a large, leafy garden compound. However, many lack hot water and cleanliness standards could be better. There's a huge restaurant that serves up pricey Western and Indonesian food (subject to a stiff 20% service charge).

It's 4km below Bromo and tours can be arranged. Room prices rise by around 25% in high season (July to September, Christmas and New Years').

Jiwa Jawa HOTEL $$$
(☎0335-541193; www.jiwajawa.com; r incl breakfast 750,000-2,250,000Rp, ste/lodge from 3,630,000/4,000,000Rp, meals from 40,000Rp;) A kind of ultra-modern mountain lodge, this excellent place has expanded its operations in recent years and was in the midst of a name change and rebranding at press time. It has a huge selection of stylish rooms (largely built from wood) that are of a high standard, though many are quite compact.

You'll also love the elevated cafe-restaurant, which has sweeping views over villages and vegetable fields. The whole place is enhanced by the oversized prints of Indonesia, taken by the talented photographer-owner.

Information

There are two entry posts as you drive uphill toward Cemoro Lawang and into Bromo-Tengger-Semeru National Park. The first will charge a mere 10,000Rp entrance fee, but the second is the real ticket. And that ticket costs 317,500Rp. Steep? Yes, but worth it. Information about trails and mountain conditions is available from the **PHKA post** (☎0335-541038; ⏲8am-3pm Tue-Sun) in Cemoro Lawang and also at the **PHKA post** (☎034-357 1048; ⏲8am-3pm Tue-Sun) on the southern outskirts of Wonokitri. Both extend their opening hours during busy periods. The park's official office is located in Malang (p169). There's a BNI ATM close to the crater lip in Cemoro Lawang.

BROMO BY BUS

Minibus trips to Gunung Bromo (and on to Bali) are very popular with travellers. However, few enjoy the experience, as the route involves a long, slow overland journey in cramped conditions. Ten-hour journeys can take 13 hours, and the air-conditioned bus promised turns out to be a rusty tin can on wheels. The most comfortable way to Bromo is to take a train (or even fly) to Surabaya and then another train or bus on to Probolinggo.

If you do decide to do the trip by minibus (from 200,000Rp, 11 to 13 hours) note that many operators often terminate short of Cemoro Lawang, and drop you off at a (poor) hostel on the way up the volcano (which is sure to be paying a commission).

Travellers also have regularly reported mysterious 'breakdowns' on the Bromo route, which cut into travelling time and mean that you don't reach Cemoro Lawang. Others have experienced problems with onward connections to Bali. Purchase your ticket from a reliable agent – we suggest Great Tours (p116) – and check up-to-date information with other travellers and on Lonely Planet's Thorn Tree internet forum.

Getting There & Away

Probolinggo is the main gateway to Bromo. Hotels in the Bromo area can book minivans to Probolinggo (35,000Rp, two hours) where you can catch long-distance buses to Yogyakarta (90,000Rp to 150,000Rp, 10 to 11 hours) and Denpasar (125,000Rp to 150,000Rp, 11 hours). Many people arrive on tours from Yogyakarta, which involves a punishing overland journey, usually in a cramped minibus. Alternatively, if you don't mind changing transport, the most comfortable (and fastest) way to cover this route is Yogyakarta to Surabaya by train, then a train or bus to Probolinggo and a minibus up to Cemoro Lawang.

Tours to Bromo are also easily organised in Malang, where you can arrange 4WD hire in hotels and travel agencies.

Gunung Semeru

Part of the huge Tengger Massif, the classic cone of Gunung Semeru is the highest peak in Java, at 3676m. Also known as Mahameru (Great Mountain), it is looked on by Hindus as the most sacred mountain of all and the father of Gunung Agung on Bali.

Semeru is one of Java's most active peaks and has been in a near-constant state of eruption since 1818 – it exploded as recently as March 2009. At the time of research the mountain was open to hikers, but periodically officials will warn against attempting the summit due to volcanic acitivity.

Trekking tours from Malang usually take two (or sometimes three) days to get to the summit and back. Helios Tours (p171) in Malang charges 750,000 per person, per day for a three-day, two-night hike including all supplies, transport, meals and an English-speaking guide.

To hike the peak independently, take an *angkot* (10,000Rp, 45 minutes) from Malang's Arjosari bus station to Tumpang. Here you can charter an *ojek*/4WD (70,000/550,000Rp) to **Ranu Pani** village, the start of the trek. There are several homestays (all around 100,000Rp per person) in Ranu Pani (2109m). Good ones include **Pak Tasrip** and **Pak Tumari**, both of which serve meals and can organise guides (150,000Rp per day), tents and sleeping bags (which are essential).

Hikers *must* register with the **PHKA post** (☎Tumpang office 034-178 7972), which is towards the lake in Ranu Pani. It will have the latest information about conditions – you may not be able to access the summit and may only make it as far as the Arcopodo campsite.

SEMERU ESSENTIALS

- Semeru is a highly active volcano and its status changes rapidly – check with the national park office, in Malang, locally in Ranu Pani village and also online at www.gunungbagging.com.
- Because several hikers have died of heart attacks climbing Semeru, officially you're supposed to have a health certificate to confirm that you should be able to make it there and back. These are best obtained in Malang in advance.
- Nights on the mountain are bitterly cold (often near-freezing) and inexperienced climbers have died of exposure. Make sure you have adequate gear and clothing.
- The best time of year to make the climb is May to October when you have a decent chance of clear skies and dry weather.

Staff might also ask you to produce a health certificate. Expect to pay a small fee for a climbing permit and entrance for the national park (317,500Rp).

Rangers will direct you to the trailhead for Semeru. The route is lined with markers for some distance and passes three shelters, so it's difficult to get lost. You'll pass pretty Ranu Kumbolo, a crater lake (2400m), 13km or 3½ hours from Ranu Pani. The trail then crosses savannah before climbing to Kalimati (three hours), at the foot of the mountain. From Kalimati it is a steep hour-or-so climb to Arcopodo, where there is a flattish campsite.

From Arcopodo, it is a short, steep climb to the start of the volcanic sands, and then a tough three-hour climb through loose scree to the peak. Semeru explodes every half-hour and the gases and belching lava make the mountain dangerous – stay well away from vents. On a clear day, there are breathtaking views of Java's north and south coasts, as well as vistas of Bali. To see the sunrise, it is necessary to start at about 1.30am for the summit.

Bondowoso

☎0332 / POP 71,000

Bondowoso, suspended between the highlands of Tengger and Ijen, is the gateway to

Bromo and Ijen and home to some of the island's best *tape*, a tasty, sweet-and-sour snack made from boiled and fermented vegetable roots.

Tape tastes vaguely alcoholic and can be found on Jl PB Sudirman, where dozens of shops sell it by the basket (15,000Rp). The '321' brand is reportedly the best.

It's mainly a transit and market town, tours to Ijen can be organised here. There are many (cramped) minibuses to Ijen (35,000Rp), all leaving before noon for the 2½-hour trip. Other destinations from Bondowoso include Jember (10,000Rp, 45 minutes), Probolinggo (20,000Rp to 30,000Rp, two hours) and Surabaya (normal/air-con 40,000/55,0000Rp, five hours).

Sleeping

Palm Hotel HOTEL $$

(☎0332-421201; www.palm-hotel.net; Jl A Yani 32; r incl breakfast with fan & mandi 190,000Rp, with air-con 320,000-610,000Rp;) Just south of the huge, grassy *alun-alun*, this good-value hotel's huge, heat-busting pool makes it a great escape from Java's punishing humidity. Take your pick from simple fan-only options with cold-water *mandi* or smart, spacious air-conditioned rooms that show a minimalist design influence. The brightest and most inviting are set toward the front of the main building. The restaurant is good. Transport to Ijen can be arranged (4WD costs 600,000Rp).

A HEAVY LOAD

The Ijen volcano produces a lot of sulphur, historically known as brimstone. Around 300 collectors (all men) work here, getting up at around 3am to hike up the crater and hack out the yellow stuff by hand. Their only protection against the cone's noxious fumes are cotton scarves, which they tie around their noses. These DIY miners then spend the next six-or-so hours scurrying back down the volcano with 60kg to 80kg loads on their backs.

It's arduous work that pays very little (around 800Rp per kilo), and yet the non-stop, physical exertion keeps the collectors incredibly fit. Few report health problems despite breathing great lungfuls of sulphurous fumes virtually every day of their lives. The sulphur collected is used for cosmetics and medicine, and is added to fertiliser and insecticides.

Ijen Plateau

The fabled Ijen Plateau is a vast volcanic region dominated by the three cones of Ijen (2368m), Merapi (2800m) and Raung (3332m). A beautiful, forested alpine area, the most dramatic scenery is yours as you wind through the rubber and clove groves, climbing up and over a pass, before dropping into an extinct crater (the so-called plateau), now home to evocative, shade-grown coffee plantations, threaded with streams and gurgling with hot springs. Along with the plantations and their company *kampung*, there are a few isolated settlements here. Gunung Ijen is Javanese for 'Lonely Mountain', after all. Access roads to the plateau are poor and perhaps because of this, visitor numbers are relatively low, though steadily increasing.

Virtually everyone who does come is here for the hike up to the spectacular crater lake of Kawah Ijen. You can see the mountain's dramatic, gaping mouth looming above the highland rim. Those kinds of sweeping vistas combined with a temperate climate make the plateau a great base for a few days up in the clouds and away from the crowds.

Sights

Java's finest coffee, both arabica and robusta varieties, is produced in the Ijen Plateau area, along with cacao, cloves and rubber. It's possible to visit coffee plantations, including **Kebun Balawan** FREE; visits will usually include a wander through coffee groves and an impromptu tour of the plantation's factory. This plantation has thermal pools and a gushing thermal waterfall (5000Rp) set amid lush jungle.

Activities

The magnificent turquoise sulphur lake of **Kawah Ijen** lies at 2148m above sea level and is surrounded by the volcano's sheer crater walls. At the edge of the lake, sulphurous smoke billows from the volcano's vent and the lake bubbles when activity increases. Ijen's last major eruption was in 1936, though due to an increased threat access was closed in late 2011, and again in March 2012 for a few weeks.

Ijen is a major sulphur-gathering centre and you'll pass the collectors as you hike up the trail. Most now ask for a fee for photographs, though a cigarette will usually be accepted as payment.

The ideal time to make the Kawah Ijen hike is in the dry season between April and October. However, while the path is steep, it's usually not too slippery, so the hike is certainly worth a try in the rainy season if you have a clear day. Make it for sunrise if you can.

The starting point for the trek to the crater is the **PHKA post** (admission weekdays/weekends 100,000/150,000Rp; ⏲7am-5pm) at Pos Paltuding, which can be reached from Bondowoso or Banyuwangi. Sign in and pay your entry fee here. The steep 3km path up to the observation post (where there's a teahouse) takes just over an hour; keep an eye out for gibbons. From the post it's a further 30-minute walk to the lip of the wind-blasted crater and its stunning views.

From the crater rim, an extremely steep, gravelly path leads down to the sulphur deposits and the steaming lake. The walk down takes around 30 minutes; the path is slippery in parts and the sulphur fumes towards the bottom can be overwhelming. Expect burning lungs and streaming eyes if you do make it to the bottom. Take great care – a French tourist fell and died here some years ago.

Back at the lip of the crater, turn left for the climb to the highest point (2368m) and magnificent views, or keep walking counterclockwise for even more expansive vistas of the lake. On the other side of the lake, opposite the vent, the trail disappears into crumbling volcanic rock and deep ravines.

Sleeping & Eating

This is a remote mountain region and, with little competition, the budget accommodation is pretty sketchy. The two guesthouses are run by coffee estates, whose owners clearly prioritise beans over beds. Few staff speak any English and email booking requests may or may not be answered. Room availability is also limited, so prepare yourself accordingly. However, if the lodge rooms are full, management can source local homestay options (125,000Rp to 150,000Rp) for you within moments.

Sempol village, home to Arabika, has a couple of warungs. Pos Paltuding has a small shop for provisions and a cafe serving little more than noodles.

Catimor is set in the village of Blawan, a hamlet gushing with hot springs and a cascading stream. It's a special place and the preferable landing spot. Book ahead.

★Catimor LODGE **$**
(☎0813 3619 9110, 0813 5799 9800; catimor_n12@yahoo.com; r 125,000-325,000Rp;) This budget lodge boasts an excellent location in the Kebun Balawan coffee plantation, close to hot springs. Unfortunately, there has been little or no maintenance for some time and the whole place is pretty creaky (especially inside the original wooden Dutch lodge, which dates back to 1894). There's also a separate block of cheap, reasonably clean, if featureless rooms.

Be sure to indulge yourself in the spring-fed hot tub, or brave the chilly swimming pool. Staff do their best here considering the remote location, and the meals are quite good. An *ojek* from Sempol is around 30,000Rp. Although management can arrange homestays if they are full, those do not include access to the hot spring.

Arabika LODGE **$**
(☎081 1350 5881, 082 8330 1347; arabica.homestay@gmail.com; r incl breakfast 175,000-325,000Rp;) This dated, usually chilly mountain lodge is managed by the Kebun Kalisat coffee plantation, which is a short walk away. Sadly, it's not in great shape these days, and cleanliness could be better – the more you pay the cleaner the rooms seem to get – but all rooms have hot water and a bathtub in which to enjoy it.

Staff are friendly, but can find it difficult to cope during busy periods. Meals are served, and there's ping-pong. It's at Sempol, 13km before Pos Paltuding on the Bondowoso side.

Pos Paltuding HUT **$**
(r 125,000Rp) The PHKA post at the start of the Kawah Ijen hike has a bare, chilly cottage with basic rooms fit for a monk. There's no hot water and blankets are not provided.

Ijen Resort HOTEL **$$$**
(☎0815 5810 4576, 0815 5810 4577; www.ijendiscovery.com; Dusun Randuagung; r/ste from US$148/238;) This top-end resort is the only luxury lodge in the Ijen region and has magnificent views over rice terraces and the foothills of the volcano. Rooms have some style, with stone or timber floors, open-air bathrooms and attractive furnishings. There's an expensive restaurant that serves local and Western food, and tours and transport can be fixed.

The resort is about 25 minutes above Banyuwangi on the road up to Ijen.

Jiwa Jawa FUSION **$$**
(Java Banana; ☎021-751 0338; java-banana.com; mains 65,000-195,000Rp) Set off the road up to Ijen from Banyuwangi, this restaurant is a stunner, with a massive ground-floor gallery and an outdoor amphitheatre with spectacular volcano views. The menu is ambitious. Expect mains such as parrotfish in Mediterranean ragu, grilled unagi (eel) with a miso beurre blanc, and a nori-crusted rack of lamb.

Lodge rooms were under constuction at research time and were expected to be open by 2016.

Getting There & Away

It is possible to travel nearly all the way to Kawah Ijen by public transport, but most visitors charter transport. Both access roads are badly potholed and slow going.

FROM BONDOWOSO

From Wonosari, 8km from Bondowoso towards Situbondo, a rough, potholed road runs via Sukosari and Sempol to Pos Paltuding. It's normally passable in any high-clearance vehicle, but sometimes a 4WD is necessary. Sign in at the coffee-plantation checkpoints (around 5000Rp) on the way. Hotels in Bondowoso can arrange day tours to Ijen for around 750,000Rp.

By public transport, several *angkot* run from Bondowoso to Sempol (25,000Rp, 2½ hours), most in the late morning, but there's a final one at 3pm. If passengers want to continue on to Pos Paltuding drivers will sometimes do so, though foreigners are regularly overcharged on this route. Otherwise, *ojek* in Sempol charge around 30,000Rp one way. At Pos Paltuding, there are usually a few drivers to take you back.

FROM BANYUWANGI

The Banyuwangi–Ijen road was in good condition at research time, though it has been known to be impossibly rutted in the past. Check locally for current conditions before setting off. There's no public transport all the way from Banyuwangi to Pos Paltuding, which is a sparsely populated region.

Jeep-style cars (650,000Rp per vehicle) can be arranged through the Banyuwangi tourist office. Chartering an *ojek* from Banyuwangi to Ijen is possible for around 200,000Rp (including a wait of four hours). *Ojek* drivers hang around the ferry terminal in Ketapang and Banyuwangi bus station, or ask at your guesthouse.

Heading back down the mountain, *ojek* charge around 75,000Rp to 100,000Rp for a one-way ride to Banyuwangi from Pos Paltuding.

Jember

☎0331 / POP 332,000

Jember is a large city and service centre for the surrounding coffee, cacao, rubber, cotton and tobacco plantations. It's relatively clean, with a futuristic mosque (it looks like a flying saucer) by its *alun-alun*, but there's no reason to linger. If you plan to go to Meru Betiri, you could drop by the **Meru Betiri National Park Office** (☎0331-335535; www.merubetiri.com; Jl Sriwidjaya 53; ⏲8am-3pm Sun-Fri), which has accommodation details and background information on the park.

Jember has an excess of transport terminals. The main one, **Tawung Alun** (or Terminal Jember), 6km west of town, has buses to Banyuwangi (27,000Rp, three hours) and Kalibaru (12,000Rp, one hour), and economy buses to Denpasar, Solo and Yogyakarta. *Angkot* run from here to **Terminal Arjesa**, which serves Bondowoso (10,000Rp, 45 minutes). There are also subterminals to the east (for Banyuwangi) and south (for Watu Ulo).

Jember is also located on the Surabaya–Banyuwangi train line; the station is in the town centre.

Kalibaru

☎0333 / POP 5000

The picturesque road from Jember to Banyuwangi winds around the foothills of Gunung Raung, through rainforest, and up to the small hill town of Kalibaru (428m).

The village itself is not much to look at, but it has a benign climate and a remarkable array of excellent midrange accommodation. It's a good base for visiting the nearby plantations around Glenmore, to the east, or the smaller, more easily visited plots of coffee and cloves to the north of Kalibaru train station.

The area has many plantations, but **Kebun Kandeng Lembu** (admission 30,000Rp; ⏲9am-noon Mon-Thu & Sat, 8.30am-noon Fri), 5km south of Glenmore, is one of the most scenic. Guides can be hired (100,000Rp) for group tours to see rubber tapping and processing, as well as cacao and coffee plantations.

Tours

Margo Utomo Resort offers several tours. English-speaking guides will show you around the estate, which is totally organic and has a butterfly park; peppercorn, cinnamon and nutmeg trees; and vanilla and cacao plants. 4WD trips to surrounding villages are on offer, and take in a waterfall and cacao factory. Excursions to Pantai Sukamade (Turtle Beach) and Alas Purwo are also possible.

Sleeping & Eating

There are warungs in town for cheap eats. Restaurants can be found at some of the area hotels.

Kalibaru Cottages BUNGALOW **$$**
(☎0333-897333; www.kalibarucottages.com; r incl breakfast 390,000-620,000Rp; ❄≋) A large, well-run resort boasting expansive, manicured grounds with a T-shaped pool that's fringed by palm trees. Faux-traditional cottages are spacious, though the restaurant is a bit pricey. It's 4km west of town on the Jember road.

Margo Utomo Resort HOTEL **$$**
(☎0333-897700; www.margoutomo.com; Jl Lapangan 10; r incl breakfast 575,000Rp; @≋) This classy former plantation enjoys a resplendent garden, bursting with shrubs and flowers (all neatly labelled). Its cottages are a bit pricey considering their simplicity, but they are tasteful and have charm. All have ceiling fans. Follow the path and you'll find a 20m pool at the rear of the grounds. There is also a restaurant.

It's popular with Dutch tour groups from June to August, when prices rise; you should book well ahead.

Getting There & Away

Buses running between Jember (12,000Rp, one hour) and Banyuwangi (22,000Rp, two hours) can drop you near the hotels. The train station is in the village centre; Kalibaru is on the main Banyuwangi–Jember–Probolinggo–Surabaya train line.

Meru Betiri National Park

The Meru Betiri National Park, covering 580 sq km between Jember and Banyuwangi districts, is an area of magnificent coastal rainforest and abundant wildlife, making it one of Java's finest parks. It's famous as one of the last refuges of the Java tiger, now almost certainly extinct. Meru Betiri is very difficult to access (often impossible in the rainy season), which keeps the number of visitors to a trickle.

The future of the park is under threat on several fronts. Illegal loggers, farmers and hunters encroach on its territory. Mining companies, and illegal miners, are also eyeing up the park after significant gold deposits were found here.

Sights & Activities

The park's major attraction is the protected turtle beach at **Sukamade**, one of Indonesia's most important turtle-spawning grounds, where several species come ashore to lay their eggs. You've a good chance of seeing a turtle here; green turtles and olive ridleys are the most common. Giant leatherbacks used to be seen between December and February, but sightings are rare these days. Mess Pantai arranges night turtle-watching trips (150,000Rp per person) and gathers eggs that are hatched inland so that wild pigs do not dig them up.

Wildlife, found mostly in the mountain forests, includes leopards, wild boars, monkeys, *banteng*, black giant squirrels, civets, reticulated pythons (the world's longest snake) and Javanese eagles. You're sure to see a lot of monkeys, monitor lizards and hornbills – maybe even the rhinoceros hornbill, which emits a bark-like honk.

Trails are limited in the park and a guide (100,000Rp) is usually necessary. There are good coastal walks but sadly there's quite a bit of trash around, on the beach and inland.

Rajegwesi, at the entrance to the park, is on a large bay with a sweeping beach and a fishing village. Past the park entrance the road climbs, giving expansive views over spectacular Teluk Hijau (Green Bay), with its cliffs and white-sand beach. A trail leads 1km from the road down to Teluk Hijau, or it is about a one-hour walk east from Mess Pantai.

Sleeping

There are guesthouses on the Sukamade plantation and in Rajegwesi, but these are some distance from the beach.

Mess Pantai BUNGALOW **$**
(☎033-133 5535; r without/with bathroom 150,000/250,000Rp) Set in the forest about 700m behind Pantai Sukamade, Mess Pantai is a basic but wonderfully located place to stay in the park, with simple, comfortable cottages. Instant noodles are usually the only food available (around 8000Rp), so it's best to stock up in Sarongan and bring your own supplies – staff will prepare it for you.

There's limited electricity and no mobile-phone coverage here, but there is bottled water for sale.

Information

The park is wet for much of the year as the coastal mountains trap the rain. Visit in the dry season from April to October, because the road into the park fords a river, which easily floods. Even in the dry season you may have to wade across the river and walk into the park.

The park's office in Jember (p190) has plenty of information; entrance to the park costs 150,000Rp.

Getting There & Away

Meru Betiri can be a tough place to reach, even by 4WD. Roads are rough and you have to ford rivers in some places. The most direct way to Sukamade from Banyuwangi or Jember is to first take a bus to Jajag, then a minibus to Pesanggaran (12,000Rp, one hour), where you'll probably have to change and get in another to Sarongan (10,000Rp, around one hour), a small town with warungs and stores where you can stock up on supplies. Watch out for the Sarongan transport mafia who will try to get you to charter a 4WD. *Ojek* to Sukamade (around 120,000Rp) can be arranged here, but generally only in the dry season; during the wet season the rivers are impassable. Otherwise, you'll have to get a truck ('taxi' in these parts), as they don't run to a fixed schedule. This should cost 30,000Rp, though foreigners are routinely overcharged. The truck has no problem with swollen rivers unless there is severe flooding.

Readers have told us they've made it all the way to Sukamade on motorcycle in the dry season; however, a dirt bike is preferable.

Alas Purwo National Park

Occupying the whole of the remote Blambangan Peninsula on the southeastern tip of Java, Alas Purwo has spectacular beaches, good opportunities for wildlife-spotting, and savannah, mangrove and lowland monsoon forests. Apart from day trippers and surfers, the park gets few visitors. Facilities are limited.

Alas Purwo means First Forest in Javanese: according to legend, this is where the earth first emerged from the ocean. Many soul-searchers and mystics flock here during the month of Suro, which marks the Javanese New Year. These pilgrims meditate in caves and pray to Nyai Loro Kidul. Pura Giri Selokah, a Hindu temple in the park, also attracts pilgrims, especially during Pagerwesi, the Hindu New Year.

The huge surf at Plengkung, on the isolated southeastern tip of the peninsula, forms one of the best left-handed waves in the world, breaking over a shallow reef in perfect barrels. Surfers have dubbed it G-Land. It's best between April and September.

Sights & Activities

A relatively flat limestone peninsula, with rolling hills that reach a peak of only 322m, Alas Purwo is dominated by lowland coastal forest. It's studded with stunning stands of mahogany but few trails to explore it. As a result, vast expanses of the eastern park are untrammelled, even by park staff, which is why big cats have survived here for so long.

You can use Trianggulasi as a base for some interesting short walks. The white-sand beach here is beautiful, but swimming is usually dangerous thanks to swirling rip tides.

Sadengan — WILDLIFE RESERVE

Down a spur that branches from the main road just after the Hindu temple, Sadengan grazing ground has the largest herd of *banteng* (wild cattle) in Java. Some of the larger bulls have birds on their back, and lovely herons often glide into the frame. *Kijang* (deer) and peacocks can also be seen here from the viewing tower. This beautiful meadow, backed by rolling, forested hills, is a 2km walk from Trianggulasi.

Alas Purwo also has a small population of *ajag* (Asiatic wild dogs), jungle fowl, leaf monkeys, muntjac deer, sambar deer and a few leopards. Some rangers even swear they've seen tigers here, which is almost certainly untrue. Or is it? Either way, they can arrange interesting (but often fruitless) nocturnal leopard-spotting expeditions for around 100,000Rp.

Ngagelan — BEACH

The turtle hatchery at Ngagelan is set in a protected, fenced-off plot behind the beach, where rangers who have collected the eggs keep them piled and dated under the brown sand, shielding them from birds and other predators. The beach itself, where four species of turtles nest – including greens and leatherbacks – is wide, majestic and 18km long. You can see the light brown sand arc along the coast all the way to G-Land.

You can't swim here though, as the rip tide is all-powerful. Turtles emerge from the sea under the cover of night, and after they lay their eggs the rangers gather them and place them in the hatchery where they will gestate for 50 days before hatching and seeking the sea. To get here it's a 6km drive from Rowobendo through lowland forest along a rough road, or a 7km walk along the beach at low tide from Trianggulasi. A ranger will gladly show you around, but he won't speak much English.

Gua Istana & Gua Padepokan CAVE
From Pancur, a trail heads 2km inland through some good forest to Gua Istana, a small cave, and another 2km further on to Gua Padepokan.

G-Land SURFING
(Plengkung) From Pancur, it's a 10km walk (two hours) around Teluk Grajagan to the fine beach at Plengkung, or G-Land, one of Asia's premier surfing spots and home to three seasonal surf camps. There are several world-class breaks here, most barrelling over a razor-sharp, shallow reef – this is mostly experts-only surf territory, though there are also some beginner waves over a sandbar bottom.

When it's firing, there can be 100 people in the water, which can feel overwhelming, but the mob usually strings out to manageable numbers as heads seek waves that suit their skill set. The surf camps offer transport to the waves from a small marina that's easy to find in the shallows. Swimmers can swim east along the reef from here, though low tide is quite low, so you may need to pick your way among the reef when you come in.

The two main surf camps are set about 500m apart in different coves. Bobby's has the more dramatic setting and offers pagodas and hammocks on the beach. Joyo's has a long bench on a rocky outcrop, along with lounges oriented toward the waves and the sunset beyond. Oh yes, those sunsets are absolutely magical!

You are in a raw and wild part of the world now. There are leopards often caught on game cameras, and one ranger swears he saw a tiger with her cub recently. The jungled coastline certainly looks like something out of Jurassic Park. No wonder G-Land is the stuff of surf legend.

Tours

There are three surf camps at Plengkung: Bobby's, Joyo's and **Raymond's** (☎036-175 0320; www.g-landsurfcamp.com). The surfing packages usually include boat transfers from Bali, accommodation and meals. Though it is possible to make your way here under your own steam, it's important to book ahead to make sure the camps have room for you. There is no other place to stay. Joyo's also offers **fishing trips** (half-day US$60) thanks to resident surfer and fisherman Mick Burke, who has lived here for 11 seasons and takes folks 2km offshore to his favourite fishing spots, searching for amberjack, Spanish mackerel and dogtooth tuna. He and his guests rarely return empty-handed. When you show up with your fish, the camp chefs will cook it up for no extra charge and your fellow guests will shower you with praise. Maybe.

Surfers take note: Mick has been riding these waves (quite well) for over a decade, and if the line-up is completely packed and you care to motor away from the crowds to unheard-of waves, he knows exactly where to go and can get you there for US$100 a head. Though the fee seems quite high, you will see a whole new stretch of coastline and be riding with just a handful of fellow surfers, which is a welcome relief on crowded days.

Sleeping & Eating

From Trianggulasi, the nearest warung (meals 10,000Rp) is at Pancur, where there are also simple rooms (100,000Rp per person). National park campsites are dusty and lack shelter from the wind and the road. We don't recommend them.

The G-Land surf camps usually have three-night minimums, but if you arrive with your own transport you may be able to negotiate a single night or two. Call ahead.

★**G-Land Joyo's Surf Camp** SURF CAMP **$$$**
(☎bookings in Bali 036-176 3166; www.g-land.com; 3-night packages from US$625; ❄📶) Joyo's has steadily upped its game over the years. It has good-quality thatched wooden bungalows with a fan or air-conditioning, a large-screen TV for sports, pool tables, internet access and table tennis. There's free yoga, fishing trips, and the crew who run the place are a blast. The price drops dramatically if you make your way here under your own steam.

The meals served here are as tasty as the food is plentiful. Price includes all meals and a free ration of two beers per day.

Bobby's Camp SURF CAMP $$$
(☎ bookings in Bali 036-175 5588; www.grajagan.com; 3-night packages US$640; ❄@📶) Right opposite the waves, this attractive camp has three standards of bungalow in shady grounds with a restaurant and bar. It has beach volleyball, ping-pong, pool tables, and boat and fishing trips can be arranged. Set back from the beach, in the jungle, the best nests are the two-storey teak cottages stilted in the trees.

Management is based in Kuta, Bali. Packages include transfers from Bali, grog and grub.

Information

The usual park entry is by road, via the village of Pasar Anyar, which has a large **national park office** (☎ 033-341 0857) and interpretive centre. Stop by to check on park accommodation and campsites; alternatively, check with the head office in Banyuwangi. You can also just show up cold, though you should book in with one of the surf camps if you intend to spend the night. The actual gateway to the park is 10km south along a bad road at Rowobendo where you need to pay your admission fee (10,000Rp per car, 150,000Rp per person). From here it's 2.5km to Trianggulasi.

Getting There & Away

Alas Purwo is a pain to get to by public transport. The best way here is to hire a motorbike or car in Banyuwangi; the access roads are poor but usually doable.

By bus, you need to get to Brawijaya bus terminal in Banyuwangi from where there are buses to Kalipahit (15,000Rp, 1½ hours). Then take an *ojek* for around 80,000Rp to the park office in Pasar Anyar to check on accommodation, before pushing on to the park. The 12km road from Pasar Anyar to Trianggulasi is badly potholed but is flat and negotiable by car.

Banyuwangi

☎ 0333 / POP 115,000

Java's land's end is a pleasant, growing city, home to a large amount of Osig people, whose roots reach back centuries in southeast Java. Most travellers simply pass through on their way to or from Bali by ferry, but the city does make a reasonable and comfortable base to explore the Ijen region and other national parks along the east coast. It's worthy of a night or two.

Point of clarification: the ferry port for Bali, the bus terminal and the train station are all some 8km north of town in **Ketapang**, though all transport states 'Banyuwangi' as their destination.

Sights

Pulau Tabuhan BEACH
A droplet of creamy white sand, topped with a tuft of scrub, this island jewel set offshore from Java, nearly halfway to Bali, is surrounded by a ring of turquoise shallows with a deep blue drop-off about 50m from shore. You'll see bait balls, schools of tropical fish and decent coral structure. The water is aquarium clear, and from the beach the volcanoes and mountains from Java and Bali are spread out in all directions.

Though the winds can rip (there's a reason an annual kite-surf contest is held here), it's possible to camp. If you do, you're likely to have the place to yourself. To get here, take a taxi or *ojek* to the Rumah Apung port, north of the ferry terminal, and hire a boat from there. It's 400,000Rp to 500,000Rp round trip.

Kongco Tan Hu Cin Jin Chinese Temple CHINESE TEMPLE
(Jl Ikam Gurani 54) One of the few sights in Banyuwangi is the Kongco Tan Hu Cin Jin Chinese temple, built in 1784. It's well worth a peek.

Blambangan Museum MUSEUM
(Jl A Yani; ⏲8am-4pm Mon-Thu, to 11am Fri) This small museum is devoted to culture from the area with batik and traditional costumes, ceramics and curios.

Festivals & Events

Banyuwangyi Festival CULTURAL
The Banyuwangyi Festival is a two-month-long series of music, arts, culture and sporting events organised by the stellar tourist office, and held on weekends in August and September. The Jazz Festival is one such event; it's held at the Jiwa Jawa amphiteatre (p190) on the slopes of Ijen.

Another standout is the magnificent kite-surf contest, the **Tabuhan Island Pro** (www.tabuhanislandpro.com), held on Tabuhan Island in late August.

Head to the local tourist office for details and transport information to any of the events.

Sleeping & Eating

For cheap eats, there are warungs on the corner of Jl MT Haryono and Jl Wahid Haysim.

Hotel Ketapang Indah HOTEL **$$**
(0333-422280; www.ketapangindahhotel.com; Jl Gatot Subroto; d from 600,000Rp;) This lovely hotel makes a peaceful place to stay. Its huge, well-kept rooms and traditional-style cottages are dotted around a sprawling garden, shaded with coconut palms and extending to the sea. The 18m pool is big enough for laps, though the restaurant is fair at best. It's 2km south of the ferry terminal.

★ **Bangsring Breeze** BOUTIQUE HOTEL **$$$**
(0813 5869 0800; www.bangsringbreeze.com; Jl Raya Situbondo Km17; r from 1,055,000Rp;) Set north of the city and just north of the ferry port, this is a boutique hotel in every respect. Each of the five rooms has been individually and tastefully designed – think high ceilings, wood floors, throw rugs, wood furnishings, flat-screens and fine art.

There is a gorgeous pool overlooking the sea and Bali's Menjangan island beyond, and a spectacular volcano rising behind the property. It's set up a hill from the beach down a little *gang*, and absolutely worth a night or two. It's a great base to explore both Menjangan or Ijen, and staff can get you down to Sukamade and Alas Purwo National Park, too.

Ikan Bakar Pesona SEAFOOD **$**
(Jl Sudarso 147; dishes 20,000-50,000Rp; 1-10pm) A classic Indonesian fish house where the tablecloths are sealed in plastic to easily wipe down the Makassar-style shrapnel after a serious feast. Famous for 10 flavours of crab (get yours Padang style), it also does grilled fish six different ways. Prices are fair and the food is delicious.

Information

Alas Purwo National Park Head Office
(0333-428675; Jl Brawijawa; 7.30am-3pm Mon-Thu, to 11am Fri) Two kilometres south of the town centre.

Banyuwangi Tourist Office (0333-424172; Jl Ahmad Yani 78; 7am-4pm Mon-Thu, to 11am Fri) Staff are helpful at this office. They speak Dutch and some English, and can organise tours.

Getting There & Away

AIR

Banyuwangi's tiny Blimbingsari airport is 9km south of the centre. **Garuda** (www.garuda-indonesia.com) and **Wings** (www.lionair.co.id) both connect the city daily with Surabaya and Denpasar from 333,000Rp. There's no public transport to the airport; a taxi will cost around 50,000Rp.

BOAT

Ferries depart around the clock for Gilimanuk in Bali (every 45 minutes, one hour). The ferry costs 7500Rp for passengers, 25,000Rp for a motorbike and 148,000 for a car (including four passengers). Through-buses between Bali and Java include the fare in the bus ticket. Pelni ships no longer call at Banyuwangi.

BUS

Banyuwangi has two bus terminals. The **Sri Tanjung terminal** is 3km north of Ketapang ferry terminal, 11km from the centre. Buses from here head along the north coast road to Baluran (10,000Rp, one hour), Probolinggo (normal/*patas* 40,000/50,000Rp, five hours) and Surabaya (46,000/66,000Rp, seven hours). Buses also go right through to Yogyakarta (*patas* 150,000Rp, 15 hours) and Denpasar (from 70,000Rp, five hours including the ferry trip). **Brawijaya terminal** (also known as Karang Ente), 4km south of town, covers buses along the southern highway to Kalibaru (22,000Rp, two hours) and Jember (27,000Rp, three hours).

TRAIN

The main Banyuwangi train station is just a few hundred metres north of the ferry terminal. The express *Mutiara Timur* leaves at 8am and 9.45pm for Probolinggo (economy/business/executive from 60,000/105,000/140,000Rp, five hours) and Surabaya (130,000Rp, seven hours).

Baluran National Park

Baluran National Park once harboured a diverse range of ecosystems in a 250-sq-km chunk of northeastern Java, though lately development has severely impacted the park. Extensive grasslands still cover parts of the park, providing grazing for *banteng* (wild cattle), *kijang* (deer) and water buffalo, and the savannah-like terrain is reminiscent of East Africa.

Sights & Activities

Baluran is home to hundreds of Timor deer and *banteng*, plus sambar deer, muntjac deer, two species of monkey and wild boars. Visit in July and August and you might see male Timor deer rutting for breeding rights.

Birdlife is also excellent, with green peafowl, red and green jungle fowl, hornbills, white-bellied woodpeckers and bee-eaters all easy to spot.

Pantai Bama BEACH

Fringed by mangroves, the sandy cove of Bama is 4km north of Bekol. It's a popular weekend retreat for local families, but usually peaceful at other times. Canoes (40,000Rp) and snorkelling gear (60,000Rp) can be hired. Watch out for the cheeky long-tailed macaques here, who have been known to pinch food.

Bekol HIKING

From the PHKA office on the highway, it's 14km down a flat gravel track to Bekol. The friendly rangers here look after a couple of lodges and can act as guides (150,000Rp per half-day). You don't need a guide to hike along a well-maintained trail to Pantai Bama (1½ hours), which follows a riverbank where deer are common.

On the hill above the guesthouses at Bekol there is a viewing tower that provides a panoramic view over a 300-hectare clearing. *Banteng* and deer can be seen here, and wild dogs can sometimes be seen hunting, usually in the early morning.

Sleeping & Eating

Most visitors tend to day-trip, so accommodation is often available, but it pays to book ahead in the peak June-to-August period.

Bungalows BUNGALOW $

(s 125,000Rp, d 175,000-225,000Rp) Pantai Bama is the preferred location as you're right on the beach and it's better set up for visitors. There is accommodation available in concrete bungalows and a warung for cheap meals (mains 9000Rp to 22,000Rp) and drinks. The rooms are functional.

Pesanggrahan GUESTHOUSE $

(☎0333-461936; per person 75,000-150,000Rp) At Bekol, this guesthouse has basic rooms in either concrete or wooden houses and simple bungalows to one side. The accommodation is basic, and you should bring your own mosquito net if you have one. You'll find a kitchen for guests or you can buy packet noodles and drinks.

Rosa's Ecolodge GUESTHOUSE $$

(☎0333-845 3005; www.rosasecolodge.com; Ds Sidomulyo RT 03/03; r incl breakfast 450,000Rp; ❄@) Rosa's spacious rooms were renovated in 2015 with private bathrooms and front porches. Rosa's is geared towards guests who join its pricey Baluran tours, and priority is given to its groups during busy times. It's on the northern edge of the park in the village of Sumberwaru. Buffet-style meals of tasty Javanese food are served here.

Information

You'll find the **PHKA office** (☎0333-461650, 0333-461936; ⏲8am-4pm) on the coastal highway in the village of Wonorejo, between Surabaya and Banyuwangi. Guides can be booked for around 250,000Rp per day. Entrance costs 105,000Rp and an extra 10,000Rp is charged for a car.

Baluran can be visited at any time of the year, but the dry season (June to November) is usually the best time because the animals congregate near the waterholes at Bekol and Bama.

Getting There & Away

A regular stream of Surabaya–Banyuwangi buses all pass right by the almost-hidden park entrance. From Banyuwangi it's a one-hour journey (10,000Rp). Coming from the west, Baluran is four hours from Probolinggo. PHKA rangers at the entrance can arrange an *ojek* (around 40,000Rp) to take you the next 12km to Bekol; the road is in pretty good shape and should be passable by most cars. A 4WD is not necessary.

Bali

POP 4.2 MILLION

Includes ➡

Best Places to Eat

- ➡ Sardine (p223)
- ➡ Mama San (p221)
- ➡ Cashew Tree (p231)
- ➡ Locavore (p261)
- ➡ Tékor Bali (p300)

Best Places to Stay

- ➡ Temple Lodge (p231)
- ➡ Bambu Indah (p258)
- ➡ Samanvaya (p270)
- ➡ Meditasi (p281)
- ➡ Sedasa (p227)

Why Go?

Impossibly green rice terraces, pounding surf, enchanting Hindu temple ceremonies, mesmerising dance performances, ribbons of beaches and truly charming people: there are as many images of Bali as there are flowers on the island's ubiquitous frangipani trees.

This small island looms large for any visit to Indonesia, and no other place is more visitor-friendly. Hotels range from surfer dives to lavish retreats in the lush mountains. You can dine on local foods bursting with flavours fresh from the markets or let world-class chefs take you on a global culinary journey. From a cold Bintang beer at sunset to an epic night of clubbing, your social whirl is limited only by your fortitude.

Small in size doesn't mean homogenous: manic Kuta segues into glitzy Seminyak; the artistic swirl of Ubud is a counterpoint to misty hikes amid volcanoes; and mellow beach towns such as Bingin, Amed and Pemuteran lie dotted along the coast.

When to Go

Denpasar

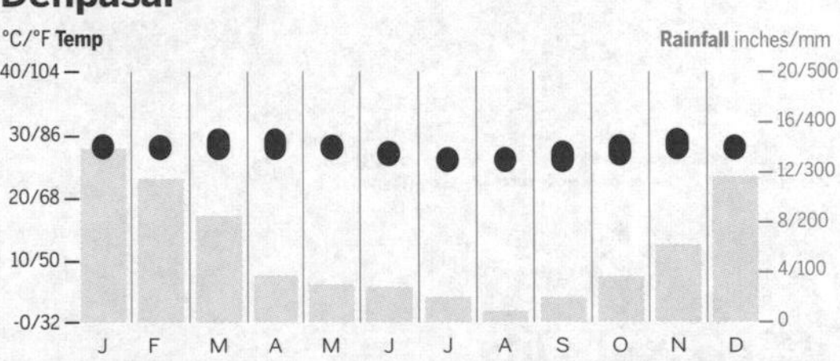

Jul & Aug High season is Bali's busiest and buzziest time. Book ahead for rooms.

May, Jun & Sep Often the best weather: slightly cooler and drier; less crowded.

Jan–Apr, Oct & Nov Low season makes spontaneous travel easy. Things go quiet for the Nyepi holiday.

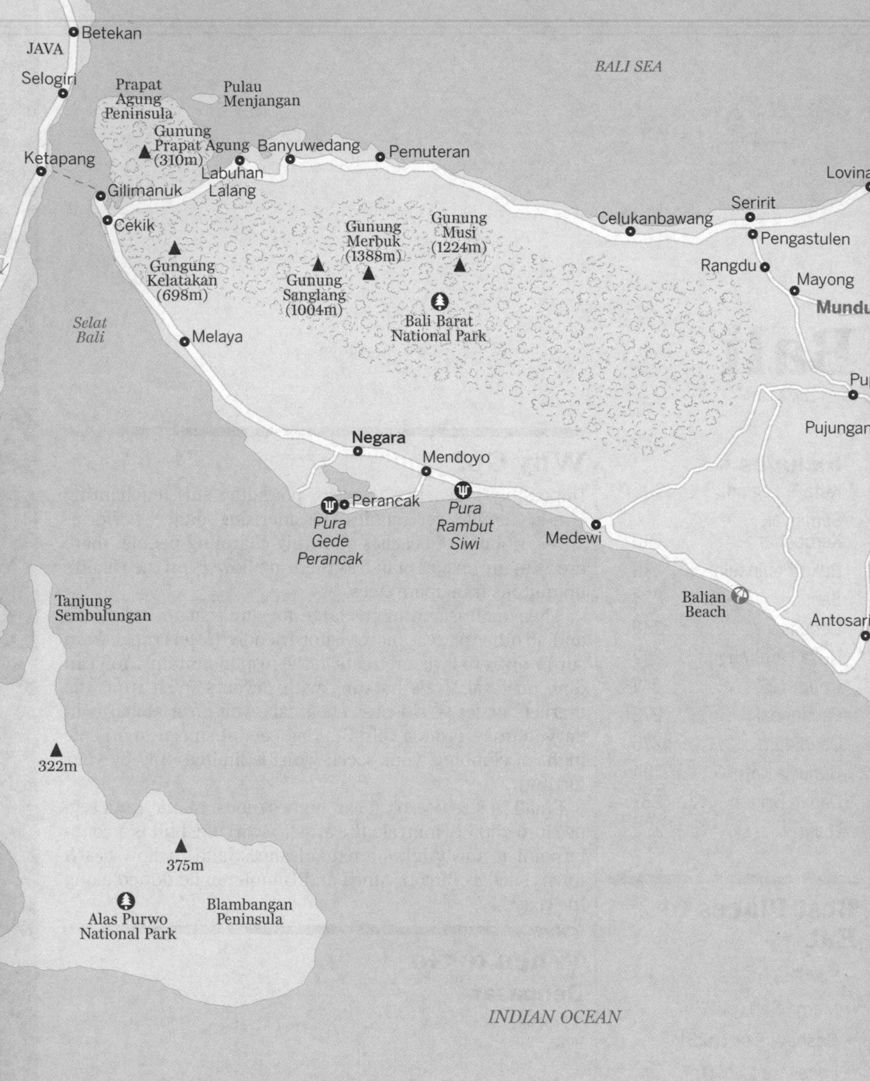

Bali Highlights

1 Shopping by day and hitting the hotspots by night in **Seminyak**, **Kerobokan** (p216) and **Canggu** (p225).

2 Discovering the beautiful string of hidden beaches in and around **Bingin** (p231), where the surfing is also fab.

3 Revelling in Bali's elaborate cultural life in **Ubud** (p247), where you can enjoy your choice of the island's iconic dance and gamelan performances nightly.

4 Zipping along the nontouristy **Sidemen road**

(p269) through verdant scenery of majestic rice fields and valleys.

5 Feeling the mist from waterfalls while hiking the lush region around **Munduk** (p288).

6 Plunging into the hedonistic nightlife of **Kuta** (p206).

7 Diving off **Nusa Lembongan** (p243) to see manta rays and mola mola (sunfish), or kicking back and enjoying island life.

History

It's certain that Bali has been populated since early prehistoric times, but the oldest human artefacts found are 3000-year-old stone tools and earthenware vessels from Cekik. Not much is known of Bali during the period when Indian traders brought Hinduism to the Indonesian archipelago; the earliest written records are stone inscriptions dating from around the 9th century. By that time, rice was being grown under the complex irrigation system known as *subak*, and there were precursors of the religious and cultural traditions that can be traced to the present day.

Hindu Influence

Hindu Java began to spread its influence into Bali during the reign of King Airlangga, from 1019 to 1042. At the age of 16, Airlangga fled into the forests of western Java when his uncle lost the throne. He gradually gained support, won back the kingdom once ruled by his uncle, and went on to become one of Java's greatest kings. Airlangga's mother had moved to Bali and remarried shortly after his birth, so when he gained the throne there was an immediate link between Java and Bali. At this time, the courtly Javanese language known as Kawi came into use among the royalty of Bali, and the stunning rock-cut memorials seen at Gunung Kawi near Tampaksiring are a clear architectural link between Bali and 11th-century Java.

After Airlangga's death, Bali retained its semi-independent status until Kertanegara became king of the Singasari dynasty in Java two centuries later. Kertanegara conquered Bali in 1284, but his power lasted only eight years until he was murdered and his kingdom collapsed. With Java in turmoil, Bali regained its autonomy and the Pejeng dynasty, centred near modern-day Ubud, rose to great power. In 1343 Gajah Mada, the legendary chief minister of the Majapahit kingdom, defeated the Pejeng king Dalem Bedaulu and brought Bali back under Javanese influence.

Although Gajah Mada brought much of the Indonesian archipelago under Majapahit control, Bali was the furthest extent of its power. Here the 'capital' moved to Gelgel, near modern-day Semarapura (Klungkung), around the late 14th century, and for the next two centuries this was the base for the 'king of Bali', the Dewa Agung.

As the Majapahit kingdom fell apart, many of its intelligentsia moved to Bali, including the priest Nirartha, who is credited with introducing many of the complexities of Balinese religion to the island. Artists, dancers, musicians and actors also fled to Bali at this time, and the island experienced an explosion of cultural activities. The final great exodus to Bali took place in 1478.

European Contact

The first Europeans to set foot in Bali were Dutch seafarers in 1597. Setting a tradition that prevails to the present, they fell in love with the island, and when Cornelius Houtman – the ship's captain – prepared to set sail from Bali, some of his crew refused to leave with him. At that time, Balinese prosperity and artistic activity, at least among the royalty, were at a peak. When the Dutch returned to Indonesia in later years, they were interested in profit, not culture, and barely gave Bali a second glance.

Dutch Conquest

In 1710 the capital of the Gelgel kingdom was shifted to nearby Klungkung, but local discontent was growing, lesser rulers were breaking away from Gelgel domination and the Dutch began to move in, using the old policy of divide and conquer. In 1846 the Dutch used Balinese salvage claims over shipwrecks as the pretext to land military forces in northern Bali. In 1894 the Dutch chose to support the Sasaks of Lombok in a rebellion against their Balinese raja. After some bloody battles, the Balinese were defeated in Lombok and, with northern Bali firmly under Dutch control, southern Bali was not to retain its independence for long.

In 1906 the Dutch commenced their final assault. The three rajas of Badung realised that they were outnumbered and outgunned, and that defeat was inevitable. Surrender and exile, however, was the worst imaginable outcome, so they decided to take the honourable path of a suicidal *puputan* – a fight to the death.

The Dutch begged the Balinese to surrender rather than make their hopeless stand, but their pleas went unheard and wave after wave of Balinese nobility marched to their deaths. In all, nearly 4000 Balinese died in the *puputan*.

The kingdoms of Karangasem and Gianyar had already capitulated to the Dutch and were allowed to retain some powers, but other kingdoms were defeated and the rulers exiled. Finally, the raja of Klungkung followed the lead of Badung and once more the Dutch faced a *puputan*. With this last

BENOA BAY RECLAMATION PROJECT

Almost 10 million tourists converge each year upon Bali, but the majority remain blissfully unaware of the environmental impact such numbers have on the island. Outside the walls of the luxury villas and five-star hotels, however, a battle is being fought by a younger generation of Balinese who hold grave concerns about the future of their homeland. Alarming shortages of water (vital for rice harvests), pollution, congestion and issues of waste management are all serious matters. Highlighting such concerns is the protest movement Tolak Reklamasi (Reject Reclamation), aligned with the ForBali (www.forbali.org/en) forum, which has generated significant awareness in its relentless drive to fight against the Benoa Bay Reclamation Project.

This controversial project would see the reclamation of 75% of Benoa Bay, a mangrove conservation area, for the creation of Dubai-style artificial islands housing luxury resorts, villas, a casino, a golf course, an amusement park and a car-racing track. The bay was a protected conservation area until outgoing Indonesia president Susilo Bambang Yudhoyono revoked its status in 2014, giving the green light for development. Not only did this decision spark outrage for its supposed murky behind-the-scenes dealings, but feasability studies suggested it will result in rising sea levels and flooding, causing genuine fear that the Benoa Bay development will mean ecological disaster.

Tolak Reklamasi has urged the younger generation to take responsibility for their homeland and 'reclaim Bali' from developers. As well as speaking to environmentalists, the movement has galvanised students, village elders, NGOs, artists, fishers, local business owners and prominent members of the community to rally against the decision. In 2015 the drummer for internationally renowned Balinese punk band Superman is Dead, Jerinx, an activist and vocal opponent of the project, met with current president Joko Widodo to discuss the matter. In this meeting, according to the Indonesia newspaper *Kompas*, Jerinx urged the president to cancel the decision, stating 'People come to Bali not looking for Disneyland or F1, but for the culture of Bali. This is what we stand for.'

While the future for Benoa Bay appears grim, groups such as Tolak Reklamasi and Bali Not for Sale (www.facebook.com/balinotforsale) are playing an important role to protect Bali's future.

obstacle disposed of, all of Bali was now under Dutch control and became part of the Dutch East Indies. Dutch rule over Bali was short-lived, however, as Indonesia fell to the Japanese in WWII.

Independence

On 17 August 1945, following the end of WWII, the Indonesian leader Sukarno proclaimed the nation's independence; however, it took four years to convince the Dutch that they were not going to get their colony back. In a virtual repeat of the *puputan* nearly half a century earlier, a Balinese resistance group was wiped out in the Battle of Marga on 20 November 1946; Bali's airport, Ngurah Rai, is named after its leader. It was not until 1949 that the Dutch recognised Indonesia's independence.

Modern Bali

The tourism boom, which started in the early 1970s, has brought many changes to Bali, and has helped pay for improvements in roads, telecommunications, education and health. Though tourism has had some marked adverse environmental and social effects, Bali's unique culture has proved to be remarkably resilient.

Bali has also been affected by global politics. In October 2002 two simultaneous bomb explosions in Kuta – targeting an area frequented by tourists – injured or killed more than 500 people. Tourism, and therefore the economy, was devastated. Soon after, the 2005 Bali bombings killed 20 and injured hundreds. Fortunately, the last decade has been peaceful, and recent years have seen Bali return to form as a tourist destination.

Culture

Bali's culture is unique, without a hint of cliché. The Balinese version of Hinduism that's practised here with great fervour exists nowhere else in the world, and has inspired fervent artistic expressions that charm visitors.

The population in Bali is almost all Indonesian; more than 90% of these are of Balinese Hindu descent and could be described as ethnic Balinese. The remaining residents are mostly from other parts of the country, predominantly Java.

The traditional Balinese society is intensely communal; the organisation of villages, the cultivation of farmlands and even the creative arts are communal efforts. A person belongs to their family, clan, caste and to the village as a whole.

Although tourism has brought much economic wealth to the island and there exists a burgeoning middle class, Bali's traditional rice-growing culture remains revered, even as swathes of land are sold for development. In 2012 Unesco recognised the island's rice-growing traditions, including the communal *subak* water distribution system.

Balinese society is held together by collective responsibility. For instance, if a woman enters a temple while menstruating, it is a kind of irreverence, an insult to the gods, and their displeasure falls not just on the transgressor but on the whole community. This collective responsibility produces considerable pressure on the individual to conform to *adat* – the traditional laws and customs that form core Balinese values.

Religion

You can't miss religion in Bali; there are temples in every village, shrines in every field and offerings made at every corner.

The Balinese are nominally Hindu, but Balinese Hinduism is half a world away from that of Indian. When the Majapahits evacuated to Bali they took with them their religion and its rituals, as well as their art, literature, music and culture. The Balinese had their own strong religious beliefs and an active cultural life, so new influences were simply overlaid on existing practices – hence the peculiar Balinese interpretation of Hinduism.

The Balinese believe that spirits are everywhere, an indication that animism is the basis of much of their religion. Good spirits dwell in the mountains and bring prosperity to the people, while giants and demons lurk beneath the sea, and bad spirits haunt the woods and desolate beaches. The people live between these two opposites and their rituals strive to maintain this middle ground. Offerings are carefully made every morning to pay homage to the good spirits, and nonchalantly placed on the ground to placate the bad ones.

Temples

The word for temple is *pura*, a Sanskrit word meaning 'a space surrounded by a wall'. As with so much of Balinese religion, temples, though nominally Hindu, owe much to the pre-Majapahit era. Their *kaja, kelod* or *kangin* (alignment towards the mountains, the sea or the sunrise) is in deference to spirits that are more animist than Hindu.

Most villages have at least three temples. The most important temple is the *pura puseh* (temple of origin), which is dedicated to the village founders and is at the *kaja* end of the village. In the middle of the village is the *pura desa* for the spirits that protect the village community in its day-to-day life. At the *kelod* end of the village is the *pura dalem* (temple of the dead). The graveyard is also here and the temple will often include representations of Durga, the terrible incarnation of Shiva's wife.

Families worship their ancestors in family temples, clans in clan temples and the whole village in the *pura puseh*. Certain temples in Bali are of such importance that they are deemed to be owned by the whole island

NYEPI

Bali's major Hindu festival, Nyepi celebrates the end of the old year and the start of the next. It's marked by inactivity – a strategy to convince evil spirits that Bali is uninhabited, so they'll leave the island alone for another year.

For the Balinese, it's a day for meditation and introspection. For foreigners, the rules are more relaxed, so long as you respect the 'Day of Silence' by not leaving your residence or hotel. If you do sneak out, you will be be escorted back to your hotel by a stern *pecalang* (village police officer). The airport also closes during Nyepi.

As daunting as it sounds, Nyepi is actually a fantastic time to be in Bali. Firstly, there's the inspired concept of being forced to do nothing. Secondly, the night before Nyepi sees the spectacle of celebrations with *ogoh-ogoh*, huge papier-mâché monsters that go up in flames.

In coming years, dates for Nyepi are 28 March 2017, 17 March 2018 and 5 April 2019.

rather than by individual villages. Overall Bali has more than 10,000 temples and shrines in all shapes and sizes.

The simple shrines or thrones you see, for example, in rice fields or next to sacred old trees are not real temples, as they are not walled. You'll find these shrines in all sorts of places, such as overlooking intersections or dangerous curves in the road to protect road users.

For much of the year Balinese temples are deserted, but on holy days it's believed that the deities and ancestral spirits descend from heaven to visit their devotees, and the temples come alive with days of frenetic activity and nights of drama and dance. Temple festivals occur at least once every Balinese year (210 days). Because most villages have at least three temples, you're assured of at least five or six annual festivals in every village. The full-moon periods, around the end of September to the beginning of October, or early to mid-April, are often times of important festivals.

Galungan-Kuningan is a 10-day festival during which *lots* of activity takes place at family and community temples all over the island.

Arts

The Balinese have no words for 'art' and 'artist' because, traditionally, art has never been regarded as something to be treasured for its own sake. Prior to the tourism boom, art was just part of everyday life, and what was produced went into temples, palaces or festivals. Although respected, the painter or carver was not considered a member of some special elite; the artist's work was not signed; and there were no galleries or craft shops.

It's a different story today, with thousands of art outlets tucked into every possible crevice. Although much Balinese art is churned out quickly as cheap souvenirs, buried beneath the reproductions of reproductions there's still much beautiful work to be found. Most visitors to the island discover the greatest concentration of the arts in and around Ubud.

Balinese Painting

The art form most influenced both by Western ideas and tourist demand is painting. Traditional painting was very limited in style and subject matter, and was used primarily for temple decoration. The arrival of Western artists after WWI introduced new subject matter and materials with which artists could work.

Traditional Balinese paintings were narratives with mythological themes, illustrating stories from Hindu epics and literature. Paintings were executed in the *wayang* style – the flat two-dimensional style that imitates *wayang kulit* (shadow puppets), with the figures invariably shown in three-quarter view. The colours that artists could use were strictly limited: red, blue, brown, yellow, and light ochre for flesh.

Bali's painting traditions remain vibrant and rich today. Ubud is the place to ponder the best paintings in museums and galleries.

Dance

Music, dance and drama are closely related in Bali. In fact, dance and drama are synonymous, though some 'dances' are more drama and less dance, and others more dance and less drama.

Many visitors are seduced by the haunting and melodic charms of a dance performance in Ubud, a quintessential Bali experience.

Balinese dance tends to be precise, shifting and jerky, like the accompanying gamelan music, which has abrupt shifts of tempo and dramatic changes between silence and crashing noise. There's virtually no physical contact in Balinese dancing – each dancer moves independently, but every movement of wrist, hand and finger is important. Even facial expressions are carefully choreographed to convey the character of the dance.

TOP BALI READS

➡ *Bali Daze – Freefall off the Tourist Trail* – Cat Wheeler's accounts of daily life in Ubud ring more true than other recent books.

➡ *Secrets of Bali: Fresh Light on the Morning of the World* – One of the most readable books about Bali, its people, its traditions and more. Authors Jonathan Copeland and Ni Wayan Murni have a winner.

➡ *Hotel K* – Serving as a cautionary tale to avoid drugs in Bali. Kathryn Bonella offers insight on life inside Kerobokan's infamous prison.

➡ *Eat, Pray, Love* – Love it or hate it, every year this bestseller lures to Bali believers hoping to capture something in Elizabeth Gilbert's prose.

WHAT'S IN A NAME

Far from being straightforward, Balinese names are as fluid as the tides. Everyone has a traditional name, but their other names often reflect events in each individual's life. They also help distinguish between people of the same name, which is perhaps nowhere more necessary than in Bali.

Traditional naming customs seem simple enough, with a predictable gender-nonspecific pattern to names. The order of names, with variations for regions and caste, is as follows:

- **First born** Wayan (Gede, Putu)
- **Second born** Made (Kadek, Nengah, Ngurah)
- **Third born** Nyoman (Komang)
- **Fourth born** Ketut (or just Tut, as in toot)

Subsequent children reuse the same set, but as many families now settle for just two children, you'll meet many Wayans and Mades.

Castes also play an important role in naming and have naming conventions that clearly denote status when added to the birth-order name. Bali's caste system is much less complicated than India's.

- **Sudra** Some 90% of Balinese are part of this, the peasant caste. Names are preceded by the title 'I' for a boy and 'Ni' for a girl.
- **Wesya** The caste of bureaucrats and merchants. Gusti Bagus (male) and Gusti Ayu (female).
- **Ksatria** A top caste, denoting royalty or warriors. I Gusti Ngurah (male) and I Gusti Ayu (female), with additional titles including Anak Agung, and Dewa.
- **Brahman** The top of the heap: teachers and priests. Ida Bagus (male) and Ida Ayu (female).

Traditional names are followed by another given name; this is where parents can get creative. Some names reflect hopes for their child, as in I Nyoman Darma Putra, who's supposed to be 'dutiful' or 'good' (dharma). Others reflect modern influences, such as I Wayan Radio who was born in the 1970s, and Ni Made Atom, who said her parents just liked the sound of this scientific term that also had a bomb named after it.

Many children are tagged for their appearance. Nyoman Darma is often called Nyoman Kopi (coffee) for the darkness of his skin compared with that of his siblings. I Wayan Rama, named after the Ramayana epic, is called Wayan Gemuk (fat) to differentiate his physique from his slighter friend Wayan Kecil (small).

Dances are a regular part of almost every temple festival, and Bali has no shortage of these. There are also dances virtually every night at tourist centres; the most authentic are found in and around Ubud.

In late 2015, nine Balinese dances were officially recognised by Unesco and added to its list of Intangible Cultural Heritage of Humanity.

Gamelan

As with Sumatran and Javanese, Balinese music is based around the gamelan orchestra. The whole gamelan orchestra is known as a *gong* – an-old-fashioned *gong gede* or a more modern *gong kebyar*. It's easy to hear gamelan music in Bali; not only is it a core part of ceremonies but groups practise regularly.

Getting There & Away

AIR

Bali is the second most common entry point to Indonesia. The only airport in Bali, **Ngurah Rai International Airport** (DPS; http://bali-airport.com), is just south of Kuta; however, it is sometimes referred to internationally as Denpasar (which is 15km north) or, on some internet flight-booking sites, as Bali. Completion of the airport's expansion and renovation has transformed it into one of Indonesia's most shiny, modern airports, with world-class facilities and restaurants.

In addition to its international flights, Bali is also a hub for domestic flights across the archipelago.

As of February 2015 departure tax is now included in all international and domestic airfares.

BUS

Mengwi bus terminal is 12km northwest of Denpasar, just off the main road to west Bali. Many long-distance buses to/from Denpasar's **Ubung bus terminal** (p241) stop here.

When travelling to/from south Bali, you can save time by using this terminal instead of Denpasar's. Metered taxis are available and fares should be 150,000Rp to 200,000Rp from Mengwi to various destinations in the south.

Ferry crossing to/from Bali is included in the services offered by numerous bus companies, many of which travel overnight to Java. It's advisable to buy tickets at least one day in advance from a travel agent or at the terminals in Denpasar (Ubung) or Mengwi. Note that flying can be as cheap as taking the bus.

Fares vary between operators; it's worth paying extra for a decent seat. All have air-con. Typical routes from Mengwi and Denpasar include Surabaya (150,000Rp, 12 hours), Yogyakarta (350,000Rp, 16 hours) and Jakarta (470,000Rp, 24 hours). You can also get buses from Singaraja in north Bali.

SEA

Ferries operate between Gilimanuk in western Bali and Ketapang in Java.

Bali is accessible by regular public ferry to Padangbai, Sanur and Amed. Fast boats for tourists serve the Gili Islands and Lombok.

Services to other islands in Indonesia are often in flux, although Pelni, the national shipping line, is reasonably reliable. It schedules large boats on long-distance runs throughout Indonesia.

For Bali, Pelni ships stop at the harbour in Benoa as part of their regular loops throughout Indonesia. Schedules and fares are found on the website. You can enquire and book at the **Pelni ticket office** (☎ 0361-763963; www.pelni.co.id; Jl Raya Kuta 299; ⏲ 8am-noon & 1-4pm Mon-Fri, 8am-1pm Sat) in Tuban.

TRAIN

There is no train service on Bali but the **State Railway Company** (☎ 0361-227131; Jl Diponegoro 150/B4; ⏲ 8am-3pm Mon-Fri, 9am-2pm Sat & Sun) does have an office in Denpasar. From here buses leave for eastern Java, where they link with trains at Banyuwangi for Surabaya, Yogyakarta and Jakarta, among other destinations. Fares and times are comparable to the bus, but the air-conditioned trains are more comfortable, even in economy class. Note: Google Translate works well on the website.

Getting Around

The best way to get around Bali is with your own transport. This gives you the flexibility to explore at will and allows you to reach many places that are otherwise inaccessible.

TO/FROM THE AIRPORT

Fixed-price taxis operate from the official counter at the airport arrivals area. Costs depend on drop-off point; however, efforts may be made to charge you the high end of the range, so it pays to know the location of your hotel.

DESTINATION	FARE (RP)
Candidasa	425,000
Canggu	225,000
Denpasar	125,000-175,000
Jimbaran	100,000-150,000
Kuta Beach	70,000-80,000
Legian	95,000
Nusa Dua	150,000
Sanur	150,000
Seminyak/Kerobokan	110,000-150,000
Ubud	300,000
Ulu Watu	200,000-225,000

Note if you have a surfboard, you'll be charged at least 35,000Rp extra.

While metered Blue Bird taxis aren't officially allowed to pick up passengers from the airport, they are allowed to drop off passengers. Hence another option is to chance your luck on the 3rd floor to see if there's a taxi waiting there.

BEMO

The bemo (a minibus or van with seats down each side) was once the dominant form of public transport in Bali. But widespread motorcycle ownership (which can be cheaper than daily bemo use) has caused the system to wither. Due to unreliable (or complete lack of) scheduling, it's uncommon to see visitors on bemos in Bali. You can certainly expect journeys to be lengthy, and you'll find that getting to many places is both time-consuming and inconvenient.

BICYCLE

Increasingly, people are touring the island by *sepeda* (bicycle). Many visitors are also using bikes around towns and for day trips in Bali.

There are plenty of bicycles for rent in the tourist areas; these cost around 30,000Rp per day.

BOAT

Boats of various sizes serve Nusa Lembongan and Nusa Penida from Sanur and Padangbai.

BALI WEBSITES

Coconuts Bali (http://bali.coconuts.co) Good source for local news, features and reviews.

InBali (www.inbali.org) Glossy site featuring articles, tips and restaurant reviews.

Bali.com (www.bali.com) Overview and practical info.

Bali Belly (www.balibelly.com) Access past editions of this excellent magazine online, which focuses on Bali youth subculture, surfing and skating.

Lonely Planet (www.lonelyplanet.com/indonesia) Destination information, hotel bookings, traveller forum and more.

BUS/TOURIST SHUTTLE

Tourist shuttles are the main mode of transport that independent travellers will use. **Perama** (☎ 0361-751170; www.peramatour.com) has a near monopoly on this service in Bali. It has offices or agents in Kuta, Sanur, Ubud, Lovina, Padangbai and Candidasa, and at least one bus a day links these tourist centres. Fares are reasonable; shuttles are air-conditioned; and it's a good way to meet other travellers.

The public bus **Trans-Sarbagita** (Map p210; Jl Imam Bonjol, Kuta; fare 3500Rp; ⏲ 5am-9pm) is suited more to locals; however, it's handy if you're heading along any of the following four routes: the bypass linking Sanur to Nusa Dua; Denpasar to Jimbaran; Tabanan to Bandara; or Mahendradata to Lebih via Sanur.

CAR & MOTORCYCLE

Car hire is easily arranged in tourist centres. A small jeep costs a negotiable 200,000Rp per day, with unlimited kilometres and very limited insurance. Nearly all vehicles have manual transmission. Petrol costs around 6500Rp per litre.

A much better option is to hire a car with a driver, which costs from 500,000Rp per day including fuel.

Renting motorbikes is a very popular means of getting around Bali, but think carefully before hiring one. It is dangerous, and every year visitors go home with lasting damage; this is no place to learn to ride. Helmet use is mandatory.

Motorbikes are easily hired, and cost around 50,000Rp a day, or less by the week. This should include minimal insurance for the motorcycle (probably with a US$100 excess), but not for additional passengers or property. Many have racks for surfboards.

TAXI

Metered taxis are common in south Bali and Denpasar (but not in Ubud). They are essential for getting around these areas and you can usually flag one down in busy areas. They're often a lot less hassle than haggling with drivers offering 'transport!'.

- Taxis are fairly cheap: Kuta to Seminyak can be just 50,000Rp.
- The best taxi company by far is **Blue Bird Taxi** (☎ 0361-701111; www.bluebirdgroup.com), which uses blue vehicles with a light on the roof bearing a stylised blue bird. Watch out for fakes – there are many. Look for 'Blue Bird' over the windscreen and the phone number. Drivers speak reasonable English and use the meter at all times. Many expats will use no other firm. Blue Bird has a slick phone app that summons a taxi to your location. Flagfall is 7000Rp, and it's 5700Rp for each additional kilometre. Waiting time is 40,000Rp per hour.
- Avoid any taxis where the driver won't use a meter, even after dark when they claim that only fixed fares apply.
- Taxi scams include: lack of change, 'broken' meter, fare-raising detours, and offers for tours, massages, prostitutes etc.

SOUTH BALI

For many people south Bali *is* Bali. Chaotic Kuta and upscale Seminyak throb around the clock. In the south, the Bukit Peninsula is home to some of the island's best hidden beaches, while in the east, Sanur follows the subdued beat of its reef-protected surf. Denpasar is a fascinating excursion into Balinese culture.

Kuta & Legian

☎ 0361

Loud, frenetic and brash are just some of the adjectives commonly used to describe Kuta and Legian, the centre of mass tourism in Bali. Only a couple of decades ago, local hotels tacked their signs up to palm trees. Amid the wall-to-wall cacophony today, such an image seems as foreign as the thought that the area was once rice fields. Parts are just plain ugly, like the unsightly strips that wend their way inland from the beach.

Although this is often the first place many visitors hit in Bali, the region is not for everyone. Kuta has narrow lanes jammed with cheap cafes, surf shops, incessant motorbikes and an uncountable number of T-shirt

South Bali

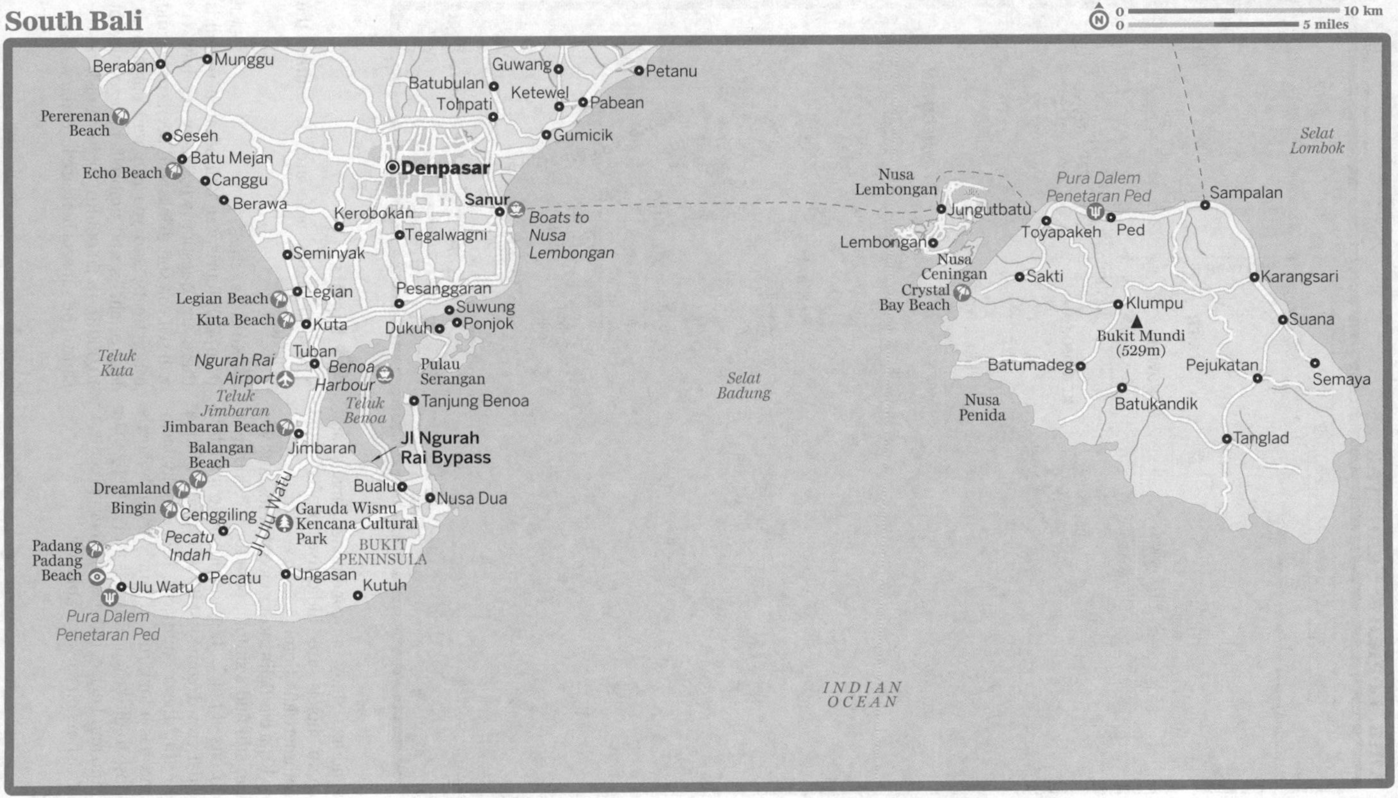

0 10 km
0 5 miles

Beraban
Munggu
Pererenan Beach
Seseh
Batu Mejan
Echo Beach
Canggu
Berawa
Guwang
Batubulan
Tohpati
Ketewel
Pabean
Petanu
Gumicik
Denpasar
Sanur
Boats to Nusa Lembongan
Kerobokan
Tegalwagni
Seminyak
Legian Beach
Legian
Kuta Beach
Kuta
Pesanggaran
Suwung
Ponjok
Dukuh
Teluk Kuta
Ngurah Rai Airport
Tuban
Benoa Harbour
Pulau Serangan
Teluk Jimbaran
Teluk Benoa
Tanjung Benoa
Jimbaran Beach
Jimbaran
Jl Ngurah Rai Bypass
Balangan Beach
Dreamland
Bingin
Cenggiling
Jl Ulu Watu
Bualu
Nusa Dua
Garuda Wisnu Kencana Cultural Park
Pecatu Indah
BUKIT PENINSULA
Padang Padang Beach
Ulu Watu
Pecatu
Ungasan
Kutuh
Pura Dalem Penetaran Ped
Selat Badung
INDIAN OCEAN
Nusa Lembongan
Jungutbatu
Lembongan
Nusa Ceningan
Crystal Bay Beach
Pura Dalem Penetaran Ped
Toyapakeh
Ped
Sampalan
Selat Lombok
Sakti
Karangsari
Klumpu
Bukit Mundi (529m)
Suana
Batumadeg
Pejukatan
Semaya
Batukandik
Nusa Penida
Tanglad

Kuta, Legian & Seminyak

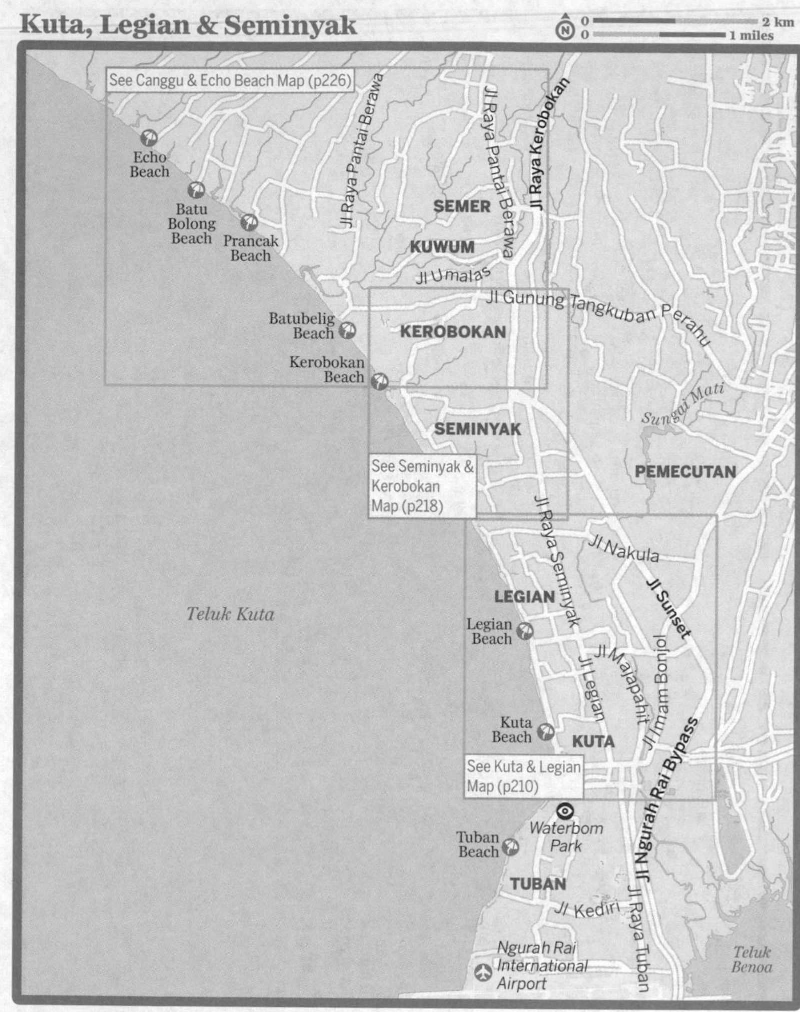

vendors. Shiny air-conditioned malls and chain hotels are indicative of its rapid commercialisation.

Kuta has Bali's most raucous clubs, and you can still find a simple room for 150,000Rp in dozens of hotels. Legian appeals to a slightly older crowd (some jest it's where fans of Kuta go after they're married). It is equally tacky and has a long row of family-friendly hotels close to the beach. Tuban is more sleepy than Kuta and Legian, but has a higher percentage of visitors on package holidays.

Sights

The real sights here are, of course, the beaches.

★Kuta Beach BEACH

(Map p210) Tourism in Bali began here and is there any question why? Low-key hawkers will sell you soft drinks and beer, snacks and other treats, and you can rent surfboards, lounge chairs and umbrellas (negotiable at 10,000Rp to 20,000Rp) or just crash on the sand. The sunsets here are legendary.

★Legian Beach BEACH

(Map p210) An extension of Kuta Beach to the south, Legian Beach is quieter thanks to the lack of a raucous road next to the sand and fewer people.

Double Six Beach BEACH

(Map p210) The beach becomes less crowded as you go north from Legian until very popular Double Six Beach, which is alive with pick-up games of football and volleyball all day long. It's a good place to meet locals.

Tuban Beach BEACH

Tuban's beach is a mixed bag. There are wide and mellow stretches of sand to the south but near the Discovery Mall it disappears entirely.

Memorial Wall MONUMENT

(Map p210; Jl Legian) This memorial wall reflects the international scope of the 2002 bombings, and people from many countries pay their respects. Listing the names of the 202 known victims, including 88 Australians and 35 Indonesians, it is starting to look just a touch faded. Across the street, a parking lot is all that is left of the destroyed **Sari Club** (Map p210).

Activities

From Kuta you can easily go surfing, diving, fishing or rafting anywhere in the southern part of Bali and still be back for the start of happy hour at sunset.

Spas have proliferated, especially in hotels.

Jamu Traditional Spa SPA

(Map p210; ☎0361-752520 ext 165; www.jamutraditionalspa.com; Jl Pantai Kuta, Alam Kul Kul; massage from 600,000Rp; ⊙9am-7pm) In serene surrounds at a resort hotel you can enjoy massage in rooms that open onto a pretty garden courtyard. If you've ever wanted to be part of a fruit cocktail, here's your chance – treatments involve tropical nuts, coconuts, papayas and more, often in fragrant baths.

Bali Sea Turtle Society TURTLE HATCHERY

(Map p210; www.baliseaturtle.org; Kuta Beach; ⊙4.30pm Apr-Oct) Lend a hand in re-releasing turtle hatchlings into the ocean from Kuta Beach around 4.30pm from April to October. The release is organised by the Bali Sea Turtle Society, a conservation group doing great work in protecting olive ridley turtles. Join the queue to collect your baby turtle, pay a small donation, and join the group to release them.

BALI FOR KIDS

There's no shortage of fun for the kids on their Bali visit.

Best Beaches

Kids of all ages will get their kicks at Bali's beaches, from the surf schools at **Kuta Beach** to kite-flying at **Sanur** (p236).

Best Water Fun

Play in the ocean at **Nusa Lembongan** (p242), or snorkel at **Pulau Menjangan** (p296). For something different, walk across the rice fields – who could resist the promise of muddy water filled with ducks, frogs and other fun critters?

Best Adventure Parks

Kids can make like monkeys at **Bali Treetop Adventure Park** (p288) in Candikuning or hit the aquatic playground of **Waterbom Park** in Tuban.

Best for Animals

Take the kids to Ubud's **Sacred Monkey Forest Sanctuary** (p251), the **Bali Bird Park** (p265) south of Ubud, and the **Elephant Safari Park** (p266) north of Ubud.

Waterbom Park WATER PARK

(☎0361-755676; www.waterbom-bali.com; Jl Kartika Plaza; adult/child 490,000/325,000Rp; ⊙9am-6pm) This watery amusement park covers 3.5 hectares of landscaped tropical gardens. It has assorted water slides (21 in total), swimming pools, a FlowRider surf machine, a supervised park for children under five years old, and a 'lazy river' ride. Other indulgences include a food court, a bar and a spa.

Sleeping

Wandering the *gang* (alleys) looking for a cheap room is a rite of passage for many visitors. Small and family-run options are still numerous even as chains and five-star resorts crowd in.

★Hotel Ayu Lili Garden HOTEL $

(Map p210; ☎0361-750557; ayuliligardenhotel@yahoo.com; off Jl Lebak Bene; r with fan/air-con from 175,000/226,000Rp; ❄ 🏊) In a *relatively* quiet area near the beach, this vintage family-run hotel has 22 bungalow-style

Kuta & Legian

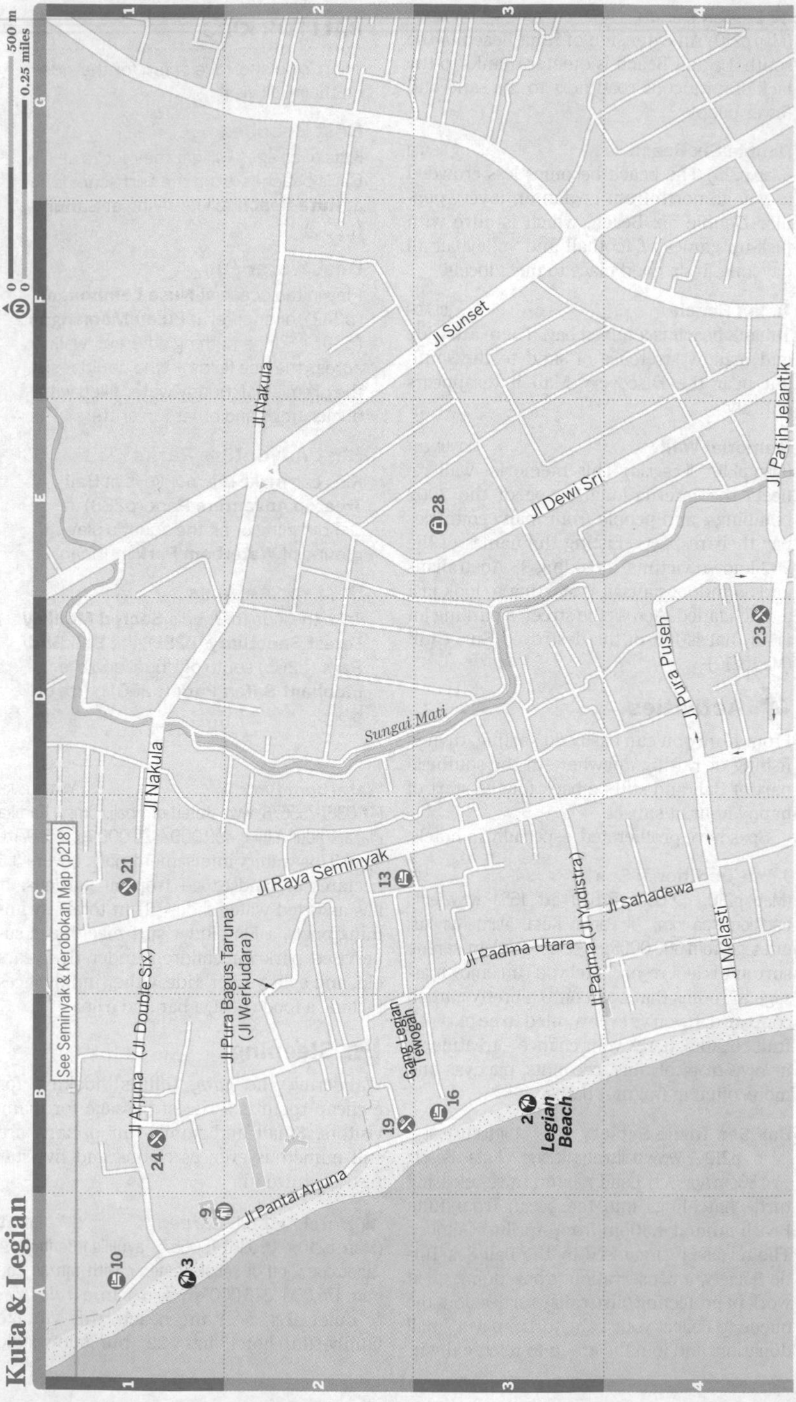

0 500 m
0 0.25 miles

A B C D E F G
1 2 3 4

See Seminyak & Kerobokan Map (p218)

10
Jl Arjuna (Jl Double Six)
21
Jl Nakula
24
3
9
Jl Pura Bagus Taruna (Jl Werkudara)
Jl Nakula
Jl Pantai Arjuna
Jl Raya Seminyak
19
13
Gang Legian Tewogah
Sungai Mati
16
28
Jl Sunset
Jl Padma Utara
2
Legian Beach
Jl Dewi Sri
Jl Padma (Jl Yudistra)
Jl Sahadewa
Jl Pura Puseh
Jl Melasti
23
Jl Patih Jelantik

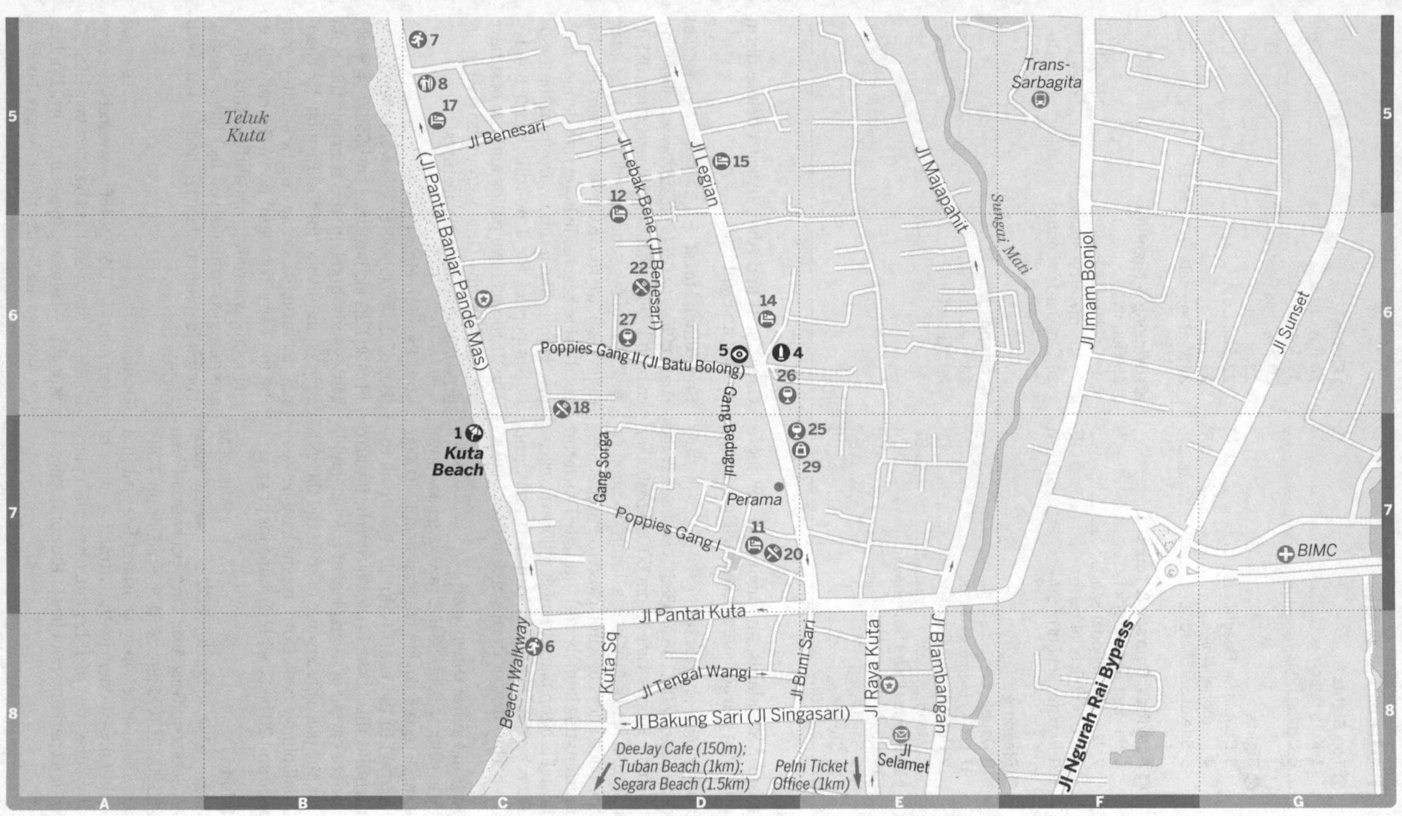
Teluk Kuta
Trans-Sarbagita
Jl Benesari
(Jl Pantai Banjar Pande Mas)
Jl Lebak Bene (Jl Benesari)
Jl Legian
Jl Majapahit
Sungai Mati
Jl Imam Bonjol
Jl Sunset
Poppies Gang II (Jl Batu Bolong)
Gang Bedugul
Gang Sorga
Kuta Beach
Perama
Poppies Gang I
BIMC
Jl Pantai Kuta
Beach Walkway
Kuta Sq
Jl Tengal Wangi
Jl Buni Sari
Jl Raya Kuta
Jl Blambangan
Jl Ngurah Rai Bypass
Jl Bakung Sari (Jl Singasari)
Jl Selamet
DeeJay Cafe (150m); Tuban Beach (1km); Segara Beach (1.5km)
Pelni Ticket Office (1km)

Kuta & Legian

Top Sights
1 Kuta Beach ... C7
2 Legian Beach ... B3

Sights
3 Double Six Beach ... A1
4 Memorial Wall ... D6
5 Site of Sari Club ... D6

Activities, Courses & Tours
6 Bali Sea Turtle Society ... C8
7 Jamu Traditional Spa ... C5
8 Pro Surf School ... C5
9 Rip Curl School of Surf ... A1

Sleeping
10 Double-Six ... A1
11 Funky Monkey Hostel ... D7
12 Hotel Ayu Lili Garden ... D5
13 Island ... C2
14 Kayun Hostel Downtown ... D6
15 Love Fashion Hotel ... D5
16 Sari Beach Hotel ... B3
17 Stones ... C5

Eating
18 Fat Chow ... C6
19 Mozzarella ... B2
20 Poppies Restaurant ... D7
21 Saleko ... C1
22 Stakz Bar & Grill ... D6
23 Take ... D4
24 Warung Asia Thai Food ... B1

Drinking & Nightlife
25 Bounty ... D7
Double-Six Rooftop ... (see 10)
Infamy@The Stones ... (see 17)
26 Sky Garden Lounge ... D6
27 Twice Bar ... D6

Shopping
28 Luke Studer ... E3
29 Surfer Girl ... E7

rooms. Standards are high and for more dosh you can add amenities such as a fridge.

Funky Monkey Hostel HOSTEL **$**
(Map p210; ☎0812 4636 4386; www.funkymonkeybali.com; Poppies Lane 1; dm 60,000-120,000Rp, r 300,000Rp;) In a lovely location in the back alleys of Kuta, close to Poppies Restaurant, this homely and intimate Dutch-run hostel is a top place to meet fellow travellers. There's a small pool, free pancakes and cheap beer. The cheaper dorms are outdoor bunks.

Kayun Hostel Downtown HOSTEL **$**
(Map p210; ☎0361-758442; www.kayun-downtown.com; Jl Legian; dm incl breakfast from 190,000Rp;) In the heart of Kuta, close to all the nightlife, this hostel is the place to be if you're here to party. Set in an elegant colonial building, the place has a sense of style and there's a small plunge pool. Dorm rooms have between four and 20 beds, with curtains for privacy.

Island GUESTHOUSE **$$**
(Map p210; ☎0361-762722; www.theislandhotelbali.com; Gang Abdi; dm/r incl breakfast from 250,000/500,000Rp;) One of Bali's few flashpacker options, Island is a real find – literally. Hidden in the attractive maze of tiny lanes west of Jl Legian, this stylish place with a sparkling pool lies at the confluence of Gang 19, 21 and Abdi. It has a deluxe dorm room with eight beds.

Sari Beach Hotel HOTEL **$$**
(Map p210; ☎0361-751635; www.saribeachinn.com; off Jl Padma Utara; r incl breakfast from US$70;) Follow your ears down a long *gang* (alleyway) to the roar of the surf at this good-value beachside hotel that defines mellow. It feels like a time warp from the 1980s but is perfect for a no-frills beach holiday. The 21 rooms have patios and the best have big soaking tubs. Grassy grounds boast many little statues and water features.

Love Fashion Hotel HOTEL **$$**
(Map p210; ☎0361-849 6688; www.lovefhotels.com; Jl Legian 121; r incl breakfast from US$100;) This gaudy hotel in the heart of the Kuta strip is an offshoot of the Fashion TV channel, featuring a design that's suitably over the top. Strut your stuff down the catwalk in the lobby, where mirrors and lighting effects are designed to make you feel like a model. There's a rooftop Jacuzzi and a bar with nightly parties.

Double-Six RESORT **$$$**
(Map p210; ☎0361-730466; www.double-six.com; Double Six Beach 66; r incl breakfast from US$350;) A colossus five-star resort, Double-Six takes a leaf out of the Vegas book of

extravagance. Fronted by a luxurious 120m pool, the spacious rooms all overlook the beach, and have 24-hour butlers and TVs in the bathrooms. It has several restaurants and an enormous rooftop bar (p215).

Stones RESORT $$$
(Map p210; ☎0361-300 5888; www.stoneshotelbali.com; Jl Pantai Kuta; r incl breakfast from US$190; ❄📶🏊) Looming across the road from Kuta Beach, this vast resort boasts a huge pool, a vertical garden and nearly 300 rooms in five-storey blocks. The design is hip and contemporary, and high-tech features such as huge HD TVs abound. It's one of the growing number of new mega-hotels along this strip; it's affiliated with Marriott.

Eating

There's a profusion of places to eat around Kuta and Legian. Tourist cafes, with their cheap menus of Indonesian standards, sandwiches and pizza, are ubiquitous. Look closely and you'll find genuine Balinese warungs (food stalls) tucked in amid it all.

Saleko INDONESIAN $
(Map p210; Jl Nakula 4; meals from 11,000Rp; ⏲8am-11pm) If you haven't tried Masakan Padang food yet, you haven't eaten proper Indonesian. Saleko is a great place to sample this simple, delicious and cheap Sumatran street food. Spicy grilled chicken and fish dare you to ladle on the volcanic sambal – not despiced for timid tourist palates. All dishes are halal; there's no alcohol.

Warung Asia Thai Food ASIAN $
(Map p210; ☎0361-742 0202; Jl Werkudara; meals from 32,000Rp; ⏲11am-late; 📶) Staffed by exceptionally friendly waiters, this popular upstairs warung serves both Indo classics and Thai fare. It gets boozy and raucous at night.

★**Fat Chow** ASIAN $$
(Map p210; ☎0361-753516; www.fatchowbali.com; Poppies Gang II; mains from 60,000Rp; ⏲10am-11pm; 📶) A stylish, modern take on the traditional open-fronted cafe, Fat Chow serves up Asian-accented fare at long picnic tables, small tables and lounges. The food is creative, with lots of options for sharing. Among the favourites: crunchy Asian salad, pork buns, Tokyo prawns and authentic pad thai.

Poppies Restaurant INDONESIAN $$
(Map p210; ☎0361-751059; www.poppiesbali.com; Poppies Gang I; mains 43,000-120,000Rp; ⏲8am-11pm; 📶) Opening its doors in 1973, Poppies was one of the first restaurants to be established in Kuta (Poppies Gang I is even named after it). It's popular for its elegant garden setting and a menu of upmarket Balinese, Western and Thai cuisine. The *rijstaffel* (selection of dishes served with rice) and seafood is popular.

Take JAPANESE $$
(Map p210; ☎0361-759745; Jl Patih Jelantik; meals 70,000-300,000Rp; ⏲11am-11pm; 📶) Flee Bali for a relaxed version of Tokyo just by ducking under the traditional fabric shield over the doorway at this ever-expanding restaurant. Hyper-fresh sushi, sashimi and more are prepared under the keen eyes of a team of chefs behind a long counter. The head chef is a stalwart at the Jimbaran fish market in the early hours.

Stakz Bar & Grill AUSTRALIAN $$
(Map p210; ☎0361-762129; www.stakzbarandgrill.com; Jl Benesari; mains 40,000-140,000Rp; ⏲8am-midnight; 📶) From Vegemite on toast and a flat white for brekkie, a potato-cake roll or a meat pie in the arvo, and an Aussie burger with the lot (including beetroot, egg and pineapple) for dinner: Stakz is a good spot to sample typical Australian tucker.

Mozzarella ITALIAN, SEAFOOD $$$
(Map p210; ☎0361-751654; www.mozzarella-resto.com; Jl Padma Utara; meals from 100,000Rp; ⏲noon-11pm; 📶) The best of the beachfront restaurants on Legian's car-free strip, Mozzarella serves Italian fare that's more authentic than most. Fresh fish also features; service is rather polished and there are various open-air areas for moonlit dining, plus a more sheltered dining room.

Drinking & Nightlife

Sunset on the beach (at around 6pm year-round) is the big attraction, perhaps while enjoying a drink at a cafe with a sea view or with a beer vendor on the beach. Later on, the legendary nightlife action heats up.

Sky Garden Lounge BAR, CLUB
(Map p210; www.skygardenbali.com; Jl Legian 61; ⏲24hr) This multilevel palace of flash flirts with height restrictions from its rooftop bar where all of Kuta twinkles around you. Look for top DJs, a ground-level cafe and paparazzi-wannabes. Munchers can enjoy a long menu of bar snacks and meals, which most people pair with shots. Roam from floor to floor in this vertical playpen.

SURFING IN BALI

Bali's legendary breaks are found right around the south side of the island. There's a large infrastructure of schools, board-hire places, cheap surfer accommodation and more that caters to the crowds.

Here are six famous spots you won't want to miss:

➡ **Kuta Beach** (p208) Where surfing came to Asia. Long, steady breaks mean this can be a good place for beginners.

➡ **Echo Beach** (p223) Northwest of Kerobokan; there's a good surfer scene here, including cafes, board rental and more.

➡ **Ulu Watu** (p232) Some of the largest – and most famous – sets in Bali. It featured in legendary surf movie *Morning of the Earth*.

➡ **Pantai Medewi** (p301) Famous point break with a ride right into a river mouth.

➡ **Pantai Keramas** (p267) This right-hander fast reef break is home to Bali's main surf event and has night surfing under floodlights.

➡ **Nusa Lembongan** (p242) The island is a mellow scene for surfers and nonsurfers alike. The breaks are accessible from accommodations.

Magic Seaweed (www.magicseaweed.com) and **Bali Waves** (www.baliwaves.com) are both good resources for surf reports, forecasts and tips.

Stalls on or near the beach hire out surfboards and boogie boards. In Kuta and around there are plenty of stores selling new and used boards; many can repair dings.

Ideal for beginners, **Pro Surf School** (Map p210; ☎0361-751200; www.prosurfschool.com; Jl Pantai Kuta; lessons from €45) is right across from the classic stretch of Kuta Beach. Facilities include semiprivate lesson areas and a hostel (dorms from €15). **Rip Curl School of Surf** (Map p210; ☎0361-735858; www.ripcurlschoolofsurf.com; Jl Arjuna; lessons from 700,000Rp) offers classes for beginners and experts alike.

Surf camps have become all the rage in south Bali, and offer packages for surf lessons and accommodation. The **Green Room** (Map p218; ☎0361-738894; www.thegreenroombali.com; Gang Puri Kubu 63B; dm incl breakfast from €20; ❄📶🏊) in Seminyak is very popular.

The World Surf League pro circuit comes to Bali with the Kommune Bali Pro held at Keramas in May, and the Quiksilver Uluwatu Challenge in August. The **Rip Curl Cup** (http://live.ripcurl.com/ripcurlcup) at Padang Padang in August is another pro event.

Bounty CLUB
(Map p210; www.bountydiscotheque.com; Jl Legian; ⏰8pm-4am) Set on a faux sailing boat amid a mini-mall of food and drink, the Bounty is a vast open-air disco that pumps all night to hip-hop, techno, house and party tracks. Foam parties, go-go dancers, drag shows and cheap shots add to the rowdiness.

Twice Bar BAR
(Map p210; Poppies Gang II; ⏰7pm-2am) Where the local cool kids hang out, Twice Bar is home to Kuta's underground music scene. It's a sweaty, dark dive that hosts local punk, indie and hardcore bands, with the occasional international act passing through. It's owned by the drummer from Balinese punk band Superman is Dead.

Infamy@The Stones LOUNGE
(Map p210; ☎0361-766100; www.thestones-kuta.com; Jl Pantai Kuta; cocktails from 85,000Rp; ⏰11am-10pm; 📶) Bring your swimming costume to enjoy Kuta's famous sunset while sipping a cocktail in a Jacuzzi at this stylish rooftop bar overlooking the ocean. There's Bintang on tap and quality food, too.

DeeJay Cafe CLUB
(Map p210; ☎0361-758880; Jl Kartika Plaza 8X, Kuta Station Hotel; ⏰midnight-9am) The choice for closing out the night (or starting the day). House DJs play tribal, underground, progressive, trance, electro and more. Beware of posers who set their alarms for 5am and arrive all fresh.

Double-Six Rooftop BAR

(Map p210; ☎0361-734300; www.doublesixrooftop.com; Double Six Beach 66; ⊙3-11pm;) Sharks swimming in aquarium-lined walls, suave lounges, a commanding location and tiki torches: this ostentatious bar above the Double-Six hotel could easily pass as a villain's lair from a Bond film. Amazing sunset views are best enjoyed from the circular booths enclosed by water – it's a minimum 1,000,000Rp spend to reserve one, but it's redeemable against food, and perfect for groups.

Shopping

Kuta has a vast concentration of cheap, tawdry shops, as well as huge, flashy surf-gear emporiums. As you head north along Jl Legian, the quality of the shops improves, and you'll start finding cute little boutiques – especially near Jl Arjuna, which has wholesale fabric, clothing and craft stores, giving it a bazaar-like feel. Large malls are also making inroads.

Surfer Girl CLOTHING

(Map p210; www.surfer-girl.com; Jl Legian 138; ⊙9am-10.30pm) A local legend, this vast store for girls of all ages has a winsome logo that says it all. Clothes, gear, bikinis and plenty of other stuff in every shade of bubblegum ever made.

Luke Studer SURFBOARDS

(Map p210; ☎0361-894 7425; www.studersurfboards.com; Jl Dewi Sri 7A; ⊙9am-8pm) Legendary board shaper Luke Studer works from this large and glossy shop. Shortboards, retro fishes, single fins and classic longboards are sold ready-made or custom-built.

Information

DANGERS & ANNOYANCES

The streets and *gang* are usually safe but there are annoyances. Your biggest irritation will likely be the chaotic traffic.

Things to watch out for:

- **Alcohol poisoning** There are ongoing reports of injuries and deaths among tourists and locals due to *arak* (the local booze, traditionally distilled from palm or cane sugar) being adulterated with methanol, a poisonous form of alcohol. Avoid offers of free cocktails and any offers of *arak*.
- **Surf** The surf can be dangerous, with a strong current on some tides, especially up north in Legian. Lifeguards patrol swimming areas of the beaches at Kuta and Legian, indicated by red-and-yellow flags. If they say the water is too rough or unsafe to swim in, they mean it. Red flags with skull and crossbones mean no swimming allowed.
- **Theft** Visitors lose things from unlocked (and some locked) hotel rooms and from the beach. Going into the water and leaving valuables on the beach is simply asking for trouble. Snatch-thefts by crooks on motorbikes are common. Valuable items can be left at your hotel reception.
- **Water pollution** The sea around Kuta is commonly contaminated by run-off from both built-up areas and surrounding farmland, especially after heavy rain. Swim far away from streams, including the often foul and smelly one at Double Six Beach.

EMERGENCY

Police Station (Map p210; ☎0361-751598; Jl Raya Kuta; ⊙24hr) Ask to speak to the tourist police.

Tourist Police Post (Map p210; ☎0361-784 5988; Jl Pantai Kuta; ⊙24hr) This is a branch of the main police station in Denpasar. It's right across from the beach; the officers have a gig that is sort of like a Balinese *Baywatch*.

INTERNET ACCESS

Most hotels and cafes have wi-fi. The back lanes of Kuta and Legian have numerous internet spots.

MEDICAL SERVICES

BIMC (Map p210; ☎0361-761263; www.bimcbali.com; Jl Ngurah Rai 100X; ⊙24hr) On the bypass road just east of Kuta near the Bali Galleria shopping mall. It's a modern Australian-run clinic that can do tests, hotel visits and arrange medical evacuation. Visits can cost US$100 or more. It has a branch in Nusa Dua.

MONEY

ATMs abound and can be found everywhere, including in the ubiquitous Circle K and Mini Mart convenience stores.

Numerous 'authorised' moneychangers are efficient, open long hours and may offer good exchange rates. Be cautious, though, where the rates are markedly better than the norm. Extra fees may apply or the moneychangers may be adeptly short-changing their customers.

POST

Postal agencies that can send mail are common.

Main Post Office (Map p210; ☎0361-754012; Jl Selamet; ⊙7am-2pm Mon-Thu, 7-11am Fri, 7am-1pm Sat) On a little road east of Jl Raya Kuta, this small and efficient post office is well practised in shipping large packages.

Getting There & Away

BEMO

Bemos (minibuses) regularly travel between Kuta and the Tegal terminal in Denpasar; the fare should be 8000Rp. The route goes from Jl Raya Kuta near Jl Pantai Kuta, looping past the beach, then on Jl Melasti and back past Bemo Corner for the trip to Denpasar.

TOURIST SHUTTLE BUS

Perama (Map p210; ☎0361-751551; www.peramatour.com; Jl Legian 39; ⏰7am-10pm) is the main shuttle-bus operation in town, and may do hotel pickups and drop-offs for an extra 10,000Rp (confirm this with the staff when making arrangements). It usually has at least one bus a day to its destinations.

DESTINATION	COST (RP)	DURATION (HR)
Candidasa	75,000	3½
Lovina	125,000	4½
Padangbai	75,000	3
Sanur	35,000	30min
Ubud	60,000	2

Getting Around

The hardest part about getting around south Bali is the traffic. Besides using taxis, you can rent a motorbike, often with a surfboard rack. One of the nicest ways to get around the area is by foot along the beach.

Seminyak & Kerobokan

Seminyak is flash, brash and arguably a bit phoney. It's also a very dynamic place, home to dozens of restaurants and a wealth of exclusive galleries, and the centre of life for hordes of the island's expats.

Seminyak seamlessly merges with Kerobokan, which is immediately north; in fact the exact border between the two is as fuzzy as most other geographic details in Bali. The many restaurants combine to give travellers the greatest choice of style and budget in Bali.

One notable landmark is the notorious **Kerobokan jail** (Map p218; Jl Gunung Tangkuban Perahu), home to prisoners both infamous and unknown.

Sights

Seminyak Beach BEACH
(Map p218) Seminyak continues the long sweep of Kuta Beach. A sunset lounger and an ice-cold Bintang on the beach at sunset is simply magical. A good stretch can be found near Pura Petitenget, and it tends to be less crowded than further south in Kuta.

Fewer crowds also means that the beach is less patrolled and the water conditions less monitored. The odds of encountering dangerous rip tides and other hazards are ever-present, especially as you head north.

Pura Petitenget HINDU TEMPLE
(Map p218; Jl Pantai Kaya Aya) FREE This is an important temple and the scene of many ceremonies. It is one of a string of sea temples that stretches from Pura Luhur Ulu Watu on the Bukit Peninsula north to Pura Tanah Lot in western Bali. Petitenget loosely translates as 'magic box'; it was a treasured belonging of the legendary 16th-century priest Nirartha, who refined the Balinese religion and visited this site often.

Batubelig Beach BEACH
(Map p226) Kerobokan's beach is equal to more famous beaches north and south. You can walk along the curving sands northwest towards popular spots as far as Echo Beach.

Activities

Seminyak's and Kerobokan's spas are among the best in Bali, and offer a huge range of treatments and therapies.

Spas

★**Jari Menari** SPA
(Map p218; ☎0361-736740; www.jarimenari.com; Jl Raya Basangkasa 47; sessions from 385,000Rp; ⏰9am-9pm) Jari Menari is true to its name, which means 'dancing fingers': your body will be one happy dance floor. The all-male staff use massage techniques that emphasise rhythm. You can book online, too.

Sundari Day Spa SPA
(Map p218; ☎0361-735073; www.sundari-dayspa.com; Jl Petitenget 7; massages from 200,000Rp; ⏰10am-10pm) This lovely spa strives to offer the services of a five-star resort without the high prices. The massage oils and other potions are organic, and there's a full menu of therapies and treatments on offer.

Amo Beauty Spa SPA
(Map p218; ☎0361-473 7943; www.amospa.com; 100 Jl Petitenget; massages from 200,000Rp; ⏰9am-9pm) With some of Asia's top models lounging about it feels like you've stumbled into a *Vogue* shoot. In addition to massages,

SEMINYAK VILLAS

Whether you're in Bali for a honeymoon, romantic getaway or you're just looking to splurge, staying in your own villa is a sublime experience. All villas offer full privacy within a compound, with front gate, private pool, garden, butler and Zen-like serenity. Seminyak is most well known for its abundance of villas, so here are a few of our favourites.

Villa Kubu (Map p218; ☎0361-731129; www.villakubu.com; Jl Raya Seminyak, Gang Plawa 33F; villa incl breakfast US$330; ❄📶🏊) A wonderful choice for those seeking that quintessential Balinese villa experience. In a residential locale, all private villas have their own pool, surrounded by landscaped Balinese gardens with frangipani. It has massive semi-outdoor bathrooms and luxurious interiors with all the mod cons. Breakfast is all you can eat and there's a free shuttle service.

Samaya (Map p218; ☎0361-731149; www.thesamayabali.com; Jl Kayu Aya; villas from US$600; ❄@📶🏊) Understated yet cultured, the Samaya is one of the best bets for a villa right on the beach in south Bali. It boasts 30 villas in a luxurious contemporary style, each featuring a private pool. The food, from breakfast onwards, is superb.

One Eleven (Map p218; ☎0361-731343; www.111resorts.com; Jl Pangkung Sari 3; villas incl breakfast from US$550; ❄📶🏊) Hidden behind the minimalist facade of a suave Japanese restaurant, these villas have a 1960s modernist feel about them: cool, sophisticated and stylish. Each has a manicured lawn, a sparkling pool, a spa pavilion and an open lounge with full kitchen, where your private butler will cook up your breakfast. Contemporary rooms have icy air-conditioning; elegant white-tone bathrooms have stand-alone tubs.

Mutiara Bali (Map p218; ☎0361-734966; www.mutiarabali.com; Jl Braban 77; r US$75-140, villas from US$155; ❄@📶🏊) The 17 private villas here are exceptionally good value, each with an open lounge area looking out to a private plunge pool. While there are also hotel-style rooms, here it's all about the villas.

services range from haircare to pedicures and unisex waxing. Book ahead.

Prana SPA
(Map p218; ☎0361-730840; www.pranaspabali.com; Jl Kunti 118X; massages from 450,000Rp; ⏰9am-10pm) A palatial Moorish fantasy that is easily the most lavishly decorated spa in Bali, Prana offers everything from basic hour-long massages to facials and all manner of beauty treatments.

Other Activities

Sate Bali COOKING COURSE
(Map p218; ☎0361-736734; Jl Kayu Aya 22; courses from 375,000Rp; ⏰9.30am-1.30pm) Restaurant Sate Bali runs this excellent Balinese cooking course. Students learn to prepare Balinese spices and sambals, which are then used to flavour duck, fish and pork dishes.

Jiwa Bikram Yoga YOGA
(Map p218; ☎0361-841 3689; www.jiwabikramyogabali.com; Jl Petitenget 78; classes from 180,000Rp; ⏰9am-8pm) In a convenient location, this no-frills place offers several different types of yoga, including bikram, hot flow and yin.

Sleeping

Seminyak has a wide range of accommodation, from world-class resorts to humble hotels hidden down backstreets.

Kerobokan and Seminyak are villa country, with walled developments running north from Seminyak and scattering among the rice fields.

Seminyak

Ned's Hide-Away GUESTHOUSE $
(Map p218; ☎0361-731270; nedshide@dps.centrin.net.id; Gang Bima 3; r with fan/air-con from 180,000/300,000Rp; ❄📶) While its standards have slipped in recent times, Ned's remains a good budget choice with its mix of basic and more plush rooms. Wi-fi is only available in the reception area.

Raja Gardens GUESTHOUSE $
(Map p218; ☎0361-730494; jdw@eksadata.com; off Jl Camplung Tanduk; r fan/air-con from 400,000/600,000Rp; ❄📶🏊) Here since 1980, this old-school guesthouse has spacious, grassy grounds with fruit trees and a quiet spot located almost on the beach. The eight

Seminyak & Kerobokan

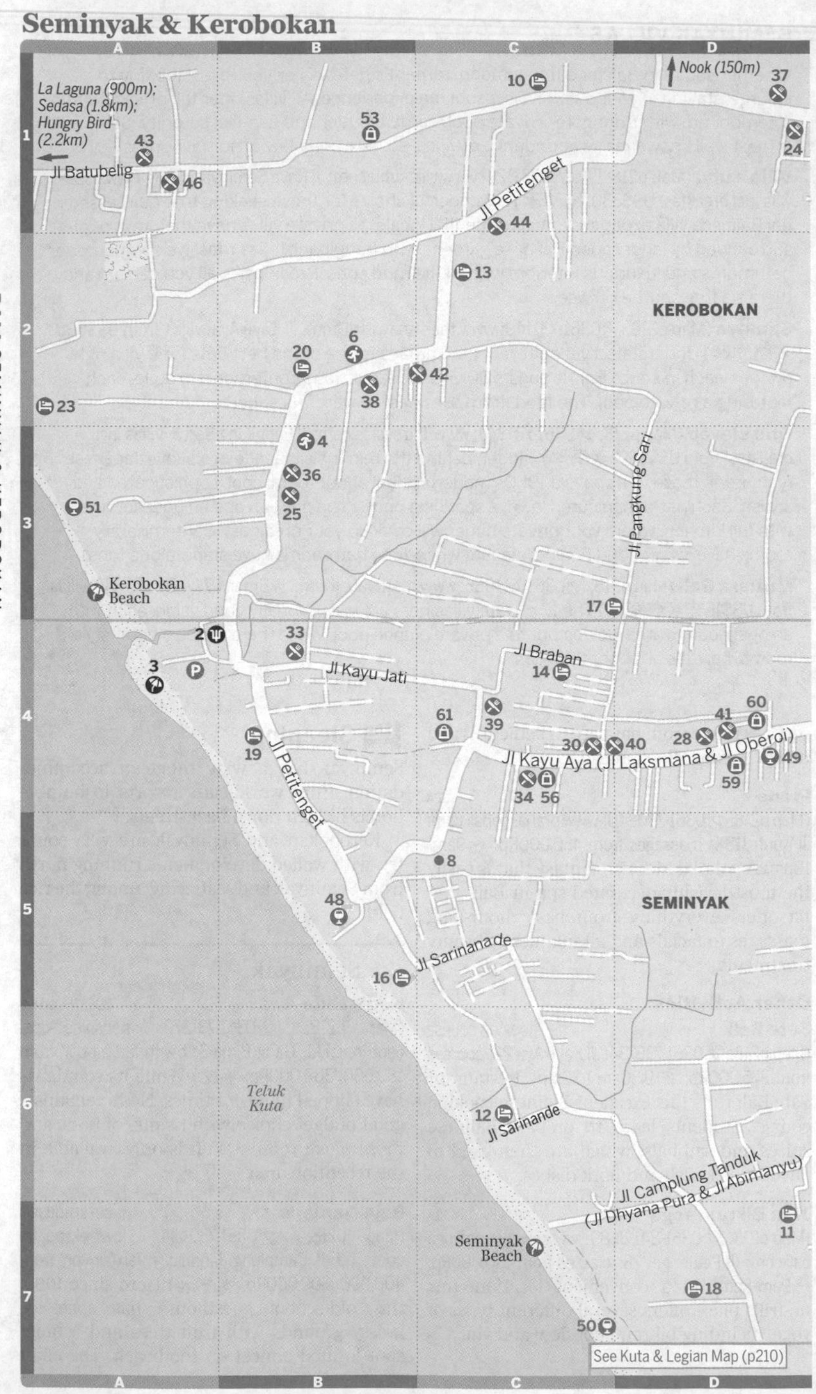

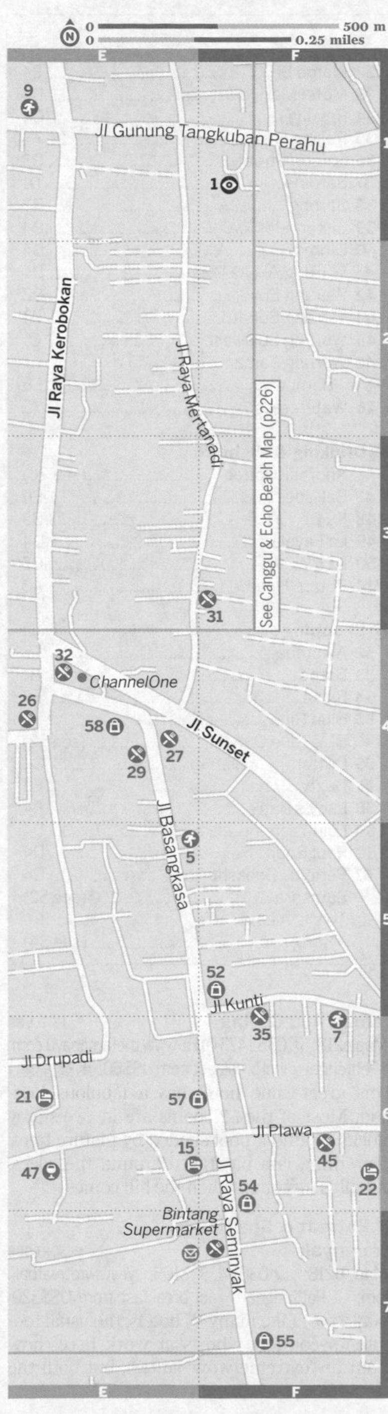

rooms are fairly basic but there are open-air bathrooms and plenty of potted plants. The pool is a nice spot to lounge by, and it's generally a mellow place popular with youngish couples.

Villa Karisa HOTEL **$$**

(Map p218; ☎0361-739395; www.villakarisabali.com; Jl Drupadi 100X; r US$89-200;) It's like visiting the gracious friends in Bali you wish you had. Ideally located on a little *gang* off busy Jl Drupadi, this large villa-style inn has a row of rooms filled with antiques and many comforts. Guests gather in the common room or around the luxurious 12m pool. Enjoy Javanese antique style in the Shiva room.

★Oberoi HOTEL **$$$**

(Map p218; ☎0361-730361; www.oberoihotels.com; Jl Kayu Aya; r incl breakfast from US$320;) The beautifully understated Oberoi has been a refined Balinese-style beachside retreat since 1971. All accommodation options have private verandas, and as you move up in price, additional features include walled villas, ocean views and private pools. From the cafe that overlooks the almost-private sweep of beach to the numerous luxuries, this is a place to spoil yourself.

Luna2 Studiotel BOUTIQUE HOTEL **$$$**

(Map p218; ☎0361-730402; www.luna2.com; Jl Sarinande 20; r incl breakfast US$300-405;) Is it Mondrian? Is it Roy Lichtenstein? We're not sure which modern artists are the inspiration for this eye-popping hotel, but we can say the results astound. The 14 boldly decorated studio apartments feature kitchens, gadgetry, balconies and have access to a rooftop bar looking over the ocean. A 16-seat cinema shows movies, and there's a Smart car for guest use.

Kerobokan

M Boutique Hostel HOSTEL **$**

(Map p218; ☎0361-473 4142; www.mboutiquehostel.com; Jl Petitenget 8; dm 150,000Rp;) A tasteful and contemporary choice for backpackers, M Boutique's beds are capsule dorms, which come with the benefit of privacy. Each has shutter blinds, a small table, a reading light and a power point. The neatly trimmed lawn and small plunge pool add charm. Rates go up slightly on weekends.

Seminyak & Kerobokan

Sights
- 1 Kerobokan Jail ... F1
- 2 Pura Petitenget ... A4
- 3 Seminyak Beach ... A4

Activities, Courses & Tours
- 4 Amo Beauty Spa ... B3
- 5 Jari Menari ... E5
- 6 Jiwa Bikram Yoga ... B2
- 7 Prana ... F6
- 8 Sate Bali ... C5
- 9 Sundari Day Spa ... E1

Sleeping
- 10 Brown Feather ... C1
- 11 Green Room ... D7
- 12 Luna2 Studiotel ... C6
- 13 M Boutique Hostel ... C2
- 14 Mutiara Bali ... C4
- 15 Ned's Hide-Away ... E6
- 16 Oberoi ... B5
- 17 One Eleven ... C3
- 18 Raja Gardens ... D7
- 19 Samaya ... B4
- 20 Taman Ayu Cottage ... B2
- 21 Villa Karisa ... E6
- 22 Villa Kubu ... F6
- 23 W Retreat & Spa Bali – Seminyak ... A2

Eating
- 24 Barbacoa ... D1
- 25 Biku ... B3
- 26 Corner House ... E4
- 27 Divine Earth ... E4
- 28 Earth Cafe & Market ... D4
- 29 Fat Gajah ... E4
- 30 Ginger Moon ... C4
- 31 Gusto Gelato & Coffee ... F3
- 32 Mama San ... E4
- 33 Motel Mexicola ... B4
- 34 Revolver ... C4
- 35 Rolling Fork ... F5
- 36 Saigon Street ... B3
- 37 Sardine ... D1
- 38 Sarong ... B2
- 39 Sisterfields ... C4
- 40 Ultimo ... D4
- 41 Warung Aneka Rasa ... D4
- 42 Warung Eny ... C2
- 43 Warung Sobat ... A1
- 44 Warung Sulawesi ... C1
- 45 Warung Taman Bambu ... F6
- 46 Watercress ... A1

Drinking & Nightlife
- Anomali Coffee ... (see 26)
- 47 Bali Joe ... E6
- 48 Ku De Ta ... B5
- 49 La Favela ... D4
- 50 La Plancha ... C7
- 51 Potato Head ... A3

Shopping
- 52 Ashitaba ... F5
- 53 Bathe ... B1
- 54 Biasa ... F6
- 55 Blue Glue ... F7
- Blue Glue Outlet ... (see 52)
- 56 Drifter ... C4
- 57 Duzty ... E6
- 58 Lucy's Batik ... E4
- 59 Lulu Yasmine ... D4
- 60 Paul Ropp ... D4
- 61 Periplus Bookshop ... C4
- Samsara ... (see 52)
- This Is A Love Song ... (see 34)

Brown Feather B&B **$$**
(Map p218; ☎0361-473 2165; www.brownfeather.com; Jl Batu Belig 100; r incl breakfast 700,000-900,000Rp; ❄☎≈) On the main road, but backing on to rice paddies, this B&B exudes a Dutch-Javanese colonial charm. Rooms mix simplicity with old-world character, such as wooden writing desks and washbasins made from old Singer sewing machines. For rice-field views, go for room 205 or 206. There's a small, attractive pool and free bicycle rental.

It's a few minutes' stroll to Kerobokan's fashionable eating strip, and a short taxi trip to the beach.

Taman Ayu Cottage HOTEL **$$**
(Map p218; ☎0361-473 0111; www.thetamanayu.com; Jl Petitenget; r incl breakfast from US$60; ❄@☎≈) This great-value hotel has a fabulous location. Most of the 52 rooms are in two-storey blocks around a pool shaded by mature trees. Everything is a bit frayed around the edges, but all is forgotten when the bill comes.

W Retreat & Spa Bali – Seminyak RESORT **$$$**
(Map p218; ☎0361-473 8106; www.wretreatbali.com; Jl Petitenget; r incl breakfast from US$320; ❄@☎≈) Like many W hotels, the usual too-cute-for-comfort vibe is at work here (how 'bout an 'extreme wow' suite?), but both the

location on a wave-tossed stretch of sand and the views are hard to quibble with. Stylish, hip bars, restaurants and smiling staff abound. The rooms all have balconies, but not all have ocean views.

Eating

Jl Kayu Aya is the focus of Seminyak eating, but there are great choices for every budget virtually everywhere. Seminyak has developed a full-on cafe culture. Kerobokan, meanwhile, boasts some of Bali's best restaurants, both budget and top end.

Seminyak

Warung Aneka Rasa INDONESIAN $
(Map p218; Jl Kayu Aya; meals from 20,000Rp; 7am-8pm) Keeping things real in the heart of Seminyak's upmarket retail ghetto, this humble warung cooks up all the Indo classics in an inviting open-front cafe.

Warung Taman Bambu BALINESE $
(Map p218; 0361-888 1567; Jl Plawa 10; mains from 25,000Rp; 9am-10pm;) This classic warung may look simple from the street but the comfy tables are – like the many fresh and spicy dishes on offer – a cut above the norm. There's a small stand for *babi guling* (suckling pig) right next door.

Revolver CAFE $
(Map p218; off Jl Kayu Aya; breakfast from 40,000Rp; 7am-6pm;) Wander down a tiny *gang* and push through narrow wooden doors to reach this matchbox of a coffee bar that does an excellent selection of brews. There are just a few tables in the creatively retro room that's styled like a Wild West saloon; nab one and enjoy tasty fresh bites for breakfast and lunch. The juices are also worth a try.

★**Mama San** FUSION $$
(Map p218; 0361-730436; www.mamasanbali.com; Jl Raya Kerobokan 135; mains 90,000-200,000Rp; noon-3pm & 6.30-11pm;) One of Seminyak's most esteemed restaurants, this stylish warehouse-sized space is split into levels, with photographs hanging from exposed brick walls. The menu has an emphasis on creative dishes from across Southeast Asia. A long cocktail list provides liquid balm for the mojito set and has lots of tropical-flavoured pours.

★**Motel Mexicola** MEXICAN $$
(Map p218; 0361-736688; www.motelmexicolabali.com; Jl Kayu Jati 9; tacos 30,000Rp, mains from 60,000Rp; 11am-1am) Far from your average taqueria, Motel Mexicola is an extravaganza that channels a tropical version of a glitzy 1940s nightclub. Its huge space is decked out in kitschy neon and palm trees. The menu includes hand-pressed soft corn tortilla tacos filled with tempura prawn or shredded pork, along with meaty mains. Cocktails, served in copper kettles, go down superbly on a balmy evening.

Earth Cafe & Market VEGETARIAN $$
(Map p218; 0361-732805; www.earthcafebali.com; Jl Kayu Aya; mains from 40,000Rp; 7am-11pm;) The good vibes are organic at this vegetarian cafe and store. Choose from creative salads, sandwiches or wholegrain vegan and raw-food goodies. It's most famous for its six-course 'Planet Platter' (75,000Rp). The beverage menu includes fresh juices and detox mixes.

Its **Divine Earth** (Map p218; 0361-731964; www.facebook.com/divineearthbali; Jl Raya Basangkasa 1200A; 7am-11pm;) restaurant is also worth visiting; it has an upstairs cinema that screens films nightly.

Rolling Fork ITALIAN $$
(Map p218; 0361-733 9633; Jl Kunti 1; mains from 75,000Rp; 8.30am-11pm;) A gnocchi-sized little trattoria, Rolling Fork serves excellent Italian fare. Breakfast features gorgeous baked goods and excellent coffees. Lunch and dinner include authentic and tasty homemade pastas, salads, seafood and more. The open-air dining room has an alluring retro charm; the Italian owners provide just the right accent.

Corner House CAFE $$
(Map p218; 0361-730276; www.cornerhousebali.com; Jl Laksmana 10A; dishes 35,000-125,000Rp; 7am-11pm;) With polished concrete floors, dangling light bulbs, distressed walls and vintage-style furniture, this cavernous cafe is typical of what's going on in Seminyak. A popular brunch spot, it does great coffee, big breakfasts, homemade sausage rolls and sirloin steak sandwiches. There's also a small shady courtyard and a more relaxed, breezy upstairs dining area.

Ultimo ITALIAN $$
(Map p218; 0361-738720; www.balinesia.co.id; Jl Kayu Aya 104; meals 40,000-210,000Rp; 5pm-1am) This vast and always popular restaurant thrives in a part of Seminyak that's as thick as a good risotto with eateries. Choose a table overlooking the street action, out the back

in one of the gardens or inside. Ponder the surprisingly authentic menu and then let the army of servers take charge.

Sisterfields CAFE $$
(Map p218; ☎0811 386 0507; www.sisterfieldsbali.com; Jl Kayu Cendana 7; mains from 60,000Rp; ⊙7am-5pm; ❄📶) Trendy Sisterfields does classic brekkies such as smashed avocado, and more inventive dishes such as truffled oyster mushrooms with duck eggs and crispy pig ears. There are also hipster faves like pulled-pork rolls and lobster sliders. Grab a seat at a booth, the counter or in the rear courtyard.

Fat Gajah ASIAN $$
(Map p218; ☎0361-868 8212; www.fatgajah.com; Jl Basangkasa 21; dumplings 52,000-80,000Rp; ⊙11am-10.30pm; 📶) Fat Gajah is all about the dumplings, prepared with mostly organic ingredients. They come fried or steamed with innovate fillings such as beef rendang, black-pepper crab, kimchi tuna or lemongrass lamb.

Ginger Moon ASIAN $$
(Map p218; ☎0361-734533; www.gingermoonbali.com; Jl Kayu Aya 7; mains 70,000-160,000Rp; ⊙11am-midnight; ❄📶) Australian Dean Keddell is one of scores of young chefs lured to Bali to set up restaurants. His creation is a very appealing, airy space, with carved wood and palms. The menu features a 'Best of' list of favourites, served in portions designed for sharing and grazing.

Kerobokan

★Nook ASIAN $
(Map p226; ☎0813 3806 0060; Jl Umalas I; mains from 35,000Rp; ⊙8am-11pm; 📶) Sublimely positioned among the rice fields, this casual, open-air cafe is popular for its creative takes on Asian fare. It's got a modern vibe mixed with tropical flavours. Good breakfasts and lunchtime sandwiches.

Warung Eny BALINESE $
(Map p218; ☎0361-473 6892; Jl Petitenget; mains from 35,000Rp; ⊙8am-11pm) The eponymous Eny cooks everything herself at this tiny open-front warung nearly hidden behind various potted plants. Look for the roadside sign that captures the vibe: 'The love cooking'. The seafood, such as large prawns smothered in garlic, is delicious and most ingredients are organic. Ask about Eny's fun cooking classes.

Gusto Gelato & Coffee GELATERIA $
(Map p218; ☎0361-552 2190; www.gusto-gelateria.com; Jl Raya Mertanadi 46; gelato from 22,000Rp; ⊙10am-10pm; ❄📶) Bali's best gelato is made fresh throughout the day, with unique flavours such as avocado choc-chip, dragonfruit, and *kamangi* (lemon basil). The classics are all here, too.

Warung Sulawesi INDONESIAN $
(Map p218; Jl Petitenget; meals from 30,000Rp; ⊙10am-6pm) Find a table in this quiet family compound and enjoy fresh Balinese and Indonesian food served in classic warung style. Choose a rice, then pick from a captivating array of dishes that are always at their peak at noon. The long beans are yum!

Warung Sobat SEAFOOD $
(Map p218; ☎0361-473 8922; Jl Batubelig 11; mains 37,000-90,000Rp; ⊙11am-11.30pm; 📶) Set in a sort of bungalow-style brick courtyard, this old-fashioned restaurant excels at fresh Balinese seafood with an Italian accent (lots of garlic!).

★Biku FUSION $$
(Map p218; ☎0361-857 0888; www.bikubali.com; Jl Petitenget 888; meals 40,000-120,000Rp; ⊙8am-11pm; 📶) Housed in a 150-year-old teak *joglo* (traditional Javanese house), hugely popular Biku retains the timeless vibe of its predecessor. The menu combines Indonesian and other Asian with Western influences; book for lunch or dinner. It's also popular for high tea (from 11am to 5pm; 220,000Rp for two people), served Asian-style – with samosa, spring rolls etc, and green or oolong tea – or traditional – with cucumber sandwiches etc.

★Watercress CAFE $$
(Map p218; ☎0851 0280 8030; www.watercressbali.com; Jl Batubelig 21A; mains from 65,000Rp; ⊙7.30am-11pm; 📶) A hit with the Bondi hipster set, this leafy roadside cafe does a roaring trade. As well as hearty breakfasts and gourmet burgers, it prides itself upon the healthy mains and salads. Excellent coffee, beer on tap and cocktails are other reasons to stop by.

Saigon Street VIETNAMESE $$
(Map p218; ☎0361-897 4007; www.saigonstreetbali.com; Jl Petitenget 77; mains 50,000-175,000Rp; ⊙11.30am-11pm; 📶) Modern, vibrant and buzzing, this new Vietnamese restaurant lures in punters with its swanky neon decor. Creative Vietnamese dishes include peppery betel leaves filled with slow-cooked octopus,

DON'T MISS

BEACHES: KEROBOKAN TO ECHO BEACH

The 4km of sand curving between Kerobokan's Batubelig Beach (p216) and Echo Beach has several uncrowded strands that can be reached by road or on foot from either direction.

Berewa Beach (Map p226; parking motorbike/car 2000/3000Rp) A greyish beach, secluded among rice fields and villas, about 2km up the sand from Seminyak. There are a couple of surfer cafes by the pounding sea.

Prancak Beach (Map p226) Marked by the large temple complex of Pura Dalem Prancak. There is usually at least one vendor at this quiet beach.

Nelayan Beach (Map p226) A collection of fishing boats and huts marks this very mellow stretch of sand that fronts 'villa-land' just inland.

Batu Bolong Beach (Map p226) The *pantai* (beach) at Batu Bolong boasts the large Pura Batumejan complex, which has a striking pagoda-like temple. There are surfboard rentals (100,000Rp per day) and impromptu lessons available, and some groovy cafes. About 200m further on there's a slightly upscale beach vendor with comfy loungers for rent and drinks for sale.

Echo Beach (Pantai Batu Mejan; Map p226) Surfers, and those who watch them, flock here for the high-tide left-hander that regularly tops 2m. The greyish sand right in front of the developments can vanish at high tide, but you'll find wide strands both east and west. Batu Bolong beach is 500m east.

Pererenan Beach (Map p226) For the moment, this laid-back northerly surf beach comprises only a few guesthouses and beach bars overlooking its dark tanned sands. It's an easy 300m walk from Echo Beach across sand and rock formations (or about 1km by road).

an impressive rice-paper roll selection, along with curries, pho and grilled meats cooked on aromatic coconut wood.

★Sardine SEAFOOD $$$
(Map p218; ☎0811 397 8111; www.sardinebali.com; Jl Petitenget 21; meals US$20-50; ⏰11.30am-4pm & 6-11pm; 📶) Seafood fresh from the famous Jimbaran market is the star at this elegant yet intimate, casual yet stylish restaurant. It's in a beautiful bamboo pavilion, with open-air tables overlooking a private rice field patrolled by Sardine's own flock of ducks. The inventive bar is a must and stays open until 1am. The menu changes to reflect what's fresh. Booking is vital.

Sarong FUSION $$$
(Map p218; ☎0361-473 7809; www.sarongbali.com; Jl Petitenget 19X; mains 120,000-180,000Rp; ⏰6.30-10.45pm; 📶) Sarong is an elegant affair by the owners of Seminyak's excellent Mama San (p221). The cuisine spans the globe, and its small plates are popular with those wishing to pace an evening and enjoy the commodious bar. No children allowed.

Barbacoa BARBECUE $$$
(Map p218; ☎0361-739235; www.barbacoabali.com; Jl Petitenget 14; mains 110,000-250,000Rp; ⏰noon-midnight; 📶) Adding another star to Jl Petitenget's fashionable culinary strip, Barbacoa is an impressive space with soaring timber ceilings, colourful mosaic tiled floors and outlooks to rice fields. The food is all about charcoal meats; the restaurant's walls are lined with firewood to cook up its menu of Latin American dishes.

Drinking & Nightlife

Like your vision at 2am, the division between restaurant, bar and club blurs in Seminyak. Although the area lacks any real hard-core clubs where you can greet the dawn (or vice versa), stalwarts can head south to the rough edges of Kuta and Legian in the wee hours.

Numerous bars popular with gay and straight crowds line Jl Camplung Tanduk.

★Potato Head BEACH CLUB
(Map p218; ☎0361-473 7979; www.ptthead.com; Jl Petitenget; ⏰11am-2am; 📶) Bali's original beach club is still one of the best. Wander up

DON'T MISS

BEACH SUNSETS

While there are plenty of fancy beach clubs and rooftop bars where you can indulge in south Bali's magical sunsets, nothing beats heading to the beach. Grab a plastic chair or a beanbag and plonk yourself on the sand with a cheap, cold Bintang in hand and enjoy the show.

off the sand or follow a long drive off Jl Petitenget and you'll find much to amuse, from an enticing pool to a swanky restaurant, plus lots of lounges and patches of lawn for chillin' the night away under the stars.

★La Favela BAR
(Map p218; ☎0361-730603; www.lafavela.com; Jl Kayu Aya 177X; ⏰noon-late; 📶) Full of bohemian flair, La Favela is one of Bali's coolest and most original nightspots. Themed rooms lead you on a confounding tour from dimly lit speakeasy cocktail lounges and antique dining rooms to graffiti-splashed bars. Tables are cleared after 11pm to make way for DJs and a dance floor.

It's equally popular for its garden restaurant, which has a Mediterranean-inspired menu.

★Anomali Coffee CAFE
(Map p218; www.anomalicoffee.com; Jl Kayu Aya 7B; coffee from 26,000Rp; ⏰6.30am-10pm; ❄📶) While there's no shortage of cafes in Seminyak, for the serious coffee drinker Anomali remains the standout. Single-origin beans are sourced from across the archipelago and roasted on-site. Take your pick of V-60 drip coffee, Aeropress, siphon or espresso made by expert baristas in cool warehouse-style surrounds. It also sells packaged ground beans.

Ku De Ta CLUB
(Map p218; ☎0361-736969; www.kudeta.net; Jl Kayu Aya 9; ⏰8am-late; 📶) Ku De Ta teems with Bali's beautiful people (including those whose status is purely aspirational). Scenesters perfect their 'bored' look over drinks during the day while gazing at the fine stretch of beach. Sunset brings out crowds, which snatch cigars at the bar or dine on eclectic fare at tables. The music throbs with increasing intensity through the night.

La Plancha BAR
(Map p218; ☎0361-730603; off Jl Camplung Tanduk; ⏰8am-midnight) The most substantial of the beach bars along the beach walk south of Jl Camplung Tanduk, La Plancha has its share of ubiquitous brightly coloured umbrellas and beanbags on the sand, plus a menu of Spanish-accented bites. After sunset, expect DJs and beach parties.

Bali Joe LGBT
(Map p218; ☎0361-847 5771; www.balijoebar.com; Jl Camplung Tanduk; ⏰3pm-3am; 📶) One of several lively LGBT venues along this strip. Drag queens and go-go dancers rock the house nightly.

Shopping

Seminyak shops could occupy days of your holiday. Designer boutiques (Bali has a thriving fashion industry), retro-chic stores, slick galleries, wholesale emporiums and family-run workshops are just some of the choices.

In Kerobokan look for boutiques interspersed with the trendy restaurants on Jl Petitenget.

★Drifter CLOTHING, ACCESSORIES
(Map p218; ☎0361-733274; www.driftersurf.com; Jl Kayu Aya 50; ⏰7.30am-11pm) High-end surf fashion, surfboards, gear, cool books and brands such as Obey and Wegener. Started by two savvy surfer dudes, the shop stocks goods noted for their individuality and high quality. There's also a small cafe-bar and a patio.

Ashitaba HANDICRAFTS
(Map p218; Jl Raya Seminyak 6; ⏰9am-9pm) Tenganan, the Aga village of east Bali, produces the intricate and beautiful rattan items sold here. Containers, bowls, purses and more (from 50,000Rp) display the very fine weaving.

Bathe BEAUTY, HOMEWARES
(Map p218; ☎0811 388 640; www.bathestore.com; Jl Batu Belig 88; ⏰7am-10pm) Double-down on your villa's romance with the handmade candles, air diffusers, aromatherapy oils, bath salts and homewares at this shop that evokes the feel of a 19th-century French dispensary.

Lulu Yasmine CLOTHING
(Map p218; ☎0361-736763; www.luluyasmine.com; Jl Kayu Aya; ⏰9am-10pm) Designer Luiza Chang gets inspiration from her worldwide travels for her elegant line of women's clothes.

Biasa CLOTHING
(Map p218; ☎0361-730308; www.biasabali.com; Jl Raya Seminyak 36; ⏰9am-9pm) This is Bali-based designer Susanna Perini's premier shop. Her line of elegant tropical wear for men and women combines cottons, silks and embroidery. The outlet store is at Jl Basangkasa 47.

Paul Ropp CLOTHING
(Map p218; ☎0361-735613; www.paulropp.com; Jl Kayu Aya; ⏰9am-9pm) The main shop of one of Bali's premier high-end fashion designers for men and women. Most goods are made in the hills above Denpasar. And what goods they are: rich silks and cottons, vivid to the point of gaudy, with hints of Ropp's roots in the tie-dyed 1960s.

Blue Glue CLOTHING
(Map p218; ☎0361-731130; www.blue-glue.com; Jl Raya Seminyak 16E; ⏰9am-9pm) 'The dream bikini of all women' is the motto of this famous brand that makes a big statement with its tiny wear. The swimwear is French designed and made right in Bali. There's also an **outlet** (Map p218; Jl Basangkasa; ⏰9am-8pm), with prices as small as its bikinis.

Lucy's Batik TEXTILES, CLOTHING
(Map p218; ☎085100951275; www.lucysbatikbali.com; Jl Raya Basangkasa 88; ⏰9.30am-9pm) Great for both men and women, Lucy's is a good spot to shop for the finest batik. Shirts, dresses, sarongs and bags are mostly handwoven or hand-painted. It also sells material by the metre.

This Is A Love Song CLOTHING
(TIALS; Map p218; www.thisisalovesong.com; Jl Kayu Aya 3; ⏰10am-10pm) One for Gen-Y fashionistas, this quirky streetwear label born out of Bali has clothed stars from Miley Cyrus to Katy Perry.

Samsara CLOTHING
(Map p218; www.samsaraboutique.com; Jl Raya Seminyak; ⏰10am-10pm) True Balinese-made textiles are increasingly rare as production moves to Java and other places with cheaper labour. But the local family behind this tidy shop still sources hand-painted Batik for a range of exquisite casual wear.

Duzty CLOTHING
(Map p218; Jl Raya Seminyak 67; ⏰9am-10pm) In an industry dominated by foreigners, it's refreshing to see a local label. T-shirts here are designed by a young Balinese lad, Rahsun. They feature edgy rock-and-roll and counter-culture themes. There are also a few women's tank tops.

Periplus Bookshop BOOKS
(Map p218; ☎0361-736851; Jl Kayu Aya, Seminyak Sq; ⏰8am-10pm) A large outlet of the island-wide chain of lavishly fitted bookshops. In addition to design books numerous enough to have you fitting out even your garage with 'Bali Style', it stocks bestsellers, magazines and newspapers.

ℹ Information

Seminyak is generally more hassle-free than nearby Kuta and Legian. But it's worth reading up on the warnings (p215), especially surf and water pollution, which also apply here.

ℹ Getting There & Around

Metered taxis are easily hailed. A trip to Seminyak from the airport with the airport taxi cartel costs about 120,000Rp; to the airport, about 50,000Rp.

Taxis from the airport to Kerobokan will cost at least 150,000Rp. In either direction at rush hour the trip may verge on an hour. Note also that Jl Raya Kerobokan can come to a fume-filled stop for extended periods.

You can beat the traffic, save the ozone and have a good stroll by walking along the beach; Legian is only about 15 minutes away from Seminyak.

Canggu & Around

The Canggu region, north and west from Kerobokan, is Bali's hippest and fastest-growing area. Much of the growth is centred along the coast, anchored by the endless swathes of beach, which, despite rampant development, remains fairly uncrowded and rice fields abound (for the moment).

In addition to long-term expats in their cloistered villas, Canggu lures a new generation of trendy, youthful and entrepreneurial expats who whisk past stooped rice farmers on their motorbikes. As well as surfers, it attracts a demographic of traveller looking for a more laid-back alternative to the mass tourism Kuta–Seminyak. In the Canggu area it's all about relaxed beach bars, yoga, organic produce and good coffee.

One of Bali's most popular surf breaks, Echo Beach has reached critical mass in popularity; it's quite the scene, with tourists, expats and locals all coming down to wet their feet at the often spectacular sunsets.

Canggu & Echo Beach

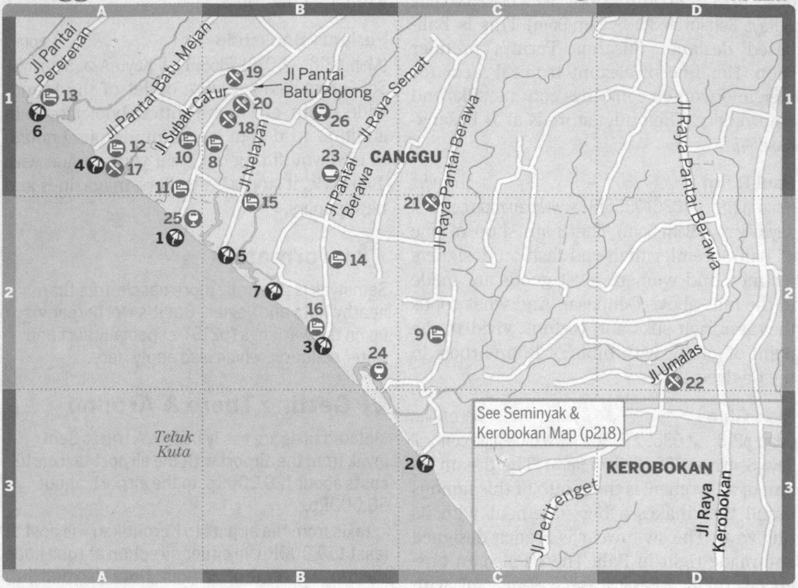

Canggu & Echo Beach

Sights

1 Batu Bolong Beach A2
2 Batubelig Beach C3
3 Berawa Beach B2
4 Echo Beach A1
5 Nelayan Beach B2
6 Pererenan Beach A1
7 Prancak Beach B2

Sleeping

8 Coconuts Guesthouse Canggu B1
9 Desa Seni C2
10 FRii Bali Echo Beach A1
11 Hotel Tugu Bali A1
12 Ketapang Guest House A1
13 Pondok Nyoman Bagus A1
14 Sedasa B2
15 Serenity Eco Guesthouse & Yoga B2
16 Widi Homestay B2

Eating

17 Beach House A1
18 Betelnut Cafe B1
Crate .... (see 18)
19 Deus Ex Machina B1
20 El Jefe Jose Cubanos B1
21 Green Ginger C2
22 Nook D2

Drinking & Nightlife

23 Hungry Bird B1
24 La Laguna B2
25 Old Man's A2
26 Pretty Poison B1

Shopping

Dylan Board Store .... (see 20)

Sleeping

Canggu

Serenity Eco Guesthouse & Yoga GUESTHOUSE $
(Map p226; ☎0361-846 9257; www.serenityecoguesthouse.com; Jl Nelayan; dm/s/d with fan 165,000/203,000/440,000Rp, d with air-con 495,000Rp;) This hotel is an oasis among the sterility of walled villas. Rooms range from shared-bath singles to quite nice doubles with bathrooms. The grounds are appealingly eccentric; Nelayan Beach is a five-minute walk. There are yoga classes

(from 100,000Rp) and you can rent surfboards, bikes, cars and more.

Widi Homestay HOMESTAY $
(Map p226; ☎0819 3303 2322; widihomestay@yahoo.co.id; Jl Pantai Berawa; r from 250,000Rp; ❄📶) There's no faux hipster vibe here, just a spotless, friendly, family-run homestay. The four rooms have hot water and air-con; the beach is barely 100m away.

★Sedasa BOUTIQUE HOTEL $$
(Map p226; ☎0361-844 6655; www.sedasa.com; Jl Raya Pantai Berawa; r incl breakfast from 875,000Rp; ❄📶🏊) Both intimate and stylish, Sedasa has an understated Balinese elegance that gives it a distinct Ubud-like feel. Large rooms overlook a small pool, and have designer furniture and travel photography on the walls. The beanbags on the rooftop make a good place to relax with a book. Downstairs there's an organic cafe with an open kitchen and cooking classes.

Coconuts Guesthouse Canggu GUESTHOUSE $$
(Map p226; ☎0878 6192 7150; www.coconutsguesthouse.com; Jl Pantai Batu Bolong; r from 650,000Rp; ❄📶🏊) The five breezy rooms at this contemporary guesthouse are very comfortable. Some have lovely views of the (surviving) rice fields, and all have fridges and a relaxed motif. Enjoy sunsets from the rooftop lounge area or take a dip in the 10m pool. Batu Bolong Beach is a 700m walk.

★Hotel Tugu Bali HOTEL $$$
(Map p226; ☎0361-473 1701; www.tuguhotels.com; Jl Pantai Batu Bolong; r incl breakfast from US$400; ❄@📶🏊) Right at Batu Bolong Beach, this exquisite hotel blurs the boundaries between accommodation and a museum-gallery, especially the Walter Spies and Le Mayeur Pavilions, where memorabilia from the artists' lives decorates the rooms. There's a spa and customised dining options.

Desa Seni HOTEL $$$
(Map p226; ☎0361-844 6392; www.desaseni.com; Jl Subak Sari 13; s/d incl breakfast from US$135/210; ❄@📶🏊) This place has been described as being like a hippy Four Seasons, and that's not far from the truth. The 10 classic wooden homes, up to two centuries old, were brought to the site from across Indonesia and turned into luxurious quarters. Guests enjoy a menu of organic and healthy cuisine plus yoga courses.

Echo Beach & Around

Ketapang Guest House GUESTHOUSE $
(Map p226; ☎0815 5843 4626; barbequw@yahoo.com; Jl Pantai Batu Mejan; s/d incl breakfast 250,000/350,000Rp; ❄) Given its proximity to Echo Beach, Ketapang offers exceptional value, with huge modern tile-floor rooms, free breakfast, air-con, hot-water showers and free drinking-water refills.

Pondok Nyoman Bagus GUESTHOUSE $$
(Map p226; ☎0361-848 2925; www.pondoknyoman.com; Jl Pantai Pererenan; r 500,000Rp; ❄📶🏊) Just behind Pererenan Beach, this popular guesthouse has 14 rooms with terraces and balconies, all set in a newish two-storey building that boasts a rooftop infinity pool and a restaurant with sensational sea views.

FRii Bali Echo Beach HOTEL $$
(Map p226; ☎0361-846 9178; www.friihotels.com; Jl Munduk Catu 32; r from 900,000Rp; ❄@📶🏊) Aspiring to appeal to the typical young, hip travellers that come to Canggu, this chain hotel feels a bit contrived in its delivery. Modern rooms have brick walls with chic-industrial trimmings and balconies. The bottom-level rooms literally open up to the pool. Head up to its rooftop deck for food, a bar and a yoga space. Free shuttle to Seminyak.

Eating

Canggu

Betelnut Cafe CAFE $
(Map p226; ☎0821 4680 7233; Jl Pantai Batu Bolong; mains from 45,000Rp; ⏲7am-10pm; ❄📶) There's a hippy-chic vibe at this thatched cafe with a mellow open-air dining room upstairs. The menu leans towards healthy, but not too healthy – you can get fries. There are juices and lots of mains featuring vegies. Good baked goods, nice shakes.

Crate CAFE $
(Map p226; www.facebook.com/cratecafebali; Jl Pantai Batu Bolong 64; coffee 20,000Rp, breakfast from 35,000Rp; ⏲7am-3pm; 📶) Set up inside a concrete bunker, this cafe is popular with Canggu scenesters who come here for coffee, avocado on sourdough or a bowl of Fruit Loops.

Green Ginger ASIAN, VEGETARIAN $
(Map p226; ☎0878 6211 2729; Jl Pantai Berawa; meals from 40,000Rp; ⏲8am-9pm; 📶🖉) An attractive little restaurant on the fast-changing strip in Canggu, Green Ginger specialises in

fresh and tasty vegetarian and noodle dishes from across Asia.

El Jefe Jose Cubanos SANDWICHES $$
(Map p226; www.facebook.com/eljefejosecanggu; cnr Jl Batu Bolong & Jl Nelayan; sandwiches 65,000Rp; ⏲ noon-midnight) At the 'Junction' leading into Canggu's most happening strip, this roadside shack serves up Cuban sandwiches filled with house-smoked pork, chicken or tempeh. It shares space with a tropical dive bar run by an Aussie larrikin and is frequented by a cast of colourful characters.

Deus Ex Machina CAFE $$
(Temple of Enthusiasm; Map p226; ☎ 0811 388 315; wwwdeuscustoms.com; Jl Batu Mejan 8; mains 60,000-115,000Rp; ⏲ 7am-10.30pm; 📶) This surreal venue standing amid Canggu's rice fields takes on many personas. If you're hungry it's a restaurant-cafe-bar; if you want to shop it's a fashion label; if you're into culture it's a contemporary-art gallery; if you're into music it's a live-gig venue (Sunday afternoons) for local punk bands; if you're a biker it's a custom-made motorcycle shop; if you want your beard trimmed, it's a barber...

Echo Beach

Beach House CAFE $$
(Echo Beach Club; Map p226; ☎ 0361-747 4604; www.echobeachhouse.com; Jl Pura Batu Mejan; mains 40,000-110,000Rp; ⏲ 7am-11pm; 📶) The most popular of Echo Beach's seafront restaurant-bars, here you can gaze out to the waves from a variety of couches and picnic tables. There's an impressive display of skewered meats and seafood ready to grill, as well as a tasty breakfast and lunch menu. Evening barbecues are popular, especially on Sundays when there's live music.

Drinking & Nightlife

★ Old Man's BEER GARDEN
(Map p226; ☎ 0361-846 9158; www.facebook.com/oldmansbali; Jl Pantai Batu Bolong; mains from 50,000Rp; ⏲ 8am-midnight) You'll have a tough time deciding just where to sit down to enjoy your drink at this popular coastal beer garden overlooking Batu Bolong Beach. The menu is aimed at surfers and surfer-wannabes: burgers, pizza, fish and chips, and, for the New Agers, salads. Wednesday nights are an institution, while Fridays (live rock and roll) and Sundays (DJs) are also big.

★ Hungry Bird CAFE
(Map p226; www.hungrybirdcoffee.com; Jl Raya Semat 86; ⏲ 8am-5pm; 📶) One of the few genuine third-wave coffee roasters in Bali, Hungry Bird does superb single-origin brews. The Javanese owner is incredibly knowledgeable on the subject, and roasts beans on-site from all over Indonesia; cupping sessions are possible if you call ahead. The food's also excellent and perfect for brunch.

La Laguna BAR
(Map p226; ☎ 0361-474 1214; Jl Pantai Kayu Putih, Berawa; ⏲ 11am-midnight; 📶) Run by the same owners as Seminyak's La Favela, La Laguna is in the same beatnik mould, but by the beach. Explore an eclectic layout, and find your place on a Chesterfield couch, a sofa-bed stacked with velvet cushions, a picnic table in the garden or within a gypsy caravan. The menu comprises cocktails, chargrilled meats and Cuban cigars.

There's a bridge leading to the ocean, so you can hang out on the beach.

Pretty Poison BAR
(Map p226; ☎ 0812 3800 6004; Jl Subak Canggu; ⏲ 5-11pm) Pretty Poison's bar overlooks an old-school '80s skate bowl, so a surfboard isn't the only board you to need to pack. While skateboarding is the focus, it's a great place to hang out, with cheap beers and bands.

Shopping

Dylan Board Store SURFBOARDS
(Map p226; ☎ 0857 3853 7402; www.dylansurfboards.com; Jl Pantai Batu Bolong; ⏲ 9.30am-9pm Mon-Sat, 10am-8pm Sun) Famed big-wave rider Dylan Longbottom runs this custom surfboard shop. A talented shaper, he creates boards for novices and pros alike. He also stocks plenty of his designs that are ready to go.

Getting There & Around

From the airport, fixed-price taxis cost 225,000Rp.

You can reach the Canggu area by road from the south by taking Jl Batubelig west in Kerobokan almost to the beach and then veering north past various huge villas and expat shops along a curved road. It's much longer to go up and around via the traffic-clogged Jl Raya Kerobokan.

Getting to the Canggu area can cost 80,000Rp or more by taxi from Kuta or Seminyak. Don't expect to find taxis cruising anywhere, although any business can call you one.

From Echo Beach a local taxi cooperative has taxis waiting to shuttle you back to Seminyak and the south for about 70,000Rp.

Bukit Peninsula

☎ 0361

Home to some of Bali's biggest waves, nicest beaches and some spectacular coastal views, the southern peninsula of Bukit is popular for good reason. Its booming west coast, with its string-of-pearls beaches, is a real hotspot for surfers and hip young beachgoers. World-famous surf breaks run all the way south to the important temple of Ulu Watu.

The east coast of Nusa Dua generally attracts a more well-heeled crowd to its five-star resorts and manicured beaches.

Jimbaran

Just south of Kuta and the airport, Teluk Jimbaran (Jimbaran Bay) is an alluring crescent of white-sand beach and blue sea, fronted by a long string of seafood warungs and ending at the southern end in a bushy headland.

Sights & Activities

Jimbaran Fish Market MARKET

(Jimbaran Beach; 6am-3pm) A popular morning stop on a Bukit Peninsula amble, this fish market is smelly, lively and frenetic – watch where you step. Brightly painted boats bob along the shore while huge cases of everything from small sardines to fearsome langoustines are hawked. The action is fast and furious.

Jimbaran Beach BEACH

One of Bali's best beaches, Jimbaran's 4km-long arc of sand is mostly clean and there is no shortage of places to get a snack, a drink, a seafood dinner or to rent a sunlounger. The bay is protected by an unbroken coral reef, which keeps the surf more mellow than at popular Kuta further north, although you can still get breaks that are fun for bodysurfing.

Eating & Drinking

Seafood is what brings most tourists to Jimbaran. Stretching along the coast, **warungs** cook fresh barbecued seafood every evening (and lunch at many). The open-sided affairs are right by the beach and perfect for enjoying sea breezes and sunsets. Arrive before sunset so you can get a good seat.

Fixed prices for seafood platters in a plethora of varieties have become common, and allow you to avoid the sport of choosing your fish and paying for it by weight while the locals break out in laughter. Should you go this latter route, be sure to agree on costs first. Generally, you can enjoy a seafood feast, sides and a couple of beers for under US$20 per person. Lobster (from US$30) will bump that figure up considerably.

Rock Bar BAR

(☎ 0361-702222; www.ayanaresort.com/rockbarbali; Jl Karang Mas Sejahtera, Ayana Resort; 4pm-1am;) Star of a thousand glossy articles written about Bali, this bar perched 14m above the crashing Indian Ocean is very popular. In fact, at sunset the wait to ride the lift down to the bar can top one hour.

Getting There & Away

Plenty of taxis wait around the beachfront warungs in the evening to take diners home (about 100,000Rp to Seminyak). Some of the seafood warungs provide free transport if you call first; look them up online.

Balangan Beach

A long, low strand at the base of rocky cliffs, Balangan Beach is covered with palm trees and fronted by a ribbon of near-white sand, picturesquely dotted with sun umbrellas. Surfer bars, cafes in shacks and slightly more permanent guesthouses precariously line the shore.

A small temple, **Pura Dalem Balangan**, sits at the northern end of the beach. Bamboo beach shacks line the southern end; visitors laze with one eye cast on the action at the fast left surf break here.

Sleeping & Eating

The string of shack restaurants perched on the hill overlooking the beach have prime wave-viewing positions and make great spots for a meal or drink. Some have basic accommodation.

Santai Bali Homestay BUNGALOW $

(☎ 0338-695942; balanganbrothers@yahoo.com; Balangan Beach; from 200,000Rp) Right on the sands of Balangan Beach, the bare-bones rooms at this shack bungalow are perfect for surfers and beach bums wanting easy access to the water. Its restaurant has tables and chairs plonked on the beach.

Balangan Beach & Ulu Watu

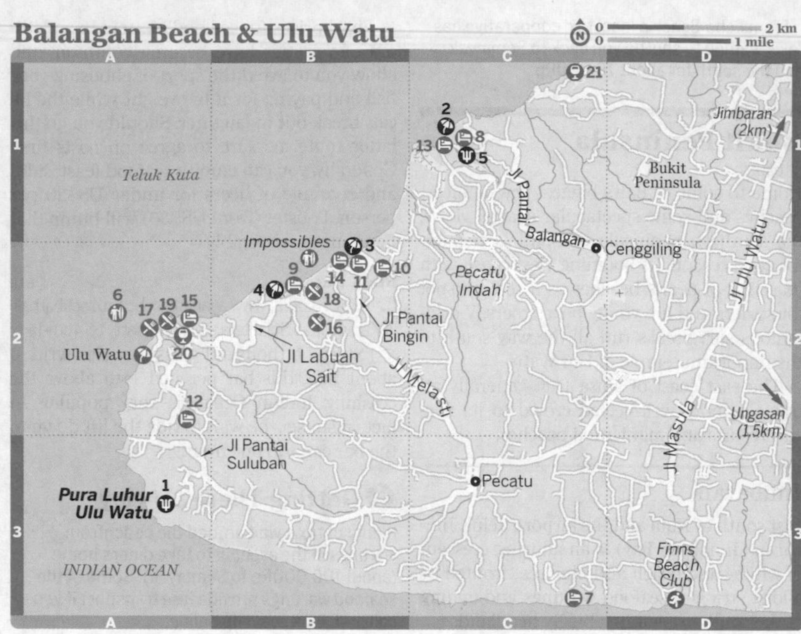

Balangan Beach & Ulu Watu

Top Sights
1 Pura Luhur Ulu Watu ... A3

Sights
2 Balangan Beach ... C1
3 Bingin Beach ... B2
4 Padang Padang Beach ... B2
5 Pura Dalem Balangan ... C1

Activities, Courses & Tours
6 Ulu Watu ... A2

Sleeping
7 Alila Villas Uluwatu ... C3
8 Balangan Sea View Bungalow ... C1
9 Bali Rocks ... B2
10 Bingin Garden ... B2
11 Chocky's Place ... B2
12 Gong ... A2
Le Sabot ... (see 9)
13 Santai Bali Homestay ... C1
Secret Garden ... (see 11)
14 Temple Lodge ... B2
15 Uluwatu Cottages ... A2

Eating
16 Buddha Soul ... B2
Cashew Tree ... (see 11)
17 Delpi ... A2
18 Om Burger ... B2
19 Single Fin ... A2

Drinking & Nightlife
20 Mamo Hotel ... A2
21 Rock Bar ... C1

Balangan Sea View Bungalow GUESTHOUSE $
(☎0851 0080 0499; www.balanganseaviewbungalow.com; off Jl Pantai Balangan; r with fan/air-con from 355,000/475,000Rp, q from 650,000Rp; ❄📶🏊) A cluster of thatched bungalows are the pick here. They surround a small pool in an attractive compound, and some have sea views.

ℹ Getting There & Away

Balangan Beach is 6.2km off Jl Ulu Watu on Jl Pantai Balangan. Turn west at the crossroads at Nirmala Supermarket.

Taxis from the Kuta area cost at least 300,000Rp for the round trip, including waiting time.

Bingin

An ever-evolving scene, Bingin comprises scores of unconventionally stylish lodgings scattered across cliffs and along the strip of white-sand **Bingin Beach** below. The scenery here is simply superb, with sylvan cliffs dropping down to surfer cafes and the foaming edge of azure sea. The beach is a five-minute walk down steep steps.

Sleeping & Eating

Numerous places to stay are scattered along and near the cliffs. All have at least simple cafes.

Chocky's Place GUESTHOUSE $
(☎0818 0530 7105; www.chockysplace.com; Bingin Beach; s/d from 100,000/200,000Rp; 📶) Down the bottom of the stairs on Bingin Beach, this classic surfer hang-out has cosy rooms varying from charming with awesome views to rudimentary with shared bathrooms. Its bamboo restaurant looks out to the beach; it's a great place to meet fellow travellers over a few cold ones.

Bingin Garden GUESTHOUSE $
(☎0816 472 2002; tommybarrell76@yahoo.com; off Jl Pantai Bingin; r with fan/air-con 300,000/400,000Rp; ❄📶🏊) There's a relaxed hacienda feel to Bingin Garden, where six bungalow-style rooms are set among an arid garden and a large pool. It's back off the cliffs and about 300m from the path down to the beach. It's run by gun local surfer Tommy Barrell and his lovely wife.

★**Temple Lodge** BOUTIQUE HOTEL $$
(☎0857 3901 1572; www.thetemplelodge.com; off Jl Pantai Bingin; r incl breakfast US$80-230; 📶🏊) 'Artsy and beautiful' just begins to describe this collection of huts and cottages made from thatch, driftwood and other natural materials. Each sits on a jutting shelf on the cliffs above the surf breaks, and there are superb views from the infinity pool and some of the seven units. You can arrange for meals, and there are morning yoga classes.

Secret Garden GUESTHOUSE $$
(☎0816 474 7255; http://homepage3.nifty.com/balisurf/secretgarden2.html; Bingin; r from 443,000Rp; 📶) Tasteful and ultra laid-back, this guesthouse has open-plan bamboo bungalows with futon beds, and a design that incorporates its natural environment. It's run by a Japanese surfer-photographer who has good knowledge of local waves. It's at the top of the hill near the path leading down to the beach.

★**Cashew Tree** CAFE $
(☎0353-218157; www.facebook.com/the-cashew-tree; Jl Pantai Bingan; meals from 40,000Rp; ⏰8am-10pm; 📶🖉) The Cashew Tree is *the* place to hang out in Bingin. Surfers and beachgoers gather for tasty vegan and vegetarian meals. Expect the likes of tempeh rice-paper rolls with tahini dipping sauce, and smoothies with banana, raw cacao and cashews. It's also a good spot for a drink; Thursday nights especially go off, attracting folk from up and down the coast.

Padang Padang

Slight in size but not in perfection, **Padang Padang Beach** is a cute little cove. As well as having great surf, its popularity has surged since appearing in *Eat, Pray, Love*, the film based on the bestselling book by Elizabeth Gilbert. The Saturday-night beach parties here are legendary. The beach is a short walk through a temple and down a well-paved trail.

If you're feeling adventurous, you can enjoy a much longer stretch of nearly deserted white sand that begins on the west side of the river. Ask locals how to get there.

Sleeping & Eating

Bali Rocks GUESTHOUSE $
(☎0817 344788; www.facebook.com/balirockspadang; r 200,000Rp) Down the cliff face, this thatched bit of wonder has dead-simple rooms with stunning views of the surf breaks and the ocean. Showers and toilets are down a couple of flights of stairs from the rooms. At high tide you can jump directly into the water.

★**Le Sabot** BUNGALOW $$
(☎0812 3768 0414; www.lesabotbali.com; r from 700,000Rp) Revel in a 1960s surfer fantasy on the Bukit cliffs at these open-plan bungalow-style units. There's hot water, electricity, fridges, large beds and decks with some of Bali's finest views. Room 3 is the pick. Bungalows are quite a slog down the cliff face.

Buddha Soul CAFE $$
(www.buddhasoul.com.au; Jl Labaunsait; breakfast from 50,000Rp, mains 65,000-150,000Rp; ⏰7.30am-10pm; 📶) This chilled-out roadside cafe has an outdoor deck where you can enjoy healthy, organic meals such as grilled calamari, chicken salad and lentil burgers. Closer to the beach,

BUKIT PARTY CIRCUIT

Though it's the beaches and waves that bring tourists to Bukit, the area's beginning to gain a reputation as a place to party. The fun is shared along the peninsula, with a different spot hosting each evening. Sunday nights are the most well known on the social calendar: this is when beautiful people descend in mass upon Ulu Watu's Single Fin for DJs and sunset sounds; Wednesdays are also popular. On Saturdays it's Padang Padang (p231)'s turn to host its famed evening beach parties. On Thursdays things get lively with live bands at the Cashew Tree (p231) at Bingin, while Fridays it's back to Ulu Watu for the rooftop bash at **Mamo Hotel** (☎0361-769882; www.mamohoteluluwatu.com; Jl Labuan Sait;).

the same team also runs **Om Burger** (☎0812-391 3617; Jl Labuan Sait; burgers from 65,000Rp; 7am-10pm;), which has an excellent selection of burgers.

Getting There & Away

A metered taxi from Kuta will cost about 150,000Rp and take an hour, depending on traffic.

Ulu Watu & Around

Ulu Watu has become the generic name for the southwestern tip of the Bukit Peninsula. It includes the much-revered temple and the fabled namesake surf breaks.

About 2km north of Ulu Watu temple, there is a dramatic cliff from where steps lead to the legendary Ulu Watu surf breaks. All manner of cafes and surf shops spill down the almost sheer face to the water below. Views are stellar, and it is quite the scene.

Sights & Activities

★Pura Luhur Ulu Watu HINDU TEMPLE

(Jl Ulu Watu; admission incl sarong & sash rental adult/child 10,000/10,000Rp; 8am-7pm) This important temple is perched precipitously on the southwestern tip of the peninsula, atop sheer cliffs that drop straight into the ceaseless surf. You enter through an unusual arched gateway flanked by statues of Ganesha. Inside, the walls of coral bricks are covered with intricate carvings of Bali's mythological menagerie.

Only Hindu worshippers can enter the small inner temple that is built onto the jutting tip of land. However, the views of the endless swells of the Indian Ocean from the cliffs are almost spiritual. At sunset, walk around the clifftop to the left (south) of the temple to lose some of the crowd.

Ulu Watu is one of several important temples to the spirits of the sea along the south coast of Bali. In the 11th century the Javanese priest Empu Kuturan first established a temple here. The complex was added to by Nirartha, another Javanese priest who is known for the seafront temples at Tanah Lot, Rambut Siwi and Pura Sakenan. Nirartha retreated to Ulu Watu for his final days when he attained *moksa* (freedom from earthly desires).

A popular Kecak dance is held in the temple grounds at sunset (100,000Rp), when traffic jams form during high season.

Ulu Watu SURFING

On its day, Ulu Watu is Bali's biggest and most powerful wave. It's the stuff of dreams and nightmares, and definitely not one for beginners! Since the early 1970s when it featured in the legendary surf flick *Morning of the Earth,* Ulu Watu has drawn surfers from around the world for left breaks that seem to go on forever.

Sleeping & Eating

Gong GUESTHOUSE $

(☎0361-769976; www.thegonguluwatubali.com; Jl Pantai Suluban; r from 220,000Rp;) The 12 tidy rooms here have good ventilation and hot water, and face a small compound with a lovely pool. Some 2nd-floor units have distant ocean views. It's about 1km south of the Ulu Watu cliffside cafes; the host family is lovely.

Uluwatu Cottages BUNGALOW $$

(☎0361-207 9547; www.uluwatucottage.com; off Jl Labuan Sait; r from US$75;) Fourteen bungalows are spread across a large site right on the cliff, just 400m east of the Ulu Watu cafes (about 200m off Jl Labuan Sait). The units are comfortable and the views are superb.

Delpi CAFE $

(meals 40,000-60,000Rp; 7am-7pm;) A relaxed cafe-bar sitting on a cliff away from other cafe spots, with stunning views. There are also simple rooms for rent (with fan/air-con US$35/40).

★ **Single Fin** CAFE $$

(☎0361-769941; www.singlefinbali.com; Jl Mamo; mains 65,000-150,000Rp; ⌚8am-11pm; 📶) The views of the surf action from this triple-level cafe are breathtaking. Watch the never-ending swells march in across the Indian Ocean from this cliffside perch; it's a great spot to spectate surfers carving it up when the waves are big. Drinks here aren't cheap and the food is merely passable, but come sunset, who cares?

Its Sunday session is a big event, when all the beautiful people come here in full force for a night out.

Getting There & Away

The best way to see the Ulu Watu region is with your own wheels. Otherwise a taxi ride out here will cost at least 200,000Rp from Seminyak and take more than hour in the coagulated traffic.

Ungasan & Around

If nearby Ulu Watu is all about celebrating surf culture, Ungasan is all about celebrating oneself. From crossroads near this otherwise nondescript village, roads radiate to the south coast, where some of Bali's most exclusive oceanside resorts can be found. With the infinite turquoise waters of the Indian Ocean rolling hypnotically in the distance, it's hard not to think you've reached the end of the world, albeit a very comfortable end.

Bali's southernmost **beach** can be found at the end of a 3km-long road from Ungasan village. Newish concrete steps lead down the 200m cliff to a sweet crescent of sand edging the pounding ocean.

Sleeping

★ **Alila Villas Uluwatu** RESORT $$$

(☎0361-848 2166; www.alilahotels.com/uluwatu; Jl Belimbing Sari; r incl breakfast from US$750; ❄@📶🏊) Visually stunning, this vast resort has an artful contemporary style that is at once light and airy while still conveying a sense of luxury. The 85-unit Alila offers gracious service in a setting where the blue of the ocean contrasts with the green of the surrounding (hotel-tended) rice fields. It's 2km off Jl Ulu Watu.

Nusa Dua

Nusa Dua translates literally as 'Two Islands' – although they are actually small raised headlands, each with a small temple. But Nusa Dua is much better known as Bali's gated compound of resort hotels. Gone is the hustle, bustle and engaging chaos of the rest of the island.

Nusa Dua is very spread out. You enter the enclave through one of the big gateways, and inside there are expansive lawns, manicured gardens and sweeping driveways leading to the lobbies of large hotels.

Sights

★ **Pasifika Museum** MUSEUM

(☎0361-774559; www.museum-pasifika.com; Bali Collection shopping centre, Block P; admission 70,000Rp; ⌚10am-6pm) When groups from the nearby resorts aren't around, you'll probably have this large museum to yourself. A collection of art from Pacific Ocean cultures spans several centuries and includes more than 600 paintings (don't miss the tikis). The influential wave of European artists who thrived in Bali in the early 20th century is well represented. Look for works by Arie Smit, Adrien-Jean Le Mayeur de Merpres and Theo Meier. There are also works by Matisse and Gauguin.

Sleeping & Eating

Nusa Dua resorts are similar in several ways: they are all big (some are huge) and almost every major international brand is represented. Most are right on the placid beach.

If you're considering a stay at Nusa Dua, search for deals.

Sofitel Bali Nusa Dua Beach Resort RESORT $$$

(☎0361-849 2888; www.sofitelbalinusadua.com; Jl Nusa Dua; r from US$246; ❄@📶🏊) Making up a part of the resort strip, the Sofitel has a vast pool that meanders past the 415 rooms, some of which have terraces with direct pool access. The room blocks are huge; many rooms have at least a glimpse of the water. The Sofitel's lavish Sunday brunch (11am to 3pm) is one of Bali's best; it costs from 400,000Rp.

St Regis Bali Resort RESORT $$$

(☎0361-847 8111; www.stregisbali.com; ste from US$600; ❄@📶🏊) This lavish Nusa Dua resort leaves most of the others in the sand. Every conceivable luxury is provided, from electronics to the furnishings, the marble and the personal butler. Pools abound and units are huge. Go for the pool suite with ocean views if you want to relax in style.

Nusa Dua Beach Grill INTERNATIONAL $$

(☎0851 0043 4779; Jl Pura Gegar; meals 65,000-250,000Rp; ⌚8am-10.30pm) A good spot for day trippers, this hidden, warm-hued cafe is south of Gegar Beach and the huge Mulia resort. The drinks menu is long, the seafood fresh and the atmosphere heavy with assignations.

Getting There & Around

The Bali Mandara Toll Road (car/motorcycle 11,000/4000Rp) greatly speeds up journeys between Nusa Dua and the airport and Sanur.

The fixed taxi fare from the airport is 150,000Rp; a metered taxi to the airport will be much less. Metered taxis to/from Seminyak average 90,000Rp.

A free **shuttle bus** (☎0361-771662; www.bali-collection.com/shuttle-bus; ⊙9am-10pm) connects Nusa Dua and Tanjung Benoa resort hotels with the Bali Collection shopping centre in Nusa Dua about every hour.

You can walk the delightful beach promenade that leads to Tanjung Benoa.

Tanjung Benoa

The peninsula of Tanjung Benoa extends about 4km north from Nusa Dua to Benoa village. It's flat and lined with family-friendly resort hotels, most of midrange calibre. By day the waters buzz with the roar of dozens of motorised water-sports craft. It's popular with domestic travellers, and group tours arrive by the busload for a day's aquatic excitement, such as straddling a banana boat among other thrills.

Tanjung Benoa is a good base for budget travellers wanting to utilise Nusa Dua's beaches.

Sights

Amble the narrow lanes of the peninsula's tip for a multicultural feast. Within 100m of each other you'll find a brightly coloured **Chinese Buddhist temple**, a domed **mosque** and a **Hindu temple** with a nicely carved triple entrance.

Sleeping & Eating

Pondok Hasan Inn GUESTHOUSE $

(☎0361-772456; hasanhomestay@yahoo.com; Jl Pratama; r incl breakfast 200,000Rp; ❄📶) Back 20m off the main road, this friendly family-run homestay has nine immaculate hot-water rooms that include breakfast. The tiles on the outdoor veranda gleam; it's shared by the rooms, and there is a small garden.

Rumah Bali GUESTHOUSE $$

(☎0361-771256; www.balifoods.com; off Jl Pratama; r incl breakfast from US$110, villas from US$270; ❄@📶🏊) Rumah Bali is a luxurious interpretation of a Balinese village by cookbook author Heinz von Holzen, who also runs local restaurant Bumbu Bali. Guests choose from large family rooms or individual villas (some have three bedrooms) with their own plunge pools and kitchens. In addition to a large communal pool, there's also a tennis court. The beach is a short walk away.

★**Bumbu Bali** BALINESE $$

(☎0361-774502; www.balifoods.com; Jl Pratama; mains from 90,000Rp, set menus from 270,000Rp; ⊙noon-9pm) Long-time resident and cookbook author Heinz von Holzen, his wife Puji, and well-trained and enthusiastic staff serve exquisitely flavoured dishes at this superb restaurant. Many diners opt for one of several lavish set menus. Cooking classes on Mondays, Wednesdays and Fridays (from US$103) are highly recommended.

Whacko Beach Club INTERNATIONAL $$

(☎0361-771384; Jl Pratama; mains 80,000-180,000Rp; ⊙9am-10pm; 📶) There's nothing whacko about this beachside hang-out. Instead it's a laid-back, family-friendly spot. Spend the day lazing by the pool, in the restaurant, at the bar or on sunloungers looking out to the water. The menu offers burgers, grilled seafood, pizzas and Indonesian dishes.

Getting There & Around

Taxis from the airport cost 150,000Rp. A free **shuttle bus** (☎0361-771662; www.bali-collection.com/shuttle-bus; ⊙9am-10pm) connects Nusa Dua and Tanjung Benoa resort hotels with Nusa Dua's Bali Collection shopping centre. You can stroll the beach promenade along to Nusa Dua.

Sanur

☎0361

Sanur is a genteel alternative to raucous Kuta. It's low-key surf experience and the area's status as a haven for expat retirees contributes to Sanur's nickname, 'Snore'. Parents tend to enjoy the beach at Sanur because its calmness makes it a good place for small children to play.

Sanur stretches for about 5km along an east-facing coastline, with the lush and green landscaped grounds of resorts fronting right onto the sandy beach. West of the beachfront hotels, the busy main drag, Jl Danau Tamblingan, has hotel entrances and oodles of tourist shops, restaurants and cafes.

Sights

Sanur's 4km **beachfront walk** follows the sand south as it curves to the west. Lots of cafes with tables on the sand will give you plenty of reason to pause and enjoy the views.

Sanur is also a good base for taking in nearby Denpasar's museums and galleries.

★Museum Le Mayeur MUSEUM
(☎0361-286201; Jl Hang Tuah; adult/child 20,000/10,000Rp; ⏲8am-3.30pm Sat-Thu, 8.30am-12.30pm Fri) Artist Adrien-Jean Le Mayeur de Merpres (1880–1958) arrived in Bali in 1932, and married the beautiful Legong dancer Ni Polok three years later, when she was just 15. They lived in this compound back when Sanur was still a quiet fishing village. After the artist's death, Ni Polok lived in the house until she died in 1985. Despite security (some of Le Mayeur's paintings have sold for US$150,000) and conservation problems, almost 90 of Le Mayeur's paintings are displayed.

The house is an interesting example of Balinese-style architecture. Notice the beautifully carved window shutters that recount the story of Rama and Sita from the Ramayana. The museum also has a naturalistic Balinese interior of woven fibres.

Activities

Sanur's calm waters and steady breezes make it a natural centre for windsurfing and kitesurfing. Sanur's fickle surf breaks (tide conditions often don't produce waves) are offshore along the reef. The best breaks are **Sanur Reef**, a right break in front of Inna Grand Bali Beach Hotel, and **Hyatt Reef**, in front of, you guessed it, the Bali Hyatt Regency.

Rip Curl School of Surf KITESURFING
(☎0361-287749; www.ripcurlschoolofsurf.com; Beachfront Walk, Sanur Beach Hotel; lessons from 1,100,000Rp, rental per hr from 550,000Rp; ⏲8am-5pm) Sanur's reef-protected waters and regular offshore breezes make for good kitesurfing. The season runs from June to October. Rip Curl also rents boards for windsurfing and stand-up paddle boarding (SUP; including yoga SUP for 300,000Rp per hour).

Sanur

Top Sights
1 Museum Le Mayeur B2

Activities, Courses & Tours
2 Balinese Cooking Class A7
3 Crystal Divers B5

Sleeping
4 Fairmont Sanur Beach Bali B7
5 Hotel La Taverna B3
6 Pollok & Le Mayeur Inn B1
7 Tandjung Sari B4
8 Yulia 1 Homestay A3

Eating
9 Byrdhouse Beach Club B3
10 Char Ming A6
11 Manik Organik B5
12 Massimo A6
Minami .... (see 9)
13 Three Monkeys Cafe B4
Warung Little Bird .... (see 8)
14 Warung Pantai Indah B6

Drinking & Nightlife
15 Kalimantan A3

Shopping
16 A-Krea B4
17 Ganesha Bookshop B4

Crystal Divers DIVING
(☎0361-286737; www.crystal-divers.com; Jl Danau Tamblingan 168; dives from US$65) This slick diving operation has its own hotel (the Santai) and a large diving pool. It's recommended for beginners; the shop offers a long list of courses, including PADI open-water (US$500).

Balinese Cooking Class COOKING COURSE
(☎0361-288009; www.santrian.com; Puri Santrian, Beachfront Walk; 1½hr class without/with market visit US$55/70; ⏲Wed & Fri) With a kitchen that's set on the beachfront, this is a memorable spot to learn to cook Balinese food. For a bit extra you can visit the market to source ingredients.

★ **Power of Now Oasis** YOGA
(☎0813 3831 5032; www.powerofnowoasis.com; Beachfront Walk, Hotel Mercure; classes from 100,000Rp) Enjoy a yoga class in this atmospheric bamboo pavilion looking out to Sanur Beach. Several levels are offered. Sunrise yoga is a popular choice.

Sleeping

Yulia 1 Homestay GUESTHOUSE $
(☎0361-288089; yulia1homestay@gmail.com; Jl Danau Tamblingan 38; r incl breakfast with fan & cold water 170,000-220,000Rp, with air-con 300,000-350,000Rp; ❄📶🏊) Run by a friendly family, this mellow guesthouse is set in a lovely bird-filled garden full of palms and flowers. Rooms vary in standards (some cold water, fan only), but all come with minibars. The plunge pool is a nice area for relaxing.

Pollok & Le Mayeur Inn HOMESTAY $
(☎0361-289847; pollokinn@yahoo.com; Jl Hang Tuah, Museum Le Mayeur; r fan/air-con from 250,000/350,000Rp; ❄📶) The grandchildren of the late artist Le Mayeur de Merpes and his wife Ni Polok run this small homestay. It's within the Le Mayeur museum compound (p235), and offers a good budget option on the beachfront. The 17 rooms vary in size; ask to see a few.

★ **Hotel La Taverna** HOTEL $$
(☎0361-288497; www.latavernahotel.com; Jl Danau Tamblingan 29; r US$100-200, ste from US$150; ❄@📶🏊) One of Sanur's first hotels, La Taverna has been thoughtfully updated while retaining its artful, simple charm. The pretty grounds and paths that link the buildings hum with a creative energy, infusing the 36 vintage bungalow-style units with an air of understated luxury. Art and antiques abound; views beckon.

★ **Fairmont Sanur Beach Bali** RESORT $$$
(☎0361-3011888; www.fairmont.com; Jl Kesumasari 8; r from US$315; ❄@📶🏊) Looming over Sanur's beachfront, this massive hotel has 120 elegant suites and villas on a sprawling site that includes a 50m infinity pool. The design is strikingly modern, and high-tech pleasures abound. There are also lavish spas and restaurants, and a state-of-the-art gym. Kids get their own pool and play area.

Tandjung Sari HOTEL $$$
(☎0361-288441; www.tandjungsarihotel.com; Jl Danau Tamblingan 29; bungalows incl breakfast from

US$225; ❄@📶≋) One of Bali's first boutique hotels, Tandjung Sari has flourished since it opened in 1967 and continues to be lauded for its style. The 28 traditional-style bungalows are beautifully decorated with crafts and antiques. The gracious staff are a delight. Free Balinese dance classes (Wednesdays at 3pm) are taught by one of Bali's best dancers.

Eating & Drinking

Although there are plenty of uninspiring places on Jl Danau Tamblingan, there are also some gems.

Many of Sanur's drinking establishments cater to retired expats and are, thankfully, air-conditioned.

Beachfront

The beach path has restaurants, cafes and bars where you can catch a meal, a drink or a sea breeze.

Warung Pantai Indah CAFE $$
(Beachfront Walk; mains 30,000-110,000Rp; 9am-9pm) Sit at battered tables and chairs with your toes in the sand at this timeless beach cafe. It specialises in fresh barbecue-grilled seafood and cheap local dishes.

Minami JAPANESE $$
(0812 8613 4471; Beachfront Walk; mains from 56,000Rp; 10am-11pm) With its minimalist white decor, bright open-air atmosphere and a vast range of ultrafresh fish, this authentic Japanese place is a great find on Sanur Beach.

Byrdhouse Beach Club INTERNATIONAL $$
(0361-288407; Segara Village; mains from 60,000Rp; 6am-midnight; 📶) With loungers, a swimming pool, a restaurant and bar, wi-fi and table tennis on-site, one could happily spend the entire day here by the beach. Check the club's Facebook page for upcoming events, including outdoor-cinema screenings and street-food stalls.

Jalan Danau Tamblingan

Warung Little Bird INDONESIAN $
(0361-745 4968; Jl Danau Tamblingan 34; mains from 25,000Rp; 10am-10pm) The charming Little Bird does tasty Indonesian dishes including beef *rendang* (coconut curry), and Balinese specialities such as *ayam betutu* (slow-cooked chicken stuffed with Balinese spices), which you'll need to reserve in advance. Its inviting little bar makes it a good spot for a drink, too.

★ **Massimo** ITALIAN $$
(0361-288942; www.massimobali.com; Jl Danau Tamblingan 206; meals 80,000-200,000Rp; 11am-11pm) The interior is like an open-air Milan cafe; the outside is like a Balinese garden – it's a combo that goes together like spaghetti and meatballs. Pasta, pizza and more are prepared with authentic Italian flair. No time for a meal? Nab some gelato from the counter up the front.

Manik Organik HEALTH FOOD $$
(0821 4416 8228; www.manikorganikbali.com; Jl Danau Tamblingan 85; meals from 55,000Rp; 9am-11pm;) Trees shade the serene terrace at this creative and healthful cafe that smells of lemongrass. Vegetarians and raw-food enthusiasts are well cared for, but there are also meaty dishes made with free-range chicken and the like. Smoothies include the fortifying 'immune tonic'.

Char Ming ASIAN $$
(0361-288029; www.charming-bali.com; Jl Danau Tamblingan 97; meals 100,000-200,000Rp; 5-11pm) Asian fusion with a French accent. A daily menu board lists the fresh seafood available for grilling. Look for regional dishes, many with modern flair. The highly stylised location features lush plantings and carved-wood details from vintage Javanese and Balinese structures.

Three Monkeys Cafe ASIAN $$
(0361-286002; www.threemonkeyscafebali.com; Jl Danau Tamblingan; meals 62,000-200,000Rp; 11am-11pm; 📶) This branch of the splendid Ubud original is no mere knock-off. The creative menu has homemade pastas, wood-oven lamb rack and pan-Asian creations. Healthy salads and juices are also recommended.

Kalimantan BAR
(Borneo Bob's; 0361-289291; Jl Pantai Sindhu 11; mains from 40,000Rp; 7.30am-11pm) This veteran boozer has an old *South Pacific* thatched charm and is one of several casual bars on this street. Enjoy cheap drinks under the palms in the large, shady garden. The Mexican-style food features homegrown chilli peppers.

Shopping

Sanur is no shopping haven like Seminyak, but a few designers from there are opening branches here.

A-Krea CLOTHING
(☎0361-286101; Jl Danau Tamblingan 51; ⏲9am-9pm) An excellent spot for souvenirs, A-Krea has a range of items designed and made in Bali in its attractive store. Clothes, accessories, homewares and more are all handmade.

Ganesha Bookshop BOOKS
(www.ganeshabooksbali.com; Jl Danau Tamblingan 42; ⏲8am-9pm) A branch of Bali's best bookshop for serious readers.

Information

There are numerous ATMs and banks along Jl Danau Tamblingan.

Getting There & Away

BEMO

Green bemos go along Jl Hang Tuah to the Kereneng Bemo Terminal in Denpasar (7000Rp).

BOAT

➡ Myriad **fast boats** to Nusa Lembongan, Nusa Penida, Lombok and the Gili Islands depart from a strip of beach south of Jl Hang Tuah. None of these services uses a dock: be prepared to wade to the boat. Note that most companies offer free hotel pickup and drop-off from destinations between Kuta and Ubud.

➡ Recommended fast-boat companies include **Rocky Fast Cruises** (☎0361-283624; www.rockyfastcruise.com; Jl Hang Tuah 41; ⏲8am-8pm) to Nusa Lembongan (one way/return US$30/50, 30 minutes, four daily), and **Scoot** (☎0361-285522; www.scootcruise.com; Jl Hang Tuah; ⏲8am-8pm) to Nusa Lembongan (one way/return 400,000/600,000Rp, 30 minutes, four daily), and to Sengigi and the Gilis (one way 700,000Rp, two hours, departing 9.30am) on Lombok.

➡ Regular **public boats** head to Nusa Lembongan: a slow boat (100,000Rp, 1½ hours) at 10.30am or fast boats (175,000Rp, 30 minutes, four daily). A boat to Nusa Penida (175,000Rp, 35 minutes) departs at 7am.

TOURIST SHUTTLE BUS

The **Perama office** (☎0361-285592; www.peramatour.com; Jl Hang Tuah 39; ⏲7am-10pm) is at Warung Pojok at the northern end of town. Tourist shuttle destinations include Kuta (35,000Rp, 45 minutes), Ubud (50,000Rp, one hour), Padangbai (75,000Rp, two hours) and Lovina (125,000Rp, four hours).

Getting Around

Taxis from the airport cartel cost 150,000Rp.

Bemos go up and down Jl Danau Tamblingan and Jl Danau Poso for 5000Rp, offering a greener way to shuttle about the strip than a taxi.

Denpasar

☎0361

Sprawling, hectic and ever-growing, Bali's capital has been the focus of a lot of the island's growth and wealth over the last five decades. It can seem a daunting and chaotic place, but spend a little time on its tree-lined streets in the relatively affluent government and business district of Renon and you'll discover a more genteel side.

Denpasar might not be a tropical paradise, but it's as much a part of 'the real Bali' as the rice paddies and clifftop temples. This is the hub of the island for 800,000 locals and here you will find their shopping malls and parks. Most enticing, however, is the growing range of authentic and tasty restaurants and cafes aimed at the burgeoning middle class. You'll also want to sample Denpasar's markets, its important museum and its purely modern Balinese vibe.

Sights

★**Museum Negeri Propinsi Bali** MUSEUM
(☎0361-222680; adult/child 20,000/10,000Rp; ⏲8am-4pm Sat-Thu, 8.30am-12.30pm Fri) Think of this as the British Museum or the Smithsonian of Balinese culture. It's all here, but unlike those world-class institutions, you have to work at sorting it out; the museum could use a dose of curatorial energy. Most displays are labelled in English. The museum comprises several buildings and pavilions, including many examples of Balinese architecture, housing prehistoric pieces, traditional artefacts, Barong (mythical lion-dog creatures), ceremonial objects and rich displays of textiles.

Pura Jagatnatha HINDU TEMPLE
(Jl Surapati) FREE The state temple, built in 1953, is dedicated to the supreme god, Sanghyang Widi. Part of its significance is its statement of monotheism. Although the Balinese recognise many gods, the belief in one supreme god (who can have many manifestations) brings Balinese Hinduism into conformity with the first principle of Pancasila – the 'Belief in One God'.

★**Bajra Sandhi Monument** MONUMENT
(Monument to the Struggle of the People of Bali; ☎0361-264517; Jl Raya Puputan, Renon; adult/child 20,000/10,000Rp; ⏲9am-6pm) The centrepiece

to a popular park, this huge monument is as big as its name. Inside the vaguely Borobudur-like structure are dioramas tracing Bali's history. Note that in the portrayal of the 1906 battle with the Dutch, the King of Badung is literally a sitting target. Take the spiral stairs to the top for 360-degree views.

Festivals & Events

★Bali Arts Festival PERFORMING ARTS
(www.baliartsfestival.com; Taman Wedhi Budaya; mid-Jun–mid-Jul) This annual festival, based at the Taman Wedhi Budaya arts centre, is an easy way to see a wide variety of traditional dance, music and crafts. The productions of the Ramayana and Mahabharata ballets are grand, and the opening ceremony and parade in Denpasar are spectacles. Tickets are usually available before performances; schedules are available online and at the Denpasar tourist office.

Sleeping

Spending a night in Denpasar will appeal to those seeking a more localised cultural experience outside the tourist areas.

★Nakula Familiar Inn GUESTHOUSE $
(0361-226446; www.nakulafamiliarinn.com; Jl Nakula 4; s with fan/air-con 175,000/225,000Rp, d 200,000/250,000Rp;) The eight rooms at this sprightly urban family compound, a longtime traveller favourite, are clean and have small balconies. There is a nice courtyard and cafe in the middle. Tegal–Kereneng bemos go along Jl Nakula.

Eating & Drinking

Denpasar has the island's best range of Indonesian and Balinese food. Savvy locals and expats each have their own favourite warungs and restaurants.

★Café Teduh INDONESIAN $
(0361-221631; off Jl Diponegoro; mains 12,000-23,000Rp; 10am-10pm;) An oasis hidden down a tiny lane, with hanging orchids, trees, flowers and ponds with fountains. Try *ayam dabu-dabu* (grilled chicken with chilli paste, tomatoes, shallots, lemongrass and spices) or *nasi bakar cumi hitam* (rice and marinated squid wrapped in banana leaf and grilled).

Cak Asmo INDONESIAN $
(Jl Tukad Gangga; meals from 15,000Rp; 9.30am-10.30pm) Join the government workers and students from the nearby university for superb dishes cooked to order in the bustling kitchen. Order the buttery and crispy *cumi cumi* (calamari) battered in *telor asin* (a heavenly mixture of eggs and garlic). Fruity ice drinks are a cooling treat. An English-language menu makes ordering a breeze. It's halal, so there's no alcohol.

Warung Wardani INDONESIAN $
(0361-224398; Jl Yudistira 2; nasi campur from 35,000Rp; 8am-4pm) Don't be deceived by the small dining room at the entrance: there's another vastly larger one out the back. The top-notch *nasi campur* (rice with side dishes) draws in the masses for lunch daily.

Shopping

★Pasar Badung MARKET
(Jl Gajah Mada; 6am-5pm) Bali's largest food market is busy in the mornings and evenings; it's a great place to browse and bargain. You'll find produce and food from all over the island. Allow yourself to get lost here and revel in the range of fruits and spices on offer. The shops lining the side streets of the market are famous for textiles.

Sadly, a fire ripped through the market in early 2016 as this guidebook was going to press and it was unclear if/when it would be rebuilt.

Information

All major Indonesian banks have offices in Denpasar, and most have ATMs. Several are on Jl Gajah Mada, near the corner of Jl Arjuna.

Main Post Office (0361-223565; Jl Raya Puputan; 8am-9pm Mon-Fri, to 8pm Sat) Your best option for unusual postal needs. Has a photocopy centre and ATMs.

RSUP Sanglah Hospital (Rumah Sakit Umum Propinsi Sanglah; 0361-227911; www.sanglahhospitalbali.com; Jl Diponegoro; 24hr) The city's general hospital has English-speaking staff and an ER. It's the best hospital on the island, although standards are not the same as those in developed countries. It has a special wing for well-insured foreigners, **Paviliun Amerta Wing International** (0361-740 5474, 0361-257477).

Getting There & Away

Denpasar is a hub of public transport in Bali. You'll find buses and minibuses bound for all corners of the island.

BEMO

With most locals now preferring to travel by motorbike, note that the bemo network is spluttering. The total lack of schedules, and long waiting times, mean it's generally not suitable for tourists.

Denpasar

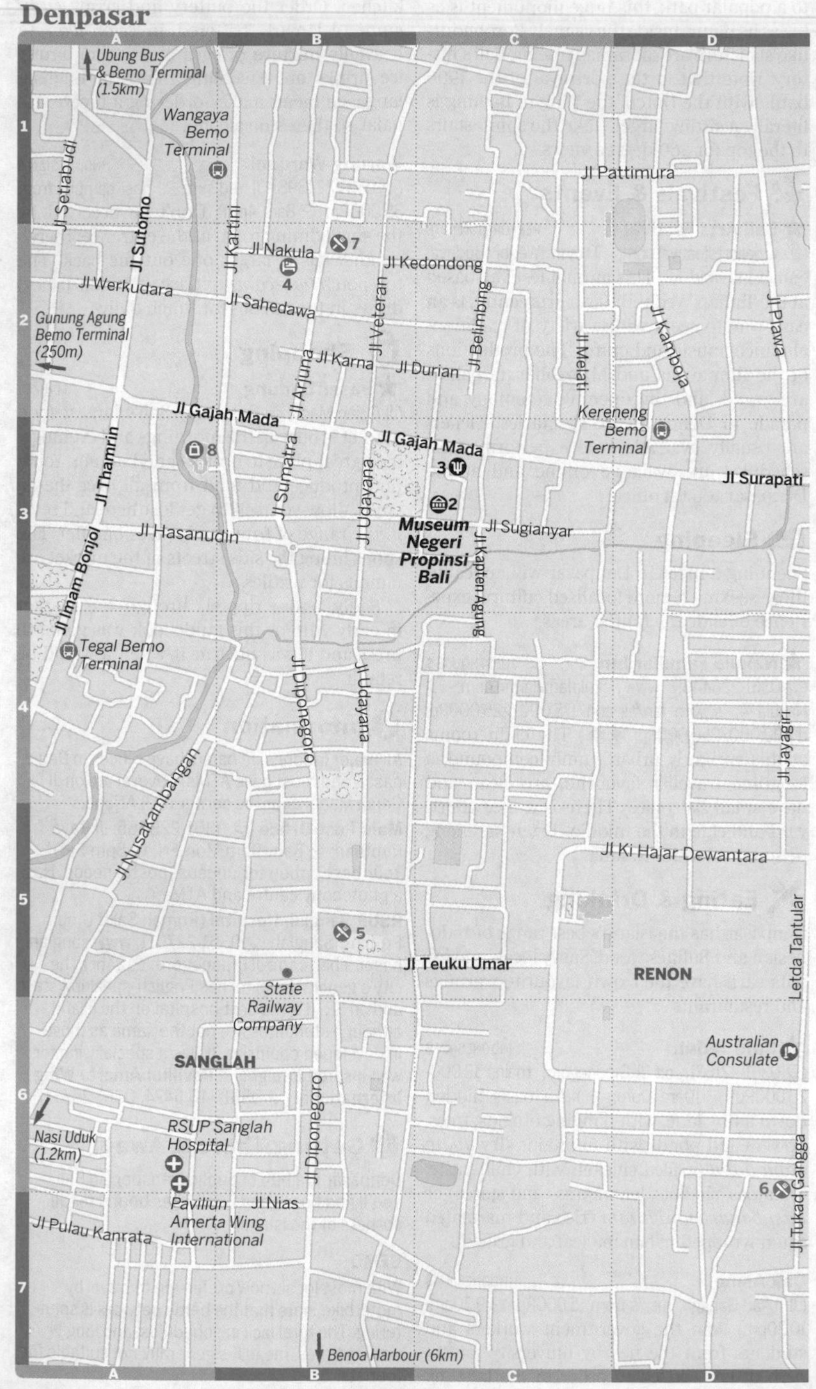

A
B
C
D
1
2
3
4
5
6
7
Ubung Bus & Bemo Terminal (1.5km)
Wangaya Bemo Terminal
Jl Setiabudi
Jl Sutomo
Jl Kartini
Jl Nakula
7
4
Jl Kedondong
Jl Werkudara
Jl Sahedawa
Jl Veteran
Jl Belimbing
Jl Melati
Jl Kamboja
Jl Plawa
Jl Pattimura
Gunung Agung Bemo Terminal (250m)
Jl Karna
Jl Durian
Jl Arjuna
Jl Gajah Mada
Jl Gajah Mada
Kereneng Bemo Terminal
Jl Thamrin
8
3
Jl Surapati
Jl Sumatra
Jl Udayana
2
Museum Negeri Propinsi Bali
Jl Sugianyar
Jl Hasanudin
Jl Kapten Agung
Jl Imam Bonjol
Tegal Bemo Terminal
Jl Diponegoro
Jl Udayana
Jl Jayagiri
Jl Nusakambangan
Jl Ki Hajar Dewantara
Letda Tantular
5
Jl Teuku Umar
RENON
State Railway Company
SANGLAH
Australian Consulate
RSUP Sanglah Hospital
Nasi Uduk (1.2km)
Jl Diponegoro
6
Jl Tukad Gangga
Pavilium Amerta Wing International
Jl Nias
Jl Pulau Kanrata
Benoa Harbour (6km)

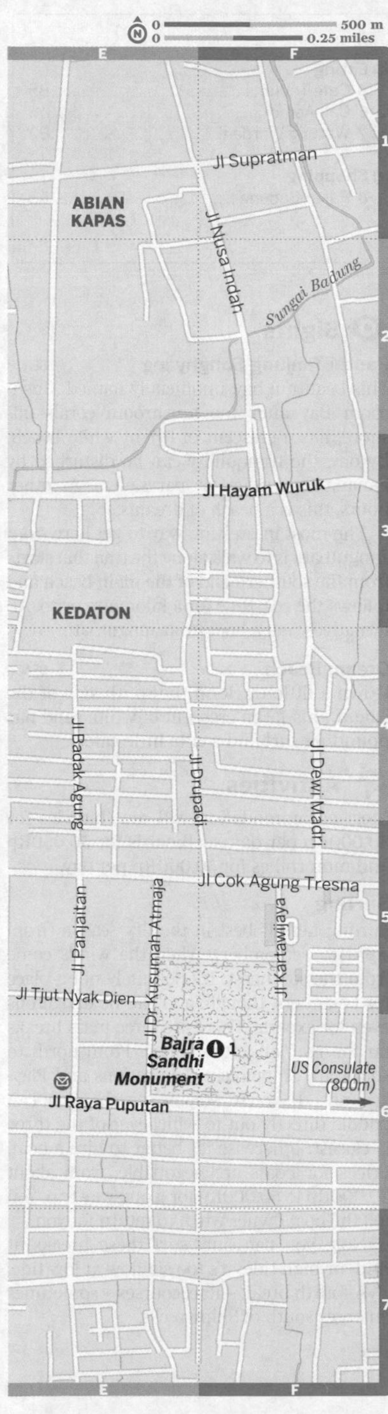

The terminals for transport around Bali are Ubung, Batubulan and Tegal, while Kereneng serves destinations in and around Denpasar. Each terminal has regular bemo connections to the other terminals in Denpasar for 7000Rp.

Fares are approximate and at times completely subjective. Drivers often try to charge nonlocals at least 25% more.

Ubung

Well north of town, on the road to Gilimanuk, the **Ubung Bus & Bemo Terminal** is the hub for northern and western Bali. It has long-distance buses in addition to those serving the bus terminal 12km northwest in Mengwi.

DESTINATION	FARE (RP)
Gilimanuk (for the ferry to Java)	30,000
Mengwi bus terminal	15,000
Munduk	22,000
Singaraja (via Pupuan or Bedugul)	25,000

Batubulan

Located a very inconvenient 6km northeast of Denpasar on a road to Ubud, the **Batubulan Bus & Bemo Terminal** is for destinations in eastern and central Bali.

DESTINATION	FARE (RP)
Amlapura	25,000
Padangbai (for the Lombok ferry)	18,000
Sanur	7000
Ubud	13,000

Tegal

On the western side of town on Jl Iman Bonjol, **Tegal Bemo Terminal** is the terminal for Kuta and the Bukit Peninsula.

DESTINATION	FARE (RP)
Airport	15,000
Jimbaran	17,000
Kuta	13,000

Gunung Agung

This **terminal** (Jl Gunung Agung), at the northwestern corner of town (look for orange bemos), has bemos to Kerobokan and Canggu (10,000Rp).

Kereneng

East of the town centre, **Kereneng Bemo Terminal** has bemos to Sanur (7000Rp).

Denpasar

Top Sights
1 Bajra Sandhi Monument........................F6
2 Museum Negeri Propinsi Bali................C3

Sights
3 Pura Jagatnatha......................................C3

Sleeping
4 Nakula Familiar Inn.................................B2

Eating
5 Café Teduh...B5
6 Cak Asmo..D6
7 Warung Wardani.......................................B2

Shopping
8 Pasar Badung...A3

Wangaya

Near the centre of town, this small **terminal** is the departure point for bemo services to northern Denpasar and the outlying Ubung Bus and Bemo Terminal (8000Rp).

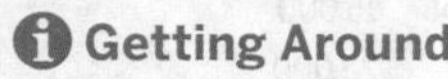

Getting Around

Blue Bird Taxi (☎0361-701111; www.bluebirdgroup.com)

NUSA LEMBONGAN & ISLANDS

Look towards the open ocean southeast of Bali and the hazy bulk of Nusa Penida dominates the view. But for many visitors the real focus is Nusa Lembongan, which lurks in the shadow of its vastly larger neighbour. It offers amazing diving, languorous beaches, great surfing and the kind of laid-back vibe travellers cherish.

Once ignored, Nusa Penida is now attracting visitors, but its dramatic vistas and unchanged village life are still yours to explore. Tiny Nusa Ceningan huddles between the larger islands. It's a quick and popular jaunt from Lembongan.

The main cash crop here has been seaweed, although the big harvest now comes on two legs.

Nusa Lembongan

☎0366

Once the domain of shack-staying surfers, Nusa Lembongan has hit the big time. Yes, you can still get a simple room with a view of the surf breaks and the gorgeous sunsets, but now you can also stay in a boutique hotel and have a fabulous meal. But even as Nusa Lembongan grows in popularity each year, it remains a mellow place.

Sights

Pantai Tanjung Sanghyang BEACH

This beautiful bay, unofficially named Mushroom Bay after the mushroom corals offshore, has a crescent of bright white beach. By day, the tranquillity can be disturbed by banana-boat riders or parasailers. At other hours, this is a beach of dreams.

The most interesting way to get here from Jungutbatu is to walk along the trail that starts from the southern end of the main beach and follows the coastline for a kilometre or so. Alternatively, get a boat from Jungutbatu.

Dream Beach BEACH

Down a little track on the south side of the island, this 150m crescent of white sand has pounding surf and a cute little cafe.

Activities

Most accommodation will rent bicycles for 30,000Rp per day, surfboards for 50,000Rp and motorbikes for 50,000Rp per day.

Surfing

Surfing here is best in the dry season (from April to September), when the winds come from the southeast. It's definitely not a place for beginners, though, and can be dangerous even for experts. There are three main breaks on the reef, all aptly named. From north to south are Shipwrecks, Lacerations and Playgrounds. If you're staying nearby, you can paddle directly out to whichever of the three is closest; otherwise it's better to hire a boat. Prices for boats are negotiable, from about 30,000Rp to 50,000Rp for a one-way trip. You tell the boat owner when to return for you.

Note you can only surf these breaks at mid- or high tide; it's too shallow at low tide.

A fourth break – Racecourses – sometimes emerges south of Shipwrecks.

Diving

You'll have plenty of choice for diving around Nusa Lembongan and the islands (see more on p243).

World Diving DIVING
(☎0812 390 0686; www.world-diving.com; Jungutbatu Beach; 2 dives excl equipment from 1,200,000Rp, open-water course 5,500,000Rp) World Diving, based at Pondok Baruna, is very well regarded. It offers a complete range of courses, plus diving trips to dive sites all around the three islands. Equipment is first-rate.

Bali Diving Academy DIVING
(☎0361-270252; www.scubali.com; Bungalow Number 7; 2 dives excl equipment US$79, PADI US$415) The long-running and very professional Bali Diving Academy is a recommended dive operation, which has long experience in the waters around Lembongan and Penida. It has a full range of courses.

Snorkelling

Good snorkelling can be had just off Tanjung Sanghyang (Mushroom Bay) and Bounty pontoons off Jungutbatu Beach, as well as in areas off the north coast of the island. You can charter a boat from 150,000Rp per hour, depending on demand, distance and the number of passengers.

A trip to the challenging waters of Nusa Penida costs 400,000Rp for three hours, and to the nearby mangroves costs about 300,000Rp. Snorkelling gear can be rented for about 30,000Rp per day. World Diving allows snorkellers to join dive trips and charges 250,000Rp for a four-hour trip.

Sleeping & Eating

Rooms and amenities generally become increasingly posh as you head south and west along the water to Tanjung Sanghyang (Mushroom Bay).

Jungutbatu

★**Pondok Baruna** GUESTHOUSE $
(☎0812 394 0992; www.pondokbaruna.com; Jungutbatu Beach; r 250,000-650,000Rp;) Associated with World Diving, a local dive

DIVING NUSA LEMBONGAN & ISLANDS

There are great diving possibilities around Nusa Lembongan, Nusa Penida and Nusa Ceningan, from shallow and sheltered reefs, mainly on the northern side of Lembongan and Penida, to very demanding drift dives in the channel between Penida and the other two islands. Vigilant locals have protected their waters from dynamite bombing by renegade fishing boats, so the reefs are relatively intact. And a side benefit of local seaweed farming is that locals no longer rely so much on fishing. The islands were designated a marine conservation district in 2012.

If you arrange a dive trip from Padangbai or south Bali, stick with the most reputable operators, as conditions here can be tricky and local knowledge is essential. Diving accidents regularly happen and people die diving in the waters around the islands every year.

Using one of the recommended operators on Nusa Lembongan puts you close to the action from the start. A particular attraction are the large marine animals, including turtles, sharks and manta rays. The large (3m, fin to fin) and unusual mola mola (sunfish) are regularly seen around the islands between mid-July and October, while manta rays are often seen south of Nusa Penida.

The best dive sites include Blue Corner and Jackfish Point off Nusa Lembongan and Ceningan Point at the tip of Nusa Ceningan. The channel between Ceningan and Penida is renowned for drift diving, but it is essential you are with a good operator who can judge fast-changing currents and other conditions. Upswells can bring cold water from the open ocean to sites such as Ceningan Wall. This is one of the world's deepest natural channels and attracts all manner and sizes of fish.

Sites close to Nusa Penida include Crystal Bay, SD, Pura Ped, Manta Point and Batu Aba. Of these, Crystal Bay, SD and Pura Ped are suitable for novice divers and are good for snorkelling.

For a fascinating look into the marine species that inhabit these waters, check out the website of ecological group Aquatic Alliance (www.aquaticalliance.org). The group gives free talks on Tuesdays and Thursdays at 6.30pm at Secret Garden Bungalows (up the road from World Diving), which are worth attending.

Nusa Lembongan

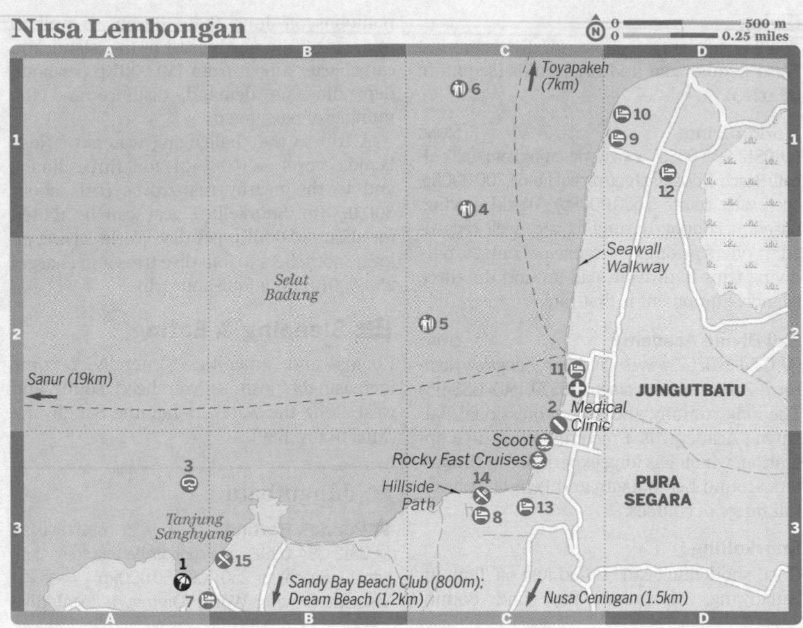

Nusa Lembongan

Sights
1 Pantai Tanjung Sanghyang A3

Activities, Courses & Tours
2 Bali Diving Academy C2
3 Bounty Pontoon A3
4 Lacerations C1
5 Playgrounds C2
6 Shipwrecks C1
World Diving .... (see 11)

Sleeping
7 Alam Nusa Huts A3
8 Batu Karang C3
9 Indiana Kenanga D1
10 Pemedal Beach D1
11 Pondok Baruna C2
12 Pondok Baruna Frangipani D1
13 Ware-Ware C3

Eating
14 Deck Cafe & Bar C3
15 Hai Bar & Grill B3

operator, this place offers fantastic rooms with terraces facing the ocean. Plusher rooms surround a dive pool behind the beach. There are another eight rooms at sister site **Pondok Baruna Frangipani** (☎0812 394 0992; www.pondokbaruna.com; s/d incl breakfast 600,000/650,000Rp; ❄📶🏊), set back in the palm trees around a large pool. Staff members, led by Putu, are charmers.

Pemedal Beach GUESTHOUSE $$
(☎0822 4441 4888; www.pemedalbeach.com; Jungutbatu Beach; r from 500,000Rp; ❄📶🏊) A lovely affordable option if you want to be near a sandy beach; the 11 bungalows are set back a bit with a nice pool.

Indiana Kenanga BOUTIQUE HOTEL $$$
(☎0828 9708 4367; www.indiana-kenanga-villas.com; Jungutbatu Beach; r US$200-490; ❄📶🏊) Two posh villas and 16 stylish suites shelter near a pool behind the beach at Lembongan's most upscale digs. The French designer-owner has decorated the place with Buddhist statues, purple armchairs and other whimsical touches. The restaurant has an all-day menu of seafood and various surprises cooked up by the skilled chef, plus there's a poolside creperie!

Hillside

The steep hillside just south of Jungutbatu offers great views and an ever-increasing number of luxurious rooms.

Ware-Ware GUESTHOUSE $$
(0812 397 0572; r incl breakfast from 700,000Rp;) The nine units at this hillside place are a mix of square and circular numbers with thatched roofs. The large rooms (some with fan only) have rattan couches and big bathrooms. The cafe scores with its spectacular, breezy location on a cliffside wooden deck.

Batu Karang HOTEL $$$
(0366-559 6376; www.batukaranglembongan.com; r incl breakfast from US$270;) This upmarket resort perched on a terraced hillside has a large infinity pool. Some of its 25 luxury units are villa-style and have multiple rooms and private plunge pools. All have open-air bathrooms and wooden terraces with sweeping views. Right on the hillside path, **Deck Cafe & Bar** (http://thedecklembongan.com; snacks from 20,000Rp; 7.30am-11pm;) is a good pause for a gourmet snack or a drink.

Tanjung Sanghyang (Mushroom Bay)

It's your own treasure island. This shallow bay has a nice beach, plenty of overhanging trees and some of the nicest lodgings on Lembongan.

Alam Nusa Huts GUESTHOUSE $
(0819 1662 6336; www.alamnusahuts.com; Tanjung Sanghyang; r from US$40;) This small property is less than 100m from the beach. Four bungalows sit in a small, lush garden; each has an open-air bathroom and a secluded terrace. The interiors feature a lot of rich wood and bamboo. The staff are especially welcoming.

★ **Hai Bar & Grill** INTERNATIONAL $$
(0361-720331; www.haitidebeachresort.com/hai-bar-and-grill; Tanjung Sanghyang, Hai Tide Beach Resort; mains from 60,000-125,000Rp; 7am-10.30pm;) This wide-open bar with wide-open views of the bay and sunsets is the most stylish restaurant bar along Tanjung Sanghyang. The menu mixes Asian and Western dishes, and there are comforts such as fresh-baked muffins. You can use the pool if you eat here, and open-air movies screen some nights. Call for pickup from Jungutbatu.

Elsewhere on Lembongan

Dream Beach Huts GUESTHOUSE $$
(0821 4508 3170; www.dreambeachlembongan.com; Dream Beach; r incl breakfast from 650,000Rp;) Overlooking Lembongan's best beach, this guesthouse truly does have a dream location. The traditionally styled thatched-roof huts are no-frills, with outdoor bathrooms and cold-water showers, so it won't suit those seeking luxury. On the flip side, its grounds are a delight, with a double-tiered swimming pool, ping-pong tables, hammocks and beanbags.

The restaurant (mains from 55,000Rp) is popular with day trippers, so service can be on the slow side.

Sandy Bay Beach Club INTERNATIONAL $$
(0828 9700 5656; www.sandybaylembongan.com; Sunset Bay; mains from 55,000Rp; 8.30am-10.30pm;) Pushing the distressed bleached-wood look for all its worth, this appealing beach club occupies a fine position on a sweet pocket of sand most call Sunset Beach (unless you're this place and call it Sandy Bay...). The menu spans Asia and Europe, with a detour to Burgerville. The evening seafood barbecues are popular.

Information

It's vital that you bring sufficient cash in rupiah for your stay, as there is only one ATM and it won't accept most foreign cards, even when it actually has cash to dispense.

Getting There & Away

There are numerous options for getting to/from Nusa Lembongan, some quite fast. Note: anyone with money to buy a speedboat is getting into the fast-boat act here; be wary of fly-by-night operators with fly-by-night safety standards. Boats anchor offshore, so be prepared to get your feet wet. There are a number of fast boats heading to/from Sanur; recommended operators include **Scoot** (0361-285522; www.scootcruise.com) and **Rocky Fast Cruises** (0361-283624; www.rockyfastcruise.com; Jungutbatu Beach).

Nusa Penida boats take locals between Jungutbatu and Toyapakeh (one hour) between 5.30am and 6am for 30,000Rp. Otherwise, charter a boat for 150,000Rp one way.

Getting Around

The island is fairly small and you can walk to most places. There are no cars (although pickup trucks are proliferating); bicycles (30,000Rp per day) and small motorcycles (50,000Rp per day) are widely available for hire. One unwelcome development has been the arrival of SUV-sized golf carts.

One-way rides on motorcycles or trucks cost 20,000Rp and up.

Nusa Ceningan

There is an atmospheric, narrow **suspension bridge** crossing the lagoon between Nusa Lembongan and Nusa Ceningan, which makes it quite easy to explore the island. In addition to the lagoon that's filled with frames for seaweed farming, you'll see several small agricultural plots and a fishing village. The island is quite hilly and, if you're up for it, you can get glimpses of great scenery while wandering or cycling around.

Activities

The **Mahana Point** cliff jump (50,000Rp for three jumps) is a popular activity.

JED CULTURAL TOUR
(Village Ecotourism Network; 0361-366 9951; www.jed.or.id; per person US$130) To really savour Nusa Ceningan, take an overnight tour of the island with JED, a cultural organisation that gives people an in-depth look at village and cultural life. Trips include family accommodation in a village, local meals, a fascinating tour with seaweed workers and transport to/from mainland Bali.

Sleeping & Eating

Le Pirate Beach Club GUESTHOUSE $$
(0361-487240; www.lepirate-beachclub.com; Nusa Ceningan; r incl breakfast from 900,000Rp;) With a colour scheme of sprightly white and blue, the theme here is retro-chic island kitsch. The accommodation consists of air-conditioned beach boxes, which range from bunk beds that sleep four to doubles. The popular restaurant looks over the small kidney-shaped pool and has broad views of the channel. Two-night minimum.

Sea Breeze Warung INDONESIAN $
(Nusa Ceningan; mains 30,000-70,000Rp; 8am-10pm) The charming Sea Breeze has a great location overlooking the water and the seaweed harvest, and an attractive open-air setting decorated with plants. It offers an excellent seafood selection, and does a tasty *nasi campur*.

Nusa Penida

0366

Largely overlooked by tourists, Nusa Penida awaits discovery. It's an untrammelled place that answers the question: what would Bali be like if tourists never came?

Nusa Penida was once used as a place of banishment for criminals and other undesirables from the kingdom of Klungkung. It's thought to be home to demons. Life is simple here and there are not a lot of formal activities or sights; rather, you go to Nusa Penida to explore and relax.

Sights & Activities

Nusa Penida has world-class **diving** (see p243). Most people make arrangements through dive shops on Nusa Lembongan.

Between Toyapakeh and Sampalan there is excellent **cycling** on the beautiful, flat coastal road. The roads elsewhere are good for mountain bikes. Ask around to rent a bike, which should cost about 25,000Rp per day.

At **Batukandik**, a rough road and a 1.5km track lead to a spectacular waterfall (Air Terjun), which crashes onto a small beach.

★Pura Dalem Penetaran Ped HINDU TEMPLE
FREE The important temple of Pura Dalem Penetaran Ped is near the beach at Ped, 3.5km east of Toyapakeh. It houses a shrine for the demon Jero Gede Macaling that is a source of power for practitioners of black magic, and a place of pilgrimage for those seeking protection from sickness and evil.

Octopus Dive DIVING
(0878 6268 0888; www.octopusdive-pelabuhanratu.com; Bodong; 2-tank dives from 1,000,000Rp) A small and enthusiastic local dive operator.

Penida Tours CULTURAL TOUR
(0852 0587 1291; www.penidatours.com; Bodong, Ped; tours from 500,000Rp; 9am-6pm) A great local operation that arranges cultural tours around Penida, covering anything from black magic to seaweed farming. It's a bit on the pricey side, but few leave disappointed. The office is located next door to Gallery cafe.

Sleeping & Eating

Ped

Just 600m west of the Balinese temple, the tiny village of Bodong has a burgeoning traveller scene.

Jero Rawa HOMESTAY $

(☎0852 0586 6886; www.jerorawa.com; Jl Raya Ped; r incl breakfast with fan/air-con 175,000/275,000Rp) Run by a delightful family, this laid-back guesthouse has clean bungalow-style rooms just across the street from the beach.

Ring Sameton Inn GUESTHOUSE $$

(☎0813 798 5141; www.ringsameton-nusapenida.com; Bodong; r incl breakfast 500,000Rp; ❄📶🏊) If you're seeking comfort, this is easily the best place to stay on Penida. As well as spiffy business-style rooms with air-con and wi-fi, there's a pool, an atmospheric restaurant and quick beach access.

★**Gallery** CAFE $

(☎0819 9988 7205; Bodong; mains 25,000Rp; ⏰7.30am-9pm) A popular spot for volunteers at the NGOs, this small cafe and shop is run by the ever-charming Mike, a Brit who is a font of Penida knowledge. There's art on the walls, hand-roasted filter coffee and a Western menu of breakfasts items and sandwiches.

Penida Colada CAFE $

(www.facebook.com/penidacolada; Bodong; mains 35,000-60,000Rp; ⏰9am-late; 📶) The cocktails at this charming seaside-shack cafe, run by an Indo–Aussie husband-wife team, are a must have. Fresh, creative concoctions include aloe-lime mojitos and dragon-fruit daiquiris to go with a menu of grilled fish, BLT toasties and handcut chips with aioli. There's often a seafood barbecue in the evenings.

Warung Pondok Nusa Penida INDONESIAN $

(Bodong; mains from 27,000Rp; ⏰9am-9pm) A cute little breezy place right on the beach. Enjoy well-prepared Indo classics and seafood (plus the odd international item) while taking in the views to Bali. Try the 'seaweed mocktail' dessert.

Sampalan

Sampalan, the main town on Penida, is a surprisingly hectic strip full of commerce.

MaeMae Beach House GUESTHOUSE $

(☎0817 479 4176; maemaebeachhouse2015@gmail.com; Kutampi; r with fan/air-con 250,000/300,000Rp; ❄📶) In the town of Kutampi just outside Sampalan, this guesthouse is convenient for the main harbour. The manager Agus speaks excellent English and is a wealth of knowledge about everything Penida. Rooms are modern, but with a few rough edges. The chilled-out warung does decent food and is close to the water.

Information

Services are limited to small shops in the main towns. There are a few ATMs, but it's wise to bring enough cash and anything else you'll need.

Getting There & Away

Speedboats on Penida depart from Buyuk harbour in Kutampi village, heading to Sanur (175,000Rp, 45 minutes) and Padangbai (110,000Rp, 25 minutes). A car ferry also operates daily (passenger/motorcycle 27,300/39,000Rp, two hours) to/from Padangbai.

If you come by boat from Nusa Lembongan, you'll probably be dropped at the beach at Toyapakeh, a pretty village with lots of shady trees. Public boats run between Jungutbatu and Toyapakeh (30,000Rp, one hour) between 5.30am and 6am and there are also several trips a day between Lembongan village and Toyapakeh on fast boats (50,000Rp). Otherwise, charter a boat for 400,000Rp return.

Getting Around

To see the island you can rent a motorbike, or charter a private vehicle with driver from 350,000Rp for a half-day.

UBUD

☎0361

Serving as the perfect antidote to the fun-lovin' beaches of the south, Ubud is the place to go once you're done partying hard and need some spiritual cleansing and detox. Framed by stunning green rice fields, lush jungles, ravines and rivers, the town of Ubud is justifiably one of Asia's most famous tourist towns. Though its main streets are often clogged with traffic, all it takes is a short stroll (or better yet, a long hike) and you'll find yourself immersed in its idyllic green surrounds.

A patron of the arts as well as a cradle for Balinese culture, Ubud showcases traditional Balinese dance and artworks, and its ornate architecture is on show in its many palaces, Hindu temples and shrines. And despite its touristy make-up, Ubud remains a wonderful place to observe traditional Balinese life through its daily offerings and Hindu rituals.

It also beckons as a spiritual retreat. Yoga is the big draw, and many relaxation and wellness centres offer every kind of treatment. Food is another highlight: Ubud has some of the most creative restaurants in Indonesia. While you'll find a big emphasis on organic and vegetarian fare, don't miss the traditional Balinese food here.

Ubud Area

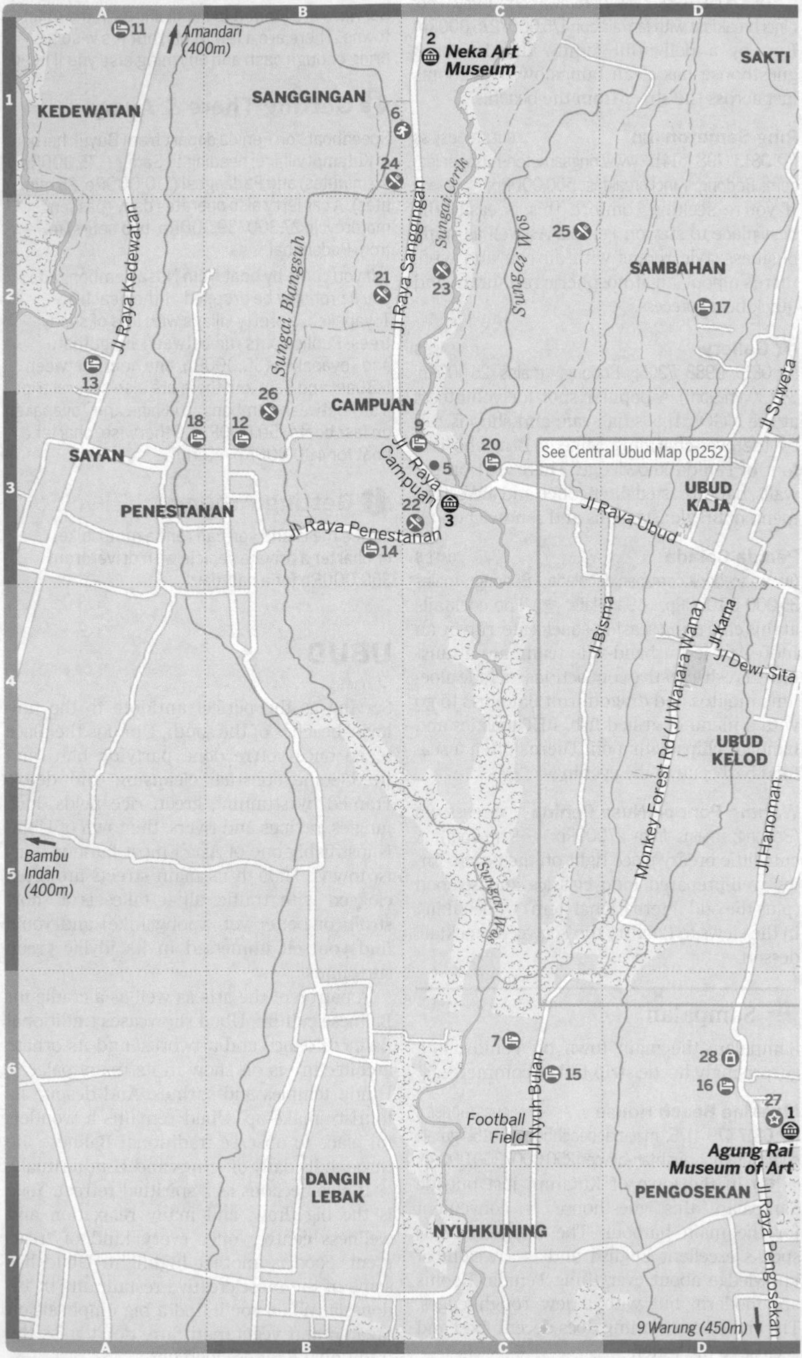

A B C D

1 2 3 4 5 6 7

11 Amandari (400m)

2 **Neka Art Museum**

SAKTI

SANGGINGAN

KEDEWATAN

6

24

25

Sungai Cerik

Sungai Wos

Jl Raya Kedewatan

Sungai Blangsuh

Jl Raya Sanggingan

21

23

SAMBAHAN

17

13

26

CAMPUAN

Jl Suweta

9

18

12

20

SAYAN

Jl Raya Campuan

5

See Central Ubud Map (p252)

UBUD KAJA

PENESTANAN

22

3

Jl Raya Ubud

Jl Raya Penestanan

14

Jl Bisma

Monkey Forest Rd (Jl Wanara Wana)

Jl Karna

Jl Dewi Sita

UBUD KELOD

Bambu Indah (400m)

Sungai Wos

Jl Hanoman

7

15

28

16

27

1

Football Field

Jl Nyuh Bulan

Agung Rai Museum of Art

DANGIN LEBAK

PENGOSEKAN

Jl Raya Pengosekan

NYUHKUNING

9 Warung (450m)

Spend a few days in Ubud to appreciate it properly. Ubud is one of those places where days can become weeks and weeks become months, as the noticeable expat community demonstrates.

Sights

★Museum Puri Lukisan MUSEUM

(Museum of Fine Arts; Map p252; ☎0361-975136; www.museumpurilukisan.com; off Jl Raya Ubud; adult/child incl drink 85,000Rp/free; ⏰9am-5pm) It was in Ubud that the modern Balinese art movement started, when artists first began to abandon purely religious themes and court subjects for scenes of everyday life. This museum displays fine examples of all schools of Balinese art, and all are well labelled in English. It was set up by Rudolf Bonnet, with Cokorda Gede Agung Sukawati (a prince of Ubud's royal family) and Walter Spies.

The **East Building** to the right upon entry has a collection of early works from Ubud and surrounding villages. These include examples of classical 16th-century cloth *wayang*-style paintings (art influenced by shadow puppetry). The **North Building** features fine ink drawings by I Gusti Nyoman Lempad and paintings by Pita Maha artists. Notice the level of detail in Lempad's *The Dream of Dharmawangsa*. Classic works from the 1930s heyday of expats are also here. The **West Building** has vibrant postwar modern art by Balinese painters, while the **South Building** is used for special exhibitions.

The museum has a good bookshop and a cafe. The lush, garden-like grounds alone are worth a visit.

Ubud Palace PALACE

(Map p252; cnr Jl Raya Ubud & Jl Suweta; ⏰8am-7pm) FREE The palace and its temple, **Puri Saren Agung**, share a space in the heart of Ubud. The compound was mostly built after the 1917 earthquake and the local royal family still lives here. You can wander around most of the large compound and explore the many traditional, though not excessively ornate, buildings.

Take time to appreciate the stone carvings, many by noted local artists such as I Gusti Nyoman Lempad. On many nights you can watch a dance performance here.

Just north, **Pura Marajan Agung** (Map p252; Jl Suweta) FREE has one of the finest gates you'll find and is the private temple for the royal family. The compound across from the palace has a magnificent banyan tree, and is also used as a residence for the family.

Ubud Area

Top Sights

1	Agung Rai Museum of Art	D6
2	Neka Art Museum	C1

Sights

3	Blanco Renaissance Museum	C3
4	Museum Rudana	F7

Activities, Courses & Tours

5	Bali Bird Walks	C3
6	Bali Botanica Day Spa	C1

Sleeping

7	Alam Indah	C6
8	Bali Asli Lodge	E2
9	Hotel Tjampuhan	C3
10	Ketut's Place	E2
11	Mandapa Ritz Carlton	A1
12	Santra Putra	B3
13	Sayan Terrace	A2
14	Shift	B3
15	Swasti Eco Cottages	C6
16	Tegal Sari	D6
17	Ubud Sari Health Resort	D2
18	Villa Nirvana	A3
19	Wapa di Ume	E1
20	Warwick Ibah Luxury Villas	C3

Eating

	Alchemy	(see 14)
21	Bintang Supermarket	B2
22	Element	C3
23	Elephant	C2
24	Mozaic	B1
25	Sari Organik	C2
26	Yellow Flower Cafe	B3

Entertainment

27	Arma Open Stage	D6

Shopping

28	Goddess on the Go!	D6
	Rumble	(see 3)

Pura Desa Ubud HINDU TEMPLE
(Map p252; Jl Raya Ubud) FREE The main temple for the Ubud community. It is often closed but comes alive for ceremonies.

★**Pura Taman Saraswati** HINDU TEMPLE
(Map p252; Jl Raya Ubud) FREE Waters from the temple at the rear of this site feed the pond in the front, which overflows with pretty lotus blossoms. There are carvings that honour Dewi Saraswati, the goddess of wisdom and the arts, who has clearly given her blessing to Ubud. There are regular dance performances by night.

★**Neka Art Museum** GALLERY
(Map p248; ☎0361-975074; www.museumneka.com; Jl Raya Sanggingan; adult/child 50,000Rp/free; ⏰9am-5pm Mon-Sat, noon-5pm Sun) The creation of Suteja Neka, a private collector and dealer in Balinese art, Neka Art Museum has an excellent and diverse collection. It's a good place to learn about the development of painting in Bali. You can get an overview of the myriad local painting styles in the **Balinese Painting Hall**. Look for the *wayang* works.

The **Arie Smit Pavilion** features Smit's works on the upper level, and examples of the Young Artist school, which he inspired, on the lower level. Look for the Bruegel-like *The Wedding Ceremony* by I Nyoman Tjarka.

The **Lempad Pavilion** houses Bali's largest collection of works by the master I Gusti Nyoman Lempad.

The **Contemporary Indonesian Art Hall** has paintings by artists from other parts of Indonesia, including stunning works by Affandi. The upper floor of the **East-West Art Annexe** is devoted to the work of foreign artists, such as Louise Koke, Miguel Covarrubias, Rudolf Bonnet, Han Snel, Donald Friend and Antonio Blanco.

The temporary exhibition hall has changing displays, while the **Photography Archive Centre** features black-and-white photography of Bali in the early 1930s and '40s. Head upstairs in the lobby to see the large collection of ceremonial kris (daggers).

★**Agung Rai Museum of Art** GALLERY
(ARMA; Map p248; ☎0361-976659; www.armabali.com; Jl Raya Pengosekan; adult/child incl drink 60,000Rp/free; ⏰9am-6pm, Balinese dancing 3-5pm Mon-Fri, classes 10am Sun) Founded by art patron Agung Rai as an art museum, cultural centre, botanical gardens and hotel, the impressive ARMA features a world-class collection of Balinese, Indonesian and European artists. The collection is well labelled in English. Exhibits include classical Kamasan paintings, Batuan-style work from the 1930s and '40s, and works by Lempad, Affandi, Sadali, Hofker, Bonnet and Le Mayeur. The museum is housed in several traditional

buildings set in gardens with water coursing through channels.

It's fun to visit ARMA when local children practise Balinese dancing and during gamelan practice.

Museum Rudana GALLERY

(Map p248; ☎0361-975779; www.museumrudana.com; Jl Raya Mas; admission incl drink & souvenir 100,000Rp; ⏲9.30am-5pm) This imposing museum overlooking rice fields is the creation of local politician and art-lover Nyoman Rudana and his wife, Ni Wayan Olasthini. The three floors contain more than 400 traditional paintings, including a calendar dated to the 1840s, some Lempad drawings and more-modern pieces. The museum is beside the Rudana Gallery, which has a large selection of paintings for sale. Photography is prohibited.

Blanco Renaissance Museum MUSEUM

(Map p248; ☎0361-975502; www.blancomuseum.com; Jl Raya Campuan; adult/child 80,000Rp/free; ⏲9am-5pm) The picture of Antonio Blanco (1912–99) mugging with Michael Jackson says it all. His surreal palatial neo-renaissance home and namesake museum captures the artist's theatrical spirit. Blanco came to Bali from Spain via the Philippines. Playing the role of an eccentric artist à la Dalí, he is known for his expressionist art and illustrated poetry that incorporates a mix of styles and mediums. Enjoy the waterfall and exotic birds on the way in, and good views over the river.

Neka Gallery GALLERY

(Map p252; ☎0361-975034; Jl Raya Ubud; ⏲8am-5pm) FREE Operated by Suteja Neka since 1966, the low-key Neka Gallery is a separate entity from the other gallery bearing Neka's name, Neka Art Museum. It has an extensive selection from all the schools of Balinese art, as well as works by European residents, such as the renowned Arie Smit.

Activities

Ubud has established itself in recent years as one of the best places in Southeast Asia to practise yoga. All forms of yoga are on offer and for all levels.

It also brims with salons and spas, where you can heal, pamper, rejuvenate or otherwise focus on your personal needs, both physical and mental.

White-Water Rafting

The nearby Sungai Ayung (Ayung River) is the most popular river in Bali for white-water rafting. **Bali Adventure Tours** (☎0361-721480; www.baliadventuretours.com; rafting trips adult/child from $79/52) and **Bio** (☎0361-270949; www.bioadventurer.com; adult/child from US$79/65) are two reputable operators.

Yoga & Wellness

Yoga Barn YOGA

(Map p252; ☎0361-971236; www.theyogabarn.com; off Jl Raya Pengosekan; classes from 120,000Rp; ⏲7am-8pm) The chakra for the yoga revolution in Ubud, the Yoga Barn sits in its own lotus position amid trees back near a river valley. The name exactly describes what you'll find: a huge range of classes in yoga, Pilates, dance and life-affirming offshoots, held throughout the week.

DON'T MISS

UBUD MONKEY FOREST

One of Ubud's most famous sights (or should that be *infamous*) is the **Sacred Monkey Forest Sanctuary** (Mandala Wisata Wanara Wana; Map p252; ☎0361-971304; www.monkeyforestubud.com; Monkey Forest Rd; adult/child 30,000/20,000Rp; ⏲8.30am-6pm). It's a cool and dense swathe of jungle inhabited by a band of grey-haired and greedy long-tailed Balinese macaques. They are nothing like the innocent-looking doe-eyed monkeys on the brochures. Monkeys keep a keen eye on passing tourists in hope of handouts (or an opportunity to help themselves). Don't feed these creatures; avoid eye contact and showing your teeth, including smiling, which is interpreted as a sign of aggression.

The forest sanctuary houses three holy temples. The interesting **Pura Dalem Agung** (Map p252) FREE has a real *Indiana Jones* feel to it; the entrance to the inner temple features Rangda figures devouring children.

You can enter the monkey forest through one of three gates: the main one at the southern end of Monkey Forest Rd; from 100m further east, near the car park; or from the southern side, on the lane from Nyuhkuning.

Central Ubud

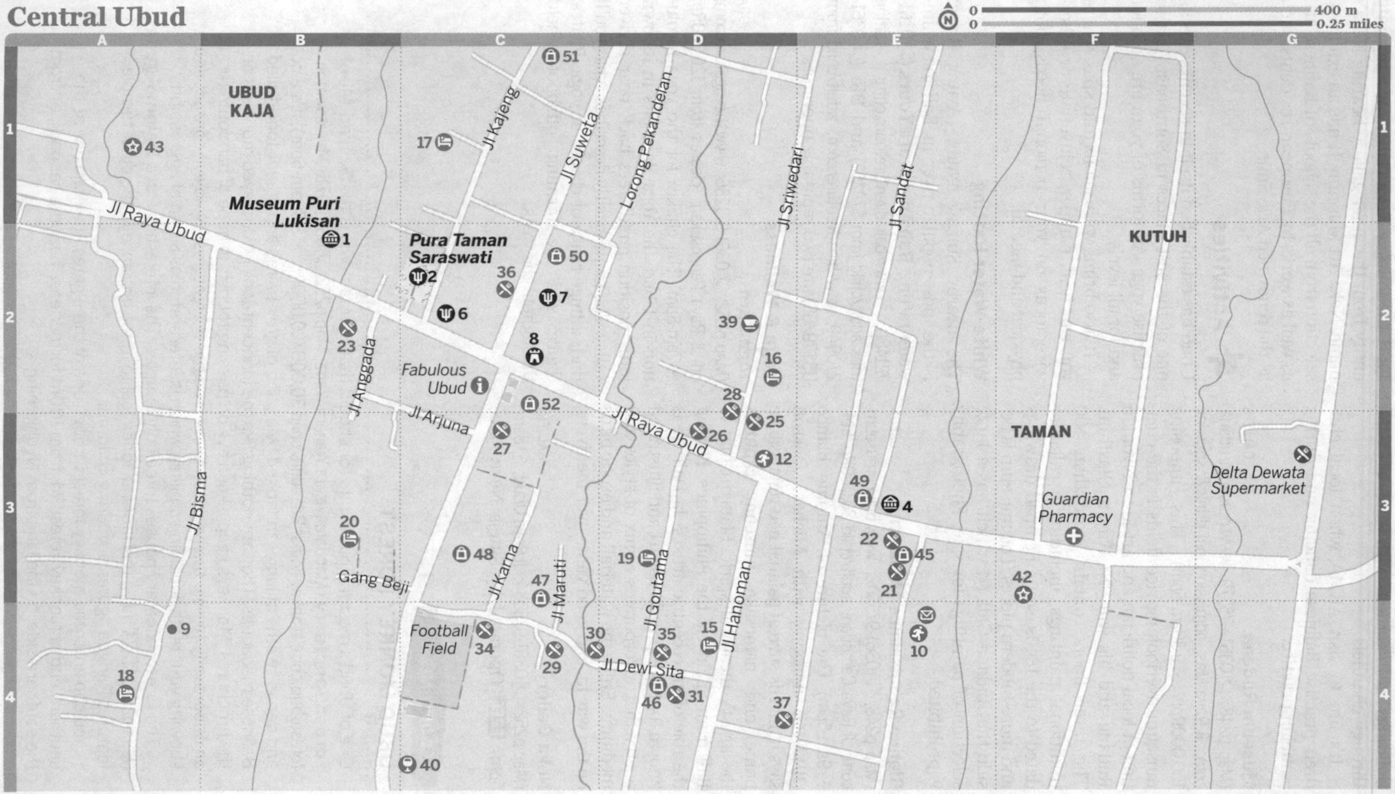

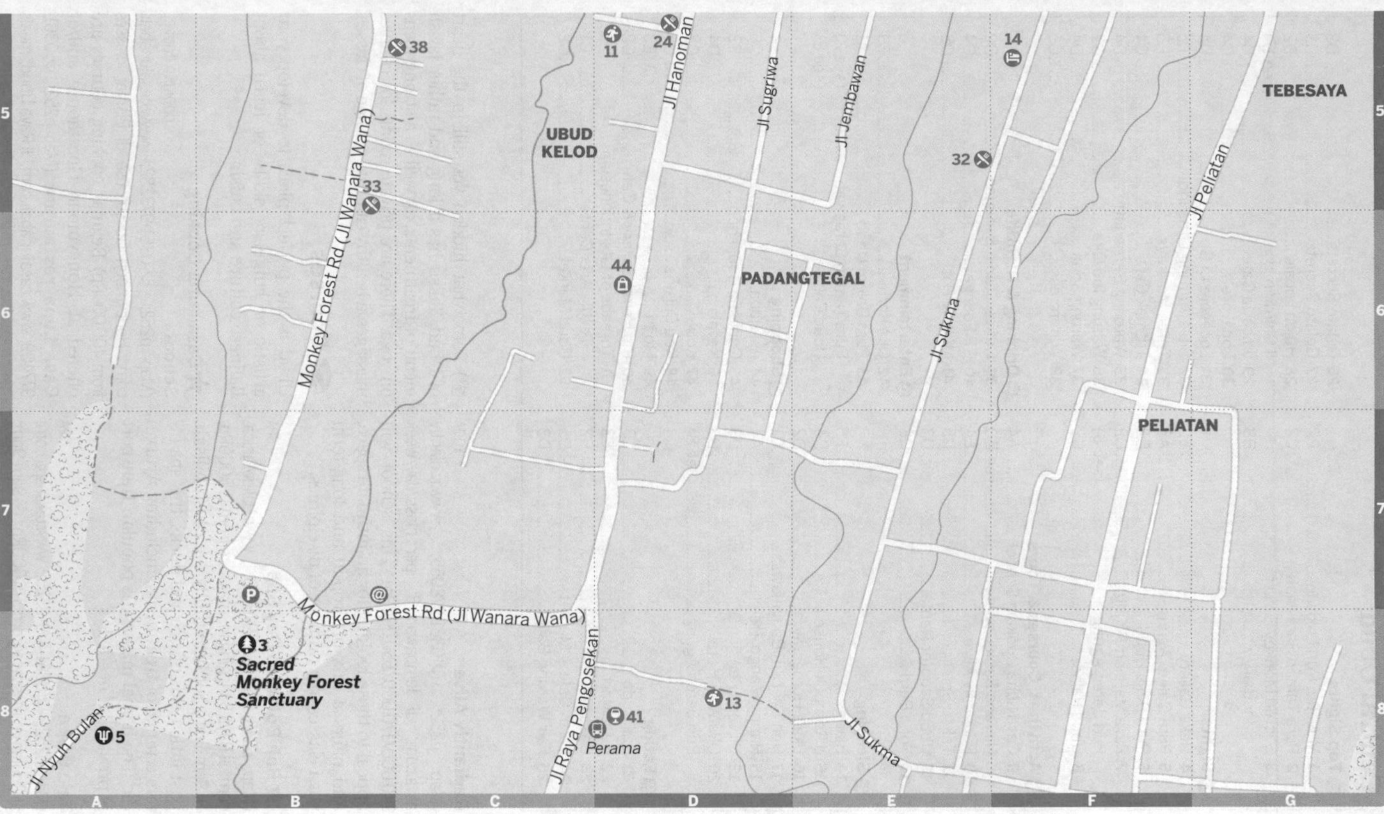
38
11
24
Jl Hanoman
Jl Sugriwa
Jl Jembawan
14
TEBESAYA
Monkey Forest Rd (Jl Wanara Wana)
UBUD KELOD
32
Jl Peliatan
33
44
PADANGTEGAL
Jl Sukma
PELIATAN
Monkey Forest Rd (Jl Wanara Wana)
3
Sacred Monkey Forest Sanctuary
Jl Raya Pengosekan
13
41
Perama
Jl Sukma
Jl Nyuh Bulan
5
5
6
7
8
A
B
C
D
E
F
G

Central Ubud

Top Sights

1 Museum Puri Lukisan ... B2
2 Pura Taman Saraswati ... C2
3 Sacred Monkey Forest Sanctuary ... B8

Sights

4 Neka Gallery ... E3
5 Pura Dalem Agung ... A8
6 Pura Desa Ubud ... C2
7 Pura Marajan Agung ... C2
Puri Saren Agung ... (see 8)
8 Ubud Palace ... C2

Activities, Courses & Tours

9 Casa Luna Cooking School ... A4
Nirvana Batik Course ... (see 19)
10 Radiantly Alive ... E4
11 Taksu Spa ... D5
12 Ubud Scooter Rental ... D3
13 Yoga Barn ... D8

Sleeping

14 Biangs ... F5
15 d'Rompok House ... D4
16 Eka's Homestay ... D2
17 Han Snel Siti Bungalows ... C1
18 Happy Mango Tree ... A4
19 Nirvana Pension ... D3
20 Oka Wati Hotel ... B3
Puri Saren Agung ... (see 8)

Eating

21 Bali Buda ... E3
22 BudaMart ... E3
23 Casa Luna ... B2
24 Earth Cafe & Market ... D5
25 Fair Warung Balé ... D3
26 Gelato Secrets ... D3
27 Gelato Secrets ... C3
28 Hujon Locale ... D2
Il Giardino ... (see 17)
29 Juice Ja Cafe ... C4
30 Locavore ... C4
31 Locavore to Go ... D4
32 Siti's Warung Little India ... E5
33 Three Monkeys ... B5
34 Tutmak Cafe ... C4
35 Waroeng Bernadette ... D4
36 Warung Ibu Oka ... C2
37 Warung Sopa ... D4
38 Watercress ... C5

Drinking & Nightlife

39 Coffee Studio Seniman ... D2
40 CP Lounge ... C4
41 Melting Pot ... D8

Entertainment

42 Oka Kartini ... F3
43 Pura Dalem Ubud ... A1
Pura Taman Saraswati ... (see 2)
Ubud Palace ... (see 8)

Shopping

44 Ashitaba ... D6
45 Ganesha Bookshop ... E3
46 Kevala ... D4
47 Kou ... C3
48 Kou Cuisine ... C3
49 Moari ... E3
50 Rio Helmi Gallery & Cafe ... C2
51 Threads of Life Indonesian Textile Arts Center ... C1
52 Ubud Market ... C2

Radiantly Alive YOGA
(Map p252; ☎0361-978055; www.radiantlyalive.com; Jl Jembawan 3; per class/day/week 140,000/170,000/550,000Rp) This school will appeal to those looking for an intimate space, and offers a mix of drop-in and long-term yoga classes in a number of disciplines.

★ **Bali Botanica Day Spa** SPA
(Map p248; ☎0361-976739; www.balibotanica.com; Jl Raya Sanggingan; massage from 155,000Rp; ⏰9am-9pm) Set beautifully on a lush hillside past little fields of rice and ducks, this spa offers a range of treatments, including Ayurvedic. The herbal massage is popular. Transport is provided if needed.

Taksu Spa SPA
(Map p252; ☎0361-479 2525; www.taksuspa.com; Jl Goutama; massage from 375,000Rp; ⏰9am-9pm; 📶) Somewhat hidden yet still in the heart of Ubud, Taksu has a long and rather lavish menu of treatments, as well as a strong focus on yoga. There are private rooms for couples massages, a healthy cafe and a range of classes.

Courses

Ubud is the perfect place to develop your artistic or language skills, or learn about Balinese culture and cuisine.

★ **Casa Luna Cooking School** COOKING COURSE
(Map p252; ☎0361-973282; www.casalunabali.com; Honeymoon Guesthouse, Jl Bisma; classes from 400,000Rp) Regular cooking courses are offered at Honeymoon Guesthouse and/or **Casa Luna restaurant** (Map p252; ☎0361-977409; www.casalunabali.com; Jl Raya Ubud; meals

from 50,000Rp; ⏲8am-10pm). Half-day courses cover ingredients, cooking techniques and the cultural background of the Balinese kitchen (note, not all courses include a visit to the market). Tours are also offered, including a good one to the Gianyar night market or to a Kintamani coffee plantation.

Nirvana Batik Course ARTS
(Map p252; ☎0361-975415; www.nirvanaku.com; Nirvana Pension, Jl Goutama 10; classes from 480,000Rp; ⏲classes 10am-2pm Mon-Sat) Nyoman Suradnya teaches these highly regarded batik courses.

Tours

Day tours around Ubud are popular, especially ones that involve activities or themed programs.

Bali Nature Herbal Walks WALKING TOUR
(☎0812 381 6024; www.baliherbalwalk.com; walks per person 200,000Rp; ⏲8.30am) Three-hour walks through lush Bali landscapes. Medicinal and cooking herbs and plants are identified and explained in their natural environment. Includes herbal drinks.

Banyan Tree Cycling Tours BICYCLE TOUR
(☎0813 3879 8516; www.banyantreebiketours.com; tours adult/child from 550,000/350,000Rp) Enjoy day-long tours of remote villages in the hills above Ubud. The tours are very popular, and emphasise interaction with villagers. Hiking and rafting trips are also available.

Bali Bird Walks BIRDWATCHING
(Map p248; ☎0361-975009; www.balibirdwalk.com; Jl Raya Campuan; tour incl lunch US$37; ⏲9am-12.30pm Tue, Fri, Sat & Sun) Started by Victor Mason more than three decades ago, this tour, ideal for keen birders, is still going strong. On a gentle morning's walk (from the long-closed Beggar's Bush Bar) you may see up to 30 of the 100-odd local species.

Festivals & Events

The Ubud area is one of the best places to see the many religious and cultural events celebrated in Bali each year. The tourist office is unmatched for its comprehensive information on events each week.

Bali Spirit Festival DANCE, MUSIC
(www.balispiritfestival.com; day pass US$156; ⏲late Mar/early Apr) A popular yoga, dance and music festival from the people behind the Yoga Barn, a local yoga hub. There are more than 100 workshops and concerts, plus a market and more.

Ubud Writers & Readers Festival LITERATURE
(www.ubudwritersfestival.com; 1-day pass 1,200,000Rp; ⏲late Oct/early Nov) Brings together scores of writers and readers from around the world in a celebration of writing – especially writing that touches on Bali. A major event on the Ubud calendar.

Sleeping

Ubud has the best and most appealing range of places to stay in Bali, including fabled resorts, artful guesthouses, and charming, simple homestays.

It enjoys cool mountain air at night, so air-con isn't necessary, and with your windows open you'll hear the symphony of sounds off the rice fields and river valleys.

Central Ubud

Happy Mango Tree HOSTEL $
(Map p252; ☎0812 3844 5498; www.thehappymangotree.com; Jl Bisma 27; dm/d from 100,000/250,000Rp; 📶) This bright and bubbly hostel revels in its hippy vibe. Bright colours abound inside the rooms and out on the various terraces, some of which have rice-field views. Mixed dorms have four or five beds; doubles come with names (and matching decor) such as Love Shack and Ceiling Museum. There's a social bar and a restaurant, too.

Han Snel Siti Bungalows GUESTHOUSE $
(Map p252; ☎0361-975699; www.sitibungalow.com; Jl Kajeng 3; r incl breakfast with fan/air-con from 250,000/350,000Rp; ❄📶🏊) Owned by the family of the late Han Snel, a well-known Dutch painter, Siti Bungalows is one of Ubud's original guesthouses. While its standards have slipped, it remains excellent value and a wonderful choice for those seeking somewhere with character, a delightful garden and spacious bungalows – some of which overlook the river gorge.

d'Rompok House GUESTHOUSE $
(Map p252; ☎0353-344837; drompokhouse@yahoo.com; Jl Hanoman 39; r incl breakfast 250,000Rp; ❄📶) Tucked down a tight *gang*, the well-priced d'Rompok is more suave than your usual homestay, with large modern rooms decorated with contemporary art. Go for one of the top-floor rooms with views of the rice fields.

WALKS AROUND UBUD

Though Ubud has become traffic-clogged and tourist-choked, fortunately it's easy to escape. With only a short walk you'll find yourself immersed in verdant rice fields. There are lots of awe-inspiring walks to surrounding villages or through the rice paddies.

For a short jaunt head down a little track heading north off Jl Raya Ubud that goes past Abangan Bungalows, then follow the path through the lush rice fields; you'll pass numerous charming eateries, including Sari Organik (p260). You can keep heading north as long as your interest or endurance lasts. Look for little offshoot trails to either side that lead to small rivers. Similarly, you can head down Jl Kajeng past Threads of Life (p262) and soon be transported to emerald surrounds.

For longer walks it's good to start at daybreak, before it gets too hot.

The 8.5km **Campuan Ridge walk** leaves Jl Raya Campuan at the Warwick Ibah Luxury Villas. Enter the hotel driveway and take the path to the left, where a walkway crosses the river to Pura Gunung Lebah. From there follow the concrete path north, climbing up onto the ridge between the two rivers. It passes over the lush river valley of Sungai Wos, offering views of Gunung Agung and glimpses of small village communities and rice fields.

Continuing north along the Campuan ridge, the road improves as it passes through rice paddies and the small village of **Bangkiang Sidem**. On the outskirts of the village, an unsigned road heads west, which winds down to Sungai Cerik (the west branch of Sungai Wos), then climbs steeply up to **Payogan**. From here you can walk south to the main road and on to the centre of Ubud.

Eka's Homestay HOMESTAY $
(Map p252; ☎0361-970550; eka_sutawan@yahoo.com; Jl Sriwedari 8; s/d incl breakfast 200,000/250,000Rp; wi-fi) Follow your ears to this nice little family compound with seven basic rooms. Eka's is the home of Wayan Pasek Sucipta, a teacher of Balinese music. It's in a nice sunny spot on a quiet road (well, except during practice times).

Biangs HOMESTAY $
(Map p252; ☎0361-976520; wah_oeboed@yahoo.com; Jl Sukma 28; s/d with fan 100,000/200,000Rp, r with air-con 300,000Rp; air-con wi-fi) In a little garden, Biangs (meaning 'mama') homestay has six well-maintained rooms, with hot water. The friendly family makes it feel like a genuine homestay, and its residential street has a local feel.

Nirvana Pension GUESTHOUSE $
(Map p252; ☎0361-975415; www.nirvanaku.com; Jl Goutama 10; s/d/tr with fan 250,000/350,000/500,000Rp, s/d with air-con 350,000/450,000Rp; air-con wi-fi) Nirvana has *alang-alang* (thatched roofs), a plethora of paintings, ornate doorways and six rooms with modern bathrooms, all set in a shady, secluded locale next to a large family temple. Batik courses are also held here. It's a great location, back off trendy Goutama.

★ **Oka Wati Hotel** HOTEL $$
(Map p252; ☎0361-973386; www.okawatihotel.com; off Monkey Forest Rd; r incl breakfast US$65-115; air-con wi-fi pool) Owner Oka Wati is a lovely lady who grew up near the Ubud Palace. Go for a room in the old wing, where the decor features vintage detail and some rooms have views over a small rice field and river valley. Rooms have large verandas, where the delightful staff will deliver your choice of breakfast (don't miss the house-made yogurt).

Tegal Sari HOTEL $$
(Map p248; ☎0361-973318; www.tegalsari-ubud.com; Jl Raya Pengosekan; r 330,000-990,000Rp; air-con @ wi-fi pool) Though literally a stone's throw from the hectic main road, here rice fields (along with ducks) miraculously materialize. Go for a superdeluxe cottage (770,000Rp) with bathtub looking out to wonderful bucolic views. Units in the new brick buildings, on the other hand, are stark. It has two pools, including one on the rooftop, and a yoga space.

Shift DESIGN HOTEL $$
(Map p248; www.theshifthotelbali.com; Jl Raya Penestanan Kelod; r incl breakfast US$49-79; air-con wi-fi) Set in an old renovated apartment, this hipster, vegan hotel has your classic motel configuration but with plenty of rock-and-roll panache. The modern rooms are comfortable

and include minibars and fibre-optic wi-fi. The rooftop deck has sunloungers, a restaurant, a single-origin speciality cafe, a raw vegan sushi bar and a yoga space that's also used for movies and dance parties.

Puri Saren Agung GUESTHOUSE **$$**
(Map p252; 0361-975057; Jl Suweta 1; r US$75;) Part of the Ubud royal family's historic palace, three rooms are tucked behind the courtyard where the dance performances are held. Accommodation is in traditional Balinese pavilions, with big verandas, four-poster beds, antique furnishings and hot water. Give a royal wave to wandering tourists from your patio.

Sambahan & Sakti

Going north from Jl Raya Ubud, you are soon in rolling terraces of rice fields. Tucked away here you'll find interesting and often luxurious hotels, and you can have a beautiful walk to the centre.

Bali Asli Lodge HOMESTAY **$**
(Map p248; 0361-970537; www.baliaslilodge.com; Jl Suweta; r incl breakfast 300,000Rp;) Escape the central Ubud hubbub here. Made is your friendly host, and her four rooms are in traditional Balinese stone-and-brick houses set on verdant gardens. There are terraces where you can let the hours pass; interiors are clean and comfy. Town is a 15-minute walk.

Ketut's Place GUESTHOUSE **$$**
(Map p248; 0361-975304; www.ketutsplace.com; Jl Suweta 40; r incl breakfast with fan 500,000Rp, with air-con 600,000Rp;) A step up from the usual temple compound homestays, here the rooms all have artful accents and river-valley views. A dramatic pool shimmers down the hillside. Rooms range from basic with fans to deluxe versions with air-con and bathtubs.

Ubud Sari Health Resort GUESTHOUSE **$$**
(Map p248; 0361-974393; www.ubudsari.com; Jl Kajeng; r/villa from US$50/60;) Overlooking a bubbling stream and surrounded by forest, the 21 rooms at this noted health spa have a name that says it all: Zen Village. The plants in the gardens are labelled for their medicinal qualities, and the cafe serves organic, vegetarian fare. Guests can use the health facilities, including the sauna and whirlpool.

Wapa di Ume RESORT **$$$**
(Map p248; 0361-973178; www.wapadiumeubud.com; Jl Suweta; r incl breakfast & activities from US$280, villas from US$417;) Located a gentle 2.5km uphill from the centre, this elegant compound enjoys engrossing verdant views across rice fields. New and old styles mix in the 33 large units; go for a villa with a view. Service is superb yet relaxed. Listening to gamelan practice echoing across the fields at night is quite magical. There's a shuttle bus on the hour to central Ubud.

Nyuhkuning

A popular area just south of the Monkey Forest, Nyuhkuning has some creative guesthouses and hotels, yet is not a long walk to the centre.

Swasti Eco Cottages GUESTHOUSE **$$**
(Map p248; 0361-974079; www.baliswasti.com; Jl Nyuh Bulan; r incl breakfast with fan/air-con from 650,000/750,000Rp;) A five-minute walk from the south entrance to the Monkey Forest, this guesthouse and bungalow compound has large grounds that feature an organic garden (produce is used in the cafe). Some of the rooms are in simple two-storey blocks; others are in vintage traditional houses brought here from across Bali. Swasti also offers a mix of Balinese classes and workshops.

Alam Indah HOTEL **$$**
(Map p248; 0361-974629; www.alamindahbali.com; Jl Nyuh Bulan; r incl breakfast US$65-135;) Just south of the Monkey Forest, this isolated and spacious resort has 16 rooms that are beautifully finished in natural materials to traditional designs. The Wos Valley views are entrancing, especially from the multilevel pool area. There's a free shuttle into central Ubud.

Campuan & Sanggingan

The long sloping road that takes its names from these two communities has a number of upscale properties on its east side that overlook a lush river valley.

Hotel Tjampuhan HOTEL **$$**
(Map p248; 0361-975368; www.tjampuhan-bali.com; Jl Raya Campuan; r incl breakfast US$95-180;) This venerable 69-room place overlooks the confluence of Sungai Wos (Wos

River) and Campuan. The influential German artist Walter Spies lived here in the 1930s, and his former home, which sleeps four people, is part of the hotel. Bungalow-style units spill down the hill and enjoy mesmerising valley and temple views.

★**Warwick Ibah Luxury Villas** HOTEL **$$$**
(Map p248; ☎0361-974466; www.warwickibah.com; off Jl Raya Campuan; ste/villa incl breakfast from US$255/440; ❄📶🏊) Overlooking the rushing waters and rice-clad hills of the Wos Valley, the Ibah offers refined luxury in spacious, stylish individual suites and villas that combine ancient and modern details. Each could be a feature in an interior-design magazine. The swimming pool is set into the hillside amid gardens and lavish stone carvings.

Penestanan

Just west of the Campuan bridge, steep Jl Raya Penestanan branches off to the left and climbs up and around to Penestanan, a large plateau of rice fields and lodgings.

★**Santra Putra** GUESTHOUSE **$**
(Map p248; ☎0361-977810; wayankarja@gmail.com; off Jl Raya Campuan; r incl breakfast 300,000-400,000Rp; 📶) Run by internationally exhibited abstract artist I Wayan Karja (whose studio-gallery is also on-site), this place has 11 big, open, airy rooms with hot water. Enjoy paddy-field views from all vantage points. Painting and drawing classes are offered by the artist.

Villa Nirvana BOUTIQUE HOTEL **$$**
(Map p248; ☎0361-979419; www.villanirvanabali.com; Penestanan; r incl breakfast US$120-250; ❄📶🏊) You may find nirvana reaching Villa Nirvana: access is along a 150m path through a small river valley from the west or along a rice-field path from the top of steep steps from the east. The eight-room compound, designed by local architect Awan Sukhro Edhi, is a serene retreat. Rates include shuttle service and free loan of a mobile phone.

Sayan & Ayung Valley

Two kilometres west of Ubud, the fast-flowing Sungai Ayung (Ayung River) has carved out a deep valley, its sides sculpted into terraced paddy fields or draped in thick rainforest. Overlooking this verdant valley are some of Bali's best hotels.

★**Bambu Indah** BOUTIQUE HOTEL **$$**
(☎0361-975124; www.bambuindah.com; Banjar Baung; s/d incl breakfast US$110/150; 📶🏊) Famed expat entrepreneur John Hardy sold his jewellery company in 2007 and became a hotelier. On a ridge near Sayan and his beloved Sungai Ayung, he's assembled a compound of 100-year-old royal Javanese houses and a stunning Sumbanese thatched house; each space is furnished with style and flair. Several outbuildings create a timeless village with underpinnings of luxury. Free shuttle into central Ubud.

Sayan Terrace HOTEL **$$**
(Map p248; ☎0361-974384; www.sayanterraceresort.com; Jl Raya Sayan; r/villa incl breakfast from US$100/175; ❄@📶🏊) Gaze into the Sayan Valley from this venerable, but slightly dated, hotel and you'll understand why this was the site of composer Colin McPhee's book *A House in Bali*. Stay here while your neighbours housed in luxury resorts pay far more. The 12 rooms and villas are simply decorated but are large and have *that* view. Rates include afternoon tea.

Mandapa Ritz Carlton VILLA **$$$**
(Map p248; ☎0361-4792777; www.ritzcarlton.com; Jl Kedewatan; ste/villa incl breakfast & activities from US$575/870; ❄📶) Epic doesn't even begin to describe the extent to which this stunning resort soars. Sprawling over 5.5 hectares, it's the size of a small village, and set in a spectacular valley enclosed by rice fields. The stars of the show are the villas on the riverfront, but you can't go wrong in any of the villas or suites.

Kubu restaurant is worth a visit even if you're not staying here, both for its scenic riverfront location and its five-course degustation menu.

Amandari HOTEL **$$$**
(☎0361-975333; www.amanresorts.com; Sayan; ste incl breakfast from US$950; ❄@📶🏊) In Kedewatan village, the storied Amandari does everything with the charm and grace of a classical Balinese dancer. Superb views over the jungle and down to the river – the 30m green-tiled swimming pool seems to drop right over the edge – are just some of the inducements. The 30 private pavilions may prove inescapable.

Peliatan

Located 3km east of Ubud Palace, the Peliatan area has a relaxed rural feel, sans traffic jams and tourists.

★ **Maya Ubud** HOTEL $$$
(0361-977888; www.mayaubud.com; Jl Gunung Sari Peliatan; r/villa incl breakfast & activities from US$330/545;) One of the most beautiful large hotels around Ubud, this massive 10-hectare property is superbly integrated into its surrounding river valley and rice fields. The 108 rooms and villas have the sort of open and light feeling combined with traditional materials that defines the concept of 'Bali style'. The infinity pool overlooking the jungle is wonderful, as is its spa complex.

Eating

Ubud's cafes and restaurants are some of the best in Bali. Local and expat chefs produce a bounty of authentic Balinese dishes, as well as inventive Asian and international cuisines. It's also known for its organic and vegetarian fare (p260).

Central Ubud

Warung Ibu Oka BALINESE $
(Map p252; Jl Suweta; mains from 50,000Rp; 11am-7pm) Opposite Ubud Palace, lunchtime crowds are waiting for one thing: Balinese-style roast *babi guling* (suckling pig). Order a *spesial* to get the best cut.

Tutmak Cafe CAFE $
(Map p252; 0361-975754; www.tutmak.com; Jl Dewi Sita; mains 30,000-90,000Rp; 8am-11pm;) This smart, breezy multilevel terrace restaurant is a popular place for a refreshing drink or something to munch on from the menu of Indo classics. The *nasi campur* with fresh tuna is one of Ubud's finest.

Gelato Secrets GELATERIA $
(Map p252; www.gelatosecrets.com; Jl Raya Ubud; from 25,000Rp; 10.30am-11pm) On Ubud's main drag, this temple to frozen goodness has fresh flavours made from local fruits and spices, such as dragonfruit cinnamon or cashew black sesame. It also has a branch on **Monkey Forest Road** (Map p252; www.gelatosecrets.com; Monkey Forest Rd; 10am-10.30pm).

★ **Waroeng Bernadette** INDONESIAN $$
(Map p252; 0821-4742 4779; Jl Goutama; mains from 60,000Rp; 11am-11pm;) It's not called the 'Home of Rendang' for nothing. The west Sumatran classic dish of long-marinated meats (beef is the true classic, but here there's also a vegie jackfruit variety) is pulled off with colour and flair. Other dishes have a zesty zing missing from lacklustre versions served elsewhere. The elevated dining room is a vision of kitsch.

Hujon Locale INDONESIAN $$
(Map p252; 0361-849 3092; www.hujanlocale.com; Jl Sriwedari 5; mains 110,000-200,000Rp; noon-10pm;) From the team of the critically acclaimed Mama San in Seminyak, Hujon Locale is one of Ubud's finest restaurants. The menu mixes traditional Indonesian dishes with modern, creative flair, from Sulawesi salt-baked barramundi, Achenese prawn curry to slow-braised Sumatran lamb curry. The setting within a chic colonial-style two-storey bungalow is made for a balmy evening.

Watercress CAFE $$
(Map p252; www.watercressubud.com; Monkey Forest Rd; mains 90,000-150,000Rp; 7.30am-11pm;) Riding on the success of the hip Canggu cafe, the Ubud version attracts a young fashionable crowd for quality Western food. It has a stylish double-level open-air setting, does creative all-day breakfasts, and offers a menu leaning towards Modern Australian: fresh salads, awesome fish burgers with crispy chat potatoes, king prawn linguine and charred lamp chops.

Siti's Warung Little India INDIAN $$
(Map p252; 0819 9962 4555; Jl Sukma 36; mains from 45,000Rp; 10am-10pm) Run by the delightful Siti, this character-filled Indian restaurant is decked out in vintage Bollywood posters and accompanied by a soundtrack of Hindi pop. Its thalis, samosas and masala chai are all delicious and authentic. Also delivers tiffins.

Fair Warung Balé INTERNATIONAL $$
(Map p252; 0361-975370; www.fairfuturefoundation.org; Jl Sriwedari 6; mains 45,000-75,000Rp; 11am-10pm) Mellow by day, hotspot by night; there are often queues in the evenings to get a table at this attractive upstairs restaurant. It's run by a Swiss-based NGO and 100% of proceeds go to healthcare in the local community. Food ranges from local curries to freshly baked baguettes with tuna tartare.

HEALTHY & ORGANIC UBUD

With its beautiful surrounds, fresh climate and status as champion of the arts, Ubud has long been a place travellers come to nourish the soul. As a current hotspot for yoga, meditation and organic healthy living, it's also the place for all things vegetarian, vegan, raw food and detox.

The **Ubud Organic Market** (www.ubudorganicmarket.com; ⌚9am-1pm Wed & Sat) operates twice a week: Wednesdays at Warung Sopa and Saturdays at Pizza Bagus. Bali Buda's **BudaMart** (Map p252; www.balibuda.com; Jl Raya Ubud; ⌚8am-8pm) is a good source for organic, seasonal produce.

Raw Food Bali (www.rawfoodbali.com) is an excellent resource for everything healthy and organic in Ubud and beyond.

Sari Organik (Warung Bodag Maliah; Map p248; ☎0361-972087; Subak Sok Wayah; meals from 38,000Rp; ⌚8am-8pm) In a beautiful location on a plateau overlooking rice terraces and river valleys, this attractive cafe is in the middle of a big organic farm. The food's healthy and the drinks are cool and refreshing. The walk through the rice fields means half the fun is getting here.

Warung Sopa (Map p252; ☎0361-276 5897; Jl Sugriwa 36; mains 30,000-60,000Rp; ⌚8am-9.30pm; 📶✎) This popular open-air place in a residential street captures the Ubud vibe with creative and (more importantly) tasty vegetarian fare with a Balinese twist. Look for specials of the day on display; the ever-changing *nasi campur* is a treat.

Bali Buda (Map p252; ☎0361-976324; www.balibuda.com; Jl Jembawan 1; meals from 30,000Rp; ⌚7.30am-10pm; ✎) This breezy upper-floor place offers a full range of vegetarian *jamu* (health tonics), salads, sandwiches, savoury crepes, pizzas and gelato. The bulletin board downstairs is packed with idiosyncratic Ubud notices.

Earth Cafe & Market (Map p252; www.dtebali.com/earth-cafe-market-ubud; Jl Gotama Selatan; meals from 30,000Rp; 📶✎) 'Eliminate Free Radicals' is but one of many healthy drinks at this hard-core outpost for vegetarian organic dining and drinking. The seemingly endless menu has a plethora of soups, salads and platters that are heavy on Med flavours. There's a market on the main floor.

Alchemy (Map p248; ☎0361-971981; www.alchemybali.com; Jl Raya Penestanan 75; mains from 50,000Rp; ⌚7am-9pm; 📶✎) A prototypical 100% vegan Ubud restaurant, Alchemy features a vast customised salad menu as well as cashew-milk drinks, durian smoothies, ice cream, fennel juice and a lot more. The raw-chocolate desserts are addictive.

Juice Ja Cafe (Map p252; ☎0361-971056; Jl Dewi Sita; mains from 30,000Rp; ⌚8am-10pm; 📶) Glass of spirulina? Dash of wheatgrass with your papaya juice? Organic fruits and vegetables go into the food at this funky bakery-cafe. Little brochures explain the provenance of items such as the organic cashew nuts. Enjoy the patio.

Yellow Flower Cafe (Map p248; ☎0361-889 9865; off Jl Raya Campuan; mains from 30,000Rp; ⌚8am-9pm; 📶) New Age Indonesian right up in Penestanan along a little path through the rice fields. Organic mains such as *nasi campur* or rice pancakes are good; snackers will delight in the decent coffees, cakes and smoothies. From 5.30pm Sunday evenings there's an excellent Balinese buffet (99,000Rp).

9 Warung (☎0817 776 768; Jl Lodtunduh; per item 3000Rp; ⌚10.30am-9.30pm; ✎) A unique self-service system where customers serve themselves vegetarian and vegan dishes (3000Rp per spoonful), wash their own dishes and calculate the bill before paying using a trust system.

Elephant (Map p248; ☎0361-716 1907; www.elephantbali.com; Jl Raya Sanggingan; mains 60,000-150,000Rp; ⌚8am-9.30pm; 📶✎) High-concept vegetarian dining with gorgeous views across the Sungai Cerik valley. Foods are well seasoned, interesting and topped off with an especially good dessert menu.

Three Monkeys FUSION **$$**
(Map p252; www.threemonkeyscafebali.com; Monkey Forest Rd; meals from 60,000Rp; ⏲8am-10pm; 📶) Order a kaffir-lime mojito and settle back amid the frog symphony of the rice fields. Add the glow of tiki torches for a magical effect. By day there are sandwiches, salads and gelato. At night there's a fusion menu of Asian classics. The staff are very friendly.

Il Giardino ITALIAN **$$**
(Map p252; ☎0361-974271; www.ilgiardinobali.com; Jl Kajeng; mains 60,000Rp-150,000Rp; ⏲5-10.30pm; 📶) This romantic outdoor Italian restaurant has a beautiful setting overlooking a lily pond and the gallery of Dutch painter Han Snel. It does *aperitivo,* wood-fired pizzas, homemade pastas and hearty Italian mains.

Element INTERNATIONAL **$$**
(Map p248; ☎0821 4419 7198; Jl Penestanan; mains 55,000-105,000Rp; ⏲7am-11pm; 📶) A charming little roadside eatery hidden on the backstreets, Element does fresh lunches such as house-smoked ham baguettes or grilled tuna burgers. The locally inspired Kintamani pork belly is popular. Look out for the amusing 'thought for the day' on the chalkboard outside.

★**Locavore** FUSION **$$$**
(Map p252; ☎0361-977733; www.restaurantlocavore.com; Jl Dewi Sita; 5-/7-course degustation 475,000/575,000Rp; ⏲noon-2pm & 6-10pm; ❄📶) *The* foodie heaven in Ubud, this temple to locally sourced, ultra-creative foods is the town's toughest table. Book weeks in advance. Meals are degustation and can top out at nine courses; expect this cuisine nirvana to last upwards of three hours. Chefs Eelke Plasmeijer and Ray Adriansyah in the open kitchen are magicians; enjoy the show.

Up the road there is also **Locavore to Go** (Map p252; ☎0361-977733; Jl Dewi Sita; from 75,000Rp; ⏲8.30am-6pm; 📶), which is good for brunch, with the likes of breakfast burgers and banh mi.

★**Mozaic** FUSION **$$$**
(Map p248; ☎0361-975768; www.mozaic-bali.com; Jl Raya Sanggingan; 6-course menu 700,000Rp; ⏲6-10pm; 📶) Chef Chris Salans oversees this much-lauded top-end restaurant. Fine French fusion cuisine features on a constantly changing seasonal menu that takes its influences from tropical Asia. Dine in an elegant garden or an ornate pavilion. Choose from four tasting menus, one of which is a surprise.

Drinking & Nightlife

No one comes to Ubud for wild nightlife. A few bars get lively around sunset and later in the night, but the venues often close by 11pm.

★**Coffee Studio Seniman** CAFE
(Map p252; ☎0361-972085; www.senimancoffee.com; Jl Sriwedari; coffee 30,000Rp; ⏲8am-10pm; ❄📶) That 'coffee studio' moniker isn't for show; all the equipment is on display at this temple of single-origin coffee. Take a seat on the designer rocker chairs and choose from an array of pourovers, siphon, Aeropress or espresso using a range of quality Indonesian beans. It's also popular for food (mains from 40,000Rp) and drinks in the evening.

CP Lounge BAR, CLUB
(Map p252; www.cp-lounge.com; Monkey Forest Rd; ⏲11am-4am) Open till early morning, CP is the place to kick on once everything else has closed. It has garden seating, live bands and a club with DJ and sound system.

Melting Pot SPORTS BAR
(Map p252; ☎0858 5748 0230; www.meltingpotbali.com; Jl Raya Pengosekan 22; ⏲11am-2am) While a sports bar may seem at odds with artsy Ubud, this Texan-run pool hall does a good job of catering to expat needs with live AFL, NRL, Premier League and American sports. It attracts a diverse crowd through its quality diner food (awesome cheeseburgers), pool tables and rock and roll.

Entertainment

Few travel experiences are more magical than attending a Balinese dance performance, especially while in Ubud.

In a week in Ubud you can see Kecak, Legong and Barong dances, *wayang kulit* shadow puppets, gamelan orchestras and more.

Fabulous Ubud (p263) has performance information and sells tickets (usually 80,000Rp). For performances outside Ubud, transport is often included in the price. Tickets are also sold at the venues and by street vendors who hang around outside Ubud Palace; all tickets cost the same price.

DON'T MISS

BALINESE DANCE

Dance and musical performances are the result of an ever-evolving culture with a legacy that's centuries long. Rigid choreography and discipline are hallmarks of beautiful, melodic Balinese dance, a performance of which no visitor should miss.

Kecak

Probably the best-known dance. With its spellbinding, hair-raising atmosphere, the Kecak features a 'choir' of men and boys who sit in concentric circles and slip into a trance as they chant and sing 'chak-a-chak-a-chak', imitating a troupe of monkeys. Sometimes called the 'vocal gamelan', this is the only music to accompany the dance re-enactment from the Hindu epic Ramayana, the familiar love story about Prince Rama and his Princess Sita.

Barong & Rangda

The Barong is a good but mischievous and fun-loving shaggy dog-lion, with huge eyes and a mouth that clacks away to much dramatic effect. Because this character is the protector of a village, the actors playing the Barong (who are utterly lost under layers of fur-clad costume) will emote a variety of winsome antics.

Meanwhile, the widow-witch Rangda is bad through and through. The Queen of Black Magic, the character's monstrous persona can include flames shooting out her ears, a tongue dripping with fire, a mane of wild hair and large breasts.

The story features a duel between the Rangda and the Barong, whose supporters draw their kris (traditional dagger) and rush in to help. The long-tongued, sharp-fanged Rangda throws them into a trance, making them stab themselves. It's quite a spectacle. Thankfully, the Barong casts a spell that neutralises the kris power so it cannot harm them.

Legong

Characterised by flashing eyes and quivering hands, this most graceful of Balinese dances is performed by young girls. Their talent is so revered that in old age, a classic dancer will be remembered as a 'great Legong'.

Peliatan's famous dance troupe, Gunung Sari, often seen in Ubud, is particularly noted for its Legong Keraton (Legong of the Palace). The very stylised and symbolic story involves two Legong dancing in mirror image. They are elaborately made up and dressed in gold brocade, relating a story about a king who takes a maiden captive and consequently starts a war, in which he dies.

Ubud Palace DANCE
(Map p252; Jl Raya Ubud) Performances are held here almost nightly against a beautiful backdrop.

Pura Dalem Ubud DANCE
(Map p252; Jl Raya Ubud) At the west end of Jl Raya Ubud, this open-air venue has a flame-lit carved-stone backdrop and is one of the most evocative places to see a dance performance.

Pura Taman Saraswati DANCE
(Ubud Water Palace; Map p252; Jl Raya Ubud) The beauty of the setting may distract you from the dancers, although at night you can't see the lily pads and lotus flowers that are such an attraction by day.

Arma Open Stage DANCE
(Map p248; ☎0361-976659; Jl Raya Pengosekan) Has among the best troupes performing Kecak and Legong dance.

Oka Kartini PERFORMING ARTS
(Map p252; ☎0361-975193; Jl Raya Ubud; adult/child 100,000/50,000Rp; ⏲8pm Wed, Fri & Sun) Regular shadow-puppet shows are held at Oka Kartini, which also has an art gallery.

Shopping

Ubud has myriad art shops, boutiques and galleries. Many offer clever and unique items made in and around the area. It's the ideal base for exploring the enormous number of craft galleries, studios and workshops in villages north and south. For indie boutiques, your best bet is Jl Hanoman and Jl Dewi Sita.

★Threads of Life Indonesian Textile Arts Center TEXTILES
(Map p252; ☎0361-972187; www.threadsoflife.com; Jl Kajeng 24; ⏲10am-7pm) This small, professional textile gallery and shop sponsors the production of naturally dyed, handmade

ritual textiles from around Indonesia. It exists to help recover skills in danger of being lost to modern dyeing and weaving methods. Commissioned pieces are displayed in the gallery, which has good explanatory material. Also runs regular textile appreciation courses.

★ Rio Helmi Gallery & Cafe ARTS
(Map p252; ☎0361-978773; www.riohelmi.com; Jl Suweta 06B; ⏲7am-7pm) Noted photographer and Ubud resident Rio Helmi has a small commercial gallery where you can admire or purchase examples of his journalistic and artistic work.

Kevala CERAMICS
(Map p252; www.kevalaceramics.com; Jl Dewi Sita; ⏲9am-7.30pm) Fitting right in along this boutiquey strip, Kevala is famous for its handmade and handpainted contemporary ceramic designs and homewares.

Ubud Market SOUVENIRS
(Pasar Seni; Map p252; Jl Raya Ubud; ⏲7am-8pm) The large Ubud Market is your one-stop shop for kitschy souvenirs, clothing and presents for back home. It's inside a large complex; stallholders set up across several buildings, and also along Jl Karna.

Ganesha Bookshop BOOKS
(Map p252; www.ganeshabooksbali.com; Jl Raya Ubud; ⏲9am-8pm) A quality bookshop with an excellent selection of titles on Indonesian studies, travel, arts, music, fiction (including used books) and maps. Good staff recommendations.

Kou BEAUTY
(Map p252; ☎0361-971905; Jl Dewi Sita; ⏲9am-8pm) The perfume of luxurious locally handmade organic soaps wafts as you enter. Put some in your undies drawer and it'll smell fine for weeks. The range is unlike that found in chain stores selling luxe soap. It also operates **Kou Cuisine** (Map p252; ☎0361-972319; Monkey Forest Rd; ⏲10am-8pm), which specialises in homemade jams.

Ashitaba HOMEWARES
(Map p252; ☎0361-464922; Jl Hanoman; ⏲10am-8pm) Tenganan, the Aga village of east Bali, is where the beautiful rattan items sold here are produced. Containers, bowls, purses and more (from US$5) display the fine and intricate weaving.

Goddess on the Go! CLOTHING
(Map p248; ☎0361-976084; www.goddessonthego.net; Jl Raya Pengosekan; ⏲9am-8pm) A large selection of ecofriendly women's clothes made to be supercomfortable with modal fibre.

Rumble CLOTHING
(Rmbl; Map p248; www.xrmblx.co; Jl Raya Campuhan; ⏲9am-10pm) Owned by the drummer of reputed Balinese punk act Superman is Dead, Rumble stocks a cool selection of locally designed streetwear.

Moari MUSIC
(Map p252; ☎0361-977367; Jl Raya Ubud; ⏲10am-8pm) New and restored Balinese musical instruments are sold here. Splurge on a cute little bamboo flute for 30,000Rp.

ℹ Information

Along the main roads you'll find most services you need, including lots of ATMs.

Fabulous Ubud (Yaysan Bina Wisata; Map p252; ☎0361-973285; www.fabulousubud.com; Jl Raya Ubud; ⏲8am-8pm) Set up by the Ubud royal family, this is the one really useful tourist office in Bali. It has a good range of information and a noticeboard listing current happenings and activities. The staff can answer most regional questions and have up-to-date information on ceremonies and traditional dances held in the area; dance tickets are sold here.

Hubud (Map p252; ☎0361-978073; www.hubud.org; Monkey Forest Rd; per month from US$60; ⏲24hr Mon-Fri, 9am-midnight Sat & Sun; @📶) One for the digital nomads, this co-working space and digital hub has ultrafast web connections, developer seminars and much more. Take in rice-field views as you create a billion-dollar app.

ℹ Getting There & Away

BEMO

Ubud is on two bemo routes. Bemos travel to Gianyar (10,000Rp) and Batubulan terminal in Denpasar (13,000Rp). Ubud doesn't have a bemo terminal; there are bemo stops on Jl Suweta near the market in the centre of town.

TOURIST SHUTTLE BUS

Perama (Map p252; ☎0361-973316; www.peramatours.com; Jl Raya Pengosekan; ⏲9am-9pm) is the major tourist-shuttle operator. Destinations include Kuta (60,000Rp, two hours), Sanur (50,000Rp, one hour), Padangbai (75,000Rp, two hours), Lovina (125,000Rp, three hours) and Amed (175,000Rp, 3½ hours).

Getting Around

TO/FROM THE AIRPORT

Taxis with the cartel from the airport to Ubud cost 300,000Rp. A car with driver *to* the airport will cost around 250,000Rp. The Perama (p263) shuttle leaves Ubud three times a day (60,000Rp, two hours).

BICYCLE

Shops renting bikes have their cycles on display along the main roads. Ubud Scooter Rental (p264) is a good, central bet.

CAR & MOTORCYCLE

With numerous nearby attractions, many of which are difficult to reach by bemo, renting a vehicle is sensible.

Ubud Scooter Rental (Map p252; ☎0361-972170; www.ubudbikerental.com; Jl Raya Ubud; bicycle/motorbike per day 25,000Rp/50,000Rp; ⏰9am-5pm) A reputable operator renting bicycles, scooters and motorbikes.

TAXI

There are no metered taxis based in Ubud; those that are honking their horns at you have usually dropped off passengers from southern Bali in Ubud and are hoping for a fare back. Instead you'll use one of the ubiquitous drivers with private vehicles hanging around on the streets hectoring passer-by (the better drivers politely hold up signs that say 'transport').

Most of the drivers charge very fairly; a few – often from out of the area – not so much. If you find a driver you like, get their number and call them for rides during your stay. From central Ubud to, say, Sanggingan should cost about 50,000Rp, which is rather steep. A ride from the palace to the end of Jl Hanoman should cost about 30,000Rp.

It's easy to get a ride on the back of a motorbike; rates are half those of cars.

AROUND UBUD

☎0361

The immediate region surrounding Ubud has many of the most ancient monuments and relics in Bali. Some of them predate the Majapahit era and raise as-yet unanswered questions about Bali's history. Others are more recent, and in other instances newer structures have been built on and around the ancient remains.

South of Ubud

The roads between Ubud and south Bali are lined with little shops that make and sell handicrafts. Many visitors shop along the route as they head to and from Ubud, sometimes by the busload. Much of the craftwork, though, is actually done in small workshops and family compounds on quiet back roads.

Bedulu

Bedulu was once the capital of a great kingdom. The legendary Dalem Bedaulu ruled the Pejeng dynasty from here, and was the last Balinese king to withstand the onslaught of the powerful Majapahit from Java. He was defeated by Gajah Mada in 1343. The capital shifted several times after this, to Gelgel and then later to Semarapura (Klungkung).

Sights

Goa Gajah CAVE

(Elephant Cave; Jl Raya Goa Gajah; adult/child 15,000/7500Rp, parking motorcycle/car 2000/5000Rp; ⏰8am-5.30pm) There were never any elephants in Bali (until tourist attractions changed that); ancient Goa Gajah probably takes its name from the nearby Sungai Petanu, which at one time was known as Elephant River, or perhaps because the face over the cave entrance might resemble an elephant. It's located some 2km southeast of Ubud on the road to Bedulu.

The origins of the cave are uncertain; one tale relates that it was created by the fingernail of the legendary giant Kebo Iwa. It probably dates to the 11th century, and was certainly in existence during the Majapahit takeover of Bali. The cave was rediscovered by Dutch archaeologists in 1923, but the fountains and pool were not found until 1954.

The cave is carved into a rock face and you enter through the cavernous mouth of a demon. Inside the T-shaped cave you can see fragmentary remains of the lingam, the phallic symbol of the Hindu god Shiva, and its female counterpart the yoni, plus a statue of Shiva's son, the elephant-headed god Ganesha. In the courtyard in front of the cave are two square bathing pools with water trickling into them from waterspouts held by six female figures.

From Goa Gajah you can clamber down through the rice paddies to Sungai Petanu, where there are crumbling rock carvings of

DON'T MISS

BALI'S CHOCOLATE FACTORY

You might think Swiss or Belgian when you think chocolate, but soon you could be thinking Bali. **Big Tree Farms** (☎0361-846 3327; www.bigtreefarms.com; Sibang; tours with/without bookings 40,000/60,000Rp; ⏲tours 2pm Mon-Fri) , a local producer of quality foodstuffs that has made a big splash internationally, has built a chocolate factory about 10km southwest of Ubud in the village of Sibang.

And this is not just any factory: rather it is a huge and architecturally stunning creation made sustainably from bamboo. This emphasis on sustainable practice extends to the company's very philosophy.

The chocolate made here comes from cocoa beans grown by more than 13,000 farmers across Indonesia. The result is a very high-quality chocolate that you can watch being made on a tour.

Just seeing one of the world's largest bamboo structures is an attraction in itself; toss in getting to sample the chocolate – from raw cacao to the finished product – and you've landed an all-round delectable experience.

Reaching the factory is easy as Sibang is on one of the roads linking Ubud to south Bali. A taxi here is around 100,000Rp, including waiting time.

stupas (domes for housing Buddhist relics) on a cliff face, and a small cave.

Try to get here before 10am, which is when the big tourist buses begin lumbering into the large souvenir-stall-filled parking lot like, well, elephants.

Yeh Pulu HISTORIC SITE
(adult/child 15,000/7500Rp; ⏲8am-5.30pm) A man having his hand munched by a boar is one of the scenes on the 25m-long carved cliff face known as Yeh Pulu, believed to be a hermitage from the late 14th century. Apart from the figure of Ganesha, the elephant-headed son of Hindu god Shiva, most of the scenes deal with everyday life, although the position and movement of the figures suggest that it could be read from left to right as a story. One theory is that they are events from the life of Krishna, the Hindu god.

Even if your interest in carved Hindu art is minor, this site is quite lovely and rarely will you have much company. From the entrance, it's a 300m lush, tropical walk to Yeh Pulu.

ℹ Getting There & Away

About 3km east of Teges, the road from Ubud reaches a junction where you can turn south to Gianyar or north to Pejeng, Tampaksiring and Penelokan; for Bedulu follow the signs to Goa Gajah.

Bali Bird Park

Bali Bird Park BIRD SANCTUARY
(☎0316-299352; www.bali-bird-park.com; Jl Serma Cok Ngurah Gambir; adult/child 2-12yr 432,000/216,000Rp; ⏲9am-5.30pm) More than 1000 birds from 250 species flit about here, including rare cendrawasih (birds of paradise) from West Papua and the all-but-vanished Bali starlings. Many are housed in special walk-through aviaries; in one of the aviaries you follow a walk at tree-level, or what some with feathers might say is bird-level. A **reptile section** includes a Komodo dragon. It's popular with kids; allow at least two hours. It's located in Batubulan, halfway between Ubud and Denpasar.

Sukawati

Sukawati is a centre for the manufacture of wind chimes, temple umbrellas and masks.

Wayang kulit and *topeng* (wooden masks used in funerary dances) are also made in the backstreets of Sukawati, about 1km northwest of the main road.

★Sukawati Market MARKET
(Jl Raya Sukawati, Sukawati; ⏲6am-8pm) Sukawati Market is a highlight of any visit to the area. Always lively, this large market is a major source of the flowers, baskets, fruits, knickknacks and other items used in temple offerings. It's a riot of colour.

Mas

Mas means 'gold', but woodcarving, particularly mask carving, is the craft practised here. The road through Mas is lined with craft shops for the tour buses, but there are plenty of smaller carving operations in the back lanes.

The galleries become ever-more glitzy the further north and closer to Ubud you get.

Sights

★Setia Darma House of Masks & Puppets MUSEUM
(☎0361-898 7493; Jl Tegal Bingin; suggested donation 35,000Rp; ⏲8am-4pm) FREE This is one of the best museums in the Ubud area, home to more than 7000 ceremonial masks and puppets from Bali, Indonesia, Asia and beyond. All are beautifully displayed in a series of renovated historic buildings. Among the many treasures, look for the golden Jero Luh Mask, and the faces of royalty, mythical monsters and even common people. The museum is about 2km northeast of the main Mas crossroads.

North of Ubud

Tampaksiring

Tampaksiring is a small village, about 18km northeast of Ubud. It has a large and important temple, Tirta Empul, and the most impressive ancient site in Bali, Gunung Kawi. It sits in the Pakerisan Valley, and the entire area has been nominated for Unesco recognition.

Sights

★Gunung Kawi MONUMENT
(adult/child incl sarong 15,000/7500Rp, parking 2000Rp; ⏲7am-6pm) At the bottom of a lush green river valley lies one of Bali's oldest and largest ancient monuments. Gunung Kawi consists of 10 rock-cut *candi* (shrines) – memorials cut out of the rock face in imitation of actual statues. They stand in awe-inspiring 8m-high sheltered niches cut into the sheer cliff face. Be prepared for long climbs – there are more than 270 steps. The views as you walk through ancient terraced rice fields are as fine as any in Bali.

Tirta Empul MONUMENT
(adult/child 15,000/7500Rp, parking 2000Rp; ⏲7am-6pm) A well-signposted fork in the road north of Tampaksiring leads to the popular holy springs at Tirta Empul, discovered in AD 962 and believed to have magical powers. The springs bubble up into a large, crystal-clear pool within the temple and gush out through waterspouts into a bathing pool.

Getting There & Away

Tampaksiring is an easy day trip from Ubud, or a stop between Ubud and Danau Batur. Tirta Empul and Gunung Kawi are easy to find along the Penelokan–Ubud road, and are only about 1.5km apart.

Elephant Safari Park

Elephant Safari Park WILDLIFE RESERVE
(☎0361-721480; www.baliadventuretours.com; Taro; tours incl transport adult/child US$65/44; ⏲8am-6pm) Abandoned and abused logging elephants from Sumatra have been given refuge at this camp in the cool, wet highlands of Taro (14km north of Ubud). Besides seeing a full complement of exhibits about elephants, you can ride one of 31 residents for an extra fee. Be aware that animal welfare groups claim elephant rides are harmful for the pachyderms, so it's worth reading up on the issues involved if you're considering that option.

While far from a perfect model (metal 'gancho' hooks are used on the elephants, which are chained up when unattended), this park has been praised for its conservation efforts. Be careful you don't end up at one of the rogue copycat parks, designed to divert the unwary to less salubrious elephant encounters.

EAST BALI

The eastern side of Bali is dominated by the mighty 3142m Gunung Agung, the 'navel of the world' and Bali's 'mother mountain'. The slopes of this and the other peaks at this end of the island hold some of the most verdant rice fields and tropical vistas you can imagine. East Bali is a good place to have your own transport, as you can have the freedom to 'get lost' wandering side roads and to revel in the exquisite scenery.

The coast is dotted with beaches, many rough, rugged and untrammelled. Add in some ancient cultural sites and the popular areas of Sidemen, Padangbai and Amed, and you have an area that will lure you from the south Bali–Ubud juggernaut.

Gianyar

☎0361

This is the affluent administrative capital and main market town of the Gianyar district, which also includes Ubud. The town has a number of factories producing batik and ikat fabrics, and its compact centre offers some excellent food, especially at the famous night market.

Eating

★Night Market MARKET
(Jl Ngurah Rai; dishes from 15,000Rp; ⌚5-11pm) The sound of hundreds of cooking pots and the glare of bright lights add a frenetic and festive clamour to Gianyar's delicious night market, which any local will tell you has some of the best food in Bali. Scores of stalls set up each night in the centre and cook up a mouth-watering and jaw-dropping range of dishes.

Shopping

At the western end of Gianyar on the main Ubud road you'll find textile factories, including the large **Tenun Ikat Setia Cili** (☎0361-943409; Jl Astina Utara; ⌚9am-5pm) and **Cap Togog** (☎0361-943046; Jl Astina Utara 11; ⌚8am-5pm). Both are on the main drag west of the centre, about 500m apart. The latter has a fascinating production area below it; follow the sound of dozens of clacking wooden looms.

Getting There & Away

Regular bemos run between Batubulan terminal near Denpasar and Gianyar's main terminal (15,000Rp), which is behind the main market. Bemos to and from Ubud (10,000Rp) use the bemo stop across the road from the main market.

A driver from Ubud will charge 120,000Rp, including waiting time, for a night-market excursion. It's a 20-minute drive.

Bangli

☎0366

Halfway up the slope to Penelokan, Bangli was once the capital of a kingdom. Nowadays it's a humble market town noteworthy for its sprawling temple, Pura Kehen, which is on a beautiful jungle road that runs east past rice terraces and connects at Sekar with roads to Rendang and Sidemen.

Sights

★Pura Kehen HINDU TEMPLE
(adult/child incl sarong 30,000Rp/free; ⌚9am-5pm) The state temple of the Bangli kingdom, Pura Kehen is one of the finest temples in eastern Bali; it is a miniature version of Pura Besakih, Bali's most important temple. It's terraced up the hillside, with a flight of steps leading to the beautifully decorated entrance. The first courtyard has a huge banyan tree with a *kulkul* (hollow tree-trunk drum used to sound a warning) entwined in its branches.

The inner courtyard has an 11-roof *meru* (multi-tiered shrine), and there are other shrines with thrones for the Hindu trinity: Brahma, Shiva and Vishnu. The carvings are particularly intricate. See if you can count all 43 altars.

Pura Dalem Penunggekan HINDU TEMPLE
(Jl Merdeka) FREE The exterior wall of this fascinating temple of the dead features vivid relief carvings of evil-doers getting their just deserts in the afterlife. One panel addresses the lurid fate of adulterers (men in particular may find the viewing uncomfortable). Other panels portray sinners as monkeys, while another is a good representation of sinners begging to be spared the fires of hell. It's 3km south of the centre of Bangli.

> WORTH A TRIP
>
> ### SURFING KERAMAS
>
> As you head east on the coast from Sanur, pretty much any side street leading off the main road will end up at a beach. Most notable is the surf beach **Pantai Keramas**, a powerful right-hand break known for its barrels. It's home of the **Komune Bali Pro** (www.worldsurfleague.com) in May, when the world's best professional surfers battle it out. It's also famous for night surfing, with floodlights erected by the **Komune Bali** (☎0361-301 8888; www.komuneresorts.com; Jl Pantai Keramas; r from US$90; ❄📶🏊) surf resort. Only six surfers are allowed out at a time, and you'll need to book in advance (US$24 per hour; 8pm to 10pm).

Semarapura (Klungkung)

☎0366

A tidy regional capital, Semarapura should be on your itinerary for its fascinating Kertha Gosa complex, a relic of Bali from the time before the Dutch. Once the centre of Bali's most important kingdom, Semarapura is still commonly called by its old name, Klungkung.

It's a good place to stroll and get a feel for modern Balinese life. The markets are large, the shops many and the streets are reasonably calm.

East Bali

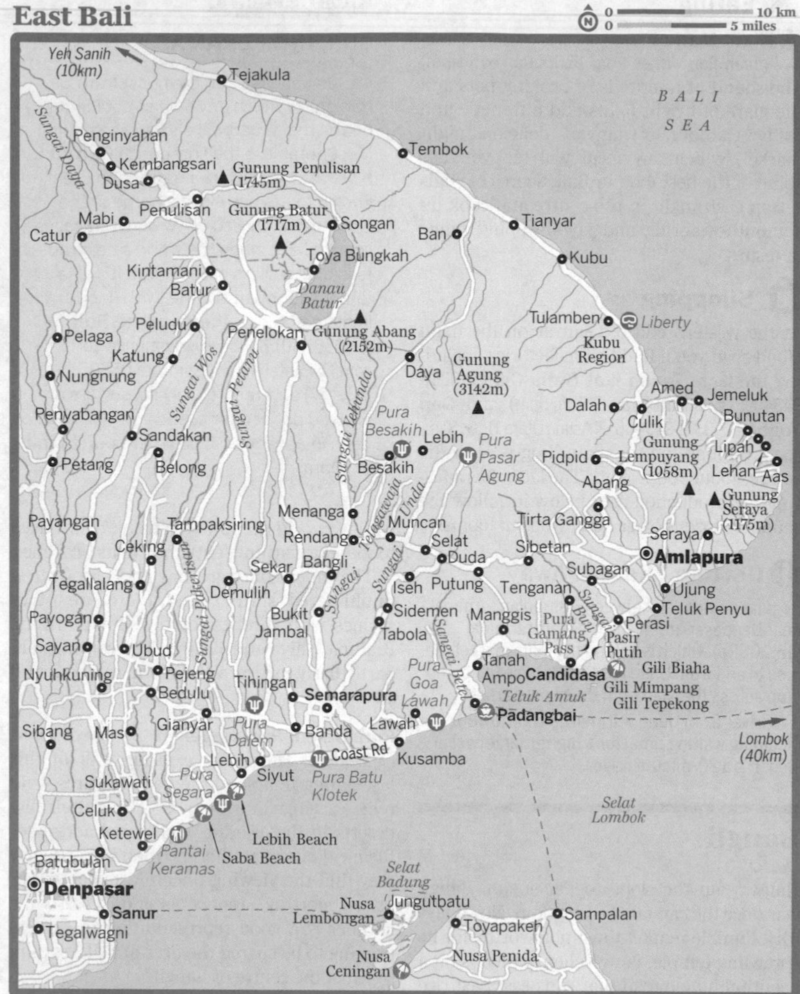

Sights

★Klungkung Palace HISTORIC BUILDING

(Jl Puputan; adult/child 12,000/6000Rp; ⌚6am-6pm) When the Dewa Agung dynasty moved here in 1710, the Semara Pura was established. The palace was laid out as a large square, believed to be in the form of a mandala, with courtyards, gardens, pavilions and moats. The complex is sometimes referred to as Taman Gili (Island Garden). Most of the original palace and grounds were destroyed by the 1908 Dutch attacks; the **Pemedal Agung**, the gateway on the south side of the square, is all that remains of the palace itself – check out its carvings.

Two important buildings are preserved in a restored section of the grounds, and, along with a museum, they comprise the remains of the palace complex.

➡ Kertha Gosa

(Hall of Justice) In the northeastern corner of the complex, the Kertha Gosa was effectively the supreme court of the Klungkung kingdom, where disputes and cases that could not be settled at the village level were eventually brought. This open-sided pavilion is a superb example of

Klungkung architecture. The ceiling is completely covered with fine paintings in the Klungkung style. The paintings, done on asbestos sheeting, were installed in the 1940s, replacing cloth paintings that had deteriorated.

The rows of ceiling panels depict several themes. The lowest level illustrates five tales from Bali's answer to the *Arabian Nights,* where a girl called Tantri spins a different yarn every night. The next two rows are scenes from Bima's travels in the afterlife, where he witnesses the torment of evil-doers. The gruesome tortures are shown clearly, but there are different interpretations of which punishment goes with what crime. (There's an authoritative explanation in *The Epic of Life – A Balinese Journey of the Soul* by Idanna Pucci, available for reference in the pavilion.) The fourth row of panels depicts the story of the search of the *garuda* (mythical man-bird) for the elixir of life, while the fifth row shows events on the Balinese astrological calendar. The next three rows return to the story of Bima, this time depicting him travelling in heaven, with doves and a lotus flower at the apex of the ceiling.

➡ Bale Kambang

(Taman Kertha Gosa) The ceiling of the beautiful Bale Kambang (aka the Floating Pavilion) is painted in Klungkung style. Again, the different rows of paintings deal with various subjects. The first row is based on the astrological calendar, the second on the folk tale of Pan and Men Brayut and their 18 children, and the upper rows on the adventures of the hero Sutasona.

➡ Museum Semarajaya

The diverting museum has an interesting collection of archaeological and other pieces. There are exhibits of *songket* (silver- or gold-threaded cloth) weaving and palm toddy (palm wine) and palm-sugar extraction. Don't miss the moving display about the 1908 *puputan* (fight to the death against an enemy), along with some interesting old photos of the royal court. The exhibit on salt-making gives you a good idea of the hard work involved.

Semarapura Market MARKET

(Jl Diponegoro; ⏲6am-5pm) Semarapura's sprawling market is a vibrant hub of commerce and a meeting place for people of the region. You can easily spend an hour wandering about the warren of stalls on three levels. It's grimy, yes, but also endlessly fascinating. Huge straw baskets of lemons, limes, tomatoes and other produce are islands of colour amid the chaos. A plethora of locally made snacks are offered in profusion; try several.

Getting There & Away

The best way to visit Semarapura is with your own transport and as part of a circuit taking in other sites up the mountains and along the coast.

If you're lucky, a bemo from Denpasar (Batubulan terminal) may pass through Semarapura (13,000Rp) on the way to points further east. They can be hailed from near the Puputan Monument, but don't count on it.

Sidemen Road

☎0366

Winding through one of Bali's most beautiful river valleys, the Sidemen road offers marvellous paddy-field scenery, a delightful rural character and extraordinary views of Gunung Agung (when the clouds permit). Each year the region becomes more popular as a verdant escape, where a walk in any direction is a communion with nature.

There are many **walks** through the rice and chilli fields and along streams in the multihued green valley. One involves a spectacular three-hour round-trip climb up to **Pura Bukit Tageh**, a small temple with big views. No matter where you stay, you'll be able to arrange guides for in-depth hiking (about 80,000Rp per hour), or just set out on your own exploration.

Sleeping & Eating

Views throughout the area are sweeping, taking in both terraced green hills and Gunung Agung. It can get cool and misty at night. Most inns have cafes.

Near the centre of Sidemen, a small road heads west for 500m to a fork and a signpost that lists the names of many places to stay.

★ Khrisna Home Stay HOMESTAY $

(☎0815 5832 1543; pinpinaryadi@yahoo.com; Jl Tebola; r incl breakfast 300,000Rp; wifi) Why go to a market for fruit when you can sleep among it? This wonderful seven-room homestay is surrounded by all-organic trees and plants growing guava, bananas, passion fruit, papaya, oranges and more. Needless to say, breakfasts are excellent. The rooms are comfortable (with terraces) and the owners lovely.

Pondok Wisata Lihat Sawah GUESTHOUSE $

(0852 0511 0916; www.lihatsawah.com; r incl breakfast 300,000-500,000Rp;) Translating as 'See the Ricefields', this guesthouse lives up to its name: all 12 rooms have views of the surrounding rice fields, valley and mountain. All have hot water – nice after a morning hike – and the best have lovely wooden verandas. There are also three bungalows. The cafe has wi-fi and serves Thai and Indo dishes (mains from 15,000Rp). From near the centre of Sidemen, take the right fork in the road to reach this guesthouse.

★ **Samanvaya** INN $$

(0821 4710 3884; www.samanvaya-bali.com; r incl breakfast US$65-156;) An attractive boutique inn with sweeping views over the rice fields, all the way south to the ocean. The Brit owners are steadily expanding the complex: it has a stunning new bamboo yoga space, spa pavilion and restaurant. Bamboo bungalows are the pick, but units with thatched roofs and deep, wooden terraces are also nice. The landscaped garden, infinity pool and hot tub are a dream.

Darmada GUESTHOUSE $$

(0853 3803 2100; www.darmadabali.com; r incl breakfast from 600,000Rp;) Beautifully set in a small river valley on spacious, lush grounds, this seven-room guesthouse has a large pool lined with tiles in gentle shades of green. Rooms have hammocks on the patio near the babbling waters, and there's a natural-water swimming pool. The small warung has food made with vegetables and fruit grown on the grounds.

Joglo d'Uma BALINESE $

(0819 1566 6456; mains from 45,000Rp; 11am-8pm;) This restaurant is a wonderful spot to sit back and take in stunning views of rice fields and verdant hills. Order a bottle of locally made crisp white wine, order a few Balinese dishes, and marvel at how good life is. It's just across from the Samanvaya inn.

Pura Besakih

Perched nearly 1000m up the side of Gunung Agung is Bali's most important temple, Pura Besakih. In fact, it is an extensive complex of 23 separate but related temples, with the largest and most important being Pura Penataran Agung. Unfortunately, many people find it a disappointing (and dispiriting) experience due to the avarice of various local characters.

Sights

The largest and most important temple is Pura Penataran Agung. The other Besakih temples – all of which have individual significance and are often closed to visitors – are markedly less scenic. When it's mist-free, the view down to the coast is sublime.

Pura Penataran Agung HINDU TEMPLE

(admission per person 15,000Rp, plus per vehicle 5000Rp) Pura Penataran Agung, the most important temple in the Pura Basakih temple complex, is built on six levels, terraced up the slope, with the entrance approached from below, up a flight of steps. This entrance is an imposing *candi bentar* (split gateway), and beyond it, the even more impressive *kori agung* is the gateway to the second courtyard.

AN UNHOLY EXPERIENCE

So intrusive are the scams and irritations faced by visitors to Pura Besakih that many wish they had skipped the complex altogether. What follows are some of the ploys you should be aware of before a visit.

- Near the main parking area at the bottom of the hill is a 'guide' office, where guides hang around looking for visitors. Guides here may emphatically tell you that you need their services and quote a ridiculously high price of US$25 for a short visit. You don't need them: you may walk freely and independently among the temples, and no 'guide' can get you into a closed temple.
- Other 'guides' may foist their services on you throughout your visit. There have been reports of people agreeing to a guide's services only to be hit with a huge fee at the end.
- Once inside the complex, you may receive offers to 'come pray with me'. Visitors who seize on this chance to get into a forbidden temple can face demands of 100,000Rp or more.

You will find that it's most enjoyable during one of the frequent festivals, when hundreds or even thousands of gorgeously dressed devotees turn up with beautifully arranged offerings. Note that tourists are not allowed inside this temple.

Information

The temple's **main ticket office** is 2km south of the complex on the road from Menanga and the south. Admission is 15,000/10,000Rp per adult/child plus sarong rental 10,000Rp and 5000Rp per vehicle. Pay no more than 50,000Rp for a guide.

About 200m past the ticket office, there is a fork in the road with a sign indicating Besakih to the right and Kintamani to the left. Go left, because going to the right puts you in the **main parking area** at the bottom of a hill some 300m from the complex. Going past the road to Kintamani, where there is a **west ticket office**, puts you in the **north parking area** only 50m from the complex, and away from scammers at the main entrance.

Getting There & Away

The best way to visit is with your own transport; it's easily done as a day trip from Ubud or Sidemen, which allows you to explore the many gorgeous drives in the area.

Rendang to Amlapura Road

A fascinating road goes around the southern slopes of Gunung Agung from Rendang almost to Amlapura. It runs through some superb countryside, descending more or less gradually as it heads east.

Starting in the west, Rendang is an attractive town that is easily reached either by bemo from Semarapura or via a particularly pretty minor road from Bangli. About 4km along a winding road from Rendang is the old-fashioned village of **Muncan** with its quaint shingle roofs.

The road then passes through some of the most attractive rice country in Bali before reaching **Selat**, where you turn north to get to Pura Pasar Agung, a starting point for climbing Gunung Agung.

Further on is **Duda**, where the scenic Sidemen road branches southwest to Semarapura.

Continuing east, **Sibetan** is famous for growing *salak*, the delicious fruit with a curious 'snakeskin' covering, which you can buy between December and April. *Salak* are the spiky low palm trees you'll see, and the fruit grows in clusters at the base of the trunks. Sibetan is also able to be visited as part of a recommended cultural tour with **JED** (Village Ecotourism Network; 0361-366 9951; www.jed.or.id; day trips US$75, overnight stays US$125).

Gunung Agung

Bali's highest and most revered mountain, Gunung Agung is an imposing peak seen from most of south and east Bali, although it's often obscured by cloud and mist. Many sources say it's 3142m high, but some say it lost its summit in the 1963 eruption. The summit is an oval crater, about 700m across, with its highest point on the western edge above Besakih.

Activities

It's best to climb during the dry season (April to September); July to September are the most reliable months. At other times the paths can be slippery and dangerous, and the views are clouded over (especially true in January and February). Climbing Gunung Agung is not permitted when major religious events are being held at Pura Besakih, which generally includes most of April.

Guides

Trips with guides on either of the routes up Gunung Agung generally include breakfast and other meals, but be sure to confirm all details in advance.

Most of the places to stay in the region, including those at Selat, along the Sidemen road and at Tirta Gangga, will recommend guides for Gunung Agung climbs. Expect to pay a negotiable 900,000Rp to 1,000,000Rp for one to four people for your climb.

Gung Bawa Trekking TREKKING
(0812 387 8168; www.gungbawatrekking.com) Experienced and reliable trekking guide.

Ketut Uriada TREKKING
(0812 364 6426; ketut.uriada@gmail.com) This knowledgeable guide can arrange transport for an extra fee. Look for his small sign on the road east of Muncan.

Wayan Tegteg TREKKING
(0813 3852 5677; tegtegwayan@yahoo.co.id) A recommended guide who wins plaudits from hikers.

TIPS FOR CLIMBING GUNUNG AGUNG

- Use a guide.
- Respect your guide's pauses for prayers at shrines on the sacred mountain.
- Get to the top before 8am – clouds that often obscure the view *of* Agung also obscure the view *from* Agung.
- Take a strong torch (flashlight), extra batteries, plenty of water (2L per person), snack food, waterproof clothing and a warm jumper (sweater).
- Wear strong shoes or boots and keep your toenails short: the trail is very steep and the descent is especially hard on your feet.
- This is a hard climb; don't fool yourself.
- Take frequent rests and don't be afraid to ask your guide to slow down.

Routes

It's possible to climb Agung from various directions. The two most popular routes leave from the following places:

- **Pura Pasar Agung** (on the southern slopes; about eight hours) This route involves the least walking, because Pura Pasar Agung (Agung Market Temple) is high on the southern slopes of the mountain (around 1500m) and can be reached by a good road north from Selat.
- **Pura Besakih** (on the southwest side of the mountain; about 12 hours) This climb is much tougher than the already demanding southern approach and is only for the very physically fit. For the best chance of a clear view before the clouds close in you should start at midnight.

Either route can take you to the summit, although most people on the shorter route go just to the crater rim (2866m).

Sleeping

Pondok Wisata Puri Agung Inn GUESTHOUSE $
(☎0857 3857 4850; Jl Raya Selat; r incl breakfast 250,000-300,000Rp; 📶) Located in relaxed Selat, convenient for climbs up Gunung Agung or rice-field walks, this attractive inn has comfortable budget rooms. Room 2 is the pick for both size and views of the rice fields. A pool was being built at the time of research.

Kusamba to Padangbai

A small road at the east end of the coast road from Sanur goes south to Kusamba, a fishing and salt-making village, where you'll see lines of colourful fishing *perahu* (boats) lined up on the beach. The thatched roofs of salt-making huts can be seen along the beach.

Sights

Pura Goa Lawah CAVE
(Bat Cave Temple; Jl Raya Goa Lawah; adult/child 6000/4000Rp, sarong 4000Rp, car park 1000Rp; ⏱7am-6pm) Three kilometres east of Kusamba, Pura Goa Lawah is one of nine directional temples in Bali. The cave in the cliff face is packed, crammed and jammed full of bats, and the complex is equally overcrowded with worshippers and tour groups. Ceremonies are regularly held here, hence it's a good spot to observe Balinese Hindu rituals; however, be sure to maintain a respectful distance and read any etiquette guidelines before entering.

Padangbai

☎0363

There's a real traveller vibe about this little beach town. It attracts travellers for two mains reasons: for diving or to catch a ferry to the Gili Islands in Lombok. Either way it's an attractive place, sitting on a small bay with a nice little curve of sand. A compact seaside backpacker hub offers cheap places to stay and some fun cafes. For beachgoers, just around the bend there is the attractive Blue Lagoon Beach.

Sights

Padangbai is interesting for a stroll. At the west end of town near the post office there's a small **mosque** (Jl Penataran Agung) and a temple, **Pura Desa** (Jl Pelabuhan). Towards the middle of town are two more temples, **Pura Dalem** (Gang Segara II) and **Pura Segara** (off Jl Silayukti).

Padangbai

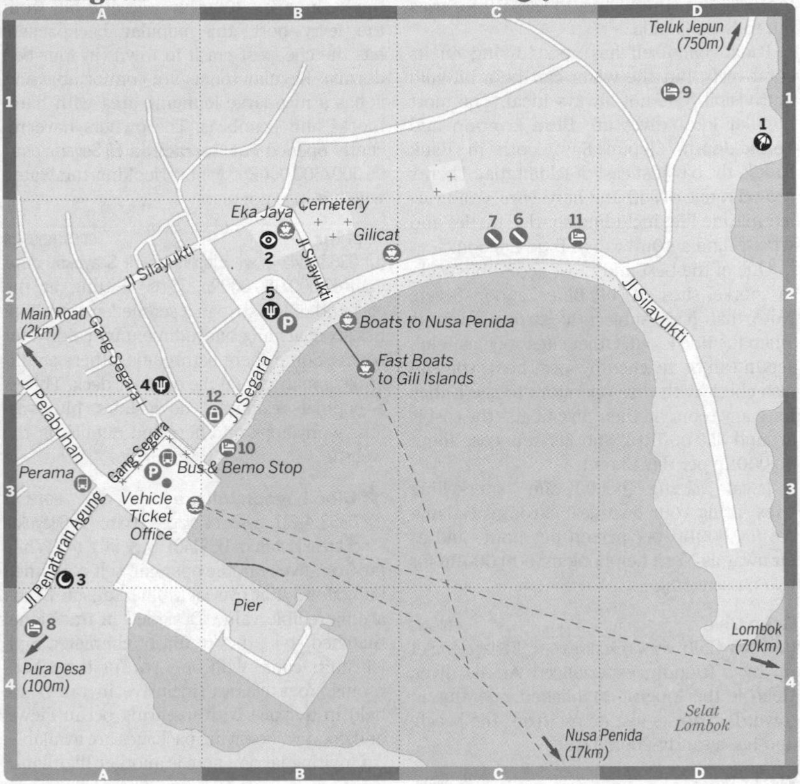

Teluk Jepun (750m)
Cemetery
Eka Jaya
Gilicat
Jl Silayukti
Main Road (2km)
Gang Segara
Jl Segara
Boats to Nusa Penida
Fast Boats to Gili Islands
Jl Pelabuhan
Perama
Bus & Bemo Stop
Vehicle Ticket Office
Jl Penataran Agung
Pier
Pura Desa (100m)
Lombok (70km)
Selat Lombok
Nusa Penida (17km)

Padangbai

Sights

1 Blue Lagoon Beach D1
2 Central Market B2
3 Mosque A3
4 Pura Dalem A2
5 Pura Segara B2

Activities, Courses & Tours

6 Geko Dive C2
7 Water Worx C2

Sleeping

8 Bamboo Paradise A4
9 Bloo Lagoon Village D1
10 Fat Barracuda B3
11 Topi Inn C2

Eating

Topi Inn .... (see 11)

Shopping

12 Ryan Shop B3

Central Market MARKET

(Jl Silayukti) This market near the middle of town is home to numerous vendors and cafes.

Blue Lagoon Beach BEACH

On the far side of Padangbai's eastern headland is the small, light-sand Blue Lagoon Beach, an idyllic place with a couple of cafes and gentle, family-friendly surf.

Activities

Diving & Snorkelling

Padangbai makes an excellent base for divers wanting to access Bali's best dive sites. Many local outfits offer diving trips to see mola mola (sunfish) and rays in Nusa Penida, go wreck-diving in Tulamben and then head on to Gili Tepekong and Gili Biaha. All dive prices are competitive, costing from US$65 for local dives in the area to US$110 for trips out to Nusa Penida.

Padangbai itself has good diving on its coral reefs, but the water can be a bit cold and visibility is not always ideal. The most popular local dives are **Blue Lagoon** and **Teluk Jepun** (Jepun Bay), both in Teluk Amuk, the bay just east of Padangbai. There's a good range of soft and hard corals and varied marine life, including sharks, turtles and wrasse, and a 40m wall at Blue Lagoon.

One of the best and most accessible walk-in snorkel sites sits off Blue Lagoon Beach. Note that it is subject to strong currents when the tide is out. Other sites such as Teluk Jepun can be reached by local boat; you can also check with dive operators to see if they have any room on their dive boats (the cost is around 350,000Rp). Snorkel sets cost about 30,000Rp per day to rent.

Local *jukung* (boats) offer snorkelling trips (bring your own gear) around Padangbai (90,000Rp per person per hour) and as far away as Nusa Lembongan (500,000Rp for two passengers).

Geko Dive DIVING

(0363-41516; www.gekodive.com; Jl Silayukti) Set up by a friendly, experienced Aussie diver, Geko is the longest-established operator in town. Its base is just across from the beach, and has a sandy-floored cafe.

Water Worx DIVING

(0363-41220; www.waterworxbali.com; Jl Silayukti) A well-regarded German-run dive operator offering trips to surrounding areas, plus PADI and SSI courses. Can also arrange dives for travellers with disabilities.

Sleeping & Eating

Accommodation in Padangbai – like the town itself – is pretty laid-back. It's easy to wander around comparing rooms before choosing one; up the hill just above the port are many budget options.

Beach fare and backpacker staples are mostly what's on offer in Padangbai – lots of fresh seafood, Indonesian classics, pizza and, yes, banana pancakes.

Bamboo Paradise GUESTHOUSE $

(0822 6630 4330; www.bambooparadisebali.com; Jl Penataran Agung; dm incl breakfast with air-con 95,000Rp, r incl breakfast with fan/air-con from 200,000/300,000Rp;) Away from the main strip, 200m up a gentle hill from the ferry port, this popular backpackers has the cheapest crash in town (in four-bed dorms). Regular rooms are comfortable and it has a nice large lounging area with hammocks and beanbags. The owners have recently opened **Fat Barracuda** (Jl Segara; dm/r 95,000/300,000Rp;) overlooking the water, which is also popular.

Topi Inn GUESTHOUSE $

(0363-41424; www.topiinn.nl; Jl Silayukti; dm/r from 60,000/150,000Rp;) Sitting at the east end of the strip in a serene location, Topi has six charming but rudimentary cold-water rooms. Some share bathrooms, others are literally a mattress on the outdoor deck. There's a popular restaurant downstairs, plus various workshops on offer; find details on the website.

★**Bloo Lagoon Village** HOTEL $$

(0363-41211; www.bloolagoon.com; Jl Silayukti; r incl breakfast from US$140;) While far from five-star, the open-air, self-contained bungalows that overlook Blue Lagoon Beach are incredible value. Designed in traditional thatched style, they're full of character. Stylish units come with one, two or three bedrooms. Yoga classes (inclusive in rates) are held in a space with inspiring ocean views, and good-value diving packages are available. An inviting lagoon pool is another highlight.

Topi Inn CAFE $

(0363-41424; Jl Silayukti; mains from 50,000Rp; 7.30am-10pm) Juices, shakes and good coffees are served up throughout the day. Breakfasts are big, and whatever is landed by the fishing boats outside the front door during the day is grilled by night. Refill your water bottle here for 2000Rp. It also has an atmospheric bamboo bar selling Balinese wines and cheap beers.

Shopping

Ryan Shop MARKET

(0363-41215; Jl Segara 38; 8am-8pm) The perennial pleasures of the Ryan Shop can't be underestimated. It has good used paperbacks and sundries.

Information

There are several ATMs around town.

Getting There & Away

BEMO

Padangbai is 2km south of the main Semarapura–Amlapura road. If you're lucky, but it's unlikely, there will be a bemo leaving from the car park in front of the port; some go east via Candidasa to Amlapura (10,000Rp); others go west to Semarapura (10,000Rp).

BOAT

There are two options for travel between Bali and Lombok and the Gilis: fast boats or public ferry. Be sure to consider important safety information. Boats also head to Nusa Lembongan.

- Public ferries (child/adult/motorbike/car 29,000/44,000/123,000/879,000Rp, four hours) travel between Padangbai and Lembar (Lombok) every hour from 5am to 3pm. Passenger tickets are sold near the pier. Note that these boats don't have the best safety record, and have in the past caught on fire and run aground.
- Fast boats to the Gilis (one way 660,000Rp to 700,000Rp, 1½ hours) and Nusa Lembongan (300,000Rp, 30 minutes) are a safer option. Most prices include hotel transfer from south Bali.

Eka Jaya (0361-849 6222; www.baliekajaya.com) A reputable fast-boat company running three morning services to the Gili Islands (one way/return 660,000/1,200,000Rp) and an afternoon boat to Nusa Lembongan (one way/return 300,000/550,000Rp, 30 minutes).

Gilicat (0363-41441; www.gilicat.com; Made's Homestay, Jl Silayukti) The most established of the fast-boat operators has an office at the waterfront. Trips to the Gili Islands cost adult/child one way 700,000/490,000Rp.

TOURIST SHUTTLE BUS

Perama (0363-41419; Jl Pelabuhan; 7am-8pm) services destinations around the east coast including Candidasa (35,000Rp, 30 minutes), Kuta (75,000Rp, three hours), Sanur (75,000Rp, two hours), Ubud (75,000Rp, two hours) and Amed (100,000Rp, 2½ hours).

Padangbai to Candidasa

It's 11km along the main road from the Padangbai turn-off to the tourist town of Candidasa. Between the two towns is an attractive stretch of coast, which has some tourist development and a large oil-storage depot in Teluk Amuk.

Coming from the west, there are hotels and guesthouses well off the main road at **Mendira**, about 2.5km before you reach Candidasa. Although the beach has all but vanished and unsightly sea walls have been constructed, this area is a good choice for a quiet getaway if you have your own transport. Think views, breezes and a good book.

Sleeping & Eating

★ Amarta Beach Cottages HOTEL $
(0363-41230; www.amartabeachcottages.com; Jl Raya Mendira, Mendira; d incl breakfast with fan/air-con from 400,0000/500,000Rp, ste from 800,000Rp;) In a panoramic seaside setting, the rooms here are right on the water and are good value. The more expensive ones have modern style and open-air bathrooms. The delightful **Sea Side restaurant** (mains from 40,000Rp; 8am-10pm;) looks out to Nusa Penida – it's a great choice for lunch, whether you are staying here or not.

Candi Beach Resort & Spa RESORT $$$
(0363-41234; www.candibeachbali.com; Jl Raya Mendira, Mendira; r incl breakfast $US130-330;) This large beach resort has 84 comfortable rooms and cute individual bungalows. The pool has a nice beige-stone look, framed by the sea view and palm trees, and is located just up from a semi-decent beach. The much-lauded **Bali Conservancy** (0822 3739 8415; www.bali-conservancy.com; walks from adult/child US$40/30) runs nature tours in conjunction with the hotel.

Tenganan

Step back several centuries with a visit to Tenganan, home of the Bali Aga people – the descendants of the original Balinese who inhabited Bali before the Majapahit arrival in the 11th century.

The Bali Aga are reputed to be exceptionally conservative and resistant to change. Well, that's only partially true: TVs and other modern conveniences are hidden away in the traditional houses. But it is fair to say that the village has a much more traditional feel than most other villages in Bali. Cars and motorcycles are forbidden from entering. It should also be noted that this is a real village, not a creation for tourists.

The most striking feature of Tenganan is its postcard-like beauty, with the hills providing a photogenic backdrop to its setting. The compact 500m by 250m village is surrounded by a wall, and basically consists of two rows of identical houses stretching up the gentle slope of a hill. As you enter the village (10,000Rp donation) through one of only three gates, you'll likely be greeted by a guide who will take you on a tour – and generally lead you back to their family compound to look at textiles and *lontar* strips (specially prepared palm leaves). However, there's no pressure to buy anything.

A peculiar, old-fashioned version of the gamelan known as the *gamelan selunding* is still played here, and girls dance an equally ancient dance known as the Rejang. There are other Bali Aga villages nearby, including **Tenganan Dauh Tenkad**, 1.5km west off the Tenganan road, which has several weaving workshops and a charming, old-fashioned ambience.

Getting There & Away

Tenganan is 3.2km up a side road just west of Candidasa. At the turn-off where bemos stop, motorcycle riders offer rides on *ojeks* (motorcycles that take passengers) to the village for about 25,000Rp. A nice option is to take an *ojek* up to Tenganan, and enjoy a shady downhill walk back to the main road, which has a Bali rarity: wide footpaths.

Candidasa

0363

Candidasa is a relaxed spot on the route east, with hotels and some decent restaurants. However, it also has problems stemming from decisions made three decades ago that should serve as cautionary notes to any previously undiscovered place that suddenly finds itself on the map.

Until the 1970s, Candidasa was just a quiet little fishing village, then beachside losmen (budget accommodation) and restaurants sprang up, and suddenly it was *the* new beach sensation in Bali. As the facilities developed, the beach eroded – unthinkingly, offshore barrier-reef corals were harvested to produce lime for cement in the orgy of construction that took place – and by the late 1980s Candidasa was a beach resort with no beach.

Mining stopped in 1991, and concrete sea walls and breakwaters have limited erosion and now provide some tiny pockets of sand. The relaxed seaside ambience and sweeping views from the hotels built right on the water appeal to a more mature crowd of visitors. Candidasa is a good base from which to explore the interior of east Bali on a walk; it's also a place to spend some quiet time.

While Candidasa lacks a decent beach, fortunately nearby **Pasir Putih** (p279) is a wonderful spot to hang out for the day.

Activities

Gili Tepekong has a series of coral heads at the top of a sheer drop-off and is the best local dive site. It offers the chance to see lots of fish, including some larger marine life, but it's recommended for experienced divers only.

Hotels rent snorkel sets for about 30,000Rp per day. For the best snorkelling, take a boat to offshore sites or to **Gili Mimpang** (a one-hour boat trip should cost about 100,000Rp for up to three people).

Dive Lite DIVING
(0363-41660; www.divelite.com; Jl Raya Candidasa; dives from US$90) Best option in town for the local area or nearby sites such as Penida. The Intro to Diving course is an excellent deal: US$90 gets you a dive with basic instruction followed by a supervised fun dive. It's a great way to see if diving is for you. Night dives to the *Liberty* wreck are available, as are snorkelling trips (US$30).

★**Trekking Candidasa** WALKING TOUR
(0878 6145 2001; www.trekkingcandidasa.com; walks from 250,000Rp) The delightful Somat leads walks through the verdant hills behind Candidasa. One popular route takes 90 minutes and follows rice-field paths to Tenganan.

Sleeping & Eating

Candidasa's busy main drag is well supplied with seaside accommodation, as well as restaurants and other tourist facilities. Quieter places can be found east of the centre along Jl Pantai Indah. These are nicely relaxed and often have a sliver of beach.

Rama Shinta Hotel HOTEL $
(0363-41778; www.ramashintahotel.com; off Jl Raya Candidasa; r incl breakfast 400,000-600,000Rp;) On a little lane near the lagoon and ocean, Rama Shinta's 15 rooms are split between a two-storey stone structure and bungalows. They've been nicely updated with outdoor bathrooms. It's worth upgrading to an upstairs room for views of the lagoon and its birdlife. The pool area is an inviting spot for lounging.

Ari Home Stay GUESTHOUSE $
(0817 970 7339; www.arihomestay.com; Jl Raya Candidasa; r with fan/air-con 150,000/300,000Rp;) Run by the ebullient Gary and his

Candidasa

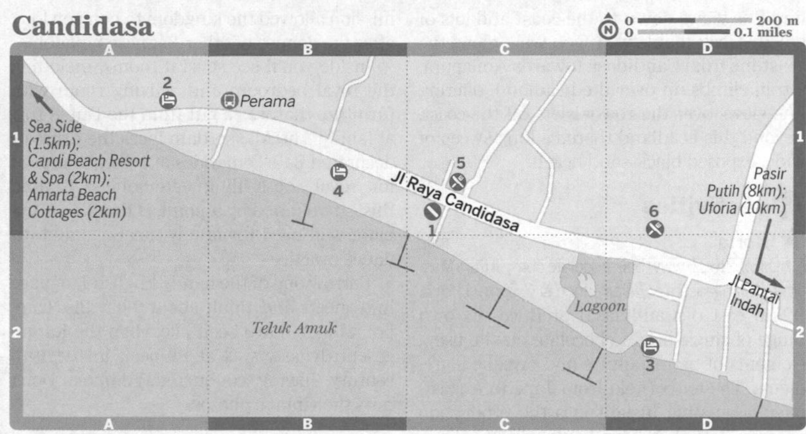

Candidasa

Activities, Courses & Tours
1 Dive Lite ... C1

Sleeping
2 Ari Home Stay ... A1
3 Rama Shinta Hotel ... D2
4 Seaside Cottages ... B1

Eating
5 Crazy Kangaroo ... C1
6 Vincent's ... D1

family, Ari Home Stay has rooms that ramble over the compound, and range from cold-water with fans to air-con with hot water. Its position on the main road across from the water isn't ideal, but very cold beer is always available and there's a pleasurable shack hot-dog restaurant, too.

Seaside Cottages GUESTHOUSE $
(☎0363-41629; www.balibeachfront-cottages.com; Jl Raya Candidasa; cottages 190,000-550,000Rp;) A well-established, popular choice, the 15 rooms here are in cottages and span the gamut from cold-water basic with ineffectual fans, to restful units with air-con and tropical bathrooms. The seafront has loungers right along the breakwater. The Temple Café is a well-regarded restaurant; eat there or dine on tables set along the water.

★**Vincent's** INTERNATIONAL $$
(☎0363-41368; www.vincentsbali.com; Jl Raya Candidasa; meals 60,000-150,000Rp; 8am-11pm;) One of east Bali's classiest restaurants, Vincent's has several distinct open-air rooms, and a large and lovely rear garden with rattan furniture. The bar is an oasis of jazz. The menu combines excellent and inventive Balinese, fresh seafood and European dishes. Thursday evenings there's live music.

Crazy Kangaroo PUB FOOD $$
(☎0363-41996; www.crazy-kangaroo.com; Jl Raya Candidasa; mains 40,000-120,000Rp; 10am-late;) Wild by local standards, this pub is full of characters propped up at the bar to watch sports on the telly, shooting pool or grabbing a feed. The food is good, cooked in an open kitchen that mixes Western and local dishes with tasty seafood specials. There are often performances in the evening, from fire dancing to live music.

Information

Candidasa has many ATMs.

Getting There & Away

Candidasa is on the main road between Amlapura and south Bali, but there's no terminal, so hail bemos, as buses probably won't stop. You'll need to change in either Padangbai or Semarapura going west.

Perama (☎0363-41114; Jl Raya Candidasa; 7am-7pm) is at the western end of the strip. Shuttle-bus destinations include Kuta (75,000Rp, three hours), Sanur (75,000Rp, 2½ hours) and Ubud (75,000Rp, two hours).

Candidasa to Amlapura

The main road east of Candidasa curves up to **Pura Gamang Pass** (*gamang* means 'to get dizzy' – an overstatement), from where you'll find fine views down to the coast and lots of greedy-faced monkeys. If you walk along the coastline from Candidasa towards Amlapura, a trail climbs up over the headland, offering fine views over the rocky islets off the coast. Beyond this headland there's a long sweep of wide, exposed black-sand beach.

Activities

★Uforia TOUR

(☎0363-21687; www.balichocolate.com; Jl Pura Mastima, Karangaasem; ⏰9am-noon & 2-5pm) Uforia (12km east of Candidasa) produces its own range of single-origin chocolate on-site using elements of permaculture and organic ingredients. The tours (held from June to August) offer fascinating insight into the production process; call ahead for bookings and directions. Each Saturday you can take part in a workshop where you make your own personalised chocolate bars from scratch using a choice of ingredients.

Other times stop by the showroom for generous tastings and to stock up on goods.

Amlapura

☎0363

Amlapura is the tidy capital of Karangasem district, and the main town and transport junction in eastern Bali. It's the smallest of Bali's district capitals, and features quaint, wide, leafy residential streets and colonial architecture. It's a multicultural place, with Chinese shophouses and several mosques, and has confusing one-way streets. It's worth a stop to see the royal palaces.

Sights

Amlapura's atmospheric palaces, on Jl Teuku Umar, are vintage reminders of Karangasem at its most important, as a kingdom supported by Dutch colonial power in the late 19th and early 20th centuries.

Puri Agung Karangasem PALACE

(Jl Teuku Umar; adult/child 10,000/5000Rp; ⏰8am-5pm) Outside the orderly Puri Agung Karangasem there are beautifully sculpted panels and an impressive multi-tiered **entry gate**. After you pass through the entry courtyard (all entrances point you towards the rising sun in the east), a left turn takes you to the main building, known as the **Maskerdam** (Amsterdam), because it was built by the Dutch as a reward for the Karangasem kingdom's acquiescence to Dutch rule. This submission allowed the kingdom to hang on long after the demise of other Balinese kingdoms.

Inside you'll see several rooms, including the royal bedroom and a living room with furniture that was a gift from the Dutch royal family. The Maskerdam faces the ornately decorated Bale Pemandesan, which was used for royal tooth-filing ceremonies. Beyond this, surrounded by a pond, is the Bale Kambang, still used for family meetings and for dance practice.

Borrow one of the handy English-language info sheets and think about what this compound must have been like when the Karangasem dynasty was at its peak in the 19th century, having conquered Lombok. Don't miss the vintage photos.

Puri Gede PALACE

(Jl Teuku Umar; ⏰8am-6pm) FREE Puri Gede is still used by the royal family. Surrounded by long walls, the palace grounds feature many brick buildings dating from the Dutch colonial period. Look for 19th-century stone carvings and woodcarvings. The **Rangki**, the main palace building, has been returned to its glory and is surrounded by fish ponds.

Getting There & Away

Amlapura is a major transport hub. Minibuses and bemos regularly ply the main road towards Denpasar's Batubulan terminal (35,000Rp, roughly three hours) via Candidasa (10,000Rp), Padangbai and Gianyar. Plenty of minibuses also go around the north coast to Singaraja (about 30,000Rp) via Tirta Gangga, Amed and Tulamben.

Tirta Gangga

☎0363

Tirta Gangga (Water of the Ganges) is the site of a holy temple, some great water features and some of the best views of rice fields and the sea beyond in east Bali. Capping a sweep of green flowing down to the distant sea, it is a relaxing place to stop for an hour or a few days. With more time you can hike the surrounding terraced countryside, which ripples with coursing water and is dotted with temples.

Sights

★Taman Tirta Gangga PALACE

(admission 20,000Rp, parking 2000Rp; ⏰site 24hr, ticket office 7am-6pm) Amlapura's water-loving rajah, after completing his lost masterpiece at Ujung, had another go at building the

WORTH A TRIP

PASIR PUTIH

The most popular 'secret' beach on Bali, Pasir Putih (aka Dream Beach, aka Virgin Beach) is an idyllic white-sand beach whose name indeed means 'White Sand'. When we first visited in 2004, it was empty, save for a row of fishing boats at one end. Now it's an ongoing lab in seaside economic development.

A dozen thatched beach warungs (food stalls) and cafes now line the sand. You can get nasi goreng (fried rice) or grilled fish. Bintang is of course on ice and loungers await bikini-clad bottoms. The beach itself is truly lovely: a long crescent of white sand backed by coconut trees. At one end cliffs provide shade. The surf is often mellow; you can rent snorkelling gear to explore the waters.

The one thing saving Pasir Putih from being swamped is the difficult access. Look for crude signs with the various monikers near the village of Perasi. Turn off the main road (8km east of Candidasa) and follow a pretty paved track for about 1.5km to a temple, where locals will collect a fee for entry (3000Rp per person) and parking (10,000Rp per vehicle).

water palace of his dreams in 1948. He succeeded at Taman Tirta Gangga, which has a stunning crescent of rice-terrace-lined hills for a backdrop.

This multilevel aquatic fantasy features two swimming ponds that are popular on weekends, and ornamental water features filled with huge koi and lotus blossoms, which serve as a fascinating reminder of the old days of the Balinese rajahs. Look for the 11-tiered *meru* fountain, and plop down under the huge old banyans and enjoy the views.

Activities

Hiking in the surrounding hills is recommended: the rice terraces around Tirta Gangga are some of the most beautiful in Bali. Back roads and walking paths take you to many picturesque traditional villages, or you can ascend the side of Gunung Agung. **Guides** are a good idea. Ask at your accommodation, especially Homestay Rijasa. A local guide who comes with good marks is **Komang Gede Sutama** (☎0813 3877 0893). Guide rates average about 75,000Rp per hour for one or two people.

Among the possible hikes is a walk to **Pura Lempuyang**, one of Bali's nine directional temples, perched on a hilltop on the side of Gunung Lempuyang (1058m); it's around 1½ hours' walk from Tirta Gangga. Another hike is a six-hour loop to Tenganan village, and there are shorter ones across the local hills, which include visits to remote temples and all the stunning vistas you can handle.

★Bung Bung Adventure Biking BICYCLE TOUR
(☎0813 3840 2132, 0363-21873; bungbungbikeadventure@gmail.com; Tirta Gangga; half-/full-day tours from 250,000/300,000Rp) Ride downhill through the simply gorgeous rice fields, terraces and river valleys around Tirta Gangga with this grassroots tour company. Itineraries last from two to four hours, and include use of a mountain bike and helmet, water and plenty of local encounters. The office is at Homestay Rijasa, across from the Tirta Gangga entrance. Book in advance.

Sleeping & Eating

You can overnight in luxury in old royal quarters overlooking the water palace, or lodge in humble surrounds in anticipation of an early-morning hike.

Pondok Lembah Dukah GUESTHOUSE $
(☎0813 3829 5142; dukuhstay@gmail.com; s/d/f 150,000/200,000/350,000Rp) Atop a hill with divine views over the rice fields, this guesthouse has charming bungalows. Rooms are basic but a stay here is a good chance to get close to local life. It's a 10-minute walk from the palace, down the path to the right of Good Karma guesthouse; follow the signs for 300m along the rice field and then up a steep set of steps.

Homestay Rijasa HOMESTAY $
(☎0363-21873; Jl Tirta Gangga; s/d incl breakfast from 100,000/150,000Rp; Wi-Fi) With elaborately planted grounds, this well-run homestay is located opposite the water palace entrance. Expect to pay around double the price for rooms with hot water, which is good for the large soaking tubs. It has a fantastic little warung at the front.

Tirta Ayu Hotel HOTEL $$
(☎0363-22503; www.hoteltirtagangga.com; Pura Tirta Gangga; villas incl breakfast US$125-200;

) Right in the palace compound, this hotel has two pleasant villas and three rooms that have plenty of royal decor. Enjoy the hotel's private pool or use the vast palace facilities. The **restaurant** (mains from 65,000Rp; 7am-9pm) is a tad upscale and serves creative takes on local classics, which come with great water-palace views.

Getting There & Away

Having your own transport is by far the best means. Unreliable bemos and minibuses making the east-coast haul between Amlapura (7000Rp) and Singaraja stop at Tirta Gangga, which is 6km northwest of Amlapura.

Amed & the Far East Coast

0363

Stretching from Amed to Bali's far eastern tip, this semi-arid coast draws visitors with its succession of small, scalloped, grey-sand beaches (some more rocks than sand), a relaxed atmosphere and excellent diving and snorkelling.

The coast here is often called simply 'Amed' but this is a misnomer, as the coast is a series of seaside *dusun* (small villages) that starts with the actual Amed in the north and then runs southeast to Aas. Everything is spread out, so you never feel like you're in the middle of anything, though each township certainly has plenty of signs of a low-key tourist scene.

Traditionally this area has been quite poor, with thin soils, low rainfall and very limited infrastructure. Salt production is still carried out on the beach at Amed. Villages further east rely on fishing, and colourful *jukung* (traditional boats) line up on every available piece of beach. Inland, the steep hillsides are generally too dry for rice; corn, peanuts and vegetables are the main crops.

Activities

Diving & Snorkelling

Snorkelling is excellent along the coast. Jemeluk is a protected area where you can admire live coral and plentiful fish within 100m of the beach. There are a few bits of wood remaining from a **sunken Japanese fishing boat** at Banyuning – just offshore from Eka Purnama bungalows – and you'll find coral gardens and colourful marine life at Selang. Snorkelling equipment rents for about 30,000Rp per day.

Diving is also good, with dive sites off Jemeluk, Lipah and Selang featuring coral slopes and drop-offs with soft and hard corals, and abundant fish. Some sites are accessible from the beach, while others require a short boat ride. The *Liberty* wreck at Tulamben is only a 20-minute drive away.

Several dive operators have shown a commitment to the communities by organising regular beach clean-ups and educating locals on the need for conservation. All operators have similar prices for a long list of offerings (eg local dives from about US$80 and open-water dive courses from about US$400).

Eco-Dive DIVING
(0363-23482; www.ecodivebali.com; Jemeluk Beach;) Full-service dive operator with simple, cheap accommodation for clients. Has led the way on environmental issues.

Hiking

Quite a few trails go inland from the coast, up the slopes of **Gunung Seraya** (1175m) and to some little-visited villages. The countryside is sparsely vegetated and most trails are well defined, so you won't need a guide for shorter walks; if you get lost, just follow a ridge-top back down to the coast road. Allow a good three hours to get to the top of Seraya, starting from the rocky ridge just east of Jemeluk Bay; ask for directions. Sunrise is spectacular but requires a climb in the dark; ask at your hotel about a guide.

Sleeping

The Amed region is very spread out, so take this into consideration when choosing accommodation. You will also need to choose between staying in the little beachside villages or on the sunny and dry headlands connecting the inlets. The former puts you right on the sand and offers a small amount of community life while the latter gives you broad, sweeping vistas and isolation.

Jemeluk

You might say what's now called Amed started here.

Hoky Home Stay & Cafe HOMESTAY $
(0819 1646 3701; madejoro@yahoo.com; Jemeluk; r incl breakfast 200,000Rp;) This place near the beach offers great cheap rooms with fans and hot water. The owner, Made, is tuned in to budget travellers' needs. The **cafe** (mains 25,000Rp; 8am-10pm) has fresh and creative local foods, especially seafood. Bikes for rent (30,000Rp per day).

Galang Kangin Bungalows GUESTHOUSE $
(0363-23480; bali_amed_gk@yahoo.co.jp; Jemeluk; r incl breakfast with fan/air-con from 300,000/500,000Rp;) Set on the hill side of the road amid a nice garden, the 10 rooms here mix and match fans, cold water, hot water and air-con. The modern air-con rooms open to the beach, while the fan rooms across the road have a more traditional, ornate Balinese style.

Bunutan

These places are on a sun-drenched, arid stretch of highland.

★ **Wawa-Wewe II** HOTEL $$
(0363-23522; www.bali-wawawewe.com; Bunutan; r incl breakfast 400,000-700,000Rp;) This restful place has 10 bungalow-style rooms on lush grounds that shamble down to the water's edge. The natural-stone infinity pool is shaped like a Buddha and is near the sea, as are two rooms with fine ocean views.

Santai HOTEL $$
(0363-23487; www.santaibali.com; Bunutan Beach; r incl breakfast US$87-163;) This lovely option is set on a slight hill down to the beach. The name means 'relax', and that's just what you'll do here. A series of authentic traditional thatched bungalows gathered from around the archipelago holds 10 rooms with four-poster beds, open-air bathrooms and big balcony sofas. A swimming pool, fringed by purple bougainvillea, snakes through the property.

Lipah

This coastal village is just large enough for you to go wandering – briefly.

Coral View Villas HOTEL $$
(www.coralviewvillas.com; Lipah; r from US$90;) Lush grounds surrounding a naturalistic pool set this tidy property apart from other more arid places. The 19 rooms are in bungalow-style units and have nice terraces outside; inside, the rooms are large and there are stone-lined open-air bathrooms.

Lehan

Quiet, beachy Lehan has some of Amed's nicest boutique-style accommodation.

Palm Garden HOTEL $$
(0828 9769 1850; www.palmgardenamed.com; Lehan; r incl breakfast US$110-250;) This oceanfront villa hotel verges on elegant. Certainly it has the best beach in Amed. The 10 units have large patios and the grounds are lined with palm trees, including one growing from its own island in the pool. There's a two-night minimum stay in high season.

Aas

The last community of any size on the road from Amed, Aas is very quiet.

★ **Meditasi** GUESTHOUSE $
(0828 372 2738; www.meditasibungalows.blogspot.com; Aas; r 300,000-500,000Rp) Get off the grid at this chilled-out and charming hideaway. Meditation and yoga help you relax, and the eight rooms are well situated for good swimming and snorkelling. By far the best bet are the villa-style bungalows, complete with private garden, open-air bathrooms and balconies with superb sea views. Elizabeth Gilbert, author of *Eat, Pray, Love,* stayed in room 7.

Eating & Drinking

Most accommodation also has a cafe.

★ **Warung Enak** BALINESE $
(0819 1567 9019; Jemeluk; mains from 50,000Rp; 9am-11pm) Black rice pudding and other less-common local treats are the specialities of this dead-simple and supertasty little eatery. Also does a fresh catch of the day and homemade ice cream.

★ **Smiling Buddha Restaurant** BALINESE $
(0828 372 2738; Aas; meals from 30,000Rp; 8am-10pm;) The restaurant at this highly recommended guesthouse has excellent organic fare, much sourced from its own garden. Balinese and Western dishes are excellent and original, and there are good views out to sea. The place even manages some full-moon fun. Happy hour is from 7pm to 8pm.

Green Leaf Cafe CAFE $
(0812 3826 7356; www.apneista.com; Jemeluk; mains from 35,000Rp; 8.30am-6.30pm;) After you've chilled out, chill out some more. This excellent cafe has a good vegetarian menu, with many specials. There's a wide range of coffees, teas and juices. Sit at a table inside or on loungers outside. This is also a hub for yoga and freediving.

Wawa-Wewe I BAR
(0363-23506; Lipah; 8am-late;) You won't know your wawas from your wewes if you

spend the evening here trying the local *arak* (distilled palm wine) made with palm fronds. This is the coast's most raucous bar – which by local standards means that sometimes it gets sorta loud. Local bands jam on Wednesday and Saturday nights. Meals are served (from 35,000Rp) and it also has budget rooms.

Information

You may be charged a tourist tax to enter the area. Enforcement of a 5000Rp per-person fee at a tollbooth on the outskirts of Amed is sporadic. There are several ATMs, but best not to rely on them. Wi-fi is nearly universal.

Getting There & Around

Most people drive here via the main highway from Amlapura and Culik. The spectacular road going all the way around the twin peaks of Lempuyang and Seraya from Aas to Ujung makes a good circle.

You can arrange for a driver and car to/from south Bali and the airport for about 500,000Rp.

Public transport is difficult. Minibuses and bemos between Singaraja and Amlapura pass through Culik, the turn-off for the coast. Infrequent bemos go from Culik to Amed (3.5km), and some continue to Seraya until 1pm. Fares average 10,000Rp.

You can also charter transport from Culik for a negotiable 50,000Rp (by *ojek* it's less than half). Specify which hotel you wish to go to; agree just on 'Amed' and you could come up short in Amed village.

Amed Sea Express (☎ 0878 6306 4799; www.gili-sea-express.com; Jemeluk; per person from 300,000Rp) and **Kuda Hitam Express** (☎ 0852 3869 2853; www.kudahitamexpress.com; Jemeluk) are two reputable companies that make crossings to Gili Trawangan and Gili Air in less than an hour for around 250,000Rp to 300,000Rp. Both can arrange hotel pickup.

Tulamben

☎ 0363

The big attraction here sunk more than 60 years ago. The wreck of the US cargo ship *Liberty* is among the best and most popular dive sites in Bali, and this has given rise to an entire town based on scuba diving. Even snorkellers can easily swim out and enjoy the wreck and the coral.

But if you don't plan to explore the briny waves, don't expect to hang out on the beach either. The shore is made up of rather beautiful, large washed stones, the kind that cost a fortune at a DIY store.

For nonaquatic delights, check out the **morning market** in Tulamben village, 1.5km north of the dive site.

Activities

Diving and **snorkelling** are the reason Tulamben exists.

The **shipwreck Liberty** is about 50m directly offshore from Puri Madha Beach Bungalows (where you can park); look for the schools of black snorkels. Swim straight out and you'll see the stern rearing up from the depths, heavily encrusted with coral and swarming with dozens of species of colourful fish – and with scuba divers most of the day. The ship is more than 100m long, but the hull is broken into sections and it's easy for divers to get inside. The bow is in quite good shape; the midship's region is badly mangled; and the stern is almost intact – the best parts are between 15m and 30m deep. You will want at least two dives to really explore the wreck.

FREEDIVING

For those wanting to dive but not deal with all the cumbersome breathing apparatus, decompression etc (not to mention high costs), freediving is a good alternative. This form of diving involves learning techniques to allow you to hold your breath for several minutes and reach similar depths to diving with equipment.

Several operators along the east Bali coast offer both beginner and advance courses in freediving.

Apnea Bali (☎ 0822 6612 5814; www.apneabali.com; Jl Kubu-Abang; lessons from US$60) This polished operator on Tulamben's main strip specialises in a variety of freediving courses and trips, including down to the *Liberty* wreck.

Apneista (☎ 0812 3826 7356; www.apneista.com; Green Leaf Cafe, Jemeluk; 2-day courses US$200; ⌚ 8.30am-10pm) Set up in Jemeluk's popular Green Leaf Cafe, Apneista has run freediving courses and trips out of Amed for several years.

Many divers commute to Tulamben from Amed, Candidasa or Lovina, and in busy times it can get quite crowded between 11am and 4pm, with 50 or more divers at a time around the wreck. Stay the night in Tulamben or in nearby Amed and get an early start.

Most hotels have their own diving centre, and some offer good-value packages if you dive with them as well.

Expect to pay from US$80 for two dives at Tulamben, and a little more for night dives around Amed. Snorkelling gear is rented everywhere for 30,000Rp.

Tauch Terminal DIVING
(☎0363-774504, 0363-22911; www.tauch-terminal.com; 1/2 dives €29/55) Among the many dive operators, Tauch Terminal is one of the longest-established in Bali. It also offers unlimited 24-hour nonboat diving for €105; you need to book this in advance. A four-day SSI open-water certificate course costs €420. It also runs its own dive resort.

Sleeping & Eating

Tulamben is a quiet place, and is essentially built around the wreck. Hotels, all with cafes and many with dive shops, are spread along a 4km stretch either side of the main road. You have your choice of places roadside (cheaper) or by the water (nicer). At high tide even the rocky shore vanishes.

Dive Concepts GUESTHOUSE $
(☎0812 3684 5440; www.diveconcepts.com; dm 50,000Rp, r 100,000-300,000Rp;) A great place to meet other divers, this busy French-run dive shop has an old-school guesthouse with 12 rooms in a variety of flavours (from cold water and fan to hot water and air-con), including six-bed dorms. It has barbecue and film nights, too.

Deep Blue Studio GUESTHOUSE $
(☎0363-22919; www.diving-bali.com; s/d/tr incl breakfast US$28/44/60;) Owned by Czechs, this dive operation has 10 rooms in two-storey buildings on the hill side of the road. It's an attractive place and is well set up for dive classes and chilling out after a day in the depths. Rooms have fans and balconies. A variety of packages are available with the affiliated dive shop.

Puri Madha Beach Bungalows HOTEL $$
(☎0363-22921; www.purimadhabeachhotel.weebly.com; r 500,000-600,000Rp;) Re-styled bungalow-style units lying directly opposite the *Liberty* wreck dive site offshore. The best of the 21 rooms have air-con and hot water. The spacious grounds feel like a public park, and there is a swish pool area overlooking the ocean. You can't beat getting out of bed and swimming right out to a famous shipwreck.

THE WRECK OF THE LIBERTY

In January 1942 the small US Navy cargo ship USAT *Liberty* was torpedoed by a Japanese submarine near Lombok. Taken in tow, it was beached at Tulamben so that its cargo of rubber and railway parts could be saved. The Japanese invasion prevented this, however, and the ship sat on the beach until the 1963 eruption of Gunung Agung broke it in two and left it just off the shoreline, much to the delight of scores of divers.

Getting There & Away

Plenty of buses and bemos travel between Amlapura and Singaraja and will stop anywhere along the Tulamben road, but they're infrequent after 2pm. Expect to pay 12,000Rp to either town.

CENTRAL MOUNTAINS

Most of Bali's mountains are volcanoes; some are dormant, but some are definitely active. The mountains divide the gentle sweep of fertile land to the south from the narrow, more arid strip to the north. Northwest of Gunung Agung is the stark and spectacular caldera that contains the volcanic cone of Gunung Batur (1717m), the waters of Danau Batur and numerous smaller craters. In central Bali, around Bedugul, there's another complex of volcanic craters and lakes, with much lusher vegetation.

It's all a big change if you've come from the coastal areas. Temperatures fall and you may need something warmer than shorts. There are two main routes through the mountains to the north coast (via Gunung Batur and via Bedugul), which allow you to make a circuit. There are hikes to do, clear lake waters to enjoy, and a few other natural and sacred sites of note, especially the mysterious temple Pura Luhur Batukau, the nearby Unesco-recognised ancient rice terraces in and around Jatiluwih, and stupendous hiking around the old colonial village of Munduk.

Gunung Batur

☎ 0366

Most day visitors come on organised tours and stop at the crater rim at Penelokan for views and lunch; most overnight visitors stay in the villages around the lake. The views both from above and from lake level are truly wonderful – if you hit the area on a clear day.

Activities

The setting for Gunung Batur is other worldly: it's like a giant dish, with the bottom half covered with water and a set of volcanic cones growing in the middle. Visit the area on a clear day and you'll understand what all the fuss is about. Soaring up in the centre of the huge outer crater is the cone of Gunung Batur (1717m), formed by a 1917 eruption. A cluster of smaller cones lies beside, created variously by eruptions in 1926, 1963, 1974 and 1994. The last eruption was in 2000.

But is it worthwhile to go through the hassle and the expense of making the climb? You'll get some amazing photos and come close to volcanic action not easily seen anywhere. But the flipside is that it's costly; you have to deal with various characters; and at some point you may just say, 'I could have enjoyed all this from the car-park viewpoint in Penelokan.'

Even reputable and highly competent adventure tour operators from elsewhere in Bali cannot take their customers up Gunung Batur without paying the PPPGB and using one of its guides, so these tours are relatively expensive.

Pretty much all the accommodation in the area can help you put a trek together. They can also recommend hassle-free alternatives to Batur, such as the outer rim of the crater, or trips to other mountains such as Gunung Agung.

Trips from Ubud are also easily arranged, from where you have the advantage of joining other trekkers in order to share costs.

PPPGB HIKING

(Mt Batur Tour Guides Association; ☎ 0366-52362; Toya Bungkah; ⏱ 3am-6pm) The PPPGB (formerly HPPGB) has a monopoly on guided climbs up Gunung Batur. It requires all trekking agencies to hire at least one of its guides for trips up the mountain, and has a reputation for tough tactics in requiring climbers to use its guides. A simple ascent costs 350,000Rp; the main crater 500,000Rp; exploration of additional volcanic cones 650,000Rp; plus an additional 10,000Rp per person. Prices are fixed and inclusive for groups of four.

Equipment

If you're climbing before sunrise, take a torch (flashlight) or be absolutely sure that your guide will provide you with one. You'll need good strong footwear, a hat, a jumper (sweater) and drinking water.

Routes

Most travellers use one of two trails that start near Toya Bungkah. The shorter one is straight up (three to four hours return), while a longer trek (five to six hours return) links the summit climb with the other craters. Climbers have reported that they have easily made this journey without a PPPGB guide, although it shouldn't be tried while it's dark. The major obstacle is actually avoiding any hassle from the guides themselves.

There are a few separate paths at first, but they all rejoin sooner or later and after about 30 minutes you'll be on a ridge with quite a well-defined track. It gets pretty steep towards the top and it can be hard walking over the loose volcanic sand – you'll be climbing up three steps and sliding back two. Allow about two hours to get to the top.

There's also a third track, which enables you to use private transport to within about 45 minutes' walk of the top. From Toya Bungkah, take the road northeast towards Songan and take the left fork after about 3.5km at Serongga, just before Songan. Follow this inner-rim road for another 1.7km to a well-signposted track on the left, which climbs another 1km or so to a car park. From here, the walking track is easy to follow to the top.

Information

Gunung Batur has developed a well-deserved reputation as a money-grubbing place where visitors (mainly around Penelokan) are hassled by touts and wannabe mountain guides (mainly around the lake area). Of course, the guides themselves can be a problem, too. Don't leave valuables in your car, especially at any car park at the start of a volcano trail. Don't even leave a helmet with a motorcycle.

Getting There & Around

From Batubulan terminal in Denpasar, bemos make regular trips to Kintamani (18,000Rp). You can also get a bus on the busy Denpasar Batabulan–Singaraja route, which makes stops in both Penelokan and Kintamani (about

Gunung Batur Area

Gunung Batur Area

Sights

1 Pura Batur A3
2 Pura Puncak Penulisan A1

Activities, Courses & Tours

3 Batur Natural Hot Spring C3
C.Bali .... (see 5)
4 PPPGB C3

Sleeping

5 Hotel Segara C4
6 Under the Volcano III C3

Eating

7 Kedisan Floating Hotel C4
8 Pulu Mujung Warung B4

18,000Rp). Alternatively, you can hire a car or use a driver. From south Bali expect to pay around 500,000Rp. Bemos shuttle between Penelokan and Kintamani (about 10,000Rp to Toya Bungkah). Later in the day, you may have to charter transport (50,000Rp or more).

Around Gunung Batur

As of 2015 there's a 30,000Rp entrance fee (plus 5000Rp per vehicle) to access the area, which you'll be stopped to pay at the roadside ticket office.

Penelokan

Appropriately, Penelokan means 'place to look', and you'll be stunned by the view across to Gunung Batur and down to the lake at the bottom of the crater (check out the large lava flow on Gunung Batur).

Eating

Although the huge tourist restaurants on the road from Penelokan to Kintamani disappoint, there are some acceptable choices here, including many humble open-air joints where you can sit on a plastic chair and have a simple, freshly cooked meal while enjoying a priceless view.

★ **Pulu Mujung Warung** INDONESIAN **$$**
(☎0813 3864 4037; Penelokan; mains 38,000-65,000Rp; ⏰9am-6pm) Easily the best option for a meal in the area, this fantastic cafe has epic volcano views. It's affiliated with the much-loved Sari Organik (p260) restaurant in Ubud. Soups are enjoyable in the cool mountain air, and you can also choose from salads, pizzas, Indo specials, homemade wines, juices, smoothies and more.

Kintamani & Batur

The villages of Kintamani and Batur now virtually run together. Kintamani is famed for its large and colourful **market**, which is held every three days. The town is like a string bean: long, with pods of development. Activity starts early, and by 11am everything's all packed up. If you don't want to go on a hike, the sunrise view from the road here is good.

Spiritually, Gunung Batur is the second most important mountain in Bali (only Gunung Agung outranks it), so the temple, **Pura Batur** (admission 10,000Rp, sarong & sash rental 3000Rp), is of considerable importance. It's a great stop for the architectural spectacle. Within the complex is a Taoist shrine.

Penulisan

The road gradually climbs along the crater rim beyond Kintamani, and is often shrouded in clouds, mist or rain. Penulisan is where the road bends sharply and heads down towards the north coast and the remote scenic drive to Bedugul. A **viewpoint** about 400m south of here offers an amazing panorama over three mountains: Gunung Batur, Gunung Abang and Gunung Agung.

Near the road junction, several steep flights of steps lead to Bali's highest temple, **Pura Puncak Penulisan** FREE, at 1745m. Some of the sculptures date back to the 11th century.

Around Danau Batur

The farming villages down on the lakeside grow onions and other aromatic crops. It's a crisp setting with often superb lake and mountain views.

Kedisan & Buahan

A hairpin-bend road winds its way down from Penelokan to Kedisan on the shore of the lake.

Activities

★ **C.Bali** ADVENTURE TOUR
(☎info only 0813 5342 0541; www.c-bali.com; Hotel Segara, Kedisan; tours from adult/child 450,000/350,000Rp) Operated by an Australian–Dutch couple, C.Bali offers bike tours around the region and canoe tours on Danau Batur. Prices include pickup across south Bali. Packages also include multiday trips. A very important note: these tours often fill up in advance, so book ahead through the website.

Sleeping & Eating

Hotel Segara GUESTHOUSE **$**
(☎0366-51136; www.batur-segarahotel.com; Kedisan; r incl breakfast 250,000-600,000Rp; 📶) The popular Segara has bungalows set around a cafe and courtyard. The cheapest of the 32 rooms have cold water; the best rooms have hot water and bathtubs – perfect for soaking after an early trek.

Kedisan Floating Hotel BALINESE **$**
(☎0813 3775 5411, 0366-51627; Kedisan; meals from 25,000Rp; ⏰8am-8pm; 📶) This hotel on the shores of Danau Batur is hugely popular for its daily lunches. On weekends tourists vie with day trippers from Denpasar for tables out on the piers over the lake. The Balinese food, which features fresh lake fish, is excellent. You can also stay here: the best rooms are cottages at the water's edge (from 400,000Rp).

Toya Bungkah

The main tourist centre for the area is Toya Bungkah, which is scruffy but has a cute charm and a serene lakeside setting.

Activities

Hot springs bubble in a couple of spots, and have long been used for bathing pools.

Batur Natural Hot Spring HOT SPRINGS
(☎0813 3832 5552; Toya Bungkah; admission from 150,000Rp; ⏰8am-6pm) This ever-expanding complex is on the edge of Danau Batur. The three pools have different temperatures, so you can simmer yourself successively. The

overall feel of the hot springs matches the slightly shabby feel of the entire region. Lockers and towels are included with admission, and the simple cafe has good views.

Sleeping

Under the Volcano III GUESTHOUSE $
(0813 3860 0081; Toya Bungkah; s/d incl breakfast 150,000/200,000Rp;) Featuring a lovely, quiet lakeside location opposite chilli plots, this inn has six clean and simple rooms; go for room 1 right on the water. There are two other nearby inns in the Volcano empire, all run by the same lovely family.

Danau Bratan

0368

Approaching from south Bali, you gradually leave the rice terraces behind and ascend into the mountain country around Danau Bratan. Candikuning is the main village in the area, and has an important and picturesque temple, Pura Ulun Danu Bratan. Munduk anchors the region with fine hiking to waterfalls and cloud-cloaked forests and to nearby Danau Tamblingan. Note that it is often misty and can get chilly up here.

On Sundays and public holidays the lakeside can be crowded with courting couples and Toyotas bursting with day-tripping families.

Wherever you go, you are likely to see the tasty local strawberries on offer.

Candikuning

Sights & Activities

Pura Ulun Danu Bratan TEMPLE
(off Jl Raya Denpasar-Singaraja; adult/child 30,000/15,000Rp, parking 5000Rp; 6am-6pm) An iconic image of Bali, depicted on the 50,000Rp note, this important Hindu-Buddhist temple was founded in the 17th century. It is dedicated to Dewi Danu, the goddess of the waters, and is built on small islands. Pilgrimages and ceremonies are held here to ensure that there is a supply of water for farmers all over Bali as part of the Unesco-recognised *subak* system. The tableau includes classical Hindu thatch-roofed *meru* (multi-tiered shrines) reflected in the water and silhouetted against the often-cloudy mountain backdrop.

Bali Botanic Garden GARDENS
(0368-2033211; www.balibotanicgarden.org; Kebun Raya Eka Karya Bali; entry 18,000Rp, parking 6000Rp; 7am-6pm) Established in 1959 as a branch of the national botanic gardens at Bogor, near Jakarta, these gardens cover

Danau Bratan Area

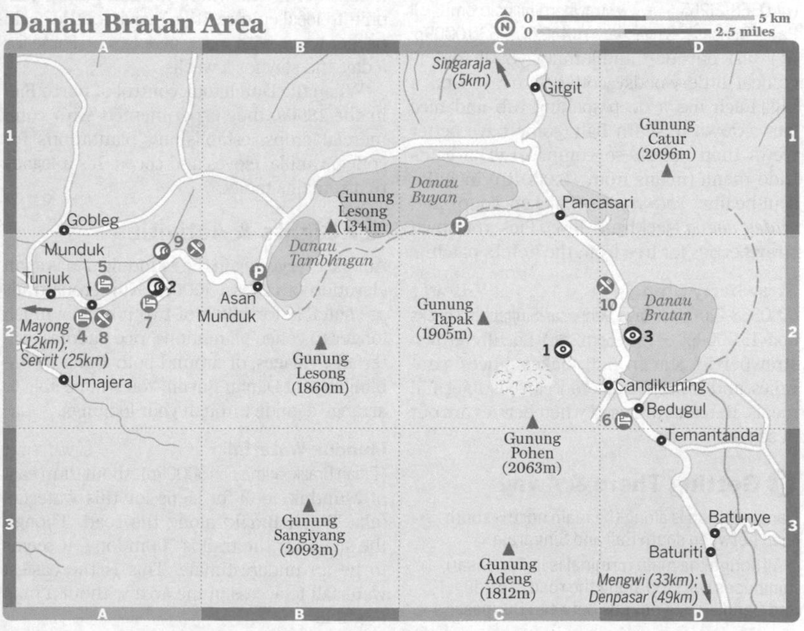

Danau Bratan Area

Sights
1 Bali Botanic Garden C2
2 Munduk Waterfall A2
3 Pura Ulun Danu Bratan D2

Activities, Courses & Tours
Bali Treetop Adventure Park .... (see 1)

Sleeping
4 Meme Surung A2
5 Puri Lumbung Cottages A2
6 Strawberry Hill D2
7 Villa Dua Bintang A2

Eating
8 Don Biyu A2
9 Ngiring Ngewedang A2
10 Strawberry Stop D2

more than 154 hectares on the lower slopes of Gunung Pohen. Don't miss the Panca Yadnya Garden (Garden of Five Offerings), which preserves plants used in ancient Hindu ceremonies.

Within the park, the **Bali Treetop Adventure Park** (0361-934 0009; www.balitreetop.com; Kebun Raya Eka Karya Bali; adult/child US$24/16; 9.30am-6pm) has ropes, nets and the like, which let you explore the forest well above the ground.

Sleeping & Eating

The choice of accommodation near the lake is limited but nearby Munduk has many excellent inns.

★ **Strawberry Hill** GUESTHOUSE $$
(0368-21265; www.strawberryhillbali.com; Jl Raya Denpasar-Singaraja; r 450,000-600,000Rp; wi-fi) Just outside Candikuning you'll find 17 conical little woodsy cottages arrayed on a hill. Each has a deep soaking tub and nice views down to south Bali (some have better views than others, so compare). The cafe's Indo menu (mains from 40,000Rp) includes soul-healing *soto ayam* (chicken soup) and *gudeg yogya* (jackfruit stew). Pick your own strawberries for free from the hotel's patch.

Strawberry Stop CAFE $
(0368-21060; Jl Raya Denpasar-Singaraja; snacks from 15,000Rp; 9am-6pm; wi-fi) Locally grown strawberries star in milkshakes, juices, pancakes and other treats. You can also get full meals. Bananas are used when berries are out of season.

Getting There & Away

Danau Bratan is along the main north–south road between south Bali and Singaraja.

Although the main terminal is in Pancasari, minibuses will stop along the road in Bedugul and Candikuning on runs between Denpasar's Ubung terminal (20,000Rp) and Singaraja's Sangket terminal (20,000Rp).

Generally, though, you'll want your own transport to get around the scattered attractions of the region.

Munduk & Around

0362

The simple village of Munduk is one of Bali's most appealing mountain retreats. It has a cool, misty ambience and is set among lush hillsides covered with jungle, rice fields, fruit trees and pretty much anything else that grows on the island. **Waterfalls** tumble off precipices by the dozen. There are hikes and treks galore and a number of really nice places to stay, from old Dutch colonial summer homes to retreats where you can plunge full-on into local culture. It's a thriving little backpacker town, with many people who come for a day and stay for a week.

When the Dutch took control of north Bali in the 1890s, they experimented with commercial crops, establishing plantations for coffee, vanilla, cloves and cocoa. It's a legacy that remains today.

Sights & Activities

Almost everything in the Munduk area is at an elevation of at least 1000m. Numerous trails are suitable for **hikes** of two hours or much longer to coffee plantations, rice paddies, waterfalls, villages, or around both Danau Tamblingan and Danau Buyan. You will be able to arrange a guide through your lodgings.

Munduk Waterfall WATERFALL
(Tanah Braak; admission 5000Rp) About 2km east of Munduk, look for signs for this waterfall (aka Tanah Braak) along the road. Though the signs say the trail is 700m long, it seems to be an underestimate. This is the easiest waterfall to access in the area without a map or guide.

Sleeping & Eating

The hikes around Munduk draw many visitors, and consequently there are many places for them to stay. Enjoy simple old Dutch houses in the village or more naturalistic places in the countryside. Most have cafes, usually serving good local fare. There are a couple of cute warungs in the village and a few stores with very basic supplies (including bug spray).

Meme Surung GUESTHOUSE $
(0851 0001 2887; www.memesurung.com; r incl breakfast from 200,000Rp;) Two atmospheric old Dutch houses adjoin to form a compound of 11 rooms, immersed among an English-style garden. The decor is traditional and simple; the view from the long wooden veranda is both the focus and joy here. It's located along the main strip of Munduk's township.

★Puri Lumbung Cottages GUESTHOUSE $$
(0851 0021 0675; www.purilumbung.com; cottages incl breakfast US$83-173;) Founded by Nyoman Bagiarta to develop sustainable tourism, this lovely hotel has 43 bright two-storey thatched cottages and rooms set among rice fields. Enjoy intoxicating views (units 32 to 35 have the best) from the upstairs balconies. Dozens of trekking options and courses are offered.

Villa Dua Bintang GUESTHOUSE $$
(0812 3700 5593, 0361-401 1416; www.villaduabintang.com; Jl Batu Galih; r incl breakfast 800,000Rp;) Hidden 500m down a tree-shaded lane that's off the main road, 1km east of Munduk. Four gorgeous rooms are elaborately built amid fruit trees and forest (two rooms are family-size). The scent of cloves and nutmeg hangs in the air from the porch. There's a cafe, and the family who owns it is lovely.

Don Biyu CAFE $
(0812 3709 3949; www.donbiyu.com; mains 26,000-80,000Rp; 7.30am-10pm;) Catch up on your blog; enjoy good coffee; zone out before the sublime views; and choose from a mix of Western and interesting Asian fare. Dishes are served in mellow open-air pavilions. It also has six double rooms (600,000Rp), all with balconies and views. It's on the main road leading into Munduk.

Ngiring Ngewedang CAFE $
(0812 380 7010; www.ngiringngewedang.com; snacks 15,000-40,000Rp; 10am-5pm) Stop in at this coffeehouse, 5km east of Munduk; it grows its own coffee on the surrounding slopes.

Getting There & Away

Minibuses leave Ubung terminal in Denpasar for Munduk (22,000Rp) but only if there are enough passengers. Driving to the north coast, the main road west of Munduk goes through a number of picturesque villages to Mayong (where you can head south to west Bali). The road then goes down to the sea at Seririt in north Bali.

Gunung Batukau Area

Often overlooked (probably a good thing, given what the vendor hordes have done to Gunung Agung in the east), Gunung Batukau is Bali's second-highest mountain (2276m), the third most spiritually significant of Bali's three major mountains and the holy peak of the island's western end. Enjoy a magical visit to one of the island's holiest and most evocative temples, Pura Luhur Batukau, and revel in the ancient rice-terrace greenery around Jatiluwih.

Sights

★Pura Luhur Batukau HINDU TEMPLE
(donation 20,000Rp; 8am-6pm) On the slopes of Gunung Batukau, Pura Luhur Batukau was the state temple when Tabanan was an independent kingdom. It has a seven-roofed *meru* dedicated to Maha Dewa, the mountain's guardian spirit, as well as shrines for Bratan, Buyan and Tamblingan lakes. This is certainly the most spiritual temple you can easily visit in Bali. Outside the compound, the temple is surrounded by forest, and the atmosphere is cool and misty; the chants of priests are backed by singing birds.

Rice Fields VIEWPOINT
(per person 20,000Rp, plus per car 5000Rp) At Jatiluwih, which means 'Truly Marvellous', you'll be rewarded with vistas of centuries-old rice terraces that exhaust your ability to describe green. The terraces have received Unesco World Heritage status, listed in recognition of the ancient rice-growing culture. You'll understand why just by viewing the panorama from the narrow, twisting 18km road leading in and out of town, but do get

out for a rice-field walk. Follow the water as it runs through channels and bamboo pipes from one plot to the next.

There's a road toll for visitors.

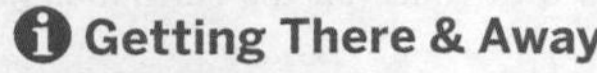

Getting There & Away

The only realistic way to explore the Gunung Batukau area is with your own transport.

NORTH BALI

The land on the other side of the map, that's north Bali. Although one-sixth of the island's population lives here, the vast region is overlooked by many visitors who stay trapped in the south Bali–Ubud axis.

The big draw here is the incredible diving and snorkelling at Pulau Menjangan. Arcing around a nearby bay, Pemuteran may be Bali's best beach town. To the east is Lovina, a sleepy beach strip with cheap hotels and even cheaper sunset beer specials. All along the north coast are interesting little boutique hotels, while inland you'll find quiet treks to waterfalls.

Getting to north Bali for once lives up to the cliché: it's half the fun. Routes follow the thinly populated coastlines east and west, or you can go up and over the mountains by any number of routes, marvelling at crater lakes and maybe stopping for a trek on the way.

Singaraja

☎0362

With a population of more than 120,000 people, Singaraja (which means 'Lion King') is Bali's second-largest city and the capital of Buleleng Regency, which covers much of the north. With its tree-lined streets, Dutch colonial buildings and charmingly sleepy waterfront area north of Jl Erlangga, it's worth exploring for a couple of hours. Most people stay in nearby Lovina.

Singaraja was the centre of Dutch power in Bali and remained the administrative centre for the Lesser Sunda Islands (Bali through to Timor) until 1953. Today, Singaraja is a major educational and cultural centre.

Sights

At the old harbour and waterfront along the canals you can still get a little feel of the colonial port that was the main entrance to Bali before WWII.

Check out the cinematically decrepit **old Dutch warehouses** opposite the water. A couple of warungs have been built on stilts over the water. Walk up Jl Imam Bonjol and you'll see the art deco lines of late-colonial Dutch buildings.

Museum Buleleng MUSEUM
(Jl Veteran 23; ⏲9am-4pm Mon-Fri) **FREE** Museum Buleleng recalls the life of the last *radja* (rajah; prince) of Buleleng, Pandji Tisna, who is credited with developing tourism in Lovina to the west. Among the items here is the Royal (brand) typewriter he used during his career as a travel writer before his death in 1978. It also traces the history of the region back to when there was no history.

Gedong Kirtya Library LIBRARY
(☎0362-22645; Jl Veteran 23; ⏲8am-4pm Mon-Thu, 8am-1pm Fri) This small historical library was established in 1928 by Dutch colonialists and named after the Sanskrit for 'to try'. It has a collection of *lontar* (dried palm leaf) books, as well as some even older written works in the form of inscribed copper plates called *prasasti*. Dutch publications, dating back to 1901, may interest students of the colonial period. It's on the same grounds as Museum Buleleng.

Eating

Manalagi BALINESE $
(Jl Sahadewa 8A; mains from 12,000Rp; ⏲8am-10pm) Down a pretty tree-shaded street, this recently remodelled Balinese restaurant sits in its own compound and is very popular with locals looking for a special meal that includes fresh fish.

Getting There & Away

Singaraja is the main transport hub for the northern coast, with three bemo/bus terminals. From the **Sangket terminal**, 6km south of town on the main road, minibuses go to Denpasar (Ubung terminal; 25,000Rp) via Bedugul/Pancasari sporadically.

The **Banyuasri terminal**, on the western side of town, has buses heading to Gilimanuk (25,000Rp, two hours) and bemos to Lovina (8000Rp). For Java, several companies have services, which include the ferry trip across the Bali Strait. Buses go as far as Yogyakarta (from 360,000Rp, 16 hours) and Jakarta (from 455,000Rp, 24 hours) – book at the Banyuasri terminal a day before.

North Bali

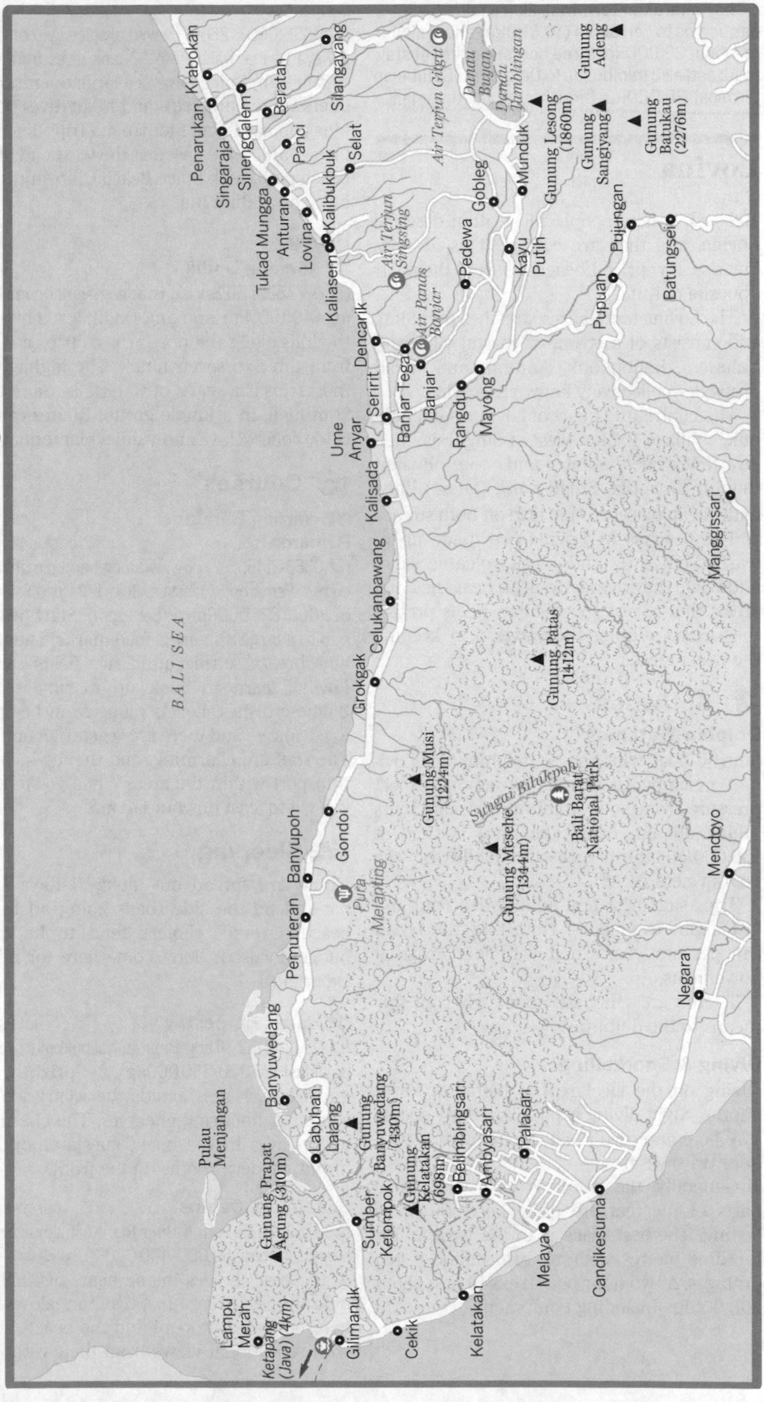

0 — 20 km
0 — 10 miles

BALI SEA

Pulau Menjangan
Lampu Merah
Ketapang (Java) (4km)
Gunung Prapat Agung (310m)
Banyuwedang
Pemuteran
Banyupoh
Labuhan Lalang
Gilimanuk
Sumber Kelompok
Gunung Banyuwedang (430m)
Gondoi
Pura Melanting
Cekik
Gunung Kelatakan (698m)
Belimbingsari
Kelatakan
Ambyasari
Palasari
Melaya
Candikesuma
Negara
Mendoyo
Gunung Musi (1224m)
Gunung Mesehe (1344m)
Sungai Bilukpoh
Bali Barat National Park
Gunung Patas (1412m)
Grokgak
Celukanbawang
Kalisada
Ume Anyar
Seririt
Dencarik
Banjar Tega
Banjar
Air Panas Banjar
Air Terjun Singsing
Rangdu
Mayong
Pedewa
Manggissari
Penarukan
Krabokan
Singaraja
Sinengdalem
Tukad Mungga
Anturan
Beratan
Panci
Lovina
Kaliasem
Kalibukbuk
Selat
Silangayang
Air Terjun Gitgit
Gobleg
Danau Buyan
Danau Tamblingan
Kayu Putih
Munduk
Gunung Lesong (1860m)
Pupuan
Pujungan
Batungsei
Gunung Sangiyang
Gunung Adeng
Gunung Batukau (2276m)

The **Penarukan terminal**, 2km east of town, has bemos to Yeh Sanih (10,000Rp) and Amlapura (about 20,000Rp, three hours) via the coastal road; and also minibuses to Denpasar (Batubulan terminal, 30,000Rp, three hours) via Kintamani.

Lovina

☎0362

'Relaxed' is how people most often describe Lovina, and they are correct. This low-key, low-rise, low-priced beach resort is the polar opposite of Kuta.

The Lovina tourist area stretches over 8km, and consists of a string of coastal villages – Kaliasem, Kalibukbuk, Anturan and Tukad Mungga – collectively known as Lovina.

The 'centre' and heart of Lovina is Kalibukbuk, a village 10.5km west of Singaraja. Mellow Jl Mawar is quieter and more pleasant than Jl Bina Ria. Small *gang* (alleys) lined with cheap places to stay lead off both streets.

The beaches in Lovina are made up of washed-out grey and black volcanic sand, and while they're mostly clean near the hotel areas, they're not spectacular. Reefs protect the shore, calming the waves and keeping the water clear.

Activities

Dolphin-Watching

Sunrise boat trips to see dolphins are Lovina's much-hyped tourist attraction. Expect pressure from your hotel and various touts selling dolphin trips. The price is fixed at 100,000/50,000Rp per adult/child by the boat-owners' cartel.

Trips start at a non-holiday-like 6am and last about two hours. Note that the ocean can get pretty crowded with loud, roaring powerboats.

There's great debate about what all this means to the dolphins.

Diving & Snorkelling

Diving on the local reef is better at lower depths. Night diving is popular. Many people stay here and dive Pulau Menjangan, a two-hour drive west.

Generally, the water is clear and some parts of the reef are quite good for snorkelling. The best place is to the west, a few hundred metres offshore from Billibo Beach Cottages. A two-hour boat trip will cost about 200,000Rp, including equipment.

Spice Dive DIVING

(☎0851 0001 2666; www.balispicedive.com; off Jl Raya Lovina, Kalibukbuk; 2-tank dives from €40; ⏲8am-9pm) Spice Dive is a large operation. It offers snorkelling trips and night dives (€60), plus popular Pulau Menjangan trips (snorkel/dive €55/80). It's based at the west end of the beach path, with Spice Beach Club, and at an office on Jl Bina Ria.

Hiking

★**Komang Dodik** HIKING

(☎0877 6291 5128; lovina.tracking@gmail.com; hikes from 400,000Rp) Komang Dodik leads hikes in the hills along the north coast. Trips can last from three to seven hours. The highlight of most trips is a series of waterfalls, more than 20m high, in a jungle grotto. Routes can include coffee, clove and vanilla plantations.

Courses

★**Warung Bambu Pemaron** COOKING COURSE

(☎0362-31455; www.warung-bambu.mahanara.com; Pemaron; classes for 1/2 people from 620,000/825,000Rp; ⏲8am-1pm) Start with a trip to a large Singaraja food market and then, in a breezy setting amid rice fields east of Lovina, learn to cook up to nine classic Balinese dishes. Levels range from beginner to advanced, and there are vegetarian options. The staff are charming, and the fee includes transport within the area. When you're done you get to feast on your labours.

Sleeping

Hotels are spread out along Jl Raya Lovina, and on the side roads going off to the beach. Overall, choices tend to be more budget-focused; don't come here for a luxe experience.

★**Harris Homestay** HOMESTAY $

(☎0362-41152; Gang Binaria, Kalibukbuk; s/d incl breakfast 130,000/150,000Rp; 📶) Sprightly, tidy and white, Harris avoids the weary look of some neighbouring cheapies. The charming family lives in the back; guests enjoy four bright, modern rooms up the front.

Sea Breeze Cabins GUESTHOUSE $

(☎0362-41138; off Jl Bina Ria, Kalibukbuk; r incl breakfast from 350,000-400,000Rp; ❄📶🏊) One of the best choices in the heart of Kalibukbuk, the Sea Breeze has five bungalows and two rooms by the pool and the beach, some with sensational views from their verandas.

The only downside is that it can get noisy from nearby bars at night.

Padang Lovina GUESTHOUSE $
(☎0362-41302; padanglovina@yahoo.com; Gang Binaria, Kalibukbuk; r with fan/air-con 250,000/300,000Rp;) Down a narrow lane in the very heart of Kalibukbuk, 12 comfortable, unpretentious bungalow-style rooms are set around spacious grounds teeming with flowers. The nicest rooms have air-con and bathtubs. There's wi-fi by the pool.

Villa Taman Ganesha GUESTHOUSE $$
(☎0362-41272; www.taman-ganesha-lovina.com; Jl Kartika 45; r €30-60;) This lovely guesthouse is down a quiet lane lined with Balinese family compounds. The grounds are lush and fragrant with frangipani from around the world that have been collected by the owner, a landscape architect from Germany. The four units are private and comfortable. The beach is 400m away and it's a 10-minute walk along the sand to Kalibukbuk.

Eating

Just about every hotel has a cafe or restaurant. Walk along the beach footpath to choose from a selection of basic places for cold beer, standard food and sunsets.

A small **night market** (Jl Raya Lovina, Kalibukbuk; mains from 15,000Rp; 5-11pm) is a good choice for fresh and cheap local food.

Warung Music INDONESIAN $
(off Jl Bina Ria, Kalibukbuk; mains from 25,000Rp; 8am-late) A humble store with a few tables and chairs out front, Warung Music does tasty inexpensive meals. It has a great local feel and is the place to hang out with a cheap drink before hitting the bars. The staff are exceptionally friendly and it's a good spot to meet new friends, locals and tourists alike.

Global Village Kafe CAFE $
(☎0362-41928; Jl Raya Lovina, Kalibukbuk; mains from 19,000Rp; 8am-10pm;) Che Guevara, Mikhail Gorbachev and Nelson Mandela are just some of the figures depicted in the paintings lining the walls of this artsy cafe. The baked goods, fruit drinks, pizzas, breakfasts and much more are excellent. There are free book and DVD exchanges, plus a selection of local handicrafts. Watch for art-house movie nights.

DON'T MISS

WATERFALLS

About 5km west of Lovina, a sign points to Air Terjun Singsing (Daybreak Waterfall). About 1km off the main road, there's a warung (food stall) on the left and a car park on the right. Walk past the warung and along the path for about 200m to the lower falls. The waterfall isn't huge, but the pool underneath is ideal for swimming, though not crystal-clear. The water, cooler than the sea, is very refreshing.

The area is thick with tropical forest and makes a nice day trip from Lovina. The falls are more spectacular in the wet season (October to March), and may be just a trickle at other times.

Akar VEGETARIAN $
(☎0817 972 4717; Jl Bina Ria, Kalibukbuk; mains 40,000-65,000Rp; 7am-10pm;) The many shades of green at this vegetarian cafe aren't just for show. They reflect the earth-friendly ethics of the owners. Enjoy organic smoothies, house-made gelato, and fresh international dishes, such as chargrilled aubergine filled with feta and chilli.

★**Jasmine Kitchen** THAI $$
(☎0362-41565; Gang Binaria, Kalibukbuk; mains from 55,000Rp; 11am-10pm;) The Thai fare at this elegant two-level restaurant is excellent. The menu is authentic, and the staff are gracious. Try the homemade ice cream for dessert and enjoy to the sounds of soft jazz. You can refill water bottles here for 2000Rp. The ground-floor coffee bar is a fine stop.

★**Seyu** JAPANESE $$
(☎0362-41050; www.seyulovina.com; Gang Binaria, Kalibukbuk; dishes from 50,000Rp; 11am-10pm;) This authentic Japanese place has a skilled sushi chef and a solid list of fresh nigiri and sashimi choices. The dining room is suitably spare and uncomplicated.

Drinking & Nightlife

In the evenings, Lovina shrugs off its sleepy daytime demeanour to offer a suprisingly spirited nightlife.

Lovina

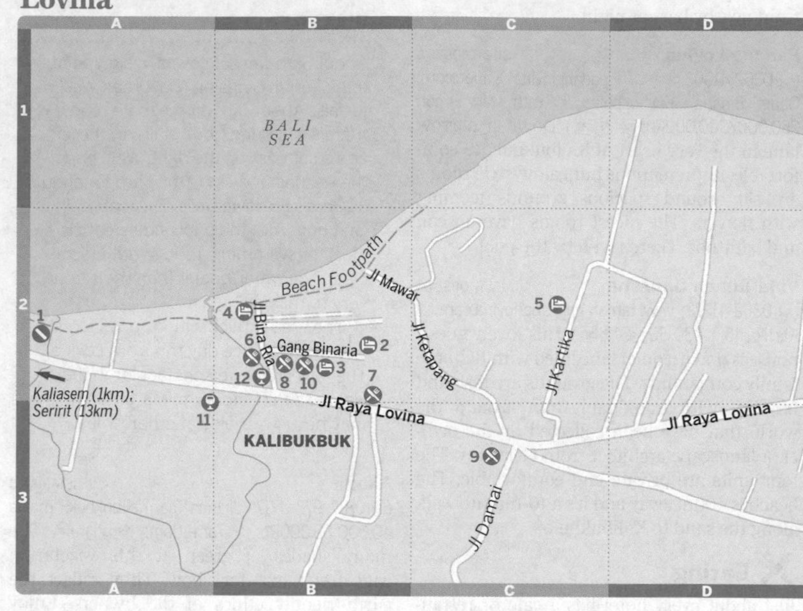

Lovina

Activities, Courses & Tours
1 Spice Dive A2

Sleeping
2 Harris Homestay B2
3 Padang Lovina B2
4 Sea Breeze Cabins B2
5 Villa Taman Ganesha C2

Eating
6 Akar B2
7 Global Village Kafe B2
8 Jasmine Kitchen B2
9 Night Market C3
10 Seyu B2
Warung Music .... (see 6)

Drinking & Nightlife
11 Kantin 21 .... A3
12 Poco Lounge B2

Kantin 21 BAR
(☎0812 460 7791; Jl Raya Lovina, Kalibukbuk; ⊙11pm-late; 📶) The place to head for a night out on 'the town', this open-air venue has a long drinks list, fresh juices and a few local snacks. On many nights, a local band plays after 9pm.

Poco Lounge BAR
(☎0362-41535; Jl Bina Ria, Kalibukbuk; ⊙2pm-2am; 📶) Cover bands perform nightly at this popular bar-cafe. Classic traveller fare is served at tables open to street life at the front and the river at the back.

Information

Kalibukbuk has ATMs, book stalls, internet places and pharmacies.

Getting There & Away

BUS & BEMO

To reach Lovina from south Bali by public transport, you'll need to change twice in Singaraja. Regular bemos go from Singaraja's Banyuasri terminal to Kalibukbuk (about 8000Rp) – you can flag them down anywhere on the main road.

If you're coming by long-distance bus from the west you can ask to be dropped off anywhere along the main road.

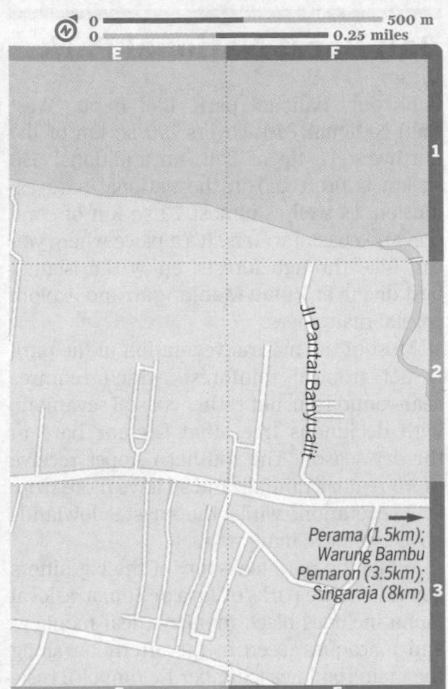

TOURIST SHUTTLE BUS

Perama (☎0362-41161; www.peramatour.com; Jl Raya Lovina) buses stop in Anturan. Passengers are then ferried to other points on the Lovina strip (10,000Rp). There's a morning bus to/from the south, including Kuta, Sanur and Ubud (all 125,000Rp).

Getting Around

The Lovina strip is *very* spread out, but you can easily travel back and forth on bemos (5000Rp).

West of Lovina

The main road west of Lovina passes temples, farms and towns while it follows the thinly developed coast. You'll see many vineyards, home to Bali's wine industry.

Pemuteran

☎0362

This popular oasis in the northwest corner of Bali has a number of artful resorts set on a little dogbone-shaped bay that's alive with local life such as kids playing soccer until dark. Pemuteran offers a real beach getaway. Most people dive or snorkel the underwater wonders at nearby Pulau Menjangan while here.

Sights

Project Penyu TURTLE HATCHERY
(☎0362-93001; www.reefseenbali.com; Reef Seen; donation 20,000Rp; 8am-5pm) Run by Reef Seen Divers' Resort, this nonprofit turtle hatchery project collects turtle eggs, which are looked after until they're ready for ocean release. More than 7000 turtles have been released since 1994.

Activities

Diving is the main reason people come to Pemuteran. It's the ideal base for diving and snorkelling **Pulau Menjangan** (p297). Banyuwedang's harbour is just 7km west of town, so you have only a short ride before you're on a boat for the relaxing and pretty 30-minute journey to Menjangan.

Pemuteran itself also has extensive coral reefs about 3km offshore at Pemuteran Bay; there's varied marine life, coral gardens and walls. There's also a sunken underwater Hindu temple and 41 statues.

Dive shops and local hotels run snorkelling trips that cost US$35 to US$60; two-tank dive trips cost from US$80; snorkelling gear rents from 40,000Rp.

★ **Reef Seen Divers' Resort** DIVING
(☎0362-93001; www.reefseenbali.com; shore/boat dives from 315,000/555,000Rp) Right on the beach in a laid-back resort, Reef Seen is a PADI dive centre and has a full complement of classes. It also offers **pony rides** on the beach for kids (from 200,000Rp for 30 minutes). Some dive packages include accommodation at the resort. The company is active in local preservation efforts.

Easy Divers DIVING
(☎0813 5319 8766; www.easy-divers.eu; Jl Singaraja-Gilimanuk; introductory dives from €50, Pulau Menjangan snorkelling €35) Easy Divers' founder, Dusan Repic, has befriended many a diver new to Bali, and this shop is well recommended. It's near Taman Selini and Pondok Sari hotels.

Sleeping & Eating

Pemuteran has one of the nicest selections of beachside hotels in Bali plus a growing number of budget guesthouses. Many have a sense of style and all are low-key and relaxed, with easy access to the beach.

★Kubuku Ecolodge GUESTHOUSE $
(☎0362-343 7302; www.kubukuhotel.com; Jl Singaraja-Gilimanuk; r incl breakfast with fan/air-con from 350,000/450,000Rp; ❄📶) A slice of Seminyak style in Pemuteran, Kubuku has a chic pool and bar with an inviting patch of lawn. Comfortable rooms are excellent value, and the restaurant serves tasty organic meals. There are also yoga and cooking classes, and bike hire.

Jubawa Homestay GUESTHOUSE $
(☎0362-94745; www.jubawa-pemuteran.com; r 300,000-600,000Rp; ❄📶🏊) One of Pemuteran's originals, Jubawa is a rather plush budget choice. The 24 rooms are set in expansive gardens around a pool. The popular cafe-bar serves Balinese and Thai food.

Double You Homestay GUESTHOUSE $
(☎0813 3842 7000; www.doubleyoubali.com; off Jl Singaraja-Gilimanuk; r incl breakfast 400,000-600,000Rp; ❄📶) On a small lane south of the main road, this stylish guesthouse is a good example of the many well-priced new accommodations springing up in Pemuteran. The four immaculate units are set in a garden and have hot water and other comforts.

★Taman Selini Beach Bungalows BOUTIQUE HOTEL $$
(☎0362-94746; www.tamanselini.com; Jl Singaraja-Gilimanuk; r incl breakfast US$90-160; ❄📶🏊) The 11 bungalows here recall an older, refined Bali, from the quaint thatched roofs down to the antique carved doors and detailed stonework. Rooms, which open onto a large garden running down to the beach, have four-poster beds and large outdoor bathrooms. The outdoor daybeds can be addictive. It's immediately east of Pondok Sari hotel, on the beach and off the main road.

La Casa Kita PIZZA $$
(☎0852 3889 0253; Jl Gilimanuk-Seririk; pizzas 58,000-75,000Rp; ⏲2-10pm) Grab a table and a cold Bintang on the outdoor lawn and choose from an excellent selection of thin-crust wood-fired pizzas. Other Western and Indonesian options are good, too; the chef knows their stuff. It's on the main road across from Easy Divers.

ℹ Getting There & Away

Pemuteran is served by any of the buses and bemo on the Gilimanuk–Lovina run. Labuhan Lalang and Bali Barat National Park are 12km west. It's a three- to four-hour drive from south Bali, either over the hills or around the west coast.

Bali Barat National Park

☎0365

Bali's only national park, Bali Barat (West Bali) National Park covers 190 sq km of the northwestern tip of Bali. An additional 550 sq km is protected in the national park extension, as well as almost 70 sq km of coral reef and coastal waters. It's a place where you can hike through forests, enjoy the island's best diving at **Pulau Menjangan** and explore coastal mangroves.

Most of the natural vegetation in the park is not tropical rainforest, which requires year-round rain, but rather coastal savannah, with deciduous trees that become bare in the dry season. The southern slopes receive more-regular rainfall, and so have more tropical vegetation, while the coastal lowlands have extensive mangroves.

While the park lacks any of the big hitters you find in the parks of Java or Sumatra, local fauna includes black monkeys, leaf monkeys and macaques (seen in the afternoon along the main road near Sumber Kelompok); rusa, barking, sambar, Java and muncak (mouse) deer; wild boar, leopard cats, giant squirrels, porcupine, buffalo, iguanas, cobras, pythons and green snakes. There were once tigers, but the last confirmed sighting was in 1937 – and that one was shot. The best time for wildlife-watching is during the dry season from May to October.

The birdlife is prolific, with around 200 species found here, including the very rare Bali starling (which can also be spotted flying about at the park headquarters' breeding centre in Cekik).

There are more than 200 species of plants growing in the park.

Activities

Whether by land, by boat or underwater, to explore the park you'll need a guide, which can be arranged at the park offices in Cekik or Labuhan Lalang.

In 2014 permits were increased to a hefty 200,000Rp per person, per day. Given this doesn't include activities or guides, visiting the park can become a costly affair when accommodation and transport are factored in.

Boat Trips

To explore the mangroves of Teluk Gilimanuk (Gilimanuk Bay) or the west side of Prapat Agung you'll need to charter a 10-seater boat (525,000Rp per three hours), plus a guide

DON'T MISS

DIVING PULAU MENJANGAN

Bali's best-known dive area, Pulau Menjangan has a dozen superb dive sites. The diving is excellent – iconic tropical fish, soft corals, great visibility (usually), caves and a spectacular drop-off. One of the few complaints we've ever heard came from a reader who said that while snorkelling she kept getting water in her mouth because she was 'smiling so much'.

Most dive sites are close to shore and suitable for snorkellers or diving novices. Some decent snorkelling spots are not far from the jetty; ask the boatman where to go. Venture a bit out, however, and the depths turn inky black as the shallows drop off in dramatic cliffs, a magnet for experienced divers looking for wall dives. The Anker Wreck, a mysterious sunken ship, challenges even experts.

The closest and most convenient dive operators are found at Pemuteran. Trips leave from the tiny dock at Labuhan Lalang (just across the turquoise water from Menjangan), where you'll pay the 200,000Rp park permit. Given the high costs of renting boats and guides (and a whole host of other ludicrous fees), independent snorkellers are best advised to join one of the dive companies heading from Pemuteran.

(250,000Rp), pay the entrance fee (200,000Rp) and miscellaneous costs such as insurance (4000Rp) and toilet fees (10,000Rp)! But this is the ideal way to see birdlife, including kingfishers, Javanese herons and more.

Hiking

All hikers must be accompanied by an authorised guide. It's best to arrive the day before you want to hike, and to make enquiries at the park offices in Cekik or Labuhan Lalang.

The set rates for guides in the park depend on the size of the group and the length of the hike; with one or two people it's 350,000Rp for one or two hours, with rates steadily increasing from there. You'll also need to pay 200,000Rp for a permit per person.

Early morning, say 6am, is the best time to start; it's cooler and you're more likely to see some wildlife. The following are two of the more popular treks:

From a trail west of Labuhan Lalang, hike around the mangroves at Teluk Terima. Then partially follow Sungai Terima into the hills and walk back down to the road along the steps at Makam Jayaprana. You may see grey macaques, deer and black monkeys. Allow two to three hours.

From Sumber Kelompok, go up **Gunung Kelatakan** (698m), then down to the main road near Kelatakan village (six to seven hours). Clear streams abound in the woods.

Iwan Melali (☎0819 3167 5011; iwan_melali@yahoo.com) is a recommended guide who's knowledgeable about birdlife, animals and hiking routes.

Sleeping

★Menjangan RESORT **$$$**
(☎0362-94700; www.themenjangan.com; Jl Raya Gilimanuk-Singaraja, Km 17; r/ste/villas incl breakfast US$250/350/500;) Just within the buffer zone of Bali Barat National Park, this five-star resort is the perfect spot for those wanting to see both sides of the national park. Spread out over 382 hectares, it has two entities: the **Monsoon Lodge** has rooms set in the bush section and will suit those seeking wildlife encounters; and the **Beach Villas** overlook the mangroves and sparkling water, just across from Pulau Menjangan.

Regardless of which section you decide upon, guests can utilise all facilities, whether hiking in the park or lazing on the private beach looking out to the turquoise water. Horse-riding safaris are available to explore the park (also available to nonguests) from 600,000Rp per hour. Other activities include guided hikes, birdwatching, kayaking and diving.

Information

The **park headquarters** (☎0365-61060; Jl Raya Cekik; 24hr) at Cekik displays a topographic model of the park area, and has a little information about plants and wildlife. The **Labuhan Lalang Information Office** (Jl Singaraja-Gilimanuk; 7am-7pm) is in a hut located in the parking area where boats leave for Pulau Menjangan.

Getting There & Away

If you don't have transport, any Gilimanuk-bound bus or bemo from north or west Bali can drop you at park headquarters at Cekik. Those from north Bali can also drop you at the Labuhan Lalang visitor centre.

Gilimanuk

0365

Gilimanuk is the terminus for ferries that shuttle back and forth across the narrow strait to Java. Most travellers get an onward ferry or bus straight away, and won't hang around.

Getting There & Around

Car ferries to Ketapang on Java (adult/child 7500/5500Rp, motorcycle/car 24,500/148,000Rp, 30 minutes) depart every 12 minutes and run around the clock.

Frequent buses run between Gilimanuk's large depot and Denpasar's Ubung terminal (40,000Rp, two to three hours), or along the north-coast road to Lovina (38,000Rp), Amed (60,000Rp) and Padangbai (61,000Rp) departing every 30 minutes between 6am and 5pm.

WEST BALI

Even as development from south Bali creeps ever further west, via hotspots such as Canggu, Bali's true west, which is off the busy main road from Tabanan to Gilimanuk, remains mostly little-visited. It's easy to find serenity amid its wild beaches, jungle and rice fields.

On the coast, surfers hit the breaks at Balian and Medewi. Some of Bali's most sacred sites are here, too, from the ever-thronged Pura Tanah Lot to Pura Taman Ayun and on to the wonderful isolation of Pura Rambut Siwi.

The tidy town of Tabanan is at the hub of Bali's Unesco-listed *subak*, the system of irrigation that ensures everybody gets a fair share of the water. On narrow back roads you can cruise beside rushing streams with bamboo arching overhead and fruit piling up below.

Pura Tanah Lot

0361

An excessively popular day trip, **Pura Tanah Lot** (adult/child 30,000/15,000Rp, parking cars/motorbikes 5000/2000Rp; 7am-7pm) is the most visited and photographed temple in Bali, especially at sunset when crowds and traffic overwhelm the site. However, it has all the authenticity of a stage set – even the tower of rock that the temple sits upon is an artful reconstruction (the entire structure was crumbling) and more than one-third of the rock is artificial.

For the Balinese, Pura Tanah Lot is one of the most important and venerated sea temples. Like Pura Luhur Ulu Watu, at the tip of the southern Bukit Peninsula, and Pura Rambut Siwi to the west, it is closely associated with the Majapahit priest Nirartha. It's said that each of the sea temples was intended to be within sight of the next, so they formed a chain along Bali's southwestern coast; from Pura Tanah Lot you can usually see the clifftop site of Pura Luhur Ulu Watu far to the south, and the long sweep of seashore west to Perancak, near Negara. There are restaurants on the clifftop overlooking the temple.

Aim to coincide your visit with high tide, when the temple is marooned at sea; at low tide you can walk over to the temple itself, but non-Balinese people are not allowed to enter.

There are evening Kecak and fire dance performances (50,000Rp) from 6.30pm.

To reach the temple, walkways run from the vast parking lots through a mind-boggling sideshow of tacky souvenir shops down to the sea. Clamorous announcements screech from loudspeakers.

Getting There & Away

If coming from south Bali take the coastal road west from Kerobokan and follow the signs. From other parts of Bali, turn off the Denpasar–Gilimanuk road near Kediri and follow the signs. During the pre- and post-sunset rush, traffic is awful.

Tabanan

0361

Tabanan, like most regional capitals in Bali, is a large, well-organised place. The verdant surrounding rice fields are emblematic of Bali's rice-growing traditions and are part of its Unesco recognition.

Playing a critical role in rural Bali life, the *subak* is a village association that deals with water, water rights and irrigation. With water passing through many, many scores of rice fields before it drains away for good, there is always the chance that growers near the source would be water-rich while those at the bottom would be selling carved wooden critters at Tanah Lot. Regulating a system that apportions a fair share to everyone is a model of mutual cooperation and an insight

West Bali

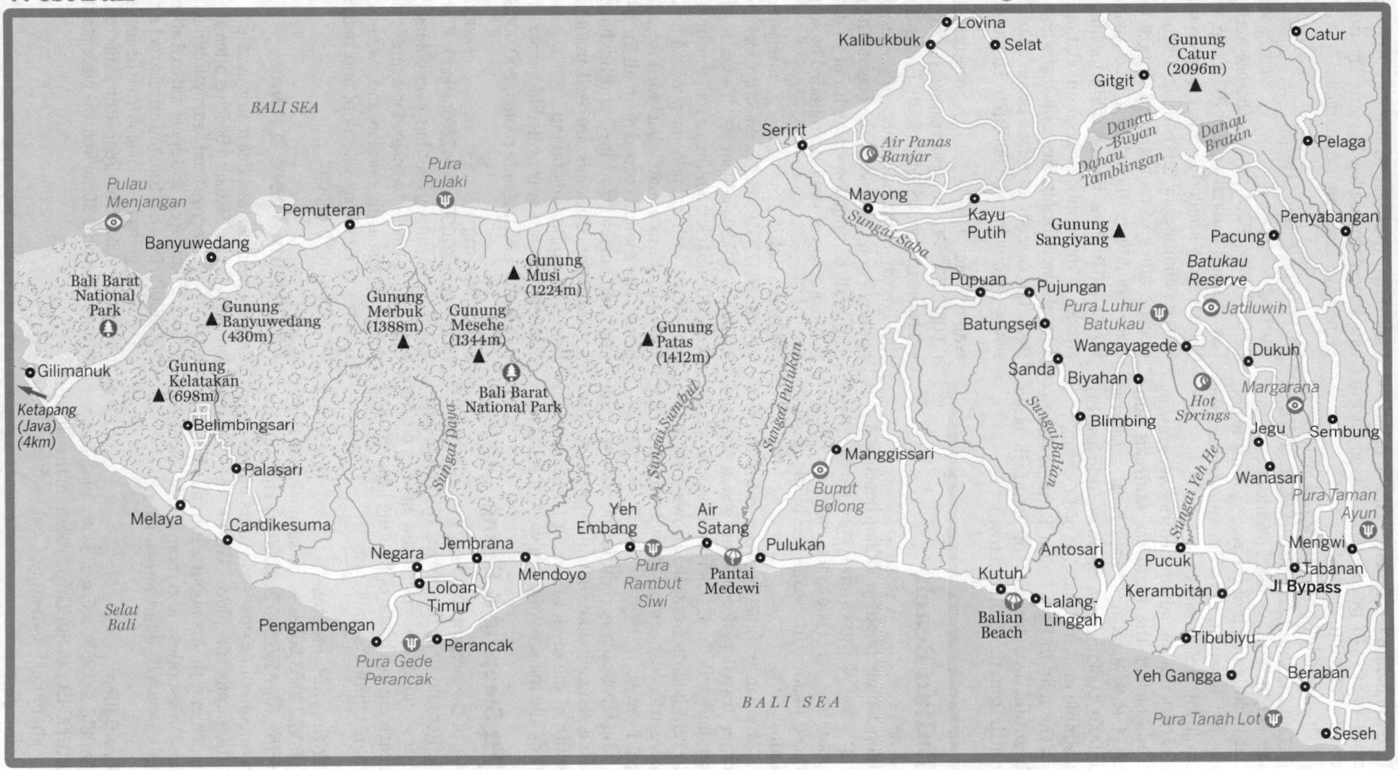

0 — 20 km
0 — 10 miles

BALI SEA
Lovina
Kalibukbuk
Selat
Catur
Gunung Catur (2096m)
Gitgit
Danau Buyan
Danau Bratan
Danau Tamblingan
Pelaga
Seririt
Air Panas Banjar
Pura Pulaki
Pulau Menjangan
Pemuteran
Banyuwedang
Mayong
Kayu Putih
Sungai Saba
Gunung Sangiyang
Penyabangan
Pacung
Batukau Reserve
Bali Barat National Park
Gunung Banyuwedang (430m)
Gunung Musi (1224m)
Gunung Merbuk (1388m)
Gunung Mesehe (1344m)
Gunung Patas (1412m)
Pupuan
Pujungan
Pura Luhur Batukau
Jatiluwih
Batungsei
Wangayagede
Dukuh
Gilimanuk
Gunung Kelatakan (698m)
Ketapang (Java) (4km)
Bali Barat National Park
Sanda
Biyahan
Margarana
Hot Springs
Blimbing
Jegu
Sembung
Belimbingsari
Sungai Daya
Sungai Sumbul
Sungai Pulukan
Sungai Balian
Manggissari
Sungai Yeh He
Wanasari
Palasari
Bunut Bolong
Pura Taman Ayun
Melaya
Candikesuma
Yeh Embang
Air Satang
Pulukan
Antosari
Pucuk
Mengwi
Negara
Jembrana
Mendoyo
Pura Rambut Siwi
Pantai Medewi
Kutuh
Tabanan
Loloan Timur
Balian Beach
Lalang-Linggah
Kerambitan
Jl Bypass
Selat Bali
Pengambengan
Perancak
Pura Gede Perancak
Tibubiyu
Yeh Gangga
Beraban
BALI SEA
Pura Tanah Lot
Seseh

into the Balinese character. (One of the strategies used is to put the last person on the water channel in control.)

This complex and vital social system was recognised by Unesco in 2012 and added to the World Heritage list. Specific sites singled out include much of the rice-growing region around Tabanan, Pura Taman Ayun and the Jatiluwih rice terraces.

Learn more about Bali's rice-growing traditions at the **Mandala Mathika Subak** (Subak Museum; Jl Raya Kediri; adult/child 15,000/7500Rp; ⌚8am-5pm Mon-Fri, to 1pm Sat), a simple museum just east of Tabanan.

The road to Pura Luhur Batukau and the beautiful rice terraces of Jatiluwih heads north from the centre of town.

Balian Beach

☎0361

Increasingly popular, Balian Beach is a rolling area of dunes and knolls overlooking pounding surf. It attracts both surfers and those looking to escape the bustle of south Bali.

You can wander between cafes and join other travellers for a beer, watch the sunset and talk surf. There are simple places to rent boards along the brown-sand beach; nonsurfers can simply enjoy bodysurfing the wild waves.

Balian Beach is right at the mouth of the wide Sungai Balian (Balian River). It is 800m south of the town of Lalang-Linggah, which is on the main road 10km west of Antosari.

Sleeping & Eating

All of the accommodation is fairly close together and near the beach. Warungs, simple cafes and a few restaurant shacks on the beach mean a bottle of Bintang is never more than a minute's walk away.

★Surya Homestay GUESTHOUSE $
(☎0813 3868 5643; wayan.suratni@gmail.com; r incl breakfast 150,000-200,000Rp) There are five rooms in bungalow-style units at this sweet little family-run place (Wayan and Putu are charmers) that is about 200m along a small lane. It's spotless, and rooms have cold water and fans. Ask about long-term rates.

Ayu Balian HOMESTAY $
(☎0812 399 353; Jl Pantai Balian; r incl breakfast 100,000-150,000Rp) The 15 rooms in this slightly shambolic two-storey cold-water block look down the road to the surf. The small cafe serves crowd-pleasing fare. The friendly owner Ayu is a genuine character.

★Pondok Pitaya: Hotel, Surfing & Yoga GUESTHOUSE $$
(☎0819 9984 9054; www.pondokpitaya.com; Jl Pantai Balian; r incl breakfast from 750,000Rp; 📶🏊) With a spray-scented location right on wave-tossed Balian Beach, this complex features an eclectic range of rooms: from vintage Indonesian buildings (including a 1950 Javanese house and an 1860 Balinese alligator hunter's shack) to more modest accommodation. It's a great place for families as it has a popular pool. The cafe serves juices, organic fare and pizzas (mains from 35,000Rp to 120,000Rp).

Gajah Mina BOUTIQUE HOTEL $$
(☎0812 381 1630; www.gajahminaresort.com; villas incl breakfast from US$140; ❄🏊) Designed by the French architect-owner, this eight-unit boutique hotel is close to the ocean. The private, walled bungalows march out to a dramatic outcrop of stone surrounded by surf.

★Tékor Bali INTERNATIONAL $
(☎0815 5832 3330; off Jl Pantai Balian; mains from 30,000Rp; ⌚7.30am-10pm; 📶) Down a small lane 100m back from the beach, this inviting restaurant with a grassy lawn feels a bit like you've come to a mate's backyard for a barbecue. The menu is broad, with all the usual local and surfer favourites., and the burgers are excellent. Cocktails are well made and there's cheap Bintang on tap.

Accommodation is available in two small cold-water and fan-only rooms (200,000Rp).

Deki's Warung INDONESIAN $
(mains from 30,000Rp; ⌚7.30am-9pm) With a spectacular hill top setting overlooking the water, this place is *the* place for a sunset view. It has the usual Indonesian and Western favourites, a good bar selection, and makes a lively evening hang-out.

Getting There & Away

Because the main west Bali road is usually jammed with traffic, Balian Beach is often at least a two-hour drive from Seminyak or the airport (55km). A car and driver will cost about 500,000Rp for a day trip. You can also get a bus (20,000Rp) going to Gilimanuk from Denpasar's Ubung terminal and be dropped off at the road entrance, which is 800m from the places to stay.

DON'T MISS

PURA TAMAN AYUN

The huge royal water temple of **Pura Taman Ayun** (adult/child 15,000/7500Rp; ⏲8am-6pm), surrounded by a wide, elegant moat, was the main temple of the Mengwi kingdom, which survived until 1891, when it was conquered by the neighbouring kingdoms of Tabanan and Badung. The large temple was built in 1634 and extensively renovated in 1937. It's a spacious place to wander around and you'll be able to get away from speed-obsessed group-tour mobs.

The first courtyard is a large, open, grassy expanse and the inner courtyard has a multitude of *meru* (multi-tiered shrines). Lotus-blossoms fill the pools; the temple is part of the *subak* (complex rice-field irrigation system) sites recognised by Unesco in 2012.

Pura Taman Ayun is an easy stop on a drive to/from Bedugal and the Jatiluwih rice terraces. It is a stop-off on many organised tours.

Jembrana Coast

About 34km west of Tabanan you cross into Bali's most sparsely populated district, Jembrana. The main road follows the south coast most of the way to Negara. There's some beautiful scenery and little tourist development, with the exception of the surfing action at Medewi.

Medewi

On the main road, a large sign points down the short paved road (200m) to the surfing mecca of **Pantai Medewi** and its *long* left-hand wave. Rides of 200m to 400m are common. There's no beach here, instead it's a stretch of huge, smooth grey rocks interspersed among round black pebbles. Cattle graze by the shore, paying no heed to the spectators watching the action out on the water.

Sleeping & Eating

You'll find accommodation along the main lane to the surf break and down other lanes about 2km east of the main surf break.

Warung Gede & Homestay GUESTHOUSE $
(☎0812 397 6668; s/d 80,000/100,000Rp) From the simple open-air cafe (meals from 15,000Rp; open 6am to 10pm) you can watch the breaks and enjoy basic Indonesian fare as well as good Western breakfasts. Rooms are surfer-simple: cold water and fans.

Surf Villa Mukks GUESTHOUSE $
(☎0812 397 3431; www.surfvillamukks.com; Pulukan; r incl breakfast with fan/air-con 250,000/400,000Rp; ❄📶) About 900m east of the Medewi surf break at Pulukan, this Japanese-owned guesthouse has modern rooms overlooking rice fields and distant surf. It's a superchilled spot where some rooms have large bamboo blinds instead of doors. It rents boards and offers surf lessons.

Medewi Beach Cottages HOTEL $$
(☎0361-852 8521; www.medewibeachcottages.com; r from US$80; ❄📶🏊) A large pool anchors 27 comfortable, modern rooms (with satellite TV) scattered about nice gardens right down by the surf break. It has a small annex nearby for surfers, with cold-water, fan-only rooms for 200,000Rp.

Puri Dajuma Cottages HOTEL $$$
(☎0811 388 709; www.dajuma.com; cottages from US$160; ❄@📶🏊) Coming from the east on the main road, you won't be able to miss this seaside resort, thanks to its prolific signage. Happily, the 18 cottages actually live up to the billing. Each has a private garden, hammock, ocean view and a walled outdoor bathroom. The Medewi surf break is 2km west.

Getting There & Away

Medewi Beach is 75km from the airport. A car and driver will cost about 600,000Rp for a day trip. You can also get a bus (25,000Rp) going to Gilimanuk from Denpasar's Ubung terminal and be dropped off at the road entrance.

Nusa Tenggara

POP 9.7 MILLION

Includes ➡

Best Resorts

- Pearl Beach (p309)
- Tugu Lombok (p313)
- Amanwana Resort (p346)
- La Petite Kepa (p381)
- Malole Surf House (p393)

Best Beaches

- Pantai Segar (p322)
- Mawi (p323)
- Pantai Koka (p375)
- Nemberala (p392)
- Pantai Etreat (p404)

Why Go?

If you're seeking white sand, azure bays, hot springs and hidden traditional villages, Nusa Tenggara is your wonderland. Here's an arc of islands that is lush and jungle-green in the north, and more arid savannah in the south. In-between are some of the world's best diving spots, limitless surf breaks and technicolour volcanic lakes. It's a land of pink-sand beaches, schooling sharks and rays, and swaggering dragons.

You'll also find a cultural diversity that is unmatched elsewhere in Indonesia. Animist rituals and tribal traditions still thrive alongside the countless minarets, temples, convents and chapels, and though Bahasa Indonesia is a unifying tongue, each main island has at least one native language, which is often subdivided into dialects. Whether your wish is to drop into the easy, tourist-ready life of a car-free Gili island, or you crave something, somewhere less comfortable, more challenging and a shade deeper, you're exactly where you're supposed to be.

When to Go

Mataram

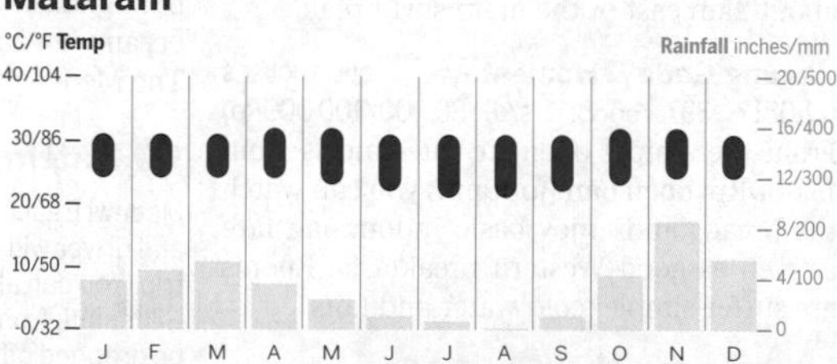

Apr–Sep The dry season brings great diving visibility; travellers flock to Komodo and other locales.

May & Oct Epic waves and thin crowds in Rote and Sumbawa.

Oct–Mar Sumba's spectacular Pasola festival, in February, is reason enough to visit in the wetter months.

Nusa Tenggara Highlights

1. Seeing dragons on land, then snorkelling or diving with underwater critters in **Komodo National Park** (p352).

2. Trekking up the slopes of the sacred volcano that dominates northern Lombok, **Gunung Rinjani** (p315).

3. Exploring Flores from one end to another – a world of ancient cultures, volcanoes, rainforests and beaches such as **Pantai Naga** (p375).

4. Discovering the remote villages of West Timor, characterised by their beehive-shaped clan houses, such as otherworldly **Temkessi** (p390).

5. Diving on the **Alor Archipelago** (p378), which feels like one stop before the end of the world.

6. Plunging into watery pleasures by day, and then choosing between many at night, on **Gili Trawangan** (p326).

7. Bouncing between one sensational beach and the next in West Sumba, then pausing at the ancient village of **Ratenggaro** (p406).

Getting There & Around

Overland travel is slow in mountainous Nusa Tenggara. Busy Lombok, Sumbawa, Flores and Timor have fairly decent, surfaced main roads and relatively comfortable bus services. Get off the highways, and things slow down considerably. Ferry services are regular and consistent in the dry season, but in the wet season, when seas get rough, your ship may be cancelled for days on end. Overland travel across all of Nusa Tenggara is time-consuming, with stretches of tedium offset by areas of interest.

Several airlines cover interisland routes, many of which start in Bali. All the important towns and cities have regular – and expanding – air service. Lombok and Kupang are hubs, while airports such as Labuanbajo in Flores and Tambolaka in Sumba boast new and improved facilities.

LOMBOK

Long overshadowed by its superstar neighbour across the Lombok Strait, Lombok has a steady hum about it that catches the ear of travellers looking for something different from Bali. Blessed with exquisite white-sand beaches, epic surf, a lush forested interior, and hiking trails through tobacco and rice fields, Lombok is fully loaded with equatorial allure. Oh, and you'll probably notice mighty Gunung Rinjani, Indonesia's second-highest volcano, its summit complete with hot springs and a dazzling crater lake.

And there's much more. Lombok's southern coastline is nature on a very grand scale: breathtaking turquoise bays, world-class surf breaks and massive headlands.

Transport options are good in Lombok and the mood could not be more laid-back. If you're planning to head further east in Nusa Tenggara, you can pass through Lombok overland to Sumbawa, or catch a boat to Flores (p354).

Getting There & Away

AIR

Lombok International Airport (p319), near Praya, is ever-more busy. There is good service to Bali and Java, with fewer services going east into Nusa Tenggara. Flights also serve the international hubs of Singapore and Kuala Lumpur. You'll find travel agents for airline tickets in Kuta, Mataram and Senggigi.

DON'T MISS

BEST OF LOMBOK

- Surfing (or learning to surf) in **Gerupuk** (p322).
- Scaling **Gunung Rinjani** (p315) Lombok's incomparable sacred peak.
- Setting eyes on idyllic **Mawan** (p323) beach for the very first time.
- Picking your own deserted-cove beach north of **Senggigi** (p309).

BOAT

Public ferries connect Lembar (p307) on Lombok's west coast with Bali, and Labuhan Lombok (p324) on its east coast with Sumbawa. Numerous fast-boat companies link Lombok with the Gili Islands and Bali. These are mostly centred on Senggigi (p309).

PUBLIC BUS

Mandalika Terminal (p307) in Mataram is the departure point for major cities in Sumbawa, Bali and Java, via interisland ferries. For long-distance services, book tickets a day or two ahead at the terminal, or from a travel agent. If you get to the terminal before 8am without a reservation, there may indeed be a spare seat on a bus going in your direction, but don't count on it, especially during holidays.

TOURIST SHUTTLE BUS

There are tourist shuttle-bus services between the main tourist centres in Lombok (Senggigi and Kuta) and most tourist centres in Bali (Ubud, Sanur and the Kuta region) and the Gilis. Typically these combine a minibus with public ferries. Tickets can be booked directly or at a travel agent. These schemes are heavily marketed.

Getting Around

There is a good – though often traffic-clogged – road across the middle of the island, between Mataram and Labuhan Lombok. The Mataram–Praya–Kuta road is multilane and quick. The Lembar–Mataram–Senggigi–Anyar route is in very good condition. Elsewhere you'll find mostly decent sealed roads, with a few notable exceptions such as the beaches of southwest Lombok. Public transport is generally restricted to the main routes; away from these, you need a car or motorbike, or to charter an *ojek* (motorcycle taxi).

BUS & BEMO

Mandalika Terminal is 3km east of central Mataram; other regional terminals are in Praya, Anyar and Pancor (near Selong). You may have to go via one or more of these terminals to get from one part of Lombok to another. Fixed fares should be displayed. Public transport becomes scarce in the late afternoon and normally ceases after dark.

CAR & MOTORCYCLE

It's easy to hire a car in all the tourist areas (with/without driver per day from 600,000/300,000Rp). Motorbikes are also widely available from about 70,000Rp per day. Check your insurance arrangements carefully. Some agencies do not offer any coverage at all, and others offer only basic coverage. Even insured Balinese vehicles are often not covered in Lombok.

There's little reason to bring a car or motorbike from Bali when you can avoid the ferry charges and easily rent your own wheels on Lombok.

Mataram

0370 / POP 420,000

Lombok's capital is a blended sprawl of several (once separate) towns with fuzzy borders: Ampenan (the port); Mataram (the administrative centre); Cakranegara (the business centre, often called simply 'Cakra'); and Bertais and Sweta to the east, where you'll find the bus terminal. Stretching for 12km from east to west, it's home to half a million people.

There aren't many tourist attractions, yet Mataram's broad tree-lined avenues buzz with traffic, thrum with motorbikes and are teeming with classic markets and malls. If you're hungry for a blast of Indo realism, you'll find it here.

Sights

★Pura Meru HINDU TEMPLE

(Jl Selaparang; admission 10,000Rp; 8am-5pm) Pura Meru is the largest and second most important Hindu temple on Lombok. Built in 1720, it's dedicated to the Hindu trinity of Brahma, Vishnu and Shiva. The inner court has 33 small shrines and three thatched, teak-wood *meru* (multi-tiered shrines). The central *meru*, with 11 tiers, is Shiva's house;

Lombok

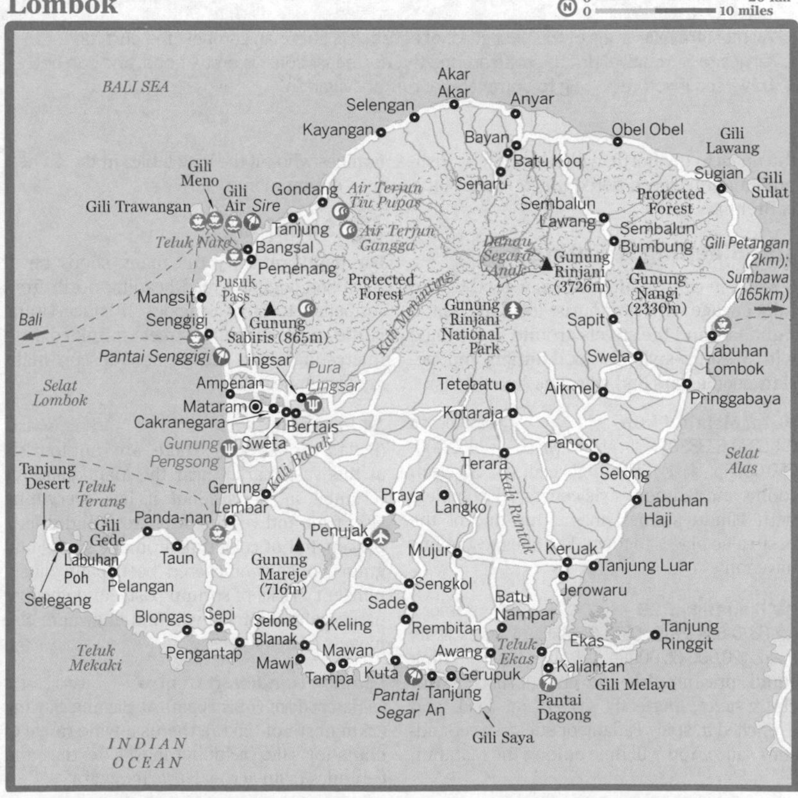

LOMBOK'S REGIONS

West Lombok

The region's biggest city, Mataram, just keeps growing with the economy of West Nusa Tenggara. Meanwhile the famed beach resort Senggigi remains in a 1990s time warp. The greatest allure is southwest of Lembar port, where the peninsula bends forward and back, the seas are placid, bucolic offshore islands beckon and surf breaks such as Tanjung Desert await.

North & Central Lombok

Lush and fertile, Lombok's scenic interior is stitched together with rice terraces, lush forest, undulating tobacco fields, and fruit and nut orchards, and is crowned by sacred Gunung Rinjani. Entwined in all this big nature are traditional Sasak settlements, some of which are known for their handicrafts. Public transport is neither frequent nor consistent enough to rely on.

South Lombok

Beaches just don't get much better: the water is warm, striped turquoise and curls into barrels, and the sand is silky and snow-white, framed by massive headlands and sheer cliffs that recall Bali's Bukit Peninsula 30 years ago. Village life is still vibrant in south Lombok as well, with unique festivals. The south is noticeably drier than the rest of Lombok and more sparsely populated. But, with Lombok's international airport now located here and with greatly improved roads, change has arrived. This is now the centre of Lombok's tourism development.

East Lombok

All most travellers see of the east coast of Lombok is Labuhan Lombok, the port for ferries to Sumbawa. But the road around the northeast coast is pretty good, and can be traversed if you're hoping to complete a circumnavigation.

the *meru* to the north, with nine tiers, is Vishnu's; and the seven-tiered *meru* to the south is Brahma's.

Sleeping & Eating

Staying in central Mataram is a good way to fully engage with nontourist local life. Mataram Mall, and the streets around it, are lined with Western-style fast-food outlets, Indonesian noodle bars and warungs (food stalls).

Hotel Melati Viktor GUESTHOUSE $
(☎0370-633830; Jl Abimanyu 1; r 150,000-250,000Rp; ❄📶) The high ceilings, 37 clean rooms and Balinese-style courtyard, complete with Hindu statues, make this one of the best-value places in town. The cheapest rooms have fans.

★Ikan Bakar 99 SEAFOOD $
(☎0370-664 2819, 0370-643335; Jl Subak III 10; mains 20,000-55,000Rp; ⏰11am-10pm) Think squid, prawns, fish and crab, brushed with chilli sauce, perfectly grilled or fried, and drenched in spicy Padang or sticky sweet-and-sour sauce. You will dine among the Mataram families who fill the long tables in the arched, tiled dining room.

Shopping

For handicrafts try the many shops on Jl Raya Senggigi, the road heading north from Ampenan towards Senggigi. Jl Panca Usaha is the main shopping street, sprinkled with interesting shops. Large new air-con malls are also appearing.

★Pasar Mandalika MARKET
(Bertais; ⏰7am-5pm) There are no tourists at this vast market near the Mandalika bus terminal in Bertais, but it has everything else: fruit and veggies, fish (fresh and dried), baskets full of colourful, aromatic spices and grains, freshly butchered beef, palm sugar, pungent bricks of shrimp paste, and cheaper handicrafts than you will find anywhere else in west Lombok.

Lombok Handicraft Centre HANDICRAFTS
(Jl Hasanuddin; ⏰9am-6pm) At Sayang Sayang (2km north of Cakra), there's a wide range of crafts for sale, including masks, textiles and ceramics from across Nusa Tenggara.

Mataram Mall MALL
(Jl Selaparang; ⏲7am-9pm; ❄) A multistorey shopping mall with a supermarket, department stores, electronics and clothes shops, and some good restaurants.

Information

You'll find plenty of banks with ATMs across Mataram.

Kantor Imigrasi (Immigration Office; ☎0370-632520; Jl Udayana 2; ⏲8am-3pm Mon-Fri) Government office for renewing your visa.

Rumah Sakit Harapan Keluarga (☎0370-670000; www.harapankeluarga.co.id; Jl Ahmad Yani 9; ⏲24hr) The best private hospital on Lombok is just east of downtown Mataram and has English-speaking doctors.

Getting There & Around

Mataram's airport was closed after the new one near Praya opened in 2011.

BEMO

Mataram is *very* spread out. Bemos (minibuses) shuttle between the Kebon Roek bemo terminal in Ampenan and the Mandalika terminal in Bertais (10km away) along the two main thoroughfares via the centre (5000Rp).

Outside the Pasar Cakranegara there is a handy bemo stop for services to Bertais, Ampenan, Sweta and Lembar. Kebon Roek has bemos to Bertais (3000Rp) and Senggigi (5000Rp).

BUS

The chaotic **Mandalika Terminal** is 3km from the centre and is a bus and bemo hub. It's surrounded by the city's chaotic main market. Use the official ticket office to avoid touts. Bemos shuttle to the centre (4000Rp).

TAXI

For a reliable metered taxi, call a Blue Bird **Lombok Taksi** (☎627000).

Around Mataram

As well as Lombok's most important temple, sights around Mataram include the old port town of **Ampenan**. Although most people buzz through on their way to or from Senggigi, if you pause you'll discover a still-tangible sense of the Dutch colonial era in the tree-lined main street and the older buildings.

Pura Lingsar HINDU TEMPLE
(off Jl Gora II; grounds free, temple admission by donation; ⏲7am-6pm) This large temple compound is the holiest in Lombok. Built in 1714 by King Anak Agung Ngurah, and nestled beautifully in lush rice fields, it's multidenominational, with a temple for Balinese Hindus (Pura Gaduh), and one for followers of Lombok's mystical take on Islam, the Wektu Telu religion.

It's just 6km northeast of Mataram in the village of Lingsar. Take a bemo from the Mandalika terminal to Narmada, then another to Lingsar. Ask to be dropped off near the entrance to the temple complex.

Pura Gaduh has four shrines: one orientated to Gunung Rinjani (seat of the gods on Lombok), one to Gunung Agung (seat of the gods in Bali), and a double shrine representing the union between the two islands.

The Wektu Telu temple is noted for its enclosed and lily-covered pond devoted to Lord Vishnu, and for the holy eels, which can be enticed from their lair with hard-boiled eggs (available at stalls). It's considered good luck to feed them.

BUSES FROM MATARAM

Services to Other Islands

DESTINATION	FARE (RP)	DURATION (HR)
Bima (Sumbawa)	250,000	15
Denpasar (Bali)	175,000	8

Services Across Lombok

DESTINATION	FARE (RP)	DURATION (HR)
Airport	25,000	45min
Kuta (via Praya & Sengkol)	25,000	2
Labuhan Lombok	35,000	2½
Lembar	25,000	30min

You will be expected to rent a sash and/or sarong (or bring your own) to enter the shrines.

Lembar

Lembar is Lombok's main port for ferries, tankers and Pelni liners coming in from Bali and beyond. Though the ferry port itself is scruffy, the setting – think azure inlets ringed by soaring green hills – is stunning. If you need cash there are ATMs near the harbour entrance.

Public ferries (child/adult/motorbike/car 27,000/40,000/112,000/773,000Rp, five to six hours) travel nonstop between Padangbai (Bali) and Lembar. Passenger tickets are sold near the pier. Boats supposedly run 24 hours and leave about every 90 minutes, but the service can be unreliable – boats have caught on fire and run aground.

Bemo and bus connections are abundant, and bemos run regularly to the Mandalika bus/bemo terminal (25,000Rp), so there's no reason to linger. Taxis cost 80,000Rp to Mataram, and 150,000Rp to Senggigi.

Southwestern Peninsula

0370

The sweeping coastline that stretches west of Lembar is blessed with boutique sleeps on deserted beaches and tranquil offshore islands. You can while away weeks here among the pearl farms, salty old mosques, friendly locals and relatively pristine islands.

Of the dozen islands off the coast here, **Gili Gede** is a favourite. Although popular with day-tripping snorkellers and divers from across Lombok, the island itself is utterly serene and has a couple of isolated places to stay and unwind.

Gili Asahan is another idyllic spot: soothing winds gust, birds flutter and gather in the grass just before sunset, muted calls to prayer rumble, and the stars and moon light up the sky.

The only off-note on the landscape is the dull town of **Sekotong**, which you have to pass through on your way west. Otherwise, you follow the narrow coastal road along the contours of the peninsula, skirting white-sand beach after white-sand beach on your way to the village of Bangko Bangko and one of Asia's legendary surf breaks, **Tanjung Desert** (Desert Point), which has one of the world's longest left-hand barrels.

Although winding, the road is in good shape almost until the end, when suddenly it switches to deeply rutted gravel and dirt. You can traverse it with a car or motorbike but you'll have to drive at a walking pace. After 2km you'll reach a fork; turn right for the fishing village of Bangko Bangko. Turn left for another 1km of road misery that ends at the oceanic wonders of Tanjung Desert. Your reward for enduring the horrible last 3km of road to Tanjung Desert? An entrance fee of 10,000Rp per person and 5000Rp per vehicle.

Sleeping & Eating

There are a few hotels and resorts sprinkled along the northern coast of the peninsula, though the most atmospheric beaches and lodging are on the offshore islands. You'll eat where you sleep. Top-end places have dive operations.

At Tanjung Desert, you'll discover a strip of white sand and a row of flimsy bamboo cafes where you can scarf down simple meals, quaff cold beer and gaze out at the break. Phone service is dodgy and the area gets very crowded during peak surfing season (May to October) so you may or may not find room at the very basic inns. A number of dirt-simple (sand-simple?) no-name warungs will let you crash for about 100,000Rp a night.

Desert Point Lodge BUNGALOW $
(0819 1605 4320; www.desertpoint-lodge.com; west of Pelangan; r from 300,000Rp) A solid choice near Tanjung Desert, with seven woven-bamboo and thatched bungalows with bamboo beds, hammocks on the porch and private baths attached. Surfing may be king here but you can also dive.

Madak Belo BUNGALOW $
(0818 0554 9637; www.madak-belo.com; Gili Gede; r/bungalows from 200,000/400,000Rp; @) Here's a sensational French hippy-chic island paradise, with ooh-la-la views and three basic rooms upstairs in the main wooden and bamboo lodge. They share a bath and a bamboo lounge area strung with hammocks. It also has two private bungalows with queen beds and private bathrooms.

Desert Point Bungalows BUNGALOW $
(0878 6585 5310; nurbaya_sari@yahoo.com; Tanjung Desert; r from 300,000Rp) The most upscale place to stay right at Tanjung Desert (that's

because there's a phone number you can try calling) has 10 rather shacky bungalows. A generator provides power at certain times and there's a two-level surf-viewing platform.

★ Pearl Beach BUNGALOW $$
(☎0819 0724 7696; www.pearlbeach-resort.com; Gili Asahan; cottages/bungalows from US$44/80; 📶) A private-island resort; cottages are simple, bamboo affairs with outdoor baths and a hammock on the porch. The bungalows are chic, with polished concrete floors, soaring ceilings, gorgeous outdoor bathrooms, and fabulous daybed swings on the wooden porches. There's great diving, kayaks and more.

Cocotino's RESORT $$$
(☎0819 0797 2401; www.cocotinos-sekotong.com; Jl Raya Palangan Sekotong, Tanjung Empat; r/villas from US$100/$275; ❄@📶🏊) This walled compound along the main road has an oceanfront location, a private beach and 36 high-quality bungalows (some with lovely outdoor bathrooms, some with sea views). It offers deals via its website. The setting is a sublime tropical idyll.

ℹ Getting There & Away

BEMO

Bemos run between Lembar and Pelangan (10,000Rp, 1½ hours) via Sekotong and Tembowong every 30 minutes until 5pm. West of Pelangan transport is less regular, but the route is still served by infrequent bemos until Selegang. Private wheels are your best transport option.

TAXI BOATS

Taxi boats (per person 20,000Rp) shuttle from Tembowong on the mainland to Gili Gede. You'll see them near the Pertamina gas station. Chartered boats also connect Tembowong with the islands of Gili Gede and Gili Asahan (from 300,000Rp return).

Senggigi

☎0370

Lombok's traditional tourist resort, Senggigi enjoys a fine location along a series of sweeping bays, with light-sand beaches sitting pretty below a backdrop of jungle-clad mountains and coconut palms. In the late afternoon a setting blood-red sun sinks into the surf next to the giant triangular cone of Bali's Gunung Agung.

Tourist numbers are relatively modest here and you'll find some good-value hotels and restaurants. Still, the tacky main strip could be more appealing, the noticeable influx of bar girls is sleazy, and the resident beach hawkers can be over-persistent.

The Senggigi area spans 10km of coastal road; the upscale neighbourhood of Mangsit is 3km north of central Senggigi.

Sights

Pura Batu Bolong HINDU TEMPLE
(off Jl Raya Senggigi; admission by donation; ⏲7am-7pm) It's not the grandest, but Pura Batu Bolong is Lombok's most appealing Hindu temple, and particularly lovely at sunset. Join an ever-welcoming Balinese community as they leave offerings at the 14 altars and pagodas that tumble down a rocky volcanic outcropping into the foaming sea about 2km south of central Senggigi. The rock underneath the temple has a natural hole, hence the name (*batu bolong* literally means 'rock with hole').

Activities

Snorkelling & Diving

There's reasonable snorkelling off the point in Senggigi, 3km north of the town. You can rent gear (per day 50,000Rp) from several spots on the beach. Diving trips from Senggigi usually visit the Gili Islands. The dive shops we list also offer courses.

Blue Marlin DIVING
(☎0370-613 2424, 0370-693719; www.bluemarlindive.com; Holiday Resort Lombok, Jl Raya Senggigi; single dive trips 490,000Rp) The local branch of a well-regarded Gili Trawangan dive shop; offers dive courses and trips.

Dream Divers DIVING
(☎0370-693738; www.dreamdivers.com; Jl Raya Senggigi; intro dives 910,000Rp) The Senggigi office of the Gili diving original. Runs snorkelling trips out to the Gilis for 400,000Rp. It also organises activities such as Rinjani treks, and dive courses.

Trekking

Rinjani Trekking Club ADVENTURE SPORTS
(☎0817 573 0415, 0370-693202; www.info2lombok.com; Jl Raya Senggigi; ⏲9am-8pm) Well informed about routes and trail conditions on Gunung Rinjani, and offers a wide choice of guided hikes. It's the best of the many places hawking Rinjani treks along the strip.

Massages & Spas

Very determined local masseurs, armed with mats, oils and attitude, hunt for business

Senggigi

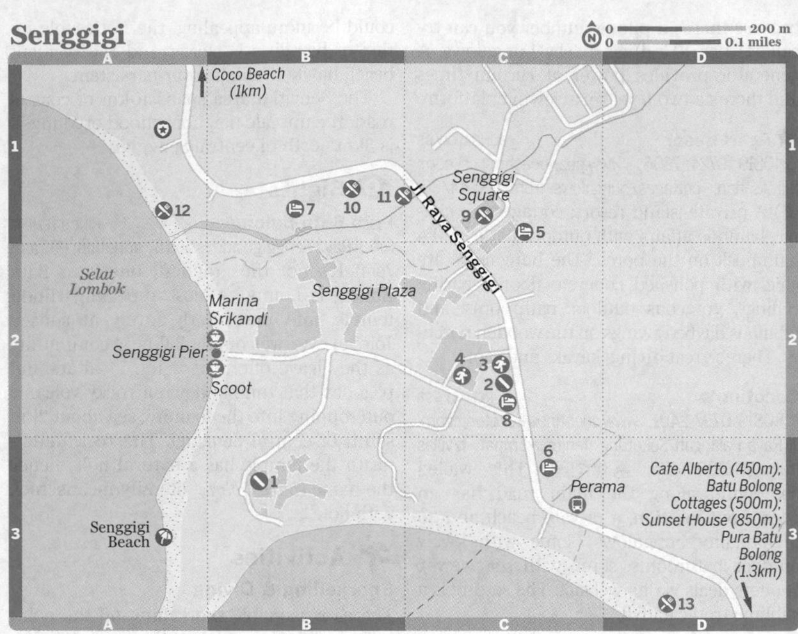

Senggigi

Activities, Courses & Tours
1 Blue Marlin ... B3
2 Dream Divers ... C2
3 Rinjani Trekking Club ... C2
4 Royal Spa ... C2

Sleeping
5 Hotel Elen ... C1
6 Sendok Hotel ... C3
7 Sonya Homestay ... B1
8 Wira ... C2

Eating
9 Bambu Lounge ... C1
10 Banana Tree Cafe ... B1
11 Cafe Tenda Cak Poer ... B1
12 Office ... A1
13 Warung Menega ... D3

on Senggigi's beaches. Expect to pay about 60,000Rp for one hour after bargaining. Most hotels can arrange for a masseur to visit your room; rates start at about 75,000Rp. Be warned, many of the street-side 'salons' you'll find are fronts for more salacious services.

★Qamboja Spa SPA
(☎0370-693800; www.quncivillas.com; Qunci Villas, Mangsit; massages from US$30; ⏲8am-10pm) Gorgeous hotel spa where you select your choice of oil (uplifting, harmony...) depending on the effect and mood you require from your massage; types available include Thai, Balinese and shiatsu.

Royal Spa SPA
(☎0370-660 8777; off Jl Raya Senggigi, Senggigi Plaza; massages from 110,000Rp; ⏲10am-9pm) A professional yet inexpensive spa with a tempting range of scrubs, massages and treatments. The *lulur* massage is a real treat and includes a body mask.

Sleeping

Senggigi's accommodation is very spread out. But even if you're located a few kilometres away (say, in Mangsit) you're not isolated as many restaurants offer free rides to diners and taxis are very inexpensive.

Heavy discounts of up to 50% are common in midrange and top-end places outside the July–August peak season.

Senggigi

★Wira GUESTHOUSE $
(0370-692153; www.thewira.com; Jl Raya Senggigi; dm from 100,000Rp, r 250,000-450,000Rp;) This boutique losmen (a type of budget accommodation) is on the beach side of the main Senggigi strip. It has 11 simple, sizeable rooms with bamboo furnishings and private porches out back. There is also a 10-bed fan-cooled dorm room. Use the quiet entrance on the side street, away from Jl Raya Senggigi.

Hotel Elen HOTEL $
(0370-693077; Jl Raya Senggigi; r fan/air-con from 120,000/200,000Rp;) Elen is the long-time backpackers' choice. Rooms are very basic, but those facing the waterfall fountain and koi pond come with spacious tiled patios that catch the ocean breeze.

Sendok Hotel INN $
(0370-693176; www.sendokhotellombok.com; Jl Raya Senggigi; r fan/air-con from 250,000/400,000Rp;) This guesthouse is more attractive than the (friendly) pub it sits behind. The 28 rooms pair lovely Javanese antiques with garish tiles, and have high ceilings and decent bathrooms; all are bright and airy with their own private front porch. Some rooms have hot water.

Sonya Homestay HOMESTAY $
(0813 3989 9878; Jl Raya Senggigi; r 100,000-160,000Rp;) A shady family-run enclave of nine very simple rooms (the cheapest are fan-only) with nice patios. Nathan, the owner, offers driving tours of Mataram and the surrounding area. It's off the road amid a small garden.

Batu Bolong Cottages HOTEL $$
(0370-693065, 0370-693198; bbcresort_lombok@yahoo.com; Jl Raya Senggigi; r 400,000-800,000Rp;) Charming two-level bungalow-style rooms by the sand are the best bets at this well-run hotel, which straddles both sides of the road south of the centre. The beachfront rooms have quaint touches such as carved doors, and there's a lovely pool area. The rest of the rooms are in more standard two-storey blocks. Good breakfast.

Sunset House HOTEL $$
(0370-692020; www.sunsethouse-lombok.com; Jl Raya Senggigi 66; r 500,000-800,000Rp;) Offers 35 rooms, all with a tasteful, well-equipped simplicity, in a quiet oceanfront location towards Pura Batu Bolong. Rooms on the upper floors have sweeping ocean views towards Bali. Wi-fi is only available in public areas.

Chandi Boutique Resort RESORT $$$
(0370-692198; www.the-chandi.com; Batu Bolong; r 1,800,000-2,200,000Rp;) This stylish boutique hotel that still manages a lot of thatch is about 1km south of Pura Batu Bolong. Each of the 15 rooms has an outdoor living room, and a hip modern interior with high ceilings and groovy outdoor bathrooms. The ample oceanfront perch is likely to absorb your daylight hours.

Mangsit

★Qunci Villas RESORT $$$
(0370-693800; www.quncivillas.com; Mangsit; r US$140-250;) A spectacular, lovingly imagined property that comes close to a luxe experience. Everything, from the food to the lovely pool area to the spa, and especially the sea views (160m of beachfront), is magical. It has 78 rooms that, together with the other diversions here, give you little reason to leave.

Jeeva Klui RESORT $$$
(0370-693035; www.jeevaklui.com; Jl Raya Klui Beach; r from US$160, villas from US$250;) This is why you came to the tropics: a palm-shaded, shimmering infinity pool and a lovely, almost private, beach, sheltered by a rocky outcrop. The 35 rooms are stylishly thatched, and have bamboo columns and private porches. Villas are luxurious, private and have their own pools. It's one bay north of Mangsit.

Eating & Drinking

Senggigi's dining scene ranges from tourist-friendly dining to simple warungs. Many places offer free transport for evening diners – phone for a ride. Few visitors miss the chance to enjoy a sunset beverage at one of the many low-key places along the beach.

Not long ago, Senggigi's bar scene was pretty vanilla with most cafes and restaurants doing double duty. However, now, like something out of a Pattaya fever-dream, huge breeze-block buildings have been built on the outskirts of the centre, and feature arrays of 'karaoke' joints and massage parlours.

Senggigi

★Cafe Tenda Cak Poer INDONESIAN $
(Jl Raya Senggigi; mains 12,000-20,000Rp; ⏲6pm-late) Barely enclosed, this roadside warung wows the stool-sitting masses with hot-outta-the-wok Indo classics. Get the nasi goreng (fried rice) made extra hot *(ekstra pedas)* and with extra garlic *(bawang putih ekstra)* and you'll be smiling through tears *and* sweating.

Office INTERNATIONAL $
(☎0370-693162; Jl Raya Senggigi, Pasar Seni; mains 25,000-70,000Rp; ⏲9am-10pm) This pub near the euphemistic 'art market' offers typical Indonesian and Western choices along with pool tables, ball games and barflies. It also has a Thai menu, which is the choice of those in the know. Tables on the sand near fishing boats are among Senggigi's best places for a relaxed sunset drink.

★Warung Menega SEAFOOD $$
(☎0370-663 4422; Jl Raya Senggigi, Pantai Batu Layar; meals 80,000-250,000Rp; ⏲11am-11pm) If you fled Bali before experiencing the Jimbaran fish grills, you can make up for it at this beachside seafood barbecue. Choose from a daily catch of barracuda, squid, snapper, grouper, lobster, tuna and prawns – all of which are grilled over smouldering coconut husks and served on candlelit tables on the sand.

Banana Tree Cafe INTERNATIONAL $$
(Jl Raya Senggigi; mains 30,000-120,000Rp; ⏲8am-10pm) One of the better choices in the centre, this cheery cafe is set back from the road buzz and has a nice seating area to the rear. It's number-one appeal is the coffee bar operated by skilful baristas. Food spans the globe, from Indo classics to Italian to seafood. It's all fresh and tasty.

Bambu Lounge INTERNATIONAL $$
(☎0877 6547 7443; off Jl Raya Senggigi, Senggigi Square; mains 30,000-120,000Rp; 📶) Indo, Indian, Greek, the list goes on! The talented chef-owner here serves up an eclectic menu of favourites that are actually quite good. Find repose at a table surrounded by potted plants outside or in the cute interior. Enjoy a cold drink and merrily graze away.

Cafe Alberto ITALIAN $$
(☎0370-693039; Jl Raya Senggigi; mains from 50,000Rp; ⏲8am-11pm) A long-standing, beachside Italian kitchen, this place serves a variety of pasta dishes but is known for its pizza. It offers free transport to and from your hotel. Best bet: wiggling your toes in the sand while sipping a cold one under the moonlight.

North of Senggigi

★Coco Beach INDONESIAN $$
(☎0817 578 0055; Pantai Kerandangan; mains from 60,000Rp; ⏲noon-10pm; 🖉) This wonderful beachside restaurant has a blissfully secluded setting off the main road. It's pretty and stylish, with many choices for vegetarians. The nasi goreng is locally renowned and the seafood is the best in the area. It has a full bar and blends its own authentic *jamu* (herbal medicines) tonics. It's about 2km north of central Senggigi.

ℹ Information

The nearest hospitals are in Mataram. ATMs abound.

Tourist Police (☎0370-632733)

ℹ Getting There & Away

BEMO & TAXI

➡ Regular bemos travel between Senggigi and Ampenan's Kebon Roek terminal (3000Rp), where you can connect to Mataram. Wave them down on the main drag.

➡ A taxi to Lembar is 150,000Rp.

➡ Metered taxis to the airport in Praya cost about 150,000Rp and take an hour.

➡ There's no public bemo service north to Bangsal Harbour. A metered taxi costs about 90,000Rp.

BOAT

Fast boats to Bali leave from the large pier right in the centre of the beach. A ticket office is out on the pier.

Marina Srikandi (☎0361 729818; marinasrikandi.com; Senggigi Pier; one-way from 375,000Rp) Has daily fast boats to Padangbai.

Perama (☎0370-693008; www.peramatour.com; Jl Raya Senggigi; ⏲8am-8pm) Has an economical shuttle-bus service that connects with the public ferry from Lembar to Padangbai, Bali (125,000Rp), from where there are onward shuttle-bus connections to Sanur, Kuta and Ubud (all 175,000Rp). These trips can take eight or more hours. It also offers a bus-and-boat connection to the Gilis for a reasonable 150,000Rp (two hours). It saves some hassle at Bangsal Harbour.

Scoot (☎0828 9701 5565; www.scootcruise.com; Senggigi Pier; one-way US$60) Has daily fast boats to Padangbai and Sanur on Bali.

Getting Around

Senggigi's central area is easy to negotiate on foot. If you're staying further from the centre, many restaurants offer a free lift for diners. Otherwise, hop a metered Blue Bird Lombok Taksi.

Senggigi to Bangsal

As you head north along the scalloped coast from Senggigi, you catch glimpses of the white-sand-ringed Gilis glowing in the sun. The bays that make up the coast here are undeveloped, picture-perfect crescents backed by palm trees.

About 20km north of Senggigi is the wide bay of **Teluk Nare/Teluk Kade**. This is where several fast-boat companies stop as part of their service linking Bali and the Gilis. Private boats belonging to Gili Trawangan resorts use private docks here.

Another 5km brings you to the turn for Bangsal Harbour (p326) and the busy public boats serving the Gilis.

Bangsal to Bayan

☎0370

Lombok quickly becomes uncommercial and almost pastoral as you head north from Bangsal. Watch for Rinjani views.

Public transport north from Bangsal is infrequent. Several minibuses a day go from the Mandalika terminal in Mataram to Bayan, but you'll have to get connections in Pemenang and/or Anyar, which can be difficult to navigate. Simplify things and get your own wheels.

Sire

A hidden upmarket enclave, the jutting Sire (or Sira) peninsula seems to be squirting the three Gilis out of its tip. It's blessed with gorgeous, broad white-sand **beaches** and good snorkelling offshore. Several resorts are now established here, alongside a couple of fishing villages and some amazing private villas.

Sleeping

★Rinjani Beach Eco Resort BOUTIQUE HOTEL $$

(☎0819 3677 5960; www.lombok-adventures.com; Karang Atas; bungalows 350,000-900,000Rp; ❄≋) This gem has bamboo bungalows and villas, each with its own theme; hammocks on private porches; and access to a pool on the black-sand beach. Two cheaper, smaller cold-water bungalows cater to budget travellers. There is also a dive shop and a restaurant, plus sea kayaks and mountain bikes. Waste water is treated and used to water the lush grounds.

★Tugu Lombok RESORT $$$

(☎0819 3799 5566, 0370-612 0111; www.tuguhotels.com; bungalows from US$250, villas from US$330; ❄☎≋) An astonishing hotel, this larger-than-life amalgamation of luxury accommodation, eclectic design and spiritual Indonesian heritage sits on a wonderful white-sand beach. Room decor is a fantasy of Indonesian artistic heritage, while the exquisite spa is modelled on Java's Buddhist Borobudur. Smart green practices abound.

Gondang & Around

Just northeast of Gondang village, a 6km trail heads inland to **Air Terjun Tiu Pupas**, a 30m waterfall (per person 30,000Rp) that's only worth seeing in the wet season. Trails continue from here to other wet-season waterfalls, including **Air Terjun Gangga**, the most beautiful of all. A guide (about 90,000Rp) is useful to navigate the confusing trails in these parts.

Bayan

Wektu Telu, Lombok's animist-tinted form of Islam, was born in humble thatched mosques nestled in these Rinjani foothills. The best example is **Masjid Kuno Bayan Beleq**, next to the village of Beleq. Its low-slung roof, dirt floors and bamboo walls reportedly date from 1634, making this mosque the oldest on Lombok. Inside is a huge old drum which served as the call to prayer before PA systems.

Senaru

☎0370

One of the major gateways to Gunung Rinjani, the scenic villages that make up Senaru merge into one along a steep road with sweeping Rinjani and sea views. Most visitors here are volcano-bound, but beautiful walking trails and spectacular waterfalls beckon to those who aren't.

Senaru derives its name from *sinaru*, which means light. As you ascend the hill towards the sky and clouds, you'll see just why this makes sense.

WEKTU TELU

Wektu Telu is a complex mixture of Hindu, Islamic and animist beliefs, though it's now officially classified as a sect of Islam. At its forefront is a physical concept of the Holy Trinity. The sun, moon and stars represent heaven, earth and water, while the head, body and limbs represent creativity, sensitivity and control.

As recently as 1965 the vast majority of Sasaks in northern Lombok were Wektu Telu, but under Suharto's 'New Order' government, indigenous religious beliefs were discouraged, and enormous pressure was placed on Wektu Telu to become Wektu Lima (Muslims who pray five times a day). But in the Wektu Telu heartland around Bayan, locals have been able to maintain their unique beliefs by differentiating their cultural traditions (Wektu Telu) from religion (Islam). Most do not fast for the full month of Ramadan and only attend the mosque for special occasions, and there's widespread consumption of *brem* (alcoholic rice wine).

Sights & Activities

Air Terjun Sindang Gila (10,000Rp) is a spectacular set of falls 20 minutes' walk from Senaru via a lovely forest and hillside trail. The hardy make for the creek, edge close and then get pounded by the hard, foaming cascade that explodes over black volcanic stone 40m above.

A further 50 minutes or so uphill is **Air Terjun Tiu Kelep**, another waterfall with a swimming hole. The track is steep and guides are compulsory (60,000Rp). Long-tailed macaques (locals call them *kera*) and the much rarer silvered leaf monkey sometimes appear.

In the traditional Sasak village of **Dusun Senaru**, at the top of the road, locals will invite you to chew betel nut (or tobacco) and show you around for a donation.

Guided walks and community tourism activities can be arranged at most guesthouses – they include a **rice-terrace and waterfalls walk** (per person 150,000Rp), which takes in Sindang Gila, rice paddies and an old bamboo mosque, and the **Senaru panorama walk** (per person 150,000Rp), which incorporates stunning views and insights into local traditions.

You do not need a guide to reach Air Terjun Sindang Gila; it's on a well-marked path. A guide to the second waterfall is recommended. However, anyone lurking around the waterfall ticket office is likely not an official guide. Avoid them. Legitimate guides are easy to find in town, especially in the small collection of shops by the entrance to Air Terjun Sindang Gila.

Sleeping & Eating

All of Senaru's places to stay and eat are strung along the 6.5km-long road that starts in Bayan and runs uphill via Batu Koq to the main Gunung Rinjani park office and Rinjani Trek Centre.

Most of the dozen or so places here are simple mountain lodges, and the cool altitude means you won't need air-con.

★ **Rinjani Lighthouse** GUESTHOUSE $
(☎0818 0548 5480; www.rinjanilighthouse.mm.st; r 350,000-800,000Rp;) Set on a wide plateau just 200m from the Rinjani park office, this impressive guesthouse (with hot water) has thatched-roof bungalows in sizes ranging from double to family. The owners are founts of Rinjani info.

Pondok Senaru & Restaurant LODGE $
(☎0818 0362 4129; pondoksenaru@yahoo.com; r 250,000-700,000Rp;) This place has 14 lovely little cottages (most fan-only) with terracotta-tiled roofs, and some well-equipped superior rooms with such niceties as hot water. The restaurant, with tables perched on the edge of a rice-terraced valley, is a sublime place for a meal. It's at the waterfall entrance.

Sinar Rinjani LODGE $
(☎0818 540 673; www.senarutrekking.com; r 200,000-350,000Rp;) The eight rooms here are huge and offer rain showers and king-sized beds; some have hot water and air-con. The rooftop restaurant has outstanding views. The lodge offers good trekking packages, and is 2.1km from the top of the road.

Information

Rinjani Trek Centre (RTC; ☎0817 572 4863, 0878 6432 3094; 6am-4pm) The local guiding and mountaineering collective; a good stop for information and planning.

Getting There & Away

From Mandalika terminal in Mataram, catch a bus to Anyar (25,000Rp to 30,000Rp, 2½ hours). Bemos no longer run from Anyar to Senaru, so you'll have to charter an *ojek* (per person from 20,000Rp, depending on your luggage).

Sembalun Valley

☎0376

High on the eastern side of Gunung Rinjani is what could be the mythical Shangri-La: the beautiful Sembalun Valley. This high plateau is ringed by volcanoes and peaks. It's a rich farming region where the golden foothills turn vivid green in the wet season. When the high clouds part, Rinjani goes full frontal from all angles.

The valley has two main settlements, Sembalun Lawang and Sembalun Bumbung, tranquil breadbaskets primarily concerned with growing cabbage, potatoes, strawberries and, above all, garlic – though trekking tourism brings in a little income, too.

Activities

Rinjani Information Centre HIKING

(RIC; ☎0818 0572 5754; Sembalun Lawang; ⏰6am-6pm) The Rinjani Information Centre is the place to enquire about Rinjani treks. It has well-informed English-speaking staff and lots of fascinating information panels about the area's flora, fauna, geology and history. It also offers a four-hour **Village Walk** (per person 150,000Rp, minimum two people) and a two-day rambling **Wildflower Walk** (per person including guide, porters, meals and camping gear 550,000Rp) past flowery grasslands.

Camping and trekking gear is available for hire. The centre is right by a huge garlic statue on the main road.

Sleeping & Eating

Sembalun Lawang village is rustic; most guesthouses will heat *mandi* water for a fee. The Rinjani Information Centre (RIC) can direct you to small homestays where rooms cost between 150,000Rp and 500,000Rp.

Lembah Rinjani LODGE $

(☎0818 0365 2511, 0852 3954 3279; Sembalun Lawang; r 300,000-400,000Rp) This property has 15 basic, clean tiled rooms with private porches and breathtaking mountain and sunrise views.

Maria Guesthouse GUESTHOUSE $

(☎0852 3956 1340; Sembalun Lawang; r from 250,000Rp) Choose one of three large tin-roofed bungalows at the rear of a family compound. Digs are bright with vibrantly tiled floors; the family vibe is fun and the garden location sweet.

Getting There & Away

From Mandalika bus terminal in Mataram, take a bus to Aikmel (20,000Rp) and change there for a bemo to Sembalun Lawang (15,000Rp).

There's no public transport between Sembalun Lawang and Senaru, so you'll have to charter an *ojek* for a potentially uncomfortable ride costing about 200,000Rp.

Gunung Rinjani

Lording over the northern half of Lombok, Gunung Rinjani (3726m) is Indonesia's second-tallest volcano. It's an astonishing peak, sacred to Hindus and Sasaks who make pilgrimages to the summit and lake to leave offerings for the gods and spirits. To the Balinese, Rinjani is one of three sacred mountains, along with Bali's Agung and Java's Bromo. Sasaks ascend throughout the year around the full moon.

The mountain also has climatic significance. Its peak attracts a steady stream of swirling rain clouds, while its ash emissions bring fertility to the island's rice fields and tobacco crops, feeding a tapestry of paddies, fields, and cashew and mango orchards.

Inside the immense caldera, sitting 600m below the rim, is a stunning, 6km-wide, turquoise crescent lake, **Danau Segara Anak** (Child of the Sea). The Balinese toss gold and jewellery into the lake in a ceremony called *pekelan,* before they slog their way towards the sacred summit.

The mountain's newest cone, the minor peak of **Gunung Baru** (2351m), emerged just a couple of hundred years ago; its scarred, smouldering profile rising above the lake is an ominous reminder of the apocalyptic power of nature. This peak has been erupting fitfully for the last decade, periodically belching plumes of smoke and ash over the entire Rinjani caldera. Also in the crater are natural hot springs known as **Aiq Kalak**. Locals suffering from skin diseases trek here with a satchel of medicinal herbs in order to bathe and scrub in the bubbling mineral water.

Activities

Organised Hikes

Treks to the rim, lake and peak should not be taken lightly, and guides are mandatory. Climbing Rinjani during the wet season

Gunung Rinjani

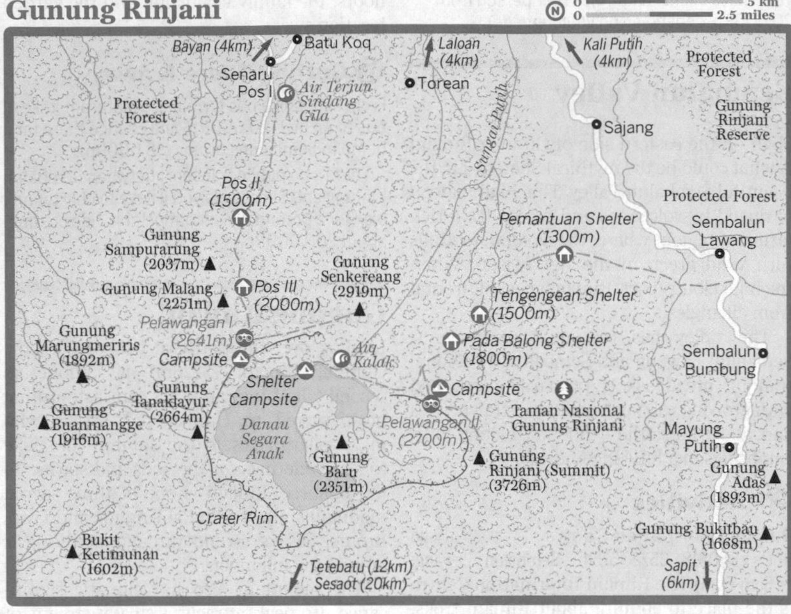

(November to March) is usually completely forbidden due to the risk of landslide. June to August is the only time you are (almost) guaranteed minimal rain or clouds. Be prepared with layers and a fleece because it can get cold at the rim (and near-freezing at the summit) at any time of year.

Roughly the same trek packages and prices are offered by all operators (base guide and porter prices are set by RTC and RIC), though some outfitters have a 'luxury' option. Treks from Senaru to Sembalun Lawang via the lake summit are very popular, and the return hike from Sembalun Lawang to the summit is another well-trodden trail.

Prices get cheaper the larger the party. A three-day hike (including food, equipment, guide, porters, park fee and transport back to Senaru) to the summit and lake costs from US$300 per person based on a group of two to four. An overnight trek to the crater rim costs about US$150 to US$200. Note that almost all the costs are negotiable.

Operators

In addition to local companies, operators in Mataram, Senggigi and the Gili Islands can organise Rinjani treks too, with return transport from the point of origin. Recommendations include Rinjani Information Centre (p315), Rinjani Trek Centre (p314) and Rinjani Trekking Club (p318).

John's Adventures HIKING
(☎0817 578 8018; www.rinjanimaster.com; Senaru) John's Adventures is a very experienced outfitter that has toilet tents, thick sleeping mats, and itineraries that start from either Senaru or Sembalun. The Senaru office is 2km below the park office.

Rudy Trekker HIKING
(☎0818 0365 2874; www.rudytrekker.com; Senaru) Rudy Trekker is a conscientious organisation based in Senaru. It has a variety of itineraries; most hikers prefer the three-day, two-night package starting from Sembalun Lawang. The office is near the entrance to Air Terjun Sindang Gila. It has a great list of what to pack displayed on the wall.

Sinaru Trekking HIKING
(☎0818 540 673) The monosyllabically named Gul is an excellent Rinjani guide. He offers 5% off his fees if you'll help him carry trash down from the mountain.

Guides & Porters

Hiking independently is simply not allowed, and deeply unwise. People have died on Rinjani, with or without guides, and only the

CLIMBING GUNUNG RINJANI

The most popular way to climb Gunung Rinjani is the five-day trek that starts at Senaru and finishes at Sembalun Lawang. Other possibilities include a summit attempt from Sembalun, which sits higher on the slope and can be done as a gruelling two-day return hike.

Day One: Senaru Pos I to Pos III (five to six hours)

At the southern end of Senaru is the **Rinjani Trek Centre** (Pos I, 601m), where you register, organise your guide and porters, and pay the park fee. Just beyond the post, you'll head right when the trail forks. The trail climbs steadily through scrubby farmland for about half an hour to the entrance of **Gunung Rinjani National Park** (Taman Nasional Gunung Rinjani). The wide trail climbs for another 2½ hours until you reach Pos II (1500m), where there's a shelter. Another 1½ hours' steady walk uphill brings you to Pos III (2000m), where there are two shelters in disrepair. Pos III is usually the place to camp at the end of the first day.

Day Two: Pos III to Danau Segara Anak & Aiq Kalak (four hours)

From Pos III, it takes about 1½ hours to reach the rim, **Pelawangan I** (2641m). Setting off very early promises a stunning sunrise. It's possible to camp at Pelawangan I, but level sites are limited, there's no water and it can be very blustery.

It takes about two hours to descend to **Danau Segara Anak** and over to the hot springs, **Aiq Kalak**. The first hour is a very steep descent and involves a bit of bouldering. From the bottom of the crater wall it's an easy 30-minute walk across undulating terrain around the lake's edge. There are several places to camp, but most locals prefer to be near the hot springs to soak their weary bodies.

Day Three: Aiq Kalak to Pelawangan II (three to four hours)

The trail starts beside the last shelter at the hot springs and heads away from the lake for about 100m before veering right. It then traverses the northern slope of the crater, and it's an easy one-hour walk along the grassy slopes before you hit a steep, unforgiving rise; from the lake it takes about three hours to reach the crater rim (2639m). At the rim, a sign points the way back to Danau Segara Anak. The trail forks here – straight on to Sembalun or along the rim to the campsite of **Pelawangan II** (2700m).

Day Four: Pelawangan II to Rinjani Summit (five to six hours return)

Gunung Rinjani's summit arcs above the campsite at Pelawangan II and looks deceptively close. You'll start the climb around 3am to reach it by sunrise. Depending on wind conditions, it may not be possible to attempt the summit at all, as the trail is along an exposed ridge.

It takes about 45 minutes to clamber up a steep, slippery and indistinct trail to the ridge that leads to Rinjani. Once on the ridge it's a relatively steady walk uphill. After about an hour heading towards a false peak, the real **summit of Rinjani** (3726m) looms. The trail then gets increasingly steeper. About 350m before the summit, the scree is composed of loose, fist-sized rocks. This section can take about an hour. The views from the top are truly magnificent. In total it takes around three hours to reach the summit, and two to return.

Day Four/Five: Pelawangan II to Sembalun Lawang (six to seven hours)

From the Pelawangan II campsite, it's a steep descent to Sembalun; you'll feel it in your knees. From the campsite, you head back along the crater rim. Shortly after the turn-off to Danau Segara Anak, there's a signposted right turn down to **Pada Balong** (also called Pos 3, 1800m). The trail is easy to follow; it takes around two hours to reach Pada Balong shelter.

The trail then undulates toward the **Sembalun Lawang** savannah, via **Tengengean** (Pos 2, 1500m) shelter, beautifully situated in a river valley. It's another 30 minutes through long grass to lonely **Pemantuan** (Pos 1, 1300m), and two more hours along a dirt track to Sembalun Lawang.through long grass to lonely **Pemantuan** (Pos 1, 1300m), and two more hours along a dirt track to Sembalun Lawang.

most skilled climbers should consider themselves qualified to undertake such a journey.

Guides and porters operate on loosely fixed fees, which are included in whatever trekking package you purchase. Tips of 30,000Rp to 50,000Rp per day are sufficient and can be paid at the end of the trip.

Entrance Fee & Equipment

Entrance to Gunung Rinjani National Park is 150,000Rp *per day* – you register and pay with your trek organiser or at the park office. Note that there are proposals to raise these fees even higher.

Sleeping bags and tents are essential and can usually be hired from your trek organiser. Decent footwear, warm clothing, wet-weather gear, gloves, cooking equipment and a torch are important (all can be hired if necessary). Expect to pay upwards of 100,000Rp a head per day for all your hired gear. Muscle balm (to ease aching legs) and a swimming costume (for the lake and hot springs) could also be packed. Discuss what to bring with your trekking organisation or guide.

Bring home your rubbish, including toilet tissue. Sadly several Rinjani camps are litter-strewn.

Food & Supplies

Trek organisers will arrange trekking food. Mataram is cheapest for supplies, but many provisions are available in Senaru and Sembalun Lawang, too. Take more water than seems reasonable (dehydration can spur altitude sickness), extra batteries (as altitude can wreak havoc on those, as well) and a back-up lighter.

Information

Rinjani National Park (Taman Nasional Gunung Rinjani; 0370-660 8874; www.rinjaninationalpark.com) The official website for the park has good maps, info and a useful section on reported scams by dodgy hiking operators.

Rinjani Trekking Club (0370-693202; www.info2lombok.com; Jl Raya Senggigi, Senggigi) This group sells treks on the mountain but it also has a very worthwhile website and organises sustainable programs.

Tetebatu

0376

Laced with Rinjani spring-fed streams and blessed with rich volcanic soil, Tetebatu is a Sasak breadbasket. The surrounding countryside is quilted with tobacco and rice fields, fruit orchards and cow pastures that fade into remnant monkey forest gushing with waterfalls. Tetebatu's sweet climate is ideal for long country walks (at 400m it's high enough to mute that hot, sticky coastal mercury). Dark nights come saturated with sound courtesy of a frog orchestra accompanied by countless gurgling brooks. Even insomniacs snore here.

The town is spread out, with facilities on roads north and east (nicknamed 'waterfall road') of the central *ojek* stop, which happens to be the town's main intersection and a basis for all directions.

Sights & Activities

A shady 4km track leading from the main road, just north of the mosque, heads into the **Taman Wisata Tetebatu** (Monkey Forest) with black monkeys and waterfalls – you'll need a guide.

On the southern slopes of Rinjani, there are two **waterfalls**. Both are accessible by private transport or a spectacular two-hour walk (one way) through rice fields from Tetebatu. If walking, hire a guide (150,000Rp) through your guesthouse.

A steep 2km hike from the car park at the end of the access road to Gunung Rinjani National Park leads to beautiful **Air Terjun Jukut**, an impressive 20m drop to a deep pool surrounded by lush forest.

Sleeping & Eating

Cendrawasih Cottages COTTAGE $

(0878 6418 7063; r from 250,000Rp) Sweet little *lumbung* (rice barn)–style brick cottages with bamboo beds and private porches, nestled in the rice fields. Sit on floor cushions in the stunning stilted restaurant (mains 20,000Rp to 45,000Rp; open 8am to 9pm), which has Sasak, Indonesian and Western fare, and take in 360-degree rice-field views. It's about 500m east of the intersection.

Pondok Tetebatu LODGE $

(0818 0576 7153; r 150,000-250,000Rp; wi-fi) These 12 detached, ranch-style rooms set around a flower garden 500m north of the intersection are basic. The lodge offers guided walks through farming villages to the falls.

★**Tetebatu Mountain Resort** LODGE $$

(0819 1771 6440, 0812 372 4040; r 450,000-650,000Rp; wi-fi) These two-storey Sasak bungalows with 23 rooms in total are the best digs in town. There are separate bedrooms

NUSA TENGGARA TETEBATU

on both floors – perfect for travelling buddies – and a top-floor balcony with magical rice-field views.

Getting There & Around

All cross-island buses pass Pomotong (15,000Rp from Mandalika terminal) on the main east–west highway. Get off here and you can hop on an *ojek* (from 20,000Rp) to Tetebatu.

Praya

0370

Sprawling Praya is the main town in the south, with tree-lined streets and the odd crumbling Dutch colonial relic. The bemo terminal is on the northwest side of town.

Lombok International Airport

Surrounded by rice fields and 5km south of Praya proper, the modern Lombok International Airport (www.lombok-airport.co.id) has become an attraction in its own right: on weekends you'll see vast crowds of locals sitting around watching and snacking. They're not waiting on anyone, rather they are hanging out for the day enjoying the spectacle of people flying in and out.

The airport is not huge, but is very modern and has a full range of services such as ATMs (and convenience stores with ludicrous prices). There is a useful **NTT Tourist Office** in the arrivals area with maps and brochures.

FLIGHTS FROM LOMBOK

DESTINATION	AIRLINE	DURATION	FREQUENCY
Bali	Garuda, Lion Air/ Wings Air	20min	several daily
Bima (Sumbawa)	Garuda	45min	daily
Jakarta	Garuda, Lion Air	2hr	several daily
Kuala Lumpur	Air Asia	3hr	daily
Makassar	Garuda	1¾hr	daily
Singapore	Silk Air	3hr	daily
Sumbawa Besar	Garuda	30min	daily
Surabaya	Citilink, Lion Air	1½hr	several daily

Getting There & Away

Thanks to wide new roads, the airport is only 30 minutes' drive from both Mataram and Kuta, and is well linked to the rest of the island. Note that some airport road signs simply say 'BIL', an acronym for the Bahasa Indonesia name, Bandera Internasional Lombok'.

Bus Damri operates tourist buses; buy tickets in the arrivals area. Destinations: Mataram's Mandalika terminal (25,000Rp) and Senggigi (35,000Rp).

Taxi The airport taxi cartel offers fixed-price rides to destinations that include: Kuta (100,000Rp, 30 minutes), Mataram (165,000Rp, 30 minutes), Senggigi (200,000Rp, one hour) and Bangsal (260,000Rp, 90 minutes), from where you can access the Gili Islands.

Around Praya

Penujak

Penujak is well known for its traditional *gerabah* pottery. Made from chocolatey terracotta-tinted local clay, it's hand-burnished and topped with braided bamboo. Huge floor vases cost US$6 or so, and there are also plates and cups on offer from the potters' humble home studios, most of which huddle around the eerie village cemetery. Any bemo from Praya to Kuta will drop you off here.

Rembitan & Sade

The area from Sengkol down to Kuta is a centre for Sasak culture – traditional villages full of towering *lumbung* (rice barns) and *bale tani* (family houses, made from bamboo, mud, and cow and buffalo dung). Regular bemos cover this route.

Sade's **Sasak Village** has been extensively renovated and has some fascinating *bale tani*. Further south, **Rembitan** has more of an authentic feel to it. It boasts a cluster of houses and *lumbung*, and the 100-year-old **Masjid Kuno**, an ancient thatched-roof mosque that is a pilgrimage destination for Lombok's Muslims.

Both villages are worth a look but it's not possible without a guide (around 40,000Rp).

Kuta

0370

What could be a better gateway to the wonderful beaches of south Lombok? Imagine a crescent bay, turquoise in the shallows and deep blue further out. It licks a huge, white-sand beach, as wide as a football pitch and framed by headlands. Now imagine a coastline of nearly a dozen such bays, all backed by a rugged range of coastal hills spotted with lush patches of banana trees and tobacco fields, and you'll have a notion of Kuta's immediate appeal.

Kuta's original attraction was the limitless world-class breaks, and now even as developers lick their chops, the sets still keep rolling in.

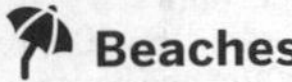

Beaches

Kuta's main beach can easily snare you and keep you from looking elsewhere. It's got ideal white sand and all those views. Plus the surf is just right for swimming. But even here change looms: most of the beach cafes that used to line the sand have been demolished and the local government has planted some trees. (Although a few bamboo joints have snuck back in to vend beer at night.) It's slightly bleak, but then again, there's that water…

Activities

There's a whole row of activity sales agents across the road from Lamancha Homestay. They can set you up on anything from surf tours to snorkelling in obscure locations. Bargain hard.

Surfing

For surfing, stellar lefts and rights break on the reefs off Kuta Bay (Telek Kuta) and east of Tanjung An. Boatmen will take you out for around 150,000Rp. Seven kilometres east of Kuta is the fishing village of **Gerupuk** (p322), where there's a series of reef breaks, both close to the shore and further out, but they require a boat, at a negotiable 300,000Rp per day. However, savvy surfers buzz past Gerupuk and take the road to **Ekas** (p322), where crowds are thin and surf is plentiful. West of Kuta you'll find **Mawan** (p323), a stunning swimming beach (the first left after Astari), and **Mawi** (p323), a popular surf paradise with world-class swells and a strong rip tide.

Kimen Surf SURFING
(☎0370-655064; www.kuta-lombok.net; Jl ke Mawan; board rental per day 100,000Rp, lessons per person from 500,000Rp; ⏲9am-8pm) Swell forecasts, tips, kitesurfing, board rental, repairs and lessons. It runs guided excursions to breaks such as Gerupuk (400,000Rp).

NYALE FESTIVAL

On the 19th day of the tenth month in the Sasak calendar (generally February or March), hundreds of Sasaks gather on the beach at Kuta, Lombok. When night falls, fires are built and teens sit around competing in a Sasak poetry slam, where they spit rhyming couplets called *pantun* back and forth. At dawn the next day, the first of millions of *nyale* (wormlike fish that appear here annually) are caught, then teenage girls and boys take to the sea separately in decorated boats, and chase one another with lots of noise and laughter. The *nyale* are eaten raw or grilled, and are considered to be an aphrodisiac. A good catch is a sign that a bumper crop of rice is coming.

Diving

Scuba Froggy DIVING
(☎0877 6510 6945; www.scubafroggy.com; Jl ke Mawan; open-water course US$360; ⏲9am-8pm) Runs local trips to a dozen sites, most no deeper than 18m. From June to November it also runs trips to the spectacular and challenging ocean pinnacles in Blongas Bay, famous for schooling hammerheads and mobula rays. Snorkelling trips are 150,000Rp.

Discovery Divers Lombok DIVING
(☎0812 3629 4178; www.discoverydiverslombok.com; Jl ke Mawan; 2 local dives from 1,200,000Rp; ⏲8am-9pm) A big, glossy operation, this dive shop has a full slate of courses, and runs tours through the region. It also has a very nice and welcoming cafe.

Sleeping

Prices increase markedly in the July–August high season. Beware of ageing, run-down hotels along Jl Raya Pantai Kuta.

★**Bombara Bungalows** GUESTHOUSE $
(☎0370-615 8056; bomborabungalows@yahoo.com; Jl Raya Kuta; r 350,000-450,000Rp; ❄☜☒) One of the best places for a low-cost stay in Kuta, these eight (some fan-cooled) bungalows are built around a lovely pool area. Coconut palms shade loungers and the entire place feels like an escape from the hubbub of town. The staff understand the needs of surfers, and everyone else for that matter.

Bule Homestay GUESTHOUSE $
(☎0819 1799 6256; bulehomestay.com; Jl Raya Bypass; r 250,000-300,000Rp;) Although it's about 2km back from the beach near the junction of Jl Raya Kuta and Jl Raya Bypass, this eight-bungalow complex is worth consideration simply for the snappy way it's run. Dirt doesn't dare enter the small compound, where rooms gleam with a hospital white. It is surrounded by a wall that could have been in *The Flintstones*.

Sekar Kuning INN $
(☎0370-615 4856; Jl Raya Pantai Kuta; r from 200,000Rp;) A charming beach-road inn. Tiled rooms have high ceilings, pastel paintjobs, ceiling fans, and bamboo furniture on the patio. Top-floor rooms have ocean views and are more expensive.

Mimpi Manis B&B $
(☎0818 369 950; www.mimpimanis.com; off Jl Raya Kuta; r 150,000-350,000Rp;) An inviting English–Balinese-owned B&B in a two-storey house with three spotless rooms (one with air-con), with en-suite showers, TVs and DVD players. There are plenty of good books to browse and DVDs to borrow. It's 1km inland from the beach; the owners offer a free drop-off service to the beach and town, and arrange bike and motorbike rental.

★**Yuli's Homestay** HOMESTAY $$
(☎0819 1710 0983; www.yulishomestay.com; off Jl Raya Kuta; r 400,000-500,000Rp;) A popular choice, the 13 rooms here are immaculately clean, spacious and nicely furnished with huge beds and wardrobes. They also have big front terraces, and cold-water bathrooms. There's a guest kitchen, and a garden and pool to enjoy.

Novotel Lombok Resort & Villas RESORT $$$
(☎0370-615 3333; www.novotel.com; r/villas from US$120/250;) One of the nicest beach resorts in NTT, this appealing, Sasak-themed four-star resort spills onto a superb beach less than 3km east of the junction. The 102 rooms have high sloping roofs and modern interiors. There are two pools, a spa, resort-style restaurants, a swanky bar and a plethora of activities on offer. Note: wi-fi doesn't work in the rooms.

Eating & Drinking

Kuta's dining scene has improved with growth, but at most local joints the Indo nosh or fresh seafood are the smart choices. The **market** (off Jl Raya Kuta; ⏲Sun & Wed) sells an ever-changing variety of foodstuffs and basic necessities.

Full Moon Cafe CAFE $
(Jl Raya Pantai Kuta; mains from 30,000Rp; ⏲8am-late;) Right across from the beach, the second-floor cafe here is like a tree house with killer ocean views. The menu has all the standards, from banana pancakes to various Indo rice creations. Come for the view and sunset, then hang out.

★**Warung Bule** SEAFOOD $$
(☎0819 1799 6256; Jl Raya Pantai Kuta; mains 40,000-250,000Rp; ⏲8am-10pm;) Arguably the best restaurant in Kuta, founded by the long-time executive chef at the Novotel, who delivers tropical seafood tastes at an affordable price. We like the tempura starter. His trio of lobster, prawns and mahi mahi might have you cooing. It gets very busy in high season, so be prepared for a wait.

El Bazar MEDITERRANEAN $$
(☎0819 9911 3026; Jl Raya Kuta; mains 30,000-150,000Rp; ⏲8am-11pm) A small cafe that's big on flavour. Pass by the flowers at the entrance and you'll be entranced by authentic tastes from around the Mediterranean. Hearty soups, salads, luscious aubergine, Moroccan tagines and more.

★**Warung Rasta** BAR
(☎0882 1907 1744; Jl Raya Pantai Kuta; ⏲8am-late) The local owners of this barely-there shack of a bar have created a laid-back party vibe that draws in crowds each night. Guitars get strummed and surfers compete in 'strawpedo' contests that involve beer-chugging with the strategic aid of straws. Hungry? Enjoy cheap Indo standards.

Surfer's Bar BAR
(☎0878 6456 8195; www.facebook.com/surfersbarkutalombok; Jl Raya Pantai Kuta; ⏲9am-late) Tables are scattered across the sand at this thumping dive bar, which has frequent live music.

Information

ATMs are common, as is wi-fi.

DANGERS & ANNOYANCES

➡ If you decide to rent a bicycle or motorbike, take care when selecting a supplier – arrangements are informal and no rental contracts are exchanged. We have received occasional reports of some visitors having motorbikes stolen, and then having to pay substantial sums of money as compensation to the owner (who may or may not have arranged the 'theft' themselves). Renting a motorbike from your guesthouse is safest.

- As you drive up the coastal road west and east of Kuta, watch your back – especially after dark. There have been reports of muggings in the area.
- Throngs of vendors – many children – are relentless.

Getting There & Away

You'll need at least three bemos to get here just from Mataram. Take one from Mataram's Mandalika terminal to Praya (15,000Rp), another to Sengkol (5000Rp) and a third to Kuta (5000Rp).

Simpler are the daily tourist buses serving Mataram (125,000Rp) plus Senggigi and Lembar (both 150,000Rp).

A taxi to the airport costs 60,000Rp.

Ride-share cars are widely advertised around town. Destinations include: Bangsal for Gili Islands public boats (160,000Rp), Seminyak (Bali) via the public ferry (200,000Rp), and Senaru (400,000Rp).

Getting Around

Guesthouses rent motorbikes for about 60,000Rp to 70,000Rp per day.

Ojeks congregate around the junction.

East of Kuta

A good paved road runs along the coast to the east and Ekas, passing a seemingly endless series of beautiful bays punctuated by headlands. It's a terrific motorbike ride.

Pantai Segar & Tanjung An

Pantai Segar, a lovely beach about 2km east of Kuta around the first headland, has unbelievably turquoise water, decent swimming (though no shade) and a break 200m offshore.

Continuing 3km east on an increasingly rough road, Tanjung An (or variously Aan or Ann) is a spectacular sight: a giant horseshoe bay with two sweeping arcs of fine sand with the ends punctuated by waves crashing on the rocks. Swimming is good here and there's a little shade under trees and shelters, plus safe parking (for a small charge). Bamboo warungs offer meals, beers, beach chairs and more.

Construction of the long-rumoured huge international resort here has finally begun. Vast boulevards are in the works for the former marshlands behind the beach and other developments will follow. Expect the area to change greatly in the next few years.

Gerupuk

Just 1.6km past Tanjung An, Gerupuk is a fascinating little ramshackle coastal village where the thousand or so local souls earn their keep from fishing, seaweed harvesting and lobster exports. Oh, and guiding and ferrying surfers to the five exceptional **surf breaks** in its huge bay.

To surf here you'll need to hire a boat to ferry you from the fishing harbour, skirting the netted lobster farms, to the break (200,000Rp). The boatman will help you find the right wave and wait patiently. There are four waves inside and a left break outside on the point. All can get head-high or bigger when the swell hits.

Sleeping & Eating

There is a growing number of hotels and warungs popular with surfers in Gerupuk.

Surf Camp Lombok SURF CAMP $
(☎0819 1608 6876; www.surfcampindonesia.com; Gerupuk; 1 week from €650) Lodging at this fun surf resort at the eastern end of Gerupuk village is in a bamboo Borneo-style longhouse, albeit with lots of high-tech diversions. The beach setting feels lush and remote. All meals are included plus surf lessons, yoga and more. Rooms sleep four, except for one double. Recycling and other eco-friendly practices are embraced.

Edo Homestay INN $
(☎0818 0371 0521; Gerupuk; r 150,000-600,000Rp;) Right in the village, this place offers 18 clean rooms (some fan-cooled). Most have colourful drapes and double beds; top-end rooms are in a villa. It has a decent restaurant and a surf shop too (boards per day 100,000Rp).

Ekas

Ekas is an uncrowded find, where the breaks and soaring cliffs recall Bali's Ulu Watu – but an almost deserted Ulu Watu. It's easy to drive here from both the west and the north. From Kuta, it's under 90 minutes on a scooter.

Ekas itself is a sleepy little village, but head south into the peninsula and you'll soon make the sorts of jaw-dropping discoveries that will have you tweeting like mad. Start by driving all the way south (6.5km from Ekas) over the rough but passable road to **Pantai Dagong**. Here, you'll find an utterly empty and seemingly endless white beach backed by azure breakers.

Ask directions to **Heaven Beach** for another bit of sandy wonder. It's a stunning little pocket of white sand and surf about 4km from Ekas. Despite the omnipresent resort, you're free to access the shore: all Indonesian beaches are public.

Sleeping & Eating

There are posh boutique resorts hidden on the beautiful coves south of Ekas. Also look out for new and simple guesthouses along the rural roads.

Heaven on the Planet BOUTIQUE HOTEL **$$$**
(☎0812 375 1103; www.sanctuaryinlombok.com; per person all-inclusive US$160-225;) The aptly named Heaven on the Planet has five units scattered along a cliff's edge, from where you'll have spectacular bird's-eye views of the sea and swell lines. Heaven is primarily a surf resort (you can even surf at night here thanks to ocean spotlights) but kitesurfing, scuba diving and snorkelling are also possible.

West of Kuta

West of Kuta is a series of awesome beaches and ideal surf breaks. Developers are nosing around here, and land has changed hands, but for now it remains almost pristine and the region has a raw beauty. In anticipation of future developments, the road has been much improved and electrical wires strung. It meanders inland, skirting tobacco, sweet potato and rice fields in between turn-offs to the sand and glimpses of the gorgeous coast.

Mawan

How's this for a vision of sandy paradise? Just 600m off the main road (9km from Kuta), this half-moon cove is framed by soaring headlands with azure water and a swathe of empty sand (save a fishing village of a dozen thatched homes). It's a terrific swimming beach. There's paved parking (car/motorbike 10,000/5000Rp) and some modest cafes.

Mawi

Some 16km west of Kuta, look for a small road down to Mawi. This is a surf paradise: a stunning scene, with legendary barrels and several beaches scattered around the great bay. Watch out for the strong rip tide. There's parking (car/motorbike 10,000/5000Rp) and vendors.

> **LOMBOK & SUMBAWA DURING RAMADAN**
>
> Ramadan, the month of fasting, is the ninth month of the Muslim calendar. During daylight hours, many restaurants are closed in Mataram and in conservative east and south Lombok (excepting Kuta and the coast). The same goes for all of the next island east, Sumbawa. At this time, foreigners eating, drinking (especially alcohol) and smoking in public may attract a negative reaction in these areas.

Selong Blanak

West of Mawi, and just when you think you've seen the most beautiful beaches Kuta has to offer, you reach Selong Blanak. Behold the wide, sugar-white beach with water streaked a thousand shades of blue, ideal for swimming. You can rent surfboards (per day 100,000Rp) and arrange for a boat out to area breaks (three hours from 500,000Rp). The parking lot (car/motorbike 10,000/5000Rp) is just 400m off the main drag on a good road.

Sleeping & Eating

Sempiak Villas RESORT **$$$**
(☎0821 4430 3337; www.sempiakvillas.com; Selong Blanak; villas from 1,200,000Rp;) Tucked away on the cliffs, this fabulous boutique resort is one of the Kuta area's most upscale properties. The six villas are built into the hillside above the beach and feature antique wood; some have covered decks with stupendous views.

★**Laut Biru Bar & Restaurant** SEAFOOD **$$**
(☎0821 4430 3339; Selong Blanak; mains 40,000-80,000Rp; 8am-10pm;) On the beach, this light and airy haven is part of the cliffside Sempiak Villas but is open to all-comers. Breakfasts feature muesli and yogurt, banana pancakes and eggs on toast. Lunch and dinner have global influences, and include local and Thai dishes plus seafood. It's a beautiful place, and you can dine on the sand.

Blongas & Around

From **Pengantap**, the road climbs across a headland then descends to a superb bay; follow this around for 1km then look out for the turn-off west to **Blongas** – a steep and winding road with breathtaking scenery. Blongas is set on a secluded namesake bay that is positively beautiful.

Dive Zone (☎0812 3924 1560, 0819 0785 2073; www.divezone-lombok.com; Blongas Bay; 2 dives from US$100) focuses on the famed nearby dive sites **Magnet** and **Cathedrals**. Spotting conditions peak in mid-September when you may see schooling mobula rays in addition to hammerheads, which school around the pinnacle (a towering rock that breaks the surface of the ocean and is the heart of the dive sites) from June to November. It's not an easy dive, so you must be experienced and prepared for heavy current.

Labuhan Lombok

☎0376

Labuhan Lombok (also known as Labuhan Kayangan or Tanjung Kayangan) is the port for ferries and boats to Sumbawa. The town centre of Labuhan Lombok, 3km west of the ferry terminal, is a scruffy place but it does have great views of Gunung Rinjani.

Getting There & Away

BUS & BEMO

Regular buses and bemos buzz between Mandalika terminal in Mataram and Labuhan Lombok; the journey takes 2½ hours (35,000Rp). Some buses will only drop you off at the port entrance road from where you can catch another bemo to the ferry terminal. Don't walk – it's too far.

FERRY

Ferries run hourly, 24 hours a day, between Labuhan Lombok and Poto Tano, Sumbawa (passengers 19,000Rp, 1½ hours). Cars cost 466,000Rp, motorbikes 54,000Rp. Through buses to points east from Bali and Lombok include the ferry fare.

South of Labuhan Lombok

Selong, the capital of the east Lombok administrative district, has some dusty Dutch colonial buildings. The transport junction for the region is just to the west of Selong at **Pancor**, where you can catch bemos to most points south.

Tanjung Luar is one of Lombok's main fishing ports (and home to one of Indonesia's most egregious shark-finning operations) and has lots of Bugis-style houses on stilts. From here, the road swings west to **Keruak**, where wooden boats are built, and continues past the turn to **Sukaraja**, a traditional Sasak village where you can buy woodcarvings. Just west of Keruak a road leads south to **Jerowaru** and the spectacular southeastern peninsula. You'll need your own transport; be warned that it's easy to lose your way around here, but the main roads are good.

GILI ISLANDS

☎0370

Picture three miniscule desert islands, fringed by white-sand beaches and coconut palms, sitting in a turquoise sea: the Gilis are a vision of paradise. These islets have exploded in popularity, and are booming like nowhere else in Indonesia – speedboats now zip visitors direct from Bali and a hip new hotel opens practically every month.

It's not hard to understand the Gilis' unique appeal, for a serenity endures (no motorbikes or dogs!) and a green consciousness is growing. Development has been more tasteful than rapacious and there are few concrete eyesores.

Each island has its own special character. Trawangan (universally known as Gili T) is by far the most cosmopolitan, its bar and party scene vibrant, its accommodation and restaurants close to definitive tropical chic. Gili Air has the strongest local character, but also a perfect mix of buzz and languor. Gili Meno is simply a desert-island getaway, albeit one with some buzz.

Getting There & Away

FROM BALI

Fast boats advertise swift connections (about two hours) between Bali and Gili Trawangan. They leave from several departure points in Bali, including Benoa Harbour, Sanur, Padangbai and Amed. Some go via Nusa Lembongan. Many dock at Teluk Nare/Teluk Kade on Lombok north of Senggigi before continuing on to Air and Trawangan (you'll have to transfer for Meno).

The website **Gili Bookings** (www.gilibookings.com) presents a range of boat operators and prices in response to your booking request. It's useful for getting an idea of the services offered, but it is not comprehensive and you may get a better price by buying direct from the operator.

> **HOTEL TRANSPORT**
>
> Most hotels and many guesthouses will be happy to help you sort out your transportation options to and from the Gilis as part of your reservation. If you use an online booking website, contact the hotel directly afterwards. Some high-end resorts have their own boats for transporting guests.

Other considerations:

- Fares are not fixed; especially in quiet times, you should be able to get discounts on published fares.
- If you don't need transport to/from the boat, ask for a discount.
- The advertised times are illusionary. Boats are cancelled, unplanned stops are made or they simply run very late.
- Book ahead in July and August.
- The sea between Bali and Lombok can get very rough (particularly during rainy season).
- The fast boats are unregulated, and operating and safety standards vary widely. There have been some major accidents and boats have sunk.

Amed Sea Express (☎0878 6306 4799; www.gili-sea-express.com; per person from 600,000Rp) Makes 75-minute crossings to Amed on a large speedboat; this makes many interesting itineraries possible. Also serves Sanur.

Blue Water Express (☎0361-895 1111; www.bluewater-express.com; one-way from 750,000Rp) From Serangan and Padangbai (Bali), to Teluk Kade, Gili T and Gili Air.

Gili Cat (Map p329; ☎0361-271680; www.gilicat.com; adult/child 700,000/550,000Rp; ⊙Gili T office 9am-9pm) Well-established company linking Padangbai, Gili T and Teluk Kade.

Gili Getaway (Map p329; ☎0813 3707 4147; www.giligetaway.com; one-way from 675,000Rp; ⊙Gili T office 9am-8pm) Very professional; links Serangan on Bali with Gili T and Gili Air.

Perama (☎0361-750808; www.peramatour.com; per person 225,000Rp; ⊙Gili T office 9am-8pm) Links Padangbai, the Gilis and Senggigi by a not-so-fast boat.

Scoot (Map p329; www.scootcruise.com; one-way from 700,000Rp; ⊙Gili T office 9am-9pm) Boats link Sanur, Padangbai, Nusa Lembongan and the Gilis.

Semaya One (☎0361-877 8166; www.semayacruise.com; adult/child 650,000/550,000Rp) Network of services linking Sanur, Nusa Penida, Padangbai, Teluk Kade, Gili Air and Gili T.

FROM LOMBOK

Coming from Lombok, you can travel on one of the fast boats from Teluk Nare/Teluk Kade north of Senggigi. However most people use the public boats that leave from **Bangsal Harbour**.

Boat tickets at Bangsal Harbour are sold at the port's large ticket office which has posted prices, and which is where you can also charter a boat. Buy a ticket elsewhere and you're getting played.

Public boats run to all three islands before 11am, after that you may only find one to Gili T or Gili Air. Public boats in both directions leave when the boat is full – about 30 people. When no public boat is running to your Gili, you may have to charter a boat (400,000Rp to 500,000Rp, carries up to 25 people).

One-way fares are 10,000Rp to Gili Air, 12,000Rp to Gili Meno and 15,000Rp to Gili Trawangan. Boats often pull up on the beaches; be prepared to wade ashore. Public fast boats

Gili Islands

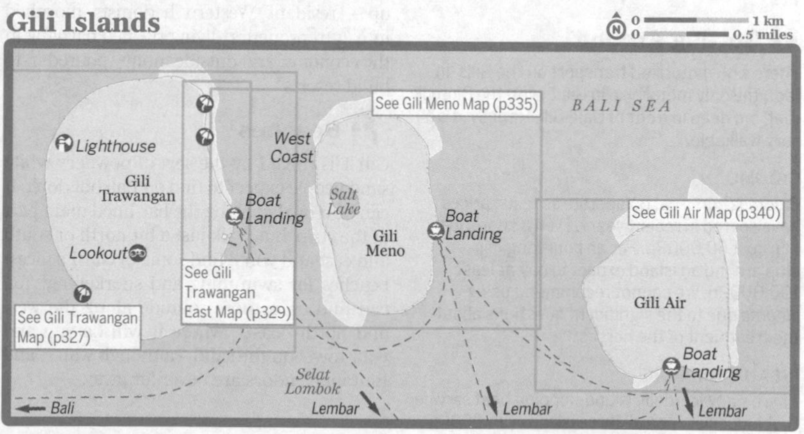

DON'T MISS

BEST OF THE GILI ISLANDS

- Snorkelling with hawksbill and green turtles off **Gili Meno** (p335).
- Dancing all night at one of **Gili Trawangan's** (p334) (in)famous parties.
- Finding serenity on **Gili Meno's** (p334) west coast.
- Learning to freedive on **Gili T** (p328).
- Spending a day walking around **Gili Air** (p338), pausing endlessly for swims and refreshments.
- Diving with reef sharks at **Shark Point** (p336).

also link Gili T, Gili Air and Bangsal; they run several times a day and cost 100,000Rp.

Although it had a bad reputation for years, Bangsal Harbour hassles are much reduced. Still, avoid touts and note that anyone who helps you with bags deserves a tip (10,000Rp per bag is appropriate). There are ATMs.

Coming by public transport via Mataram and Senggigi, catch a bus or bemo to Pemenang, from where it's a 1.2km walk (5000Rp by *ojek*) to Bangsal Harbour. A metered taxi to the port will take you to the harbour. From Senggigi, Perama offers a bus and boat connection to the Gilis for a reasonable 150,000Rp (two hours).

Arriving in Bangsal, you'll be offered rides in shared vehicles at the port. To Senggigi, 100,000Rp is a fair price. Otherwise, walk 500m down the access road past the huge new tsunami shelter to the Blue Bird Lombok Taksi stand (always the best taxi choice) for metered rides to Senggigi (90,000Rp), the airport (200,000Rp) and Kuta (300,000Rp).

Getting Around

There's no motorised transport on the Gilis. In fact, the only motorbike in Gili T is on the Biorock reef, 5m deep in front of Cafe Gili. Happily, it's all very walkable.

CIDOMO

Cidomo (horse carts) operate as taxis; prices have soared in recent years. Even a short ride can cost 50,000Rp. For an hour-long clip-clop around an island expect to pay at least 100,000Rp. We cannot recommend using *cidomo* due to the significant questions about the treatment of the horses.

ISLAND-HOPPING

There's a twice-daily island-hopping boat service that loops between all three islands (35,000Rp to 40,000Rp), so you can sample another Gili's pleasures for the day – although you can't hit all three in one day by public boat. Check the latest timetable at the islands' docks. You can also always charter boats between the islands (400,000Rp to 450,000Rp).

Gili Trawangan

Gili Trawangan is a paradise of global repute, ranking alongside Bali and Borobudur as one of Indonesia's top destinations. Trawangan's heaving main drag, busy with bikes, horse carts and mobs of scantily clad visitors, can surprise those expecting some languid tropical retreat. Instead, a wall-to-wall roster of lounge bars, hip guesthouses, ambitious restaurants, minimarts and dive schools clamour for attention.

And yet behind this glitzy facade, a bohemian character endures, with rickety warungs and reggae joints surviving between the cocktail tables, and quiet retreats dotting the much-less-busy north coast. Even as massive 200-room-plus hotels begin to colonise the still mostly wild and ragged west coast, you can head just inland to a village laced with sandy lanes roamed by free-range roosters, kibbutzing *ibu* (mothers) and wild-haired kids playing hopscotch. Here the call of the *muezzin,* not happy hour, defines the time of day.

Settled just over 50 years ago (by Bugis fishers from Sulawesi), Gili T was discovered by travellers in the 1980s, seduced by the white-sand beaches and coral reefs. By the 1990s Trawangan had mutated into a kind of tropical Ibiza, a stoney idyll where you could rave away from the eyes of the Indonesian police. And then the island began to grow up – resident Western hedonists morphed into entrepreneurs, diving rivalled partying in the economy, and outside money poured in to build resorts.

Beaches

Gili T is ringed by the sort of powdery white sand people expect to find on Bali but don't. It can be crowded along the bar-lined main part of the strip, but walk just a bit north or south and east and you'll find some of Gili T's nicest beaches for swimming and snorkelling. You can find even more solitude along the west and north coasts, where it will be you and your towel on the sand – although water- and Bintang-vendors are never far away.

Gili Trawangan

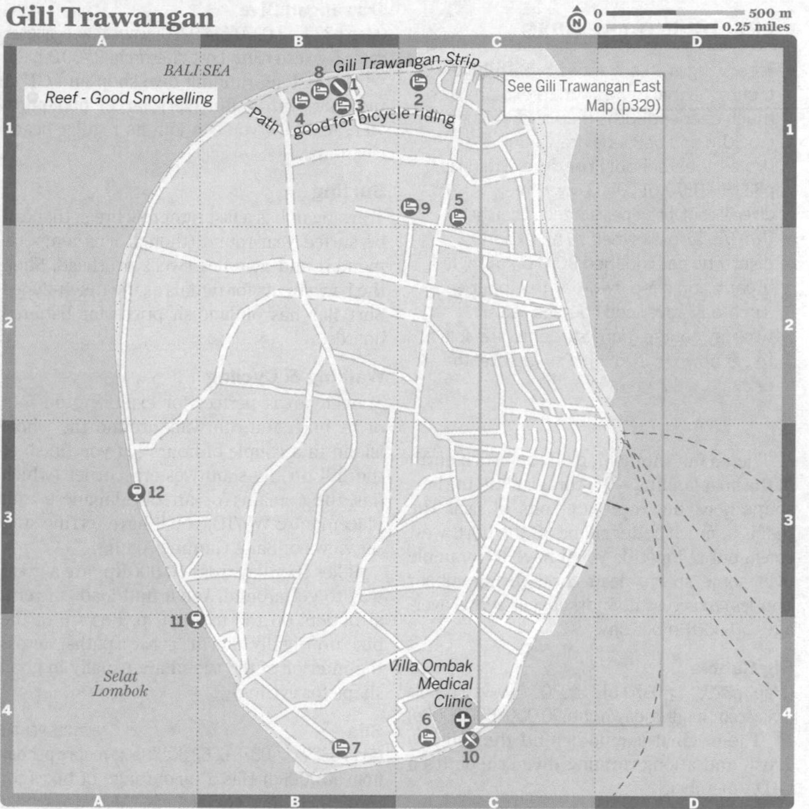

Gili Trawangan

Activities, Courses & Tours

1 Lutwala Dive B1

Sleeping

2 Alam Gili C1
3 Eden Cottages B1
4 Gili Eco Villas B1
5 Indigo Bungalows C1
6 Kokomo C4
7 Pondok Santi B4
8 Wilson's Retreat B1
9 Woodstock C1

Eating

10 Pearl Beach Lounge C4

Drinking & Nightlife

11 Exile A4
12 Vintage Sunset Beach A3

Note that at low tide large portions of the west and north coasts have rocks and coral near the surface, which makes trying to get off the shore deeply unpleasant. And the beach has eroded to oblivion on the northeast corner.

Many people simply enjoy the sensational views of Lombok and Gunung Rinjani, and of Bali and Gunung Agung.

Activities

Almost everything to do on Gili T will involve the water at some point.

Diving & Snorkelling

Trawangan is a diving polestar, with over a dozen professional scuba schools and one of Asia's only freediving schools. Most dive schools and shops have good accommodation for clients who want to book a package.

FREEDIVING THE GILIS

Freediving is an advanced breath-hold technique that allows you to explore much deeper depths than snorkelling (to 30m and beyond). Trawangan's professional school **Freedive Gili** (Map p329; ☎0370-614 0503; www.freedivegili.com; beginner/advanced courses US$275/375) is owned by an expert diver who has touched 90m on a single breath, and offers two-day beginner and three-day advanced courses. After a two-day course many students are able to get down to 20m on a single breath of air.

There's fun snorkelling off the beach north of the boat landing – the coral isn't in the best shape here, but there are tons of fish. The reef is in much better shape off the northwest coast, but at low tide you'll have to scramble over some sharp, dead coral (bring rubber booties) to access it. Snorkel gear rental averages 50,000Rp per day.

Big Bubble DIVING
(Map p329; ☎0370-612 5020; www.bigbubblediving.com; fun dives day/night 490,000/600,000Rp) The original engine behind the Gili Eco Trust, and a long-running dive school. It's a GIDA member.

Blue Marlin Dive Centre DIVING
(Map p329; ☎0370-613 2424; www.bluemarlindive.com; 10-dive nitrox package 5,100,000Rp) Gili T's original dive shop, and one of the best tech diving schools in the world. It's a GIDA member *and* home to one Gili T's classic bars.

★**Lutwala Dive** DIVING
(Map p327; ☎0877 65492615; www.lutwala.com; divemaster courses 14,000,000Rp) A nitrox and five-star PADI centre owned by Fern Perry, who held the women's world-record for deepest open-circuit dive (190m). A GIDA member, it also rents top-quality snorkelling gear.

Manta Dive DIVING
(Map p329; ☎0370-614 3649; www.manta-dive.com; open-water courses 5,500,000Rp) The biggest and still one of the best dive schools on the island. It has a large compound that spans the main road and a pool. It is a GIDA member and has special kids programs.

Trawangan Dive DIVING
(Map p329; ☎0370-614 9220; www.trawangandive.com; 5 guided nitrox boat dives from 2,700,000Rp) A top, long-running dive shop and GIDA member with a fun (very large) pool-party vibe. Ask how you can join its regular beach clean-ups.

Surfing

Trawangan has a fast right reef break that can be surfed year-round (though it is temperamental) and at times swells overhead. Shop the backstreets for rentals as the much-hyped Surf Bar has outlandish prices for battered boards.

Walking & Cycling

Trawangan is perfect for exploring on foot or by bike. You can walk around the whole island in a couple of hours – if you finish at the hill on the southwestern corner (which has the remains of an old Japanese gun placement c WWII), you'll have terrific sunset views of Bali's Gunung Agung.

Bikes (per day from 50,000Rp) are a great way to get around. You'll find loads of rental outlets on the main strip. Beware of the bike-unfriendly north coast; paths across the interior of the island are usually in good shape for cycling.

Sila BICYCLE RENTAL
(Map p329; ☎0878 6562 3015; bike rentals per day from 50,000Rp) Has a huge range of bikes for rent, including two-seaters. Also does boat trips.

Yoga & Wellness

Gili Yoga YOGA
(Map p329; ☎0370-614 0503; www.giliyoga.com; per person from 100,000Rp) Runs daily vinyasa classes, and is part of Freedive Gili.

Xqisit Spa SPA
(Map p329; ☎0370-612 9405; www.exqisit.com; 1hr massages from 180,000Rp; ⏲10am-10pm) A day spa on the waterfront with curtained-off treatment rooms for massage, and leather seats for mani-pedi or reflexology. Also has a coffee bar. The long list of services includes shiatsu and an 'extreme hangover recovery' massage treatment (700,000Rp) – talk about tapping into market demand.

Courses

Gili Cooking Classes COOKING COURSE
(Map p329; ☎087763241215; www.gilicookingclasses.com; classes from 275,000Rp; ⏲11.30am, 4pm, 8pm) This slick operation has a large

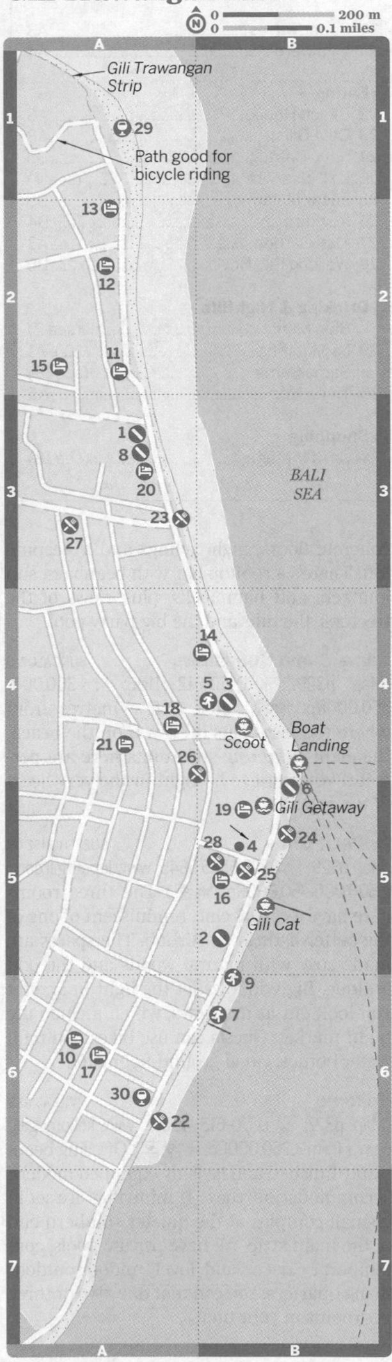

kitchen for classes right on the strip. You have a range of options for what you'll learn to cook – choose wisely as you'll be eating your work.

Sleeping

Gili T has over 5000 rooms and more than 200 places to stay, ranging from thatched huts to sleek, air-conditioned villas with private pools. Yet, in peak season the entire island is often booked; reserve your room well ahead to arrive with a relaxed attitude.

Many places are owned by local families with little or no experience of running hotels. Virtually all dive schools offer really good midrange accommodation, which may come with price breaks on diving packages. The cheapest digs are in the village, where the mosque is everyone's alarm clock. Head to the north or west coasts to escape the crowds.

The high-season rates quoted can drop a bit off-peak, but Gili T's popularity means that rates are mostly zooming upwards.

Village

Pondok Gili Gecko GUESTHOUSE $

(Map p329; ☎0818 0573 2814; r from 250,000Rp;) An inviting guesthouse with a charming gecko motif. The four rooms are super-clean, and have ceiling fans and private tiled patios overlooking the garden.

★Indigo Bungalows GUESTHOUSE $$

(Map p327; ☎0818 0371 0909; www.facebook.com/IndigoGiliT; r from 550,000Rp;) In the crowded Gili T midrange market, Indigo stands out for its attention to detail. The four rooms have hot water, patios and views of the pool or gardens. It's got a nice, quiet compound feel.

★Woodstock BUNGALOW $$

(Map p327; ☎0821 4765 5877; www.woodstockgili.com; r from 540,000-600,000Rp;) The hippest spot on Trawangan. Commune with the spirit of the Dead, Baez and Hendrix in 12 pristine rooms with tribal accents, private porches and outdoor baths, which surround a laid-back pool area.

Alexyane Paradise BUNGALOW $$

(Map p329; ☎0878 6599 9645; r from 400,000Rp;) Five great-quality dark-wood cottages with high ceilings, bamboo beds, and lovely light-flooded outdoor baths sprouting foliage.

Gili Trawangan East

Activities, Courses & Tours
1 Big Bubble ... A3
2 Blue Marlin Dive Centre ... B5
3 Freedive Gili ... B4
4 Gili Cooking Classes ... B5
5 Gili Yoga ... B4
6 Manta Dive ... B5
7 Sila ... B6
8 Trawangan Dive ... A3
9 Xqisit Spa ... B6

Sleeping
10 Alexyane Paradise ... A6
11 Balé Sampan ... A2
12 Blu da Mare ... A2
13 Danima Resort ... A2
14 Gili Hostel ... B4
15 Gili Joglo ... A2
16 Le Petit Gili ... B5
17 Oceane Paradise ... A6
18 Pondok Gili Gecko ... A4
19 Sama Sama Bungalows ... B5
20 Soundwaves ... A3
21 Villa Nero ... A4

Eating
22 Beach House ... A6
23 Cafe Gili ... A3
24 Kayu Café ... B5
La Dolce Vita ... (see 4)
25 Pasar Malam ... B5
26 Regina ... B4
27 Thai Garden ... A3
28 Warung Kiki Novi ... B5

Drinking & Nightlife
Blue Marlin ... (see 2)
29 La Moomba ... A1
Sama Sama ... (see 19)
30 Tir na Nog ... A6

Shopping
Casa Vintage ... (see 18)

Oceane Paradise COTTAGE $$
(Map p329; ☎0812 3779 3533; r from 500,000Rp; ❄📶) A terrific compound of nine wooden cottages with stylish outdoor bathrooms.

★Villa Nero VILLA $$$
(Map p329; ☎0819 0904 8000; www.thevillanero.com; villas from US$250; ❄📶🏊) One of the best-run and most luxurious places to stay on Gili T. Each of the 10 large units has multiple rooms and a large lounging patio. The scheme is refreshingly minimalist, with accents of art and green plants. Among the many amenities: free bike use.

Gili Joglo VILLA $$$
(Map p329; ☎0813 5678 4741; www.gilijoglo.com; villas from 1,400,000Rp; ❄📶) Three fabulous villas. One is crafted out of an antique *joglo* (traditional Javanese house) with polished concrete floors, two bedrooms and a massive indoor-outdoor great room. Though slightly smaller, we prefer the one built from two 1950s *gladaks* (middle-class homes). Rooms come with butler service.

Main Strip

★Gili Hostel HOSTEL $
(Map p329; ☎0877 6526 7037; www.gilihostel.com; dm from 175,000Rp; ❄📶🏊) This co-ed dorm complex has a shaggy Torajan-style roof. The seven rooms each sleep seven, and have concrete floors, high ceilings and a sleeping loft. There's a rooftop bar with beanbags, sun loungers and hammocks, plus views of the treetops, the hills and the big party pool.

Sama Sama Bungalows BUNGALOW $
(Map p329; ☎0370-612 1106; r 300,000-550,000Rp; ❄📶) Just a few metres from where the fast boats drop you on the beach, the eight *lumbung*-style units here are perfect if you want to be right in the very heart of the action.

Le Petit Gili GUESTHOUSE $$
(Map p329; ☎0878 6585 5545; www.lepetitgili.com; r 500,000-750,000Rp; ❄📶) The three rooms here have a casual chic, reminiscent of one of the better listings on Airbnb. The spaces are made cosy with natural woods and the odd antique. Big windows let the light in and let you look out at the views, which include the night market. Guests can use bikes and refill water bottles. Good ground-floor cafe.

Kokomo VILLAS $$$
(Map p327; ☎0370-613 4920; www.kokomogilit.com; r from 3,250,000Rp; ❄📶🏊) Offering beautifully finished and lavishly equipped modern accommodation, these 11 minivillas are set in a small complex at the quieter southern end of the main strip. All have private pools, contemporary decor and lovely indoor-outdoor living quarters. You can rent one, two or three bedrooms in your unit.

Beachside

Blu da Mare BUNGALOW $$
(Map p329; ☎0858 8866 2490; www.bludamare.it; r from 900,000Rp; ❄📶) At Blu da Mare you can bed down in one of five lovely, antique *joglo* from 1920s Java. Features include gorgeous old wood floors, queen beds, and freshwater showers in a sunken bath. It has a fine, Euro-accented cafe.

Balé Sampan HOTEL $$
(Map p329; ☎0812 3702 4048; www.balesampanbungalows.com; r garden/pool US$88/94; ❄📶🏊) On a nice wide-open stretch of beach. The 14 fine modern-edge rooms have Yogja stone baths and plush duvet covers. Other highlights include a freshwater pool and a proper English breakfast.

Soundwaves BUNGALOW $$
(Map p329; ☎0819 3673 2404; www.soundwavesresort.com; r 400,000-700,000Rp; ❄📶) The 13 rooms here are simple and clean with tiled floors. Some are set in wooden A-frames, others in a two-storey concrete building with staggered and recessed patios offering beach views from each room. Some rooms are fan-only.

North, South & West Coasts

★**Eden Cottages** COTTAGE $$
(Map p327; ☎0819 1799 6151; www.edencottages.com; cottages 550,000-850,000Rp; ❄🏊) Six clean, thatched concrete bungalows wrapped around a pool, fringed by a garden and shaded by a coconut grove. Rooms have tasteful furnishings, stone baths, TV-DVD and fresh cold-water showers. The owner avoids wi-fi, which only increases the serenity.

Alam Gili HOTEL $$
(Map p327; ☎0370-613 0466; www.alamgili.com; r US$65-125; ❄📶🏊) A lush mature garden and a quiet beach location are the main

GREEN GILI

When you pay your hotel or diving bill on the Gilis you may be offered the chance to pay an 'Eco Tax' (50,000Rp per person). It's a voluntary donation, set up by the pioneering **Gili Eco Trust** (www.giliecotrust.com) to improve the island's environment.

It's a worthy cause. The environmental pressure on the Gilis as their popularity has grown is enormous. Intensive development and rubbish plus offshore reef damage from fishers using cyanide and dynamite to harvest fish have been just some of the problems. Up to 10,000 visitors and workers arrive on the islands each day.

Eco Trust has several initiatives to help:

➡ Distributing free reusable shopping bags to cut down on plastic-bag use, and encouraging restaurants to stop using plastic straws.

➡ An aggressive education campaign to get locals and business owners to recycle their rubbish. There are now over 1000 recycling bins on the islands.

➡ A long-term scheme to recycle virtually all the rubbish on the islands. Ground was broken for a sorting centre on Gili T in 2015.

➡ Care of the islands' horses – vet clinics are offered and there are driver education programs in horse care.

➡ Biorock, a reef restoration program that now has over 120 installations around the islands.

There are many ways visitors to the Gilis can help, besides just paying the Eco Tax:

Clean up the beach Eco Trust and Trawangan Dive both organise weekly beach clean-ups and more hands are always needed. Admire the white sand and azure waters as you do your own freelance beach clean-up. Toss anything you find in a recycling bin.

Report horse mistreatment Anyone seeing a *cidomo* driver mistreating a horse can get the number of the cart and report it to Eco Trust (☎0370-625020 or ☎0813 3960 0553), which will follow up with the driver. Unfortunately, many transport carts with their heavy loads of construction supplies and Bintang have no cart numbers for reporting.

Build a reef For US$600 you'll get two dives a day for two weeks and can help build a Biorock installation. Eco Trust has details.

CULTURAL RESPECT

As almost all locals on the Gilis Islands are Muslim; visitors should keep these cultural considerations in mind:

➡ It's not at all acceptable to wander the village lanes in a bikini, no matter how many others you see doing so. Cover up away from the beach or hotel pool.

➡ Nude or topless sunbathing anywhere is offensive.

➡ During the month of Ramadan many locals fast during daylight hours and there are no all-night parties on Gili Trawangan.

draws here. The nine rooms and villas in a small compound boast elegant lashings of old-school Balinese style. There's a small pool and a cafe on the beach.

★Wilson's Retreat RESORT **$$$**
(Map p327; 0370-612 0060; www.wilsons-retreat.com; r from 1,750,000Rp;) A fine new addition to the north shore, Wilson's has 20 rooms plus four villas with private pools. Even though the setting is expansive and classy, it still manages some Gili languor. The excellent cafe overlooks a fine stretch of beach.

Gili Eco Villas VILLA **$$$**
(Map p327; 0361-847 6419; www.giliecovillas.com; r/villas from US$150/190;) Nineteen classy rooms and villas, made from recycled teak salvaged from old Javanese colonial buildings, are set back from the beach on Trawangan's idyllic north coast. Comfort and style are combined with solid green principles (water is recycled, there's an organic vegetable garden, and solar and wind energy provide most of the power).

Pondok Santi RESORT **$$$**
(Map p327; 0370-714 0711; www.pondoksanti.com; r from US$300;) Six gorgeous bungalows are set well apart on this old coconut plantation. Lawns now cover the grounds, and this is easily the classiest-looking resort on Gili T. The units have outdoor showers and rich, traditional wood decor. It's on a great beach and *just* close enough to the strip.

Danima Resort GUESTHOUSE **$$$**
(Map p329; 0878 6087 2506; www.giliresortdanima.com; r from 1,600,000Rp;) An intimate four-room boutique property. Nests are blessed with floating beds, vaulted ceilings, tasteful lighting, rattan deck seating and rain showers. It has a romantic pool and beach area, too.

Eating

In the evenings, numerous places on the main strip display and grill delicious fresh seafood. There's not much to distinguish them – pick by what looks good and how much chilli and garlic you like in your marinade.

Elsewhere on the strip, you'll find timeless beach bars with lots of Indo standards, which you can enjoy with a cold Bintang and your feet in the sand. There's also a growing number of high-concept cafes.

★Pasar Malam MARKET **$**
(Night Market; Map p329; mains 15,000-30,000Rp; 6pm-midnight) Blooming every evening in front of Gili T's market, this night market is the place to indulge in ample local eats, including tangy noodle soup, savoury fried treats, scrumptious *ayam goreng* (fried chicken) and grilled fresh catch. Just wandering around the stalls (we like Green Cafe) looking at all the dishes vying for your attention will get you drooling. Seating is at long tables.

La Dolce Vita ITALIAN **$**
(Map p329; mains 20,000-40,000Rp; 7.30am-5pm Tue-Sun;) There comes that moment when another nasi goreng will just make you turn nasty. Don't delay, hop right on over to this little cafe that's not much bigger than one of its excellent espressos. Slices of authentic pizza and a whole range of pastries are joined by daily specials to sate the ravenous.

Warung Kiki Novi INDONESIAN **$**
(Map p329; mains from 15,000Rp; 8am-10pm) Long-time islanders will tell you that this is the best place for *nasi campur* (rice with a choice of side dishes) in the Gilis, and they are right; this cheery dining room is the scene of budget-dining nirvana. Besides fine Indo mains there's a smattering of Western sandwiches and salads.

★Kayu Café CAFE **$$**
(Map p329; 0878 6239 1308; mains 40,000-80,000Rp; 8am-10pm;) There are two options here: the main cafe on the inland side of the strip has a lovely array of healthy baked goods, salads, sandwiches and the island's best juices, all served in air-con comfort.

Across the road the beach cafe is all open-air and exposed wood. Service on the sand can be slow – head inside to order.

Regina PIZZA $$
(Map p329; ☎0877 6506 6255; mains 40,000-100,000Rp; ⏰5-11pm) The wood-fired oven rarely gets a break at this excellent Italian joint, just inland. At busy times there's a long line for takeaway pizzas, but a better option is to find a bamboo table in the garden and have some cold ones with the fine thin-crust pies. A sign announces: 'no pizza pineapple'. Ahh, the sound of authenticity...

Thai Garden THAI $$
(Map p329; ☎0878 6453 1253; mains 50,000-120,000Rp; ⏰3-10pm) Who needs Bangkok when you have Gili T? The most authentic Thai food this side of Phuket is served up in a cute little garden. The flavours are spot on thanks to regular deliveries of key spices. Here's the place to beat the Indo rice blues.

Cafe Gili INTERNATIONAL $$
(Map p329; mains 35,000-70,000Rp; ⏰8am-10pm; 📶) Think: cushioned beachside seating, candlelight, and some cool and housey music playing. The kitchen spills from a shabby-chic whitewashed dining room and rambles across the street to the shore. The menu meanders from eggs Florentine and breakfast baguettes, to deli sandwiches and salads, to decent pasta and seafood dishes.

Pearl Beach Lounge INTERNATIONAL $$
(Map p327; ☎0370-613 7788; www.pearlbeachlounge.com; mains 60,000-180,000Rp; ⏰8am-11pm; 📶) The bamboo flows only a little less fluidly than the beer at this high-concept beachside lounge and restaurant. During the day, spending 100,000Rp on food and drink from the burger-filled menu gets you access to a pool and comfy beach loungers. At night the striking bamboo main pavilion comes alive, and more complex steak and seafood mains are on offer.

Beach House INTERNATIONAL $$
(Map p329; ☎0370-614 2352; www.beachhousegilit.com; mains 75,000-250,000Rp; ⏰11am-10pm; 📶) Boasts an elegant marina terrace, a wonderful nightly barbecue, a salad bar and fine wine. Among much competition, it's a contender for the best barbecued seafood around and is always popular. Book ahead.

Drinking & Nightlife

The island has oodles of beachside drinking dens, ranging from sleek lounge bars to simple shacks. Parties are held several nights a week, shifting between mainstay bars such as Tir na Nog and Rudy's Pub, and various other upstarts. The strip south of the Pasar Malam is the centre for raucous nightlife.

★**La Moomba** BAR
(Map p329; ⏰10am-midnight) If you wish to chill on a luscious white beach, with bamboo

DANGERS & ANNOYANCES ON THE GILIS

➡ Although it's rare, some foreign women have experienced sexual harassment and even assault while on the Gilis – it's best not to walk home alone to the quieter parts of the islands.

➡ As tranquil as these seas appear, currents are strong in the channels between the islands. Do not try to swim between Gili islands as it can be deadly.

➡ The drug trade remains endemic in Trawangan. You'll get offers of mushrooms, meth and other drugs. But remember, Indonesia has a strong antidrugs policy; those found in possession of or taking drugs risk jail or worse.

➡ Tourists have been injured and killed by adulterated *arak* (colourless, distilled palm wine) on the Gilis; skip it.

➡ Bike riders (almost entirely tourists) regularly plough into and injure people on Gili T's main drag. *Cidomo* hauling construction goods are almost as bad.

➡ There are seldom police on any of the Gilis (though this is changing). Report thefts to the island *kepala desa* (village head) immediately, who will deal with the issue; staff at the dive schools will direct you to him.

➡ For trouble on Gili Trawangan, contact Satgas, the community organisation that runs island affairs, via your hotel or dive centre. Satgas tries to resolve problems and track down stolen property.

lounges and reggae pumping from the tiki bar, head to La Moomba, Trawangan's best beach bar.

Vintage Sunset Beach BAR
(Map p327; ⏲11am-10pm) The kind of sunset bar that you won't want to leave after the sun has set. While strains of Billie Holiday add mellifluous accents to the lapping surf, enjoy excellent Jamaican food (the spicy chicken, yum!; mains from 60,000Rp). Or just let the sand caress your toes as you hang low in a hammock.

Tir na Nog PUB
(Map p329; ☎0370-613 9463; ⏲7am-2am Thu-Tue, to 4am Wed; 📶) Known simply as 'The Irish', this hanger of hangovers has a sports-bar interior with big screens. Enjoy tasty chow such as kebabs (mains 35,000Rp to 80,000Rp). Its shoreside open-air bar is probably the busiest meeting spot on the island. Jovial mayhem reigns on Wednesday nights when the DJ takes over.

Blue Marlin BAR
(Map p329; ⏲8am–very late) Of all the party bars, this upper-level venue has the largest dance floor and the meanest sound system – it pumps trance and tribal beats on Mondays.

Sama Sama BAR
(Map p329; ⏲hours vary) An overly decorated reggae bar–slash–roadhouse with a top-end sound system, a killer live band (playing the same set list) at least six nights a week, and a beer garden on the beach.

Exile BAR
(Map p327; ☎0819 0772 1858; ⏲noon-late; @) This beach bar has a party vibe at all hours. It's Indonesian owned and 20 minutes from the main strip on foot, or an easy bike ride. There is also a compound of 10 woven bamboo bungalows with rooms from 450,000Rp here, just in case home seems too far.

Shopping

Gili Trawangan was once the domain of cheap knick-knack stalls and not much else, but a stream of refinement is rapidly taking root. Outlets of Bali boutiques are popping up along the main strip near the Pasar Malam.

★Casa Vintage CLOTHING
(Map p329; ⏲9am-9pm) The best boutique on Gili T is tucked on a backstreet near Il Pirata. It's a treasure trove of vintage fashion sourced internationally, and displayed with grace. Browse chunky earrings, superb leather hand- and shoulderbags, baby-doll dresses, and John Lennon shades.

Information

EMERGENCY

There's a few very basic health clinics around, including **Vila Ombak Medical Clinic** (Map p327; ⏲24hr). For security issues contact **Satgas**, a community organisation, via your hotel or dive shop.

INTERNET & TELEPHONE

Wi-fi is common. There is 3G data service.

MONEY

Gili T has abundant ATMs on the main strip and even on the west coast.

Getting There & Away

You can buy tickets and catch public and island-hopping boats at the **boat landing** (Map p329). While you wait for your ship to sail, note the amazing amount of Bintang bottles arriving full and leaving empty. Several of the fast-boat companies have offices (p325) on Gili T.

Gili Meno

Gili Meno is the smallest of the three islands and a good setting for your desert-island fantasy. Meno has a certain Robinson Crusoe charm, although new resorts under construction will mean Crusoe will want to don some Ray-Bans.

Most accommodation is strung out along the east coast, near the most picturesque beach. Inland you'll find scattered homesteads, coconut plantations and a salty lake. The once lonely west coast is seeing some high-profile development, including an enormous beachside condo project called Bask (www.baskgilimeno.com) that is slated to have over 130 rooms when it opens in 2017. It's got some powerful Australian backers and a high-profile pitchman, ex-*Baywatch* star David Hasselhoff (aka 'The Hoff'). The effect of this huge resort on little Gili Meno is likely to be profound.

Beaches

Ringed by sand, Gili Meno has one of the best strips of beach in the Gilis at its southeast corner. The sand is wide and powdery white, while the swimming is excellent. The west coast is rockier with crushed coral, and a lot of rocks and coral near the surface at low tide.

Gili Meno

Gili Meno

Sights
1 Turtle Sanctuary C3

Activities, Courses & Tours
2 Blue Marlin Dive Centre C2
3 Divine Divers B1
4 Gili Meno Divers C3
5 Mao Meno C3

Sleeping
6 Ana Bungalow C1
7 Gili Meno Eco Hostel C1
8 Jepun Bungalows C2
9 Kebun Kupu Kupu B2
10 Mallias Bungalows C3
11 Seri Resort C1
12 Tao Kombo C3

Eating
13 Sasak Cafe B2
14 Webe Café B1
15 Ya Ya Warung C2

Drinking & Nightlife
16 Diana Café B2

Shopping
17 Art Shop Botol C3

Meno's northeast also has nice sand, although erosion is a problem in parts. It takes around two hours to circumnavigate Meno on foot.

Sights

Unique to Gili Meno, the large inland salt lake is home to imposing white egrets, which make it an intriguing natural attraction.

Turtle Sanctuary TURTLE HATCHERY

(Map p335; www.gilimenoturtles.com; donations accepted; ⏲office 9am-6pm) Meno's turtle sanctuary consists of an assortment of little pools and bathtubs on the beach, bubbling with filters and teeming with baby green and loggerhead turtles. They're nurtured here until they're around eight months old, and then released. The impact of the hatchery on turtle populations has been considerable. With a simple snorkel you're all but guaranteed a sighting. Try to attend one of the regular releases.

Activities

Like the other Gilis, most of the fun here involves getting wet. **Walking** around the island is scenic and takes less than two hours.

Although you can rent **bikes** for 50,000Rp per day, you won't get far. The beach path

DIVING THE GILIS

The Gili Islands are a superb dive destination as the marine life is plentiful and varied. Turtles and black- and white-tip reef sharks are common, and the macro life (small stuff) is excellent, with seahorses, pipefish and lots of crustaceans. Around the full moon, large schools of bumphead parrotfish appear to feast on coral spawn; at other times of year manta rays cruise past dive sites.

Though years of bomb fishing and an El Niño–induced bleaching damaged corals above 18m, the reefs are now well into a profound recovery and haven't looked this great in years. The Gilis also have their share of virgin coral.

Safety standards are reasonably high on the Gilis, but with the proliferation of new dive schools, several have formed the Gili Island Dive Association (GIDA), which comes together for monthly meetings on conservation and dive impact issues, and all mind a written list of standards that considers the safety of their divers, a limitation on number of divers per day, and preservation of the sites to be paramount concerns, which is why we highly recommend diving with GIDA-associated shops (identifiable by a logo). All GIDA shops carry oxygen on their boats and have working radios. They also have a price agreement for fun dives, training and certification. Sample prices:

- Introductory dives – 900,000Rp
- Open Water Diver course – 5,500,000Rp
- Rescue Diver course – 5,500,000Rp

Some of the best dive sites include the following:

Deep Halik A canyonlike site ideally suited to drift diving. Black- and white-tip sharks are often seen at 28m to 30m.

Deep Turbo At around 30m, this site is ideally suited to nitrox diving. It has impressive sea fans and leopard sharks hidden in the crevasses.

Mirko's Reef Named for a beloved dive instructor who passed away, this canyon was never bombed and has vibrant, pristine soft and table coral formations.

Japanese Wreck For experienced divers only (it lies at 45m), this shipwreck of a Japanese patrol boat (c WWII) is ideal for tech divers.

Shark Point Perhaps the most exhilarating Gili dive: reef sharks and turtles are very regularly encountered, and there are schools of bumphead parrotfish and mantas.

Sunset (Manta Point) Some impressive table coral; sharks and large pelagics are frequently encountered.

from the southern tip right round up the west coast to the top of the salt lake is a shadeless dry-sand path that will have you walking your wheels. You can go for a little jaunt to the northwest coast on the good path along the north side of the lake, but again soft sand along the very north will stymie riding further.

Diving & Snorkelling

Snorkelling is good off the northeast coast; on the west coast towards the north; and also around the site of the vast new Bask hotel on the west coast (which claims it will install an underwater sculpture garden, no idea if the Hoff – or Pamela Anderson for that matter – will be depicted).

Gear is available from 40,000Rp per day.

Blue Marlin Dive Centre DIVING
(Map p335; ☎0370-639980; www.bluemarlindive.com; guided boat dives 490,000Rp) The Meno shingle of the Trawangan original. There are rooms here, too.

Divine Divers DIVING
(Map p335; ☎0852 4057 0777; www.divinedivers.com; guided dives from 500,000Rp) This Meno-only dive shop is on a sweet slice of beach on the west coast. It has rooms and offers some good dive/stay packages.

Gili Meno Divers DIVING
(Map p335; ☎0878 6536 7551; www.giliairdivers.com; Kontiki Cottages; introductory dives from 900,000Rp; ⏰9am-5pm) French and Indonesian owned; offers a range of courses including some good ones in underwater photography.

Yoga

Mao Meno YOGA

(Map p335; ☎0819 9937 8359; www.mao-meno.com; classes from US$9) Offers daily classes in styles that include ashtanga and vinyasa. It has simple cottages in its inland compound that rent from US$45 per night.

Sleeping

As you can see with all the west-coast development, Meno is not immune from Gili growth. New properties are also appearing in the north – some of them rather posh. But you can still find a simple beachfront retreat.

★Gili Meno Eco Hostel HOSTEL $

(Map p335; ☎0878 6249 2062; gilimenoecohostel.com; dm/r from 90,000/200,000Rp;) A fantasy in driftwood, this is the place you dream about staying when you're stuck in the snow waiting for a train. A volleyball court, groovy lounge, tree house, beach bar and much more open right onto the sand. Recycling and other ecofriendly practices, such as using sustainable construction materials, are a feature.

Tao Kombo BUNGALOW $

(Map p335; ☎0878 6033 1373; www.tao-kombo.com; r 200,000-400,000Rp;) This innovatively designed place has seven *lumbung* cottages with thatched roofs, stone floors and outdoor bathrooms. It's home to the popular Jungle Bar, and is 200m inland from the main strip. The owners are heavily involved in community projects; the whole place is run with an eye to sustainability.

★Kebun Kupu Kupu GUESTHOUSE $$

(Map p335; ☎0819 0742 8165; www.kupumenoresort.com; r from 800,000Rp;) Situated 300m from the beach, this collection of bungalows (the ones made from wood are lovely) has a great pool, palm trees overhead and a quiet spot near the salt lake. The French owners honour their heritage by serving excellent food (the crème brûlée is particularly good).

Ana Bungalow BUNGALOW $$

(Map p335; ☎0878 6169 6315; www.anawarung.com; r fan/air-con from 500,000/800,000Rp;) Four sweet, peaked-roof, thatch-and-bamboo bungalows with picture windows, and pebbled floors in the outdoor bathrooms. This family-run place has a cute used-book exchange on the beach next to its four lovely dining *berugas* (open-sided pavilions) lit with paper lanterns. Seafood dinners are excellent.

Jepun Bungalows BUNGALOW $$

(Map p335; ☎0819 1739 4736; www.jepunbungalows.com; bungalows fan/air-con 500,000/600,000Rp;) Just 100m from the main beach path and harbour, with charming accommodation dotted around a garden. Choose from six lovely thatched *lumbung*, bungalows, or book the family house; all have bathrooms with fresh (hot) water and good-quality beds. Three have air-con.

Seri Resort RESORT $$

(Map p335; ☎0878 6109 6374; www.seriresortgilimeno.com; r 550,000-1,600,000Rp;) It's a tough call, but we think this beachfront resort is just *that* much whiter than the surrounding sand. There is an interesting range of rooms here, from budget huts that share bathrooms, to suites in three-storey blocks, to luxurious beach villas. Service is good, and the atmosphere high-end.

Mallias Bungalows INN $$

(Map p335; ☎0819 1732 3327; www.malliasgili.com; r 500,000-1,200,000Rp;) This location right on Meno's best beach can't be beaten. The bungalows are simple – although some have air-con – really just bamboo and thatch. As such they are a good deal at the lower end of the price range. Then again, swinging on a hammock on your porch overlooking the beach is priceless.

Eating & Drinking

Almost all of Meno's restaurants have absorbing sea views. Here 'dressing for dinner' simply means putting on clothes.

★Sasak Cafe INDONESIAN $

(Map p335; mains 25,000-80,000Rp; kitchen 7am-9pm, bar till late) Considering its out-of-the-way location, this bamboo-and-thatch, island-casual hang-out has tasty Indo standards, which literally take on a rosy glow when the sun sets. The tunes and the drinks flow late into the night.

Webe Café INDONESIAN $

(Map p335; ☎0821 4776 3187; mains from 25,000Rp; 8am-10pm;) A wonderful location for a meal, Webe Café has low tables sunk in the sand, with the turquoise water just a metre away. It scores well for Sasak and Indonesian food such as *kelak kuning* (snapper in yellow spice); staff fire up a seafood barbecue most nights, too. There are also basic bungalows for rent (from 400,000Rp).

Ya Ya Warung INDONESIAN $
(Map p335; dishes 15,000-30,000Rp; ⏲8am-10pm) Ramshackle warung-on-the-beach that serves up Indonesian faves, curries, pancakes and plenty of pasta, along with the views you came to Meno to enjoy.

Diana Café BAR
(Map p335; ⏲8am-9pm) If you find the pace of life on Meno too busy, head to this intoxicating little tiki bar par excellence. Diana couldn't be simpler: a wobbly-looking bamboo-and-thatch bar, a few tables on the sand, a shack offering tattoos, a hammock or two, reggae on the stereo and a chill-out zone.

Shopping

Art Shop Botol HANDICRAFTS
(Map p335; ⏲hours vary) Art Shop Botol is a large handicrafts stall just south of Kontiki Meno hotel. Choose from masks, Sasak water baskets, woodcarvings and gourds. It's run by an elderly shopkeeper with 11 children and countless grandchildren.

Information

There is one ATM; it's near the boat landing and is often out of currency. Given that few places take credit cards, bring cash.

Getting There & Away

The **boat landing** (Map p335) is a sleepy hub. Check the public boat schedules carefully as Meno's small size means that waiting for a boat to fill can take a long time. None of the fast boats directly serve Meno, although some provide connections. Otherwise, you need to go to Trawangan or Air to catch a Bali boat.

Gili Air

Closest to Lombok, Gili Air falls between Gili T's sophistication and less-is-less Meno, and is for many just right. The white-sand beaches here are arguably the best of the Gili bunch and there's just enough buzz to provide a dash of nightlife. Snorkelling is good right from the main strip – a lovely sandy lane dotted with bamboo bungalows and little restaurants where you can eat virtually on top of a turquoise sea.

Though tourism dominates Gili Air's economy, coconuts, fishing and creating the fake-distressed fishing-boat wood vital to any stylish Gili guesthouse are important income streams. A buzzy little strip has developed along the beach in the southeast, although the lane is still more sandy than paved.

Beaches

The entire east side of the island has great beaches with powdery white sand and a gentle slope into beautiful turquoise water, with a foot-friendly sandy bottom. There are also good, private spots the rest of the way around Air, but low-tide rocks and coral are a problem.

Activities

Water Sports

The entire east coast has an offshore reef teeming with colourful fish; there's a drop-off about 100m to 200m out. Snorkelling gear is easily hired for about 50,000Rp per day.

The island has an excellent collection of dive shops which charge the standard Gili rates.

Blue Marine Dive Centre DIVING
(Map p340; ☎0812 377 0288; www.bluemarinedive.com; night dives 570,000Rp) Has a nice location on the beautiful northeast corner of the island. Offers free diving courses. The owner is very active in reef preservation efforts.

Oceans 5 DIVING
(Map p340; ☎0813 3877 7144; www.oceans5dive.com; fun dives from 500,000Rp) Has a 25m training pool, an in-house marine biologist and nice hotel rooms. Also offers a program of yoga diving, and emphasises sustainable diving practices to its guests.

7 Seas DIVING
(Map p340; ☎0370-663 2150; www.7seasdivegili.com; 4-day TEC diving packages 6,400,000Rp) A vast dive shop with a range of accommodation and a good pool for training or just playing. A local leader in recycling.

Oriental Land KAYAKING
(Map p340; ☎0878 6546 1505; 1/2hr rental 150,000/270,000Rp) Rent a kayak made from clear plastic and not only can you explore the reef-protected waters around Air, but you can see the reefs right under you.

DON'T MISS

SNORKELLING THE GILIS

Ringed by coral reefs, the Gilis offer superb snorkelling. Masks, snorkels and fins are widely available and can be hired for about 40,000Rp per day. It's important to check your mask fits properly: just press it gently to your face, let go and if it's a good fit the suction should hold it in place.

Snorkelling trips – many on glass-bottomed boats – are very popular. Typically, you'll pay about 200,000Rp per person. Expect to leave at about 10am and visit three or more sites, possibly with a stop for lunch on another island. On Gili T there are many places selling these trips along the main strip; prices are very negotiable.

On Trawangan and Meno turtles very regularly appear on the reefs right off the beach. You'll likely drift with the current, so be prepared to walk back to the starting line. Over on Air, the walls off the east coast are good too.

It's not hard to escape the crowds. Each island has a less-developed side, usually where access to the water is obstructed by shallow patches of coral. Using rubber shoes makes it much easier to get into the water. Try not to stamp all over the coral but ease yourself in, and then swim, keeping your body as horizontal as possible.

Among the many reasons to snorkel in the Gilis are the high odds you'll encounter hawksbill and green sea turtles. Top overall snorkelling spots include the following:

- Gili Meno Wall
- The north end of Gili T's beach
- Gili Air Wall

Cycling

Bikes can be rented for 50,000Rp a day but large sections of the coastal path in the north and west are annoying, as long slogs of deep sand swallow the trail at times. Inland lanes, however, are mostly concrete and very rideable. Some shops have bikes with huge tyres which actually aren't any easier to pedal.

Yoga & Wellness

H2O Yoga YOGA

(Map p340; ☎0877 6103 8836; www.h2oyogaandmeditation.com; classes 100,000Rp, 3hr workshops 300,000Rp) This wonderful yoga and meditation retreat centre is set back from the beach on a well-signed path in the village. Top-quality classes are held in a lovely circular *beruga* (open-sided pavilion). Massage is also available, and there's candlelight yoga at 5pm.

Harmony Spa SPA

(Map p340; ☎0812 386 5883; massages from 150,000Rp; ⏲10am-7pm) The beautiful north-coast location alone will make you feel renewed. Facials, body treatments and more are on offer. Call first.

Sleeping

Gili Air's 50 or so places to stay are mostly located on the east coast. You'll find more isolation in the west.

★Gili Air Hostel HOSTEL $

(Map p340; www.giliairhostel.com; dm/r from 125,000/350,000Rp; ⏲reception 7.30am-7pm; ❄📶) A great addition to the island. Beds here are in two- to seven-bed rooms, all of which share bathrooms. The decor defines cheery, and there's a cool bar, a huge frangipani tree and even a climbing wall.

Bintang Beach 2 BUNGALOW $

(Map p340; ☎0877 6522 2554; r from 350,000Rp; ❄) On Gili Air's quiet northwest coast, this sandy but tidy compound has basic rooms and bungalows that range from budget-friendly and fan-cooled to mildly snazzy. The bar area is a delight. This enterprising clan has a few other guesthouses nearby.

★Villa Casa Mio BUNGALOW $$

(Map p340; ☎0370-646160; www.villacasamio.com; cottages from 900,000Rp; ❄📶🏊) Casa Mio has fine cottages with pretty garden bathrooms, as well as a riot of knick-knacks (from the artistic to the kitsch). Rooms have fridges, stereos and nice sun decks with loungers. The *casa* also boasts a lovely beach area, and good access via a paved portion of the beach lane from the boat landing. Several competitors have sprung up nearby.

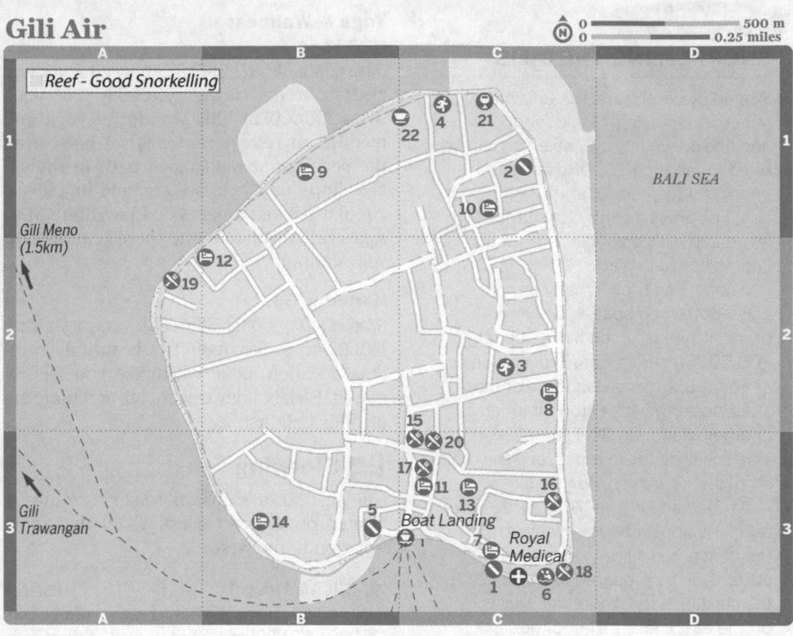

Gili Air

Activities, Courses & Tours

1 7 Seas ... C3
2 Blue Marine Dive Centre ... C1
3 H2O Yoga ... C2
4 Harmony Spa ... C1
5 Oceans 5 ... B3
6 Oriental Land ... C3

Sleeping

7 7 Seas ... C3
8 Biba Beach Village ... C2
9 Bintang Beach 2 ... B1
10 Damai ... C1
11 Gili Air Hostel ... C3
12 Grand Sunset ... B2
13 Rival Village ... C3
14 Villa Casa Mio ... B3

Eating

15 Eazy Gili Waroeng ... C3
16 Le Cirque ... C3
17 Pasar Malam ... C3
18 Scallywags Beach Club ... C3
Siti Shop ... (see 15)
19 Sunset Lounge ... A2
20 Warung Sasak II ... C3

Drinking & Nightlife

21 Legend Bar ... C1
22 Little Bar ... C1

★ **Rival Village** GUESTHOUSE **$$**

(Map p340; ☎0819 0734 9148; www.facebook.com/rivalvillagegiliair; r 500,000-600,000Rp; ❄📶) This modest four-room guesthouse just gets everything right. The French owners have created a sparkling-clean little compound amid family houses off one of the village's main paths. Rooms are large, the bathrooms are open-air, breakfast is delicious, everything works. Très bon!

Damai GUESTHOUSE **$$**

(Map p340; ☎0878 6142 0416; www.facebook.com/damaihomestay.giliair; r 450,000-650,000Rp; ❄📶) It's worth seeking out this thatched enclave. The 11 rooms range from basic bungalows to deluxe crash pads, which are tasteful and open onto a garden. The cosy dining patio has cushioned seating, and is elegantly lit with paper lanterns.

Biba Beach Village BUNGALOW $$
(Map p340; ☎0819 1727 4648; www.bibabeach.com; bungalows from 700,000Rp;) Biba offers nine lovely, spacious bungalows with large verandas, and grottolike bathrooms that have walls inlaid with shells and coral. The gorgeous garden has little chill-out zones. Biba is also home to a good Italian restaurant. The best rooms have sea views.

Grand Sunset BUNGALOW $$
(Map p340; ☎0859 3610 3847; www.grandsunsetgiliair.com; r 700,000-900,000Rp;) These solidly built, bungalow-style rooms reflect the ethos of this modest resort: solid. Bathrooms are well designed and open-air, rooms have all the basic comforts, the wi-fi works, the pool is large and refreshing, and the beachside loungers have superb views. Plus there's the quiet that comes with the location on the sunset side of Air.

7 Seas HOTEL $$
(Map p340; ☎0819 0700 3240; www.7seas-cottages.com; dm from 80,000Rp, r 450,000-800,000Rp;) Part of the 7 Seas dive empire, this is an attractive bungalow compound in a great location. Rooms are tidy and comfy; cottages have soaring ceilings and thatch. There are also fan-cooled, bamboo, loftlike hostel rooms.

Eating

Most places on Gili Air are locally owned and offer an unbeatable setting for a meal, with tables right over the water.

★**Eazy Gili Waroeng** INDONESIAN $
(Map p340; mains 25,000-40,000Rp; 8am-10pm) In the buzzy main village, this spotless corner cafe serves up local fare aimed at visitors. It's the slightly Westernised face of the beloved Warung Muslim, immediately to the east. It also does breakfasts, sandwiches and a superb *pisang goreng* (fried banana).

Warung Sasak II INDONESIAN $
(Map p340; mains from 15,000Rp; 8am-10pm) A fine find in the village, this dead-simple warung has excellent versions of all the standards such as chicken satay and fish curry. It also has many variations on *parapek*, a Sasak speciality where foods are cooked in a spicy sauce.

Pasar Malam MARKET $
(Night Market; Map p340; mains from 15,000Rp; 6-11pm) Inspired by the wild success of the night market on Gili T, Air's has the requisite stalls with fresh Indo fare arrayed around open-air tables. It gets lively after 8pm. Half the fun is just browsing.

★**Le Cirque** FRENCH, BAKERY $$
(Map p340; ☎0819 1601 0360; www.lecirque-giliair.com; mains 35,000-120,000Rp; 7am-10pm;) A clever French-accented culinary vision with a scrumptious bakery and tables spanning the path right up to the shore. The dinner menu is ambitious and there are nightly seafood specials. Kids get their own menu with tasty treats such as 'pizza circus'.

★**Scallywags Beach Club** INTERNATIONAL $$
(Map p340; ☎0370-645301; www.scallywagsresort.com; mains 45,000-150,000Rp; 8am-10pm;) Set on Gili Air's softest and widest beach, there's elegant decor, upscale comfort food, great barbecue, homemade gelato and superb cocktails here. But the best feature is the alluring beach dotted with loungers. The choice of sambals is sublime.

Sunset Lounge SEAFOOD $$
(Map p340; mains 40,000-120,000Rp; 9am-11pm) More ambitious than your usual beachside bamboo hang-outs, Sunset offers a nightly seafood barbecue and an ever-changing line-up of fresh fare. Good pasta shows what the Italians can do with *mie* (noodles). Come for drinks, stay for sunset and then have a moonlit meal. (On a bike, buzz over on the paved interior lanes.)

Drinking & Nightlife

Gili Air is usually a mellow place, but there are full-moon parties and things can rev up on the strip in the southeast in high season. Still, where late-night Gili T is all about parties, Gili Air's hotspot is the waffle-cone stand.

★**Legend Bar** BAR
(Map p340; 7am-late) Painted the requisite Rasta colours of red, green and gold, this raffish reggae bar has a large dance party every full moon.

Little Bar CAFE
(Map p340; 9am-late) Set on a sublime stretch of beach with technicolour sunsets, there is no better place for a sundowner than Little Bar. The menu includes snacks and veggie options.

Information

There are **ATMs** along the southeast strip.

Royal Medical (Map p340; ☎0878 6442 1212; ⏲phone service 24hr) has a simple clinic.

There's a good general store, **Siti Shop** (Map p340; ⏲8am-8pm), in the village.

ℹ Getting There & Away

The **boat landing** (Map p340) is busy. Gili Air's commerce and popularity mean that public boats fill rather quickly for the 15-minute ride to Bangsal. The ticket office has a shady waiting area. Clipboard-toting staff handle fast-boat check-ins.

SUMBAWA

Elaborately contorted and sprawling into the sea, Sumbawa is all volcanic ridges, terraced rice fields, dry expanses and sheltered bays. Two main areas draw visitors: the southwest coast from Maluk is essentially a layered series of headlands and wide, white beaches with renowned surf, while in the southeast, Lakey Peak has become Sumbawa's premier year-round surf magnet. Elsewhere, massive, climbable Gunung Tambora (2850m), which once had an explosion so large it changed the climate of the planet, looms in the north.

Though well connected to Bali and Lombok, Sumbawa is a very different sort of place. It's far less developed, mostly very dry, much poorer, extremely conservative, and split between two distinct peoples. Those who speak Sumbawanese probably reached the west of the island from Lombok. Bimanese speakers dominate the Tambora Peninsula and the east. Although Sumbawa is an overwhelmingly Islamic island, in remote parts underground *adat* (traditional laws and regulations) still thrive. During festivals you may come across traditional Sumbawan fighting, a sort of bare-fisted boxing called *berempah*. Dynamic horse and water-buffalo races, best glimpsed in Bima each August, are held before the rice is planted.

Transport connections off the trans-Sumbawa road are infrequent and uncomfortable, and most overland travellers don't even get off the bus in Sumbawa as they float and roll from Lombok to Flores. For now, it's the domain of surfers, miners and mullahs.

ℹ Dangers & Annoyances

Most Sumbawans are hospitable, albeit taciturn, but you may encounter some tension. In the past, protests against foreign-owned mining operations have turned violent. The island is also much more conservative in terms of religion than neighbouring Lombok or Flores; behave modestly at all times. Indonesia's anti-terrorism police make raids and arrests around Bima.

DON'T MISS

BEST OF SUMBAWA

Pantai Lakey A genuine beach town, with cool guesthouses and cafes linked by a sandy path overlooking awesome surf.

Rantung A low-key collection of classic surfer dives, great breaks and a fine beach.

Trans-Sumbawa Highway Mostly traffic-free and in great shape; good for speeding between Lombok and Flores.

ℹ Getting Around

Sumbawa's main highway is in good condition and runs from Taliwang (near the west coast) through Sumbawa Besar, Dompu and Bima to Sape (the ferry port on the east coast). It's relatively traffic-free – a relief if you've made the trek through Java, Bali and Lombok. Fleets of long-distance buses, most of them air-conditioned, run between the west-coast ferry port of Porto Tano and Sape, serving all the major towns between.

Car hire is possible through hotels: prices are about 600,000Rp to 800,000Rp per day, including a driver. Motorbikes cost 50,000Rp to 80,000Rp a day.

West Sumbawa

☎0372

West Sumbawa is dry and rolling. Beaches are wide, sugar-white, and framed with domed headlands. Bays are enormous and dynamic: they can be tranquil one hour and fold into overhead barrels the next. Sumbawa Besar is a humble Muslim town with a good morning market. Pulau Moyo, a lush jewel off the northern shore, has revered diving and snorkelling, but it's difficult to access on a budget. Watch for small Balinese villages near the coasts.

Poto Tano

Poto Tano, the main port for ferries to/from Lombok, is a ramshackle harbour, fringed by stilt-fishing villages with tremendous views of Gunung Rinjani. Pretty place, but there's no need to sleep here.

Getting There & Away

Ferries run hourly, 24 hours a day, between Labuhan Lombok and Poto Tano (passengers 19,000Rp, 1½ hours). Cars cost 466,000Rp, motorbikes 54,000Rp. Through buses to Lombok, Bali and Java include the ferry fare.

Buses meet the ferry and go to Taliwang (20,000Rp, one hour) and Sumbawa Besar (30,000Rp, two hours).

Taliwang & Around

It may be the regional capital and transport hub, but Taliwang is just a small, conservative village, 30km south of Poto Tano. There are ATMs along the main road, plenty of Padang warungs (food stalls), and no reasons to hang around.

From Taliwang, bemos (minibuses) and trucks also run 11km south to **Jereweh**, your gateway to the remarkable beach and enormous horseshoe bay at **Jelenga**, a humble country village with rice fields, goat farms and a world-class left break known as **Scar Reef**.

Sleeping & Eating

★ **Scar Reef Hotel** SURF CAMP **$$**
(☎0813 3774 2679; www.scarreefhotel.com; r 500,000-900,000Rp; ❄) A modern lodge for surfers. The four rooms, which each sleep up to four, have soaring ceilings, wood furnishings, air-con, and a common beachside porch and lounge area with satellite TV. Two have ocean views. There's also a cafe.

Getting There & Away

Buses go from Taliwang to Poto Tano (20,000Rp) almost hourly, where you can hop on a bus to Mataram or Sumbawa Besar. Hourly bemos head to Maluk (20,000Rp, two hours).

Maluk, Sekongkang & Rantung

South of Taliwang, the beaches and bays try to outdo one another. Your first stop is the working-class commercial district of **Maluk**, 30km south of Taliwang. Yes, the town is ugly, but the beach is superb. The sand is a blend of white and gold, and the bay is buffered by two headlands. There's good swimming in the shallows, and when the swell hits, the reef further out sculpts perfect barrels.

One of the world's largest copper mines, about 30km inland of Maluk, has driven a wave of development and attracted scores of employees from the US, Australia and Java. The Newmont Mining Corporation employs about 8000 workers, and has had a huge impact on the area (you'll see its vast port facilities along the coastal road). Most of the expat restaurant and bar traffic is in **Townside**, a private company enclave complete with golf courses and other amenities. Casual visits are discouraged.

Directly south of Maluk, within walking distance of the beach (though it is a long walk) is **Supersuck**, consistently rated as the best left the world. Surfers descend regularly from Hawaii's North Shore to surf here – which should tell you something – and many lifelong surfers have proclaimed it the finest barrel of their lives. It really pumps in the dry season (May to October).

About a 10km serpentine drive further south, the spread-out settlement of **Sekongkang** includes three superb beaches with another handful of surf breaks. It also has the

Sumbawa

best range of accommodation and a gorgeous all-natural vibe. **Pantai Rantung** (commonly called Rantung Beach), 2km downhill from Sekongkang Atas, spills onto a secluded and majestic bay framed by 100m-high headlands. The water is crystal-clear and waves roll in year-round at **Yo Yo's**, a right break at the north end of the bay. **Hook**, which breaks at the edge of the northern bluff, is also a terrific right. **Supershit** breaks straight in front of the Rantung Beach Hotel, and is a consistent year-round beginner's break, though it gets heavy and delivers a long left when the swell comes in. The next bay down is where you'll find **Tropical**, another phenomenal beach (named for the nearby resort) and home to great left and right breaks that beginners will enjoy.

North of Rantung is **Pantai Lawar**, a tree-shaded stretch of white sand on a turquoise lagoon sheltered by volcanic bluffs draped in jungle. When the surf is flat, come here to swim and snorkel.

Sleeping & Eating

Maluk's fun beachside marketplace is packed with warungs selling everything from *soto ayam* (chicken soup) to coffees, juices and *ikan bakar* (grilled fish).

Bars and restaurants on Rantung Beach get crowded with expat mine workers on weekends. Most everything here is in easy walking distance, and it has a classic surfer feel.

★Santai Beach Bungalows GUESTHOUSE $
(0878 6393 5758; Rantung Beach; r 100,000-200,000Rp; @) The choice budget spot in the area offers a collection of 12 spacious, well-tended tiled rooms. Those with private bath have sensational sea views from the front porch, and all have access to amazing views from the thatched restaurant (dishes 30,000Rp to 60,000Rp), where there's a pool table. Book ahead: when that swell hits it's full for weeks. It is close to several other places.

Maluk Resort HOTEL $
(0372-635424; Jl Pasir Putih, Maluk; r 225,000-425,000Rp;) One block west of the main road, and steps from the sand, is this decent collection of 10 rooms. Garden rooms surround a small pool and most have a private terrace. Upstairs deluxe rooms are slightly larger, with bathtubs and a better view.

Rantung Beach Hotel GUESTHOUSE $
(0878 3905 4999; www.surfindo.com.au; Rantung Beach; r from 150,000Rp) Located on a small point overlooking the best part of the breaks, this 12-room surfer crash pad makes up for its dishevelled appearance with a great, welcoming spirit. The view from the cafe (dishes 30,000Rp to 60,000Rp) and bar are stunning. Rooms have fans and simple bamboo furniture. The hotel organises various surfing packages, including transport from Bali.

Rantung Beach Bar & Cottages BUNGALOW $$
(0819 1700 7481; Rantung Beach; cottages from 550,000Rp;) The mining crowd has enjoyed more than a few sundowners at the vast and open beachside cafe here (dishes 40,000Rp to 80,000Rp); the food always delivers (we love the crunchy cassava chips and huge burgers). Five refined, spacious cottages have queen beds and leafy private decks with sea views. Cheaper surfer crash pads are planned.

Yo Yo's Hotel RESORT $$
(0819 9895 5377; yoyoshotel@yahoo.co.id; Rantung Beach; dm 100,000, s/d from 250,000/450,000Rp; @) A vast beachfront complex with a range of 20 rooms. Deluxe rooms are quite large and well appointed with wood furnishings. Standard rooms are smaller, and a bit worn, but still good value. The 'surf camp' is a clean, hostel-like, fan-only bunkhouse with five bright, air-conditioned rooms (five beds each).

A large two-storey bar and cafe (dishes 30,000Rp to 80,000Rp) overlooks the surf. Monkeys wander the grounds, possibly lured by the Australian Rules Football (AFL) signs.

Information

Maluk has services. There's a BNI bank with ATM on Jl Raya Maluk, adjacent to the Trophy Hotel. Internet access is hobbled in Rantung Beach by the lack of a proper phone line: once this is installed, expect fast wi-fi everywhere.

Getting There & Around

Bemos travel between Taliwang and Maluk (20,000Rp, two hours) almost hourly from 7am to 6pm. Three daily buses leave Terminal Maluk, north of town across from the entrance to the Newmont mine (look for the big gates and massive parking area), for Sumbawa Besar (40,000Rp, four hours).

From Benete Harbour, just north of Maluk, a fast ferry run by the Newmont mine (125,000Rp,

90 minutes) goes to/from Labuhan Lombok one or two times daily. Check times with the Rantung Beach guesthouses.

Sumbawa Besar

☎0371 / POP 54,000

Sumbawa Besar, often shortened to 'Sumbawa', is the principal market town of the island's west. It's leafy, devoutly Muslim (that legion of nearby karaoke bars notwithstanding), and runs on the bushels of beans, rice and corn cultivated on the outskirts. There's not much to see here aside from the old palace and a lively morning market. Trips to Pulau Moyo and to nearby villages are worthwhile but take time and money, which is why most travellers simply consider this town a respite on the trans-Sumbawa highway.

Traffic runs in a high-speed Jl Hasanuddin–Jl Diponegoro loop. The best sleeping and eating options are clustered along Jl Hasanuddin.

Sights

Dalam Loka PALACE
(Sultan's Palace; Jl Dalam Loka 1; 8am-noon & 1-5pm Mon-Fri, 8-11am & 1.30-5pm Sat & Sun) FREE Originally built over 200 years ago for Sultan Mohammad Jalaluddin III, the remains of the Dalam Loka, a once-imposing structure that covers an entire city block, are in fair condition and are still used for political events. You can wander the grounds (unadorned except for some fenced-in deer). Inside the palace are old photos of the royal family, antique parasols and carriages.

Pasar Syketeng MARKET
(off Jl Diponegoro; 7am-4pm) Rise early and hit the steamy, exotic Pasar Syketeng. Its dank alleyways come alive as young and old descend to barter and haggle for every conceivable item, from fish to household goods to live chickens.

Sleeping & Eating

Basic hotels congregate on Jl Hasanuddin, although there is little reason to overnight in Sumbawa Besar.

Sumbawa Transit Hotel HOTEL $$
(☎0371-21754; Jl Garuda 41; r 250,000-600,000Rp;) Conveniently located across the main road and to the left as you emerge from the airport, rooms in this low-rise compound are spacious with high ceilings, cheery bathroom tiles and a nice private terrace out front. VIP rooms are larger, quieter and have hot water.

★ **Cipta Sari Bakery** BAKERY $
(☎0371-21496; Jl Hasanuddin 47; snacks from 20,000Rp; 8am-5pm) Don't pass through town without a stop at this excellent bakery on a shady stretch of the main drag. Pause for coffee or a cold drink, and be sure to stock up for your journey: the various baked goods, pastries and savoury treats are the best you'll find between here and Bima.

Aneka Rasa Jaya CHINESE $
(☎0371-21291; Jl Hasanuddin 14; mains from 25,000Rp; 8am-3pm & 6-10pm) Clean and popular, this Chinese seafood house plates tender fish fillets, shrimp, squid, crab and scallops in oyster, Szechuan, and sweet-and-sour sauce. The *soto kepiting* (crab soup) is good, as is anything with noodles.

Information

There are numerous banks and ATMs all along Jl Hasanuddin.

Kantor Imigrasi (Immigration Office; Jl Garuda 131; 8am-3pm Mon-Thu, to noon Fri) Extend your tourist visa; it'll take at least two days.

Klinik Lawang Gali (☎0371-626567; Jl Sudirman 18-20; 24hr) Hospital with ambulance services.

Getting There & Away

AIR

The airport is very close to the centre. **Transnusa** (☎0371-7162 6161; Jl Garuda 41) has flights to Bali, and Garuda has flights to Lombok.

BUS

Sumbawa Besar's main long-distance bus station is **Terminal Sumur Payung**, 5.5km northwest of town on the highway. You can book tickets at the station and at **Tiara Mas** (☎0371-21241; Jl Yos Sudarso; 9am-6pm). Destinations served include the following:

Bima 80,000Rp, seven hours, several daily

Mataram (Lombok) 80,000Rp (including ferry ticket), six hours, several daily

Poto Tano 30,000Rp, three hours, hourly from 8am to midnight

Getting Around

It's easy to walk into town from the airport, just turn to your right as you exit the terminal. The walk is less than 1km. Alternatively, you can arrange transport with local guesthouses.

Bemos cost 3000Rp for trips anywhere around town.

Around Sumbawa Besar

You'll need private transport to navigate Sumbawa's outskirts effectively. Some of the best ikat and *songket* (silver or gold-threaded cloth) sarongs are made by members of a women's weaving *klompok* (collective) in the conservative mountain village of **Poto**, 12km east of Sumbawa Besar and 2km from the small town of Moyo. Traditional designs include the *prahu* (outrigger boat). You'll hear the clack of weavers' looms from the street and are welcome to duck into their humble huts. The most intricate pieces take up to 45 days to produce.

If you're doing the trans-Sumbawa slog with your own wheels, stop for lunch at **Warung Santong** (Pantai Santong; meals 30,000-60,000Rp; 24hr), a tasty fish shack teetering on the rocky shore at the island's midway point. Dine on fresh catch, grilled or fried, in the 'dining room', or in one of the stilted pagodas at the water's edge.

Pulau Moyo

A gently arcing crescent of jungled volcanic rock, Moyo – all 36,000 hectares of it – floats atop the gorgeous azure seas north of Sumbawa Besar. The same size as Singapore, it has almost no commercial development and is peopled by just six small villages. The majority of the island, and its rich reefs, form a nature reserve laced with trails, dripping with waterfalls and offering some of the best diving west of Komodo. Loggerhead and green turtles hatch on the beaches, long-tail macaques patrol the canopy, and wild pigs, barking deer and a diverse bird population all call Moyo home.

Accommodation is limited to just one luxury resort, although there are plans to develop more modest options. It is possible to visit Moyo on a day trip from Sumbawa Besar.

Activities

Boats from the mainland will take you to the **snorkelling** spot **Air Manis**, and the even better **Tanjung Pasir** (it has a great beach). Good reefs with a plunging wall can be found all around the island if you are prepared to charter your boat for a bit longer. Just northeast of Pulau Moyo is small Pulau Satonda, which also has good beaches and tremendous snorkelling. There are no places in the area to rent snorkelling gear, so bring your own.

There are only two ways to **dive** at Pulau Moyo. You can join a Bali- or Lombok-based, Komodo-bound liveaboard, or checkin to the luscious Amanwana, the swankiest dive camp on the planet.

The seas around Moyo get turbulent from December to March and boat captains understandably may refuse to risk a journey.

Sleeping

★ **Amanwana Resort** RESORT $$$
(0361-772333, 0371-22233; www.amanresorts.com; all-inclusive jungle/ocean-view tents from US$1100/1300;) On Moyo's western side, Amanwana is the ultimate island hideaway. Guests stay in lavish permanent tents with antique wood furnishings, king-sized beds and, of course, air-con. But nature still rules here. The resort is built around diving, hiking and mountain biking. Guests arrive by private seaplane or helicopter from Bali, or from mainland Sumbawa on an Amanwana boat.

The resort sponsors turtle hatcheries, deer breeding and reef-protection projects. There's a full-service spa and a dive school with private courses and dive trips. You can charter a luxury liveaboard for private seven-day cruises to Komodo National Park and further on to the Bandas in Maluku and Papua's Raja Ampat archipelago.

Information

The website www.moyoisland.com has info about the island, which is the centre of much speculation regarding future tourism development.

Getting There & Away

Take a public bemo (10,000Rp, one hour) or your own wheels to Air Bari, a small harbour 22km northeast of Sumbawa Besar. You can charter a boat here for a day trip to Pulau Moyo. Bargain hard for a journey to Tanjung Pasir (from 1,500,000Rp), which is the closest place to Air Bari, about 3km across the water. You may also be able to hitch a ride on one of the regular service boats (from 200,000Rp).

East Sumbawa

0373

Twisted into a shape all its own, and linguistically and culturally distinct from the west, the eastern half of Sumbawa sees the most visitors thanks to accessible year-round surf near Hu'u village. Adventurous souls may also want to tackle majestic Gunung Tambora, a mountain that changed the world.

Gunung Tambora

☎0373

Looming over central Sumbawa is the 2850m volcano Gunung Tambora. Its peak was obliterated during the epic eruption of April 1815.

But you're here to surmount the peak. From the summit you'll have spectacular views of the 6km-wide caldera, which contains a two-coloured lake, and endless ocean vistas that stretch as far as Gunung Rinjani (Lombok). A basic climb to the crater rim takes at least two days; if you want to venture down into the spectacular crater – one of the world's deepest – add another five days. Much of the mountain was declared a national park in 2015.

The base for ascents is the remote village of **Pancasila** near the town of **Calabai** on the western slope. Here you can organise climbs. Contacts include **Pak Saiful** (☎0859 3703 0848, 0823 4069 9138; Pancasila) and **Rik Stoetman** (☎0813 5337 0951; visittambora.wordpress.com; near Pancasila). Both can rent rooms (from 100,000Rp to 200,000Rp), and handle transport and logistical issues. Guides and porters cost about 200,000Rp to 300,000Rp per day.

Getting There & Away

The road along the peninsula from the trans-Sumbawa highway to Calabai is much improved. You can cover the 57km in under two hours with your own wheels, or hop on a very crowded bus from Dompu (40,000Rp, four to five hours) to Calabai. From Calabai take an *ojek* (motorcycle that takes passengers; 30,000Rp) to Pancasila.

Pantai Lakey & Hu'u

☎0373

Pantai Lakey, a gentle crescent of golden sand, is where Sumbawa's tourist pulse beats, thanks to seven world-class surf breaks that curl and crash in one massive bay, and a string of modest beach guesthouses, all linked by a beachside path which contributes to the fun atmosphere.

Hu'u is a small, poor and very friendly fishing village, 3km north of Lakey. It's suffused with the scent of drying fish and blessed with breathtaking pink sunsets.

The area is the centre of a recent push to increase tourism on Sumbawa. New roads hint at future large projects; you can now easily drive east from Hu'u, and north to Bima via Parado, enjoying some superb sea views along the way.

Activities

This is one of Indonesia's best **surfing** destinations. **Lakey Peak** and **Lakey Pipe** are the best-known waves and are within paddling distance of the various hotels and guesthouses. You'll need to rent a motorbike or hire an *ojek* to get to **Nungas**, **Cobblestone** and **Nangadoro**. **Periscope** is 150m from the sand at the far north end of the bay near **Maci Point**, which is another good spot. When the swell gets really big, there's a beach break at Hu'u, as well.

Most surfers share the cost of a boat (from 800,000Rp, maximum five people) to get to the breaks and back. Waves can be very good (and very big) year-round, but the most consistent swell arrives between June and August. From August to October the wind gusts,

THE YEAR WITHOUT SUMMER

After a few days of tremors the top blew off Gunung Tambora on 10 April 1815 in what is the most powerful eruption in modern history. Tens of thousands of Sumbawans were killed, molten rock was sent more than 40km into the sky, and the explosion was heard 2000km away (by comparison, the 1873 eruption of Krakatau (p78) was one-tenth the size).

In the months and years that followed, weather was affected worldwide as the cloud of ash blotted out the sun. In Europe 1816 came to be known as 'the year without summer'. Crops failed, temperatures plummeted, disease spread and tens of thousands died across the globe. Historical evidence is everywhere, including in the works of JMW Turner, whose paintings from the period feature shocking orange colours in the dim, ash-filled skies.

Two books vividly illustrate how Tambora's eruption changed the planet: *Tambora* by Gillen D'Arcy Wood and *Tambora: Travels to Sumbawa and the Mountain that Changed the Earth* by Derek Pugh. The latter author has a lot of useful information for climbing Tambora today on his website (www.derekpugh.com.au).

which turns Pantai Lakey into Indonesia's best **kitesurfing** destination – it's regarded as one of the 10 best in the world. Kites descend on Lakey Pipe and Nungas when it's pumping.

Inexperienced surfers should be cautious. Waves break over a shallow reef, and serious accidents do happen.

Joey Barrel's Board Shop SURFING
(Jl Raya Hu'u; hours vary) Out on the main drag, this small shop offers ding repairs, board rental (per day from 50,000Rp), surfing supplies and board sales. It's open when the owner isn't at the breaks.

Sleeping & Eating

There are plenty of decent-value digs strung along Pantai Lakey; most have their own cafes and bars. A paved beach walk follows the shore, linking guesthouses. It has stands selling refreshments and a few simple warungs.

Puma Bungalows & Restaurant BUNGALOW $
(0373-623061; Jl Raya Hu'u; r 90,000-350,000Rp;) Expect 23 colourful concrete bungalows with tiled roofs and shady front porches, plus sprawling, palm-shaded grounds with fabulous views. Cheaper rooms are fan-only. The two-storey cafe (mains 30,000Rp to 50,000Rp) has sweeping views and a rickety, bamboo vibe; the ginger prawns are popular. On some days yoga classes are held.

Lakey Beach Inn GUESTHOUSE $
(0373-623576; www.lakey-beach-inn.com; Jl Raya Hu'u; r 90,000-250,000Rp;) Enjoy tasty homestyle fish dinners, pizza and Indo classics at the large and driftwoody waterfront cafe (mains 25,000Rp to 60,000Rp). Rooms are basic – the cheapest have fans and cold water. French owner Rachel is a legendary local character.

★**Vivian's Lakey Peak Homestay** HOMESTAY $$
(0878 6698 1277; www.lakeypeakhomestay.com; off Jl Raya Hu'u; r 250,000-300,000Rp;) Set along a little lane between the beach and the main road, this five-room family compound offers the area's warmest welcome. Rooms are newish and large with nice furnishings. The yard is shaded by banana trees and there's a genial cafe-cum-dayroom.

Aman Gati Hotel RESORT $$
(0373-623031, 0821 4473 4511; www.amangati-hotel.com; Jl Raya Hu'u; r 600,000-750,000Rp, oceanfront villas from 1,000,000Rp;) The most upscale place on the beach, this Balinese-run, three-star resort has 57 attractive modern rooms. Some are perfectly oriented to the break; others, in the cheaper older building, have higher ceilings and bigger beds. All come with wood furnishings, hot water and satellite TV.

Surf Houses Lakey Peak HOUSE $$
(www.lakeypeaksurf.com; small/big houses from 290,000/320,000Rp;) Bertrand Fleury, a world-class kitesurfer, hosts kite pros from July to November for the wind season. When he's gone he rents out his two excellent wooden houses, set right on the Nungas break. Each sleeps up to five with full kitchen, private decks and outdoor baths. Rates vary greatly by the number of people and length of stay.

Blue Lagoon BUNGALOW $$
(0813 3982 3018; Jl Rya Hu'u; r 200,000-350,000Rp;) A vast one-storey complex that stretches back from the beach, Blue Lagoon has well-looked-after, tiled rooms with private patios. All are spacious, but some are in better shape than others. The most expensive rooms have air-con, hot water and satellite TV. The waterfront restaurant (mains 30,000Rp to 50,000Rp) and bar draws a crowd.

Mama's INDONESIAN $
(Beach Path; mains 20,000-30,000Rp; 8am-7pm) The namesake owner sits out front of this simple little stall all day peeling veggies for her excellent local fare. Choose a few mains, serve yourself and lap up classic homestyle cooking. It's right on the beach path near the vast Blue Lagoon complex.

★**Fat Mah's** INTERNATIONAL $$
(off Jl Raya Hu'u; mains 40,000-80,000Rp; 6am-11pm) Lakey's best kitchen turns out creative fare throughout the day and night. Tables sit in a raised bleached-wood house overlooking the beach. There's a bit of style to everything, from the granola and muffins at breakfast, to the juices and cocktails, and on to the sandwiches and nightly seafood and pasta specials.

Information

There is community wi-fi, although some places offer their own (faster) service.

The nearest ATMs are 37km north in Dompu.

Getting There & Away

From Dompu there are two daily (slow) buses as far as Hu'u (25,000Rp, 1½ hours), where you can hire an *ojek* (15,000Rp) to Pantai Lakey. *Ojeks* to/from Dompu on the trans-Sumbawa highway cost 150,000Rp.

Try doing this with a surfboard and you'll see why so many people take a taxi from Bima airport (around 800,000Rp, four people). Buses to/from Bima cost from 50,000Rp (one to two daily).

The *ojek* cartel is omnipresent in Lakey; rates to the breaks range from 30,000Rp to 80,000Rp.

Bima

0374 / POP 149,000

East Sumbawa's largest metropolitan centre is a conservative Islamic place with few sights, and it's nobody's favourite getaway. The streets can be traffic-choked, the architecture is charmless and crumbling, and the vibe is unappealing after dark. If you're heading to Pantai Lakey there's no need to stop here, but if you want a morning ferry to Flores, you're better off staying here than in Sape, for the greater range of sleeping options alone.

Sights

Museum Asi Mbojo MUSEUM

(Jl Sultan Ibrahim; admission 2000Rp; 8am-5pm Mon-Sat) The old Sultan's Palace, former home of Bima's rulers, still reflects the colonial style of a 1927 renovation. Past the large verandas, the interior is home to a grab bag of dusty curios, including a royal crown, battle flags and weapons. A modest wooden building next to the palace has an evocative and traditional look. The weedy grounds are large; the area outside the northern fence is a favourite night-time spot for prostitutes.

Festivals & Events

Horse racing is held four times a year, in May, July, August and December, at the Desa Panda horse stadium, 14km west of town on the trans-Sumbawa highway. There's a large grandstand, a gaggle of warungs, and plenty of cheering as horses thunder around a dusty track. Action peaks on 17 August as independence fever kicks in.

Sleeping

Hotel Lila Graha HOTEL $

(0374-42740; Jl Lombok 20; r 200,000-350,000Rp;) One of two four-storey, block-long hotels, each with a wide range of rooms; ground-floor suite rooms are newest and nicest. There's wi-fi in the lobby only. It's right in the centre.

★ **Marina Hotel** HOTEL $$

(0374-42072; www.marinabima.com; Jl Sultan Kaharuddin 41; r 390,000-450,000Rp;) Bima's best sleep is very central. The 52 rooms in this three-storey building (there's an elevator) are bright and airy, with large flat-screen TVs, glassed-in showers and plush bed linens. All rooms get plenty of light, though some have more windows than others. There are sweeping views from the common lounge.

Eating

★ **Rumah Makan Sabar Sabur** SEAFOOD $

(0374-646236; Jl Salahudin, Bandara; mains from 20,000Rp; 7am-7pm) Out by the airport, off the trans-Sumbawa highway, the long wooden tables here are always crowded with locals who come to munch *bandeng goreng* (a flash-fried freshwater fish). Like herring, you can eat it whole, bones and all. It's best combined with their fiery crushed-tomato sambal, torn leaves of lemon basil and a bit of rice.

Pasar Malam MARKET $

(Night Market; Jl Sultan Ibrahaim; 6pm-11pm) Dine cheaply at the night market: there's fish and chicken *sate* (satay), *mie goreng* (fried noodles) and nasi goreng (fried rice), *bakso* (meatball soup) and various deep-fried treats, including bananas aplenty.

Rumah Makan Arema Raya PADANG $

(0374-44960; Jl Sultan Hasanuddin; mains 20,000-30,000Rp; 7am-10pm) The cleanest and most central Padang food depot in town. Pick and mix from an array of curried, baked and fried fish and chicken dishes. Note: it gets quite spicy here. When the day's fresh fare runs out (about 6pm), head upstairs for some just-fair pizza.

Warung Taliwang INDONESIAN $

(Jl Sulawesi; mains 20,000-40,000Rp; 11am-11pm) On the ground floor of a building that still has some colonial style, this open-air warung serves up seafood and chicken dishes fresh from the woks. Settle in at the street-side rows of long tables.

Information

There are plenty of banks and ATMs in Bima, especially along the town's main drag, Jl Sultan Hasanuddin.

PT Man Jaya Executive Tours (0819 0901 2555; Jl Sultan Kaharuddin 36; 8am-6pm Mon-Sat) West of the centre and on the main road, this full-service agency is the best place for Pelni and ferry tickets.

Travel Lancar Jaya (0374-43737; Jl Sultan Hasanuddin 11) Bima's Lion Air agent offers a range of services. It's across from the largest supermarket in the town centre.

Getting There & Away

AIR

Bima is the main airport for travellers to Pantai Lakey. During peak season (June to August), when flights from Labuanbajo (Flores) are often fully booked, you can make the 10-hour ferry and bus trip from Labuanbajo to Bima to find a seat on a less-packed Bima-Bali flight. Services include the following:

Bali Garuda, Lion Air, 1¼ hours, daily

Makassar (Sulawesi) Garuda, 1½ hours, daily

BOAT

Pelni boats travel twice monthly from Bima to Waingapu, Ende and Kupang, Benoa (Bali) and Sulawesi.

Travel agencies in town can organise tickets, since the **Pelni office** (0374-42625; Jl Kesatria 2) is at Bima port.

BUS

Buses heading west leave from the Bima bus terminal, a 10-minute walk south along Jl Sultan Kaharuddin from the centre of town. You can buy a ticket in advance from bus-company offices on Jl Sultan Kaharuddin. Buses for Sape depart from the Kumbe terminal in Raba (a 3000Rp bemo ride away). Routes include the following:

Dompu 25,000Rp, two hours, almost hourly from 6am to 5pm

Mataram 250,000Rp, 11 to 14 hours, two daily

Sape 35,000, two hours, almost hourly from 6am to 5pm

Sumbawa Besar 80,000, seven hours, several daily

Getting Around

The airport sits amid salt flats 17km west from the centre on the way to Dompu and the road to Pantai Lakey. You can walk out to the main road and catch a passing bus. Alternatively, taxis meet arrivals, charging 100,000Rp to Bima or 800,000Rp to Pantai Lakey.

A bemo around town costs 3000Rp per person.

Sape

0374

Sape's got a tumbledown port-town vibe, perfumed with the conspicuous scent of drying cuttlefish. The outskirts are quilted in rice fields backed by jungled hills, and the streets are busy with *benhur* (horse-drawn carts) and early-morning commerce. There's decent food and doable lodging here too, so if you are catching a morning ferry, consider this an alternative to Bima.

Sleeping & Eating

The ferry port is 3km east of Sape's diminutive centre.

Losmen Mutiara GUESTHOUSE $

(0374-71337; Jl Pelabuhan Sape; r 60,000-160,000Rp;) Despite little competition, Losmen Mutiara, right next to the port gates and last bus stop, is a decent place to stay. Twenty rooms are spread across two floors, with the most expensive having air-con.

Rumah Makan Citra Minang INDONESIAN $

(Jl Pelabuhan Sape; mains 20,000-30,000Rp; 8am-9pm) The smiling ladies here bring the finest and spiciest Padang dishes to life. The shabby interior belies the quality and flavour of the food. It's mere steps from the boats and last bus stop.

Getting There & Around

BOAT

Regular breakdowns and big water disrupt ferry services – always double-check the latest schedules in Bima and Sape. Ferries from Sape include the following:

Labuanbajo 60,000Rp, six to seven hours, one to two daily

Waikelo (Sumba) 65,000Rp, eight hours, two weekly

BUS

Express buses with service to Lombok and Bali meet arriving ferries.

Buses leave every hour for Bima (35,000Rp, two hours), where you can catch local buses to other Sumbawa destinations.

Taxi drivers may claim that buses have stopped running and you must charter their vehicle to Bima (350,000Rp, 1½ hours); this is usually not true.

KOMODO & RINCA ISLANDS

Nestled between Sumbawa and Flores, the islands of Komodo and Rinca are the main components of Unesco-recognised Komodo National Park, whose rapidly increasing popularity is helping drive the booming tourism economy of Flores.

The island's jagged hills, carpeted with savannah and fringed with mangroves, are home to the legendary Komodo dragon. The world's largest lizard, known locally as *ora*, it can reach over 3m in length. It hunts alone and feeds on animals as large as deer and buffalo, both of which are found here.

These isolated islands are surrounded by some of the most tempestuous waters in Indonesia. The convergence of warm and cold currents breeds nutritious thermal climes, rip tides and whirlpools that attract large schools of pelagics, from dolphins and sharks to manta rays and blue whales. The coral here is mostly pristine. Add it all up and you have some of the best diving in the world (p360), which is why dozens of liveaboards ply these waters between April and September when the water is smooth and the diving at its finest.

Komodo

Spectacular Komodo, its steep hillsides jade in the short wet season, frazzled by the sun and winds to a deep rusty red for most of the year, is the largest island in the national park. A succession of eastern peninsulas spread out like so many fingers, fringed in pink sand, thanks to the abundance of red coral offshore. The main camp of **Loh Liang** and the PHKA office, where boats dock and guided walks and treks start, is on the east coast.

The fishing village of **Kampung Komodo** is an hour-long walk south of Loh Liang. It's a friendly stilted Bugis village that's full of goats, chickens and children. The inhabitants are said to be descendants of convicts exiled to the island in the 19th century by one of the sultans in Sumbawa. The residents here are used to seeing tourists and you can spend a fair bit of time absorbing village life and gazing out over the water.

Activities

Walking & Trekking

The 80,000Rp entrance fee at Komodo includes a choice of three walks: the **short walk** (1.5km, 45 minutes), which includes a stop at an artificial waterhole that attracts the diminutive local deer – and of course

Komodo & Rinca Islands

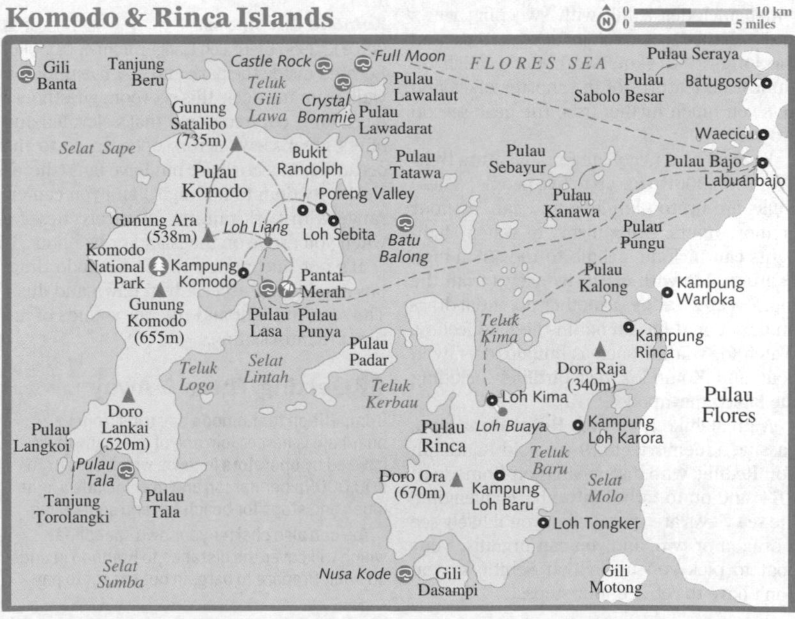

VISITING KOMODO NATIONAL PARK

Komodo National Park (www.komodo-park.com), established in 1980, encompasses Komodo, Rinca, several neighbouring islands, and the rich marine ecosystem within its 1817 sq km.

Fees for visitors add up quickly:

- Landing fee per person for Komodo and Rinca islands: 50,000Rp
- Basic guided walk fee per person: 80,000Rp
- Diving fee per person per day: Monday to Saturday/Sunday 175,000/250,000Rp
- Snorkelling fee per person per day: Monday to Saturday/Sunday 165,000/240,000Rp

Tour operators (including dive shops) usually collect the fees in advance. If not, you pay them in the park offices on Komodo or Rinca, or in Labuanbajo (p362).

At both Komodo and Rinca you have a choice of walks, from short to long, which you arrange with a ranger when you arrive at the relevant island's park office.

ora; the **medium walk** (2.5km, 90 minutes), which includes a hill with sweeping views and a chance to see colourful cockatoos; and the **long trek** (4km, two hours), which includes the features of the shorter hikes and gets you much further from the peak-season crowds.

You can also negotiate for adventure treks (from 500,000Rp for up to five people). These walks are up to 9km long and can last four or more hours. Bring plenty of water. Highlights can include a climb to the 538m-high **Gunung Ara** with expansive views from the top. **Poreng Valley** is another potential dragon haunt, and has an out-in-the-wild feeling. Watch for wildlife such as buffalo, deer, wild boar and Komodo's rich birdlife, including the fabled megapodes.

A great hike goes over **Bukit Randolph**, passing a memorial to 79-year-old Randolph Von Reding, who disappeared on Komodo in 1974, and on to **Loh Sebita**. It's challenging, the sea views are spectacular, you'll likely see a dragon or two, and you can organise your boat to pick you up in Loh Sebita, so you don't have to retrace your steps.

Water Sports

Almost everybody who visits Komodo hires a boat in Labuanbajo or visits as part of a liveaboard itinerary. Day trips always offer snorkelling (gear included) as part of the itinerary as well as a stop at an island beach. Many snorkel around the small island of **Pulau Lasa** near Kampung Komodo, and just off the pink sands of **Pantai Merah** (Red Beach), which is just an hour's walk from Loh Liang.

People who stay on Komodo can arrange for kayaking and sunrise dolphin tours.

Sleeping & Eating

Although it is easy to visit Komodo on a day trip from Labuanbajo, there are definite advantages to spending the night on the island. In the park you can spot *ora* during their active postdawn rambles and before the first tour boats arrive at 9am. Late in the afternoon, you can enjoy near-solitude after the day's visitors have left, leaving you to absorb nature's rhythm and delight in Komodo's pastoral charms. Any place you stay will provide simple meals.

In the village of Kampung Komodo, you'll find a few very casual homestays that give you a basic bed and some meals. Either just turn up and let locals guide you to one (rooms from about 200,000Rp per night) or arrange your stay in advance with **Usman Ranger** (☎0812 3956 6140; Komodo).

Komodo Guesthouse GUESTHOUSE **$$**
(☎0812 3956 6140; Loh Liang; r from 400,000Rp) Located inside the park and just five minutes' walk from the dock, this six-room guesthouse has a long, covered porch that's elevated and offers great views across open space to the ocean. Rooms are basic but have fans (there's electricity 6pm to midnight) and you can arrange with park rangers for meals. Reserve when you arrive on the island or by phone.

It's not uncommon to see Komodo dragons amble past, especially at dawn and dusk. The stars at night and the raw sounds of nature are intoxicating.

Getting There & Away

Competition for Komodo day trips from Labuanbajo is fierce. Join one of the many tours hawked by operators in town, which cost from 300,000Rp per person and may include a light lunch and stops for beach fun and snorkelling.

You can also charter your own speedboat which will cover the distance to Komodo in under an hour. Prepare to bargain but expect to pay around 7,000,000Rp for up to four people for a full day out (which can include stops at both Komodo and Rinca).

The many liveaboard schemes almost always include a stop at Komodo at some point, as do the private boats making the run between Flores and Lombok and Bali.

Rinca

Rinca is slightly smaller than Komodo, close to Labuanbajo, and easily done in a day trip. It packs a lot into a small space and for many it is more convenient but just as worthy a destination as Komodo. The island combines mangroves, light forest and sun-drenched hills, as well as – of course – Komodo dragons.

Activities

From the boat dock, it's a 10-minute walk across tidal flats, home to long-tail macaques and wild water buffalo, to the PHKA station camp at **Loh Buaya**. Three basic types of guided walks are included in the 80,000Rp admission fee: the **short walk** (500m, one hour) takes in mangroves and some *ora* nesting sites; the **medium walk** (1.5km, 90 minutes) is literally just right as it includes the shady lowlands plus a trip up a hillside where the views across the arid landscape to palm-dotted ridges, achingly turquoise waters and pearly white specks of beach are spectacular; and the **long walk** (4km,

KOMODO DRAGONS

The Komodo dragon *(ora)* is a monitor lizard, albeit one on steroids. Growing up to 3m in length and weighing up to 100kg, they are an awesome sight and make a visit to Komodo National Park well worth the effort. Lounging about lethargically in the sun, these are actually as fearsome as their looks imply. Park rangers keep them from attacking tourists; random encounters are a bad idea. Some dragon details:

- They are omnivorous, and enjoy eating their young. Juvenile dragons live in trees to avoid becoming a meal for adults.
- *Ora* often rise up on their hind legs just before attacking, and the tail can deliver well-aimed blows that knock down their prey.
- Long thought to be a type of bacteria, venom (located in glands between the dragons' teeth) are their secret weapon. One bite from a dragon leads to septic infections that inevitably kill the victim. The huge lizard lopes along after its victim waiting for it to die, which can take up to two weeks.
- Komodos will feed on mammals weighing up to 100kg. They do this at one sitting and then retire for up to a month to digest the massive meal.
- On Komodo, *ora* have been seen chasing deer into the ocean and then waiting on shore while the hapless deer tries to come back ashore. Eventually the exhausted animal staggers onto the beach, where the dragon inflicts its ultimately deadly bite.
- There is no accepted reason why the dragons are only found in this small area of Indonesia, although it's thought that their ancestors came from Australia four million years ago. There are about 4000 in the wild today.
- A recent discovery has biologists baffled: female dragons kept isolated from other dragons their entire lives have recently been observed in zoos giving birth to fertilised eggs.

Spotting Dragons

At both Komodo and Rinca your odds of seeing dragons are very good. Although claims are made that there is no feeding of the *ora*, invariably you'll see a few specimens hanging around the ranger stations, especially at the kitchens. There are further opportunities on the actual walks, where you are likely to see the animals in purely natural surroundings.

Rangers carry a forked staff as their only protection; you may get quite close to *ora*. A telephoto lens is handy but not essential. Still, treat the seemingly slow-moving *ora* with great respect: two villagers have been killed in the last two decades.

Peak months for komodo-spotting are September to December, when both sexes are out and about. The worst months are June to August, which is mating season for the males, which causes the females to go into hiding.

BOAT TOURS BETWEEN LOMBOK & FLORES

Travelling by sea between Lombok and Labuanbajo is a popular way to get to Flores, as you'll glimpse more of the region's spectacular coastline and dodge the slog by bus across Sumbawa. Typical three- and four-day itineraries take in snorkelling at Pulau Satonda or Pulau Moyo off the coast of Sumbawa, and a dragon-spotting hike on Komodo or Rinca.

But note, this is usually no luxury cruise – a lot depends on the boat, the crew and your fellow travellers. Some operators have reneged on 'all-inclusive' deals en route, and others operate decrepit old tugs without life jackets or radio. And this crossing can be hazardous during the rainy season (October to January), when the seas are rough.

Most travellers enjoy the journey though, whether it involves bedding down on a mattress on deck or in a tiny cabin. The cost for a three- to four-day itinerary ranges from about US$170 to US$400 per person and includes all meals, basic beverages and use of snorkelling gear.

Other considerations:

- Carefully vet your boat for safety (p780).
- Understand what's included and not included in the price. For instance, if drinking water is included, how much is provided? If you need more, can you buy it on the boat or do you need to bring your own?
- If you are flexible, you can often save money by travelling west from Flores, as travelling eastwards to Flores is more popular. Look for deals at agents once you're in Labuanbajo.

Kencana Adventure (☎0370-693432; www.kencanaadventure.com; Jl Soekarno Hatta, front of Gardena Hotel, Labuanbajo; one-way deck/cabin from 1,750,000/4,500,000Rp) Offers basic boat trips between Lombok and Labuanbajo with deck accommodation as well as cabins that sleep two. Also has a **branch** in Sengiggi, Lombok (Jl Raya Senggigi).

Perama Tour (☎0361-750808; www.peramatour.com; Jl Soekarno Hatta, Labuanbajo; one-way deck/cabin from 1,300,000/2,000,000Rp) Runs basic boat trips between Lombok and Labuanbajo with deck accommodation as well as small two-person cabins. Also has a branch in Kuta, Bali (Jl Raya Legian 39).

three hours) which takes in all the island's attractions.

Besides dragons, you may see tiny Timor deer, snakes, monkeys, wild boar and myriad birds. There are supposedly no set dragon-feeding places on Rinca, but there are often a half-dozen massive beasts near the camp kitchen at Loh Buaya, so you do the math.

Sleeping & Eating

You can stay in a spare room in the ranger's dorm (from 300,000Rp), but there's little reason to as the site lacks charm.

There is a simple daytime **cafe** at the ranger station where you can stock up on water, enjoy a cold beer while watching grazing deer nervously eyeing *ora*, and have a snack.

Getting There & Away

Day trips to Rinca cost from about 300,000Rp and choices are many. Chartering a speedboat to Rinca costs at least 3,000,000Rp from Labuanbajo and takes less than an hour each way. Boats usually return via small island beaches and snorkelling spots.

At Rinca, boats dock at the sheltered lagoon at Loh Kima, which at busy times may have over two dozen wooden vessels tied together.

FLORES

Flores, the island named 'flowers' by 16th-century Portuguese colonists, has become Indonesia's 'Next Big Thing'. In the far west, Labuanbajo is a booming tourist town that combines tropical beauty with nearby attractions such as Komodo National Park, myriad superb dive spots and beach-dappled little islands.

The often lush interior is attracting an ever-greater river of travellers who, in just a few days' journey overland, encounter smoking volcanoes, spectacular rice fields and lakes, exotic cultures and hidden beaches. You'll even see plenty of steeples, as away from the port towns most people are nominally Catholic. And many more people are part of cultures and groups that date back centuries, and live in traditional villages seemingly unchanged in millennia.

The 670km serpentine, yet rapidly improving, Trans-Flores Hwy skirts knife-edge ridges that sheer into spectacular river canyons, brushes by dozens of traditional villages, and always seems to have a perfectly conical volcano in view. Roads of varying quality branch off into areas few tourists have explored.

Culture

The island's 1.9 million people are divided into five main linguistic and cultural groups. From west to east, these are the Manggarai (main town Ruteng), the Ngada (Bajawa), the closely related Ende and Lio peoples (Ende), the Sikkanese (Maumere) and the Lamaholot (Larantuka). In remote areas, especially those accessible only by trail, some older people don't speak a word of Bahasa Indonesia, and their parents grew up in purely animist societies.

Around 85% of the people are Catholic, but in rural areas Christianity is welded onto *adat*. Animist rituals are still used for births, marriages and deaths, and to mark important points in the agricultural calendar. Even educated, English-speaking Florinese participate in the odd chicken, pig or buffalo sacrifice to the ancestors when rice is planted.

Muslims congregate in fishing villages and coastal towns such as Ende (where they make up half the population) and Labuanbajo.

Information

Foreign aid money has funded an excellent string of tourist offices in key towns across Flores. Their enthusiastic information is backed by an excellent website (www.florestourism.com), free town maps and several publications well worth their modest price, including a huge, detailed island map, and books covering activities and culture.

Getting There & Away

Air You can easily get flights connecting Flores and Bali, Lombok and Kupang (West Timor), among other destinations. Labuanbajo is the main gateway, while Maumere and Ende are also serviced by daily flights. It's easy to fly into, say, Labuanbajo, tour the island, and fly out of Maumere. However, note that the booming popularity of Flores means that flights are booked solid at peak times.

SEVEN DAYS ON FLORES

You can take as long as you like exploring Flores, but a common trip for the visa-expiry-date-conscious using a hired car and driver goes like this:

- Three days in Labuanbajo and the surrounding Komodo National Park and waters
- One day driving to the hill town of Bajawa with time to explore the surrounding Ngada villages
- One day driving to the sweet mountain village of Moni via the Ngada village of Bena and the steamy port town of Ende
- One day exploring the area around Moni, including Kelimutu National Park
- One day driving to Maumere, with a stop at the beach in Paga

You can fly out of Maumere and you can do this trip in either direction, although it's easiest to find a driver you'll like in Labuanbajo. Add a couple of extra days to the schedule above if you're sticking to buses.

Boat Daily ferries connect Labuanbajo with Sape (Sumbawa). From Larantuka, infrequent ferries go to Kupang (West Timor). From Ende and Aimere, boats will take you to Waingapu (Sumba).

Getting Around

The Trans-Flores Hwy is the spine of the island. It is rapidly being improved, so much so that you can expect delays for major roadworks. It twists and turns through the beautiful countryside, loops around volcanoes and passes untouched beaches.

The improving roads mean that more and more visitors are simply hiring motorbikes in Labuanbajo and heading east. This can cost from 50,000Rp per day plus petrol. But note that this is not for the faint of heart: driving conditions can be hazardous and exhausting.

Regular buses run between Labuanbajo and Maumere. They're cheap and cramped. Much more comfortable and only somewhat more expensive are public minibuses (often a Toyota Kijang), which link major towns in air-con comfort. Many travellers hire a car and driver, which costs from 600,000Rp to 800,000Rp per day. If you have a group of six, this is a fair deal; some drivers also work as guides, and can arrange fascinating and detailed island-wide itineraries.

Flores

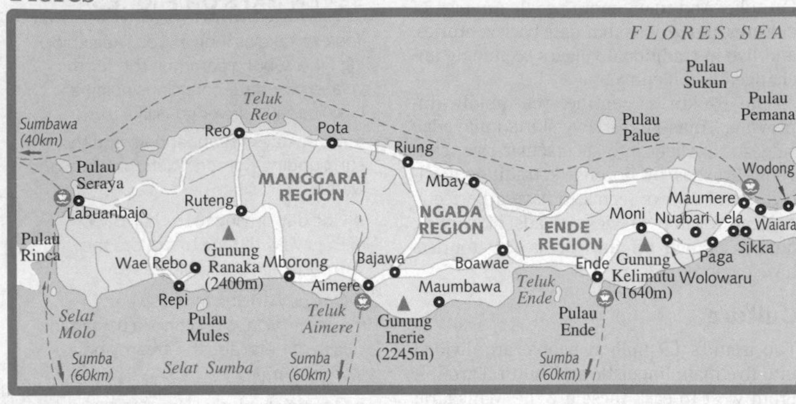

Your accommodation will usually have details on all the above options.

Andy Rona (☎ 0813 3798 0855; andyrona7@gmail.com) An excellent driver and guide, who has a network of reliable colleagues.

Philip Neto (☎ 0813 3903 1877, WhatsApp 184-791; philip.neto@yahoo.com) Based in Bajawa and has island-wide experience. Excellent for treks to remote villages.

Labuanbajo

☎ 0385

Ever-more travellers are descending on this gorgeous, slightly ramshackle harbour town, freckled with offshore islands and blessed with idyllic views that offer surrealist sunsets.

Labuanbajo's main drag, Jl Soekarno Hatta, is lined with cool cafes, guesthouses, travel agents and a few hopping bars. The waterfront is spiffed-up and the connections to other parts of Indonesia are excellent. With the many beguiling islands just offshore, you may find Labuanbajo (or Bajo as it's commonly called) hard to leave, even as the draw of Flores proper lures you east.

Note, however, that Bajo is at a crossroads: with its new popularity, growth has spiralled upwards. How the new development along the coast is handled will say much about whether the town remains a traveller's idyll or becomes just another trashed hotspot.

Activities

Excursions to nearby islands make great day trips, offering the chance to snorkel or lounge on a deserted beach. **Pulau Bidadari**, for instance, offers lovely coral and crystalline water. You can snooze on **Pantai Waecicu** and snorkel around the tiny offshore islet of **Kukusan Kecil**. **Pulau Seraya** and **Pulau Kanawa** are both gorgeous and have excellent beaches.

Some of the islands have hotels offering free transport, and day trips abound. You'll find no shortage of offers in Labuanbajo – many focused on Rinca and Komodo Islands. Decent trips with snorkelling, beach time and maybe a Komodo dragon or two start at 250,000Rp.

Diving & Snorkelling

With dive sites around the islands near Labuanbajo and the proximity of Komodo National Park, there are some excellent scuba opportunities here. We're talking about some of the best sites on earth, which explains the ever-increasing number of dive shops and liveaboards. Also note that **freediving** is becoming as popular locally as it is in the Gilis.

Labuanbajo dive shops have similar prices. For instance, it costs around 1,100,000Rp for two dives on a day trip. Some shops offer Open Water Diver certification and Divemaster programs (from about US$500). You'll need to have Advanced Open Water to hit the best sites. Custom dive safaris to the brilliant northern Komodo sites are also available.

Dive shops line Jl Soekarno Hatta. It's best to shop around first, and survey equipment and boats before you make a decision. Bring your own computer or anything else you deem essential.

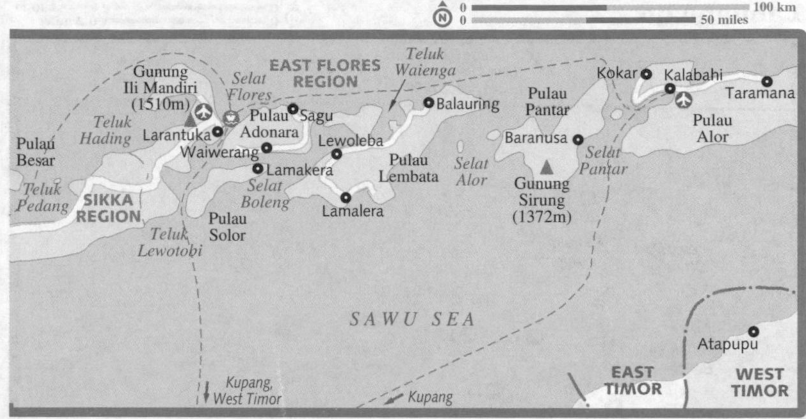

Dive operators – and many others, including some hotels – rent snorkelling gear. July and August is peak season, with ever-larger crowds. In March, April and September crowds thin and the diving is magical.

★ Wicked Diving DIVING
(☎0812 3964 1143; www.wickeddiving.com/komodo; Jl Soekarno Hatta; floating dm per night from US$100; ⏰8am-8pm) Offers popular multiday liveaboards on a classic Bugis schooner and has a 'floating hostel' set among the northern islands of Komodo National Park. Its day trips are justifiably popular and the company wins plaudits for nurturing local divers, promoting strong green practices and giving back to the community. Accommodation rates include dives and transport.

Blue Marlin DIVING
(☎0385-41789; www.bluemarlindivekomodo.com; Jl Soekarno Hatta; day trips from 1,100,000Rp; ⏰8am-8pm) Long before the boom this dive shop was running liveaboards between the Gilis and Labuanbajo, and it has great experience in the Komodos. Staff are also expert tech divers. Its custom, fibreglass 15m boat allows for three dives per day instead of the two on a standard day trip. The bay-front compound includes a swimming pool used for instruction.

Uber Scuba DIVING
(☎0812 3653 6749; uberscubakomodo.com; Jl Soekarno Hatta; three-dive fun dive 1,400,000Rp; ⏰8am-8pm) This new dive shop is riding the wave of ever-increasing visitor numbers to the Komodo area. Besides extensive courses, it offers a full range of free diving excursions and instruction.

Bajo Dive Club DIVING
(☎0385-41503; www.komododiver.com; Jl Soekarno Hatta; day trips from 950,000Rp; ⏰8am-8pm) A popular, long-running choice with a large day-trip boat, which means comfortable voyages to the national park sites. It also offers dive safaris and courses.

CNDive DIVING
(☎0823 3908 0808; www.cndivekomodo.com; Jl Soekarno Hatta; per person per day from US$150; ⏰8am-8pm) Condo Subagyo, the proprietor of CNDive, is the area's original Indonesian dive operator and a former Komodo National Park ranger. The staff are all locals who have been thoroughly trained and have intimate knowledge of over 100 dive sites.

Komodo Dive Center DIVING
(☎0812 3630 3644; www.komododivecenter.com; Jl Soekarno Hatta; day trips from 1,200,000Rp; ⏰8am-8pm) Offers a full range of day trips, multiday tours and courses. Promotes its use of nitrox and its extensive range of gear rentals.

Current Junkies DIVING
(www.currentjunkies.com; 6-day, 5-nights liveaboards from US$1000) One of the most interesting liveaboards in the area, Current Junkies does not shy away from a ripping current. It dives into them, because the current brings pelagics. Trips are six days and five nights, and include 14 dives. It only accepts five divers per trip, and no beginners. Online bookings only; the boat departs from Labuanbajo.

Labuanbajo

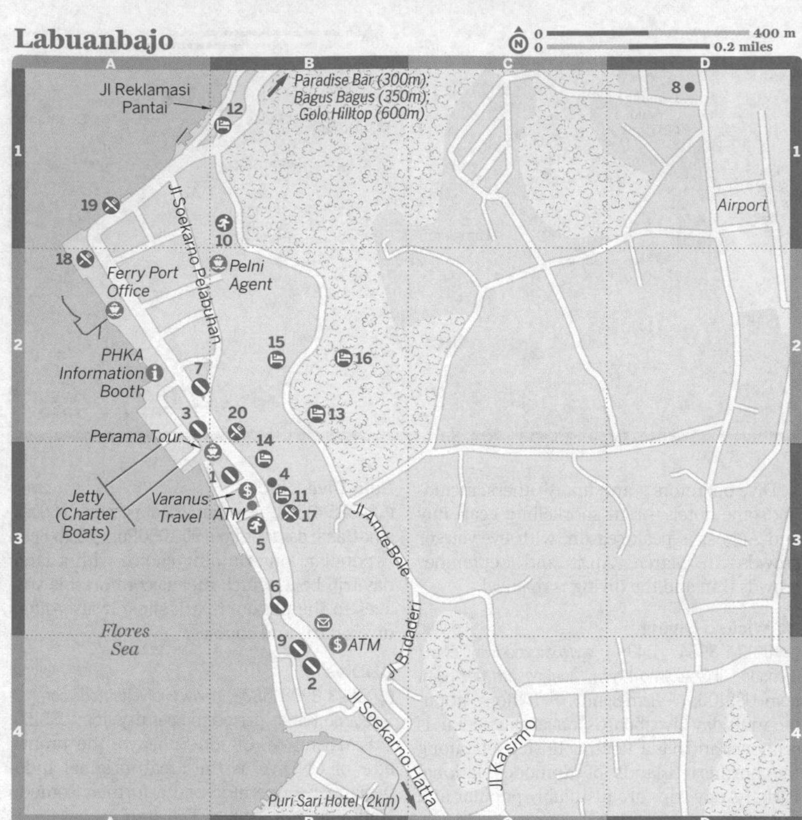

Labuanbajo

Activities, Courses & Tours

1	Bajo Dive Club	B3
2	Blue Marlin	B4
3	CNDive	A2
4	Flores Komodo Expedition	B3
5	Flores Spa	B3
6	Komodo Dive Center	B3
7	Uber Scuba	A2
8	Wicked Adventures	D1
9	Wicked Diving	B4
10	Yayasan Ayo Mandiri	B1

Sleeping

11	Bajo Beach Hotel	B3
12	Bajo Sunset Hostel	B1
13	Bayview Gardens Hotel	B2
14	Green Hill Hotel	B3
15	Palulu Garden Homestay	B2
16	Villa Seirama Alam	B2

Eating

17	Bajo Bakery	B3
	Cafe in Hit	(see 14)
18	Daily Market	A2
	Lounge	(see 14)
	Made In Italy	(see 11)
	Mediterrano	(see 1)
19	Pasar Malam	A1
	Tree Top	(see 9)
20	Warung Mama	B2

Climbing & Canyoning

Opportunities for exploration on land abound east of Labuanbajo. Tour operators can organise these and countless more trips.

Climbing up the rainforested slopes of **Gunung Mbeliling** (1239m) is popular. The trip usually takes two days, and includes about eight hours of hiking, sunrise at the summit and a stop-off at Cunca Rami Air

Terjun, a cooling cascade with freshwater swimming holes.

If you like canyoning, you'll enjoy the **Cunca Wulang Cascades**, where local guides lead you down natural rock water slides, off 7m rock jumps and into swimming holes beneath a series of waterfalls. Trips generally last half a day.

Massage & Spa

Flores Spa SPA

(☎0385-42089; www.floresspa.com; Jl Soekarno Hatta; massages from 120,000Rp; ⊙10am-8pm Mon-Sat, 1-8pm Sun) A shopfront spa with recommended treatments such as the jasmine body scrub, reflexology, full body massage and sunburn relief.

Yayasan Ayo Mandiri SPA

(☎0385-041318; www.yam-flores.com; Jl Puncak Waringin; 70min massages 120,000Rp; ⊙9am-12.30pm & 3-8pm Mon-Sat) Enjoy a massage at the hands of a gifted, sightless therapist. A home for the blind, this spa offers top-quality treatments including acupressure, hot stone and reflexology. Look for the big red 'massage' sign.

Tours

In addition to the dedicated tour companies, drivers can also plan and lead trips.

Wicked Adventures ADVENTURE TOUR

(☎0812 3607 9641; www.wickedadventures.com; Arah BTN depan Bandara; 1-day kayak trips from US$100; ⊙10am-6pm) An offshoot of the recommended Wicked Diving (p357), this group runs very enjoyable kayak trips with local guides in Komodo National Park. Other adventures include Wae Rebo trekking and trips to Wicked's turtle conservation camp on a south Flores beach. The office is across from the airport.

Flores Komodo Expedition ADVENTURE TOUR

(☎0385-42127; www.floreskomodoexpedition.com; Jl Soekarno Hatta; 2-day Wae Rebo tours for 2 people 1,800,000Rp; ⊙10am-7pm) Organises all manner of trips around Flores. Themes include birdwatching, ancient villages, jungle-trekking, Komodo National Park and much more, and can be customised to suit. Also rents motorbikes for 90,000Rp per day.

Sleeping

It seems every week there is a new place to stay in Labuanbajo. Still, during peak season in July and August book ahead lest you be one of the sad groups trooping along the streets looking for a room while the already accommodated look down on you from cafes with ill-disguised pity.

If you can swing it, consider one of the superb resorts on the nearby islands.

DIVING INTO THE FUTURE

The fact that the waters in and around Komodo National Park have both Unesco World Heritage status and official protection from the Indonesian government doesn't mean that they are not constantly under threat.

Reports of dynamite fishing – although decreasing – continue, even as the PHKA park administration has become more aggressive in protecting the region. Fortunately, the huge popularity of the waters means that there is no shortage of diving operators and divers watching out for transgressions. These efforts have been aided by the increasing economic incentives for people in the fishing industry to switch to the tourism industry. It also helps that some dive shops have proactive programs to hire and train locals from across the region, who then become conservation ambassadors in their home villages.

Central Area

★**Bajo Sunset Hostel** HOSTEL $

(☎0812 3799 3814; bajosunset.wordpress.com; Jl Reklamasi Pantai; dm/r from 150,000/250,000Rp; ❄📶) A great new addition to the Bajo scene, this newly built guesthouse sits on reclaimed land on the waterfront. There is a modest cafe and a large open-air common area with great views out to sea. Accommodation is in a 14-bed dorm and four-bed rooms. Smaller private rooms are planned.

Palulu Garden Homestay HOMESTAY $

(☎0822 3658 4279; palulugarden.wordpress.com; off Jl Ande Bole; r economy/budget/air-con from 140,000/200,000/350,000Rp; ❄) Long-time local guide Kornelis Gega and his family run this four-room homestay just a short walk above the centre. The cheapest room shares a bathroom, while the top room has air-con. It's pure Flores throughout, and utterly spic and span. Kornelis can help with your trip planning and arrange transport etc.

DIVING & SNORKELLING AROUND KOMODO & LABUANBAJO

Komodo National Park has some of the most exhilarating scuba diving in Indonesia, especially around the many islands in the north. It's a region swept by strong currents and cold upswells, created by the convergence of the warmer Flores Sea and the cooler Selat Sumba (Sumba Strait) – conditions that create rich plankton soup and an astonishing diversity of marine life. Mantas and whales are drawn here to feed on the plankton during their migration from the Indian Ocean to the South China Sea. Dolphins are also common in the waters between Komodo and Flores.

The following are among the several dozen dive sites mapped in the park and in the waters and islands around Labuanbajo:

Batu Balong A split pinnacle with pristine coral and a relatively light current. The small rock jutting above the water only hints at the wealth of life below.

Crystal Bommie (aka Crystal Rock) Has electric soft corals, turtles, schooling pelagics and strong currents.

Castle Rock (aka Tako Toko Toko) A tremendous sunrise dive site where, with a little luck, you'll dive with dolphins or see magnificent pinwheels of tropical fish amid strong currents.

Makassar Reef A shallow drift dive over moonscape rubble where massive manta rays school and clean themselves on the rocks. If you've never seen mantas before, dive here. It's (almost) guaranteed.

Multiple shark sightings on a single dive are common (there are a lot of grey reef sharks as well as the humongous plankton-eating whale sharks).

You'll have your pick of excellent dive shops in Labuanbajo and at some of the island resorts. Myriad day trips and liveaboard schemes are on offer.

Bajo Beach Hotel GUESTHOUSE $

(0385-41008; Jl Soekarno Hatta; r 150,000-250,000Rp;) A fine cheapie in the city centre with 16 basic but spacious tiled older rooms that are clean and well tended. Each has a private seating area out front. You'll get the same room either way, but pay a bit more for air-con.

Golo Hilltop BUNGALOW $$

(0385-41337; www.golohilltop.com; Jl Binongko; r 450,000-525,000Rp;) The pool just makes this 10-room nest even sweeter. Expect modern, super-clean concrete bungalows in a hilltop garden setting with magnificent views of Teluk Labuanbajo (but not of the harbour). Deluxe rooms are on the top ridge; standard rooms are fan-cooled. You must reserve ahead.

Bagus Bagus GUESTHOUSE $$

(0812 386 0084; stefankomodo@gmail.com; off Jl Binongko; r from 250,000Rp) Accessed from the walkway that leads to Paradise Bar, these fine, spacious, tiled rooms have wooden beds, mosquito nets, high woven-bamboo and beamed ceilings, open-air baths, and exquisite sunset views from the common porch. The owner is a major promoter of recycling.

Bayview Gardens Hotel INN $$

(0385-41549; www.bayview-gardens.com; Jl Ande Bole; r from 500,000Rp;) A lovely nine-room inn notched onto the hillside above town with epic sunset and harbour views, and a lovely grey-water-fed garden with over 450 plant species. Breakfast is served in your room, which isn't fancy but is sweet with an outdoor living room, separate indoor bedroom and huge bathroom. Wi-fi is only in the lobby; reserve in advance.

Green Hill Hotel GUESTHOUSE $$

(0385-41289; www.greenhillboutiquehotel.com; Jl Soekarno Hatta; r from 500,000Rp;) The communal terrace bar with its view of the town, bay and sunsets makes this an excellent choice. The 11 rooms are a brief climb from the very centre of town and range from scruffy and older to sprightly and newer. Breakfasts are excellent.

Villa Seirama Alam HOTEL $$$

(0813 5377 9942; www.villaseiramaalam.com; off Jl Ande Bole; villas from US$165;) Enjoy the home you'd live in if you called Bajo home. This two-storey, three-bedroom house is set on lush grounds and has brilliant views across the harbour and islands. Everything is rather stylish and made of wood. Ask about cheaper rates if you only rent part of the villa.

By the Beach

This crescent of sand south of the centre may be the future of Labuanbajo tourism. The massive Jayakarta Hotel opened its 200-room resort in 2011, followed by the slightly shambolic Laprima, signalling the coming dawn of mass tourism in Labuanbajo.

Puri Sari Hotel BOUTIQUE HOTEL **$$$**
(0385-244 3710; www.purisarihotel.com; Jl Pantai Pede; r from 850,000Rp;) A two-storey ranch-style hotel with a boutique feel. There's a shady garden, a beachside pool, and warm and friendly management. The 21 rooms are lovely with queen-sized wooden beds, bowl sinks and a wide private terrace. It offers free shuttles to and from the airport, and a daily shuttle to town.

Island Hotels

Although close to Labuanbajo, the surrounding island hotels and resorts feel like a world apart. All offer some form of boat transfer to/from town – in an hour or less you can escape to your own tropical paradise. And most have their own excellent dive operations (Kanawa is a notable exception).

★ **Scuba Junkie Komodo Beach Resort** DIVE RESORT **$$**
(0812 3601 8523; www.scubajunkiekomodo.com; Warloka Flores; 3-night all-inclusive packages dm/s/d from US$390/550/900) This fantastically run new dive resort is on an isolated bay about 45 minutes south of Bajo by boat. Rinca Island is nearby as are oodles of fine dive sites, which is good as staying here is all about underwater adventures. On land, accommodation is in fine four-bed dorms or breezy beach bungalows. Food and drink are excellent. Diving is included in package prices.

Kanawa Beach Bungalows BUNGALOW **$$**
(0813 3823 3312, 0385-41252; kanawaisland resort.com; Pulau Kanawa; bungalows s/d from 550,000/700,000Rp) There's no denying this beach hideaway its loveliness. There's an elegant strip of white sand, a turquoise lagoon with magnificent snorkelling, endless island views and a long crooked jetty that is the tropical romantic ideal. However, conditions can be shambolic and getting close to nature can mean bedding down with bugs.

If you're an intrepid backpacker you might love the adventure; if you can't be separated from your roll-aboard luggage, you may flee screaming.

★ **Angel Island Resort** RESORT **$$$**
(0385-41443; www.angelisleflores.com; Pulau Bidadari; d per person from €145;) Set on its own 15-hectare island and linked to Labuanbajo by private boat, this resort has 10 sweet villas scattered about the trees behind one of three white-sand beaches. All meals are included; the food and service are casual and superb. You can easily while away your days here on the deserted beaches, or out snorkelling, diving and visiting the park. Minimum two-night stay.

Komodo Resort Diving Club RESORT **$$$**
(0385-42095; www.komodoresort.com; Pulau Sebayur; d per person all-inclusive €140;) With 14 *lumbung*-style bungalows spread along the white-sand beach on Pulau Sebayur, this is one of our favourite island resorts. Bungalows have wood floors, queen beds, plush linens, 24-hour electricity, tented marble bathrooms with hot water, and more. Rates include three excellent meals. There's a spa and a fun beach bar. Minimum three-night stay.

Seraya Hotel & Resort RESORT **$$$**
(0821 4647 1362; www.serayahotel.com; Pulau Seraya; d per person from €105) Get-away-from-it-all bliss exists on Pulau Seraya. Stay in utterly casual, whitewashed, weathered wood-and-thatch-bungalows set on a white-sand beach, with offshore snorkelling and a rugged hilltop where you can wonder at spectacular sunsets for days on end. It's only 20 minutes by boat from Bajo. Minimum three-night stay.

Eating & Drinking

Labuanbajo punches way above its weight in the food department. Browse the local bounty of fruits, vegetables, fish and other market fare at the **daily market** (Jl Soekarno Hatta; 7am-4pm) at the north end of the waterfront.

★ **Pasar Malam** INDONESIAN **$**
(Night Market; Jl Soekarno Hatta; mains from 20,000Rp; 6pm-midnight) At sunset, grab a tarp-shaded table at Bajo's waterfront night market, as a dozen stalls come alive with all manner of Indo classics, fried delights and grilled seafood. Get cold beer from the market across the road.

Cafe in Hit CAFE $
(☎0813 5367 3884; Jl Soekarno Hatta; mains from 40,000Rp; ⊙7am-10pm; ❄📶) You may forget you're in Bajo, let alone Flores, at this semislick coffee house. Let the air-con cool you while you choose a drink from the blackboards, which could be in any upscale hipster cafe worldwide. Food is well executed and includes sandwiches, baked goods, brownies and more. Breakfasts are heavy on wholegrains and fruit.

Bajo Bakery BAKERY $
(Jl Soekarno Hatta; mains 20,000-40,000Rp; ⊙7am-7pm Mon-Sat; ❄) Expect good fresh breads, seductive banana muffins, tasty breakfasts, a few sandwiches and a quiche of the day. Good coffee.

Warung Mama INDONESIAN $
(☎0822 3926 4747; Jl Soekarno Hatta; mains from 30,000Rp; ⊙8am-10pm) Set slightly above Bajo's main drag, this bamboo haven offers cheap and cheerful local fare to discerning budget eaters. There's no MSG, the veggies aren't cooked to death, the juices are fresh, and standards such as the *rendang* (beef coconut curry) are very well done.

★**Made In Italy** ITALIAN $$
(☎0385-41366; www.miirestaurants.com; Jl Soekarno Hatta; mains 50,000-90,000Rp; ⊙11am-11pm; 📶) A fun and stylish indoor–outdoor dining room known the island over for its fantastic pizza and pasta. In fact we'll just say it: it's some of the best pizza we've ever had anywhere – wafer thin and crunchy with perfectly delectable toppings. You'll dig the rattan lighting, custom wood furnishings, ceiling fans and long drinks menu.

Mediterrano ITALIAN $$
(☎0385-42218; www.mediterraneoinn.com; Jl Soekarno Hatta; mains 40,000-120,000Rp; ⊙7am-midnight; 📶) Enjoy pastas, pizzas and excellent seafood amid a beach-chic interior, which rambles beneath whitewashed rafters dangling with woven rattan lanterns. Grab an upcycled wooden table or sink into a beanbag, read or play board games for as long as you wish, or simply gaze out over the harbour.

Tree Top INDONESIAN $$
(Jl Soekarno Hatta; mains 30,000-100,000Rp; ⊙9am-11pm; 📶) This fun, triple-decker cafe offers a pub vibe and billiards table downstairs, and fine harbour and island views from the split-level upstairs dining rooms where it serves tasty, spicy Indonesian seafood. Many bar seats face the sunset.

Lounge INTERNATIONAL $$
(☎0385-41962; Jl Soekarno Hatta; mains 35,000-80,000Rp; ⊙8am-11pm; 📶) This hill-climbing cafe is where you come for holy comfort food. Think: burgers that demand two hands, knife and fork calzoni, fish and chips, panini and salads. Staff mix cocktails from a bar stocked with premium liquids, and there are cushy built-in loungers. Live music features cover bands of varying talents. You can't beat the views from the top-level Sky Bar.

★**Paradise Bar** BAR
(☎0823 3935 4854; off Jl Binongko; ⊙11am-2am) Set on a hilltop, Paradise satisfies all the requirements of a definitive tropical watering hole. There's ample deck space, a mesmerising sea view, a natural wood bar serving ice-cold beer, and live music. There's food too – mains run between 22,000Rp and 60,000Rp. This is as wild as it gets for Bajo nightlife – divers get up early. It's a 10-minute walk uphill from the centre.

Information

Banks, ATMs and shops line Jl Soekarno Hatta.

PHKA Information Booth (☎0385-41005; Jl Soekarno Hatta; ⊙8am-2.30pm Mon-Thu, to 11am Fri) PHKA administers the Komodo National Park, and provides information and permits for Komodo and Rinca islands.

Tourist Office (www.florestourism.com; Jl Soekarno Pelabuhan; ⊙8.30am-4.30pm Mon-Sat) This excellent office has details on local activities, updated maps and books plus all the transport info – and tickets – you'll need. The porch has comfy chairs you can use while you plot out your visit.

Varanus Travel (☎0385-41709; Jl Soekarno Hatta; ⊙8am-6pm) Full-service travel agent; can book airline and bus tickets.

Getting There & Away

AIR

Labuanbajo's **Komodo Airport** (LBJ) has a huge new airport terminal as well as a newly lengthened runway, which gives some idea of the expected tourism growth.

Garuda, Transnusa and Wings Air serve the airport and have counters in the terminal. There are several daily flights to/from Bali but these are booked solid at busy times. Don't just expect to turn up and go. Garuda also flies to Kupang five times weekly.

BOAT

The ASDP ferry from Labuanbajo to Sape (60,000Rp, six to seven hours) has a morning run and often another in the afternoon. Confirm all times carefully. Buy your tickets the day of departure at the **ferry port office** (Jl Soekarno Hatta; ⌚7am-5pm).

Agents for the boats running between Labuanbajo and Lombok (p354) line Jl Soekarno Hatta.

Pelni Agent (☎0385-41106; off Jl Mutiara; ⌚hours vary) Easily missed on a side street, this agency run by Varanus Travel is the place to get tickets for long-distance boat travel. Schedules posted in the windows outline twice-monthly services, which include Makassar and the east coast of Sulawesi as well as Bima, Lembar and Benoa (Bali).

BUS

With no bus terminal in Labuanbajo, most people book their tickets through a hotel or agency. If you get an advance ticket, the bus will pick you up from your hotel. All buses run via Ruteng, so no matter where you're headed just take the first available east-bound bus.

Ticket sellers for **long-distance buses** to Lombok and Bali work the ferry port office. The fares include all ferries (three to Bali!) and air-con buses in between.

Getting Around

The airport is 1.5km from the town. Many hotels and dive shops offer free rides into town. A private taxi to town costs a fixed flat rate of 70,000Rp.

In town itself you can walk to most places. An *ojek* costs 5000Rp to 10,000Rp. Bemos (3000Rp) do continual loops around the centre, following the one-way traffic.

Manggarai Country

☎0385

To compare gradations of beauty on Flores is as futile as it is fun. And if you do get into such a debate, know that if you've explored Manggarai's lush rainforests, studded with towering stands of bamboo and elegant tree ferns, and climbed its steep mountains to isolated traditional villages accessible only by trail, you may have the trump card.

Rapidly improving roads are opening up new areas for easy exploration, such as the beach-lined south coast.

Ruteng

The staid and sprawling market city of Ruteng is the area's base of operations. It's barely four hours by car from Labuanbajo. Should you take in a few sights, you'll be overnighting here.

Sights

★Spiderweb Rice Fields VIEWPOINT
(Linko; off Trans-Flores Hwy) The greatest local site is actually 20km west of Ruteng near the village of Cancar. The legendary Spiderweb Rice Fields are vast creations that are shaped exactly as their name implies. The surrounding region is beautifully lush with paddies.

For the best view, stop at a small house (drivers all know this place), tip the genial owners about 10,000Rp, borrow a walking stick and ascend a dirt path to a ridge where the surreal shapes of the rice fields can be fully appreciated.

Pasar MARKET
(Market; Jl Bhayangkara; ⌚7am-5pm) Don't miss the lively, sprawling market, a vital lifeline for villagers in the surrounding hills. Much of it is underground – look for the entrance next to the supermarket.

Sleeping & Eating

Ruteng is somewhat elevated compared to Bajo, so it can get almost chilly at night.

★Kongregasi Santa Maria Berdukacita GUESTHOUSE $
(☎0385-22834; Jl A Yani 45; r 160,000-350,000Rp) The best local sleep is in one of the 15 rooms at this convent, where the rooms are huge and spotless, service is excellent, smoking is prohibited, and there is a 9pm curfew. Among the other constraints: breakfast *ends* at 7.30am and checkout is at 9am. It's on a hillside a little south of the centre.

Homestay Mbeliling GUESTHOUSE $$
(☎0385-22323; homestaymbeliling@yahoo.com; Jl Mbeliling 14; s/d from 225,000/300,000Rp; wi-fi) Set up a modest hill in a quiet neighbourhood south of the centre, this six-room retreat is perfectly calm and tidy. Rooms are large and you can snooze away amid the serenity (and leafy garden).

Rumah Makan Cha Cha INDONESIAN $
(☎0385-21489; Jl Diponegoro 12; mains 15,000-30,000Rp; ⌚8am-10pm) Perched on a hillside overlooking the broad valley, this wooden restaurant is a 15-minute walk from the convent Kongregasi Santa Maria Berdukacita. The Indo standards are well prepared and it's a relaxing place.

Agape Café INDONESIAN $
(☎0385-22561; Jl Bhayangkara; dishes 8000-30,000Rp; ⏰8am-10pm; 📶) Ruteng makes a fine lunch stop thanks to this cafe that's popular with both locals and seemingly every traveller who drives past. The dining area is bright and airy, with a high ceiling. The standard Indonesian fare is well prepared.

ℹ Information

ATMs dot the centre.

ℹ Getting There & Away

The bus terminal for eastern destinations is located 3.5km and a 3000Rp bemo ride out of Ruteng. Local buses heading west still run from the central bus/bemo terminal near the police station. Regular buses head to Bajawa (60,000Rp, five hours) and Labuanbajo (60,000Rp, four hours).

Liang Bua

The limestone cave of Liang Bua, where the remains of the **Flores 'hobbit'** were famously found in 2003, is about 14km north of Ruteng, down a rough dirt track that is often impassable. Archaeologists believe that the lip along the entrance permitted sediments to build up steadily as water flowed through the cave over the millennia, sealing in the remains of the humans and animals that lived and died here. It's a rather evocative spot, with the arching entrance to the cave having an otherworldly feel. Local guides, whose service is included in your 30,000Rp entry fee, will meet you at the cave's entrance and explain why Liang Bua is considered sacred. To get here take an *ojek* (80,000Rp) from Ruteng.

Wae Rebo

Wae Rebo is the best of Manggarai's traditional villages. Recent road improvements have opened up the area, although it is still very remote.

A village visit involves a splendid but challenging 10km **hike** that takes four hours and winds past waterfalls and swimming holes, as well as spectacular views of the Savu Sea. Once you arrive in the village you will be treated to indigenous music and dance, and a demonstration of local weaving practices, then bed down in a *mbaru tembong* (traditional home). All this hospitality deserves a gift of at least 200,000Rp per person.

The next morning you can retrace your steps or choose to hike another six hours over a pass to another trailhead; arrange for pickup here in advance.

You can arrange for guides (400,000Rp) and porters (250,000Rp) at the local guesthouses. Be sure to start very early, to avoid the sweltering heat of midday. Bring water.

🛏 Sleeping

Given that early morning is the optimal time to start the trek to Wae Rebo, you'll want to stay near the trailhead as opposed to in Ruteng.

Wae Rebo Lodge GUESTHOUSE $
(☎0852 3934 4046; martin_anggo@yahoo.com; Dintor; r per person per night 220,000Rp) A purpose-built lodge run by a local from Wae Rebo. It sits serenely amid rice fields and is some 9km from the trailhead. Meals are included in the rates and you can make all trekking arrangements here.

Wae Rebo Homestay HOMESTAY $
(☎0813 3935 0775; Denge; r per person per night 200,000Rp) Right at the trailhead, this is the original place to sleep for people making the Wae Rebo trek. The owners are helpful in arranging village visits and transport. Rates include meals and very basic accommodation.

ℹ Getting There & Away

It's about a three-hour drive from Ruteng to the village trailhead in Denge. You'll need your own wheels for this.

Repi

The southwest coast of Flores is like a Morse code of beaches: a dot of sand here, a dash there. Improving roads mean it's easier than ever to visit these pristine white beaches, where the only footprints you find might belong to a turtle.

The tiny village of Repi is typical. Impoverished locals have for aeons harvested turtle eggs and engaged in destructive practices such as dynamite fishing in order to survive. Now an innovative program run by Wicked Diving in Labuanbajo is helping to change that. At a beachside bamboo-and-brick outpost called Pante Hera, locals are getting paid for the eggs they find as well as learning how revenue from visitors – who want healthy reefs – can be used to build a reliable water supply and make other improvements. It's an innovative and privately funded effort that's

THE FLORES 'HOBBIT'

The Manggarai have long told folk tales of *ebo gogo* – hairy little people with flat foreheads who once roamed the jungle. Nobody paid them much attention until September 2003, when archaeologists made a stunning find.

Excavating the limestone cave at Liang Bua, they unearthed a skeleton the size of a three-year-old child but with the worn-down teeth and bone structure of an adult. Six more remains appeared to confirm that the team had unearthed a new species of human, *Homo floresiensis*, which reached around 1m in height and was nicknamed the 'hobbit'.

Lab tests brought another surprise. The hominid with the nutcracker jaw and gangly, chimplike arms lived until 12,000 years ago, practically yesterday in evolutionary terms, when a cataclysmic volcanic eruption is thought to have wiped out the little people and devastated the island of Flores.

But not all scientists are convinced on the origins of the Flores species. The prevailing school of thought argues that the Flores hominids are descendants of *Homo erectus*, a species that fled Africa around two million years ago and spread throughout Asia. Until recently it was thought that the arrival of *Homo sapiens* in Asia led to the demise of *Homo erectus* around 50,000 years ago. Flores humans could indicate that the species survived in isolated places.

Rival anthropologists suggest that the Flores find could represent *Homo sapiens* (who were known to be travelling between Australia and New Guinea 35,000 years ago) that suffered from microcephaly – a neurological disorder causing stunted head growth, and often dwarfism, that runs in families.

But the momentum still seems to be with the original theory, given that the bones of at least eight more individuals have been found at the site with similar characteristics to the first discovery. And with tools very similar to those found in Liang Bua reportedly unearthed in Timor, and possibly in Sulawesi, more little people could yet emerge from the evolutionary backwoods.

making the beautiful 3km-long beach a haven for leatherback, hawksbill and green turtles.

You can enjoy basic accommodation and meals at **Pante Hera** (Turtle Beach; ☎0822 2572 0562; Repi; tent pads for 4 people 300,000Rp, dm per person from 225,000Rp) – meals are included in room rates. There is snorkelling, hiking and cycling plus interactions with locals that often include welcoming ceremonies. Plans are afoot to build private rooms and generally develop the place with the community.

Arrange your stay with Wicked Adventures (p359) in Labuanbajo, or visit via your own wheels – but book first so they know you're coming.

Bajawa

☎0384

Framed by forested volcanoes and blessed with a pleasant climate, Bajawa, a laid-back hill town at 1100m, is a great base from which to explore dozens of traditional villages that are home to the local Ngada people. Bajawa is the Ngada's de facto trading post, and you'll mingle with the locals as you stroll these quiet streets edged by blooming gardens. Gunung Inerie (2245m), a perfectly conical volcano, looms to the south, where you'll also find some hot springs. The recently emerged volcano, Wawo Muda, with its Kelimutu-esque lakes, is another favourite. Bajawa is a key base for exploring the region's traditional villages.

Sleeping

Thanks to a growth spurt in Bajawa tourism, local accommodation has been happily spruced up. All prices include breakfast.

★**Hotel Happy Happy** GUESTHOUSE **$$**
(☎0384-421763, 0853 3370 4455; www.hotelhappyhappy.com; Jl Sudirman; r 300,000-350,000Rp; 📶)
A simple yet classy guesthouse with seven immaculate tiled rooms, brushed with lavender walls, dressed with high-quality linen – a scarcity in Bajawa. There's an amiable sitting area on the patio, free water-bottle refills and an excellent included breakfast. It's a short walk from the main cluster of tourist businesses.

Sanian Hotel Bajawa HOTEL $$
(☎0384-21777; www.sanianhotelbajawa.com; Jl DI Panjaitan; r 350,000-550,000Rp;) Bajawa's newest place to stay has 11 rooms in a two-storey building near the town centre and market. Rooms are refreshingly spare of extraneous decor. Those upstairs have nice views from the shared balcony.

Villa Silverin LODGE $$
(☎0384-222 3865, 0852 5345 3298; www.villasilverinhotel.com; Jl Bajawa; r 350,000-450,000Rp;) A fine hillside lodge 3km outside town on the road to Ende, with beckoning verandas and jaw-dropping valley views. VIP rooms are bright with queen beds and hot water.

Hotel Bintang Wisata HOTEL $$
(☎0384-21744; Jl Palapa 4; r 200,000-350,000Rp;) In a central two-storey block, 24 basic tiled rooms are set in an arc around a parking lot where drivers lounge about awaiting their charges. Upstairs VIP rooms have terraces, hot water and great views of the surrounding hills. The cheapest rooms are cold-water only – a bracing prospect as nights can get chilly.

Eating

Bajawa's best places to eat are clustered around other visitor services just south of the centre.

Dito's INDONESIAN $
(☎0384-21162; Jl Ahmad Yani; mains 25,000-50,000Rp; ⊗8am-10pm) Dito's does a brisk business serving pork and chicken *sate* and fresh tuna *bakar,* which is sourced from nearby Aimere and grilled to perfection. The tamarillo juice is *delish*.

Camellia INDONESIAN $
(☎0384-21458; Jl Ahmad Yani 74; mains 20,000-35,000Rp; ⊗8am-10pm) The dining room is brightly lit, the better for reading your guidebook. There are Western dishes, but try the chicken *sate* – it comes with a unique sweet, smoky pepper sauce.

Lucas INDONESIAN $
(☎0384-21340; Jl Ahmad Yani; mains 20,000-35,000Rp; ⊗8am-10pm) This long-running favourite has a new 2nd-floor location, which puts you above traffic and in the midst of pleasant breezes. It serves fine pork sate and other local faves in an appealing wooden dining room.

WORTH A TRIP

HOT SPRINGS

In this cool, lush and palpably volcanic region, it's no surprise that the Bajawa area has a few hot springs on offer. The most accessible is **Air Panas Soa** (per person 5000Rp; ⊗6.30am-6pm), situated just east of town on the rough road to Riung. There are two clean and fresh pools here; one is a scintillating 45°C, and the other a more pedestrian 35–40°C. It has modern buildings and gets busy with locals on weekends.

The most natural springs are found 6km from Bena at Air Panas Malange. At the base of one of the many volcanoes, two streams – one hot, one cold – mix together in one temperate pool. Soak amid the scents of coconut, hazelnut, vanilla and clove.

Information

BNI Bank (Jl Pierre Tendean; ⊗8am-3pm Mon-Fri, to 12.30pm Sat) In the centre; has an ATM and exchanges dollars. There are several more ATMs around town.

Tourist Office (www.florestourism.com; Jl Ahmad Yani; ⊗8.30am-4.30pm Mon-Sat) Small but highly useful; good for Ngada info. Various trekking and travel agencies have shops nearby.

Getting There & Away

There are buses and bemos to various destinations. Buses don't necessarily leave on time, only when the bus is almost full. Kijangs, or travel cars, also leave throughout the day from the bemo **terminal** (Jl Basoeki Rahmat). Rates are about 20% more than bus fares. Bus services include the following:

Ende 60,000Rp, several times daily
Labuanbajo 120,000Rp, several times daily
Ruteng 60,000Rp, frequent services from 8am to 11am

Getting Around

Bemos (3000Rp) cruise town, but it is easy to walk almost everywhere except to the bus terminals.

Treks (trucks) serve remote routes, most leaving traditional villages in the morning and returning in the afternoon.

Motorbikes cost 60,000Rp to 80,000Rp a day. A private vehicle (with driver) is 700,000Rp. Most hotels can arrange rental.

The airport is 25km from Bajawa and about 6km outside Soa.

Around Bajawa

Bajawa's big draw is the chance to explore traditional villages in the gorgeous countryside. Their fascinating architecture features carved poles supporting a conical thatched roof. It is certainly possible to visit the area alone, but you'll learn a lot more about the culture and customs (such as the caste system) with a guide. Some organise meals in their home villages, others will suggest treks to seldom-visited villages accessible only by trail.

Guides linger around hotels and can arrange day trips from 600,000Rp per person with transport, village entry fees and lunch. A classic one-day itinerary would start in Bajawa and include Bena, Luba, Tolo Lela and Air Panas Malange hot springs.

Bena

Resting on Inerie's flank, Bena is one of the most traditional Ngada villages. It's home to nine clans, and its fabulous stone monuments are the region's best. Houses with high thatched roofs line up in two rows on a ridge, the space between them filled with fine *ngadhu, bhaga* (smeared with sacrificial blood) and megalithic tomblike structures (see p368). Most houses have male or female figurines on their roofs, while doorways are decorated with buffalo horns and jawbones – a sign of the family's prosperity.

Bena is the most visited Ngada village, and weavings and souvenir stalls line the front of houses. Although the village is crowded when tour groups arrive during high season, and all villagers are now officially Catholic and attend a local missionary school, traditional beliefs and customs endure. Sacrifices are held three times each year, and village elders still talk about a rigidly enforced caste system that prevented 'mixed' relationships, with those defying the *adat* facing possible death.

Visitors are asked to make a donation of 10,000Rp to 20,000Rp. You can spend the night for 125,000Rp per person, which includes meals of boiled cassava and banana.

Getting There & Away

Bena is reached by a good 12km road from Langa, a traditional town 7km from Bajawa. An *ojek* ride here costs about 70,000Rp.

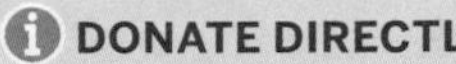

DONATE DIRECTLY

It's customary to make a donation to the head of traditional villages you visit. It's better to do this directly rather than through a guide, so as to ensure the money is received in full.

Luba

Tucked into the jungle like a beautiful secret, the traditional village of Luba is about 2km from Bena and much more intimate. Just four very welcoming clans live here in a baker's dozen homes. You'll see four *ngadhu* and *bhaga* in the common courtyard, and within the local population are a few artists whose houses are decorated with depictions of horses, buffalo and snakes, which translate as symbols of power, status and protection. Photography is welcomed by most; leave a donation of 10,000Rp to 20,000Rp.

Getting There & Away

You can hire an *ojek* from Bajawa for around 70,000Rp. With guides and hired cars, it's common to visit both Bena and Luba in one trip.

Tolo Lela

A mere 4km walk from Bena (about 90 minutes) brings you to this seldom-visited Ngada settlement which consists of three linked traditional villages. Residents love receiving visitors (donate at least 20,000Rp per person) and you can sip simple refreshments while everyone satisfies their mutual curiosity. A highlight is watching an elderly villager making traditional gongs.

Belaragi

Most visitors to the Bajawa area rely on hired vehicles to whisk them between traditional villages. But it's much more fulfilling to trek through the rainforest to villages such as Belaragi, accessible only by trail. Your trek will begin in **Pauleni Village**, approximately 45km (90 minutes) from Bajawa by car. From there it's a steep 90-minute hike to the village itself. Here are more than a dozen traditional homes and welcoming villagers. It can be done in a day trip, but you'll be tired by now, so you may as well stay the night. The Kepala Kampung (village head) offers a bed and meals for 250,000Rp per person. You can't

THE NGADA

Over 60,000 Ngada people inhabit the upland Bajawa plateau and the slopes around Gunung Inerie. Most practise a fusion of animism and Christianity, worshipping Gae Dewa, a god who unites Dewa Zeta (the heavens) and Nitu Sale (the earth).

The most evident symbols of continuing Ngada tradition are pairs of *ngadhu* and *bhaga*. The *ngadhu* is a parasol-like structure about 3m high, consisting of a carved wooden pole and thatched 'roof', and the *bhaga* is a miniature thatched-roof house.

The *ngadhu* is 'male' and the *bhaga* is 'female'. Each pair is associated with a particular family group within a village. Some were built over 100 years ago to commemorate ancestors killed in long-past battles.

Agricultural fertility rites continue (sometimes involving gory buffalo sacrifices), as well as ceremonies marking birth, marriage, death and house building – always a communal event. The major annual festival is the six-day Reba ceremony at Bena, held in late December or early January. Villagers wear specially made all-black ikat, sacrifice buffalo, and sing and dance through the night.

Although the Ngada are not matriarchal (the village elders are men), they are matrilineal, which means that property passes down through women.

find the village on your own, but most Bajawa area guides can arrange the trip.

Wawo Muda

Wawo Muda (1753m) is the latest volcano to emerge in Flores, exploding in 2001 and leaving behind a mini-Kelimutu, complete with several small crater lakes coloured variously burnt-orange, yellow and green. Pine trees charred by the eruption stand in isolated patches, and there are spectacular views of Gunung Inerie.

The area is best visited in the wet season from November to March, if the trails are not too muddy. The lakes usually evaporate in the dry season.

Getting There & Away

To reach Wawo Muda, take one of the regular bemos from Bajawa (10,000Rp, 50 minutes) or an *ojek* to the village of Ngoranale, near Menge, then walk an hour up an easy-to-follow trail. Some *ojek* drivers may offer to take you the whole way up, as the path is doable on a motorbike. A car and driver will cost 600,000Rp round trip.

Gunung Inerie

One of the gorgeous volcanoes looming above Bajawa, Gunung Inerie (2245m), 19km from town, beckons all would-be climbers. Or does she taunt them? The journey is difficult, but then this spectacularly jagged cone is worth sweating and suffering for. You can do it as a 10-hour round trip but it's also possible to camp by the lake. You'll need a guide, and remember to bring extra water even if your guide says he has that covered; you'll require more hydration than any local guide can possibly imagine.

Getting There & Away

With an English-speaking guide and transport from Bajawa, expect to pay about 800,000Rp for one and 1,000,000Rp for two people.

Riung

Riung is a wonderful little town, lush and isolated, stitched with rice fields, stilted with fishers' shacks and framed with coconut palms. Coming from Ende you'll drive along a parched and arid coastline that skirts a spectacularly blasted volcano before a sudden burst of foliage swallows the road as it winds into town. The effect makes Riung – a classic 'end-of-the-road' destination, feel like an island unto itself, part of some whole other time and place.

Guesthouses are homey, the quiet streets are made for walking, and the waterfront is a gateway to a marine park. Only its relative inaccessibility (read: challenging roads) keep it from profound development.

The closest beach to Riung is a 1km walk. There is no local dive shop.

Sights & Activities

The main Riung attraction is the **Seventeen Islands Marine Park**. There are actually 23 islands, all uninhabited, but government authorities decided on the number as a convenient tie-in with Indonesia's Independence Day (17 August).

Three or four islands are usually included in a boat trip, and the first is almost always **Pulau Ontoloe**, a mangrove isle where a massive colony of flying foxes roosts and mewl (these huge fruit bats blacken the sky around Riung at sunset). There are also a few resident Komodo dragons. **Pulau Rutong** is popular for its lovely wide white-sand beach. **Pulau Temba** is another slender slice of white sand, tucked against a rugged hillside – picturesque and wild, it tends to escape the crowds. **Pulau Tiga** is likewise not to be missed. The sea is a glassy turquoise, the hard corals off the east coast nourish schools of tropical fish, and the long sweep of white sand is perfect for barefoot strolls. An offshore site called **Laingjawa** has excellent snorkelling. Mingling among the hard corals are schools of bumpheads, some colourful cuttlefish, an occasional blacktip shark and at least two resident turtles. **Pulau Bakau** has above-average coral.

Be aware that the park's coral was impacted by the El Niño bleaching in 2002. While visibility is quite good – frequently at least 10m to 15m – don't expect colourful corals. Still, the number and variety of fish here is special.

VISITING SEVENTEEN ISLANDS MARINE PARK

Guides will appear at your hotel offering to organise **boat trips** to the islands. We recommend Al Itchan, owner of **Del Mar Cafe**. Al is one of Riung's most experienced guides and has a team of colleagues. They have excellent knowledge of the snorkelling spots.

Before going to the islands you must sign in and pay 100,000Rp per person at a separate booth by the dock. Your captain or guide should pay the anchorage fees for your boat.

Tour options include the following:

- A boat-only day trip without a guide for four to six people costs 500,000Rp to 600,000Rp. However captains often don't know the best spots to take the plunge.
- A boat day trip with at least four snorkelling stops, a guide and a beach barbecue for four people is organised by Itchan for 1,500,000Rp.
- Overnight camping on Palau Rutong, organised by Itchan, costs 3,000,000Rp for two people and includes boat rides, snorkelling and meals.

Sleeping & Eating

★Eco Eden GUESTHOUSE $

(☎0852 3751 4582; Watulagar; r 250,000Rp) Some 16km east of Riung and 2.5km off the main road, this new thatched Robinson Crusoe fantasy has a 3km-long beach to itself (although perhaps not for long). The nine bungalows are simply built of bamboo (any sound you make will be enjoyed by all, unless the surf drowns it out) with a bathroom behind.

Seafood barbecues are the night-time fare; mains cost from 20,000Rp to 40,000Rp. Snorkelling trips can be arranged.

Pondok SVD GUESTHOUSE $

(☎0813 3934 1572; www.pondoksvdriung.com; r 200,000-400,000Rp; ❄) Here are 21 clean rooms with desks, reading lights and Western toilets, set down a gravel road from the port. However, it is right next door to the town generator. The cheapest rooms are fan-only.

Del Mar Cafe GUESTHOUSE $$

(☎0812 4659 8232, 0813 8759 0964; r 300,000-400,000Rp) The hippest warung (mains 30,000Rp to 50,000Rp; open 7am to 10pm) in Riung, this tiki bar, strung with shell strands and Christmas lights, rumbles with rock and roll, and grills a fresh catch over smouldering coconut husks. Owned by the area's top guide, Al Itchan, it has four large and clean fan-only rooms, plus a few watchful monkeys wandering about.

Nirwana BUNGALOW $$

(☎0813 3852 8529; bungalows 375,000-450,000Rp; ❄) Eight fun, detached hippy shacks with thatched roofs, private patios and outdoor baths set in a quiet garden surrounded by coco palms near the port. There's no cafe. The engaging owner offers guided trips to the islands.

Rumah Makan Murah Muriah INDONESIAN $$
(☎0813 3717 2918; mains 25,000-50,000Rp; ⏰7am-10pm) The house speciality here is the *sop ikan asam pedas,* Nusa Tenggara Timor's endemic spicy-and-sour tamarind fish soup. This one is as good as it gets. It also does grilled fish, fried squid and vegies, chicken *sate,* fried noodles and much more.

Information

There's a BRI ATM but it doesn't accept foreign cards, and there's no official currency exchange facilities in Riung; come with ample rupiah.

There's no useful internet access but there is 3G data.

Getting There & Away

Riung is 75km (about two hours) over rough roads from the turn-off the Trans-Flores Hwy at Boawae. There is a *much* worse 79km road to Riung from Bajawa that takes about four hours by bus (40,000Rp, one daily), slightly quicker by car (600,000Rp). Ende is also four hours by bus (60,000Rp, one daily).

If you can't bear the Trans-Flores Hwy for another second, consider chartering a boat from Riung all the way to Labuanbajo (2,800,000Rp, seven to 10 hours). It's a bit pricey, but you'll enjoy a coastline most visitors never see, stopping in virgin coves and snorkelling along the way. Just bring headphones or earplugs. Those outboard motors are loud!

Ende

☎0381 / POP 65,000

The most obvious merit of this muggy port town is its spectacular setting. The eye-catching cones of Gunung Meja (661m) and Gunung Iya (637m) loom over the city and the nearby black-sand and cobblestone coastline. The views get even better just northeast of Ende as the road to Kelimutu rises along a ridge opposite misty peaks, overlooking a roaring river and gushing with ribbons of waterfalls in the wet season. Throw in the jade rice terraces and you have some of Flores' most jaw-dropping scenery.

Ende itself is worth more than a pause at its traffic circles. It has a compact and atmospheric centre, and an intriguing grittiness.

Sights

The black-sand beach at the waterfront won't win any tidy town awards, but the views are dramatic and there's always something of interest tied up at the pier.

Pasar MARKET
(Market; Jl Pasar; ⏰7am-6pm) Meander through the aromatic waterfront market with the requisite fruit pyramids and an astonishing fish section. The adjacent **ikat market** (cnr Jls Pabean & Pasar; ⏰9am-5pm) sells hand-woven tapestries from across Flores and Sumba.

Musium Bung Karno MUSEUM
(Jl Perwira; admission by donation; ⏰7am-noon Mon-Sat) History buffs can visit Sukarno's wood-shuttered house of exile (1934–38). Most of the original period furnishings remain. This is where the beloved revolutionary penned the *Frankenstein* knock-off, *Doctor Satan.*

Sleeping

Accommodation is spread around town. Although many people blow through Ende on their way east to Moni, you can spend a night here enjoying the good sleeping and eating options, and then hit the sights of Moni in the morning.

Guesthouse Alhidayah GUESTHOUSE $
(☎0381-23707; Jl Yos Sudarso; r 150,000-250,000Rp; ❄) This spot offers seven sparkling, but otherwise basic, tiled rooms with high ceilings and a private porch area. Priciest rooms have air-con and hot water, and are decent value. It's a solid budget choice.

★ **Dasi Guest House** GUESTHOUSE $$
(☎0381-262 7049; yosdam@yahoo.co.id; Jl Durian Atas 2; s/d from 200,000/225,000Rp; ❄📶) This excellent family-run guesthouse has 15 rooms in a new building. Some are dark, some are bright, but all have air-con and TV. There's a pleasant common room with views south. It's located about 3km east of the centre in a residential neighbourhood.

Hotel Mentari HOTEL $$
(☎0381-21802; Jl Pahlawan 19; r 250,000-400,000Rp; ❄📶) Well-run Mentari has 11 clean rooms with high ceilings; some have garden views and catch a bit of breeze. The priciest have air-con.

Ende

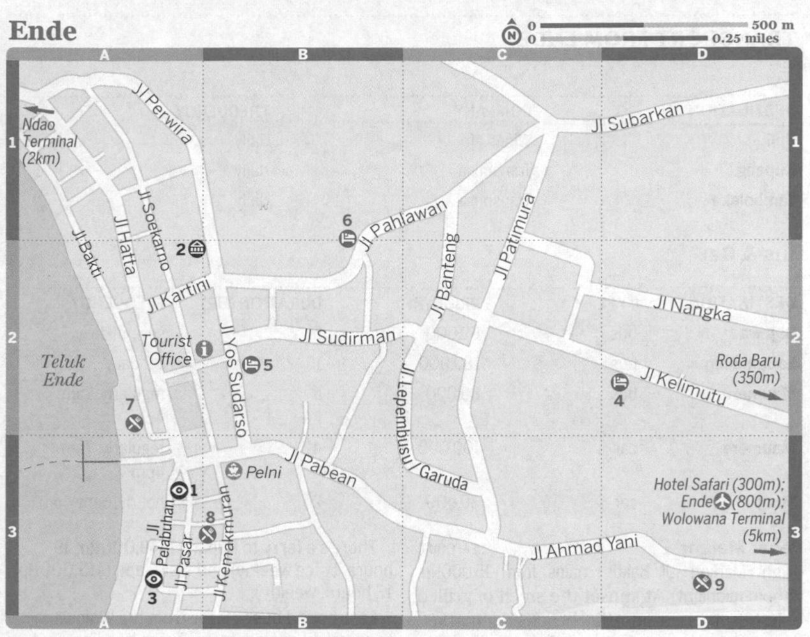

NUSA TENGGARA ENDE

Ende

Sights
1 Ikat Market A3
2 Musium Bung Karno A2
3 Pasar A3

Sleeping
4 Grand Wisata D2
5 Guesthouse Alhidayah B2
6 Hotel Mentari B1

Eating
7 Pasar Malam A2
8 Rumah Makan Istana Bambu B3
9 Sari Rasa D3

Grand Wisata HOTEL $$
(☎0381-22974; www.grandwisatahotel-ende.com; Jl Kelimutu 32; r 500,000-700,000Rp; ❄🛜🏊) Be warned, some rooms here can be dark and cramped, and the price category doesn't necessarily correlate with room size, so have a look around. Rooms on the 2nd floor have views of the 15m lap pool with the epic Gunung Meja looming beyond. It's walking distance to the airport.

Eating

★ Sari Rasa INDONESIAN $
(Jl Ahmad Yani; mains 13,000-26,000Rp; ⏲6pm-midnight) One of the best restaurants not just in Ende, but in all of Nusa Tenggara. Looks are deceiving: just a few plastic stools at fluorescent-lit metal tables. But once the food arrives, you'll understand. The menu is short but shows the incredible care of the family in the kitchen.

The *ayam goreng* (fried chicken) uses special 'village' chickens known for their rich flavour, the *mie ayam special* is a savoury bowl of homemade noodles in broth that is cooked each day for hours, and the *bakso cinta* (love meatballs) has heart-shaped meatballs in an amazing sauce. The genial owner delights in explaining his food to patrons.

Roda Baru PADANG $
(☎0381-24135; Jl Kelimutu; mains 20,000-30,000Rp; ⏲9am-midnight) You can trust the cleanliness and care of this spotless pick-and-mix Padang diner. The fish, chicken and shrimp are all fried or grilled and sauced five ways, the beef *rendang* is locally beloved, and the tasty sambal brings everything to life.

TRANSPORT FROM ENDE

Air

DESTINATION	COMPANY	FREQUENCY
Bali	Wings Air	daily
Kupang	Transnusa	daily
Tambolaka	Transnusa	daily

Bus & Car

DESTINATION	TYPE	PRICE (RP)	DURATION (HR)	FREQUENCY
Bajawa	bus	60,000	5	several daily
Labuanbajo	bus	180,000	15	1-2 daily
Maumere	bus	80,000	5	regularly, 7am-4pm
Maumere	car	100,000	4½	regularly, 7am-4pm
Moni	car	30,000	2	hourly, 6am-4pm

Pasar Malam SEAFOOD $
(Night Market; Jl Bakti; mains from 15,000Rp; 5pm-midnight) At sunset the smell of grilled fish fills the air at this beachside market. Browse the many stalls and feast on what looks best.

Rumah Makan Istana Bambu SEAFOOD $
(0381-21921; Jl Kemakmuran 30A; mains 25,000-50,000Rp; 8am-10pm) Here's a classic, funkified Chinese fish house. It's old-fashioned and dark but the fresh fish, squid, prawns and lobster, and the spicy sambal (which they bottle and sell), are all tops.

Information

ATMs and banks dot the centre.

Tourist Office (www.florestourism.com; Jl Bakti; 8.30am-4.30pm Mon-Sat) The enthusiastic staff here dispense up-to-date transport information.

Getting There & Away

Air and ferry schedules in East Nusa Tenggara are historically fluid, and it's best to confirm all times and carriers prior to planning your trip. Wings Air and Transnusa serve **Ende Airport** (Jl Ahmad Yani), which is right in the centre.

Pelni has boats every two weeks to Waingapu, Benoa and Surabaya, then east to Kupang and Sabu. Visit the helpful **Pelni office** (0381-21043; Jl Kathedral 2; 8am-noon & 2-4pm Mon-Sat).

There's a ferry to Kupang (149,000Rp, 19 hours, twice weekly) and Waingapu (115,000Rp, 13 hours, weekly).

East-bound buses leave from the Wolowana terminal, 5km from town. Buses heading west leave from the Ndao terminal, 2km north of town on the beach road.

Getting Around

Airport taxis to most hotels cost around 60,000Rp.

Bemos run frequently to just about everywhere for a flat rate of 3000Rp.

Kelimutu

There aren't many better reasons to wake up before dawn than to witness the sun cresting Kelimutu's western rim, filtering mist into the sky and revealing three deep, volcanic lakes – nicknamed the tricoloured lakes because for years each one was a different striking shade.

Kelimutu National Park (0381-23405; Jl El Tari 16; admission per person Mon-Sat/Sun 150,000/225,000Rp, per ojek/car 5000/10,000Rp; ticket office 5am-5pm) is a Nusa Tenggara must. The lakes' colours are spectacular, shifting between turquoise, olive green and rust. The colours are so dense that the lakes' waters seem to have the thickness of paint. It's thought that dissolving minerals (a process that can accelerate in the rainy season) account for the chameleonic colour scheme – although the colour of one of the turquoise lakes never changes.

The summit's moonscape gives Kelimutu an ethereal atmosphere, especially when clouds billow across the craters and sunlight shafts burn luminescent pinpoints to the water's surface.

Kelimutu is sacred to local people, and legend has it that the souls of the dead migrate here: young people's souls go to the warmth of Tiwu Nuwa Muri Koo Fai (Turquoise Lake), old people's to the cold of Tiwu Ata Polo (Brown Lake) and those of the wicked to Tiwi Ata Mbupu (Black Lake).

Ever since locals led early Dutch settlers here, sightseers have made the sunrise trek. Most visitors glimpse the lakes at dawn, leaving nearby Moni at 4am for early-morning views after the predawn mist rises, and before clouds drift in. Afternoons are usually empty and peaceful at the top of Mt Kelimutu, and when the sun is high the colours sparkle.

There's a staircase up to the highest lookout, **Inspiration Point**, from where all three lakes are visible. It's not advisable to scramble around the craters' loose scree. The footing's so bad and the drop so steep, a few careless hikers have perished here.

Activities

For a beautiful **walk** through the lush local landscape, hire transport one-way to the lakes and then walk back to Moni. The stroll down the mountain, through the village, past rice fields and along cascading streams takes about three hours and isn't too taxing. A *jalan potong* (shortcut) leaves the road back to Moni 3km south of the ticket office and goes through Manukako village, then meanders back to the main road 750m uphill from Moni. A second shortcut diverges from the trail and goes through Tomo, Mboti, Topo Mboti, Kolorongo and Koposili villages, skirts a waterfall and returns to Moni without rejoining the highway.

Getting There & Away

The ticket office is 8.5km up the paved access road from the Trans-Flores Hwy. The turn is 2km west of Moni. The parking area for the lake is another 4km. From the car park it's a nice 20-minute walk up through the pines to Inspiration Point. To get here from Moni, hire an *ojek* (50,000Rp one way) or car (300,000Rp return, maximum five people).

Moni

Moni is a picturesque village sprinkled with upcountry rice fields, ringed by soaring volcanic peaks and blessed with distant sea views. It's a slow-paced, easy-going, cool breeze of a town that serves as a gateway to Kelimutu. On clear, dark-moon nights, you'll walk the silent streets beneath a black-dome universe. The Monday market, held on the soccer pitch, is a major local draw and a good place to snare local ikat.

Activities

Apart from the trek to/from **Kelimutu**, there are several other walks from Moni. About 750m along the Ende road from the centre of Moni, paths lead down to a 10m **air terjun** (waterfall), with a swimming hole and **air panas** (hot springs) near the falls. The trail branches to the left of Rainbow Cafe. There are more gorgeous hot springs in the middle of the rice fields at **Kolorongo** (3.5km from Moni) on the way to Kelimutu. Or walk south past the church to **Potu** and **Woloara** (about 2.5km from Moni).

Sleeping & Eating

Most Moni accommodation is budget to low-midrange, and is sprinkled along the Trans-Flores Hwy (the town's only road). Guesthouses may book up in the June to August high season, so reserve ahead. Many are in shabby shape; prepare to compare.

Local specialities tend to be hearty, to ward off the chilly nights. Try a 'Moni cake', a starchy mashed-potato pie topped with cheese.

Watugana Bungalows BUNGALOW $
(☎0813 3916 7408; Jl Trans Flores; r 150,000-350,000Rp) Downstairs rooms are older and kept reasonably clean, though they are dark and the bathrooms are a bit moist. The newish rooms upstairs are bright and have hot water.

Daniel Lodge GUESTHOUSE $$
(☎0812 4602 8875; wanggeyanto@yahoo.co.id; r from 250,000Rp) A sprightly new guesthouse with three bungalow-style rooms, where you can bed down to the whoosh of a running stream. The yard is scented with myriad flowers. Relax on comfy bamboo chairs on the porches.

TRANSPORT FROM MONI

DESTINATION	TYPE	FARE (RP)	DURATION (HR)	FREQUENCY
Ende	bus	30,000	2	regularly, 7am-4pm
Ende	car	40,000	1½	regularly, 7am-9pm
Maumere	bus	50,000	3	regularly, 9am-6pm
Maumere	car	80,000	2½	regularly, 8am-9pm

Bintang Lodge GUESTHOUSE $$
(☎0852 3790 6259, 0812 3761 6940; Jl Trans Flores km 54; r 350,000-400,000Rp; ❄@) Easily the best of the old guesthouse standbys, the four rooms here are the cleanest and largest in the town centre. They also have hot water, which is nice on chilly mornings and evenings. The cafe (mains from 25,000Rp) has a great open terrace with views over the green surrounds. Real travellers order the garlic sandwich for breakfast.

Hidayah GUESTHOUSE $$
(☎0853 3901 1310; briandanros@gmail.com; Jl Trans Flores; r 350,000Rp) Seven huge rooms with outstanding mountain and valley views from the common porch. The owner is a great source of trekking information, and organises car trips to west and east Flores. The relaxed indoor-outdoor cafe (mains from 25,000Rp) serves Indo basics, and a take on the Moni cake called the Hidayah cake.

★**Kelimutu Ecolodge** LODGE $$$
(☎0361-747 4205, 0813 5399 9311; www.ecolodgesindonesia.com; r from 800,000Rp; ❄) Easily the nicest spot in Moni. At the east end of town, nestled by the riverside, you'll find 16 lodge rooms, all with pebbled tiles, hot water, solar power and outdoor sitting areas. Let the sounds of babbling streams lull you to sleep. The restaurant (mains from 40,000Rp) serves local specialities and has a bar.

Chenty Café INDONESIAN $
(dishes 15,000-40,000Rp; ⏰8am-9pm; @) Long-running, popular place with a nice porch overlooking the rice fields. The special here is the Moni cake. Another local dish is *rumpu rampe,* which combines cassava, beans, various leaves, rice, chilli, garlic and onions.

Getting There & Away

It's always best to travel in the morning, when buses are often half-empty. Afternoon buses are usually overcrowded. Don't book through your homestay – hail the bus as it passes through town.

Bintang Lodge (p374) rents motorbikes (per day 100,000Rp).

Local drivers charge 700,000Rp per day.

Detusoko

Wedged into the misty peaks above an emerald valley blanketed with rice fields is the friendly village of Detusoko. Located halfway between Ende and Moni, and just a 45-minute drive from Kelimutu, it's a misty, cool hill town.

The roads here are lined with tarps where the area's agricultural treasures are laid out to dry. Cloves scent the air, while cocoa beans promise future pleasures. Look for stands selling all manner of fruits and vegetables.

Paga

Halfway between Moni and Maumere are a string of beaches that are the stuff of fantasy. As accommodation options grow, Paga may soon be another must-stop town on the trans-Flores shuffle. The Trans-Flores Hwy swoops down to the shore at this rice-farming and fishing hamlet, where the wide rushing river meets the placid bay.

Sights & Activities

The lush land lures you inland from the beautiful beaches. You can hike to megalithic stone graves and amazing ocean views at the nearby village of Nuabari. Agustinus Naban of Restaurant Laryss will guide you for 500,000Rp per day.

★Pantai Koka BEACH

(admission per car 20,000Rp) One of the nicest beaches in Flores has a split personality – literally. About 5km west of Pantai Naga, look for a small partially paved road that runs for 2km through a cocoa plantation to a stunning double bay. Facing a promontory, on the right is a perfect crescent of sand with calm, protected water. On the left is another perfect crescent, but with lively surf and views out to sea.

Vendors offer cold drinks, beer, coconuts, snacks and grilled fish (15,000Rp) under shady trees.

Pantai Naga BEACH

The Trans-Flores Hwy parallels this beautiful long stretch of white sand. The water is perfect for swimming and you can easily lounge away an afternoon.

Sleeping & Eating

As locals ponder the bonanza of tourism, some are converting what could be stables into rooms. Beware.

Fajar Gunawan GUESTHOUSE $

(☎0812 3752 1597; r 150,000Rp) By far the best of the new crop of Naga flophouses, this purpose-built wooden gem is on the inland side of the road but still close to the beach. The four rooms share bathrooms.

★Restaurant Laryss SEAFOOD $$

(☎0852 5334 2802; www.floresgids.com; Jl Raya Maumere-Ende; mains from 50,000Rp; ⊙kitchen 8am-8pm) Don't miss lunch at this fabulous restaurant, a tumbledown, beachfront fish joint that is one of the best places to eat in Flores. Owner Agustinus Naban serves snapper or tuna, plucked fresh out of the sea that morning, rubbed generously with turmeric and ginger, squeezed with lime and roasted on an open flame flavoured with coconut shells.

Beautifully prepared by his wife Cecilia, meals are served with red rice and a buttery sambal that is hot, but not scalding, and full flavoured. Or get the soul-stirring *ikan kuah assam* (tamarind fish soup) – an oily, savoury, spicy broth swimming with a chunk of steamed fish.

Two very basic rooms (200,000Rp) match the ad hoc architecture but open directly onto the sand.

Getting There & Away

Flag down passing buses, which run regularly during daylight hours. East to Maumere costs 15,000Rp; west to Moni costs 30,000Rp.

Sikka & Lela

Just off the Trans-Flores Hwy, 20km south of Maumere, a paved road descends 2km through coconut and banana groves to the south-coast weaving and fishing village of Lela. Villagers live in bamboo huts sprinkled on a rocky black-sand beach.

Around 4km further is the charming seaside village of Sikka, one of Flores' first Portuguese settlements. Its kings dominated the Maumere region until the 20th century. You'll be swarmed by ikat-*wallahs* as soon as you enter town, but they're a charming bunch. Buy even one piece and all of them will smile. For a 75,000Rp donation you can watch them work the looms. But the big draw is Sikka's gorgeous, narrow Catholic **cathedral**, which dates from 1899. The open windows in the arched, beamed eaves allow the sound of crashing waves to echo through the sanctuary.

Maumere

☎0382 / POP 54,000

Blessed with a long, languid coastline backed by layered hills, Maumere is one of the main gateways to Flores and the logical start or stop to a trans-Flores tour. It's well connected with Bali and Timor, so you'll probably wind up here for a night. Yet it's not exactly a charming urban destination. Thankfully, you don't have to stay in the city, as there are options along the coast.

Sleeping

There's a couple of decent options in town and along the coast to the west. Also, given that the airport is east of Maumere, the many well-regarded oceanfront hotels in Waiara (p377) and to the east are both viable and appealing options before or after a flight.

Hotel Wini Rai II HOTEL $

(☎0382-21362; Jl Soetomo; s/d fan-only 100,000/150,000Rp, s/d with air-con 150,000/200,000Rp; ❄) Maumere's best budget option (and the competition is *not* fierce) is barebones but very friendly. Small rooms face a covered courtyard. The cheapest are fan-only and can get steamy. It's close to various eating options.

★Wailiti Hotel HOTEL $$
(☎0382-23416; Jl Raya Don Silva; r 400,000-500,000Rp; ❄@☏≋) Rooms at Maumere's most pleasant accommodation are in one-storey blocks and bungalows. The flash-free vibe here extends to the spacious grounds, large pool and narrow black-sand beach with views of off shore islands. The simple cafe serves superb seafood and some amazingly good aubergine fritters. It's 6.5km west of the centre; airport transport costs 100,000Rp and is reliable.

Hotel Sylvia HOTEL $$
(☎0382-21829; www.sylviahotelmaumere.com; Jl Gajah Mada 88; r from 400,000Rp; ❄☏≋) Yes, it is a bit too shabby, as modern as this hotel is. But the service is sincere, the rooms are spacious, breakfast is a good buffet, and you can get decent food if you can't face hitting town for something more interesting.

Eating

Maumere is known for its seafood, although transiting travellers tend to eat at their hotels.

Pasar Malam SEAFOOD $
(Night Market; off Jl Slamet Riyadi; mains from 12,000Rp; ⊙5-11pm) Maumere's large night market not surprisingly has plenty of stalls grilling fresh fish.

Restaurant Gazebo SEAFOOD $$
(☎0382-22212; Jl Yos Sudarso 73; mains 30,000-80,000Rp; ⊙9am-10pm) A reasonably priced fish house. The spicy, *kuah assam* soup is delicious and the *ikan bakar* (grilled fish) is nice, too. It's just across the road from the rather shambolic waterfront.

Golden Fish Restaurant SEAFOOD $$
(☎0382-21667; Jl Hasanuddin; mains 30,000-120,000Rp; ⊙9am-9pm) Walk through the open kitchen and peruse the day's live catch – including crab and lobster – on your way to the breezy second-storey dining room with a classic harbour view.

Information

Banks and ATMs dot the centre.

Getting There & Away

Air Maumere is connected to Bali and Kupang. Airline offices and travel agents are clustered in the centre on Jl Pasar Baru Timur.

Bus & Kijang There are two bus terminals. Buses and Kijang heading east to Larantuka leave from the Lokaria (or Timur) terminal, 3km east of town. The Ende Terminal (off Jl Gajah Mada), 1km southwest of town, is the place for westbound departures. Schedules are rarely precise – be prepare d to wait around until there are sufficient passengers.

Getting Around

TO/FROM THE AIRPORT

Maumere's **Wai Oti Airport** (MOF) is 3km east of town, 800m off the Maumere–Larantuka road.

A taxi to/from town is a non-negotiable, flat fee of 70,000Rp.

TRANSPORT FROM MAUMERE

Air

DESTINATION	COMPANY	DURATION (HR)	FREQUENCY
Bali	Kalstar, Wings Air	2	daily
Kupang	Kalstar, Wings Air	1	daily

Bus & Car

DESTINATION	TYPE	PRICE (RP)	DURATION (HR)	FREQUENCY
Ende	bus	80,000	5	several daily
Ende	car	100,000	4½	several daily
Larantuka	bus	60,000	4	several daily
Larantuka	car	80,000	3	several daily
Moni	bus	50,000	3	several daily
Moni	car	80,000	3	several daily

CAR & MOTORCYCLE

Renting a car costs 600,000Rp to 800,000Rp per day, including driver and fuel. You can organise vehicle and motorbike (80,000Rp) rental at **hotels** (for more information, see p355).

Around Maumere

Heading east from Maumere, you rapidly leave the Flores tourism boom behind. But perhaps not for long, as there are lovely beaches and good diving all along the coast.

Waiara & Around

Waiara is the departure point for the Maumere 'sea gardens', once regarded as one of Asia's finest dive destinations. The 1992 earthquake and tidal wave destroyed the reefs around Pulau Penman and Pulau Besar, but they've now recovered.

Sleeping

★Budi Sun Flores Diving Resort DIVE RESORT $$
(0813 5323 7327; www.budi-sun-resort.com; Wairita; r €45-70;) This Indonesian-German venture is one of the best-run resorts along the coast east of Maumere. It sits on a nice strip of grey sand with good views. The pool is large and partially shaded, while the restaurant has excellent local and European food. The bungalow-style rooms are bright and pristine; some have sea views.

The in-house dive operation is excellent (two-tank dives €60), although many people stay here before early-morning flights. The airport is a 15-minute drive.

Sea World Club RESORT $$
(Pondok Dunia Laut; 0382-242 5089; www.sea-world-club.com; Waiara; s/d cottages from US$40/45, beachfront bungalows from US$75/80;) Just off the Larantuka road you'll find this modest 26-room beach resort. It's an Indo-German Christian collaboration started to provide local jobs and build tourism. There are simple, thatched cottages, and more modern and comfortable air-conditioned bungalows, on a quiet black-sand beach. The restaurant is decent, and it has a dive shop (US$75 for two dives including gear).

Getting There & Away

To get to Waiara, catch any Talibura- or Larantuka-bound bus from Maumere to Waiara (3000Rp). Resorts are signposted from the highway.

Wodong & Around

The pod of beaches and resorts just east of Waiara centres on Wodong, 26km east of Maumere. The narrow, palm-dappled beaches here, which include Ahuwair, Wodong and Waiterang, are tranquil and beautiful.

There's an impressive variety of dive and snorkelling sites with plenty of marine life offshore around Pulau Babi and Pulau Pangabaton, a sunken Japanese WWII ship, and colourful microlife in the 'muck' (shallow mudflats). Happy Dive at Ankermi bungalows is an excellent operator. In November whale-watching trips are also offered, although you'll probably see migrating sperm whales spout from the beach.

Sleeping

Most accommodation options are located down trails 10m to 500m from the road; they are signposted from the highway.

★Lena House BUNGALOW $
(0813 3940 7733; www.lenahouseflores.com; Wodong; r from 150,000Rp) Chill out in one of eight clean bamboo bungalows, operated by a sweet family and set on a spectacular stretch of beach, with jungled mountains painted against the eastern horizon. The owners arrange snorkelling trips, but you may be just as happy to let your mind drift as you watch local fishers ply the glassy bay in their dugouts.

Sunset Cottages BUNGALOW $
(0812 4602 3954, 0821 4768 7254; Maumere-Larantuka Rd Km 25; r without/with bathroom from 150,000/250,000Rp) Nestled on a secluded black-sand beach, with views of offshore islands, Sunset Cottages is shaded by swaying coco palms. The thatched, coconut-wood and bamboo bungalows of varying ages have Western toilets and *mandis* (Indonesian baths), with decks overlooking the sea. Snorkel gear is available for hire; order ahead for fresh fish.

Ankermi BUNGALOW $$
(0812 466 9667; www.ankermi-happydive.com; r 300,000-400,000Rp;) These cute, tiled and thatched bungalows have private porches with stunning sea views (fan-only) or garden views (with air-con). The dive shop, Happy Dive, is the best in the Maumere area (two-tank dives from €65). They grow their own organic rice and vegetables on-site, and meals are fresh and delicious.

Getting There & Away

Wodong, the main village in the area, is on the Maumere–Larantuka road. Take any Talibura, Nangahale or Larantuka bemo or bus from the Lokaria terminal in Maumere (3000Rp). A bemo from Wodong to Waiterang costs another 1000Rp. A taxi or chartered bemo from Maumere is around 80,000Rp. Buses pass by throughout the day.

Larantuka

0383

A bustling little port of rusted tin roofs at the easternmost end of Flores, Larantuka rests against the base of **Gunung Ili Mandiri** (1510m), separated by a narrow strait from Pulau Solor and Pulau Adonara. It has a fun street-market vibe at dusk, when streets come alive with the commerce of fresh fruit and fish, but most visitors stay just one night on their way to Kupang or Alor. Easter is a particularly good time to be in this Christian-majority town, as there are huge processions of penitents and cross-bearers.

Sleeping & Eating

★Asa Hotel & Restaurant HOTEL **$$**
(0383-232 5018; asahotel-larantuka.com; Jl Soekarno Hatta; r from 360,000Rp, mains from 25,000Rp;) The best place to stay has an impressive complex overlooking the harbour, 5km east of the centre. The 27 modern and well-designed rooms are in one- and two-storey blocks, and have fridges and balconies. There is a good restaurant (mains from 25,000Rp), and a bar with views.

Hotel Lesthari GUESTHOUSE **$$**
(0383-232 5517, 0852 5303 1152; Jl Yos Sudarso; r 250,000-300,000Rp;) Choose from 11 clean rooms, some with double beds dressed in colourful sheets. Rooms have private patios and are within walking distance of the pier; the more expensive ones have hot water.

Rumah Makan Nirwana INDONESIAN **$**
(Jl Yos Sudarso; mains 15,000-30,000Rp; 7am-9pm) Still the best choice in the heart of town, just don't expect miracles. The *soto ayam* (chicken soup) is tasty and the house sambal scintillating.

Information

The ferry pier, shipping offices and the main bus terminal are in the southern part of town. **Bank BNI** (Jl Fernandez 93) has multiple ATMs around town.

Getting There & Away

Ferries run to Kupang (105,000Rp to 154,000Rp, 15 hours, two per week) and Kalabahi (economy 115,000RP, VIP 170,000Rp, 24 hours, one per week).

The main bus terminal is 5km west of town. Buses (60,000Rp, four hours) and cars (80,000Rp, three hours) to Maumere run frequently between 7am and 5pm.

Getting Around

Bemos (3000Rp) run up and down Jl Niaga and Jl Pasar, and to outlying villages.

Ojeks also run to the pier and bus terminal for about 10,000Rp.

ALOR ARCHIPELAGO

The final link of the island chain that stretches east of Java is wild, volcanic and drop-dead gorgeous. There are crumbling red-clay roads, jagged peaks, white-sand beaches, and crystal-clear bays that have some remarkable diving – with plenty of pelagics and sheer walls draped in vast eye-popping coral gardens.

The cultural diversity here is simply staggering. In this tiny archipelago alone there are over 100 tribes who, by some accounts, speak eight languages and 52 dialects. The terrain and lack of roads isolated the 200,000 inhabitants from one another and the outside world for centuries. Although the Dutch installed local rajas along the coastal regions after 1908, they had little influence over the interior, where people were still taking heads into the 1950s, and indigenous animist traditions endure.

Though a network of simple roads now covers Pulau Alor, boats are still a common form of transport. The few visitors who land here tend to linger on nearby Pulau Kepa or dive these waters from liveaboards.

Kalabahi

0386 / POP 61,000

Kalabahi is the chief town on Pulau Alor, located at the end of a spectacular 15km-long, palm-fringed bay on the west coast. Yet the town's main drag is a long, concrete sprawl that doesn't so much as hint at the sea. Thanks to the punishing heat, the streets only come to life in the morning, and again an hour before sundown.

ALOR OFFSHORE

Alor's dive operators regularly visit upwards of 40 dive sites, sprinkled throughout the archipelago. There are wall dives, slopes, caves, pinnacles and really good muck diving in the Alor bay. What makes Alor special isn't the huge number of pelagics, but rather the completely unspoiled reefs with intact hard and vibrant soft corals. The water is absolutely crystal-clear. Dive sites are never crowded, and pelagic disclaimer aside, you may well see a thresher shark, a pod of dolphins or even migrating sperm whales wander past. Just know, there is frequently unpredictable current and the water can be cold (as low as 22°C), which is what keeps the coral well nourished and spectacular. It's best to have 30 dives under your belt before venturing into these waters.

All divers must pay a marine park fee of 35,000Rp per day to fund the management of a 400,000-hectare marine park. For several years the WWF has been trying to influence the government to develop a park management plan, but so far without success.

Sandwiched between Pulaus Pantar and Alor is **Pulau Pura**, which has some of Alor's best dive sites. **Pulau Ternate**, not to be confused with the Maluku version, also has some magnificent dive and snorkel sites. (Who are we kidding, it's all magical here.) **Uma Pura** is an interesting weaving village on Ternate, with a rather prominent wooden church. To get there charter a boat from Alor Besar or Alor Kecil (150,000Rp).

Sights & Activities

Hanging around the docks, which are closer to the heart of town than is immediately apparent, is the perfect way to absorb the remote, off-the-grid, languid tropical vibe.

Pantai Maimol BEACH

The best beach near Kalabahi is this ribbon of white sand 10km out of town on the airport road. You can easily laze away a few hours here. Plans are in the works for a bungalow resort.

Museum Seribu Moko MUSEUM

(Museum of 1000 Drums; Jl Diponegoro; 8am-2pm Mon-Fri) FREE Named for its collection of *moko* (bronze drums; the 1000 is purely figurative), this humble museum located just west of the market has some good English booklets about the collection, which includes fine ikat, ceremonial clothes made from bark and, yes, drums (some of which bear designs dating to Southeast Asia in 700 BC).

Alor Dive DIVING

(0386-222 2663, 0813 3964 8148; www.alor-dive.com; Jl Suharto; 2-tank dives from €80; 8am-4pm) This long-running dive shop run by a German expat organises all manner of diving trips, from one day to a week or more. It has years of experience in the beautiful local waters.

Sleeping & Eating

Kalabahi's choice of accommodation is unlikely to persuade you to linger. You can spend an enjoyable evening around the main dock, when several warungs set up shop and serve excellent fish and other Indo treats.

★Cantik Homestay HOMESTAY $

(0813 3229 9336, 0386-21030; Jl Dahlia 12; r 150,000-200,000Rp;) Seven simple, tiled rooms in a family home, tucked into a shady, compact residential neighbourhood. The owner rents motorbikes; room rates include breakfast.

The lady of the house cooks lunch and dinner (meals 20,000Rp to 25,000Rp), which can mean ridiculously good fish, fried to crispy, moist perfection and served with a stunning veggie dish made out of papaya flower. It's served simply at one long table.

Hotel Pelangi Indah HOTEL $

(0386-21251; Jl Diponegoro 34; s/d with fan 90,000/180,000Rp, s/d with air-con 150,000/300,000Rp, s/d VIP 250,000/325,000Rp;) Set on the main drag, these reasonably well-tended rooms flank a leafy courtyard. Many of the rooms are dark, however the VIP ones have private bathrooms and small terraces out front.

Pagi Mart SUPERMARKET $

(Jl Suharto; 8am-8pm) Alor's one supermarket is where you can get any vital supply you might need (beer, ice cream, sunscreen…) while here at – if not the end of the world – then almost the end of Nusa Tenggara.

★Restaurant Mama INDONESIAN $$

(0386-222 2845, 0813 5382 3280; mains 25,000-65,000Rp; 10am-10pm) Alor's best views are from this wood-and-bamboo dining room perched over the bay on stilts, 50m west of the big waterfront market. It does all the seafood delights and competent Indo fare such as nasi goreng. The house special is *ikan kuah assam mama,* an addictive local fish soup with a fiery, tamarind-inflected broth.

Information

Bank BNI (Jl Sutomo; 8am-4pm Mon-Fri) has an ATM.

Getting There & Away

Transnusa and Wings Air make the one-hour flight to Kupang. The tiny **airport** is comically disorganised, and 13km from Kalabahi. Check in early to avoid the mad scrum that often develops.

Ferries leave from the **ferry terminal** 1km southwest of the town centre; it's a 10-minute walk or a 3000Rp bemo ride. There are two weekly to Kupang (116,000Rp to 170,000Rp, 18 hours), and one to Larantuka (115,000Rp to 170,000Rp, 24 hours).

Pelni (0386-21195; Jl Cokroaminoto 5, ticket office; 8am-2pm Mon-Sat) ships leave from the main pier in the centre of town (the Pelni office is opposite the pier) and visit Rote, Ende, Bima, Bali and more on a monthly schedule. ADSP ferries serve Kupang and Larantuka.

Getting Around

The airport is 13km from town. Taxis cost a fixed 100,000Rp.

Transport around town is by bemo (3000Rp).

Rent a motorbike at **Cantik Homestay** (p379) for 100,000Rp per day.

Ojeks are easily hired for 120,000Rp per day.

Pak Marlon is the best local guide. He can organise trips across Alor and his English is excellent.

Drivers charge from 300,000Rp per day.

Around Kalabahi

Takpala is a stunning traditional village etched into a hillside about 13km east of Kalabahi. There are several *lopo* (traditional high-roofed houses), held together with lashings, scattered beneath mango, papaya and banana trees. The villagers are charming, and will be more than happy to teach you how to use a traditional bow and arrow, or to roll you one of their home-cured cigarettes, which go well with a pinch of betel. To get here take a Mabu bus (5000Rp) from the terminal at Kalabahi market. Walk about 1km uphill on a sealed road from where the bus drops you off.

OFF THE BEATEN TRACK

PANTAR

The second-largest island of the Alor group is way off the beaten track. A daily ferry from Kalabahi (45,000Rp, two hours) docks at **Baranusa**, the island's sleepy main town, with a straggle of coconut palms, a homestay, and a couple of general stores. Smouldering Gunung Sirung (1372m) draws a few hearty climbers each year. From Baranusa take a truck to Kakamauta and walk for three hours to Sirung's crater. Bring water from Baranusa and stay with the *kepala desa* (village head; 50,000Rp) in **Kakamauta**.

Pantar is also home to an upscale dive resort. **Alor Divers** (0813 1780 4133; www.alor-divers.com; week-long dive packages from €1000), built and operated by a French-Slovenian couple on the island's eastern shore, caters exclusively to divers and their plus-ones. Guests stay in smart, thatched bungalows, and dive at least twice daily. Orcas, and sperm and pilot whales migrate off the west coast in June and December.

You can also do a fascinating village tour of Alor's bird's head – the island's distinctively shaped northern peninsula. From Kalabahi head to **Mombang**, up through the clove trees and coffee plots of **Kopidil** (where they make ceremonial clothes out of tree bark) to **Tulta**, and then down to the stunning sweep of white sand and coconut palms that is **Batu Putih**. It's backed by granite bluffs and cornfields, and cradles a turquoise and emerald lagoon 10km north of Mali. You'll either need to hire a motorbike (100,000Rp) or charter an *ojek* (150,000Rp per day) for this. Bring plenty of water, a boxed lunch, *pinang* (betel nut), smokes, a few essential food items, and the best Bahasa Indonesia you've got to share with your new friends. Or ease the process considerably and hire **Pak Marlon** (0853 3896 1214; marlon.adang@yahoo.co.id; per day 200,000Rp), an excellent guide.

For hikers or motorcyclists who like rugged backcountry, consider a longer trip; two or three days hiking along the verdant, mountainous spine of Central Alor. One route connects **Mainang** with **Kelaisi** and on to **Apui**. Another loop begins in **Ateng**, stops in **Melang** and ends in **Lakwati**. These are all very poor, purely traditional villages.

The roads and trails are very bad, so these are not easy journeys. You'll be sleeping in basic village accommodation (per person from 50,000Rp), and meals will be extremely basic too. Not all villages have latrines, and you'll need to bring extra food and water. Be prepared.

The fishing village of **Alor Besar** is where you'll find **Al Quaran Tua**, a 12th-century Quran integral to the seeding of Islam in the Alor archipelago. Take care if you choose to handle the handmade parchment. It's held at the town mosque, **Masjid Jami Babussholah**, which is open to tourists by donation from sunrise to sundown.

There are also nice white-sand beaches in both Alor Besar and nearby **Alor Kecil**, with excellent snorkelling. The best is at **Sebanjar**, 3km north of Alor Kecil. The water here is wonderfully cool, with a gorgeous soft-coral garden offshore. Alor Kecil is also the jumping-off point for beautiful Pulau Kepa.

Sleeping

★La Petite Kepa DIVE RESORT **$$**
(SMS only 0813 3910 2403; www.la-petite-kepa.com; bungalows incl meals per person 225,000-450,000Rp, dives from €32) The top destination in the Alor archipelago is this French-owned, solar-powered dive resort, which offers 10 bungalows, three of which are replicas of traditional Alor homes and have shared baths. The delicious meals, crafted from fresh ingredients (the sambal could launch a thousand ships), are eaten family-style. The resort has a boat for the quick shuttle from Alor Kecil.

Most of the bungalows are standard thatched bamboo casitas with attached outdoor baths. All have sea and island views. There are two beaches, including an exquisite sliver of white sand on the west side with spectacular sunset views and good snorkelling offshore. Snorkelling equipment is available, and snorkellers can join the dive boat for 100,000Rp per day. In July and August divers get priority for bookings. Reserve your room well in advance.

The resort recycles, and conserves water and power.

Getting There & Away

Buses and bemos to Alor Kecil (3000Rp, 30 minutes) and Alor Besar leave from the Kalabahi Pasar Inpres (market). You can also take a taxi from the airport (150,000Rp to 200,000Rp).

WEST TIMOR

With amazing traditional villages, rugged countryside and empty beaches, West Timor is an undiscovered gem. Deep within its mountainous, *lontar*-palm-studded interior, animist traditions persist alongside tribal dialects, and ikat-clad, betel-nut-chewing chiefs govern beehive-hut villages. Hit one of the many weekly markets in tribal country and you'll get a feel for rural Timor life, while eavesdropping on several of some 14 languages spoken on the island. In West Timor even Bahasa Indonesia is often a foreign tongue. Except, of course, in Kupang, the coastal capital and East Nusa Tenggara's top metropolis, which buzzes to a frenetic Indonesian beat.

EXPLORING WEST TIMOR

Kupang is a gateway to West Timor's fascinating and welcoming traditional villages. Bahasa Indonesia – let alone English – is often not spoken. In addition, the traditional villages can be a minefield – albeit a friendly minefield – of cultural dos and don'ts. A local guide is essential.

Oney Meda (0813 3940 4204; per day from 300,000Rp) An English-speaking guide with nearly two decades of experience organising anthropological tours and treks throughout West Timor and Alor. Meda's rates depend on the complexity of the itinerary.

Eben Oematan (0852 3795 8136; per day from 300,000Rp) Has over 25 years of experience. Oematan is from Kapan, which means he speaks several dialects spoken in the villages you'll want to visit. Based in Soe, he picks up guests in Kupang.

Edwin Lerrick (0812 377 0533, 0380-832256; lavalonbar@gmail.com; per day from 300,000Rp) The irrepressible owner of Kupang's Lavalon Bar & Hostel (p383) is also a sensational guide, with deep regional knowledge and connections throughout West Timor, especially in the traditional villages.

West Timor

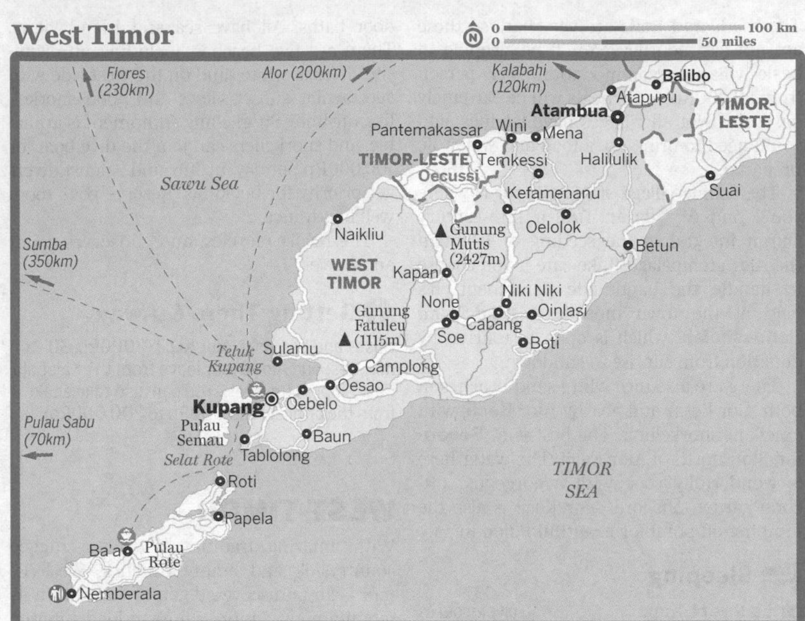

History

The Tetun (or Tetum) of central Timor are one of the largest ethnic groups on the island, and boast the dominant indigenous language. Before Portuguese and Dutch colonisation, they were fragmented into dozens of small states led by various chiefs. Conflict was common, and headhunting a popular pastime.

The first Europeans in Timor were the Portuguese, who prized its endemic *cendana* (sandalwood) trees. In the mid-17th century the Dutch landed in Kupang, beginning a prolonged battle for control of the sandalwood trade, which the Dutch eventually won. The two colonial powers divvied up the island in a series of treaties signed between 1859 and 1913. Portugal was awarded the eastern half plus the enclave of Oecussi, the island's first settlement.

Neither European power penetrated far into the interior until the 1920s, and the island's political structure was left largely intact. The colonisers spread Christianity and ruled through the native aristocracy, but some locals claim Europeans corrupted Timor's royal bloodlines by aligning with imported, and eventually triumphant, Rotenese kingdoms. When Indonesia won independence in 1949 the Dutch left West Timor, but the Portuguese still held East Timor. In 1975 East Timor declared itself independent from Indonesia; shortly afterwards Indonesia invaded, setting the stage for the tragedy that continued until the East's independence in 2002.

During August 1999, in a UN-sponsored referendum, the people of East Timor voted in favour of independence. Violence erupted when pro-Jakarta militias, backed by the Indonesian military, destroyed buildings and infrastructure across the East, leaving up to 1400 civilians dead before peacekeepers intervened. Back in West Timor, the militias were responsible for the lynching of three UN workers in Atambua in 2000, making West Timor an international pariah.

After several turbulent years, relations normalised by 2006 and road and transport links were restored.

Kupang

0380 / POP 350,000

Kupang is the capital of Nusa Tenggara Timur (NTT) and despite the city's scruffy waterfront, its sprawling gnarl of traffic, and the complete lack of endearing cultural or architectural elements, this is a place you can get used to. Chalk it up to Kupang's chaotic energy. It's a university town, after all, and there's the intangible buzz of a place on the move.

Kupang's a regional transport hub, so you will do time here. Just don't be surprised if between trips to the interior, Alor or Rote, you discover that you actually dig it. England's Captain Bligh had a similar epiphany when he spent 47 days here after that emasculating mutiny on the *Bounty* incident in 1789.

Kupang sprawls and you'll need to take bemos or *ojeks* to get around. You will likely land in one of two main areas. The waterfront district – which stretches along Jl Sumba, Jl Sumatera, Jl Garuda and Jl Siliwangi, and rambles inland with Jl Ahmad Yani – has numerous lodging options, plenty of restaurants and the night market. Jl Mohammad Hatta and Jl Sudirman to the south, is the new commercial centre with chain hotels and malls.

DON'T MISS

BEST OF WEST TIMOR

None One of many traditional villages; they only stopped hunting heads here in 1945.

Boti An ancient village doing its best to make sure time forgets it.

Temkessi A magical, mystical outpost of centuries-old culture atop a limestone promontory.

Oinlasi Ikat in colours and patterns you didn't think possible is sold by the women who made it at this huge weekly market.

Sights

The very heart of old Kupang centres on the **old port area** and its surrounding cacophonous market. Look closely and you'll see a few traces of Dutch colonial times, when Kupang was considered a genteel tropical idyll.

Museum Nusa Tenggara Timur MUSEUM
(0380-832471; Jl Frans Seda; admission by donation; 8am-3pm Mon-Sat) Renovations are rapidly improving the regional museum. It has skulls, seashells, stone tools, swords, gourds and antique looms from across the province, plus an entire blue whale skeleton. Displays (some in English) cover historical moments and cultural topics such as which plants provide dyes for traditional fabrics.

Sleeping

Near the airport and the new commercial district there are several large and bland chain hotels such as the Neo Aston and the Amaris. Any of the properties on the waterfront will be much more pleasant, and will enjoy ocean breezes and views.

★**Lavalon Bar & Hostel** HOSTEL $
(0812 377 0533, 0380-832256; www.lavalontouristinfo.com; Jl Sumatera 44; dm 50,000Rp, r 150,000-250,000Rp;) The best value in town with clean rooms and Western-style bathrooms. Excellent meals and cold beer are served in the open-air common area, which has fine views. It's run by the much-loved living NTT encyclopedia and former Indonesian film star Edwin Lerrick. Expansion plans will bring more private rooms to this prime waterfront location.

Hotel Maliana GUESTHOUSE $
(0380-821879; Jl Sumatera 35; r with fan/air-con 175,000/250,000Rp;) These 14 basic yet comfy motel rooms are a popular budget choice. Rooms are clean and have ocean glimpses from the front porch, which dangles with vines. Breakfast is included.

★**Swiss Belinn Kristal Kupang** HOTEL $$
(0380-843 0300; www.swiss-belhotel.com; Jl Timor Raya 59; r from 670,000Rp;) Recently renovated and well managed, this hotel is the most appealing in town. The beachfront location and resort feel makes this the preferred hotel of the transiting Alor and Rote set. Rooms are spacious and carpeted, and equipped with a minibar, bathtub and satellite TV. Ask for one with a sea view. The pool area is lovely. It's 2km east of the centre.

Evergreen Homestay GUESTHOUSE $$
(0380-805 0015; Jl Sapta Marga 1/10; r 175,000-300,000Rp;) Confusingly located off Jl Mohammad Hatta in a residential neighbourhood, this compound is actually quite central. The 13 rooms are basic, large and clean. All have air-con, some have hot water.

Hotel La Hasienda HOTEL $$
(0380-800 4333; hotellahasienda.com; Jl Adi Sucipto; s/d from 325,000/380,000Rp;) Rather improbably, this three-storey family-run hotel has a faux Mexican motif. Although they get points for trying, if not succeeding, where they really score is in their attention to detail and hospitality. The 22 rooms are spotless and bright. It's near the airport and there is shuttle service as well as a restaurant with a diverse menu.

Kupang

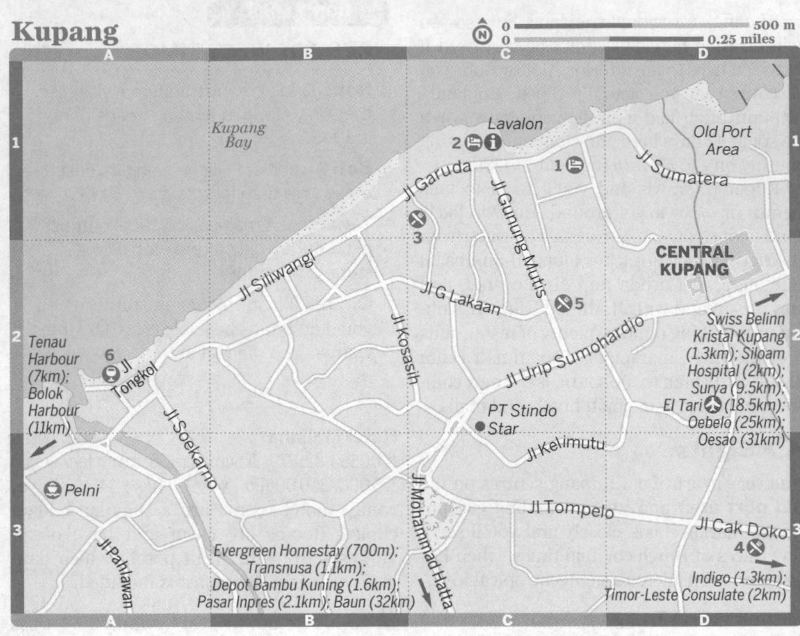

Kupang

Sleeping

1 Hotel Maliana C1
2 Lavalon Bar & Hostel C1

Eating

Lavalon Bar & Hostel .... (see 2)
3 Pasar Malam C1
4 Rumah Makan Palembang D3
5 Rumah Makan Wahyu Putra Solo C2

Drinking & Nightlife

6 999 Restaurant & Bar A2

Eating & Drinking

As you'd expect, seafood is big in Kupang. Another local speciality is succulent *sei babi* (smoked pork); it's used as the base for various sauces, and is served with noodles.

★Pasar Malam MARKET $

(Night Market; Jl Garuda; mains from 12,000Rp; ⏲6-11pm) Kupang was never considered a good eating town until this wonderful, lamp-lit market launched and turned a lane off Jl Garuda over to street-side grill and wok chefs, who expertly prepare inexpensive dishes. The seafood selection is vast, the grilling superb.

Depot Bambu Kuning INDONESIAN $

(☎0380-832302; Jl Soekarno 19; ⏲10am-10pm) The place in Kupang for *sei babi*. You have your choice of chopped-up meat or ribs. Either way the sides are rice and rich pork soup with red beans. This simple shopfront gets jammed with happy locals at lunch, so try other times.

Rumah Makan Palembang CHINESE $

(☎0821 4796 6011; Jl Cak Doko; dishes 20,000-90,000Rp; ⏲10am-2.30pm & 6-11pm) This is first-rate Chinese Indonesian food. Get the *ikan bakar rica rica* (grilled fish with chilli sauce); its sauce is a sweet, smoky wonder. The squid and shrimp are fresh daily, the veggies are perfectly cooked, and do not skimp on that beautiful cucumber sambal. If you like a spicy pickle, you'll be thrilled.

Rumah Makan Wahyu Putra Solo INDONESIAN $

(☎0380-821552; Jl Gunung Mutis 31; meals 10,000-25,000Rp; ⏲7am-9pm; 🖉) Kupang's best pick-and-mix Padang-style warung offers beef, chicken, fish, potatoes and greens, deep- and stir-fried, stewed in coconut sauce, and chilli-rubbed and roasted. Vegetarians will find something tasty here.

Lavalon Bar & Hostel BURGERS $

(☎0380-832256, 0812 377 0533; www.lavalontouristinfo.com; Jl Sumatera 44; mains from 30,000Rp; ⏰7am-late; 📶) The heart of the Lavalon empire occupies the same sweet spot as the hostel. Edwin Lerrick and his chatty crew dish up excellent burgers and chips plus Indo standards through the day and evening. The ocean laps at the shore 10m away, and you can lounge back in a hammock with a cold Bintang in hand.

Indigo INTERNATIONAL $$

(☎0811 228 1318; Jl Suprapto 30; mains 40,000-100,000Rp; ⏰noon-10pm; ❄📶) There's a slick industrial chic at this popular restaurant and bar, which does good pizza as well as pasta and local dishes such as the ubiquitous nasi goreng. Everything is well prepared and the beer is even colder than the chilled air-con surrounds.

999 Restaurant & Bar BAR

(☎0380-802 0999; 999-kupang.com; Jl Tongkol 3; ⏰10am-late; 📶) In the shadow of an old fort, this tropical bar has an expansive thatched roof, no walls, views of the shabby beach and the ever-present sound of rolling surf. There's a pool table, a full bar including a menu of dayglo cocktails, and a decent menu. Just east, waterfront vendors sell corn on the cob.

Shopping

Sandalwood oil is something of a local speciality. You can buy oils of varying quality at the shops in the old town, off Jl Garuda. The purest oils are upwards of 300,000Rp for a small vial.

Pasar Inpres MARKET

(off Jl Soeharto; ⏰7am-4pm) The main market is the rambling Pasar Inpres in the south of the city. It's mostly fruit and vegetables, but some ikat and handicrafts can be found near the terminal. Bizarre *ti'i langga* (conical hats) from Rote make a fun purchase, but try fitting one in your backpack. Take bemo 1 or 2 and follow the crowd.

Ina Ndao TEXTILES

(☎0380-821178; Jl Kebun Raya II; ⏰8am-7pm Mon-Sat) It's worth seeking out this neighbourhood ikat shop. Textile lovers should be pleased with the wares sourced from across NTT. It offers naturally and chemically dyed varieties, and demonstrates the weaving process upon request.

Information

MEDICAL SERVICES

Siloam Hospital (☎1-500-911; off Jl Eltari; ⏰24hr) A new and upscale hospital attached to the Lippo Plaza shopping mall.

MONEY

Kupang has scores of banks and ATMs throughout town.

TOURIST INFORMATION

Lavalon (☎0380-832256, 0812 377 0533; www.lavalontouristinfo.com; Jl Sumatera 44; ⏰8am-late; 📶) Edwin Lerrick, the proprietor, is a vital source for the latest transport information, as well as cultural attractions throughout NTT. His website is a must-read for information.

TIMOR-LESTE VISA RUN

Hitting Dili in Timor-Leste is one way to renew your Indonesian visa from Nusa Tenggara. If you decide to go, be aware that Timor-Leste is considerably more expensive than Indonesia, and the return trip normally takes more than a week by the time you get to Dili, wait for your Indonesian visa and return to West Timor.

Apply for your visa to Timor-Leste at the **Timor-Leste Consulate** (☎0813-3936 7558; Jl Eltari II; ⏰8am-4pm Mon-Thu, to 2pm Fri) in Kupang with a valid passport, a photocopy and passport photos. It costs US$30 and takes one to three working days to process.

In Dili head to the Indonesia Consulate for your new tourist visa (US$50). Travellers have been issued with 60-day visas here upon request. Visas take four working days to issue and you'll need to visit the office three times (the first time just to make an appointment for the process).

Direct minibuses (10 to 11 hours) to Dili are operated by **Timor Tour & Travel** (☎0380-881543; one-way 230,000Rp) and **Paradise** (☎0380-830414, 0813 3944 7183; one-way 230,000Rp). Call for a hotel pickup. Departures can be as early as 5am, so brace yourself.

TRAVEL AGENCIES

PT Stindo Star (☎0380-809 0584, 0380-809 0583; Jl Urip Sumohardjo 2; ⏲9am-6pm) An efficient travel agency that sells airline tickets.

Getting There & Away

AIR

Kupang is the most important hub for air travel in Nusa Tenggara. There are frequent flights to Bali and a web of services across the region.

FERRY

Tenau Harbour, 7km west of the centre, is where the fast ferry to Rote and Pelni ships dock. Bolok Harbour, where you get regular ferries to Kalabahi, Larantuka, Rote and Waingapu, is 11km west of the centre.

Pelni (☎0380-824357; Jl Pahlawan 3; ⏲8.30am-3pm Mon-Sat, 9-11am Sun) serves Kupang on a twice-monthly loop that includes Larantuka and Maumere. Its office is near the waterfront.

Getting Around

TO/FROM THE AIRPORT

Kupang's El Tari Airport is 15km east of the town centre.

Taxis from the airport to town cost a fixed 60,000Rp. For public transport, turn left out of the terminal and walk 1km to the junction with the main highway, from where bemos to town cost 3000Rp.

Going to the airport, take the *Penfui* bemo to the junction and walk.

BEMO

A ride in one of Kupang's unique bass-thumping hip-hop bemos (2000Rp) is one of the city's essential experiences (Kupang is too spread out to walk). Windscreens are festooned with either girlie silhouettes, Jesus of Nazareth, his mum, or English football stars. The low-rider paint job is of the *Fast & Furious* technicolour variety, while banks of subwoofers will have your ass involuntarily shaking to the driver's C-list hip-hop soundtrack.

Bemos stop running by 9pm. The bemo hub is the Kota Kupang terminal. Useful bemo routes:

➡ **1 & 2** Kuanino–Oepura; passing many popular hotels.

➡ **5** Oebobo–Airnona–Bakunase; passing the main post office.

➡ **6** Goes to the Flobamora shopping mall and the post office.

➡ **10** Kelapa Lima–Walikota; from Kota Kupang terminal to the tourist office, Oebobo bus terminal and Museum Nusa Tenggara Timur.

Several bemos use names instead of numbers. *Tenau* and *Belok Harbour* bemos run to the docks. The *Penfui* bemo links to the airport.

CAR & MOTORCYCLE

It's possible to rent a car with a driver from 400,000Rp to 750,000Rp per day, depending upon the destination. Motorcycles cost around 60,000Rp per day. You can arrange one at your hotel or Lavalon (p385).

Around Kupang

Oenesu

Hidden in this sleepy farming village just off the Kupang–Tablolong road is an impressive three-stage, turquoise-tinted **waterfall** (admission 2000Rp). There's a nice swimming hole beneath the last cascade. Locals love it, which explains the profound rubbish issue. The turn-off is 13km from Kupang near Tapa village, serviced by regular bemos from Tabun. From the main road it's a 2.5km walk to the falls. Take the road to Sumlili; after the Immanuel church turn and walk 800m along a rough road.

Oebelo & Oesao

Oebelo, a small salt-mining town 22km from Kupang on the Soe road, is notable for a terrific Rotenese musical-instrument workshop, **Sasandu** (☎0852 3948 7808; Jl Timor Raya; ⏲9am-6pm), run by Pak Pah and his family. Traditional 20-stringed harps, aka *sasando,* are made and played in all sizes. Pak may treat you to a haunting instrumental number, or a cover of 'Country Road.'

Oesao is another 6km down the road and is a mandatory stop for one marvellous reason: **Inzana** (Jl Timor Raya; bag of treats 10,000Rp; ⏲4am-10pm), a roadside sweet shop located just east of the main market that serves a variety of traditional Timorese cakes. Our favourites are the pancakes stuffed with coconut cream, and the sublime (and still warm) flying-saucer-shaped discs of fried dough stuffed with candied rice. Your driver will know the place. Stock up for the road. Ignore the lesser competition nearby.

Soe

☎0388 / POP 32,000

About 110km east from Kupang, the cool, leafy market town of Soe (800m) makes a decent base from which to explore West Timor's interior. The traditional villages scattered throughout the interior are some of the most intriguing sights in NTT.

Sights

★Air Terjun Oehala WATERFALL

One of the prettiest waterfalls we've seen in Indonesia is close to Soe. Look for a road going north off the main highway, drive 6km and turn east at a sign for 'Oehala'. After another 3km you'll find a parking area where a short walk brings you down to a series of white ribbons of tumbling water. The best section sees the water diffusing over huge boulders in a silvery sheen. It's popular with locals at weekends, deserted other times.

Sleeping

Hotel Bahagia I GUESTHOUSE $

(0853 3830 3809; Jl Diponegoro; r 120,000-275,000Rp;) Right in the centre, there are a range of rooms here – from small, dark cold-water ones, to airy air-con retreats. It's a compact courtyard building with a little breezy terrace offering valley views.

★Timor Megah Hotel HOTEL $$

(0388-22280; Jl Gajah Mada; r 250,000-400,000Rp;) This new hotel block just west of the centre is Soe's best place to stay. There is a range of large rooms in a L-shaped three-storey block. The cheapest have fans and hot water, the best add air-con and fridges.

Hotel Gajah Mada HOTEL $$

(0388-21197; Jl Gajah Mada; r standard/VIP 250,000/450,000Rp) Well situated near the centre of town. The 38 rooms are large, comfortable and clean with queen beds, TV and hot water. There are nice mountain views from the second-storey terrace.

Eating

★Depot Remaja INDONESIAN $

(Jl Gajah Mada; mains from 20,000Rp; 10am-10pm;) This modest yet very clean diner is *the* place to try succulent *sei babi*, the iconic local smoked pork. But the fun doesn't stop there; try the warming pork soup – which is more stew than soup – and the *jantung pisang* (banana-flower salad). Everything is superb and there are many veggie options such as papaya salad.

Bundo Kanduang INDONESIAN $

(0813 3947 0896; Jl Gajah Mada; meals 25,000-35,000Rp; 24hr) If you've been waiting to find a fresh spot to try Padang food, this is it. There are devilled eggs with chilli, fried and curried fish, *rendang*, stewed vegies and potato cakes. Almost everything is spicy and it all rocks. It's 1.5km west of Soe centre.

Shopping

Timor Art Shop HANDICRAFTS

(0853 3351 8929; Jl Bill Nope 17; by appointment) If you're interested in antiques and handicrafts, don't miss this shop that could be a museum. You'll find Timor's best selection of masks, sculpture, hand-spun fabrics and carvings at unbelievable prices. There's no sign, so call owner Alfred Maku first. He speaks excellent English.

Information

There are **Bank BNI** ATMs around town, including right across from Hotel Bahagia on Jl Diponegoro.

Tourist Information Centre (0368-21149; Jl Diponegoro; 9am-3pm Mon-Fri) Has good detail on the surrounding area and is a good place to arrange guides.

Getting There & Away

The Haumeni bus terminal is 4km west of town (3000Rp by bemo). Regular buses go from Soe to Kupang (30,000Rp, three hours), Kefamenanu (20,000Rp, 2½ hours) and Oinlasi (20,000Rp, 2½ hours), while bemos cover Niki Niki (10,000Rp).

Around Soe

None

None is Kefamenanu's last headhunting village and one of the area's best attractions. A trail runs for 900m from where the bemo drops you off on the main road. Stroll past corn and bean fields and hop over a meandering stream (often dry) and you'll reach scattered *ume bubu* (traditional beehive huts), home to 56 families that have lived here for nine generations. Parents still bury their baby's placenta in the centre of their hut, and the village is protected by a native rock fort, which abuts a sheer cliff.

At the cliff's edge you'll find a 200-year-old banyan tree and a **totem pole** where shamans once met with warriors before they left on headhunting expeditions (the last was in 1945). The wise ones consulted chicken eggs and their wooden staff before predicting if the warriors would prevail.

TRADITIONAL HOUSES

Central West Timor is dotted with ubiquitous *ume bubu* (beehive-shaped hut) villages that are home to local Dawan people. With no windows and only a 1m-high doorway, *ume bubu* are cramped and smoky. Government authorities have deemed them a health hazard and are in the process of replacing them with cold concrete boxes, which the Dawan have deemed a health hazard. They've built new *ume bubu* – or rehabbed their old ones – behind the approved houses, and live there.

Villagers are warm and welcoming, and break out their looms at the village *lopo* (meeting place) for weaving demonstrations upon request. It is so peaceful here that it's hard to believe they were taking heads just two generations ago. You can arrange for traditional dances or even stay the night. Be sure to leave an offering of at least 20,000Rp each.

Getting There & Away

You can reach None, 18km east of Soe, on an *ojek* (30,000Rp), or hop on a Soe–Niki Niki bemo for 5,000Rp. If driving, you can get close to the village, but consider doing the access walk from the main road to soak up the atmosphere.

Oinlasi

We'll let others speculate about why local governments keep the road to the important market town of Oinlasi in such miserable condition. But the painful drive is worth it, especially on Tuesdays, when a **traditional market** spreads for over 400m along a ridge overlooking two valleys. Villagers from the surrounding hills, many of whom wear traditional ikat, descend to barter, buy and sell weavings, carvings, masks and elaborately carved betel-nut containers, along with fruit, livestock, local sweets and some of the worst popular music ever recorded. The market starts early in the morning and continues until 2pm, but is at its best before 10am.

If you want to immerse yourself in Timor life or troll the surrounding villages for handicrafts, stay the night 1.5km from Oinlasi at **Sungar Budaya** (Desa Anin; r incl 3 meals 150,000Rp), a simple homestay in Desa Anin. It has just two clean rooms with concrete floors.

Getting There & Away

Regular buses from Soe (20,000Rp, two hours) make the 51km trip along the twisted, rutted mountain road to Oinlasi. Turn south off the main highway at Cabang, which is 5km east of the turn for None.

Boti

Hidden out of sight on an isolated mountain ridge and accessible only by a degrading mountain road that's often impassable without a 4WD, is the traditional, almost orthodox, sun-dappled village of Boti. Here, the charismatic *kepala suku* (chief), often referred to as the last king in West Timor, has vowed to maintain the strict laws of *adat*. He's also the only king we've ever heard of who works the fields side by side with his people.

The Boti people maintain their own language, live off their own land (they grow bananas, corn, papaya, rice, pumpkin, coconuts and a cash crop of peanuts) their own way (they live by a nine-day week and always rest on that ninth day), and steadfastly refuse government assistance of any kind. Their autonomy was given an early assist when the Dutch colonial powers failed to find Boti. So did the headhunters before them, which allowed the Boti to live peacefully in an isolated corner of Timor, unmolested, for centuries.

Villagers wear shirts, ikat sarongs and shawls made only from locally grown and hand-spun cotton thread coloured with natural dyes. Men are encouraged to marry outside the village and bring their new wife back into the fold. After marriage the men must let their hair grow long. Similar to Rastafarians, they view their hair as their connection to nature. Their head is like the mountain, they say, and their hair, like the trees. Cutting their hair-trees is considered a bad omen and carries a fine, payable to the… well, to the king.

Women, on the other hand, are forever shunned if they marry outside the village, and children are allowed to attend only primary school. High school is forbidden, as it is considered by elders to be the key to unhappiness, which may sound familiar. Boti's over 300 villagers (76 families) still follow ancient animist rituals, though another 700 neighbouring families who live in Boti's geographical sphere of influence have adopted Protestantism and attend public schools.

The village has been hosting guests since 1981, but sees fewer than 400 visitors per year. Make sure you're one of them. This place is magical, the people pretence-free and with great sincerity. On arrival you will be led to the king's house, where, in keeping with tradition, you will offer betel nut to the chief as a gift. You'll then enjoy coffee, tea and snacks (banana chips, a delectable version of doughnuts, steamed cassava etc) prepared and served by the king's sister.

It's possible to stay in the leafy, cool, charming village, in your own simple *lontar* guesthouse, and sleep on beds swathed with local ikat. All meals are provided for 100,000Rp per person, and for another 100,000Rp the wives and mothers will play their early-days gamelan (traditional orchestra) and sing a haunting tune. The king will strum his indigenous ukelele and young women will twirl in the village courtyard before the young men demonstrate their war dance. Day trippers are expected to contribute a donation, as well (50,000Rp should work).

The Boti king requests that you do not visit independently; bring a guide from Kupang or Soe conversant with local *adat*.

Getting There & Away

You have two ways to reach Boti: you can go via a tortuous road that passes through Oinlasi from Cabang, or you can take a tortuous road directly from Cabang. The best solution is to simply do a loop, so you can fully partake of the rugged countryside and avoid repetition. (Note that you can't drive the 12km between Oinlasi and Boti in the rainy season because a bridgeless river crossing floods.)

You can go directly to Boti from the bus stop in Cabang on an *ojek* for 80,000Rp.

Kefamenanu

0388 / POP 35,000

A former Portuguese stronghold, Kefamenanu is mostly a quiet hill town, although you'll see some traces of the manganese mining boom in full effect in the form of somewhat more ribald night-time commerce than you might expect.

Still, it remains devoutly Catholic and has a couple of impressive colonial churches. Most importantly it's the jumping-off point for Temkessi, one of West Timor's 'can't miss' villages. Known locally as Kefa, the town lies at the heart of an important weaving region. Prepare to haggle with the ikat cartel.

DON'T MISS

IKAT MARKETS

Women in small villages across West Timor produce some of the most beautiful traditional ikat cloth in all of Indonesia. They sell their wares at weekly markets near their homes at prices one-tenth of what you'll pay at a boutique in Bali. Top markets include the following:

Oinlasi – Tuesday

Niki Niki – Wednesday

Ayotupas – Thursday

Sleeping & Eating

Hotel Ariesta HOTEL $

(0388-31007; Jl Basuki Rahman 29; r economy/superior/ste 100,000/250,000/400,000Rp;) Set on a leafy backstreet, this long-time budget joint sprawls across 44 rooms in a modern annex and a weathered original block. Economy rooms are scruffy. The all-suite annex boasts plenty of light, hot water, air-con and a private porch, but the cheaper superior rooms hit the sweet spot with air-con, hot water and nice porches.

Victory Hotel HOTEL $$

(0388-31349; Jl Sudirman 10; r 250,000-500,000Rp;) Newly built, this two-storey block has rooms ranging from windowless cells to spacious, light-filled retreats. The small breakfast buffet is above average. The check-in area doubles as a jewellery shop.

Hotel Livero HOTEL $$

(0388-233 2222; Jl El Tari; r 300,000-500,000Rp;) The airy lobby has grace, and the 38 rooms are decent with wooden bed-frames and flat-screen TVs. A few have private terraces in the treetops, but some have no windows at all, or have been tainted by nicotine. There's a nightclub popular with miners and a nice open-air cafe.

★**Defi Natalina** INDONESIAN $

(Jl Semangka 2; snacks under 10,000Rp; 9am-6pm) Stalls selling fried snacks in Indonesia are myriad but this little corner operation is superb. It's near the bus terminal and on the main road to Timor-Leste. The hard-working lady prepares *tempe goreng* (succulent tofu fritters) and *pisang goreng* (banana fritters) that are just that much better. Buy by the bagful.

THE STORY OF SEVEN

Ethnic Timorese are known as the 'people of the sunrise' and trace their ancestry back to seven sisters who came down to earth from the sun for a bath. A lustful man watched as they bathed, and hid the most beautiful sister's robes. Naked and ashamed, she was left behind, and eventually became mother of the Timorese people.

The number seven permeates Timor. Their sacred swords have seven lines, special rituals are carried out every seven years, and seven also symbolises completion of the human life cycle; from birth, through childhood and adulthood, to marriage and the cultivation of wisdom, and finally death and the merging of the soul back into the universe.

Rumah Makan Nusantara INDONESIAN **$**
(☎0852 3638 8814; Jl El Tari 99; mains 10,000-25,000Rp; ⏰7am-9pm) You'll enjoy a cheery 'Merry Christmas' year-round thanks to the decor at this high-ceilinged, large and popular restaurant. The full range of Indo foods are on offer, both cooked to order and served Padang-style. The house-made sambal is smooth and spicy.

ℹ Information

Kefa stretches in all directions from the old market, *pasar lama*, which is around 2.5km north of the bus terminal.

Use the Visa-compatible ATM at the gleaming new **Danamon Bank** (Jl Kartini).

The tourist office, **Dinas Pariwisata** (☎0388-21520; Jl Sudirman), is opposite the field north of the highway and can help locate a guide.

ℹ Getting There & Away

The bus terminal is in Kefamenanu's centre, 50m from the Jl El Tari market, which blooms most days. From here there are regular buses to Kupang (50,000Rp, 5½ hours), Soe (20,000Rp, 2½ hours) and Atambua (20,000Rp, two hours), on the Timor-Leste border, from 6am until about 4pm.

Hotel Ariesta (p389) rents motorbikes for 70,000Rp per day. Rental cars in Kefa cost 600,000Rp per day with driver.

Timor Tour & Travel (☎0388-31320) You can join express minibuses running between Kupang (95,000Rp, five hours) and Dili in Timor-Leste (180,000Rp, 7½ hours). Tickets are sold at an office 4km east of the centre on the main highway; pickups are made at hotels.

Around Kefamenanu

Oelolok

Oelolok, a weaving village 26km from Kefa by bus and a further 3km by bemo, is home to **Istana Rajah Taolin**, a massive beehive hut with a huge outdoor patio and carved beams dangling with corn from decades of harvests. Royals have lived here for five generations, and its current residents are more than happy to share the myths and legends of their culture and kingdom. Ask about the power of the 'sword with seven lines'.

Temkessi & Around

Accessible through a keyhole between jutting limestone cliffs, 50km northeast of Kefa, Temkessi is one of West Timor's most isolated and best-preserved villages.

The drive across windswept ridges, with distant views out to sea, sets the otherworldly mood. Just when you think you've left civilisation far behind, a giggle betrays some little kids spying on you.

From a parking area, you walk 300m up a path paved with enormous cobblestones under a canopy of trees until you find a grouping of stone buildings that looks like something out of *Star Wars*.

The **raja's house** overlooks the village. Clamber up the stone steps that lace the village to meet the day's designated dignitary, where you'll offer gifts of betel nut, make a donation (50,000Rp per person) and pay your respects. After that you can shoot pictures of the low-slung beehive huts built into the bedrock and connected by red clay paths that ramble to the edge of a precipice (just don't take a picture of one conical hut that is the designated home of evil spirits, lest your camera explode – so the locals solemnly intone). If you drop something, don't pick it up. Let local villagers do it, unless you want bad vibes in your life.

You won't be able to miss the soaring and utterly alien-looking limestone rocks. At least once every seven years, young warriors climb its face, sans rope, with a red goat strapped to their back. They slaughter the animal on top and can't come down until they roast and eat it in full. This Natamamausa ritual is performed to give thanks for a good harvest or to stop or start the rain.

Very little Bahasa Indonesia is spoken here, so a guide is essential. A few villagers will guide your guide and the overall mood is warm and welcoming. Once settled into this surreal setting, with the wind rustling the trees in what feels like the top of the world, you may find it hard to leave.

Back along the road from the main highway, 19km from Kefa, **Maubesi** is home to the Kefa regency's best textile market. Market day is Thursday, when goods are spread beneath riverside shade trees. Sometimes cockfights break out. **Maubesi Art Shop** (☎0852 8508 5867; ⌚hours vary) has a terrific selection of local ikat, antique masks and statues, plus carved beams, reliefs and doors from old Timorese homes. Prices are quite low. Look for the plain yellow-and-black 'Textile' sign.

ℹ Getting There & Away

Regular buses run from Kefa to Manufui, about 8km from Temkessi. On market day in Manufui (Saturday), trucks or buses should run through to Temkessi. Otherwise, charter an *ojek*, or better, secure your own wheels.

ROTE

A slender, rain-starved limestone jewel with powdery white-sand beaches and epic surf, Rote floats just southwest of West Timor, but has an identity all of its own. For tourists it's all about the surf, which can be gentle enough for beginners and wild enough for experts.

Stunning Pantai Nemberala is home to the world-renowned T-Land break, and there are dozens of hidden white-sand beaches, aquamarine lagoons and seldom-surfed waves on the beaches south and north of Nemberala. To find them you'll roll through thatched traditional villages, over natural limestone bridges and through an undulating savannah that turns from green in the November to March 'wet season' to gold in the 'dry season', which also happens to be when the offshore winds fold swells into barrels. The whole experience has a nostalgic *Endless Summer* feel. And don't overlook the tiny offshore islands where you can find gorgeous ikat, more silky white sand and life-affirming turquoise bays, and, of course, more surf.

Historically, the simple local economy revolved around the majestic and nutritious *lontar* palm. Then in the late 17th century, after a bloody campaign, Rote became the source of slaves and supplies for the Dutch. But the Rotenese also took advantage of the Dutch presence, adopted Christianity and, with Dutch support, established a school system that eventually turned them into NTT's best-educated islanders. This allowed them to influence the much larger island of Timor both politically and economically for generations.

ℹ Information

Internet Access Sparse, but you can get 3G data in some places, including Nemberala.

Money There's a BRI ATM in Ba'a but it usually refuses foreign cards. Bring plenty of rupiah as exchanging cash is difficult.

ℹ Getting There & Away

AIR

Wings Air operates a flight between Kupang and Ba'a (30 minutes, three times weekly). It usually leaves in the afternoon, which can allow for a same-day connection from Bali, although transporting surfboards can complicate the transfer and add to the costs (Wings Air charges 200,000Rp per board).

BOAT

The swiftest and most comfortable way to reach Rote is via the **Baharai Express** (executive/VIP 160,000/190,000Rp, two hours), a fast ferry that departs from Kupang at 9am daily, docks at Ba'a and returns at 11am. Book your ticket in advance and arrive at the dock by 8.30am. Be warned, this service is sometimes cancelled due to rough seas.

There's also a daily slow ferry (54,000Rp to 65,000Rp, five hours) that docks at Pantai Baru, north of Ba'a.

ℹ Getting Around

Local touts will try to convince you that to get to Nemberala from the fast-boat port in Ba'a you'll have to charter a bemo (from 300,000Rp, two hours), or hire an *ojek* (from 150,000Rp). But just outside the harbour gates you can easily flag down a public bemo (with/without surfboard 30,000/60,000Rp). You can also arrange with

LONTAR PALM

Rote remains dependent on the drought-resistant *lontar* palm. The palm is extremely versatile; its tough yet flexible leaves are woven to make sacks and bags, hats and sandals, roofs and dividing walls. *Lontar* wood is fashioned into furniture and floorboards. But what nourishes the islanders is the milky, frothy *nirah* (sap) tapped from the *tankai* (orange-stemmed inflorescences) that grow from the crown of the *lontar*. Drunk straight from the tree, the *nirah* is refreshing, nutritious and energising. If left to ferment for hours, it becomes *laru* (palm wine), which is hawked around the lanes of Rote. With a further distillation, the juice is distilled into a gin-like *sopi* – the power behind many a wild Rote night.

your hotel for a car to pick you up for about 400,000Rp.

Many of the resorts offer transfer packages from Kupang's airport via the fast ferry and on to the resort. These are undeniably seamless, but can cost US$100 or more.

Once you're in Nemberala, hire a motorbike (80,000Rp per day) through your hotel or guesthouse, and explore.

Ba'a

Ba'a, Rote's commercial centre, is a sleepy port town that snakes south along the island's west coast among banyan trees, and banana and coconut groves. The fast ferry and flights land here. Some houses have boat-shaped thatched roofs. The town doesn't offer enough of a reason to linger, although the coast from the ferry port at Pantai Baru south to Ba'a is sparsely populated and has some superb beaches.

Nemberala

Nemberala is a chilled-out fishing village on an exquisite white-sand beach. It's sheltered by a reef that helps form the legendary 'left', T-Land. Don't expect an isolated vibe here as there's been an influx of visitors, expats and vacation home owners who have bought up large swatches of beachfront in the area. New businesses are opening to serve these new devotees.

Still, Nemberala hasn't gone all flash: the local pigs, goats, cows, chicken and other critters still freely wander the beach and resorts, and you still need to avoid getting conked on the head by a falling coconut.

Activities

The **T-Land** wave gets big, especially between June and August, but it's not heavy, so the fear factor isn't ridiculous. Like other once-undiscovered waves in east Indo, the surfing line-up gets busy in the high season.

If you rent a motorbike and drive the spectacularly rutted coastal road north or south, you'll notice that you're within reach of a half-dozen other desolate beaches and a few superb uncharted surf breaks. Beginners take note: just north of the Nemberala fishing-boat harbour is a terrific novice break called Squealers.

Many resorts rent high-quality boards from about 100,000Rp per day.

Sleeping & Eating

The surf season peaks between June and September. Accommodation range and value are solid, but there isn't a lot of rooms – book ahead. While most of the lodges and guesthouses are all-inclusive, some local warungs have appeared, so you do have options to vary up your vittles.

Ti Rosa BUNGALOW **$**

(☎0821 4633 7016; per person incl meals from 200,000Rp) Run by sweet Ibu Martine, this fine collection of eight lime-green, concrete bungalows is super clean, shaded by palms and is the cheapest beach option available. Budget surfers love it so much, some book rooms for the whole season. Turn right at the first intersection in town, and head north along the dirt road for 500m.

Lualemba Bungalows BUNGALOW **$$**

(☎0812 3947 8823; www.lualemba.com; s/d incl meals 500,000/900,000Rp) This highly recommended spot is set 500m inland from the beach. Attractive, thatched *lontar* bungalows feature stone foundations, and private verandas strung with hammocks. Rates include boat rides to the surf break and neighbouring islands, three meals and use of mountain bikes. The restaurant (mains from 40,000Rp) is open to nonguests and serves fine, hearty chow and excellent ice cream.

Anugrah Surf & Dive Resort BUNGALOW $$
(☎0813 5334 3993, 0852 3916 2645; surfdiverote.com; s/d incl meals from 500,000/800,000Rp;) The 28 cute, compact, *lontar*-palm bungalows here range from newish to older, and come with a variety of patios and *mandis,* wooden furniture, outdoor bathrooms and more. It's right on the beach opposite T-Land. The restaurant, which is decked out with ikat tablecloths, serves *ikan bakar* (grilled fish) amid a menu that changes daily. Reserve ahead during surf season.

★ **Malole Surf House** SURF CAMP $$$
(☎0813 5317 7264, 0813 3776 7412; www.rotesurfhouse.com; per person incl 3 meals US$140-200;) Built by surf legend Felipe Pomar, this surf lodge blends comfort, cuisine and style better than anywhere else in Rote. The four rooms are set in a large wooden house and guesthouse with daybeds, ikat bedspreads, limitless laundry and more. You'll hit the right waves at the right time via the house boat. Closed during the wet season.

Sublime international seafood is but one highlight of the kitchen, which carves fresh sashimi, bakes fresh bread, and blends spectacular soups and curries. Mountain bikes, fishing trips and island excursions are also on offer.

The level of comfort and elegance here feels effortless (it isn't) and belies its extremely remote location.

Nemberala Beach Resort RESORT $$$
(☎0813 3773 1851; www.nemberalabeachresort.com; s/d surfers from US$275/380, nonsurfers US$235/340;) Right on the ocean, this relaxed four-star, all-inclusive spot has spacious slate-and-timber bungalows with ceiling fans, outdoor baths and freshwater showers. There's a swimming pool, volleyball court and pool table, and a terrific beach bar where sundowners can easily phase into late-night cocktails. It's closed during the wet season.

The food has received mixed reviews of late, but it does have a speedboat to whisk you out to nearby surf breaks, and it offers excursions to limestone caves and tidal lagoons. Fishing trips for dog-toothed tuna and mackerel can also be arranged.

Villa Santai BUNGALOW $$$
(☎0812 3941 4568; surfroteisland.com; s/d incl meals from US$120/210) Hugely popular for its highly personalised service, this small resort started with two luxurious bungalows and added a third in 2015. The top one has sweeping views of the powdery white sand and T-Land. The food is fresh, local and copious. There's a full bar and many end their day with a G&T sundowner, soaking up the surf action.

Around Nemberala

You really must explore this lonely limestone coast by motorbike in order to absorb its majesty. If you prefer a heavier, hollow wave, your first stop should be 3km north of Nemberala at **Suckie Mama's**.

About 8km south of Nemberala, **Bo'a** has a spectacular white-sand beach and consistent off-season surf. Set on a notch in the headland that bisects this absurdly wide and almost unjustly beautiful bay, **Bo'a Hill Surf House** (☎0813 3935 1165; www.surfrote.com; per person incl meals 800,000Rp) has lovely bungalows set on a 3-hectare site with gorgeous views. The eco-cred is strong here. The owner grows fruit and herbs, raises pigs and ducks, collects honey, and is a superb guide to local delights on land and sea.

From Bo'a continue south over the dry rocky road – look out for monkeys – and after you traverse the natural limestone bridge, negotiate the descent and reach **Oeseli** village. Then make a right on the dirt road, which leads to another superb beach with some good waves, and a huge natural tidal lagoon that shelters local fishing boats and floods limestone bat caves. There's an ideal kitesurf launch here, too.

The southernmost island in Indonesia, **Pulau Ndana** can be reached by local fishing boat from Nemberala. It's currently a military camp, but for years it was uninhabited. Legend has it that the entire population was murdered in a 17th-century revenge act, staining the island's small lake with the victims' blood. Ndana has wild deer and a wide variety of birds. Its beaches are prime turtle-nesting territory, and the snorkelling here is superb.

Boni is about 15km from Nemberala, near the northern coast, and is one of the last villages on Rote where traditional religion is still followed. Market day is Thursday. To get here, rent a motorcycle in Nemberala.

Pulau Do'o is a flat spit of pale golden sand with terrific though finicky surf. You can see it from Pantai Nemberala. Further on is the stunning **Pulau Ndao**, which has more powdery white-sand beaches, limestone bluffs, and a tidy, charming, ikat-weaving, *lontar*-tapping fishing village that is home to nearly 600 people who speak their own indigenous dialect, Bahasa Ndao. There are some fantastic swimming beaches up the west and east coast, and good though inconsistent surf off the southern point. Ndao is 10km west of Nemberala. To get here you'll have to charter a boat (800,000Rp to 1,000,000Rp, maximum five people). You could easily do both islands in one trip.

SUMBA

Sumba is a dynamic mystery. With its rugged undulating savannah and low limestone hills knitted together with more maize and cassava than rice, physically it looks nothing like Indonesia's volcanic islands to the north. Sprinkled throughout the countryside are hilltop villages with thatched clan houses clustered around megalithic tombs, where villagers claim to be Protestant but still pay homage to their indigenous *marapu* with bloody sacrificial rites. Throw in outstanding hand-spun, naturally dyed ikat, and the annual Pasola festival (p405) – where bareback horsemen ritualise old tribal conflicts as they battle one another with hand-carved spears – and it's easy to see that Sumba runs deep.

It's one of the poorest islands in Indonesia, but an influx of welcome government and NGO investment has brought recent improvements in infrastructure – best seen in Tambolaka, the island's version of a boomtown. And change has trickled down to traditional villages, as well. Thatched roofs have been switched to tin, tombs are now made from concrete, traditional dress is rare, and remote villagers expect larger donations from visitors. Some traditions persist, however. Sumba's extensive grasslands make it one of Indonesia's leading horse-breeding islands. Horses still serve as a mode of transport in more rugged regions, they remain a symbol of wealth and status, and they can still win a bride.

History

According to local legend, a great ladder once connected heaven and earth. Down it clambered the original earthlings to Sumba, where they settled at Tanjung Sasar, on the northern tip of the island.

Though 14th-century Javanese chronicles place Sumba under Majapahit control, Sumbanese history is more a saga of internal wars over land and trading rights between small kingdoms. Despite their mutual hostility, they often depended on each other economically. The inland regions produced horses, timber, betel nut, rice, fruit and dyewoods, while coastal people concentrated on ikat production and trade with other islands.

The Dutch initially paid little attention to Sumba because it lacked commercial possibilities. But in the early 20th century they finally decided to bring Sumba under their control and invaded the island. In 1913 a civilian administration was set up, but Sumbanese nobility continued to reign as the Dutch ruled through them. When the Indonesian republic ceased to recognise the native rulers' authority, many of them became government officials. These long-time ruling clans continued to exert hegemony by monopolising local government appointments.

It all came to a head during the 1998 Waikabubak riots. Initially sparked by demonstrations against such nepotism, and Suharto-era corruption in general, the bad political blood developed into a full-scale tribal conflict perpetrated by a horseback posse of at least 3000 men. Armed with machetes, they rode through town killing at least 26 people.

These days Sumba is benefiting from outside interest and investment. Better air links to Denpasar and Kupang point to a more connected future.

Culture

Ikat

Sumbanese ikat is the most dramatic and arguably best executed in Indonesia. Natural dyes are still preferred by weavers who sell their wares to serious collectors in Bali and beyond. The earthy orange-red colour comes from *kombu* tree bark, indigo-blue and yellow tones are derived from *loba* leaves. Some motifs are historical: a record of tribal wars and precolonial village life. Others depict animals and mythical creatures, such as *marapu*.

Traditionally, ikat cloth was only worn ceremonially. Less than 100 years ago, only members of Sumba's highest clans and their personal attendants could make or wear it. Dutch conquest broke the Sumbanese royal ikat monopoly and opened up an external market, which increased production. In the late 19th century ikat was collected by Dutch ethnographers and museums, and by the 1920s visitors were already noting the introduction of nontraditional designs, such as lions from the Dutch coat of arms.

Sumba

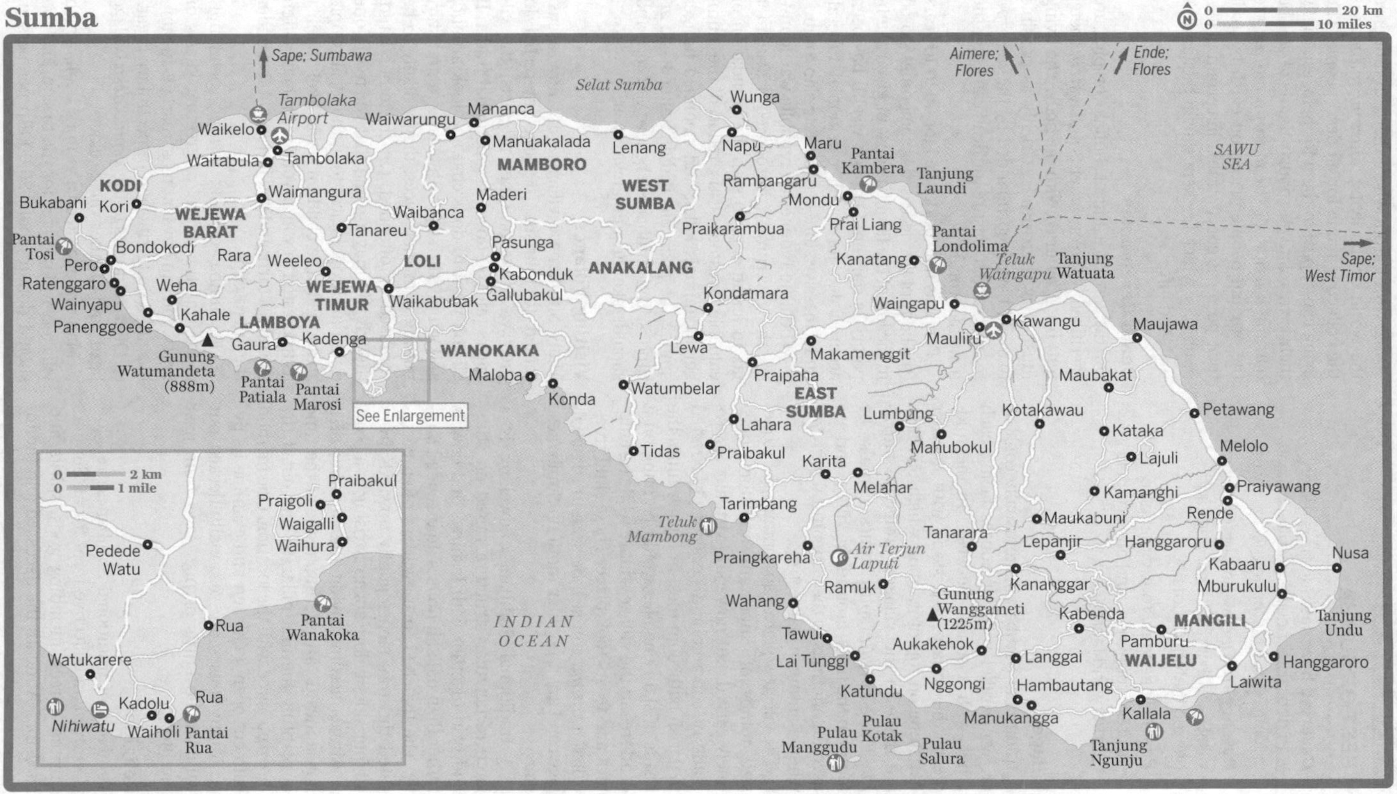

0 – 20 km
0 – 10 miles

Sape; Sumbawa
Selat Sumba
Aimere; Flores
Ende; Flores
SAWU SEA
Sape; West Timor
INDIAN OCEAN

KODI
WEJEWA BARAT
WEJEWA TIMUR
LOLI
LAMBOYA
MAMBORO
WANOKAKA
WEST SUMBA
ANAKALANG
EAST SUMBA
MANGILI
WAIJELU

Tambolaka Airport
Waikelo
Waitabula
Tambolaka
Waiwarungu
Mananca
Manuakalada
Lenang
Wunga
Napu
Maru
Pantai Kambera
Tanjung Laundi
Rambangaru
Mondu
Prai Liang
Praikarambua
Bukabani
Kori
Waimangura
Maderi
Waibanca
Tanareu
Pantai Tosi
Bondokodi
Pero
Ratenggaro
Wainyapu
Panenggoede
Rara
Weeleo
Weha
Kahale
Gunung Watumandeta (888m)
Gaura
Kadenga
Pantai Patiala
Pantai Marosi
Pasunga
Kabonduk
Gallubakul
Waikabubak
Maloba
Konda
Kondamara
Lewa
Watumbelar
Tidas
Praipaha
Lahara
Praibakul
Makamenggit
Kanatang
Pantai Londolima
Teluk Waingapu
Tanjung Watuata
Waingapu
Kawangu
Mauliru
Maujawa
Maubakat
Kotakawau
Lumbung
Mahubokul
Karita
Melahar
Tarimbang
Teluk Mambong
Praingkareha
Air Terjun Laputi
Tanarara
Lepanjir
Kananggar
Ramuk
Wahang
Gunung Wanggameti (1225m)
Tawui
Lai Tunggi
Aukakehok
Katundu
Nggongi
Langgai
Hambautang
Manukangga
Pulau Kotak
Pulau Manggudu
Pulau Salura
Petawang
Kataka
Lajuli
Melolo
Kamanghi
Praiyawang
Maukabuni
Rende
Hanggaroru
Kabaaru
Nusa
Mburukulu
Kabenda
Pamburu
Tanjung Undu
Hanggaroro
Laiwita
Kallala
Tanjung Ngunju

See Enlargement

0 – 2 km
0 – 1 mile
Praibakul
Praigoli
Waigalli
Waihura
Pedede Watu
Rua
Pantai Wanakoka
Watukarere
Kadolu
Rua
Nihiwatu
Waiholi
Pantai Rua

DON'T MISS

BEST OF SUMBA

Deserted beaches Sumba is ringed with ribbons of powdery white sand, including Pantai Marosi in the southwest.

Ratenggaro One of the best traditional villages, with intricate carvings and peaked thatched roofs.

Pasola Legendary tournaments to measure toughness and bravery, held in February and March.

Villages

A traditional Sumba village usually consists of two parallel rows of houses facing each other, with a square between. In the middle of the square is a stone with another flat stone on top of it, upon which offerings are made to the village's protective *marapu*. These *kateda* (spirit stones) can also be found in the fields around the village and are used for offerings to the agricultural *marapu* when planting or harvesting.

The village square also contains the stone-slab tombs of important ancestors, once finely carved, but nowadays virtually always made of concrete and occasionally covered in garish bathroom tiles. In former times the heads of slain enemies would be hung on a dead tree in the village square while ceremonies and feasts took place. These skull trees, called *andung*, can still be seen in some villages and are a popular motif on Sumbanese ikat.

A traditional Sumbanese dwelling is a large rectangular structure raised on stilts, and held together with lashings and dowels rather than nails: it houses an extended family. The thatched (or nowadays often corrugated tin) roof slopes gently upwards from all four sides before abruptly rising to a peak.

Rituals accompanying the building of a house include an offering, made at the time of planting the first pillar, to find out if the *marapu* agree with the location. One method is to cut open a chicken and examine its liver. Many houses are seasonally decked out with buffalo horns or pigs' jaws from past sacrifices.

Religion

The basis of traditional Sumbanese religion is *marapu*, a collective term for all Sumba's spiritual forces, including gods, spirits and ancestors. At death the deceased join the invisible world, from where they can influence the world of the living. *Marapu mameti* is the collective name for all dead people. The living can appeal to them for help, especially their own relatives, though the dead can be harmful if irritated. The *marapu maluri* are the original people placed on earth by god; their power is concentrated in certain places or objects, which are kept safe in the family's thatched loft.

Death Ceremonies

On the day of a burial, buffalo or pigs are sacrificed while ornaments and a *sirih* (betel nut) bag are buried with the body. The living must bury their dead as richly as possible to avoid being reprimanded by the *marapu mameti* and to ensure the dead can enter the invisible world.

Funerals may be delayed for up to 10 years (the body of the deceased is sometimes stored in the loft of the family's house or given a temporary burial) until enough wealth has been accumulated for a full ceremonial funeral, and a massive stone- or concrete-slab tomb.

When the Indonesian republic was founded, the government introduced a slaughter tax in an attempt to stop the liquidation of valuable livestock. This reduced the number of animals killed and stemmed hunger among the poor, but it didn't alter basic attitudes. The Sumbanese believe you *can*, and should, take the animal with you.

Visiting Villages

Many Sumbanese villagers are now accustomed to tourists. If you're interested in their weavings or other artefacts, the villagers put you down as a potential trader. If all you want to do is chat and look around, and simply turn up with a camera and start putting it in their faces, they're likely to be confused or offended. On the other hand, though you may assume that you're the one on an anthropological tour, the local people – especially the children – will likely be just as interested in you as you are in them. Often the tables turn, and you just might feel under the microscope.

On Sumba, offering *pinang* (betel nut) is the traditional way of greeting guests or hosts. You can buy it at most markets in Sumba, and it's a terrific and respectful ice breaker. Offer your gifts to the *kepala desa* (village head) and to other village elders.

Many villages keep a visitors' book, which villagers will produce for you to sign, and you should donate about 20,000Rp per person.

SUMBA'S BEST WEBSITE

A true labour of love by Matthias Jungk, a German, www.sumba-information.com is a vast compendium for all things Sumba. You can buy a 64-page pdf version of the website for €5; in addition Jungk has created a superbly detailed *and* accurate map of Sumba which you can use online or buy. Best of all, this invaluable resource is continually updated.

Hiring a guide to the isolated villages is a big help and offers some protection from getting into the wrong situation. No matter where you go, taking the time to chat with the villagers helps them see you more as a guest than a customer or visiting alien.

Getting There & Away

Sumba's links to greater Indonesia are improving. Airports in Tambolaka and Waingapu have daily flights to Bali and Kupang in West Timor. Ferries run to Flores and Kupang.

Waingapu

0387 / POP 55,000

Waingapu is a leafy, laid-back town that is plenty walkable and makes a decent base from which to explore the surrounding villages. It became an administrative centre after the Dutch military 'pacified' the island in 1906 and has long been Sumba's main trading post for textiles, prized Sumbanese horses, dyewoods and lumber. The town has a groovy harbourfront dining scene, and a few ikat shops and workshops. Traders with bundles of textiles and carvings hang around hotels or walk the streets touting for rupiah.

Sleeping

Breakfast and free airport transfer (if you call in advance) are usually included in accommodation rates.

★Tanto Hotel GUESTHOUSE $
(0387-61048, 0387-62500; Jl Prof Dr WZ Yohanes;) The newest hotel in town is also the best. Bright, fresh rooms and good service set the Tanto apart from most of its competition. The decor is primarily white, with natural wood and vivid-red accents. Many rooms have fridges; the breakfast is good.

Hotel Merlin HOTEL $
(0387-61300; Jl Panjaitan 25; r 110,000-220,000Rp, mains 15,000-35,000Rp;) This long-standing travellers' favourite has a decent assortment of rooms over three floors, with Flores views from the rooftop restaurant (mains 15,000Rp to 35,000Rp). Rooms are large, with wood furnishings, but they vary in quality. Ask to see a few before deciding. Guides lurk out front.

Hotel Kaliuda HOTEL $
(0387-61264; Jl Lalamentik 3; r 150,000-250,000Rp) This reasonably clean, quiet motel has six basic rooms with fans offering decent value (an expansion is planned). It also has a small antique collection and motorbikes for rent.

Eating

Good restaurants are thin on the ground in Waingapu, but you can do all right for a night or two.

★Pasar Malam INDONESIAN $
(Night Market; off Jl Yos Sudarso; mains from 12,000Rp; 6-11pm) The best dinner option is the night market at the old wharf, where a couple of permanent warungs and half a dozen gas-lit carts set up to grill, fry and sauté seafood on the cheap. It's especially nice when the moon glows. You can also get various *sate* as well as postdinner treats such as *pisang goreng* (banana fritters).

Warung Enjoy Aja SEAFOOD $
(Pelabuhan; mains 15,000-45,000Rp; 6-11pm) Part of the harbour night market, this is the last warung before the pier on the east side. The fish and squid are expertly grilled and served with three types of sambal and a sea-salt garnish.

Mr Cafe INDONESIAN $
(0387-61605; Jl Umbu Tipuk Marisi 1; mains 15,000-30,000Rp; 8am-10pm) The interior is simple, with comfy plastic chairs and wood tables, which is fitting as the fare is also simple. But the meatballs, fried chicken and various rice dishes are well prepared and there's a big selection. You can bring in beer from the small shop around the corner (they have an opener).

If you're wondering about the lives of expat NGO workers on Sumba, just drop by here.

Yenny's Bakery BAKERY $

(☎0387-62449; Komplek Ruko; treats 3000-12,000Rp; ⏰8am-6pm) Got a sweet tooth? Peruse the shelves of doughnuts, cakes, pastries and breads at this friendly bakery. Staff will pack a box for the road.

Shopping

Waingapu has a few 'art shops' selling Sumbanese ikat and artefacts. Vendors also descend on hotels – some will squat patiently all day. Prices are fair, and there's far more choice here than in the countryside.

★ **Ama Tukang** TEXTILES

(☎0852 3747 4140; Jl Hawan Waruk 53; ⏰9am-6pm) Do not miss this ikat workshop. You'll see the whole process from motif design to colouring to weaving, and the collection – featuring *marapu*, village scenes, horsemen and buffalo – is arguably the best in all of Indonesia. To get there, head south of the bridge on the southern side of Waingapu and turn left onto Jl Hawan Waruk.

Information

There are several BNI ATMs around town.

Getting There & Away

TX Waingapu (☎0387-61534; www.txtravel.com; Jl Beringin 12; ⏰9am-6pm) books airline tickets.

Pelni (☎0387-61665; www.pelni.co.id; Jl Hasanuddin; ⏰9am-4pm) ships leave from the newer Darmaga dock to the west of town but the ticket office is at the old port. Ferry schedules are subject to change: check the **ASDP** (☎0214-288 2233) hotline or see the schedules at the port.

The terminal for eastbound buses is in the southern part of town, close to the market. The West Sumba terminal (aka Terminal Kota) is about 5km west of town.

Getting Around

Sumba has some of the highest car-hire rates in Nusa Tenggara. Even after bargaining, 700,000Rp is a good price per day, including driver and petrol. The Sandle Wood and Merlin hotels can help sort you out. Virtually any hotel worker can arrange a motorbike (from 80,000Rp per day).

TO/FROM THE AIRPORT

The airport is 6km south on the Melolo road. A taxi into town costs a standard 60,000Rp, but most hotels offer a free pickup and drop-off service for guests. It's 3000Rp for a bemo ride to any destination around town, and 5000Rp to the western bus terminal.

Around Waingapu

Londolima, a sliver of sand about 7km northwest of Waingapu, is a favourite local swimming spot on weekends and holidays. The bay is turquoise and glassy; the beach isn't so magical. Bemos from Waingapu's Terminal Kota pass by regularly. Continue along this road and you'll reach an even better beach, **Puru Kambera**, where you can stay the night at the **Villa Cemara** (☎0812 2465 4448, 0812 384 2178; Puru Kambera; r from 400,000Rp; ❄📶) resort in lavishly decorated wood cottages on the beach, with pebbled baths. It's close to the traditional **Prai Liang** and **Prai Natang** villages, which are just 15 minutes from the resort. Three daily buses (12,000Rp) go to/from Waingapu.

Three kilometres east of Waingapu, **Prailiu** is an ikat-weaving centre that's worth a quick look. Alongside traditional thatched houses are some concrete tombs bearing carvings of crocodiles and turtles, as well as empty graves that will be filled when the deceased's family can afford the funeral. Visitors are asked for a cash donation. Bemos to Prailiu run from Waingapu's main bus and bemo terminal. Continuing east, it's a further 7km to **Kawangu**, which has two massive stone-slab tombs in the pasture, 300m off the road to Melolo. There are good beaches and mangroves close by.

East Sumba

Southeast of Waingapu, nestled in dry undulating savannah interspersed with cashew orchards, are several traditional villages, some with striking ancestral tombs. This area produces some of Sumba's best ikat. Most villages are quite used to tourists – you'll have to pay to visit (give at least 20,000Rp), and be prepared for plenty of attention from handicraft vendors.

Praiyawang & Rende

Nestled in a beautiful shallow valley between grassy hills, **Praiyawang** is a traditional compound of Sumbanese houses and is the ceremonial focus of the more modern village of **Rende**, located 7km south of Melolo. It has an imposing line-up of nine big stone-slab tombs. The largest is that of a former chief.

Shaped like a buffalo, it consists of four stone pillars 2m high, supporting a monstrous slab about 5m long, 2.5m wide and 1m thick. Two stone tablets stand atop the main slab, carved with figures. A massive Sumbanese house with concrete pillars faces the tombs, along with a number of older *rumah adat* (traditional houses).

Several buses go from Waingapu to Rende (20,000Rp), starting at about 7am. The last bus back to Waingapu leaves at 3pm.

Kallala

Kallala, 126km from Waingapu and 2km down a dirt road from the nearby village of **Baing**, has emerged as the surf capital of East Sumba. It's an absolutely stunning stretch of white-sand beach that arcs toward the coastal mountains, which tumble down to form East Sumba's southernmost point. Waves break 500m offshore.

Only the most hard-core will tolerate the area's one place to stay: the once-renowned **Mr David's Surf Camp** (Kalala Beach; ☎0813 5397 6282; www.kalalabeach.com; all-inclusive bungalows from 400,000Rp). Mr David passed on in 2012 and this eponymous place seems likely to follow. Conditions are crude at best; however the location right on the beach is excellent and some will cheerfully overlook the many downsides. One saving grace is Yohanna, who is an excellent cook.

Several buses a day go to Baing (40,000Rp, four hours) from Waingapu. The road is sealed all the way but is bumpy past Melolo. A dirt track with many branches runs from Baing to Kallala. Buses will drop you off at the beach if you ask.

South-Central Sumba

This part of the island is gorgeous, but difficult to access. Although there are daily buses from Waingapu to Tarimbang and trucks to Praingkareha, getting around may require a 4WD or motorcycle and, often, some hiking.

If you're looking for more deserted waves, check out **Tarimbang**, a life-altering crescent of white sand framed by a massive limestone bluff 88km southwest of Waingapu. The beach thumps with terrific surf, there's some nearby snorkelling, and rustic accommodation is available at the 18-bed **Marthen's Homestay** (☎0852 8116 5137; r from 150,000Rp) and the *kepala desa*'s six-room place. Daily trucks to Tarimbang leave Waingapu in the morning (40,000Rp, five hours).

Waikabubak

☎0387 / POP 22,000

A country market town, home to both thatched clan houses and rows of concrete shops, administrative buildings and tin-roof homes sprouting satellite dishes, Waikabubak makes Waingapu feel like a metropolis. It's a welcoming place, surrounded by thick stands of mahogany, and at about 600m above sea level, it's a little cooler than the east and a good base for exploring the traditional villages of West Sumba. The big market is on Saturday.

Sights

Within the town are some friendly and quite traditional *kampung* (villages) with stone-slab tombs and thatched houses. You don't need a guide here. Locals will love to show off their spacious homes lashed with old ironwood columns and beams. Charming children will mug for the camera. Old folks will offer betel nuts. Bring gifts (cigarettes), offer a donation (10,000Rp to 20,000Rp), or buy a handicraft or two, and the villagers will beam with gratitude and pride.

Kampung Tambelar, just off Jl Sudirman, has very impressive tombs, but the most interesting *kampung* are on the western edge of town. It's only a short stroll from most hotels to **Prai Klembung** and then up the slippery slope that juts from the centre of town to **Tarung**, **Waitabar** and **Belakilu**, three villages that bleed into one.

In November Kampung Tarung, reached by a concrete path off Jl Manda Elu, is the scene of an important month-long ritual, the **Wula Podhu**. This is an austere period when even weeping for the dead is prohibited. Rites consist mainly of offerings to the spirits (the day before the ritual ends, hundreds of chickens are sacrificed), and people sing and dance for the entire final day. Tarung is home to five tribes, each with their own small, thatched shrine where only the local priest is allowed to pray and commune with the *marapu*.

Other interesting *kampung* occupying ridge or hilltop positions outside town include **Praiijing**, with traditional huts set around some cool primitive stone tombs, and surrounded by coconut palm and bamboo

Waikabubak

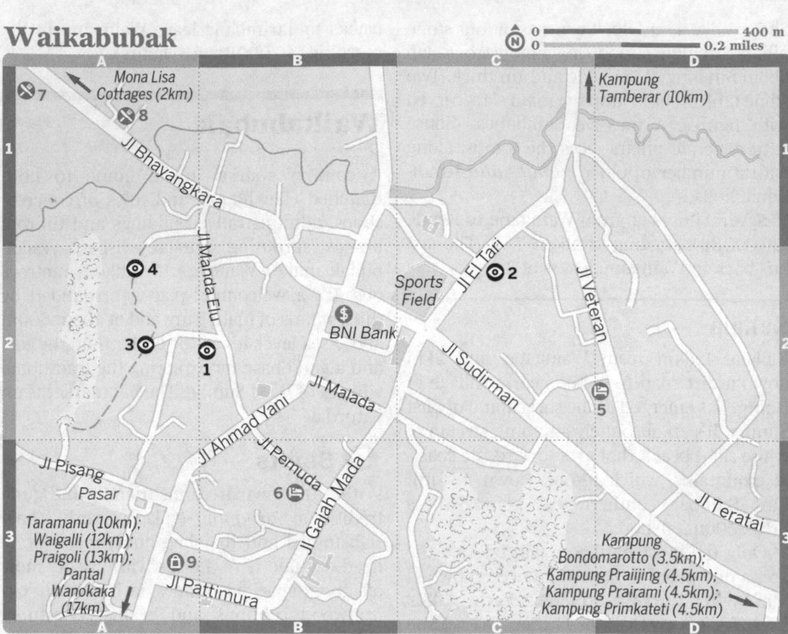

Waikabubak

Sights
1 Kampung Prai Klembung B2
2 Kampung Tambelar C2
3 Kampung Tarung A2
4 Kampung Waitabar A2

Sleeping
5 Hotel Artha D2
6 Hotel Manandang B3

Eating
7 Rumah Makan Fanny A1
8 Rumah Makan Gloria A1

Shopping
9 A Hamid Algadi Art Shop A3

groves. **Bondomarotto**, **Kampung Prairami** and **Kampung Primkateti** are also beautifully located on adjacent hilltops. You can take a bemo to the turn-off for Praiijing (3000Rp).

Tours

Yuliana Ledatara GUIDE
(☎0852 3918 1410; yuli.sumba@gmail.com; Kampung Tarung, Waikabubak; per day from 450,000Rp) A wonderful local English- and French-speaking guide who lives in Tarung – Waikabubak's hilltop traditional village – Yuliana can organise tours of traditional villages throughout West Sumba, where she sniffs out funerals and sacrifices, takes horse tours through rice fields, and can arrange village homestays too. She's one of Indonesia's very few female guides, and she's a good one.

Sleeping

Karanu Hotel GUESTHOUSE $
(☎0387-21645; Jl Sudirman 43; r 150,000-250,000Rp) A bright garden hotel east of the downtown swirl and within view of nearby rice fields. Rooms are clean if worn. They don't have air-con, but there is a fading *Last Supper* rug tacked to the lobby wall.

★ **Mona Lisa Cottages** BUNGALOW $$
(☎0387-21364; www.monalisacottages-sumba.com; Jl Adhyaska 30; r 120,000-720,000Rp; ❄@☜) You'll find the best night's sleep 2km northwest of town, across from the rice fields. It includes attractive, fan-cooled budget rooms, and a few higher-end units as well. The cottages all have peaked tin roofs, private patios with bamboo furnishings and fridges; some

have air-con. The deluxe cottage has a king-sized bed, DVD player and bathtub.

Hotel Manandang HOTEL **$$**
(☎0387-21197; Jl Pemuda 4; r 285,000-435,000Rp; ❄📶) Some 33 tidy, good-value rooms cluster around a pleasant back garden, and management works hard to keep it that way. The cheapest rooms have cold water; more money brings air-con and yet more brings hot water.

Hotel Artha GUESTHOUSE **$$**
(☎0387-21112; Jl Veteran 11; r 200,000-400,000Rp; 📶) Spacious rooms horseshoe the flower-filled courtyard, and though some of the 15 are a bit dark and walls can be scuffed, the tiled floors and bathrooms are super clean. VIP rooms even have fresh bathroom tiles. Good value.

Eating

Rumah Makan Gloria INDONESIAN **$**
(☎0387-21140; Jl Bhayangkara 46; meals 15,000-50,000Rp; ⏲8am-10pm) Cute and cheerful, with chequered tablecloths, silk flowers and colourful handwritten menus offering an array of Indonesian classics. Consider just three: *soto ayam* (chicken soup) is uber-turmericy, truly excellent; *ikan kuah assam* (tamarind fish soup); and, if you specially order it, *ayam kafir,* a Sumba-style fire-roasted chicken, salted and served with a sublime, super-spicy sambal.

Rumah Makan Fanny INDONESIAN **$**
(☎0387-21389; Jl Bhayangkara 55; mains 15,000-50,000Rp; ⏲8am-9pm) A pint-sized Waikabubak staple, favoured for flavourful but crazy-spicy *ikan kuah assam* – one is enough to feed two. It also has assorted Chinese-Indo seafood dishes and a house special fried chicken.

★**D' Sumba Ate** INTERNATIONAL **$$**
(☎0857 3775 6606; Jl Ahmad Yani 148; mains 20,000-70,000Rp; ⏲10am-10pm) A welcome addition to the West Sumba food scene, this excellent restaurant cooks up wood-fired pizzas, pasta, burgers and the usual Indo suspects. There's a cool open-air bamboo vibe and a competent bar, plus Sumba's cleanest toilets!

Shopping

Traders gather at hotels with ikat from East Sumba, locally made bone, wood, horn and stone carvings, and jewellery. Tarung (p399) is known for beaded jewellery, which you can easily find on a walk through the village.

A Hamid Algadi Art Shop HANDICRAFTS
(☎0387-21170; Jl Ahmad Yani 99; ⏲9am-6pm Mon-Sat) Fantastic stone carvings in the front yard, plus wooden antiques, some cool old stone grinders and bronze jewellery indoors. Not to mention its all-natural ikat. Your Sumbanese treasure hunt starts here.

Information

BNI Bank (Jl Ahmad Yani; ⏲8am-3.30pm Mon-Fri) Has an ATM and offers fair exchange rates.
Tourist Office (☎0387-21240; Jl Teratai 1; ⏲8am-3pm Mon-Sat) The staff here have info about forthcoming funerals and cultural events. It's on the eastern outskirts of town.

Getting There & Away

Tambolaka, 42km northwest of Waikabubak, is the closest airport. A bus to the Waitabula (an older town being swallowed by Tambolaka) terminal and a bemo or *ojek* from there is the cheapest way, but most people get a taxi from Waitabula or charter a bemo (around 100,000Rp) from Waikabubak.

Bemos, trucks and minibuses service most other towns and villages in West Sumba. Generally, it's best to leave early in the day, when they tend to fill up and depart quickest. There are several daily buses to Waingapu (50,000Rp, five hours).

Waikabubak is the place to rent a motorbike for exploring West Sumba. Expect to pay 80,000Rp a day. Hotels can set you up with car rental (700,000Rp with driver).

West Sumba

☎0387

If you're hungry for traditional Sumba culture, head west into the golden rice fields that crawl up blue mountains, carved by rivers and sprouting with bamboo and coconut palms. *Kampung* of high-roofed houses are still clustered on their hilltops (a place of defence in times past), surrounding the large stone tombs of their ancestors. Rituals and ceremonies for events such as house building and marriage often involve animal sacrifices and can take place at any time. Outsiders are welcome at these events, but be sure to make a donation – your guide will know how much (usually 20,000Rp to 50,000Rp).

Even though *kampung* seem accustomed to visiting foreigners, gifts of betel nut help warm the waters with the older crowd and are a sign of respect.

Give yourself a few days around West Sumba. Once you have learned some basic manners as a guest arriving in a village – hopefully armed with some Bahasa Indonesia – it's possible to do it without a guide, though it always helps to have one.

Getting Around

If you have limited time and want to explore remote villages and the wild coast without having to worry about transport schedules or language barriers, call **Sumba Adventure** (☎ 0387-21727, 0813 3710 7845; www.sumbarentcar.com; Tambolaka). The team of drivers (most of whom speak English) have good cars, are trustworthy and know Sumba well. An SUV with driver and guide per day is 1,000,000Rp for up to four people.

For a much cheaper drive around the west, you can hire an *ojek* for the day (100,000Rp).

Tambolaka & Around

☎ 0387

Located 42km northwest of Waikabubak, this once-sleepy market town has become West Sumba's main transport hub – it's booming and it's got a whole new name, at least in tourism brochures and other government literature. We've followed suit, even if many locals of a certain age still refer to it as Waitabula. While still in the early stages of growth, Tambolaka is easily accessible from Bali, and is the gateway to the island's sensational western half.

Future visitor growth seems inevitable; beachfront 'for sale' signs are common and a new school to train locals in tourism is opening east of the airport.

Sights

Tambolaka's big market day is Saturday.

★Lembaga Studi & Pelestarian Budaya Sumba MUSEUM
(☎ 0813 3936 2164; www.sumbaculture.org; museum by donation; ⊙ 8am-4pm Mon-Sat) Just 3km outside of town, this Catholic-run NGO is in a working coconut plantation and has an excellent cultural museum. It was developed by Fr Robert Ramone, who noticed how, once they are baptised, Sumbanese frequently break clean from their old culture and develop negative associations with the *marapu* and other totems. In addition to displays of old photographs, money and pottery, there is an ongoing project showing how tombs are carved. The website is a brilliant cultural resource.

The complex also has five basic rooms for rent (300,000Rp to 600,000Rp). Sit on one of the private porches and let the quiet envelop you.

Tours

Sumba Adventure Tours & Travel TOUR
(☎ 0813 3710 7845; sumbaadventure@yahoo.com; Desa Kalena Wanno, Tambolaka; guiding services per day 250,000Rp, per day with car & driver 850,000Rp) With an office close to the airport, experienced guide Philip Renggi is one of the best in West Sumba. He and his team of guides lead trips into seldom-explored villages, including his native Manuakalada and Waiwarungu, where there are several sacred *marapu* houses that only shaman can enter. He can arrange itineraries, set you up for Pasola, rent cars etc.

Sleeping & Eating

Penginapan Melati GUESTHOUSE $
(☎ 0813 5396 6066, 0387-24055; Jl Waitabula; r with fan/air-con 150,000/250,000Rp; ❄ 📶) Shaded by a huge tree, the 15 rooms here are simple but immaculate with fresh paint and tile throughout. They even have rain shower heads in the *mandi*. There's a simple Padang-style restaurant right next door.

★Oro Beach Houses & Restaurant BUNGALOW $$
(☎ 0813 3911 0068, 0813 5378 9946; www.oro-beachbungalows.com; r US$45-60) Think: three wild beachfront acres owned by a special family (she used to run an NGO, he's an architect with a disaster-relief background), where you can nest in a circular thatched bungalow blessed with a canopied driftwood bed and outdoor bath. They offer excellent meals, mountain biking and snorkelling just off their stunning 200m long beach.

Low-lying bluffs, lilac dawns, smouldering sunsets and starry night skies are just some of the highlights, and you can enjoy them from the new open-air beachside bar. It's all placidly low-key.

The airport is 20 minutes by potholed road.

Hotel Sinar Tambolaka HOTEL $$
(☎ 0387-253 4088; Jl Tambolaka; r 200,000-450,000Rp; ❄ 📶) Set on a sunken plateau below Jl Tambolaka, perched on the edge of a green valley, is this 80-room hotel. Standard rooms are cramped, fan-cooled and have twin beds, but VIP rooms have views and numerous luxuries. It also has a restaurant (mains 15,000Rp to 35,000, open 9am to 10pm)

recommended by locals, and lovely views. Guests get free airport transfers.

★ **Warung Gula Garam** INTERNATIONAL $
(☎0387-252 4019; Bandara Udara; mains 12,000-100,000Rp; ⏰10am-11pm; 📶) 'They have a wood-burning pizza oven!' exclaimed more than one expat as they enthused about this stylish new cafe in an open-air pavilion near the airport. Elsewhere, a full coffee and juice bar, plus a menu of organic salads, pastas and burgers would raise nary an eyebrow, but here it's revolutionary.

Warungku INDONESIAN $
(☎0812 5250 5000; Jl Ranggaroko; mains 20,000-45,000Rp; ⏰9am-10pm) Set back from the main road in a walled compound, this open-air restaurant has excellent versions of Indo classics. It's a pretty garden setting, and you can while away a few hours grazing the menu and enjoying cold beverages.

ℹ Information

BNI Bank (Jl El Tari; ⏰8am-5pm Mon-Thu, 7.30am-4pm Fri) Has an ATM and exchanges money.

ℹ Getting There & Away

AIR

Tambolaka's airport terminal is shiny and modern. There are daily flights to Bali and Kupang (West Timor) by Garuda and Wings Air. Note that on some websites it is listed as 'Waikabubak'.

BOAT

Waikelo, a small and predominantly Muslim town north of Tambolaka, has a small picturesque harbour that is the main port for West Sumba and offers ferry service to Sape (Sumbawa) twice a week (65,000Rp, eight hours).

BUS

Buses leave throughout the day for Waikabubak (10,000Rp to 15,000Rp, one hour), departing from the centre of town.

Anakalang Villages

Set in a fertile valley carpeted in rice fields, the Anakalang district (east of Waikabubak) has some exceptional stone megaliths that are worth seeing. Historically the seat of West Sumbanese power (though geographically it is in the island's centre), Anakalang royals ruled for centuries. During colonisation only royal children were educated, so when government bureaucracies took hold the royals still ruled thanks to wealth and educational access bias. Eventually educational access evened out, and the government diversified.

Right beside the main road to Waingapu, 22km east of Waikabubak, **Kampung Pasunga** boasts one of Sumba's most impressive tombs. The grave of particular interest consists of an upright stone slab carved with images of a chief and his wife with their hands on their hips. This monument dates from 1926 and took six months to carve; 150 buffalo were sacrificed for the funeral ceremony. It is visible from the road. Pasunga's *kepala desa,* whose house has racks of buffalo horns, is friendly if you share some *sirih* or cigarettes with him. He will ask you to sign the visitors' book and leave a donation.

At **Gallubakul**, 2.5km down the road from the modernising village of **Kabonduk** (as elsewhere, metal roofs predominate), tombs are largely crafted from concrete and cheesy tile, but it's also home to Sumba's heaviest tomb, weighing in at 70 tonnes. It is said that 6000 workers took three years to chisel the Umbu Sawola tomb out of a hillside and drag it 3km to town. The tomb is a single piece of carved stone, about 5m long, 4m wide and nearly 1m thick. At its eastern end is a separate upright slab with carvings of the raja and queen who are buried here, as well as buffalo and cockerel motifs. The raja's son lives right by the tomb with his wife and can tell its story. He'll also ask you to sign in and make a donation.

Regular minibuses run between Waikabubak and Anakalang (fewer after 1pm). Buses to Waingapu can drop you off on the highway.

North of Waikabubak

Head north from the Anakalang villages along the mostly paved road and you will traverse mountains sprouting with bamboo, palms and wild fruit trees, over a pass and down into a river valley home to a number of rarely visited *kampung*. **Memboro**, set right on the river, is one of the largest. It used to be a huddle of field houses – places the farmers slept during the planting and harvest seasons – but lately it's grown into a somewhat modern place where people live full-time because of its wide blue river and abundant water supply. **Manuakalada** is a traditional thatched village nearby, but most of the residents have abandoned it in favour of Memboro. The entire area is verdant green during the rainy season, November to May.

Waiwarungu, accessible by a decent road from Memboro, is a proper traditional village – and one that is very remote and quite poor. There are over 20 thatched houses, one *marapu* house and nearly three dozen slab tombs, all within view of the sea. Pigs rut under the houses, and puppies and children run and play everywhere. Still, it's hard, unforgiving country, especially in the parched dry season.

There's at least one daily bus from Waikabubak to Memboro (20,000Rp, one hour), but to get to Waiwarungu you'll need wheels and a guide.

Along the busy (by Sumba standards) road between Waikabubak and Tambolaka, **Waimangura** is the site of one of Sumba's markets. Every Saturday scores of people gather to haggle over fruits, vegetables, ikat fabric, horses and much more. Even in the mobile-phone era, this is still the primary place where people meet up and share stories and gossip.

South of Waikabubak

The Wanokaka district south of Waikabubak has stunning mountain and coastal scenery and several very traditional *kampung*. It's a gorgeous drive from Waikabubak, taking a sealed but narrow road that splits at Padede Weri junction 6km from town. This is where golden, white-headed eagles soar over mountains, which tumble to the azure sea. Turn left at the junction, and the road passes through the riverside settlement of **Taramanu**, 4km further on. About 2km further downhill you'll meet a good road that leads to **Waigalli**, a huddle of about 30 thatched peak roof houses around a fabulous stone grave site on a promontory above the sea. You'll see slabs blanketed with corn kernels drying in the sun, women weaving or children pounding rice in the old timber grinder, and a marvellous view of the rice fields in the valley below. A few families have traded the thatched roof for tin. You'll be asked to make a donation (20,000Rp per person will suffice) and sign the guestbook.

You'll find the nearly 200-year-old Watu Kajiwa tomb in the deeply traditional and isolated, though sprawling, village of **Praigoli**, notched in the dusty, leafy hills above Sumba's southwest coast. From here it's just a short drive further on to lovely **Pantai Wanakoka**, where there's a crescent of sand, craggy palm-dotted cliffs and massive bluffs to the south, a bay bobbing with fishing boats, and a beachfront Pasola site. In the rocky coves west of the beach, the water becomes clearer and rolls into decent, if inconsistent, surf. But the wind is consistent, which makes for interesting kitesurf possibilities. Most of the action gathers around the concrete public fishers house, where you can see their catch in the morning and watch them mend their nets in late afternoon. Nearby is the traditional village of **Wangli**, with views of rice fields, a river, the sea and coastal mountains, and another stone tomb with a 2.5m-tall fleur-de-lis.

Rua, the next in a series of luscious south Sumba beaches, is 5km southwest of the Padede Weri junction. It's yet another tumbledown rustic fishing village with a failed jetty bisecting its wide bay. At one time the Bima ferry docked here but a big storm trashed the jetty and the new dock was situated in Waikelo. Expect more lovely pale-golden sand, turquoise water, and great waves when the swell hits between June and September. There looks to be a point break in the south and stiff onshore wind in the afternoon. There's only one very basic lodging option.

Heading west again, the road passes through the village of **Lemboya**, with its gorgeous rice fields scalloped into the inland side of the rugged coastal mountains. Lemboya boasts one of Sumba's greatest Pasola fields. Set on a rolling grassland it's big and wide and attracts thousands of people in February. From here there's yet another turn-off south to the idyllic white sands of **Pantai Marosi**, 32km from Waikabubak. Set on a ridge above the coast is the sweet Sumba Nautil resort. Nearby is **Pantai Etreat**, a secluded, powdery gem that stands out even amongst some tough competition, and the glassy seas of **Pantai Tarikaha**. Offshore is **Magic Mountain**, a coral-draped underwater volcano that is Sumba's best dive site. Just before Sumba Nautil, the road forks. If you take the right fork you'll reach *kampung* **Litikaha**, where there is now a graded gravel road to **Tokahale**, **Kahale** and **Malisu**, three hilltop villages with spectacular panoramas. It's a 15-minute 4WD drive to the villages, or you can park on the road and walk to all three in about two hours.

The world-class surf spot known as **Occy's Left**, featured in the film *The Green Iguana,* is on **Pantai Nihiwatu**, east of Marosi on another absolutely stunning stretch of sand buffered by a limestone headland. Unfortunately, only Nihiwatu Resort's paying

PASOLA: LET THE BATTLES BEGIN

A riotous tournament between two teams of spear-wielding, ikat-clad horsemen, the Pasola has to be one of the most extravagant (and bloodiest) harvest festivals in Asia. Held annually in February and March, it takes the form of a ritual battle – not so much a quarrel between opposing forces as a need for human blood to run to keep the spirits happy and bring a good harvest. The riders gallop at each other, hurling their *holas* (spears) at rival riders (it's not permitted to use a spear as a lance). Despite the blunt spears, there will be blood, and sometimes deaths (of riders and horses) still do occur. Accidentally, of course.

Pasola takes place in four areas, its exact timing determined by the arrival on nearby coasts of a certain type of sea worm called *nyale*. Two days before the main events, brutal boxing matches called *pajura* are held, with the combatants' fists bound in razor-sharp local grasses.

Before the Pasola can begin, priests in full ceremonial dress must first wade into the ocean to examine the worms at dawn; they're usually found on the eighth or ninth day after a full moon. Fighting begins on the beach, and continues further inland later that same day. Opposing 'armies' are drawn from coastal and inland villages.

In February, Pasola is celebrated in the Kodi area (centred on Kampung Tosi) and the Lemboya area (Kampung Sodan); in March it's in the Wanokaka area (Kampung Waigalli) and the remote Gaura area, west of Lamboya (Kampung Ubu Olehka). Exact dates are known two weeks before Pasola. Check with the guides and hotels in Waikabubak and Tambolaka, as well as NTT expert Edwin Lerrick at Lavalon (p385) in Kupang.

guests are allowed onto this beach and the number of surfers is capped at 10. At slow times nonguest surfers can ask the manager for permission to ride the break. Thankfully, there are a few more lefts and rights scattered within a 30-minute boat ride of both Marosi and Nihiwatu.

Sleeping

Ama Homestay HOMESTAY $

(☎0821 4716 2012; Rua; per person incl all meals 300,000Rp) Just five basic, tiled rooms in a sweet guesthouse made from breeze blocks and woven bamboo. Rooms are just big enough for a double bed and mosquito net. Sheltered by palms and lots of potted plants, this is a perfect surfer crash pad. The drawbacks: electricity is cut at midnight, and all rooms share just one *mandi*.

The beach is only 100m away. You can hire a boat to haul you to the best breaks (250,000Rp per two hours).

★Sumba Nautil RESORT $$$

(☎0813 3747 1670, 0387-21806; www.sumbanautilresort.com; cottages from US$136, r without/with bathroom 450,000/650,000Rp; ❄≋) One of the best-situated resorts in all of Nusa Tenggara, Sumba Nautil sits on the rugged coastal hills with panoramic views of Pantai Marosi and the bluffs that roll north in a series of jutting headlands. Stay in a plush brick cottage with outrageous sea views or a more affordable villa room. A car will shuttle you to beaches and breaks.

The menu is French with North African flair, just like the owner, who makes his own pastas, breads, ice cream and chocolate. Meals are served in a marvellous open-air dining room (mains from US$5).

It has trail maps for hikers, and village visits can be organised. Diving must be arranged well in advance. Rates include breakfast.

Nihiwatu Resort RESORT $$$

(☎reservations 0361-757149; www.nihiwatu.com; bungalows & villas from US$550; ❄📶≋) Hefty price tag notwithstanding, you can certainly understand the draw of this place. There's a virgin beach crashing with head-high (or higher) surf that folds into turquoise barrels on the rugged, beautiful, tribal, raw west coast of Sumba. Every detail is posh, and junket-seeking glossy magazine writers can't seem to stay away. Few luxuries are excluded.

However, what is excluded are nonguests. The current American owners maintain strict restrictions on who can access the beach and breaks.

Amenities are myriad – it even has its own freediving pro. Accommodation is limited to 30 units and there is a multiday minimum stay. Guests are hauled around West Sumba in African safari vehicles; as one local said to us: 'I guess we are the zebras.'

Getting There & Away

A few buses run between Waikabubak and the many villages, but by far the best way to visit the area is by car or motorbike. Most roads are sealed and traffic is light. The hills south of Waikabubak are a taxing yet exhilarating ride for cyclists.

Pero

Pero is a small Muslim fishing village, with a natural harbour inlet sheltered by a sandbar and mangroves. The village does tend to waft with the scent of drying squid, but the all-natural beach just north of town has blonde sand, a palm and scrubby grass backdrop, and a sneaky good left-hand break just offshore, as well as ideal side shore wind for kitesurfers. From here you won't hit land again until Africa. The long-running **Homestay Stori** (☎0813 3755 7272; per person incl all meals 250,000Rp) is run by a hospitable family, and has eight rooms in a rather frayed concrete home with peeling linoleum floors and shared unpleasant *mandis* in the backyard. But, hey, it's the only surf crash pad in the area and it's cheap. It's on the main drag in town, on the right side of the street as you head toward the sea. To visit traditional *kampung*, go north or south along the coastline.

From Tambolaka there are frequent bemos and trucks to Pero.

Ratenggaro & Around

One of Sumba's best villages is close to Pero. Take the paved road from **Bondokodi**, or go off-road for about 3km along **Pantai Radukapal** – a sliver of white sand along a pasture – and you'll come to the *kampung* of Ratenggaro, framed by a low rock wall. Rebuilt after a 2012 fire, it is a remarkable place. There are 11 houses supported by intricately carved columns, one for each cardinal point. The tall, peaked roof homes are situated on a grassy lawn on a bluff above the mouth of **Sungai Rateboya** (Crocodile River), with an absolutely breathtaking view along the coconut-palm-fringed shoreline. You can easily pass hours watching the waves of **Miller's Point** (a famous surf break) pound the rocks, with the high roofs of **Wainyapu**, a collection of 12 *kampung* and more than 40 homes, peeking out above the trees across the river. On the near side of the river mouth – where the mocha river meets the turquoise sea – Wainyapu's unusual stone tombs occupy a small headland. Visitors are asked to contribute a donation (20,000Rp will suffice). The villagers here are full of life, and after a few minutes you'll realise that you're not here to check them out, or to inspect another exotic culture. Rather you are here to be inspected yourself. To get to Wainyapu, you'll have to wade across the river at low tide.

On the way to Ratenggaro, look out for the thinner, high-peaked roofs of **Kampung Paranobaroro** through the trees, about 1km inland. The best of these have enormous timber columns intricately carved and cured by an almost perpetually smouldering cooking fire in the centre of the raised bamboo platform. Stone statues decorate the public space. During the day only women and children are in the village. Women are often weaving and are happy to chat. During ceremonial times you may see pig jaws and buffalo horns displayed on the front porch.

Maluku

POP 2.6 MILLION

Includes ➡

Best Places to Eat

- Floridas (p415)
- Cilu Bintang Estate (p440)
- Delfika Cafe (p440)
- Savana Cottages (p448)
- Beta Rumah (p426)

Best Places to Stay

- Cilu Bintang Estate (p440)
- CDS Bungalow (p443)
- Bela International Hotel (p413)
- Coaster Cottages (p448)
- Maluku Divers (p431)

Why Go?

Welcome to the original Spice Islands. Back in the 16th century when nutmeg, cloves and mace were global commodities that grew nowhere else, money really did 'grow on trees'. It was the search for the Moluccas' (Maluku's) valuable spices that kick-started European colonialism and, thanks to a series of wrong turns and one auspicious land swap, shaped the modern world. When the islands' monopoly on cloves and nutmeg was broken in the 18th century, Maluku settled into gentle obscurity.

What remains is a scattering of idyllic islands where the complex web of cultures envelops visitors with an effusive, almost Polynesian charm. While transport can prove infuriatingly inconvenient, with flexibility and patience you can explore pristine reefs, stroll empty stretches of powdery white sand, book idyllic overwater bungalows, scale 16th-century fort walls, snap endless photos of perfectly formed volcanoes, and revel in a tropical discovery that seems almost too good to be true.

When to Go

Ambon

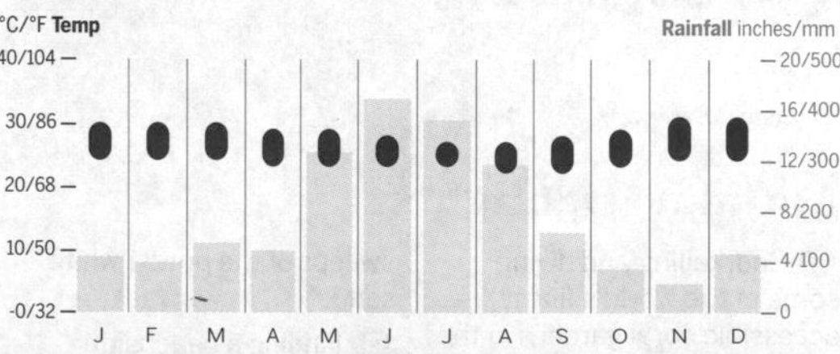

Nov–Mar The dry season is the best time to visit, with consistently spectacular diving.

Apr–May & Sep–Oct The shoulder seasons are a good alternative, especially for the Banda and Kei Islands.

Jun–Aug Monsoons prevail during the wet season, upsetting transport and shuttering dive shops.

Maluku Highlights

1. Snorkelling and diving some of the world's finest accessible coral gardens in the historically fascinating **Banda Islands** (p437).

2. Unwinding at **Ohoidertawun** (p447) or **Pasir Panjang** (p448) in the Kei Islands, two stunning sweeps of the purest white sand.

3. Finding a beachside homestay with coral at your doorstep on **Pulau Hatta** (p442).

4. Staying at one of the offbeat getaways on **Pulau Saparua** (p431) before mainstream tourism discovers the island's white-sand beaches, friendly villages and extensive diving potential.

5. Plunging into the muck with **Maluku Divers** (p431), Pulau Ambon's finest dive operator and most appealing resort.

Getting There & Away

AIR

Ambon and Ternate are the region's air hubs. Both have several daily connections to Jakarta, some direct and some via Makassar, Manado (Sulawesi) or Surabaya. There are several connections from Ambon to Papua.

SEA

Four Pelni liners visit Ambon on biweekly cycles from Bau Bau (22 hours), Makassar (40 hours), Surabaya (70 hours) and/or Jakarta (four days). The *Tidar* handily continues east via the Banda and Kei Islands, as does the infinitely slower *Kelimutu*, which is reportedly infested with roaches. These ships, along with the *Nggapulu*, continue on to various ports in Papua. The *Sinabung* instead swings north via Ternate and Bitung.

Getting Around

AIR

Garuda and Xpress Air fly major routes within Maluku, including a new daily Ambon–Langgur service and connections from Ternate to Halmahera and Ambon. Smaller routes are handled by Wings, Susi (which currently has the Banda contract), Lion and Merpati. Bad weather, low passenger loads and engine trouble make cancellations quite frequent.

BOAT

Pelni's patchy North Maluku services change each month, but you can count on the routes that connect Ambon with the Banda Islands and onward to the Kei Islands. Some medium-range hops are served by uncomfortable ASDP ferries or by wooden boats known as *kapal motor*. Perintis cargo boats are bigger but not at all designed with passengers in mind (bring waterproof clothes). Speedboats link nearby islands and roadless villages.

Locals use very specific terms for boat types: if there isn't a *spid* (covered multi-engine speedboat) to your destination, there might still be a *Johnson* (outboard-powered longboat) or a *ketingting/lape-lape* (smaller, short-hop motorised outrigger canoe).

Regular speedboats connect short and midrange destinations (eg Ternate–Tidore, Ternate–Halmahera, Ambon–Lease Islands, Ambon–Seram). The longer rides are only available in the dry season and are best early in the morning when seas are calmest. Chartering is widely available.

ROAD TRANSPORT

In mountainous Maluku, the few asphalted roads can be surprisingly good, but some areas have only mud tracks or no roads at all. Shorter routes are generally operated by *bemo* (minibus), also known as *mobil*. On Halmahera and Seram, shared Kijangs (fancy seven-seat Toyotas) predominate. Renting an *ojek* (motorcycle taxi) can be a pleasant, inexpensive way to travel.

NORTH MALUKU

North Maluku's historically and politically most significant islands are the pyramidal volcanic cones of Ternate and Tidore. These ancient Islamic sultanates were once the world's only source of cloves, enormously valued in medieval Europe as food preservatives and 'cures' for everything from toothache to halitosis to sexual dysfunction. Funded by the spice trade, these islands' sultans became the most powerful rulers in medieval Maluku, yet wasted much of their wealth fighting each other.

In 1511 the first Portuguese settlers arrived in Ternate. Tidore quickly responded by inviting in the Spaniards. Both islands found their hospitality rapidly exhausted as the Europeans tried to corner the spice market and preach Christianity. When Ternate's Muslim population – already offended by the Europeans' imported pigs and heavy-handed 'justice' – rebelled in 1570, Ternate's Sultan Hairun (Khairun) was executed and his head exhibited on a pike. The besieged Portuguese held out in their citadel until 1575 when the new Ternatean sultan – the same Babullah whose name graces Ternate's airport – took it over as his palace.

The Spaniards, and later the Dutch, made themselves equally unpopular. In a history that's as fascinating as it is complicated, they played Ternate off against Tidore and also confronted one another for control of an elusive clove monopoly. The Dutch prevailed eventually, though the sultanates survived, remaining well-respected institutions to this day.

Ternate is still today the main hub of North Maluku (Maluku Utara, or 'Malut'), though in 2007 Sofifi on Halmahera was named the province's official capital, and many government *kantor* (offices) have relocated there. Few islands in North Maluku have any real history of tourism, so visits beyond Ternate will often prove to be something of an adventure.

Pulau Ternate

☎ 0921

The dramatic volcanic cone of Gunung Api Gamalama (1721m) dominates Pulau Ternate. Settlements are sprinkled around its lower coastal slopes with villages on the east coast coalescing into North Maluku's biggest town, Kota Ternate. The city makes a useful transport gateway for the region and has fishing harbours filled with colourful boats and a few remnant stilt-house neighbourhoods.

Kota Ternate

POP 172,000

Ternate is gorgeous, swathed in jungle and wild clove trees. However, when you first land here, in the looming shadow of Gamalama, with several more volcanic islands dotting the deep blue channel beyond, you may be shocked by its frenetic pace. Traditionally the bureaucratic heart of Malut, Kota Ternate is grudgingly relinquishing some *kantor* to the new capital, Sofifi on nearby Halmahera. It's the transport hub of the region, but it's worth a visit in its own right for its 16th-century forts, thronging markets and superb seafood.

Sights

Kota Ternate's three fortresses were rebuilt by the Dutch between 1606 and 1610. They've been over-renovated since falling into decrepitude by the 1990s, but moves towards more sensitive restoration are afoot.

Benteng Tolukko FORTRESS

(Map p412; admission by 10,000Rp donation) A tiny, beautifully situated fort surrounded by a vivid tropical garden, Benteng Tolukko was the first Portuguese stronghold on Ternate (1512). It's better-preserved that the town's two other *benteng*, inviting a stroll on the battlements for yet another stunning view across to Tidore and Halmahera. If it's locked, knock on the door of the family home next door; they'll have the key.

Keraton MUSEUM

(Istana Kesultan; Map p412; ☎ 0921-312 1166; admission by donation; ⏲ 9am-5pm Mon-Fri, to 3pm Sat, to 1pm Sun) Built in 1834 and restored in semi-colonial style, the Sultan's Palace is still a family home. There's a museum section with a small but interesting collection of historic weaponry and memorabilia from the reigns of past sultans, whose lineage dates back to 1257. Unfortunately, the Keraton is sometimes closed during advertised hours, and an adjoining purpose-built museum was two years behind schedule at the time of research.

You need a special invitation from the sultan to see the famous *mahkota* (royal crown). Topped with cassowary feathers, it supposedly has magical powers such as growing 'hair', and keeping the volcano in check. The *mahkota* is only worn at coronations and during the **Legu Gam**, or 'People's Festival'. Ternate's main festival is held in April, culminating on the late sultan's birthday (he passed away in early 2015) and involves traditional performers, the Gam Maracahaya (a torch-lit flotilla) and a ritual scaling of Gamalama.

Royal Mosque MOSQUE

(Map p412; Jl Sultan Babullah) On the 27th evening of Ramadan, Lailat-ul-Qadr celebrations see the sultan's procession arrive to a mass of flaming torches at the Royal Mosque, which has impressive heavy interior timberwork.

Benteng Oranye FORTRESS

(Map p414) Known to the Portuguese as Fort Malayo, the Dutch-built Benteng Oranye, which dates from the early 17th century, is a largely ruinous complex inhabited by goats, rusted cannon and…the army. Once home to the Dutch governor, it's now overgrown, neglected and (in parts) unsympathetically concreted. You can still wander some sections of cannon-topped bastion, accessed through a restored gateway arch, and its current tenants (the army, not the goats) are aiding efforts to restore some of its former grandeur.

Majolica Ulama Indonesia MOSQUE

(Masjid Al Munawwah; Map p414; Jl Sultan Djabir Sjah) It's hardly the Hagia Sophia, and the seaward minarets have been reclaimed by the sea (only the crumbled footings remain), but this concrete-and-tile mosque dominates the central foreshore of Kota Ternate, and has been listed amongst the most impressive mosques in all Indonesia. Its architectural highlight is the centralised dome, covered in the repeating name of Allah picked out in Arabic calligraphy.

Benteng Kalamata FORTRESS

(Map p412) The 1540 Benteng Kalamata is dramatically situated on the waterfront 1km southwest of Bastiong, staring down Ternate's old foe, Tidore. You can wander the unusual angular geometry of its outer walls, but may have to slip the grumpy caretaker 5000Rp for the privilege.

Pulau Ternate

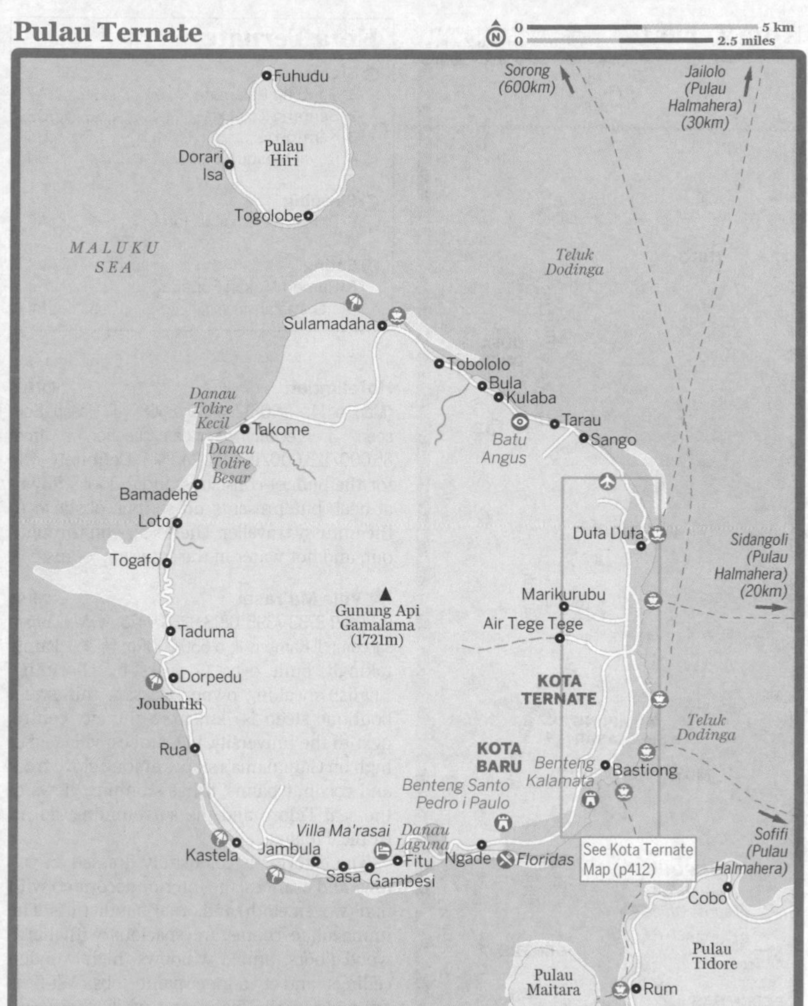

Sleeping

Prices have risen quite sharply in Ternate over recent years, but remain very affordable. Accommodation under 150,000Rp can still be found, but conditions are often very basic. You'll value a room with air-con, given the oppressive heat and humidity.

Seqavia Guesthouse GUESTHOUSE $
(Map p414; ☎0921-311 1147; Jl Kampung Kodok; r 150,000Rp; ❄) Tucked away from the two-stroke mayhem of the main roads, Seqavia is a basic, good-value option. Unfinished renovations (including the intriguing stairs-to-nowhere) and faded fittings explain the low prices, but many at this level wouldn't come with air-con in all rooms.

Tiara Inn GUESTHOUSE $
(Map p414; ☎0921-311 1017; Jl Salim Fabanyo 1; s/d/superior r 200,000/220,000/250,000Rp; ❄) Popular for its good value, the Tiara is a little tarnished, but ticks all the boxes of adequate, dependable accommodation. Behind the standard Ternate lobby of polished tiles, chattering TV and idling smokers you'll find simple, clean rooms and effective air-conditioning.

Kota Ternate

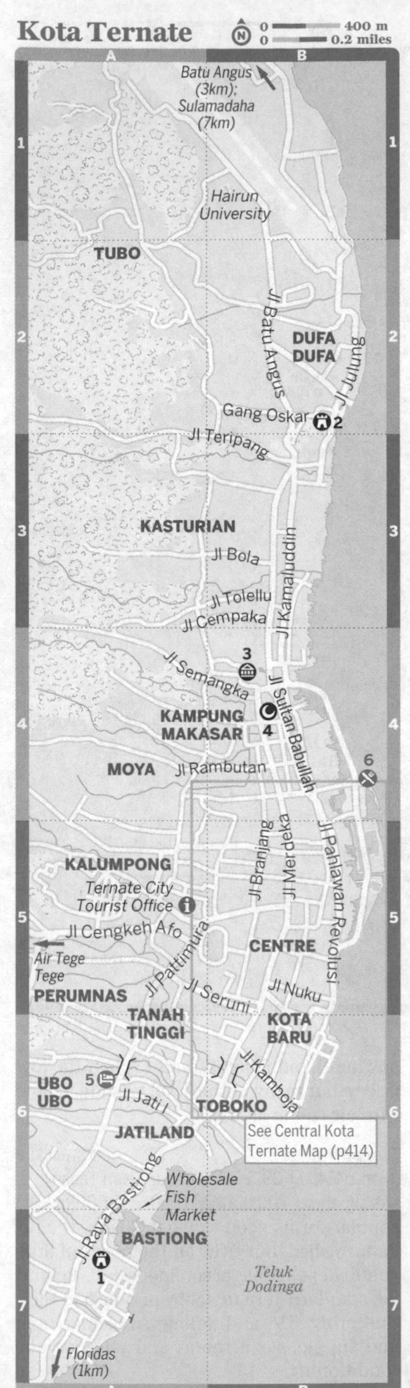

Kota Ternate

Sights

1 Benteng Kalamata A7
2 Benteng Tolukko B2
3 Keraton B4
4 Royal Mosque B4

Sleeping

5 Bela International Hotel A6

Eating

6 Rumah Makan Popeda Gamalama B4

Hotel Indah HOTEL $

(Map p414; ☎0812 4499 8668; Jl Hasan Boesoeri 3; economy/standard/superior r from 85,000/125,000/150,000Rp; ❄) Definitely one for the budget-conscious, Indah looks down-at-heel, but presents no serious obstacle to the unfussy traveller. There's air-con throughout, and hot water in the superior rooms.

★**Villa Ma'rasai** INN $$

(☎0821 3733 7395, 0813 9288 9475; www.vilamarasai.com; Jl Kampus II; d 650,000Rp; ❄📶) Painstakingly built over 15 years by charming, English-speaking owner Hassan, this sweet boutique sleep is 7km from the city centre, next to the university, in Gambesi village. Set high on Gamalama's slopes among clove trees and coconut palms, it has stunning views of the sea, Tidore and the surrounding riot of tropical foliage.

The exterior is colourfully dressed in yellows and oranges, the interior decorated with ikat (woven cloth) and other handicrafts. The immaculate rooms are spacious with hardwood floors, ample windows, high wooden ceilings and two-tone paint jobs. Wi-fi is available in the lobby, and while there's no hot water, the alternative is 'cold' in name only. Meals, primarily fish, are exceptional, and Hassan, himself a fount of knowledge about Malut, can organise bikes, cars and tours of Ternate's jungles (and beyond). All told, a delightful place to unwind beyond the grit and bustle of Ternate.

Hotel Archie HOTEL $$

(Map p414; ☎0921-311 0555; Jl Nuku 6; standard/superior r 300,000/330,000Rp; ❄) Archie's empire now comprises three hotels within spitting distance of each other: the original, always better than most equivalently priced competitors; **Archie 2** (Map p414; ☎0921-312 1197; Jl Nuku 100; d 350,000Rp; ❄), across the road and with similar (if less charismatic) features; and the new flagship, **Archie Menara** (Map p414; ☎0921-312 2100; archiehotelmenara@gmail.com; Jl Nuku 101; standard r 425,000Rp; ❄ 📶) aimed at higher-end and business travellers – it's comfortable, clean, and good value. All three are close to the action.

Emerald Hotel HOTEL **$$**
(Map p414; ☎0921-312 8188/8288; emeraldternate@yahoo.com; Jl Branjang 28; standard/superior/deluxe r 390,000/490,000/590,000Rp; ❄ 📶) On a quieter side street off Jl Pattimura, lined with food vendors, you'll find the Emerald, one of the newest and nicest hotels in town. It's pushing towards the upper end of mid-range, but the wi-fi, cool comfortable rooms, super-friendly staff and (slightly bizarre) gleaming equestrian statuary in the lobby make it feel like decent value.

Boulevard Hotel HOTEL **$$**
(Map p414; ☎0921-311 0777, 0921-311 0666; Jatiland BS; standard/business/deluxe r 330,000/395,000/475,000Rp; ❄ 📶) Usefully located near both a modern shopping centre and the traditional markets, the Boulevard is a comfortable, reasonably upmarket option. Behind the standard Ternate lobby of tiles, TVs and plastic orchids you'll find clean if slightly stale-smelling rooms with TVs, wi-fi, air-conditioning and Western-style bathrooms.

★ **Bela International Hotel** HOTEL **$$$**
(Map p412; ☎0921-312 1800; www.belainternationalhotel.com; Jl Jati Raya 500; deluxe/executive r 1,350,000/2,250,000Rp; ❄ 📶 🏊) A little out of the centre, the Bela is the place to go for an 'international' hotel experience. In fact, it's the swankiest of its kind in Maluku: 195 rooms of flashy fittings, paddling-pool-sized beds, and flunkies hurrying down endless corridors. It's not the most charismatic or best-value place in town, but it comes with all the trimmings.

Eating

Rumah makan (eating houses) offer cheap eats throughout town, with high concentrations around the markets. Several shacks north of the bemo terminal serve local specialities such as *ikan gohu* (raw tuna 'cooked' in citrus) and *popeda* (Malukan sago congee) as part of 30,000Rp all-you-can-eat spreads, including fish, cassava and a dozen other side dishes.

Self-caterers should head to the supermarkets at Jatiland (p415) and Ternate (p415) malls, or **Golden Bakery** (Map p414; Jl Pattimura; ⏲9am-10pm), which bakes a decent selection of fresh bread and pastries.

Rumah Makan Popeda Gamalama INDONESIAN **$**
(Map p412; mains 30,000Rp; ⏲5am-5pm) This wonderful little market shack is the choice spot to try *popeda* in Ternate. An array of fish, stewed greens, mushrooms, pumpkin and sambals accompanies the mucilaginous sago-flour glue that is *popeda*. Leave your textural food fears at the door: the locals will be thrilled to have you, and you may even like it!

Rumah Makan Joyo INDONESIAN **$**
(Map p414; Jl Nuri; mains 35,000-55,000Rp; ⏲9am-midnight) Joyo has joyously bright decor (think mermaids and waterdragons) and is a joy to seafood lovers. Choose from the catch of the day, stashed in polystyrene coolers for your rummaging convenience. *Udang* and *kepiting* (prawn and crab) dishes are wonderful, and wonderfully cheap.

Kedai Mita INDONESIAN **$**
(Map p414; Jl Stadion; mains 15,000-60,000Rp; ⏲10am-10pm) One of the best places in town to sample Malukan staples (alongside classic Indo fare), Kedai Mita is a covered, open-air eating house in the lee of Ternate's stadium. Try the *ikan gohu* (raw tuna 'cooked' in *calamansi* juice with chillies, basil and steamed cassava) or the *popeda*.

Lauk Pauk INDONESIAN **$**
(Map p414; Jl Pattimura; mains 12,000-25,000Rp; ⏲6am-8pm) This looks like just another what-you-see-is-what-you-get *rumah makan*, but locals know it's one of the best. Multiple styles of *ikan* (perhaps *woku* – braised in a lemongrass paste – or *kayu* – sun-dried, Acehnese style) and *ayam* (chicken fried, or in an *acari* sauce of Indian pickling spices) all repay the adventurous orderer.

Bakso Lapangan Tembak Senayan INDONESIAN **$**
(Map p414; ☎0921-326 028; Jl Mononutu; mains 20,000-43,000Rp; ⏲10am-10pm) Vaguely Japanese in decor, this fan-cooled, brick-and-timber eating house specialises in *bakso* (meatballs) various ways, including fried or bobbing in clear soup. The other Indonesian staples – noodles, fried rice, flour-dusted squid and the like – can all be depended on.

Central Kota Ternate

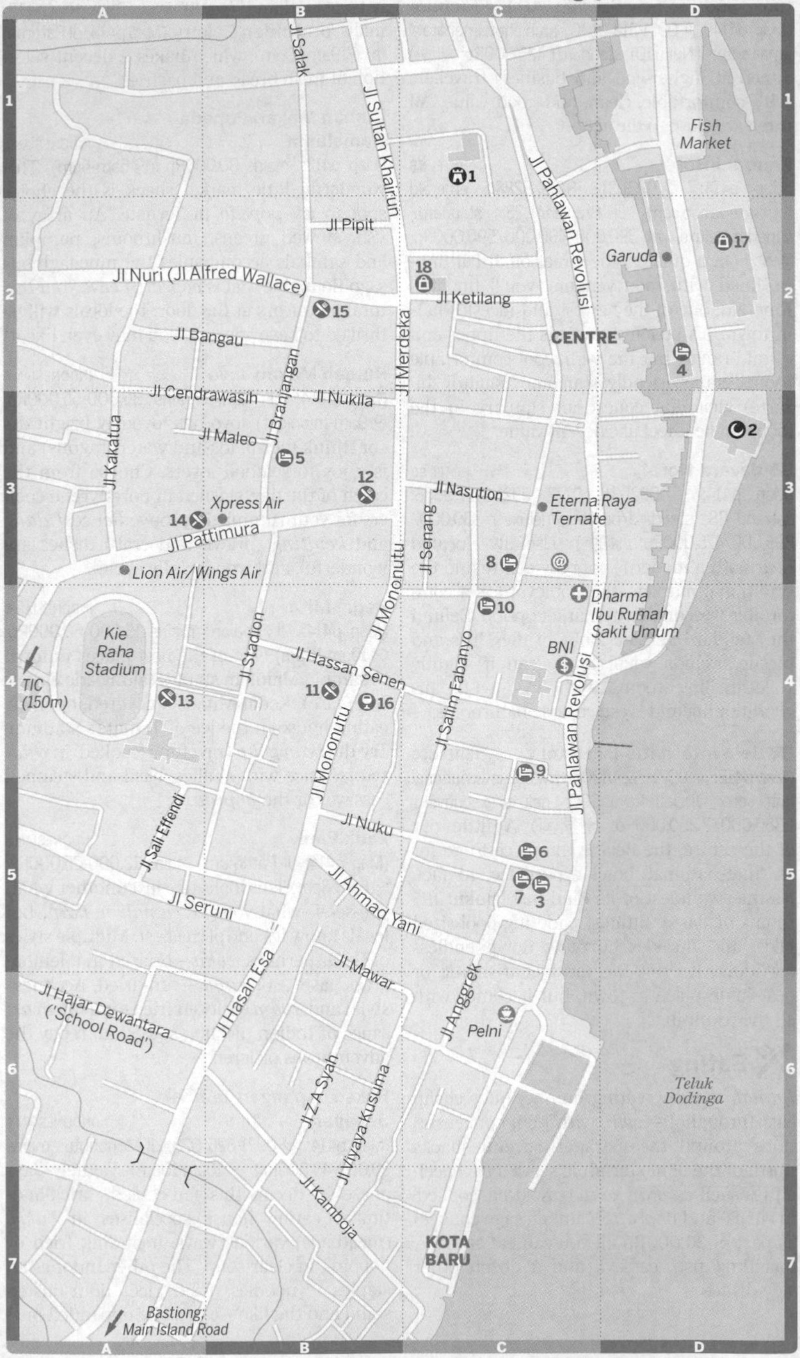

0 200 m
0 0.1 miles

A B C D
1 2 3 4 5 6 7

Jl Salak
Jl Sultan Khairun
Jl Pahlawan Revolusi
Fish Market
1
Jl Pipit
17
Garuda
18
Jl Nuri (Jl Alfred Wallace)
Jl Ketilang
15
Jl Bangau
CENTRE
4
Jl Merdeka
Jl Branjangan
Jl Cendrawasih
Jl Nukila
2
Jl Maleo
Jl Kakatua
5
12
Jl Nasution
Xpress Air
14
Eterna Raya Ternate
Jl Senang
Jl Pattimura
Jl Mononutu
8
Lion Air/Wings Air
Dharma Ibu Rumah Sakit Umum
10
Kie Raha Stadium
Jl Stadion
BNI
Jl Hassan Senen
TIC (150m)
11
16
13
Jl Salim Fabanyo
Jl Mononutu
9
Jl Pahlawan Revolusi
Jl Sali Effendi
Jl Nuku
6
Jl Ahmad Yani
7
3
Jl Seruni
Jl Mawar
Jl Hasan Esa
Jl Hajar Dewantara ('School Road')
Jl Anggrek
Pelni
Teluk Dodinga
Jl Z A Syah
Jl Viyaya Kusuma
Jl Kamboja
KOTA BARU
Bastiong; Main Island Road

Central Kota Ternate

Sights
- 1 Benteng Oranye C1
- 2 Majolica Ulama Indonesia D3

Sleeping
- 3 Archie Menara C5
- 4 Boulevard Hotel D2
- 5 Emerald Hotel B3
- 6 Hotel Archie C5
- 7 Hotel Archie 2 .... C5
- 8 Hotel Indah C3
- 9 Seqavia Guesthouse C4
- 10 Tiara Inn C4

Eating
- 11 Bakso Lapangan Tembak Senayan B4
- 12 Golden Bakery B3
- 13 Kedai Mita A4
- 14 Lauk Pauk A3
- 15 Rumah Makan Joyo B2

Drinking & Nightlife
- 16 New Laguna Executive Club B4

Shopping
- 17 Jatiland Mall D2
- 18 Ternate Mall C2

★**Floridas** SEAFOOD $$
(0921-321 4430; mains 20,000-700,000Rp; 10am-11pm) Floridas is a locally famous seafood restaurant. Get yourself a balcony table with peerless views to Tidore and Maitara, and tuck into *ikan woku balanga*: fish steak roasted in *kenari* nut, chilli, lemongrass and other aromatics. The lobster may be pricy by local standards, but is well worth it.

Drinking & Nightlife

In deference to Ternate's Muslim majority, alcohol may not be sold in restaurants, and beer (prohibitively expensive by local standards) is available only in karaoke bars. Translation: pack a flask.

New Laguna Executive Club CLUB
(Map p414; Jl Mononutu; 10pm-4am Mon-Sat) Don't be put off by the title – the Laguna isn't just for executives; in fact, it jauntily boasts 'we never stop the party!' Behind a looming facade on Jl Mononutu you'll find live bands, three DJs on rotation, and one of the few places in Ternate to buy (expensive) beer.

Shopping

Jatiland Mall MALL
(Map p414; Jl Sultan M Djabir Shah; 10am-10pm) The bustling new waterfront Jatiland Mall is not going to give Surabaya or Jakarta or even Medan mall envy. However, you can find cafes with wi-fi, a Graha Media bookshop, a Multi Mart outlet and even a gym, all in air-conditioned, middle-class comfort.

Ternate Mall SHOPPING CENTRE
(Map p414; cnr Jl Merdeka & Ketilang; 8am-10pm) A small, serviceable shopping centre with a supermarket, pharmacy and food and clothing outlets. One of the few places in Ternate to buy sunscreen and insect repellent.

Information

A town-wide rash of new, air-conditioned ATM cabinets attests to Ternate's growing prosperity, but only the **BNI** (Map p414; Jl Pahlawan Revolusi; 8am-3pm Mon-Thu, to noon Fri) changes money (and then only US dollars in new, unfolded $100 bills). Carry cards compatible with Indonesian ATMs, and you'll never be caught short.

Dharma Ibu Rumah Sakit Umum (Map p414; Jl Pahlawan Revolusi) Ternate's principal hospital is a Dutch-founded holdover from the colonial days, set in the original 80-year-old building. There are multiple doctors, but English may be limited, so it's best to bring a translator where possible.

Ternate City Tourist Office (Map p412; 0921-311 1211, 0813 222 7667; Jl Pattimura 160; 8am-2.30pm Mon-Fri) There's not a great deal of information in English, but the staff are knowledgeable and will do all they can to help. Look for the office signed '*Dinas Pariwisata*', opposite the police station.

Warnet Online (Map p414; Jl Hasan Boesoeri; per hr 6000Rp; 8am-10pm; @) A very basic (but functional) internet cafe open into the evening.

Getting There & Away

There's a **Pelni office** (Map p414; 0921-312 1434; www.pelni.com; 9am-4pm Mon-Sat) near the port.

Flight schedules and carriers shift frequently. If you want a current, comprehensive view of exactly who is flying where and when, find **Eterna Raya Ternate** (Map p414; 0921-312 1651; Jl Hasan Boesoeri 109; 8am-5pm), the best travel agent in Ternate. Departure tax is 16,000Rp.

A number of airlines have offices in town.

Xpress Air (Map p414; ☎0921-312 2846; Jl Pattimura 24; ⏰9am-6pm Mon-Sat)

Garuda (Map p414; ☎0921-312 8030, 0921-331 8757, 0823 4694 0800; Jl Boulevard Raya 43, Ruko Jatiland Business Centre; ⏰9am-6pm Mon-Sat)

Lion Air/Wings Air (Almas Mega Travel; Map p414; ☎0921-327 005, 021-6379 8000; Jl Pattimura 125; ⏰8am-6pm Mon-Sat)

Getting Around

Taxis charge an exorbitant 100,000Rp for the 6km from Babullah Airport to central Ternate. *Ojeks* will do this run for as little as 10,000Rp, however, and bemos (from outside Hairun University, 10 minutes' walk south) cost only 5000Rp to the central market. From there, bemos run in all directions (5000Rp) but *ojeks* (from 5000Rp per ride) are generally more convenient.

Around Pulau Ternate

Head out of Kota Ternate via **Batu Angus** (a gnarled 300-year-old lava flow) and you'll reach **Sulamadaha** (entrance 5000Rp), a popular if somewhat litter-strewn black-sand beach with heavy swells and sadly ruined coral. From a cove 800m east, public longboats (5000Rp per person) cross to the offshore volcanic cone of **Pulau Hiri** almost hourly from dusk till dawn. Hiri was the last step of the sultan's family's *Sound of Music*–style escape from Ternate during WWII.

Back on Ternate, beyond the village of Takome, the main road returns to the coast beside the small, muddy Danau Tolire Kecil. Less than a kilometre further, a paved side lane (2000Rp fee) climbs to the rim of **Danau Tolire Besar**. Startlingly sheer cliffs plummet down to the lugubriously green, crocodile-infested waters of this deep crater lake. Locals offer guide services should you want to descend (1½ hours return on foot).

TRANSPORT FROM PULAU TERNATE

Air

DESTINATION	AIRLINE	FREQUENCY
Ambon	Garuda, Xpress Air	3 weekly
Galela (Pulau Halmahera)	Xpress Air	3 weekly
Makassar	Xpress Air, Garuda, Sriwijaya	daily
Manado	Lion Air/Wings Air, Garuda	daily
Surabaya	Batavia Air, Xpress Air	daily

Boat

DESTINATION	PORT	TYPE	FARE (RP)	FREQUENCY
Ambon via Namlea	Ahmad Yani	Pelni	varies	2 monthly
Jailolo (Pulau Halmahera)	Dufa Dufa	*kapal motor*	35,000	3 daily
Jailolo (Pulau Halmahera)	Dufa Dufa	speedboat	50,000	when full
Rum	Bastiong Ferry Port	car ferry	5,000	7am, 1pm, 4pm, 6pm
Rum	Bastiong Ferry Port	speedboat	10,000, charters 70,000	when full
Sidangoli (Pulau Halmahera)	Mesjid Raya	speedboat	50,000, charters 350,000	when full
Sofifi (Pulau Halmahera)	Kota Baru	speedboat	30,000-50,000	when full
Sorong	Ahmad Yani	Pelni	varies	2 monthly

A footpath from the southern edge of Dorpedu leads down to **Jouburiki**, the beach where Ternate's very first sultan was supposedly crowned in 1257. **Danau Laguna** is a pleasant, spring-fed bowl lake with a lushly forested perimeter (and plans to introduce aquaculture and fishing). Across the straits lie the conical islands of Tidore and Maitara, as featured on Indonesia's 1000Rp notes. Those volcanoes align perfectly when viewed from Floridas (p415) restaurant just beyond Ngade. Across the road are the stubby roadside remnants of **Benteng Santo Pedro i Paulo**, once Ternate's main line of defence against a 1606 Spanish attack.

GUNUNG API GAMALAMA

Ternate's central volcano laid waste to the island in 1840, and periodic eruptions continue to this day. While it's not considered imminently dangerous, it's currently prohibited to bag its peak. There are pleasant, shorter clove-grove hikes from Air Tege Tege village (near the transmitter tower), or from Villa Ma'rasai (p412) in Kampung Gambesi (it arranges day hikes), but even here it gets very steep rapidly. The tourist office (p415) can help you find a guide.

Getting Around

From Kota Ternate's central terminal, bemos run frequently to Sulamadaha (5000Rp, counter-clockwise) and Kastela (5000Rp, clockwise). No single bemo goes right around the island but some north-route vehicles drive as far as Togafo (10,000Rp). From there it's a pleasantly twisty 2km walk to Taduma, where the longest south-route bemos start. Consider chartering an *ojek* to loop around the island with photo stops (from 100,000Rp).

Pulau Tidore

0921

Less populous, less mercantile and less frenetic than Ternate, Tidore makes a refreshing escape from the bustle of its historical enemy. The sultanate – which endured from 1109 until the Sukarno era – was re-established in 1999. Today, the 36th sultan presides over a sublime volcanic island dotted with painted wooden homes bordered by flower gardens, shaded by mango trees and coconut palms, and scented by sheets of cloves and nutmeg sun-drying in the street.

Pulau Tidore

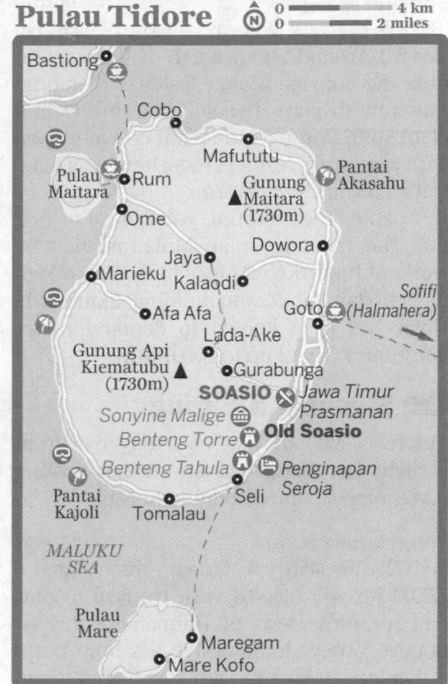

In Tidorean dialect *sukur dofu* means 'thank you', *saki* means 'delicious' and *sterek* (*lau*) means '(very) good'. Hire an *ojek*, spin all the way around, and you'll come out smiling.

Soasio

Drowsy and exceptionally friendly for a capital, Soasio has fewer shops than nearby port-town Goto, but a monopoly on Tidore's cultural and historical sights.

Sights

Benteng Tahula FORT

(Jl Lain) FREE A legacy of Spain's short-lived presence in Tidore, this early 17-century fort is well preserved, with orderly market gardens within and spectacular views to Halmahera without. It's a steep climb to the top, and the fort is always open.

Benteng Torre FORT

FREE No less spectacular than its nearby twin, Benteng Tahula, Torre was bult by the Spanish in the early 17th century. Broken lava flows, vivid tropical foliage and commanding views of southern approaches to the island make this a worthy, picturesque traipse up the hill from the centre of Soasio.

Sonyine Malige MUSEUM

(Sultan's Memorial Museum; Jl Lain; ⌚9am-2pm Mon-Fri) Around 200m north of Benteng Tahula the Sonyine Malige Sultan's Memorial Museum displays the sultan's throne and giant spittoons, plus the royal crown topped with cassowary feathers (considered as magical as Ternate's *mahkota*).

To enter the museum, you'll have to first find the curator, Umar Muhammad, who works at the DIKNAS office in the Dinas Pendidikan dan Kebudayan building, 2km north. Umar has been known to demand rather hefty entry fees of up to 100,000Rp.

Sleeping & Eating

Tidore is easy to visit as a day trip from Ternate, but Soasio has one rather inviting *penginapan* (simple lodging house).

Penginapan Seroja HOMESTAY $$

(☎0921-316 1456; Jl Sultan Hassanuddin; d 275,000Rp; ❄) Blessed with tropical blooms and stunning views of Halmahera, this attractive waterside homestay lies 50m north of Benteng Tahula in Old Soasio, and is run by a charming *ibu* (lady) who can really cook. Its air-con twin rooms are acceptable, but not terribly clean or comfortable; try to grab one with a balcony overlooking the water.

Jawa Timur Prasmanan INDONESIAN $

(Jl Soasio; mains 15,000-20,000Rp; ⌚9am-9pm Mon-Sat) One kilometre north of Benteng Tahula and opposite the Transport Ministry office, this place does good renditions of Indonesian hawker staples, including nasi goreng *ikan asin* (salty fish) and *mie goreng* (fried noodles).

Information

The BNI branch in Soasio has an ATM – it's one of the few places to get or change cash on the island, along with ATMs in Rum, Tomalau and Goto.

Around Tidore

Tidore's villages are little more than sleepy clusters of houses, bedecked with woven mats of cloves and nutmeg, blackening in the sun. There are some reasonable beaches: **Pantai Akasahu** isn't spectacular, but is popular for its modest hot-spring pool. From here the quiet road to **Rum** is attractive, with fine views over Ternate. A three-minute speedboat hop from Rum, **Pulau Maitara** has clear blue waters for better snorkelling and swimming. On Tidore's southern coast, **Pantai Kajoli** is a slender white-sand beach – the island's best – that kisses turquoise shallows. **Pulau Mare**, just offshore, is famed for its attractive, no-frills pottery. Boat charters (100,000Rp) to and from the island are available from Kajoli or Seli.

Getting There & Around

Frequent bemos run from Rum to Soasio to Goto (50,000Rp, for the entire 45-minute trip) using the south-coast road. No bemos use the quiet Rum to Mafututu route, but that pretty road is now asphalted. *Ojeks* circumnavigate the island for negotiable rates (around 150,000Rp).

Pulau Halmahera

Maluku's biggest island is comprised of four mountainous peninsulas, several volcanic cones and dozens of offshore islands. As it's sparsely populated and hard to get around, Halmahera's potential for diving, birdwatching and beach tourism remains almost entirely untapped. But the creation of new regional capitals at Weda (Central Halmahera) and Jailolo (Western Halmahera), along with the recent naming of Sofifi as provincial capital of North Maluku, is stimulating local building booms. The movement of government functions from Ternate and Tidore may finally reverse a history throughout which those tiny islands have dominated Halmahera.

BOATS FROM PULAU TIDORE

DESTINATION	PORT	TYPE	FARE (RP)	FREQUENCY
Bastiong	Rum	ferry	5,000	3 daily
Bastiong	Rum	speedboat	10,000	when full
Sofifi (Pulau Halmahera)	Goto	speedboat	50,000	when full 7-9am

Pulau Halmahera

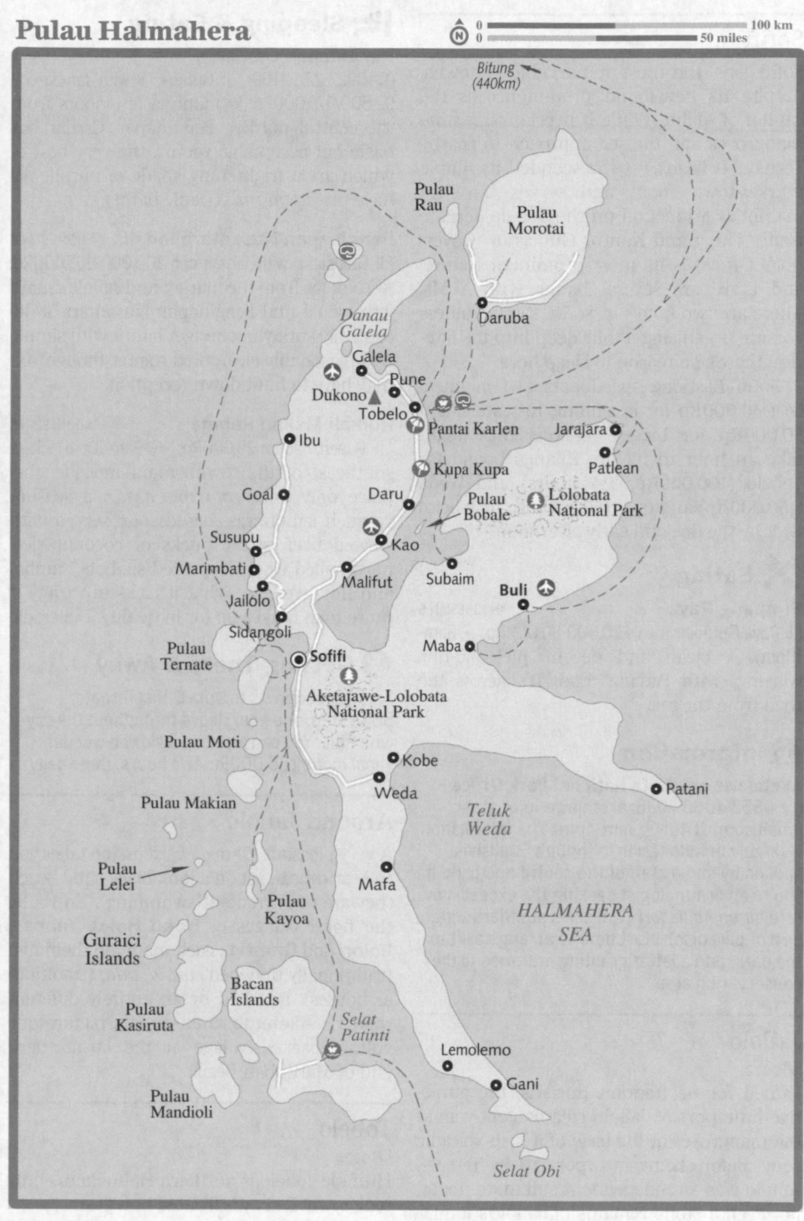

Getting There & Away

Xpress Air flies to Galela and Kao. Pelni's *Sangiang* liner loops around Halmahera once or twice a month from Ternate and/or Bitung (Sulawesi). But by far the most popular access is by speedboat from Ternate. For the northwestern coast head for Jailolo. For Tobelo, Galela and the east, cross initially to Sofifi or Sidangoli. The public boats to Sidangoli (50,000Rp, 30 minutes, leaving when full) are lighter than those that make the Jailolo run and get tossed around by the sea when the swell rises in the afternoon. You can also charter one for 350,000Rp.

Sofifi

Sofifi isn't the most remarkable of towns, despite its new-found prominence as the capital of Malut. While it overlooks pristine mangroves and the sea approach to nearby Ternate, it hasn't yet transcended its simple market-town roots, and serves travellers mainly as a junction on the Tobelo–Ternate route. The grand Kantor Gubernur (Governor's Office) is its most prominent feature, and there are several banks with ATMs. There are two hotels in Sofifi, though unless you are organising a tour deep into the interior, there's no reason to sleep here.

Sofifi–Bastiong speedboats (40 minutes) cost 50,000Rp for fast-filling 12-seaters, and 30,000Rp for bigger versions that might take an hour to fill up. Kijangs bound for Tobelo (100,000Rp, 3½ hours) and Weda (150,000Rp) and taxis (500,000Rp to Tobelo) wait by the dock till early afternoon.

Eating

Simpang Raya INDONESIAN $

(Jl Raya Gurapin; meals 20,000-30,000Rp; 8am-10pm) A clean and decent pick-and-mix warung, with Padang food. It's across the road from the sea.

Information

Aketajawe-Lolobata National Park Office

(0852 4003 7036; aketajawe-lolobata@gmail.com; Jl 40; 9am-4pm) The information is largely in Indonesian, although English is spoken by some staff of the centre and park. If you're an ornithologist seeking the exceedingly rare *burung bidadari* (Wallace's standard-wing bird of paradise), start here to arrange a lift to the park, and a letter granting entrance to the conservation area.

Jailolo

0922

Famed for its fragrant durians, the attractive little port of Jailolo steams gently amid the mangroves at the base of a lush volcanic cone. Before being incorporated by Ternate, Jailolo was an independent sultanate. Today, not even a stone remains of Jailolo's former *keraton* (palace), abandoned in the 1730s. However, the sultan was reinstated in 2003 and now lives in a modest beachfront villa in Marimbati.

Sleeping & Eating

Penginapan Camar INN $

(0922-222 1100; Jl Gufasa; r with fan/air-con 92,500/175,000Rp;) Only a few doors from the central market, Penginapan Camar has basic but acceptable rooms, the very best of which are a frightening shade of purple. All have private *mandis* (ladle baths).

Penginapan Nusantara Indah HOMESTAY $

(Jl Gufasa; r with fan/air-con 100,000/165,000Rp;) Not far from the market and Jailolo's main jetty, you'll find Penginapan Nusantara, a deceptively sprawling budget haunt with simple and reasonably clean tiled rooms, though you may have to hunt down reception.

Rumah Makan Rahma INDONESIAN $

(Jl Puaen; soup 29,000Rp; 9am-10pm) Just southeast of the town's main mosque, this place only does *coto makassar*, a season-yourself lemongrass-based soup served with stewed beef, sticky pucks of coconut rice, hard-boiled eggs, deep-fried shallots, sambal and lime wedges. What it lacks in variety it more than makes up for in quality. Delicious!

Getting There & Away

Large speedboats to Dufa Dufa (Ternate, 50,000Rp, one hour) leave throughout the day when full. You can also hop a slower, wooden *kapal motor* (35,000Rp, two hours, three daily).

Around Jailolo

A very pleasant 12km *ojek* excursion takes you to **Marimbati**, set on a long black-sand beach (beware of currents if swimming). En route, the floral villages of **Hoku Hoku**, **Taboso**, **Lolori** and **Gamtala** each maintain their own traditionally thatched *rumah adat* (traditional houses). Reached by an entirely different road via **Akelamo**, **Susupu** is a picturesque volcano-backed village at the far-northern end of Marimbati Beach.

Tobelo

0924

Humble Tobelo is northern Halmahera's only real 'town'. Its bay is fronted by a pretty jigsaw of atolls, all ringed with pale, sandy beaches. The most accessible are Tagalaya and Kakara, where you can stay in a sadly neglected government-built diving centre.

Sleeping

Penginapan Asean Jaya GUESTHOUSE $
(☎0924-262 1051; Jl Pelabuhan; s/d 75,000/100,000Rp) Super-clean budget rooms with fresh paint, spotless floors and linens, and small shared *mandis*. Anis, the delightful owner, speaks English, but his staff don't.

Bianda Hotel HOTEL $$
(☎0924-262 2123; Jl Kemakmuran; standard/superior/deluxe r 330,000/360,000/450,000Rp; ❄) Super-friendly, English-speaking staff are a drawcard at Bianda, the freshest and newest place on the block. The spacious rooms have white tiled floors, flat-screens, recessed lighting, modern wooden furniture, and air-con throughout. Superior and deluxe rooms have hot water.

Elizabeth Inn HOTEL $$
(☎0924-262 1165, 0813 5546 9999; Jl Kemakmuran; r 330,000Rp; ❄) The Elizabeth is one of several decent midrange options ranged on the seaward side of Jl Kemakmuran. Behind the cool, beige tiles of its lobby you'll find clean rooms with comfortable beds, TVs and air-con. There's an internet cafe adjoining the hotel.

Kakara Island Resort RESORT $$
(☎0852 4084 2579; www.halmaherautara.com; per person 250,000Rp, meals 50,000Rp) This 'resort', tucked into the mangroves west of the only settlement on this tiny, gorgeous, sadly litter-strewn atoll, could be so much more. Built as a dive centre by the government in 2011, it now offers no diving (many of Halmahera's reefs are quite damaged anyway) and rudimentary accommodation that's nonetheless the only option.

Eating

Waroeng Famili INDONESIAN $
(☎0924-262 1238; Jl Kemakmuran; mains 40,000Rp) Locals push through the carved wooden doors, hunker down under pastel walls adorned with patterned fans, and scratch their heads over the choice: either *ikan bakar* (grilled fish) or *ayam goreng* (fried chicken). Both come with sambal, steamed cassava and garlic-sautéed water spinach, and both are delicious.

Pondok Indah Restaurant INDONESIAN $$
(☎0924-262 2061/1968; Jl Tobelo, Pitu Village; mains 15,000-100,000Rp; ⏲10am-10pm Mon-Sat) Technically located in Pitu village, on the southern outskirts of Tobelo, this roomy place threatens to morph into a reception/karaoke venue at night, but maintains high standards on the food front. The *ikan bakar* is a particularly fine example of the genre.

Information

There are ATMs dotted around the centre of town (the Jl Kemakmuran/Pelabuhan junction) but no exchange facilities.

Kantor Pariwisata Halmahera Utara (www.halmaherautara.com; Jl Bhayangkara, Kantor Bupati, 2nd fl; ⏲8am-noon & 1-4pm Mon-Fri) An essential depository of information on Halmahera Utara, including diving sites and guides, natural attractions and WWII relics. The charming staff speak English well, and dress in traditional Halmaheran costume on Wednesdays.

The local handicrafts on display, including patterned scarves and traditional dress, are for sale. You'll also find what tourist literature there is on the region (some in English; more in Bahasa Indonesia) and get personal recommendations for places to eat and stay. If you're looking for advice on diving sites, this is the place – they'll put you in touch with North Halmahera's two best diving guides, Messrs Yus (☎0852 4684 2579) and Firman (☎0812 4215 1172).

Getting There & Away

There are daily Kijangs to Sofifi and Jailolo (4am and 1pm; 100,000Rp) from the bemo terminal in Wosia (a 5000Rp *ojek* fare out of Tobelo) or you can charter a taxi for 500,000Rp. Bemos to Kao and Daru are 25,000Rp and 15,000Rp, respectively.

Within town, *ojeks* and *bentor* (motorcycle-rickshaws) cost 5000Rp to 10,000Rp. The nearest airport, in Galela, handles flights to Ternate.

BOATS FROM TOBELO

DESTINATION	TYPE	FARE (RP)	FREQUENCY
Bitung	Pelni	varies	2 monthly
Morotai	speedboat	100,000	8am, 9am, 10am
Morotai	speedboat	100,000	8am, 9am, 10am
Pulau Ternate	Pelni	varies	2 monthly

WORTH A TRIP

PULAU MOROTAI

A minor Japanese base during WWII, Morotai leapt to prominence when it was captured by the Allies and used to bomb Manila to bits. Among the Japanese defenders who retreated to Morotai's crumpled mountain hinterland was the famous Private Nakamura: only in 1973 did he discover that the war was over. A WWII US amphibious tank still lies rusting in a hidden palm grove, a five-minute *ojek* ride behind Morotai's village capital **Daruba**.

There are attractive palm-backed fishing beaches along the narrow **Nefelves Peninsula**, stretching south from Daruba. But for better beaches explore the array of offshore islands in Morotai's sparkling turquoise waters (day charter on a decent longboat is 400,000Rp to 750,000Rp). Speedboats leave Tobelo (Halmahera) for Morotai (100,000Rp, two hours) at 8am, 9am and 10am, and there's a *kapal motor* at 1pm (50,000Rp, four hours). They return at the same times.

South of Tobelo

The drive south from Tobelo follows a long, languid coastline, alternating between white- and black-sand beaches, simple villages and lush coconut groves which ramble to the edge of a vast mangrove estuary where black jungle rivers foam into rapids.

Pantai Karlen is a beach of strikingly pure black sand, 1km east of Pitu and 5km south of Tobelo. Around 10km further south, then 2km off the main road, **Kupa Kupa** has a white-sand swimming beach, heavily shaded with mature trees. It's very photogenic when looking north, less so looking south thanks to the Pertamina Oil Terminal next door. There's good snorkelling, just 500m north of the Pantai Kupa Kupa Cottages resort.

There's also reputedly good snorkelling off the sandy southern tip of **Pulau Bobale**, accessed by a 10,000Rp shared boat from **Daru**, the departure point for speedboats to eastern Halmahera.

A shipwrecked Japanese freighter, one of many WWII relics in the Kao region, lies just off Pantai Sosol at **Malifut**. Keep heading south, past the turn-off towards Sofifi, and you'll reach the port town of **Sidangoli**.

Sleeping

Pantai Kupa Kupa Cottages BUNGALOW **$$**
(☎0812 4477 6773; kupakupacottages@gmail.com; Kupa Kupa; bungalows/family cottages 250,000/500,000Rp) Deliciously laid-back Pantai Kupa Kupa Cottages offers plenty of reasons to stay a night or three in its rather lovely shaggy-haired Halmahera-style bungalows, decorated with Papuan handicrafts. There are also rooms in the main house with shared bathrooms and the whole property is surrounded by a lush garden.

There's a fabulous beach cafe where you can sink into a coconut-wood chair, sip superb coffee and enjoy views of the amazing Halmahera peninsula, which wraps around the bay and looks like distant bay islands.

North of Tobelo

The road north is well surfaced with several very attractive woodland sections, glimpses of coast and a fine brief view (8km) of **Dukono**, an active volcano that spewed ash over Tobelo in 2012. There are Japanese WWII cannon at **Pune** (10km), while **Luari** (13km) has a pretty horseshoe-shaped bay beach. Turning 1.5km inland at Galela (25km) you come to **Danau Galela** (aka Danau Duma), a sizeable lake lined with villages that suffered particularly in the 1999 troubles. Several burnt-out church ruins remain. Ox carts are common on the lake's 16km 'ring' road.

Eastern Halmahera

Way off the tourism radar, eastern Halmahera appeals to travellers who fancy plunging into the remote **Aketajawe-Lolobata National Park**, passes for which must be organised in advance at the office in Sofifi (p420), or in being an area's first foreigner in a generation. Deep in the riverine hinterland, at least a two-day trek from Subaim, Jarajara or Patlean, live the nomadic Togutil people. The fine sandy beach and coral reef at **Jarajara** have swimming and diving possibilities.

Boats from Tobelo run to Subaim (Tuesday and Thursday), Patlean (Sunday), Jarajara (some Tuesdays) and Maba (three weekly). If you organise in advance, you can arrange longboat transfers that allow hop-offs at intermediate villages en route.

PULAU AMBON

Maluku's most prominent island is lush and gently mountainous, indented with two great hoops of bay. Around capital Kota Ambon, villages merge into a long, green, suburban ribbon. West of the airport, this gives way to a string of charming coastal villages where, if you take the time to explore, you'll discover Ambon is not just an unavoidable step on the road to the lovely Lease, Kei and Banda Islands. In fact it's a significant underwater mecca: the bay is known for excellent muck-diving, while the southern coast has clear waters and intact coral.

The more developed southern part of Ambon is called Leitimur. It's joined to the northern Leihitu part by a narrow neck of land at Passo.

History

Until 1512 Ambon was ruled by Ternate. The sultans brought the civilising force of Islam to the island's north coast and developed Hitu Lama as a major spice-trading port. When the Portuguese displaced the Ternateans, they found Ambon's less developed, non-Islamicised south more receptive to Christianity, and built the fortress around which Kota Ambon would eventually evolve. The Portuguese never established perfect control over Ambon or the Banda nutmeg trade, and were easily displaced by the Dutch in the early 17th century. Ambon briefly served the VOC (Dutch East India Company) as its pre-Jakarta capital, and the island became the world's largest producer of cloves.

During WWII, when Kota Ambon was a Japanese military headquarters, Allied bombing destroyed most of its once-attractive colonial architecture. In 1950, the island was briefly the centre of the southern Malukan independence movement, extinguished within a few months by the Indonesian military.

From 1999 until mid-2002, Ambon was ripped apart by Christian–Muslim intercommunal violence, leaving Kota Ambon looking like 1980s Beirut. After a stable nine years or so, which allowed for a strong economic resurgence that wiped away almost every visible scar of that tragic era, there were once again frayed nerves. In both 2011 and early 2012 sectarian violence flared, showing the persistent Muslim–Christian divide beneath the veneer of peace. But while the darkest years were organised and overwhelming, these were only a handful of guys on either side, throwing bottles and rocks at each other, and (mostly) missing, while everyone else got on with their lives.

Pulau Ambon

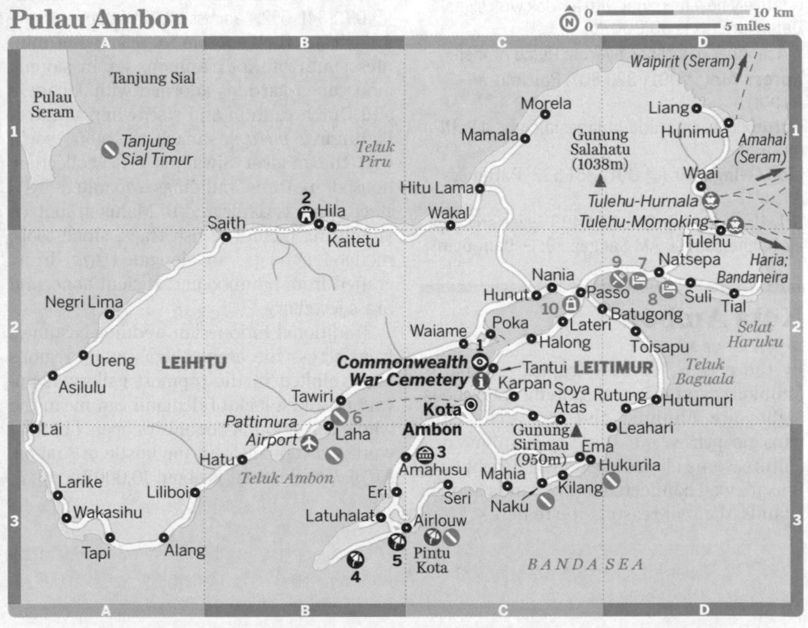

Pulau Ambon

Getting There & Away

Ambon's airport, Bandara Pattimura, has a relatively new terminal with a weak wi-fi signal. Departure tax is 30,000Rp.

A number of airlines fly from Pulau Ambon.

Xpress Air (☎0911-323 807; Pattimura Airport)

Garuda (www.garuda-indonesia.com; Jl Pattimura 5)

Lion/Wings Air (☎0911-351 532; Pattimura Airport)

Sriwijaya Air (☎0911-354 498; www.sriwijayaair-online.com; Jl AM Sangaji 79; ⏲9am-6pm)

Kota Ambon

☎0911 / POP 331,000

By the region's dreamy tropical standards, Maluku's capital is a throbbing metropolis. Sights are minimal and the architecture wins no prizes, but there is a unique cafe culture, some choice sleeps and decent food. Plus it's well connected to the Banda and Kei Islands, the real reasons you're here.

Sights

★Commonwealth War Cemetery CEMETERY
(Tantui) Known to locals as the 'Australian Cemetery', this trim and neatly manicured cemetery was designed by a British landscape architect in honour of Allied servicemen who died in Maluku and the Celebes in WWII. Adding poignancy, it's built on the site of a former POW camp.

Benteng Victoria FORTRESS
Undramatic Benteng Victoria (out of bounds due to army use) is a Dutch-era fortress. The site of Indonesian national hero Pattimura's hanging, it's fronted by a gilded statue of Slamet Riyadi, an Indonesian commander who died retaking the place in 1950.

Masjid Raya al-Fatah MOSQUE
(Jl Sultan Babullah) The town's biggest mosque, Masjid Raya al-Fatah is a modern concrete affair, its gold-and-brown onion dome visible across much of central Ambon.

Francis Xavier Cathedral CHURCH
(Jl Pattimura) FREE Named for the Basque missionary who visited Maluku in the 16th century, Francis Xavier Cathedral has a facade crusted with saint statues and glimmering steeples.

Museum Siwalima MUSEUM
(☎0911-341 652; admission 10,000Rp; ⏲8am-4.30pm Mon-Fri, 10am-3pm Sat & Sun) Ten minutes south of Kota Ambon, set in sloping landscaped gardens adorned with Japanese and Dutch cannon and a scowling statue of Pattimura, *parang* (machete) aloft, you'll find the modest Siwalima. The collection, housed in three buildings separated by a steep road, is dedicated to Malukan material culture, including fish traps, stone tools, model longboats, an elongated *tifa* drum, crafted from bamboo and ancient bone, and brass jewellery.

Traditional Indonesian wedding costumes from across the archipelago's many regions are exhibited in the topmost gallery. Renovations and a lack of demand can mean the whole collection is not always open, but it's a worthy diversion from the hustle of Ambon. An *ojek* to the door is about 10,000Rp.

Kota Ambon

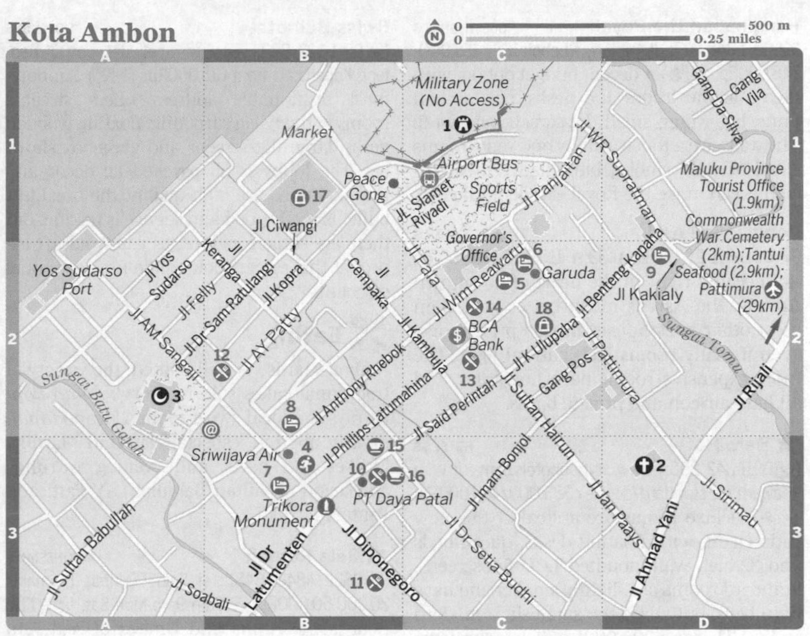

Activities

Aside from idling in *rumah kopi* (coffee houses) and plotting your escape to the Banda or Kei Islands, there's not a great deal to do in Ambon.

Nakamura SPA

(☎0911-345 557; www.nakamura-info.com; Jl Phillips Latumahina SK 5/7; treatments 60,000-215,000Rp; ⏰10am-10pm; ❄) This Japanese-style spa, replete with gurgling fountains, trilling birdsong and rice-paper massage cubicles, is the ideal antidote to the sweat and bustle of Ambon. They take their acupressure and shiatsu therapy seriously here, even checking your blood pressure before getting down to business.

Sleeping

Ambon has recently benefited from a growth in choice, affordable accommodation.

Penginapan the Royal GUESTHOUSE $
(☎0911-348 077; Jl Anthony Rhebok 1D; r 165,000-248,000Rp; ❄📶) A decent budget option, with Ikea-chic wardrobes and desks, new air-con units, hot water, small flat-screens and wi-fi. The walls are a touch grubby and some rooms smell of stale smoke, but unadvertised discounts can make the Royal excellent value.

Penginapan Asri GUESTHOUSE $
(☎0911-311 217; Jl Baru 33; r 110,000-180,000Rp; ❄) Located right in the heart of downtown Ambon, the Asri is much better kept than most other guesthouses in this price range, even if many rooms lack natural light. The more expensive rooms have hot water, and all have air-con and private baths.

★**Hero Hotel** HOTEL $$
(☎0911-342 898; www.cityhubhotels.com; Jl Wim Reawaru 7B; standard/deluxe r 385,000/480,000Rp; ❄📶) Deluxe rooms are a steal at this new Indo chain, with floating desks, queen beds and 32-inch wall-mounted LCD flat-screens. Standard rooms are slightly smaller and have twin beds, but share the same slick, modern styling. There's a 200,000Rp cash security deposit upon check-in, and wi-fi throughout the hotel. Breakfast is 25,000Rp extra.

Orchid Hotel HOTEL $$
(☎0911-346 363; Jl Pattimura 5; standard/superior r 350,000/400,000Rp; ❄📶) Sharing a lobby with Garuda's Ambon office, the Orchid is another of the city's terrific-value modern sleeps. It has large rooms with high ceilings, wood furnishings, queen beds, minibar, wi-fi and ample natural light. The friendly reception staff also sell Ambon Manise ('Sweet Ambon') T-shirts and souvenirs.

Swiss-Belhotel HOTEL $$$
(☎0911-322 888; www.swiss-belhotel.com; Jl Benteng Kapaha; d from 615,000Rp; ❄📶) Ambon's most fashionable address offers sizeable rooms with stylish carpeting, floating wooden desks, large flat-screens and glass-box showers. The lobby is all psychedelic decor and muzak, linens are high quality, the breakfast buffet is really good and service is terrific. But there are some rough edges you wouldn't expect at this price. Book online for substantial discounts.

Eating

Ambon Manise is well named: the variety of traditional cakes sold in every *rumah kopi* betrays the local sweet tooth. Cheap *rumah makan* abound, especially around Mardika Market and ports, and evening warungs appear on Jl Sultan Babullah, AY Patti and Pantai Mardika.

★**Beta Rumah** INDONESIAN $
(☎0822 4840 5481; Jl Said Perintah 1; mains 20,000-50,000Rp; ⏲9am-9pm Mon-Sat; 🖉) The Beta is the Alpha and Omega of real Ambonese food. Laid out in simple *rumah makan* style beneath a glass sneeze shield, you'll find local delicacies such as *kohu-kohu*, made with smoked skipjack tuna, green beans and shaved coconut, or squid with papaya leaves, steamed in a banana leaf with *kenari* nuts and *colo colo* (citrus dip).

Rumah Makan Nifia INDONESIAN $
(Jl AY Patti 66; meals 15,000-30,000Rp; ⏲9am-9pm Mon-Sat) A superior pick-and-mix warung with alarming lime-and-orange decor and a devoted following. Dishes are fresh, rotate frequently, and include several varieties of

THE MALUKAN PALATE

Despite what you'll see in most restaurants, Maluku's traditional staple isn't rice but *kasbi* (boiled cassava) or *papeda* (sago congee, called *popeda* in Ternate), a thick, colourless, sodium-packed goo that you ladle into plates of *kuah ikan* (fish soup), then suck down as though trying to swallow a live jellyfish. Odd, but surprisingly good when accompanied with *sayur garu* (papaya flower), *kohu-kohu* (smoked fish with green beans and fresh coconut), *papari* (a unique mixed vegetable), *keladi*-root, and cassava leaf. For protein, fish and seafood are king, typically served with a chilli, shallot and citrus dip called *colo colo* or *dabu dabu*.

Originally unique to the Banda Islands, the spice-yielding kernel of nutmeg *(pala)* grows within a fruit that itself makes deliciously tart jams and distinctive sweet 'wine', available at Ambon's Sibu-Sibu cafe (p427). Nutmeg grows best in the shade of magnificent *kenari* trees, which themselves yield an almond-like nut (used locally in confectionery and sauces) and timber (for *kora kora* canoes). *Kenari*-nut chunks also float atop *rarobang*, a distinctive hot spiced coffee.

roasted and baked fish, fried chicken, fried tempeh, curried and stir-fried vegetables, beef *rendang* (cooked in spicy coconut milk), and a tasty *soto ayam* (chicken soup), ideal for monsoon season.

Tantui Seafood SEAFOOD $
(☎0852 3223 7888; Jl Tantui; mains from 25,000Rp; ⊙11am-11pm; ❄) Sit inside on faintly silly, bow-wrapped chairs or out on the waterside terrace for generous portions of shrimp-rich nasi goreng or spicy squid *(cumi bakar)*. A little out of town, but well situated on the bay.

Sarinda BAKERY $
(☎0911-355 109; Jl Sultan Hairun 11; pastries from 6500Rp; ⊙8am-9.30pm) With its lovely Dutch-colonial windows, ample garden seating and central location, this is a great place to select pastries presented on dozens of oven-warm racks. Now that it also does coffee, it's perfect for a late-morning fuel-stop.

Ratu Gurih SEAFOOD $$
(☎0911-341 202, 0813 4338 8883; Jl Diponegoro 26; meals 35,000-190,000Rp; ⊙9am-11pm Mon-Sat; 📶) It has fluorescent tiles and the atmosphere is bland, but the fish – perfectly grilled by the coal-stoking chef, smothered in chilli and served alongside three tasty sambals – is fall-off-the-bone fresh. If you're tired of Indonesian fare, it offers Chinese, Thai and Japanese choices too. Try the *tom yam* (spicy, clear soup) or get fancy with lobster.

Sari Gurih SEAFOOD $$
(☎0911-341 888; Jl PH Latumahina; mains 35,000-80,000Rp; ⊙9am-11pm) More like a Western idea of a restaurant than is common in Maluku – complete with more Western clientele and prices – Sari Gurih is nonetheless a great place to eat Malukan seafood. Ice-chests keep the catch fresh while the grill never stops. Unfortunately, in the evenings, neither does the karaoke. Accepts cards.

Drinking & Nightlife

Although proper bars are *instiututa non-grata* in sweaty old Ambon, you must tip your cap to a town that embraces cafe culture. *Rumah kopi* (coffee houses), each with their own (often eccentric) style, abound.

★**Sibu-Sibu** CAFE
(☎0911-312 525; Jl Said Perintah 47A; snacks from 3000Rp, breakfasts from 20,000Rp; ⊙7am-10pm; 📶) Ambonese stars of screen and song deck the walls of this sweet little coffee shop, which plays Malukan and Hawaiian music to accompany local snacks such as the wonderful *koyabu* (cassava cake, 3000Rp), and *lopis pulut* (sticky rice with palm jaggery). It also has free wi-fi, good full breakfasts, fried breadfruit that you'll dip into melted palm sugar, and rocket-fuelled ginger coffee.

Kopi Tradisi Joas CAFE
(☎0911-341 518; Jl Said Perintah; coffee 5000-11,000Rp; ⊙7.30am-8.30pm Mon-Sat) There's a convivial murmur throughout this local institution, where bigwigs talk politics for hours over rich mocha-style 'secret-recipe' coffees and slices of deep-fried breadfruit (*sukun goreng*, 2000Rp). Get a table out back, under the avocado tree, away from the fumes of the *jalan*.

Shopping

Plaza Ambon MALL
(Jl Sam Ratulangi; ⊙9am-10pm) Plaza Ambon is the city's cross between a proper shopping mall and old-school market. In addition to byzantine market stalls, it has the requisite fast-food choices, a Matahari store, and a big Foodmart grocer for self-caterers.

Ambon City Center MALL
(☎0911-362 957; amboncitycenter.cs@gmail.com; Jl Wolter Monginsidi; ⊙8am-10pm) Don't be fooled by the name: the shiny new Ambon City Center is actually in Passo, some way out of town. It's the biggest mall in Maluku, and the place to reconnect with your favourite brands or stock up on groceries at its enormous Hypermart. It's also a reassuring sign of normality and progress to the strife-weary Ambonese.

Ud Inti ALCOHOL
(Jl K Ulupaha; ⊙8am-9pm) A tiny, blink-and-you'll-miss-it minimart, this is one of only two places in town where you can buy beer, apart from in a restaurant. It even has Guinness.

Information

Change or withdraw enough money in Ambon for trips to outlying islands where there are no exchange facilities. ATMs are sprinkled throughout bustling, mercantile Ambon.

BCA Bank (Bank Central Asia; Jl Sultan Hairun 24; ⊙9am-3pm Mon-Fri) Exchanges euros and Australian and US dollars from 10am, but you may have to wait. Its battalion of ATMs allows 2,500,000Rp or 1,250,000Rp withdrawals, depending on denomination.

Maluku Province Tourist Office (Dinas Pariwisata; ☎0911-312 300; Jl Jenderal Sudirman; ⏰8am-4pm Mon-Fri) A handy source of info on Ambon, the Bandas, Seram and other neighbouring islands, some in English.

PT Daya Patal (☎0911-353 344; spicetr@gmail.com; Jl Said Perintah 53A; ⏰9am-7pm Mon-Sat) Ever-obliging agency with several knowledgeable English-speaking staff. Sells airline, speedboat and Pelni tickets and can advise on schedules to the Banda and Kei Islands. Charges 50,000Rp commission on ticket sales, and occasionally opens Sundays.

Reno.net (Jl Sultan Babullah; per hr 5000Rp; ⏰10am-midnight) Across from Ambon's Grand Mosque, Reno.net is central and reliable for internet access.

Tourist Info Desk (☎0813 4302 8872; erenst_michael@yahoo.co.id; Pattimura Airport, Arrivals Hall; ⏰Mon-Sat) An unmarked but useful desk, straight ahead once you leave baggage claim, and open to meet flights. The desk is run by Michael, Ambon's greatest ambassador. He has reams of information for you, a ready smile and an inexpensive nearby homestay. If you're after information, he's the island's best source.

Getting There & Away

Road transport (including buses to Seram via the Hunimua car ferry) starts from various points along Jl Pantai Mardika. For Natsepa (5000Rp), Tulehu-Momoking (7000Rp) and Tulehu-Hurnala (10,000Rp) take Waai or Darussalam bemos. Latuhalat (5000Rp) and Amahusu bemos also pick up passengers beside the Trikora monument on Jl Dr Latumenten.

Getting Around

TO/FROM THE AIRPORT

Pattimura Airport is 37km round the bay from central Kota Ambon. Hatu- and Liliboi-bound bemos pass the airport gates (10,000Rp, 70 minutes from Mardika). There is a ferry (per person/motorbike/car 2000/5000/20,000Rp) across Teluk Ambon to the airport side of the bay. If you time it right and use the ferry and an *ojek*, it would be comfortable and inexpensive (80,000Rp), so worth considering. A taxi costs up to 200,000Rp to/from the airport. A new bridge is expected to connect the airport directly with the city centre; at research time it was still incomplete.

TRANSPORT FROM PULAU AMBON

Air

DESTINATION	AIRLINE	FREQUENCY
Bandaneira	Susi	3 weekly
Jakarta	Lion/Wings Air, Garuda, Sriwijaya	daily
Langgur	Garuda, Lion/Wings Air	daily
Makassar	Lion/Wings Air, Garuda	daily
Sorong	Garuda, Lion/Wings Air, Xpress Air	daily
Ternate	Garuda, Xpress Air	3 weekly

Boat

DESTINATION	PORT	TYPE	FARE (RP)	FREQUENCY
Amahai (Pulau Seram)	Tulehu	Bahari Express	economy/VIP 91,000/150,000	9am, 4pm daily
Bandaneira	Tulehu	Bahari Express	economy/VIP 300,000/400,000	2 weekly
Haria (Pulau Saparua)	Tulehu	Bahari Express	economy/VIP 50,000/75,000	8am daily
Haria (Pulau Saparua)	Tulehu-Momoking	speedboat	30,000	when full
Papus	Kota Ambon	Pelni	varies	2 weekly
Tual	Kota Ambon	Pelni	varies	2 weekly
Waipirit (Pulau Seram)	Hunimua	car ferry	varies	3 daily

There is also an **airport bus** (per person 35,000Rp) that leaves from landward side of the Peace Gong four times daily (4.30am, 5am, 10am and 1pm – timed to feed airline departures). It departs from the airport for the city centre after the inbound flights land (approximately 7am, 8am, 1pm and 4pm).

BEMO

Green bemos circulate within the city centre and blue bemos head out of town. Traffic jams near Mardika Market (the terminus) can be bad – consider getting off 200m away.

Ultrafrequent Lin III bemos *(mobils)* head southwest down Jl Pantai Mardika and either Jl Dr Sam Ratulangi or Jl AY Patty, swinging around the Trikora monument onto Jl Dr Latumenten. After 2km they loop back via Jl Sultan Babullah and Jl Yos Sudarso.

Tantui bemos run northeast from Mardika, passing the Commonwealth War Cemetery and Tantui Seafood, then looping back past the tourist office.

Southern Leitimur

Latuhalat straddles a low pass culminating in a pair of popular, well-shaded 'Sunday beaches' – **Santai** (admission 2000Rp) and **Namalatu** (admission 2000Rp). Neither offers great swimming but both have hotels. Walk between the two in 15 minutes or take a *becak* (bicycle-rickshaw). No dive operations are based here anymore, but coral sites off the southern coast can be reached with Maluku Divers (p431) or Blue Rose (p430), both based on Teluk Ambon.

Getting There & Away

Green 'Lt Halat' bemos from Kota Ambon (5000Rp, 40 minutes) run to Namalatu along a pretty waterside road through Eri.

Eastern Leihitu

Teluk Baguala and **Natsepa** beach are two of eastern Leihitu's beauty spots, popular with the locals for weekend swims and roadside *rujak* (fruit salad in a spicy chilli, tamarind and shrimp-paste dressing).

Waai is famous for its 'lucky' *bulut* (moray eels). For 10,000Rp, a 'guide' tempts the eels from dark recesses in a concrete-sided pond (Jl Air Waysikaka) by feeding them raw eggs. To find the pond, take a Waai bemo and get off one block before the thatched *baileu* (open hut), and head two blocks inland.

Bemos from Mardika (Kota Ambon) run frequently to Waai and Tulehu, via Natsepa (5000Rp to 10,000Rp).

Activities

Dive into Ambon DIVING
(http://diveintoambon.com; The Natsepa; 3 dives with lunch US$160; ⏲Sep-Jun) Based at the swanky Natsepa, Dive into Ambon has more direct access to the coral sites of the island's southern coast than Ambon's other operators. It also takes its big, covered, wi-fi-equipped boats into the bay to get into the muck with the critters.

Sleeping & Eating

Baguala Bay Resort RESORT $$
(☎0911-362 717; www.bagualabayresort.wordpress.com; Jl Raya Waitatiri; deluxe r 350,000, cottage 450,000Rp; ❄@≋) Family-friendly Baguala Bay Resort is set around a swimming pool in a lovely waterfront palm garden, especially enchanting at night. Rooms are outwardly nice with close proximity to the sea, though they can be musty; cottages are larger and fresher. Baguala also has a good-value seafront cafe serving Western and local food, and runs a superb retreat in Seram.

It was closed for renovations at the time of research.

★**The Natsepa** RESORT $$$
(☎0911-362 555; www.thenatsepa.com; Jl Raya Natsepa 36; r/ste 890,000/1,800,000Rp; ❄📶≋) With a stylish lobby big enough for local birds to take exercise, big modern rooms tricked out in custard and apricot decor, and carefully-tended lawns meeting a stunning bay location, the Natsepa is Ambon's best hotel. It also has the in-house Dive into Ambon dive centre, open to outsiders and well placed for the limpid coral waters of southern Leitimur.

Some rooms can smell damp, and the four-star polish is a little worn in some corners, but those seeking an international hotel experience, complete with satellite TV, wi-fi (LAN in the rooms) and an endless (if slightly lacklustre) breakfast buffet shouldn't be too disappointed.

Gaba Gaba INDONESIAN $
(Jl Propinsi; mains 20-35Rp; ⏲10am-10pm) The friendly, spanking-new Gaba Gaba 'resto-cafe' makes great use of stunning bay views, serving good Indo-Chinese grub in a scattering of wooden pagodas shaded by coconut palms. The menu of grilled fish, rice and noodles may

be familiar, but the setting, complete with kids' play equipment and a view of fishermen casting their nets in Natsepa bay, is delightful.

Northern & Western Leihitu

Western Leihitu is home to some of Ambon's most picturesque and archetypal coastal villages.

Laha is a cute, quaint, almost prim little town. It has small concrete houses brushed in pastels, fenced-in front yards blooming with flowers, and a mangrove-shrouded natural harbour right in front of Pondok Patra guesthouse. It's also the hub of muck-diving in Ambon, and is handy for the airport. If you're here to dive, and seeking an alternative to the Kota Ambon bustle, this is it.

In **Alang**, at the southern tip of Leihitu, a traditional thatched *baileu*, rebuilt in 2004, sports a carved crocodile. In photogenic **Wakasihu** village, elders while the day away at seaside platforms, with views of an offshore, tree-topped mini-island.

A sharper rock shard appears at the roadside beyond **Larike**, where there are 30 to 40 massive eels living under a big boulder in the river. Before you arrive, buy some sardines in the market, so you can lure them to the surface. Compared to the concrete pool and raw-egg feeding in Waai, this is a much more beautiful and natural setting in which to observe them, and you can even walk in the river beside them. The village charges 5000Rp per person for the eel tour.

In north **Asilulu** there are multiple boat racks and fine views across to Seram's Tanjung Sial. Offshore lies **Pulau Tiga**, a trio of islands around which lie several diving and snorkelling spots.

In **Hila**, the 1649 **Benteng Amsterdam** (20,000Rp; ⏲8am-6pm) is an impressive, old, walled fort. Though the walls are obviously rebuilt with concrete, the inner tower, with its brick floors and thick walls, is fluttering with resident swallows. Gates were open when we visited but you may have to seek out the keymaster in town. About a block from here you'll find **Gereja Tua Hila**, an ancient, all-wood, thatched Catholic church, built by the Portuguese. It's closed to the public but is still a good photo op. A five-minute walk further inland, and then across a school football field, is Kaitetu's pretty little thatch-roofed **Mesjid Wapaue**. Originally built in 1414 on nearby Gunung Wawane, the mosque was supposedly transferred to the present site in 1664 by 'supernatural powers'.

Activities

Dive Bluemotion DIVING
(☎0812 3871 9813; www.dive-bluemotion.com; Laha; 1 dive/1 day's equipment 330,000/150,000Rp; ⏲Sep-May) Banda's Bluemotion has now set up shop in Laha, lured by Teluk Ambon's critters and the folks who'll pay to see them. With perhaps the Bay's best dive site on its doorstep, Bluemotion gives its divers greater freedom to come and go at their leisure. The more you dive, the less you pay.

Blue Rose Divers DIVING
(☎0852 5462 3354; www.bluerosedivers.com; Jl Laha; 1 dive 350,000Rp; ⏲Sep-Apr; ❄) Blue Rose has relocated to Laha on Ambon Bay, although it will still take groups to visit the coral south of Leitimur, weather and fuel surcharge permitting. It's a local operation, the cheapest way to dive Laha, Pulau Tiga,

DIVING AMBON

Ambon's wide urban bay – as deep as 500m in some places – and abundance of underwater life make it a celebrated muck-diving location. There are as many as 30 dive sites within the bay alone, plus 16 reef dives around the coast and nearby **Tiga Islands**.

Highlights include coral-crusted volcanic pinnacles off **Mahia**, the blue hole at **Hukurila**, a huge underwater arch at **Pintu Kota**, and the **Duke of Sparta shipwreck**, which was allegedly sunk by the CIA in 1958. Also, during action-packed drift dives between the Tiga Islands you'll meet bumphead parrotfish, Napoleons, dogtooth tuna, vast schools of fusiliers, dolphins, sharks and turtles. You can also glimpse the big stuff at **Tanjung Sial Timur** (Bad Corner), where strong currents attract pelagic fish off the southern tip of Seram.

But as special as those sites can be, it's the muck that draws the crowds for such oddities as the psychedelic frogfish, 15 varieties of rhinopia, manta shrimp, zebra crabs, banded pipefish, pygmy squid and seahorses. Plan your trip between October and April.

the WWII wreck off Waiame, and the other delights Ambon has to offer. It also has basic, clean accommodation (standard/deluxe room 300,000/400,000Rp).

Maluku Divers DIVING
(www.divingmaluku.com; Jl Air Manis, Laha; 2/3 dives US$115/155; reef/island surcharge US$15/20; ⏲Sep–late May) Maluku Divers is the most professionally run operation in Ambon, and is largely responsible for embedding Ambon into the greater scuba zeitgeist. Its local and expat divemasters know thc spots intimately, and its brand-new resort, geared to serious divers and underwater photographers, is marvellous. It isn't cheap, however it does accept day trippers.

The private deck out front offers capacity for 20 divers, with a maximum of seven per dive boat. It also now has a private jetty, once the only thing missing from the slickest diving operation in Maluku. Non-guests can pay per dive (from US$65).

Sleeping & Eating

Several simple options cater for travellers taking early flights from Pattimura Airport, or diving in Ambon Bay.

Penginapan Michael HOMESTAY $
(☎0813 4302 8872; erenst_michael@yahoo.co.id; Jl Propinsi, Laha; r 100,000Rp) Opposite the runway, this homestay is run by the ever warm and welcoming Michael, Ambon's finest tourism ambassador. In addition to his duties at the tourist info desk (p428) in baggage claim, he offers three tidy rooms just a short *ojek* ride, or longer stroll, to the terminal. Rooms share a bathroom, and include breakfast.

Pondok Patra GUESTHOUSE $
(☎0813 4323 0559; Laha; r 150,000-300,000Rp; ❄) Hidden in quaint Laha village, Pondok Patra has a pleasant little rear sitting area on stilts, overlooking a boat-and-mangrove-filled inlet. You can stay here and dive with one of the three operations based in town.

★**Maluku Divers** RESORT $$$
(☎0911-336 5307; www.divingmaluku.com; Jl Raya Air Manis, Laha; all-inclusive per person US$285; bungalow US$145; garden-view r US$95; ⏲Sep-Jun; ❄📶) Snuggled on a palm-dappled sliver of coastline near the mouth of the bay in Laha, Maluku Divers offers quality chalets and 'garden-view' rooms with timber ceilings, ceiling fans, air-con, turbo hot-water showers and two desks. The price includes three dives per day.

In addition, there are professional-grade camera and equipment rooms, excellent dive photography throughout, and lovely lounge and dining areas with dangling lanterns, icy beer, tasty cuisine, and excellent service.

Getting There & Away

Bemos (5000Rp) leave from Hunut to Hila and from Kota Ambon to Liliboi. To close the loop, charter an *ojek* from near the airport. The road is mostly new asphalt, but landslides are relatively frequent in monsoon season, which means circumnavigation doesn't always pan out.

LEASE ISLANDS

☎0931

Pronounced 'leh-*a*-say', these conveniently accessible yet delightfully laid-back islands have a scattering of old-world villages, lovely bays, and a couple of great-value budget beach retreats. Foreign tourists remain very rare and little English is spoken, but Saparua has some existing tourism inroads.

Pulau Saparua

Saparua is the island escape of choice for the Ambonese, and it's easy to see why. Blessed with good coral- and muck-diving, significant historical remains, white beaches and dense forests, it's also only 90 minutes from Tulehu.

Getting There & Away

Predawn speedboats run from Itawaka (50,000Rp) to Tulehu-Momoking (Ambon) and from Ihamahu (50,000Rp, one hour) to Namano near Masohi (Seram). Arrive from 4.30am, get your name on the passenger list, and then pay for the ticket when your name is called.

From Haria to Ambon, Bahari Express runs an 8am *kapal motor* (economy/VIP 50,000/75,000Rp, two hours) and during the dry season there are also several speedboats (mostly early morning, 30,000Rp, leave when full). During monsoon months there is just the one daily boat, and waves do crash over the bow, so get that VIP ticket.

Kota Saparua

Suffused with durian musk, the ramshackle, jungle-island town of Kota Saparua has an extremely friendly countenance, and charm aplenty. Along Jl Muka Pasar are a few *rumah makan,* the **market** (Jl Muka Pasar; ⏲Wed & Sat) and a Telkom building, directly behind which is the **bemo terminal** (Jl Belakang).

Lease Islands

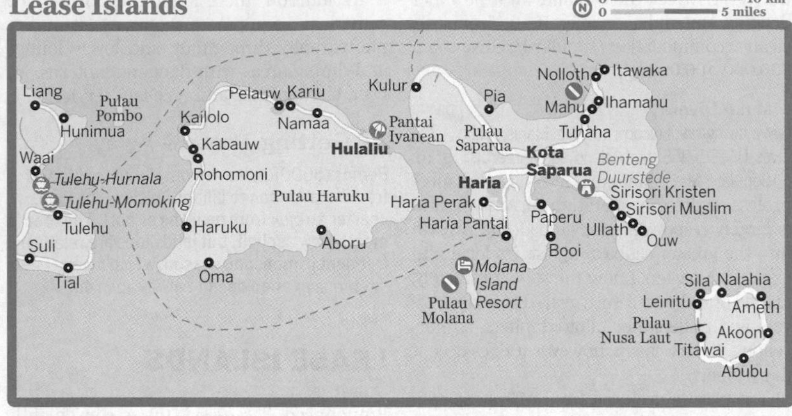

Sights

Benteng Duurstede FORTRESS

FREE The low-walled 1676 Benteng Duurstede, famously besieged by Pattimura in 1817, has been refaced with mouldering grey concrete, but the (locked) gateway is original and the cannon-studded ramparts survey a gorgeous sweep of turquoise bay.

Sleeping & Eating

Penginapan Mandiri GUESTHOUSE $

(☎0931-21063; Jl Muka Pasar; r with fan/air-con 110,000/132,000Rp; ❄) Adjacent to the market, and on the 2nd floor, Mandiri is the town's newest choice. Rooms are all cheerily painted and have spotless *mandis* and Disney cabinetry. No, seriously. Its greatest asset is the gorgeous terrace overlooking the fort and the bay beyond.

Penginapan Lease Indah GUESTHOUSE $

(☎0931-21069; Jl Muka Pasar; d 120,000-220,000Rp; ❄) The Penginapan Lease Indah is a sleepy garden guesthouse haunted by chickens and butterflies the size of bats. Opt for a basic, clean and fan-cooled, tiled room in the old wing, over those in the gaudy, columned new building (unless you must have TV, air-con and hot water).

RM Dulang Radja INDONESIAN $

(Jl Muka Pasar; mains 15,000-27,000Rp; ⊙10am-10pm Mon-Sat) Fronted by by an ornamental longboat, this open-sided *rumah makan* doesn't stray from the repertoire of Indonesian staples, but does those well. The *nasi ikan telur* (rice with egg, fresh tuna, tempeh and beans) is a good, healthy option.

Getting There & Away

Kota Saparua's access port is Haria (where you'll find an interesting *baileu*). From Kota Saparua *ojek* fares include Haria (10,000Rp), Itawaka (15,000Rp), Ouw (20,000Rp) and Kulur (35,000Rp). If you can manage to find a bemo, it will cost 5000Rp for most places.

Mahu

There's good muck-diving off Mahu in Saparua's north.

Sleeping

★**Mahu Lodge** LODGE $

(☎0811 977 232; mahu_lodge@yahoo.com; per person half-board 175,000Rp; ❄) The 15-room Mahu Lodge, set in the mangrove fishing village of Mahu, offers basic, tiled and very clean rooms. The price includes breakfast and dinner, and the concrete jetty offers easy swimming access in a placid bay. There's no coral, but good muck-diving (two tanks 800,000Rp to 1,000,000Rp), and the chance to see dolphins, sharks and (in January and February) sperm whales.

It also has a full-fledged dive operation (September to April), a dive boat that will get you to the stunning reefs of Nusa Laut, Itawaka and Pulau Molana, a pool for dive instruction, and snorkelling gear for hire (30,000Rp to 50,000Rp). The resort is owned by an English speaker born locally, though he lived and worked for much of his life in Jakarta. Check its Facebook page for information.

Around Pulau Saparua

Nolloth in the island's northeast has Saparua's most impressive *baileu*, and some beautiful beaches with views to Seram

On the southeastern flank, **Ullath** also has a traditional *baileu*, while **Ouw** boasts a small tumbledown fort, and is famous for its elegantly simple pottery *(sempe)*. None is obviously on show but any local can lead you to a workshop, where 10,000Rp to 20,000Rp is a reasonable donation to watch sweet *ibu* throw pots in back-porch studios, serenaded by the surf. Their clay comes from Saparua's mountain, it's spun on a wheel, sculpted with a thick chunk of green papaya, and tamped at the rim with a bamboo rod.

Pulau Molana

Uninhabited, roadless Pulau Molana has several great diving spots. There's great swimming on soft white sand at the island's northernmost tip, while directly west a coral wall offers excellent snorkelling.

Sleeping

★ **Molana Island Resort** BUNGALOW $$$
(☎0813 4307 7423, 0817 762 833; www.molanaisland.com; 3 nights per person US$178) This blissful island hideaway, which only opens its three bungalows in the dry season when guests are expected, would be ideal for a small group of friends. The resort can arrange everything: meals, transfers from Haria or Ambon, boats to dive sites – and fishing trips, jungle treks and beachside barbecues are all enticing possibilities.

PULAU SERAM

☎0914

Some Malukans call Seram 'Nusa Ina' (Mother Island), believing that all life sprang from 'Nunusaku', a mythical peak ambiguously located in the island's western mountains. The best known of Seram's indigenous minority tribes, the Nua-ulu (Upper River) or Alifuro people, sport red-bandana headgear and were headhunters as recently as the 1940s. The tribe lives in Seram's wild, mountainous interior where thick forests are alive with cockatoos and colourful parrots. Seeing them usually requires a masochistic trek into the remote Manusela National Park, for which you'll need guides and extra permits. Seram's greatest tourist attraction is dramatic Teluk Sawai on the northern coast.

Getting There & Away

The Amahai-bound *Bahari Express* (economy/VIP 120,000/255,000Rp, 2½ hours) depart Tulehu-Hurnala (Ambon) at 9am and 4pm, returning at 8am and 2pm (no Sunday service). Grab an *ojek* into Masohi (10,000Rp), then hop a Masohi–Sawai Kijang (per person/vehicle 150,000/700,000Rp, 2½ hours). You can also make the Masohi–Sawai run by *ojek* (around 200,000Rp), with insane jungle views en route. If you're headed to Ora Beach Resort (p435), get off in Saleman village, and hop on a small motorboat from there to your secluded bay retreat. By prior arrangement management can also arrange private transport in a Kijang from the Amahai harbour to Saleman village, where you'll meet the boat.

Pulau Seram

PATTIMURA & TIAHAHU

In 1817, the Dutch faced a small but emotionally charged uprising led by Thomas Matulessy, who briefly managed to gain control of Saparua's Benteng Duurstede (p432). He killed all the fortress defenders but spared a six-year-old Dutch boy. For this 'mercy' Matulessy was popularly dubbed Pattimura ('big-hearted'). The rebels were rapidly defeated and dispatched to the gallows but have since been immortalised as symbols of anticolonial resistance. Today, their statues dot the whole of Maluku and Pattimura even features on Indonesia's 1000Rp banknotes.

A much-romanticised heroine of the same saga is Martha Christina Tiahahu, whose father supported Pattimura. After his execution on Nusa Laut, Martha was put on a ship to Java but, grief-stricken, she starved herself to death. Her remains were thrown into the sea but her memory lingers on.

Masohi, Namano & Amahai

Masohi, the purpose-built capital of Central Maluku, is only really useful to travellers as a transport interchange. There's a warnet (internet cafe), modest shopping mall, bemo terminal and several ATMs. The main street, Jl Soulissa, becomes Jl Martha Tiahahu as it continues 6km through Namano to Amahai.

Sleeping & Eating

Hotel-Restaurant Isabela HOTEL $
(☎0914-22637; Jl Manusela 17; s with fan 95,000-105,000Rp, d with air-con from 205,000Rp; ❄🏊) The Isabela's cracked concrete forecourt doesn't look promising, but its comfortable 'executive' rooms have windows, hot showers and settee seating. A sizeable swimming pool, open to nonguests, is plonked oddly in the car park.

Penginapan Irene GUESTHOUSE $
(☎0914-21238; Jl MC Tiahahu; r with fan/air-con 135,000/330,000Rp; ❄) The Irene (pronounced 'ee-reh-neh') is friendly, professionally run and suffers less road noise than most. Many cheaper rooms are windowless; it's worth the extra for the nicer ones. Look it up on Facebook.

Afsal INDONESIAN $
(Jl Binaya; mains 18,000-35,000Rp; ⌚7.30am-10.30pm) This clean, slightly upscale pick-and-mix joint has Masohi's most appealing interior with solid black furniture, mirrored wall panels and chequerboard floors. The food's not bad either.

Information

Central Maluku Tourist Office (Dinas Kebudayan & Parawisata; ☎0914-21462; Jl Imam Bonjol; ⌚8am-2pm Mon-Sat) The staff are friendly, but there's little information on offer in either spoken or written English. This is the place to begin the three-stage application for permits to visit Manusela National Park.

Northern Seram

Seram's most accessible scenic highlight is **Teluk Sawai**, a beautiful wide bay backed by soaring cliffs and rugged, forested peaks. Hidden from the best views by a headland, the photogenic stilt-house village of **Sawai** is a great place to unwind and contemplate the moonlit sea.

Snorkelling is possible in offshore coral gardens (bring your own gear) though the reefs show signs of bomb-fishing damage. Other possible activities include boat rides to **Pulau Raja** or to the bay's spectacular western side, where dramatic cliffs rise up above the picturesque village of **Saleman**. It's famed for flocks of bat-like Lusiala birds, which emerge at dusk, supposedly bearing the souls of human ancestors. En route, tempting little **Ora** is a handkerchief of marvellously spongy, white-sand beach, where you'll find Seram's very best nest, the Ora Beach Resort.

Sleeping

Penginapan Lisar Bahari HOMESTAY $
(☎0852 3050 5806; Sawai; per person incl full board 250,000Rp) Perched romantically above the water, rooms at this age-old traveller favourite are predictably somewhat damp (bring a

sleeping mat) and showers in the basic en-suite bathrooms are salty. There's no phone, but call the owner's cousin Wati – he speaks good English and can help organise your stay. Cost includes fish dinners, assorted snacks and endless tea.

★ Ora Beach Resort BUNGALOW **$$**
(☎0817 083 3554, 0813 3363 3338; www.bagualabayresort.wordpress.com; Ora Beach; beachfront/overwater 500,000/700,000Rp, meals per day 250,000Rp) Grab one of eight beachfront rooms, one of seven brand-new romantically rustic overwater bungalows, or even the 'floating house'. Activities include snorkelling tours to offshore islands and trips up the Salawai River into the exotic and remote Manusela National Park. Packages are available, and rooms can be booked ahead through Baguala Bay Resort (p429) in Ambon.

BANDA ISLANDS

☎0910 / POP 22,000

Combining raw natural beauty, a warm local heart, and a palpable and fascinating history, this remote cluster of 10 picturesque islands isn't just Maluku's choice travel destination, it's one of the very best in all of Indonesia. Particularly impressive undersea drop-offs are vibrantly plastered with multicoloured coral gardens offering superlative snorkelling and tasty diving. The central islands – Pulau Neira (with the capital Bandaneira sprinkled with relics) and Pulau Banda Besar (the great nutmeg island) – curl in picturesque crescents around a pocket-sized tropical Mt Fuji (Gunung Api, 656m).

Outlying Hatta, Ai and Neilaka each have utterly undeveloped picture-postcard beaches. And Run, her gnarled limestone sprouting with nutmeg and cloves, is one drop-dead-gorgeous historical footnote. Banda became a region (no longer a subdistrict) in 2015, bringing national investment, rising transport and communication standards, and (inevitably) more visitors. The new fast-boat service from Ambon is already making Banda more accessible; it's time to get there before everyone else does!

History

Nutmeg, once produced almost exclusively in the Banda Islands, was one of the medieval world's most expensive commodities. Its cultivation takes knowledge but minimal effort, so the drudgery of manual labour was virtually unknown in the Bandas. Food, cloth and all necessities of life could be easily traded for spices with eager Arab, Chinese, Javanese and Bugis merchants, who queued up to do business. Things started to go wrong when the Europeans arrived; the Portuguese in 1512, then (especially) the Dutch from 1599.

These strange barbarians had no foodstuffs to trade, just knives, impractical woollens and useless trinkets of mere novelty value. So when the Dutch demanded a trade monopoly, the notion was laughable. However, since they were dangerously armed, some *orang kaya* (elders) signed a 'contract' to keep them quiet. Nobody took it at all seriously. The Dutch sailed away and were promptly forgotten. But a few years later they were back, furious to find the English merrily trading nutmeg on Pulau Run and Pulau Ai. Entrenching themselves by force, the dominant Dutch played cat and mouse with the deliberately provocative English, while trying unsuccessfully to enforce their mythical monopoly on the locals. In 1621, Jan Pieterszoon Coen, the new governor general of the VOC (Dutch East India Company), ordered the virtual genocide of the Bandanese. Just a few hundred survivors escaped to the Kei Islands.

Coen's VOC thereupon provided slaves and land grants to oddball Dutch applicants in return for a promise that they'd settle permanently in the Bandas and produce fixed-price spices exclusively for the company. These folk, known as *perkeniers* (from the Dutch word *perk*, meaning 'ground' or 'garden'), established nearly 70 plantations, mostly on Banda Besar and Ai.

This system survived for almost 200 years but corruption and mismanagement meant that the monopoly was never as profitable as it might have been. By the 1930s, the Bandas were a place of genteel exile for better-behaved anti-Dutch dissidents, including Mohammed Hatta (future Indonesian vice president) and Sutan Syahrir (later prime minister). The small school they organised while in Bandaneira inspired a whole generation of anticolonial youth.

In the 1998–99 troubles, churches were burnt and at least five people were killed at Walang including the 'last *perkenier*', Wim de Broeke. Most of the Christian minority fled to Seram or Ambon, but the islands rapidly returned to their delightful calm.

Banda Islands

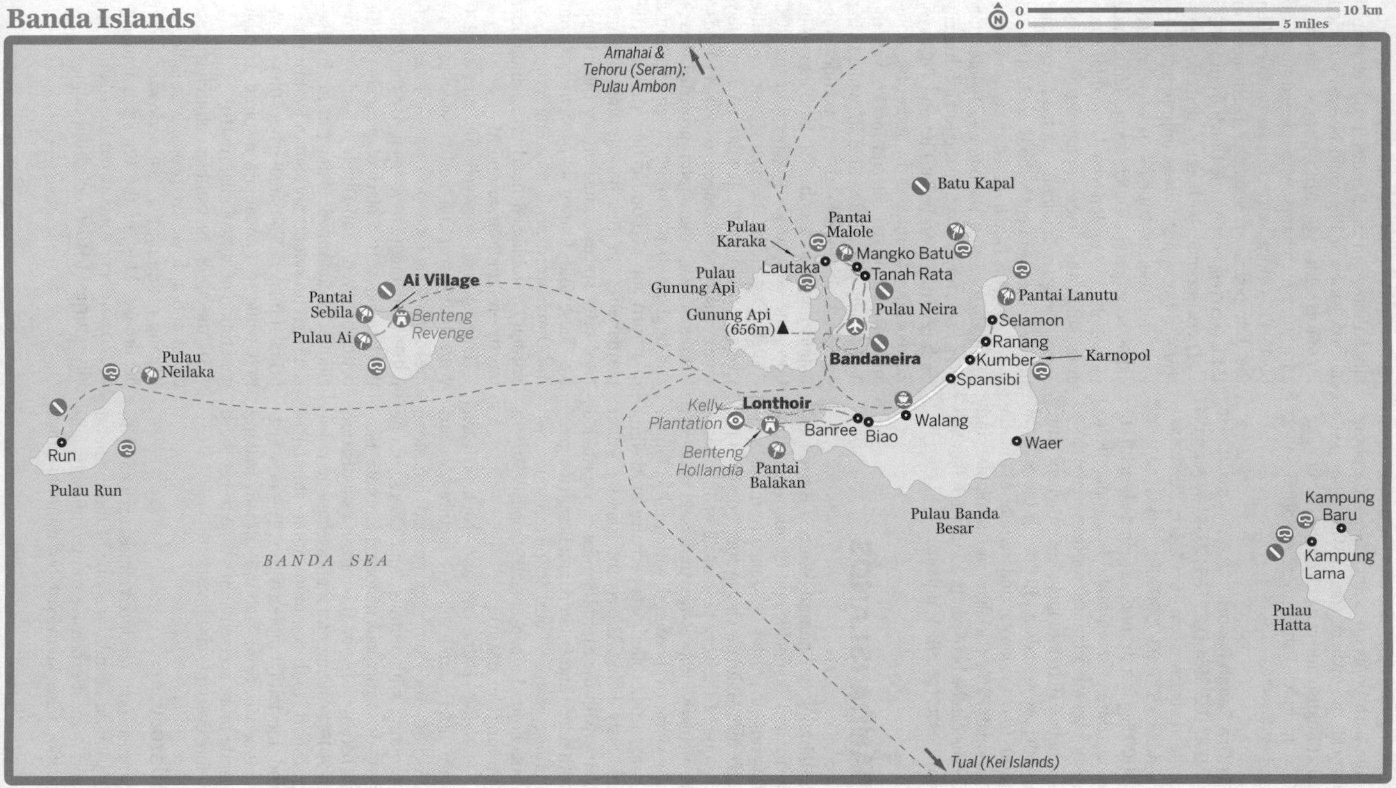

0 10 km
0 5 miles

Amahai & Tehoru (Seram); Pulau Ambon

Batu Kapal

Pulau Karaka

Pantai Malole

Mangko Batu

Lautaka

Tanah Rata

Pulau Gunung Api

Pantai Lanutu

Pulau Neira

Gunung Api (656m)

Selamon

Ranang

Bandaneira

Kumber

Karnopol

Spansibi

Ai Village

Pantai Sebila

Benteng Revenge

Pulau Ai

Pulau Neilaka

Kelly Plantation

Lonthoir

Walang

Banree

Biao

Waer

Run

Benteng Hollandia

Pantai Balakan

Pulau Run

Pulau Banda Besar

Kampung Baru

Kampung Lama

Pulau Hatta

BANDA SEA

Tual (Kei Islands)

Activities

Crystal-clear seas, shallow-water drop-offs and coral gardens teeming with multi-coloured reef life offer magnificently pristine snorkelling off Hatta, Banda Besar and Ai. Some Bandaneira homestays rent fins and snorkels to guests (30,000Rp per day).

Liveaboards also descend on the Bandas en route from Komodo Island to the Raja Ampat Islands. In addition to all the popular sites around Run, Hatta, Ai and the lava flow off the coast of Pulau Gunung Api, they often enjoy muck-diving the channel between Bandaneira, Api and Banda Besar.

Dive Bluemotion DIVING
(☎0812 4714 3922; www.dive-bluemotion.com; Jl Pelabuhan, Laguna Inn; dives from 350,000Rp; equipment per day from 100,000Rp; ⏰Feb-May & Aug-Dec) Bluemotion is one of only two land-based dive operations in the Bandas, and now has an outlet in Ambon (p430). It has new, well-maintained gear, a good speedboat and fair prices (cheaper as more dives are taken). Surcharges for Run and Hatta apply, and trips include lunch. It's closed during the unsettled months of January, June and July.

Naira Dive DIVING
(☎0813 4490 2298; www.nairadive.com; Jl Pelabuhan; per dive 400,000Rp; ⏰7am-6pm; diving Feb-May & Aug-Dec) The new kid in town, Naira Dive is an Indonesian operation catering to the expanding dive clientele of Banda. It visits all the principal Banda dive sites (there's a fuel surcharge for taking groups of fewer than five to Run and Hatta) and can arrange snorkelling trips. There's a two-dive minimum.

Bandaneira

POP 9,000

Little Bandaneira has always been the Bandas' main port and administrative centre. In the Dutch era the *perkeniers* virtually bankrupted themselves maintaining a European lifestyle, even after the lost nutmeg monopoly made it untenable. Today, Bandaneira's sleepy, flower-filled streets are so quiet that two becak count as a traffic jam. It's a charming place to wander aimlessly, admire tumbledown Dutch villas, ponder mouldering ruins, watch glorious cloudscapes over Gunung Api and trip over discarded cannon lolling in the grass.

Sights

Several Dutch-era buildings have been restored. If you manage to gain access (knock and hope!), much of the fun is hearing the fascinating life stories of the septuagenarian caretakers, assuming your Bahasa Indonesia is up to the task. Donations (around 10,000Rp per person) are appropriate.

Benteng Belgica FORTRESS
(admission by donation) A classic star fort, the Unesco-nominated Benteng Belgica was built on the hill above Nassau in 1611, when it became apparent the lower bastion was an inadequate defence. The five massive sharp-pointed bastions were expensively crafted to deflect the cannon fire of a potential English naval bombardment.

It caused quite a scandal in Holland when, in 1796, the Brits managed to seize it (albeit briefly) without firing a shot. The fort is open sporadically; to reach the upper ramparts (with great views), take the second arch on the left from the central courtyard. Be sure to look for the old jail, where locals were imprisoned if they dared sell their spices to the English.

Benteng Nassau FORTRESS
Nassau, quietly crumbling amongst tropical foliage now, was the scene of the Banda Massacre, the greatest enormity in the violent history of Dutch Banda. It was built in 1609, against the wishes of the *orang kaya* (local leaders) by Dutch Admiral Verhoeff, on foundations abandoned by the Portuguese 80 years earlier.

The Bandanese, fearing Dutch control, ambushed and executed some 40 Dutch 'negotiators', including Verhoeff himself. Unfortunately, the party also contained Jan Pieterszoon Coen, who was to become the fourth governor general of the Dutch East Indies, and who retaliated (in 1621) with the infamous beheading and quartering of 44 *orang kaya* within the fortress. What followed was the virtual genocide of the Bandanese population.

Hatta's House HISTORIC BUILDING
(Jl Hatta; admission by donation) Of three early-20th-century 'exile houses', Mohammed Hatta's House is the most appealing. It's partly furnished and photos of the dissident, his typewriter, distinctive spectacles and neatly folded suit are all on display. In the courtyard, where there are vintage clay cisterns

Bandaneira

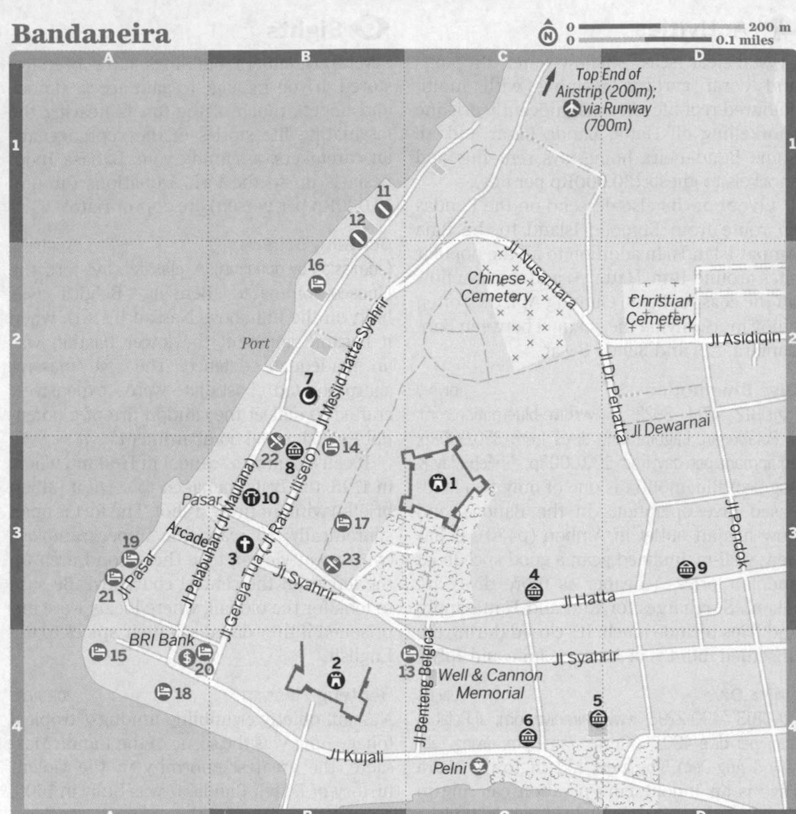

Bandaneira

Sights
1 Benteng Belgica ... C3
2 Benteng Nassau ... B4
3 Church ... B3
4 Hatta's House ... C3
5 Istana Mini ... C4
6 Makatita Hall ... C4
7 Mesjid Hatta-Syahrir ... B2
8 Rumah Budaya ... B3
9 Schelling House ... D3
10 Sun Tien Kong Chinese Temple ... B3

Activities, Courses & Tours
11 Dive Bluemotion ... B1
12 Naira Dive ... B1

Sleeping
13 Cilu Bintang Estate ... C4
14 Delfika ... B3
15 Delfika 2 ... A4
16 Hotel Maulana ... B2
17 Mutiara Guesthouse ... B3
18 Pantai Nassau Guesthouse ... A4
19 Penginapan Babbu Sallam ... A3
20 Penginapan Gamalama ... A4
21 Vita Guesthouse ... A3

Eating
Cilu Bintang Estate ... (see 13)
Delfika Cafe ... (see 14)
22 Namasawar ... B3
23 Nutmeg Cafe ... B3

and an old brick well sprouting with bromeliads, you'll also find a schoolhouse that Hatta founded during his exile. It's literally built into the hillside.

Schelling House HISTORIC BUILDING
(Jl Hatta; by apointment) This massive, columned house, owned by the daughter of the last Banda king, will inspire 'I could live

here' fantasies. It has a leafy courtyard, high ceilings and, in the the master bathroom, a stone tub resting against an exposed coral wall. And definitely wander up to that special shuttered loft in the rear courtyard.

Istana Mini HISTORIC BUILDING
(Jl Kujali) Little in Banda gives a sense of the scale of the Dutch enterprise like this grand, atmospheric yet largely empty 1820s mansion. Once a residence of the colonial governors, it's now shrouded in benign neglect. You can find 19th-century plaques and a bust of Willem III in the shady courtyard.

Makatita Hall HISTORIC BUILDING
(Jl Kujali) Makatita Hall occupies the site of the former Harmonie Club (aka 'the Soc') that once boasted seven snooker tables and was the focus of colonial-era social events. Now it's home to chickens and furtive graffiti.

Rumah Budaya MUSEUM
(Jl Gereja Tua; admission 20,000Rp; ⌚9am-5pm, by appointment) Bandaneira's little museum is worth a quick visit. It's dusty, and only haphazardly 'curated', but you can see colonial artefacts including coins, silverware, crockery, pipes, swords and flintlock pistols and muskets. There's also a smattering of Bandanese stuff, including the *parang* (machete) and *kapsete* (helmet) used in the *cakalele* (the warrior dance once performed by up to 50 young males that went underground following the 1621 massacre). The key is available from the caretaker: ask for Mrs Feni or Iqbal.

Mesjid Hatta-Syahrir MOSQUE
(Jl Mesjid Hatta-Syahrir) Behind the main port is the eye-catching minaret of the Mesjid Hatta-Syahrir. Some locals claim this was converted into a mosque from the mansion that first accommodated Hatta and Syahrir on their arrival in 1936.

Sun Tien Kong Chinese Temple CHINESE TEMPLE
(Jl Pelabuhan) The 300-year-old Sun Tien Kong Chinese Temple is testament to the ancient Chinese involvement in the Banda spice trade. Ask at the antique shop across the road for the key, or you'll have to glimpse its dim, lantern-lit interior through round, latticed windows.

Church CHURCH
(Jl Gereja Tua) The restored 1852 Dutch church has a portico of four chubby columns, a decorative bell-clock and an antique stone floor.

Activities

Though not Banda's best place for snorkelling, **Pulau Neira** has pleasant (if distressingly litter-strewn) coral gardens at the southern end of **Tanah Rata** village, off the eastern end of the airstrip and to the northeast off **Pantai Malole**. A notable marine attraction is to spot populations of mandarin fish that emerge at dusk from rubble piles within Neira harbour. Snorkellers can find them near Vita Guesthouse (p440), and divers can find deeper-water populations just off the Hotel Maulana (p440), where most of the muck-diving happens. Bring underwater torches.

Sleeping

More than a dozen family guesthouses and homestays offer simple but clean rooms, almost all with en-suite *mandi*. Cilu Bintang, Mutiara and Delfika are best set up for foreign travellers, offering spoken English, snorkelling gear and help with boat hire.

Mutiara Guesthouse GUESTHOUSE $
(☎0910-21344, 0813 3034 3377; www.banda-mutiara.com; r with fan/air-con from 150,000/200,000Rp; ❄📶) A special boutique hotel disguised as a homestay, Mutiara is the first venture of Abba, the tirelessly helpful and well-connected owner of Cilu Bintang (p440). The front garden is a wonderful spot for an afternoon snooze, or to catch the resident cuscus raiding the cinnamon tree at night.

Delfika GUESTHOUSE $
(☎0910-21027; delfika1@yahoo.com; Jl Gereja Tua; r with fan 100,000-150,000Rp, with air-con 175,000-250,000Rp; ❄) Built around a shady courtyard, the charming Delfika has a range of mostly well-renovated rooms on the main village drag. There's also a bric-a-brac-stuffed sitting room and an attached cafe (p440), one of Banda's best.

Delfika 2 GUESTHOUSE $
(☎0910-21127; r with fan/air-con 150,000/225,000Rp) A little out of the way, located down a twisting alley between the market and the water, Delfika 2 has particularly fine bay views from its upper-storey rooms. You can knock 25,000Rp off the price if you avoid using the air-con, or add 75,000Rp to sleep an extra person in your room.

Pantai Nassau Guesthouse GUESTHOUSE $
(☎0813 4326 6771; Jl Kujali; r with fan/air-con 150,000/200,000Rp) The location's the thing that elevates this establishment, perched on a

black-sand beach with harbour and Gunung Api views. The four rooms are bright and clean with double beds, but toilets are all Indo squat-pots and only breakfast is served.

Penginapan Babbu Sallam GUESTHOUSE **$**
(☎0910-21043; Jl Nairam Bessy; r with fan/air-con 150,000/200,000Rp; ❄) Newly-renovated, with vibrant papaya-coloured paintwork and a patio and a deck overlooking the bay, this guesthouse is another of Neira's good cheap sleeps. Breakfast is included.

Vita Guesthouse GUESTHOUSE **$**
(Fita; ☎0910-21332, 0812 4706 7099; allan darman@gmail.com; Jl Pasar; d with fan/air-con from 140,000/175,000Rp; ❄) Popular with Euro backpackers, Vita offers a great bayside location with seven comfortable rooms set in a colonnaded L-shape around a waterfront palm garden (ideal for an evening beer, contemplating Gunung Api). The beds are adequate, there's some decent wooden furniture in the rooms, and it has Western-style toilets.

Penginapan Gamalama GUESTHOUSE **$**
(☎0910-21053; Jl Gereja Tua; tw 150,000Rp; ❄) The Gamalama offers functional, relatively large rooms beyond a lobby decked out in concrete trees. The air-con is a little primitive, but all told, with breakfast included, it's good value.

★**Cilu Bintang Estate** BOUTIQUE HOTEL **$$**
(☎0813 3034 3377, 0910-21604; www.cilubintang.com; Jl Benteng Belgica; d 300,000-400,000Rp, VIP 750,000Rp; ❄📶) After storming the charts with his first guesthouse, the still-excellent Mutiara (p439), Abba (Rizal, the owner) has outdone himself with the difficult sophomore release. Cilu Bintang is head and shoulders above any other accommodation in all the Banda Islands – an immaculate, breezy Dutch-colonial reproduction with superb rooms, beds, food and company.

While it's a little pricier than most other options in Neira, Cilu Bintang remains exceptional value. Even the basic rooms come with carved (and very comfy) four-poster beds, well-equipped bathrooms, air-con and lovely nutmeg-themed furnishings. The evening meal, a convivial buffet cooked for guests and drop-ins, may just be the best food you eat in Maluku. Add to that Abba's unmatched ability to organise just about anything you might like to do in Banda, and you have the perfect base to explore one of Indonesia's most stunning locations.

Hotel Maulana HOTEL **$$**
(☎0910-21022; r/presidential ste 350,000/1,500,000Rp; ❄) Once Neira's finest hotel, this rebuilt Dutch-colonial hotel is now resting on its laurels to some extent, relying on travellers attracted to its plumb location in Neira harbour, rather than providing professional service. It does have a lovely veranda overlooking the waterfront between palms and shaggy ketapang trees, and the top-floor suites (no elevators) have spectacular views. The dive centre moved out to Laguna, as Hotel Maulana was too chaotic.

Eating

Frequent cups of tea and a light breakfast are generally included in room prices, and almost every place will serve lunch or dinner (35,000Rp to 90,000Rp per person) on advance request. Street vendors sell presmoked fish on a stick (10,000Rp), sticky rice, dried nutmeg-fruit slices, and delicious *halua-kenari* almond brittle.

★**Delfika Cafe** INDONESIAN **$**
(Jl Gereja Tua; mains 15,000-50,000Rp; ⏲10am-9pm) Attached to the *penginapan* (p439) of the same name, Delfika serves seasonal fruit juices, delicious nutmeg-jam pancakes, *soto ayam*, *nasi ikan* and a variety of fried noodle and vegetable dishes. Look out for local favourites such as fish in nutmeg sauce and eggplant with *kenari*-almond sauce. No alcohol.

Namasawar INDONESIAN **$**
(☎0910-21136; Jl Pelabuhan; mains 20,000-80,000Rp; ⏲10am-10pm) Opening onto the courtyard of the owner's house, this simple little *rumah makan* offers ice cream and some Western dishes, alongside well-executed Indonesian staples. Some of these come with a distinctive Bandanese twist: the *nasi ikan telur* (rice with fish and egg) is accompanied by an unusual dish of bitter melon stuffed with nutmeg-scented forcemeat.

Nutmeg Cafe INDONESIAN **$**
(Jl Hatta; mains 15,000-40,000Rp; ⏲8am-9pm) Bolted onto a family home, the sleepy, shuttered Nutmeg is a charmer. It does noodles, juices, fish and rice, a good *soto ayam* and thick pancakes to slather with house-jarred nutmeg jam.

★**Cilu Bintang Estate** INDONESIAN **$$**
(☎0910-21604, 0813 3034 3377; www.cilubintang.com; Jl Benteng Belgica; buffet 90,000Rp; ⏲7-9pm) The best place to stay in Bandaneira is also the best place to eat, hands-down. Abba's

charming wife Dila works all day to produce a magnificent evening buffet of spanking-fresh baked fish, soups liberally spiced with Banda nutmeg and cinnamon, curries, fritters, salads and more. Classes and a cookbook are also available.

Information

There's no tourist office, but several guesthouses have helpful English-speaking owners. Delfika, Mutiara and Cilu Bintang give guests a free, basic island map and offer slow web access as well (15,000Rp per hour).

BRI Bank (Jl Kujali) Now has a 24-hour ATM (which only accepts MasterCard) but still no exchange facilities.

Getting There & Away

The new fast ferry from Ambon has really opened up the Banda Islands.

AIR

Susi Air (http://fly.susiair.com) is the latest to win the Ambon–Bandaneira route. Its small, twin-prop plane makes the trip on Wednesday, Thursday and some Friday mornings (300,000Rp, 40 minutes). It's wise to organise your (return) ticket at least 10 days in advance, and cancellations (for weather and lack of passengers) are common. However, if it lands in Bandaneira on any given morning, it will fly back to Ambon for sure.

BOAT

Banda is expecting a visitor surge, with a new, fast ferry greatly simplifying connections to Ambon. The *Express Bahari 2B* leaves Tulehu for Bandaneira at 9am on Monday and Friday, returning at the same time on Tuesday and Saturday. The trip takes six hours, and the VIP tickets (400,000Rp) aren't really necessary (the 300,000Rp seats are comfortable enough).

If you take the **Pelni** (☎0910-21196; www.pelni.co.id; Jl Kujali; ticket from 100,000Rp; ⏲8.30am-1pm & 4-6pm Mon-Sat), hop on the *Tidar* or *Kelimutu*, both of which leave Ambon on Sunday to arrive early morning in Banda, before a circuit of the Kei and Aru islands. Economy adult tickets are 112,000Rp and there are four classes, plus discounts for children, the elderly, and babies (!). Bear in mind that Pelni timetables (issued online) change monthly, and beware of pickpockets at any Pelni embarkation.

Getting Around

The island is small and walkable but *ojeks* save sweat at 3000Rp for a short trip, 10,000Rp to the airport or 15,000Rp to Pantai Malole. Cilu Bintang rents old pushbikes (50,000Rp per day). Several guesthouses offer free airport pickups.

Typical boat-charter rates for full-day trips include snorkelling stops on Ai (350,000Rp), Hatta (600,000Rp), Karnopol and Pisang (400,000Rp), or Run (600,000Rp). Run trips may include a stop on Ai and Neilaka, as well.

Pulau Gunung Api

This impish little 656m volcano has always been a threat to Bandaneira, Banda Besar and anyone attempting to farm its fertile slopes. Its most recent eruption in 1988 killed three people, destroyed more than 300 houses and filled the sky with ash for days. Historically, Gunung Api's eruptions have often proven to be spookily accurate omens of approaching European invaders or traders.

The volcano can be climbed for awesome sunrise views in around three hours, but the unrelenting slope is arduous and the loose scree is scary, especially upon descent. Take more drinking water than you think you'll need. Guides (from 100,000Rp) are prepared to accompany hikers but the path up is fairly obvious. Ask a local to point out the direction when you get off your boat. Once you're on the trail it's easy.

The waters around Gunung Api are home to lurid purple-and-orange sea squirts, remarkably fast-growing table corals, leatherback turtles and concentrations of (mostly

BOATS FROM BANDANEIRA

DESTINATION	TYPE	FARE (RP)	FREQUENCY
Amahai (Pulau Seram)	*kapal malolo* (cargo)	40,000	varies
Pulau Ai	public longboat	20,000	noon, 2pm daily
Pulau Ambon	Pelni	varies	weekly
Pulau Ambon	*kapal malolo* (cargo)	50,000	varies
Pulau Banda Besar	public longboat	5,000	when full
Pulau Run	public longboat	25,000	2pm daily
Tehoru (Pulau Seram)	longboat	5,000,000	charter

harmless) sea snakes. The submerged north-coast lava flows ('New Lava') are especially good for snorkelling and shallow dives.

Pulau Banda Besar

POP 11,000

The largest island of the group, hilly Banda Besar makes a great day trip and offers some interesting woodland walks. Boats shuttle regularly from Bandaneira to several Banda Besar jetties, most frequently to **Walang** (per person/boat 5000/30,000Rp, 15 minutes). *Ojeks* (5000Rp) run via **Biao** village (home of a scraggy pet cassowary) to **Banree** where the asphalt ends.

If you walk 10 minutes west, along the narrow concrete sea-defence wall, you'll emerge at the relatively new but photogenic **Masjid Al Taqwa** mosque in **Lonthoir** (pronounced 'lon-tor'). This is Banda Besar's sleepy, steeply layered 'capital' village. Its main 'street' is actually a long stairway that starts beside **Homestay Leiden** (Jl Warataka; per person 150,000Rp). Leiden offers two neat guest rooms (thin mattresses and shared *mandi*) in the attractive house of earnest, English-speaking Usman Abubakar.

At the top of the stairway turn right – you will find the **Kelly Plantation** where centuries-old, buttressed kenari trees tower protectively over a nutmeg grove. Abba at Cilu Bintang (p440) offers wonderful three-hour tours (per person 100,000Rp) to both Kelly Plantation and **Van der Broecke Plantation**, known as the last Dutch-owned plantation on the Bandas. Slain amidst sectarian violence, the long-gone patriarch was helpful in repopulating nutmeg trees throughout the Bandas.

One of Banda's best views is to be had from **Benteng Hollandia**. Built in 1624, this was once one of the biggest Dutch fortresses in the Indies, until shattered by a devastating 1743 earthquake. The chunky overgrown ruins, high above Lonthoir, offer perfect palm-framed views of Gunung Api with a magical foreground of sapphire shallows.

Thanks to a new, smooth road, you can now take an *ojek* from Lonthoir north to **Selamon** (20,000Rp), then walk to the beach at **Timbararu** where there is superb snorkelling off a secluded white-sand beach. You can also take a public boat (5000Rp) directly from Bandaneira to Selamon, and walk from there.

Pulau Hatta

POP 800

A stunning flying-saucer-shaped island of jungle-swathed limestone, trimmed with white sand, Pulau Hatta, once known as Rozengain, had no nutmeg. Thus its only historical relevance was a comical episode where eccentric English Captain Courthope raised a flag merely to enrage the Dutch. Until very recently there was nowhere to stay on the island; now, there are four guesthouses/homestays, and Naira Dive is building a fifth. None offer snorkelling equipment, so bring your own.

Kampung Lama, where all the accommodation is based, rests on a lovely white-sand beach connected to Banda's clearest waters and richest reefs. Around 300m west of Lama the beach is empty, raw and gorgeous. Here, a natural underwater 'bridge' creates a beautiful blue hole over part of Hatta's stunning vertical drop-off. Forests of delicate soft coral alongside huge table and fern corals, clouds of reef fish and superb visibility make this Banda's top snorkelling spot. Leatherback turtles, reef sharks, trigger fish and an endless roll-call of species can easily be encountered.

From Bandaneira, count on around 600,000Rp to charter a suitably powerful boat, including stops on Hatta, eastern Banda Besar and Pisang.

Sleeping

Penginapan Tiara GUESTHOUSE $
(per person incl meals 150,000Rp) Located on the forest track between Kampungs Lama and Baru, this rude wooden guesthouse has been known to charm travellers into staying an extra week or two. There are four timbered rooms (two more are under construction), a communal table and hammock, low-pressure showers and electricity from 6pm to 11pm. On your doorstep: 400m of pristine coral, then the drop-off.

Rozengain Vitalia Guesthouse GUESTHOUSE $
(Kampung Lama; per person incl meals 150,000Rp) With four rooms, space for eight guests, and direct access to the dazzling sands and unspoilt coral of Hatta, this place tends to attract visitors for the long haul. Price includes three meals a day – Bandanese food with the accent on fruits of the sea. Electricity only from 6pm to 10pm.

Homestay Sara HOMESTAY $
(Kampung Lama; per person incl meals 150,000Rp) Offering a few bright, clean rooms with mosquito nets, communal *mandi* and all meals included, Sara is another of the new homestays on the beach in Hatta.

Bunga Karung HOMESTAY $
(Kampung Lama; per person incl meals 150,000Rp) Right on the beach, in the middle of Kampung Lama, this simple, good-value homestay is all rough wooden beams, lime-green walls and sandy floors. The food is good, and the hospitality sincere.

Pulau Ai

POP 1300

Ai's greatest attraction is snorkelling, or diving the remarkably accessible, brilliantly pristine coral drop-offs just a flipper-flap away. There's a lot to see directly in front of the village, especially in October when groups of Napoleon fish appear along with migrating dolphins and whales. Sea life is likewise impressive off Pantai Sebila, a 15-minute walk west, where an exceptionally stark wall, crusted with coral and laced with sea anemone, juts straight down.

Ai blipped on the global map in the 17th century, when English agents fortified and armed the locals against a 1615 Dutch attack. The islanders inflicted some 200 casualties on the astonished Dutch. An English–Dutch naval encounter the following year saw the Brits accept trading rights and nominal sovereignty to Run, abandoning their Ai allies. Unprotected, they were slaughtered by the Dutch, who repopulated the island with slaves and prisoners. Ai's four-pointed star fortress, now with a sweet community garden sprouting within its crumbling walls, has been poignantly known ever since as **Benteng Revenge**.

Sleeping & Eating

Ai has but a faint mobile-phone (cell) signal, accessible from the jetty, but word sent through your Bandaneira guesthouse is more reliable. There are no restaurants, but accommodation prices include three meals. The town generator provides power three hours per day.

Green Coconut GUESTHOUSE $
(☎0812 4241 0667; ayem_nasrun@yahoo.com; Jl Patalima; per person incl meals 175,000Rp) Run by a chef, the Green Coconut has the best seafront location in Ai, with a common dining room and wonderful sea views from its common balcony (if you're lucky you'll spot Napoleon fish). Renovations that were due to be completed in late 2015 when we passed through will see it get 24-hour electricity and indoor toilets.

Revenge 2 HOMESTAY $
(☎0812 4781 1028; per person incl meals 200,000Rp) Despite the slasher-movie title, this is a clean, basic homestay with a pious Muslim family. The two spacious rooms share a *mandi*.

Dua Putri Homestay HOMESTAY $
(☎0878 0644 6874; per person incl meals 100,000Rp) While there's no sign, you can't miss this new choice, first on the right after the jetty, with gorgeous sea views. There are just five basic rooms with thin mattresses, two with shared *mandi*, and all the same price.

★**CDS Bungalow** BUNGALOW $$
(per person incl meals r 250,000-300,000Rp) To find the class crash pad on Ai, walk up from the jetty, right at the T-intersection, past the fort, then 500m further past a school and pineapple plantations. Once there, you'll find two cute wooden cottages with genuine spring beds, outdoor bathrooms, and a wide veranda stilted over a secluded beach. Book through Cilu Bintang (p440).

GO ON, TAKE NEW YORK!

After the 1616 Dutch ravaging of Ai, English forces retreated to their trading post on Pulau Run and built an 'impregnable' fort on the tiny, waterless islet of Neilaka. Increasingly besieged, the same eccentric Captain Courthope who had taunted the Dutch on Hatta (formerly Rozengain), put honour above survival in a preposterously futile last stand, refusing even the most reasonable offers to leave. Somehow British sovereignty was maintained, even after the 1621 Dutch atrocities during which all of Run's nutmeg trees were systematically destroyed. The Dutch eventually took Run, so the English agreed, in 1674, to swap it for a (then equally useless) North American island. That island was Manhattan. Not a bad deal, as it turned out.

Getting There & Away

Two or three passenger boats (20,000Rp, one hour) leave Ai for Bandaneira when full at around 8am, returning between noon and 2pm. To make day trips from Bandaneira you'll have to charter (400,000Rp).

Pulau Run (Rhun)

Run, for all its historical gravitas, is simply a remote chunk of limestone, swathed in jungle and surrounded by deep blue sea. The village is an appealing little network of steps and concrete paths backed by vine-draped limestone cliffs, with attractive views between the tamarind trees from the top end of Jl Eldorado. The old **English Fort** (the one held by Nathaniel Courthope) perpetuated the Spice Wars and resulted in the great trade of Run for Manhattan (let's all go play poker in Amsterdam!). From the pier, walk to the main lower path, turn right, and follow the stairs up, up, and up to the rough track leading to the vague, overgrown ruins.

Run's main attraction is diving the wall that lies 70m to 150m off the island's northwestern coast (access by boat), known as **Depan Kampung** (next to the village). Visibility is magnificent. Alternatively, beach yourself on the picture-perfect, powdery white sands of **Pulau Neilaka**, an islet so small you explore it in 10 minutes, drinking in dazzlingly photogenic views of Gunung Api.

A morning boat (25,000Rp, two hours) leaves Run at 9am for Bandaneira, returning around 2pm. Chartering (600,000Rp return from Bandaneira) makes more sense if you're doing a day trip. You'll need a boat anyway to reach Neilaka and the offshore drop-offs, plus you can stop by Pulau Ai on your way home.

Sleeping

Manhattan 2 HOMESTAY $
(0852 4372 5784; Jl Pantei Run; per person incl meals 125,000Rp) Bedecked with kitsch figurines of 18th-century gentlefolk and lurid tropical bedspreads, this clean, super-friendly homestay offers rooms with fans and hand showers. Call the contact in Bandaneira to organise your stay.

Homestay Neilaka HOMESTAY $
(0813 4460 2095; Jl Eldorado; per person incl meals 125,000Rp) Run from a gleaming, comfortable (if small) family home, Neilaka offers three rooms with shared bathrooms in a new concrete building with wooden ceiling and tiled facade.

Homestay Manhattan HOMESTAY $
(per person incl meals 125,000Rp) Reached by steps cut into ossified coral, this proudly immaculate concrete home is located on the second 'tier' of the village. Its three rooms all have private *mandis* and squat toilets, and meals are served at the nearby Manhattan 2.

KEI ISLANDS

0916

The trump cards for the Kei Islands are kilometres of stunning white-sand beaches and a deeply hospitable population. Beneath the mostly Christian facade, Kei culture is fascinatingly distinctive with three castes, holy trees, bride prices paid in *lela* (antique table cannons) and a strong belief in *sasi* (a prohibition spell; p448). In Kei language *bokbok* means 'good', *hanarun (li)* means '(very) beautiful' and *enbal* (cassava) is a local food staple. The driest season is September to December, with *Belang* war-canoe races held in November. While the islands are all reef-fringed, illegal fishing has seen dynamite and poison take a heavy toll on coral.

Tual & Langgur

POP 65,000

Bridging the two central islands, these twin towns form the Kei Islands' main commercial centre and transport gateway. Christian Langgur is relaxed, strung along broad avenues. Tual, predominantly Muslim, is a jumble of ramshackle humanity which gives it a manic edge. Many of Tual's 'Arabs' are (mixed) descendants of a migration from the Middle East 250 years ago.

Sleeping

Tual and Langgur have ample, if basic, accommodation, though most visitors wisely head straight for the beachside options.

Hotel Dragon HOTEL $
(0916-21812; Jl Jenderal Sudirman 154; r 100,000-250,000Rp;) There's a languid, siesta-at-any-time-of-the-day feel to the Dragon, but that's not out of keeping with Langgur generally. Persist beyond the perennial Christmas decorations and toothpaste-green walls of the lobby and you'll find spacious, super-clean rooms with big beds and crisp sheets. More expensive rooms have hot water; all have air-con, TV and spring mattresses.

Tual & Langgur

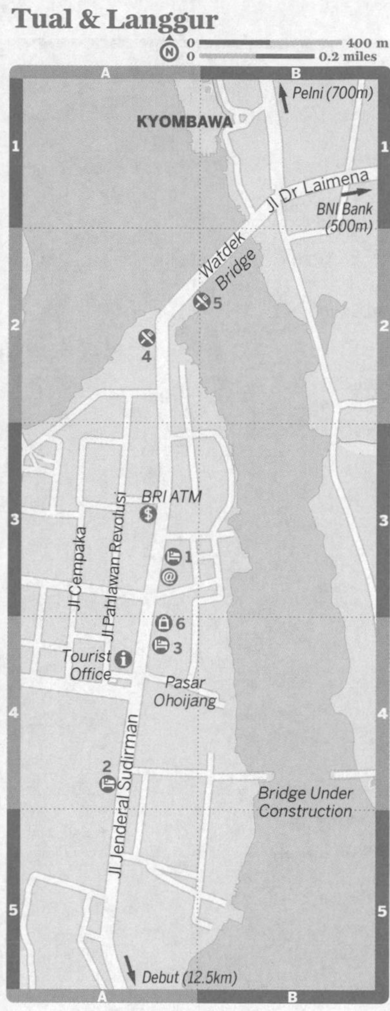

Tual & Langgur

Sleeping

1 Aurelia Hotel A3
2 Hotel Dragon A4
3 Hotel Suita A4

Eating

4 RM Ayah A2
5 Warung Serabba B2

Shopping

6 Gota A4

Hotel Suita HOTEL $$
(☎0916-24007; hotelsuitatual@telkom.net; Jl Jenderal Sudirman; d/deluxe/ste 355,000/385,000/650,000Rp;) Don't let the higher prices convince you you're buying true luxury. The Suita is comfortable enough, with ample rooms, large beds and in-room wi-fi (15,000Rp per hour) but it's faded since the days when it was clearly built to be one of Langgur's few upmarket options. You'll find the local Garuda desk in its lobby.

Aurelia Hotel HOTEL $$
(☎0916-23748; www.kimsoncenter.com; Jl Jenderal Sudirman; standard/deluxe/VIP 275,000/325,000/600,000Rp;) To one side of the bulky, tiled Kimson Center, arranged around a colonnaded courtyard, you'll find some of the more expensive rooms in Langgur, decked out in the height of 1980s beige chic. They all boast nice wood furnishings, coffee makers, crown mouldings, and free bottled water, but the carpet is threadbare and some smell, well, moist.

Eating

★Warung Serabba SEAFOOD $
(beside Watdek Bridge; mains 30,000-150,000Rp; 9am-2am) The sign's obscure, but you can't miss the rickety wooden building before the bridge, stilted over the channel with views of the mangroves. There's no menu either, so just choose your fresh catch or a lobster plucked just for you from Serabba's netted farm in the channel.

RM Ayah INDONESIAN $
(Jl Jenderal Sudirman; mains 20,000-40,000Rp; 9am-5am) Other than four hours of early-morning respite, Ayah never closes. If you should find yourself adrift in Langgur at 2am, desperate for a feed, you could do much worse than the slices of spicy omelette, chilli-stewed eggplant, fried chicken, potato patties, curries and greens at this Padang-style *rumah makan*.

Shopping

Gota DEPARTMENT STORE
(Jl Jenderal Sudirman; 9am-10pm) The only place resembling a supermarket in Langgur/Tual. Stock up on packaged food, cheap phones and clothes, and fruit at prices inverse to quality, compared to the streetside vendors everywhere.

Kei Islands

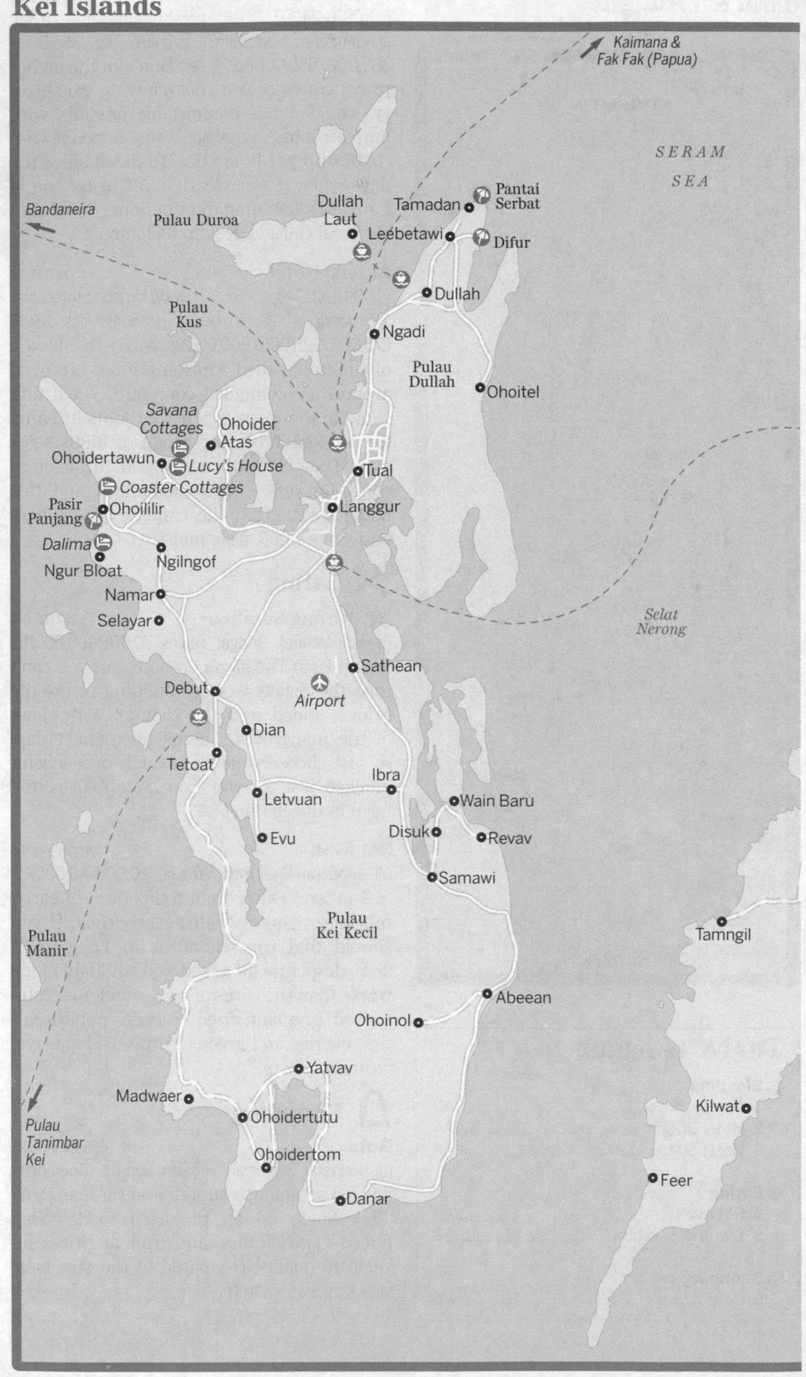
Kaimana &
Fak Fak (Papua)
SERAM
SEA
Pantai
Serbat
Tamadan
Dullah
Laut
Bandaneira
Pulau Duroa
Leebetawi
Difur
Dullah
Pulau
Kus
Ngadi
Pulau
Dullah
Ohoitel
Savana
Cottages
Ohoider
Atas
Ohoidertawun
Lucy's House
Tual
Coaster Cottages
Pasir
Panjang
Ohoililir
Langgur
Dalima
Ngur Bloat
Ngilngof
Namar
Selayar
Selat
Nerong
Sathean
Debut
Airport
Dian
Tetoat
Ibra
Letvuan
Wain Baru
Disuk
Revav
Evu
Samawi
Pulau
Kei Kecil
Pulau
Manir
Tamngil
Abeean
Ohoinol
Yatvav
Madwaer
Kilwat
Ohoidertutu
Pulau
Tanimbar
Kei
Ohoidertom
Feer
Danar

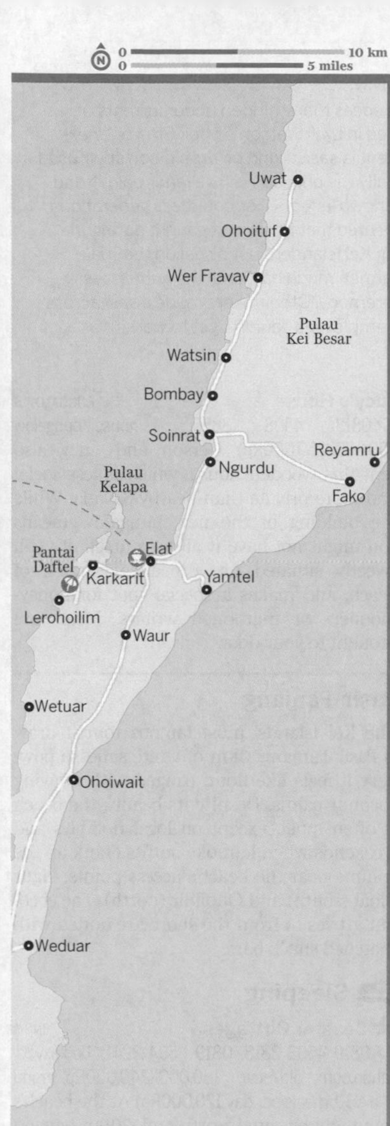

Information

Tourist Office (Dinas Parawisata; ☎0916-24063; Jl Jenderal Sudirman; ⊙8am-2.30pm Mon-Sat, to noon Fri) Answers questions and dispenses maps and brochures.

BNI Bank (Bank Negara Indonesia; Jl Dr Laimena; ⊙8am-3pm Mon-Fri) Has the only official currency exchange (terrible rates) and an ATM. Also has ATMs (Jl Jenderal Sudirman) in Langgur.

Kimson Internet (Jl Jenderal Sudirman; per hr 10,000Rp; ⊙9am-midnight) Part of the Kimson Center, it charges 10,000Rp, and connections vary.

Getting There & Away

AIR

Since the opening of Tual's new airport Garuda has started a Kei route, driving prices down (753,000Rp) and frequency up (daily). Wings Air also flies this route most days (673,000Rp). Whichever carrier you use for the 90-minute flight, aim for a southern window for gorgeous views of Tayando and Bandas en route.

BEMO (MOBIL) & OJEK

Mobil for Debut (5000Rp), and southern Kei Kecil operate from a station beside Pasar Langgur. From Langgur's Pasar Ohoijang roughly one *mobil* per hour leaves for Ohoililir (for Coaster Cottages, 5000Rp). Or you can take an *ojek* (30,000Rp, 25 minutes) or taxi (150,000Rp).

BOAT

Pelni (☎22520; Jl Pattimura; ⊙8am-2pm) liner *Tidar* links Tual to Ambon (22 hours) via Bandaneira (10 hours). Eastbound, it loops through Kaimana and Fak Fak in Papua, returning 36 hours later. The reportedly roach-infested *Kelimutu* offers a similar itinerary.

Getting Around

Bemos (from 3000Rp) are common along Jl Jenderal Sudirman, mostly continuing to Tual's big Pasar Masrun market. Southbound from Tual, 'Langgur' bemos pass Hotel Vilia and terminate at Pasar Langgur. *Ojeks* start at 5000Rp per ride. Savana Cottages (p448) in Ohoidertawun offers motorbike rental (per hour/day 10,000/50,000Rp, plus fuel).

Pulau Kei Kecil

Ohoidertawun

The charming village of Ohoidertawun surveys a lovely bay that becomes a vast, white-sand tidal flat when craftsmen sit in the palm

SASI SAVVY

Call it 'magic' or 'earth knowledge', Maluku experiences many hidden undercurrents of almost voodoo-esque beliefs, beautifully described in Lyall Watson's book *Gifts of Unexpected Things*. One such belief still widely prevalent is *sasi*, a kind of 'prohibition spell' used to protect property and prevent trespass. Physically the only barrier is a *janur* palm frond. But few would dare to break a *sasi* for fear of unknown 'effects'. For countless generations *sasi* have prevented the theft of coconuts and ensured that fish aren't caught during the breeding season. However, in 2003 some cunning Kei Islanders put a *sasi* on the Tual–Langgur bridge. With the bridge off limits the boatmen made hay, until the authorities finally stumped up the cash for a *sasi*-removal ceremony. Other jokers made a *sasi* across the access route to Tual's government offices so employees couldn't get to work.

shade carving out canoes. A holy tree on the waterfront beside Savana Cottages is believed to enforce peace or bind relationships. A footpath and stairway leads north to **Ohoider Atas** village. At low tide you can splash across the sand flats past small caves cut in the limestone cliffs (some contain human bones). After around 25 minutes you'll begin to notice the mysterious red-and-orange petroglyphs painted on the cliff faces.

Sleeping

The owners of Savana Cottages can set you up with village homestays (single/double 100,000/150,000Rp, including three meals) if you wish to go local.

★ Savana Cottages BUNGALOW $

(☎SMS only 0813 4308 3856; s/d 210,000/250,000Rp, meals 50,000-80,000Rp, beer 40,000Rp) For pure soporific serenity, few budget guesthouses in Indonesia can beat Savana Cottages. Watch the changing moods of nature, the swooping curlews and the tide retreating in the moonlight, while sipping an ice-cold beer or swinging from the hammock between sighing casuarinas. You can book by text message.

The colours on this beach, when the tide is out and the blinding white-sand flats stretch to distant ribbons of turquoise sea, are just magnificent. As for the digs, there are four simple, double-bed, bamboo-and-wood rooms, with rattan chairs on the balcony, and towels for the shared *mandis*. Mosquito nets are available and hearty breakfasts are included at the sweet cafe, which is decorated with gongs, carvings and tinkling wind chimes. Dinners, cooked by the hilarious Lucy, are excellent too. English-speaking owner Gerson is a fount of knowledge on Kei Kecil.

Lucy's House BUNGALOW $

(☎0813 4308 3856; 'house'/bungalow 200,000/250,000Rp) Gerson and Lucy also rent this wooden house, which is less social and more private than nearby Savana. While the building of the new bungalow means you might not have it all to yourself, it's still sweetly situated on a peerless stretch of beach, and makes a special spot for honeymooners or marooned writers. Meals are brought to your door.

Pasir Panjang

The Kei Islands' most famous tourist draw is Pasir Panjang, 3km of white sand so powdery it feels like flour, fringed with swaying coconut palms. Despite its beauty, the beach is often quiet, except on local holidays and weekends when karaoke outfits crank up the volume near the beach's access points: Ngur Bloat (south) and Ohoililir (north). The coconut groves in from the shore are dotted with thatched snack bars.

Sleeping

★ Coaster Cottages INN $

(☎0819 4502 2818, 0819 4504 2241; bob.azyz@yahoo.com; old/new r 180,000/240,000Rp, grand villa €60, meals per day 120,000Rp) At the beach's reputedly haunted north end, 700m beyond Ohoililir village, Coaster Cottages offers spacious new rooms with wooden furniture and shared patio, and, closer to the beach, older brick rooms with basic *mandis* that are a touch slimy. The grand villa has character to spare, but only makes sense for a family, at the price.

Dalima GUESTHOUSE $

(☎0822 3880 3711; per person 100,000Rp; breakfast/other meals 20,000/45,000Rp) Run by a sweetly hospitable Muslim family, you'll find this delightful guesthouse set in the shade of coconuts and ferns, back from the snack-huts of Pasir Panjang. The small wooden rooms come with fans, mosquito nets and an atmosphere so relaxed it's almost catatonic. Access is from the Ngur Bloat (southern) end of the beach.

Government Houses BUNGALOW **$**
(Ohoililir; d 200,000Rp) You can rent these two wooden government houses, in the shady north end of the village, through the *kepala desa* (village head).

Southern Kei Kecil

Near **Letvuan** are the striking **Goa Hawang caves**, limestone grottoes with luminous blue water, giant spiders and bats. Further south near **Evu** you'll find freshwater springs and a public pool. Get a local to guide you.

A new bridge connects **Debut** with **Tetoat**, from which a rough road continues all the way south to **Madwaer**, about 41km from Langgur, then to the island's cape, where you'll discover an absolutely magnificent sweep of powdery white sand known as **Pantai Ohoidertutu**. Given its daily access to Ambon, you may be surprised just how remote Kei Kecil is, especially the far south. The only way down here is on a horribly rutted road by *ojek* (150,000Rp round trip) or rented motorbike. And if you do make this motorbike-motocross run, bring rain gear. Folks will be joyfully surprised to see you.

Pulau Tanimbar Kei

A series of outlying islands with lovely beaches and turquoise waters surrounds Kei Kecil, the most intriguing of which is Pulau Tanimbar Kei, southwest of Ohoidertutu. Famed for its traditional village, powdery sand and magnificent snorkelling, the only way to get here is by chartering your own speedboat from Langgur or Debut (2,000,000Rp round trip) or with local villagers who come to Langgur to shop. Their powered canoes are the cheaper (25,000Rp), slower and possibly safer option. However, you will have to find your way back, which could take a few days. There's no formal accommodation on Tanimbar Kei. Upon arrival arrange a homestay with the *kepala desa* (village head) or perhaps on the Indonesian marine base.

Pulau Kei Besar

Scenic Kei Besar is a long ridge of lush, steep hills edged with remote, traditional villages and several picture-perfect beaches (better for taking photos than for swimming). Expect intense curiosity from locals and take your best *kamus* (dictionary) as nobody speaks English.

Attractively set on a bay featuring three tempting sand-fringed islets, **Elat** is Kei Besar's main village. It has a market and a few rice-and-fish *rumah makan*. All close by dusk, so eat early or snack on biscuits from the few tiny evening shops.

Southwest of Elat, a lane through palm fronds and bougainvillea leads 6km to **Pantai Daftel**, 1.8km of superb, shallow white-sand beach stretching to **Lerohoilim**, where there's a scattering of ancient graves atop a rocky outcrop called **Batu Watlus**. Other easy *ojek* excursions from Elat include picturesque **Yamtel** village (20 minutes east), **Waur** (15 minutes south), or the charming west-coast villages of **Ngurdu** (3km), **Soinrat** (4km), **Bombay** (7km) and **Watsin** (8km), all with bay views, stone stairways and rocky terraces.

The east coast has attractive, tidal rock pools but no beaches. Villages are comparatively isolated, steeped in superstitious traditions, and locals tend to speak the local Kei language rather than Bahasa Indonesia. **Banda Ely** in the extreme northeast is a settlement founded by Bandanese refugees from Dutch atrocities. Its predominantly Muslim people preserve their Bandanese culture.

Torpedo-shaped 50-seater speedboats shuttle between Watdek (Langgur) and Elat (50,000Rp, 65 to 80 minutes), leaving when full – that's roughly hourly between around 8.30am and 4pm.

Papua

Includes ➡

Best Places to Eat

- Rumah Makan Salam Manis (p465)
- Duta Cafe (p468)
- Yougwa Restaurant (p471)
- Warung Makan Bakwokah (p474)

Best Places to Stay

- Raja Ampat Biodiversity (p462)
- Lumba Lumba (p461)
- Kordiris Homestay (p462)
- Alberth Elopore's Guesthouse (p486)
- Hotel Rainbow Wamena (p478)
- Padaido Hotel (p474)

Why Go?

Even a country as full of adventure as Indonesia has its final frontier. And here it is: Papua, half of the world's second-biggest island, New Guinea. It may be the youngest part of Indonesia, but Papua's rich tribal traditions span centuries. This is a place where some people still hunt their food with bows and arrows. A place where roads are so scarce, that to travel between towns you often have no choice but to take to the air or the water. So unlike any other part of Indonesia, the province formerly known as Irian Jaya can feel like a different country – which is what many Papuans, who are Melanesian and ethnically distinct from other Indonesians, would like it to be.

Travel here is undoubtedly a challenge, and not one that comes cheap. But those who take it on rarely fail to be awed by the charm of Papua's peoples, the resilience of its cultures and the grandeur of both its dramatic landscapes and idyllic seascapes.

When to Go

Sorong

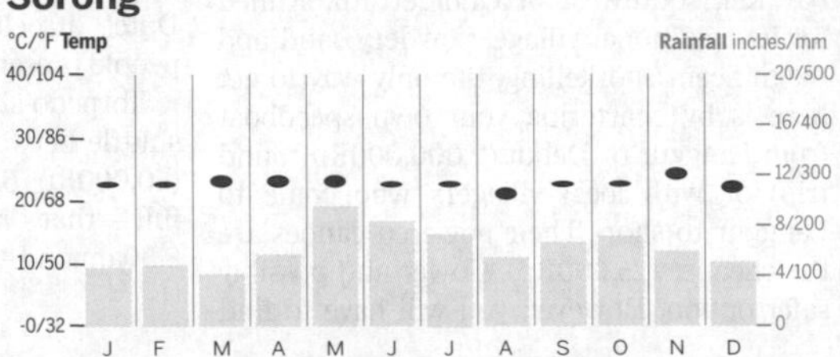

Apr–Dec Generally benign weather in the Baliem Valley; perfect for trekking.

Aug Join in with the feasting and the fun at the Baliem Valley Festival.

Nov–Mar Ideal conditions for marvelling at the aquatic wonders of the Raja Ampat Islands.

History

It's estimated that Papua has been inhabited for 30,000 or 40,000 years, but contact with the outside world was minimal until the mid-20th century. Three colonial powers agreed to divide the island of New Guinea between them in the late 19th century: Holland got the western half, and Britain and Germany got the southeastern and northeastern quarters respectively (together these two parts now comprise the country of Papua New Guinea). Dutch involvement with Papua was minimal up until WWII when Japan seized most of New Guinea in 1942. Japan was then driven out in 1944 by Allied forces under US general Douglas MacArthur.

Indonesia Takes Over

When the Netherlands withdrew from the rest of the Dutch East Indies (which became Indonesia) in 1949, it hung on to its half of New Guinea, and then began to prepare it for independence with a target date of 1970. Indonesia's President Sukarno had other ideas and in 1962 Indonesian troops began infiltrating the territory in preparation for an invasion. Under pressure from the US, which didn't want to risk a damaging defeat for its Dutch ally by the Soviet-backed Sukarno regime, the Netherlands signed the New York Agreement of 15 August 1962. Under this agreement, Papua became an Indonesian province in 1963. The Papuan people were to confirm or reject Indonesian sovereignty in a UN-supervised vote within six years. In 1969, against a background of Papuan revolt and military counter-operations that killed thousands, Indonesia decided that the sovereignty vote would involve just over 1000 selected 'representatives' of the Papuan people. Subjected to threats, the chosen few voted for integration with Indonesia in what was officially named the Act of Free Choice.

The following decades saw a steady influx of Indonesian settlers into Papua – not just officially sponsored transmigrants but also 'spontaneous' migrants in search of economic opportunity. Intermittent revolts and sporadic actions by the small, primitively armed Organisasi Papua Merdeka (Free Papua Organisation; OPM) guerrilla movement were usually followed by drastic Indonesian retaliation, which at times included bombing and strafing of Papuan villages. Indonesia invested little in Papuans' economic or educational development, while the administration, security forces and business interests extracted resources such as oil, minerals and timber.

Papua in the 21st Century

Following the fall of the Suharto regime in 1998, the *reformasi* (reform) period in Indonesian politics led many Papuans to hope that Papuan independence might be on the cards. In June 2000 the Papua People's Congress (more than 2500 Papuan delegates meeting in Jayapura) declared that Papua no longer recognised Indonesian rule and delegated a smaller body, the Papua Council Presidium, to seek a UN-sponsored referendum on Papuan independence. But the 'Papuan Spring' was short-lived. The second half of 2000 saw a big security force build-up in Papua, and attacks on pro-independence demonstrators. In 2001, the Papua Council Presidium's leader Theys Eluay was murdered by Indonesian soldiers.

The year 2001 also saw the passing of a Special Autonomy charter for Papua – Jakarta's response to Papuan grievances. The major provision was to give Papua a bigger share (70% to 80%) of the tax take from its own resources, plus more money to develop education and health. But many Papuans consider that Special Autonomy has not benefited them significantly, complaining that too much of the money disappears into the hands of the bureaucracy. They also complain that non-Papuans control Papua's economy and government in their own interests, and are exploiting Papua's natural resources with minimal benefit for the native people. The US-owned Freeport mine, digging the world's biggest recoverable lodes of gold and copper out of the mountains north of Timika, and using the Indonesian police and army as part of its security force, is often considered a classic symbol. Its troubled relationship with local communities has seen violence on numerous occasions, and its installations and workers have been targets of attacks usually attributed to the OPM.

Pro-independence activism and OPM activity have increased in Papua in recent years, and killings, torture, rape and disappearances carried out by the Indonesian security forces have continued to be reported by human-rights bodies. Papuans regularly receive jail sentences of 10 years or more for simply raising the Morning Star flag, the symbol of Papuan independence. A new meeting of the Papua People's Congress in 2011 reaffirmed its independence declaration but was broken up by troops, with six people reported killed.

Despite this, living standards in Papua's cities have risen, but the villages and countryside, where most native Papuans live, remain among Indonesia's poorest. The AIDS

Papua Highlights

1 Hiking among the thatched-hut villages, unique tribal culture and mountain grandeur of the **Baliem Valley** (p477).

2 Diving and snorkelling in the real-life tropical aquarium of the **Raja Ampat Islands** (p458).

3 Swimming with whale sharks off **Nabire** (p476).

4 Witnessing spectacular tribal festivities at the **Baliem Valley Festival** (p478) or **Festival Danau Sentani** (p471).

5 Hiking into the mountains around **Manokwari** (p463) in search of birds of paradise and other exotic wildlife.

6 Enjoying the island life among the friendly folk of **Pulau Biak** (p473).

7 Searching out the indigenous lowland culture and Australia-like flora and fauna of **Wasur National Park** (p487).

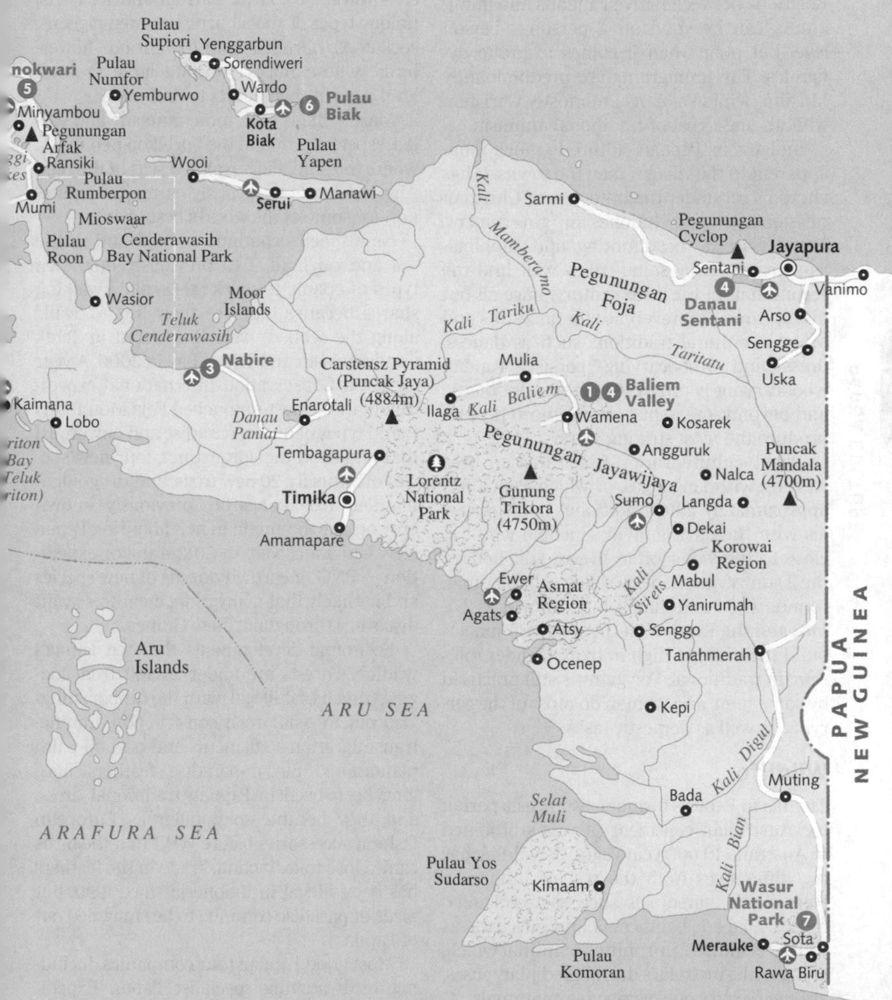

0 250 km
0 150 miles
N
PACIFIC OCEAN
Equator
Pulau Supiori
Yenggarbun
Sorendiweri
nokwari
5
Pulau Numfor
Yemburwo
Wardo
Kota Biak
6 Pulau Biak
Minyambou
Pegunungan Arfak
Ransiki
Pulau Rumberpon
Wooi
Pulau Yapen
Serui
Manawi
Mumi
Mioswaar
Pulau Roon
Cenderawasih Bay National Park
Wasior
Moor Islands
Teluk Cenderawasih
3 Nabire
Kaimana
Lobo
Danau Paniai
Enarotali
Carstensz Pyramid (Puncak Jaya) (4884m)
Tembagapura
Timika
Amamapare
Lorentz National Park
Ilaga
Kali Baliem
Mulia
Kali Tariku
Kali Mamberamo
Sarmi
Pegunungan Cyclop
Jayapura
Sentani
4 Danau Sentani
Vanimo
Pegunungan Foja
Kali Taritatu
Arso
Sengge
Uska
1 4 Baliem Valley
Wamena
Kosarek
Pegunungan Jayawijaya
Angguruk
Gunung Trikora (4750m)
Nalca
Puncak Mandala (4700m)
Sumo
Langda
Dekai
Korowai Region
Ewer
Agats
Asmat Region
Kali Sirets
Mabul
Yanirumah
Atsy
Senggo
Ocenep
Tanahmerah
Kepi
Aru Islands
ARU SEA
ARAFURA SEA
PAPUA NEW GUINEA
Kali Digul
Muting
Bada
Selat Muli
Kali Bian
Pulau Yos Sudarso
Kimaam
Wasur National Park
7
Sota
Merauke
Rawa Biru
Pulau Komoran

rate in Papua is the highest in Indonesia. Most Papuans want to be free of Indonesian rule, but their chances of that seem as slim as ever now that, by some estimates, half of Papua's four million people are non-Papuans.

Culture

Papua is a land of hundreds of cultures – those of the 200-plus indigenous peoples and those of all the immigrants from other parts of Indonesia, who dominate in the cities and now make up more than half of Papua's population. Relations between native Papuans and immigrants can be good on a person-to-person level but poor when it comes to group dynamics. The immigrants are predominantly Muslim, while Papuans are mostly Christian with an undercoat of traditional animism.

Indigenous Papuan culture is much more apparent in the villages than the towns. It has altered a lot under the influence of Christian missionaries and Indonesian government. Tribal warfare, headhunting and cannibalism, practised by some tribes well into the second half of the 20th century, have all but disappeared. But reverence for ancestors and pride in cultural traditions such as dances, dress and woodcarving persist. Papuan woodcarving is prized throughout Indonesia and beyond: the Asmat and Kamoro peoples produce the most striking work.

Tribal culture varies from area to area starting with languages, of which Papua has approximately 280. Traditional housing varies with the environment – people who live close to the water often live in stilt houses, the Dani of the Baliem Valley inhabit snug, round, wood-and-thatch huts known as *honai,* and the Korowai of the southern jungles build their homes high in trees. Gender roles remain traditional. Polygamy is still practised by some men, and women do most of the carrying as well as domestic tasks.

Wildlife

Thanks to Papua's former existence as part of the Australian continent (it was still joined to Australia 10,000 years ago), its wildlife has big differences from the rest of Indonesia. Here dwell marsupials such as tree kangaroos, wallabies, bandicoots and cuscuses, as well as echidnas, a primitive mammal which, along with Australia's duck-billed platypuses, are the world's only egg-laying mammals.

Papua is still three-quarters covered in forest. Its diverse ecosystems range from savannahs and mangroves to rainforest, montane forest and the glaciers around 4884m Carstensz Pyramid (Puncak Jaya), the highest peak in Oceania. It's home to more than half the animal and plant species in Indonesia, including more than 190 mammals, 550 breeding birds, 2650 fishes and more than 2000 types of orchid.

The megastars of the feathered tribe are the birds of paradise, whose fantastically coloured males perform weird and wonderful mating dances. Also here are large, ground-dwelling cassowaries, colourful parrots and lorikeets, unique types of kookaburra, crowned pigeons, cockatoos, hornbills, and the curious bowerbirds, whose males decorate large ground-level dens in their efforts to find mates.

Marine life is even more fantastic and varied, especially around the Vogelkop peninsula, where the still-being-explored seas of the Raja Ampat Islands are quickly earning a reputation for some of the world's best diving.

New species continue to be found in the sea and on land. Two previously unknown types of epaulette shark (also called walking sharks because they use their fins to 'walk' along the seabed) were discovered in Teluk Cenderawasih and Triton Bay in 2006. A year earlier, a Conservation International expedition in the almost-untouched Foja Mountains found types of bird of paradise and bowerbird that had been thought extinct, four new species of butterfly, 20 new frogs, and the golden-mantled tree kangaroo, previously known only on one mountain in neighbouring Papua New Guinea (PNG). In 2013 a major expedition to PNG unearthed dozens of new species and it's likely that many more creatures await discovery throughout New Guinea.

Economic developments threaten Papua's wildlife. Forests are under assault from logging (much of it illegal, with the timber smuggled out to Asia), road construction, mining, transmigration settlements and new oil-palm plantations. Bird-of-paradise feathers have long been used in Papuan traditional dress, and they became so popular as European fashion accessories before WWI that the birds came close to extinction. Trade in the feathers has been illegal in Indonesia since 1990, but birds of paradise continue to be smuggled out of Papua.

Most good Papuan tour companies, including birdwatching specialist Papua Expeditions (p456), can arrange birdwatching trips with expert local guides.

PAPUA TRAVEL PERMIT

In the fairly recent past, visiting Papua meant filling out reams of forms and obtaining a special travel permit known as a *surat keterangan jalan* (commonly called a *surat jalan*). In the past couple of years, though, permit restrictions have been eased for many areas (though this could just as easily be reversed). At the time of research in mid-2015, exactly where a *surat jalan* was required seemed to depend on whom you asked. The police in Jayapura insisted one was required for almost every town and area in Papua, but the reality was that in all but the remotest areas you now very rarely get asked to produce a *surat jalan*. To be on the safe side, however, if you're heading to the Baliem Valley, Yali country, Agats and the Korowai region it's better to get one.

A *surat jalan* is usually easily obtained from the police in the capitals of Papua's 30-odd *kabupaten* (regencies). The relevant police departments are typically open from about 8am to 2pm Monday to Saturday; times and days vary, and some departments can attend to you outside their official hours. Take your passport, two passport photos, and photocopies of your passport's personal details page and your Indonesian visa. The procedure normally takes about an hour and no payment should be requested. The duration of the permit depends on how long you request and the expiry date of your visa.

Some police stations will only issue a *surat jalan* for their own regencies or limited other destinations. The best place to obtain a wide-ranging *surat jalan* is Polresta (p469) in Jayapura, where you can present a list of every place that you intend to visit (don't omit any obscure, small, off-the-beaten-track places), and get them all listed on one *surat jalan*. You might have similar luck in other relatively large cities such as Manokwari and Sorong.

Once you have your *surat jalan*, make several photocopies of it. In remoter areas your hotel should report your arrival to the police and they will likely need photocopies of your passport and/or *surat jalan* to do so. In a few places you may need to report to the police yourself. Carry your *surat jalan* on out-of-town trips.

Some parts of Papua are sometimes off limits to tourists, usually because of Organisasi Papua Merdeka (Free Papua Organisation; OPM) activity. When you apply for a *surat jalan*, the police will tell you if anywhere on your itinerary is off limits.

Note: some Indonesian embassies may tell you that in order to visit Papua you must obtain a special permit from the Indonesian immigration authorities and/or the police department in Jakarta – some have even reportedly refused visas to applicants who said they planned to visit Papua. This is not true. In practice, as long as you have an Indonesian visa then you're free to travel to and around Papua (and don't worry, airlines never ask to see a *surat jalan*).

Tours & Guides

While travel in Papua is, in many cases, no more challenging than anywhere else in Indonesia, there are certain areas where the logistical difficulties of travel mean that it makes sense to take a guided tour. This is particularly true of the Asmat or Korowai regions or the little-explored Mamberamo basin in the north. Guided tours are essential (given the bureaucracy involved) for mountaineers wanting to climb Papua's high peaks such as Carstensz Pyramid (Puncak Jaya) or Gunung Trikora.

As well as guides and agencies with local ambits, there are several that offer trips to a range of Papua destinations.

Adventure Indonesia ADVENTURE TOUR

(www.adventureindonesia.com) Top Indonesian adventure-tourism firm that does Asmat, Carstensz Pyramid (Puncak Jaya) and Baliem Valley trips.

Andreas Ndruru TOUR

(☎0813 4496 9100; andreasndruru@hotmail.com) Andreas is a Sumatran-born, Papuan-passionate freelance guide who speaks fluent English and has huge experience of Papua and a great team (including an outstanding camp cook). He's based in Sentani but specialises in hiking trips and tours to tribal regions.

PAPUA TRAVEL WARNING

Outbreaks of civil unrest and violence do occur in Papua, but they shouldn't deter you from visiting unless the current situation changes. Political demonstrations sometimes turn violent, and acts of violence between Papuans and non-Papuans, often involving the Organisasi Papua Merdeka (Free Papua Organisation; OPM) or the Indonesian army or the police, happen most months. Many of these incidents occur in remote parts of the highlands (where the OPM is strongest), or around the Freeport mine near Timika, although the Baliem Valley and the Jayapura area also see some violence.

Localised fighting between different tribal groups sometimes occurs; these are normally disputes over land, livestock or women.

Whatever the type of violence, foreigners are rarely the targets or victims; tourists are welcomed by the great majority of people in Papua. Stay abreast of current events and ask the police if you have concerns about particular places.

Bob Palege TOUR
(☎0812 4721 0365; bobfredpalege@gmail.com) Based in Sentani, Bob Palege is something of a legend in Papuan travel circles and is arguably one of the region's most experienced and knowledgeable guides, with unsurpassed connections and contacts throughout Papua.

Discover Papua Adventure TOUR
(www.discoverpapua.com) An efficient, well-established Biak-based agency that can set up just about any trip you want throughout Papua.

Papua Expeditions BIRDWATCHING
(www.papuaexpeditions.com) This ecotourism-minded, Sorong-based company specialises in birding in all the best Papuan destinations. Its website is a great resource.

Getting There & Around

Intercity roads are still a thing of the future for Papua. Boats are an option for travelling to Papua and between its coastal towns if you have enough time, or along its rivers if you have enough money. Flying is the common way to reach Papua and to travel between its cities and towns.

AIR

To fly to Papua you must first get to Jakarta, Makassar, Denpasar, Manado or Ambon, then take a domestic flight. For the Baliem Valley, fly first to Jayapura and take an onward flight from there. Jayapura is served by four airlines from Jakarta and Makassar, and by Garuda from Denpasar (via Timika). Jakarta–Jayapura fares are not cheap and start at around 1,500,000Rp one way. For the Raja Ampat Islands, fly to nearby Sorong from Jakarta, Makassar or Manado.

Most commercial flights within Papua cost around 700,000Rp to 1,200,000Rp, plus or minus a hundred thousand or two.

Missionary airlines such as the Roman Catholic Associated Mission Aviation (AMA) and Protestant Mission Aviation Fellowship (MAF) do a lot of flying between small, remote airstrips. They will sometimes carry tourists if they have spare seats. Chartering a small plane for seven to 12 people is another option for routes not served by scheduled flights. Airlines servicing Papua include **Batik Air** (www.batikair.com), **Garuda Indonesia** (www.garuda-indonesia.com), **Lion Air** (www.lionair.co.id), **Sriwijaya Air** (www.sriwijayaair.co.id), **Susi Air** (www.susiair.com; flies small planes on local routes within Papua), **Trigana Air** (www.trigana-air.com), **Wings Air** (www.lionair.co.id) and **Xpress Air** (www.xpressair.co.id).

BOAT

Every two weeks, five Pelni liners sail into Sorong from Maluku, Sulawesi, Kalimantan or Java, continue to Jayapura via various intermediate ports along Papua's north coast, then head back out again. There are also a few sailings connecting Agats and Merauke on Papua's south coast with Sorong and ports in Maluku. We have listed economy-class prices, but other levels of comfort (at higher prices) may be available.

Various smaller, less comfortable passenger boats serve minor ports, offshore islands and routes on a few rivers such as the Mamberamo and Digul; some have more or less fixed schedules, others don't. On routes without any public service, you can charter a boat, which might be a fast, powerful speedboat, or a *longbot* (large motorised canoe) or a *ketinting* (smaller motorised canoe; long-tail boat). Charter costs are highly negotiable and depend on the boat, its fuel consumption, the distance and the petrol price.

WEST PAPUA

The province of West Papua chiefly comprises two large peninsulas – the Vogelkop (also known as Bird's Head, Kepala Burung and Semdoberai) and the more southerly Bomberai Peninsula – and several hundred offshore islands. The attractions here are primarily natural – above all, the world-class diving and gorgeous island scenery of the Raja Ampat Islands. Sorong and Manokwari are well-provided urban bases from which to launch your explorations.

Sorong

0951 / POP 190,000

Papua's second-biggest city, Sorong sits at the northwestern tip of the Vogelkop. It's a busy port and base for oil and logging operations in the region. Few travellers stay longer than it takes to get on a boat to the Raja Ampat Islands, but Sorong can be quite fun for a day or two, and there are some interesting destinations in the surrounding region.

Sleeping

JE Meridien Hotel HOTEL $$

(0951-327 999; www.hoteljemeridiensorong.blogspot.com; Jl Basuki Rahmat Km7.5; r 534,000-836,500Rp, ste from 1,009,000Rp, all incl breakfast;) Handily located opposite the airport, the Meridien offers nicely aged, slightly old-fashioned rooms of generous proportions. Rooms come with TVs and tea and coffee makers, plus you can get a free ride to the airport or the Raja Ampat ferry. The buzzing lobby has a good coffee shop and the Raja Ampat Tourism Management Office (though at the time of research this was scheduled to move).

Hotel Waigo HOTEL $$

(0951-333 500; Jl Yos Sudarso; r 489,000-705,600Rp, ste from 1,029,000Rp, all incl breakfast;) This hotel, facing the Tembok Berlin waterfront, offers fair value, large and bright (sometimes a bit *too* bright and pink!) rooms, which have a few nice touches like art and masks on the walls. The ocean-view 'suites' are massive. The in-house restaurant (mains 25,000Rp to 65,000Rp) is good value.

Swiss-Belhotel Sorong BUSINESS HOTEL $$$

(0951-321 199; www.swiss-belhotel.com; Jl Jendral Sudirman; r incl breakfast from 743,800Rp;) Opened in 2014 and setting new standards for Sorong hotels, the Swiss-Belhotel is easily the swankiest option in town – though if it were in Jakarta it wouldn't earn its four-star status. The staff are exceptionally helpful and there's a good in-house restaurant (mains 65,000Rp to 100,000Rp).

Eating

Sorong restaurants are generally better stocked with alcohol (beer, at least) than those elsewhere in Papua. For cheaper eats, dozens of seafood warungs (food stalls) set up in the evenings along waterfront Tembok Berlin (Jl Yos Sudarso).

Sunshine Beach INDONESIAN, CHINESE $$

(Jl Yos Sudarso, beside Hotel Tanjung; mains 50,000-120,000Rp; 9am-10pm Mon-Sat, 4-10pm Sun) This spacious, semi-open-air place with sparkling lights is built over the edge of the sea. It offers everything from fried rice or noodles to prawns, crab, fish, squid and beef, prepared in assorted ways. For something different dig into a plate of sea cucumber (380,000Rp). There's an air-conditioned bar, too.

Rumah Makan Ratu Sayang SEAFOOD, CHINESE $$

(Jl Yos Sudarso; grilled fish from 60,000Rp; 9am-2.30pm & 5.30-10pm) Pick up the scent of fish on the grill and head inside this two-level eatery for delicious *ikan bakar* (grilled fish). With rice, spinach, three sauces and a drink, this will set you back around 120,000Rp to 140,000Rp. It's just north of the well-signed turning to Sunshine Beach restaurant.

Information

ATMs outside Saga supermarket, at about the midpoint of Jl Yani, service Visa, Visa Electron, MasterCard, Maestro, Cirrus and Plus cards. There's also a Bank Mandiri ATM just north of Sunshine Beach and next to the huge pink church (you can't miss this!).

Polresta Sorong (0951-321 929; Jl Yani I) Head to this police station, 1km west of the airport, for a *surat jalan* (travel permit).

Raja Ampat Tourism Management Office (0811 485 2033; www.gorajaampat.com; JE Meridien Hotel, Jl Basuki Rahmat Km7.5; 9am-4pm Mon-Fri, to 1pm Sat) This incredibly helpful office can tell you almost anything you need to know about the Raja Ampat Islands, and it's the best place to buy the tag permitting you to visit the islands. It's scheduled to move to a new office next to the airport towards the end of 2015.

FLIGHTS FROM SORONG

DESTINATION	AIRLINE	FREQUENCY
Ambon	Wings Air	daily
Fak-Fak	Xpress Air	3 weekly
Jakarta	Xpress Air	daily
Jayapura	Garuda	daily
Makassar	Garuda, Sriwijaya Air	daily
Manado	Garuda, Wings Air, Xpress Air, Merpati	daily
Manokwari	Garuda, Sriwijaya Air, Xpress Air, Susi Air	daily
Timika	Garuda, Sriwijaya Air	daily

Getting There & Away

AIR

All airlines have ticket counters at the airport. Garuda and Sriwijaya Air connect Jakarta and Sorong via Makassar.

BOAT

Pelni (Jl Yani 13), near the western end of Jl Yani, has five ships sailing every two weeks east to Jayapura (via assorted intermediate ports, including Manokwari, Biak and Nabire) and west to ports in Maluku, Sulawesi and Java. Sample fares (economy class) are 263,000Rp to Biak; 299,000Rp to Jayapura; and 171,000Rp to Ambon. The *Tatamailau* heads down to Agats and Merauke (economy 395,000Rp) on Papua's south coast, every two weeks.

Getting Around

Official airport taxis charge 100,000Rp to hotels at the western end of town; on the street outside you can charter a public *taksi* for half that or less. Using the yellow public *taksi* (minibuses; 5000Rp), first get one going west outside the airport to Terminal Remu (600m), then change there to another for Jl Yos Sudarso. Short *ojek* (motorcycle) rides of 2km to 3km are 5000Rp; between the western end of town and the airport is 20,000Rp.

Raja Ampat Islands

POP 43,000

The sparsely populated Raja Ampat Islands comprise around 1000 islands just off Sorong. With their sublime scenery of steep, jungle-covered islands, scorching white-sand beaches, hidden lagoons, spooky caves, weird mushroom-shaped islets and pellucid luminous turquoise waters, Raja Ampat has to be one of the most beautiful island chains in Southeast Asia.

Pure, unadulterated beauty isn't just what draws people here, though. Raja Ampat has good birdwatching, with a couple of species of birds of paradise present, and what many call the best diving in the world. Little known until the last few years, Raja Ampat's diversity of marine life and its huge, largely pristine coral reef systems are a diver's dream come true – and fantastic for snorkellers too. It's like swimming in a tropical aquarium. In fact, the waters are so clear and fish so numerous that you hardly even need don a mask. We saw six sharks swimming around below us merely by peering out the window of an over-water hut! So great is the quantity and variety of marine life here that scientists have described Raja Ampat as a biological hotspot and believe that the reef systems here act to restock reefs throughout the South Pacific and Indian Oceans.

The four biggest islands are Waigeo (with the small but fast-growing regional capital, Waisai), Batanta, Salawati and Misool. The Dampier Strait between Waigeo and Batanta has many outstanding dive sites, so most accommodation options are on Waigeo, Batanta or three smaller islands between them: Kri, Gam and Mansuar.

Activities

Diving

You can get up close with huge manta rays and giant clams, gape at schools of barracuda, fusiliers or parrotfish, peer at tiny pygmy seahorses or multicoloured nudibranchs, and, with luck, encounter wobbegong and epaulette (walking) sharks. The reefs have hundreds of brilliantly coloured soft and hard corals, and the marine topography varies from vertical walls and pinnacles to reef flats and underwater ridges. To generalise, Raja Ampat is better suited to advanced divers; it's not exactly a learn-to-dive hotspot. There are, however, some dive spots suitable for relative novices.

Most dives are drift dives. Beware: the currents that whip you along the edge of the reefs can be very strong. You can dive year-round, although the usually smooth seas can get rough from July to September (the Raja Ampat/Sorong area gets its heavier rain from May to October). The dive resorts generally offer packages of a week or more and focus

Raja Ampat Islands

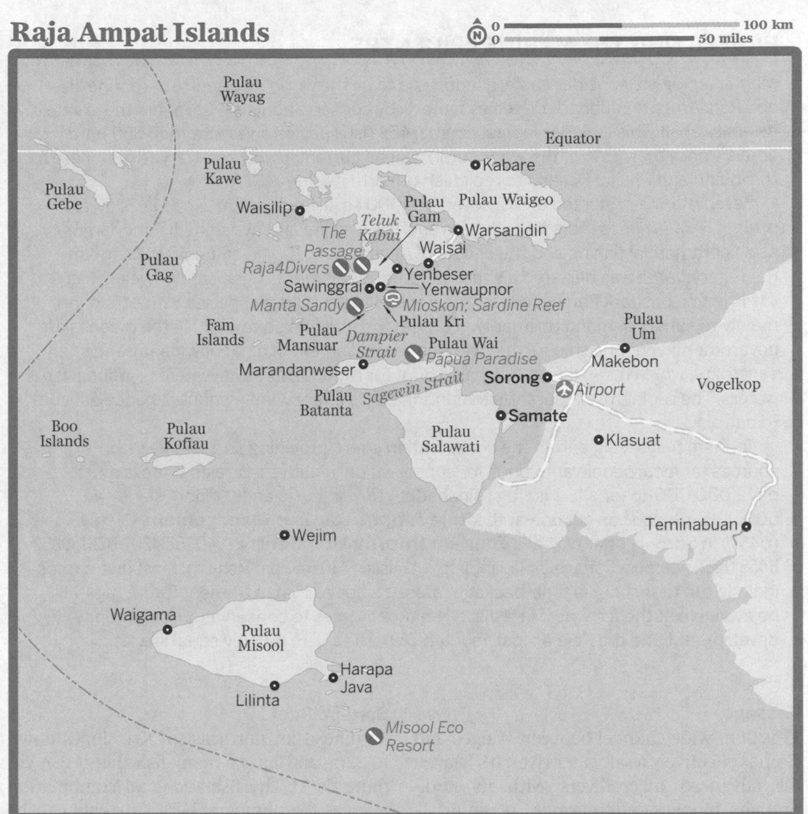

on spots within about 10km of their resort. Some will take nonguests diving if they have places available, for around €50 per dive, plus €40 to rent a complete set of equipment. Valid insurance and dive cards will be required at reputable dive operators.

Many of the ever-growing number of homestays on Pulau Kri and Pulau Gam also offer diving services, but only highly experienced divers should consider this option – the guides can be short on professional training and experience and on safety protocols and safety equipment. We've heard numerous stories of people who've signed up to dive with a homestay and run into problems, including having to be rescued by boats from the top-end dive resorts. If you do dive with a homestay ask to see its certification. There's a decompression chamber in Waisai, but the quality of the facilities here can be unreliable; the nearest quality chamber is far away in Manado, Sulawesi.

Here's a very brief selection of the top dive areas and spots, in approximate northwest-to-southeast order:

Wayag Islands — DIVING

These small, uninhabited and incredibly picturesque islands, 30km beyond Waigeo, feature heavily in Raja Ampat promotional material. It's mainly liveaboards that dive here, but Wayag also attracts nondivers for its scenery, snorkelling and the challenge of scaling its highest peak, Pindito. An all-day speedboat round trip from Waisai for six to 10 people costs around 12,000,000Rp.

Teluk Kabui — DIVING

The bay between Waigeo and Gam is packed with picturesque jungle-topped limestone islets. The Batu Lima dive spot in the bay's entrance has a great variety of fish and beautiful soft corals.

PROTECTING THE MARINE EPICENTRE

Marine biologists consider eastern Indonesia to be the world's epicentre of marine life, and Raja Ampat – dubbed a 'species factory' by conservationists – harbours the greatest diversity of all. This includes, at last count, 1459 fish species and more than 550 hard corals (more than 75% of the world total). Ocean currents carry coral larvae from here to the Indian and Pacific Oceans to replenish other reefs.

Seven marine protected areas, covering 9000 sq km, were established in 2007 to protect Raja Ampat's reefs from threats such as cyanide and dynamite fishing, large-scale commercial fishing and the effects of mining. In 2010, the entire 50,000-sq-km Raja Ampat area was declared a shark sanctuary. This was a significant move against the practice of shark finning, which threatens numerous shark species with extinction, mainly to satisfy demand (primarily in China) for shark-fin soup. In 2014 the Indonesian government went one step further with the establishment of a nationwide ray and shark sanctuary, which mean it's now illegal to hunt for rays or sharks anywhere in Indonesian waters. The problem, of course, is that Indonesia is a very watery country, hence difficult to patrol.

Tourism plays a big part in the conservation effort, providing sustainable income sources for local people and funds for conservation initiatives. Foreign visitors must pay 1,000,000Rp for a tourist tag (pin/badge) to visit the islands (Indonesians pay 500,000Rp): you can get one at the **Raja Ampat Tourism Management Office** (p457) in Sorong, or at Waisai's **Tourism Information Centre** (☎0852 4202 0251, 0852 5455 0411; Acropora Cottage, Jl Badar Dimara, Waisai; ⏱10am-2pm Mon-Fri). Most dive camps include the tourist tag in their package rates. It's hoped that in the near future tags will be available at the ferry port in Waisai. The money goes to conservation, community development and the Raja Ampat Tourism Department, in roughly equal shares.

Passage DIVING

This 20m-wide channel between Waigeo and Gam is effectively a saltwater river. It's heaven for advanced macrodivers with its nudibranchs, sponges and tunicates ('sea squirts'). Sharks, archerfish, turtles, rays and schools of bumphead parrotfish are seen here, too.

Fam Islands DIVING

Calm waters, stunning coral and masses of fish, notably at the Melissa's Garden spot.

Manta Sandy DIVING

At this famous site between Mansuar and Arborek islands, numbers of huge manta rays, some with wingspans over 5m, wait above large coral heads to be cleaned by small wrasses. Best from about October to April.

Cape Kri DIVING

The fish numbers and variety at the eastern point of Pulau Kri have to be seen to be believed. A world record of 374 fish species in one dive was counted here in 2012. Schools of barracuda, jacks, batfish and snapper coexist with small reef fish, rays, sharks, turtles and groupers. Beautiful coral too. There can be strong currents and so diving here requires a minimum of 50 logged dives.

Sardine Reef DIVING

Sardine, 4km northeast of Kri, slopes down to 33m, and has so many fish that it can get quite dark! The fish-and-coral combination is great for photographers. Currents can be strong.

Pulau Misool DIVING

This remote southern island – especially the small islands off its southeastern corner – has stunning coral. The pristine reefs attract pygmy seahorses, epaulette sharks, manta rays and a vast range of other fish.

Snorkelling

There are strong currents in some areas of the Raja Ampat Islands, but snorkellers can enjoy top dive locations including Cape Kri, Manta Sandy (although the manta rays are often a bit deep to see properly), the Fam Islands, Pulau Wai and Mioskon (10km northeast of Kri). You can also see wonderful coral and marine life just by stepping off the beach in many, many places. Most accommodation, including homestays, can rent or loan snorkelling gear.

Birdwatching

The many exotic birds on the islands include two fantastically coloured endemic birds of paradise, the red and the Wilson's.

The red male has a spectacular courtship dance in which he spreads his wings and shakes like a big butterfly. Village guides in Sawinggrai, Yenwaupnor and Yenbeser on Pulau Gam provide a relatively easy way to see this, charging 150,000Rp per person for early-morning walks to nearby display spots. Maybe the most enjoyable of these is the tour offered by **Simon Dimara** (☎0852 4301 2894), which, as well as seeing birds of paradise, also includes a boat ride up a long, narrow green-water gorge and a visit to the spot where naturalist Alfred Wallace set up camp while exploring these islands. Sorong-based Papua Expeditions (p456) offers specialised Raja Ampat birding trips.

Kayaking

★Kayak4Conservation KAYAKING
(www.kayak4conservation.com; kayak per day from €35, guesthouse per person with/without 3 meals 400,000/300,000Rp, guide per day 300,000Rp) Originally established by the forward-thinking folk at Sorido Bay Resort on Pulau Kri, Kayak4Conservation provides exciting multiday tours of Raja Ampat by kayak, with or without a guide, staying at homestays or camping. Your money goes directly to the local people providing the services.

Sleeping

Accommodation options in Raja Ampat are growing fast (some people worry that it's too fast and lacking regulation) and can be divided into three options: high-quality dedicated dive lodges, homestays and liveaboard dive boats. The typical packages with the dive resorts or liveboards include 'unlimited' diving (up to four boat dives per day within about 10km, plus house-reef dives), accommodation, meals and Sorong transfers on fixed days of the week. Transfers from Waisai are also possible. More distant dives, equipment rental and transfers on nonstandard days cost extra. Most dive resorts offer cheaper rates for nondivers.

A growing number of much-less-expensive 'homestays' are opening up on several islands – the majority on Kri and Gam. Few of them are actual homestays but groups of purposely built palm-thatch huts close to or even over the water. A few now have private bathrooms but most just have separate, shared Indonesian-style bathrooms. They all offer snorkelling, birdwatching and other outings. Three (mainly fish-based) meals a day are usually part of the deal. Homestays will normally pick you up in Waisai if you contact them a day or two ahead (best by phone or SMS), typically for 1,000,000Rp to 1,200,000Rp per boat return trip to Kri or Gam, and increasingly more distant places. Boat outings can cost anything from 400,000Rp to 1,500,000Rp, or even more, depending how far you go.

The Raja Ampat Tourism Management Office (p457) in Sorong can help you contact homestays, or visit www.stayrajaampat.com, which lists all homestays and includes contact details, rates and reviews. A warning: we've heard several tales from disappointed travellers who found promised services or meals lacking, or even nonexistent. The ones listed here are the better-established or more professional options.

Pulau Kri

★Lumba Lumba GUESTHOUSE $$
(☎081 281 009244, 082 198 294400; www.lulumba.com; r incl full board 500,000Rp) On the blissfully quiet southern shore of Pulau Kri, Lumba Lumba is one of the most professionally run guesthouses on Kri and in all of Raja Ampat. The five comfortable over-water huts are well maintained and have attractive seashell decorations. Looking over the eye-searing white sands and sheer jungle-tinged cliffs, you'll probably decide this is the perfect spot to drop out of life for a while.

Mangkur Kodon Homestay HOMESTAY $$
(☎0852 4335 9154; enzomo@libero.it; s/d incl full board 400,000/600,000Rp) This guesthouse is set where two perfect beaches meet in one tight triangle – a sight known to induce tears of joy. Combine that with friendly staff, top-class snorkelling out front, and inviting palm-thatch huts hung over the water and you've all the ingredients for happiness.

It's on the far southwestern edge of the island, and a short walk (or wade at high tide) from the other accommodation options.

Koranu Fyak Bungalows HOMESTAY $$
(☎081 344 174787, 082 238 019420; stephy_eeuu@hotmail.com; s/d incl full board 400,000/600,000Rp) This foreign-managed homestay understands the needs of backpackers and serves them up simple thatch huts with separate shared bathrooms lined up along a sparkly white beach. If you don't like dogs you probably won't like this place because there are loads of them hanging around. English and Spanish spoken.

Kri Eco Resort RESORT $$$
(☎0811 483 4614; www.papua-diving.com; Pulau Kri; 7-night unlimited diving package s/d from €1729/3038; 📶) 🍃 Operating since 1994, Kri Eco is the original Raja Ampat dive lodge. It's a professional operation with a gorgeous setting. Baby black-tip reef sharks are frequently seen swimming in the shallows below the restaurant. All 13 rooms are on stilts at the edge of the crystal-clear water but most have on-land, shared bathrooms (with *mandis*).

Sorido Bay Resort RESORT $$$
(☎0811 483 4614; www.papua-diving.com; Pulau Kri; 7-night unlimited diving package €2705-2890; ❄📶) 🍃 Sorido offers top diving standards along with Western-style comforts, such as air-con, camera workstations and hot showers in spacious, well-equipped beachfront bungalows. The tucked-away location fronting a divine beach is superb.

Owner Max Ammer pioneered diving in Raja Ampat after he stumbled upon the potential while searching the area for crashed WWII aircraft. From that you will probably quite rightly deduce that he's a real character who'll add much to your stay.

Pulau Gam

★**Kordiris Homestay** GUESTHOUSE $$
(☎085 399 040888, 081 248 569412; www.kordiris.com; Pulau Gam; per person incl full board 300,000-350,000Rp) This well-organised homestay, which sits in a secluded, dreamy bay dotted with tiny coral islands, is one of the best around. The rooms are made of palm thatch, and while some are in the cool shade of trees, others are exposed to the breezes on the salty white sand.

Mambefor Homestay HOMESTAY $$
(☎085 254 544254; Sawinggrai Village, Pulau Gam; s/d incl full board 400,000/500,000Rp) A very basic little over-water homestay that's right on the jetty in Sawinggrai village. There are three rooms with mattresses on the floor and shared bathrooms 50m away in the village. As such, a stay here is more about cultural interaction than beach lounging. Don't expect much privacy – or much beach.

★**Raja Ampat Biodiversity** LODGE $$$
(☎0821 8922 2577; www.rajaampatbiodiversity.com; Pantai Yenanas, Pulau Gam; 7 nights full board incl 14 dives s/d from €1630/2770) 🍃 Two kilometres east of Yenbeser village on Gam, Spanish-run Biodiversity is probably the overall best-value place to stay on the islands. Accommodation is in spacious, comfortable cabins filled with seashore knick-knacks. The 'budget' rooms have shared bathrooms. Good Indonesian and Western food is served, the dive operation is of a high standard, and PADI and SSI diving courses are offered, too.

Unusually for a resort it offers packages shorter than a week. Free scheduled transfers from Waisai are available.

Papua Explorers Resort RESORT $$$
(☎081 180 00511; www.papuaexplorers.com; 7-night dive package incl full board s/d €2310/3930, incl 3 boat dives daily & unlimited house-reef dives; ❄📶) One of the flashiest, newest and biggest of the dive resorts, Papua Explorers is set in a large, pretty bay and has 15 palatial over-water bungalows. It's all very polished – maybe too much for some. All bungalows have elegant furnishings and tribal decoration, hot-water bathrooms, terraces with easy sea access and in-room wi-fi.

Other Islands

Harapan Jaya Homestay HOMESTAY $$
(☎0813 4435 3030; Harapan Jaya Village; full board per person 400,000Rp) This superior-standard homestay is currently the only one on large, remote Pulau Misool (actually it's on a small offshore island). It's a great base for exploring Misool's breathtaking islands, beaches, caves and waterfalls. However, getting there is problematic. You can either charter an expensive speedboat (around US$3500) or take the weekly ferry from Sorong (departs Friday, returns Saturday).

Misool Eco Resort RESORT $$$
(www.misoolecoresort.com; Pulau Batbitim; 7-night unlimited diving package r from €2320-4390; ⏲closed Jul & Aug; ❄📶) 🍃 On a beautiful small island off southeastern Misool (a four- to five-hour trip from Sorong), this comfortable, well-run dive resort has a strong conservation and community ethos and many superb dive sites within a few minutes' boat ride. Most cottages have a veranda over the water; all have open-air bathrooms.

It maintains an 862-sq-km no-take zone in the surrounding waters. Speedboat transfers from Sorong are €300 per person.

Papua Paradise RESORT $$$
(www.papuaparadise.com; Pulau Birie; 7-night unlimited diving package s/d €2335/3994; 📶) With large, elegant over-water bungalows on a

gorgeous, pristine, small island off northern Batanta, and masses of good diving nearby, this resort is one of the best in Raja Ampat. It's also a good base for birdwatching (including the red and Wilson's birds of paradise) and offers PADI courses.

Raja4Divers RESORT **$$$**
(☎081 1485 7711; www.raja4divers.com; Pulau Pef; 7-night unlimited diving package s/d €3100/5200; @📶) A classy small resort on an idyllic island beach with a reef out front, Raja4Divers sits off western Gam, giving access to some superb dives that are beyond the normal reach of Dampier Strait resorts. The large, airy water's-edge bungalows are decked with intriguing artefacts and are as refined as they come.

There's no extra charge for distant dives here, but you do have to pay (€250 per person each way) for the scheduled Sorong transfers.

Liveaboards

The ultimate Raja Ampat experience could be cruising around on a Bugis-style schooner specially kitted out for divers. Some 40-plus Indonesian- and foreign-owned liveaboards do regular one- to two-week dive cruises, usually starting and ending in Sorong. Some itineraries combine Raja Ampat with Maluku, Teluk Cenderawasih, or Triton Bay (Teluk Triton) south of Kaimana. Most boats carry 12 to 16 passengers and some are luxurious, with air-conditioned cabins and en-suite bathrooms. Most cruises run between November and April, when Raja Ampat seas are calmest. Costs typically range between US$300 and US$500 per person per day. See www.diverajaampat.org for a full list of operators.

Grand Komodo DIVING
(www.komodoalordive.com) A long-running Indonesian operation, which has three liveaboards operating year-round and is among the least expensive.

Seven Seas DIVING
(www.thesevenseas.net) The Seven Seas is probably the last word in Raja Ampat liveaboard luxury.

Shakti DIVING
(www.shakti-raja-ampat.com) Well-established, quality operator.

Pindito DIVING
(www.pindito.com) Beautiful boat, cruising in a beautiful place.

Seahorse DIVING
(www.indocruises.com) Excellent operator around Raja Ampat and elsewhere.

Getting There & Around

Waisai has a new and impressive airport. Sadly its runway is also very short – too short, it turned out, for the full-sized passenger planes that were planned to come here. Instead there are Susi Air flights on Sunday and Friday between Sorong and Waisai, but it's just as quick (after all the messing around at the airport) to get the ferry.

Fast Marina Express passenger boats (economy/VIP 130,000/220,000Rp, two hours) and a larger, slower boat (100,000Rp, three hours) depart for Waisai from Sorong's **Pelabuhan Feri** (Pelabuhan Rakyat; Jl Feri, off Jl Sudirman) at 2pm daily. The slower boats have greater open-air deck space. The boats head back from Waisai at 2pm Sunday to Friday and at noon Saturday.

Ojeks to Pelabuhan Feri cost around 15,000Rp from the western end of Sorong or outside the airport; a taxi is around 50,000Rp. *Ojeks* between port and town in Waisai (2km) are 20,000Rp.

An overnight boat to Waigama and Lilinta on Misool leaves Pelabuhan Feri at 10pm every Friday (economy/VIP 310,000Rp/375,000), but other passenger boats to and around the islands are irregular. To arrange transport around the islands once there, your best bet is to ask at your accommodation or Waisai's Tourism Information Centre (p460). Prices depend on boat, distance and petrol price and are usually negotiable.

Manokwari

☎0986 / POP 60,000

Capital of Papua Barat (West Papua) province, Manokwari sits on Teluk Cenderawasih near the northeastern corner of the Vogelkop. It merits a visit mainly for the natural attractions in the surrounding area, notably the Pegunungan Arfak. Most travellers' facilities are in the area called Kota, on the eastern side of the Teluk Sawaisu inlet. Local transport terminals and the airport (7km from town) are to the west and southwest.

Sights & Activities

Pulau Mansinam ISLAND
Two German missionaries settled on Mansinam Island off Manokwari in 1855 and became the first to spread Christianity in Papua. The picturesque, rainforest-covered island is home to a small village, a none-too-subtle church, and a wannabe Rio statue of

Manokwari

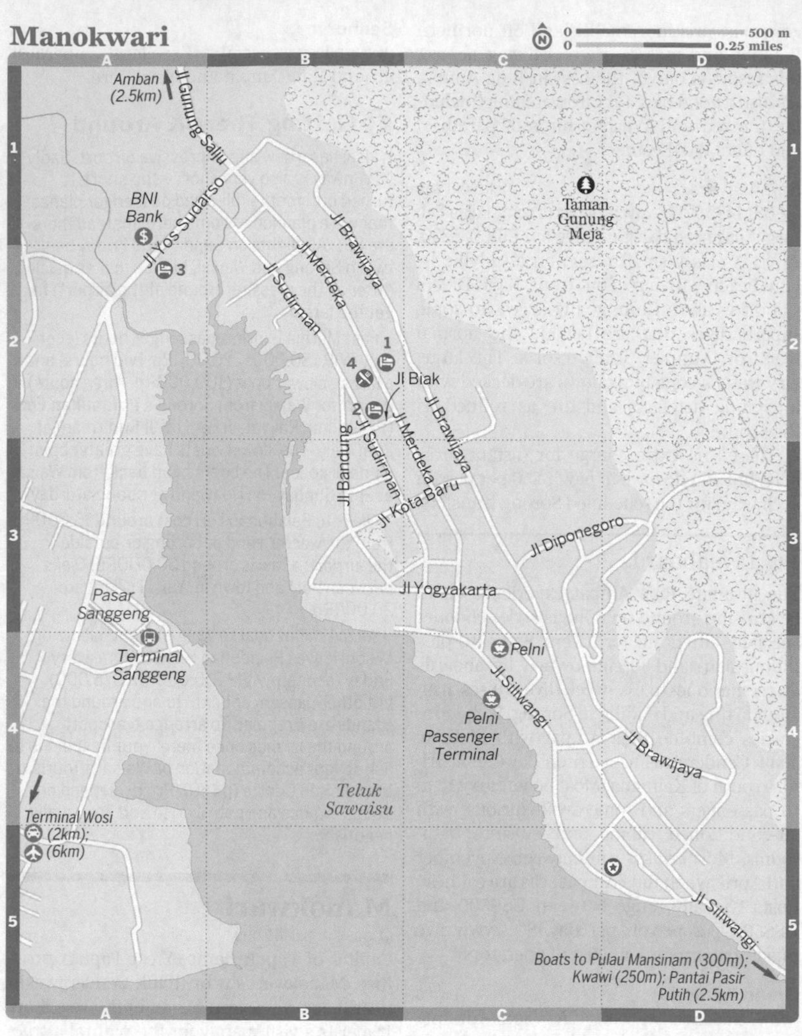

Manokwari

Sleeping

1 Billy Jaya Hotel....B2
2 Metro Hotel....B2
3 Swiss-Belhotel....A2

Eating

4 Rumah Makan Salam Manis....B2

Christ. There's also a pleasant beach along its western and southern shores. The coral reef off the southern end offers good snorkelling.

Outrigger boats (5000Rp one way) sail to Mansinam from Kwawi, 2.5km southeast of central Manokwari, when they have enough passengers.

Pantai Pasir Putih BEACH

About 5km east of town, this 600m curve of clean white sand and clear water is good for swimming, and snorkelling if you have gear. It's generally quiet – except on Sunday when half of Manokwari invades the beach.

Taman Gunung Meja WALKING

(Table Mountain Park) This protected forest makes an enjoyable walk if you start early enough to catch the birdlife and morning cool. A 1km walk up from Jl Brawijaya brings you to the white entrance gate, from where a fairly level 3km track, mostly paved, runs north through the forest.

After 800m the **Tugu Jepang**, a Japanese WWII monument, stands 100m to the left along a branch track. From the far end of the forest track, follow the paved road 600m past houses, then go left at a T-junction. This brings you in 400m to the Manokwari–Amban road, where you can catch a *taksi* or *ojek* back to town.

Sleeping

Billy Jaya Hotel HOTEL $$
(☎0986-215432; hotelbillyjaya@yahoo.com.sg; Jl Merdeka 57; r incl breakfast 200,000-400,000Rp; ❄📶) The older, cheaper rooms (up to 290,000Rp) range from small and dark to large, windowed and acceptable. The new section is much better, with shiny tiled floors and nice white bedding. The old Vespa with side car in the hotel lobby is an unusual talking point. The hotel offers free airport drop-offs (though, sadly, not in the Vespa).

Metro Hotel HOTEL $$
(☎0986-215975; Jl Biak; r incl breakfast 300,000-500,000Rp; ❄) A fair deal with small but clean rooms, with thick mattresses on the beds and pleasant staff at reception.

Swiss-Belhotel BUSINESS HOTEL $$
(www.swiss-belhotel.com; Jl Yos Sudarso 8; r incl breakfast from 686,000Rp; ❄📶🏊) The best hotel in town has comfy but surprisingly tired rooms, and the restaurant (mains 72,000Rp to 300,000Rp) provides a wide range of Asian dishes, plus steaks. It's not deserving of its four stars.

Eating

★ **Rumah Makan Salam Manis** INDONESIAN $
(Jl Merdeka; mains 20,000-40,000Rp; ⏲8.30am-10pm) Renowned far and wide for its *nasi ayam panggang lalapan* (grilled chicken with green vegetables and rice), this two-storey place is an excellent choice for a communal meal while sat cross-legged at low tables surrounded by pot plants on the 1st floor. Very popular with locals.

Information

BNI Bank (Jl Yos Sudarso) With ATM.

Police Station (Jl Bhayangkhara; ⏲9am-5pm) Grab your *surat jalan* here. It's 1km southeast of the port.

Getting There & Away

Tickets for the small planes of **Susi Air** (www.susiair.com) are only sold at the airport, 6km southwest of town, and even then the ticket office is often only open very early in the morning (like 5am early…).

Every two weeks **Pelni** (☎0986-215 167; Jl Siliwangi 24) has five sailings each to Jayapura (economy class 431,000Rp) and Sorong (126,500Rp), four to Makassar, three to Nabire, two each to Biak and Ternate, and one each to Ambon and Banda. ASDP Indonesia Ferry's *Kasuari Pasifik IV* sails to Biak (economy/1st/VIP class 50,000/120,000/150,000Rp, 15 hours) at 4pm Thursday. The *KM Napan* sails to Nabire via Wasior (economy/VIP 150,000/290,000Rp) on Tuesday at 5pm.

Getting Around

Airport taxis to town cost 100,000Rp. Some public *taksi* (5000Rp) pass the airport, bound for Terminal Wosi, halfway to the centre. At Wosi you might find another *taksi* direct to Kota (6000Rp); otherwise get one to Terminal Sanggeng, then another (or walk) to Kota. Terminal Sanggeng is the starting point for very frequent public *taksi* running through Kota and out to Kwawi and Pantai Pasir Putih.

FLIGHTS FROM MANOKWARI

DESTINATION	AIRLINE	FREQUENCY
Ambon	Wings Air	4 weekly
Biak	Susi Air	3 weekly
Jakarta	Xpress Air, Garuda, Sriwijaya Air	daily
Jayapura	Garuda, Sriwijaya Air	daily
Makassar	Garuda (not direct), Sriwijaya Air	daily
Sorong	Sriwijaya Air, Xpress Air, Garuda	daily
Kaimana	Wings Air	3 weekly

Around Manokwari

The mountains, jungles, coasts and islands around Manokwari are great for off-the-beaten-track adventures in nature. Best known for their birds of paradise and other exotic species are the mountains of the Pegunungan Arfak. The offshore islands and waters, the lowland forests and the exciting but little-known **Senopi area**, 130km west (reachable by a five-hour drive or via Susi Air flights to Kebar), are also ripe for exploring. Senopi village has the unexpectedly good **Senopi Guesthouse** (d incl full board 350,000Rp), and **Aiwatar hill**, a day's walk away, attracts thousands of birds every morning to its warm saltwater springs and coastal vegetation (40km from the sea). A guide can help you get the best out of the region.

Activities

★Charles Roring HIKING, BIRDWATCHING
(☎0813 3224 5180; www.manokwaripapua.blogspot.com) An enthusiastic guide who seeks out exciting natural destinations, Charles offers hiking, camping, birding, nature and snorkelling trips all over the Manokwari region and as far as Triton Bay (Teluk Triton) south of Kaimana. Browse his websites (goldmines of information) for ideas. His guiding fee is usually between 350,000Rp and 500,000Rp per day, depending on group size and destination.

Arfak Paradigalla Tours BIRDWATCHING, HIKING
(☎0812 4809 2764; yoris_tours@yahoo.com) This effusive, one-man, English- and Dutch-speaking outfit offers city tours as well as Arfak trips. Yoris Wanggai is very knowledgeable about the area's birds, plants and insects. He charges around 800,000Rp per day for overnight trips, not including transport, accommodation or food.

Pegunungan Arfak

The thickly forested Arfak mountains, rising to more than 2800m south of Manokwari, are a region of beautiful tropical scenery, exotic wildlife (especially birds) and a mostly indigenous Papuan population (the Hatam and other peoples), some of whom still inhabit traditional 'thousand-leg' stilt houses. The first and one of the biggest Papuan revolts against Indonesian rule happened here from 1965 to 1968.

The best-known birdwatching base is **Mokwam**, a collection of small villages a few kilometres down a side road about 50km from Manokwari, before Minyambou. There's accommodation for tourists in two of the villages, Syobri and Kwau.

In Syobri ask for **Zeth Wonggor** (☎0852 5405 3754), a highly experienced guide who has worked here with, among others, Sir David Attenborough. He has forest hides for viewing the magnificent bird of paradise, Western parotia and Arfak astrapia (also

OFF THE BEATEN TRACK

TRITON BAY

In the past few years, whispered rumours have started emerging about Triton Bay (Teluk Triton) and how, just maybe, the marine ecosystems here are even more impressive than those of Raja Ampat.

The wealth of marine life here is extraordinary. Of the many highlights are pygmy seahorses, Nursalim flasher wrasse, Triton Bay walking sharks, big pods of dolphins, marlin, groupers, sweetlips, large schools of fusiliers and surgeonfish and arguably the most spectacular soft corals in the world. And if all that weren't enough, there's also the big daddy of them all, whale sharks, which are attracted to the fishing *bagang* (platform).

So far there are around 30 identified dive sites ranging from pinnacles to shallow soft-coral gardens and drift and wall dives. The one downside is that average visibility ranges from 10m to 15m, though it can be up to 25m or as little as 5m.

Currently very few people have dived here and only a few liveaboard dive boats come through, but with the 2015 opening of the **Triton Bay Divers** (www.tritonbaydivers.com; Aiduma Island; 7-nights full board incl 15 dives s/d €2400/3800; closed Jun–mid-Sep), the first dive resort in the area, the reefs around here are about to become easier to access. The resort is set on Aiduma Island and has just four elegant, luxurious wooden cottages on a beautiful white-sand beach.

Access to Triton Bay is via Kaimana. **Wings Air** (www.lionair.co.id) connects Kaimana with Jayapura and Manokwari.

birds of paradise), the Vogelkop bowerbird and other exotic feathery species. February and March are best for observing spectacular, iridescent birdwing butterflies with wingspans of up to 25cm. Zeth has tourist accommodation (per person 100,000Rp) in a well-built wooden house. He charges 500,000Rp per day for guiding.

In Kwau village **Hans Mandacan** (☎081 344 214965) runs a similar kind of show. The very comfortable guesthouse (100,000Rp) here is surrounded by flowers and is only a five-minute walk from the nearest bird hides. Hans charges 175,000/350,000Rp per half-day/day for guiding.

You can get a 4WD double-cabin pickup to Mokwam (150,000Rp, 1½ hours) from around 7am, 100m along the street past Manokwari's Terminal Wosi. Talk to drivers the day before, or get to the stop in good time, if you don't want to end up chartering a whole vehicle for 1,200,000Rp (one way).

OFF THE BEATEN TRACK

BIRDING IN MUPI GUNUNG

Perhaps the best birding area around Manokwari, and one that so far remains very unexplored, is Mupi Gunung, south of Manokwari. The birding here is rumoured to be superb, but at the time of research only a handful of tourists had ever visited. To get there, head to the coastal village of Mupi, after which it's a six-hour hike through forest. Currently this is one excursion for which you really will need local help. Charles Roring (p466) in Manokwari can organise visits.

NORTHERN PAPUA

Papua province's capital, Jayapura, and its airport town Sentani, are hubs of Papuan travel, and there's a scattering of appealing things to see and do in and around these towns. Further west, Biak is a relaxed offshore island that's good for a spot of lazing on a beach, snorkelling and diving, and has evocative WWII sites to investigate. Nabire is the starting point for trips to swim with whale sharks.

Jayapura

☎0967 / POP 316,000

Downtown Jayapura is hot and busy with traffic, but it has a beautiful setting between steep, forested hills opening onto Teluk Imbi as well as a certain decrepit tropical air that some find appealing.

A small settlement named Hollandia was established here by the Dutch in 1910. In 1944, 80,000 Allied troops landed here to dislodge the Japanese in the largest amphibious operation of WWII in the southwestern Pacific. After WWII, Hollandia became capital of Dutch New Guinea. Following the Indonesian takeover in 1963, it was renamed Jayapura ('Victory City') in 1968. A public consultation exercise in 2010 favoured changing the name to Port Numbay, a name popular with indigenous Papuans, but this has yet to be officially ratified.

The city stretches 6km northeast from its centre, and its conurbation includes the formerly separate towns of Argapura, Hamadi, Entrop, Abepura and Waena, all south of Jayapura proper. Cenderawasih University at Abepura is a particular focus of Papuan nationalism.

Sights

Museum Loka Budaya MUSEUM
(Jl Abepura, Abepura; admission 25,000Rp; ⏲7.30am-4pm Mon-Fri) Cenderawasih University's cultural museum contains a fascinating range of Papuan artefacts including the best collection of Asmat carvings and 'devil-dance' costumes outside Agats, plus fine crafts from several other areas, historical photos and musical instruments. There's also a collection of stuffed Papuan fauna, which includes a number of birds of paradise. The museum is next to the large Auditorium Universitas Cenderawasih on the main road in Abepura.

Pantai Base G BEACH
Base G beach is nearly 3km long, sandy, clean and lined with wooden picnic platforms. The best beach easily accessible from Jayapura, it is usually near-empty, except on Sunday when locals come in droves for a bathe and a walk. Beware the many rocks in the water. Base G was the American forces' administrative HQ in 1944.

Frequent 'Base G' *taksi* (4000Rp) start from Jl Sam Ratulangi for the 5km trip; the beach is a 10-minute walk downhill from the last stop.

Jayapura

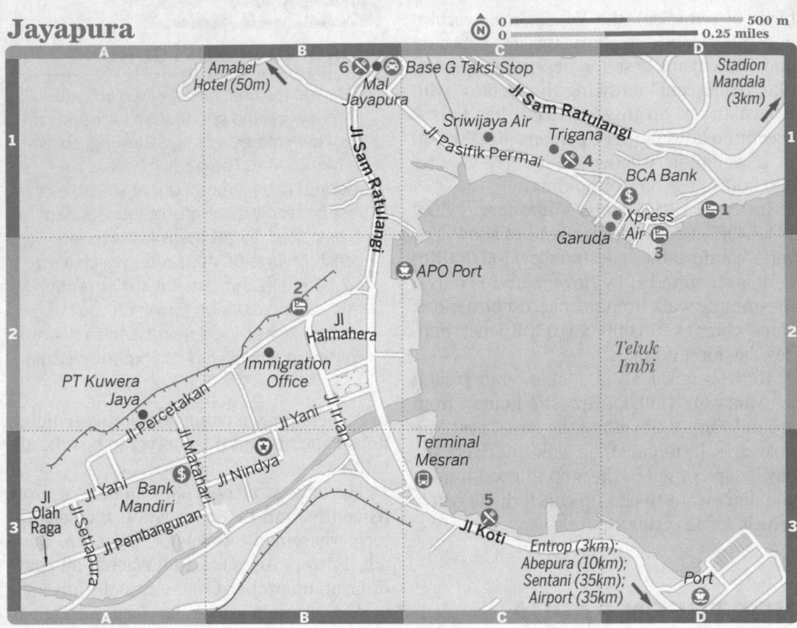

Jayapura

Sleeping

Eating

Sleeping

Amabel Hotel HOTEL $

(☎0967-522102; Jl Tugu 100; s/tw/d 253,000/297,000/363,000Rp;) Easily the best budget option, the Amabel has neat little rooms with windows and its own inexpensive restaurant. It's up a small, leafy side street, a block before the Mal Jayapura (shopping mall).

Hotel Grand View HOTEL $$

(☎0967-550646; Jl Pasifik Permai 5; r incl breakfast 450,000-750,000Rp;) A very good deal. This place has plain but bright, modern, no-frills rooms, half of which peer directly out over the waters of the bay. The downstairs cafe-restaurant is a delightfully cheery strawberry red.

Hotel Yasmin HOTEL $$$

(☎0967-533222; www.yasminjayapura.com; Jl Percetakan 8; s 700,000-1,100,000Rp, d 750,000-1,150,000Rp;) A quite classy place with well-equipped but small rooms, and a 24-hour restaurant. Some of the cheapest rooms lack windows and are dark, but head up a price band and you get smart, spacious and great-value rooms.

Swiss-Belhotel BUSINESS HOTEL $$$

(☎0967-551888; www.swiss-belhotel.com; Jl Pasifik Permai; r incl breakfast from 988,000Rp;) There's nothing very Papuan about it, but the Swiss-Bel provides high-quality, European-style comfort in a harbourside location and it has a good open-air pool. Check the website for discounts, especially at weekends.

Eating

★**Duta Cafe** SEAFOOD $$

(Duta Dji Cafe; Jl Pasifik Permai; vegetable dishes 15,000-25,000Rp, whole fish 50,000-80,000Rp; 5pm-2am) Long lines of evening warungs open along Jl Pasifik Permai, cooking up all sorts of Indonesian goodies, including seafood galore. At the large, clean Duta Cafe, halfway along the street, an excellent *ikan bakar* (grilled fish) comes with several sambals (chilli sauces) lined up on your table, and the juice drinks go down very nicely.

Don't confuse this place with another Duta Cafe further along near the Swiss-Belhotel.

Waroeng Pojok INDONESIAN $

(Mal Jayapura; mains 35,000-40,000Rp; ⏲7am-10pm) Part of a small national chain of cool, comfy, air-con restaurants serving classic Javanese cuisine and frothy milkshakes and juices. It makes a delicious change from the endless oily nasi goreng of small-town Papua or the sweet potatoes of the mountains. It's on the 2nd floor of the Mal Jayapura (shopping mall).

Resto & Cafe Rumah Laut INDONESIAN, SEAFOOD $$

(☎0967-537673; Jl Koti; mains 40,000-80,000Rp; ⏲8am-10pm) This upmarket place, built on stilts above the waters of Jayapura bay, is where locals come when they want to impress. The wide-ranging menu takes in Indonesian classics, a few Chinese options, and fish. Lots of fish. If you're not eating, at least come for a fruit juice.

Information

Bank Mandiri (Jl Yani 35; ⏲8am-3pm Mon-Fri) You can exchange US$100 notes here, and there's an ATM.

BCA Bank (Blok C, Ruko, Jl Pasifik Permai; ⏲8am-3pm Mon-Fri) Exchanges cash US dollars, euros and British pounds, with no minimum.

Immigration Office (☎0967-533647; Jl Percetakan 15; ⏲8am-4pm Mon-Fri) This office will issue one 30-day extension to a visa on arrival (VOA): apply at least one week before your visa expires. Travellers with VOAs must come here for a (free) exit stamp before crossing the land border to Vanimo, Papua New Guinea.

Polresta (Polda; Jl Yani 11; ⏲9am-3pm Mon-Fri) Police elsewhere in Papua will often only

TRANSPORT FROM JAYAPURA

Air

DESTINATION	AIRLINE	FREQUENCY
Biak	Garuda, Sriwijaya Air	daily
Denpasar	Garuda (via Timika)	daily
Jakarta	Garuda, Lion Air, Batik Air, Sriwijaya Air	daily
Kaimana	Wings Air	daily
Makassar	Garuda, Batik Air, Lion Air, Sriwijaya Air	daily
Manado	Lion Air (via Sorong), Sriwijaya Air (via Timika)	daily
Manokawri	Garuda, Sriwijaya Air	daily
Merauke	Garuda, Lion Air, Sriwijaya Air	daily
Nabire	Wings Air, Trigana	weekly
Sorong	Garuda, Lion Air	daily
Wamena	Trigana, Wings Air, Xpress Air	daily

Boat

DESTINATION	FARE (RP; ECONOMY CLASS)	DURATION	FREQUENCY (PER 2 WEEKS)
Ambon	405,000	2½–4 days	3
Banda	395,000	3½ days	1
Biak	173,500	17-25hr	3
Makassar	720,000	4-5 days	5
Manokwari	245,000/	1-2 days	5
Nabire	225,000	15-32hr	3
Sorong	325,000	1½–2½ days	6

TRAVELLING BETWEEN PAPUA & PNG

There are no flights between Papua (Indonesia) and Papua New Guinea (PNG), and the only land border crossing that is open to foreigners is at Skouw (opposite Wutung, PNG), 55km east of Jayapura and 40km west of Vanimo, PNG. This border suffers occasional temporary closures, usually due to political tensions.

To cross the land border in either direction, you need a visa beforehand. It's best to get visas in advance at Indonesian or PNG embassies elsewhere. The **PNG consulate at Jayapura** (☎0967-53 1250; Blok 6 & 7, Ruko Matoa, Jl Kelapa Dua, Entrop; ⏱9am-noon & 1-2pm Mon-Fri) issues 60-day tourist visas. If you turn up early enough in the morning then you might get it the same day. To apply, you must submit an application form; a cover letter stating where you want to go in PNG and why; a photocopy of a confirmed onward air ticket; a photocopy of your passport; and two colour photos (4cm by 6cm), with your signature on the back. Regulations and practices at both consulates change from time to time and you might also be asked to supply a sponsor's or invitation letter from PNG (if this is impossible, explain why in your letter of request). The Jayapura consulate is next to Hotel Le Premiere, 600m east of the Entrop *taksi* terminal.

Note that if you are in Indonesia with a visa on arrival (VOA), you must get an exit stamp at Jayapura's immigration office before travelling to the border to cross to PNG.

Buses and vans link Vanimo's market area with the border. Between the border and Jayapura or Sentani you usually need to charter a *taksi* for 250,000Rp to 400,000Rp; the trip takes about two hours.

issue a *surat jalan* for their own regencies, but here you can get one for everywhere you want to go in Papua (that's not off limits). They do tend to request a donation for 'administrative costs', however. Processing normally takes about one hour.

PT Kuwera Jaya (☎0967-533333; Jl Percetakan 96; ⏱8am-9pm Mon-Sat, 10am-9pm Sun) This efficient travel agency sells tickets for flights and Pelni boats from Jayapura, and also some flights from other Papuan cities.

ℹ Getting There & Away

AIR

Jayapura airport (☎0967-591 809), actually located at Sentani, 36km west, is the hub of Papuan aviation. Most flights arrive and depart between 7am and 1pm. Tickets are available at travel agencies and at the airport and Jayapura offices of the airlines.

Garuda (www.garuda-indonesia.com; Blok G 11-12, Jl Pasifik Permai)

Sriwijaya Air (www.sriwijayaair.co.id; Blok A 2, Jl Pasifik Permai)

Trigana (☎0967-535 666; www.trigana-air.com; Blok B 12B, Jl Pasifik Permai)

Xpress Air (www.xpressair.co.id; Jl Pasifik Permai)

BOAT

Six Pelni liners leave from Jayapura in every two-week period, sailing to some 20 ports in Papua, Maluku, Sulawesi, Kalimantan and Java.

The **port** (Jl Koti) is accessible by any *taksi* heading to Hamadi or Entrop. Pelni tickets are available there or at travel agencies including PT Kuwera Jaya.

Perintis boats also head along the coast as far as Manokwari, putting in at smaller ports en route and even heading to villages up rivers such as the Mamberamo. They normally leave from the **APO port** (Jl Sam Ratulangi) and typically take a week to get to Manokwari. Finding out about schedules will be a challenge! Bring food and drinks.

ℹ Getting Around

Official airport taxis from the airport at Sentani to central Jayapura cost a hefty 450,000Rp. If you organise a taxi yourself without going through the taxi booths, they will quote you the same fare but with bargaining will drop as low as 300,000Rp.

Going by public *taksi* from Sentani to Jayapura involves three changes and takes about 1½ hours if the traffic is on your side. Fortunately, each change is just a hop into another vehicle waiting at the same stop. Start with one from Sentani (outside the airport gate or heading to the right along the main road 400m straight ahead) to Waena (4000Rp, 20 to 30 minutes). Then it's Waena to Abepura (3000Rp, 10 minutes), Abepura to Entrop (3000Rp, 20 minutes) and Entrop to Jayapura (2500Rp, 20 minutes). Heading back from Jayapura, go through the same routine in reverse. You can pick up Entrop-bound *taksi* on Jl Percetakan or at **Terminal Mesran** (Jl Koti).

Sentani

0967 / POP 48,000

Sentani, the growing airport town 36km west of Jayapura, sits between the forested Pegunungan Cyclop and beautiful Danau Sentani.

Festivals & Events

Festival Danau Sentani CULTURAL
(around 18-25 Jun) The Lake Sentani Festival, inaugurated in 2008, features spectacular traditional dances and chanting as well as boat events, music, crafts and hair braiding. It's very popular with locals and lately has taken place at Kalkhote, on the lakeside 8km east of Sentani town.

Sleeping

Rasen Hotel HOTEL $$
(0967-594455; rasenhotel_papua@yahoo.com; Jl Penerangan; s/d incl breakfast 250,000/350,000-400,000Rp;) The best choice near the airport, the Rasen has small, clean rooms with hot showers and TVs, plus a decent restaurant, free airport drop-offs and even a small fish pond. Unsurprisingly, it fills up, so try to call ahead. Some staff speak English.

★ **Grand Allison Hotel** BUSINESS HOTEL $$$
(0967-592210; www.grandallisonsentani.com; Jl Raya Kemiri 282; r incl breakfast from 1,680,000Rp;) Quite possibly the single fanciest hotel in Papua, the Grand Allison is business slick with international-standard rooms, facilities and service that you won't find elsewhere. A highlight is the lovely swimming-pool complex. Book online for discounts.

Eating

★ **Yougwa Restaurant** INDONESIAN $$
(0967-571570; Jl Raya Kemiri; mains 25,000-60,000Rp; 10am-8.30pm Mon-Sat, to 4pm Sun & holidays) Sentani's most charming dining is on the Yougwa's breezy wooden terraces over

Sentani

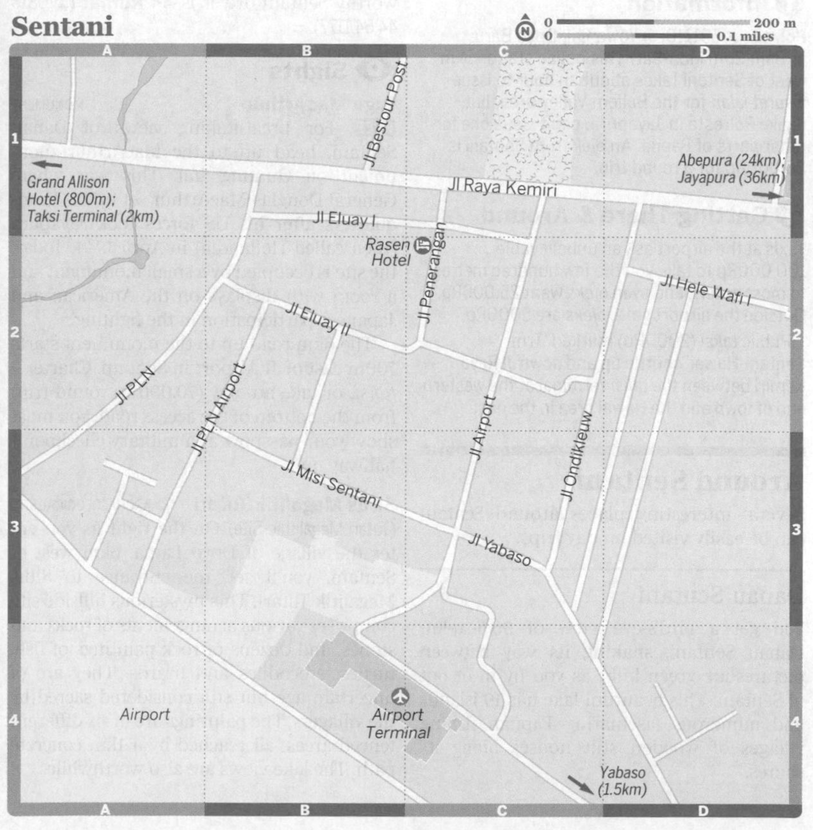

Around Jayapura & Sentani

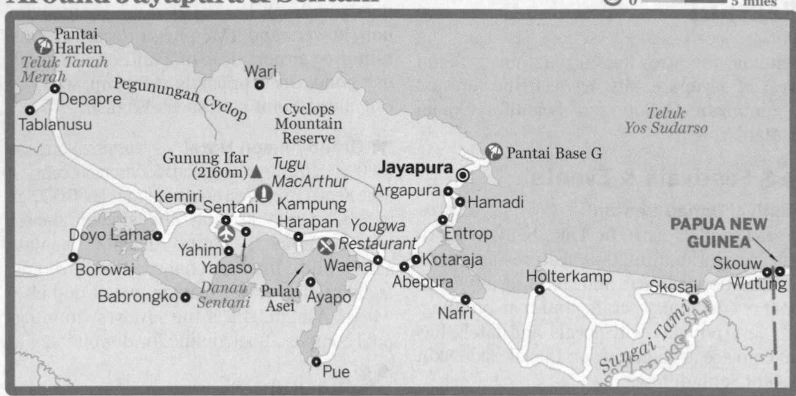

the lake, 13km east of town. Try *ikan gabus* (snakehead), a tasty lake fish that doesn't fill your mouth with little bones.

Information

Polres (591110; Jl Yowanibi, Doyo Baru; 8am-2pm Mon-Sat) This police station 5km west of Sentani takes about an hour to issue a *surat jalan* for the Baliem Valley area, but, unlike Polresta in Jayapura, can't issue one for other parts of Papua. An *ojek* from Sentani is 30,000Rp for a round trip.

Getting There & Around

Taxis at the airport ask an unbelievable 100,000Rp to take you the few hundred metres to most hotels, and even *ojeks* want 25,000Rp. Outside the airport gate, *ojeks* are 5000Rp.

Public *taksi* (2000Rp) marked 'Trm Sentani-Hawai' shuttle up and down Jl Raya Kemiri between the *taksi* terminal at the western end of town and the Hawai area in the east.

Around Sentani

Several interesting places around Sentani can be easily visited on day trips.

Danau Sentani

You get a bird's-eye view of 96.5-sq-km Danau Sentani, snaking its way between picturesque green hills, as you fly in or out of Sentani. This beautiful lake has 19 islands and numerous fascinating Papuan fishing villages of wooden stilt houses along its shores.

If you've got time between flights you can hire a taxi and driver at the airport for half a day to scoot about some of the sights. Expect to pay anywhere up to 800,000Rp. One trustworthy Sentani driver is **Ali Rumaf** (0813 44 54 1177).

Sights

Tugu MacArthur MONUMENT

FREE For breathtaking views of Danau Sentani, head up to the MacArthur monument on Gunung Ifar. This was where General Douglas MacArthur set up his headquarters after his US forces took Jayapura (then called Hollandia) in April 1944. Today, the site is occupied by a small monument and a room with displays on the American and Japanese participation in the fighting.

The 6km road up to the monument starts 700m east of Jl Airport in Sentani. Charter a *taksi*, or take an *ojek* (70,000Rp round trip) from the bottom of the access road. You must show your passport at a military checkpoint halfway up.

Situs Megalitik Tutari ARCHAEOLOGICAL SITE

(Tutari Megalithic Site) On the right as you enter the village of Doyo Lama, 6km west of Sentani, you'll see the entrance to Situs Megalitik Tutari. This mysterious hillside site comprises various arrangements of rocks and stones, and dozens of rock paintings of fish, turtles, crocodiles and lizards. They are of uncertain age but still considered sacred by the villagers. The paintings are in six different fenced areas, all reached by a 1km concrete path. The lake views are also worthwhile.

Entry is by donation. The gate man will probably ask for an optimistic amount, but 20,000Rp should do the trick. If you find the gate closed, no one is likely to mind if you climb over and enter anyway.

Pulau Asei ISLAND

Asei is the main centre for Sentani bark paintings. Originally done only on bark clothing for women of the chiefs' families, bark paintings are now a Sentani art form. To reach Asei, take a *taksi* to Kampung Harapan, then an *ojek* 2km south to the lake, then a boat to the island.

Pulau Biak

0981

Biak (1898 sq km) is one of Papua's biggest offshore islands. It's a relaxed and friendly place with good snorkelling and diving. It was once a popular destination with foreign travellers to Papua but today has been rather eclipsed by the Raja Ampat Islands.

Biak saw fierce fighting in WWII, with about 10,000 Japanese and nearly 500 Americans reported killed in the month-long Battle of Biak (1944).

Getting Around

Public *taksi* and a few buses reach most places of interest around the island. You can make things easier by chartering a car or *ojek*, or by taking a trip with Discover Papua Adventure (p475). Away from the south coast, most villages are little more than a handful of huts, with no accommodation or food for travellers.

Kota Biak

POP 38,000

This main town is your obvious, and only real, base. The airport is 3km east of the centre, along Jl Yani, which becomes Jl Prof M Yamin.

Activities

Though Biak is not in the same league as the Raja Ampat Islands as a scuba destination, there is still some good diving and snorkelling. In general you'll see most fish from May to July. East of Kota Biak there are wall dives at Marau, Saba and Wadibu, which are also good snorkelling spots, as is Anggaduber. But the best diving and snorkelling is around the offshore Padaido Islands.

The island also attracts the odd exploratory surfer between November and April.

Pulau Biak

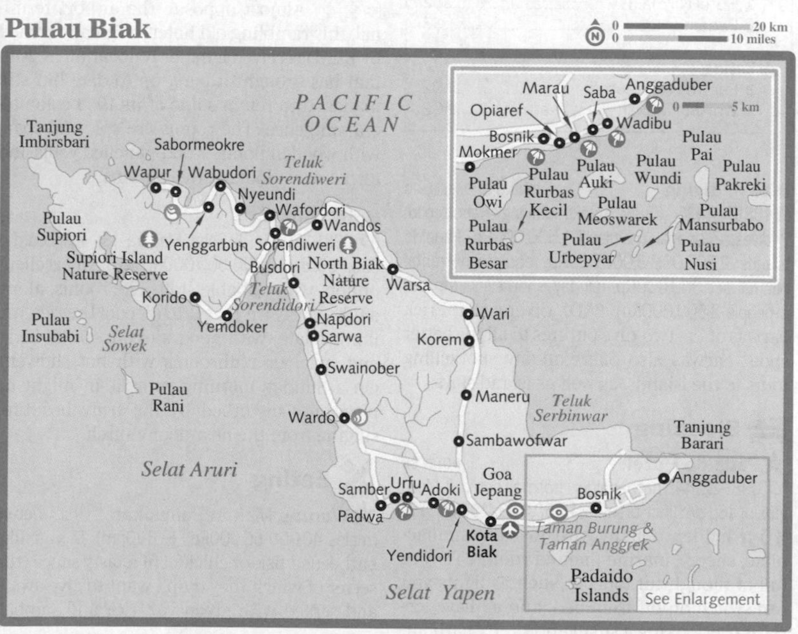

Kota Biak

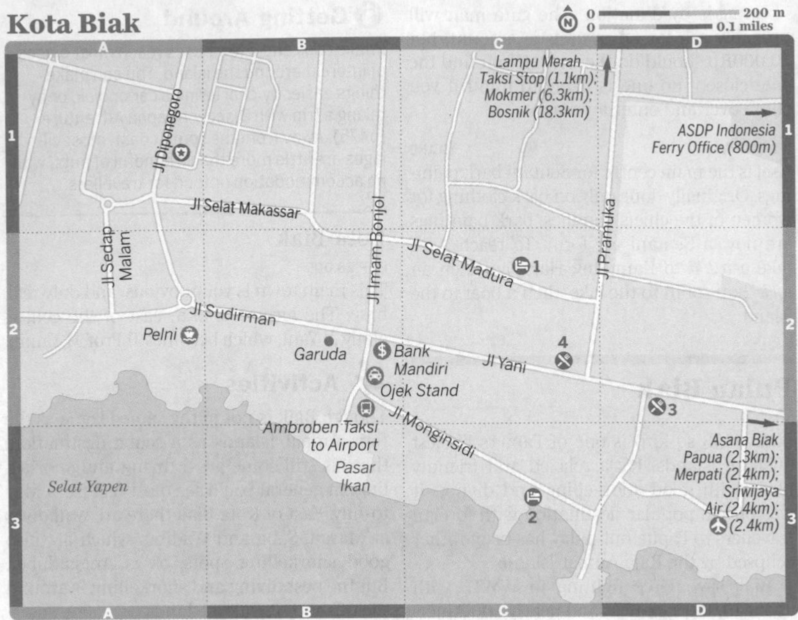

Kota Biak

Sleeping

1 Hotel Nirmala C2
2 Padaido Hotel C3

Eating

3 Furama Restaurant D2
4 Warung Makan Bakwokah C2

Biak Padiving DIVING, SNORKELLING
(☎0813 4436 6385; biakpadaiving@yahoo.co.id; 2 dives, 2 people mainland 1,500,000Rp, Padaido Islands 2,500,000-3,000,000Rp, equipment rental per full set 300,000Rp, full-day snorkelling trip per 2 people 2,500,000Rp) PADI divemaster Erick Farwas offers two-dive outings to all the better spots. Farwas also offers all-day snorkelling tours to the islands, as well as island stays.

Sleeping

★Padaido Hotel HOTEL $$
(☎0981-22144; hotpadaido@hotmail.com; Jl Monginsidi 16; s/d incl breakfast 350,000/400,000Rp; ❄) A hidden delight with just five immaculate, cheery, marine-themed rooms. They're full of thoughtful touches such as lights you can switch on/off from bed, and all have terraces overlooking a small and pretty harbour.

Asana Biak Papua HOTEL $$
(☎0981-21939; www.aerowisatahotels.com; Jl Prof M Yamin 4; r incl breakfast from 600,000Rp; ❄📶🏊) Almost opposite the airport terminal, this rambling old hotel (originally owned by KLM) received a major renovation in 2010 that has brought it bang up to date but still managed to retain some of its 1953 colonial-era ambience. The rooms are spic-and-span, with wooden floors, wood-panelled walls and terraces overlooking the gardens.

Hotel Nirmala HOTEL $$
(☎0981-22005; Jl Selat Madura 13; full board s 350,000, d 400,000-600,000Rp; ❄) An excellent option, with amiable staff. The rooms, along a tidy courtyard that catches cool breezes, are immaculate, with good air-con, comfy beds, and spacious bathrooms with hot showers. On a Sunday morning your lie-in might be pleasantly disturbed by the truly beautiful singing from the next-door church.

Eating

★Warung Makan Bakwokah SEAFOOD $$
(mains 40,000-60,000Rp; ⏲6-10pm) If you like barbecued fish or chicken in a tasty sauce (the secret of which they didn't want to give away) and served with green veg, rice and sambal,

then this eternally popular place is for you. It's cheap, simple and frankly brilliant.

Afterwards, pop over the road to the market to grab some fruit for a takeaway dessert.

Furama Restaurant INDONESIAN, CHINESE **$$**
(Jl Yani 22; mains 40,000-80,000Rp; ❄) Offers cold Guinness and Bintang as well as plenty of good-quality Chinese and Indonesian dishes. It's one of the few places in town that actually feels like a proper restaurant.

Information

Bank Mandiri (cnr Jl Imam Bonjol & Jl Yani; ⌚8am-3pm Mon-Fri) Exchanges cash US dollars and has Visa and Plus ATMs.

Discover Papua Adventure (Biak Paradise; ☎0852 4494 0860, 0981-23196; www.discoverpapua.com) A well-established agency that can set up just about any trip you want, not only around Biak but throughout Papua and beyond. The experienced, capable manager, Benny Lesomar, speaks excellent English. Call and he'll meet you in town.

Police Station (Jl Diponegoro 3; ⌚8am-4pm Mon-Sat) *Surat jalan* are issued in an hour or so here. For Biak, you normally only need one if you stay on an offshore island or visit neighbouring Pulau Supiori.

Getting There & Away

AIR

Tickets for **Garuda** (Jl Sudirman 3) and **Sriwijaya Air** (www.sriwijayaair.co.id; Jl Prof M Yamin) are sold at travel agencies as well as their offices. Tickets for the small planes of **Susi Air** (☎0967-591782; www.susiair.com; airport; ⌚6am-3pm) are sold only at the airport. Between them Garuda and Sriwijaya Air fly at least once a day to Jayapura and Jakarta. Garuda also flies daily to Makassar. Susi Air heads to Manokwari three times weekly and to Nabire daily.

BOAT

ASDP Indonesia Ferry (☎22577; Jl Suci 21) Has boats on Tuesday for Manokwari (88,000Rp) and Thursday for Nabire (130,000Rp), sailing from Mokmer, 6km east of Kota Biak.

Pelni (☎23255; Jl Sudirman 37) Every two weeks, Pelni has three liners heading east to Jayapura (economy class 173,500Rp, 18 to 27 hours) and west to Sorong (272,000Rp, 19 to 38 hours) and beyond. Some Sorong-bound sailings also call at Nabire and Manokwari.

TAKSI

Blue *taksi* to Bosnik (8000Rp, 30 to 40 minutes), passing Mokmer and Taman Burung, run every few minutes; you can catch them at the 'Lampu Merah' (Traffic Lights) stop on Jl Bosnik Raya in the northeast of town. The main terminal for other *taksi* is Terminal Darfuar, about 5km northwest of downtown. On most routes, service winds down in the afternoon.

Getting Around

Yellow public *taksi* (5000Rp) going to the right (west) outside the airport terminal head into town. Returning, take one marked 'Ambroben' from the corner of Jl Imam Bonjol and Jl Monginsidi or heading east along Jl Yani. A taxi from the airport to a downtown hotel is around 100,000Rp.

Around Kota Biak

Sights

Goa Jepang CAVE
(admission 50,000Rp; ⌚7am-5pm) The 'Japanese Cave', 4km northeast of Kota Biak, was used as a base and hideout in WWII by thousands of Japanese soldiers. A tunnel from it is said to lead 3km to the coast at Parai. In 1944, an estimated 3000 Japanese died when US forces bombed a hole in the cave roof, dropped petrol drums into it and then bombarded it from above.

From a concrete walkway, steps lead down into the spooky biggest cavern with a hole in the roof through which tree roots dangle. In and around the ticket office is a collection of Japanese and US weapons, equipment and photos.

An *ojek* from town costs 15,000Rp. Otherwise take a Bosnik-bound *taksi* and ask to be dropped at the unsigned road that leads 700m up to the cave. After heading uphill for around 300m, when you get to the top, a Japanese gun emplacement overlooks the airport. This was the focus of all the fighting.

Taman Burung & Taman Anggrek GARDENS
(Jl Bosnik Raya Km12; admission 10,000Rp; ⌚7am-6pm) At Ibdi, 12km east of Kota Biak on the Bosnik road, the Bird & Orchid Garden contains a sizeable collection of (caged) Papuan birds, including strikingly coloured lories, hornbills, cockatoos and three sad-looking cassowaries in cages that are far too small for such birds. Mixing it up with the birds are dozens of types of orchid.

Bosnik & Around

Bosnik, 18km from Kota Biak, is a laid-back village strung along the coast for 2km. Its daily morning market is busiest on Tuesday, Thursday and Saturday, when Padaido islanders come in biggest numbers. Don't get too excited about the beaches here – they're far from the best in Indonesia and at low tide a lot of 'reef hopping' is required to reach the sea, but for what it's worth the best section of beach is **Pantai Segara Indah** (admission 20,000Rp) at the eastern end.

Bosnik-route *taksi* from Kota Biak usually go as far as Opiaref, where the coast road turns inland. You can continue on foot 6km through Opiaref to Marau, Saba and Wadibu, where a road heads 500m inland to join the Anggaduber road. The coral and fish off **Pantai Marau** make for good snorkelling and diving, as do the rocky islets off **Saba**.

Padaido Islands

This lovely cluster of 36 islands and islets (only 13 of them inhabited) makes for a great day trip from Kota Biak or Bosnik, and you can stay over on some islands. Virtually all have jungle-backed, white-sand beaches with crystal-clear waters, coral reefs and plenty of marine life. The best snorkelling spots include **Pulau Wundi**, which has good coral and many fish near the surface, **Pulau Rurbas Kecil** and **Pulau Meoswarek**. Top diving sites include the western end of **Pulau Owi**, with good coral and big fish; **Pulau Rurbas Besar** for coral, sharks, turtles and more big fish; and Pulau Wundi, with a cave, a long wall and good coral.

You can charter a boat from Bosnik to the nearest and most-populated islands, Owi and Auki, for 400,000Rp to 600,000Rp round trip, or twice as much for Wundi.

Biak Padiving (p474) offers diving trips, and also sightseeing and snorkelling trips, to the islands. Padiving's Erick Farwas has a basic four-room **guesthouse** (☎0813 4436 6385; per person with/without meals 250,000/200,000Rp) on Pulau Wundi (meals must be arranged in advance).

The cheapest transport to the islands is from Bosnik on Tuesday, Thursday or Saturday afternoon, when islanders are returning from Bosnik market and you should be able to get a place in a boat for 30,000Rp to 50,000Rp. You can normally find accommodation for 100,000Rp per person in an island house or by asking the local church-keeper. Bring food.

Nabire

☎0984 / POP 52,000

For travellers the main attraction of this relatively prosperous town is swimming with whale sharks. Whale sharks can grow over 10m long and inhabit warm seas all round the world. They feed mainly on plankton but also on small fish and for this reason they hang around fishing platforms called *bagan* in the southwest of Teluk Cenderawasih, 1½ hours from Nabire by boat. Close encounters with at least a few of these harmless giants are almost guaranteed any day of the year. Don't touch or interfere with the whale sharks, and try to discourage locals from doing so as well.

Activities

Merry Yoweni SNORKELLING
(☎0821 9830 9115; merrypapua@yahoo.com; AA Hotel, Pantai Yamarel; per person 580,000Rp) Merry Yoweni offers whale-shark trips from Nabire for up to five people; the cost is slightly higher for fewer people, though it's rare that there would be fewer than five people on a boat.

Sleeping

Nabire's few hotels can fill up so booking ahead is advantageous.

AA Hotel HOTEL $$
(☎0821 9830 9115, 0853 4468 4937; merrypapua@yahoo.com; Pantai Yamarel; r incl breakfast 350,000Rp; ❄📶) Near a grey-sand beach 2.5km from the airport, this well-run and very popular hotel has neat, medium-sized rooms with hot showers and a restaurant. The enthusiastic owners also do whale-shark trips, and offer free airport pickups and drop-offs if you reserve ahead.

Getting There & Away

Wings Air flies to Ambon four times each week, while Wings Air and Trigana fly daily to Jayapura and Susi Air flies daily to Biak.

Pelni sails three times every two weeks to Jayapura (once via Biak), and three times to Manokwari, Sorong and beyond.

BALIEM VALLEY

The legendary Baliem Valley is the most popular and most accessible destination in Papua's interior. The Dani people who live here were still dependent on tools of stone, bone and wood when a natural-history expedition led by American Richard Archbold chanced upon the valley in 1938. Dani life has since changed enormously with stone axes being replaced by mobile phones and age-old belief systems with Christianity, but even so the changes are often only skin-deep and the valley and surrounding highlands remain one of the world's last fascinatingly traditional areas. Visiting the Baliem Valley and trekking through high mountain scenery, past neat and orderly Dani villages, takes you to a world far removed from Jakarta and is an honour and an experience to be savoured. For most people it is the highlight of Papua.

The main valley is about 60km long and 16km wide and bounded by high mountains on all sides. The only sizeable town, Wamena, sits at its centre at an altitude of 1650m. The powerful Kali Baliem (Baliem River), running through the valley, escapes via a narrow gorge at the southern end. Amid this spectacular scenery, the majority of Dani still live close to nature, tending their vegetable plots and pigs around villages composed of circular thatched huts called *honai*. Roads are few, and the raging mountain rivers are crossed on hanging footbridges that may be held together only by natural twine.

Christian missionaries arrived in 1954 and a Dutch government post was established in Wamena in 1956. Since the 1960s, Indonesia has added its own brand of colonialism, bringing immigrants, government schools, police, soldiers, shops, motor vehicles and becak (bicycle-rickshaws) to the valley. Big changes have been wrought in Dani life, but their identity and culture have proved resilient. Tensions between Dani and the security

Baliem Valley

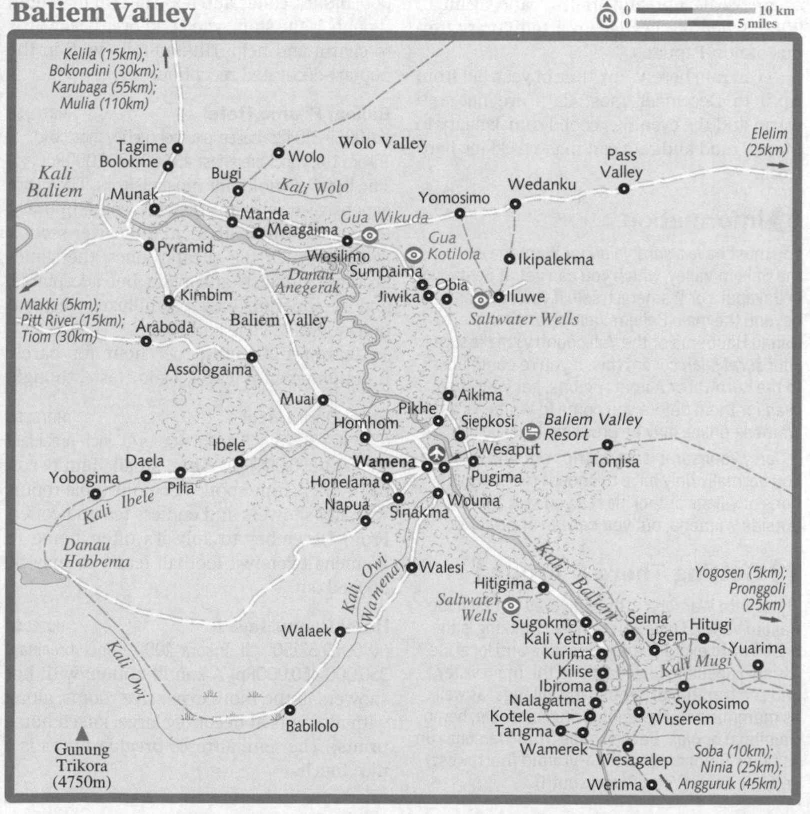

BALIEM VALLEY FESTIVAL

To coincide with the busiest tourism season, the two-day Baliem Valley Festival is held in the Baliem Valley during the second week of August. The highlight is mock tribal fighting, where village men dress up in full regalia and enact an old-fashioned tribal battle and accompanying rituals.

The festival also features pig feasts, traditional costumes, and Dani music on instruments such as the *pikon* (a kind of mouth harp). Other goings-on include pig races, tourist-only spear-throwing and archery contests.

In recent years, the main events have taken place at Wosilimo. There's an entrance fee of 250,000Rp.

forces and Indonesian immigrants periodically erupt into violence, most notably during a large-scale uprising in 1977 and again in 2000, when clashes led to a temporary exodus of non-Papuans.

It can rain here at any time of year, but from April to December most days are fine and warm and the evenings cool. From January to March, mud and rain can make trekking hard work.

Information

You must have a *surat jalan* for Wamena and the Baliem Valley, which you can get at Sentani or Jayapura or Wamena itself. If you're going beyond the main Baliem Valley (for example, to Danau Habbema or the Yali country) make sure your *surat jalan* covers this. If you're continuing to the Korowai or Asmat regions, get your *surat jalan* for them before you come to Wamena, as Wamena police may be unwilling to issue one.

Carry your *surat jalan* on trips outside Wamena. You normally only have to show it (to police stations or village authorities) if you stay overnight outside Wamena, but you can never be sure.

Getting There & Around

Flying into Wamena is the only way to reach the Baliem Valley. Once you're here, trekking is the best way to explore the landscape and local life. It's also possible to get around the main valley and see traditional people and villages, as well as mummies and hanging bridges, by car, bemo (minibus) or *ojek*. Paved roads from Wamena run as far as Bolokme (north), Pyramid (northwest) and Kali Yetni (Yetni River; south).

Wamena

☎0969 / POP 31,000

Wamena is a sprawling Indonesian creation with nothing traditional about it, but it's the obligatory base for any travels around the valley. The population is a mix of Papuans and non-Papuans and the latter run all the businesses.

Penis gourds are no longer banned here, as they were during Indonesia's 'Operasi Koteka' (an attempt to force the Dani to wear clothes) in the 1970s, but only a very few old men coming into town for the day are likely to be seen wearing them.

Sleeping

★Hotel Rainbow Wamena HOTEL **$$**
(Hotel Pelangi; ☎0969-31999; Jl Irian 28; r incl breakfast 450,000-750,000Rp; wi-fi) A great option. Rooms are excellent, clean and of a good size with aprés-trek soothing hot-water bathrooms and nice touches such as shampoo, tissues, coffee and tea. The real highlight, though, is the staff, who bend over backwards to charm and help. Hit-and-miss wi-fi in the pop-art-decorated reception.

Baliem Pilamo Hotel HOTEL **$$**
(☎0969-31043; baliempilamohotel@yahoo.co.id; Jl Trikora 114; r incl breakfast 456,000-726,000Rp; wi-fi) The hotel of choice for most visitors. The more expensive rooms are tasteful, contemporary, brown-and-white affairs in the newer section at the rear. Of the cheaper ones, the standards are smallish and plain but acceptable, and the superiors have a semi-luxury feel and quirky garden-style bathrooms.

Charging 20,000Rp per hour for barely functioning wi-fi leaves a sour taste, though.

Putri Dani Hotel HOTEL **$$**
(☎0969-31223; Jl Irian 40; s/d incl breakfast 450,000/550,000Rp) This small family-run place offers nine spotless, comfortable rooms with hot showers and endless tea and coffee. From December to July it's often home to Wamena's Persiwa football team, so may be booked out.

Hotel Rannu Jaya I HOTEL **$$**
(☎0969-32150; Jl Trikora 109; r incl breakfast 350,000-450,000Rp) A sound option, with hot showers in the more expensive rooms, along with attempts at decor (eg large, kitsch horse prints). The semi-alfresco breakfast area is a nice touch.

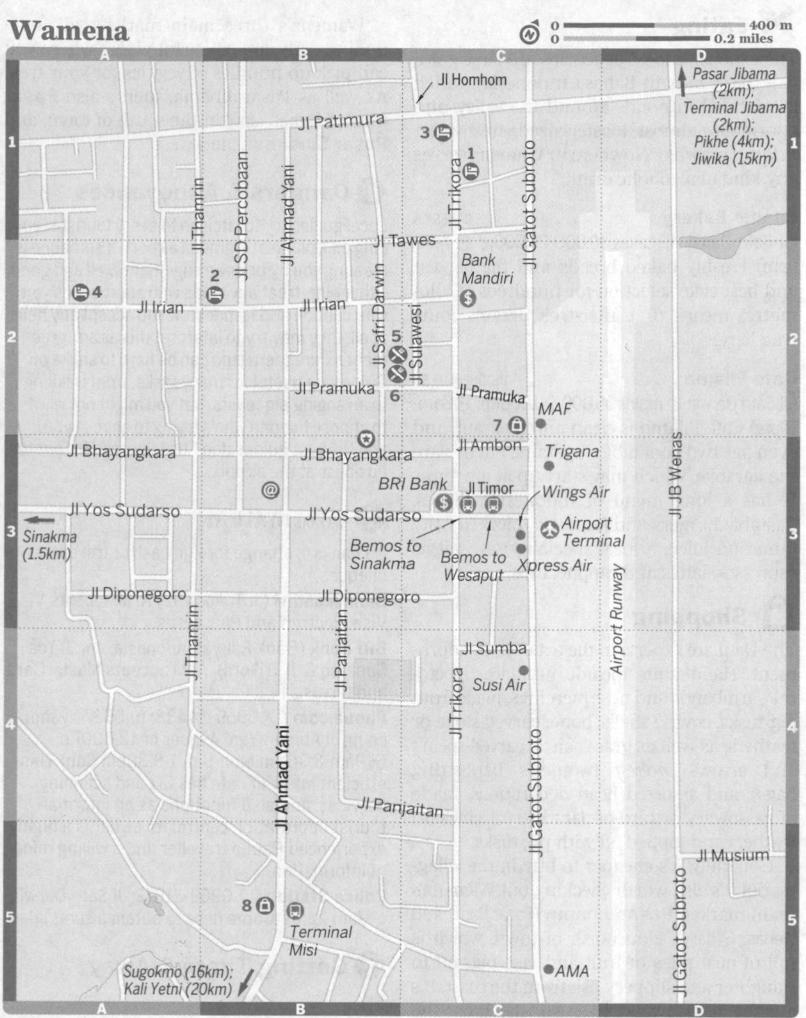

Wamena

Sleeping

1 Baliem Pilamo Hotel C1
2 Hotel Rainbow Wamena B2
3 Hotel Rannu Jaya I C1
4 Putri Dani Hotel A2

Eating

5 Cafe Pilamo B2
6 Pilamo Bakery B2

Shopping

7 Oi-Tourism C2
8 Pasar Misi B5

Baliem Valley Resort RESORT **$$$**
(☎0812 4810 0240, Germany +49 6051 61388; www.baliem-valley-resort.de; s/d incl breakfast €108/126) This surprising hotel occupies a gorgeous hillside position 21km east of Wamena, with large, rustic-style but comfortable guest cottages in picturesque grounds. A superb collection of Papuan (especially Asmat) art adorns the semi-open-air dining hall. The German owner has a wealth of Papua expertise, and offers a variety of excursions and expeditions.

Eating

The expensive local delicacies are large goldfish (*ikan mas* in Bahasa Indonesia), which are farmed in ponds around the valley, and enormous, almost lobster-sized, freshwater *udang* (prawns). Nowhere in Wamena serves any kind of alcoholic drink.

Pilamo Bakery BAKERY **$**
(Jl Safri Dawin 4; cakes 10,000-25,000p; ⌚7am-9pm) Freshly baked breads and the biggest and best cake selection for hundreds of kilometres means that after-trek dreams come true here.

Cafe Pilamo INDONESIAN **$$**
(Jl Safri Darwin 2; mains 35,000-90,000Rp; ⌚8am-10pm) Cafe Pilamo is clean and pleasant, and even has two pool tables upstairs, but beware the karaoke, which may start up at any time. It has a long menu of Indonesian dishes, passable burgers and fantastic juices (try the tamarind juice, a local speciality) as well as espressos, lattes and cappuccinos.

Shopping

The Dani are experts in the art of body adornment. Handicrafts include necklaces, pectorals, armbands and nose piercings, made from pig tusks, cowrie shells, bone, carved stone or feathers, as well as grass skirts, carved spears and arrows, *noken* (women's bark-string bags), and assorted head decorations, made of cassowary or bird-of-paradise (or chicken) feathers and topped off with pig tusks.

Generally, it's cheaper to buy in the villages, but it's also worth checking out Wamena's main market, **Pasar Jibama** (Pasar Baru; Jl JB Wenas; ⌚daily), 2km north of town, which is full of neat piles of fruit and veg, pigs off to slaughter and slippery fish from the coast. It's a sight in its own right. Also, check out the NGO-run **Oi-Tourism** (Jl Gatot Subroto; ⌚7am-5pm Mon-Sat), or the handful of craft shops on Jl Trikora north of Jl Ambon. Asmat, Korowai and PNG artefacts are also available in the souvenir shops. Avoid buying items made from bird-of-paradise or cassowary feathers and any other products made from wild animals. Not just is it pushing such creatures closer to extinction, but trade in such items is illegal and airport customs will confiscate them and perhaps fine you.

Of course, the most popular souvenir is the penis gourd. These cost from about 20,000Rp to 100,000Rp, depending on size, materials and negotiation. Changing rooms in which to try them on aren't provided!

Wamena's three main markets, all functioning daily, are colourful places where you can pick up bundles of veggies for your trek. As well as Pasar Jibama, there's also **Pasar Misi** (Jl Ahmad Yani), in the south of town, and **Pasar Sinakma**, 2km west.

Dangers & Annoyances

Local guides try to latch on to every tourist stepping off a plane at Wamena airport. If someone is meeting you by prior arrangement, well and good. Otherwise, treat any guide who approaches you with caution and firmness. If you accept any help at all, they may try to interpret this as an agreement to hire them, and can be hard to shake off. Guides are useful for many tasks, from trekking to arranging pig feasts, but you might not want to choose the one who's trying to choose you, and the best guides don't usually need to tout for business at the airport.

Information

No banks exchange foreign cash or travellers cheques.

Bank Mandiri (Jl Trikora 92) ATM accepts Visa, Visa Electron and Plus cards.

BRI Bank (Bank Rakyat Indonesia; cnr Jl Yos Sudarso & Jl Trikora) ATM accepts MasterCard and Cirrus.

Papua.com (☎0969-34488; fuj0627@yahoo.co.jp; Jl Ahmad Yani 49; per hr 12,000Rp; ⌚9am-8.30pm Mon-Sat, 1-8.30pm Sun) This efficient internet cafe has fax and scanning services, and also functions as an informal tourist information centre. Its owner is a highly experienced Papua traveller and a willing mine of information.

Police Station (☎0969-31972; Jl Safri Darwin; ⌚7am-2pm) Come here to obtain a *surat jalan*.

Getting There & Away

AIR

Flights can be heavily booked, especially in August. The carriers between Jayapura (Sentani) and Wamena are **Wings Air** (www.lionair.co.id), **Trigana** (www.trigana-air.com; airport) and **Xpress Air** (www.expressair.biz). Wings flies twice daily in either direction for 624,000Rp. Most locals suggest they are the choice operator. Trigana flies three or more times daily each way, charging from 574,0000Rp. Xpress, which uses very old Boeing planes, also flies three times daily charging 750,000Rp. **Susi Air** (☎081 3431 22002; www.susiair.com; Jl Gatot Subroto) operates small planes to remote airfields such as Dekai, Elelim, Kenyan and others. You can charter a plane with them to fly to Angguruk in Yali country for 19,470,000Rp.

BEMOS FROM WAMENA

DESTINATION	DEPARTURE POINT	FARE (RP)	DURATION
Aikima	Jibama	15000	15min
Ibele	Sinakma	20,000	1hr (departures until noon)
Jiwika	junction 600m past Jibama	15,000	30min
Kali Yetni	Misi	15,000	1hr
Kimbim	Jibama	25,000	50min
Makki	Sinakma	70,000	3hr (departures 3-5am)
Meagaima	Jibama	25,000	1hr
Sugokmo	Misi	15,000	45min
Tagime	Jibama	30,000	1¾hr
Tiom	Sinakma	120,000	4hr (departures 3-5am)
Wosilimo	Jibama	20,000	40min

Mission airlines **AMA** (Associated Mission Aviation; http://ama-papua.blogspot.com; Jl Gatot Subroto) and **MAF** (☎ 0969 31263; www.maf.org; Jl Gatot Subroto) fly small planes to many small highland airstrips. They may carry tourists if spare seats are available. There is generally much more chance of getting a seat flying back to Wamena than for outbound flights. A seat from Angguruk to Wamena, for example, costs about 700,000Rp if you are lucky enough to get one. As a rule, MAF doesn't carry tourists outbound at all.

PUBLIC BEMO

Overcrowded bemos head out along the main roads from several starting points around Wamena. Most just leave when they are full. The main terminals – **Terminal Jibama** (Jl JB Wenas), **Terminal Misi** and **Sinakma** – are at Wamena's three markets. Bemos get scarce after 3pm and are less plentiful on Sunday. Few villages or attractions are signposted, so ask the conductor to tell you where to get off.

CHARTERED BEMO & CAR

For more comfort than the public bemos, consider chartering a vehicle for out-of-town trips. A bemo costs 200,000Rp to 300,000Rp one way to Kali Yetni (a common trek starting point), or 400,000Rp to 500,000Rp for a return trip of about three hours to Jiwika. Cars (parked opposite the airport) cost 800,000Rp to 1,000,000Rp a day (possibly 1,500,000Rp in August) for a full-day trip around the northern ends of the valley.

Getting Around

For trips within town, *ojeks* generally charge 10,000Rp and becak 5000Rp to 10,000Rp. Bemos marked 'A2' (5000Rp) run from BRI Bank to Jl Irian and up Jl Trikora to Terminal Jibama. An *ojek* to Terminal Jibama is 15,000Rp.

Northeastern Baliem Valley

Several interesting places along the northeastern Baliem Valley are within day-trip reach of Wamena, and some side valleys offer good hiking.

Aikima

About 8km from Wamena, nondescript Aikima is famous for its **Werapak Elosak mummy** (admission 100,000Rp), the 300-year-old corpse of a great chief, which was preserved (by smoking) to retain some of his power for the village. You'll probably be asked to pay 100,000Rp per person for a viewing, but this price can be quickly bargained down to more like 50,000Rp.

Jiwika & Around

Jiwika (pronounced Yiwika) is a local administrative centre and home to the celebrated **Wimontok Mabel mummy** (admission 130,000Rp). The mummy is kept at the tiny settlement of **Sumpaima**, 300m north along the main road from the main Jiwika village entrance (look for the black 'Mummy' sign). Wimontok Mabel was a powerful 18th-century chief here and his blackened corpse is the best preserved and most accessible of its kind near Wamena. You will likely be asked around 130,000Rp per person for a viewing. You could try bargaining but don't expect much of a reduction. Sumpaima is something of a 'cultural' village and you will be greeted by fantastically dressed people in traditional garb.

HIKING & TREKKING THE BALIEM VALLEY

Beyond the reach of roads in the Baliem Valley, you come closer to traditional Dani life. In one day, you may climb narrow rainforest trails, stroll well-graded paths past terraces of purple-leafed sweet-potato plants, wend through villages of grass-roofed *honai* (circular thatched huts), cross rivers on wobbly hanging footbridges, and traverse hillsides where the only sounds are birds, wind and water far below.

The classic trekking area, offering up to a week of walking, is in the south of the valley (beyond Kali Yetni), along with branch valleys to the east and west. Dani life here is still relatively traditional, the scenery gorgeous and the walking varied.

Accommodation is available in nearly all villages. Some have dedicated guesthouses (sometimes in *honai*-style huts); elsewhere you can often stay in a teacher's house, the school or other houses. Either way you'll usually be asked a standard 120,000Rp per person (guides and porters excluded). You sleep on the floor, but it may be softened with dried grass (so not very soft at all!) and you may get a mat. It gets surprisingly cold at night. It's a good idea to bring a decent sleeping bag and some thermals and fleeces. Other items worth bringing along include a torch, spare batteries for cameras etc (there's little or no electricity in any of the villages), a book (evenings can be long) and water purifying pills (you'll be refilling from streams a lot of the time). Good hiking boots are an essential and walking poles a good idea. Sunscreen, sunglasses, a sun hat and wet-weather gear (including gators or trousers) are also essential.

Larger villages have kiosks selling basics such as biscuits, noodles and rice (the final reliable supplies are at Manda and Kimbim in the north and Kurima in the south) and you can obtain sweet potatoes, other vegetables or fruit here and there. But to be on the safe side you need to take enough food with you from Wamena. Villages can normally supply firewood for cooking, for 20,000Rp a load.

Guides & Porters

In the more frequented trekking areas it's technically possible to head off alone and ask the way as you go, or pick up a local porter-cum-guide for 80,000Rp to 100,000Rp a day if you need one. However, you would need to have excellent Bahasa Indonesia language abilities and, ideally, a grasp of the local Dani language to really pull this off. Trails are unmarked and often faint and confusing and there's frequently nobody around to point out the correct route. It would be very easy for a foreign trekker walking alone to get very lost. To summarise: get a guide!

Some people might describe it as a tourist trap, but for exotic, and fairly pain-free, photos it's great. The going rate is 10,000Rp per shot or negotiate a fee based on time spent photographing a person (around 200,000Rp per person for up to an hour is fair).

Anemangi, just behind Sumpaima, and **Obia** (Isinapma) to the south of Jiwika, are among villages where traditional Dani pig feasts and colourful warrior dances based on ritual warfare can be staged for tourists, if requested a day or two ahead. A typical price for a warrior dance alone is about 1,500,000Rp depending on number of dancers. For the pig feast you'll pay more like 2,000,000Rp plus you buy the pig (and these aren't cheap).

At Iluwe, 1½ hours up a steep path from Jiwika, is **Air Garam**, a group of saltwater wells. Villagers soak sections of banana trunk in the water, then dry and burn them and use the resulting ashes as salt. Village boys will show you the way for around 30,000Rp, but to see the process at work, try to find a woman who will accompany you (50,000Rp). To avoid climbing in the midday heat, start from Jiwika before 10am.

The road north from Jiwika is flanked by rocky hills with several caves. **Gua Kotilola** (admission 100,000Rp; ⌚8am-4pm) is a sizeable cavern up a short, pretty path behind a Dani compound, about 5km north of Jiwika. It contains the bones of past tribal-war victims – though they don't show these to outsiders. It's hard to justify the high entry fee.

Finding a good, reliable guide can be a challenge. You should allow at least one day to find a guide you're happy with and make trek preparations. Tricks played by unscrupulous guides may include pocketing some of the money you've given them to get supplies (go with them or get the supplies yourself); sending a junior replacement at the last minute; asking for more money mid-trek and refusing to continue without it; or disappearing and leaving you in the hands of a porter.

A good source of recommendations for reliable guides in Wamena is **Papua.com** (p480). It's worth seeking out one of the Baliem Valley's 20 or so officially licensed guides. These are not the only good guides around, but they usually speak reasonable English, and have a professional reputation to look after.

There are no fixed prices in the Baliem trekking world. Hard bargaining is the norm. Don't be put off by glum faces and do insist on clarifying any grey areas. No decent guide will agree to anything he's unhappy about. Official licensed guides request 700,000Rp per day (and more for harder treks to, for example, the Yali or Korowai areas), but some decent, English-speaking guides will work for less. You'll find a number of dependable agencies and individual guides in Wamena. There are also excellent trekking guides based elsewhere in Papua who will always be happy to act as a guide in the Baliem Valley; try **Andreas Ndruru** (p455) and **Bob Palege** (p456).

In addition to a guide, porters are a good idea and cost 200,000Rp each per day, depending partly on the toughness of the trek. A cook costs 250,000Rp per day, but guides or porters can cook if you're looking to cut costs. You'll have to provide enough food for the whole team (for two trekkers, a guide and two porters doing a one-week trek this is likely to cost around 2,500,000Rp to 3,000,000Rp in total) and probably cigarettes for them and your village hosts. It's a good idea to have the whole agreement written down and signed by your guide before you start, and it's normal to pay some money up front and the rest at the end. A 10% tip at the end is also expected for each member of the team.

Jonas Wenda (☎0852 4422 0825; jonas.wenda@yahoo.com; Wamena) Highly experienced (your author first trekked with him in 1986) and notably knowledgeable on flora and fauna.

Kosman Kogoya (☎0852 4472 7810; kogoyakosmam@gmail.com; Wamena) A popular, reliable guide who will quote reasonable prices from the outset and won't waste your time bargaining.

Trek-Papua Tours & Travel (☎0812 4762 8708; www.papuatravels.com; Jl Airport, Sentani) A young but energetic, internet-wise agency, which also offers tours to other parts of Papua.

Wosilimo

Wosilimo ('Wosi') is a relatively major village with a couple of kiosks. The cave here, **Gua Wikuda** (admission 30,000Rp), is said to be several kilometres long, with an underground river that reaches Danau Anegerak. It's possible to visit about the first 100m of the cave, which has a few stalagmites and 'tites. Ask for the lights to be turned on. There are some small **guest honai** (per person 150,000Rp) near the cave entrance, which have straw floors, sleeping mats and a filthy shared *mandi* with squat toilet. Bring food and the people there will cook for you. It's handy during the Baliem Valley Festival but is otherwise avoidable.

Two kilometres south from Wosi, along the main road, a path starting in front of a church leads half an hour southwest to a small lake, **Danau Anegerak**, crossing a hanging bridge over Kali Baliem on the way. It's a pleasant walk, though during wet weather it may be impassable.

Pass Valley Area

A rough road heads up over the hills from Wosilimo to Pass Valley, then descends to Elelim, about 60km from Wosi. The small **Wedanku valley** between Wosilimo and Pass Valley still retains a traditional Dani culture. Wedanku village's Catholic mission can provide accommodation and from there you can hike one day up through the forest to **Ikipalekma** (where you can find accommodation in local houses), then on the next day to Jiwika, via the Iluwe wells.

Northwestern Baliem Valley

The western side of the valley is less scenic than the eastern. **Kimbim** is a pleasant administrative centre with a few shops and the main market outside Wamena, busiest on Monday and Saturday. An hour's walk away, **Araboda** houses the 250-year-old **Alongga Huby mummy**; viewings cost around 50,000Rp. About 7km past Kimbim is **Pyramid**, a graceful mission village named after the shape of a nearby hill, with a theological college and sloping airstrip.

Danau Habbema

This beautiful lake, 30km west of Wamena as the crow flies, sits amid alpine grasslands at 3400m altitude, with dramatic, snow-capped mountains in view (4750m Gunung Trikora rises to the south). The fauna and flora are a big draw for nature lovers. It's possible to visit Habbema as a day trip from Wamena – the drive is around two hours each way. You can rent a 4WD and driver in Wamena for around 4,000,000Rp round trip. The road is paved as far as the military post at Napua, 7km from Wamena.

THE DANI

Dani is an umbrella name for around 30 clans in the main Baliem Valley and its side-valleys and some Mamberamo tributary valleys to the north. They number somewhere over 200,000 people in total.

Most Dani speak Bahasa Indonesia but appreciate a greeting in their own language. Around Wamena, the general greeting is *la'uk* to one person, and *la'uk nyak* to more than one – except that men say *nayak* to one other man and *nayak lak* to more than one man. *Wa, wa* is another common greeting expressing respect or offering thanks.

Many older Dani men still wear a penis sheath (*horim* in Dani, *koteka* in Bahasa Indonesia) made from a cultivated gourd, and little else apart from a few neck, head or arm adornments. Others now prefer T-shirts and trousers or shorts. In the past women used to go bare-breasted, but it would be a very rare day to see that nowadays, though some still sport grass skirts. Women often still carry string bags called *noken* on their backs, strapped over the head and heavily laden with vegetables, babies or pigs. *Noken* are made from shredded tree bark, rolled into thread. Some Dani wear pig fat in their hair and cover their bodies in pig fat and soot for warmth.

Most Dani are now Christian and one traditional pastime that has gone out the window is village warfare. Villages used to go to war over land disputes, wife stealing or even pig stealing, with combat happening in brief, semi-ritualised clashes (with a few woundings and deaths nevertheless). Today, such quarrels are normally settled by other, usually legalistic, means.

Villages are mostly composed of extended-family compounds, each containing a few *honai* (circular thatched huts). The men sleep in a dedicated men's hut, visiting the women's huts only for sex. *Honai* interiors have a lower level with a fire for warmth and sometimes cooking, and an upper platform for sleeping.

After a birth, sex is taboo for the mother for two to five years, apparently to give the child exclusive use of her milk. Some Dani are still polygamous: the standard bride price is four or five pigs, and a man's status is measured partly by how many wives and pigs he has. One of the more unusual (and now prohibited, though it still happens) Dani customs is to amputate one or two joints of a finger when a spouse or child dies. This is most frequently done by battering the finger with a rock. Many older Dani have the ends of fingers missing.

One thing that hasn't changed, and probably never will, is the Dani's love for the sweet potato, grown on extensive plots and terraces all over the valley. The Dani don't mess about with fancy sauces or curries to go with their potatoes. They like them plain, steamed and, if possible, for each and every meal. If you spend long in the villages you'll likely grow to hate the things!

The ideal way to visit Habbema is to drive there and trek back (three to four days). To do this you will need a guide; find one in Wamena. Much of the route is through rainforest. The usual route starting from the lake is via Yobogima (a forest clearing) and then through a spectacular gorge to Daela village and on to Pilia and Ibele.

Yali Country

Over the eastern walls of the Baliem Valley, amid scenery that is often just as stunning, lies the home of the Yali people. They are one of the more traditional highland peoples, although traditional dress is now much less common than it was 15 years ago. The men may wear 'skirts' of rattan hoops, with penis gourds protruding from underneath. Missionaries provide much of the infrastructure here, such as schools and transport.

Yali country is a great destination for more adventurous trekkers with enough time. You need about a week to walk there (the Yali themselves can do it, barefoot, in two days) and you should allow at least two or three days to explore once there. You might be able to get on a mission flight back to Wamena, but otherwise you'll have to walk back or charter a plane. Villages with airstrips include Angguruk, Pronggoli, Kosarek and Welarek.

The most direct route runs from Sugokmo or Kurima to Ugem, then up the Mugi Valley, over 3500m-plus Gunung Elit with at least one night (but often two) camping, then down to Abiyangge, Piliam and Pronggoli in Yali country. There are sections of long, steep ascent, and the upper reaches over Gunung Elit involve climbing up and down several rustic wooden ladders. From Pronggoli to Angguruk, the biggest Yali village (with a large market twice a week), takes another one or two days.

An easier but longer option, about eight days from Sugokmo to Angguruk and still with plenty of up and down, is the southern loop via Wesagalep, Werima, Soba and Ninia.

Whichever route you take you should have an experienced guide. You should be able to organise one in Wamena.

Beyond Yali country it's possible to trek southeastwards into the country of the Mek people, similarly small in stature to the Yali (their main village is Nalca), and even to cross Papua's north–south watershed to Langda, the main village of the Una people (considered pygmies).

THE SOUTH

Few travellers make it to the low-lying, river-strewn south, but Wasur National Park is one of Papua's best wildlife destinations (for a few months a year), while the Asmat region provides a fascinating taste of life along jungle rivers with a headhunting past and marvellous woodcarving artisanry.

Merauke

☎0971 / POP 87,000

Merauke is a reasonably prosperous and orderly town of wide, straight streets, renowned as the most southeasterly settlement in Indonesia. The best reason to visit is nearby Wasur National Park, which is like a small slice of Australian bush in Indonesia, wallabies and all.

It's 6km from the airport at the southeast end of town to the port on Sungai Maro at the northwest end. The main street, running almost the whole way, is Jl Raya Mandala.

Sleeping & Eating

Marina Hotel HOTEL **$**
(☎0971-326240; Jl Raya Mandala 23; s/d 165,000/220,000Rp) Acceptable, clean rooms with cold showers.

Hotel Megaria HOTEL **$$**
(☎0971-321932; Jl Raya Mandala 166; r incl breakfast from 250,000Rp; ❄) The Megaria has a selection of large, well-furnished rooms that wouldn't win awards for being at the cutting edge of style but are otherwise OK. Get one as far away from the motorbike-infested road as possible.

Swiss-Belhotel BUSINESS HOTEL **$$$**
(☎0971-326333; www.swiss-belhotel.com; Jl Raya Mandala 53; r incl breakfast from 1,005,000Rp; ❄📶🏊) Stylish, luxurious and by far the best option in town, the Swiss-Belhotel offers all the business-class frills.

Information

Police Station (Jl Brawijaya 27) Come here to get a *surat jalan* (travel permit). Located opposite the main market.

Getting There & Around

Garuda and Lion Air fly daily to Jayapura and Sriwijaya Air flies thrice weekly. Garuda also offers a direct Jakarta to Merauke flight but travelling in the other direction involves flying via Jayapura. Airport taxis cost 50,000Rp into town. Yellow

HIKING THE SOUTHERN BALIEM VALLEY

South of Wamena, the Baliem Valley narrows and Kali Baliem (Baliem River) becomes a ferocious torrent. For the small number of hikers who come to Papua the southern Baliem Valley is easily the most popular hiking destination. The scenery is spectacular, the walking exhilarating and the cultural village-life fascinating.

From Kurima, the first village most trekkers reach, you can access a network of trails linking villages on the west side of the Baliem, or cross the river for the trails and villages on the eastern side. A good circular route of six or seven days links both sides.

You can lengthen the trek by continuing further up the Mugi Valley from Yuarima, or heading south from Wesagalep to Pukam and Werima. For a shorter hike, on day one you could head from Kurima to Kilise, Ibiroma, Wamerek and Wesagalep (six to seven hours), and on day two from Wesagalep to Wamerek. On day three, diverge from the Wamerek–Syokosimo path to cross Kali Mugi by a hanging bridge, not far upstream from its confluence with Kali Baliem. Then continue up the Baliem to Kurima or Seima (three hours from Wamerek).

Walking times are based on an average 'tourist pace', including rest stops.

Day One

The paved road from Wamena passes through Sugokmo village after 16km (you may have to change vehicle here) and ends at the small but fast and turbulent Kali Yetni. This is where you start walking. The only way across the Yetni is on precarious logs for which you need a helping hand from a guide. It's a 45-minute walk from the Yetni to Kurima, a largish village with a police station (show your *surat jalan* here).

If you don't have someone to help you over the Yetni, start walking from Sugokmo, from where it's a 20-minute walk down to a metal hanging bridge over the Baliem. A path then leads down the east bank to neat Seima (1½ hours), from where you can descend to Kurima in 30 minutes, recrossing the Baliem by another hanging bridge. One hour south (uphill) from Kurima you reach Kilise, a *honai* village with glorious views.

Alberth Elopore's Guesthouse (per person 120,000Rp) in Kilise is one of the best in the area, with cosy *honai*-style huts and a wonderful grotto-like kamar *mandi (water-tank bath)*. Total walk time: two hours.

Day Two

From Kilise follow the gently rising and falling trail for an hour to the pretty village of Ibiroma, which offers splendid views up the imposing looking Mugi Valley on the other side of the river. After a further hour of walking, the trail descends very steeply to Nalagatma with its attractive wooden church on a grassy plain. From here the trail narrows and disappears in and out of thick vegetation as it descends all the way to the Kali Baliem.

Continue 50 minutes further on and you reach the thatched *honai* of tiny Kotele where the trail bends and provides the first views of the massive mountains to the south through which you will pass in a few days. It's now just a 40-minute walk very steeply downwards along a trail that is treacherously slippery after rain to a stream, small bridge and delightful Wamerek, where the knowledgeable Mr Yeki runs the *honai*-style **Kulugima Guesthouse** (per person 120,000Rp). Total walk time: four to five hours.

Day Three

Today is a long, hard slog, but by the end of it you will really feel in the high mountains. One hour of walking from Wamerek will bring you to a rickety wooden bridge over the angry Kali Baliem. One look at this bridge, with its missing wooden planks and gentle sway in the

public *taksi* (4000Rp) from the airport parking area, or the road just outside, run along Jl Raya Mandala.

Every two weeks Pelni's *Tatamailau* sails from Merauke to Agats (economy class 183,000Rp) and Sorong (484,000Rp). The *Kelimutu* sails to Agats then through southern and central Maluku to Sulawesi, every four weeks. Smaller boats run up and down the coast to Agats and as far inland as Tanahmerah.

breeze, might be enough to make some people decide they don't like hiking after all. Assuming you make it over the river, it's about a three-hour unrelentingly steep uphill slog to almost the very top of the mountain (look out for the high waterfall near the top where you can take an exhilarating shower). Reaching a small level it's another 20 minutes uphill to a small hamlet of perfectly formed huts which are often half-hidden under a cold mist. The path continues up through the mist-soaked mountains to Wesagalep village which is situated on a small, cold ridge with remarkable mountain vistas. Overnight in the village school/hall. Total walk time: five to six hours.

Day Four

Day four starts rudely with a steep, breathless 20-minute climb to a low pass. Don't follow the obvious trail straight ahead (this just leads to gardens), but instead turn right along the fainter trail. After 45 minutes of steep climbing through muddy, muggy jungle the reward is a narrow, grassy ridge with endless views in all directions. The path skips along a spur before plummeting downwards for about three hours to the Kali Lubuk where you can reward yourself with a refreshing (read: bloody freezing) dip.

The path then climbs up another ridge dipping in and out of often very boggy forest before reaching a final ridge and dropping down to Wuserem village where accommodation is available in either a wooden hut in the first, higher part of the village by the church or, 20 minutes further on in the main part of the village, in the village school. Total walk time: five to six hours.

Day Five

This is a fairly short and gentle day though the temperature and humidity rise fast as you descend. From Wuserem work your way along a spur for half an hour, from where there are memorable views to the north up toward Wamena. By now the track is fairly wide and well maintained and more and more villages start appearing. Descend gently and turn to the east into the Mugi Valley. From this point it's just 45 minutes to an hour down to riverside Syokosimo, which has a nice wooden hut to stay in. You can have a dip in the river and enjoy an afternoon of rest. Total walk time: four hours.

Day Six

From Syokosimo follow the trail along the river heading further up the Mugi Valley. After 20 minutes you'll come to Yuarima and a small bridge, built only of vines and tree branches, that crosses the river. From the other side a gentle climb takes you through beautiful meadows and past little farmsteads. Soon you'll be out of the Mugi Valley and back into the Baliem Valley proper and the village of Hitugi (1½ hours after setting off). The path wends downhill for just over an hour to Ugem village. Both villages have accommodation.

Continue onwards and nearly five hours after setting out that morning you reach Seima. On the opposite bank of the Kali Baliem you'll be able to see where you started trekking several days ago. You could stop in Seima for the night but most people choose to press on for a further 1½ hours. From Seima continue along the track heading north. It wends in and out of forest and farmland before dropping down to the river, which you eventually cross on a scary yellow hanging bridge, built of metal and sticks (most of which are missing). Ten minutes uphill walk and you'll reach the tarmac road, the village of Sugokmo and transport back to Wamena. Total walk time: six to seven hours.

Wasur National Park

The 4130-sq-km Wasur National Park, stretching between Merauke and the PNG border, will fascinate anyone with an interest in wildlife, especially birds and marsupials. But come in the later part of the dry season (mid-July to early November), otherwise most of Wasur's tracks will be impassable.

Part of the Trans-Fly biome straddling the Indonesia–PNG border, Wasur is a low-lying area of savannahs, swamps, forests and

OFF THE BEATEN TRACK

MOUNTAIN CLIMBING IN PAPUA

Papua contains the biggest mountains in Oceania including the biggest of them all, the 4884m **Carstensz Pyramid** (Puncak Jaya) and the 4750m **Gunung Trikora**, which comes in at number two. The Carstensz Pyramid has a fast-receding glacier and both mountains are frequently dusted in snow.

Climbing either mountain is possible, though basic mountaineering skills are needed for Carstensz Pyramid. Both require several nights camping at high, cold altitudes and both require a stash of permits and the services of a recognised Indonesian tour company.

Altitude sickness can be a real danger and this risk is increased by the fact that many of the standard 'package' climbing tours don't tend to include an acclimatisation day before attempting the summit.

Adventure Indonesia (p455) is one reliable operator offering expeditions up both mountains.

slow-moving rivers that inundate much of the land during the wet season. Wasur's marsupials includes at least three species of wallaby (locals call them all *kangguru*), though illegal hunting means numbers of wallaby are falling. There are also nocturnal cuscuses and sugar gliders. Among the 400 birds are cassowaries, kookaburras, cockatoos, brolgas, magpie geese and three types of bird of paradise.

The southern part of the park is the best for wildlife-spotting as it has more open grasslands and coastal areas. At **Rawa Biru**, an indigenous village 45km east of Merauke (300,000Rp one way by *ojek*, or 2,500,000Rp to 4,000,000Rp round trip in a rented 4WD vehicle with driver), you can stay in local houses for 100,000Rp to 150,000Rp person (bring food and mosquito nets). From Rawa Biru it's a two- to three-hour walk to **Prem**, with a small savannah surrounded by water, and a good chance of seeing wallabies and various waterbirds. Also within reach (20km) is **Yakiu**, where chances are high of seeing the greater, king and red birds of paradise in the early morning and late afternoon.

Bony Kondahon (☎0813 4458 3646; bonykondahon@rocketmail.com), an excellent, English-speaking, Merauke-based Papuan guide, can help with arrangements and show you the park. He charges 300,000Rp to 350,000Rp per day for guiding and cooking.

Asmat Region

The Asmat region is a massive, remote, low-lying area of muddy, snaking rivers, mangrove forests and tidal swamps, where many villages, including their streets, are built entirely on stilts. The Asmat people, formerly feared for their headhunting and cannibalism, are now most celebrated for their woodcarvings – the most spectacular of Papuan art. It's a fascinating area to explore but it requires time, money and patience.

Most visitors who do make it here spend time boating along the jungle-lined rivers to different villages, seeing and buying Asmat artefacts, and maybe seeing a traditional dance or ceremony.

Villages to visit for their carving include Atsy, Ambisu and Jow, all south of Agats. Fos and Awok, east of Agats up Kali Sirets (Sirets River), and Ocenep, south of Agats, are places where traditional Asmat celebrations can be laid on for a significant sum of cash.

Agats

Capital of the Asmat Region is the overgrown village of Agats, on the Aswet estuary. Due to the extraordinary tides and location, its streets are raised boardwalks. It's a curious place to wander round, with markets, shops, mosque, churches and questionable monuments, just like any other Papuan town.

Don't miss the **Museum Kebudayaan dan Kemajuan Asmat** (Asmat Museum of Culture & Progress; http://asmatmuseum.com; Jl Missi; admission by donation; ⏲8am-3pm Mon-Sat), which has a fantastic collection of Asmat art and artefacts, from *bis* poles and skulls to full-body dance outfits.

The government-run **Hotel Assedu** (☎0821 9831 2611; Jl Pemda 1; s/d incl breakfast 265,000/290,000Rp; ❄) has clean rooms with comfy beds, almost-tasteful plastic flowers and the best restaurant in town.

Getting There & Away

Unfortunately, actually getting to Agats can be problematic as there are few reliable scheduled flights. **Susi Air** (www.susiair.com) flies to Agats from Merauke via the island of Pulau Yos Sudarso but the service is rather infrequent. **Trigana** (www.trigana-air.com) has twice-weekly flights between Agats and Timika from where you can connect to Jayapura and other cities, but these flights seem to be booked up weeks in advance.

Pelni's *Tatamailau* leaves Agats every two weeks for Merauke (economy class 178,000Rp) southbound, and Timika, Tual and Sorong northbound. The *Kelimutu* comes every four weeks, to Merauke southbound and Timika and Maluku northbound.

Korowai Region

Far inland, in the region of the Dairam and upper Sirets rivers, live the Korowai people, seminomadic dwellers in tree houses perched 10m to 20m high as refuges against animals, enemies, floods and mosquitoes. The Korowai were not contacted by missionaries until the 1970s, and though some have since settled in new villages of ground-level houses, others still live their traditional way of life, wearing few clothes and employing stone and bone tools.

Most Papua-based tour companies offer tours to this area (an organised tour is, for all intents and purposes, the only feasible way of currently visiting). Tours typically fly from Jayapura or Wamena to Dekai, then boat down Kali Brazza and up Kali Pulau to the first Korowai village, Mabul. You then spend some days walking along muddy, slippery trails through hot, humid jungles, sleeping in tents, huts or tree houses, and witnessing tribal life, often including some prearranged festivities. You're looking at approximately €2000 to €2500 for a seven- to 10-day trip, with perhaps half that time actually in Korowai territory.

Sumatra

POP 50.37 MILLION

Includes ➡

Best Places to Eat

- ➡ Bixio Cafe (p529)
- ➡ Pak Tri's (p541)
- ➡ Marola (p567)
- ➡ Jenny's Restaurant (p512)
- ➡ Pondok Kelapa (p576)

Best Places to Stay

- ➡ Horas Family Home (p512)
- ➡ Pondok Tailana (p533)
- ➡ Freddies (p527)
- ➡ Abdi Homestay (p558)
- ➡ Nachelle Homestay (p507)

Why Go?

Few isles tempt the imagination with the lure of adventure quite like the fierce land of Sumatra. An island of extraordinary beauty, it bubbles with life and vibrates under the power of nature. Eruptions, earthquakes and tsunamis are Sumatran headline grabbers. Steaming volcanoes brew and bluster while standing guard over lakes that sleepily lap the edges of craters. Orangutan-filled jungles host not only our red-haired cousins, but also tigers, rhinos and elephants. And down at sea level, idyllic deserted beaches are bombarded by clear barrels of surf.

As varied as the land, the people of Sumatra are a spicy broth of mixed cultures, from the devout Muslims in Aceh to the hedonistic Batak Christians around Danau Toba and the matrilineal Minangkabau of Padang. All are unified by a fear, respect and love of the wild and wondrous land of Sumatra.

When to Go

Padang

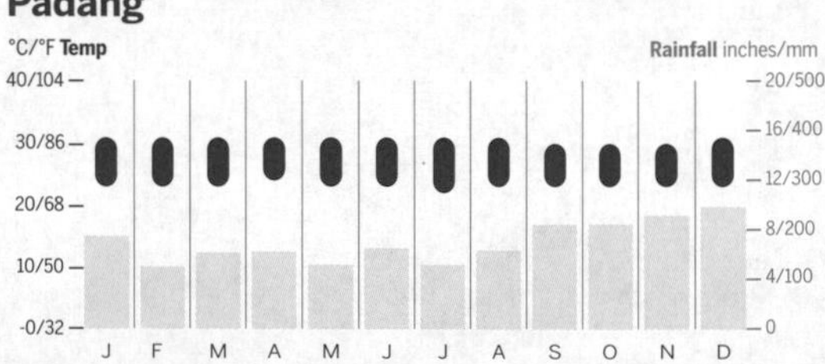

Apr–Oct Hit the waves on the Mentawais, Nias and the Banyaks.

Mid-Jun Take in the chaotic canoe races at the Danau Toba Festival.

Feb–Aug Travelling during the dry season maximises wildlife sightings in the jungle.

History

Pre-Islamic history is often more myth than fact, but archaeological evidence suggests that Sumatra was the gateway for migrating tribes from mainland Southeast Asia.

The Strait of Melaka, an important trade route between China and India, exposed the east coast of Sumatra to the region's superpowers and cultural influences such as Islam. The kingdom of Sriwijaya emerged as a local player at the end of the 7th century, with its capital presumably based near the modern city of Palembang. After Sriwijaya's influence waned, Aceh, at the northern tip of Sumatra, assumed control of trade through the strait. The era of Aceh's sultanate prevailed until the beginning of the 17th century, when Dutch traders claimed a piece of the spice trade.

The most influential port of the day, Samudra, near Lhokseumawe, eventually became the name that traders used to refer to the entire island. It was Marco Polo who corrupted the name to 'Sumatra' in his 1292 report on the area.

Throughout the colonial era, Sumatra saw many foreign powers stake a claim in its resources: the Dutch based themselves in the west Sumatran port of Padang, the British ruled in Bencoolen (now Bengkulu), American traders monopolised pepper exports from Aceh, and the Chinese exploited the reserves on the islands of Bangka and Belitung, east of Palembang.

In the early 19th century, the Dutch attempted to assert military control over all of Sumatra, a move met with resistance by its disparate tribes. In 1863 the Dutch finally established authority over Pulau Nias. Treaties and alliances brought other areas of Sumatra under Dutch rule.

The Dutch were never welcomed in Sumatra, which contributed several key figures to the independence struggle. Yet Sumatra was dissatisfied with Jakarta's rule. Between 1958 and 1961, rebel groups based in Bukittinggi and the mountains of south Sumatra resisted centralisation, which led to clashes with the Indonesian military. Fiercely independent Aceh proved to be Jakarta's most troublesome region. Aceh's separatist movement started in the late 1970s and continued until 2006.

No human conflict could compare to the destruction that occurred on Boxing Day in 2004, when a 9.0-plus-magnitude earthquake off the northwestern coast of Sumatra triggered a region-wide tsunami, killing over 170,000 people, mainly in Aceh. The one silver lining to the disaster was that the rescue and reconstruction efforts have brought peace to region and it largely holds to date.

ℹ Getting There & Away

These days, most travellers reach Sumatra via budget airline flight or ferry from Java. The old sea routes are largely redundant.

Keep in mind that Sumatra is one hour behind Singapore and Malaysia.

AIR

Medan is Sumatra's primary international hub, with frequent flights from its new airport to mainland Southeast Asian cities such as Singapore, Kuala Lumpur and Penang with **Silk Air** (www.silkair.com), **AirAsia** (www.airasia.com) and **Malaysia Airlines** (www.malaysiaairlines.com), respectively. In West Sumatra, Padang receives flights from Kuala Lumpur. Banda Aceh, Palembang, Pulau Batam and Pekanbaru also receive international flights from mainland Southeast Asia.

You can hop on a plane from Jakarta to every major Sumatran city aboard **Garuda** (www.garuda-indonesia.com), **Lion Air** (www.lionair.co.id) or **Sriwijaya Air** (www.sriwijayaair.co.id), among others. Flights from Sumatra to other parts of Indonesia typically connect through Jakarta.

A word of warning: when oil-palm plantations on Sumatra's east coast are burned (annually, usually during dry season), the smoke frequently results in the closure of Pekanbaru and Jambi airports.

BOAT

Ferries run between Dumai on Sumatra's east coast and Melaka and Klang (for Kuala Lumpur) in Malaysia, Singapore and Pulau Batam, but Dumai is only useful if you have your heart set on an international boat journey or if you're transporting a motorbike between Sumatra and Malaysia.

From Singapore, ferries make the quick hop to Pulau Batam and Pulau Bintan, the primary islands in the Riau archipelago. From Batam, boats set sail for Dumai, Palembang and Pekanbaru, but few travellers use these routes.

Ferries cross the narrow Sunda Strait, which links the southeastern tip of Sumatra at Bakauheni to Java's westernmost point of Merak. The sea crossing is a brief dip in a day-long voyage that requires several hours' worth of bus transport from both ports to Jakarta and, on the Sumatra side, Bandarlampung.

Sumatra Highlights

1 Delving into the fascinating Batak culture on the shores of **Danau Toba** (p508).

2 Ogling orangutans in the jungles of **Bukit Lawang** (p501).

3 Finding your desert island paradise among the **Banyak Islands** (p531) and snorkelling Sumatra's best reefs.

4 Swimming with sharks and turtles in the coral garden off **Pulau Weh** (p526).

5 Searching for tigers and pristine lakes and hiking up volcanoes in **Kerinci Seblat National Park** (p563).

6 Exploring the heartland of the Minangkabau from the sleepy **Harau Valley** (p558) to spectacular **Danau Maninjau** (p558).

7 Getting the real jungle experience around **Ketambe** (p535), at the heart of the Gunung Leuser National Park.

8 Living the surfer dream around the **Mentawai** (p544), **Nias** (p515) and **Banyak** (p531) Islands.

9 Rock climbing and hiking in the countryside around **Bengkulu** (p566), Sumatra's most pleasant city.

10 Hiking to a steaming volcanic peak around the hill town of **Berastagi** (p505).

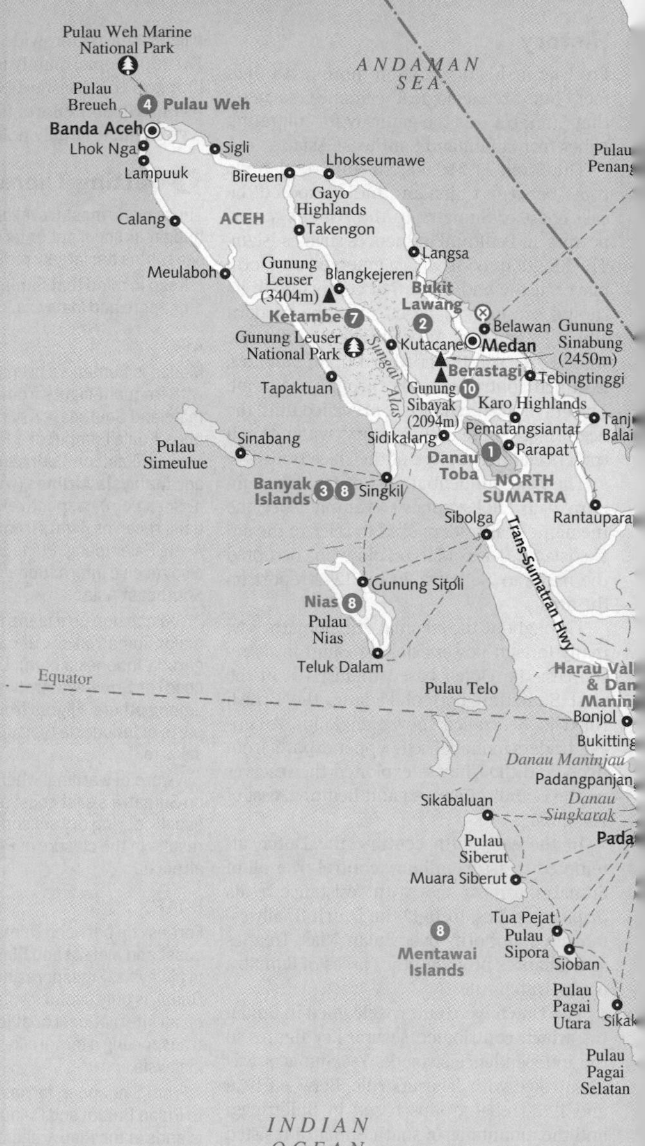

SOUTH CHINA SEA
THAILAND
MALAYSIA
Ipoh
Lumut
KUALA LUMPUR
Pelabuhan (Port) Klang
Strait of Melaka
Melaka
Pulau Rupat
Dumai
Duri
Pulau Bengkalis
Pulau Rangsang
Tanjung Buton
Pulau Kalimun
SINGAPORE
Pulau Bintan
Pulau Batam
Nongsa
Selat Panjang
Siak
Siakinderapura
Tanjung Samak
Tanjung Balai
Tanjung Pinang
Kijang
Pulau Tebingtinggi
Pulau Mendol
Pulau Kundur
RIAU
Pulau Penuba
Daik
Pulau Lingga
Sungai Buluh
Dabo
LINGGA ISLANDS
Pulau Singkep
Bukit Tigapuluh National Park
Kerinci Seblat National Park
JAMBI
Muara Jambi
Tujuh Islands
Selat Berhala
Muarabungo
Jambi
Bubus
Kerinci Valley
Bangko
Bukit Duabelas National Park
Muntok
Sungailiat
Pangkal Pinang
Kerinci Seblat National Park
Pegunungan Bukit Barisan
Sungai Musi
Pulau Bangka
Mukomuko
Ipuh
BENGKULU
Lubuklinggau
Palembang
Perabumulih
Kayuagung
SOUTH SUMATRA
Lais
Curup
Lahat
Bengkulu
Pasemah Highlands
Pagaralam
Baturaja
Manna
LAMPUNG
Danau Ranau
Bintuhan
Kotabumi
Bukit Barisan Selatan National Park
Simpang Sinder
Krui
Metro
Way Kanan
Way Kambas National Park
Pulau Enggano
Jepara
Bandarlampung
Pulau Seribu
Kota Agung
Kalianda
Bakauheni
Gunung Krakatau
Merak
Sunda Strait
JAKARTA
JAVA
Pulau Laut
Pulau Matak
Pulau Natuna Besar
Pulau Terempa
Pulau Jemaja
Pulau Midai
Pulau Subi
ANAMBAS ISLANDS
Pulau Serasan
NATUNA SEA
Pulau Mendarik
Pulau Dumdum
TAMBELAN ISLANDS
KALIMANTAN
Equator
Pulau Pejantan
Tanjung Pandan
Pulau Belitung

Getting Around

Most travellers bus around northern Sumatra and then hop on a plane to Java, largely avoiding Sumatra's highway system. Most of the island is mountainous jungle and the poorly maintained roads form a twisted pile of spaghetti on the undulating landscape. Don't count on getting anywhere very quickly on Sumatra.

AIR

Short plane journeys can be an attractive alternative to spending an eternity on packed buses. Competition between domestic carriers means internal flights are inexpensive and largely reliable, with the exception of Susi Air and their small planes which are particularly susceptible to bad weather. Dry-season smog affects planes along the east coast.

Medan to Pulau Weh, Medan to Padang, Palembang to Jambi, Medan to Banda Aceh, and Pulau Batam to Padang and Bengkulu are useful air hops.

BOAT

Most boat travel within Sumatra connects the main island with the many satellite islands lining the coast. The most commonly used routes link Banda Aceh with Pulau Weh; Singkil and Sibolga with Pulau Nias; and Padang with the Mentawai Islands. Most long-distance ferries have several classes, ranging from dilapidated and crowded to air-conditioned, dilapidated and less crowded. The Mentawai Islands are now served by a comfortable large speedboat.

BUS

Bus is the most common mode of transport around Sumatra, and in some cases it's the only option for intercity travel. But it is far from efficient or comfortable, since all types of buses – from economy sardine cans to modern air-con coaches – are subject to the same traffic snarls along Sumatra's single carriageways, potholes the size of Cumbria and endless stops to pick up or drop off passengers. At the top of the class structure are super-executive buses with reclining seats, deep-freeze air-con, toilets and an all-night serenade of The Scorpions' greatest hits. Many passengers come prepared with a jacket and earplugs.

In some towns, you can go straight to the bus terminal to buy tickets and board buses, while other towns rely on bus-company offices located outside the terminals. Ticket prices vary greatly depending on the quality of the bus and the perceived gullibility of the traveller; ask at your guesthouse how much a ticket is supposed to cost.

LOCAL TRANSPORT

The usual Indonesian forms of transport – bemo or *angkot* (small minibus), becak (motorcycle-rickshaw or bicycle-rickshaw) and *bendi* (two-person horse-drawn cart) – are available in Sumatran towns and cities. Establish a price for a becak ride before climbing aboard. For an *angkot*, you pay after you disembark.

MINIBUS

For midrange and shorter journeys, many locals and travellers prefer to use minibus and shared car services, which can be more convenient than hustling out to the bus terminal as they run intercity and door-to-door. They are not necessarily faster, but more comfortable and convenient.

TRAIN

The only three useful train services in Sumatra run from Medan's new airport to the centre of Medan, and from Bandarlampung to Palembang and Lahat (for the Pasemah Highlands).

NORTH SUMATRA

For many visitors, this is the sole slice of Sumatra they'll taste. And with good reason: here you can ogle the orangutans in Bukit Lawang, veer over the volcanoes of Berastagi, laze away on the shores of Danau Toba, skim the waves off the Banyaks and Nias, and go underwater on Pulau Weh. Overall, North Sumatra is a well-trodden but extremely worthy circuit that centres on gateway metropolis Medan.

North Sumatra stretches from the Indian Ocean to the Strait of Melaka. From sea to shining sea, it is anything but homogeneous. The rolling landscape varies from sweaty plains to cool highlands, while the houses of worship switch between the metal domes of mosques to the arrow-straight steeples of Christian churches. The coastal Malays, relatives of peoples from mainland Southeast Asia, live along the Strait of Melaka and are the largest ethnic group. In the highlands around Danau Toba are the delightful Batak, and then there's the megalithic culture of Pulau Nias.

Medan

☎061 / POP 2.2 MILLION

Sumatra's major metropolis, and Indonesia's third-largest city, is seen as a necessary evil by many Sumatra-bound travellers. It's almost inevitably a place to pass through en route to more exciting destinations and also, for some, a welcome return to the trappings of 'civilisation' in the shape of modern malls and restaurants. It's a brash urban sprawl, chocked by streams of cars and becaks, but it would also be fair to say that this is a city with real Indonesian character. So get over the culture shock, give Medan a bit of time and discover an amenity-filled, modern city with more than a hint of crumbling Dutch-colonial-era charm and a couple of worthwhile museums.

Sights

Ghosts of Medan's colonial-era mercantile past are still visible along Jl Ahmad Yani from Jl Palang Merah north to Lapangan Merdeka, a former parade ground surrounded by handsome colonial-era buildings, such as the Bank Indonesia, **Balai Kota** (Town Hall; Jl Balai Kota) and the main post office.

★Museum of North Sumatra MUSEUM
(Museum Negeri Privinci Sumatera Utara; Jl HM Joni 51; admission 10,000Rp; 8am-4pm Tue-Thu, to 3.30pm Fri-Sun) Housed in a striking traditional building, this museum has a well-presented collection ranging from early North Sumatran civilisations to Hindu, Buddhist and Islamic periods to Dutch colonial-era and military history. There are also sections devoted to traditional occupations such as fishing and farming. Highlights include fine stone carvings and extravagantly carved wooden dragon coffins from Nias, Batak scrolls for fending off misfortune, fine textiles and a *keris* (ornamental dagger) collection. It's a short way east of the centre.

Tjong A Fie Mansion HISTORIC BUILDING
(Jl Ahmad Yani 105; admission incl guide 35,000Rp; 9am-5pm) The former house of a famous Chinese merchant who died in 1921 – formerly the wealthiest resident of Medan – mixes Victorian and Chinese style. The original hand-painted ceilings, Tjong's huge bedroom, imported dark-wood furniture inlaid with marble and mother-of-pearl, interesting art pieces, an upstairs ballroom and Taoist temples help to make it one of the most impressive historic buildings in town.

Istana Maimoon PALACE
(Jl Katamso; admission 5000Rp; 8am-5pm) The grand, 30-room Maimoon Palace was built by the sultan of Deli in 1888 and features Malay, Mughal and Italian influences. Only the main room, which features the lavish inauguration throne, is open to the public. Here you can check out a modest collection of ceremonial *kerises* and dress up in traditional Malay costume.

The back wing of the palace is occupied by members of the sultan's family. The current sultan, Aria Mahmud Lamanjiji, was only eight years old when he was installed as the 14th Sultan of Deli in 2005, replacing his father, who died in a plane crash. He is the youngest sultan in Deli history. He currently resides in Sulawesi with his mother, and his role is purely ceremonial.

Traditional music performances take place at 10am and 2pm Monday to Friday and at 2pm on Saturday and Sunday. Note that punctuality isn't the musicians' strong point.

Mesjid Raya MOSQUE
(cnr Jl Mesjid Raya & SM Raja; admission by donation; 9am-5pm, except during prayer times) The impressive Grand Mosque was commissioned by the sultan in 1906. The Moroccan-style building has a grand entrance, towering ceilings, ornate carvings, Italian marble and stained glass from China.

Tours

Tri Jaya Tour & Travel TOUR
(061-703 2967; www.trijaya-travel.com; Hotel Deli River, Jl Raya Namorambe 129; 2-person tour US$70) Superb historic city tours as well as multiday tours of Sumatra. You can also pick up the book *Tours Through Historic Medan and Its Surroundings,* written by the owner of this company.

Sleeping

Pondok Wisata Angel GUESTHOUSE $
(061-732 0702; a_zelsy_travel@yahoo.com; Jl SM Raja 70; s with fan 70,000Rp, d with fan/air-con 100,000/130,000Rp;) The best backpacker option in town. Angel's clean rooms are a swirl of vivid blues and yellows, a colour scheme that almost succeeds in offsetting the noisy traffic. It has a sociable street-front cafe.

Residence Hotel HOTEL $
(061-732 1249; www.residencehotelmedan.com; Jl Tengah 1; r 70,000-150,000Rp;) The lime-green Residence has enough rooms, at a range of different prices, to suit both your mood and your pockets. Warning: the cheaper rooms are top-floor, windowless cells with a Dickensian prison vibe and they get hot. The pricier rooms are pleasant.

Medan

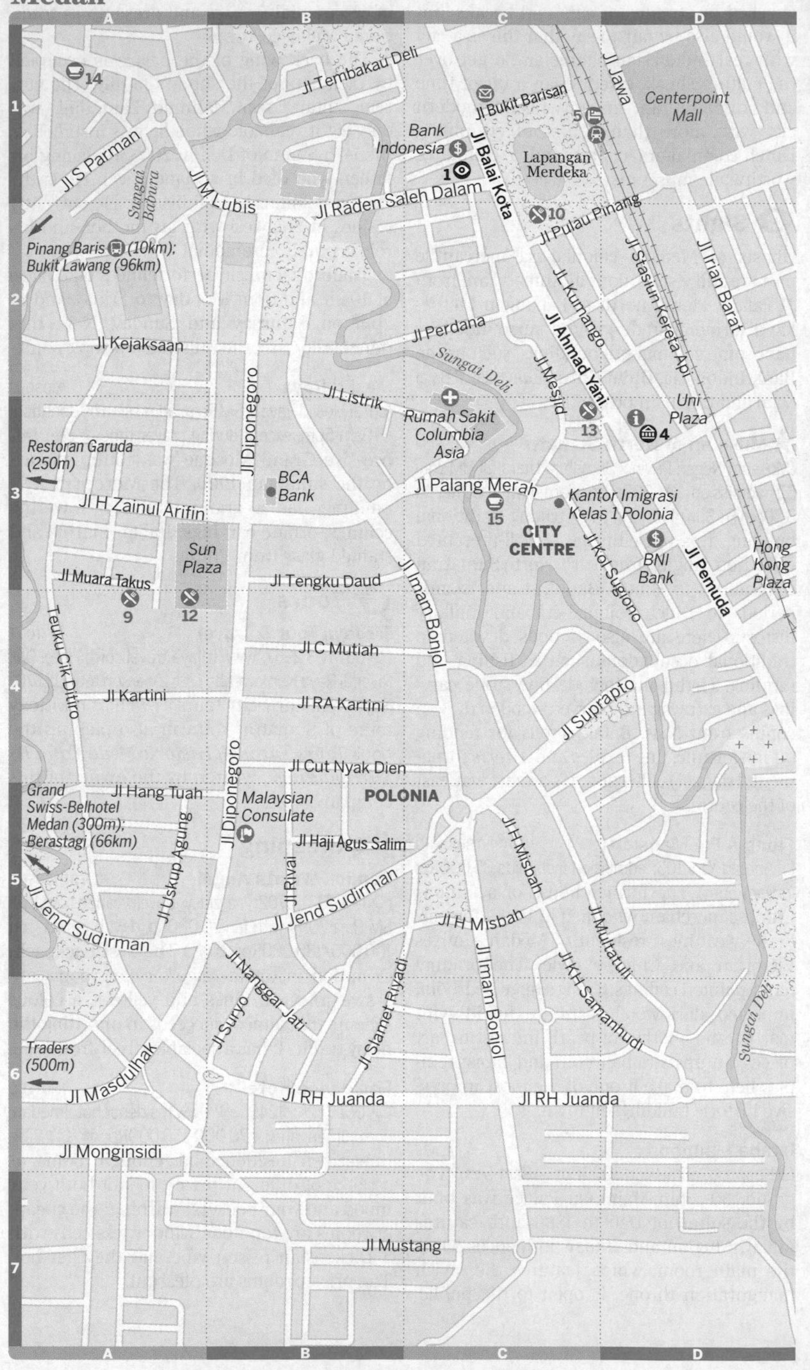

A
B
C
D
1
2
3
4
5
6
7
Jl Tembakau Deli
Jl Bukit Barisan
Jl Jawa
Centerpoint Mall
Bank Indonesia
Jl Balai Kota
Lapangan Merdeka
Jl S Parman
Sungai Babura
Jl M Lubis
Jl Raden Saleh Dalam
Jl Pulau Pinang
Pinang Baris (10km); Bukit Lawang (96km)
Jl Stasiun Kereta Api
Jl Irian Barat
Jl Kumango
Jl Perdana
Jl Ahmad Yani
Jl Kejaksaan
Sungai Deli
Jl Mesjid
Jl Diponegoro
Jl Listrik
Rumah Sakit Columbia Asia
Uni Plaza
Restoran Garuda (250m)
BCA Bank
Jl Palang Merah
Kantor Imigrasi Kelas 1 Polonia
Jl H Zainul Arifin
CITY CENTRE
Sun Plaza
BNI Bank
Jl Pemuda
Hong Kong Plaza
Jl Muara Takus
Jl Tengku Daud
Jl Imam Bonjol
Jl Kol Sugiono
Teuku Cik Ditiro
Jl C Mutiah
Jl Kartini
Jl RA Kartini
Jl Suprapto
Jl Cut Nyak Dien
Grand Swiss-Belhotel Medan (300m); Berastagi (66km)
Jl Hang Tuah
Malaysian Consulate
POLONIA
Jl Uskup Agung
Jl Haji Agus Salim
Jl H Misbah
Jl Rivai
Jl Jend Sudirman
Jl Multatuli
Jl Nanggar Jati
Jl Slamet Riyadi
Jl KH Samanhudi
Jl Suryo
Traders (500m)
Jl Masdulhak
Jl RH Juanda
Jl Monginsidi
Jl Mustang
1
4
5
9
10
12
13
14
15

K77 Guest House GUESTHOUSE **$$**

(061-736 7087, 0813 9653 8897; http://k77guesthousemedan.blogspot.com; Jl Seto 6B; r/f 250,000/300,000Rp;) This backpacker haven is not in the city centre. Instead, you get a typical residential neighbourhood experience, and the hosts, Johan and Lola, go out of their way to make it a good one. Rooms are clean, snug and cool, and Johan can organise pickup and all manner of tours.

Gandhi Inn HOTEL **$$**

(061-733 2330; www.gandhiinn.com; Jl Gandhi 125 A-B; r 338,000-598,000Rp;) Decked out in sedate creams and browns, rooms at this budget (for Medan!) hotel are compact, comfortable and just a short walk from Thamsin Plaza Mall and the Pasar Ramai market. The owner and his team do their best to assist guests and recommend local culinary secrets. A place to chill out in between Sumatra adventures, do laundry and sleep.

D'Prima Hotel HOTEL **$$**

(061-456 1077; www.dprimahotelmedan.com; Jl Stasiun Kereta Api 1; r 395,000-550,000Rp;) Occupying the top floors of the train station and surprisingly quiet, given the location, this slick hotel is super convenient for train departures to the airport. Rooms are somewhat anonymous, but they are ultra-clean and come with flat-screen TVs, kettles and powerful hot showers.

Swiss-Belinn Medan BUSINESS HOTEL **$$**

(061-452 0505; www.swiss-belhotel.com; Jl Surabaya 88; r 416,000-500,000Rp;) Smart, busy hotel that almost verges on earning a boutique label. The rooms have lovely cool, dark-slate floors and bathrooms, rough white-washed walls, subdued art and deliciously comfortable beds. There's a good range of facilities, including a popular restaurant, but some rooms are windowless and the air-con could be more powerful.

Hotel Deli River HOTEL **$$$**

(061-703 2964; www.hotel-deliriver.com; Jl Raya Namorambe 129; r 750,000-950,000Rp, f 1,400,000Rp, all incl breakfast;) This colonial-style retreat, consisting of luxury cottages and rooms, shaded by fruit trees and overlooking the Deli River, provides respite from the city smog while remaining within striking distance (12km) of Medan. A wonderfully tranquil setting, but we were underwhelmed by the restaurant offerings.

Medan

Sights
1 Balai Kota C1
2 Istana Maimoon E5
3 Mesjid Raya F5
4 Tjong A Fie Mansion D3

Sleeping
5 D'Prima Hotel C1
6 Pondok Wisata Angel F6
7 Residence Hotel F6
8 Swiss-Belinn Medan E3

Eating
9 Bollywood Food Centre A4
10 Merdeka Walk C2
11 Mie Tiong Sim Selat Panjang E3
12 Sushi Tei A4
13 Tip Top Restaurant C3

Drinking & Nightlife
14 Macehat Coffee A1
15 Royale Coffee Shop C3

Grand Swiss-Belhotel Medan BUSINESS HOTEL $$$
(☎061-457 6999; www.swiss-belhotel.com; Jl S Parman 217; d incl breakfast from 847,000Rp;) This huge, modern hotel follows the standard business-class formula of great facilities, an array of different restaurants and a guaranteed good night's sleep. But it also throws in a see-through, glass-walled swimming pool and floor-to-ceiling windows that offer great city views from the upper floors.

Eating

Medan has the most varied selection of cuisines in Sumatra, from basic Malay-style *mie* (noodle) and nasi (rice) joints, to top-class hotel restaurants.

Lots of simple warungs (food stalls) occupy the front courtyards of the houses in the little lanes around Mesjid Raya. Medan's numerous malls also have decent food courts.

★Merdeka Walk SOUTHEAST ASIAN $
(Lapangan Merdeka, Jl Balai Kota; dishes 10,000-35,000Rp; 5-11pm;) Inspired by Singapore's alfresco dining, this collection of outdoor eateries in Lapangan Merdeka offers everything from doughnut stalls to breezy sit-down restaurants serving grilled seafood and Malaysian-style noodles. There is also what may possibly be the world's glitziest Pizza Hut.

Bollywood Food Centre INDIAN $
(☎061-453 6494; Jl Muara Takus 7; dishes from 15,000Rp; lunch & dinner;) Locals are adamant that this tucked-away little place, which is more like someone's front room with a family atmosphere to match, serves the most authentic Indian cuisine in the city. There are several Malay-Indian roti shops located nearby.

Mie Tiong Sim Selat Panjang NOODLES $
(Jl Selat Panjang 7; meals around 70,000Rp; 10am-10pm) This stall, on a street of food stalls, is locally (and justifiably) famous for its *mie tiong sim* (soft, handmade noodles topped with sweet, flavourful char siu pork). The chicken noodle is almost equally as good, as are the wontons. It's behind the Hotel Swiss-Belinn.

Pasar Ramai MARKET $
(Ramani Market; Jl Thamrin) The main fruit market is a profusion of colour and smells, and has an impressive selection of local and imported tropical fruit. It's next to Thamrin Plaza.

★Sushi Tei JAPANESE $$
(www.sushitei.co.id; Sun Plaza; meals 60,000-200,000; 11am-10pm) At the back of Sun Plaza mall, on the ground floor, this celebrated chain serves some of Medan's best sushi as well as an extensive array of tonkatsu, tempura, yakitori, sashimi platters and bowls of udon. We're quite partial to the spicy maguro rolls and the stuffed crab. The virgin cocktails and imaginative drinks really hit the spot, too.

Restoran Garuda INDONESIAN $$
(www.restorangaruda.com; Jl Gajah Mada 8; meals around 80,000Rp; lunch & dinner) A venerable Medan institution for nearly 40 years, Restoran Garuda specialises in Minang dishes (similar to Padang cuisine), so you get to sample a variety of small, fiery, flavourful platefuls during the course of a meal.

Traders INTERNATIONAL $$
(Jl Kapten Pattimura 423; mains 80,000-200,000Rp; noon-midnight;) Plush Traders is very much a high-society kind of place. It's the perfect spot to blow your dining budget on sushi, lobster dishes or Australian Angus steaks; the restaurant is particularly known for expertly grilling your chosen cuts of meat.

Tip Top Restaurant INTERNATIONAL $$
(Jl Ahmad Yani 92; dishes 15,000-45,000Rp; lunch & dinner;) Only the prices have changed at this colonial-era relic, which dates back to 1934 and is great for a taste of bygone imperialism. It offers an array of Indonesian, Chinese and international dishes, but it's the old-school ice cream that's really worth a try. Focus on the setting and atmosphere and overlook the poor service.

Drinking

Macehat Coffee COFFEE
(www.macehatcoffee.com; Jl Karo 20; 10am-8pm) Not only do these guys roast their own, but this cafe is a magnet for bean connoisseurs wanting to sample some of Sumatra's best – Mandheling Arabica from the Danau Toba area. For something a bit more unusual, try the avocado coffee blend.

Royale Coffee Shop COFFEE
(Jl Palang Merah 4; 9am-7pm) *The* home of Medan's latte art and award-winning baristas. Good for sampling blends from all over Sumatra.

Traders COCKTAIL BAR
(Jl Kapten Pattimura 423; noon-midnight) With its long and glamorous list of cocktails and equally glamorous people, swanky Traders is the place to be seen in Medan.

Information

Medan has branches of just about every bank operating in Indonesia, including **Bank Indonesia** (Jl Balai Kota), **BCA Bank** (Bank Central Asia; cnr Jl Diponegoro & Jl H Zainal Arifin) and **BNI Bank** (Bank Negara Indonesia; Jl Pemuda). Most bank headquarters sit along the junction of Jl Diponegoro and Jl H Zainal Arifin.

There is a basic tourist information booth at Medan's new airport.

Kantor Imigrasi Kelas 1 Polonia (061-453 3117; 2nd fl, Jl Mangkubumi 2; 8am-4pm Mon-Fri) For visa extensions. Technically the process takes three days, costs 350,000Rp and cannot be done until a few days before your current visa expires. Bring photocopies of your passport and Indonesian visa, as well as your onward ticket. The office you need is on the 2nd floor.

Main Post Office (Jl Bukit Barisan; 8am-6pm) Located in an old Dutch building on the main square.

North Sumatra Tourist Office (061-452 8436; Jl Ahmad Yani 107; 8am-4pm Mon-Fri) Brochures, maps and basic information.

Rumah Sakit Columbia Asia (061-456 6730; www.columbiaasia.com; Jl Listrik 2A; 24hr) The best hospital in the city, with a 24-hour walk-in clinic and pharmacy, as well as English-speaking doctors and specialists.

Getting There & Away

Medan is Sumatra's main international arrival and departure point.

AIR

Kualanamu International Airport (061-8888 0300; www.kualanamu-airport.co.id), which opened in 2014, is 39km from the city centre and handily connected to central Medan by frequent trains and buses.

BUS

There are two major bus terminals in Medan. Purchase tickets from ticket offices outside the terminals.

The **Amplas bus terminal** (Jl SM Raja), which serves southern destinations, is 6.5km south of the city centre. Almost any *angkot* heading south on Jl SM Raja will get you to Amplas (5000Rp).

The **Pinang Baris bus terminal** (Jl Gatot Subroto), 10km west of the city centre, serves Bukit Lawang, Berastagi and Banda Aceh (the latter is also served by buses from Amplas).

Singkil Raya (Jl Bintan), near the caged-bird shops, is one of the companies running daily morning and evening trips to Singkil, the departure point for boats to the Banyak Islands. Nearby you'll also find a bus at 7.30pm to Ketambe. Take *angkot* 53 from Jl SM Raja to Medan Mall.

Most lodgings and numerous travel agencies along Jl Katamso can arrange a space for you on a shared door-to-door minibus to popular destinations such as Bukit Lawang, Berastagi and Danau Toba; it's pricier than a bus but faster and more comfortable.

TRAIN

Rail services are very limited. The only one that's useful to travellers is the airport train.

Getting Around

TO/FROM THE AIRPORT

The fastest and most comfortable way to reach central Medan from the airport is by air-conditioned train (100,000Rp, 45 minutes, 5am to 11.30pm). From Medan city centre, trains run between 4am and 9.20pm.

Taxis from the airport charge a basic fare of 6000Rp, with an additional 3500Rp per kilometre. A journey to the city centre costs at least 150,000Rp.

Paradep (061-77123029; one way 60,000Rp) and **Damri** (061-7865466; one-way

TRANSPORT FROM MEDAN

Air

DESTINATION	AIRLINE	FREQUENCY
Banda Aceh	Garuda, Lion Air	4 daily
Bandung	Citilink, Lion Air	4 daily
Bangkok	Indonesia AirAsia	daily
Denpasar	Garuda	daily
Gunung Sitoli	Garuda, Wings Air	8 daily
Jakarta	Batik Air, Citilink, Garuda, Indonesia AirAsia, Lion Air, Sriwijaya Air	45 daily
Kuala Lumpur	AirAsia, Indonesia AirAsia, Malaysia Airlines	9 daily
Meulaboh	Garuda, Wings Air	2 daily
Padang	Lion Air, Sriwaya Air	3 daily
Palembang	Indonesia AirAsia	daily
Penang	AirAsia, Indonesia AirAsia, Lion Air, Sriwijaya Air	8 daily
Pekanbaru	Lion Air	2 daily
Pulau Batam	Citilink, Lion Air, NAM Air	5 daily
Pulau Simeulue	Susi Air	2 daily
Sibolga	Wings Air	3 daily
Silangit	Susi Air	daily
Singapore	Jetstar, Silk Air	5 daily
Surabaya	Lion Air	2 daily
Yogykarta	Indonesia AirAsia	daily

Bus

DESTINATION	FARE (RP)	DURATION (HR)	FREQUENCY
Banda Aceh	150,000-210,000	12	several daily
Berastagi	15,000Rp	3-4	numerous daily
Bukittinggi	200,000-320,000	16-20	several daily
Bukit Lawang	30,000	4-5	twice daily
Ketambe	150,000	7	daily
Padang	250,000	18-22	several daily
Parapat (Danau Toba)	30,000	5-6	several daily
Sibolga	100,000-130,000	11	several daily
Singkil	90,000-110,000	9	several daily

50,000Rp) shuttles through the city centre en route from the airport.

PUBLIC TRANSPORT

Medan's got more *angkot* than you can shake a spoon player at. The going rate is 5000Rp per ride. A few helpful routes include the white Mr X from Jl SM Raja to Kesawan Sq, Lapangan Merdeka and the train station, and the yellow 64 from Maimoon Palace to Sun Plaza. Becak journeys across the city centre cost between 15,000Rp and 20,000Rp.

Bukit Lawang

☎061 / POP 30,000

This sweet little town, 96km northwest of Medan, next to dense Sumatran jungle, is built around the popularity of its orangutan-spotting opportunities. But Bukit Lawang has much more to offer beyond our red-haired cousins. It's very easy to while away a few days lounging in hammocks, splashing in the river and hiking in the jungle. The forests surrounding Bukit Lawang are part of the vast Gunung Leuser National Park, which is one of the richest tropical-forest ecosystems in the world. The park as a whole is home to eight species of primate plus tigers, rhinos, elephants and leopards. However, aside from orangutans, baboons, various macaque species and the elusive Thomas leaf monkey, you'd have to be very lucky to see any other large mammals here, as oil-palm plantations extend right up to the edge of the village. At weekends, when foreign tourists are joined by masses of domestic visitors, Bukit Lawang can feel rather overrun, so try to arrive on a weekday.

Bukit Lawang became famous as a site to view orangutans largely due to the activities of its (now sadly closed) orangutan rehabilitation and feeding centre.

The centre was set up in 1973 to help primates readjust to the wild after captivity or displacement through land clearing, and during its decades-long operation it introduced around 200 orangutans into the surrounding jungle. Visitors will likely spot some of these semi-wild apes on treks.

Many of them had been kept as caged pets, and the centre taught them how to forage for food in the wild, build nests, climb trees and other essentials for survival after release. The orangutans were also treated for diseases that they contracted during contact with humans.

Vestiges of the centre can still be seen. The main office, reached by an inflatable boat crossing upriver from the village, still issues permits for Gunung Leuser National Park and shows a film about the continuing conservation efforts of the centre. There are also some faded information panels advising on the responsible way to behave around the apes (worth a read). Some treks pass the old feeding platform where pregnant and vulnerable orangutans were provided with milk and bananas twice a day as a way to help them transition to their new wild circumstances.

Activities

Hiking

Treks into the Gunung Leuser National Park require a permit and guide and can last anywhere from three hours to several days. Most people opt for two days so they can spend the night in the jungle, which increases their likelihood of seeing orangutans and other wildlife. It's best to hike in the smallest group possible and to set off early.

Orangutan sightings are highly likely, but not guaranteed. When you do come across them, always keep a safe distance and do not attempt to feed or touch the animals. Not only are orangutans susceptible to many human illnesses, but those in pursuit of that perfect selfie risk having their backpacks or phones snatched away or even getting attacked. Don't forget that these are wild, immensely strong animals that can crack your head like a coconut if they wish to: keep your distance.

That said, a sighting of these comical red hairy creatures, swinging freely through the trees, is nothing short of magical, and visitors are often surprised at how close they do come.

Take your time in choosing a guide as jungle practices are not as regulated as they should be. Talk to returning hikers and decide how much jungle time you really need. If you just want a few souvenir pictures and stories, find a guide you like. People who trekked with guides from the village have mainly positive feedback, with the greatest kudos going to the nightly meals and campfire socials. Common complaints include guides who don't know much about the flora and fauna, the bunching together of trekking groups and the feeding of orangutans.

'Rafting' (an extra 150,000Rp per person) back to town, which actually involves sitting on rubber tubes tied together, is a popular option that allows you to trek deeper into the jungle and makes for a fun and relaxing way to finish your trek. Prices include basic meals, guide fees, camping equipment and the park

JUNGLE TREKKING FEES

Guide rates are fixed by the Sumatra Guide Association. Prices are based on a three person minimum; if there is less than three people, then the cost based on three people must be paid in full by the couple or the solo traveller.

DURATION	COST (RP) PER PERSON
Half day	395,000
1 day	550,000
2 days	945,000
3 days	1,340,000
4 days	1,970,000
5 days	2,290,000

permit. Camping involves a tarpaulin sheet thrown over bamboo poles, with everyone sleeping in the same tent.

Hiking in the jungle is no stroll in the park. You'll encounter steep, slippery ascents and precipitous drops amid intense humidity, so a good level of fitness is essential. The trails can be well-worn paths or barely visible breaks in the underbrush. Pack at least two bottles of water per day and wear sturdy footwear.

Tubing

On the river, en route to the orangutan centre, you'll find a shed renting inflated truck inner tubes (20,000Rp per day), which can be used to ride the Sungai Bohorok rapids. On weekends the river near the bridge resembles a water theme park, but don't underestimate the river. Currents are extremely strong, and when the water is high, tubing is officially off limits, though few will tell you this. Avoid the very last section as you approach the village centre.

Sleeping

The further upriver you go, the more likely you are to ogle the swinging monkeys and apes from your porch hammock. Only a few guesthouses have hot water; some provide fans.

Green Hill GUESTHOUSE $

(0813 7034 9124; www.greenhillbukitlawang.com; r incl breakfast 100,000-300,000Rp; wi-fi) Run by an English conservation scientist and her Sumatran husband, Green Hill has three lovely stilt-high rooms ideal for couples, with ensuite bamboo-shoot showers that afford stunning jungle views while you wash, as well as a few-frills budget room. The restaurant serves some of the tastiest sambal in the village (among other dishes) and the service is friendly and prompt.

Back to Nature GUESTHOUSE $

(0821 7055 6999, 0813 7540 0921; www.backtonature.asia; r 150,000-200,000Rp; wi-fi) Preserving a giant patch of jungle otherwise destined to become an oil-palm plantation, the eco-minded owner has built this lodge on a gorgeous bend in the river. The comfortable wooden rooms, raised off the ground on stilts, are a half-hour walk upstream from the river crossing for the orangutan feeding centre. Jungle treks and pick ups from Bukit Lawang are offered.

Rainforest Guesthouse GUESTHOUSE $

(Nora's; 0813 6207 0656; www.bukitlawang.com; d 50,000-150,000Rp) This cluster of wooden rooms set close to the gurgling river equals backpacker bliss. Cheaper rooms have a mattress on the floor and shared bathrooms, but pricier rooms come with bathrooms and fans. There's a friendly dining area (with Western meals like pasta, burgers and all the rest) and it's a super place to hook up with other travellers.

The place is still known locally as Nora's, though Nora passed away in 2014.

Garden Inn GUESTHOUSE $

(0813 9600 0571; www.bukitlawang-garden-inn.com; r 100,000-250,000Rp; wi-fi) A popular backpacker choice, the ever-growing Garden Inn empire spreads over several buildings, which house a variety of different rooms, from cosy, wooden jungle shacks to pristine, modern white rooms. There's a sweet little cafe for swapping ape-spotting tales.

Sam's Bungalows GUESTHOUSE $

(0813 7009 3597; www.bukitlawangaccommodation.com; r 150,000-300,000Rp) There's an excellent range of wooden tree houses here as well as more solidly built rooms painted in sunny Mediterranean colours. Rooms have four-poster beds, huge bathrooms and Italian rain showers.

★ **On the Rocks** BUNGALOW $$

(0812 6303 1119; www.ontherocksbl.com; r 200,000-500,000Rp; wi-fi) More on the hill than on the rocks, the six 'tribal' huts here verge on being luxurious in a rustic kind of way. Each hut has a veranda and sunken bathroom, and all are shrouded in peace and beautiful views. It's across the river and a fair hike from the main strip, so it's a good thing it serves decent meals!

EcoTravel Cottages LODGE **$$**
(☎0813 7089 5186; www.sumatra-ecotravel.com; r 345,000-690,000Rp; ❄📶) With huge four-poster beds, immense rooms, hammocks on porches and immaculate hot-water bathrooms, this riverfront lodge combines the ultimate in creature comforts with professionally run tours by Sumatra Ecotravel. Multiday trips into the jungle and further afield connections to Danau Toba and Tangakhan.

Jungle Inn GUESTHOUSE **$$**
(☎0853 7342 2405; www.jungleinnbukitlawang.com; d 150,000-500,000Rp) The last guesthouse along the strip near the park entrance, Jungle Inn is an old favourite of many a Lonely Planet reader. One room overlooks a waterfall, while another incorporates the hill's rock face, and the bathroom sprouts a shower from living ferns.

Eating & Drinking

Most guesthouses along the river en route to the park entrance serve a mix of Western and Indonesian food and have a laid-back ambience.

Lawang Inn INDONESIAN **$**
(mains from 25,000Rp; ⏲breakfast, lunch & dinner; 📶🌿) Located in the heart of the village, the Inn's congenial Dutch owner serves large portions of curries, sambal dishes and more. The friendly staff can kick the spice factor up to eye-watering Indonesian levels if you ask nicely. Vegetarians are well-catered for and treats include homemade brown bread and avocado-and-chocolate shakes.

Jungle Hill INDONESIAN **$**
(mains 15,000-27,000Rp, pizza 80,000Rp; ⏲breakfast, lunch & dinner; 🌿) This chilled-out, family-run spot overlooking the river is good for chowing down on curry, *rendang* and sambal dishes. Classics such as *mie goreng*, some unusual delights (pumpkin noodles, cow skin sambal) and genuinely good pizza are also on the menu.

Dangers & Annoyances

There's a proliferation of guides in Bukit Lawang, and if you haven't prebooked a tour before your arrival in town, they may be keen to escort you to a guesthouse and sign you up for a jungle hike. Be polite and feel no obligation to book anything unless you want to. There's also little reason to sign up for cut-price trekking tours organised by Medan's budget hotels; everything can be organised within moments of arriving in Bukit Lawang.

Information

The nearby village of Gotong Royong, 2km southeast of Sungai Bohorok, is where most of the nontourist-related facilities can be found. If you arrive by public bus it's about a 1km walk north to where the Bukit Lawang accommodation begins. There are no banks, but you'll find moneychangers along the strip and if you need a post office you can buy stamps from the shops and use a local postbox. There is a market on Friday and Sunday in Bohorok town, 15km away, where you will also find the nearest police station and medical clinic.

Bukit Lawang Guide Association (⏲8am-2pm) This place can arrange guides and distributes the official guide rate sheet. Located in the centre of the village.

Bukit Lawang Visitors Centre (⏲7am-3pm) Park tickets are sold here. There's also displays of the flora and fauna found in Gunung Leuser National Park, plus a book of medicinal plants and their uses. Past visitors often record reviews of guides in the sign-in book. It's located down in the heart of the village.

Getting There & Away

Direct public buses go to Medan's Pinang Baris bus terminal (30,000Rp, four hours, half-hourly) between 5.30am and 5pm. There are also tourist minibuses (120,000Rp, three hours, daily at 8am). For Berastagi, there's a daily public bus (38,000Rp, six to seven hours) and tourist bus (170,000Rp, four to five hours, daily 8.30am) Tourist minibuses also go to Medan Airport (190,000Rp, around four hours, daily 8am) and Parapat (for Danau Toba; 180,000Rp, six hours, daily 8.30am).

Bukit Lawang is also a handy jumping off-point for day trips or onward travel to Tangakhan.

Tangkahan

The word is out: tiny Tangkahan has become synonymous with elephants, and visitors trickle in from nearby Bukit Lawang and Medan to get up close and personal with the mighty pachyderms.

Towards the end of the 1990s, a few foreign ecologists and conscientious locals decided to take a stand against the oil-palm loggers working in this wild part of northern Sumatra. Armed with a few rifles and machetes, and using elephants to patrol the jungle against loggers and poachers, the locals have gradually lobbied the government into declaring the region a protected area. Fast-forward almost two decades and the once-doomed region is still home to all manner of apes, monkeys and, of course, elephants.

Tangkahan is not so much a village as a bus stop, a park entrance and a handful of basic riverside bungalows on the wild banks of the Kualsa Buluh River. A small community of amiable loggers-turned-guides lives on the edge of untamed jungle.

Activities

Elephant Interaction ELEPHANT INTERACTION
(elephant bathing 250,000Rp; elephant bathing 8.30am & 3.30pm Tue, Wed & Fri-Sun) For many, the elephants are the main draw in Tangkahan. While elephant rides are available here, consider opting for the more sustainable (and pachyderm-friendly) option of giving them their daily bath. On Mondays, Thursdays and public holidays there are no elephant-based activities. Elephant activities are booked directly through the CTO visitor centre.

Note that elephants (even 'domesticated' ones) kill hundreds of people every year and you should exercise extreme caution in their vicinity. It's also worth reading up on the significant animal welfare issues associated with elephant rides before choosing that option.

Jungle Hikes HIKING
The CTO visitor centre can arrange a park permit and guide to take you hiking in the Gunung Leuser National Park. A 2½ hour 'taster' is 360,000Rp for two people, while the full-day option for serious hikers is 990,000Rp for up to three people. Good footwear is a must; prepare to get very muddy.

Tubing TUBING
A popular activity with locals is renting a rubber tube (10,000Rp) and floating down the shallow river below Jungle Lodge and Dreamland Resort. Longer tubing adventures can be arranged by the CTO visitor centre.

Sleeping & Eating

Accommodation in Tangkahan is limited and is concentrated on the opposite side of the river from where transport drops you off. All guesthouses serve simple meals.

Mega Inn GUESTHOUSE $
(0813 7021 1009; www.mega-inn-tangkahan.op-het-web.be; r 200,000Rp) The first place you come to after the river crossing has pretty bungalows made of twisted wood. Some of the bathrooms contain such a mass of foliage they could almost be classed as jungles themselves. The restaurant is a good spot for gobbling down fried noodles.

Dreamland Resort BUNGALOW $
(0812 6963 1400; bungalow 150,000-170,000Rp;) Run by two friendly young brothers who speak good English, Dreamland has three appealing A-frame cottages with private bathroom sitting partially hidden amid lush greenery. The cafe gives you a bird's-eye view of the river.

Jungle Lodge GUESTHOUSE $
(0813 7633 4787; www.junglelodge.net; r 120,000-170,000Rp) The bungalows (two single and two double) at this popular place are scattered across the attractive gardens. Some have fab river views. There's a large, thatched restaurant overlooking the bubbling river, and staff are friendly.

Information

CTO Visitor Centre (0852 7560 5865, 0813 6142 3245; www.tangkahanecotourism.com; 8am-4pm) Across the river from the lodges and near the bus terminal, this visitor centre organises everything from elephant bathing to jungle treks and caving; pay your fees here.

Getting There & Away

Two direct, daily buses go to Medan's Pinang Baris terminal (20,000Rp, four hours) at 5.30am and 7.30am.

To get to Tangkahan from Bukit Lawang, you have two options. The slow, cheap, roundabout way: take one of the many buses to Binjai (12,000Rp to 15,000Rp, 2½ hours), then connect to one of the twice-daily buses directly to Tangkahan (30,000Rp, 2½ hours) if you time it well, or take a bus to Tittamangga (26,000Rp, two hours) and from there hop on the back of a motorbike to Tangkahan (70,000Rp). The fast, pricier way: get a guide to take you directly from

Bukit Lawang on a motorbike (one way/return 200,000/300,000Rp, two hours) – but be warned that the road is unpaved. Alternatively, team up with other travellers to hire a 4WD (550,000Rp to 650,00Rp, 2½ hours). Most Medan-based travel agents can also arrange 4WD transport (around 1,000,000Rp, 3½ to four hours).

Berastagi

0628 / POP 43,000

To escape the heat of sea-level Medan, the colonial Dutch traders climbed high into the lush, cool, volcanic hills. They took one look at the verdant, undulating landscape and decided to build a rural retreat where Berastagi (also called Brastagi) now stands at an altitude of 1300m.

Today, weekending Medan folk and foreign visitors alike sigh with relief upon arriving in this highland town, where the climate is deliciously cool. Others contemplate the endless, noisy traffic of this agricultural town with resignation but console themselves with the excellent hiking prospects and visits to the outlying villages, where vestiges of indigenous Karo Batak culture remain in the shape of the immense wooden houses with their soaring thatched roofs and cattle horn adornments.

Beyond the town are the green fields of the Karo Highlands, dominated by Sumatra's two most accessible volcanoes: Gunung Sinabung to the west and the smoking Gunung Sibayak to the north. You won't find lava in Sibayak, but Sinabung took everyone by surprise by spewing ash and lava in the summer of 2015, causing the evacuation of thousands of people resident on its foothills. Sinabung volcano is off-limits to hikers indefinitely.

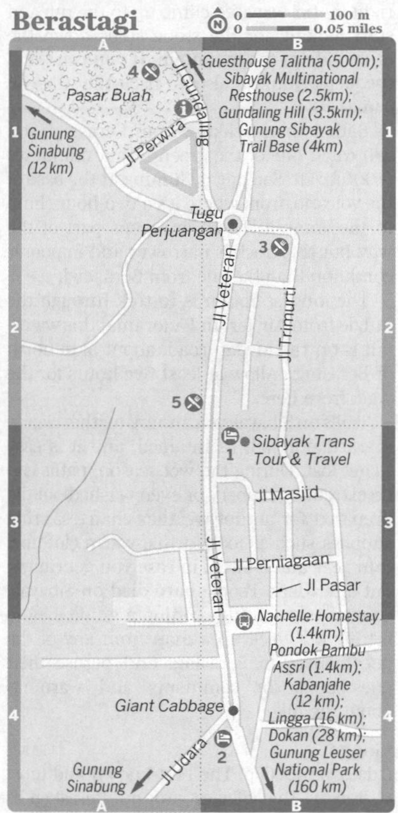

Berastagi

Sleeping
1 Losmen Sibayak Guesthouse B3
2 Wisma Sibayak B4

Eating
3 Café Raymond B2
4 Produce Market A1
5 Ruma Makan Eropah A2

Sights & Activities

There are some fine examples of traditional Karo Batak architecture in the villages around Berastagi. Most of the houses are no more than 60 years old – or possibly 100, but certainly not 400, as claimed by some guides.

★ Gunung Sibayak VOLCANO

(guide along the road 400,000Rp, through the jungle 650,000Rp) At 2094m, Gunung Sibayak is one of Indonesia's most accessible volcanoes. There are three ways to tackle the climb, depending on your energy level; a guide is only essential if taking the route through the jungle, but if you're trekking alone it's a good idea. The hike can be done in five hours return, and you should set out as early as possible.

The easiest way is to take the track that starts to the northwest of Berastagi, a 10-minute walk past the Sibayak Multinational Resthouse. Take the left-hand path beside the hut where you pay the entrance fee. From here, it's 7km (about three hours) to the top and fairly easy to follow, mostly along a road. Finding the path down is a little tricky. When you reach the crater, turn 90 degrees to the right (anticlockwise), climb up to the rim and start looking for the stone steps down the other side of the mountain. If you can't find the steps, you can also go back the way you came.

Rather than trekking from Berastagi, you can catch one of the green Kama minibuses (4000Rp) to Semangat Gunung at the base of the volcano, from where it's a two-hour climb to the summit. There are steps part of the way, but this track is narrower and in poorer condition than the one from Berastagi.

The longest option is to trek through the jungle from Air Terjun Panorama; this waterfall is on the Medan road, about 5km north of Berastagi. Allow at least five hours for the walk from here.

Trails on Sibayak volcano are neither clearly marked nor well maintained, and it is easy to get lost. During the wet season, paths can be extremely slippery or even washed out. Be prepared for abrupt weather changes, bring supplies such as food, drink, warm clothing, rain gear and a torch, in case you get caught out after dark. People have died on Sibayak, so seriously consider getting a guide. Before setting out, pick up a map from any of the guesthouses in Berastagi and peruse their guestbooks for comments and warnings about the hike.

Lingga VILLAGE

(admission 4000Rp) The best-known and most visited of the villages around Berastagi is Lingga, a few kilometres northwest of Kabanjahe. There are about half-a-dozen traditional houses here with characteristic soaring thatched roofs topped with cattle horns. To get here, take a yellow KT minibus from Berastagi (7000Rp, 45 minutes). Some only go as far as Kabanjahe, so check first if you'll have to change.

Some of the houses, such as the *rumah rajah* (king's house), are occupied (by several families) and are in good condition. Others, including the *sapo ganjang* (house for young unmarried men), are unused and in various stages of decay. There may or may not be someone around to charge you for looking at their exteriors; ignore the enterprising ticket man if he offers to show you the inside of one of the houses for 50,000Rp; approach the inhabitants directly if you wish to take a peek.

Dokan VILLAGE

The charming little village of Dokan is approximately 16km south of Kabanjahe. Around half-a-dozen traditional houses can be found here and they are all occupied, which immediately gives the place more interest than any of the museum-like traditional buildings you might have seen elsewhere. However, as they remain family homes you're unlikely to be invited inside to look around. You can get here by the occasional direct minibus from Kabanjahe (7000Rp).

Rumah Bolon PALACE

(admission 5000Rp; ⏲8am-6pm) This impressive, well-tended palace complex on the edge of the village of Pematang Purba was the home of the Simalungan Batak chiefs until 1947 when the last one died. Public transport to the site is scarce, but it's an easy stop-off on a journey between Berastagi and Danau Toba by private car.

The site consists of a large main building that functioned as the king's quarters and a harem. The buffalo skulls inside the main building symbolise the power of the chief. The remainder of the complex consists of meeting halls, assistants' houses and rice-storage areas.

Gundaling Hill HILL

Around 4km north of the War Monument, tree-shaded Gundaling Hill provides a unique vantage point from which you can see both Gunung Sinabung and Gunung Sibayak. It's a 45-minute walk past the turnoff towards Sibayak or you can catch a green Bintang Karo (4000Rp) minibus from halfway along the main street.

Air Terjun Sipiso-Piso WATERFALL

These narrow but impressive falls cascade 120m down to the northern end of Danau Toba, 24km from Kabanjahe and about 300m from the main road. It's fairly easy to get here by yourself; take a bus from Kabanjahe to Merek (12,000Rp) and then walk or take an *ojek* the remaining few hundred metres.

Hot Springs

On the descent from Gunung Sibayak, you can stop off at the various hot springs (admission 5000Rp to 15,000Rp) in **Semangat Gunung** on the road towards Berastagi. You'll be disappointed if you're expecting natural springs; instead, you'll find a complex of small concrete pools. They are best visited on the weekend; on weekdays public transport stops around 3pm or 4pm and you may face a long walk to the main road.

Sleeping

Jl Veteran sees heavy traffic and many rooms along the main road can be very noisy. With one notable exception, the quality of accommodation in Berastagi leaves much to be desired.

Guesthouse Talitha HOMESTAY $
(☎0813 7066 4252; Jl Kolam Renang 60B; r incl breakfast 100,000-150,000Rp; 📶) A 15-minute walk north of the centre is this tranquil family-run guesthouse. The rooms could use a facelift, but there are hot-water showers in the pricier rooms and the friendly owners perk you up with good home-brewed coffee.

Wisma Sibayak GUESTHOUSE $
(☎0628-91104; Jl Udara 1; r without bathroom 70,000-90,000Rp, with bathroom 120,000-250,000Rp; @📶) The pros: lots of travel information, a friendly family feel, spacious rooms, a central location and a decent restaurant. The cons: it's on the main street, so some rooms are noisy, hot-water showers cost extra even in the priciest room, and there's a 10pm curfew.

Losmen Sibayak Guesthouse GUESTHOUSE $
(☎0628-91122; dicksonpelawi@yahoo.com; Jl Veteran 119; r with/without bathroom 100,000/70,000Rp; @📶) These passable, ultra-central cheapies have a lot of Indonesian personality, making the place feel more like a homestay. However, the cheapest rooms overlook the main road and are very noisy. Wi-fi in the lobby.

★ **Nachelle Homestay** HOMESTAY $$
(☎0821 6275 7658, 0813 6242 9977; nachellehomestay@gmail.com; r without bathroom 225,000Rp, r with bathroom 275,000-400,000Rp; 📶) The friendliest of Berastagi's lodgings is run by Mery and Abdy, who speak excellent English and will issue you with a map of the area; Abdy guides guests up Gunung Sibaya. Rooms are new and plush; the loveliest have king-sized beds and volcano views. Nachelle is 1.5km south of the giant cabbage landmark on Jl Veteran; email for directions.

Sibayak Multinational Resthouse GUESTHOUSE $$
(☎0628-91031; Jl Pendidikan 93; r with/without bathroom 350,000/250,000Rp) Set in immaculate gardens and with a hill-country vibe (as long as the dogs aren't barking), the vast, modern rooms here are a decent, if overpriced, bet. Pricier rooms have hot water. Avoid the restaurant. The hotel is a short *angkot* ride north of town towards Gunung Sibayak. We won't nominate the owner for any friendly service awards.

Eating & Drinking

The rich volcanic soils of the surrounding countryside supply much of North Sumatra's produce, which passes through Berastagi's colourful **produce markets**. Passionfruit is a local speciality, as is *marquisa Bandung* (a large, sweet, yellow-skinned fruit). The *marquisa asam manis* (a purple-skinned fruit) makes delicious drinks.

Most hotels have restaurants, but head into town for more diversity. Along Jl Veteran, there's a variety of evening food stalls, as well as simple restaurants specialising in *tionghoa* (Chinese food). Because this is a largely Christian community, get your *babi* (pork) fix here. Another local favourite is *pisang goreng* (fried banana).

Ruma Makan Eropah CHINESE $
(Jl Veteran 20; mains 20,000-40,000Rp; ⏲11am-10pm; 📝) Feast on pork belly soup, pork with green chilli, sweet and sour fish or a host of noodle and rice dishes at this friendly Chinese place.

Pondok Bambu Assri INDONESIAN $
(mains 20,000-30,000Rp; ⏲11am-midnight; 📶) Around 1.5km south of town, right near Nachelle Homestay, this excellent restaurant serves classic fish assam, prawn dishes, roast chicken and local greens, as well as an array of juices (soursop, *marquisa* etc). And – miracle of miracles! – there's reliable wi-fi.

Café Raymond INTERNATIONAL $
(Jl Trimurti 49; mains 12,000-30,000Rp; ⏲7am-midnight; 📝) Berastagi's local bohemians hang out at Café Raymond, which serves fruit juices, beer and a mix of Indonesian and Western food, with a few Indian dishes thrown in for good measure. Enquire here about shared cars to Bukit Lawang, Medan and Lake Toba.

Information

There are several ATMs and banks halfway between the giant cabbage landmark and the War Memorial.

Sibayak Trans Tour & Travel (☎0628-91122; dicksonpelawi@yahoo.com; Jl Veteran 119; ⏲8am-5pm) A solid port of call for almost any onward travel advice as well as local tours.

Tourist Information Centre (☎0628-91084; Jl Gundaling 1; ⏲8am-5pm Mon-Sat) Has maps and can arrange trekking guides, as well as private transport to Medan, Danau Toba and Kutacane. Opening hours are rather flexible.

Getting There & Away

The **bus terminal** (Jl Veteran) is conveniently located near the centre of town. Long-distance buses pass through Berastagi en route to Kabanjahe, the local hub. You can catch buses to Medan's Padang Bulan (15,000Rp, three to four hours) anywhere along the main street between 6am and 8pm.

The cheapest way to reach Danau Toba is to catch an *angkot* to Kabanjahe (5000Rp, 20 minutes), change to a bus for Pematangsiantar (28,000Rp, three hours), then connect with a Parapat-bound bus (15,000Rp, 1½ hours). For Bukit Lawang, take a bus to Pinangbari (13,000Rp, two hours) and change for Bukit Lawang (25,000Rp, three hours). Berastagi is the southern approach for visits to Gunung Leuser National Park; catch a bus to Kutacane.

A couple of private companies run a shared minibus or car service, connecting Berastagi to Bukit Lawang (170,000Rp, three to four hours), Danau Toba (to Parapat; 150,000Rp, 3½ to four hours), Medan's Padang Bulan (100,000Rp, 2½ hours) and Medan airport (150,000Rp, three hours).

Getting Around

Angkot to the surrounding villages leave from the bus terminal. They run every few minutes between Berastagi and Kabanjahe (10,000Rp), the major population and transport centre of the highlands. You can wave them down anywhere along the main road.

Parapat

0625

The mainland departure point for Danau Toba, Parapat has everything a transiting tourist needs (transport, lodging and supplies). But unless you get here too late to catch a boat to Tuk Tuk, there's no reason to overnight here.

The commercial sector of the town is clumped along the Trans-Sumatran Hwy (Jl SM Raja) and has banks, ATMs and plenty of eateries. Most buses pick up and drop off passengers at ticket agents along the highway or at the pier.

Sleeping

Melissa Palace HOTEL $

(0813 9223 6383; Jl Nelson Purba 28; r from 190,000Rp) Melissa Palace is a friendly cheapie with featureless tiled rooms and temperamental plumbing. It's ideal for catching the morning ferry if you get in too late to catch the last boat to Tuk Tuk.

Atsari Hotel HOTEL $$

(0852 7607 5316; Jl Kol. TPR Sinaga 9; r incl breakfast 550,000-950,000Rp;) Across the road from the lakefront, this hotel is a good overnighter with clean, spacious rooms and ample breakfast.

Getting There & Away

The **bus terminal** (Jl SM Raja) is about 2km east of town on the way to Bukittinggi, but it's infrequently used by travellers. From here you could, however, make your way by public bus to Berastagi (48,000Rp, with two changes), Bukit Lawang (170,000Rp, seven hours), Medan (35,000Rp, five to six hours) and Sibolga (70,000Rp, seven hours).

PT Bagus Holiday (0812 8083 8222, 0625-41747) is one of several operators next to the ferry pier that arrange tourist minibuses and car transfers to the most popular destinations. Tourist minibuses go to Berastagi (150,000Rp, four hours), Bukittinggi (180,000Rp, 16 hours), Bukit Lawang (230,000Rp, six hours), Medan (80,000Rp to 100,000Rp, four hours), Padang (285,000, 18 hours) and Sibolga (100,000Rp, six hours).

Getting Around

Angkot shuttle constantly between the ferry dock and the bus terminal (3000Rp).

Danau Toba

0625 / POP 305,000

Danau Toba has been part of traveller folklore for decades. This grand ocean-blue lake, found high up among Sumatra's volcanic peaks, is where the amiable Christian Batak people reside. The secret of this almost mythical place was opened up to others by intrepid travellers, and Tuk Tuk – the village on the lake's inner island – is still one of the undisputed highlights of Sumatra.

Danau Toba is the largest lake in Southeast Asia, covering a massive 1707 sq km. In the middle of this huge expanse is Pulau Samosir, a wedge-shaped island almost as big as Singapore that was created by an eruption between 30,000 and 75,000 years ago. In fact, Samosir isn't an island at all. It's linked to the mainland by a narrow isthmus at the town of Pangururan – and then cut again by a canal.

Directly facing Parapat is another peninsula occupied by the village of Tuk Tuk, which has Samosir's greatest concentration of tourist facilities. Tomok, a few kilometres south of Tuk Tuk, is the main village on the east coast of the island.

THE BATAKS

British traveller William Marsden astonished the 'civilised' world in 1783 when he returned to London with an account of a cannibalistic kingdom in the interior of Sumatra that, nevertheless, had a highly developed culture and a system of writing. The Bataks have been a subject of fascination ever since.

The Bataks are a Proto-Malay people descended from Neolithic mountain tribes from northern Thailand and Myanmar (Burma) who were driven out by migrating Mongolian and Siamese tribes. When the Bataks arrived in Sumatra they trekked inland, making their first settlements around Danau Toba, where the surrounding mountains provided a natural protective barrier. They lived in virtual isolation for centuries.

The Bataks were among the most warlike peoples in Sumatra and villages were constantly feuding. They were so mistrustful that they did not build or maintain natural paths between villages, or construct bridges. The practice of ritual cannibalism, which involved eating the flesh of a slain enemy or a person found guilty of a serious breach of *adat* (traditional law), survived among the Toba Bataks until 1816.

Today, there are more than six million Bataks, divided into six main linguistic groups, and their lands extend 200km north and 300km south of Danau Toba. Technically, they are only supposed to marry other Bataks (if outside their own clan) but over the years several foreigners have married in; they had to be 'adopted' by a Batak clan first.

The Bataks have long been squeezed between the Islamic strongholds of Aceh and West Sumatra, and despite several Acehnese attempts to conquer and convert, it was the European missionaries who finally quelled the waters with Christianity.

The majority of today's Bataks are Protestant Christians, although many still practise elements of traditional animist belief and ritual, particularly when it comes to honouring dead ancestors, who are buried in elaborate tombs and dug up after 10 to 15 years so that their bones can be cleaned, polished and reburied. The Bataks also believe the banyan to be the tree of life; they tell a legend of their omnipotent god Ompung, who created all living creatures by dislodging decayed branches of a huge banyan into the sea.

Music is a great part of Batak culture and a Batak man is never far from his guitar. The Bataks are also famous for their powerful and emotive hymn singing. Most of their musical instruments are similar to those found elsewhere in Indonesia – cloth-covered copper gongs in varying sizes struck with wooden hammers; a small two-stringed violin, which makes a pure but harsh sound; and a kind of reedy clarinet.

Sights

The following sights and activities are located on or near Samosir Island.

King Sidabutar Grave HISTORIC SITE

(Samosir Island; admission by donation; ⏲dawn-dusk) The Batak king who adopted Christianity is buried in Tomok village, 5km southeast of Tuk Tuk. The king's image is carved on his tombstone, along with those of his bodyguard and Anteng Melila Senega, the woman the king is said to have loved for many years without fulfilment. The tomb is also decorated with carvings of *singa* (mythical creatures with grotesque three-horned heads and bulging eyes). To get here, look out for the small brown signpost shortly after you pass through Tomok.

Next to the king's tomb is the tomb of the missionary who converted the tribe in the 19th century and an older Batak royal tomb, which souvenir vendors say is used as a multilingual fertility shrine for childless couples.

Very close by are some well-preserved traditional Batak houses.

Stone Chairs HISTORIC SITE

(Samosir Island; admission by donation, guide 20,000Rp; ⏲8am-6pm) Ambarita, 5km north of Tuk Tuk, features a group of 300-year-old stone chairs where important matters were discussed among village elders. Here wrongdoers were tried and led to a further group of stone furnishings where they were bound, blindfolded, sliced, rubbed with garlic and chilli, and then beheaded.

Rumours abound that the story is the product of an overactive imagination and that the chairs are just 60 years old. On the premises you can peek into a traditional Batak kitchen.

Danau Toba

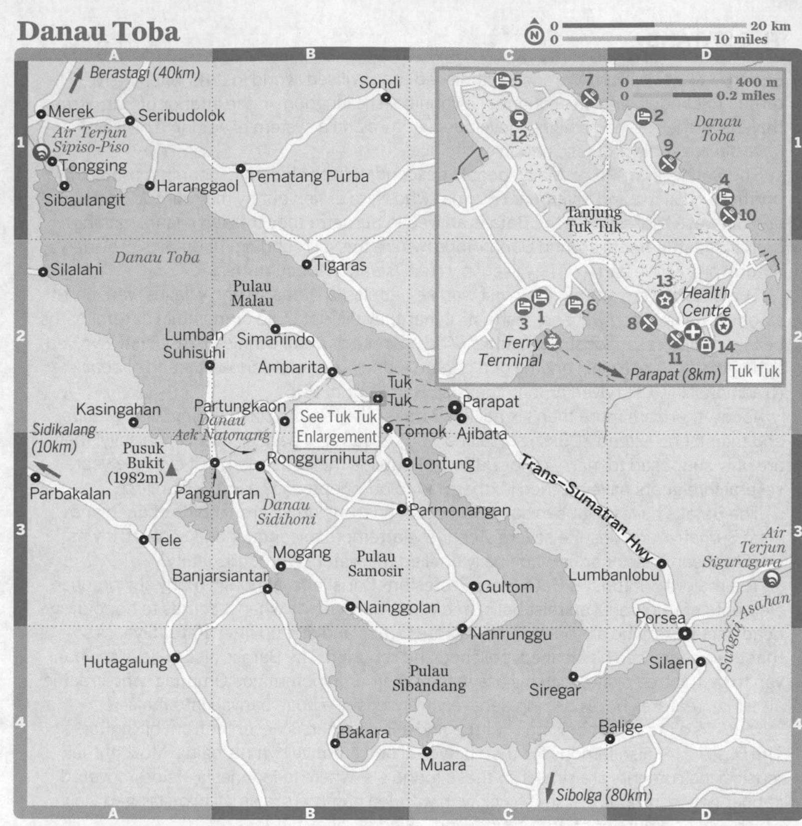

Danau Toba

Sleeping

1 Bagus Bay Homestay C2
2 Harriara Guesthouse D1
3 Liberta Homestay C2
4 Merlyn Guesthouse D1
Romlan Guesthouse .... (see 4)
5 Samosir Cottages C1
6 Tabo Cottages C2

Eating

7 Jenny's Restaurant C1
8 Juwita Cafe D2
9 Maruba D1
10 Rumba Pizzeria D1
11 Today's Cafe D2

Drinking & Nightlife

12 Brando's Blues Bar C1

Entertainment

13 Roy's Pub D2

Shopping

14 Penny's Books D2

Museum Huta Bolon Simanindo MUSEUM
(Samosir Island; admission 50,000Rp; ⏲10am-5pm) At Samosir's northern tip, in the village of Simanindo, 15km north of Tuk Tuk, there's a beautifully restored traditional house that now functions as a museum. It was formerly the home of Rajah Simalungun, a Batak king, and his 14 wives. The roof was originally decorated with 10 buffalo horns, representing the 10 generations of the dynasty. The museum has a small, interesting collection of brass cooking utensils, weapons, Mula Jadi sculptures and Batak carvings.

Lacklustre displays of traditional Batak dancing are performed at 10.30am from Monday to Saturday if enough people show up; audience participation tends to be required.

Batak Graves HISTORIC SITE

The road that follows the northern rind of Samosir between Simanindo and the town of Pangururan is a scenic ride through the Bataks' embrace of life after death. In the midst of the fertile rice fields are large multistorey graves decorated with the distinctive miniature Batak-style house and a simple white cross. Batak graves reflect the animistic attitudes of sheltering the dead (who are dug out 10 years after the original internment and reburied after the polishing of the bones).

Cigarettes and cakes are offered to the deceased as memorials or as petitions for favours. Typical Christian holidays, such as Christmas, dictate special attention to the graves. Some of newer graves are particularly showy.

Activities

Cycling & Motorcycling

Pulau Samosir's sleepy roads make the island perfect for exploring by motorbike or bicycle (p514). Zipping through the scenic countryside enclosed by lush volcanic mountains and the stunning lake is the highlight of many who visit. The rice paddies and friendly villages are cultivated around sober Protestant-style churches and tombs merging traditional Batak architecture and Christian crosses.

Swimming

Danau Toba reaches a depth of 450m in places and is refreshingly cool. The best swimming on the south coast is said to be at Carolina Cottages, and many cottages on the north coast maintain weed-free swimming. There are also a couple of attractive beaches on Samosir's north coast.

Hiking

There are several worthwhile hikes on Samosir Island and around Danau Toba. The trails aren't well marked and can be difficult to find, so check with your guesthouse which ones are doable and ask for a map. In the wet season (December to March) the steep inclines are very muddy and slippery.

The central highlands of Samosir are about 700m above the lake and on a clear day afford stunning views of mist-cloaked mountains. The top of the escarpment forms a large plateau and at its heart is a small lake, Danau Sidihoni. Much of the plateau is covered with cinnamon, clove and coffee plantations, interspersed with pine forest and the odd waterfall.

Guides aren't essential but they are a good idea if you're alone as visitors have gotten lost in the past. The going rate is around 200,000Rp; Liberta Homestay and Tabo Cottages (p512) can arrange one.

Pusuk Buhit TREKKING

(Holy Mountain) Just to the west of Samosir Island rises Pusuk Buhit (1981m), the holy mountain sacred to Batak creation myths. Its ascent makes for a straightforward day trip and there are all-encompassing views of Danau Toba from its summit. It's about four or five hours to the top; start early. Tabo Cottages can arrange a guide.

Festivals & Events

Harvest Festival CULTURAL

Taking place in June in Sianjur Mula Mula village, at the foot of the Bataks' Holy Mountain, this harvest festival incorporates traditional singing and dancing, as well as the symbolic planting of the Tree of Life and the sacrifice of a young bull to ensure future harvests. The villagers are disarmingly friendly and visitors are very much encouraged to attend.

Danau Toba Festival CULTURAL

The weeklong Danau Toba Festival is held every year in mid-June. Canoe races are a highlight of the festival, but there are also Batak cultural performances.

Sleeping

Liberta Homestay GUESTHOUSE $

(☎0625-451035; liberta_homestay@yahoo.com.co.id; r without bathroom 50,000Rp, with bathroom 70,000-90,000Rp; wi-fi) This backpacker fave may have only limited lake views, but a chill universe is created here by a lush garden and arty versions of traditional Batak houses. Crawling around the balconies and shortened doors of the rooms makes you feel like being a deckhand on a Chinese junk (or a Hobbit). The popular Mr Moon is a great source of travel information.

Merlyn Guesthouse GUESTHOUSE $

(☎0625-451057, 0813 6116 9130; Rio@merlynguesthouse.com; r 80,000-90,000Rp; wi-fi) Situated right on the lake shore, this German-Indonesian-run place has traditional, characterful wooden Batak houses with dwarf-sized

BATAK PUPPET DANCE

A purely Batak tradition is the *sigalegale* puppet dance, once performed at funerals but now more often a part of wedding ceremonies. The life-sized puppet, carved from the wood of a banyan tree, is dressed in the traditional costume of red turban, loose shirt and blue sarong. The *sigalegale* stand up on long, wooden boxes where the operator makes them dance to *gamelan* (percussion orchestra) music accompanied by flute and drums.

One story of the origin of the *sigalegale* puppet concerns a widow who lived on Samosir. Bereft and lonely after the death of her husband, she made a wooden image of him and whenever she felt lonely hired a *dalang* (puppeteer and storyteller) to make the puppet dance and a *dukun* (mystic) to communicate with the soul of her husband.

Whatever its origins, the *sigalegale* soon became part of Batak culture and were used at funeral ceremonies to revive the souls of the dead and to communicate with them. Personal possessions of the deceased were used to decorate the puppet, and the *dukun* would invite the deceased's soul to enter the wooden puppet as it danced on top of the grave.

doors and shared bathrooms, as well as modern rooms in sunny colours with hot-water bathrooms.

Harriara Guesthouse GUESTHOUSE **$**
(☎0625-451183; http://hariara-guesthouse.webs.com; Tuk Tuk; r 150,000Rp;) This guesthouse has a top-notch lakeside setting, riotous tropical flower gardens and sparkling rooms with mozzie nets and porches overlooking the water. There's good swimming from here, too. If there's nobody at the reception enquire at the nearby restaurants.

Romlan Guesthouse GUESTHOUSE **$**
(☎0625-451386; www.romlantuktuk.com; Tuk Tuk; r 80,000-150,000;) Run by a German-Indonesian family, this waterfront guesthouse is one of the original places to stay in Tuk Tuk and it's still going strong. Choose between a Western-style room with hot shower and veranda, one of two traditional Batak houses, or save your pennies in the budget room.

★**Tabo Cottages** BUNGALOW **$$**
(☎0625-451318; www.tabocottages.com; r 350,000-390,000, cottage 500,000-950,000Rp;) The swankiest accommodation on the island, this German-run lakeside place has beautiful traditional-style Batak houses that come with huge bathrooms and hammocks swinging lazily on the terrace. Simpler rooms have shaded porches. Owner Annette is a treasure trove of information on Batak culture, and the homemade bread and cakes are worthy of mention as well.

Samosir Cottages HOTEL **$$**
(☎0625-451170; www.samosircottages.com; Tuk Tuk; r 100,000-425,000Rp;) A good choice for travellers who want to hang out with young like-minded folk and boisterous young staff. The fully refurbished, squeaky-clean rooms span a wide variety of prices and styles, and range from smaller, tiled cheapies to quite plush rooms. It has every traveller service you can imagine – travel agency, tour guides, sun loungers, and a busy restaurant.

★**Horas Family Home** COTTAGE **$$$**
(☎0813 6105 1419; www.holidaysumatra.com; cottage 700,000-1,000,000Rp;) Stay in a gorgeous, renovated traditional Batak house, complete with original furnishings, or opt for the smaller Horas Indah. Hosts Berend and Mian are exceptionally helpful and knowledgeable about Batak culture. The superb meals incorporate fresh fish, freshwater prawns and organic vegetables grown in the garden. Transfers and tours organised on request.

Eating

The guesthouses tend to mix eating and entertainment in the evening. Many restaurants serve the Batak speciality of barbecued carp (most from fish farms), sometimes accompanied by traditional dance performances.

Magic or 'special' omelettes are commonly seen on restaurant menus. We probably don't need to tell you that the mushrooms contained in these are not of the sort that you can buy at your local supermarket.

★**Jenny's Restaurant** INTERNATIONAL **$**
(Tuk Tuk; mains 26,000-55,000Rp; ⏲5-10pm) There are lots of different options on the menu at Jenny's, but one dish really shines – lake fish grilled right in front of you and served with chips and salad. Follow it up with the generously portioned fruit pancake.

Juwita Cafe INDONESIAN $
(mains 25,000-46,000Rp; ⏲ lunch & dinner) This cosy family restaurant does Batak and other Indonesian dishes extremely well. We're particularly big fans of the aubergine sambal. Friendly matriarch Heddy also hosts cooking courses; a three-hour course includes a chicken, fish and vegetable dish, as well as dessert. Book a day in advance.

Today's Cafe INTERNATIONAL $
(Tuk Tuk; mains 30,000-50,000Rp; ⏲ breakfast, lunch & dinner; ✎) This little wooden shack has a laid-back vibe in keeping with Tuk Tuk life. It's run by a couple of friendly ladies who whip up some fabulous and eclectic dishes such as *sak sang* (chopped pork with brown coconut sauce, cream and a wealth of spices), aubergine curry and chapatis with guacamole.

Rumba Pizzeria INTERNATIONAL $$
(Tuk Tuk; mains 35,000-80,000Rp; ⏲ lunch & dinner; ✎) Rumba stays open late on Saturday to show English Premier League football (soccer). Delicious pick-your-own-ingredients pizzas are served.

★ **Maruba** INDONESIAN $$
(mains 40,000-125,000Rp; ⏲ lunch & dinner) Tucked away between Amartoba Hotel and Rodeo guesthouse, Maruba is well worth seeking out for peerless Batak dishes cooked by the talented proprietress. River crabs, *na neura* (raw fish marinated with candlenut, lime juice and spices) and *saksang* (chopped pork cooked with spices and pig's blood) are real local treats. There's also gool ol' roast chicken for the less adventurous.

Drinking & Entertainment

On most nights, music and spirits fill the night air with the kind of camaraderie that only grows in small villages. The Toba Bataks are extremely musical, and passionate choruses erupt from invisible corners. The parties are all local – celebrating a wedding, a new addition on a house or the return of a Toba expat. Invitations are gladly given and should be cordially accepted.

Bagus Bay Homestay (☎ 0625-451287; www.bagusbay.com) and Samosir Cottages both have traditional Batak music and dance performances on Wednesday and Saturday evenings at 8.15pm.

Brando's Blues Bar BAR
(☎ 0625-451084; Tuk Tuk; ⏲ 6pm-late) One of a handful of foreigner-oriented bars that gets particularly lively on weekends. Happy hour is a civilised 6pm to 10pm and you can take to the small dance floor during the reggae and house sets.

Roy's Pub LIVE MUSIC
(Tuk Tuk; ⏲ 9pm-1am) Has live music (normally local rock bands) on Tuesday, Thursday and Saturday nights in a graffiti-splattered building. Great, alcohol-fuelled fun.

Shopping

In Tuk Tuk's many souvenir shops, look out for local Gayo embroidery made into a range of bags, cushion covers and place mats.

Around Tuk Tuk there are numerous woodcarvers selling a variety of figures, masks, boxes and *porhalaan* (traditional Batak calendars made of wood and buffalo bone). You'll also find some traditional musical instruments and elaborately carved totem poles that untwist into several sections for easier transportation.

Roganda CRAFTS
(Tuk Tuk; ⏲ 10am-8pm) The best selection of wood carvings in Tuk Tuk, particularly Batak calendars, elaborate totem poles and fine musical instruments. Bargain hard. We're not too sure about the authenticity of some of the 'antique' items in the shop.

Penny's Books BOOKS
(Tuk Tuk; ⏲ 10am-7pm) An extensive selection of used books for sale.

Information

BRI Bank (Tuk Tuk; ⏲ 9am-5pm) On the northern approach to Tuk Tuk. Only accepts MasterCard, and not all foreign ones at that. Bring plenty of cash.

Health Centre (☎ 0625-451075; Tuk Tuk) Small 24-hour place at the southern end of the peninsula, equipped to cope with minor problems.

Police Station There's a small police station near the main road at the northern approach to Tuk Tuk.

Post Office (Ambarita; ⏲ 8am-2pm) Samosir's only post office is in Ambarita, 5km north of Tuk Tuk, but several shops in Tuk Tuk sell stamps and have postboxes.

Getting There & Away

BOAT

Ferries between Parapat and Tuk Tuk (15,000Rp, 11 daily) operate about every hour from 8.30am to 7pm. Ferries stop at Bagus Bay (35 minutes); other stops are by request. The first and last ferries from Tuk Tuk leave at 7am and 5.30pm respectively; check exact times with your lodgings. When leaving for Parapat, stand on your hotel jetty and wave a ferry down. Fourteen ferries a day shuttle motorbikes and people between Parapat and Tomok (10,000Rp), from 7am to 7pm.

BUS

To get to Berastagi from Samosir via public bus, catch a bus from Tomok to Pangururan (16,000Rp, 45 minutes), then take another bus to Berastagi (48,000Rp, three hours). This bus goes via Sidikalang, which is also a transfer point to Kutacane. Most guesthouses and travel agencies can pre-book the pricier, direct shared minibus tickets from Parapat for you.

Getting Around

Local buses serve the whole of Samosir except Tuk Tuk. Minibuses run between Tomok and Ambarita (5000Rp), continuing to Simanindo (10,000Rp) and Pangururan (15,000Rp); flag them down on the main road. Services dry up after 5pm. The peaceful, generally well-maintained (yet narrow) island roads are good for travelling by motorbike (80,000Rp to 100,000Rp per day) or bicycle (30,000Rp per day), both easily rented in Tuk Tuk.

Sibolga

☎0631 / POP 84,000

Sibolga is one of two jump-off points for boats to Nias (the other being Singkil), with daily departures to the island. It's not a particularly pleasant port town and is renowned for its touts. Dragging around surf gear can invite inflated prices: bargain hard or accept a degree of extra 'service.' Arrive as early in the day as possible to ensure a place on a boat departing that evening.

If you absolutely must stay overnight, **Hotel Wisata Indah** (☎0631-23688; Jl Katamso 51; r incl breakfast from 450,000Rp;), near the airstrip and well past its prime, is the pick of a pretty uninspiring lot. Its dated rooms offer sea views and staff are helpful but don't speak English. At the grungy end of the accommodation spectrum are the insalubrious losmen (basic accommodation) near the ferry terminal: for hardcore shoestringers only.

There are plenty of Padang restaurants directly across the street from the harbour. **Sibolga Square** (mains 10,000-25,000Rp; 5-10pm) is a semi-pedestrianised street that fills with food hawkers and street stalls come evening.

There are numerous ATMs. **BNI Bank** (Jl Katamso) is a good bet, as options on Pulau Nias are limited if you arrive in Teluk Dalam.

Getting There & Away

AIR

Sibolga is linked to Medan by three daily flights with **Wings Air** (www.lionair.co.id) and to Jakarta by a daily **Garuda** (www.garuda-indonesia.com) flight.

BOAT

Ferries to Pulau Nias leave from the harbour at the end of Jl Horas. **ASDP** (☎0631-25076) runs daily services to Gunung Sitoli at 8pm (economy/VIP 80,000/115,000Rp, 11 to 13 hours) and Teluk Dalam (economy/VIP 100,000/150,000Rp, 12 to 14 hours) on Sunday, Tuesday and Friday, also at 8pm. VIP is air-conditioned; if travelling economy, get there early to claim your seat. Ferries generally leave one to two hours late. If you arrive in Sibolga and are told you have just missed the boat it is often worth going to the harbour yourself to verify this. Surfboards sometimes incur extra charges.

BUS

The bus terminal is on Jl SM Raja, 2km from the harbour. You can ask the bus driver to drop you off at the harbour. A becak between the two should be around 10,000Rp.

BUSES FROM SIBOLGA

DESTINATION	BUS (FARE/DURATION)	TOURIST MINIBUS (FARE/DURATION)
Bukittinggi	110,000Rp/13-14hr	170,000Rp/12hr
Medan	100,000Rp–130,000/11hr	150,000Rp/10hr
Padang	140,000Rp/14hr	180,000Rp/14hr
Parapat	70,000Rp/7hr	100,000Rp/6hr
Singkil	75,000Rp/7-8hr	120,000Rp/6hr

WORTH A TRIP

SURFING'S REMOTE FRONTIERS

If Nias was the original surfers' paradise and the Mentawai Islands are currently in vogue, then tomorrow's slice of surfing paradise could be the **Telo Islands**. This group of islands sits to the north of the main Mentawain island of Siberut and until recently it was almost completely unknown to the outside world.

Today, liveaboard surf-charter boats have started adding the islands to their more ambitious itineraries, though the islands' relative remoteness still means uncrowded waves. The two best-known luxury surf camps here, **Telo Island Lodge** (www.teloislandlodge.com; 10-night package from US$5500;) and **Resort Latitude Zero** (www.resortlatitudezero.com;), have luxury beachside cottages, swimming pools, trained chefs and private plane and speedboat transfers. For a more affordable, but still very comfortable, option, try **Surfing Village** (www.surfing-village.com; s/d US$250/330;), which is run by the ever-helpful Brazilian transplant Mario Fernandes. Nonsurfing travellers are very rare visitors to the Telo Islands, but if you have patience and a sense of adventure, they offer enormous potential for beach lounging, village living and snorkelling. Ferries travel from Nias every other day to the Telo Islands and irregular boats sail between the Telo Islands and Padang. Cheap and basic losmen (basic accommodation) can be found in the small towns and hiring a boat to check out the islands shouldn't prove difficult.

But if surfing the Telo Islands sounds a bit tame, you can head inland for potentially the most adventurous surf destination in all of Indonesia. **Bono** (Seven Ghosts; www.bonosurf.com) is a tidal bore wave that breaks halfway up the mud-brown Kampar river, somewhere in the jungles north of Pekanbaru in the remotest reaches of Riau state. Its phenomenal river-bore waves, which put many ocean-borne waves to shame, can be ridden by determined surfers prepared to venture to the surf camp in the jungle. Bono Surf Camp can provide boat transfers here from Pekanbaru.

Pioneered by surfer Antony Colas in 2010, Bono's barrels were surfed by pros Tom Curren, Dean Brady, Bruno Santos, Tyler Larronde and Ohney Anwar in 2011 and captured on film. Though tidal bore surfing is nothing new, and Bono is no bigger than some of the world-famous bores, the river's unique conditions conspire to produce the longest and the most consistent bore ride. Longboarder Bagé currently holds the longest continuous ride record on the Bono (one hour and two minutes).

PULAU NIAS

The Indian Ocean roars onto Indonesia, arriving in one of the world's most spectacular surf breaks here on lonely Pulau Nias: a sizeable but solitary rock off the northern Sumatran coast. Surfers have been coming here for decades for the waves on superb Teluk Sorake, which has deservedly kept this far-flung island on the international surfing circuit. Away from the waves, the ancient megalithic monuments and traditional architecture has great appeal for the anthropologically inclined.

History

Local legend has it that Niassans are the descendants of six gods who came to earth and settled in the central highlands. Anthropologists link them to just about everyone: the Bataks of Sumatra, the Naga of Assam in India, the aborigines of Taiwan and various Dayak groups in Kalimantan.

Nias' history is the stuff of campfire tales, with prominent themes of headhunting, dark magic and human sacrifice; but this isn't ancient history – the first Aussie surfers to ride Sorake's waves in the 1970s were stalked by a rogue shaman bent on collecting a human head.

Traditionally, Niassan villages were presided over by a village chief, who headed a council of elders. Beneath the aristocratic upper caste were the common people, and below them the slaves, who were often traded. Until the first years of the 19th century, Nias' only connection with the outside world was through the slave trade.

Sometimes villages would band together to form federations which often fought each other. Prior to the Dutch conquest and the arrival of missionaries, intervillage warfare was fast and furious, spurred on by the desire for revenge, slaves or human heads. Heads were needed for stately burials, wedding dowries and the construction of new villages.

When the people weren't warring, they were farming, a tradition that continues today. They cultivated yams, rice, maize and taro, despite the thick jungle, and raised pigs as a source of food and a symbol of wealth and prestige; the more pigs you had, the higher your status in the village. Gold and copper work, as well as woodcarving, were important industries.

The indigenous religion was thought to have been a combination of animism and ancestor worship, with some Hindu influences. Today, the dominant religions on Nias are Christianity and Islam, overlaid with traditional beliefs.

The island did not come under full Dutch control until 1914. Today's population of about 656,000 is spread through more than 650 villages, some inaccessible by road.

Dangers & Annoyances

Nias is one of the few places in Sumatra where visiting surfers can expect a bit of aggression in the water. Experiencing surf rage is never pleasant, but if our local breaks pumped like this, we probably wouldn't want to share the lineups with a boatload of tourists either.

Renting surf gear on the island can be an issue. Be sure you pay a fair price; if it is too cheap, you'll probably pay for it at the end with inflated damage costs.

Chloroquine-resistant malaria has been reported on Nias, so be sure to take appropriate precautions.

Getting There & Away

AIR

Binaka airport is served by six daily flights from Medan (four with Wings Air and two with Garuda Indonesia). Extra charges apply to surfboards. The government plans to expand the runway by early 2016 to allow large planes to access Nias.

Pulau Nias

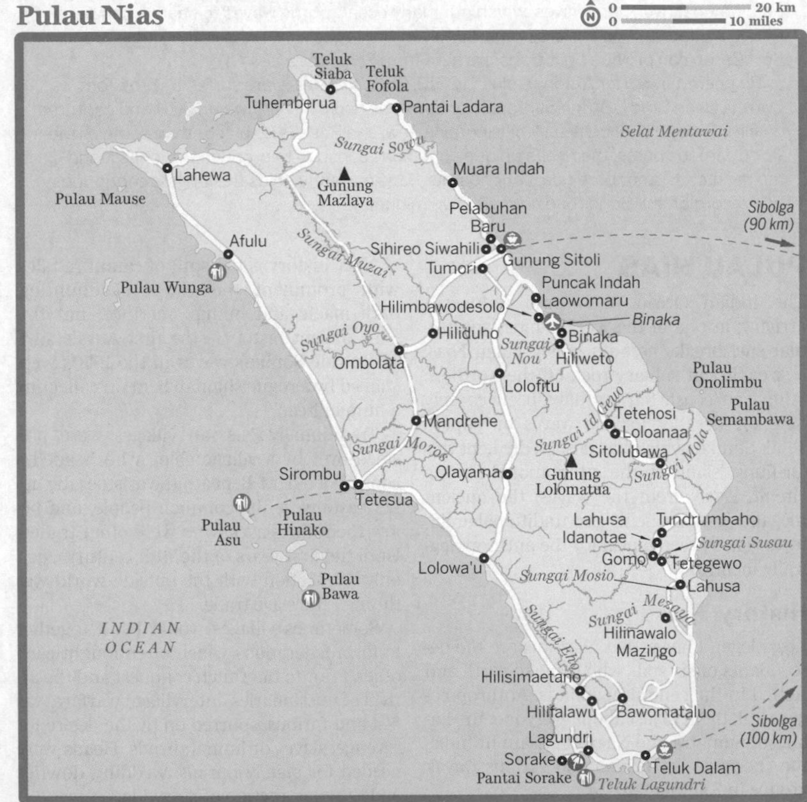

EARTH-SHAKING SUMATRA

If you tally up the sheer number of natural disasters that have occurred on the island, few land masses can claim to have literally moved the planet in the same way as Sumatra.

Take for instance the 1883 eruption of Krakatau, 40km off the southern Sumatra coast. This volcanic explosion was equivalent to that from 200 megatonnes of TNT, and more powerful than the A-bomb dropped on Hiroshima. So much ash was hurled into the atmosphere that the sky was darkened for days and global temperatures were reduced by an average of 1.2°C for several years.

It is said that the blast that created Danau Toba some 100,000 years ago would have made Krakatau look like an after-dinner belch.

Then there was the 2004 Boxing Day earthquake, the world's second-largest recorded earthquake (magnitude 9.3). The resulting tsunami hit more than a dozen countries around the Indian Ocean, leaving more than 300,000 people dead or missing and millions displaced. The force of the event is said to have caused the earth to wobble on its axis and shifted surrounding land masses southwest by up to 36m.

BOAT

Ferries link Nias with the mainland towns of Sibolga and Singkil. Twice-weekly ferries from Singkil (economy 55,000Rp, seven hours) arrive on Monday and Thursday mornings and depart the same days around 9pm.

ASDP (Jl Yos Sudarso) ferries to Sibolga leave Gunung Sitoli daily at around 9pm (economy/VIP 80,000/115,000Rp, 11 to 13 hours) and Teluk Dalam (economy/VIP 100,000/150,000Rp, 12 to 14 hours) on Monday, Wednesday and Saturday at 8pm. ASDP ferries also connect Teluk Dalam with the Telo Islands (40,000Rp, five hours) to the south on Tuesday, Thursday and Friday.

Pelni (Jl Chengkeh) has an irregular monthly boat to and from Padang.

Getting Around

The Binaka airport is 19.5km south of Gunung Sitoli. Becaks to the airport cost around 50,000Rp to 70,000Rp.

Gunung Sitoli's bus terminal is 1.5km south of the centre of town; an *angkot* from the pier costs 3000Rp. From Gunung Sitoli, there are infrequent and mostly morning departures to Teluk Dalam (80,000Rp, three hours), which has transport to Lagundri, 13km away. There are even less frequent minibuses to Afulu on the west coast. If you've booked accommodation in Sorake, price tends to include transfers from Gunung Sitoli airport; ask about transfers from the town itself. On public transport you're most likely to be charged extra for a surfboard. To get to Sorake or Lagundri from Teluk Dalam, catch a local bus from the town centre (7000Rp). Losmen owners or staff will also hunt the town looking for new arrivals and usually charge 12,000Rp to 15,000Rp for motorbike transfer.

It's easy to hire motorbikes in Sorake. If you're after a car and driver, **Fritz** (☎0812 6913 3399) in Gunung Sitoli speaks good English. Negotiate.

Gunung Sitoli

☎0639

Gunung Sitoli, on the northeastern coast of Nias, is the island's main, rather spread-out town. Rebuilt after the 2005 tsunami, it serves merely as the main entrance and exit point to Nias, though its excellent museum is reason enough to linger a little longer if you're interested in indigenous culture.

Sights

★ Museum Pusaka Nias MUSEUM

(☎0639-21920; Jl Yos Sudarso 134A; admission 20,000Rp; ⏲8am-11.30am & 1.30pm-4.30pm Mon-Sat, 1pm-5pm Sun) This superb museum, housed inside several traditional-style buildings, offers an in-depth introduction to the indigenous culture of Nias. The displays run the gamut from jewellery worn by noblemen, weapons, crocodile-hide battle armour, traditional fishing and hunting equipment to headhunting sculptures and paraphernalia, wood carvings used in ancestor worship, ceremonial drums, *nifolasara* (boat-like) coffins with dragon heads, and microliths (anthropomorphic stone figures found on top of megaliths throughout the island). One room features beautiful scale models of traditional houses.

Outside is a restored traditional house, typical of North and West Nias, and a depressing zoo that's best avoided.

Sleeping & Eating

If you need to stay on the north coast to catch a departing flight or boat, there are a few options outside the town centre.

Wisma Soliga Resort Hotel RESORT **$**
(☎0613-21815; Jl Diponegoro; d from 150,000Rp; ❄📶) Located 4km south of town, this place has spacious, motel-style rooms with reliable wi-fi and the world's smallest toilet seats. The service is friendly but erratic, the mattresses uncomfortable, and the restaurant mediocre, but it'll do in a pinch. Price goes up depending on the number of amenities in-room.

Miga Beach Bungalows RESORT **$$**
(☎0813 9764 8200, 0639-21460; migabeachhotel@yahoo.com; Ji Diponegoro; d incl breakfast from 220,000Rp; ❄📶) About 1.5km out of town, Miga sits right on a small beach with comfortable rooms that are given a sense of place with driftwood furnishings, individual touches and earthy tones.

★ **Rapi Seafood** SEAFOOD **$$**
(☎0639-22247; Jl Kelapa 15; mains 30,000-60,000Rp; ⏲from 6pm) This nondescript eatery in central Gunung Sitoli is responsible for some of the best, freshest fish and seafood we've ever had in Sumatra. Choose your dinner, then have it grilled, with sweet and spicy sauce or otherwise. Squid also comes with different sauces and the monster-sized grilled prawns are sheer perfection. Speaking some Bahasa Indonesia is a definite boon.

Information

Bank Sumut (Jl Hatta) Has a Mastercard-accessible ATM.

BNI Bank (Jl Diponegoro) Accepts Visa and Mastercard. Allows you to withdraw up to 2,000,000Rp at a time.

Post Office (cnr Jl Gomo & Hatta; ⏲8am-2pm) Main post office.

Public Hospital (☎0639-21271; Jl Cipto M Kusomo) For dealing with minor emergencies.

Teluk Dalam

☎0631

This squat little port town is as loud and chaotic as much larger cities. You'll need to pass through Teluk Dalam for transit connections to/from Sorake beach or to pick up provisions. About half a block from the main road, **Mari Rasa** (Jl Pelita; mains 25,000Rp; ⏲lunch & dinner) is locally famous for its *babi panggang* (grilled pork) and *lomok-lomok* (pork belly) served with rice, local greens, a dark chilli sauce and a bowlful of flavourful, spicy broth. A great place to hit if you're waiting for a night boat or pickup.

WEST COAST SURFING

Given Sorake's consistent (and sometimes overwhelming) popularity, adventurous surfers are heading to Nias' west coast in search of empty waves and as yet undiscovered spots.

Much of the west coast is still a DIY adventure; some surfers stay in losmen (basic accommodation) around the village of Afulu and hire local boats to take them up and down the coast. **Walo Beach Bungalows** (☎0823 0416 2558; www.northniastourism.com/where-to-stay/afulu; r 100,000Rp; ❄), just north of Afulu, and surrounded by a bamboo stockade, is the best of the west coast surfing lodgings. Choose between one of the three breezy bungalows with private outdoor bathroom or bunk with fellow surfers in a basic shared room. The owners cook up massive platters of fish.

Further afield are the islands of Asu and Bawa. More exposed than Nias itself, the islands see bigger and more consistent waves. With a left-hander at Asu and a strong right-hander at Bawa, good surf is almost guaranteed regardless of wind direction. The risk of malaria is high on these islands, particularly Bawa, which has a large swamp in its interior.

Bawa has several simple losmen. **Asu Surf Resort** (☎0852 8561 0931; www.asucamp.com; Asu; per person per night A$220; ❄📶), a luxurious surf camp, gets rave reviews from surfers for its excellent food and vibe and nearby uncrowded waves. Price includes speedboat transfers to top surfing spots.

Sirombu on Nias' west coast is the jumping-off point for the islands. Ask around to see if any public buses will be heading there; otherwise you can charter transport for about 600,000Rp. From Sirombu there are cargo boats (100,000Rp). You can also charter boats (600,000Rp, maximum 10 people) from local fishermen at Teluk Dalam and save yourself the hassle of getting to Sirombu.

Pantai Sorake & Teluk Lagundri

☎0630

A fish-hook piece of land creates the perfect horseshoe bay of Teluk Lagundri and the Point surf break at Pantai Sorake, which is generally regarded as one of the best right-handers in the world. The main surfing season is June to October, with a peak in July and August when the waves can be very solid. Folks refer to this area interchangeably as Sorake or Lagundri.

The waves discovered here in 1975 by Aussie surfers Kevin Lovett and John Giesel have become shallower and more perfectly shaped and powerful following the 2004 earthquake and tsunami. With a couple of exceptions, all accommodation sits cheek by jowl along Pantai Sorake, which is considered to be more protected from possible future disasters.

Activities

Surfing is the island's tourism raison d'être. Sorake's famous right consistently unrolls between June and October. Access to the wave is a quick paddle from the Keyhole, a break in the coral reef that lies between the beach and the bay.

Although swells are often much smaller between November and March and the winds less favourable, you can still get some good days with far fewer surfers. Whatever time of year, Nias is not a good place to learn how to surf – it's just not a beginner's wave.

Most surfers will arrive with their own gear, but if you need to, it's possible to rent equipment from several surf camps.

Sleeping & Eating

The western part of the bay, known as Pantai Sorake, is the primary location for lodging, though there are also a couple of surf camps in nearby Lagundri. Many of the better places prefer you to take a multiday package, which includes airport transfers and all meals, but they'll always rent a room by the night. Rates at these places are officially quoted in US dollars but payment is always in rupiah. Check out www.sorakebeach.com for helpful info.

Lagundri Beach House GUESTHOUSE $
(☎0813 9656 7202; ian@lagundri.net; r 150,000-250,000Rp; ❄📶) One of only two lodgings on Lagundri Beach, this friendly losmen is run by the knowledgeable Impian ('Ian'), who can show you around the traditional villages, point you to the waves, and cook up a seafood storm if you ask him in advance. Four fan-cooled rooms have breezy terraces.

STORMRIDER SURF STORIES

Even if you're not a surfer, *Stormrider Surf Stories* by Chris Goodnow (2014) allows you to delve deep into the surfer subculture. You can learn about the initial discovery of Sorake's waves, how the surfers were stalked by a shaman who practised dark magic, what it's like to be a surfing doctor on the Mentawais and how to ride Sumatra's strangest wave.

Sanali Losmen GUESTHOUSE $
(☎0812 6516 0312; http://sanalilosmen.jimdo.com; per person 200,000Rp) Simple rooms and no real pressure to book a longer stay package. Like many places it can organise boat trips to surf spots further afield.

Key Hole Surf Camp SURF CAMP $$
(☎0813 7469 2530; www.niaskeyholesurfcamp.com; per person incl full board US$60; 📶) Key Hole Surf Camp, right in the thick of things, has eight comfortable rooms and the restaurant serves anything from pizza to lobster. Airport pickup is included in the 10-day package and guests can borrow motorcycles for free.

Home @ Nias GUESTHOUSE $$
(☎0852 7529 0363; www.niassurfaccommodation.com.au; per person incl full board US$40; ❄📶) Right in front of the Keyhole, an easy paddle from the Point and Indicator, this shiny new place, run by a friendly local surfer, consists of two spacious rooms and two garden bungalows with hammocks swinging on the terrace. There are boards for hire.

Traditional Villages

For hundreds of years, Nias residents built elaborate villages around cobblestone streets lined with rows of shiplike wooden houses. The traditional homes were balanced on tall wooden pylons and topped by a steep, thatched roof. Some say the boat motif was inspired by Dutch spice ships. Constructed from local teak and held together with hand-hewn wooden pegs, the houses are adorned with symbolic wooden carvings. The technology of traditional architecture proved quite absorbent and these structures fared better in the 2005 earthquake than modern concrete buildings.

Reflecting the island's defensive strategies, villages were typically built on high ground reached by dozens of stone steps. A protective stone wall usually encircled the village. Stone was also used for carved bathing pools, staircases, benches, chairs and memorials.

The island has geographic diversity when it comes to traditional houses. In northern Nias, homes are free-standing, oblong structures on stilts, while in the south they are built shoulder to shoulder on either side of a long, paved courtyard. Emphasising the roof as the primary feature, southern Niassan houses are constructed using pylons and cross-beams slotted together without the use of bindings or nails.

Gomo & Around

The villages around Gomo, in the central highlands, contain some of the island's best examples of stone carvings and *menhirs* (single standing stones), some thought to be 3000 years old. Such examples can be found in the village of **Tundrumbaho**, 5km from Gomo; **Lahusa Idanotae**, halfway between Gomo and Tundrumbaho; and at **Tetegewo**, 7km south of Gomo. Getting there is a bit of a challenge, since the roads are in poor condition.

Hilinawalo Mazingo

Omo Hada ARCHITECTURE

(Chieftain's House) One of only five such surviving buildings on the island, the Omo Hada is situated in the prestigious 'upstream' direction of the remote Hilinawalo Mazingo village, garnering the first rays of morning light. It still serves its traditional purpose as a meeting hall for seven neighbouring villages. In order to repair damages from age and climate, villagers have been trained in traditional carpentry skills, in turn preserving crafts that were nearing extinction. You need a local guide and sturdy motorbike to negotiate the bad roads.

Bawomataluo

Perched on a hill about 400m above sea level, Bawomataluo (Sun Hill) is the most famous, and the most accessible, of the southern villages. It is also the setting for *lompat batu* (stone jumping). The final approach is up 88 steep stone steps flanked by stone dragons and houses are arranged along two main stone-paved avenues. Bawomataluo is well worth exploring, but be prepared for eager knick-knack sellers.

The village's two street meet opposite the impressive **chief's house**, which is thought to be both the oldest and the largest on Nias. You can poke around its heavy wooden-beamed interior and admire the drum that signals the beginning and end of meetings, as well as the original wooden carvings and rows of pigs' jawbones. Outside is the chief's stone throne next to a large stone phallus and stone tables where dead bodies were once left to decay.

Stone jumping was once a form of war training; the jumpers had to leap over a 1.8m-high stone wall, traditionally topped with pointed sticks. These days the sticks are left off – and the motivation is financial (200,000Rp per jump outside ceremonial occasions). There are also cultural displays of war dances, traditionally performed by young, single males.

From Bawomataluo, you can see the rooftops of nearby **Orihili**. A stone staircase and a trail lead downhill to the village.

Bawomataluo is 15km from Teluk Dalam and is accessible by public transport (7000Rp); guesthouses in Sorake can also arrange transfers.

Hilisimaetano

Hilisimaetano VILLAGE

There are more than 100 traditional houses in this large village, 16km northwest of Teluk Dalam. Stone jumping and traditional dancing are performed here during special events. Hilisimaetano can be reached by infrequent public transport from Teluk Dalam (7000Rp).

Botohili & Hilimaeta

Botohili VILLAGE

This small village on the hillside above the peninsula of Pantai Lagundri has two rows of traditional houses, with a number of new houses breaking up the skyline. The remains of the original entrance, stone chairs and paving can still be seen.

Hilimaetaniha VILLAGE

A 2km walk or ride from Lagundri along a steep, partially paved road, this traditional village is one of the quietest. Friendly locals sit by their traditional houses, some of them brightly tiled or painted, and children fly kites along the only street. The *lompat batu* pylon can still be seen here and there are a number of stone monuments, including a 2m-high stone penis. A long pathway of stone steps leads uphill to the village.

ACEH

Over the years, this far-flung corner of the Indonesian archipelago has grabbed headlines for all the wrong reasons. Earthquakes, tsunamis, civil war and sharia law are the main associations people have with Sumatra's northernmost state. With the reconstruction from the 2004 Boxing Day tsunami long completed, post-tsunami Aceh is slowly healing the social wounds incurred by the natural disaster and the previous civil war. Still, while the guns have been laid down and a degree of autonomy has been granted to the province, there are occasional blips on the road to peace such, as the April 2015 murder of two Indonesian soldiers, the government threat to send the army in once more, and the prevailing belief in the rest of Sumatra that the people of Aceh are keen to spread their conservative Islamic ways across the whole country.

Undeterred by the province's reputation, some intrepid travellers to the region are unearthing wildlife-rich jungle, misty mountain peaks and endless swathes of empty beach, not to mention the rainbow of pristine coral beneath the sea. Tangible remains of the 2004 tsunami can still be seen.

History

In the days of sailing ships, Aceh competed with Melaka on the Malay Peninsula for control of the important spice-trade route, the influx of traders and immigrants, and the province's strategic position contributing to Aceh's wealth and importance. Aceh was also Islam's entry to the archipelago, while the capital, Banda Aceh, was a centre of Islamic learning and a gateway for Mecca-bound pilgrims.

Though Aceh's power began to decline towards the end of the 17th century, the province remained independent of the Dutch until war was declared in 1871. It was 35 years before the fighting stopped and the last of the sultans, Tuanku Muhamat Dawot, surrendered.

In 1951 the Indonesian government incorporated Aceh's territory into the province of North Sumatra. The prominent Islamic Party was angered at being lumped together with the Christian Bataks, and proclaimed Aceh an independent Islamic Republic in September 1953. Prolonged conflict ensued, and in 1959 the government was forced to give Aceh 'special district' status, granting a high degree of autonomy in religious, cultural and educational matters.

The formation of Gerakan Aceh Merdeka (GAM; Free Aceh Movement) in December 1976 and subsequent struggle with the Indonesian military led to nearly 30 years of deaths, torture, and disappearances occurring on an almost daily basis, perpetuated by both sides against the civilian population, with thousands displaced.

At the turn of the millennium, there was a brief ceasefire and Aceh was granted the right to implement sharia law, followed by an escalation of conflict, the imposition of martial law and a full-scale military assault on the separatists, which was brought to an abrupt end by the 2004 tsunami. The province remains largely peaceful, in spite of occasional bouts of unrest, courtesy of a GAM rebel splinter group that remains disaffected with former colleagues who now run the province.

Banda Aceh

☎0651 / POP 223,000

Indonesian cities are rarely coupled with pleasant descriptions, but Banda Aceh breaks the mould. The laid-back provincial capital is a pleasant enough spot to spend a couple of days and pedestrians will notice with delight that the city has actual pavements.

Given that Banda Aceh bore the brunt of the 2004 tsunami, with 61,000 killed here, and that much of the city had to be rebuilt, it's little wonder that it looks well maintained and affluent. The aid workers have long gone, and it remains to be seen how much of an impact direct flights between Medan and Pulau Weh will have on tourism, now that visitors no longer have to pass through the city to reach the island.

Banda Aceh is a fiercely religious city and the ornate mosques are at the centre of daily life. Respectfully dressed visitors shouldn't face any hassles and most travellers find the Acehnese to be friendly and extremely hospitable.

Aceh

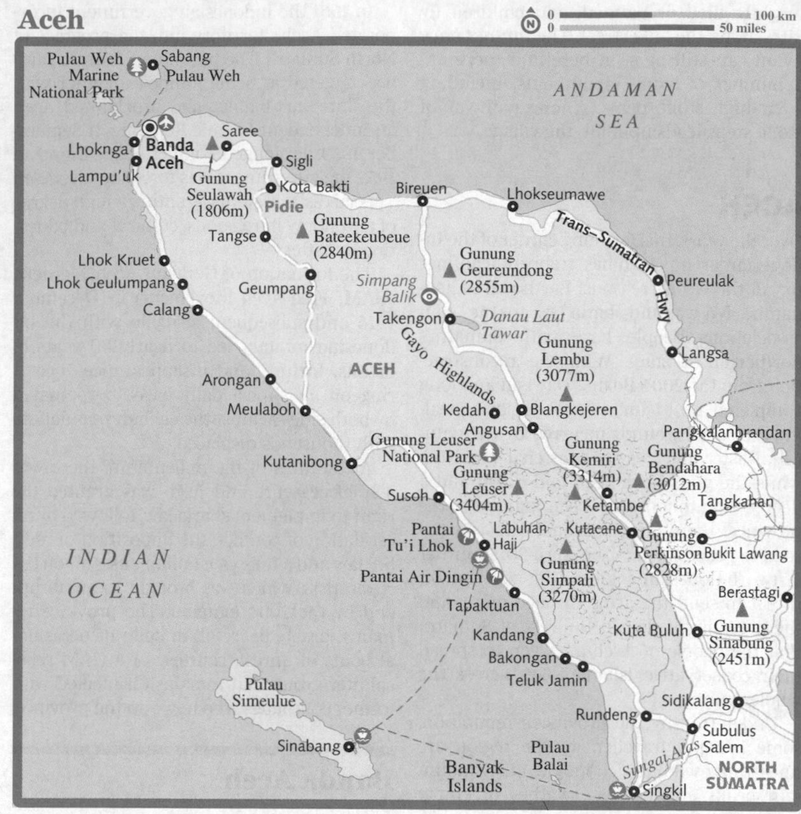

Sights & Activities

Mesjid Raya Baiturrahman MOSQUE

(admission by donation; 7-11am & 1.30-4pm) With its brilliant-white walls, ebony-black domes and towering minaret, the 19th-century Mesjid Raya Baiturrahman is a dazzling sight. The best time to visit the mosque is during Friday afternoon prayers, when the entire building and yard are filled with people. A headscarf is required for women.

The first section of the mosque was built by the Dutch in 1879 as a conciliatory gesture towards the Acehnese after the original one burnt down. Two more domes – one on either side of the first – were added by the Dutch in 1936 and another two by the Indonesian government in 1957. The mosque survived intact after the 2004 earthquake and tsunami, a sign interpreted by many residents as direct intervention by the Divine. During this time the mosque served as an unofficial crisis centre for survivors, and bodies awaiting identification were laid on the public square in front of the mosque.

Museum Negeri Banda Aceh MUSEUM

(0651-23144; Jl Alauddin Mahmudsyah 12; admission 10,000Rp; 8am-noon & 2-5pm Tue-Sun) The Museum Negeri Banda Aceh has displays of Acehnese weaponry, household furnishings, ceremonial costumes, everyday clothing, gold jewellery, calligraphy and some magnificently carved *recong* (Acehnese daggers) and swords. It also has a display of a baby two-headed buffalo. At research time, the museum was closed for renovation.

Rumah Aceh MUSEUM

(Jl Alauddin Mahmudsyah 12; admission 5000Rp; 8am-noon & 2-5pm Tue-Sun) In the same compound as the Museum Negeri Banda

Aceh is the Rumah Aceh, a fine example of traditional Acehnese architecture, built without nails and held together with cord and pegs. Inside is a typical traditional kitchen and living area with hanging crib. Other displays include wedding paraphernalia and a small weaponry collection. Out front is a huge cast-iron bell, the Cakra Donya, said to have been a gift from a Chinese emperor in the 15th century.

Gunongan HISTORIC BUILDING

(Jl Teuku Umar; ⏲8am-6pm) All that remains of Aceh's powerful sultanates today is on view at Gunongan. Built by Sultan Iskandar Muda (1607–36) as a gift for his Malay princess wife, it was intended as a private playground and bathing place. The building consists of a series of frosty peaks with narrow stairways and a walkway leading to ridges, which represent the hills of the princess' native land. Ask around for someone to unlock the gate for you.

Directly across from the Gunongan is a low vaulted gate, in the traditional Pintu Aceh style, which provided access to the sultan's palace – supposedly for the use of royalty only.

Kherkhof CEMETERY

(Dutch Cemetery; Jl Teuku Umar; ⏲8am-6pm) The Kherkhof is the last resting place of more than 2000 Dutch and Indonesian soldiers who died fighting the Acehnese. The entrance is around 50m west of the Tsunami Museum. Tablets set into the walls by the entrance gate are inscribed with the names of the dead soldiers and the plain white crosses in the eastern part of the cemetery have replaced the gravestones destroyed by the tsunami.

Sleeping

There is very little in the way of budget accommodation here; the cheapies on Jl Khairil Anwar don't seem to accept foreign guests. Shoestringers may find themselves racing straight through Banda Aceh and out to the mellower prices of Pulau Weh.

★Hotel Sei HOTEL **$$**

(☎0651-21866; www.seihotelaceh.com; Jl Tanoh Abe 71, Kampung Mulia; d 550,000Rp; ❄📶) This new lemon-yellow hotel down a quiet side street is one of Banda Aceh's swankiest options. Expect compact rooms with reliable wi-fi, the arctic chill of the air-con, a pleasant respite from the outdoors, as well as friendly

REMEMBERING THE TSUNAMI

On December 26, 2004, an immense tsunami swept inland in Aceh, killing 170,000 people and altering the physical and emotional landscape of the province forever. In spite of the extensive rebuilding that has removed most signs of physical damage, stark reminders of the devastation remain in the form of many memorials that both honour those killed and allow visitors to comprehend the full horror of what transpired.

For many residents of the province the tsunami is a sensitive subject as many lost loved ones. However, if interest is expressed in a delicate manner, no offence is taken.

Tsunami Museum (Jl Iskandar Muda; ⏲9am-4.15pm Sat-Thu, noon-2pm Fri) A visit to this museum commences with a walk through a dark, dripping tunnel that symbolises the tsunami waves, with plaintive, terrified voices and the sound of rushing water all around you. This is followed by a powerful set of images of the devastation projected from tombstone-like receptacles, and a circular chamber engraved with the names of the lost. Upstairs a very graphic short film is aired, along with photographs of rebuilding, loss, hopefulness, displacement and reunited families.

Other displays explain how earthquakes and tsunamis are created and how Aceh's landscapes were altered by this one (look out for 'before' and 'after' scale models of the city).

Mass Graves There are four mass graves around Banda Aceh where the dead in the province were buried, post-tsunami. The largest site is Lambaro, located on the road to the airport, where 46,000 unidentified bodies were buried. Other grave sites include Meuraxa, Lhok Nga and Darusalam, where another 54,000 bodies were interred. Families who wish to mourn their unlocated loved ones choose one of the mass graves based on geographic proximity; they have no other evidence of where to offer their prayers.

Lampulo Boat The most famous of the tsunami sights is the boat in the house in Lampulo, and the 2500-tonne power-generator vessel that was carried 4km inland by a wave.

Banda Aceh

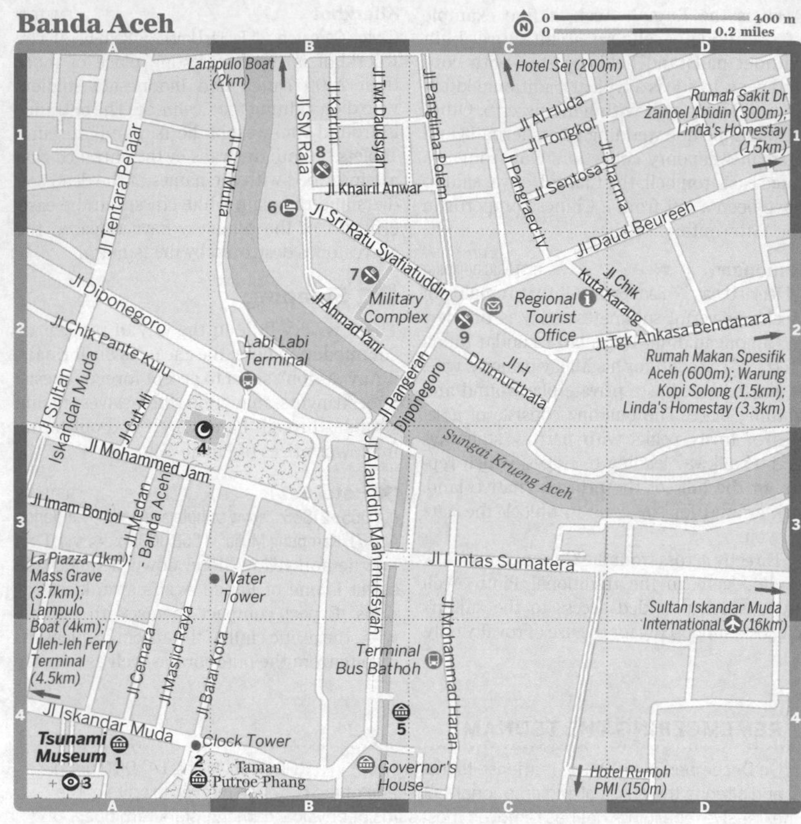

Banda Aceh

Top Sights
1 Tsunami Museum A4

Sights
2 Gunongan A4
3 Kherkhof A4
4 Mesjid Raya Baiturrahman A3
5 Museum Negeri Banda Aceh B4
Rumah Aceh .... (see 5)

Sleeping
6 Hotel Medan B1

Eating
7 Country Steakhouse B2
8 Pasar Malam Rek B1
9 Restoran Bunda C2

but erratic service and a seemingly deserted but actually decent restaurant.

Linda's Homestay HOMESTAY **$$**
(☎0823 6436 4130, 0811 680 305; http://lindas-homestay.blogspot.com; Jl Mata Lorong Rahmat 3, Lambneu Barat; r 350,000-400,000Rp; ❄📶) Staying in the home of hospitable Linda, 4km out of town, is a good way of experiencing local life and many travellers rave about her. Linda cooks up a storm of Acehnese food and her sons are on hand to give you a tour of the city. However, some travellers report misunderstandings about prices and ensuing bad feelings.

Hotel Rumoh PMI HOTEL **$$**
(☎0651-33292; Jl Nyak Adam Kamil II 1, Kampong Ateuk Mungjing; r 300,000Rp; ❄📶) This hotel, in a residential area southwest of the centre,

is a 15-minute walk to the Tsunami Museum (p523). Rooms could use some sprucing up, but on the whole they are clean and pleasantly chilly, the staff are friendly and helpful, and pickup from the airport or ferry can be arranged in advance. A stopover rather than a place to linger.

Hotel Medan HOTEL **$$**
(0651-21501; www.hotel-medan.com; Jl Ahmad Yani 17; r incl breakfast 330,000-550,000Rp;) We're in two minds about this business-class hotel. On the one hand, the central location is very handy and the tiled rooms are clean and comfortable. On the other, the furniture is aged, the wi-fi unpredictable, breakfast choices are limited, rooms facing the road are noisy and it's overpriced for what it is.

Eating

Pasar Malam Rek MARKET **$**
(cnr Jl Ahmad Yani & Jl Khairil Anwar; dishes from 10,000Rp; 5-10pm) The square at the junction of Jl Ahmad Yani and Jl Khairil Anwar is the setting for the Pasar Malam Rek, Banda Aceh's lively night food market featuring noodle and *sate* stalls.

Rumah Makan Spesifik Aceh INDONESIAN **$**
(Jl T Hasan Dek; mains from 30,000Rp; 11am-10pm) An excellent introduction to Acehnese cuisine, with such delights as *asam keeng* (hot and sour soup), *mie aceh* (spicy noodle dish), *udang goreng kunyit* (turmeric shrimp), and curried fish.

★ **La Piazza** ITALIAN **$$**
(Jl Iskandar Muda 308 & 309; mains from 40,000Rp; 11am-11pm;) Authentic Italian food is on the menu at this outpost belonging to Freddie from Pulau Weh. You're not limited to pasta and pizza, though; the seafood dishes are also one of the strong points. Romance your sweetie by candlelight at this garden restaurant on the 3rd floor. Discreetly open all day during Ramadan.

Restoran Bunda INDONESIAN **$$**
(Jl Pante Pirak 7-9; meals around 70,000Rp; 11am-10pm;) Think bright lights, a shiny canteen and uniformed waiters piling endless plates of sublime *masakan minang* (basically the same as Padang food) dishes onto your table and you get this popular 'posh warung' style restaurant. It also does a takeaway service – ideal if you have a long bus ride ahead.

Country Steakhouse STEAK **$$**
(0651-24213; off Jl Sri Ratu Safiatuddin 45B; mains 25,000-130,000Rp; noon-10pm;) Well hidden down an alley, this wood-panelled restaurant used to feed the international aid workers. It's now added a few Indonesian standards to the menu that features New Zealand steaks, snapper and hand-cut chips; specify how you want your steak or be prepared for the default ('well done'). Also has beer and Australian red wine.

Drinking

Because of sharia law, alcohol is not available as openly here as elsewhere in Indonesia, but a few of the more expensive restaurants and hotels discreetly serve beer.

Warung Kopi Solong CAFE
(Jl Teuku Iskandar 13-14; 9am-7pm;) Aceh's most famous coffee house has been doing business since 1974. It's an excellent place to try *kopi sanger* (coffee with condensed milk) – with the coffee strained through a sock! You can buy 250g and 500g bags of finely ground, locally grown Ulee Kareng robusta coffee to take away. Noodle dishes and other snacks available. Take a taxi.

Information

There are lots of ATMs around town, mainly on Jl Panglima Polem and Jl Sri Ratu Safiatuddin.

Post Office (Jl H Bendahara 33; 8am-4pm Mon-Fri) A short walk from the centre.

Regional Tourist Office (Dinas Parawisata; 0651-852020; www.bandaacehtourism.com; Jl Chik Kuta Karang 3) The staff are exceptionally friendly and sometimes have free copies of an excellent guidebook to the province. On the 1st floor of a government building.

Rumah Sakit Dr Zainoel Abidin (0651-34565; Jl Daud Beureuch 108) One of the best hospitals in town. Located just east of the centre.

Getting There & Away

AIR

Banda Aceh's **Sultan Iskandar Muda International Airport** is 16km southeast of the centre.

BOAT

Boats serving Pulau Weh depart from the port at Uleh-leh, 5km northwest of Banda Aceh's city centre.

BUS

Terminal Bus Bathoh (Jl Mohammed Hasan) is located 2km south of the city centre. Large

TRANSPORT FROM BANDA ACEH

Air

DESTINATION	AIRLINE	FREQUENCY
Jakarta	Garuda	2 daily
Kuala Lumpur	AirAsia	daily
Kutacane	Susi Air	2 weekly
Medan	Garuda, Lion Air	3 daily
Penang	Firefly, Malaysia Airlines	3 weekly

Bus

DESTINATION	FARE (RP)	DURATION (HR)	FREQUENCY
Ketambe/Kutacane	220,000	15-18	daily
Medan	210,000	12	hourly until 10pm
Singkil	230,000	15	daily

buses to Medan aside, most accommodation can arrange for the relevant minibus to pick you up.

Getting Around

Taxis from the airport to the city centre charge around 100,000Rp. A taxi from the airport to the Uleh-leh port will cost around 130,000Rp.

Labi labi are the main form of transport around town and cost 2500Rp. The **labi labi terminal** (Jl Diponegoro) is that special breed of Indonesian mayhem. For Uleh-leh (10,000Rp, 35 minutes), take the blue *labi labi* signed 'Uleh-leh.' You can also reach Lhok Nga and Lampu'uk (16,000Rp).

From the bus terminal, a becak into town will cost around 25,000Rp. A becak around town should cost between 10,000Rp and 20,000Rp, depending on your destination. A becak to Uleh-leh from the city centre is 30,000Rp and a taxi 60,000Rp.

Pulau Weh

0652 / POP 25,000

A tiny tropical rock off the tip of Sumatra, Pulau Weh is a small slice of beach and jungle that rewards travellers who've journeyed up through the turbulent greater mainland below. After you've hiked around the mainland's jungles, volcanoes and lakes, it's time to jump into the languid waters of the Indian Ocean. Snorkellers and divers bubble through the great walls of swaying sea fans, deep canyons and rock pinnacles, ogling the dazzling kaleidoscope of marine life, including manta rays and whale sharks. Both figuratively and geographically, Pulau Weh is the cherry on top for many visitors to Sumatra.

Pulau Weh is shaped roughly like a horseshoe. On the northeastern leg is the port town of Sabang, where most of Weh's population lives. The primary tourist beaches are Gapang and Iboih, which are about 20km heading towards the northwestern leg. In the bendy-palms and sandy-toes stakes, Iboih probably just outclasses Gapang, but for the best beaches of all, pack a towel and head to Pantai Sumur Tiga near Sabang and Long Beach, a little way north of Iboih.

Activities

Most travellers come to Weh for the diving and snorkelling, which is considered some of the best in the Indian Ocean. On an average day, you're likely to spot morays, lionfish and stingrays. During plankton blooms, whale sharks come to graze. Unlike at other dive sites, the coral fields take a back seat to the sea life and landscapes. There are close to 20 dive sites around the island, most in and around Iboih and Gapang where dive operators are based.

Snorkelling gear can be hired almost anywhere for around 30,000Rp per day.

Getting There & Away

AIR

The small, new **Maimun Saleh Airport**, 2km south of Sabang, is connected to Medan by Garuda Indonesia on Wednesday, Friday and Sunday, departing Medan at 8.50am and returning from Sabang at 10.40am.

BOAT

Slow car ferries and express passenger ferries ply the route between Uleh-leh, 5km northwest of Banda Aceh on the mainland, and Balohan port, around 8km south of Sabang on Pulau Weh. You should get to the port at least 45 minutes before departure to get a ticket. Ferry service is weather pending.

Car ferries (economy/air-con 25,000/50,000, two hours) leave Pulau Weh daily at 8am, returning from Uleh Leh on the mainland at 11am. On Monday, Wednesday, Saturday and Sunday, there's an additional service from Pulau Weh at 1.30pm, returning from Uleh Leh at 4pm.

The **Express Ferry** (☎ 0651-43791, 0652-332 4800; business/executive/VIP 125,000/150,000/165,000Rp) departs Banda Aceh for Pulau Weh at 9.30am and 4pm daily (45 minutes to one hour). Services from Pulau Weh to Banda Aceh depart at 8am and 2.30pm daily.

Getting Around

From the Balohan port, there are regular minibuses to Sabang (25,000Rp, 15 minutes), and Gapang and Iboih (60,000Rp, 40 minutes). You can catch a minibus from Jl Perdagangan in Sabang to Gapang and Iboih (40,000Rp). Becaks and taxis charge around 80,000Rp from the port to Gapang and Iboih and around 70,000Rp from Sumur Tiga near Sabang to Gapang and Iboih.

A taxi from Sumur Tiga to the airport is 30,000Rp; from Gapang/Iboih it's around 70,000Rp to 80,000Rp.

Many lodgings rent out motorbikes for around 100,000Rp per day.

Sabang

The island's main township is a mix of traditional fishing village and old colonial-era villas. During Dutch rule, Sabang was a major coal and water depot for steamships. The town enjoyed a brief revival in the 1970s as a duty-free port, but is now a sleepy town whose inhabitants either fish or make rattan furniture.

If staying on the Sabang side of the island, visitors make a beeline for the beautiful Sumur Tiga beach, 5km east of town.

Sleeping & Eating

★ Freddies LODGE **$$**
(☎ 0813 602 5501; www.santai-sabang.com; Pantai Sumur Tiga; r 300,000Rp; ❄ 📶) This delightful cluster of breezy rooms sit above a pretty stretch of white-sand beach with a coral reef. It's perfect for those content with snorkelling off the strategically placed pontoon and swinging in a hammock. Freddie, the South African owner, is responsible both for the delicious, varied buffet dinners (65,000Rp) and for the genuine feeling of camaraderie among the guests.

★ Casa Nemo BUNGALOW **$$**
(☎ 0812 1735 4141; www.casanemo.com; Pantai Sumur Tiga; cottage 275,000-300,000Rp; ❄ 📶) Sitting on the balcony of your luxurious thatched beach bungalow (which in some cases comes complete with a stone bath) and looking down on a day-glow blue ocean, you'll probably find it impossible to wipe the smile off your face.

Information

The **BRI bank** (Jl Perdagangan) has an ATM, as do a couple of other banks.

Gapang

Occupying a sandy cove, with a great reef for snorkelling just offshore, Gapang is an appealing stretch of beach lined with shack restaurants and simple guesthouses.

Activities

Lumba Lumba Diving Centre DIVING
(☎ 0811 682 787; www.lumbalumba.com; discover dive/Open Water Diver course €45/300) The professional Dutch-run Lumba Lumba Diving Centre has been introducing divers to Pulau Weh's underwater world for two decades now and is the only PADI-certified diving centre on the island. The owners Ton and Marjan Egbers maintain a helpful website with detailed descriptions of dives and need-to-know information. Highly recommended.

Monster Divers DIVING
(☎ 0812 6960 6857; www.monsterdivers.com; discover dive/day trip incl dives €40/60) A popular, professional new diving outfit consisting of three friendly Barcelonians and one local PADI diving instructor.

Sleeping & Eating

Gapang is much less lively than nearby Iboih and the accommodation consists largely of basic beach huts (100,000Rp) with only one notable exception. Beachside cafes serving very standard Western and Indonesian food absorb the evening breezes and post-dive appetites.

ISLAND TOUR ON TWO WHEELS

Pulau Weh is a delight to explore either by motorbike or by bicycle (if you happen to have brought one along) due to its relatively compact size, light traffic and picturesque scenery.

If you start from Ipoih and follow the road all the way north through the forest reserve, you'll reach Kilometer 0, a brash orange marker indicating the westernmost tip of Indonesia. The road itself is hilly, winding and beautiful, with an excellent chance of spotting monkeys and snakes. Head back south until you almost reach Gapang; the westbound turnoff leads to **Lhong Anden**, a beach ideal for sunset watching. Head back and go southeast past Gapang; just before you reach the village of Pria Laot, a rough road leads south to a waterfall that you can bathe in, and possibly spot flying foxes and monkeys. East past Pria Laot, you hit a T-junction; take the southbound branch and you pass between **Gunung Kulan**, the island's highest volcano, on your right, and **Gunung Merapi**, a semiactive volcano which holds boiling water in its caldera and occasionally puffs smoke, on your left.

Head east along the coast and you pass some sulphurous hot springs near Kaunekai village. Carry on to Balohan port and take the less-peopled road north across the island, toward Sabang, passing **Danau Anak Laut**, a serene freshwater lake that supplies the island with its drinking water. Near Sabang, it's worth seeking out the old **Merbabu cemetery**, where there are Dutch, French, Javanese, Acehnese and Japanese laid to rest.

If you don't want to motorbike around the island alone, call English-speaking guide Andy (☎0852 7644 9599; per person 150,000Rp) for a day-long tour.

Lumba Lumba RESORT **$$**
(☎0811 682 787; www.lumbalumba.com; r without bathroom €13.50, r with bathroom €20-32; @ wi-fi) Dutch-owned Lumba Lumba offers the best-quality accommodation in Gapang. Wood-decked cottages have tiled rooms, fans and Western toilets, while simpler rooms have shared bathrooms. Accommodation is mostly for divers, but they will happily rent out any spare rooms. A new restaurant is on the way.

Mama Donut INDONESIAN **$**
Mama Donut has been a local institution for a couple of decades, walking the sand selling delicious vegetable samosas, doughnuts and fried bananas to divers. On her days off, Daughter Donut takes over.

Iboih

More spread out than Gapang, Iboih (*ee*-boh) follows a rocky headland with a string of simple bungalows along a forested footpath. A small path leads through a stone gateway past the village well, and up and over a small hill to the bungalow strip. The village itself is conservative and traditional, so no swimwear beyond the bungalow strip.

Sights & Activities

Rubiah Tirta Divers DIVING
(☎0652-332 4555; www.rubiahdivers.com; discover dive/Open Water Diver course €40/270) Local-run Rubiah Tirta Divers is the oldest dive operation on the island and gets consistently good feedback from travellers.

Sea Garden DIVING
Opposite Iboih, 100m offshore, is Pulau Rubiah, a densely forested island surrounded by spectacular coral reefs known as the Sea Garden. It is a favourite snorkelling and diving spot. The coral has been destroyed in places but there is still plenty to see, including turtles, manta ray, lionfish, tigerfish and occasional sharks.

If you are a strong swimmer it is possible to make your own way there. Beware of strong currents, especially at the southern tip of the island.

Sleeping & Eating

Iboih, with its simple palm-thatch bungalows, many built on stilts and overlooking crystal-clear water, is Pulau Weh's backpacker hang out par excellence. There's a handful of places to stay with little differentiating them. If you stay for several days you can normally negotiate a discount on the daily rates.

Just off the main road are a few shops selling sundries, Indonesian lunches and coffee in front of a small beach.

Yulia's HUT **$**
(☎0821 6856 4383; r with/without bathroom 280,000/120,000Rp; wi-fi) A 500m trudge past

the rest of the guesthouses rewards you with cheerful green huts, some excellent front-door snorkelling and a pink restaurant serving a mix of Indonesian and Western dishes.

Olala HUT $
(☎0852 6060 7311; r 70,000-150,000Rp; 📶) Offering cheap and cheerful huts on stilts, Olala caters both to shoestringers (basic digs with shared bathrooms) and splurgers who want their own bathroom and fan. Its restaurant (open to all) is a popular traveller hang out and receives an equal amount of praise.

Oong's Bungalows HUT $
(☎0813 6070 0150; r 80,000-160,000Rp) Good value rooms, although the tin roof heats things up. Cheaper options share bathrooms. The on-site restaurant, Norma's, serves seafood and beer amid diving chat.

Iboih Inn BUNGALOW $$
(☎0812 6904 8397; www.iboihinn.com; r incl breakfast 250,000-550,000Rp; ❄📶) The top-dog huts at Iboih's only upmarket option come with hot-water showers, air-con and fab sea views, though they are somewhat regimental and grey. The further the huts are from the seafront, the lower the price and the quality, until you get to simple wooden shacks with thin partitioning walls that make you feel as if you're in bed with your neighbours.

Dee Dee's Kitchen INTERNATIONAL $
(mains 25,000-40,000Rp; ⏰8am-9pm; 📶✎) On the same strip of beach as Rubiah Divers, Dee Dee cooks up an eclectic selection of dishes, from the excellent homemade chapati with guacamole and tofu burgers with french fries to chicken cooked in coconut milk. Easily Iboih's most imaginative dining venue.

Long Beach

Sleeping & Eating

Stone Park BUNGALOW $
(☎0852 6258 1111, 0652-3324688; Long Beach; r 200,000Rp; ❄📶) Overlooking a private lagoon with excellent snorkelling, these two rustic cabins are run by a friendly British-Indonesian couple, Katie and Ali. Cabins are spacious, fan-cooled and equipped with mosquito nets; they also have attached kitchens if you don't feel like dining out. Located at the southern end of Long Beach.

★Bixio Cafe ITALIAN $$
(meals around 120,000Rp; ⏰noon-10pm Wed-Mon) Who would have thought Sumatra's best Italian food is hiding in a remote corner of Pulau Weh! Sit by the lapping waves and dig into Luca and Eva's wonderful authentic and freshly made gnocchi and pasta with fresh and imaginative sauces – but leave room for the divine tiramisu. There are three appealing bungalows (150,000Rp) for rent if you wish to linger longer.

Aceh's West Coast

Rounding the northwestern tip of Sumatra's finger of land is a string of little villages and endless beaches backed by densely forested hills. Most of the houses along the coast are identical in design, having been rebuilt after the tsunami. For the moment, the attractive west coast attracts the more intrepid travellers heading overland between Singkil and Banda Aceh, as well as surfers and kitesurfers in search of wind and waves.

Lhok Nga & Lampu'uk

☎0656

Comprehensively rebuilt after the 2004 tsunami, the coastal weekend spots in Lampu'uk are beginning to attract more surfers and kitesurfers as the word spreads. Surfing season is from October to April, while the rest of the year brings favourable kiting winds. Lhok Nga has decent waves too, and it's becoming particularly popular with kitesurfers.

Take *labi labi* number 04 (30,000Rp, 20 minutes) from the *angkot* terminal in Banda Aceh for both Lhok Nga and Lampu'uk. A becak costs 80,000Rp to 100,000Rp.

Joel's Bungalows BUNGALOW $
(☎0813 7528 7765; Lampu'uk; r 150,000-300,000Rp) Joel's Bungalows is the area's legendary surfer hangout. Its huts have been built into and around the cliff face and overlook a drop-dead-gorgeous beach (though the waves there are not suitable for surfing and can be dangerous for swimming). Rooms come in an array of sizes and styles and its on-site restaurant is known far and wide as the place to come for a wood-fired pizza.

Joel's Bungalows 2 (☎0813 7528 7765; r 150,000-300,000Rp), further south along the main beach at Lampu'uk, is ideal for kitesurfers due to its location.

Aceh Kitecamp SURF CAMP $$
(☎0812 6942 7770; www.aceh-kitecamp.com; Lhok Nga; s 150,000Rp, d 200,000-500,000Rp; ❄📶) Aceh Kitecamp in Lhok Nga is the best place

to learn to kitesurf in Sumatra. This clutch of comfortable bungalows comes with its own kiting school (one hour €60, full course €310). In the downtime, you can have a go at paddle boarding (150,000Rp for half a day).

Eddie's Homestay HOMESTAY $
(☎0813 7588 3445, 0811 688 682; ediguenzalo@yahoo.com; Lhok Nga; r 70,000-120,000; ❄) Run by a local surfer, Eddie's gets consistently good feedback from the surfing crowd both for its laid-back vibe and its comfy rooms (the cheaper ones share facilities).

Pulau Simeulue

☎0650 / POP 85,000

The isolated island of Simeulue, about 150km west of Tapaktuan, is a rocky volcanic outcrop blanketed in rainforest and fringed with clove and coconut plantations. An increasing number of surfers make it out here (although wave quality is generally not considered to be as high as on some other offshore Sumatran islands), but nonsurfing travellers are a rare breed indeed. This is a pity because the island holds decent potential for genuine, off-the-beaten-track adventure, and is relatively easy to get around: the ring road around the island is mostly accessible by local minibuses.

You'll find simple losmen (50,000Rp to 165,000Rp) in Sinabang and Sibigo, or if you have a tent, you can camp on the beach. A half-dozen or so surf camps take advantage of the as yet uncrowded waves. **Surf Camp Sumatra** (www.surfcampsumatra.com; bungalow US$75-85; 📶🍴) is a small, new camp that lodges up to eight guests, in a quiet bay on the west coast of Simeulue. You sleep in a simple, fan-cooled bungalow right in front of the island's most consistent break, Dylan's Right. Meals and airport transfers are included.

Bring lots of cash as the island's ATMs are not to be depended on.

Susi Air (☎061-785 2169; www.susiair.com) has two flights daily from Medan. A ferry from Simelue's port town of Sinabang to Singkil (75,000Rp to 150,000Rp, 12 hours) runs on Wednesday and Saturday at 5pm.

Singkil

☎0658 / POP 17,000

Singkil is a remote, sleepy port town with welcoming locals at the mouth of Sungai Alas. It's the departure point for island adventures in the Banyaks, Pulau Nias and Pulau Simelue, but it's worth lingering here for a day or two to explore the swampy surroundings – which are home to crocodiles, wild orangutans and more.

Unusually for Indonesia, Singkil is very spread out and has no real centre.

Activities

Swamp Tour BOAT TOUR
(per person 700,000Rp) A rewarding day trip from Singkil involves taking a single-engine canoe up the Gedang River, past two friendly waterfront villages and deeper into the great morass in search of wild orangutans and monkeys. Start out as early as possible to maximise your chances of seeing riverside wildlife. Book via Mr Darmawan at Banyak Island Travel.

The riverside villages are worth a visit, to meet the friendly locals and their inquisitive kids. Note the contrast between the enormous satellite TV dishes and the bathroom shacks right on the river. Beyond the villages, the river gives way to narrow waterways, lined with tall swamp plants and with the odd orangutan nest near the water.

Sleeping & Eating

★**Sapo Belen Lodge** LODGE $
(☎0813 6196 0997; d 150,000Rp) Sapo Belen Lodge is the nicest crash pad for travellers in town, just off the main street. It consists of characterful, antique-filled rooms with mosquito nets and local-style bathrooms; the largest room has a four-poster bed and a Western toilet. The friendly proprietor answers text messages with the help of English-speaking guides, including Mr Darmawan, his nephew.

Hotel Dina Amalia GUESTHOUSE $
(☎0821 6164 2013; elviandi_rs@yahoo.com; Jl Bahari; r 150,000-270,000Rp; ❄) The plusher rooms at this basic hotel on the main street have air-con. The manager speaks a little English. It's not far from Baroka warung.

Baroka INDONESIAN $
(mains 20,000Rp; ⏲lunch & dinner) Cheap as chips and friendly to boot, this simple warung on the main street lets you load up on gargantuan portions of rice with chicken and fish sambal and more.

Information

There's a single BRI Bank with an ATM that only accepts Mastercard (and not all foreign cards), so bring plenty of cash.

BUSES FROM SINGKIL

DESTINATION	FARE (RP)	DURATION (HR)	FREQUENCY
Medan	120,000	9-10	several daily
Banda Aceh	230,000	15	daily at 3pm
Ketambe	180,000	10	daily at 7pm
Sibolga	120,000	7-8	daily at 8am

Banyak Island Travel (☎ 0813 7721 9667, 0813 6017 0808; dmawan_skl76@yahoo.com) Your first point of contact in Singkil should be Mr Darmawan at Banyak Island Travel, who can organise any and all forms of onward transport, including speed boats to the Banyaks, minibuses and private cars to almost anywhere, and local tours. In fact, he deserves the Stranded Traveller Guardian Angel Award for helping more than a few travellers in distress!

Sumatra Ecotourism (www.sumatraecotourism.com) A very useful website with regards to Singkil, the Banyaks and other destinations in North Sumatra and Aceh. Rega maintains the Sumatra Ecotourism website and works in partnership with Mr Darmawan.

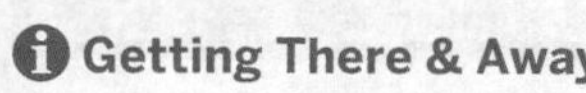

Getting There & Away

AIR

Susi Air (www.susiair.com) has twice-weekly flights on 12-seater planes between Singkil and Medan. Schedules are very changeable, so check in advance.

BOAT

From the ferry port off the main street, overnight ferries depart on Thursday and Sunday for Gunung Sitoli (75,000Rp, six hours) on Pulau Nias at 11pm. Ferries also head to Sinabang on Pulau Simeulue (75,000Rp to 150,000Rp, 12 hours) on the same days at 5pm. Get to the port an hour before departure to secure a seat.

Local boats to Pulau Balai in the Banyaks depart from the jetty at the end of the main street.

BUS & CAR

There are daily minibuses from Singkil to various destinations. You can also charter a car to any destination; this is particularly worthwhile if you're heading for Tuk Tuk on Danau Toba (1,400,000Rp to 1,600,000, seven hours) since getting there by public transport requires three bus changes and takes at least 12 hours. Private cars to Medan cost around 800,000Rp.

Banyak Islands

POP 5000

If you've ever dreamt about having a tropical island entirely to yourself, complete with palm trees, powdery white beaches and crystal-clear waters, the Banyak Islands are a great place to fulfil your Robinson Crusoe fantasy. A cluster of 99 mostly uninhabited islands, the Banyak (Many) Islands are situated about 30km west of Singkil. Remote they might be, but they are now very much on the radar of surfers and growing in popularity with paradise-seeking travellers. As well as having arguably the finest beaches in Sumatra and a handful of quality surf spots, the Banyaks feature Sumatra's best snorkelling with beautiful underwater forests of colourful coral (at least where there has been no dynamite fishing in the past). Maybe one day the dive operators will move in...

Only two of the islands are properly inhabited. The main town on the island of Pulau Balai is the main entry point to the islands. Low-key Haloban on Pulau Tuangku is the other main village.

Sights

Pulau Asok ISLAND

A crescent-shaped, uninhabited island with pristine beaches on either side as well as excellent snorkelling.

Pulau Laman ISLAND

There's fantastic snorkelling between Pulau Laman and Pulau Laureh, with some remarkable growths of vivid blue coral.

Pulau Palambak ISLAND

Rather out of the way, this medium-sized island is covered in coconut trees, has a couple of jungle paths you can walk and a gorgeous stretch of beach. The snorkelling is not great, though, since the coral has been largely destroyed by dynamite fishing.

Pulau Balai ISLAND

One of two inhabited islands, connected to the mainland by frequent public boats. No attractions of its own, but useful as a transfer point.

Pulau Bangkaru ISLAND

The second-largest of the Banyaks is home to a turtle conservation project, so visits are

Banyak Islands

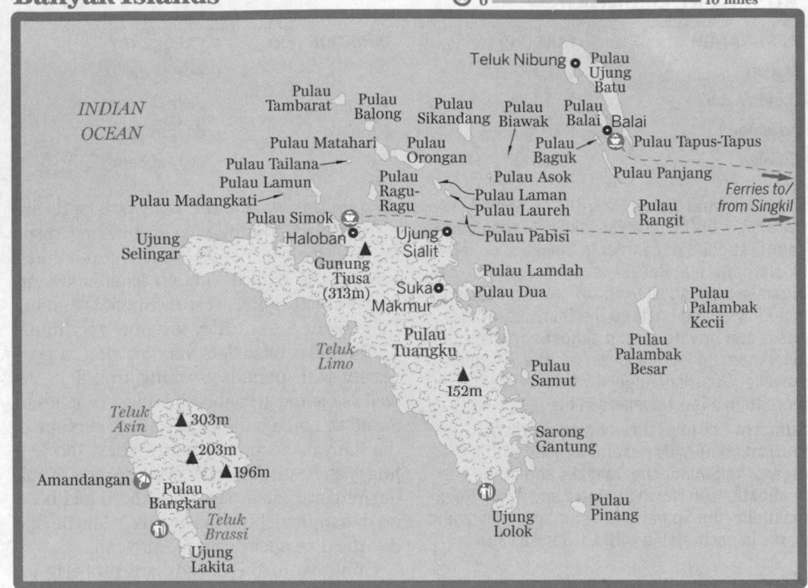

strictly controlled and you're only allowed on the island with a certified guide. The conservation project is up in the air with the demise of the previous management body, so check what's happening with Rega from **Sumatra Ecotourism** (p531).

There are pristine beaches, excellent surfing off the south coast and plenty of scope for jungle trekking. Three day, two night stays for two people cost 2,500,000Rp.

Pulau Tuangku ISLAND
Covered in dense jungle, Pulau Tuangku is the largest of the Banyaks. Surfers head to Ujung Lolok, the headland at the south of the island, complete with several world-class breaks. In the northern part of the island is Haloban, a friendly village; Suka Makmur, a Christian village, is further south. With a guide it's possible to summit Gunung Tiusa (313m) for an epic view of the surrounding islands (five hours return) and visit a cave full of stalagmites.

Pulau Tailanda ISLAND
The small island of Palau Tailana is renowned for reefs that are waves of colour.

Pulau Sikandang ISLAND
This large-ish island, with pristine beaches, takes a couple of hours to walk around. Snorkelling is possible but there's a steep dropoff near the shore off the main beach.

Pulau Ragu-Ragu ISLAND
Offers some excellent snorkelling offshore. Dugongs are sometimes sighted in the mornings off the island's north shore.

Pulau Lambodong ISLAND
A small island with a coconut collector's shack hiding in the palm thicket. The white-sand beach is strewn with storm-brought flotsam and jetsam.

Activities

Kayaking KAYAKING
(☎0852 7771 1108, 0821 6199 7974; kayak hire per day 150,000Rp) Kayaking the calm, crystal-clear waters between dozens of idyllic islands is a great way to explore the Banyaks. With Rega and Anhar, you can arrange anything from beginner routes to multiday challenges for experienced kayakers for around 350,000Rp per person per day.

Snorkelling
The reefs in the Banyaks teem with colourful fish and corals and there are some fabulous snorkelling possibilities off almost any island. The visibility is excellent and most lodgings rent snorkelling masks.

Surfing

Many visitors to the Banyaks are surfers and there are some world-class surf spots here off Pulau Tuangku and Pulau Bangkaru, as well as some more average waves. However, the waves can get rather crowded, particularly around Ujung Lolok, with up to 30 surfers regularly fighting over one peak.

It's mostly surfers who flock to the island's southernmost tip, **Ujung Lolok**. Many come on liveaboard surfing charter boats, while others do it the way surf trips are supposed to be done, by renting a local fishing boat and living on it.

Sleeping & Eating

Sleeping options on the Banyaks consist of rather basic beach bungalows, limited to five islands and with all meals included in the cost. You can also live out your castaway fantasies by camping wild on one of the numerous uninhabited islands. Tents can be arranged through Mr Darmawan at Banyak Island Travel (p531); bring all your food and water with you – stock up in Singkil or Balai, or catch your own dinner!

Pulau Balai

Balai, which oozes a hot, lazy-day ambience, is a pretty village of quiet streets lined with wood-panelled houses inhabited by friendly locals.

Losmen Putri GUESTHOUSE $
(☎0812 6313 5099; r 60,000-150,000Rp; ❄) If you get stuck on Balai, arguably the best accommodation is found here. Go for the cheapest rooms with shared bathrooms or splurge on one with a bucket shower and air-con. To get here, take a left at Homestay Lae Kombih and walk for five minutes.

Homestay Lae Kombih GUESTHOUSE $
(☎0852 9689 5929; Jl Iskandar Muda; r 50,000Rp) This guesthouse overlooks the water and has hot and stuffy rooms. But for this price, what do you expect? The owner is very friendly and speaks English.

Pulau Palambak Basar

Lyla's Bungalows BUNGALOW $
(☎0813 6017 0808, 0811 604 794; r 200,000Rp) Pulau Palambak Basar's only accommodation is at these seven basic bungalows with shared bathrooms fronting a stunning beach. Australian owner David can arrange transfers and speedboat pickup from Singkil (1,600,000Rp), where he also has a guesthouse. A bit of jungle trekking in the island interior is possible, but snorkelling is not great due to damage caused by dynamite fishing.

Pulau Tailana

★**Pondok Tailana** BUNGALOW $
(☎0813 7721 9667, 0822 770 0791; www.tailana.webs.com; r 100,000Rp) Pulau Tailana is the best place to be based in the Banyaks for nonsurfers, with island-hopping, incredible snorkelling and jungle trekking on offer and decent fish-filled reefs just offshore. Wonderfully friendly staff feed you the freshest fish, grilled over a wood fire (meals 100,000Rp per person per day) and lodging consists of seven simple beach huts with shared bathrooms.

Pulau Sikandang

Nina's Bungalows BUNGALOW $
(☎0852 7086 8591; www.banyak-island-bungalow.com; r 150,000-200,000Rp; ❄) A good bet for island-hopping trips, the only lodgings on Sikandang Island consist of five spacious, thatched bungalows (with electricity!) with hammocks swinging on shady porches and helpful manager Rius taking good care of the guests. In front of the bungalows, the drop off is steep and pretty near the shoreline.

Pulau Tuangku

The main village of Haloban has one basic losmen (100,000Rp per person); what the locals lack in English-speaking skills they more than make up for with enthusiasm and friendliness.

The southern tip of the island attracts almost exclusively a surfing crowd.

Banyak Island Lodge LODGE $$$
(☎+61 407 018 708; www.banyaksurfbungalows.com; 8-/11-night package AU$2200/2500) The only land-based accommodation is the Banyak Island Lodge, situated in the so-called Bay of Plenty. Rates include internal flights, transfers and full board. There are five fan-cooled bungalows with twin beds and mozzie nets overlooking Gunters and Camel Back waves out front. The lounge serves local and Western dishes to the accompaniment of surf chat.

Floating Surf House SURF CAMP $$$
(www.floatingsurfhouse.com; 10 nights US$1600; ❄📶) Sitting in the calm waters of the Bay

of Plenty, near Ujung Lolok and within easy reach of Dindos, Gunters and Lolok Point waves, this surf-camp-on-a-raft provides unique accommodation for those chasing the waves. Owned by local surfer Erwin, it has two basic three-bed rooms for solo guests, two doubles and a stilt house.

Getting There & Around

There are two car ferries a week (Tuesday 10am and Friday 1pm) between the mainland port of Singkil and Balai (40,000Rp to 50,000Rp, 3½ to four hours), returning on Wednesday and Saturday at 2pm. Local boats depart Singkil (30,000Rp, four to five hours) daily between 8am and noon (depending on the tides), returning in the afternoon. During the worst of the rough seas in October and November, boats may not run for days.

By far the most convenient – but expensive – way to reach the islands is to charter a speedboat from Singkil (one way 1,500,000Rp, two hours); most lodgings offer this services and can arrange speedboat pickup from Balai.

Enquire in Balai about hiring a fishing boat (from 600,000Rp to 2,500,000Rp per day, depending on boat size, with all the rice and fish you can eat). Mr Darmawan at Banyak Island Travel (p531) can also assist.

Gunung Leuser National Park

☎0629

The Aceh section of Gunung Leuser National Park has slipped under the tourist radar for years, seeing only a trickle of visitors as the masses head to the more-hyped Bukit Lawang. Its jungle is basically the same minus the well-worn paths and tourists clambering about trying to spot semiwild orangutans. This is the place for the *real* jungle experience.

The Unesco-listed Gunung Leuser National Park is one of the world's most important and biologically diverse conservation areas. It is often described as a complete ecosystem laboratory because of the range of forest and species types.

Within the park's boundaries live some of the planet's most endangered and exotic species: tigers, rhinoceros, elephants and orangutans. Although your chances of seeing these celebrity animals are remote, you have a reasonable chance of seeing orangutans, and you can be sure of encountering plenty of other primates. The most common is the white-breasted Thomas leaf monkey, which sports a brilliant, crested punk hairdo.

Habitats range from the swamp forests of the west coast to the dense lowland rainforests of the interior. Much of the area around Ketambe is virgin forest. Above 1500m, the permanent mist has created moss forests rich in epiphytes and orchids. Rare flora includes two members of the rafflesia family, *Rafflesia acehensis* and *Rafflesia zippelnii*, which are found along Sungai Alas.

More than 300 bird species have been recorded in the park, including the bizarre rhinoceros hornbill, the helmeted hornbill and woodpeckers.

The park faces a great number of challenges. Poachers have virtually wiped out the crocodile population and have severely reduced the number of tigers and rhinoceros. According to the Indonesian Forum for the Environment, over a fifth of the park has been adversely affected by illegal logging and road construction. A highly controversial road project called Ladia Galaska runs through the park, linking the east and west coasts of the province. Furthermore, during the civil conflict in Aceh, the jungle was a stronghold of GAM militants, and the national park saw fighting between GAM and Indonesian troops.

This park receives a lot of rain throughout the year, but rain showers tend to lessen in frequency and duration between December and March.

Kedah

Located 15km west of the scrappy town of Blangkejeren, the small village of Kedah has seen very few visitors since the conflict in Aceh, making it ripe for off-the-beaten-track travel. At the northern edge of Gunung Leuser National Park, Kedah is a magnificent starting point for treks into the jungle, which is home to orangutans, gibbons and other exotic wildlife, birds and plants.

Rainforest Lodge (☎0812 699 2732, 0813 6229 1844; www.gunung-leuser-trek.net; r without bathroom 100,000Rp) has simple but pleasant bungalows in beautiful jungle surrounds, with plenty of opportunity for wildlife-spotting. The lack of electricity adds greatly to its charm. Firstly, let Mr Jally know in advance that you're coming. The Rainforest Lodge is an hour's walk from Kedah village and is literally in the middle of nowhere. Mr Jally can organise jungle treks for around 450,000Rp per day, including food and guide; these are serious adventures, from the three-day summit of Gunung Angkosan peak to a six-day expedition to an immense waterfall in the upper Alas valley. Shorter treks can also be arranged, including night treks. Park permit fees are collected intermittently and the cost is not included.

To get here catch a bus to Blangkejeren, from where you can take an *ojek* (50,000Rp, 20 minutes) to Kedah.

Ketambe

Ketambe, in the heart of the Alas Valley, is the main tourist centre of the national park. A handful of guesthouses spread along the road, hemmed in between the river and the jungle. It's one of the most chilled-out places in North Sumatra and a few lazy days relaxing beside the river and partaking in some jungle hikes is likely to be a highlight of your Sumatran adventures.

Activities

Rafting

Rafting (half/full day 450,000/800,000Rp) is a fun way to see the forest and keep cool at the same time. Most guesthouses can help organise this.

Trekking

For serious trekkers and jungle enthusiasts, the trekking (half-/full-day/overnight 350,000/500,000/900,000Rp) around Ketambe offers a much more authentic experience than that near Bukit Lawang. Be prepared for extreme terrain, leeches and mosquitoes, and bring plenty of water. Guides can tailor a trip to specific requests. One of the more popular hikes is a three-day walk to some hot springs deep in the forest.

Gurah Recreation Forest TREKKING

The *hutan wisata* (recreation forest) at Gurah is a small, riverside picnic area, but guides lead half- and full-day hikes in the forest that surrounds this and the village. There's a pretty good chance of seeing gibbons, Thomas leaf monkeys and orangutans here.

Bukit Lawang TREKKING

Starting one-hour south of Kutacane, this six-day trek through tough terrain passes over 20 river crossings. You have a good chance of seeing orangutans and gibbons, and the trek passes through areas that elephants are known to inhabit. You can arrange to have your luggage delivered to Bukit Lawang separately.

Gunung Kemiri TREKKING

At 3314m, this is the second-highest peak in Gunung Leuser National Park. The return trek takes five to six days, starting from the village of Gumpang, north of Ketambe. It takes in some of the park's richest primate habitat, with orangutans, macaques, siamangs and gibbons.

Gunung Leuser TREKKING

The park's highest peak is, of course, Gunung Leuser (3404m). Only the fit should attempt the 14-day return trek to the summit (eight days up, six days down). The walk starts from the village of Angusan, northwest of Blangkejeran.

Sleeping & Eating

Accommodation is scattered along the only road through Ketambe; there are six guesthouses in total and each has its own small restaurant.

KETAMBE RESEARCH STATION

The Ketambe Research Station has been conducting extensive studies of the flora and fauna of Gunung Leuser National Park for almost 30 years.

In the early 1970s, Ketambe was home to Sumatra's orangutan rehabilitation program, but the project was relocated to Bukit Lawang to allow researchers to study the Ketambe region without the disruption of tourists. Nowadays the station's primary concern is hard-core conservation, research and species cataloguing. Both the centre and the surrounding forest are off limits to almost everyone except the Indonesian and international researchers.

The 450-hectare protected area consists mainly of primary lowland tropical forest and is home to a large number of primates, as well as Sumatran tigers, rhinoceros, sun bears, hornbills and snakes. Despite its protected status, well over a third of the area has been lost to illegal logging since 1999.

★Thousand Hills Guest House BUNGALOW $

(☎0812 6417 6752; www.thousandhillsketambe.com; r 80,000-120,000Rp, bungalow 150,000Rp) The most upmarket of Ketambe's options, and the first guesthouse you come across if approaching Ketambe from the south, consists of cute thatched bungalows hiding in the lush vegetation. Monkeys may peek in on you as you perform your ablutions in the outdoor bathrooms. The indomitable Joseph is full of advice and can organise jungle guides.

Wisma Cinta Alam GUESTHOUSE $

(☎0852 7086 4580; www.gunung-leuser-trek.net; r 100,000-150,000Rp) The cheaper rooms sit in a row in a barrack-like construction, while the pricier ones are little bungalows in their own right; both now come with showers and real beds. Excellent, knowledgeable guides can be organised here. It's also a good choice for those keen on rafting.

Friendship Guesthouse GUESTHOUSE $

(☎0852 9688 3624; www.ketambe.com; r 100,000Rp; 📶) This spot has a beautiful riverside location with charming wooden bungalows equipped with Western toilets. The main hang-out area is decked out with photos of travellers engaging in jungle stuff. Staff are very friendly, and there are usually jungle guides lurking on the doorstep.

Wisma Sadar Wisata GUESTHOUSE $

(☎0852 7615 5741; r 60,000-80,000Rp) Here you'll find a range of good-value bungalows; some overlook the river, as does the cafe. The owner's daughter, Mira, is an excellent cook and can hook you up with a jungle guide.

ℹ Information

Ketambe is one of the main access points to Gunung Leuser National Park. Directly across the river is Ketambe Research Station, a world-renowned conservation research station, which is off limits to tourists. Kutacane, 43km from Ketambe, is the closest town of any note and is the place to go for transport, ATMs and internet. Permits to the park (150,000Rp per day) can be arranged at guesthouses in Ketambe. Guides can be hired from any guesthouse in Ketambe; ask other travellers for recommendations.

ℹ Getting There & Around

There are two weekly flights between Kutacane and Banda Aceh with **Susi Air** (www.susiair.com).

From Kutacane there are countless *labi labi* to Ketambe (10,000Rp, one hour), but they stop running around 6pm; arrange pickup with your guesthouse if arriving later. All north-bound buses from Kutacane pass through Ketambe. If you want to arrive in Takengon during daylight hours, catch a minibus to Blankejeren around 8am by standing ready on the main road; with later ones, you miss the 11am connection and will be stuck in Blangkejeren until 4pm or 5pm, when a minibus leaves for Banda Aceh via Takengon.

If travelling south to Danau Toba, catch a Sidikalang-bound bus from Kutacane, then another to Pangururan, and then one to Samosir Island. For Berastagi, there's a direct minibus from Kutacane.

WEST SUMATRA

In Sumatra Barat (West Sumatra), fertile uplands ring jungle-clad volcanoes, waterfalls cascade into deep ravines and nature takes a breath in deep, still lakes. Rainforest still clings to the steepest slopes, while rice, tapioca, cinnamon and coffee bring in the wealth.

This is the heartland of the matriarchal Minangkabau, an intelligent, culturally rich and politically savvy people who have successfully exported their culture, language, cuisine and beliefs throughout Indonesia and whose soaring architecture dominates the cities and villages.

BUSES FROM KUTACANE

DESTINATION	FARE (RP)	DURATION (HR)	FREQUENCY
Banda Aceh	220,000	18	daily
Berastagi	60,000	6	daily
Blangkejeren	50,000	3	2-3 daily
Medan	70,000	7	several daily
Sidikalang	40,000	3½	daily
Singkil	180,000	8	daily

THE MINANGKABAU

Legend has it that the Minangkabau are descended from the wandering Macedonian tyrant Alexander the Great. According to the story, the ancestors of the Minangkabau arrived in Sumatra under the leadership of King Maharjo Dirajo, the youngest son of Alexander.

Anthropologists, however, suggest that the Minangkabau arrived in West Sumatra from the Malay Peninsula some time between 1000 and 2000 BC, probably by following Sungai Batang Hari upstream from the Strait of Melaka to the highlands of the Bukit Barisan mountains.

Even if they don't have Alexander's bloodline, the Minangkabau reflect his wanderlust and love of battle, albeit in the milder form of buffalo fighting. Their success in buffalo fighting is believed to have bestowed the people with their tribal name, and the horns of the beast are the focus of their architecture and traditional costumes.

The legend of how the Minangkabau named themselves begins with an imminent attack by a Javanese king. Rather than pit two armies against each other, the Minangkabau proposed a fight between two bulls. When the time came, the West Sumatrans dispatched a tiny calf to fight the enormous Javanese bull, but the half-starved calf was outfitted with sharp metal spears to its horns. Believing the Javanese bull to be its mother, the calf rushed to suckle and ripped the bull's belly to shreds. When the bull finally dropped dead, the people of West Sumatra shouted '*Minangkabau, minangkabau!*', which literally means, 'The buffalo wins, the buffalo wins!'

Linguistic sticklers, though, prefer the far more prosaic explanation that Minangkabau is a combination of two words: *minanga,* which means 'a river,' and *kerbau,* which means 'buffalo.' A third theory suggests that it comes from the archaic expression *pinang kabhu,* which means 'original home' – Minangkabau being the cradle of Malay civilisation.

Bustling Padang, on the Indian Ocean, is a popular pit stop for surfers, trekkers and indigenous culture enthusiasts bound for the Mentawai Islands. Nestling in the cool highlands north of Padang, scenic Bukittinggi is surrounded by picturesque villages where traditional artisans still ply their trades, with the gorgeous Danau Maninjau and the secluded Harau Valley providing plenty of scope for outdoor adventure. Nature lovers also head south to explore Sumatra's largest national park in Kerinci, the last stronghold of the Sumatran tiger and with hidden lakes, volcanoes and jungle trekking galore.

History

Little is known about the area's history before the arrival of Islam in the 14th century. However, the abundance of megalithic remains around the towns of Batu Sangkar and Payakumbuh, near Bukittinggi, suggest that the central highlands supported a sizeable community some 2000 years ago.

After the arrival of Islam, the region was split into small Muslim states ruled by sultans. It remained this way until the beginning of the 19th century, when war erupted between followers of the Islamic fundamentalist Padri movement and supporters of the local chiefs, adherents to the Minangkabau *adat* (traditional laws and regulations). The Padris were so named because their leaders were haji, pilgrims who had made their way to Mecca via the Acehnese port of Pedir. They returned from the haj determined to establish a true Islamic society and stamp out the pre-Islamic ways that dominated the ruling houses.

The Padris had won control of much of the highlands by 1821 when the Dutch decided to join the fray in support of the Minangkabau traditional leaders. The fighting dragged on until 1837, when the Dutch overcame the equator town of Bonjol, the stronghold of the Padri leader Imam Bonjol, whose name adorns street signs all over Indonesia. In today's Minangkabau society, a curious fusion of traditional beliefs and Islam is practised.

Padang

0751 / POP 877,000

An urbo-Indonesian sprawl of traffic and smog, Padang sits astride one of the planet's most powerful seismic zones, centrally located on the tectonic hotspot where the Indo-Australian plate plunges under the Eurasian plate. Significant tremors occur on an almost annual basis, the most recent being in 2012.

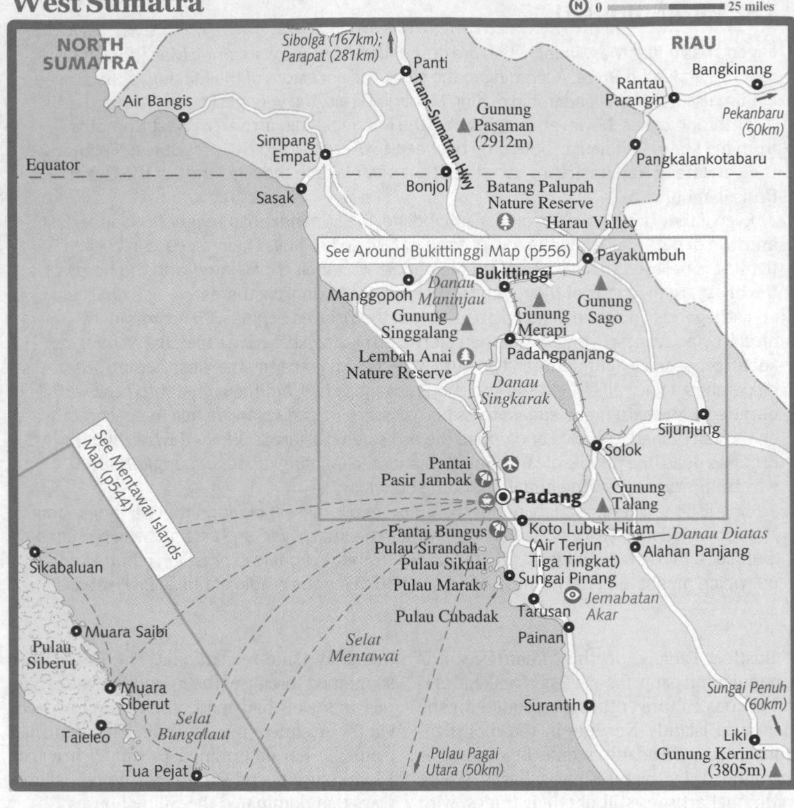

Padang is to West Sumatra what Medan is to the North – a handy transport hub with excellent connections to major regional attractions, including Mentawai islands, Bukittinggi, Danau Maninjau and the Kerinci Highlands. Due to the sheer volume of backpacker and surfer traffic passing through, it also has an above-average amount of good budget accommodation and an excellent dining scene, with regional food the most globally famous of Indonesian culinary offerings.

Sights

Colonial Quarter NEIGHBOURHOOD
Although damaged in the 2009 earthquake, Padang's colonial-era quarter around Jl Batang Arau is still worth a lazy stroll. Old Dutch and Chinese warehouses back onto a river brimming with fishing boats. The beach along Jl Samudera is the best place to watch the sunset.

Adityawarman Museum MUSEUM
(Jl Diponegoro; admission 2500Rp; 8am-4pm Tue-Sun) Adityawarman Museum, built in the Minangkabau tradition, has pleasant grounds and the exhibits are a thorough introduction to everyday Minangkabau life. A healthy imagination helps, since the exhibits are in Bahasa Indonesia. The entrance is on Jl Gereja.

Tours

Padang is the launching point for tours of the Mentawai Islands, which are famous for their hunter-gatherer culture, endemic flora and fauna, and world-class surfing. Local travel agencies can also arrange tours around the surrounding Minangkabau heartland of West Sumatra.

★Regina Adventures TOUR, SURFING
(☎0751-781 0835, 0812 6774 5464; www.regina adventures.com; 10-day surf packages per person from US$450) Reliable local operator Elvis offers trekking on the Mentawai Islands, trips to Danau Maninjau and Bukittinggi, and ascents of Gunung Merapi and Gunung Kerinci. Check the website for good-value surf trips to Mentawai and Krui further south.

Nando Sumatra Tours CULTURAL TOUR
(☎0812 6672 8800, 0852 6335 7645; www.nando sumatratour.com; Jl Tanjung Indah I blok E; 10-day Mentawai treks from per person US$700) A young, up-and-coming company with friendly owner Nando at the helm. Arranges 10-day Mentawai cultural immersion tours, as well as tours of North and West Sumatra and trekking around Danau Maninjau.

Sumatran Surfariis SURFING
(☎0751-34878; www.sumatransurfariis.com; Komplek Pondok Indah B 12, Parak Gadang) Long-established Mentawai surf-boat charter company with three boats to whisk you off on a 10- to 14-day wave hunt to the Mentawais. Nias, Aceh, Telo and the Banyaks are also options. A 10-day 'surfari' typically costs between US$2750 and US$3300.

Festivals & Events

Pesta Budaya Tabuik CULTURAL
A West Sumatran cultural calendar highlight is Pesta Budaya Tabuik (derived from the Islamic festival of Tabut), which is held in Pariaman, 36km north of Padang. It takes place at the beginning of the month of Muharam (based on the Islamic lunar calendar, usually January or February) to honour the martyrdom of Muhammad's grandchildren, Hassan and Hussein, at the battle of Kerbala.

Central to the festival is the *bouraq* (a winged horse-like creature with the head of a woman), believed to have descended to earth to collect the souls of dead heroes and take them to heaven.

Dragon Boat Festival SPORTS
Held in July or August, this festival involves boat racing competitions between international teams. Check details on Facebook.

Sleeping

Brigitte's House HOMESTAY $
(☎0813 7425 7162; http://brigittehouse.blog spot.com; Jl Kampung Sebalah 1/14; dm/s/d from 95,000/100,000/230,000Rp; ❄📶) Brigitte's has a relaxed and homely ambience, with backpackers chilling in the common area or mingling on the porch. This residential neighbourhood is quiet and leafy, and Brigitte is a treasure trove of information on buses, ferries and Mentawai adventures (and can help you with bookings). A short walk away is the separate building with air-con rooms.

Yani's Homestay HOMESTAY $
(☎0852 6380 1686; yuliuz.caesar@gmail.com; d 80,000Rp, r 120,000-175,000Rp, all incl breakfast; ❄📶) Run by friendly young owner Yuliuz, this central homestay provides bona fide backpacker digs in the form of an air-con dorm with lockers and rooms with colourful bedspreads. If you don't want to share your bathroom, splurge on the standard double. Motorbikes are available for guest use (60,000Rp per day).

Golden Homestay HOMESTAY $
(☎0751-32616; Jl Nipah Berok 1B; r 200,000-375,000Rp; ❄📶) Spotless private rooms named after Sydney's classic surfing beaches. Grab a bed in the cheaper Bronte room, or splash out on the Bondi or Manly rooms with private bathrooms.

★New House Padang GUESTHOUSE $$
(☎0751-25982; www.newhouse.padanghostel.com; Jl HOS Cokroaminoto 104; r incl breakfast 250,000-300,000Rp; ❄📶) Now run by the same folks at Brigitte's House, this friendly and relaxed guesthouse is perfect for groups of friends and surfers. A compact Zen garden combines with colourful rooms (some with terrace), contemporary artwork and a vast common area. The owners are on hand to advise about onward travel to the islands or Bukittinggi.

HW Hotel HOTEL $$
(☎0751-893500; www.hwhotelpadang.com; Jl Hayam Wuruk 16; r incl breakfast 480,000-750,000Rp; ❄📶🏊) Modern and fairly spacious rooms in a central, post-earthquake hotel. We particularly like the compact rooftop pool and the friendliness and helpfulness of the staff. There's room for negotiation on the rates, especially on weekends.

Savali Hotel HOTEL $$
(☎0751-27660; www.savalihotel.com; Jl Hayam Wuruk 31; r incl breakfast 545,000-860,000Rp; ❄📶🏊) The centrally located Savali is just a short stroll from the beach and good restaurants. The hotel's 23 rooms are set around a Zen-style garden, English is spoken at

Padang

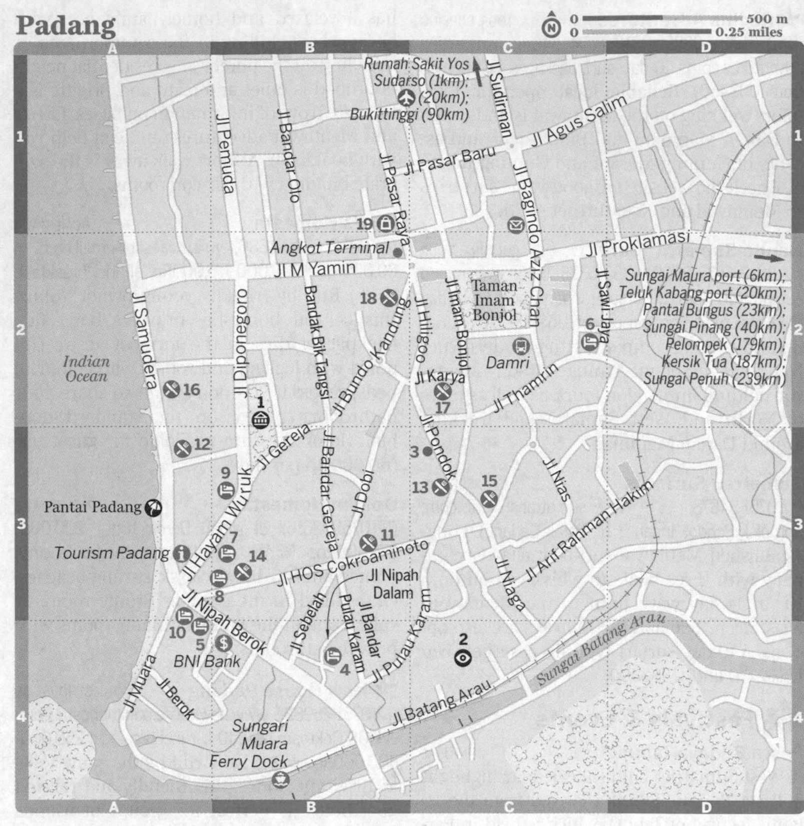

Padang

Sights

1 Adityawarman Museum ... B2
2 Colonial Quarter ... C4

Activities, Courses & Tours

3 Sumatran Surfariis ... C3

Sleeping

4 Brigitte's House ... B4
5 Golden Homestay ... A4
6 Grand Zuri Hotel ... C2
7 HW Hotel ... B3
8 New House Padang ... B3
9 Savali Hotel ... B3
10 Yani's Homestay ... A3

Eating

11 Hoya Bakery ... B3
12 Nelayan Restaurant ... A3
13 Pagi Sore ... C3
14 Pak Tri's ... B3
15 Pondok Indah Jaya ... C3
16 Safari Garden ... A2
17 Sari Raso ... C2
18 Simpang Raya ... B2

Shopping

19 Pasar Raya ... B1

reception and there's definitely an open mind to negotiation on room rates. The compact swimming pool is welcome on sultry equatorial afternoons and there's a good coffee shop next door.

Grand Zuri Hotel BUSINESS HOTEL $$$
(☎0751-894888; www.grandzuri.com/padang; Jl Thamrin; r 670,000-1,250,000Rp; ❄📶) A little out of the centre, this slick new business hotel features spacious, contemporary rooms

with polished wooden floors, large bathrooms, sumptuous mattresses and a decent 24-hour restaurant. Other perks include a gym and spa and an entire floor catering to nonsmokers. A good treat to your battered body if you've just spent a week roughing it on the Mentawais.

Eating & Drinking

Padang is the birth mother of the cuisine that migrated across Indonesia and you can pay homage to the native cooks with a visit to one of these famous franchises: **Pagi Sore** (Jl Pondok 143; dishes 9000Rp; ⏲lunch & dinner), **Sari Raso** (Jl Karya 3; dishes 10,000Rp; ⏲lunch & dinner) and **Simpang Raya** (Jl Bundo Kandung; dishes 8000Rp; ⏲lunch & dinner).

Jl Batang Arau is full of cheap warungs that spring to life at night, while discerning foodies head for Jl Pondok and Jl HOS Cokroaminoto. Juice wagons loiter near the end of Jl Hayam Wuruk. For cheap *sate* (satay), grilled seafood and a few cold Bintangs (Indonesian beer), head to the beachfront shacks lining Jl Sumadera at sunset.

Pondok Indah Jaya INDONESIAN $
(Jl Niaga 138; meals around 40,000Rp; ⏲lunch & dinner) This warung is an excellent intro to Padang cuisine, your feast of dishes including spicy tofu, beef *rendang*, *ayam* sambal and tempe. Cool the fire in your mouth with some *sirsak* (soursop), cucumber or mango juice.

Hoya Bakery BAKERY $
(Jl HOS Cokroaminoto 48; snacks/meals around 7000/20,000Rp; ⏲breakfast & lunch) Padang's go-to spot for freshly baked sweet and savoury goodies. Friendly shop assistants will guide you around the selection before steering you to a colourful table. There are also good burgers, sandwiches and pasta, and the juices and smoothies are soothing antidotes to Padang's tropical buzz.

★ **Pak Tri's** SEAFOOD $$
(Jl HOS Cokroaminoto 91; meals from 50,000Rp; ⏲5pm-late) The fish and squid are flame-grilled to perfection with a sweet, spicy sambal sauce here. The fresh-every-afternoon marine selection includes shoals of different fish and squid, with a supporting cast of *kangkung* (water spinach) and aubergine dishes. Grab a spot at the shared tables and tuck in for a quintessential Padang experience, occasionally accompanied by the serenading of street minstrels.

Nelayan Restaurant SEAFOOD $$
(Jl Samudera; mains 35,000-60,000Rp; ⏲lunch & dinner) Great seafood the Chinese way, cold beers and one of the best Padang sunset views at this three-storey establishment. Treat yourself to grilled prawns or pepper

PADANG CUISINE

With *nasi Padang* (Padang cuisine), you sit down and the whole kit and caboodle gets laid out in front of you. You decide which ones look tasty and push the others aside, only paying for what you eat.

The drawback is that you never really know what you're eating, since there's no menu. If the dish contains liquid, it is usually a coconut-milk curry, a major component of Padang cuisine. The meaty dishes are most likely beef or buffalo, occasionally offal or (less likely) even dog.

The most famous Padang dish is *rendang*, chunks of beef or buffalo simmered slowly in coconut milk until the sauce is reduced to a rich paste and the meat becomes dark and dried. Other popular dishes include *telor balado* (egg dusted with red chilli), *ikan panggang* (fish baked in coconut and chilli) and *gulai merah kambing* (red mutton curry).

Most couples pick one or two meat dishes and a vegetable, usually *kangkung* (water spinach), and load up with a plate or two of rice. Carbs are manna in Padang cuisine. Vegetarians should ask for tempe or *tahu* (tofu), which comes doctored up in a spicy sambal.

Before digging into the meal with your right hand, wash up in the provided bowl of water. Food and sauces should be spooned onto your plate of rice, then mixed together with the fingers. The rice will be easier to handle if it is a little wet. Use your fingers to scoop up the food, and your thumb to push it into your mouth. It's messy even for the locals.

Padang cuisine has an earthy spiciness that might need a little sweet tea or water as a chaser. There is usually a tumbler of lukewarm water (a sign that it has been boiled for sterilisation) on the table.

crab, but definitely ask the price before you dig in. We're pretty partial to a chilled Bintang with the *cumi asam manis* (squid in a sweet and sour sauce).

Safari Garden STEAK $$

(Jl Samudera 16; mains 50,000-350,000Rp; ⏲from 5pm; ❄📶) The menu at this bright, contemporary restaurant is the discerning carnivore's dream, with tenderloin, T-bone and sirloin dominating the list. The nice cuts of Angus and even Wagyu beef are cooked to specification, the fruit juices are unadulterated, nonsugary delights, and non-meaty options include fish and chips and pasta. The service is young, friendly and prompt.

Shopping

Pasar Raya MARKET

(Jl Pasar Raya) Pasar Raya – literally 'big market' – is the centre of Padang's shopping universe; come here for anything from fresh fruit to clothes. It's next to the large new mall.

Information

There are ATMs all over town.

BNI Bank (Jl Nipah Berok) Has an ATM dispensing up to 2,000,000Rp.

Imigrasi Office (☎0751-444511; Jl Khatib Sulaiman; ⏲8am-4pm Mon-Fri) Thirty-day visa extensions can be obtained for US$35 at the Padang Imigrasi office. It's about 5km out of town by *ojek* or taxi.

Post Office (Jl Azizchan 7; ⏲8am-4pm Mon-Fri) Near the corner of Jl M Yamin and Jl Azizchan.

Rumah Sakit Yos Sudarso (☎0751-33230; Jl Situjuh 1) Privately owned hospital.

Tourism Padang (☎0751-34186; Dinas Kebudayaan Dan Pariwisata, Jl Samudera 1; ⏲7.30am-4pm Mon-Fri, 8am-4pm Sat & Sun) Maps of town and a few English-language regional brochures.

Getting There & Away

AIR

Padang's airport, **Bandara Internasional Minangkabau** (BIM; http://minangkabau-airport.co.id; Jl Adinegoro), is located 20km north of town.

BOAT

Padang is regularly connected to the **Mentawai Islands** (p544) by boat.

BUS

Tranex (☎0751-705 8577) buses depart for Bukittinggi (20,000Rp) from the city's northern fringes, outside the Wisma Indah building. It's half the price of a door-to-door minibus but it means you have to catch any white *angkot* (3000Rp) heading north on Jl Permuda (ask for 'Tranex' or 'Wisma Indah'), and then find transport from Bukittinggi bus terminal, which is miles from the centre. In reality you save very little money.

Minibuses to Bukittinggi and other destinations depart from a variety of offices scattered around the city and offer a door-to-door service. Ask your lodgings to arrange a pick up.

The minibuses most relevant to travellers depart from Jl Jhoni Anwar. **PO Sinar Kerinci** (☎0751-783 1299; Jl Jhni Anwar Q4) has regular departures to Sungai Penuh (for Kerinci Seblat National Park). **Putra Mandau** (☎0751-782 2218;

TRANSPORT FROM PADANG

Air

DESTINATION	AIRLINE	FREQUENCY
Kuala Lumpur	AirAsia	2 daily
Jakarta	Citilink, Garuda, Lion Air, Sriwijaya Air	19 daily
Medan	Lion Air, Sriwijaya Air	3 daily
Pulau Batam	Citilink, Lion Air	5 daily

Bus

DESTINATION	FARE (RP)	DURATION (HR)	FREQUENCY
Bukittinggi	20,000	3	hourly until 6pm
Jambi	165,000-190,000	11	2 daily
Parapat (for Danau Toba)	180,000	18	daily at 1pm
Sungai Penuh	130,000	7-8	9am, 10am, 7pm, 8pm

Jl Jhoni Anwar) links Padang to Dumai if you're travelling to/from Sumatra by sea from Malaysia or Singapore. Catch an *angkot* (3000Rp) north along Jl Permuda and Jl S Parman, get off at the white mosque around 5km north of central Padang, and turn right into Jl Jhoni Anwar.

Getting Around

Airport taxis charge around 150,000Rp from the airport, but 300,000Rp to the airport. If you're travelling light, step outside the airport boundaries and hail an *ojek* to get to central Padang. White **Damri** (☎780 6335) buses (35,000Rp) are a cheaper alternative that loop through Padang, though there are no clearly designated stops and they run to an erratic schedule. If you're fortunate enough to catch one, tell the conductor your accommodation and street and they'll drop you at the right stop. If you're coming from Bukittinggi, pretty much all lodgings can arrange a cheap and convenient airport drop-off service (40,000Rp) in a shared minibus.

There are numerous *angkot* (3000Rp) around town, operating out of the **Angkot terminal** (Jl M Yamin), but you have to know where you're going.

Around Padang

If Padang's traffic is frying your brains, or you're waiting for a boat, kick back on one of the nearby beaches. **Pantai Bungus**, 23km south of Padang, is conveniently close to the ferry port of Teluk Kabung, but still sufficiently relaxed to unkink the most frazzled traveller. There's a host of nearby islands to explore, plus the odd gem in the hinterland. Further south along the coast is **Sungai Pinang** with its somnolent fishing village vibe.

To reach Pantai Bungus from Padang, take a blue *angkot* labelled 'Kabung Bungus' (15,000Rp, one hour) or a taxi (140,000Rp). There's no public transport to Sungai Pinang; it's an hour's drive along a very rough road from Bungus, so arrange transport from Padang.

Sights

Air Terjun Tiga Tingkat WATERFALL
(Three Tier Waterfall; Pantai Bungus) This spectacular three-storey waterfall is close to Teluk Kabung, by the village of Koto Lubuk Hitam. It's an hour's hike up to the base of the falls for swimming.

Pulau Pagang ISLAND
Pulau Pagang is a beautiful small island, 1½-hours offshore from Bungus, with white sandy beaches and a handful of basic bungalows. It's possible to rent a boat from Bungus and stay the night. Ask at Tin Tin Homestay, or among the local fishermen.

Sleeping

TinTin Homestay HOMESTAY $
(☎0812 6683 6668; http://tintinhomestay.blogspot.com; Pantai Bungus; r 120,000Rp) TinTin Homestay is a small, quiet, family-run losmen on Pantai Bungus offering basic, netted rooms a couple of kilometres from the port. It's run by friendly Raoul who can arrange overnight island trips and multiday trips to the Mentawais.

Jophira TinTin, reachable via a 45-minute boat ride from Pantai Bungus and owned by TinTin Homestay, is a clutch of adorable thatched bungalows on a near-pristine beach. Boat transfers cost 450,000Rp and activities include fishing and snorkelling.

Rimba Ecolodge BUNGALOW $$
(☎0821 7082 6361, 0888 0740 2278; www.rimba-ecoproject.com; r 125,000-225,000Rp) Rimba Ecolodge is an intimate French-Indonesian-run place reachable by boat from the mainland. Monkeys come to explore the beach where the breeze-cooled bungalows are situated and there's a timeless, tranquil air to the whole place. Staff are involved in coral reef and wildlife rehabilitation, working closely with the local fishing communities. The menu features plenty of fresh fish and seafood.

Cubadak Paradiso Village RESORT $$$
(☎0812 660 3766; www.cubadak-paradisovillage.com; Pulau Cubadak; r incl full board US$140-190, minimum 2 nights) Cubadak Paradiso Village is found on tranquil Pulau Cubadak where 13 bungalows perch above teal waters. You can snorkel off your front porch or go diving or canoeing. Pickup from Padang and boat transport is included.

Ricky's Beach House GUESTHOUSE $$
(☎0813 6381 1786; Sungai Pinang; r 150,000-200,000Rp; ❄ 📶) Ricky's Beach House in Sungai Pinang fishing village is the kind of place where backpackers end up extending their stay indefinitely. And why would you want to leave the Rasta-coloured beach house, the little beach bungalows or the hammock-hung bar where someone is always ready to break out the guitar and the bongos? Call ahead for transport.

Mentawai Islands

Though not a great distance from the mainland, the Mentawai Islands and its people were kept isolated until the 19th century by strong winds, unpredictable currents and razor-sharp reefs.

It's thought that the archipelago separated from Sumatra some 500,000 years ago, resulting in unique flora and fauna that sees Mentawai ranked alongside Madagascar in terms of endemic primate population. Of particular interest is *siamang kerdil,* a rare species of black-and-yellow monkey, named *simpai Mentawai* by the locals.

The largest island, Siberut, is home to the majority of the Mentawai population and is the most studied and protected island in the archipelago. About 60% of Siberut is still covered with tropical rainforest, which shelters a rich biological community that has earned it a designation as a Unesco biosphere reserve. The western half of the island is protected as the Siberut National Park.

Pulau Sipora is home to Tua Pejat, the seat of regional government and a surfer drop-off point. The archipelago's airport is located at Rokot. With only 10% original rainforest remaining, it's also the most developed of the Mentawai Islands.

Further south are the Pulau Pagai islands – Utara (North) and Selatan (South) – which rarely see independent travellers.

Change has come quickly to the Mentawai Islands. Tourism, logging, *transmigrasi* (a government-sponsored scheme enabling settlers to move from overcrowded regions to sparsely populated ones) and other government-backed attempts to mainstream the culture have separated the people from the jungle and whittled the jungle into profit. It isn't what it used to be, but it is a long way from being like everywhere else.

Surfers comprise the other island-bound pilgrims, many of whom rank the Mentawais as the ride of their life.

A magnitude 7.7 earthquake hit the islands in October 2010, with a resulting tsunami killing more than 500 people and leaving more than 8000 homeless in the archipelago's southern islands.

Activities

Hiking

The river scene from *Apocalypse Now* has a tendency to flash into your mind as you head upstream in a longboat and watch the people

Mentawai Islands

0 — 20 km
0 — 10 miles

MENTAWAI HIKING TIPS

- Dress for mud wrestling. Most of your gear will get trashed, so leave behind your finest garments and bear in mind you may need to swim across the odd river.
- Double-bag everything in plastic bags (or carry your gear in a dry bag) and keep one set of clothes dry for the evenings.
- Don't walk in flip-flops – step into deep bog and you'll never see them again. Trainers or trekking boots are a must. Keep flip-flops handy for downtime in the villages.
- Travel light. Large packs are a hindrance and anything tied to the outside is a goner.
- Prepare for poor water sanitation. The local rivers serve all purposes, so water purification (tablets or Steripen) is recommended, as is a water pump to filter out impurities. Alternatively, you can carry your weight in bottled water.
- Take precautions against chloroquine-resistant malaria which still exists on Siberut, though **SurfAid** (www.surfaidinternational.org) has been actively working to limit its spread. DDT-strength insect repellent is advisable, as are mosquito nets if you're travelling independently (tour agencies tend to provide them).
- Don't expect electricity in the evenings. A torch is your best friend, especially when it comes to negotiating your way to the local privy at night.
- Prepare for rain. May is generally the driest month, while October and November are the wettest – but it can rain at any time. The easiest thing is to just accept that you're going to get wet.
- Buy essential supplies in Padang, where there is greater choice (and cheaper prices) than in Siberut.
- Buy items for bartering and gifts. If heading to remote communities, remember that everything tends to be shared, so bring plenty of food.

and villages growing wilder by the minute. Soon you're out of the canoe and following a wild-eyed *sikerei* (shaman) covered in tattoos and a loincloth through the mud for the next few hours, passing waterfalls, balancing on slippery tree branches and swimming across rivers until you reach his humble abode on poles in the middle of nowhere.

There's been fervent discussion about the authenticity of these trips, and what actually constitutes a traditional lifestyle. There is scope for both off-the-beaten-track adventure, where you turn up in remote villages and witness Mentawai life as it really is, and more organised ventures where villagers get paid by your guide to dress up in traditional gear, show you how to fish and hunt and engage you in their daily activities.

Mainland tour agencies tend to offer multi-day treks, ranging from six to 10 days, but it's entirely possible to find your own guide, do an independent trip and decide for yourself how long you wish to go for. That said, longer hikes allow you to penetrate deeper into the island and stay in more remote villages, whereas if you opt for just a couple of nights with the Mentawai people, you're more likely to end up in a village not far removed from Muara Siberut where the villagers expect to be paid to have their photos taken.

Many hotels and guesthouses in and around Padang offer treks or can recommend guides. Blogs, forums and other travellers can be invaluable resources as well. If you have plenty of time, you can just turn up in the Mentawais and ask around at the jetty cafes in Maileppet and Siberut, though a good, recommended guide that you make advance arrangements with can be invaluable. Prices start around 300,000Rp per day, but don't include transport, food, accommodation or tips. When talking to a prospective guide, clarify exactly what is and isn't included and see if you can get a detailed breakdown of prices (guide fee per day, food, accommodation and boat), bearing in mind that accommodation prices will be the least of your expenses.

If you prefer a mainland-organised trek, prices in Bukittinggi and Padang start at around US$500 for six days and normally include a guide, accommodation, food and transport. Check for any additional costs.

Surfing

The Mentawai Islands have consistent surf year-round at dozens of legendary breaks. The season peaks between April and October, with off-season waves kinder on intermediate surfers. Mentawai waves are not for beginners; most breaks are reef breaks, some of them very shallow. Choose between staying at land-based losmen, surf camps and resorts; live-aboard boat charters head further afield.

With patience, attitude and a handful of contacts it's possible to put together your own independent surfing safari for a fraction of the cost of a package tour. Budget accommodation is on the increase throughout the Mentawais, and chartering a longboat is relatively easy.

The most consistent cluster of waves is in the Playground area, but things can get rather crowded during peak season. The most unpeopled waves are off the practically uninhabited **Pulau Pagai Selatan**; due to their remoteness, they're the premise of charter boat surfers.

Check some of the more popular surfing blogs, such as **GlobalSurfers** (www.globalsurfers.com) and **WannaSurf** (www.wannasurf.com), for the latest intel.

Tours

Tours and surf charters can be organised in Padang (p538).

Sleeping

Along with transport, accommodation will be your primary expense in the Mentawais. Trekking guides will organise family homestays for around 100,000Rp per night.

For surfers, accommodation falls roughly into three price categories: losmen (around US$35 to US$40 per night, including meals) and surf camps and resorts (US$100 to US$200 per night for a midrange place and over US$300 for top end). The best-located losmen are found on Masokut Island (in the middle of Playground), just south of Pulau Siberut; in Katiet, at the bottom of Pulau Sipora (in front of the iconic HT's break); on Pulau Pagai Utara (in front of the Macca's breaks); and facing the Telescopes break on Tua Pejat. Bring all your supplies, drinking water and mosquito nets. To get to Masokut, either bum a lift with another group, or charter a longboat from Siberut. As for the rest, interisland ferries can get you reasonably close.

Surf camp and resort prices typically include transfers to/from the nearest port (Siberut, Tua Pejat) and two speedboat outings

FIXING A SURFING SAFARI

A good fixer is worth their weight in gold. They will meet you at the airport, show you where you can procure various supplies, then get the whole lot to the port and safely stowed on the ferry. They will have already arranged your arrival day to coincide with the ferry schedule, and secured you a cabin or seat. On your return, they'll meet the ferry and get you and all your gear back to the airport.

You then need a second fixer out in the islands, who will meet your ferry, tee up a longboat, ship your gear, and drop you at a cheap losmen or basic hut somewhere close to your favourite break. They'll even arrange a cook if you want one. Of course, all this costs money, and rest assured, your fixer is taking a cut from everybody. But with careful planning and bargaining it's still going to be a whole lot cheaper than two weeks in a resort.

How do you find a fixer? Without any recommendations, your first trip will always be a learning curve. Experienced surfers come back year after year and use the same fixers, boat drivers and hut owners. All business is conducted by mobile phone, and good fixers will also have email addresses. Watch closely what other groups are doing – maybe you can share a taxi to the port, or bum a lift in a speedboat – all the time filling your mobile phone with contact numbers.

There's nothing stopping you doing all this organising yourself, but it's time and energy you'd most likely rather leave for the waves.

If you're looking to set something up before you arrive, contact **Harris Smile** (☎0821 2241 0133; harrissmile@yahoo.com), a friendly, English-speaking Tua Pejat local. But be sure to bargain hard, and if you can, ask around first about boat prices before you commit to anything.

THE MENTAWAIANS

The untouched, the unbaptised and the unphotographed have long drawn Westerners to distant corners of the globe. And the Mentawaians have seen every sort of self-anointed discoverer: the colonial entrepreneurs hoping to harness the land for profit, missionaries trading medicine for souls and modern-day tourists eager to experience life before the machine.

Very little is known about the origins of the Mentawaians, but it is assumed that they emigrated from Sumatra to Nias and made their way to Siberut from there.

At the time of contact with missionaries, the Mentawaians had their own language, *adat* (traditional laws and regulations) and religion, and were skilled boat builders. They lived a hunter-gatherer existence.

Traditional clothing was a loincloth made from the bark of the breadfruit tree for men and a bark skirt for women. Mentawaians wore bands of red-coloured rattan, beads and imported brass rings. They filed their teeth into points and decorated their bodies with tattoos.

After independence, the Indonesian government banned many of the Mentawaians' customs, such as tattoos, sharpened teeth and long hair. Although the ban has not been enforced, many villagers have adopted modern fashions.

Traditional villages are built along riverbanks and consist of one or more *uma* (communal house) surrounded by *lalep* (single-storey family houses). Several families live in the same building. Bachelors and widows have their own quarters, known as *rusuk*, identical to the family longhouse except they have no altar.

Although essentially patriarchal, society is organised on egalitarian principles. There are no inherited titles or positions and no subordinate roles. It is the *uma*, not the village itself, which is pivotal to society. It is here that discussions affecting the community take place.

The native Sibulungan religion is a form of animism, involving the worship of nature spirits and a belief in the existence of ghosts, as well as the soul. The chief nature spirits are those of the sky, the sea, the jungle and the earth. The sky spirits are considered the most influential. There are also two river spirits: Ina Oinan (Mother of Rivers) is beneficent, while Kameinan (Father's Sister) is regarded as evil.

German missionary August Lett was the first to attempt to convert the local people, but he was not entirely successful: eight years after his arrival Lett was murdered by the locals. Somehow the mission managed to survive, however, and 11 baptisms had been recorded by 1916. There are now more than 80 Protestant churches throughout the islands.

More than 50 years after the Protestants, Catholic missionaries moved in to vie for converts. They opened a mission – a combined church, school and clinic – and free medicines and clothes were given to any islander who converted.

Islam was introduced when government officials were appointed from Padang during the Dutch era. Today, more than half the population claims to be Protestant, 16% Catholic and 13% Muslim, though the number of the latter is growing due to government efforts at Islamisation. An Italian priest, Padre Pio, who has lived on the Mentawaians for decades, returned from Italy recently to find his village school in ruins, a concrete mosque in place and the headman riding a new motorbike.

per day to catch the best waves. Most top-end places include private speedboat transfer from Padang. Most operate on a package basis for around 10 days, and prebooking is required.

There's a plethora of surf resorts in the Playground and Tua Pejat areas, a couple in Katiet and just one apiece in the far-flung Pulau Pagai Utara and Pulau Pagai Selatan.

There are a couple of basic hotels in both Siberut and Tua Pejat, for the unlikely event that you get stuck waiting for a ferry.

Playground

Bintang Surf Camp SURF CAMP **$$**
(☎0812 6617 4454; Pulau Masokut; per person 400,000Rp) A short walk from Ebay on Pulau Masokut, this chilled-out surf camp is the best of the local budget lot, with basic thatched huts and shared rooms, ample portions of delicious Indonesian food and the kind of camaraderie you get when you throw 20 young Brazilians, Aussies, Irish and

Norwegians together. Can be booked through Regina Adventures (p539) in Padang.

Mentawai Surf Retreat SURF CAMP **$$**
(☎0812 6157 0187, 0751-36345; www.mentawaisurfingretreat.com; Masokut Island; 10 nights US$2500; ⏱Feb-Nov; 📶) With Pitstops breaking right in front of the four breezy Mentawai-style cottages, this intimate surf retreat has an enviable location on Masokut Island. It attracts a largely Aussie crowd with its combination of comfort (king-sized beds, large open bathrooms, delicious Indonesian food) and immediate proximity to several good waves. Manager Brent can also advise on trekking on Siberut.

Shadow Mentawai Surf Camp SURF CAMP **$$**
(www.theshadowmentawai.com; surfer/nonsurfer per day US$120/100; 📶) On tiny, lush Pulau Buasak on the outskirts of Playground, Shadow is run by friendly local surfer brothers Ade and Dodi and their crew. Solo surfers lodge in cosy two-person bunk rooms with air-con, while couples are more likely to end up in the thatched cottage with a simple outdoor Indonesian bathroom.

★**Kandui Villas** RESORT **$$$**
(☎0812 664 0941, 0751-841946; www.kanduivillas.com; Pulau Karangmajat; surfer/nonsurfer per night US$335/250; ❄📶🏊) Located on Pulau Karangmajat, American-owned Kandui Villas is a short paddle from Kandui Left, not far from the legendary Rifles and with unlimited speedboat transfers to the waves, making this the pro surfer digs of choice. Guests are lodged in 12 luxurious, breezy *umas* (Mentawai-style cottages) with king-sized beds. Nonsurfing partners and children can lounge by the infinity pool.

Wavepark Resort RESORT **$$$**
(☎0812 663 5551; www.wavepark.com; 10-night package incl meals US$3600; ❄@📶) Wavepark has a front-row view of Hideaways from its lookout tower and large, comfortable, breezy bungalows (with the best bathrooms in the Mentawais) on a private island. Nonsurfing activities (sea kayaking, snorkelling) make it a favourite with returning surfing/nonsurfing couples, and the excellent bar-restaurant screens surfing photos of the day.

Pitstop Hill Resort RESORT **$$$**
(www.pitstophill.com; Pulau Masokut; 10-day package incl meals US$3500; ❄📶) High on a hill overlooking Pitstops and around the corner from Ebay, this Aussie-run resort has six rooms in a main house, and a luxury villa for couples and families. It's wildly popular with return visitors, so book about five months ahead of time.

Pulau Sipora/Tua Pejat

★**Aloita Resort & Spa** RESORT **$$**
(☎0813 6252 7350, 0821 7015 3742; www.aloitaresort.com; surfer/nonsurfer per day from US$175/125; ❄📶) 🍃 Eight bungalows in a garden setting occupy a private beach within easy reach of Telescopes and Iceland and there's a beginner's surf break a short walk away. Italian-run Aloita contributes to the local community (by employing local staff and funding a school) and offers diving and paddle boarding. The spa and yoga terrace make it a good option for surfers planning on bringing partners or family.

Awera Island GUESTHOUSE **$$**
(www.aweraisland.com; Awera Island; per person US$120; 📶) This small guesthouse has a beach-house vibe and is just a short hop from Iceland, Suicides and other decent breaks. Accommodation is geared towards solo surfers, with airy two-bed bunk rooms, large screen projector for movie-watching, and surfing guide Pete on hand to stitch up any injuries. The beach is perfect for downtime snorkelling and jungle hikes are an option.

Uma Awera Lodge SURF CAMP **$$**
(☎0821 7086 6999; desti.sababalat@gmail.com; per person US$95) On Awera Island, within easy range of Iceland, Suicides and Telescopes, this friendly place is run by Desti and her brother. Five traditional thatched Mentawai cottages sit amid well-kept grounds, each with twin beds, fans, mosquito nets and bucket showers. Head to the dining area for impromptu music sessions and a mix of Indo and international dishes.

Oinan Surf Lodge GUESTHOUSE **$$**
(☎0821 7086 6999, 0821 2241 0133; harrissmile@yahoo.com; Jl Mappadejat Km4; r incl meals 600,000Rp; ❄📶) Not actually by the sea, the hilly Oinan Surf Lodge, around 4km from Tua Pejat, has amazing terrace views of the iconic Telescopes wave. Rooms are stylish and chic (one with private bathroom); the lodge has its own boat for easy transport to other good breaks.

★**Togat Nusa** RESORT **$$$**
(www.togatnusaretreat.com; Pitojat; d incl meals US$250; ❄📶) On the private 12-hectare

FERRIES FROM THE MENTAWAI ISLANDS

Mentawai Fast (☎0751-893 489; mentawaifast@gmail.com; one way 295,000Rp, surfboard 230,000Rp) conveniently runs from the dock in central Padang; note that when it stops at Sikabaluan en route to Siberut from Padang, the total journey time to Siberut is six hours.

DAY	DEPARTURE (LOCATION/TIME)	ARRIVAL (LOCATION/TIME)
Monday	Padang/6am	Tua Pejat/9am
Monday	Tua Pejat/3pm	Padang/6pm
Tuesday	Padang/7am	Siberut/3pm
Tuesday	Siberut/3pm	Padang/6pm
Wednesday	Padang/7am	Tua Pejat/10am
Wednesday	Tua Pejat/7am	Padang/3pm
Friday	Padang/7am	Sioban/10.30am
Friday	Sioban/noon	Tua Pejat/1pm
Friday	Tua Pejat/3pm	Padang/6pm
Saturday	Padang/7am	Siberut/11am
Saturday	Siberut/3pm	Padang/7pm

Ambu Ambu & Gambolo are the biggest ferries connecting Padang and the Mentawai islands. Options include air-conditioned VIP seats (180,000Rp), more basic economy seats (95,000Rp) and wooden berths you can lie down on (50,000Rp). Of the two, the *Gambolo* is more comfortable, though both tend to be very crowded. Both ferries leave from the Teluk Kabang port at Bungus, around 20km south of Padang.

DAY	DEPARTURE (LOCATION/TIME)	ARRIVAL (LOCATION)	VESSEL NAME
Monday	Tua Pejat/8pm	Padang	*Gambolo*
Tuesday	Padang/5pm	Sikakap	*Ambu Ambu*
Wednesday	Padang/7pm	Siberut	*Gambolo*
Thursday	Padang/7pm	Tua Pejat	*Ambu Ambu*
Thursday	Siberut/9pm	Padang	*Gambolo*
Friday	Padang/7pm	Siberut	*Gambolo*
Friday	Tua Pejat/8pm	Padang	*Ambu Ambu*
Saturday	Padang/5pm	Sikakap	*Ambu Ambu*
Saturday	Siberut/7pm	Padang	*Gambolo*
Sunday	Padang/7pm	Tua Pejat	*Gambolo*
Sunday	Sikakap/5pm	Padang	*Ambu Ambu*

Beriloga is a smaller wooden ferry that departs from the river mouth (Sungai Muara) on Sungai Batang Arau just south of central Padang. Your only option is the crowded deck class (155,000Rp). Departure times depend on the tide. Don't count on the *Bariloga* getting you back to Padang for an urgent international flight. It leaves Padang for Siberut on Monday and for Sioban on Wednesday. It returns to Padang from Siberut on Tuesday and from Sioban on Thursday.

island of Pitojat, Togat Nusa's four bungalows cater to only eight guests at a time. The funky and stylish accommodation is crafted using recycled driftwood and stained glass, and good snorkelling and romantic beach dinners make it a good option for surfing/nonsurfing couples. The excellent bar is haunted by a guest-loving langur.

Katiet

HT's Surf Resort SURF RESORT **$$$**
(☎0813 3733 7224; www.htresort.com; 9 nights from US$1200;) With an enviable location in front of the legendary HT's right-hander and just a short hop from Lance's Left, Bintangs, Cobra's and even a couple of beach

INTER-ISLAND FERRY CONNECTIONS

DEPARTURE	DESTINATION	VESSEL NAME	FREQUENCY
Maileppet	Tua Pejat	*KM Beriloga, KM Simatalu*	Monday, Thursday, Friday, Sunday
Sao (Katiet)	Sioban, Tua Pejat	*KM Simatalu*	Tuesday
Sikakap	Tua Pejat	*KM Simasini*	Wednesday, Sunday
Tua Pejat	Maileppet	*KM Beriloga, KM Simasini*	Tuesday, Wednesday, Thursday, Sunday
Tua Pejat	Sikakap	*KM Simasini*	Monday, Saturday

breaks, HT's is all about the creature comforts (hot showers, air-con, sports on cable) combined with killer views. Downtime fun includes paddle boarding, snorkelling, and snoozing under palm trees.

ℹ Information

The islands are largely undeveloped. Bring all necessities. There's an ATM in Tua Pejat, but don't rely on it.

ℹ Getting There & Away

AIR

Twelve-seater **Susi Air** (www.susiair.com) planes link Padang to Rokot airport on Pulau Sipora, but flights are unreliable, with weather delays and last-minute cancellations. Sometimes they agree to take surfboards for around US$100 per board, sometimes they refuse altogether. Book with **Regina Adventures** (p539) in Padang. Flights leave Padang on Tuesday, Thursday and Saturday, returning later the same day. The Indonesian government plans to extend the airport on Pulau Sipora to allow access by larger planes.

BOAT

The Mentawai Islands have become considerably easier to reach with the introduction of a 200-seater speedboat, *Mentawai Fast* (p549). There are also three ferries that make the overnight journey from the Sumatran mainland to the islands. Ferries take around 10 to 12 hours, depending on sea conditions. In Padang, ferries can be booked through most surfer-friendly homestays, as well as **tour agencies** (p538).

ℹ Getting Around

If you're travelling independently, travelling between islands or surfing spots is an easy way to drift into insolvency. You have three options: charter a speedboat, catch one of the three interisland ferries whose schedules are prone to changes and delay, or ask around to see if you can share a boat with another group.

Single-engine longboats can be hired from the main villages; if you want to hire a more comfortable two-engine speedboat with a roof, expect to pay considerably more. Sample charter routes (up to five passengers) include Muara Siberut to Ebay (1,500,000Rp, 1½ hours), Ebay to Playgrounds (1,000,000Rp, 30 minutes), Playgrounds to Tua Pejat (3,500,000Rp, 2½ hours) and Sioban to Katiet (1,500,000Rp, two hours). As petrol prices keep increasing, expect the charter prices to rise.

If you have more time than money, you can island-hop all the way from Siberut to Sao (near Katiet) using the three interisland ferries, *KM Beriloga*, *KM Simasini* and *KM Simatalu*; ticket prices start from 25,000Rp. That's right: a tiny fraction of speedboat costs, thanks to government subsidies. Check the latest timings with your fixer or your surf camp.

Bukittinggi

☎0752 / POP 112,000

The market town of Bukittinggi sits high above the valley mists as three sentinels – fire-breathing Merapi, benign Singgalang and distant Sago – all look on impassively. Sun-ripened crops grow large in the rich volcanic soil, as frogs call in the paddies, *bendis* (two-person horse-drawn carts) haul goods to the *pasa* (market), and the muezzin's call is heard through the town. Modern life seems far removed. Until 9am. Then the traffic starts up, and there's soon a mile-long jam around the bus terminal. The air turns the colour of diesel and the mosques counter the traffic by cranking up their amps. Such is the incongruity of modern Bukittinggi, blessed by nature, choked by mortals. Lush. Fertile. Busy. And at 930m above sea level, deliciously temperate all year round.

The town (alternatively named Tri Arga, which refers to the triumvirate of peaks) has had a chequered history, playing host at various times to Islamic reformists, Dutch colonials, Japanese invaders and Sumatran separatists. It's a good base for setting out to the Harau Valley and Danau Maninjau.

Sights

Taman Panorama VIEWPOINT
(Panorama Park; Jl Panorama; admission 10,000Rp) Taman Panorama, on the southern edge of town, overlooks the deep **Ngarai Sianok** (Sianok Canyon), where fruit bats swoop at sunset. Friendly guides will approach visitors to lead you through **Gua Jepang** (Japanese Caves), wartime defensive tunnels built by Japanese slave labour; settle on a price (around 30,000Rp) before continuing. Another path (and extra admission) gives you access to the **Koto Gadang** (Great Wall), a cheesy scaled-down Great Wall of China.

Pasar Atas MARKET
(Jl Minangkabau) Pasar Atas is a large, colourful market crammed with stalls selling fruit and vegetables, secondhand clothing and crafts. It's open daily. Find it on the east side of Jl Minangkabau.

Jam Gadang LANDMARK
(Big Clock Tower; btwn Jl Istana & Jl Sudirman) Built in the 1920s to house the clock, a gift from the Dutch queen, Jam Gadang is the town's focal point. Independence in 1945 saw the retrofit of a Minangkabau roof.

Benteng de Kock VIEWPOINT
(Benteng Fort; Jl Benteng; admission 7000Rp; 8am-5pm) Benteng de Kock was built by the Dutch during the Padri Wars. There's not much to it but it offers fine views over the town. The adjacent zoo is terrible (animals are underfed and live in cramped conditions) and we don't recommend visiting it.

Tours

Local tours fall into two categories – culture and nature – and can range from a half-day meander through neighbouring villages to a three-day jungle trek to Danau Maninjau, or an overnight assault on Gunung Merapi. For climbing in the nearby Harau Valley, contact Abdi Homestay (p558).

Full-day tours start at around 250,000Rp. Some tours have a minimum quota, though some guides and agencies also run solo tours by motorbike. If approached by a freelance guide, be clear about what you want, and what is and isn't included.

Armando DRIVING TOUR
(0812 6642 0468, 0812 674 1852; arisna_sejati@yahoo.co.id; day tour US$20-25) Armando is a helpful, knowledgeable English-speaking guide who is happy to give you cultural tours of the area around Bukittinggi on the back of his motorcycle. He also rents motorbikes if you want to ride your own.

Lite 'n' Easy Tours & Travel ADVENTURE TOUR
(0813 7453 7413; www.liteneasy.co.id; Jl Yos Sudarso 12) This friendly team offers West Sumatra tour options, including Gunung Merapi, the Harau Valley and Danau Maninjau, and trekking on the Mentawai island of Siberut.

Roni's Tour & Travel ADVENTURE TOUR
(0812 675 0688; www.ronistours.com; Orchid Hotel, Jl Teuku Umar) Based at the Orchid Hotel, Roni's can arrange everything from local tours to Danau Maninjau and the Harau Valley, to trips to further-afield locations such as the Mentawai Islands and the Kerinci Seblat National Park.

Festivals & Events

Oxen Racing SPORTS
(donation 10,000-15,000Rp) Local farmer-jockeys race twin oxen through a muddy paddy field, balancing precariously on the wooden runners. This spectacle, which animal welfare experts claim uses inhumane tactics to make the beasts run, takes place near Simasur market in Batu Sangkar, 41km southeast of Bukittinggi, on most Saturdays. Some enterprising locals try to charge foreigners 50,000Rp admission, but a donation is sufficient. Hello Guesthouse can help organise transport.

Horse Racing SPORTS
Bukittinggi holds an annual horse race at Bukit Ambacang in early March. Horses are ridden bareback and jockeys wear regional costumes, vying to win kudos for their village, and something for the onlookers' wallets. Solok and Sawahlunto also hold annual races.

Sleeping

Hotel tax is only added at top-end places and can be negotiated. On weekends and holidays, rooms can fill quickly with Indonesian visitors, but good weekday discounts can usually be negotiated. In Bukittinggi's temperate climate, hot water is more desirable than air-con.

★ **Hello Guesthouse** GUESTHOUSE $
(0752-21542; helloguesthouse12@gmail.com; Jl Teuku Umar 6b; dm/s/d from 75,000/120,000/150,000Rp;) This excellent new guesthouse with bright and modern

Bukittinggi

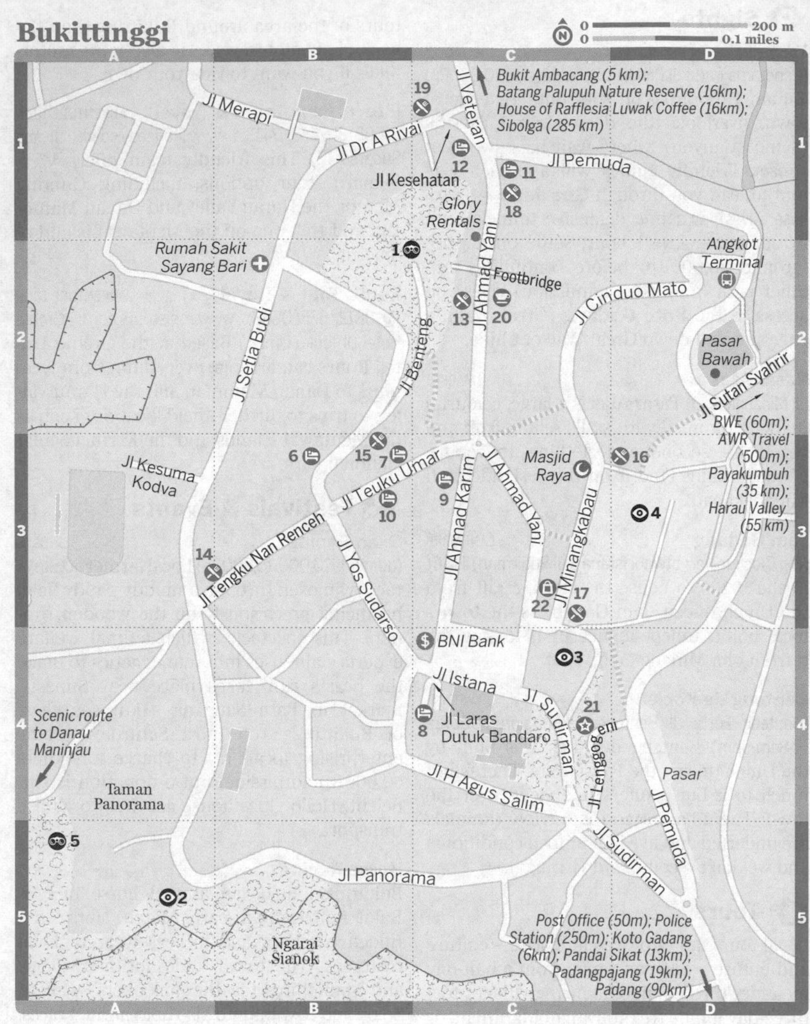

rooms is run by thoughtful owner Ling, who understands the needs of budget travellers. She is happy to provide maps of town, has displays on town attractions, and has thoughtfully kitted out her digs with super-comfy mattresses and earplugs to counter the guesthouse's proximity to a mosque. Spacious deluxe rooms come with balconies.

★Rajawali Homestay HOMESTAY $
(☎0752-31905; ulrich.rudolph@web.de; Jl Ahmad Yani 152; r 80,000Rp) The eight rooms at this friendly, central homestay are basic and come with Indonesian bathrooms. The irrepressible Ulrich is the best source of local (and regional) knowledge in town, with advice on detailed walks and motorcycle rides around Bukittinggi and excellent GPS maps. The roof terrace is perfect for sunset beers as you watch the twilight squadrons of bats flying past.

Orchid Hotel HOTEL $
(☎0752-32634; roni_orchid@hotmail.com; Jl Teuku Umar 11; r 120,000-150,000Rp; 📶) This popular backpacker inn is ground zero for arranging tours and activities with Roni's Tour & Travel (p551), which is highly praised by travellers. The rooms here could do with sprucing up though.

Bukittinggi

Sights

1 Benteng de Kock ... B2
2 Gua Jepang ... A5
3 Jam Gadang ... C4
4 Pasar Atas ... D3
5 Taman Panorama ... A5

Activities, Courses & Tours

Lite 'n' Easy Tours & Travel ... (see 13)
Roni's Tour & Travel ... (see 10)

Sleeping

6 Grand Rocky Hotel ... B3
7 Hello Guesthouse ... B3
8 Hills ... C4
9 Hotel Grand Kartini ... C3
10 Orchid Hotel ... B3
11 Rajawali Homestay ... C1
12 Treeli Hotel ... C1

Eating

13 Bedudal Cafe ... C2
14 De Kock Cafe ... A3
15 Nelayan ... B3
16 Ramadan Market ... D3
17 Simpang Raya ... C3
18 Turret Cafe ... C1
19 Waroeng Jalal Spesifik Sambal ... C1

Drinking & Nightlife

20 Rimbun Espresso & Brew Bar ... C2

Entertainment

21 Gedung Medan Nan Balinduang ... C4

Shopping

22 Makmur Arts ... C3

★Treeli Hotel BOUTIQUE HOTEL $$
(☎0752-625350; treeliboutiquehotel@gmail.com; Jl Kesehatan 36A; s/d/tr 315,000/500,000/780,000Rp; ❄📶) An excellent new addition to the rather tired midrange bunch, Treeli gets a lot of things right. Rooms are compact and quiet, with funky wallpaper, modern bathrooms and all sorts of mod cons. An excellent breakfast is served on the breezy roof terrace and the restaurant specialises in Chinese-style seafood dishes.

Hotel Grand Kartini HOTEL $$
(☎0752-33337; info@grandkartini.com; Jl Teuku Umar 5; r 375,000Rp; ❄📶) White is the predominant colour at this smart, super-central hotel. Rooms are compact yet comfortable, breakfast is good and fans can be provided if requested. Staff vary between helpful and utterly disinterested. Bring earplugs; there's a mosque next door. There's no lift.

Grand Rocky Hotel HOTEL $$$
(☎0751-627 000; www.rockyhotelsgroup.com; Jl Yos Sudarso; r incl breakfast 900,000-1,000,000Rp; ❄📶🏊) Adding a touch of Vegas glamour to Bukittinggi's top-end range, Grand Rocky stands sentinel above town, its lobby bustling with bow-tied staff. Rooms are spacious and modern, views stretch to the Sianok Canyon, and it's just a short downhill stroll to the brightish lights of central Bukittinggi. Check online for good discounts if you're keen for a mini-splurge.

Hills BUSINESS HOTEL $$$
(☎0752-35000; www.thehillshotel.com; Jl Laras Dutuk Bandaro; r 955,000-1,205,000Rp; ❄📶🏊) Commanding the heights like a Moorish citadel, Hills is usually full of VIPs and their security squads. Sports lovers can get active here with swimming, volleyball, basketball or table tennis, while the less inclined should drop by the hotel's Anai Bar for great views and relatively pricey drinks. Breakfast lets the side down, given the room price.

Eating & Drinking

Bukittinggi has long been the one place in Sumatra where weary road bums can give their poor chilli-nuked organs a chance to recover with lashings of lovingly bland Western food.

In the evenings, *sate* stalls spring up on the western side of the square, while the tents lining Jl Ahmad Yani cook up *mie* and nasi goreng (fried rice), *murtabak mesir* (filled pancake) and *roti cane* (flat bread).

Waroeng Jalal Spesifik Sambal INDONESIAN $
(Jl Kesehatan; mains 6000-20,000Rp; ⏰lunch & dinner; 📶🌶) Fans of spicy dishes will love this shady garden warung specialising mostly in sambal dishes. Squid, prawns, chicken, tofu, tempe and aubergine are all cooked in a rich, fiery chilli sauce, with *kangkung* (water spinach) providing a mild accompaniment. The beer may well be Bukittinggi's coldest. Get here early lest they run out of the most popular dishes.

MIXING BUSINESS WITH FRIENDSHIP

In Indonesia, the line between business and socialising isn't as distinct as it is in the West. We expect printed prices and obvious sales tactics. Without a price tag, we assume that it is free or done out of friendship. On the other side of the cultural divide, Sumatrans prefer business to resemble friendship: a little chit-chat, a steady sales pitch and a sort of telepathic understanding that payment is expected. They'd rather be helpful than entrepreneurial, but necessity dictates an income. The sluggish state of the Sumatran economy means that unemployment is high, with an overload of young resourceful men supporting themselves by guiding too few tourists.

Always ask about prices and don't assume that the quoted price is all-inclusive. You are expected to buy lunch and drinking water for your guide. If transport isn't included in the initial price, you should pay for this as well. A tip at the end is also welcome. Most guides are smokers and a pack costs about 10,000Rp. If all this seems steep, keep in mind that most guides don't have much more than a couple of crumpled rupiah to their name, and not a lot of other opportunity for employment.

Simpang Raya INDONESIAN $

(Jl Minangkabau; meals around 50,000Rp; lunch & dinner) The best place in town to sample the fabled Padang cuisine – spicy, flavourful dishes, with a particularly savoury *rendang* (beef coconut curry). Just ask for the assortment of what's on offer.

Ramadan Market MARKET $

(Jl Cinduo Mato; dishes from 10,000Rp; 8am-6pm) During the month of Ramadan, this car park turns into a whirlwind of culinary activity as dozens of stalls press sugar-cane juice, cook up *rendang*, concoct elaborate desserts and deep-fry all sorts of artery-clogging goodies. Locals shop here during the day in preparation for the breaking of the fast and it's a terrific place to try local dishes.

Bedudal Cafe CAFE $$

(Jl Ahmad Yani; mains 25,000-50,000Rp; lunch & dinner;) Make yourself comfortable amid the wooden carvings and posters of the Doors and order from an extensive menu of pizza, calzone, pasta, soups and whole roast chicken (250,000Rp, order in advance). The waiters break out the bongos and guitars for occasional jam sessions and it can get full.

De Kock Cafe INTERNATIONAL $$

(Jl Teuku Umar 18; mains 25,000-50,000Rp; lunch & dinner;) Under the same management as Bedudal Cafe, and with exactly the same menu, De Kock (cannon, in case you're wondering) serves a delicious mixture of Western and Indonesian dishes in arty, stone-walled surroundings. Order a roast chicken for you and your ravenous friends here.

Turret Cafe CAFE $

(Jl Ahmad Yani 140-142; mains 25,000-40,000Rp; breakfast, lunch & dinner;) A smattering of Western dishes with the odd inclusion of *mie goreng* (fried noodles) and green curry, cold beer, and the best guacamole in town. Prepare for a leisurely meal.

Nelayan SEAFOOD $$

(Jl Benteng; mains 40,000-60,000Rp; 6-11pm) Slightly more low key than its sister establishment in Padang (less neon!), Nelayan really delivers when it comes to sweet-and-sour squid, black pepper crab and other seafood delights. Portions are big enough to feed a legion. No prices on the menu, so ask before you order.

Rimbun Espresso & Brew Bar CAFE

(Jl Ahmad Yani; coffee from 25,000Rp; 9am-10pm Mon-Sat) The home of Bukittinggi's best coffee, with frappes, cappuccinos, frappuccinos and more, made with local beans. Latte art has finally made it to Bukittinggi and in the evenings this spot turns into a lively watering hole.

☆ Entertainment

Gedung Medan Nan Balinduang DANCE

(Jl Lenggogeni; tickets 50,000Rp; 8.30pm) Medan Nan Balinduang presents Minangkabau dance performances. Check with your lodgings for the latest schedule.

Shopping

Jl Minangkabau is good for shopping for woven bags and batik shirts, while upper Jl Ahmad Yani has traditional crafts and antiques.

Beautiful red and gold Minangkabau embroidery can be found in the *pasar*.

Makmur Arts ARTS & CRAFTS
(☎0752-22208; Jl Ahmad Yani 10; ⏰10am-8pm) An extensive collection of antiques, including Minangkabau brass *salapah panjang* (long boxes) used for storing lime and tobacco, silver *salapah padusi* for betel nut and lime, brass gongs, *kerises* (ceremonial daggers), 100-year-old wooden masks and heavy coconut-wood-and-brass necklaces formerly worn by local warriors.

ℹ Information

Banks and ATMs are scattered along Jl Ahmad Yani and Jl A Karim. Travel agencies line Jl Ahmad Yani for flight and bus bookings.

BNI Bank (Jl A Karim) Has ATM allowing withdrawals of up to 2,000,000Rp.

Post Office (Jl Sudirman; internet access per hr 6000Rp; ⏰8am-2pm Mon-Fri) South of town near the bus terminal.

Rumah Sakit Sayang Bari (Jl Dr Rivai) This hospital is just west of central Bukittinggi.

ℹ Getting There & Away

The chaos of the main bus terminal, Aur Kuning, 3km south of town, is easily reached by *angkot* (3000Rp); ask for 'terminal.' Heading to central Bukittinggi on arrival ask for 'Kampung China.'

The main bus terminal is useful for some bus departures but not all. Minibuses to Sibolga depart from offices on Jl Veteran, as do minibuses to Parapat.

Randy Tours & Travel (☎0813 7528 7345, 0812 6764 394; Jl Veteran 19) sells tickets for a daily 7pm service; scheduled door-to-door transfers to Padang are more convenient than waiting for a bus at the terminal. Most lodgings can point you in the right direction and assist with booking passage.

The best way to get to Dumai – for ferries to Melaka and Kuala Lupmpur in Malaysia – is with **BWE Travel** (☎0752 625 140, 0752 625 139; Jl Pemuda 81). Minibuses leave Bukittinggi nightly at 8pm, and departures are timed to link with the ferry from Dumai to Melaka. Prebooking is required. BWE can also book the ferry for you; you'll need to drop in the day before departure with your passport.

ℹ Getting Around

Angkot around town cost 3000Rp. *Bendi* start from 20,000Rp; bargain hard. An *ojek* from the bus terminal to the hotels costs 15,000Rp and a taxi costs 30,000Rp. Transfers to Padang airport can be arranged from any travel agent for around 55,000Rp. A private taxi to Padang airport is around 300,000Rp.

For motorbike rental, visit **Glory Rentals** (Tilal Bookshop, Jl Ahmad Yani; per day 60,000Rp) or enquire at your lodgings.

Around Bukittinggi

While Bukittinggi is an interesting market town, visitors come to explore the traditional architecture and craft of the Minangkabau countryside, to bag a volcano or two, or to hunt for the world's largest and smelliest flowers.

Handicraft Villages

★**Sumatera Loom** ARTS CENTRE
(☎0823 8936 8875, 0752-783 4253; www.songketminang.com; ⏰8-11am & 1-4pm Mon-Sat) Handicraft and textile fans should not miss Sumatera Loom near Simpang Bukit Batabuah, 7km southeast of Bukittinggi. Dedicated to revitalising the traditional Minangkabau art of *songket* (silver or gold-threaded cloth) weaving, the studio has trained young weavers (aged 18 to 28) in the art of producing Sumatra's finest. Replicas of heritage *songkets* based on antique cloths in museums and

BUSES FROM BUKITTINGGI

DESTINATION	FARE (RP)	DURATION (HR)	FREQUENCY
Bengkulu	125,000-150,000	18	2-3 daily
Danau Maninjau	17,000	1½	regular
Dumai	160,000	10	7pm daily
Medan	160,000-200,000	20	several daily
Padang	25,000-30,000	3-4	regular
Parapat (for Danau Toba)	180,000-200,000	16	several daily
Pekanbaru	130,000	7	6 daily
Sibolga (for Pulau Nias)	110,000-150,000	12	several daily

Around Bukittinggi

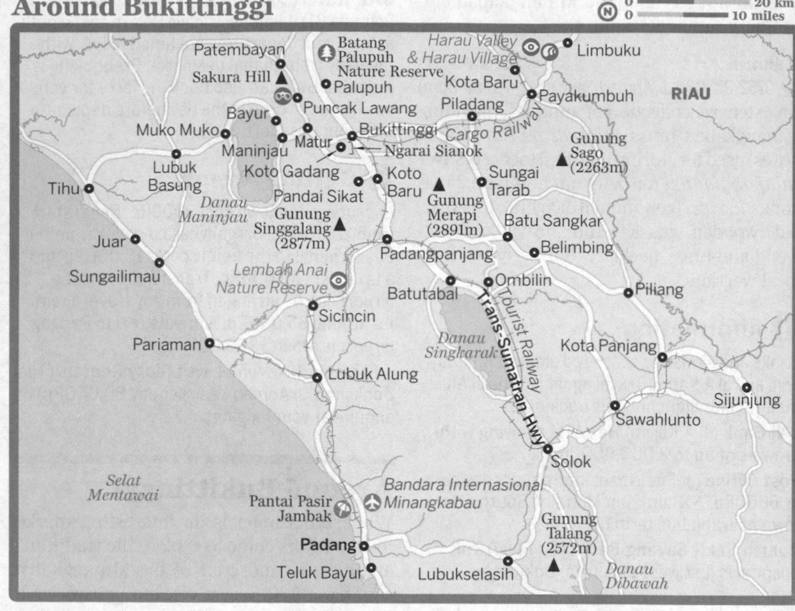

contemporary updates are both woven here. From the Aur Kuning bus terminal, catch a yellow *opelet* to Batu Taba (3500Rp), getting off at the SMKN1 (high school). Phone ahead.

This project was begun in 2005 by a Swiss architect who'd spent years studying *songkets*. The gold and silver thread used is the finest possible ordered from India rather than Singapore. You can visit the studio and watch weavers at work and purchase these extremely high-quality weavings.

Koto Gadang VILLAGE

Silversmiths occupy several old Dutch houses of Koto Gadang, 5km from Bukittinggi (an *angkot* costs 3000Rp). Alternatively, it's an hour's walk from Taman Panorama. **Silver Work** (Jln Sawahan 1) by Weli Syar Mak Wan is particularly worth seeking out for his intricate, fine models of traditional houses, delicate rings and more.

Pandai Sikat VILLAGE

Pandai Sikat (Clever Craftsmen) is famous for *songket* (silver or gold-threaded cloth) weaving and carving building decorations out of wood. The village is 13km south of Bukittinggi. Take an *angkot* (5000Rp) from Aur Kuning.

South of Bukittinggi

The rich volcanic soil of the hilly countryside around Bukittinggi oozes fertility. Stop by the roadside and you can spot cinnamon, betel nut, avocado, coffee, mango and papaya trees. Rice, tapioca and potatoes grow in terraces, while bamboo waterwheels feed irrigation ditches and drive wooden grinding mills. You may see a wedding parade. The bride and groom, dressed in full traditional regalia, are accompanied by musicians, family members and half the village. The Minangkabau tribal flags (red, black and yellow) typically mark the site of the festivities.

The sights in this area can be combined into a scenic day tour, either by renting a motorbike, taking a motorbike tour (300,000Rp) or hiring a car and driver (600,000Rp).

Rumah Gadang Pagaruyung PALACE

(King's Palace) In the village of Silinduang Bulan, 5km north of Batu Sangkar, the heartland of the red Tanah Datar clan of Minangkabau, Rumah Gadang Pagaruyung is a scaled-down replica of the former home of the rulers of the ancient Minangkabau kingdom of Payaruyung. A fire razed it to the ground in 2007, but it has been reconstructed. Batu Sangkar can be reached via public bus (22,000Rp, 1½ hours) from Bukittinggi, where you can continue by *ojek* (8,000Rp) to Silinduang Bulan.

Istano Silinduang Bulan PALACE

(Queen's Palace; admission 5000Rp) Near the King's Palace in Silinduang Bulan, 5km north of Batu Sangkar, Istano Silinduang Bulan was damaged by lightning in 2011, but has been rebuilt since. This building is still used for important clan meetings.

Conservatorium of Traditional Music ARTS CENTRE

(STSI, ASKI; Jl Bundo Kanduang 35; ⌚8am-3pm Mon-Thu, to noon Fri) Ethno-musicologists make the pilgrimage to the town of Padangpanjang, 19km south of Bukittinggi, to see the Conservatorium of Traditional Music. Minangkabau dance and music are preserved and performed here. Regular buses run between Bukittinggi and Padangpanjang (12,000Rp).

Belimbing VILLAGE

(entry by donation) Belimbing, a village southeast of Batu Sangkar, is one of the largest surviving collections of traditional architecture in the highlands. Many of the homes are 300 years old and in various states of decay. Most owners have built modern homes nearby and use the relics for ceremonial purposes.

Batang Palupuh Nature Reserve & Around

Batang Palupuh Nature Reserve NATURE RESERVE

The Batang Palupuh Nature Reserve, 16km north of Bukittinggi, is home to many orchid species, as well as the massive Rafflesia arnoldii and Amorphophallus titanium, the largest flowers on the planet – the latter endemic to Sumatra. The rafflesia blooms throughout the year, if briefly, whereas you have to be incredibly lucky to catch the Amorphophallus in bloom at all. Both flowers reek like roadkill. Local buses to Palupuh cost 8000Rp and hiring a guide to lead you to the flowers is around 100,000Rp.

The blossom of the parasitic rafflesia measures nearly a metre across and can weigh up to 11kg, while the inflorescence of Amorphophallus can extend to over 3m in circumference.

House of Rafflesia Luwak Coffee COFFEE PLANTATION

(☎0752-700 0749, 0813 7417 8971; www.rafflesialuwakcoffee.org; Desa Batang Palupuh) At this plantation in Batang Palupuh, friendly owner Umul Khairi is happy to explain the process of harvesting, drying and roasting *kopi luwak* – a smooth, earthy brew produced from coffee beans ingested and excreted by civets (cal-like mammals). While the *luwak* coffee industry has come under fire for 'farming' civets to meet demand for the brew, the House of Rafflesia still operates in the traditional way, collecting wild civet 'poo' off the jungle floor. You can also taste (20,000Rp) and purchase (from 200,000Rp) the beans. Book via the website or phone to confirm at least one day before you visit.

Minangkabau cooking classes (per person 350,000Rp) are also on offer. The multicourse menu includes beef *rendang* and chicken curry, and Umul will even run the course for solo travellers.

Joni GUIDE

(☎0813 7436 0439) Local, English-speaking, enthusiastic guide Joni is your best bet for finding the elusive rafflesia as he knows when everything is blooming and where. A morning departure from Bukittinggi is recommended to avoid the occasional influx of tour buses.

MINANGKABAU WOMEN RULE

Though Minangkabau society is Islamic, it's still matrilineal. According to Minangkabau *adat* (traditional laws and regulations), property and wealth are passed down through the female line. Every Minangkabau belongs to his or her mother's clan. At the basic level of the clan is the *sapariouk*, those matri-related kin, who eat together. These include the mother, the grandchildren and the son-in-law. The name comes from the word *periouk* (rice pot). The eldest living female is the matriarch. The most important male member of the household is the mother's eldest brother, who replaces the father in being responsible for the children's education, upbringing and marriage prospects. But consensus is at the core of the Minangkabau ruling philosophy and the division of power between the sexes is regarded as complementary – like the skin and the nail act together to form the fingertip, according to a local expression.

WORTH A TRIP

HARAU VALLEY

Heading east from Bukittinggi takes you through the tapioca-growing area of **Piladang**, famous for *keropok* (tapioca crackers), and the sprawling agricultural centre of **Payakumbuh**. Of Minangkabau's three clans, this is the territory of the 50 Kota (50 Villages) yellow branch. Rice paddies with wallowing buffalo flank the narrow road that leads to the tiny village of Harau, the volcanoes looming behind them. Venture another 3km and spectacular, vertical 100m cliffs, seemingly made of painted rock, rise up to enclose the claustrophobic Harau Valley, 15km northeast of Payakumbuh and 55km from Bukittinggi.

The most direct way to reach Harau from Bukittinggi is by renting a motorbike (65,000Rp to 80,000Rp) or taking an *ojek* (200,000Rp, two hours). Alternatively, take a Po Sarah Group minibus from the bus terminal to Tanjung Pati (15,000Rp), and then take an *ojek* the rest of the way (20,000Rp).

Lemba Harau (admission 5000Rp) and other waterfalls in the valley attract daytrippers from Bukittinggi, particularly during the rainy season; if the weather's been dry, they're reduced to mere trickles.

Rock climbing is also a big attraction in the Harau Valley, which is the best-developed rock-climbing area in Sumatra. An excellent local contact is **Ikbal** (☎0852 6378 1842) at the Abdi Homestay, who offers guided climbing excursions for US$25. Check out www.climbing.com and www.rockclimbing.com for blogs and more information.

Abdi Homestay (☎0852 6378 1842; ikbalharau@yahoo.com; Kab 50 Kota; per person 100,000-150,000Rp) Run by young and energetic owners, Ikbal and Noni, Abdi Homestay is the loveliest place to stay in the Harau Valley. Eight adorable thatched bungalows (with mosquito nets and bamboo showers) sit on the edge of verdant rice paddies and lotus ponds; the pricier ones have views. Meals include one of the best chicken *rendang* you'll ever have, and Ikbal leads day hikes (US$20 per person) to the top of the cliffs.

Lembah Echo (☎0812 6619 1501; www.lembahecho.com; Taratang Lb Limpato; r with shared bathroom 90,000Rp, r incl breakfast 150,000-600,000Rp) Sitting right under the cliffs in the narrowest part of the valley is Lembah Echo, its beautiful grounds encroached on by jungle full of monkeys. Lodgings range from very basic thatched huts that are verging on decrepit to the Minangkabau-style cottages and stylish (if dark) rooms with hardwood furniture and hot showers. Little English spoken and staff can be unhelpful.

Gunung Merapi & Gunung Singgalang

Gunung Merapi VOLCANO
(admission 10,000Rp) The smouldering summit of Gunung Merapi (2891m), Sumatra's most active volcano, looms large over Bukittinggi around 16km to the east. If Merapi is benign, then visitors typically hike overnight to view sunrise from the summit from the village of Koto Baru; it's a 12-hour round trip. You'll need good walking boots, warm clothing, a torch, food and drink and a guide. Travel agencies in Bukittinggi do guided trips to Merapi for around US$40 per person (minimum two people).

Gunung Singgalang VOLCANO
(admission 10,000Rp) Dormant Gunung Singgalang (2877m) is a more adventurous undertaking than Gunung Merapi, and it's very difficult to find someone in Bukittinggi to guide you up. Highly recommended English-speaking guide Dedi (☎0813 7425 1312), based in Pandai Sikat – the best starting point for the climb – charges 200,000Rp and the climb is an eight- to nine-hour round-trip. There are campsites by the beautiful crater lake, Telago Dewi.

Danau Maninjau

☎0752

The first glimpse of this perfectly formed volcanic lake sucks your breath away as you lurch over the caldera lip and hurtle towards the first of the 44 hairpin bends down (yep, they're numbered) to the lakeshore. Monkeys watch your progress from the crash barriers as the road takes you down from the lush rainforest of the highlands to the ever-expanding farms and paddies of the lowlands.

When the traveller tide receded from Bukittinggi, Danau Maninjau was left high and dry. The locals looked to more sustainable sources of income and aquaculture to fill the void. Fish farms now dot the lake foreshore.

Ground zero is the intersection where the Bukittinggi highway meets the lake road in the middle of Maninjau village. Turn left or right and drive 60km and you'll end up back here. The lake is 17km long, 8km wide and 460m above sea level. Most places of interest spread out north along the road to Bayur (3.5km) and beyond. If coming by bus, tell the conductor where you're staying and you'll be dropped off at the right spot.

Sights & Activities

Swimming and canoeing in the lake (warmed by subterranean springs) are still the main draw cards but there are plenty of other options.

The caldera, covered in rainforest that hides waterfalls and traditional villages, is a hiker's dream. Hike to the rim from Bayur, or cheat by catching the bus up the hill to Matur, then walking back down via the lookout at **Puncak Lawang**. Check out the map at Beach Guest House for more good trekking information.

If you want to zip around the lake on a moped that takes roughly three hours. Beach Guest House organises both guided hikes and motorbike tours.

Festivals & Events

Rakik Rakik CULTURAL

Rakik Rakik is celebrated on the night before Idul Fitri (the end of Ramadan) by building a platform to hold a replica Minangkabau house and mosque. The offering is then floated out onto the lake on canoes, accompanied by fireworks and revelry.

Sleeping

The majority of Maninjau options front onto aquaculture. There is a sprinkling of hotels, cheap losmen and restaurants between Maninjau and Bayur. Outside Maninjau village, most losmen are reached by walking along rice-paddy paths, so look for the sign by the roadside.

★ **Beach Guest House** GUESTHOUSE $

(0752-861799, 0813 6379 7005; www.beachguesthousemaninjau.com; Jl Raya Maninjau; dm 40,000, r 75,000-150,000;) Run by a friendly, energetic local couple, this is Danau Maninjau's bona fide traveller central. Owners organise excursions, from round-the-lake bicycle or motorbike jaunts to hiking the

Danau Maninjau

Danau Maninjau

Sleeping

1 Arlen Nova's Paradise A1
2 Beach Guest House B4
3 House of Annisa B5
4 Muaro Beach Bungalows B4

Eating

Bagoes Cafe .... (see 2)
5 Waterfront Zalino B3

caldera (seven hours). As for the digs, choose between bunking in the dorm or a range of rooms, the plushest lined up on the lakefront and boasting hot showers.

Muaro Beach Bungalows BUNGALOW **$**
(☎0813 3924 0042, 0752-61189; neni967@yahoo.com; Jl Muaro Pisang 53, Maninjau; r 80,000-120,000Rp; Wi-Fi) Down a maze of footpaths (about 300m northwest of the main intersection), these beachfront bungalows are the best value in Maninjau. The beach is (almost) free of aquaculture and fish farming, and there's a good restaurant that's also open to nonguests. Local tours and activities are on offer.

Arlen Nova's Paradise BUNGALOW **$**
(☎0853 7475 9288; www.nova-maninjau.id.or.id; Sungai-Rangeh; r 175,000Rp) Walk through rice paddies (5.5km north of Maninjau) to these five simple bungalows, draped in passion-fruit vines on a private beach, with nary a fish pond in sight. The setting is gorgeous and a plethora of friendly cats hang out at the on-site restaurant, but the lodgings could use some TLC.

House of Annisa HISTORIC HOTEL **$$**
(☎0857 6604 1558; Jl H Udin Rahmani, Maninjau; r 280,000Rp) This wonderful heritage Dutch villa has been lovingly restored by the great-grandchildren of the original owners. There are only three romantic rooms, one with a brass four-poster bed festooned with mirrors; bathrooms are shared. Unique touches include elegant Arabic calligraphy carved into the outside walls and a gorgeous balcony filled with antique benches and chairs. Call in advance.

Eating

Most of the guesthouses serve the usual standards such as nasi goreng and *mie goreng*, some Western favourites and freshly caught fish.

Bagoes Cafe CAFE **$**
(Maninjau; mains 20,000-30,000Rp; ⊙breakfast, lunch & dinner; Wi-Fi; vegetarian) This traveller favourite, attached to Beach House in the north part of Maninjau village, combines backpacker staples with local dishes such as vegetable gado gado and *mie goreng*. Waves lap at the deck and movie nights, accompanied by ice-cold Bintang, take place among the quirky wall art.

Waterfront Zalino INDONESIAN **$$**
(☎0815 3541 1074; mains 30,000-85,000Rp; ⊙lunch & dinner) A great lakeside location showcases some exotic local specialities like *dendeng kijang balado* (fried deer with chilli and red pepper), *udang* (freshwater lake shrimp) and grilled catfish. If you're keen to go trekking, ask if Zal – AKA 'Mr Porcupine' – is around. Waterfront Zalino is in Gasang, around 1km north of Maninjau's main intersection.

> LOCAL KNOWLEDGE
>
> ### SCENIC ROUTE TO DANAU MANINJAU
>
> If you have your own wheels, take the quiet road used by locals that zigzags picturesquely through the Sianok Canyon, passing through quiet villages and meandering around jungle-thick corners. Pause at the first bridge you come to for an excellent view of the pointed, greenery-clad Taruko karst that looms above the river. Detour along the unpaved road to the namesake restaurant with a tremendous view of it. The road eventually joins the main road down to Danau Maninjau, so you don't miss any of the hairpin bends!

Information

BRI Bank Has an ATM, but it only dispenses small amounts. Stock up on rupiah in Bukittinggi.

PT Kesuma Tour & Travel (☎0752-61422, 0812 669 9661; www.sumatratravelling.com; Jl Panurunan Air Hangat) Arranges transfers to Bukittinggii and jungle treks. Also rents outdoor equipment.

Getting There & Around

Buses run hourly between Maninjau and Bukittinggi (20,000Rp, 1¾ hours). Taxis from Bukittinggi start from 160,000Rp.

Rent mountain bikes (per day 45,000Rp), motorcycles (per day 100,000Rp) and canoes (per day 40,000Rp) from **PT Kesuma Tour & Travel** or **Waterfront Zalino**.

Minibuses (3000Rp) travel the lake road during daylight hours. An *ojek* from the intersection to Bayur will cost around 10,000Rp.

Kerinci Valley

☎0748 / POP 253,000

Kerinci is a stunning mountain valley tucked away high in the Bukit Barisan on Jambi's western border. Many of the cool, lush forests are protected as the Kerinci Seblat National Park, the last stronghold of the

Sumatran tiger. The valley's many lakes and jungle-shrouded mountains make it a big draw for hikers in search of off-the-beaten-track adventure. To the south is picturesque Danau Kerinci and a patchwork of rich farmland. Tea and cinnamon account for much of the valley's wealth, with the former ringing the higher villages and the latter forming a buffer between the farmland and rainforest.

Minangkabau and native Kerincinese make up most of the population, with a sprinkling of Batak and Javanese who are drawn by the rich soil. Kerinci is in Jambi province but has a close geographic proximity to Padang.

Getting There & Away

Safa Marwa (0748-22376; Jl Yos Sudarso 20) in Sungai Penuh is one of several companies that organises onward travel in buses and shared minibuses. If you're leaving Kersik Tua for Padang or Bukittinggi, buses can usually pick up en route from Sungai Penuh if your guesthouse books you passage in advance.

Getting Around

Most places in the valley are accessible by the white minibuses that leave the terminal and surrounding area near the market. Sample destinations and fares include Danau Kerinci (15,000Rp, 1½ hours), Kersik Tua (10,000Rp, one hour) and Pelompek (15,000Rp, 1½hours).

Sungai Penuh

Sungai Penuh (Full River) is the regional administrative centre and transport hub for the valley. There is a lively market and reliable internet, and the town makes an excellent base for ventures into the wilds of Kerinci Seblat National Park and surrounding villages.

Sights

Mesjid Agung Pondok Tinggi MOSQUE
(admission by donation) Head west up Jl Sudirman (past the post office) and turn left, where you'll find this old wooden mosque with its pagoda-style roof. Built in 1874 without a single nail, the interior contains elaborately carved beams and old Dutch tiles. Ask the caretaker for permission and cover up.

Tours

Wild Sumatra Adventures CULTURAL TOUR
(0812 6017 3651; www.wildsumatra.com; Lake Kaco hike for 2 people 1,400,000Rp, 3-day Mount Tujuh adventure for 2 people 4,500,000Rp) Based in Sungai Penuh, enthusiastic expat Luke Mackin is a passionate and knowledgeable local contact for information on the surrounding area, especially the Kerinci Seblat National Park. He has numerous alliances with local trekking guides and villages, is keen to introduce travellers to the area's many attractions and can organise guides and transport to all attractions described.

Sleeping

Budget accommodation in Sungai Penuh tends to be fairly grim. If you're looking for greater cultural immersion, Wild Sumatra Adventures can help you organise homestays in villages surrounding Sungai Penuh. Expect to pay around 50,000Rp per night to stay with a local family.

Hotel Yani HOTEL $
(0748-21409; Jl Muradi 1; r 80,000-250,000;) The pick of Sungai Penuh's cheapies has a barrack vibe, water stains on the walls, cold bucket showers and narrow, short beds most suitable. Central location but no breakfast.

★ **Hotel Kerinci** HOTEL $$
(0748-324459; Jl Muradi 28; r 120,000-425,000Rp;) By far the snazziest option in Sungai Penuh, this new and fairly central hotel consists of spotless and almost identical, business-hotel-style rooms, each with a funky purple wall and modern bathroom, with the exception of the cheapies (120,000Rp that share facilities). The suites are the largest, but otherwise the price depends on whether the room has air-con or fan.

BUSES FROM KERINCI VALLEY

DESTINATION	FARE (RP)	DURATION (HR)	FREQUENCY
Bengkulu	150,000	10-12	daily at 10am
Bukittinggi	130,000	10	daily at 7pm
Jambi	120,000-150,000	10	daily at 9am, 7pm
Padang	100,000-130,000	8	daily at 9am, 7pm

Hotel Jaya Wisata HOTEL $$
(☎0748-21221; Jl Martadinata 7; r incl breakfast 170,000-680,000Rp; ❄📶) Your options here range from rather depressing cold-water rooms downstairs that could seriously use a coat of paint, to more spacious and stylish rooms upstairs. The location is great – near the cheap eats of the night market.

Eating & Drinking

Kerinci is known for the local speciality of *dendeng batokok* (charcoal-grilled strips of pounded beef). Street stalls pop up in the evening along Jl Teuku Umar, a block from the square, and along main Jl Muradi.

Pasar Malam MARKET $
(off Jl Muradi; meals from 20,000Rp; ⏰5-10pm) The centrally located *pasar malam* (night market) is a terrific place to try local specialities, such as *martabak mesir* (square pancake filled with meat and vegetables), *mie bakso* (noodle soup with meatballs), *martabak* (sweet pancake filled with coconut or banana) and *sate* with a red gravy rather than peanut sauce.

Koi Taste Cafe INTERNATIONAL $
(Jl Muradi; mains 11,000-25,000Rp; ⏰4-10pm) This friendly new place along the main street en route to Danau Kerinci is decked out with Che Guevara posters, has low Indo-style seating and an eclectic menu. Many dishes are variations on *mie goreng* and nasi goreng, but you'll also find the more ambitious buffalo wings, tom yum soup and chicken teriyaki.

Minang Soto INDONESIAN $
(Jl Muradi; dishes from 12,000Rp; ⏰lunch & dinner) At this busy Padang-style eatery you're presented with scores of small, spicy dishes, such as the earthy *rendang* and *ayam* sambal. You're only supposed to pay for the dishes you sample from.

Q2 Cafe INTERNATIONAL $$
(mains 15,000-45,000Rp; ⏰9am-10pm) Worth a short ride from the centre, this ambitious outdoorsy restaurant mixes it up with numerous *lele* (catfish) dishes, as well as the tasty *mie* claypot and even Chicken Gordon [sic] Bleu. Splurge on the tom yum lobster and wash it down with such concoctions as Fruit My Love, cappuccino float and Moon Rever.

Wiyuka Coffee COFFEE
(Jl Kamaruddin; ⏰9am-7pm; 📶) Excellent new coffee shop giving Sungai Penuh a cosmopolitan touch. You can sample quality beans from all over Sumatra and beyond, and there's even free wi-fi. Traveller hangout potential.

Information

BNI Bank (Jl Ahmad Yani) The centrally located BNI Bank ATM dispenses up to 2,000,000Rp.

Kantor Taman Nasional Kerinci Seblat (Kerinci Seblat National Park Office, TNKS; ☎0748-22250; Jl Basuki Rahmat 11) The park headquarters sells permits; they never seem to answer the phone, so just turn up. If it's closed, you can get permits from losmen in Kersik Tua.

Post Office (Jl Sudirman 1; ⏰8am-4pm) Main post office.

Kersik Tua

At 1500m, surrounded by tea plantations and dominated by the massive cone of Gunung Kerinci (3805m), Kersik Tua makes a pleasant base for scaling the imposing volcano.

The town sprawls along one side of the main road, with tea plantations and the mountain on the other. The national park turn-off is indicated by a *harimau* (Sumatran tiger) statue.

Trekking gear, supplies, guides and transport can all be arranged here. There's a market on Saturday and a BNI Bank ATM. The village is 52km north of Sungai Penuh on the road to Padang and can be reached by any Padang–Kerinci bus. Minibuses (10,000Rp, 1½ hours) trundle north from Sungai Penuh to Kersik Tua between 8am and 5pm and north from Kersik Tua to Pelompek (5000Rp), 8km away.

There are several basic homestays spread out along the main road. Just south of the statue on the main road is **Subandi Homestay** (☎0748-357 009, 0812 7411 4273; subandi.homestay@gmail.com; r 150,000Rp), the best base camp in the village. Subandi is the only English-speaking homestay owner and a fount of local knowledge who can organise mountain, jungle and wildlife treks of varying difficulty and duration.

The southernmost option in Kersik Tua, **Family Homestay** (☎0852 6626 6992, 0748-357080; r 150,000Rp), is uphill next to the tea plantation and then left along the football field. It offers cosy carpeted rooms and hot water on request. Alternatively, **Homestay Paiman** (☎0748-357 030; r 75,000Rp), 200m south of Subandi Homestay, is your fallback option. It's a friendly place, but the beds are so ancient they're hammock-shaped.

ORANG PENDEK

Every culture that has lived among trees tells stories about elusive creatures that straddle myth and reality. Tales about leprechauns, fairies and even Sasquatch have existed for so long that it is impossible to determine which came first: the spotting or the story. The Indonesian version of these myth makers is the *orang pendek*, which has been occasionally spotted but more frequently talked about in the Kerinci forests for generations.

Villagers who claim to have seen *orang pendek* describe the creature as being about 1m tall, more ape than human, but walking upright on the ground. The creature's reclusive habits made it a celebrity in local mythology. Common folk stories say that the *orang pendek* has feet that face backwards so that it can't be tracked through the forest or that it belongs to the supernatural not the world of flesh and blood. Others say that the first-hand accounts were only spottings of sun bears.

Scientists have joined the conversation by tramping through the forest hoping to document the existence of *orang pendek*. British researchers succeeded in making a plaster cast of an animal footprint that fits the *orang pendek* description and doesn't match any other known primate. Hair samples with no other documented matches have also led researchers to believe that there is merit to the local lore. Two members of Fauna & Flora International, a British-based research team, even reported separate sightings, but were unable to collect conclusive evidence. Researchers sponsored by the National Geographic Society have resumed the search by placing motion-sensitive cameras in strategic spots in the jungle. So little is known about this region and so many areas are so remote that researchers are hopeful that the *orang pendek* will eventually wander into the frame.

If nothing else, the *orang pendek* helps illuminate aspects of Sumatrans' linguistic and cultural relationship with the jungle. Bahasa Indonesia makes little distinction between man and ape; for example, 'orang-utan' (forest man) or 'orang rimba' ('people of the forest,' the preferred term for the Kubu tribe) may reflect a perceived blood tie between forest dwellers. This imprecision is often used for comic effect. A common joke is that the *orang pendek* (which means 'short man') does indeed exist, followed by the punch line that the shortest person in the room is the missing link.

Pelompek

The small village of Pelompek, 8km north of Kersik Tua, makes a good base for a night or two if you're looking to climb Gunung Tajuh. **Homestay Gunung Tujuh** (☎0852 724 5940; r 150,000Rp) is the only place to stay in the village. Overlooking the market and a block away from the main street, its rooms are spacious, with Indonesian bucket showers, and the proprietress fusses over her guests like a mother hen in spite of the language barrier.

Buses pass along the main street fairly regularly to Kersik Tua (5000Rp) and Sungai Penuh (15,000Rp).

Kerinci Seblat National Park

The largest national park in Sumatra, Kerinci Seblat National Park (Taman Nasional Kerinci Seblat; TNKS), covers a 350km swathe of the Bukit Barisan range and protects 13,791 sq km of prime equatorial rainforest spread over four provinces, with almost 40% of the park falling within Jambi's boundaries.

Most of the protected area is dense rainforest, and its inaccessibility is the very reason the park is one of the last strongholds of the endangered *harimau* (Sumatran tiger). Kerinci Seblat National Park is known as having the highest population and occurrence of tigers anywhere in Sumatra, with 80% of the park showing signs of the species.

Because of the great elevation range within the park, Kerinci has a unique diversity of flora and fauna. Edelweiss and other high-altitude flowers grow in the forest. Lower altitudes bring pitcher plants, orchids, rafflesia and the giant *Amorphophallus*.

As with many of Sumatra's protected areas, encroachment by farmers, illegal logging and poaching are all serious issues for Kerinci, the latter dramatically on the rise in 2014. The park wardens are a passionate and dedicated lot, and they do stop a lot of the poaching, but greater numbers and more funds are desperately needed. The plight of the Sumatran tiger has recently been highlighted by Sir David Attenborough as part of Fauna & Flora International's Tiger Project (www.fauna-flora.org), aimed at saving the Sumatran tiger from extinction.

Kerinci Seblat National Park sees relatively few visitors, and the park's minimal tourist infrastructure is limited to the north around the dual attractions of Gunung Kerinci and Gunung Tujuh. While the park's northern region is more visited, the southern area features elephants – absent in the north – and also has interesting forest-edge communities living within the park's boundaries, as well as excellent trekking through pristine forests. Contact Luke Mackin of Wild Sumatra Adventures (p561) in Sungai Penuh if you're keen to explore the park's southern reaches by organising guides and treks. There are buffer areas for local cultivation and agriculture at the northern and southern edges of the park.

Permits and guides are required to enter the park. Both can be arranged at the park office (p562) in Sungai Penuh or through your losmen. There's a park office at the entrance to Danau Gunung Tujuh, but it's rarely staffed.

Permits cost 150,000Rp, guide rates are around 350,000Rp per day for an English-speaking guide, and porters can be hired for 150,000Rp to 200,000Rp per day. Be sure to clarify exactly what the rate entails, as camping gear, food and transport may be considered additional costs.

Kerinci's climate is temperate, and downright cold as you gain altitude. Bring warm clothes and rain gear.

Sights & Activities

★Gunung Kerinci VOLCANO

Dominating the northern end of the park is Gunung Kerinci (3805m), Southeast Asia's tallest volcano and one of Sumatra's most active. On clear days the summit offers fantastic views of Danau Gunung Tujuh and the surrounding valleys and mountains.

Summit treks usually start from the national park entrance, 5km from Kersik Tua, and tackle the mountain over two days, camping overnight. A fully guided trip with food, permits, transport and all gear thrown in costs around 1,500,000Rp. Fully self-sufficient parties needing only a guide will pay around 700,000Rp.

The highest camp site, at 3400m, is normally reached after six hours. The following morning, allow an hour in the predawn to reach the summit by sunrise. The path is very steep and eroded, and above the treeline the scree is extremely slippery. A guide is mandatory and you'll need full camping gear, warm and waterproof clothes, and head torch (all of which can be hired in Kersik Tua). Nights are freezing. Do not attempt the climb in wet weather.

Botanists and twitchers from around the world come for the rare flora and fauna, such as Javanese edelweiss, Schneider's pitta and the crested wood partridge. Nepthenes (pitcher plants), squirrels, geckos and long-tailed macaques can be found in the lower forest, and troops of yellow-handed mitered langurs are also seen.

While the park does have a significant tiger population, spying one in the wild is very rare, and sightings are usually restricted to paw prints and droppings. In previous centuries, local Kerinci people were thought to be weretigers (a shape-shifting synthesis of man and beast), and the tiger is still important in local mysticism and mythology.

Danau Gunung Tujuh LAKE

(Seven Mountain Lake) At 1996m, the beautiful caldera of Danau Gunung Tujuh is the highest in Southeast Asia and makes for a pleasant day ascent or part of a multiday trek. It takes 3½ hours to climb to the lake from the park entrance, which is 2km from the village of Pelompek. Camp near the lake if staying overnight. An *ojek* to the trailhead costs around 10,000Rp. Subandi Homestay (p562) in Kersik Tua can organise two- or three-day treks, including a canoe crossing.

Wildlife in this area includes tapirs and Siamang gibbons, and one of the signature sounds of the Kerinci forests is the hooting and howling call of the gibbon.

Pelompek is 8km north of Kersik Tua (bus 10,000Rp) and 60km from Sungai Penuh (15,000Rp). You'll need a park permit; if the park office is closed, ask next door at the tiny **Losmen Pak Edes** (r 70,000Rp), which also has two very basic rooms and can arrange guides.

Danau Kaco LAKE

(Glass Lake) A two- to three-hour ramble through the jungle along a largely flat (and muddy) path, Danau Kaco stops you dead in your tracks because you just can't believe the sight of this small, sapphire-coloured swimming hole, with incredible visibility down its

20m depths. The trail starts near the village of Lempur, an hour's drive from Sungai Penuh.

Danau Kerinci LAKE
Danau Kerinci, 20km south of Sungai Penuh, is a sizeable lake nestled between Gunung Raya (2535m) and rice paddies. Stone carvings around the lake suggest that the area supported a sizeable population in megalithic times. **Batu Gong** (Gong Stone), in the village of Muak, 25km from Sungai Penuh, is thought to have been carved 2000 years ago. To reach the lake, catch a public bus from Sungai Penuh to Sanggaran Agung (13,000Rp). The last return bus leaves around 4pm.

There is an annual festival held in July on the shores of the lake, with traditional Kerinci dance and music.

Gunung Kunyit VOLCANO
Visited by a fraction of hikers who take on its more famous neighbour, this active volcano, at the southern end of the Kerinci Valley, presents a wonderful challenge. It's a six-hour hike to the summit through cloud forest from the village of Talang Kumuning, passing sulphur vents en route. You can also look for the hot spring within the crater.

Goa Kasah CAVE
Considered to be the largest cave system in the Kerinci Valley, and not yet fully explored, this cave makes for a good day trek (around 2½ hours one way) from the village of Sungai Sampun. The hike isn't very strenuous, and runs largely through picturesque rice fields before ascending some forested foothills.

Air Terjun Telun Berasap WATERFALL
Impressive waterfalls dot the whole valley. The easiest to find are the **Air Terjun Telun Berasap** in the 'Letter W' village 4km north of Pelompek. Look for the 'Air Terjun Telun Berasap' sign then walk 300m to a deep, fern-lined ravine where a thunderous torrent of water crashes onto rocks below.

More impressive falls include the 75m-tall Pancuran Rayo, reachable via a half-hour drive south and then a three-hour hike from Sungai Penuh.

Night Safari SAFARI
Easily doable from Sungai Penuh, the night safari involves driving a stretch of the winding southbound road that passes through the Kerinci Seblat National Park after dark, looking for wildlife in the trees and undergrowth with torches. If you're lucky, you'll spot civets, owls and even the odd tiger. Walking is not advisable, lest you become a cat's dinner.

Renah Kemumu HIKING
This is an excellent jungle trek to the remote village of Renah Kemumu that sits in the jungle within the boundaries of the national park. It takes around 12 to 15 hours one way, to the accompaniment of Siamang gibbon calls, with plenty of bird sightings and potential large mammal sightings en route.

Hot Springs HOT SPRING
The volcanic legacy of the valley is evident in its many hot springs. These range from the semi-grotty **Air Panas** near the village of Semurup (11km north of Sungai Penuh), hugely popular with locals; **Air Panas Situs 2** across the valley is in a more natural setting. More impressive still is **Grao Sakti**, near the forest village of Renah Kemumu.

BENGKULU

Cut off from its neighbours by the Bukit Barisan range, Bengkulu remains Sumatra's most isolated province. Those travellers who make it this far are rewarded with the simple pleasures of ordinary Indonesian life and with beautiful, largely unexplored countryside and jungle around the main city.

History

Little is known of Bengkulu before it came under the influence of the Majapahits from Java at the end of the 13th century. Until then it appears to have existed in almost total isolation, divided between a number of small kingdoms such as Sungai Lebong in the Curup area. It even developed its own cuneiform script, *ka-ga-nga*.

In 1685, after having been kicked out of Banten in Java, the British moved into Bengkulu (Bencoolen, as they called it) in search of pepper. The venture was not exactly a roaring success. Isolation, boredom and constant rain sapped the British will, and malaria ravaged their numbers.

The colony was still not a likely prospect in 1818 when Sir Stamford Raffles arrived as its British-appointed ruler. In the short time he was there, Raffles made the pepper market profitable and planted cash crops of coffee, nutmeg and sugar cane. In 1824 Bengkulu was traded for the Dutch outpost of Melaka as a guarantee not to interfere with British interests in Singapore.

From 1938 to 1941 Bengkulu was a home-in-domestic-exile for Indonesia's first president, Sukarno. A series of earthquakes struck the province in 2007.

Bengkulu

0736 / POP 296,000

A real hidden gem, the quiet provincial capital of Bengkulu is quite possibly the nicest city in Sumatra. Its pedestrian-friendly streets are not desperately traffic-clogged, the beach is kept clean by locals, and there's a decent eating scene to boot. The city itself is quite light on attractions, beyond a few interesting reminders of the colonial era and an expansive beach. But travellers are beginning to discover the multiple natural attractions beyond the city limits, which make Bengkulu an excellent destination in its own right, rather than just a handy stopover between Padang and Bukittinggi to the north and Krui and Bandarlampung to the south.

Sights

Benteng Marlborough FORT

(admission 5000Rp; 8am-7pm) Set on a hill overlooking the Indian Ocean, the star-shaped Benteng Marlborough, a former British fort, became the seat of British power in Bengkulu after 1719, when it replaced nearby Fort York. Despite its sturdy defences the fort was attacked and overrun twice – once by a local rebellion just after its completion in 1719, and then by the French in 1760. The old British gravestones at the entrance make poignant reading.

There are a few interesting old engravings and copies of official correspondence from the time of British rule, and you can also see where the Dutch incarcerated Indonesia's president Sukarno during his internal exile.

Pantai Panjang BEACH

Bengkulu's main beach, Pantai Panjang, is 7km of clean white sand. Strong surf and currents make it unsafe for swimming, but there are decent surf breaks towards the northern and southern ends of the beach and, unusually for Sumatra, there's a jogging track that stretches the length of the beach.

Pulau Tikus ISLAND

Reachable from Bengkulu via a 30- to 40-minute boat ride, this small island is surrounded by coral reef, making it an excellent snorkelling destination. It's 15km west of Bengkulu; get a fishing boat to take you out here.

Tours

Wild Sumatra Adventures ADVENTURE TOUR

(0811 730 8740; www.wildsumatra.com) The indefatigable Josh and his team have done wonders in terms of opening up the Bengkulu region to adventurous travellers. Whether you're into rock climbing or trekking, or simply want to swim in pristine, remote waterfalls, these guys can help you organise your adventure.

Sleeping

Yadi Surf Camp SURF CAMP $

(8127-3309595; Jl Baai; r incl meals from 250,000Rp) At the southern end of the city, and not far from the beach, Yadi's place is the heart and soul of the local surfer community, with boards, bicycles and motorbikes for rent. Yadi and Vivi also run a good restaurant.

Vista Hotel HOTEL $

(0736-20820; Jl MT Haryono 67; r 75,000-170,000Rp;) The spic-and-span rooms with fan or air-con at this friendly cheapie are particularly useful for their location near the bus agents.

Hotel Santika BUSINESS HOTEL $$

(0736-25858; www.santika.com; Jl Raya Jati 45, Sawah Lebar; r 605,000-940,000Rp;) The latest outpost of the Santika empire is Bengkulu's smartest hotel. Expect clean, simple lines and contemporary design, complemented by such perks as a gym, pool and massage spa. The restaurant is decent and the service is attentive and friendly.

Nala Seaside Hotel HOTEL $$

(0736-344855; Jl Pariwisata 2, Pantai Panjang; bungalow 333,000Rp, d 500,000Rp;) Just across the street from Panjang Beach, in the southern part of town, this quiet hotel lets you choose between bungalow rooms with shady porches and larger, smarter rooms inside the main building.

Splash Hotel BOUTIQUE HOTEL $$$

(0736-23333; www.hotel-splash.com; Jl Sudirman 48; r incl breakfast 606,000-999,000Rp;) Bengkulu's first stab at a designer hotel is a goodie and features a colourful designer lobby and well-appointed rooms with modern bathrooms. There's an on-site cafe and restaurant and the location on one of the city's top food streets, lined with myriad stalls in the evenings, is a boon for the hungry.

Eating & Drinking

In the evening, several warungs and food tents, serving freshly grilled seafood, cause a traffic jam along Jl Sudirman, . Be sure to try the local favourites, *tempoyak* (fish with fermented durian) and *martabak* (stuffed savoury pancake). Barbecued fish is also the main feature at beachside shacks.

Saimens BAKERY $
(Jl Suprapto; mains from 15,000Rp; ⏲9am-10pm) A decent bakery chain that doesn't just go for cakes and breads – you can also get fried chicken and *mie goreng* to take away.

Sumpit Mas CHINESE $
(Jl Adam Malik 25; mains from 35,000Rp; ⏲lunch & dunner) The best Chinese in town, particularly famous for its steamboat (bring a bunch of friends). A long list of à la carte dishes are also available; seafood is their strong point.

★ **Marola** SEAFOOD $$
(Jl Pariwisata; mains around 50,000Rp; ⏲8am-8.30pm Tue-Sun, to 4pm Mon) Classic, locally famous seafood joint by the beach, near central Bengkulu. Choose from ultra-fresh giant prawns, squid and fish, pay by weight, and pick from an array of sauces you'd like your seafood cooked in. Sensational stuff.

Aloha INTERNATIONAL $$
(Jl Pariwisata; mains from 30,000Rp; ⏲9.30am-11.30pm; 🖉) This Australian-owned place is just across the street from the beach. It serves Bengkulu's best pizza and burgers as well as some Indonesian staples. A great place to nurse your Bintang, too.

Edu Coffee COFFEE
(Jl Suprapto 1-2; ⏲9am-8pm) The most central place in Bengkulu to get your caffeine fix is this cute cafe that serves decent espresso, cappuccino and other concoctions made with local beans.

Information

BNI Bank (Jl S Parman) BNI ATMs allow for the largest withdrawals, up to 2,000,000Rp.

Post Office (Jl RA Hadi 3; ⏲8am-2pm Mon-Fri) Opposite the Thomas Parr monument.

Getting There & Away

AIR

Bengkulu's airport, **Fatmawati Soekarno Airport**, has 10 daily flights to Jakarta with Citilink, Lion Air or Sriwijaya Air. Garuda has a daily flight to Palembang, and Lion Air and Wings Air have two daily flights to Pulau Batam.

BUS

Bengkulu has two bus terminals. The **Air Sebakul** terminal, 12km east of town, serves long-distance destinations, while the **Panorama** terminal, 7km east, is used by local buses. It is much easier to go to the bus company offices on Jl MT Haryono, however. Ask around and you'll quickly be steered to the most appropriate company for your destination. Jakarta is served by large buses, while other destinations are served by minibuses.

Getting Around

Bengkulu's airport is 10km southeast of town. Airport taxis charge around 80,000Rp.

Angkot fares to almost anywhere in town cost 4000Rp and *ojek* around 10,000Rp. There are no fixed routes for *angkot;* tell the driver where you want to go and specify the neighbourhood. *Angkot* and *ojek* also greet buses when they arrive at Jl MT Haryono or Jl Bali.

Around Bengkulu

The Bengkulu region has a huge wealth of attractions that are only beginning to be explored by travellers. These range from multiday volcano and jungle treks, hot springs, rock climbing and water sports on lakes and rivers to participating in elephant conservation and interacting with locals in remote villages.

BUSES FROM BENGKULU

DESTINATION	FARE(RP)	DURATION (HR)	FREQUENCY
Bandarlampung	250,000	12-14	several daily
Bukittinggi	140,000	17	several daily
Jakarta	300,000	22-30	several daily
Krui	200,000	10	several daily
Padang	140,000	15	several daily
Sungai Penuh	150,000	10-12	2 daily

Wild Sumatra Adventures (p566) is on hand to advise and organise, guided by your specific interests. Prices are based on two participants; the more participants, the cheaper it is.

South of Bengkulu, en route to Krui, there are some decent offshore surf breaks that you can stop to explore if you have your own wheels. Wild Sumatra Adventures can also help to organise homestays in Kaur, halfway along, if you wish to experience low-key, friendly village life.

Sights & Activities

Bukit Kaba VOLCANO

This active volcano with three craters makes for a relatively straightforward ascent with two trail options: an easier gravel path or tougher trail through dense jungle. Both take around three hours. From the top there are spectacular views of the surrounding countryside and a whiff of sulphur from the single active crater. Camping near the summit so you can explore the craters is highly recommended. Bukit Taba is around 30km from Curup, which is an 84km drive northeast of Bengkulu.

Bukit Daun VOLCANO

(for 2 people 3,800,000Rp) Famous for its seven multicoloured boiling pools, the whitest allegedly home to the Kawah Putri spirit who'll come if you call her, Bukit Daun makes for a challenging three-day adventure. It involves trekking through tobacco and coffee plantations and dense jungle, two nights camping in the jungle and a pit stop to wash in a small waterfall.

Seblat Elephant Conservation Centre ELEPHANT INTERACTION

(two days/one night for 2 people 6,500,000Rp) On a two-day visit to this centre, located near Mukomuko en route between Bengkulu and Sungai Penuh, you can assist the mahouts with washing the elephants, and go on elephant rides. While the Seblat Elephant Conservation Centre is one of only a handful of legitimate elephant conservation centres in Indonesia, elephant rides present various animal welfare issues worth looking into if you're considering that option. Longer visits (up to 10 days) can involve joining jungle patrols on the lookout for wild elephants and tigers, and camping overnight in the jungle.

Funds generated by visitors contribute to the care of elephants in residence, the protection of wild elephants in the region, and jungle patrols to prevent poaching.

Beringin Tiga & Curug Embun HIKING

(for 2 people 2,000,000Rp) This is a straightforward hike through coffee and palm-sugar plantations, finishing at a camp site near a hot spring. From here you can take short hikes to visit the Beringin Tiga falls and the remarkable Curug Embun falls, which comprises two falls: one cold and the other fed by hot springs, with great swimming where the two meet. Safety ropes assist descents to Curug Embun.

Bukit Kandis ROCK CLIMBING

(rock climbing 4 people 1,500,000Rp) With great views of the surrounding jungle and the Indian Ocean, this karst mountain throws down the gauntlet to serious climbers. There's also great potential for camping wild and a smaller rock face suitable for beginner climbers. It's an hour's drive from Bengkulu.

Goa Kacamata ROCK CLIMBING

(rock climbing for up to 4 people 1,500,000Rp) This 40m rock face, distinguished by two caves that look like eyes, is suitable for both beginner and intermediate climbers. It's near Muara Aman, around four hours' drive north of Bengkulu. The trip can be combined with a dip in Air Putih with its 6m cliffs and nearby hot springs.

RIAU

The landscape and character of Riau province is distinct from the northern and western rind of Sumatra. Rather than mountains and volcanoes, Riau's character was carved by rivers and narrow ocean passages. Trading towns sprang up along the important navigation route of the Strait of Melaka, across which Riau claims cultural cousins.

For the port towns, such as Pekanbaru, and the Riau Islands, proximity to Singapore and Kuala Lumpur has ensured greater access to the outside world than the towns of the interior Sumatran jungle. The discovery of oil and gas reserves has also built an educated and middle-class population in Pekanbaru, though it has failed to make the port appealing. For several months during the dry season, the Riau province (and Pekanbaru in particular) is plagued with smoke from the burning palm-oil plantations, which makes it unbearable to visit and causes flight cancellations.

The interior of the province more closely resembles Sumatra as a whole: sparse population, dense jungle, surviving pockets of nomadic peoples (including the Sakai, Kubu and Jambisal) and endangered species, such as the Sumatran rhinoceros and tiger.

History

Riau's position at the southern entrance to the Strait of Melaka, the gateway for trade between India and China, was strategically significant. From the 16th century, the Riau Islands were ruled by a variety of Malay kingdoms, which had to fight off constant attacks by pirates and the Portuguese, Dutch and English. The Dutch eventually won control over the Strait of Melaka, and mainland Riau (then known as Siak) became their colony when the Sultan of Johor surrendered in 1745. However, Dutch interest lay in international trade, and it made little effort to develop the province.

Oil was discovered around Pekanbaru by US engineers before WWII, and the country around Pekanbaru is criss-crossed by pipelines that connect the oil wells to refineries at Dumai.

Pekanbaru

☎0761 / POP 1,031,000

Indonesia's oil capital comes with all the hustle and bustle of modern cities and with the added plague of smoke from the burning oil-palm plantations that periodically shuts down the city's airport during the dry season.

The main reason to pass through Pekanbaru is if you have your heart set on an old-school journey by boat between Singapore and Sumatra or if you wish to take a boat from Dumai to Pulau Batam.

The best place to overnight is around the intersection of Jl Sudirman and Jl Teuku Umar where there are ATMs, good food and accommodation options.

Pekanbaru's best street for eating is Jl Gatot Subrato, two blocks south (from the river) of Jl Teuku Umar. There's a good food court on the top floor of the Pekanbaru Mall on the corner of Jl Teuku Umar and Jl Sudirman.

Sleeping & Eating

Red Planet Pekanbaru DESIGNER HOTEL **$$**
(☎0761-851008; www.redplanethotels.com; Jl Tengku Zainal Abidin 23; r 288,000Rp; ❄📶) This centrally located smart hotel is just a couple of blocks from the main Jl Sudirman. Its snug rooms are all blonde wood, plenty of light and contemporary furnishings.

Pondok Patin HM Yunus SEAFOOD **$$**
(Jl Kaharudin Nasution 1; mains from 50,000Rp; ⏰lunch & dinner) Worth the cab ride south of the airport, along the southern extension of Jl Sudirman, this seafood restaurant has earned a loyal contingent of local fans with its version of the hot and sour *asam pedan ikan patin*, a dish involving fresh local fish. Other fish and seafood dishes are also well worth a nibble.

DUMAI TO MELAKA BY SEA

Like most of Pekanbaru's oil, travellers enter and exit Dumai through its busy port. Ferries also link Dumai to Melaka and Port Klang (for Kuala Lumpur) and also to Pulau Batam. Buses connect Bukittinggi to Dumai if you're dead keen on transiting between Sumatra and Malaysia without flying or if you have a motorbike. (Ulrich at **Rajawali Homestay** (p552) in Bukittinggi can explain the formalities of transporting a motorbike by onion boat between the two countries).

Dumai has less-than-thrilling accommodation, but if you time it right, it's relatively straighforward to link to or from Bukittinggi without overnighting.

From Dumai there are two ferries to Melaka (per person 300,000Rp, around two to three hours), departing at 11am and 1.30pm daily. If you're travelling from Bukittinggi, **AWR Tours & Travel** (p555) has a nightly minibus (around 10 hours) linking with the ferry's morning departure.

A ferry runs from Port Klang to Dumai at 10.30am daily, returning at 1pm (270,000Rp, three hours).

If you're fresh from Malaysia, the port area is a bit of a scrum, so keep an eye out for AWR Tours & Travel, which runs shared minibuses (per person 130,000Rp) direct to Bukittinggi. There are also frequent buses from Dumai to Padang (150,000Rp, 12 hours).

Getting There & Away

AIR

Pekanbaru's airport, **Sultan Syarif Kasim II Airport** (www.sultansyarifkasim2-airport.co.id), is 10km south of the city.

BOAT

Pekanbaru's Sungai Duku port is at the end of Jl Sultan Syarif Qasyim. From the intersection of Jl Sudirman and Jl Teuku Umarit it's a short *ojek* ride.

Dumai Express (☎0765 33966; Jl Nangka 24) is one of several companies offering daily ferry services at noon from the Sungai Duku port to Sekupang port on Pulau Batam (186,000Rp, five to six hours). Minibuses do hotel pickup at around 7.30am. Combined minibus-and-boat tickets are available from Dumai Express' office at Sungai Duku port and at another main office on Jl Nangka around 4km southwest of Pekanbaru's main intersection.

BUS

All buses depart from Pekanbaru's main bus terminal, **Terminal Nangka**, 5km west of the city centre. Note, though, that buses to Bukittinggi depart between 2pm and 6pm from the southwestern outskirts of town rather than the main bus terminal. A taxi to the Bukittinggi bus departure point is around 80,000Rp.

Getting Around

Airport taxis and taxis from the bus terminal charge around 100,000Rp. The city's **Trans Metro** (rapid bus transit) service runs along Jl Sudirman to the bus terminal (5000Rp).

Pulau Batam

☎0778 / POP 1,143,000

Batam's golf resorts and casinos attract a weekender contingent both from the city-state and mainland China, while the seedier local bars provide employment for Indonesian women from impoverished parts of Sumatra and 'happy endings' for their customers. For travellers, Batam is a soft introduction to Indonesia, a handy transport hub with connections to many different parts of the country. It can also be a sort of purgatory – a cut-rate Singapore with shopping malls but none of the charm – if you're winding up your stay in Indonesia here before crossing the strait to Singapore.

Information

Most travellers to Batam arrive at the northern port of Sekupang or at Batam Centre by boat from Singapore, or else fly into Hang Nadim Airport. On Batam, Singapore dollars are as easy to spend as Indonesian rupiah.

TRANSPORT FROM PEKANBARU

Air

DESTINATION	AIRLINE	FREQUENCY
Bandung	Indonesia AirAsia	daily
Jakarta	Batik Air, Citilink, Garuda, Lion Air	19 daily
Kuala Lumpur	AirAsia	2 daily
Medan	Lion Air	2 daily
Melacca	Malindo Air	daily
Pulau Batam	Citilink, Lion Air	4 daily
Singapore	Silk Air	Mon, Fri
Surabaya	Citilink	daily
Yogyakarta	Citilink	daily

Bus

DESTINATION	FARE (RP)	DURATION (HR)	FREQUENCY
Bengkulu	210,000	15	5pm daily
Bukittinggi	60,000	8	numerous daily
Dumai	65,000	5	hourly from 7am
Jambi	260,000	12	2 daily

FLIGHTS FROM PULAU BATAM

DESTINATION	AIRLINE	FREQUENCY
Balikpapan	Lion Air	daily
Bandarlampung	Garuda	daily
Bandung	Lion Air, Wings Air	3 daily
Bengkulu	Lion Air	3 daily
Dumai	TransNusa	daily
Jakarta	Batik Air, Citilink, Garuda, Lion Air	16 daily
Jambi	Lion Air, Sriwijaya Air	3 daily
Kuala Lumpur	Malindo Air	daily
Medan	Lion Air, Sriwijaya Air	8 daily
Padang	Citilink, Lion Air	5 daily
Palembang	Citilink, Lion Air	3 daily
Pekanbaru	Lion Air	5 daily
Semarang	Lion Air	daily
Surabaya	Citilink	5 daily
Yogyakarta	Lion Air	daily

Useful websites include www.batams.com, www.enjoybatam.com and www.batamtourism.com.

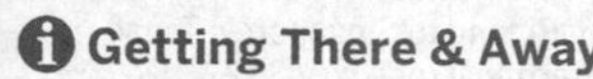

Getting There & Away

AIR

The **Hang Nadim Airport** is located on the eastern side of Pulau Batam.

BOAT

To Pulau Bintan

The ferry dock at Telaga Punggur, 30km southeast of Nagoya, is the main port for frequent speedboats to Bintan's Tanjung Pinang harbour (55,000Rp, 45 minutes) as well as the twice-daily RORO (Roll On Roll Off) car ferry that departs Batam at 10am and 4pm and Bintan at 8am and 1pm (14,500Rp, two hours). **Bintan Resort Ferries** (http://brf-batam.blogspot.com) run from Telaga Punggur to the BBT Ferry Terminal in Bintan's Lagoi resort area (110,000Rp, 1½ hours, four daily).

To Pekanbaru

From Batam's Sekupang port, **Dumai Express** (PT Lestari Indoma Bahari; ☎0765-31820; Sekupang Domestic Terminal) and **Batam Jet** (☎0765-35888; Sekupang Domestic Terminal) run daily ferries (300,000Rp to 370,000Rp, four to five hours) to the port of Tanjung Buton on mainland Sumatra. From there a minibus (around three hours) links to Pekanbaru.

To Malaysia

Passenger ferries (280,000Rp, two hours, 15 daily) run between Johor Bahru's Stulang Laut port and Batam's Sekupang.

To Singapore

Frequent **BatamFast** (www.batamfast.com), **Sindo Ferry** (www.sindoferry.com.sg) and **Majestic Fast Ferry** (www.majesticfastferry.com.sg) services connect Sekupang and Batam Centre on Pulau Batam to HarbourFront in Singapore, with departures between 6am and 9.20pm; all charge S$17 one way. There is a S$7 harbour-departure tax upon leaving Batam and an hour time difference between Indonesia and Singapore.

Getting Around

Taxis are the primary way to get around Pulau Batam. They cost around 140,000Rp to Sekupang and 100,000Rp to Nagoya.

Nagoya

This is the original boom town, showing a lot more skin than you'll find in the rest of Sumatra. The heart of town is the Nagoya Entertainment District, dotted with beer bars, shopping malls and massage parlours. It ain't pretty, but Nagoya is ultimately functional, and a good place for dining out and an overnight stay if you're travelling to or from Singapore by boat.

Sleeping & Eating

For local warungs, head to the night market or the big and raucous Pujasera Nagoya. The Nagoya Hill Mall has a specialist food street, which offers many different cuisines and there are a couple of good seafood restaurants by the mall entrance.

Hotel Sinar Bulan HOTEL **$**
(☎0778-456757; Komp Polaris Sakti Blok A 9-11; r 230,000Rp; ❄📶) Friendly hotel just a couple of blocks from the Nagoya Hill Mall and various eateries. Rooms are unmemorable but clean and air-conditioned.

Amaris Hotel Nagoya Hill HOTEL **$$**
(☎0778-743 0488; www.amarishotel.com; Komp. Ruko Nagoya Hill Blok I 1-16, Jl Teuku Umar; r 500,000-550,000Rp; ❄📶) This modern hotel is a couple of minutes' walk from Nagoya Hill Mall. Its minimalist rooms burst with mod cons and sport lime green and crimson accents.

Pulau Bintan

☎0771 / POP 173,000

Just across the water from Batam, Pulau Bintan markets itself as a high-end playground for well-heeled visitors from East Asia. Top-end resorts – mostly Singaporean-owned – huddle around the Lagoi area on the island's north coast – in close proximity to Singapore. The east coast around Pantai Trikora is more affordable and laid-back.

Check out www.welcometobintan.com and www.bintan-resorts.com.

Getting There & Away

AIR

Raja Haji Fisabilillah Airport is located to the southeast of Pulau Bintan. There are daily flights to/from Jakarta on Lion Air, Batavia Air and Sriwijaya Air.

BOAT

Bintan has two main ports and services to Pulau Batam, Singapore and other islands in the Riau archipelago. Tanjung Pinang, on the western side of the island, is the busiest harbour and the best option for folks heading for Pulau Batam or Pantai Trikora. If you're bound for the resort area of Lagoi, the **Bandar Bentan Telani (BBT) ferry terminal** is more convenient.

To Pulau Batam

Regular speedboats depart from Tanjung Pinang's main pier for Telaga Punggur on Batam (55,000Rp, 45 minutes) from 8am to 5.45pm daily, as well as two daily RORO car ferries (14,500Rp, two hours).

To Elsewhere in Indonesia

Daily ferries depart from Tanjung Pinang's main pier to other islands in the Riau chain, such as Pulau Karimum, Pulau Lingga and Pulau Penuba.

To Malaysia

There are boats to Johor Bahru in Malaysia (340,000Rp, 2½ hours, three daily) from Tanjung Pinang.

To Singapore

Sindo Ferry (www.sindoferry.com.sg) runs from Tanjung Pinang to Singapore's Tanah Merah ferry terminal (one way S$22, two hours) four times daily between 7am and 5pm.
Bintan Resort Ferries (www.brf.com.sg) connects Singapore's Tanah Merah ferry terminal (one way/return from S$45/58, one hour, five to seven daily) with the BBT ferry terminal near the Lagoi resorts area.

Tanjung Pinang

The main port town on the island is a bustling mercantile centre with more ethnic diversity than most Sumatran towns. Few travellers linger long here, but there are a couple of worthwhile attractions if you have time.

Pulau Penyenget (admission 5000Rp), reachable by frequent boats (8000Rp) from Bintan's main pier, was once the capital of the Riau rajahs. The ruins of the old palace

FERRIES TO SINGAPORE

FERRY NAME	DEPARTURE LOCATION	FREQUENCY
BatamFast	Batam Centre	12 daily
BatamFast	Sekupang	9 daily
Sindo Ferry	Batam Centre	12 daily
Sindo Ferry	Sekupang	6 daily
Majestic Fast Ferry	Batam Centre	12 daily
Majestic Fast Ferry	Sekupang	9 daily

of Rajah Ali and the tombs and graveyards of Rajah Jaafar and Rajah Ali are clearly signposted inland. The most impressive site is the sulphur-coloured mosque, with its many domes and minarets.

The star attraction of the village of **Senggarang**, just across the harbour from Tanjung Pinang, is an old Chinese temple, now suspended in the roots of a huge banyan tree.

Hotel Panorama (☎0771-22920; www.bintanpanorama.com; Jl Haji Agus Salim 12; r incl breakfast 250,000Rp; ❄@📶), a 10-minute walk from the ferry terminal, features clean and spacious rooms, with the attached Bamboo Cafe providing karaoke entertainment to Singaporean weekenders.

In the evening there are several food stalls scattered around town serving *mie bangka* (Hakka-style dumpling soup).

There are plenty of ATMs, mainly on Jl Teuku Umar. English-speaking staff at the **tourist information centre** (☎0771-31822; Jl Merdeka 5; ⏲8am-5pm) can organise tours and advise about transport.

A taxi to Pantai Trikora costs around 300,000Rp. An *ojek* to Trikora is around 150,000Rp. Another option is to rent a car (around 380,000Rp per day), which gives you flexibility in exploring the beaches around the island.

Pantai Trikora & Around

Bintan's east coast is lined with rustic beaches, the main beach being Pantai Trikora. Further north up the coast is the remote and practically deserted Mutiara Beach. The small islands off Pantai Trikora are well worth visiting and there is good snorkelling outside the monsoon season (November to March). Accommodation is laid-back and simple.

Sleeping & Eating

★Mutiara Beach Guesthouse GUESTHOUSE **$$**
(☎0821 7121 1988; www.mutiarabintan.com; Jl Trikora Km55; campsite S$8, r S$50-100; ❄📶) At this Swiss-run hideaway, gorgeous thatched bungalows with verandas sit amid unruly vegetation right by a pristine beach; its shallow waters are good for swimming.

Marjoly Beach RESORT **$$**
(☎0813 9370 0732; www.marjolybeach.com; Pantai Trikora Km33; d incl breakfast S$50-60; ❄) This laid-back resort consists of spacious thatched bungalows cooled by ocean breezes and a lack of hot water showers. Marjoly Beach is popular with kitesurfers from Singapore, and there's a good restaurant (mains 30,000Rp to 50,000Rp).

Lagoi

Bintan's resort area stretches along the northern coastline of the island along Pasir Lagoi. The beaches are sandy and swimmable, the resorts have polished four- and five-star service, and there are water sports and entertainment for all ages. Weekday discounts can be as generous as 50% off.

Sleeping

Angsana Resort & Spa Bintan RESORT **$$$**
(☎0770-693111; www.angsana.com; r incl breakfast from S$390; ❄📶🏊) The dressed-down Angsana is best suited to young professionals. The breezy common spaces are decorated in zesty citrus colours, with private rooms sporting a contemporary colonial-era style. The superior rooms are nice but the suites are super.

Banyan Tree Bintan RESORT **$$$**
(☎0770-693100; www.banyantree.com; r incl breakfast from S$650; ❄📶🏊) The private and privileged Banyan Tree has famed spa facilities and a high-powered retreat deep in the jungle. The hotel shares the 900m-long beach with Angsana Resort & Spa Bintan.

Getting Around

Most resorts organise shuttle service between the BBT Ferry Terminal and the Lagoi hotels as part of the package price.

JAMBI

The centrally located province of Jambi occupies a 53,435-sq-km slice of central Sumatra, stretching from the highest peaks of the Bukit Barisan range in the west to the coastal swamps facing the Strait of Melaka in the east.

The eastern lowlands are mainly rubber and oil-palm plantations, while in the western portion of the province is the Kerinci Seblat National Park, home to Sumatra's highest peak, Gunung Kerinci (3805m), Sumatran tigers (Jambi's faunal mascot) and rhinos. With the general improvement of roads throughout the province, it now takes only slightly longer to reach the park from Jambi than from Padang, and Jambi town is easily reached from Bandarlampung.

In the province's fast disappearing forests, the Orang Rimba are an endangered hunter-gatherer tribe.

History

The province of Jambi was the heartland of the ancient kingdom of Malayu, which first rose to prominence in the 7th century. Much of Malayu's history is closely and confusingly entwined with that of its main regional rival, the Palembang-based kingdom of Sriwijaya.

It is assumed that the temple ruins at Muara Jambi mark the site of Malayu's former capital, the ancient city of Jambi (known to the Chinese as Chan Pi). The Malayu sent their first delegation to China in 644 and the Chinese scholar I Tsing spent a month in Malayu in 672. When he returned 20 years later he found that Malayu had been conquered by Sriwijaya. The Sriwijayans appear to have remained in control until the sudden collapse of their empire at the beginning of the 11th century.

Following Sriwijaya's demise, Malayu re-emerged as an independent kingdom and stayed that way until it became a dependency of Java's Majapahit empire, which ruled from 1278 until 1520. It then came under the sway of the Minangkabau people of West Sumatra before coming under the control of the Dutch East Indian Company in 1616, who maintained a trade monopoly here until 1901 before moving its headquarters to Palembang.

Jambi

☎0741 / POP 516,000

The capital of Jambi province is a busy river port about 155km from the mouth of the Sungai Batang Hari. The large temple complex at Muara Jambi, 26km downstream from Jambi, is the single biggest attraction on Sumatra's east coast. Jambi also has a pleasantly low-key and friendly vibe, especially around the riverfront food stalls that kick off at dusk around the funky pedestrian bridge.

Sights & Activities

★Muara Jambi — RUIN

(admission 5000Rp; 8am-4pm) This scattering of ruined and partially restored temples is the most important Hindu-Buddhist site in Sumatra. The temples are believed to mark the location of the ancient city of Jambi, capital of the kingdom of Malayu 1000 years ago. Most of the *candi* (temples) date from the 9th to the 13th centuries, when Jambi's power was at its peak. You can spend the whole day wandering the forested site, crunching on ancient pottery shards and marvelling at the temple stonework.

Eight temples have been identified so far, each at the centre of its own low-walled compound. Some are accompanied by *perwara candi* (smaller side temples) and three have been restored to something close to their original form. The site is dotted with numerous *menapo* (smaller brick mounds), thought to be the ruins of other buildings – possibly dwellings for priests and other high officials.

The restored temple **Candi Gumpung**, straight ahead from the donation office, has a fiendish *makara* (demon head) guarding its steps. Excavation work here has yielded some important finds, including a *peripih* (stone box) containing sheets of gold inscribed with old Javanese characters, dating the temple back to the 9th century. A statue of Prajnyaparamita found here, and other stone carvings, are among the highlights at the small **site museum** nearby. However, the best artefacts have been taken to Jakarta.

Candi Tinggi, 200m southeast of Candi Gumpung, is the finest of the temples uncovered so far. It dates from the 9th century but is built around another, older temple. A path leads east from Candi Tinggi to **Candi Astano**, 1.5km away, passing **Candi Kembar Batu** and lots of *menapo* along the way.

The temples on the western side of the site are yet to be restored. They remain pretty much as they were found – minus the jungle, which was cleared in the 1980s. The western sites are signposted from Candi Gumpung. First stop, after 900m, is **Candi Gedong Satu**, followed 150m further on by **Candi Gedong Dua**. They are independent temples despite what their names may suggest. The path continues west for another 1.5km to **Candi Kedaton**, the largest of the temples, then a further 900m northwest to **Candi Koto Mahligai**.

The forested site covers 12 sq km along the northern bank of the Batang Hari. The entrance is through an ornate archway in the village of Muara Jambi and most places of interest are within a few minutes' walk.

Much of the site still needs excavating and there is some debate whether visitors should be allowed to clamber all over the ruins and the restored temples.

For centuries the site lay abandoned and overgrown in the jungle on the banks of the

ORANG RIMBA

Jambi's nomadic hunter-gatherers are known by many names: outsiders refer to the diverse tribes collectively as Kubu, an unflattering term, while they refer to themselves as Orang Rimba (People of the Forest) or Anak Dalam (Children of the Forest). Descended from the first wave of Malays to migrate to Sumatra, they once lived in highly mobile groups throughout Jambi's lowland forests.

As fixed communities began to dominate the province, the Orang Rimba retained their nomadic lifestyle and animistic beliefs, regarding their neighbours' adoption of Islam and agriculture as disrespectful towards the forest. Traditionally the Orang Rimba avoided contact with the outsiders, preferring to barter and trade by leaving goods on the fringes of the forest or relying on trusted intermediaries.

In the 1960s, the Indonesian government's social affairs and religion departments campaigned to assimilate the Orang Rimba into permanent camps and convert them to a monotheistic religion. Meanwhile the jungles were being transformed into rubber and oil-palm plantations during large-scale *transmigrasi* (government-sponsored scheme to encourage settlers to move from overcrowded regions to sparsely populated ones) from Java and Bali.

Some Orang Rimba assimilated and are now economically marginalised within the plantations, while others live off government funds and then return to the forests. Just over 2000 Orang Rimba retain their traditional lifestyles within the shrinking forest. The groups were given special settlement rights within Bukit Duabelas and Bukit Tigapuluh National Parks, but the protected forests are as vulnerable to illegal logging and poaching as other Sumatran parks.

According to the NGO groups that work with the Orang Rimba, it isn't a question of if the tribes will lose their jungle traditions but when. In the spirit of practical idealism, the organisation **WARSI** (www.warsi.or.id) established its alternative educational outreach. Rather than forcing educational institutions on the Orang Rimba, teachers join those that will accept an outsider and teach the children how to read, write and count – the equivalent of knowing how to hunt and forage in the settled communities.

Some of the issues highlighted during a 2015 visit by the Norwegian prime minister to Orang Rimba communities that live in a concession area were decrepit housing provided by the government, a lack of cultivable land in place of the jungle that's gone, and the inability to eat certain animals because members of Orang Rimba have been encouraged to embrace Islam.

Batang Hari. It was 'rediscovered' in 1920 by a British army expedition sent to explore the region. The dwellings of the ordinary Malayu people have been replaced by contemporary stilt houses of the Muara Jambi village residents. According to Chinese records, Malayu people once lived along the river in stilted houses or in raft huts moored to the bank.

Guntur TOUR
(☎0813 6833 0882) Highly knowledgeable, enthusiastic, English-speaking Guntur is the best tour guide you can find in Jambi if you want to go to Muara Jambi. He has an in-depth knowledge of the Kerinci Valley also.

Sleeping

Guntur or the Padmasana Foundation (p576) can arrange homestays in the village adjoining Muara Jambi, which is very worthwhile in terms of cultural immersion and also because it encourages community participation in the conservation of the ruins. Expect to pay around 150,000Rp for a room and board. There are a couple of local eateries by the river.

Hotel Duta BOUTIQUE HOTEL $$
(☎0741-755918; hotelduta@yahoo.com; Jl Sam Ratulangi 65-68; r incl breakfast 500,000-650,000Rp; ❄📶) The Duta features compact rooms with modern decor and snazzy bathrooms. Flat-screen TVs – with plenty of English-language content – and a wildly ostentatious reception area are other cosmopolitan surprises in sleepy Jambi. It's a short stroll to alfresco street food treats down on the riverbank.

Novita Hotel BUSINESS HOTEL $$
(☎0741-27208; www.novitahotel.com; Jl Gatot Subroto 44; r from 570,000Rp; ❄📶🏊) A central

location, friendly staff, pool with swim-up bar and spacious, business-style rooms are all boons at this former Novotel. The restaurant is decent if you go for the local specialities, and our only quibble is some erratic staff behaviour (waking guests up at 8am to ask if they want their laundry done, for example).

Hotel Fortuna HOTEL **$$**
(☎0741-23161; Jl Jendral Gatot Subrato; s/d 170,000/350,000Rp; ❄📶) With modern bathrooms and flat-screen TVs, your travel budget goes a long way at the Fortuna. Rooms are simple and sparsely furnished, but comfortable. The Fortuna is concealed in a quiet retail plaza near the Abadi Hotel, a local landmark, and there are Chinese noodle shops nearby for a quick breakfast. Staff won't win any congeniality prizes, though.

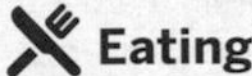

Eating

Taman Tanggo Rajo INDONESIAN **$**
(Jl Raden Pamuk; snacks from 10,000Rp) This is Jambi's essential evening destination for promenading along the attractive, curved pedestrian bridge across the river that lights up at night. Stalls sell local favourites, such as *nanas goreng* (fried pineapples), *jagung bakar* (roasted corn slathered with coconut milk and chilli) and different kinds of *sate.* Nearby is the Wiltop Trade Centre, a modern shopping mall.

Munri Food Centre INDONESIAN **$**
(Jl Sultan Agung; mains 15,000-20,000Rp; ⊙5-10pm) Night-time eats set the night ablaze at this alfresco dining area near the museum. Look for the *mie celor* and *mie pokk,* two local noodle dishes.

★ **Pondok Kelapa** SEAFOOD **$$**
(Jl Hayam Waruk; meals around 120,000Rp; ⊙lunch & dinner) Fish and seafood are the stars of the show at this appealing restaurant in a tranquil garden setting. It's a great place to try giant grilled prawns, *cumi asang manis* (squid in a sweet and sour sauce), or local specialities such as *pinang patin* (spicy fish hotpot with pineapple). Menus have pictures but no prices; check before ordering.

ℹ Information

Jambi's ATMs cluster around Jl Dr Sutomo.

Culture & Tourism Office (☎0741-445056; Jl H Agus Salim; ⊙9am-5pm Mon-Fri) Only useful if English-speaking Guntur happens to be in the office.

Padmasana Foundation (☎0852 6609 1459, 0852 6600 8969; http://padmasanafoundation.blogspot.com) The Padmasana Foundation is dedicated to the preservation and excavation of the Muara Jambi ruins and its members work together with the local community in the village next to the ruins. Staff can provide information and arrange both tours of the site and homestays in the village.

Post Office (Jl Sultan Thaha 9; ⊙8am-2pm Mon-Fri) Near the port.

TRANSPORT FROM JAMBI

Air

DESTINATION	AIRLINE	FREQUENCY
Jakarta	Citilink, Garuda, Lion Air, Sriwijaya Air	15 daily
Palembang	Garuda	daily
Pulau Batam	Lion Air, Sriwijaya Air	3 daily
Sungai Penuh (Kerinci)	Susi Air	2-3 weekly

Bus

DESTINATION	FARE (RP)	DURATION (HR)	FREQUENCY
Bengkulu	250,000	10	several daily
Padang	165,000-190,000	11	2 daily
Palembang	80,000-170,000	7	several daily
Pekanbaru	260,000	12	daily
Sungai Penuh	175,000	8	10 daily

Getting There & Away

AIR

The **Sultan Thaha Airport** (www.sultanthaha-airport.co.id) is 6km east of the centre.

BUS

Bus-ticketing offices occupy two areas of town: Simpang Rimbo, 8km west of town, and Simpang Kawat, 3.5km southwest of town on Jl M Yamin.

There are frequent economy buses to Palembang. Several minibus companies, including **Ratu Intan Permata** (☎ 0741-20784; Simpang Kawat, Jl M Yamin), offer comfortable door-to-door minibus services to Pekanbaru, Bengkulu, Palembang and Padang. **Safa Marwa** (☎ 0741-65756; Jl Pattimura 7) runs a similar service to Sungai Penuh in the Kerinci Valley. Buses depart from the companies' offices and can also pick up passengers around town.

Getting Around

Taxis from the airport charge around 50,000-70,000Rp. *Ojeks* and taxis hang around next to shopping malls. An *ojek* to the bus offices in Simpang Rimbo is around 20,000Rp. For Simpang Kawat, count on 15,000Rp.

There is no public transport to Muara Jambi. You can charter a speedboat (around 500,000Rp) from Jambi's river pier to the site. You can also hire an *ojek* (50,000Rp to 60,000Rp).

SOUTH SUMATRA

The eastern portion of South Sumatra shares a common Malay ancestry and influence with Riau and Jambi provinces from its proximity to the shipping lane of the Strait of Melaka. Rivers define the character of the eastern lowlands, while the western high peaks of the Bukit Barisan form the province's rugged underbelly. The provincial capital of Palembang was once the central seat of the Buddhist Sriwijaya empire, whose control once reached all the way up the Malay Peninsula.

Despite the province's illustrious past, it's rather light on attractions, except for Sumatra's most notorious volcano and a couple of remote nature reserves.

Palembang

☎ 0711 / POP 1.44 MILLION

Sumatra's second-largest city is a major port that sits astride Sungai Musi, the two halves of the city linked by the giant Jembatan Ampera (Ampera Bridge).

A thousand years ago Palembang was the centre of the highly developed Sriwijaya civilisation that ruled a huge slab of Southeast Asia. It covered most of Sumatra, the Malay Peninsula, southern Thailand and Cambodia, but few relics from the period remain outside the city museum.

The city's spicy fare is the subject of much debate (positive and negative) in Sumatra, and though Palembang is largely off the traveller trail, you may find yourself passing through en route to or from Jambi and Bandarlampung.

Sights

Museum Sumatera Selatan MUSEUM

(Jl Sriwijaya 1, Km5.5; admission 2000Rp; 8am-4pm Sun-Thu, to 11am Fri) Museum Sumatera Selatan houses finds from Sriwijayan times, as well as megalithic carvings from the Pasemah Highlands, including the famous *batu gajah* (elephant stone) and almost spherical fertility statue with a humongous bosom. Other worthwhile displays include a rich collection of finely woven *songkets*. There is a magnificent *rumah limas* (traditional house) behind the museum. The museum is about 5km from the town centre off the road to the airport.

Sleeping

Zuri Express BOUTIQUE HOTEL $$

(☎ 0711 710 800; www.zuriexpresshotels.com; Jl Dr Mohammed Isa 988; d incl breakfast from 350,000Rp;) Located just north of Palembang's market area, Zuri Express fills a colourful and modern building with equally colourful and contemporary accommodation. Rooms are relatively compact, but filled with all mod cons, including designer bathrooms, flat-screen TVs and wi-fi access. Downstairs is a well-priced cafe with good-value Indonesian dishes and espresso.

Red Planet Palembang BUSINESS HOTEL $$

(☎ 0711-315222; www.redplanethotels.com; Jl J Sudirman Km3.5; r 342,000Rp;) Sleek, contemporary and minimalist, with plenty of crimson accents and mod cons, this former Tune hotel received a makeover after the Red Planet takeover. The main road location is convenient for overnight stays en route to/from the airport and the on-site cafe provides sustenance.

Eating

Rumah Makan Pindang Musi Rawas INDONESIAN $

(Jl Angkatan 45 18; mains from 30,000Rp; ⌚lunch & dinner) A short ride northwest of the centre, this nondescript-looking restaurant is locally famous for its *pindang patin,* a spicy, sour, clear soup with patin fish. Other dishes are also sound ambassadors of southern Sumatran cuisine. A numbered system is used for queuing when the place gets busy.

Pagi Sore INDONESIAN $

(Jl Sudirman; meals around 45,000Rp; ⌚lunch & dinner) Palembang cuisine not your bag? Then your taste buds will thank you for this reliable Padang standby, where you will be presented with dish upon little dish of spicy, flavourful beef *rendang*, *ayam bakar* (spicy chicken), *ikan sambal* (fish sambal) and other favourites. You only pay for the ones you sample from.

EATING THE PALEMBANG WAY

Love it or hate it, Palembang fare is distinguished by its use of funky durian that sends some folks running. The best-known dishes are *ikan brengkes* (fish served with a spicy durian-based sauce) and *pindang* (a spicy, clear fish soup). Another Palembang speciality is *pempek*, a mixture of sago, fish and seasoning that is formed into balls and deep-fried or grilled. Served with a spicy sauce, *pempek* is widely available from street stalls and warungs.

Palembang food is normally served with a range of accompaniments. The main one is *sambal tempoyak*, a combination of fermented durian, *sambal terasi* (shrimp paste), lime juice and chilli that is mixed up and added to the rice. *Sambal buah* (fruit-based sambal), made with pineapple or sliced green mangoes, are also popular.

Getting There & Away

Sultan Badaruddin II airport is 12km north of town.

The **Karyajaya Bus Terminal** is 12km from the town centre, but most companies have ticket offices on Jl Kol Atmo. For door-to-door minibus services, check out the agents' offices along Jl Veteran.

Stasuin Kertapati train station is 8km from the city centre on the southern side of the river.

Getting Around

Angkot around town cost a standard 3500Rp. They leave from around the huge roundabout at the junction of Jl Sudirman and Jl Merdeka. Any *angkot* marked 'Karyajaya' (5500Rp) will get you to the bus terminal. Any *angkot* marked 'Kertapati' (5500Rp) will get you to the train station. Taxis to the airport cost around 100,000Rp. A taxi from the station to the town centre should cost around 70,000Rp.

Krui

Sweeping slithers of white sand lick the coast north and south of Krui, and the meandering coastline is dotted with surf breaks that draw an increasing number of intrepid board riders.

Most of the action is focused on the village of Tanjung Setia, 10km south of Krui. While surfers still make up most of the tourist traffic, the area's laconic and laid-back buzz is also perfect if you're overlanding to Java down Sumatra's south coast. Around midway between Bengkulu and Bandarlampung, it's a good spot to relax and recharge after one too many long Sumatran bus journeys.

Arrive fully stocked with rupiah – the nearest ATM is an hour's bus ride away in Liwa.

Activities

Karang Nyinmbor SURFING

The star attraction of Tanjung Setia is this world-renowned lefthander, right in front of the village. Depending on weather and tides, other excellent breaks up and the down the coast are also options, all easily reached by motorbike.

Hello Mister ADVENTURE SPORTS

(☎0852 6928 7811; kruimotorent@gmail.com; Jl Pantai Wisata, Tanjung Setia) Stop by and see the wisecracking Albert at Hello Mister for everything from bus transport to Krui or Bandarlampung, jungle tours (half-day per person 70,000Rp), motorbike rental (per day 65,000Rp) and surf lessons (per person 30,000Rp) on more forgiving beach breaks towards Krui village. He can also arrange longer day trips south to the Bukit Barisan Selatan National Park.

TRANSPORT FROM PALEMBANG

Air

DESTINATION	AIRLINE	FREQUENCY
Bandarlampung	Garuda	daily
Bandung	Xpressair	daily
Bengkulu	Garuda	daily
Jakarta	Batik Air, Citilink, Garuda, Lion Air, Nam Air, Sriwijaya Air	27 daily
Jambi	Garuda	daily
Kuala Lumpur	AirAsia	daily
Medan	Garuda	daily
Padang	Citilink	daily
Pulau Batam	Citilink, Lion Air	3 daily
Singapore	Silk Air	daily
Surabaya	Citilink	daily
Yogykarta	Nam Air	daily

Bus

DESTINATION	FARE (RP)	DURATION (HR)	FREQUENCY
Bandarlampung	240,000	10	2 daily
Bengkulu	185,000	8	several daily
Jambi	140,000	8	several daily
Lahat	75,000	4	hourly

Train

DESTINATION	FARE (RP)	DURATION (HR)	FREQUENCY
Bandarlampung	90,000-150,000	10	8pm daily
Lahat/Lubukliinggau	35,000-190,000	4/7	2 daily

Sleeping & Eating

Rumah Radja Losmen BUNGALOW $
(earthcraft40@gmail.com; r 150,000-170,000Rp; ❄📶) This tranquil place is run by friendly Aussie surfer, Murray. Lodgings consist of a couple of comfy bungalows that catch the breeze (with a third on the way). Only breakfast is available but there's the bonus of a guest kitchen for those who want to surf rather than be tied to a feeding schedule.

★ **Damai Bungalows** BUNGALOW $$
(☎0813 6930 7475; www.damaibungalows.com; Jl Pantai Wisata, Tanjung Setia; r incl meals 350,000Rp; ❄📶) Leafy gardens, fan-cooled bungalows with private outdoorsy bathrooms, the best surfer lodge food, and friendly underfoot dogs are defining features of this chilled-out place. There's excellent service from the Aussie-Indonesian owners, and the bar – with quite possibly Sumatra's coldest beer – provides front-row views of the iconic Karang Nyimbor left-hander. Damai is often booked by groups, but individual guests are welcome.

Lovina Krui Surf BUNGALOW $$
(☎0853 7780 2212; www.lovinakruisurf.com; Jl Pantai Wisata, Tanjung Setia; r incl meals 350,000Rp; ❄@) Divided into various room configurations (with 10 rooms in total, all with private bathrooms), Lovina Krui Surf has three lovely A-frame cottages set back from the beach. Decor and design are a big step up from Tanjung Setia's traditional focus on simple bungalows. The attached cafe and lounge is cool, cosmopolitan and serves three meals a day.

Family Losmen BUNGALOW $$
(☎0813 8043 1486; www.familylosmen.com; Jl Pantai Wisata, Tanjung Setia; per person incl meals 275,000Rp) One of Tanjung Setia's

longest-established losmen is still one of the area's best, with stylish concrete bungalows with private verandas, and a terrific rooftop viewing platform that's perfect for wave spotting and a few end-of-day Bintangs.

Lani's Resto INTERNATIONAL **$**
(Pantai Wisata, Tanjung Setia; mains from 40,000Rp; lunch & dinner) The foil to Tanjung Setia's warungs, this new joint, run by a Hawaiian-American, serves all the comfort food you've been craving after a day out on the waves: tacos, burgers and pizza, plus cold beer.

Getting There & Away

Buses between Bengkulu (100,000Rp, 10 hours, several daily) and Bandarlampung (60,000Rp, four hours, several daily) will stop on request at Tanjung Setia. A private transfer to/from Bandarlampung airport is around 1,000,000Rp. Susi Air have twice-weekly flights to Krui from Bengkulu in their 12-seater Cessna, but they either refuse to take boards or charge US$100 per board (and are very weather-dependent).

LAMPUNG

At the very tip of this bow-shaped landmass is Sumatra's southernmost province, which was not given provincial status by Jakarta until 1964. Although the Lampungese have had a long history as a distinct culture, Jakarta's gravitational force has been altering Lampung's independent streak – largely in the form of the *transmigrasi* policies, designed to off-load excess population and turn a profit in the wilds of Sumatra.

Outside the provincial capital of Bandarlampung, the province's robust coffee plantations dominate the economy and the unclaimed forests, closely followed by timber, pepper, rubber and the ever-increasing territory of oil-palm plantations.

Many Jakarta weekenders hop over to tour the Krakatau volcano or visit the elephants of Way Kambas National Park. The rugged western seaboard is ostensibly protected as the Bukit Barisan Selatan National Park.

History

Long before Jakarta became the helm of this island chain, there's evidence that Lampung was part of the Palembang-based Sriwijayan empire until the 11th century, when the Jambi-based Malayu kingdom became the dominant regional power.

Megalithic remains at Pugungraharjo, on the plains to the east of Bandarlampung, are thought to date back more than 1000 years and point to a combination of Hindu and Buddhist influences. The site is believed to have been occupied until the 16th century.

Lampung has long been famous for its prized pepper crop, which attracted the West Javanese sultanate of Banten to the area at the beginning of the 16th century and the Dutch East India Company in the late 17th century.

The Dutch finally took control of Lampung in 1856 and launched the first of the *transmigrasi* schemes that sought to ease the chronic overcrowding in Java and Bali.

Bandarlampung

0721 / POP 873,000

Perched on the hills overlooking Teluk Lampung, Bandarlampung is the region's largest city and its administrative capital. Most traveller facilties are in Tanjungkarang, including the train station and the bulk of the hotels. Krakatau and the Way Kambas National Park are the main spots to check out in the area when passing through en route to or from Java.

Sights

Krakatau Monument MONUMENT
(Jl Veteran) The Krakatau monument is a lasting memorial to the force of the 1883 eruption and resulting tidal wave. Almost half of the 36,000 victims died in the 40m-high tidal wave that funnelled up Teluk Lampung and devastated Telukbetung. The huge steel maritime buoy that comprises the monument was washed out of Teluk Lampung and deposited on this hillside.

Lampung Provincial Museum MUSEUM
(Jl Teuku Umar; admission 4000Rp; 9am-4.30pm Tue-Sun) This museum, 5km north of central Tanjungkarang, is a bit of a mixed bag, with everything from neolithic relics to stuffed animals. The few articles from the Sriwajayan empire era are worth a peek. To reach the museum, catch a grey *angkot* (3500Rp).

Sleeping

★**POP! Hotel Tanjung Karang** DESIGNER HOTEL **$$**
(0721-241742; www.pophotels.com; Jl W Monginsidi 56; r 440,000Rp;) POP! is as subtle as the giant exclamation mark decorating

the side of the building. The decor is Google meets pop art, the staff are young and helpful and the strange bathroom cubicles feature powerful showers. Our only quibbles are that the windows don't open and breakfast is a bit of a free-for-all.

Grand Citihub Hotel @Kartini BUSINESS HOTEL **$$**
(☎0721-240420; www.citihubhotels.com; Jl Kartini 41; r from 275,000Rp; ❄📶) This brand new, central hotel is a welcome addition to Bandarlampung's rather underwhelming selection. Rooms are on the snug side, but they scream 'contemporary,' with giant cityscapes splashed across the walls and powerful showers. Good coffee shop on-site, too.

Emersia Hotel & Resort RESORT **$$$**
(☎0721-258258; www.emersiahotel.com; Jl W Monginsidi 70; r 695,000-945,000Rp, ste 1,800,000-3,150,000Rp; ❄📶🏊) If you're completing your Sumatran odyssey and wish to wash the dust of the island off your feet, one of Bandarlampung's most luxurious hotels may be just the place for it. Its elevated location means that the best rooms and suites feature sea views. There's a spa for pampering and a decent restaurant to boot.

Eating

The **market stalls** around the **Bambu Kuning Plaza** offer a wide range of snacks. Food stands punctuate Jl Raden Intan after dark.

Garuda Restaurant INDONESIAN **$**
(Jl Kartini 31; meals 40,000Rp; ⏲breakfast, lunch & dinner) Come here for classic Padang dishes: choose from the likes of *udang sambal* (prawns in spicy sauce), wilted sweet potato leaves, fish curry and beef *rendang*. Staff don't speak much English but they're super helpful if you just point at what you'd like.

Kopi Oey INTERNATIONAL **$$**
(www.kopioey.com; Jl W Monginsidi 56; meals 70,000-100,000Rp) With its birdcage lights, outdoor terrace and Shanghai glamour posters, this offshoot of the Jakarta-based empire conjures an old-world vibe. The menu runs the gamut from fusion (spicy tuna spaghetti) to Javanese classics (sweet-and-spicy lamb tongseng) and *capcay* rice. Some of the drinks (iced grass jelly, hot turmeric) border on eclectic.

El's Coffee CAFE **$$**
(www.elscoffee.com; Jl Kartini 41; meals around 70,000Rp; ⏲7am-10pm) This popular coffee shop chain satisfies your caffeine cravings with a wide array of cappuccinos, lattes and frappuccinos (including the downright peculiar popcorn and avocado versions). If you're hungry, there's tiramisu, macha cake and Italian-Indonesian fusion dishes.

Shopping

Lampung produces weavings known as ship cloths (most feature ships), which use rich reds and blues to create primitive-looking geometric designs. Another type is *kain tapis*, a ceremonial cloth elaborately embroidered with gold thread.

Mulya Sari Artshop HANDICRAFTS
(Jl Thamrin 85; ⏲8am-5pm) A good collection of both ship cloths and *kain tapis* can be found here.

Information

ATMs dot central Bandarlampung; BNI Bank machines dispense up to 2,000,000Rp.

Arie Tour & Travel (☎0721-474675; www.arietour.com; Jl W Monginsidi 143; ⏲8am-5pm Mon-Sat) A helpful travel agent located outside the city centre. Trips taking in Gunung Krakatau and Way Kambas National Park can be booked here.

Post Office (Jl Kotaraja; ⏲8am-6pm Mon-Sat) The city's most central branch.

Getting There & Away

AIR

Raden Inten II Airport (☎0721-769 7114) is 24km north of the city.

BUS

There are two bus terminals in Bandarlampung. **Rajabasa bus terminal** is 10km north of town and serves long-distance destinations. **Panjang bus terminal** is 6km southeast of town along the

TRANSPORT FROM BANDARLAMPUNG

Air

DESTINATION	AIRLINE	FREQUENCY
Jakarta	Aviastar, Garuda, Lion Air, Sriwijaya Air	16 daily
Palembang	Garuda	daily
Pulau Batam	Garuda	daily
Yogykarta	Aviastar	daily

Bus

DESTINATION	FARE (RP)	DURATION (HR)	FREQUENCY
Bengkulu	150,000	12	several daily
Bukittinggi	250,000-360,000	22	daily
Jakarta	184,000-360,000	8-10	several daily
Krui	60,000	4-5	several daily
Palembang	240,000	10	2 daily

Train

DESTINATION	FARE (RP)	DURATION (HR)	FREQUENCY
Lahat/Lubklinggau	35,000-240,000	14/17	2 daily
Palembang	90,000-150,000	8	daily at 4.30am

Lampung Bay road and serves local and provincial destinations.

Damri (☎0751-780 6335) bus-boat combination tickets (184,000Rp, eight to 10 hours) are the most convenient option for heading to Jakarta. Damri buses leave from outside Bandarlampung's train station at 9am, 10am, 8pm and 9pm, shuttling passengers to the Bakahueni pier, and then picking them up at Java's Merak pier for the final transfer to Jakarta's train station.

TRAIN

The train station is in the town centre at the northern mouth of Jl Raden Intan.

Getting Around

For the airport, taxis charge around 140,000Rp for the ride to/from town. All *angkot* pass through the basement of the **Bandar Lampung Plaza** on Jl Raden Intan and the standard fare around town is 3500Rp. To reach the Rajabasa bus terminal, take a green *angkot* (4500Rp). To reach the Panjang bus terminal, take a green *angkot* to Sukaraja and then transfer to a red *angkot* (4500Rp). Taxis and *ojeks* are scarce.

Way Kambas National Park

This national park is one of the oldest reserves in Indonesia. It occupies 1300 sq km of coastal lowland forest around Sungai Way Kambas on the east coast of Lampung. What little remains of the heavily logged forests is home to endangered species of elephants, rhinos and tigers.

It is believed that around 180 wild Sumatran elephants *(Elephas maximus sumatrensis)* live in the park, but reliable estimates are uncertain and poaching and development pressures are constant. The Sumatran elephant is a subspecies of the Asian elephant and is found only in Sumatra and Kalimantan. Another rare but endemic creature in Way Kambas is the Sumatran rhino, the only two-horned rhino of the Asian species. Its hide is red in colour with a hairy coat.

The area around Way Kanan, a subdistrict of the park, is frequently visited by birdwatchers, with the white-winged duck and Storm's stork being particularly sought-after by twitchers.

Also in the park is the **Sumatra Rhino Sanctuary**, where five rhinos formerly held in captivity are introduced to wild surroundings in the hope of successful breeding, with each assigned a team of keepers to look after their health and nutritional needs.

The Sumatran rhino is a solitary animal and its habitat in the wild is so fractured that conservationists fear the species will die out without intervention. Breeding centres for rhinos are a controversial component of species-protection campaigns as they are expensive to maintain and have reported few successful births. For more information, visit the website of the **International Rhino Foundation** (www.rhinos-irf.org), one of the lead organisations involved with the centre and antipoaching patrols in the park. It's estimated that fewer than 20 wild Sumatran rhinos still survive within the park.

For the average visitor not engaged in wildlife conservation, a visit to the park is a nice break from the concrete confines of Jakarta, but it's not a true wild safari. Most visitors are led through the forest on elephants or by canoes on the Sungai Way Kanan and surrounding waterways. The most commonly spotted animals on the tour include primates and birds. Herds of elephants are seen here from time to time but sightings of the Sumatran tiger are extremely rare.

A day trip to Way Kambas costs around US$170 per person for a minimum of two people and can be arranged through tour operators in Jakarta. Bandarlampung-based tour agents include Arie Tour & Travel.

Sleeping & Eating

Tourist facilities within the park are limited. About 13km from the entrance to the park, on the main road, is **Way Kanan**, where there is a collection of simple guesthouses on the banks of Sungai Way Kanan. Food stalls nearby cater to daytrippers and close after dark, so you'll need to bring food if you're staying the night.

Satwa Elephant Ecolodge COTTAGE **$$**
(☎0812 399 5212; www.ecolodgesindonesia.com; Jl Taman Nasional Way Kambas; s/d incl breakfast US$55/60; ❄📶) This delightful ecolodge is located 500m from the park entrance. Four spacious cottages are scattered through the lodge's leafy orchard of tropical fruit trees, and activities include river trips and mountain-bike rides through the forest. The lodge is also popular with keen birdwatchers. Four-day packages departing Jakarta – including all meals and transport – are US$595 per person.

WORTH A TRIP

PASEMAH HIGHLANDS

The Pasemah Highlands, tucked away in the Bukit Barisan west of Lahat, are famous for the mysterious megalithic monuments that dot the landscape. The stones have been dated back about 3000 years, but little else is known about them or the civilisation that carved them. While the museums of Palembang and Jakarta now house the pick of the stones, there are still plenty left in situ. The main town of the highlands is Pagaralam, 68km (two hours by bus) southwest of the Trans-Sumatran Hwy town of Lahat.

If you're looking for a guide, get in touch with **Wild Sumatra Adventures** (p566) in Bengkulu, who at the time of writing were looking to start excursions into the Pasemah Highlands. There are a couple of ATMs in the town's dusty main street, and the nightly market features a lot of food stalls guaranteed to maximise your travel budget.

Every bus travelling along the Trans-Sumatran Hwy calls in at Lahat, nine hours northwest of Bandarlampung and 12 hours southeast of Padang. There are regular buses to Lahat from Palembang (75,000Rp, five hours), and the town is a stop on the train line from Palembang to Lubuklinggau. There are frequent small buses from Pagaralam to Lahat (18,000Rp, two hours) and Bengkulu (30,000Rp, six hours). There are *angkot* (3000Rp) to the villages near Pagaralam from the town centre's *stasiun taksi* (taxi station).

Tinggi Hari Tinggi Hari, 20km from Lahat, west of the small river town of Pulau Pinang, is a site featuring the best examples of early prehistoric stone sculpture in Indonesia. The Pasemah carvings fall into two distinct styles: the early style dates from around 3000 years ago and features fairly crude figures squatting with hands on knees or arms folded over chests.

The later style, incorporating expressive facial features, dates from about 2000 years ago and is far more elaborate. Examples include carvings of men riding, battling with snakes and struggling with elephants. There are also a couple of tigers – one guarding a representation of a human head between its paws. The natural curve of the rocks was used to create a three-dimensional effect, though all the sculptures are in bas-relief. Sculptures of this style are found throughout the villages around Pagaralam, although some take a bit of seeking out.

Batu Beribu In Tegurwangi, about 8km from Pagaralam on the road to Tanjung Sakti, Batu Beribu is the home of a cluster of four squat statues that sit under a small shelter by a stream. The site guardian will wander over and lead you to some nearby dolmen-style stone tombs. You can still make out a painting of three women and a dragon in one of them.

Batu Gajah (Elephant Stone) Batu Gajah sits among the rice paddies by the village of Berlubai, 3km from Pagaralam, along with tombs and statues. There is a remarkable collection of stone carvings among the paddies near Tanjung Aru. Look out for the one of a man fighting a giant serpent.

Gunung Dempo Gunung Dempo is a dormant volcano and the highest (3159m) of the peaks surrounding the Pasemah Highlands that dominate Pagaralam. Allow two full days to complete the climb. A guide is strongly recommended as trails can be difficult to find. The lower slopes are used as a tea-growing area, and there are *angkot* from Pagaralam to the tea factory.

Hotel Mirasa (☎0730-621266; Jl Muhammad Nuh 80; d 100,000-240,000Rp) There is a range of rather musty rooms to choose from and the manager can organise transport to the sites or guides to climb Gunung Dempo. The hotel is on the edge of town, about 2km from the bus terminal.

ℹ Getting There & Away

The entrance to Way Kambas is 110km from Bandarlampung. There are buses from Bandarlampung's Rajabasa bus terminal to Jepara (38,000Rp, 2½ hours). They pass the signposted entrance road to Way Kambas in the village of Rajabasalama, 10km north of Jepara. Alternatively, you can catch a bus to Metro (20,000Rp, one hour) and then another to Rajabasalama (22,000Rp, 1½ hours). From the beginning of the entrance road you can hire a motorcycle to take you to and from the park entrance.

Gunung Krakatau

Krakatau may have come closer to destroying the planet than any other volcano in recent history, when it erupted in 1883. Tens of thousands were killed either by the resulting tidal wave or by the pyroclastic flows that crossed 40km of ocean to incinerate Sumatran coastal villages. Afterwards all that was left was a smouldering caldera where a cluster of uninhabited islands had once been. Perhaps peace had come, thought local villagers. But Krakatau, like all scrappy villains, re-awoke in 1927 and resulting eruptions created a new volcanic cone, since christened Anak Krakatau (Child of Krakatau). It's estimated that Anak Krakatau is growing by around 5m every year.

Tours to the island launch from West Java or from Kalianda on the Sumatran coast. Organised day trips with Arie Tour & Travel (p582) in Bandarlampung cost around US$300 per person (based on two people). **Krakatau Tours** (www.krakatau-tour.com; 6,000,000Rp for three people) runs day tours from Jakarta, complete with English-speaking guide and powerful speedboat.

When Krakatau is rumbling, ascents are forbidden, but tour companies may not make you aware of this fact, and you'll end up paying for a very expensive boat trip. Try to check independently whether Krakatau is off-limits.

You can also join up with weekenders chartering boats from the fishing village of Canti, located outside of Kalianda, a coastal town south of Bandarlampung. Canti is reachable by frequent local buses from Bandarlampung's Rajabasa bus terminal (35,000Rp, 1½ hours). Charters usually cost around 300,000Rp per person, but with a minimum of five people. There are regular *angkot* from Kalianda to Canti (10,000Rp), and an *ojek* from Kalianda to Canti is around 30,000Rp.

Bakauheni

Bakauheni is the major ferry terminal between Java and southern Sumatra. The journey between the two islands sounds like a snap until you factor in land transport between the ferry terminals and the major towns on either side. Bakauheni is 90km from Bandarlampung, a bus journey of two or three hours. In Java, the bus transfer from the port of Merak to Jakarta is another two-hour journey. Damri (p583) runs bus-boat-bus combinations linking Sumatra and Java.

Bukit Barisan Selatan National Park

At the southern tip of Sumatra, this national park comprises one of the island's last stands of lowland forests. For this reason the World Wildlife Fund has ranked it as one of the planet's most biologically outstanding habitats and is working to conserve the park's remaining Sumatran rhinos and tigers; it is also identified as the most important forest area for tiger conservation in the world. The park is also famous for many endemic bird species that prefer foothill climates, and several species of sea turtle that nest along the park's coastal zone.

Of the 356,000 hectares originally designated as protected, less than 324,000 hectares remain untouched. The usual suspects are responsible: illegal logging, illegal encroachment of coffee, pepper and other plantations, and poachers.

Tourist infrastructure in the park is very limited and most people visit on organised tours; it may be possible to organise one from Krui. The main access point into the park is through the town of Kota Agung, 80km west of Bandarlampung.

Kantor Taman Nasional Bukit Barisan Selatan (☎0722-21095; Jl Raya Terbaya; ⏲8am-4.30pm Mon-Thu, to noon Fri) was inexplicably closed when we visited but does, in theory, sell permits into the park and can arrange guides and trekking information. However, we have also been told of incidents where visitors were not allowed access to the park at all and even surfers wishing to ride the coastal waters adjacent to the park were turned back by a boatload of serious-looking men with guns.

Kota Agung has several basic hotels. There are frequent buses from Bandarlampung to Kota Agung (16,000Rp).

Kalimantan

Includes ➡

Best Jungle River Journeys

- ➡ Sungai Bungan–Tanjung Lokan by motorised canoe (p598)
- ➡ Sungai Ohang–Tanjung Isuy to Mancong by ces (p627)
- ➡ Sungai Rungan (p605)
- ➡ Sungai Sekonyer through Tanjung Puting National Park by *klotok* (p600)
- ➡ Danau Sentarum National Park (p597)

Best Places to Stay

- ➡ Nunukan Island Resort (p634)
- ➡ Wisma Alya (p614)
- ➡ Merabu Homestay (p632)
- ➡ Hotel Gran Senyiur (p616)
- ➡ Betang Sadap (p597)

Why Go?

Skewered by the equator and roasting under a tropical sun, the steamy forests of Kalimantan serve up endless opportunities for epic rainforest exploration. The island has no volcanoes and is protected from tsunamis, which has allowed its ancient forests to grow towering trees that house some of the world's most memorable species. The noble orangutan shares the canopy with acrobatic gibbons, while prehistoric hornbills patrol the air above.

The indigenous people, collectively known as Dayak, have long lived in concert with this rich, challenging landscape. Their longhouses dot the banks of Kalimantan's many waterways, creating a sense of community unmatched elsewhere in a country already well-known for its hospitable people.

Kalimantan's natural resources have made it a prime target for exploitation; just three quarters of Borneo's lowland forests remain, and its once abundant wildlife and rich traditional cultures are rapidly disappearing. Visit this awesome wilderness as soon as you can, while you still can.

When to Go

Pontianak

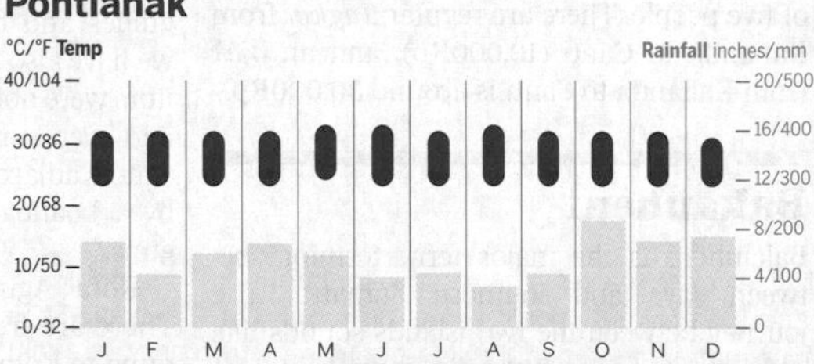

Dec–Mar Abundant fruit, including rare types of durian, brings orangutans into view.

Jul–Sep Dry season makes travelling easier, but air may be hazy from fires.

Aug–Sep Clearest water for diving in Derawan.

History & Culture

Separated from Southeast Asia's mainland 10,000 years ago by rising seas, Kalimantan was originally populated by the Dayak, who still define its public image. The culture of these diverse forest tribes once included headhunting, extensive tattooing, stretched earlobes, blowguns and longhouses – horizontal apartment buildings big enough to house an entire village. That culture has been slowly dismantled by the modern world, so that some elements, such as headhunting (thankfully), no longer exist, while others are slowly disappearing. Tribal identity persists, but many Dayak have either abandoned their traditional folk religion, Kaharingan, or combined it with Christianity (or Islam).

In addition to the Dayak, Kalimantan contains two other large ethnic groups: the Chinese and the Malay. The Chinese are the region's most successful merchants, having traded in Kalimantan since at least 300 BC. They're responsible for the bright red Confucian and Buddhist temples found in many port towns, and for a profusion of Chinese restaurants, some of Kalimantan's best dining. The Malays are predominantly Muslim, a religion that arrived with the Melaka empire in the 15th century. The most obvious signs of their presence are the grand mosques in major cities and towns, along with the call to prayer. Several palaces of Muslim sultanates, some still occupied by royal descendants, can be visited.

Since colonial times, Kalimantan has been a destination for *transmigrasi,* the government-sponsored relocation of people from more densely populated areas of the archipelago. This and an influx of jobseekers from throughout Indonesia has led to some conflict, most notably a year-long struggle between Dayak and Madurese people (from the island of Madura) in 2001, which killed 500 people, and a smaller conflict in 2010 between Dayak and Bugis in Tarakan.

Most of the struggle in Kalimantan, however, has taken place over its bountiful natural resources, and involved foreign powers. Oil, rubber, spices, timber, coal, diamonds and gold have all been pawns on the board, causing many years of intrigue, starting with British and Dutch colonial interests. During World War II oil and other resources made Borneo (the island which is home to Kalimantan) an early target for Japan, leading to a brutal occupation, in which some 21,000 people were murdered in West Kalimantan alone. In 1963 Indonesian President Sukarno led a failed attempt to take over all of Borneo by staging attacks on the Malaysian north.

Today, the struggle for Kalimantan's resources is more insidious. As one watches the endless series of enormous coal barges proceed down rivers lined with tin-roofed shacks, there is the constant sense of an ongoing plunder from which the local people benefit little, as they are outmanoeuvred by a shadowy collection of foreign businesspeople and local government officials overseen from Jakarta. Meanwhile, as palm-oil plantations spread across the landscape, the Bornean jungle recedes, never to return. Numerous conservation groups are struggling to halt the social and environmental damage, and to save some remarkable wildlife. Best to visit soon.

Wildlife

Kalimantan's flora and fauna are among the most diverse in the world. You can find more tree species in a single hectare of its rainforest than in all of the US and Canada combined. There are over 220 species of mammal and over 420 species of bird found on Borneo, many of them endemic to the island. The region is best known for its orangutans, Asia's only great ape and a rare but thrilling sight outside of Kalimantan's many rescue and rehabilitation centres. River cruising commonly reveals proboscis monkeys (unique to Borneo), macaques, gibbons, crocodiles (including gharials), monitor lizards and pythons. Hornbills are commonly seen flying overhead, and are a spiritual symbol for many Dayak. Forests harbour the rare clouded leopard, sun bears, giant moths, tarantulas, and more bizarre species of ants and spiders than you could ever conjure out of your wildest imagination. For divers, the Derawan Archipelago is renowned for its turtles, manta rays and pelagics.

ℹ Getting There & Away

The only entry points to Kalimantan that issue visas on arrival are Balikpapan's Sepinggan Airport, Pontianak's Supadio Airport and the Tebedu–Entikong land crossing between Kuching (Sarawak) and Pontianak. All other entry points require a visa issued in advance.

AIR

Most major cities can be reached from Jakarta or Surabaya. Pontianak connects with Kuching (Malaysia), while Balikpapan has direct flights to

Kalimantan Highlights

1. Completing the landmark **Cross-Borneo Trek** (p591) – if you can.
2. Meeting the orangutans of **Tanjung Puting National Park** (p600).
3. Going native in the **Kapuas Hulu** (p596) region.
4. Taking the slow boat up **Sungai Mahakam** (p623).
5. Living the (inexpensive) high life in **Balikpapan** (p615).
6. Delving into Kalimantan's near and distant past in **Merabu** (p632).
7. Exploring the **Derawan Archipelago** (p633), both under water and above.
8. Settling into village life in lovely **Loksado** (p613).
9. Witnessing the annual spectacle of **Cap Goh Meh** (p594).

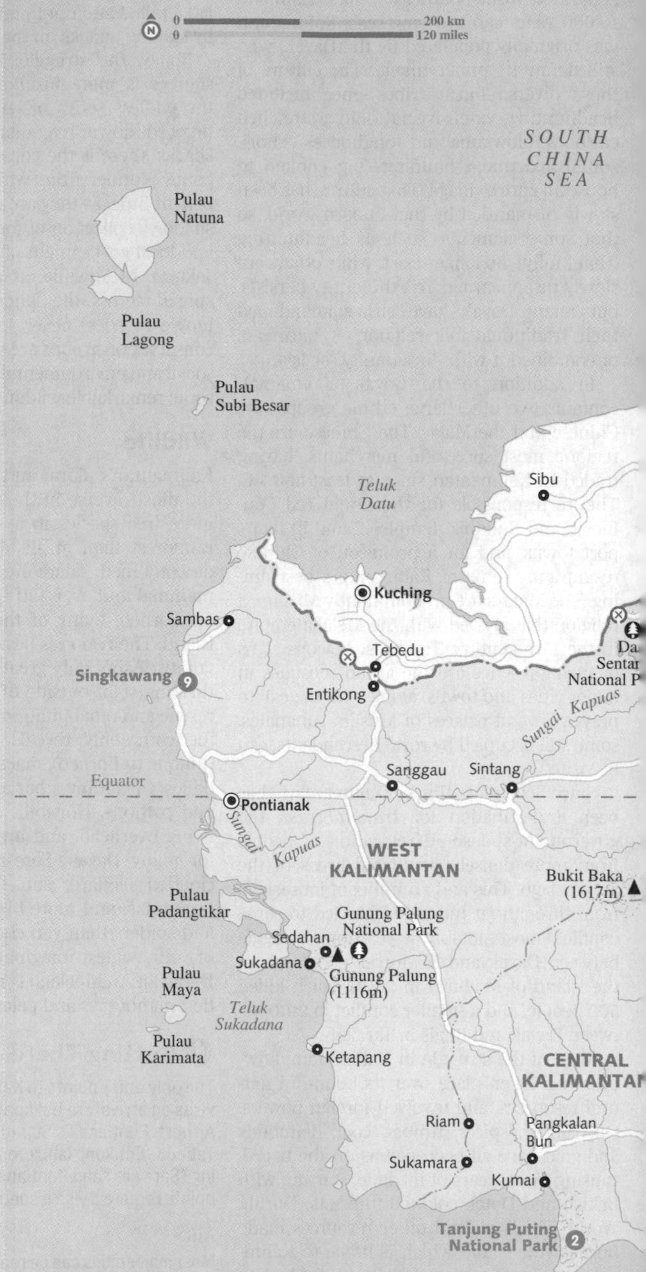

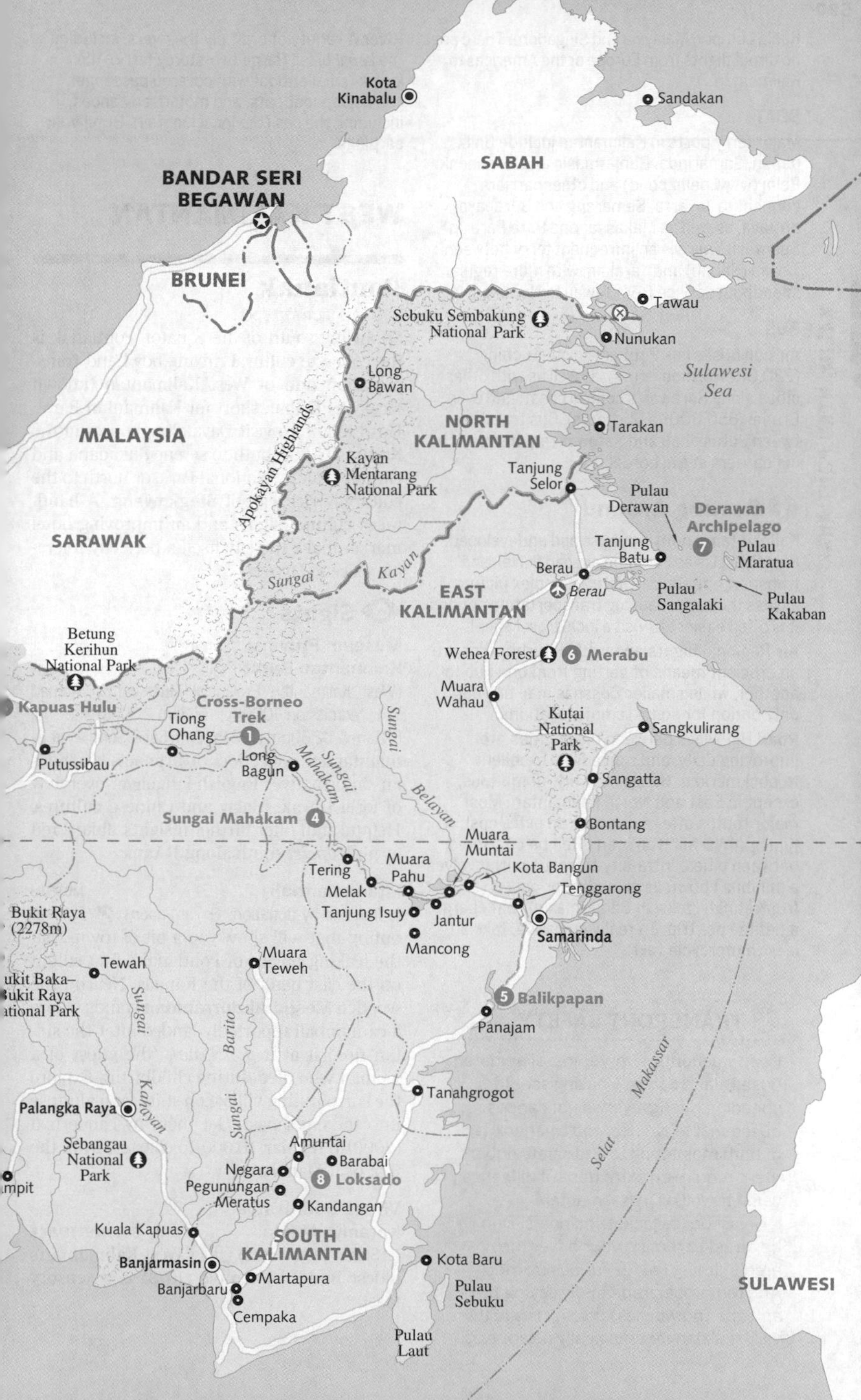

Kota Kinabalu
Sandakan
SABAH
BANDAR SERI BEGAWAN
BRUNEI
Tawau
Sebuku Sembakung National Park
Nunukan
Sulawesi Sea
Long Bawan
MALAYSIA
NORTH KALIMANTAN
Tarakan
Apokayan Highlands
Kayan Mentarang National Park
Tanjung Selor
Pulau Derawan
Derawan Archipelago
7
SARAWAK
Tanjung Batu
Pulau Maratua
Berau
Berau
Sungai
Kayan
EAST KALIMANTAN
Pulau Sangalaki
Pulau Kakaban
Betung Kerihun National Park
Wehea Forest
6
Merabu
Muara Wahau
Kapuas Hulu
Cross-Borneo Trek
1
Kutai National Park
Sangkulirang
Tiong Ohang
Putussibau
Long Bagun
Sungai Mahakam
Sungai Belayan
Sangatta
Sungai Mahakam
4
Bontang
Muara Muntai
Tering
Muara Pahu
Kota Bangun
Melak
Tenggarong
Tanjung Isuy
Jantur
Samarinda
Mancong
Bukit Raya (2278m)
Tewah
Muara Teweh
Bukit Baka–Bukit Raya National Park
Sungai Kahayan
Sungai Barito
5
Balikpapan
Panajam
Selat Makassar
Tanahgrogot
Palangka Raya
Sebangau National Park
Amuntai
Barabai
Negara
8
Loksado
Pegunungan Meratus
Kandangan
Kuala Kapuas
SOUTH KALIMANTAN
Banjarmasin
Kota Baru
Martapura
Banjarbaru
Pulau Sebuku
SULAWESI
Cempaka
Pulau Laut

Kuala Lumpur, Malaysia and Singapore. There are no direct flights from Europe or the Americas to Kalimantan.

BOAT

Major ferry ports in Kalimantan include Balikpapan, Samarinda, Banjarmasin and Pontianak. Pelni (www.pelni.co.id) and other carriers connect to Jakarta, Semarang and Surabaya on Java, as well as Makassar and Pare Pare on Sulawesi. There is an infrequent ferry between Tawau (Sabah) and Tarakan, with more regular speedboat service from Tawau to Nunukan.

BUS

Air-con buses link Pontianak with Kuching (230,000Rp, nine hours), as well as with other cities along Sarawak's central coast, and even Brunei (650,000Rp, 25 hours). Bus travel between Putussibau and Sarawak requires switching carriers at the border.

Getting Around

Kalimantan is both immense and undeveloped. River travel is as common as road travel, and transport options can form a complex picture. To assess the ever-changing transportation options it is often easiest to visit a local travel agent.

Air Regional flights aboard ATR turboprops are an efficient means of getting from one hub to another, while smaller Cessnas may be your only option for some remote locations.

Road Highways between major cities are improving daily, and range from excellent to pockmarked. Buses are fairly ubiquitous, except in East and North Kalimantan. Most major routes offer air-con for an extra cost. A Kijang (4WD minivan) can often be chartered between cities. Intra-city travel usually involves a minibus known as an *angkot* or *opelet* (or, frustratingly, *taksi* in Banjarmasin) that charges a flat fee per trip. To really go native, take an *ojek* (motorcycle taxi).

River A variety of craft ply the rivers, including the *kapal biasa* (large two-storey ferry), the *klotok* (smaller boat with covered passenger cabins), speedboats, and motorised canoes, including the *ces* (the local longtail). Bring your earplugs.

TRANSPORT SAFETY

Road washouts, river rapids, dilapidated buses, flash floods, weaving scooters, speeding Kijang, overweight canoes, questionable airlines, and a general lack of both maintenance and safety equipment require an extra dose of diligence when travelling in Kalimantan.

Insist on life jackets on boats. Don't be afraid to remind your driver they aren't filming *Fast & Furious Borneo*. And remember, repeatedly saying *tidak apa apa* (no worries) doesn't make the very real dangers magically disappear.

WEST KALIMANTAN

Pontianak

0561 / POP 570,000

Sprawling south of the equator, Pontianak is the concrete cultural mixing bowl and transportation hub of West Kalimantan (known locally as Kalbar, short for Kalimantan Barat. Head inland to visit Dayak longhouses in the **Kapuas Hulu**, south to serene Sukadana and Gunung Palung National Park, or north to the culturally rich city of **Singkawang**. A handful of cultural sights and an improving hotel market make the city itself a perfectly tolerable place to layover.

Sights

Museum Provinsi Kalimantan Barat MUSEUM

(West Kalimantan Provincial Museum; Jl Ahmad Yani; admission 1000Rp; 8am-2.30pm Tue-Thu, 8-11am & 1-2.30pm Fri, 8am-2pm Sat & Sun) A well-maintained collection of artefacts provides an informative English-language overview of local Dayak, Malay and Chinese cultures. Helpful staff offer further insights. Take a red or pink *opelet* south along Jl Yani.

Istana Kadriah MUSEUM

(admission by donation; 7am-noon) For an outing that will show you a bit of town, visit the leaking palace of Pontianak's first sultan on the east bank of the Kapuas. Nearby, the wooden **Mesjid Abdurrahman** stands where a cannonball reportedly landed after the sultan fired it at a *pontianak* (the ghost of a woman who died during childbirth). Explore the surrounding village on stilts for a glimpse into the city's past. Get there by canoe taxi (2000Rp regular, 10,000Rp charter) from the foot of Jl Mahakam.

Vihara Bodhisatva Karaniya Metta BUDDHIST TEMPLE

(Jl Sultan Muhammad) FREE West Kalimantan's oldest Buddhist temple (1673) is a sensory feast.

OFF THE BEATEN TRACK

THE CROSS-BORNEO TREK: A WORLD-CLASS ADVENTURE

Borneo offers one of the world's greatest adventure travel routes. East and West Kalimantan are divided by the Muller mountain range, which also serves as the headwaters for Indonesia's two longest rivers *(sungai)*. Sungai Kapuas snakes 1143km to the west coast near Pontianak, while Sungai Mahakam flows 930km to the east coast, by Samarinda. Thus, by travelling up one, hiking over the Muller Range, and travelling down the other, it is possible to cross the world's third-largest island. Be forewarned, however: this journey holds significant hazards, from deadly rapids to remote and brutal hiking where the smallest misstep could have life-changing consequences. This should not be your first rainforest trek.

Like all good epics, this one comes in a trilogy.

Sungai Mahakam One of Kalimantan's last great river journeys, travelling the Mahakam can easily fill several days in a succession of boats, making side trips into lakes and marshes, spotting wildlife, and visiting small river towns. The trek itself begins (or ends) at Tiong Ohang, up two boat-crushing sets of rapids from Long Bagun.

The Muller Mountains You do this jungle trek for the same reason you climb Mt Everest: because it's there. Noted for its river fording, hordes of leeches, and treacherous slopes, the route requires the knowledge of a professional guiding company. If you walk a taxing eight hours a day, you can make it across in five days, but seven is more comfortable and safer. Plan for 10.

Sungai Kapuas The *hulu* (headwater) region of the Kapuas is home to many of Kalimantan's best and most accessible longhouses. However, public-boat travel below Putussibau is nonexistent, meaning most trekkers fly or bus between Pontianak and Putussibau.

Debate rages as to which direction is preferable. The consensus seems to be that east-to-west is logistically simpler, while west-to-east is physically less brutal. Either way, success is a noteworthy achievement you'll remember for the rest of your life.

Tugu Khatulistiwa MONUMENT
(Equator Monument; Jl Khatulistiwa; 7.30am-4.30pm) If you want to stand on two hemispheres, you can formally do so here – though continental drift has moved the monument 117m south of the actual equator. The gift shop nearby has a colourful collection of T-shirts, sarongs and equator lamps. Cross the river by ferry and take an *opelet* 3km northwest on Jl Khatulistiwa.

Festivals & Events

Gawai Dayak Festival CULTURAL
(May/Jun) The Dayak harvest festival takes place in Pontianak at the end of May, but many villages hold their own sometime between April and June. These generally loud, chaotic and festive week-long affairs have plenty of dancing and food.

Tours

Canopy Indonesia ECOTOUR
(0811 574 2228, 0812 5809 2228; info.canopyindonesia@gmail.com) Energetic husband-and-wife team Deny and Venie are passionate about sustainable tourism through community engagement. They reinvest much of the proceeds from their signature Danau Sentarum National Park trips into developing new ecotourism programs throughout West Kalimantan.

Times Tours & Travel CULTURAL TOUR
(0819 560 1920; timestravell@yahoo.com; Jl Komyos Sudarso Blok H no 6) Specialising in cultural tours around Pontianak and KalBar since 1995, English-speaking owner Iwan is super-responsive and efficient. Call before visiting.

Sleeping

Green Leaf Inn HOTEL $
(0561-769622; Jl Gajah Mada 65; s/d 110,000/216,000Rp;) Large superior rooms have new paint and clean tile floors, while the 'personal' rooms barely have space for a bed. All have cold water and contortionist showers. Breakfast for one is included, but not windows.

Mess Hijas HOTEL $
(0561-744068; Jl Hijas 106; s/d 100,000/150,000Rp;) These stalwart budget digs manage to remain relevant and relatively clean. Floors three and four compensate for the hike by offering hot-water showers for

Pontianak

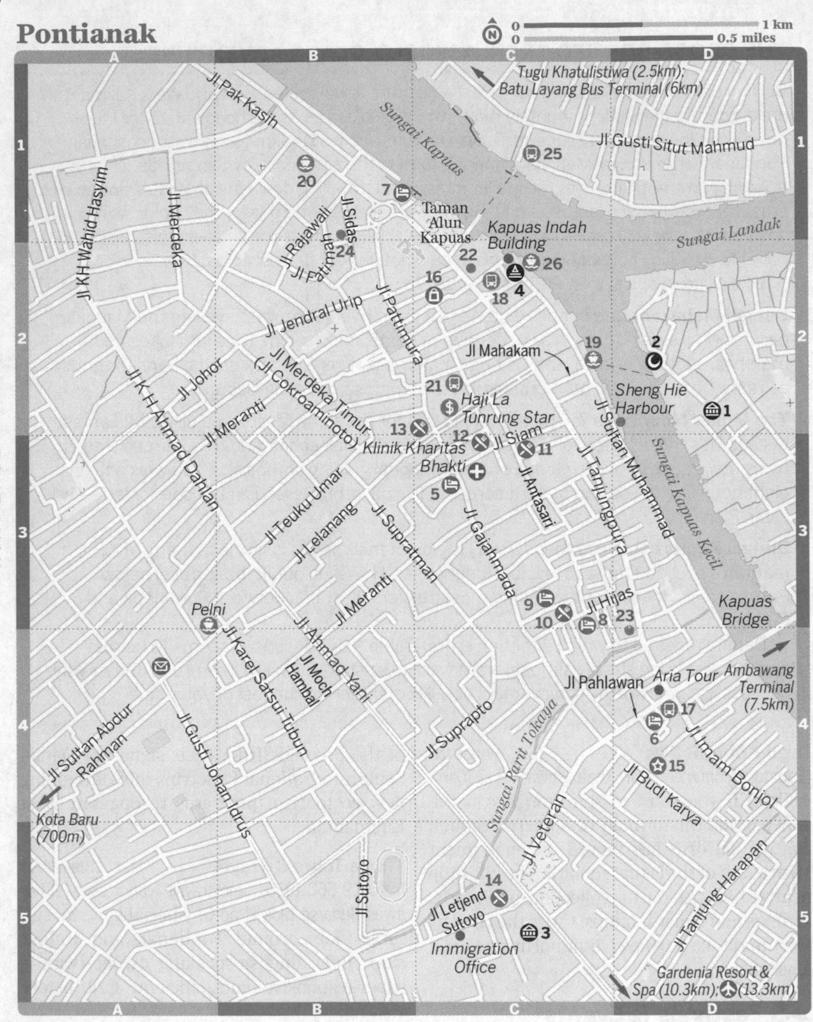

no extra cost. The front gate is locked at midnight, whether you are home or not.

Hosanna Inn HOTEL $
(0561-735052; Jl Pahlawan 224/2; s/d incl breakfast 135,000/195,000Rp;) The public spaces are pleasantly decorated and the staff are friendly, making this a good option for those taking an early DAMRI bus (next door). However, the cramped and tired budget rooms share impossibly tiny bathrooms. Room 205 has windows and access to a balcony.

Pontianak HOTEL $$
(0561-761118; Jl Gajah Mada 21; r incl breakfast 668,000-748,000Rp;) This oasis of old-school luxury and sophisticated decor is a steal at regularly discounted rates (listed here). Superiors are spacious, while the executive rooms add a bath and sofa. The RiverX entertainment complex will perk you up at night, and the substantial breakfast buffet will fuel you throughout the day.

Have a drink or two at the wine bar before shopping at the regional handicrafts shop with surprisingly reasonable prices.

Pontianak

Sights

1	Istana Kadriah	D2
2	Mesjid Abdurrahman	D2
3	Museum Provinsi Kalimantan Barat	C5
4	Vihara Bodhisatva Karaniya Metta	C2

Sleeping

5	Green Leaf Inn	C3
6	Hosanna Inn	D4
7	Kartika Hotel	B1
8	Mess Hijas	C3
9	Pontianak	C3

Eating

10	Abang Kepiting	C3
11	Ce Pien Chek	C3
12	Chai Kue Siam A-Hin	C3
13	Mie Tiau Polo	C2
14	Rumah Makan Betang	C5

Entertainment

15	Café Tisya	D4

Shopping

16	Borneo Art Shop	C2

Transport

17	ATS	D4
18	Bis Sentosa	C2
19	Canoe Taxis to Istana Kadriah	C2
	DAMRI	(see 6)
20	Dharma Lautan Utama	B1
21	Executive Buses to Kuching	C2
22	Garuda	C2
23	Kalstar	D4
24	Lion Air	B1
25	Siantan Bus & Ferry Terminal	C1
26	Speedboats to Sukadana	C2

Gardenia Resort & Spa HOTEL $$
(☎0561-672 6446; www.gardeniaresortandspa.com; Jl Ahmad Yani II; ste 750,000Rp;) The closest thing to a resort in Pontianak, the Gardenia is near the airport, making it a great option for those uninterested in the city itself. Spacious private villas connected by boardwalks to the spa and an al fresco restaurant – all built with Balinese notions – provide welcome respite from the chaos of urban Kalimantan.

Kartika Hotel HOTEL $$
(☎0561-734401; Jl Rahadi Usman 2; riverside incl breakfast 477,600Rp;) Its location on the river sets this hotel apart. Catch a breeze on the balcony as you plot upstream expeditions like an explorer of yesteryear. If the riverside rooms are full, however, give the place a miss. The open-deck Panorama Restaurant serves cold beer 24 hours.

Eating

At night Jl Gajah Mada becomes crowded with cafe culture, while seafood tents take over the Jl Diponegoro–Agus Salim median.

★Chai Kue Siam A-Hin DUMPLING $
(Jl Siam; 10 dumplings from 20,000Rp; 10am-10pm) Pork or veggies, steamed or fried – whichever you desire, you'll be waiting your turn among the mob of locals jockeying for a table or take away.

Mie Tiau Polo INDONESIAN $
(Jl Pattimura; mains 25,000Rp; 10am-9pm) Not to be confused with Apollo to the left, whose sign proudly states: 'Since 1968. Never moved.' Polo's sign retorts simply: 'Moved from next door.' The dispute is as legendary as the noodles they serve. Draw your own conclusions about which is the best … or oldest.

Ce Pien Chek VEGETARIAN $
(CPC; ☎0821 5101 8969; Jl Siam 87; mains 15,000Rp; 8.30am-9.30pm;) Piles of vegetables and fake meat served up with a small, but endearing, touch of self-righteousness.

Rumah Makan Betang DAYAK $
(Jl Letjend Sutoyo 4A; 10am-11pm;) Located behind the replica *betang* (longhouse) this small warung (food stall) cooks up traditional Dayak fare including *babi kecap,* a dish made from sautéed pork and pig fat. Wash it down with a glass of *tuak pulut,* a traditional sweet wine made from sticky rice.

Abang Kepiting SEAFOOD $$
(Jl Hijas; fish per oz 20,000Rp; 5-10pm) Buckets of iced fish out front are begging to be steamed, fried or grilled to your liking. Treat yourself to an experience and dive into a pile of smoked crabs: a full-body, all-evening affair. Come early as the place fills quickly.

Entertainment

Café Tisya LIVE MUSIC
(Jl Budi Karya; 7pm-2am) Have a few Bintang, enjoy some (loud) live music, and meet the locals, from university students to sailors on shore leave.

Shopping

For general souvenirs, visit the craft shops lining Jl Pattimura.

★**Borneo Art Shop** ANTIQUES

(☎0813 7499 6145; Jl Nusa Indah I B24; ⌚9am-5pm) Come here to enter a world of exotic curios from around Borneo including arts, antiques and etcetera. Lots of etcetera.

Information

Aria Tour (☎0561-577868; Jl Tanjungpura 36, near Hotel Garuda) Good for airline tickets and SJS buses to Kuching.

Haji La Tunrung Star (☎0561-743385; Jl Diponegoro 163) Exchange chain dealing in multiple currencies.

Immigration Office (☎0561-765576; Jl Letjend Sutoyo)

Klinik Kharitas Bhakti (☎0561-766975, 0561-734373; Jl Siam 153; ⌚7-12.30am) Emergency open 24 hours.

Main Post Office (☎0561-730641; Jl Sultan Abdur Rahman 49; ⌚7.30am-9.30pm Mon-Sat, 8am-2pm Sun)

Getting There & Away

AIR

Garuda (☎0561-734986; Jl Rahadi Usman 8A)

Kalstar (☎0561-724234, 0561-739090; Jl Tanjungpura 429)

Lion Air (☎0561-721555, 0561-742064; Mahkota Hotel, Jl Sidas)

MASwings (☎0856 5454 5016; Airport)

Sriwijaya Air (Nam Air; ☎0561-706 2400; Airport)

Trigana (☎0561-725513; Airport)

Xpress Air (☎0823 5791 9555, 0561-717 0456; Airport)

BOAT

Ships bound for Java leave from the main harbour on Jl Pak Kasih, north of the Kartika Hotel.

Dharma Lautan Utama (☎0561-765021; Jl Pak Kasih 42F)

Pelni (☎0561-748124; Jl Sultan Abdur Rahman 12)

The **Poly 2 Express** (☎0561-35864; economy 260,000Rp) jet boat to Ketapang leaves from **Sheng Hie Harbour** (Jl Barito) daily. At time of research, the **Bahari Express** (☎0561-760 820) was dry-docked for the foreseeable future.

Speedboats (☎8.30am boat 0857 5484 3414, 9.15am boat 0813 5213 4440) to Sukadana (five hours) leave from behind the Kapuas Indah Building.

There are no scheduled passenger boats upriver to Putussibau. However, if both your time and *bahasa* are abundant, negotiate a ride on a combination houseboat, freighter and general store, that can take several days to a month to make the epic 900km journey. Priceless.

BUS

International Pontianak seems determined to make international bus travel as inconvenient as possible. Malaysia and Brunei arrivals and departures take place at the massively overbuilt Ambawang Terminal, 9km east of the city. The taxi cartel has fixed the rates into town at 150,000Rp and prevents public transport from

WORTH A TRIP

SINGKAWANG, HOME OF KALBAR'S BIGGEST PARTY

Reminiscent of Shanghai 1950, Singkawang's vibrant energy is unique in Kalimantan. The largely Chinese city has some classic shop houses, ancient ceramic kilns, an impressive night market (**Pasar Malam Hongkong**), and nearly 1000 Chinese temples. The city swells beyond its streets during the **Cap Goh Meh** celebration on the 15th day of the lunar new year, when dragons and lions dance among Chinese and Dayak *tatungs* (holy men possessed by spirits who perform acts of self-mutilation and animal sacrifice). A *luar biasa* (extraordinary) spectacle.

The best rooms in town are those at the top of **Villa Bukit Mas** (☎0562 333 5666; Singkawang; s/d 560,000/600,000Rp), a sophisticated hillside hotel with wooden floors, private porches and a refined seclusion. The restaurant has grand open-air seating ringed by plumeria trees, and specialises in shabu-shabu (66,000Rp for two) and cold Bintang beer.

The extensive beaches near Singkawang offer everything from deserted paradise to garish 'resorts' with carnival atmospheres. Catch the public boat (25,000Rp, one hour, departs 8am) from the police station at **Batu Payung** to **Penata Island** for some truly off-the-beaten-path exploration.

DAMRI buses (100,000Rp, three hours) and shared taxis leave for Singkawang regularly from Pontianak's airport and Kota Baru.

TRANSPORT FROM PONTIANAK

Air

DESTINATION	COMPANY	FARE (RP)	DURATION (HR)	FREQUENCY
Balikpapan	Kalstar	1,160,000	2	Mon, Wed, Fri, Sun
Bandung	Kalstar, Xpress	1,000,000	1¼	1 daily
Batam	Lion	717,000	1¼	1 daily
Denpasar	Kalstar	1,161,000	3	Tue, Thu, Sat
Jakarta	Garuda, Lion, Sriwijaya	560,000	1½	18 daily
Ketapang	Kalstar, Trigana	440,000	40min	5 daily
Kuala Lumpur	AirAsia	399,000	2	Sun, Mon, Wed, Fri
Kuching	MASwings, Xpress	850,000	45min	1-2 daily
Palangka Raya	Garuda	1,113,000	1¾	1 daily
Pangkalan Bun	Kalstar, Trigana	854,000	1½	2 daily
Putussibau	Garuda, Kalstar	556,000	1	2 daily
Semarang	Kalstar	1,020,000	2	2 daily
Sintang	Kalstar	700,000	45min	2 daily
Surabaya	Kalstar	923,000	1¼	2 daily
Yogyakarta	Nam, Xpress	1,000,000	1½	1-2 daily

Boat

DESTINATION	COMPANY	FARE (RP)	DURATION (HR)	FREQUENCY
Jakarta	Pelni	288,000	36	weekly
Ketapang (jet boat)	Bahari Express, Poly 2 Express	260,000	8	daily
Natuna Islands	Pelni	184,000	28	weekly
Semarang	Pelni, Dharma Lautan Utama	280,000	40	weekly
Sukadana (long boat)	multiple operators	240,000	5	daily
Surabaya	Pelni	334,000	44	weekly

Bus

DESTINATION	COMPANY	FARE (RP)	DURATION (HR)	FREQUENCY
Brunei	ATS, DAMRI, SJS	650,000	26	daily
Kuching	ATS, Bintang Jaya, Bus Asia, DAMRI, EVA	230,000	9	daily
Pangkalan Bun	DAMRI	350,000	20	daily
Putussibau	Bis Sentosa	200,000-300,000	12	daily
Sambas	DAMRI, local minibus	45,000-90,0000	5	daily
Singkawang	DAMRI, local minibus	35,000-100,000	3	daily
Sintang	ATS, DAMRI	160,000-200,000	6	daily

serving the terminal. Buy international tickets from **ATS** (☎0561-706 8670; Jl Pahlawan 58), **DAMRI** (☎0561-744859, SMS 0812 5420 6001; Jl Pahlawan 226), or one of several companies along Jl Sisingamangaraja.

Domestic On the bright side, improved roads and newer fleets make bus travel within Kalimantan faster and leagues more comfortable than in the past. Regional buses still depart from within the city, with **Bis Sentosa** (☎0856 502 1219; Jl Kopten Marsan B5) serving Putussibau, and DAMRI Pangkalan Bun. Few minibuses depart from Batu Layang terminal these days, instead picking up passengers for Sambas and Singkawang on their way past the Siantan ferry terminal.

CAR

A car with driver costs 450,000Rp per day within the city. Private charters to Singkawang and points north start at 700,000Rp per day.

Getting Around

- Airport taxis cost 110,000Rp to town (17km). Alternately, take a DAMRI bus to the Kota Baru neighbourhood (35,000Rp, every two hours), then an *opelet* (3000Rp) downtown from there.
- *Opelet* (3000Rp) routes converge around Jl Sisingamangaraja.
- Becak (bicycle rickshaws) are available, but are a dying breed.
- Taxis are unmetered and scarce.

Sungai Kapuas

Indonesia's longest river, Sungai Kapuas, begins in the foothills of the Muller range and snakes 1143km west to the sea. Along the way it passes by some of Kalimantan's oldest, friendliest, and most vibrant longhouse communities, the photographer's paradise of Danau Sentarum, and – waaay off in the distance – Bukit Raya, the tallest peak in Kalimantan. Unlike the Mahakam, there is no *kapal biasa* service, making river travel impractical, but improving roads between Pontianak and Putussibau make bus trips manageable.

Sintang

☎0565

Sintang sits at the confluence of Sungai Kapuas and Sungai Melawi, where the sentinel peak of Bukit Kelam looms between you and the **Kapuas Hulu**. A phenomenal weaving **gallery** (☎0565-21098; koperasijmm@ymail.com; ⏲8am-4pm Mon-Fri, to noon Sat) in a replica longhouse and a well-meaning **museum** (Jl Sintang-Putussibau Km14; ⏲8am-3pm Mon-Fri, 9am-3pm Sat-Sun) FREE make it a good choice for breaking up your bus journey between Pontianak and Putussibau.

Start here for trips to **Bukit Baka–Bukit Raya National Park** and the seven-day expedition to climb Kalimantan's tallest mountain. Register (mandatory) at the **park office** (☎0565-23521; bukitbakabukitraya.org; Jl Wahidin Sudirohusodo 75) next to the police compound, where they'll explain transport options.

The best lodging near town is the inconveniently located **Bagoes Guesthouse** (☎0565-23733; Jl Dharma Putra 16; r 215,000-389,000Rp), southeast of the five-way intersection *(simpang lima)*.

Getting There & Away

Air Kalstar flies twice daily to Pontianak (700,000Rp, 40 minutes), and Aviastar connects to Ketapang (410,000Rp, Tue and Sat).

Bus Services run daily to/from Pontianak (160,000Rp, 10 hours) from Terminal Sungai Durian, and Putussibau-bound buses pass the Jl Deponegoro/Jl Bhayangkara roundabout. For trips to **Danau Sentarum**, go straight to the park office in Semitau on a minibus from Pasar Inpres (200,000Rp, five hours). Or take a Putussibau-bound bus to Simpang Pala Kota (100,000Rp, 3½ hours) and wait for any vehicle to Semitau.

Getting Around

White *angkot* (5000Rp) connect Terminal Pasar Inpres on the east bank and Terminal Sungai Durian on the west bank, passing most major landmarks.

OFF THE BEATEN TRACK

KALIMANTAN'S FINAL FRONTIER: BETUNG KERIHUN NATIONAL PARK

If you're the type to spend hours poring over satellite images to find the darkest green patches up the furthest reaches of jungle rivers, ripe for exploration, then you've noticed the northeast corner of KalBar. Four major watersheds draining the border with Malaysia are protected as **Betung Kerihun National Park** (☎0567-21935; betungkerihun.dephut.go.id; Jl P Tendean, Putussibau), an expanse of mountains and old-growth forests where trekkers and boaters can spend lifetimes exploring. Facilities are few and river travel expensive; this is raw adventure of a kind increasingly hard to find in Kalimantan.

Putussibau

0567

This lively river town is the last stop for airlines and long-distance buses, as well as the last chance for an ATM, before launching into the wilderness.

Sights & Activities

You can't swing a *mandau* (Dayak machete) around Putussibau without hitting a *betang* (the local word for longhouse). Some of these traditional Dayak dwellings house 30 families or more. Stand at one end of the communal front porch, and the other end disappears into converging lines interrupted occasionally by sleeping dogs or playing children. *Betang* range from historic and ornate affairs elevated on ironwood pillars, to almost nondescript row houses resembling company barracks.

Many, but not all, *betang* welcome casual visitors, with overnight stays often possible. Ask permission before entering or taking photographs. Expect to be introduced to the headman or cultural liaison, who will invariably insist you join them for a cup of overly sweet coffee or tea, the modern equivalent of a welcoming ceremony. Homestays, where available, may simply be a mat on the community room floor and a bite of whatever is cooking. You stay here for the experience, not the luxury.

Betang Buana Tengah LONGHOUSE

(homestay 35,000Rp) Built in 1864, this *betang* is home to Tamambaloh Apalin Dayak. Debate over whether it is the oldest longhouse in the region (if not Kalimantan) abruptly ended in 2014, when neighbouring contender Betang Uluk Palin tragically burned to the ground. The floor looms 4.5m above the earth, supported by the original weathered ironwood columns. Take the Badau bus 50km northwest of Putussibau, then an *ojek* 4km southwest on a gravel road.

Betang Sadap LONGHOUSE

(homestay 120,000Rp, meals 20,000Rp) Not the oldest, nor the most picturesque, but perhaps the most welcoming longhouse community. An ecotourism effort spearheaded by Januar, an Iban Matthew Broderick lookalike, will have you angling for prize-winning semah fish or splashing up the cascading rainforest creeks of their community forest. Why pay millions of rupiah for a boat trip to Betung Kerihun when you can have it all here?

Melapi 1 LONGHOUSE

The Taman Dayak longhouses of Melapi 1 to 5 stretch along the Kapuas upriver of Putussibau. As per usual, the sequels don't quite live up to the original. To find Melapi 1, borrow bicycles or a motorbike and head 10km southeast of town on Jl Lintas Timur. Turn left at the church and hail a canoe taxi across the river. A homestay may be negotiable.

OFF THE BEATEN TRACK

DANAU SENTARUM NATIONAL PARK

To avoid accusations of hyperbole, we'll let the numbers describe Danau Sentarum National Park: 4m to 6m of rainfall each year causes water levels to fluctuate by up to 12m – higher than a three-story building. As the water recedes, the lake's 240 fish species are funnelled into narrowing channels, where they must contend with 800km of gill net, 20,000 traps, and 500,000 hooks placed by fishers occupying 20 villages, who haul out as much as 13,000 tons of fish a year. Meanwhile, 237 bird and 143 mammal species inhabit the 1320 sq km of peat swamp, lowland forest and seasonal grasslands so compelling you'll be thankful for packing that extra memory card for your camera.

Enter the park's network of lakes, creeks and channels from Lanjak in the north near Putussibau, or Semitau in the south near Sintang. Be sure to register with the park office at either town (150,000Rp per person per day). Boats run 400,000Rp to 700,000Rp per day, and guides cost 150,000Rp per day. Highlights include staying at **Pelaik** (120,000Rp per room) – the isolated longhouse tucked away in the forest at the end of a hidden lake; fishing at nearby **Meliau** (300,000Rp); watching the sunrise from **Tekenang** hill; and hunting for honey with the villagers at **Semangit**. Arrange a tour through Canopy Indonesia (see p591) in Pontianak, or Kompakh (p598) in Putussibau. Getting here takes some time, so plan to stay a while.

Tours

Kompakh ADVENTURE TOUR
(☎0852 4545 0852; www.kompakh.or.id; Jl Kenanga Komp Ruko Pemda 3D) The folks at this WWF-supported ecotourism initiative know everything about Kapuas Hulu and offer tours ranging from Danau Sentarum National Park to longhouse visits to river cruising to jungle treks, including the Cross-Borneo Trek (p591).

Sleeping

Rindu Kapuas HOTEL $
(☎0567-21010; Jl Merdeka 11; r 165,000-198,000Rp; ❄) Nice rooms, each with air-con and TV, arrayed around the central living area of a large single-level house. From the traditional market, head south toward the river and turn west on Jl Merdeka (which continues under Jl A Yani at the river bridge.)

Aman Sentosa Hotel MOTEL $
(☎0567-21691; Jl Diponegoro 14; r 110,000-352,000Rp; ❄📶) A variety of clean concrete rooms ring a central parking courtyard. They don't serve breakfast, but do have wi-fi in the lobby and motorbikes for rent (75,000Rp).

Eating & Drinking

Pondok Meranti INDONESIAN $
(☎0567-21454; Jl Yos Sudarso; mains 15,000Rp; ⊙10am-10pm) A big, blue, open warehouse full of polished wooden tables where a limited menu of Indonesian staples, drinks and juice is served. Try the 'extra jos susu' for an afternoon jolt of tachycardia.

Cafe Amanda CAFE
(Alun Park; mains 20,000Rp; ⊙3pm-midnight) This al fresco cafe occupies the riverside park near the bridge, making it a uniquely popular place to hang out.

Information

Rafly Cyber (Jl Yos Sudarso 127; internet access per hour 4000Rp; ⊙7am-10pm)

RS Diponegoro (☎0567-21052; Jl Yos Sudarso 42) Local hospital.

Getting There & Away

Air Kalstar (☎0821 5202 2213; Jl Lintas Selatan 42B) and **Garuda** (☎0567-21870; Jl KS Tubun 7A) offer once daily flights to Pontianak (546,000Rp, one hour). Taxis from the airport (3½km) cost 50,000Rp, an *ojek* 25,000Rp.

Bus Services leave from **Sentosa** (☎0567-22628; Jl Rahadi Usman) and **Perintis** (☎0567-21237; Jl Yos Sudarso 71) offices for Sintang (140,000Rp, nine hours, 6am) and Pontianak (200,000Rp, 12 hours, six daily 10am to 1.30pm). For Badau and Lanjak (120,000Rp, four hours, 10.30am) head to the bus terminal north of the market.

Boat The pier is on Sungai Kapuas east of the bridge.

Getting Around

The only way to get around Putussibau is to hire a motorbike (75,000Rp per day), as *angkot* have gone way.

Tanjung Lokan & Sungai Bungan

Cross-Borneo treks start or end at the village of Tanjung Lokan, a small group of huts located on Sungai Bungan, a rapid-filled tributary of the Kapuas. There is a basic lodge (50,000Rp) and a few guides for hire, but English is hard to come by.

The expense, challenge, and risk of travelling through this section of churning river is not to be underestimated, or underappreciated. Expect to walk around some sections. The cost of the seven-hour downriver trip to Putussibau has been officially set at 1,000,000Rp per seat and up to 4,000,000Rp per per boat. Upstream takes twice as long due to the current, and costs twice as much.

Sukadana

☎0534 / POP 22,000

Sukadana is a most welcome surprise, all the more so because few people seem to know about it. Half the fun is just getting here, commonly via a scenic five-hour speedboat ride from Pontianak through tributaries, estuaries, and the mangrove wonderland near **Batu Ampar**. The region is full of forested hills and attractive islands dotted with isolated fishing villages begging for exploration. Finally you reach wide Melano Bay on the South China Sea and skirt the coastline, passing **Batu Daya**, a vertical wall of rock soaring in the distance as you approach the mountains of **Gunung Palung National Park**.

Sukadana is hidden in a fold of coastline betrayed by its major landmark, the Mahkota Kayong, a completely out of place hotel built over the water. South of town, an attractive beach, surrounded by rolling rainforested hills where gibbons usher in the dawn with melodic duets, helps make this an excellent getaway.

GUNUNG PALUNG: A PARK THAT'S HARD TO LOVE

Gunung Palung's mountain landscape, wildlife diversity and accessibility should make it *the* premier rainforest trekking location in Kalimantan. With a large population of wild orangutans, hundreds of acrobatic gibbons, sun bears, clouded leopards, and old-growth trees so large four people can't reach around them, the park is one of the last great pockets of primary rainforest on the island. Unfortunately, a history of mismanagement coupled with a monopoly on tourism by the park-employee-owned company **Nasalis Tour and Travel** (☎0534-772 2701; www.nasalistour.com; Jl Gajah Mada 34, Ketapang) has long made visiting this unspoiled gem financially challenging. But there may be hope.

Now operating under a new administrator, Gunung Palung has made laudable progress toward both curbing illegal logging, and opening the tourism market to local communities and outside companies. After a nearly four-year struggle, the village of **Sedahan** has regained permission to take visitors to the Swiss Family Robinson camp at **Lubuk Baji** in the foothills behind their home, and Canopy Indonesia (p591) is poised to begin offering the trip as well. Unfortunately, official park zoning makes the primary forests at **Cabang Panti** research camp explicitly off-limits to tourism (though somehow Nasalis still advertises trips there via a Gunung Palung summit trek – for a price.)

Tourism is in its infancy, but USAID-advised ecotourism initiatives in the nearby village of Sedahan, and an increasing focus on the **Karimata Islands**, are putting this undiscovered coastal mountain town solidly on the radar.

Sights

Pulau Datok Beach BEACH

A well-kept town beach, encircled by rainforested hills and looking out on some alluring islands. Dining options come and go as randomly as the Sunda Shelf tides, but you can usually find a few warung serving fresh coconut, assorted juices or satay. During low tide, join a pick-up game of football on the mudflats and meet the locals.

Sedahan Village VILLAGE

(☎Pak Naza, village head 0896 3411 1189, Rachel, an English-speaker 0852 5255 5678) Known for its high-quality rice, this verdant village at the foot of Gunung Palung – 10km northeast of Sukadana – has a unique attitude and aesthetic due to the Balinese *transmigrants*, whose culture blends with the local flavour. A nascent ecotourism initiative, including a community homestay (single 150,000Rp, double 200,000Rp), has opened new opportunities. Local guides can arrange trips to Lubuk Baji in Gunung Palung National Park (p599).

Sleeping & Eating

Sukadana has one very interesting hotel and several budget losmen. For meals, the Mahkota and Anugrah hotels have decent options, and warung can be found near the dock.

Penginapan Family GUESTHOUSE $

(Jl Tanjungpura; r with fan 50,000Rp, s/d with air-con 175,000/190,000Rp; ❄) Among the nicest people you could ever rent a room from, this family is eager to accommodate even when they're not sure what you want. Larger VIP rooms are quieter, set back from the road. Economy rooms are a bit dreary. Bicycle/motorbike/auto rental available (30,000/75,000/300,000Rp).

Mahkota Kayong Hotel HOTEL $$

(☎0534-772 2777; www.mahkotakayonghotel.com; Jl Irama Laut; r/ste 400,000/800,000Rp; ❄📶) Built on piles over the water, this grand anomaly dwarfs anything in town. It is usually empty outside of occasional government conventions, which seems to make some staff forget why they are here. Sea-facing rooms get blazingly hot until the sun sets with predictably stunning displays.

It's worth visiting at low-tide to watch the bizarre skin-breathing mudskippers scurry beneath the building.

Shopping

Gallery Dekranasda HANDICRAFTS

(☎0858 2001 6977; Jl Tanjungpura; 9am-noon & 2-4pm) Locally sourced handicrafts and wares, some made with unexpected refinement. And T-shirts. Find it 500m east from the durian monument.

Getting There & Around

There is no public transport within town. Most commerce is found between the dock and the durian monument. For the beach and points around, rent a bike from Penginapan Family or you could try hitching.

Speedboats (☎ Bersoul 0812 5613 3570, Synergy 0823 5737 0151; 175,000Rp; ⏲ departs 9am) to Pontianak depart Sukadana harbour twice each morning; the trip takes five hours. Sukadana can also be reached by Ketapang via bus (25,000Rp, 1½ hours, up to four daily) or **taxi** (☎ Eki, no English 0853 4524 3869); Ketapang has an airport that connects to Pontianak and Pangkalan Bun (for Tanjung Puting).

CENTRAL KALIMANTAN

Tanjung Puting National Park

Tanjung Puting is the most popular tourist destination in Kalimantan, and for good reasons. A near guarantee you'll see free-roaming orangutans, combined with a storybook journey up a winding jungle river, accessed by direct flights to Surabaya and Jakarta, give this adventure world-class appeal.

Tanjung Puting was initially set aside as a wildlife preserve by the Dutch in 1939. It gained park status and its international reputation largely thanks to Dr Biruté Galdikas, one of Leakey's Angels – the trio of female primatologists, including Dian Fossey and Jane Goodall, trained by Louis Leakey. Working from Camp Leakey since 1971, Galdikas has made such seminal discoveries as the great ape's eight-year birth cycle, which makes the species highly vulnerable to extinction. Her controversial hands-on approach to orangutan care may have lost her some supporters in the academic and conservation communities, but there is no denying the impact she has had on our understanding and appreciation of these amazing creatures and the threats they face.

The park is best seen from a *klotok,* a two-storey romantic liveaboard boat that travels up Sungai Sekonyer to Camp Leakey. During the day you lounge on deck surveying the jungle with binoculars in one hand and a drink in the other as the boat chugs along its narrowing channel. Watch for the quick flash of the colorful kingfisher, and scan the shallows for the toothy false gharail as your cook serves up fantastic meals. In the evening, you can spot proboscis monkeys bedding down in the treetops with the river at their backs for protection. These curious golden-haired, round-bellied, bulbous-nosed primates are found only on Borneo and are sometimes called *monyet belanda* (Dutch monkey – for some reason…) At night, you tie up on the river, set mattresses and mosquito nets on deck, and enjoy the finest sleep, while the hum of the rainforest purifies your ears.

Klotok call at several stations where rangers stack piles of bananas and buckets of milk to feed the resident population of ex-captive and semiwild orangutans. There are no fences or cages, but you'll be kept at a distance by ropes: a boundary ignored by the animals themselves who often wander nonchalantly through the shutter-snapping crowd on their way to lunch. While some orangutans appear deceptively tame, do not attempt to touch or feed them, and do not get between a mother and child. Orangutans are several times more powerful than you, and may bite if provoked.

Visitation has increased rapidly in recent years. There are now over 60 *klotok* running nearly nonstop during the busy dry season (June through September), with no plans by the park to limit the impact. Toilets flush directly into the creek, a questionable practice anywhere, but even more concerning given the high traffic. Some *klotok* are now outfitted with freshwater tanks, which they fill in town for showers and dish washing – a wise addition.

Despite the visitor numbers, the trip is still a fine introduction to the rainforest, and one of the most memorable experiences you'll have on the island. The park's 200 varieties of wild orchid bloom mainly from January to March, although the abundance of March fruit may lure orangutans away from feeding platforms. At any time, bring rain protection and insect repellent.

Sights & Activities

Sungai Sekonyer is opposite the port town of Kumai, where you meet your *klotok*. It is largely muddy due to upstream mining operations, although it eventually forks into a naturally tea-coloured tributary, typical of peat swamp waterways. The upriver journey contains several noteworthy stops; you won't necessarily see everything, nor in this order.

Tanjung Harapan is an orangutan feeding station with decaying interpretation centre; feedings at 3pm daily.

Sekonyer Village is a small village that arose around Tanjung Harapan, but has since been relocated across the river. There's a small souvenir shop and lodgings.

ORANGUTANS 101

Four great ape species belong to the Hominidae family: orangutans, chimpanzees, gorillas and humans. Although our auburn-haired cousins branched off from the family tree long ago, spend any time observing these *orang hutan* (Bahasa Indonesia for forest person, a name likely bestowed by the Dutch) and you'll notice similarities between us that are as striking as the differences.

The bond between a mother and her young is among the strongest in the animal kingdom. For the first two years infants are entirely dependant and carried everywhere. For up to seven years mothers continue to teach them how to thrive in the rainforest, including how to climb through the canopy and build a nest at night, the medicinal qualities of plants, what foods are poisonous, which critters they should avoid, and how to locate reliable feeding trees.

The territorial males are entirely absent from child rearing, living mostly solitary lives punctuated by sometimes violent battles for alpha status. Once a young male secures a territory, he rapidly undergoes physical changes, growing impressive cheek pads and throat pouches. He advertises his dominion by issuing booming long calls that echo through the forest for kilometres. The call both induces stress in younger males – suppressing their sexual development – and attracts females ready for breeding. It is one of dozens of vocalisations orangutans use to interact with each other and their surroundings.

Both species of orangutan, Sumatran and Bornean, are endangered. Much of their habitat is being converted to oil palm plantations. Mothers are frequently shot, their infants sold as pets. If these animals are lucky enough to be rescued, rehabilitation is long and difficult, and finding suitable places to release them is becoming nearly impossible. Currently, all of the orangutan rescue and rehabilitation centres in Indonesia are operating at or above capacity.

For more information on orangutan conservation efforts and volunteer opportunities in Kalimantan, check out the following:

Friends of the National Parks Foundation (www.fnpf.org) Funds forest restoration at Pasalat.

Orangutan Foundation International (www.orangutan.org) Founded by Biruté Galdikas; runs the park's feeding stations.

Orangutan Foundation UK (www.orangutan.org.uk) UK organisation focused on saving orangutan habitats.

Orangutan Land Trust (www.forests4orangutans.org) Influences policy and supports a wide range of organisations dedicated to the long-term survival of orangutans.

Pasalat is a reforestation camp where Pak Ledan single-handedly plants 180 saplings a month and maintains the medicinal plant garden. Be careful on the 800m forest boardwalk badly in need of donations for repairs.

Pondok Tanggui is a feeding station; feedings at 9am daily.

Pondok Ambung is popular for spotting tarantulas and glowing mushrooms on night hikes.

Camp Leakey Feedings here occur at 2pm daily at station with visitor information.

The ideal journey length is three days and two nights, giving you ample time to see everything. If you only have one day, you should take a speedboat from Kumai. A *klotok* can reach Camp Leakey in 4½ hours, making a return trip possible in one day if you leave at 6am, but this is not recommended.

During the dry season, an overnight trek from Pondok Tanggui to Pasalat (1,500,000Rp all inclusive, 22km) is a unique chance to see nocturnal wildlife. Talk to Pak Bana at Flora Homestay (p602) in Sekonyer village.

Tours

You have the choice of hiring both a *klotok* and a guide yourself, or having a tour operator do it for you. The former is moderately cheaper, the latter leagues easier. Beware: some companies advertise under multiple websites (which never list who's behind them), and others are just resellers who double the price.

Organised Tours

★Jenie Subaru ADVENTURE TOUR

(☎0857 6422 0991; jeniesubaru@gmail.com) It is a shame the passionate and charismatic Jenie does few trips these days, instead (admirably) devoting much of his time to training the next batch of local guides in sustainable tourism. Proceeds from his trips go toward buying land along the park's border to protect orangutan habitat.

Orangutan House Boat Tours ADVENTURE TOUR

(☎0857 5134 9756; www.orangutanhouseboattour.com) Local resident Fardi may be young, but he's hard-working and passionate about both his homeland and orangutans.

Borneo Orangutan Adventure Tour ADVENTURE TOUR

(☎0852 4930 9250; www.orangutantravel.com) Run by the excellent Ahmad Yani, the first official guide in the area.

Orangutan Green Tours ADVENTURE TOUR

(Harry Yacht Service; ☎0812 508 6105; www.orangutangreentours.com) Excellent at logistics for large groups, long-time guiding pioneer Herry Roustaman is also your point of contact if you're coming to Kumai aboard a yacht.

DIY Tours

Guides are now mandated for all visitors to Tanjung Puting. Fortunately, with nearly 90 guides registered with the park, they are relatively easy to come by. Unfortunately, they are not all created equal. To acquire a licence, a guide must speak basic English, undergo survival training and demonstrate basic wildlife knowledge. For some that is as far as it goes. If you are arranging a trip yourself on the ground, take the time to meet as many guides as you can (they'll find you) before choosing one.

The cost of hiring a *klotok* varies with its size. They range from small (two to four passengers, 450,000Rp to 550,000Rp per day) to large (eight to 10 passengers, 650,000Rp to 1,000,000Rp per day), including captain, mate and fuel. Cooks are an additional 100,000Rp per day, with food on top of that. When you factor in a guide (150,000Rp to 250,000Rp per day), permits (150,000Rp per person per day) and boat parking fees (100,000Rp per boat per day) the total cost for a three-day, two-night guided trip for two people easily tops 4,000,000Rp, even if you painstakingly haggle every step of the way.

Considering these prices, the hassle, transport to and from the airport, and all the other moving parts, the additional cost you may pay going through a reasonably priced company suddenly feels more affordable.

Sleeping

If you're looking to stay outside the park (typically before or after your cruise), try Kumai or Pangkalan Bun; the latter offers the only upscale accommodation in the area.

★Flora Homestay HOMESTAY $$

(☎0812 516 4727; r 500,000Rp, set meals 75,000Rp) Located directly on the river at the end of Sekonyer village, these rough-hewn wood cabins provide everything you need for a truly immersive Borneo experience. Pak Bana is eager to please, even offering to boil up water if you require a hot shower. Tours to a feeding station, canoe trips and jungle trekking are all available.

Rimba Lodge HOTEL $$$

(☎0361-747 4205; www.rimbaecolodge.com; s incl breakfast US$100-140, d incl breakfast US$110-150; ❄) Toeing a delicate line between resort and forest hut, Rimba achieves success in design and comfort, but falls short in maintenance and staff attentiveness. Although it is located near Sekonyer, access to the village is via a sketchy balance-beam path hidden behind the maintenance shed. The recent addition of solar panels lends more credence to the eco-claims.

Getting There & Around

- Tanjung Puting is typically reached via a flight to nearby Pangkalan Bun, then taxi to Kumai (150,000Rp, 20 minutes).
- Independent travellers must register at Pangkalan Bun police station upon arrival. Bring photocopies of your passport and visa (airport taxi drivers know the steps). This can also be organised by your guide.
- Speedboats from Kumai cost 700,000Rp per day, and take about two hours to reach Camp Leakey, but this is pure transport, not wildlife-spotting.
- For the cheapest route to Sekonyer village, take a ferry from Kumai across the bay (5000Rp), then an *ojek* (25,000Rp, 30 minutes) to the village.
- Canoes are a quiet alternative for exploring the river's shallow tributaries, and can be rented at Sekonyer village store for 50,000Rp per day.

Kumai

☎0532 / POP 25,000

The port of departure for Tanjung Puting National Park, Kumai is also known for its bird's-nest business, which fills the town with screeching warehouses. A handful of guesthouses and warungs line the main street, Jl HM Idris. Backpackers sometimes meet here to share the price of a *klotok*. There is an ATM downriver near the port, and the national park dock is upriver on the edge of town.

Sleeping & Eating

Permata Hijau GUESTHOUSE $
(☎0532-61325; Jl HM Idris, near Bank BNI; r with fan/air-con 100,000/175,000Rp; ❄) These budget rooms are clean, though you might find the electrical wiring a touch shocking. Located in the middle of the busy dockside nightlife, where food stalls and high jinks abound.

Mentari Hotel HOTEL $
(Jl Gerliya 98; r with cold mandi/hot shower 150,000/200,000Rp; ❄) Basic concrete boxes, although they do have windows and air-con. It's 600m away from the river.

Majid Hotel HOTEL $$
(☎0532-61740; Jl HM Idris; r incl breakfast 250,000Rp) The first place in town built with Western tourists in mind has all the right amenities. Owner Majid also has several *klotok* and can help solo travellers find shared boats. Upriver near the park dock.

★ **Acil Laila** INDONESIAN $
(Jl Gerilya 5; mains 15,000Rp; ⏲7.30am-10pm) Don't let the oodles of offal waiting to be skewered throw you off: this place does a mean grilled chicken and a divine *nasi bakar* (seasoned rice wrapped in a banana leaf and charred to perfection).

Getting There & Away

- Get to Kumai from Pangkalan Bun via the morning minibus (20,000Rp, 20 minutes), an *ojek* (50,000Rp), or Kijang (100,000Rp).
- Taxis from Pangkalan Bun airport to Kumai cost 150,000Rp, maximum three people.
- **Pelni** (☎0532-24420; Jl HM Idris; ⏲on days when boats arrive 8-11am & 2-4pm) and **Dharma Lautan Utama** (☎0532-61520; Jl Bahari 561) runs ferries connecting Kumai with Semarang (200,000Rp, 28 hours) once or twice weekly, and Surabaya (220,000Rp, 26 hours) almost daily.
- **Anggun Jaya Travel** (☎0532-61096, 0812 5366 2967; Jl Gerilya) sells boat, plane and **Yessoe Travel** (p605) bus tickets.

Pangkalan Bun

☎0532 / POP 200,000

Pangkalan Bun is largely a transit city, but with a few hidden surprises. Unlike many Kalimantan towns, the residents here have embraced the river instead of turning their backs on it, making a stroll up the boardwalk a colourful and engaging experience. If you want something better than backpacker digs before or after visiting Tanjung Puting, you'll only find it here.

Sights & Activities

Wander downriver along the Sungai Arut boardwalk to experience life before concrete and asphalt. Brightly painted *ces* (long-tail canoes) are parked between equally festive floating outhouses and fish farms. In the afternoon, children swim or fly kites while women pound spices. If you tire from walking, wave to almost any boat to take you back (negotiable, roughly 50,000Rp per hour)

Istana Kuning PALACE
(Yellow Palace; donations accepted; ⏲8am-1pm Mon-Fri, to 11am Sat, closed Sun) The mostly empty hilltop palace overlooking Pangkalan Bun

FLIGHTS FROM PANGKALAN BUN

DESTINATION	COMPANY	FARE (RP)	DURATION	FREQUENCY
Banjarmasin	Kalstar, Trigana	520,000	1½hr	1-2 daily
Jakarta	Kalstar, Trigana	700,000	1¼hr	2 daily
Ketapang	Kalstar, Trigana	400,000	40min	2 daily
Pontianak	Kalstar, Trigana	700,000	2hr	2 daily
Sampit	Kalstar	400,000	30min	1 daily
Semarang	Kalstar, Trigana	500,000	45min	2 daily
Surabaya	Kalstar, Trigana	600,000	1hr	2 daily

Pangkalan Bun

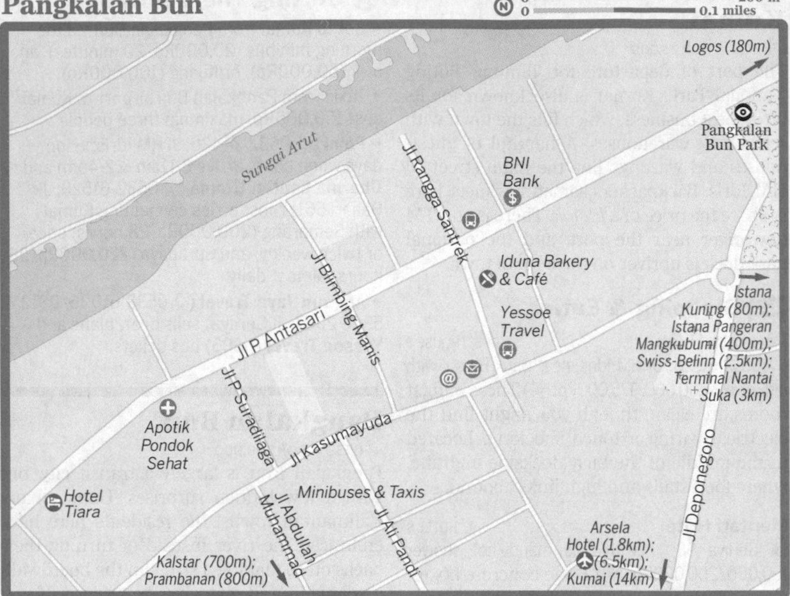

Park celebrates three architectural traditions of the sultans' assorted wives: Chinese, Dayak and Malay. Built in 1806 (and rebuilt in 1990 after a deranged woman burned it to the ground) it is not yellow, but was traditionally draped in yellow fabric.

Nearby, rambling **Istana Pangeran Mangkubumi** (open by luck, or by appointment), built to house the sultan's seven daughters, fights against gravity among well-kept gardens.

Sleeping & Eating

Hotel Tiara HOTEL **$**
(0532-22717; Jl P Antasari 16; r fan/air-con 120,000/170,000Rp;) With its high-ceilinged, well-maintained, convenient and cheap rooms, Hotel Tiara is a great backpacker stay. A new addition next door promises to provide even more options.

★ **Yayorin Homestay** HOMESTAY **$$**
(Yayasan Orangutan Indonesia; 0532-29057; info@yayorin.com; Jl Bhayangkara Km1; r incl breakfast 300,000Rp) Woven rattan walls. Solar-powered lights. Verdant woodland setting. These peaceful cottages are a fund-raising effort by Yayorin, a local NGO working to preserve Kalimantan's forests through education and community engagement. About 7km south of town; take Jl HM Rafi'i at the paratrooper roundabout.

Arsela Hotel BOUTIQUE HOTEL **$$**
(0532-28808; www.arselahotel.com; Jl Iskandar 15; r superior/deluxe incl breakfast 435,000/495,000Rp;) This architecturally compelling building with attached cafe sat empty for years before being lovingly brought back to life as a comfortable boutique hotel with lots of class. Set back from the road, the upstairs rooms have wood accents, rattan furniture, and a luxurious rain shower in the well-trimmed bathroom.

Swiss-Belinn HOTEL **$$**
(0532-27888; www.swiss-belhotel.com; Jl Ahmad Yani Km2; r incl breakfast 750,000-1,200,000Rp;) Lacking originality or charm, this chain hotel sits on the far edge of town, hoping its impressive breakfast buffet (95,000Rp for nonguests, 6am to 9am) and polished service will compensate for the fraying edges and dearth of character. The Royal Suite (2,700,000Rp) does get you a bathtub for a long soak after your rainforest adventure.

Iduna Bakery & Café BAKERY **$**
(0532-21031; Jl Rangga Santrek 42; snacks/mains 20,000/30,000Rp; 9am-9pm;) Choose from a variety of fresh pastries next door,

before sliding into a contemporary, air-conditioned space with stuffed chairs and cool lighting. Good luck explaining the concept of an Americano.

Prambanan SEAFOOD $
(☎0532-2126; Jl Hasanudin; mains 40,000Rp; ⏰7am-9pm) Average chicken. Above average fish. Next to Hotel Andika, this semi-al-fresco restaurant is renowned among locals and expats. The low-key, friendly vibe epitomises Pangkalan Bun.

Information

Many businesses close late in the afternoon and reopen after dark.

Apotik Pondok Sehat (☎0532-21167; Jl P Antasari 86) Well-stocked pharmacy with doctors' offices.

BNI Bank (Jl P Antasari) Buys crisp US$100 notes only.

Pahala Net (Jl Kasumayuda; per hour 4000Rp; ⏰8.30am-9pm; ❄) Quick internet connection.

Post Office (Jl Kasumayuda 29)

Getting There & Away

AIR

Kalstar (☎0532-21266; Jl Hassanudin 39)

Trigana (☎0532-27115; Jl Iskandar 3; ⏰8am-4.30pm & 6.30-9.30pm)

BUS

DAMRI's (☎0812 5186 3651; Nantai Suka Terminal) service to Pontianak (350,000Rp, 13 hours, daily at 7am) and all **Logos** (☎0532-24954; Jl Pangeran Antasari) buses depart from **Terminal Nantai Suka** (Jl Jend A Yani), while **Yessoe Travel** (☎0532-21276; Jl Kawitan 68) services depart from its own office. Destinations aboard Logos and Yessoe include Sampit (85,000Rp, six hours), Palangka Raya (125,000Rp, 12 hours), and Banjarmasin (175,000Rp to 290,000Rp, 16 hours).

Getting Around

Taxis to/from the airport (8km) cost 70,000Rp. Taxis to Kumai start at 100,000Rp.

Opelet around town cost 10,000Rp.

Minibuses to Kumai (20,000Rp, 20 minutes) leave across from Hotel Abadi.

Palangka Raya

☎0536 / POP 220,000

Originally envisioned by President Sukarno as a new capital city for Indonesia – and even for a pan-Asian state – Palangka Raya was built beginning in 1957. It shows in the refreshingly ordered streets and wide boulevards. While Sukarno's dream died, the city has a few surprises in store, including Kalimantan's only high-end jungle river cruise, two luxury hotels, some trendy cafes and a spot of nightlife. The market and old town are east, while government buildings and sprawl are west.

Sights

Museum Balanga MUSEUM
(Jl Cilik Riwut Km2.5; admission 15,000Rp; ⏰7.30am-3pm Mon-Fri, 8am-2pm Sat & Sun) An excellent, if small, museum introducing just enough Dayak ritual, custom and livelihood to inspire you to head into the forest in search of the real thing.

Old Town AREA
This network of boardwalks connecting wooden shops and houses lines the riverbank downstream of the planned city. The atmosphere here is more relaxed, and the smiles bigger.

Pasar Malam MARKET
The food stalls around Jl Halmahera and Jl Jawa run all day, but the the maze of shops here comes alive at night.

Borneo Orangutan Survival Foundation WILDLIFE RESERVE
(☎0536-330 8416; www.orangutan.or.id; Jl Cilik Riwut Km28; admission by donation; ⏰9am-3pm Sat & Sun) The centre is typically closed to visitors, in order to increase the rehabilitation success of its some 600 orangutans. The tiny visitor's centre opens on the weekends; you can see a few caged animals through its large windows. It is 2km from the main road. Follow signs for the arboretum.

Tours

★**Wow Borneo** BOAT TOUR
(☎0536-322 2099; www.wowborneo.com; Jl Barito 11; ⏰9am-5pm Mon-Fri, to 3pm Sat) Take everything you think you know about river travel in Kalimantan and throw it in the water. Wow Borneo's river cruises up the Sungai Rungan prove that exploring the jungle and its inhabitants doesn't have to be an exercise in stoic suffering. Built on the hulls of traditional wooden boats, their fleet of four cruisers offers amenities such as air-conditioned en-suite cabins and rattan sofas on the split-level decks.

Palangka Raya

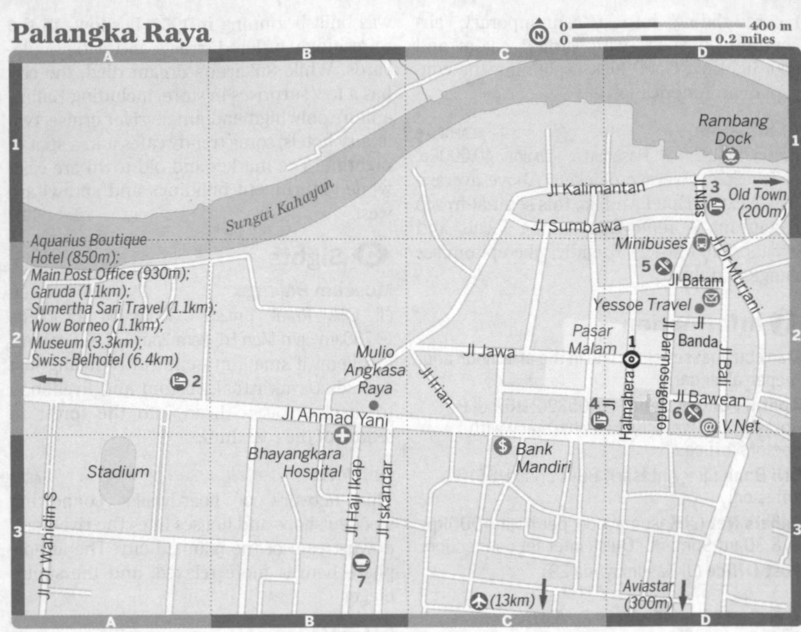

Palangka Raya

Sights
1 Pasar Malam D2

Sleeping
2 Hotel Dian Wisata A2
3 Hotel Mahkota D1
4 Hotel Sakura C2

Eating
5 Al Mu'Minun D2
6 Family D2

Drinking & Nightlife
7 Coffee Garage B3

Blue Betang ADVENTURE TOUR
(0813 4965 5021; blubetang_eventorganizer@yahoo.co.id; 9916 Jl Beliang 29) Honest and earnest guide Dodi specialises in hands-on, immersive, affordable, go-anywhere travel deep into Dayak country. Also provides day trips in the immediate vicinity of Palangka Raya.

Sleeping

Hotel Mahkota HOTEL $
(0536-322 1672; Jl Nias 5; r fan/air-con 100,000/190,000-375,000Rp;) Popular with students and families, this hotel offers a range of ageing basic, clean rooms in a good location for exploring the market, river and old town. Hot-water showers start with the VIP rooms (275,000Rp). Wi-fi in lobby only.

Hotel Dian Wisata HOTEL $
(0536-322 1241; Jl Ahmad Yani 68; r with fan/air-con incl breakfast 150,000/230,000Rp;) The odd design of this hotel, with its central well-lit atrium and colourful stairwell leading down to subterranean rooms, separates it from the boring concrete boxes that define its competition.

Hotel Sakura HOTEL $$
(0536-322 1680; Jl Ahmad Yani 87; r incl breakfast 300,000-400,000Rp;) This hotel's courtyard, populated with concrete critters, offers a welcome respite from the city. Some of the rooms have two-person tubs; the best overlook the courtyard.

Aquarius Boutique Hotel HOTEL $$
(0536-324 2121; www.aquariusboutiquehotels.com; Jl Imam Bonjol 5; d incl breakfast 685,000-950,000Rp;) A rooftop pool with a view. A 2nd-floor restaurant with a waterfall. A three-storey lounge, dance club, and karaoke complex. This hotel has all the trimmings, if a lack of upkeep. All room classes

are the same size, but have increasingly plush details. Avoid floors five and six due to noise.

★ Swiss-Belhotel Danum HOTEL **$$$**
(☎0536-323 2777; www.swiss-belhotel.com; Jl Tjilik Km5; r with breakfast from 850,000Rp;) This luxury property with resort intentions raises the local bar. The vast marble lobby drops to the restaurant (which serves an excellent buffet breakfast) before opening into the courtyard with its winding pool and palm trees. The place is trimmed with fractal Dayak motifs, and the rooms are well-thought out with attention to style and comfort.

Options range from entry-level standards to the 8,400,000Rp presidential suite with a whirlpool bathtub for two. The fitness centre is extensive with modern machines and free weights. Walk-in promo rates are often lower than even the internet discounts.

Eating & Drinking

At night, seafood and nasi goreng (fried rice) stalls sprout along Jl Yos Sudarso near the *bundaran besar* (large roundabout) – the place to see and be seen.

Al Mu'Minun INDONESIAN **$**
(☎0536-322 8659; Jl Darmosugondo 5; mains 20,000Rp; ⏲7am-8pm) Meaty chunks of fish are grilled up at this local favourite.

Family CHINESE **$**
(☎0536-322 9560; Jl Bawean 16; mains 25,000Rp; ⏲8am-10pm;) The best Chinese food in the city, with a standard menu. Known for its *ikan jelawat* (90,000Rp), a river fish cooked many ways. Serves beer.

★ Coffee Garage CAFE
(Jl Haji Ikap 22; coffee 10,000Rp; ⏲5.30pm-midnight;) A rare find, this trendy cafe comes alive at night serving all manner of coffee drinks in a colourfully painted house, garage included. It offers free wi-fi, basic food (spaghetti, desserts), outdoor seating and live music.

☆ Entertainment

For nightlife in Palangka Raya, the entertainment complex at the Aquarius Boutique Hotel is the only game in town. It includes **Blu Music Hall** (Jl Imam Bonjol 5; ⏲8pm-1am), a small but atmospheric blues bar, the adjacent **Vino Club** (Jl Imam Bonjol 5; ⏲10pm-3am), a cosy DJ club which doubles as the city's major performance venue, and **Luna Karaoke** (Jl Imam Bonjol 5; ⏲2pm-3am), which provides more traditional local entertainment. This is where the city's style-conscious young professionals come to hang out, representing a new wave of urban life.

Shopping

A collection of Dayak carvings and woven rattan crafts can be found in several shops along Jl Batam.

MEGA RICE DISASTER

On the drive between Palangka Raya and Banjarmasin you might notice a conspicuous lack of two things: forests and rice fields. The former is alarming since this was once a densely treed home to orangutans. The latter is tragic because the promise of rice destroyed the forest, leading to one of Indonesia's largest environmental disasters.

In the 1990s, President Suharto decided to boost Indonesia's food production by converting one million hectares of 'unproductive' peat forest into verdant rice fields. After the trees were cleared and 4600km of canals dug to drain the swamps, 60,000 transmigrants were relocated from Java to discover one small but important detail Suharto overlooked: nothing grows on the acidic soils of drained peat.

As peat dries it collapses and oxidises, releasing sulphuric acid into the water and carbon dioxide into the atmosphere. Further, when it rains, compacted peat floods. Catastrophically. When it stops raining, dried peat burns. Unstoppably. During the powerful El Nino drought of 1997, mega fires released over a billion tons of carbon dioxide into the environment.

Today, the area remains a wasteland. Some transmigrant communities have turned to illegal logging to try and make a living. Oil palm companies eye the land for planting. Local NGOs try to block the drainage channels in a noble attempt to right the horrific wrong. Meanwhile, Indonesia continues to import over one million metric tonnes of rice every year.

Information

Bank Mandiri (Jl Ahmad Yani; ⏲8am-3pm Mon-Fri) Currency exchange.

Bhayangkara Hospital (☎0536-322 1520; Jl Ahmad Yani 22)

Mulio Angkasa Raya (☎0536-322 1031; Jl Ahmad Yani 55) Offers booking for flights, car rental and Kijang. Not many staff speak English, though.

Sumertha Sari Travel (☎0536-322 1033; Jalan Tjilik Riwut Km0.5) Kijang transport and charter.

Post Office (Jl Batam) Branch office. Main office is located on Jl Imam Bonjol.

V.Net (Jl Ahmad Yani 99; per hour 4000Rp; ⏲8.30am-2am) Internet access.

Yessoe Travel (☎0852 4679 8939, 0536-322 1436; Jl Banda 7) All things bus.

Getting There & Away

AIR

For smaller regional destinations, try Susi Air and Aviastar. Airlines no longer sell tickets at the airport.

Aviastar (☎0536-323 8848; Jl PM Noor 5)

Garuda (☎0536-322 3573; Jl Kinibalu 1, PALMA mall)

Lion Air (Airport)

Susi Air (Jl Adonis Samad Gang Damai 9) South of town, in a residential area.

BUS & KIJANG

All long-haul buses deposit passengers at the new terminal 10km south of town, which annoyingly has no public transport options to the city. If you're coming from Banjarmasin, have them drop you at the Bangkirai four-way intersection 1.5km east of the terminal, and wait for an *angkot* heading north. Otherwise, an *ojek* will cost 50,000Rp. **Yessoe Travel** offers departing passengers free transport to the terminal from their office on Jl Batam, near the market.

Sumertha Sari Travel Kijang serve the same destinations, with higher costs and more exhaust fumes per passenger.

Getting Around

- Yellow minibuses (*angkot* or 'taxis', 5000Rp) ply major thoroughfares, converging at Jl Darmosugondo near the market.
- Airport service (13km, 20 minutes) costs 80,000Rp.
- Hire a boat at **Rambang dock** (Dermaga Rambang) to tour around, or head further upriver.

SOUTH KALIMANTAN

Banjarmasin

☎0511 / POP 625,000

Banjarmasin capitalises on its waterways and river life. But, as more locals board up their back porches to bathe without fear of prying eyes and snapping cameras, and as the government buys up waterfront property for parks and mixed commerce, the riverfront dynamic is slowly changing, perhaps for

TRANSPORT FROM PALANGKA RAYA

Air

DESTINATION	COMPANY	FARE (RP)	DURATION (HR)	FREQUENCY
Balikpapan	Garuda	670,000	1¼	daily
Jakarta	Garuda, Lion	680,000	1¾	4 daily
Ketapang	Aviastar	666,000	1¼	Mon, Fri
Muara Tewah	Susi Air	500,000	1	Wed, Fri, Sun
Pangkalan Bun	Susi Air	495,000	1	Wed, Fri, Sun
Pontianak	Garuda	910,000	1¼	daily
Surabaya	Citilink, Lion	520,000	1¼	3 daily

Bus

DESTINATION	FARE (RP)	DURATION (HR)	FREQUENCY
Banjarmasin	80,000	6	3am & 8am daily
Pangkalan Bun	100,000-200,000	10	7am & 4pm daily
Sampit	60,000-100,000	5	7am & 4pm daily

WORTH A TRIP

SEBANGAU NATIONAL PARK: MEET PEAT

Spared the destruction of the Mega Rice Disaster (p607), this area of peat swamp forest was gazetted as Sebangau National Park in 2004. Although it has seen its share of degradation, Sebangau is still home to over 5000 wild orangutans, and the forest itself is a fascinating draw.

Peat forms over thousands of years as organic material accumulates in seasonally flooded regions. The semidecayed material can extend as deep as 20m below the surface, and contains more carbon than the forest growing above. Due to habitat loss, nearly half of the mammals and one-third of the bird species found in peat swamps are endangered or threatened.

Travelling through a peat forest ranges from delightfully challenging to extremely adventurous. During the dry season, the uneven spongy trail will occasionally give way as your foot plunges into a pocket of wet peat. During the rainy season, you may spend significant stretches submerged to your knees or chest as you hunt for hornbills, red leaf and proboscis monkeys, and sun bears. Travelling by boat between ranger posts and dry hills makes for an extraordinary adventure through the true wilds of Borneo.

The closest access from Palangka Raya is **Sungai Koran** on the north edge of the park. Take a regular *angkot* (10,000Rp, 40 minutes) south to **Dermaga Kereng Bangkirai** and talk to the rangers at the national park post. If nobody is around, try calling Pak Ian (☎0852 2191 9160). Expenses include 150,000Rp per day for park entrance, 150,000Rp per day for a guide, and 250,000Rp per day for boat rental plus fuel. If you wish to stay overnight at any of the ranger posts (recommended), you'll also need a cook (90,000Rp) and food. The west edge of the park is less degraded and is accessible via a two-hour drive to **Baun Bango**, where you can check in with the park rangers and arrange a boat to the outpost on **Punggualas Lake**.

the best. The rest of the city is a sprawling beast, with the chaotic commerce of downtown turning eerily quiet at night, save for the night market holding out against the megamalls sprouting up in the suburbs.

Sights

Mesjid Raya Sabilal Muhtadin MOSQUE
(Jl Sudirman) FREE This large flat-domed mosque looks like something off a *Star Wars* set. During Ramadan, the famous **Pasar Wadai** (Cake Fair) runs along the adjacent riverfront.

Masjid Sultan Suriansyah MOSQUE
FREE Though it marks the first Islamic place of worship in Borneo, the beautiful angular wooden building was reconstructed in 1746, leaving the oldest physical mosque accolade to Banua Lawas from the Tabalong Regency (1625). Take a Kuin *angkot* to the end of the line.

Soetji Nurani Temple BUDDHIST TEMPLE
(Jl Niaga Timur 45) FREE Step into this 1898 temple, and the hobbit-sized candles and incense coils that smoulder for days will transport you 3000km north to China.

Tours

See Banjarmasin in a single journey: arrange a predawn boat near Jembatan Merdeka (Merdeka Bridge) to the floating markets. It takes an hour or so to navigate the canals lined with ramshackle homes, where the day is just beginning with a bath and tooth-brushing in the murky trash-strewn water. It feels a touch invasive until the waves and beaming smiles betray an unflappable Indonesian pride.

There are two markets: **Kuin** is closer, but by all accounts **Lok Baintan** is more traditional. At the markets, women paddle canoes brimming with exotic produce in search of a buyer among the tourist boats bristling with selfie-sticks. If it all sounds a bit bizarre, that's because it is, but it's also profoundly educational, and astoundingly beautiful.

Trips can be combined with a stop at **Kembang Island** (tours from 100,000Rp), where macaques walk the boardwalk, or at Masjid Sultan Suriansyah, site of the first (but not oldest) mosque in Kalimantan.

You'll need a guide (who will secure a boat as well) to explain what you're seeing on the floating markets tour (such as the significance of how women tie their sarongs). Tours

Central Banjarmasin

Central Banjarmasin

Sights
1 Mesjid Raya Sabilal Muhtadin B1
2 Soetji Nurani Temple C1

Sleeping
3 Hotel Biuti A2
4 Hotel Perdana B2
5 Hotel SAS A2
6 NASA Hotel A2
7 Swiss-Belhotel Borneo C3

Eating
8 Cendrawasih Sarahai B2
9 Said Abdullah C1

Drinking & Nightlife
10 People's Place C1

Entertainment
11 Dynasty B1

including a guide cost about 200,000Rp, and run from 5.30am to 9.30am.

Some Banjarmasin guides tour up into the Meratus Mountains, too, though we recommend supporting local guides in places such as Loksado.

Sarkani Gambi GUIDE
(☎0813 5187 7858; kani286@yahoo.com) Friendly and informative Sarkani runs tours for large foreign groups as well as customised trips for individuals.

Mulyadi Yasin GUIDE
(☎0813 5193 6200; yadi_yasin@yahoo.co.id) Professional and responsive.

Muhammad Yusuf GUIDE
(☎0813 4732 5958; yusuf_guidekalimantan@yahoo.co.id) The energetic head of the thriving South Kalimantan Guiding Association can also help you find other guides in a pinch.

Sleeping

A few questionable sub-100,000Rp options exist near Jl Hasanudin.

★Hotel SAS HOTEL $
(☎0511-335 3054; Jl Kacapiring Besar 2; r incl breakfast 190,000-279,000Rp; ❄) A delightful find off a quiet side street, this hotel is built around an imposing Banjar home with towering roof and central stair. The *mandiangin* rooms are newly renovated to good effect – avoid the others. Head down Jl Cempaka and turn left at the old woman selling bananas.

Hotel Biuti HOTEL $
(☎0511-335 4493; Jl Haryono MT 21; r incl breakfast 210,000-300,000Rp; ❄📶) Biuti has some of the more beautiful and colourful rooms in its class, with decorative wood walls, comfortable artistic public spaces and clean bathrooms. Even the fake lobby trees work (sort of). Cheaper rooms are in the older wing. Upgrade and be happy.

Hotel Perdana HOTEL $
(☎0511-335 3276; hotelperdana@plasa.com; Jl Katamso 8; r 120,000-300,000Rp; ❄) This rambling Escher-esque complex has a variety of musty multicoloured rooms popular with backpackers. Out front is a cacophony of commerce by day, and a reasonably entertaining night market after dark. English-speaking Linda can point you in whichever direction you need pointing, or find guides. Beware of mosquitoes.

NASA Hotel HOTEL $$
(☎0511-336 6868; Jl H Djok Mentaya 8; r incl breakfast 490,000-560,000Rp; ❄📶) Aimed at modern business travellers, the spotless superior rooms don't have any windows, but do have modern art and safety deposit boxes. The staff are efficient – sometimes to a fault. Live music in the lounge and the attached karaoke complex may appeal to some.

Swiss-Belhotel Borneo HOTEL $$
(☎0511-327 1111; www.swiss-belhotel.com; Jl Pangeran Antasari 86A; r incl breakfast 600,000-700,000Rp, ste incl breakfast 1,300,0000Rp; ❄📶) This traditional boutique-style hotel with warm wooden accents is undergoing a tasteful renovation. The deluxe is a significant upgrade in style for not much money. Rooms come with a free trip to the Kuin floating market (no guide) for one guest, additional guests are 100,000Rp. Boat leaves at 5am.

Eating & Drinking

Seek out the local speciality *soto Banjar*, a delicious soup found across the city. The Kawasan Wisata Kuliner (tourist food region), riverside between the Merdeka and Dewi bridges, has many good, but not great, options.

★ **People's Place** PUB $
(☎0511-327 7007; Jl Veteran 3, Summer B&B rooftop; beer 30,000Rp, snacks 20,000Rp; ⏲11am-11pm; 📶) With 270 degrees of floor-to-ceiling windows and an open-air porch overlooking the river and mosque, this is *the* best hangout in town. An eclectic Anglophilic atmosphere and live acoustic music draws a crowd. The lychee beer is embarrassingly refreshing.

Pondok Bahari INDONESIAN $
(☎0511-325 3688; Jl Simpang Pierre Tendean 108; mains from 20,000Rp; ⏲24hr) Pull up some floor space near the fountain and sink your teeth into some *ketupat*, sticky rice cooked in woven banana-leaf packets. Locals recommend the *rowon daging* soup, a Banjar take on an east Java favourite. Patient staff bring reinforcements to help you translate the menu.

Cendrawasih Sarahai SEAFOOD $
(Jl Pangeran Samudera; mains 20,000Rp; ⏲9am-10pm) Delve deeper into Banjar cuisine at this renowned spot (not to be confused with the mediocre other Cendrawasih, established next door to the right by a competitive relative.) Pick fish, seafood or chicken grilled to order. Please avoid (and politely shame them for) the endangered turtle eggs.

Said Abdullah INDONESIAN $
(Jl Ahmad Yani Km1; mains 25,000Rp; ⏲10am-11.30pm) Locals say the *nasi kuning* (saffron rice) at this unassuming place is Banjarmasin's best. You can restock your supply of propolis and Tahitian Noni elixir while you're here.

Entertainment

Dynasty KARAOKE
(Hotel Aria Barito, Jl Haryono MT; admission male/female 50,000/25,000Rp) This entertainment complex with disco, bar, and karaoke tries… and, at times, succeeds.

Information

Adat Tours (☎0821 4888 8801; Jl Hasanudin 27) Flight bookings, some tours, little English.

BNI Bank (Bank Negara Indonesia; Jl Lambung Mangkurat)

Haji La Tunrung (☎0511-336 5559; Jl Haryono MT 24) Exchange chain dealing in multiple currencies.

Internet (Jl Haryono MT 24; per hour 3000Rp; ⏲3pm-late)

Main Post Office (Jl Lambung Mangkurat)

Rumah Sakit Ulin (☎0511-252180; Jl Ahmad Yani 42) Medical centre.

Getting There & Away

AIR

Garuda (☎0511-336 6747; Jl Hasanudin 31)

Kalstar (☎0511-327 2470; Jl Ahmad Yani Km6 553)

Lion Air (☎0511-747 7480; Jl Ahmad Yani Km6, Efa Hotel lobby; ⏱9.30am-7.30pm)

Sriwijaya Air (☎0511-327 2377; Jl Ahmad Yani Km3.5; ⏱9am-5pm)

BOAT

Ocean ferries depart from Trisakti Pinisi Harbour (3km west on Jl Soetoyo). Pelni services Semarang (420,000Rp, 24 hours, weekly), while Dharma Lautan Utama services Surabaya (260,000Rp, 22 hours, five services a week). For boats to the interior, take a bus to Muara Tewah and start your journey there.

Dharma Lautan Utama (☎0511-441 0555; www.dluonline.co.id; Jl Yos Sudarso 4C, next to Hotel Queen)

Pelni (☎0511-335 3077; Jl Martadinata 10)

BUS

All buses leave from the Kilo Enam terminal at Jl Ahmad Yani Km6, southeast of downtown, accessible by *angkot*.

ℹ Getting Around

Angkot (5000Rp) routes are labelled by their destination, and fan out from terminals at Jl Pangeran Samudera circle, in the city core, and Antasari Centre, to the east. Becak and *ojeks* for hire gather around market areas. Taxis to/from Syamsuddin Noor Airport (26km) cost 120,000Rp.

Kandangan

☎0517 / POP 45,000

A local transport hub, Kandagan is also a fairly attractive town worth exploring. Tidy and well planned, it has decent budget hotels, a bustling market and numerous restaurants. It is also the gateway to the mountain oasis of Loksado and the buffalo herds of Nagara. Reserve ahead as rooms are few.

Sleeping & Eating

The Kandangan bus terminal doubles as a food court, and is lined with warungs to keep you well fed for days.

★Wisma Duta HOTEL **$**
(☎0571-21073; Jl Permuda 9; r fan/air-con with breakfast 130,000/250,000Rp; ❄📶) This converted country home is a rare and welcome find. Rattan walls are a nice touch, even when adorned with assorted glass armaments. Head down the alley northeast from the bus terminal and turn left.

Hotel Mutia HOTEL **$**
(☎0517-21270; Jl Soeprapto; r incl breakfast 200,000-330,000Rp; ❄📶) Basic box rooms, convenient to the bus station and market.

TRANSPORT FROM BANJARMASIN

Air

DESTINATION	COMPANY	PRICE (RP)	DURATION (HR)	FREQUENCY
Balikpapan	Lion, Sriwijaya	400,000	1	daily
Jakarta	Citilink, Garuda, Lion	600,000	1¾	daily
Makassar	Sriwijaya	680,000	1¼	Mon, Wed, Fri, Sun
Pangkalan Bun	Kalstar, Trigana	700,000	1	1-2 daily
Surabaya	Citilink, Garuda	450,000	1	daily
Yogyakarta	Garuda, Lion	660,000	1¼	daily

Bus

DESTINATION	PRICE (RP)	DURATION (HR)	FREQUENCY
Balikpapan	155,000-185,000	12	4 daily 2-5pm
Kandangan	50,000	4	several daily 9am-6pm
Muara Tewah	110,000	12	2 daily
Negara	60,000	5	several daily 9am-6pm
Palangka Raya	70,000-85,000	5	5 daily 5-11am
Pangkalan Bun	180,000-235,000	12	5 daily 5-11am
Samarinda	180,000-215,000	15	4 daily 2-5pm

Medina HOTEL $$

(☎0517-21219; Jl M Johansyah 26; r incl breakfast 350,000Rp) The newest concrete box in town is clean, if uninspired. Hot showers. Just up the block from the bus terminal.

Getting There & Around

Minibuses run frequently to/from Banjarmasin's Km6 terminal (50,000Rp, four hours) until midafternoon. Buses for Balikpapan and Samarinda (125,000Rp to 165,000Rp) pass the Kandangan terminal regularly. *Ojek* are abundant, while becak are slowly dwindling.

Pick-up trucks for Loksado (30,000Rp, 1½ hours, 9am) leave from **Muara Bilui**, a nondescript stop on a residential street 800m east of the bus terminal.

Negara

Northwest of Kandangan, the riverside town of Negara is the gateway to a vast wetland ranch, where water buffalo swim from their elevated corrals at sunrise in search of grazing areas and are herded back at dusk by cowboys in canoes – an intriguing sight if you're there in late afternoon. Rent a boat at the dock near the mosque to see the swimming herds (200,000Rp).

The trip to Negara is memorable, too, along an elevated road through seasonally flooded wetlands lined with communities on stilts. To get here from Kandagan take a public minibus (15,000Rp, one hour) or taxi (150,000Rp return). Annoyingly there is no hotel in town.

Loksado

Nestled at the end of the road in the foothills of the Meratus Mountains, Loksado is as close to an earthly Elysium as you'll find in Kalimantan. The main village sits inside a large bend in the clear chattering stream which acts as a moat protecting it from the onslaught of the modern world. Numerous trails – some paved – connect remote villages with even more remote settlements, making the area ideal for adventurers with a habit of wandering to the end of things. A mountain bike would be the perfect tool for exploration, but alas, nobody rents them in town (yet). Base here for treks to mountain peaks, waterfalls, or remote Dayak villages. Or do none of the above and just enjoy carefree mountain-town life Kalimantan style.

Activities

Muara Tanuhi Hot Springs HOT SPRING

(admission 5000Rp) These developed hot springs, located in an undermaintained resort 7km west of Loksado, make a relaxing end to a long trek. Stay across the street at Pondok Bamboo (100,000Rp) and enjoy all-night access to the pools.

Mountain Hikes

Hiking trails in the Meratus combine forest, villages, rivers, suspension bridges and *balai adat* (community house) visits. One-day walks from Loksado reach a seemingly endless number of waterfalls, and range from moderate to billy-goating up the side of impossible slopes. A long history of shifting cultivation means it is a good five-hour walk to primary forest, but there's still plenty of picture-worthy scenery closer to town. For all but the closest destinations, a local guide is highly recommended. A popular multiday trek includes summiting **Gunung Besar** (aka Halau Halau, 1901m, three to four days) the tallest mountain in the Meratus range and one of the few Kalimantan peaks with a view.

Be prepared for your particular route, read up on jungle trekking (see boxed text, p629), and don't be afraid to rein in your guide if the pace or terrain is beyond your skill level.

Bamboo Rafting

Being poled downriver on a narrow hand-tied bamboo raft ranges from relaxing to spirited, depending on water levels. Three hours (300,000Rp) might test your attention span, but the 90-minute option is just about right.

Guides

Although guides from Banjarmasin range into this area, nothing beats the perspective of a local. English speakers are smart for more involved trips, but day treks can be a world of fun with a dictionary, sign language, and an enthusiastic villager.

Pak Amat GUIDE

(☎0813 4876 6573) An English-speaking, personable Dayak and long-standing Loksado resident, with complete knowledge of the area.

Samuil Noil GUIDE

(☎0812 5127 3802) Unassuming and with a great attitude, Loksado native Noil will happily put his gardening on hold to show you the land he is so passionate about. Speaks English.

WORTH A TRIP

BANJARBARU

Three curious stops accessible from the Banjarbaru roundabout (20,000Rp, 38km southeast of Banjarmasin) can be seen in a half-day return from Banjarmasin or on your way to or from Kandangan.

Cempaka Diamond Fields (Desa Pumpung; Sat-Thu) Wooden sluices filter muck from pits where men stand chest deep blasting away at the sediment with water cannons. Mining at its most basic, cheapest, picturesque, and – for the bold – participatory. At the Banjarbaru roundabout take a green passenger truck southbound to Desa Pumpung (6000Rp, 15 minutes, 7km), then walk 700m south from the main road.

Museum Lambung Mangkurat (051 1477 2453; Jl Ahmad Yani 36; admission 5000Rp; 8am-4pm Sun-Thu, 8.30-11am Fri, 8.30am-3.30pm Sat) An above-average museum of local arts and history with approximate English translations providing nuggets of information about pivotal events – like the Banjar people sinking a Dutch warship in 1860, armed with only canoes and knives. Also, learn the architectural differences between a scholar's and a married princess' house. Head 1km west of the Banjarbaru roundabout.

Penggosokkan Intan (Diamond Polishing and Information Center; 9am-4pm Sat-Thu) Lots of shops polish diamonds, but this is the official place for tourists to watch; 700m north of the Banjarbaru roundabout.

Shady GUIDE
(0821 5306 0515; www.borneo-discoverytours.com) A young and enthusiastic English-speaking guide from Kandangan with extensive trekking experience and a great sense of humour.

Sleeping & Eating

Sleeping options are expanding, with two new losmen opening near the tourist info centre, and a bona fide resort downriver. Avoid the sad concrete Wisma Loksado hotel on the eroding island.

A smattering of warung along the river provide basic Indonesian fare, with the best one found across the street from Mount Martuas Resort.

★ **Wisma Alya** GUESTHOUSE $
(0821 5330 8276; r 150,000Rp) This two-storey backpackers haven, with just five bare wooden rooms, hangs over the rushing Sungai Amandit, making the upstairs porch the best hang-out in town. Don't let them slough you off to the *cabang* (branch lodge) down river; it's set back from the road and removed from the village.

New competition nearby puts you in a good negotiating position, but the husband and wife team are so helpful for finding guides and other services, you may feel guilty about haggling.

Mangkuraksa Malaris HOMESTAY $
(0856 5129 8492; floor space 150,000Rp) At tiny Loklahong village, 2km downriver from Loksado, you can sleep with the locals in a breezy bamboo-walled hut next to the *balai adat*. You'll only get a chunk of floor in the living room, but you'll also meet some phenomenal folks, and have one of Kalimantan's premier swimming holes at the end of your block.

Mount Martuas Resort HOTEL $$
(0812 5150 4866; r/villa 400,000/1,500,000Rp;) Loksado's official entrant into the near-luxury class. Located 800m downriver from town, it's not in the thick of village life, but you will have your own private bend of the river here. The well-crafted, rough-wood rooms come with fans and open-air stone bathrooms. Add 50,000Rp to upgrade to hot water.

The two villas are set back from the river, and offer air-con and a large kitchen/living area. Dine at the open-air restaurant, or at the tasty warung across the street.

Getting There & Around

Pick-up trucks leave for Loksado from **Muara Bilui** in Kandangan (30,000Rp, 1½ hours, 9am). They leave Loksado for Kandangan at 7am. Enquire at Wisma Alya for an *ojek* to trailheads.

EAST KALIMANTAN

Balikpapan

☎ 0542 / POP 560,000

As Kalimantan's only cosmopolitan city, Balikpapan is almost worthy of being considered a destination unto itself. A long history of oil money and foreign workers has had a tremendous impact, bringing Western aesthetics to this Eastern port town. The city is clean and vibrant, with several enormous shopping areas and some decent beaches. High-end hotels with reasonable rates abound, and the nightlife surprises. The city sprawls in all directions, but most of the action takes place in the centre off Jl Sudirman, which comes alive at night. Overall the city makes a fine weekend break, and a great place to begin or end more adventurous travels. See how many sun bear motifs you can spot.

Sights

Most sights of note lie outside of Balikpapan's borders (see boxed text, p619).

Kemala Beach BEACH
(Jl Sudirman) A clean, white-sand beach with adjacent cafes and restaurants, and a laid-back vibe. If you need a break from the jungle (urban or natural) this is your best local option. Although it gets hot at midday, you probably won't want to swim in the polluted waters.

Masjid Agung At-Taqwa MOSQUE
(Jl Sudirman) FREE An impressive sight, this mosque is adorned with a complex sheath of Islamic geometrical patterns, and is lit up in multicoloured splendour at night.

Tours

Rusdiansyah GUIDE
(☎0812 5331 2333; www.borneokalimantan.com) Now chair of the East Borneo Guiding Association, Pak Rusdy has been guiding throughout the island for 20 years and knows the land well.

Indra GUIDE
(☎081 2585 9800; indrahadi91@yahoo.com) The first choice for Japanese tourists; his English is serviceable, too.

Sleeping

The budget digs here are generally dismal and depressing, and we can't recommend them. Splurge. Ask about discounts everywhere.

★ **Wisma Kemala Bhayangkari** HOTEL $$
(☎0812 5490 2392, 0542-421260; Jl Sudirman 6; r250,000-385,000Rp; ❄) Recently re-established as public lodging after a period as the residence of the police chief (who moved into a new mansion next door), this place is a steal for its clean and simple rooms on the beach. Don't come expecting luxury (there is no hot water), but the VIP rooms up front are spacious and freshly painted. On *angkot* route 3.

Access Kemala Beach and its cafes just off the back lawn.

Ibis Hotel HOTEL $$
(☎0542-820821; www.ibishotels.com; Jl Suparjan 2; r 350,000Rp; ❄@🛜🏊) Balikpapan's great steal. The cosy, design-conscious rooms are stylish and sophisticated, with bursts of bright colour and funky space-station bathrooms. Best of all, guests are welcome to use the considerable amenities of the adjoining five-star Novotel. Basically, you're staying at the Novotel for a third of the price. Breakfast 60,000Rp.

Hotel Pacific HOTEL $$
(☎0542-750888; Jl Ahmad Yani 33; d incl breakfast 400,000-500,000Rp; ❄🛜) An excellent, classic Asian hotel with very accommodating staff and a convenient location for food options. The wooden floor and dark trim are dated, but manage to be warming rather than foreboding. Spotless bathrooms all come with bathtubs.

Hotel Gajah Mada HOTEL $$
(☎0542-734634; Jl Sudirman 328; s 229,000-418,000Rp, d 270,000-467,000Rp; ❄) These clean, bare rooms are located on prime real estate next to Balikpapan Plaza. Cheaper rooms have fans only, but the ocean breeze down the shotgun hallway keeps things cool. A large back deck overlooks the ocean, with a filthy beach next door.

Aiqo Hotel HOTEL $$
(☎0542-750288; Jl Pranoto 9; s 248,000Rp, d 268,000-328,000Rp; ❄🛜) A clean midmarket option with tiny soak-everything-when-you-shower bathrooms. The 30,000Rp surcharge for a superior room adds nothing but an in-room coffee maker. Wi-fi in the lobby only.

Balikpapan

Balikpapan

Sights

1 Masjid Agung At-Taqwa....B3

Sleeping

2 Aiqo Hotel....C2
3 Hotel Gajah Mada....C3
4 Hotel Gran Senyiur....B2
5 Hotel Pacific....C2
6 Ibis Hotel....C2
7 Novotel Balikpapan....C2

Eating

8 Bondy....C2
9 Ocean's Resto....C3
10 Sky Bar/Sky Grill....B2
11 Soto Queen....C1

Drinking & Nightlife

12 Book Cafe....B3
13 Ruko Bandar....B3

Shopping

14 Balikpapan Plaza....C3

Information

15 Aero Travel....C2
16 Kantorimigrasi Kelas....A3
17 New Sedayu Wisata....A3
18 Totogasono Sekawan....C2

★**Hotel Gran Senyiur** HOTEL $$$
(0542-820211; gran.senyiurhotels.com; Jl ARS Muhammad 7; r incl breakfast from 860,000Rp;) Unique in Kalimantan, this old-world Asian luxury hotel proves to the younger generic business hotels that experience and wisdom count ... a lot. Fine woodwork warms spaces throughout, and rooms are priced well for their elevated class. From the lobby lounge to the world-class Sky Bar, which adds a modern note to the roof, everything is upscale without being ostentatious.

Deluxe rooms are really just superior rooms with a useless kitchen space. For those in a suite mood, the opulent 'governor's room' has Victorian furniture, while the 'executive' gets you the exact same layout and killer view, with a slight downgrade in furniture.

Le Grandeur Balikpapan HOTEL $$$
(0542-420155; Jl Sudirman; r with breakfast from 870,000Rp;) A venerable luxury hotel, oozing sophistication. The 4th-floor business-class rooms have been renovated to great effect, while open-air waterfront dining

and live jazz make for a classy stay. Unfortunately, an abundance of trash tarnishes the beachfront location. On Jl Sudirman about 2km east of Plaza Balikpapan.

Novotel Balikpapan HOTEL $$$
(0542-820820; www.novotel.com/asia; Jl Suparjan 2; r incl breakfast 985,000-1,160,000Rp;) A family-friendly hotel, with an ubermodern interior and all amenities, including a patisserie, cafe, gym and 2nd-floor rooftop pool with a swim-up bar (50,000Rp to nonguests). However, the stained superior rooms with laminate furniture don't quite live up to the price.

The fitness centre has multiple modern machines and free weights. Parents are liberated by the free kids club.

Eating

★Soto Queen INDONESIAN $
(Warung Kuin Abduh, SQ; Jl Ahmad Yani; soto Banjar 15,000Rp; 2-11pm) We're not sure if they serve anything besides *soto Banjar* (chicken soup seasoned with a delicate blend of spices including cinnamon)… we've never felt the need to ask. You'll likely have to wait for a seat.

Jimbaran BALINESE $
(Dapur Bali; Jl Sudirman, Kemala Beach; mains 25,000Rp; 10am-11pm) Billowing white curtains beckon you to this open-air Balinese restaurant at the end of Kemala Beach. Locals swear by the *ayam taliwang*, a fried-grilled chicken from Lombok, and the *ayam betutu*, a spicy recipe that will transport you to Bali. Live music Saturday and Monday.

Bondy INTERNATIONAL $
(0542-424285; Jl Ahmad Yani 1; mains 35,000Rp; 10am-10pm) Dine among sculpted trees and thriving flowers in a tranquil courtyard in the middle of the city. Popular with locals and expats, mostly for their extensive homemade ice cream menu. A banana split is 30,000Rp; steaks start at 90,000Rp.

★Ocean's Resto SEAFOOD, INTERNATIONAL $$
(0542-739439; Ruko Bandar; mains 40,000Rp; 9am-11pm;) An entire reef's worth of fish, steaks aplenty, plus burgers, pizza, and 14 types of fried rice all served above the surf. Ocean's anchors a row of cafes along the waterfront, and is (deservedly) the most popular. The tiny open-air 2nd-floor curry house is a good place for appetisers.

Pondok Kelapa SEAFOOD $$
(0542-733956; Jl Yos Sudarso 72; mains 35,000Rp; 11am-10pm) Strategically located on the tip of Balikpapan bay, come here for epic sunset dining; watch the oil tankers pass while dining on gigantic *udang gala* (river prawns).

Sky Bar / Sky Grill SEAFOOD $$
(Jl ARS Muhammad, Grand Senyiur Hotel; mains 55,000Rp; 3-11pm) The Grand Senyiur Hotel has an awesome rooftop, combining glass-walled al fresco dining and a sophisticated piano bar with panoramic city views.

Open House INTERNATIONAL $$$
(0542-744823; Jl Puncak Markoni Atas 88; mains from 160,000Rp; 11am-11pm) Balikpapan's most romantic place to blow your last rupiah on a date is defined by architecturally dizzying spaces atop a prominent hill. Reserve your *puncak* (summit) table for two at the top of the spiral staircase. The above-average food blends Mediterranean, international and Indian menus; bring your own wine. A blanket 20% discount on weekdays drops to 15% on weekends.

Drinking & Nightlife

Balikpapan's expat community has fuelled a more relaxed attitude toward alcohol and nightlife than is found in other parts of Kalimantan. Most hotels serve spirits, and package liquor is available (for a price) at the Swiss-Belhotel. To get the pulse of the local scene, head to the **Ruko Bandar** (Jl Sudirman, waterfront) complex.

Book Cafe COFFEE
(0542-739168; Ruko Bandar; snacks 15,000Rp; 10am-midnight;) Monopoly anyone? A chill nonalcoholic hang-out in the Ruko Bandar complex, Book Cafe has games aplenty and, yes, books in English and Bahasa Indonesia to buy, borrow or trade. For a truly humbling experience, get trounced by a local student in a game of Scrabble… in English.

Shopping

Shopping is concentrated around **Balikpapan Plaza** (cnr Jls Sudirman & Ahmad Yani) which has a Hypermart (for groceries).

Pasar Kebun Sayur SOUVENIRS
(9am-6pm) An eclectic market for local handicrafts, gemstones and souvenirs. North of the city centre on yellow *angkot* 5.

Information

Aero Travel (0542-443350; Jl Ahmad Yani 19) Airline tickets.

Haji La Tunrung (☎0542-731975; Jl Ahmad Yani 6A; ⏰7.30am-9pm) Exchange chain dealing in multiple currencies.

Kantorimigrasi Kelas (☎0542-421175; Jl Sudirman 23) Immigration office.

New Sedayu Wisata (NSW; ☎0542-420601; Jl Sudirman 2B) Best source for all things ferry.

Pertamina Hospital (☎0542-421212; Jl Sudirman 1)

Rebel Net Internet (off Jl Ahmad Yani; per hour 5000Rp)

Totogasono Sekawan (☎0542-421539; tour@totogasono.com; Jl Ahmad Yani 40) Efficient English-speaking agent for airline bookings. Has contracts with **Pak Rusdy** (p615) for trips up the Mahakam and beyond.

Getting There & Away

AIR

Citilink (☎0542-764362; Airport)

Garuda (☎0542-766844; Airport)

Kalstar (☎0542-737473; Jl Marsaiswahyudi 12)

Lion Air (☎0542-703 3761; Airport)

SilkAir (☎0542-730800; Jl Jend Sudirman 37, BRI Tower 6th fl)

Sriwijaya (☎0542-749777; Airport)

Susi Air (☎0542-761196; Airport)

TRANSPORT FROM BALIKPAPAN

Air

DESTINATION	COMPANY	FARE (RP)	DURATION	FREQUENCY
Banjarmasin	Garuda, Lion	465,000	50min	4 daily
Berau	Garuda, Sriwijaya, Wings	470,000	50min	7 daily
Denpasar	Citilink	770,000	1½hr	Mon, Fri, Sun
Jakarta	Cililink, Garuda, Lion, Sriwijaya	810,000	2hr	many daily
Kuala Lumpur	Air Asia	550,000	2½hr	Mon, Wed, Fri, Sun
Makassar	Citilink, Garuda, Lion, Sriwijaya	480,000	1¼hr	7 daily
Melak	Kalstar	760,000	30min	2 daily
Pontianak	Kalstar	1,200,000	2hr	1 daily
Samarinda	Kalstar, Susi	350,000	20min	3 daily
Singapore	Silk	3,500,000	2¼hr	Mon, Wed, Fri, Sat
Surabaya	Citilink, Garuda, Lion, Sriwijaya	620,000	1½hr	many daily
Tarakan	Garuda, Lion, Sriwijaya	500,000	1hr	many daily
Yogyakarta	Citilink, Garuda, Lion	720,000	1¾hr	6 daily

Boat

DESTINATION	COMPANY	PRICE (RP)	DURATION (HR)	FREQUENCY
Makassar	Dharma Lautan Utama, Prima Visat, Pelni	215,000	24	5-6 weekly
Pare Pare	Prima Vista, Pelni	295,000	18	almost daily
Surabaya	Dharma Lautan Utama, Prima Vista, Pelni	400,000	40	almost daily
Tarakan-Nunukan	Pelni	273,000	12	3 weekly

WORTH A TRIP

AROUND BALIKPAPAN

A potpourri of sights around Balikpapan make for fine day trips. Some are accessible by public transit while others will require a vehicle. A guide can help.

KWPLH Balikpapan (☎0542-710 8304; www.beruangmadu.org; Jl Soekarno-Hatta Km23; ⏰9am-5pm, feedings 9am & 3pm) This informative sun bear conservation centre is surprisingly straight to the point about the heart-breaking plight of all of Kalimantan's animals. Seven resident bears hide in their 1.3-hectare walled enclosure until feeding time, when you can observe them near the clinic. Take *angkot* 8 to the large gate at Km23 (7000Rp), then walk or hitch 1.7km south.

Samboja Lestari (☎0542-702 3600; www.orangutan.or.id; Jl Balikpapan-Handil Km44; adult incl meal morning/afternoon 550,000/800,000Rp, child incl meal morning/afternoon 275,000/475,000Rp) A Borneo Orangutan Survival Foundation (p605) project, Samboja Lestari houses around 200 orangutans and 50 sun bears. Half day tours (9am to 1pm and 2pm to 8pm, reserve ahead) show off the centre's residents and accomplishments; or stay overnight at the stunning lodge.

Sungai Wain (☎Agus 0812 580 6329; agusdin_wain@yahoo.co.id; mandatory guides 100,000Rp) In the mid-'90s, 82 orangutans were released in this protected forest, but fires and illegal logging have taken their toll. Get a 6am start to maximise wildlife viewing. Take *angkot* 8 to Km15 (6000Rp), and an *ojek* 6km west.

BOAT

Semayang Harbour, at the entrance to the gulf, is the main cargo and passenger port.

Dharma Lautan Utama (☎0542-442222; Jl Soekarno-Hatta Km0.5)

Pelni (☎0542-422110; Jl Yos Sudarso, near Pelabuhan Semayang)

Prima Vista (☎0542-428888; Jl Sudirman 138)

BUS

Buses to Samarinda (30,000Rp, three hours, departing every 15 minutes, 5.30am-8pm) and minibuses to points north leave from Batu Ampar Terminal on *angkot* route 3 (light blue). Your best company for Banjarmasin (150,000Rp to 205,000Rp, 15 hours, eight daily, noon-8pm) is **Pulau Indah** (☎0542-420289; Jl Soekarno-Hatta Km 2.5).

Getting Around

- Taxis to the city centre from the airport cost 70,000Rp. Alternately, walk 150m to the road, and hail a green-and-white *angkot* 7 heading west (5000Rp).
- City *angkot* run regular routes converging at Balikpapan Plaza, and charge 5000Rp a ride.

Samarinda

☎0541 / POP 840,000

Samarinda! The very name oozes exoticism. And happily you will find some of that here in this sprawling riverfront city, including the enormous mosque of the new Islamic Center, which stands like a sentinel at the gates of the mighty Sungai Mahakam (Mahakam River), a most impressive sight. But as with many fairy tales, there is a dark side to this story. Over half of Samarinda's land has been opened for coal mining, resulting in numerous health and environmental effects, and causing hotels to advertise their 'flood-free event halls.' Meanwhile, a proliferation of monster malls has been gutting downtown, leaving some streets eerily vacant; take a taxi after dark.

Sights

Islamic Center MOSQUE
(Masjid Baitul Muttaqien; Jl Slamet Riyadi; mosque/tower free/10,000Rp; ⏰8am-6pm) The western skyline of Samarinda is dominated by this must-see complex containing an ornate and colourful mosque with adjacent observation tower. The latter is the highest point in the city, offering panoramic views up and down a great bend in the Mahakam. The muezzin's sunset call is a captivating moment.

Masjid Shirathal Mustaqiem MOSQUE
(Samarinda Seberang) FREE Built in 1881 to tame a neighbourhood notorious for gambling and drinking, the mosque's four main pillars were reportedly set by a mysterious elderly woman while nobody was looking. The yellow ironwood minaret is a distinct Kalimantan-Muslim take on the pagoda. Take

Samarinda

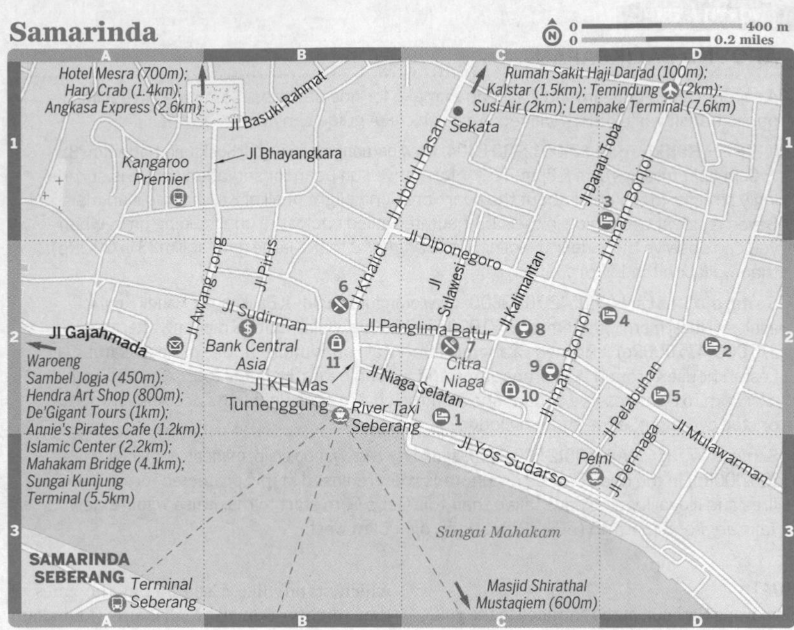

Samarinda

Sleeping
1 Akasia 8 Guesthouse C2
2 Aston Samarinda D2
3 Horison D1
4 Kost Samarinda D2
5 Swiss-Belhotel D2

Eating
6 Hero Supermarket B2
7 Sari Pacific Restaurant C2

Drinking & Nightlife
8 Dejavu Kitchen Bar & KTV C2
9 Maximum C2

Shopping
10 Citra Niaga C2
11 Pasar Pagi B2

a boat (25,000Rp, five minutes) direct to the mosque in Samarinda Seberang.

Tours

Abdullah GUIDE
(0813 4727 2817, 0821 5772 0171; doe1L@yahoo.com) Friendly, resourceful and realistic. Abdullah speaks excellent English, and understands backpackers. Also a Dayak antiques agent.

Rustam GUIDE
(0812 585 4915; rustam_kalimantan@yahoo.co.id) Rustam universally gets good reviews.

Suryadi GUIDE
(0816 459 8263) Even after guiding for almost 30 years, wise Pak Suryadi is probably still in better shape than you are. Speaks German as well as English.

De'Gigant Tours ADVENTURE TOUR
(0812 584 6578; www.borneotourgigant.com; Jl Martadinata Raudah 21) De'Gigant (also X-Treme Borneo and Kalimantan Tours) specialises in trips in East Kalimantan and has safely shepherded dozens of clients through the renowned Cross-Borneo Trek. However, readers report inconsistent guide quality.

Sleeping

Top-end hotels can be good value, but suffer from inattention. The almost-finished Ibis/Mercure megacomplex will likely reset the hospitality bar.

★ Kost Samarinda HOTEL $
(Samarinda Guesthouse; ☎0541-734337; www.kostsamarinda.com; s/d 125,000/200,000Rp; ❄📶) The excessively accommodating owners understand what backpackers need: a clean, cheap, friendly, no-frills place strategically located in the middle of the action. Rooms share a large cold-water *mandi* (Indonesian bath, consisting of a large water tank from which water is ladled over the body) and speedy wi-fi. The icing: motorbikes for rent (50,000Rp).

Akasia 8 Guesthouse GUESTHOUSE $
(☎0541-701 9590; Jl Yos Sudarso 34; s/d with breakfast 145,000/180,000Rp) The overly small *mandi* at this clean and bare dockside losmen will torment your inner claustrophobe; spring for the en suite option to buy some wiggle room.

Hotel Mesra HOTEL $$
(☎0541-732772; www.hotelmesrasamarinda.com; Jl Pahlawan 1; s incl breakfast 425,000Rp, d incl breakfast 525,000-925,000Rp; ❄📶🏊) This polished resort, owned by the Mesra Coal conglomerate, is located on a private hilltop downtown. Some rooms have balconies overlooking the manicured grounds, which include two pools open to the public (50,000Rp), gardens, tennis courts, a spa and minigolf. It's worth coming just for the breakfast (125,000Rp) – assuming you don't mind dining under the watchful eye of an enormous *garuda* (mythical bird.)

Rooms here vary greatly, even in the same building, so inspect a few before committing.

Aston Samarinda HOTEL $$
(☎0541-732600; www.astonsamarinda.com; Jl P Hidayatullah; r/ste with breakfast 700,000/830,000Rp; ❄📶🏊) This attractive, well-designed hotel is the place to come for spotless luxury. The colonnaded pool with its two-storey waterfall may be ostentatious, but the rooms have just the right amount of style and comfort. Some superiors have grand views of the river, while others have no windows but extra space. Fine dining and an in-house spa round out the scene nicely.

Horison HOTEL $$
(☎0541-727 2900; www.myhorison.com; Jl Imam Bonjol 9; r incl breakfast 685,000Rp; ❄📶🏊) This chain hotel adds a touch of class to the otherwise standard business hotel market. The fresh rooms all have work desks, flat-screen TVs and bone-chilling central air-con. The top-floor indoor pool has expansive views, while the bottom-floor lobby has batik demonstrations.

WORTH A TRIP

PAMPANG DAYAK CEREMONIES

Every Sunday at 2pm, the Kenyah Dayak village of Pampang (relocated here from the highlands in the 1970s), puts on a show (5000Rp) of traditional dances aimed squarely at camera-toting tourists. Enjoy it for what it is: an engaging, staged performance that allows a long-marginalised group to benefit economically from their rich heritage. It is also one of the last places to see women with traditional long earlobes (photos 25,000Rp). Take a public minibus (15,000Rp) from Lempake Terminal to the intersection 25km north of Samarinda.

Swiss-Belhotel HOTEL $$
(☎0541-200888; www.swiss-belhotel.com; Jl Mulawarman 6; r incl breakfast 500,000-954,000Rp; ❄📶🏊) The rooms at this business hotel are all the same size. An upgrade in price gets you touches such as a river view and face towel. The executive rooms were being nicely renovated when we visited, while the rest have touches of style, as well as touches of bathroom mould and mildly stained bed sheets.

Eating

Samarinda's food scene is a bit spread out, though there are some great options you won't regret walking for.

Annie's Pirates Cafe INDONESIAN $
(☎0541-739009; Jl Martadinata 7; mains 30,000Rp, coffee drinks 25,000Rp; ⏰3-11pm) While piracy off the shores of Samarinda has declined in recent years, Annie's business is still booming. This creatively themed resto maximises its rooftop river-breeze dining with an extensive menu, including a hogshead of rum (flavoured) drinks. Yarr.

Hero Supermarket SUPERMARKET $
(Mesra Indah Mall; ⏰10am-9pm) Good place to stock up on snacks before heading upriver.

★ Waroeng Sambel Jogja INDONESIAN $$
(☎0541-743913; Jl Gaja Madah 1; mains from 25,000Rp) Serving eight very different varieties of sambal (salsa) designed to knock your socks off, this large complex near the riverfront is packed on the weekends. Their house speciality, the onion-y sambel bawang Jogja,

was a bit salty for our liking, but the sambel tempe lit us up right.

Hary Crab SEAFOOD **$$**

(Jl Pahlawan 41; crab 75,000Rp; ⏲6-10pm) A unique local institution, these streetside outdoor benches are generally packed with people who believe dinner should be a fully immersive affair. Wear your bib.

Sari Pacific Restaurant INTERNATIONAL **$$**

(Jl Panglima Batur; mains from 35,000Rp; ⏲9am-10pm) Features a selection of New Zealand steaks (120,000Rp) as well as burgers, chicken and fish – all in frustratingly small portions. The house favourite, Ikan Patin bakar (grilled fish), is pure greasy deliciousness. Bonus: fried ice cream!

Drinking & Nightlife

Dejavu Kitchen Bar & KTV BAR

(☎0541-747880; Jl Panglima Batur 9; ⏲10pm-2am) This complex contains a booming nightclub (admission 75,000Rp) with lots of security, while a separate classy dinner restaurant is frequented by a hip and dressy crowd. The menu includes international cuisine plus a spectrum of cocktails at premium prices.

Maximum CLUB

(Jl Niaga Timur 21; ⏲8pm-late) In Plaza 21, this ear-splitter is one of the more popular dance clubs in the city. Go after midnight. Taxis available around the corner.

Shopping

★**Hendra Art Shop** ANTIQUES

(☎0541-734949; hendra.art@gmail.com; Jl Martadinata; ⏲9am-5pm) The two storeys of curios, antiques, and other Borneo exotica found in this shop can't be beat. Haggling, and an eye for authenticity, are required. Shipping is available, but that 6m carved longhouse ladder will cost you.

Citra Niaga MARKET

This daily market contains several souvenir shops offering batik sarongs and Dayak carvings. Food stalls serve *amplang* (famous crunchy fishy puffs) and standard Indonesian fare (mains 25,000Rp).

TRANSPORT FROM SAMARINDA

Air

Several airlines have planned additional routes when (if) the new airport 23km north of town is ever completed.

DESTINATION	COMPANY	FARE (RP)	DURATION	FREQUENCY
Balikpapan	Kalstar, Susi	300,000	20min	4 daily
Berau	Kalstar	830,000	45min	2 daily
Melak	Susi	500,000	40min	Mon, Wed, Fri, Sat
Tanjung Selor	Kalstar	1,140,000	1hr	1 daily

Bus

DESTINATION	TERMINAL	FARE (RP)	DURATION (HR)	FREQUENCY
Balikpapan	Sungai Kunjang	35,000	2	every 10min, 6am-8pm
Banjarmasin	Samarinda Seberang	175,000-235,000	16	8 daily 9am-5pm
Berau	Lempake	200,000	17	call ☎0812 5417 3997
Bontang	Lempake	35,000	3	every 25min, 7am-7pm
Kota Bangun	Sungai Kunjang	35,000	3½	6 daily, 7am-3pm
Melak	Sungai Kunjang	110,000	9	3 daily
Sangatta	Lampake	42,000	4	every 25min, 6am-5pm
Tenggarong	roadside across bridge	25,000	1	regular when full

Pasar Pagi MARKET
(Morning Market; Jl Sudirman) A wonderfully chaotic morning market.

Information

Angkasa Express (0541-200280; Plaza Lembuswana D3; 8am-9pm Mon-Fri, to 1pm Sat) Air tickets.

Bank Central Asia (BCA; Jl Sudirman; 8am-3pm Mon-Fri) Foreign exchange.

Main Post Office (cnr Jls Gajah Mada & Awang Long)

Rumah Sakit Haji Darjad (0541-732698; Jl Dahlia 4) Large hospital off Jl Basuki Rahmat.

Sekata (0541-742098; Jl Abdul Hasan 59) Airline tickets and car transport. English spoken.

Getting There & Away

AIR

Kalstar (0541-743780; Jl Gatot Subroto 80)

Susi Air (Airport)

BOAT

Mahakam ferries *(kapal biasa)* leave at 7am from Sungai Kunjang terminal, 6km upriver on green *angkot* A (5000Rp). At time of research, **Pelni** (0541-741402; Jl Yos Sudarso 76) ferries were no longer serving Samarinda, but the office will sell tickets for Balikpapan departures.

Cross-Mahakam ferries to Samarinda Seberang (5000Rp) leave from the end of Jl Tumenggung.

BUS

Samarinda has three main bus terminals:

Sungai Kunjang terminal (6km west on green *angkot* A) serves Mahakam river destinations as well as points south.

Lempake terminal (8km north on red *angkot* B) serves all points north, including an irregular daily bus to Berau. *Taksi gelap* (unlicensed taxis) for Berau troll the terminal, effectively killing the public bus market.

Terminal Seberang (cross the river via water taxi) serves Banjarmasin.

Minibuses for Tenggarong leave from the east side of the Mahakam Bridge. Cross it on *angkot* G and head south 500m where buses gather opposite the PLTD electric station.

Kangaroo Premier (0812 555 1199; www.kangaroo.id; Jl WR Supratman 7A) sends minibuses to Balikpapan airport every 10 minutes.

Getting Around

Angkot (5000Rp) converge at Pasar Pagi market. Taxis from Tumindung Airport (3km) cost 60,000Rp. Alternatively, walk 200m to Jl Gatot Subroto, turn left and catch *angkot* B south into town.

Sungai Mahakam

The second-largest river in Indonesia, the mighty Mahakam is a microcosm of Kalimantan. As you float upriver in search of the 'Heart of Borneo', you'll pass countless barges hauling it downriver to sell to the highest bidder. You'll see centuries-old villages just around the bend from coal mines and logging camps, and impossibly tall trees looming next to oil palm plantations. You'll pass imposing government offices with flash SUVs parked out front on your way to haggle over the price of a hand-carved *mandau* (machete) with a man who's barely keeping his family fed. This is Kalimantan in all of its conflicting, powerful, confusing and compelling beauty. And, there is no better way to see it than a trip up the Mahakam: a journey you'll remember for a lifetime.

Activities

Travelling up this major artery of Kalimantan is a journey in the fullest sense of the word. As you head away from the industrial centre of Samarinda you slip deeper into the interior, and into Borneo's past. You won't be alone (there is a daily public boat, after all) but you won't see many other foreigners – if any.

Opportunities for exploration abound, from towns and longhouses, to huge lakes, wetlands and side creeks. Wildlife is abundant, but elusive. Your odds of meeting river otters, pythons, macaques, proboscis monkeys, monitor lizards or hornbills increase exponentially with your distance from the main corridor. Jump off the boat at any random village and wait for the next one, even if it means staying overnight – especially if. The Mahakam is one of those places where you shouldn't worry too much about the details. Homestays materialise, 'my brother's boat' appears, closed stores open. Hospitality is the *lingua franca*, and the people are universally welcoming.

Heading up the main river gets you into the interior, but taking any tributary will open up a whole new world of adventures and experiences.

Stages of Travel

The Mahakam stretches from Samarinda to the highlands through several distinct regions:

Lower Mahakam: Samarinda to Kota Bangun Many travellers opt to cover this fairly developed stretch by land. Otherwise, it is an eight-hour journey from Samarinda by *kapal biasa,* which depart Samarinda every morning at 7am. Notable stops include the former Kutai sultanate in Tenggarong city.

The Lake District: Kota Bangun to Melak This diverse section of rivers, lakes and marshes is full of wildlife and dotted with villages, each completely unique in its own way. Base out of Muara Muntai for day trips to Lake Jempang, or take creative side passages upriver to Muara Pahu.

Middle Mahakam: Melak to Long Bagun The upper reach of the *kapal biasa* begins to feel like the wild Kalimantan you've dreamed about.

Upper Mahakam: Long Bagun to Tiong Ohang The most exhilarating and dangerous part of the river includes two major sets of rapids that claim multiple lives each year.

Note that *kapal biasa* reach Long Bagun when water levels permit. Otherwise they stop in Tering or Long Iram, at which point speed boats will surround your boat looking for passengers for Long Bagun.

Guides

As you head further upriver, Bahasa skills become more essential as English is almost nonexistent. You can get by with rudimentary phrases, but your travel options will be limited and your understanding of the area restricted to surface observations.

Most guides prefer package trips with preset costs, and tend not to deviate from their scripted route. However, some may agree to a more flexible itinerary for a daily fee, with you covering their food, lodging and transport as well. Independent guiding fees range from 150,000Rp to 350,000Rp per day depending on experience, skill and demand. The best guides will look out for their client's financial interests, negotiating on your behalf and making savings which may defray their fee.

Take the time to find a suitable guide in Samarinda (p620) or Balikpapan (p615), where they are relatively plentiful. An interview is essential to confirm language skills and identify personality [in]compatibilities that can make or break a long trip together.

Tenggarong

0541 / POP 75,000

Once the capital of the mighty Kutai sultanate, Tenggarong has been attempting to recreate its past glory, with mixed results. Flush with mining profits, the government has invested heavily in infrastructure – good. However, development largely focused on turning Kumala Island into a gaudy tourist attraction, which now lies abandoned and bankrupt, plagued by a corruption scandal – bad. Far worse, in 2011 the 10-year-old bridge across the Mahakam, dubbed 'Indonesia's Golden Gate', suddenly collapsed into the river, killing 36 people. Most travellers come for the lively annual Erau Festival, otherwise the informative museum is your primary draw.

Sights

Mulawarman Museum MUSEUM

(Jl Diponegoro; admission 5000Rp; 9am-4pm, closed Mon & Fri) The former sultan's palace, built by the Dutch in 1937, is now a decent museum chronicling the culture, natural history and industry of Indonesia's oldest kingdom – as evidenced by 5th-century Sanskrit engravings (originals in Jakarta). The ornate Yuan and Ming Dynasty ceramics are compelling, while the wedding headwear from around Indonesia is entertaining. (Ladies, get married in West Sumatra. Gentlemen, South Kalimantan.) The architecturally incongruous building is itself an attraction, with strong parallel lines reminiscent of Frank Lloyd Wright's work.

Don't miss the exquisitely decorative wooden palace out back, which stands empty outside of the Erau Festival, when the current sultan takes up residence.

Festivals & Events

Erau International Folk & Art Festival CULTURAL

(EIFAF; www.facebook.com/EIFAF) Originally held in celebration of a sultan's coronation, the Erau (from the Kutai word *eroh,* meaning joyful, boisterous crowd) became a biannual, then annual, gathering to celebrate Dayak culture and custom. It's usually in August, occasionally in June. Book lodging in advance.

The event has recently joined with the International Folk & Art Festival to expand the menu of twirling dancers in traditional costume to include 17 countries from Bulgaria to South Korea to Venezuela.

THE LAST IRRAWADDY DOLPHINS

Once common along the Mahakam, the population of the Critically Endangered freshwater Irrawaddy dolphin *(pesut)* has declined precipitously in recent years. Today, there are less than 90 left, and they must dodge gill nets and ship rotors in an increasingly murky river polluted with coal mine and oil palm plantation run-off. The playful, round-faced survivors can often be seen in the Pela/Lake Semayang area.

Sleeping & Eating

Hotel Karya Tapin HOTEL $
(☎0541-661258; Jl Maduningrat 29; r incl breakfast 245,000Rp; ❄) Spotless lavender-striped rooms at this small hotel include high ceilings, TVs, showers and homely touches. Head west on Jl Kartini along the south bank of the creek beside the Keraton to Jl Maduningrat. Hot water is extra (when it's working). Hot water rooms are 50,000Rp extra, even if it's not working.

Grand Elty Singgasana Hotel HOTEL $$
(☎0541-664703; Jl Pahlawan 1; r incl breakfast 694,000-814,000Rp; ❄📶🏊) Located on a beautiful hillside south of town, the stately wood-trimmed rooms are marred by peeling paint, broken walkways, and staff who seem surprised to discover someone is actually staying here. The pool (35,000Rp for nonguests) has a phenomenal view. Transport into town is 100,000Rp a trip.

Etam Fried Chicken INDONESIAN $
(☎0541-665701; Jl Muchsin Timbau; mains 20,000Rp; ⏰11am-10pm) The local recommendation for tasty fried (and more) chicken; 2km south of the museum.

Getting There & Away

Boat The *kapal biasa* dock (Pelabuhan Mangkurawang) is 2.5km north of town, with *angkot* (5000Rp) service to the centre. Boats pass heading downriver to Samarinda around 7am daily (25,000Rp, two hours) and for Kota Bangun at 9am daily (50,000Rp, six hours).

Bus Timbau bus terminal is 4km south of the museum area, with *angkot* service to the centre (5000Rp). Buses depart hourly from 9am to 4pm for Samarinda (25,000Rp) but you'll need to hail passing Kota Bangun–bound buses (30,000Rp) or Kijang (150,000Rp) on the street.

Kota Bangun

This small town is where many Mahakam journeys begin. From here, take the *kapal biasa* direct to Muara Muntai on the river, or hire a *ces* to get there via the northern scenic route through Lakes Semayang and Melintang. You'll twist and turn through narrow channels, cross endless marshes, and pass through forests of silver-barked trees, pausing for the odd monkey or some of the last Irrawaddy dolphins.

Sleeping & Eating

Warung Etam and Warung Maskur, next to the dock, serve excellent grilled chicken and chicken soup respectively. Pak Maskur speaks passable English and can help in a pinch.

Penginapan Etam GUESTHOUSE $
(Jl HM Aini H 19; r fan/air-con 60,000/120,000Rp; ❄) If you enjoyed visiting grandmother's house, you'll enjoy staying at this friendly upstairs guesthouse. Enjoy the foot-massaging floors in the clean shared *mandi*. It's 140m upriver of the *kapal biasa* dock.

Penginapan Mukjizat GUESTHOUSE $
(☎0541-666 3586; Jl A Yani 5; s/d 50,000/100,000Rp) The chill rear balcony above the river is a plus. Its proximity to the megaphonic mosque, not so much. It's 200m downriver from the *kapal biasa* dock.

Getting There & Around

Kapal biasa pass in the afternoon heading upriver, and in the predawn morning heading down. Buses to Samarinda (35,000Rp, four hours) leave at least three times daily between 7am and 2pm. Regular *ces* service runs to Muara Pela (30,000Rp), Semayang (50,000Rp) and Melintang (65,000Rp) three times daily starting at 11am. Charter a private *ces* for **dolphin watching at Pela** (☎Pak Darwis 0852 5065 0961; 2hrs 200,000Rp), or for the back-channel journey to Muara Muntai (1,000,000Rp per day).

Muara Muntai

Considering the price of ironwood these days, the streets of Muara Muntai might as well be paved with gold. This riverside town's nearly 20km network of richly weathered boardwalks clack loudly with passing motorbikes, adding to the rich Mahakam soundscape. The sound of money has also caught the attention of unscrupulous traders who offer to replace the boardwalks at cost, then sell the 'reclaimed' lumber to builders in Bali, circumventing restrictions on the trade of new ironwood. Base yourself here for day trips to Lakes Jempang or Melintang.

Sleeping

Penginapan Sri Muntai GUESTHOUSE $
(☎0853 4963 0030; s/d 50,000/100,000Rp) Bright-green Sri Muntai wins the award for best front porch: a breezy hang-out above the street. Wide hallways and clean rooms are also a nice touch.

Penginapan Adi Guna GUESTHOUSE $
(☎0823 5241 8233; r 50,000Rp) Basic fan-cooled rooms and large, shared *mandi*.

Getting There & Away

- *Kapal biasa* pass in the afternoon heading upriver, and around midnight heading down.
- A *ces* to/from Kota Bangun (the nearest bus) runs 200,000Rp for the two-hour journey.
- Charter a *ces* (400,000Rp to 700,000Rp) to Lake Jempang country, to visit villages and longhouses, with the impeccably cheerful **Udin Ban** (☎0813 3241 2089).

Lake Jempang

Located south of the Mahakam, seasonally flooded Jempang is the largest of the three major wetlands in the lake region. This birdwatcher's paradise is home to over 57 waterbird, 12 birds of prey and six kingfisher species. The fishing village of Jantur occupies the main outlet (sometimes inlet) on the east end, while the Dayak villages of Tanjung Isuy and Mancong are hidden on the southwest end. During high water, *ces* can cut back to the main river at Muara Pahu from the west edge of the lake.

JANTUR

During the wet season, Jantur appears to be floating in the middle of Lake Jempang. It is built entirely on stilts in the marshy wetlands which disappear under 6m of water in the rainy season. During the dry season, floating mats of water hyacinth can choke the channel through town, creating a transportation nightmare.

Gardening here may be difficult, but the residents do have fish – plenty of fish – producing more *ikan kering* (dried fish) than any other village in the regency. The boardwalks and rooftops are typically covered with thousands of splayed fish, some protected under the watchful eye of meter-tall pet storks.

If you can manage a homestay, you'll find Jantur is a pleasant village filled with friendly people. At the very least, stroll the boardwalk and say hello to the groups of laughing Banjarese women squatting by the river processing the morning's catch.

TANJUNG ISUY

Tranquil Tanjung Isuy is the first Dayak village most people visit on their Mahakam journey. A fire took out the waterfront in 2015, giving the new mosque skyline supremacy. The historical longhouse, Louu Taman Jamrud, still stands as a sort of museum/craft shop/losmen.

Sights

Lamin Batu Bura HISTORIC BUILDING
Few *lamin* (the local word for longhouse) around here are occupied outside of community ceremonies these days, but this Benuaq Dayak house is bucking the trend. While the men are off in the fields, women sit on the split bamboo floor weaving naturally died

BOAT TRAVEL ON THE SUNGAI MAHAKAM

Distances, costs and duration are based on a Samarinda start point. Be aware that travel times fluctuate significantly based on water levels and the number of stops. Consult locally for current conditions.

DESTINATION	DISTANCE (KM)	FARE (RP)	DURATION (HR)
Tenggarong	35	50,000	2
Kota Bangun	153	75,000	8
Muara Muntai	195	100,000	11
Muara Pahu	256	130,000	15
Melak	303	150,000	19
Tering	381	200,000	25
Long Bagung (if possible)	539	380,000	37

fibres of the doyo leaf into beautiful decorative cloth called *ulap doyo*. Walk 1.5km south of Tanjung Isuy, staying left at the fork.

Sleeping

Louu Taman Jamrud LONGHOUSE $
(Jl Indonesia Australia; r 110,000Rp) Vacated in the 1970s and refurbished as a tourist hostel by the provincial government, this stately longhouse is guarded by an impressive array of carved totems (some of which may be NSFW.) Travellers can commission a Dayak dance for 600,000Rp to 1,000,000Rp, depending on how many performers you require.

Losmen Wisata LONGHOUSE $
(Jl Indonesia Australia; r 110,000Rp) Long, but not culturally significant, this lodge's common areas have wall-to-wall windows giving you a superior view of the lake; views that formerly were enjoyed by Louu Taman Jamrud next door.

Getting There & Away

- Charter a *ces* in Muara Muntai to get here via Jantur, or in Muara Pahu to get here via the Sungai Baroh (Baroh River), if the water level permits.
- Tanjung Isuy is 25 minutes by Kijang or *ojek* from Mancong.
- A truck leaves in the morning for the intersection with the main road between Samarinda and Melak, where you can hop on a bus.

MANCONG

For optimum jungle drama Mancong is best reached by boat on the Ohong creek from Lake Jempang. You'll meander past monitor lizards, sapphire-hued kingfishers, bulb-nosed proboscis monkeys, banded kraits and marauding macaques. They'll see you, but whether or not you see them... The journey beneath towering banyan trees is as much a part of the experience as your arrival.

Sights

Mancong Longhouse HISTORIC BUILDING
This exquisitely restored 1930s longhouse is flanked by intricately carved totems. Those with chickens represent a healing ceremony. The souvenir shop across the parking lot can rustle up blankets and mosquito nets if you absolutely must sleep in the otherwise vacant building (75,000Rp).

FLOATING HOMESTAY

Floating houses and shops are a defining feature of the Sungai Mahakam. Where basic buildings are constructed on logs pulled from the river, people live lives as recognisable as they are different. Children jump into the river to bathe before putting on class uniforms. Their school bus is a canoe. Satellite dishes sit on roofs made from cast-off lumber. Homestays are basic, and involve sleeping on a mat and using the river outhouse, like everyone else. But, sitting at river level with a cup of coffee, watching river traffic at sunset, is an inimitable and unforgettable experience. **Murni** (☎ no English 0813 5042 8447; Melak; r incl dinner & breakfast per person 50,000Rp) offers a homestay in his floating house directly across from the Melak harbour with free transport in his *ces*. Additional sightseeing trips are negotiable.

Getting There & Away

To visit Mancong from Tanjung Isuy, charter a *ces* (500,000Rp return, three hours each way) or take an *ojek* (100,000Rp, 10km, 25 minutes).

Muara Pahu

Lining one side of a big curve in the Mahakam, this town is the upriver exit point from Lake Jempang when the water is high enough. You can stroll the boardwalk, or sit and watch the tugboats haul coal downriver while waiting for the evening *kapal biasa*.

Sleeping

Pension Anna GUESTHOUSE $
(s/d 50,000/100,000Rp) Four rooms in a small signless home, 90m upstream of the Sungai Baroh bridge.

Getting There & Around

Although dolphins are increasingly rare here, you can still charter a *ces* (700,000Rp per day) to explore the primate and bird life of Sungai Baroh, which leads to Lake Jempang and Tanjung Isuy. **Pak Aco** (☎ 0813 4652 3132) knows how to slow down for wildlife. *Kapal biasa* pass after 8pm heading both up and down river.

Melak

Melak could be anywhere in Indonesia. **Sendawar**, the regency seat next door, is trying to out-develop itself, with each new government building more massive than the last. It is all very disorienting, and somewhat alarming considering this is likely a preview of what's to come upriver.

That being said, however, centuries of culture can't be erased with a few years of coal money. Start your wandering with the still-occupied longhouse at **Eheng** (30km southwest of Melak) or the **Kersik Luway** (8am-4pm) FREE orchid preserve.

Sleeping & Eating

Despite (or perhaps because of) the development around Melak, the lodging options here are limited and uninspired. Instead, consider spending the night in a floating homestay (p627), or see about negotiating sparse accommodation at Eheng longhouse.

Basic food stalls can be found along Jl Pierre Tendean. Head downriver from the dock and turn right at the next major road.

Hotel Flamboyan HOTEL $
(0545-41033; Jl A Yani; r fan/air-con 115,000/165,000Rp;) Offers private *mandi* with Western toilets. Clean, but definitely not flamboyant.

Hotel Monita HOTEL $$
(0545-41798; Jl Dr Sutomo 76; r incl breakfast 240,000-360,000Rp;) The best option in town, but about 2km uphill from the *kapal biasa* dock. It's often full with mining clients, so book ahead.

Rumah Makan Jawah Indah SEAFOOD, INDONESIAN $
(Jl A Yani; mains 25,000-35,000Rp; 24hr;) Ready to cook any Javanese food you desire at any hour you require. Across from the dock.

Information

88 Net (Jl Pierre Tendean 58; per hr 5000Rp) Internet access. Head downriver 150m from the dock, and turn right on Jl Pierre Tendean; it's next to hotel Anugerah.

Getting There & Away

Air Kalstar flies to Balikpapan twice daily (720,000Rp, 30 minutes), while Susi Air services Samarinda (544,000Rp, Mon and Wed) and Data Dawai (390,000Rp, Mon and Wed).

Boat *Kapal biasa* leave for Samarinda daily at 8pm or 10pm and pass heading upriver at 1am. Charter a *ces* for 500,000Rp to 800,000Rp per day depending on your negotiating skills.

Bus Two buses for Samarinda depart in the morning (100,000Rp, nine hours).

Kijang Run to Samarinda (200,000Rp, eight hours), Balikpapan (275,000Rp, 12 hours), and Tering (150,000Rp, one hour).

DON'T MISS

THE WAY TO BORNEO'S HEART

From Long Bagun you embark upon the most thrilling ride on the Mahakam: the longboat to **Tiong Ohang** (800,000Rp, four hours). This serpentine adventure takes you through some spectacular gorges with scenic waterfalls and ancient volcanic peaks. At some undefined point, the uncanny realisation strikes... you've entered the heart of Borneo.

Be warned, however. Two major sets of rapids bar the way. Riam Udang is dangerous at high water, while Riam Panjang gets nasty at low water. In 2015 yet another boat broke apart in the tumultuous waters killing five passengers including one foreign backpacker and her guide. Insist on, and wear, a life jacket *(baju pelampung)*.

A nearly completed dirt road from **Long Bagun** to **Long Apari** (three hours upriver from Tiong Ohang) will likely be paved in a few years, changing the mystique of this journey entirely.

Tering

A planned community deep in gold-mining country, Tering is sometimes the last stop for *kapal biasa*, depending on the water level. It is really two settlements straddling the river: **Tering Baru**, a Malay village where the *kapal biasa* docks, and **Tering Lama**, a Bahau Dayak village on the northern bank, where a magnificent wooden church with intricate painted pillars has a bell tower supported by totem poles.

Kapal biasa arrive at 9am. Even during low water, they sometimes continue to Long Iram, an hour further upriver. Downriver *kapal biasa* leave around noon. A speedboat to Long Bagun is 300,000Rp for the four-hour journey. Kijang depart from the dock for Samarinda (300,000Rp) and Melak (150,000Rp).

Long Bagun

The misty mountain village of Long Bagun is the end of the *kapal biasa* route at high water and is a fine terminus for your Mahakam adventure. Somewhere in the village, a local entrepreneur is bent over a grinder, polishing a semi-precious stone into a pendant… a Chinese shopkeeper is sweating over a forge, melting gold from nearby mines to sell in Samarinda… a group of women is tying intricate beadwork for their children's next traditional dance performance… and you can see it all, or simply sit beside the river with a cup of coffee and just be.

Sleeping

★**Penginapan Polewali** GUESTHOUSE $
(081 350 538 997; r 100,000Rp) This mountain lodge with traditional furnishings is a breath of fresh air after the concrete boxes downriver. In fact, it is the best hotel on the upper Mahakam. Rooms are small, and bathrooms shared, but a nice breeze on the porch keeps you outside. Find it at the upriver edge of town, across from the longhouse.

Getting There & Away

Boats now pause at Ujoh Bilang, 3km downriver from Long Bagun, where you'll be required to register with the tourism office on the dock.

Speedboats heading up- and downriver troll for passengers along the waterfront in the morning. We've heard of at least one intrepid Huck Finn building a bamboo raft and floating back to Samarinda.

Tiong Ohang

Divided by the Mahakam, Tiong Ohang is united by its creaking suspension bridge which offers scenic views of the surrounding hills. This is the last stop before starting, or ending, the second stage of the Cross-Borneo Trek (p591) in the Muller Mountains. This is where local guides and porters are assembled, but these services are best arranged in advance by a tour company. The trailhead is two hours upriver by *ces* (1,000,000Rp).

Sleeping

Putra Apari GUESTHOUSE $
(r 60,000Rp) The only accommodation in town. Rooms have no fan and share *mandi*, but there is a nice porch with a cross-breeze, overlooking main street.

The Muller Mountains

The second stage of the Cross-Borneo Trek (p591), the journey across the Muller Mountains, is a very different experience from what precedes it. This is neither a cultural tour nor a wildlife-spotting expedition. In fact, views of any kind are scarce. This is a purpose-driven rainforest trek, and a difficult one.

Most people do the crossing in seven or more long, wet days. The trek follows a narrow path – if that – through a green maze

MULLER TREK SAFETY REQUIREMENTS

- Choose a professional local tour company. Do not even think of organising this yourself.
- Ensure that someone in your party has a complete first-aid kit and knows how to use it. Pack epinephrine, and know why.
- Wear proper shoes. The trail will be extremely greasy at times. Your feet will be constantly wet. The locals wear rubber sneakers with cleats. A sturdy pair of trail runners is a good option. Leather will quickly disintegrate. Take care of your feet.
- Wear proper leech protection. Tucking your trousers into two pairs of tight-knit socks is fairly effective. Some people swear by spandex, which can also help with chafing.
- Be firm about setting the pace at which you walk. Local guides and porters are not always aware of the difference between their skill level and your own. It is also in their interest to get across and back as soon as possible. Be sure to spread walking hours evenly among the days of the journey.
- Do not trek at night. Locals have no problem with this, but it greatly magnifies the risk, particularly if it is raining.
- Bring 10 days' worth of food. If there is a problem midway, you'll need enough to last until someone walks to the nearest village and returns with help.

with uncertain footing and nearly constant creek crossings, some chest high. Campsites are a tarp. Cooking is done over an open fire. There will be blood – from leeches if nothing else. They are harmless, but their bites easily become infected in the damp environment.

All things considered, the experience hasn't changed much since George Muller first crossed his namesake range in 1825. While that first trek ended with the locals cutting off Muller's head (likely at the behest of the Sultan of Kutai), the primary risk today is breaking a leg or merely twisting an ankle so far from outside help. To that end, heed all the precautions, and choose an experienced tour company or guide, which has considered the concept of risk management.

The Muller Trek is a horizontal Everest. You tackle it for the same reasons you climb. And when you succeed, it is both a lifetime memory and a noteworthy achievement.

Kutai National Park

Kutai National Park has seen its share of troubles. All but abandoned in the late '90s as a conservation failure ransacked by logging and fires, new studies are showing all is not lost. The wild orangutan population has recovered to as many as 2000 individuals, and pockets of forest are still relatively intact. Research is happening at the north end of the park, while Prevab station near Sangatta offers Kalimantan's best chance to see truly wild orangutans.

There are plans to restore the unfortunately abandoned Kakap Camp at Prevab, but until then, you can stay in the bare musty rooms of the ranger station. From there, several kilometres of trail fan out through decent secondary forest, where large buttressed trees still provide plenty of hiding spots for orangutans. The rangers are experts at moving slowly and listening for the telltale rustle of the canopy that betrays a critter's location. Bring mosquito repellent.

Call the lead ranger, Pak Supiani (0813 4634 8803), before visiting so he can organise your permit and a boat. To get here, take a bus from Samarinda to Sangatta (42,000Rp, four hours) and a taxi to Kabo Jaya, where a park boat will ferry you to the ranger station (300,000Rp return, 15 minutes). Park permits are 150,000Rp per day (225,000Rp during holidays). Guides (required) cost 120,000Rp per two-hour trek.

Berau

0554 / POP 63,000

Once the inspiration for Joseph Conrad's first novel, *Almayer's Folly,* Berau now only inspires you to move on to your ultimate destination. Fortunately, you have two great choices: the Derawan Archipelago to the east, or the karst wonderland of Merabu to the south. Choose wisely, as neither option is cheap nor easy to get to – but both are immensely rewarding.

Sights

Museum Batiwakkal MUSEUM

(Gunung Tabur Keraton; admission by donation; 8am-2pm Mon-Sat) Located at the site of Berau's original Keraton, this 1981 building houses an eclectic collection of sultan-obilia starting from the 17th century.

Keraton Sambaliung MUSEUM

(Sambaliung; 9am-1pm Mon-Sat) FREE This 215 year-old Keraton was built after descendants of brothers from other mothers (same father: the 9th sultan) got tired of alternating rule at Gunung Tabor and split the sultanate. The colossal crocodile of questionable taxidermy is an impressive, if somewhat random, addition.

Sleeping & Eating

Rooms in Tanjung Redeb (the main district of Berau) often fill with mine workers. Book in advance.

Hotel Mitra HOTEL $

(0812 5315 0715; Jl Gajah Mada 531A; r incl breakfast 220,000-240,000Rp;) Immaculate with friendly staff, Mitra feels less like a hotel and more like a giant homestay. As a long-standing favourite with local NGOs, Mitra has a staff well-used to dealing with foreigners. All rooms have air-con and cold water only.

Room 505 in the corner has the best natural light. Bikes are available for a quick jaunt around town, and motorbikes rent for 75,000Rp a day.

★ **Rumah Kedaung** GUESTHOUSE $$

(0821 5326 6291; rumahkedaung@yahoo.com; Jl Kedaung, Borneo IV, Sei Bedungun; r incl breakfast 320,000Rp;) Located between the airport and Tanjung Redeb, this guesthouse sits on top of a small treed hill. The common areas are decked out with Dayak art, and the rough wood duplex bungalows have a creaky charm.

Berau

Berau

Sights
1 Museum Batiwakkal A1

Sleeping
2 Hotel Mitra B1
3 Hotel Palmy B2

Eating
4 De Bunda Cafe B2

Drinking & Nightlife
5 Club BP B2

The cafe serves up solid local fare – a plus since there is not much nearby. Wi-fi is spotty.

Hotel Palmy HOTEL $$
(☎0554-202 0333; palmyhotel@yahoo.com; Jl Pangeran Antasari 26; r incl breakfast 500,000Rp; ❄📶) The newest and sharpest offering catering to jet-setting business managers. The top two floors have the best, indeed only, views. Expect to be upcharged by any taxi picking you up here.

★ **De Bunda Cafe** BAKERY $
(☎0554-21305; Jl Pangeran Antasari 5; mains 15,000-30,000Rp; ⏰7am-8pm; 📶) Owner, Ibu Ayu, is well travelled and understands your needs. She speaks English and vegetarian, and is happy to make omelettes and other off-menu dishes by request. Worth the walk.

Sari Ponti Restaurant CHINESE $
(☎0554-26688; Jl Durian II 36; mains 40,000Rp; ⏰8am-9pm) A reliable Chinese mainstay with an extensive menu. A genuine bird's-nest drink will set you back 150,000Rp – it's good for curing pretty much everything, including cancer…apparently.

Drinking & Nightlife

Club BP CLUB
(Jl Antasari, Hotel Berau Plaza; 7pm-2am) The most popular nightclub in the city.

Information

BNI Bank (Jl Maulana) Foreign exchange.
Mailbox Warnet (Jl Aminuddin; per hour 5000Rp; ⏰9am-late) Internet access.
THM Travel (☎0554-21238; Jl Niaga I) Some English-speaking staff.

Getting There & Away

AIR

Garuda (☎0554-202 0285; Jl Panglima Batur 396, Hotel Derawan Indah; ⏰8am-4.30pm Mon-Fri, 9am-3pm Sat & Sun; ❄)
Kalstar (☎0554-21007; Jl Maulana 45)

FLIGHTS FROM BERAU

Destinations serviced from Berau include the following:

Balikpapan Garuda, Sriwijaya, Wings; 450,000Rp; one hour; seven daily

Samarinda Kalstar, 674,000Rp, 45 minutes, two daily

Tarakan Kalstar, 540,000Rp, 25 minutes, one daily

Sriwijaya Air (☎0554-202 8777; Jl Pemuda 50; ⏰8am-5pm)
Wings Air (Airport)

BUS & KIJANG

Until recently, buses in this corner of Kalimantan were all but nonexistent. Transport is handled by *taksi gelap* (dark taxis), a cartel of Kijang operators, many of whom are unlicensed, inexperienced, or downright dangerous drivers. However, new bus services by DAMRI to Tanjung Selor, and a single private **bus to Samarinda** (☎0812 5417 3997; 200,000Rp; 17 hours) are signs of slow improvement.

Kijang gather in the morning across from the former bus terminal and demand a minimum of three passengers; you can buy multiple seats to leave faster. Destinations include Tanjung Batu (100,000Rp, 2½ hours), Tanjung Selor (120,000Rp, three hours), Samarinda (300,000Rp, 14 hours), and Balikpapan (400,000Rp, over 20 hours).

Getting Around

- Taxis to the airport (9km) cost 80,000Rp.
- *Angkot* cost 5000Rp to 10,000Rp, depending on distance.
- River crossings by canoe cost 5000Rp, or canoes can be chartered for 30,000Rp per hour.

Merabu

Isolated between a small river and a fortress of karst pinnacles, the Dayak Lebo villagers of Merabu never worried much about politics or the outside world. So they were understandably shocked the day they found bulldozers clearing nearby forests for an oil palm plantation, and confused to learn their gardens were soon to become a coal mine.

Rather than be bought off, however, they waged a long (and occasionally ugly) battle for their homeland. Finally, in 2014, they became the first village in Berau District to gain official recognition of their village forest, an important step towards securing the rights of indigenous communities. As part of their new forest management plan, Merabu has also opened its doors to ecotourism – an activity they are particularly well-positioned to provide.

The jagged limestone forest in their backyard is one of the least-explored and least-accessible regions in Kalimantan, meaning its wildlife has largely been spared from over hunting. Orangutan dwell in the lowlands while clouded leopard prowl the mountainsides. From the village you can arrange multiday expeditions to **Lake Tebo**, deep in the interior, or spend an afternoon climbing to **Puncak Ketepu** to whet your appetite before plunging into the vivid turquoise waters of **Nyadeng spring**. The drawcard site, however, is **Goa Beloyot**, a cliff-side cavern full of stencilled handprints thousands of years old, accessed by a half-day trek worthy of Indiana Jones (bring a torch).

Homestays run 200,000Rp per night per room, with meals provided at 25,000Rp a pop. Guides cost 100,000Rp a trip while a boat to Nyadeng and Ketepu is 175,000Rp. Additionally, there is a required 200,000Rp donation to the village, and you have the option to adopt a tree in the community forest for 1,500,000Rp for three years. The expenses add up, but remember this is one way the visionaries in the community demonstrate to their neighbours that the forest has value as it is.

It takes a bit of work to get here, but once you do, you may never want leave.

Getting There & Away

Before visiting, contact the village head, Franly Oley (☎0878 1030 3330, franlyoley@gmail.com), who speaks passable English. Your best transport option is to come from Berau to the north. Charter a Kijang (1,800,000Rp) for the four-hour dirt-road journey through Lesan village. Driver Pak Asri (☎0853 4135 9088) is familiar with the route.

From Muara Wahau, to the south, the route is a little more tricky. You'll want a 4WD or a motorbike for the sketchy road. Head 55km north to the Merapun gate (Garpu Dayak Merapun), then turn east into the oil palm plantation. At the first major fork (15km), head left to Merapun to hire a boat to Merabu (price negotiable, 1½ hours) or turn right to continue 40km over land (impassable when wet) to the Lesan road where you'll make a hard right. Just under 4km beyond, you'll arrive at the river. Merabu is opposite.

Once you arrive at the end of the road, shout across the river for a *ketinting* (canoe ferry; 25,000Rp).

Derawan Archipelago

Completely different from the rest of Kalimantan, the classic tropical islands of the Derawan Archipelago are where you go to trade jungle trekking and orangutans for beach combing and manta rays. Of the 31 named islands found here, the four most accessible to visitors are the crowded weekend getaway of Derawan, the peaceful paradise of Maratua atoll, and the wildernesses of Sangalaki and Kakaban. The scuba diving and snorkelling rank among the best in Indonesia, offering an assortment of reef and pelagic species including barracuda, sharks, mantas and turtles, all the way down. Travel between the islands is expensive, so plan your trip carefully and find friends with which to share costs. There are no ATMs on the islands. Seas are rough in January and February, limiting diving and increasing travel risks.

Getting There & Around

Most trips to the islands leave from the coastal town of Tanjung Batu, accessible from Berau by road (500,000Rp charter, 100,000Rp regular seat, 2½ hours). From there, a regular morning boat takes passengers to Pulau Derawan (100,000Rp per person, 30 minutes); otherwise your must charter a speedboat (300,000Rp, seats four).

A charter to Maratua is 1,300,000Rp for the 1½-hour journey from Tanjung Batu, or 1,100,000Rp for the one-hour trip from Derawan. Prices are sometimes negotiable.

A full-day snorkelling trip in the area runs between 1,500,000Rp to 2,000,000Rp depending on how far you go. It is four hours of spine-compressing travel from Derawan to the popular snorkelling areas around Kakaban and Sangalaki, return.

The cheapest, and slowest, way to get between islands is by *klotok*, a local open fishing boat with a noisy little engine. You can arrange this in any village, but be aware of the time involved, as you may be bobbing around in the sun for hours. Having said that, it is a fun way to get between nearby islands, such as Maratua and Nabucco.

On Friday, take a direct speed boat from Tarakan to Pulau Derawan (250,000Rp, 2pm, three hours), and return Sunday.

The new airport on Maratua is sure to change the travel dynamic considerably, but routes were still unconfirmed at time of research.

Do not attempt any passages if seas are rough. Insist on life jackets, and carry a compass or GPS – basic equipment your boat will undoubtedly lack.

Pulau Derawan

The tiny, funky backpacker's magnet of Derawan is the best known of the islands, and the closest to the mainland. It is also increasingly crowded and dirty. Along the waterfront newer guesthouses clamber over the old, reaching out into the ocean like a sprawling octopus. However, despite the near constant presence of tourists, the locals still maintain a friendly attitude and kids are eager to steal high-fives. You'll compete for solitude with local tourists on banana boats during weekends and holidays. For more idyllic surroundings, consider Maratua instead.

Sleeping & Eating

New guesthouses appear and just as quickly succumb to the ravages of the ocean. Evaluate your options before committing.

★ Miranda Homestay HOMESTAY $
(0813 4662 3550; r 200,000Rp) Tucked back toward shore with not much of a view, these two spotless rooms are still great value. Pak Marudi's spacious and relaxing *klotok* is at your disposal for slow coffee-filled snorkelling excursions (700,000Rp per day), or transport to Tanjung Batu (100,000Rp per person).

Sari Cottages GUESTHOUSE $$
(0813 4653 8448; r 350,000Rp; ❄) Centrally located Sari has 22 freshly painted rooms, strung along two parallel piers connected by a footbridge. The large, private back porches all have (as yet) unobstructed views, and the restaurant has the best location in town. Turn off the street at the sign for 'Pinades,' and keep walking the plank.

Mirroliz Pelangi Guesthouse GUESTHOUSE $$
(0813 4780 7078; r with fan/air-con 275,000/380,000Rp; ❄) With its brightly painted rooms and creative lighting, the festive Pelangi may be showing signs of age, but it still retains a chill hang-out vibe. Watch the sunset from the open-air, over-water restaurant as turtles ply the shallows beneath. The further you go out to sea, the more expensive the stay. On the west edge of town.

Derawan Dive Lodge LODGE $$$
(0431-824445; www.derawandivelodge.com; s/d incl breakfast US$80/95) A small enclave of 10 comfortable, individually designed rooms, with a cosy outdoor cafe and private beach, at the west end of the island. If you want to combine a dive holiday with some island life, this is your top choice on Derawan.

DERAWAN DIVING HIGHLIGHTS

Pulau Sangalaki Famous for its manta rays, which are present throughout the year. Turtles also abound.

Pulau Kakaban Big pelagic fish and a cave dive offshore; a rare lake full of nonstinging jellyfish inland.

Pulau Maratua Known for 'the channel' frequented by big pelagic fish, eagle rays and huge schools of barracuda. Occasional thresher sharks.

Pulau Derawan Small creatures draw photographers: ghostpipe fish, frogfish, harlequin shrimp, jawfish, and blue-ringed octopus.

Rumah Makan Nur INDONESIAN $
(☎ 0853 4689 7827; mains 30,000Rp) Nur's serves up tasty Indonesian favourites with creative twists such as shrimp and coconut aubergine with rice. The large juice menu is welcome on a hot day – as are the set prices.

Pulau Maratua

For those with time on their hands, Maratua is a slice of heaven. This enormous U-shaped atoll is almost completely untouched by tourism. Four tiny fishing villages are evenly spaced along the narrow strip of land, three of which are connected by a paved 15km path. Central to the island, near the northern end of the road, the large village of Tanjung Harapan offers several homestays, bicycle rental, and access to the island's only upscale lodging options. Bohe Silian, at the southern end of both road and island, also has a few homestays, pleasant sea views and Sembat cave – the coolest swimming hole on the island.

Hire a scooter for a day (150,000Rp) and explore to your heart's content, passing over bridges between islets, chasing green parakeets and swimming in the lagoon. Local guides (150,000Rp per day) can direct you to the island's hidden caves and private beaches. Add a special someone and a visit here could easily stretch into days…

However, the new airport and tourism port are likely to rapidly change the character of the place forever – so go now.

Diving (single dive €43) can be arranged through Nabucco Island Resort, 30 minutes across the lagoon.

Sleeping

★ **Maratua Guesthouse** GUESTHOUSE
(www.maratuaguesthouse.com; d & tw cabins US$59) Nestled in a limestone forest between the island's cleanest beach and an inland tidal pond, this complex boasts a commanding view of the Celebes Sea from its open-air restaurant out front, and shady private cabins out back. The rooms all come with a mosquito net, fan, and front porch from which to watch the resident kingfishers and parakeets.

Nabucco & Nunukan Island Resorts

These two small islets in the mouth of the Maratua atoll are owned by Extra Divers, a German dive resort operator providing a refinement and attention to detail rarely experienced in Kalimantan. The owner works closely with scientists and the local leadership to continually improve the resorts' environmental and social sustainability. When we visited, the finishing touches were being put on a third even more luxurious resort, connected to Nunukan by a 1km boardwalk.

Sleeping

★ **Nabucco Island Resort** RESORT $$$
(☎ 0812 540 6636; www.extradivers-worldwide.com; r per person incl full board s/d €131/99; ❄ 📶) The sign above the dock at Nabucco says 'Welcome to Paradise': a fair sentiment. At the edge of the Maratua lagoon, this compact island dive resort packs plenty into a tiny manicured space. Surrounding a central common area, each varnished duplex bungalow shares an ocean-view porch with access to mangroves, a white-sand beach, or a slice of house reef.

Nunukan Island Resort RESORT $$$
(☎ 0812 340 3451; www.extradivers-worldwide.com; r per person incl full board s/d €131/99) From the long jetty welcoming you across the 4km house reef, to the common areas hovering over razor-sharp limestone, there is nothing typical – and everything exotic – about this island resort. The luxurious beachfront bungalows have spacious porches with sofa beds begging you to soak in the serenity. Inside, you'll find four-poster beds and inventive showers with one-way windows to the sea.

NORTH KALIMANTAN TRANSIT OPTIONS

Navigating through the province can be confusing. Consult the table below for transit options for moving from north to south.

FROM	TO	VIA	FARE	DURATION	FREQUENCY
Tawau (Sabah)	Nunukan	speedboat	RM75	1½hr	frequent
Tawau (Sabah)	Tarakan	plane (MASwings)	1,600,000Rp	40min	Mon, Wed, Thu, Sat, Sun
Tawau (Sabah)	Tarakan	ferry	RM130	4hr	10am Mon, Wed, Fri
Nunukan	Tarakan	speedboat	240,000Rp	2½hr	5 daily from 7am-1.30pm
Tarakan	Long Bawan	plane (Susi Air)	460,000Rp	1hr	Mon, Fri, Sat, Sun
Tarakan	Derawan	speedboat	250,000Rp	3hr	2pm Fri only
Tarakan	Tanjung Selor	speedboat	120,000Rp	1hr	frequent 7am-2.30pm
Tanjung Selor	Long Pujungan	longboat	800,000Rp	2 days	weekly
Tanjung Selor	Berau (Tanjung Redeb)	Kijang	120,000Rp	3hr	when full
Tanjung Selor	Berau (Tanjung Redeb)	bus (DAMRI)	50,000Rp	3hr	9am Mon, Wed, Fri

Pulau Kakaban & Pulau Sangalaki

These two undeveloped islands 40 minutes southwest of Maratua and an hour southeast of Derawan are popular day-trip destinations. Pulau Sangalaki has decent diving but is known primarily for its consistent manta ray spotting. For a close encounter of the eerie kind, visit the inland lake of Pulau Kakaban and swim through an ethereal swarm of millions of stingless jellyfish, some as tiny as your fingertip. If tides permit, snorkel through Kakaban's tidal cave tunnel to a hidden outcrop of protected pristine coral.

NORTH KALIMANTAN

☎0551

Due to its isolation, North Kalimantan contains some of the most pristine forests on Borneo, making it one of the last and best frontiers for hardcore jungle trekking. The 1.36 million hectare **Kayan Mentarang National Park** represents a significant chunk of the heart of Borneo, and contains a dizzying diversity of life, with new species still being discovered. When it comes to travelling here, the rewards are returned in direct proportion with the level of difficulty.

The two best places to access the park are via **Long Bawan** to the north, and **Long Punjungan** to the south. Many of the ecotourism initiatives developed by WWF (www.borneoecotourism.com) have been left fallow, but the information they provide is a great orientation to the area.

In Long Bawan, contact English-speaking Alex Balang (☎0852 4705 7469, alexbalang@hotmail.com) to get the lay of the land and to arrange treks further afield.

To the south, the path is even more untrodden, and Bahasa Indonesia is essential. Start your journey at **Tanjung Selor**, where sizeable longboats powered by multiple outboard engines load wares for the long haul upstream to **Long Punjungan**. Pak Muming at Hotel Asoy (☎0812 540 4256) and Pak Heri (☎0822 5053 8995) both regularly make the trip.

North Kalimantan is also a common, though convoluted, transit option for those travelling to or from Malaysian Borneo. Take note: there is no visa on arrival service at the borders on Nunukan or Tarakan, but the Indonesian consulate in Tawau, Sabah, is among the most efficient we have worked with.

Sulawesi

POP 18.8 MILLION

Includes ➡

Best Places to Eat

- Lae Lae (p644)
- Raja Sate (p687)
- Lesehan Jetpur (p653)
- Rumah Makan Green Garden (p687)

Best Places to Stay

- Living Colours (p690)
- Hoga Island Dive Resort (p700)
- Ge Jac Mart (p641)
- Cosmos Bungalows (p651)
- Pia's Poppies Hotel (p657)

Why Go?

If you think Sulawesi's geography looks fantastic on the map, just wait until you see it for real. The massive island's multi-limbed coastline is drawn with sandy beaches that fringe coral reefs and a mind-boggling variety of fish. Meanwhile, its interior is shaded by impenetrable mountains and jungles that are thick with wildlife, such as rare nocturnal tarsiers and flamboyantly colourful maleo birds. Cultures have been able to independently evolve here, cut off from the rest of the world by the dramatic topography. Meet the Toraja highlanders, with their elaborate funeral ceremonies in which buffaloes are sacrificed and *balok* (palm sugar wine) flows freely; the Minahasans in the far north, who offer spicy dishes of everything from stewed forest rat to grilled fish; and the Bugis, who are mainly found inhabiting Sulawesi's coastal regions and are Indonesia's most famous seafarers.

When to Go

Makassar

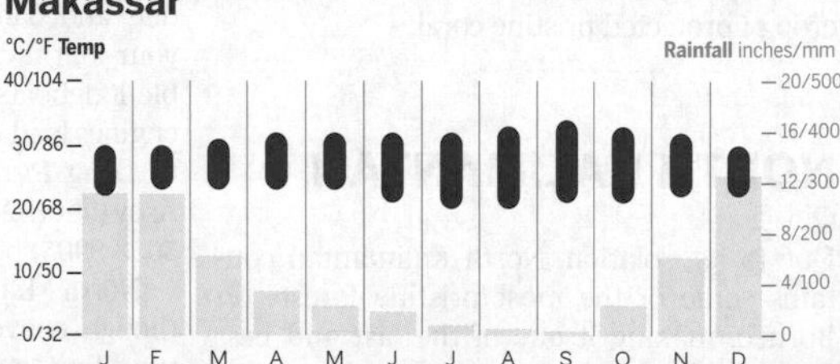

Apr–Oct It's peak season for scuba diving, with calm seas and incredible visibility.

Nov–Mar Lembeh Strait critters tend to come out of the muck more in the wet season.

Jun–Aug The best months to experience Tana Toraja's biggest funeral ceremonies.

History

The interior of Sulawesi provided a refuge for some of Indonesia's earliest inhabitants, some of whom preserved elements of their rich cultures well into the 20th century. The Makassarese and Bugis of the southwestern peninsula and the Christian Minahasans of the far north are the dominant groups in Sulawesi. The unique traditions, architecture and ceremonies of the Toraja people make the interior of South Sulawesi a deservedly popular destination.

Other minorities, particularly Bajau sea nomads, have played an integral role in the island's history. The rise of the kingdom of Gowa – Sulawesi's first major power – from the mid-16th century was partly due to its trading alliance with the Bajau. The Bajau supplied valuable sea produce, especially the Chinese delicacy trepang (sea cucumber), tortoiseshell, birds' nests and pearls, which attracted international traders to Gowa's capital, Makassar.

Makassar quickly became known as a cosmopolitan, tolerant and secure entrepôt that allowed traders to bypass the Dutch monopoly over the spice trade in the east – a considerable concern to the Dutch. In 1660 the Dutch sunk six Portuguese ships in Makassar harbour, captured the fort and in 1667 forced Gowa's ruler, Sultan Hasanuddin, into an alliance. Eventually, the Dutch managed to exclude all other foreign traders from Makassar, effectively shutting down the port.

Indonesia won its independence from the Dutch in 1945, but ongoing civil strife hampered Sulawesi's attempts at post-WWII reconstruction until well into the 1960s. A period of uninterrupted peace delivered unprecedented and accelerating development, particularly evident in the ever-growing Makassar metropolis.

Tragically, the Poso region in Central Sulawesi fell into a cycle of intercommunal violence in 1998, though things have calmed down considerably since. Since 2013 the development of the Trans-Sulawesi highway and the upgrading of several regional airports have improved the island's transport connections, boosting trade and tourism.

Getting There & Away

AIR

Domestic

The two main transport hubs are Makassar and Manado, which are well connected with the rest of Indonesia. Palu is the third most important airport. In recent years Gorontalo, Luwuk, Poso and Kendari have all seen an increase in air traffic; minor airports at towns such as Ampana, Selayar and Naha (Sangihe-Talaud Islands) also provide useful links for travellers.

There are direct flights to Java, Bali, Kalimantan, Maluku and Papua. Lion Air, Garuda Indonesia, Wings Air, Batik Air, Citilink, XpressAir, Sriwijaya Air are the main carriers.

International

Silk Air flies between Manado and Singapore four days per week for around US$210 (one way). Air Asia flies from Makassar to Kuala Lumpur from US$80.

THE WALLACE LINE

Detailed surveys of Borneo and Sulawesi in the 1850s by English naturalist Alfred Russel Wallace resulted in some inspired correspondence with Charles Darwin. Wallace was struck by the marked differences in wildlife, despite the two islands' proximity and similarities in climate and geography. His letters to Darwin, detailing evidence of his theory that the Indonesian archipelago was inhabited by one distinct fauna in the east and one in the west, prompted Darwin to publish similar observations from his own travels. The subsequent debate on species distribution and evolution transformed modern thought.

Wallace refined his theory in 1859, drawing a boundary between the two regions of fauna. The Wallace Line, as it became known, divided Sulawesi and Lombok to the east, and Borneo and Bali to the west. He believed that islands to the west of the line had once been part of Asia, and those to the east had been linked to a Pacific–Australian continent. Sulawesi's wildlife was so unusual that Wallace suspected it was once part of both, a fact that geologists have since proven to be true.

Other analyses of where Australian-type fauna begin to outnumber Asian fauna have placed the line further east. Lydekker's Line, which lies east of Maluku and Timor, is generally accepted as the western boundary of strictly Australian fauna, while Wallace Line marks the eastern boundary of Asian fauna.

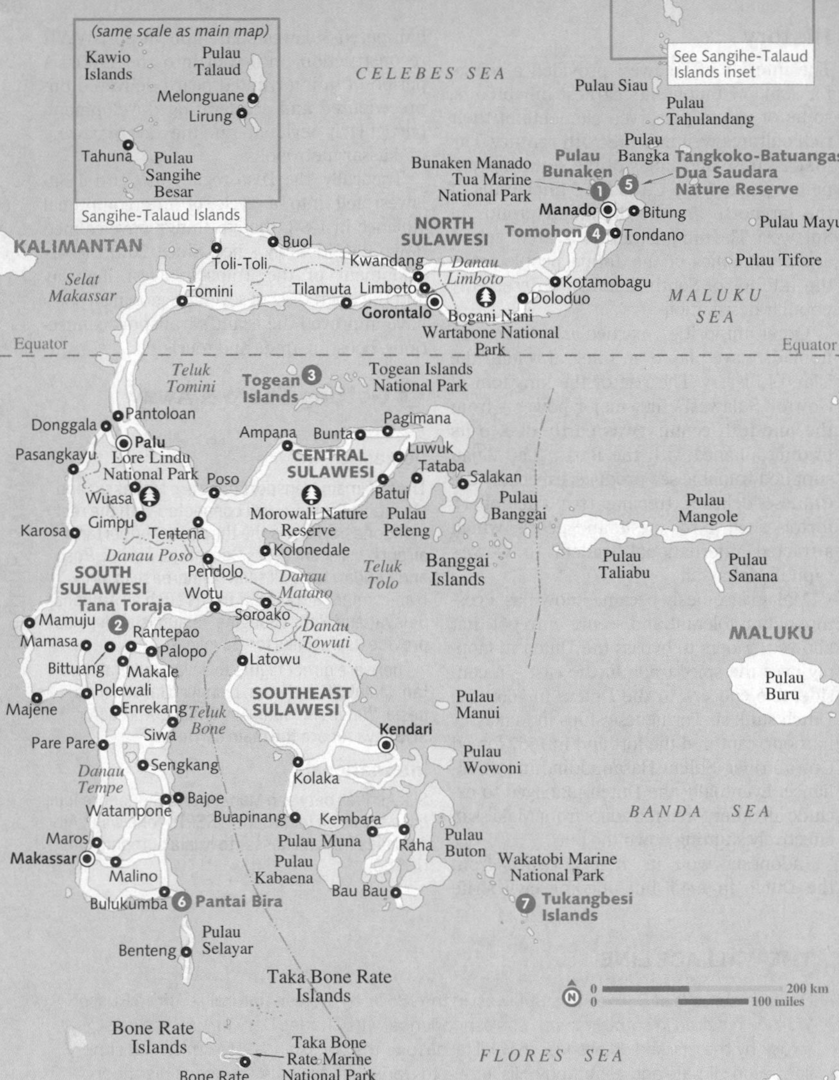

Sulawesi Highlights

1. Snorkelling or diving along unbelievably rich coral drop-offs – some of Asia's best – around chilled-out **Pulau Bunaken** (p688).
2. Witnessing the ritual and tradition of an elaborate funeral ceremony in **Tana Toraja** (p654).
3. Finding barefoot bliss in the off-grid, paradisaical **Togean Islands** (p677).
4. Hiking, cycling and birdwatching in the stunning volcanic region around **Tomohon** (p692).
5. Spotting sprightly tarsiers, black macaques and a bevy of birds at **Tangkoko-Batuangas Dua Saudara Nature Reserve** (p695).
6. Walking the beaches, diving the waters and exploring the diverse countryside around **Pantai Bira** (p647).
7. Seeking out one of Jacques Cousteau's favourite diving haunts: the rarely visited **Tukangbesi Islands** (p699).

BOAT

Sulawesi is well connected, with around half the Pelni ferry fleet calling at Makassar, Bitung (the seaport for Manado), Pare Pare and Toli-Toli, as well as a few other minor towns. Some of the more important boats that stop at Makassar and/or Bitung (for Manado) include the following:

BOAT	DESTINATIONS
Bukit Siguntang	East Kalimantan, Nusa Tenggara
Ciremai	Maluku, Papua, Java
Kelimutu	Java, Bali, Nusa Tenggara, Maluku
Kerinci	East Kalimantan
Labobar	Java, Papua
Lambelu	Java, Maluku, Northern Maluku
Sirimau	Nusa Tenggara, Java, East Kalimantan
Tilongkabila	Nusa Tenggara, Bali

Getting Around

AIR

Wings Air, Garuda Indonesia, XpressAir, Batik Air, Aviastar and Sriwijaya Air are the main carriers for getting around Sulawesi.

BOAT

With the proliferation of affordable flights in Sulawesi, very few travellers now use Pelni ferries. However, there are some useful links from Makassar to Malaku and Kalimantan and from Bitung in the north.

The *Tilongkabila* ferry sails every two weeks from Makassar to Bau Bau, Raha and Kendari, up to Kolonedale, Luwuk, Gorontalo and Bitung and returns the same way to Makassar.

Elsewhere along the coast creaky old ferries and wooden boats run to destinations including the Togean Islands. Speedboats are occasionally available for charter. Around the southeastern peninsula, the *kapal cepat* (fast boats) and the 'superjet' are the way to go.

BUS, BEMO AND KIJANG

Excellent air-conditioned buses connect Rantepao with Makassar. Elsewhere you're looking at pretty clapped-out local buses that stop every few minutes. There are some decent long-distance bemo (minibus) services, particularly on the road across Central Sulawesi connecting Luwuk and Palu.

Shared Kijang (a type of taxi) are also common; these are quicker than buses, and cost a bit more, but aren't necessarily more comfortable.

In towns minibuses called *mikrolet* or *petepete* are the main mode of transport for locals.

SOUTH SULAWESI

South Sulawesi is huge. Makassar in the far south is the capital of the island and is fittingly tumultuous yet friendly. Stop here for a day or two to feast on some of the best seafood on the island. From Makassar consider heading southeast to sleepy Pantai Bira, which has world-class diving and fine sandy beaches, or do what most people do and go directly to Tana Toraja.

The spectacular Toraja highlands should not be missed: a dizzying blend of mountains carved with rice paddies, outlandish funeral ceremonies involving animal sacrifices and some of the most fantastical local-style architecture in Asia. En route from Makassar you'll pass coastal salt farms and inland coffee, cotton and sugarcane plantations.

The estimated eight million or so inhabitants include the Bugis (who make up two-thirds of the population), the Makassarese (a quarter) and the Toraja. The Bugis and Makassarese are both seafaring people, who for centuries were active in trade, sailing to Flores, Timor and Sumba, and even as far afield as the northern coast of Australia. Islam is the dominant religion, except in Toraja, but all cultures retain vestiges of traditional beliefs.

History

The dominant powers in the south were long the Makassarese kingdom of Gowa (around the port of Makassar) and the Bugis kingdom of Bone. By the mid-16th century, Gowa had established itself at the head of a major trading bloc in eastern Indonesia. The king of Gowa adopted Islam in 1605 and Bone was soon subdued, spreading Islam to the whole Bugis–Makassarese area.

The Dutch United East India Company found Gowa a considerable hindrance to its plans to monopolise the spice trade until a deal was struck with the exiled Bugis prince Arung Palakka. The Dutch sponsored Palakka's return to Bone in 1666, prompting Bone to rise against the Makassarese. A year of fighting ensued and Sultan Hasanuddin of Gowa was forced to sign the Treaty of Bungaya in 1667, which severely reduced Gowa's power. Bone, under Palakka, then became the supreme state of South Sulawesi.

Rivalry between Bone and the other Bugis states continually reshaped the political landscape. After their brief absence during the Napoleonic Wars, the Dutch returned to a Bugis revolt led by the queen of Bone.

This was suppressed, but rebellions continued until Makassarese and Bugis resistance was finally broken in the early years of the 20th century. Unrest lingered on until the early 1930s, and revolts against the central Indonesian government occurred again in the 1950s.

The Makassarese and Bugis are staunchly Islamic and independently minded. Makassar and Pare Pare are still the first to protest when the political or economic situation is uncertain.

Today, a period of prosperity has brought stability, however, and Makassar's importance continues to grow as eastern Indonesia's foremost city.

Makassar

☎0411 / POP 1.71 MILLION

The gritty metropolis of Makassar is one of the nation's greatest ports. It's a seething maelstrom of commerce and shipping, with a polyglot population of Makassarese, Bugis and Chinese residents. But as the city has few sights, and the tropical heat and pollution is pretty unremitting, few travellers stay more than a night or two.

Makassar was the gateway to eastern Indonesia for centuries, and it was from here that the Dutch controlled much of the trade that passed between the West and the East. You can investigate the city's historical core, which retains considerable colonial charm, around Fort Rotterdam, which includes the remains of an ancient Gowanese fort and some striking Dutch buildings.

The locals are a hospitable and sociable bunch: mix with them in the city's famous seafood warung (food stalls) or join them for a stroll along Pantai Losari. This kilometre-long promenade stretches south to the 'floating mosque' Masjid Amirul Mukminin. It's a good place to catch some sea air and mingle with snacking families.

The city is expanding with new suburbs in every direction. Tanjung Bunga looms to the southwest of the city and may become the centre one day, while Panukkukang to the east is chock-a-block with mighty, modern shopping malls.

Sights

★Fort Rotterdam HISTORIC SITE

(Jl Pasar Ikan; 8am-6pm) FREE One of the best-preserved examples of Dutch architecture in Indonesia, Fort Rotterdam continues to guard the harbour of Makassar. A Gowanese fort dating back to 1545 once stood here, but failed to keep out the Dutch. The original fort was rebuilt in Dutch style, and includes many fine, well-restored colonial structures. You can walk the enclave's ramparts and see sections of the original walls.

Inside you'll find the **Museum Negeri La Galigo** (Jl Pasar Ikan, Fort Rotterdam; admission Rp10,000; 8am-6pm Tue-Sun), the collection of which is divided between two buildings.

The museum has an assortment of exhibits, including sailing boats, rice bowls from Tana Toraja, kitchen tools, musical instruments and ethnic costumes.

Pelabuhan Paotere PORT

(Paotere Harbour; admission 5000Rp) Pelabuhan Paotere, 4km north of the city centre, is a large port where Bugis sailing ships berth. There's usually lots of activity on the dock and in the huge **fish market** a few streets south, which is one of Indonesia's biggest.

ROAD TRIPS

The road network in Sulawesi has improved in recent years, and there's now (in theory) a 'Trans-Sulawesi Highway' connecting Makassar with Manado. However, it's not really a highway in the Western sense; it consists mostly of a two-laned paved road that passes through towns, over innumerable mountain ranges and is affected by landslides during heavy rains. It's very slow-going: expect to average no more than 35kph most of the time.

Roads around Makassar and the southwestern peninsula, and around Manado and the northeastern peninsula are in reasonable shape, though heavy traffic inevitably means slow journey times. A new toll road connecting Manado and Bitung is partially built. Road links have also been upgraded between Rantepao and Ampana. There's an excellent new road along the west coast between Watampone and Bulukumba.

Many travellers club together and hire a car and a driver to speed up travel in Sulawesi. The Rantepao–Ampana stretch (510km), which takes a minimum of two days, is a popular route.

WHAT'S IN A NAME?

From the early 1970s until 1999 the official name of Makassar was Ujung Pandang. During his final days as president, BJ Habibie made the popular decision to change the name back to Makassar. In reality both names are still used, as they have been for centuries, and neither title is politically charged.

Pelabuhan Paotere is one of the most atmospheric parts of the city from dawn until mid-morning, when giant tuna and every sea creature imaginable are traded.

Masjid Amirul Mukminin MOSQUE
(Jl Pasar Ikan) FREE Rising above the sea at the southern end of Pantai Losari, this elegant twin-domed structure (constructed using concrete piles driven into the seabed) is known as the 'floating mosque'. Visitors of all faiths are welcome. Built in 2009 it enjoys fine coastal views, and the landscaped area around the mosque is *the* place to break the daily fast during Ramadan.

Benteng Sungguminasa FORT
(Jl KH Wahid Hasyim; 8am-4pm) FREE This ancient fort, once the seat of the Sultan of Gowa, is 12km south of Makassar town centre at Sungguminasa. The complex here includes examples of traditional Sulawesi architecture and houses the rather dilapidated **Museum Balla Lompoa**, which displays local artefacts. Unfortunately it's all rather unloved and forgotten.

Red *pete-pete* marked 'S Minasa' head to Sungguminasa from Makassar Mall.

Makam Sultan Hasanuddin TOMB
(Jl Pallantiang, off Jl Sultan Hasanuddin) FREE Seven kilometres from town on the southeastern outskirts of Makassar, Makam Sultan Hasanuddin memorialises a 17th-century ruler of Gowa. Outside the tomb compound you'll find the Pelantikan Stone, on which the kings of Gowa were crowned. To get here take a red *pete-pete* marked 'S Minasa' from Makassar Mall to the turn-off for the 1km walk to the tomb.

Sleeping

Makassar's sleeping options are improving but still quite limited, and good budget places are hard to find. A number of excellent new midrange hotels have opened in recent years, and more are under construction.

Most of the best options are within walking distance of the waterfront.

★ **Dodo's Homestay** HOMESTAY $
(0812 412 9913; http://dodopenman.blogspot.co.uk; Jl Abdul Kadir Komplex Hartaco Indah Blok 1Y/25; s/d incl breakfast 75,000/100,000Rp;) An excellent homestay owned by Dodo, a superfriendly local who's been assisting travellers for more than 20 years. His home is a spacious, air-conditioned house in a quiet neighbourhood 4km south of the centre; one of the rooms has an en-suite bathroom. There's free tea and coffee, and Dodo arranges transport (including motorbike and car rental) and tours around Sulawesi.

The homestay can be reached by public transport; contact Dodo for exact directions.

New Legend Hotel HOTEL $
(0411-363-2123; http://newlegendhotel.com; Jl Jampea 1; dm/r/ste incl breakfast from 123,000/242,000/440,000Rp;) In a convenient Chinatown location, this new place is owned by the same helpful people who used to run Makassar's only hostel. Their new venture is primarily a modern hotel, with clean, well-presented rooms, all with TV/DVD, aircon and en-suite bathrooms (with hot water), though the cheapest lack windows. The city's only dorms are fan cooled and have shared bathrooms.

★ **Ge Jac Mart** HOMESTAY $$
(0411-859-421; http://ge-jacmart-homestay.blogspot.co.uk; Jl Rambutan 3; r incl breakfast 290,000Rp;) This is a wonderful place to stay, just off the seafront. It's run by the Pongrekun family (originally from Tana Toraja), who are hospitable, speak good English and enjoy looking after guests. The modern, immaculately clean family home has whitewashed walls and a splashes of art, and the seven very comfortable rooms each include a private bathroom with hot water.

It's located on a quiet lane just south of Jalan Kenari, near the Masjid Amirul Mukminin, the 'floating mosque'.

Makassar

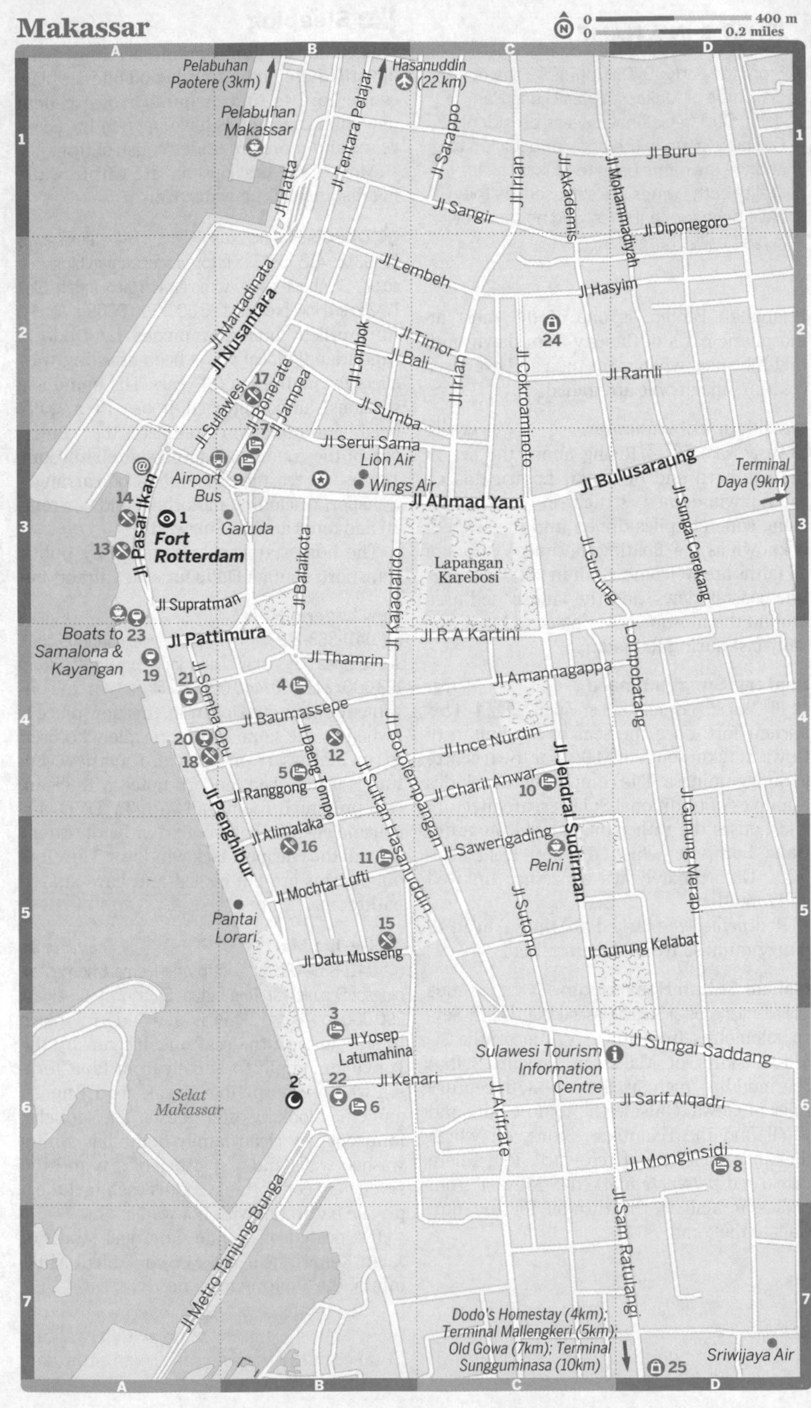

SULAWESI MAKASSAR

Makassar

Novotel Makassar Grand Shayla HOTEL $$
(☎0411-361-9444; www.novotel.com; Jl Charil Anwar 28; r incl breakfast from 640,000Rp; ❄📶🏊) This sleek, new contemporary hotel makes a fine base in the city, offering guests a 25m pool, a gym, a spa and really well equipped modern rooms that have fast wi-fi and luxury bedding. It's located about a 10-minute walk from the waterfront.

Favehotel Daeng Tompo HOTEL $$
(☎0411-363-9777; www.favehotels.com; Jl Daeng Tompo 28-36; r incl breakfast from 368,000Rp; ❄@📶) The boutique-style Favehotel represents good value given its fine location on a quiet street five minutes' walk from the beach. Rooms are not huge, but they are modish and inviting, and have quality beds with crisp linen and hip en-suite shower rooms. There's a cafe-restaurant onsite.

Santika Hotel HOTEL $$
(☎0411-363-2233; www.santika.com; Jl Sultan Hasanuddin 40; r incl breakfast from 642,000Rp; ❄@📶) The modern, slightly edgily designed Santika isn't well located for views, but the rooms are plush and have calming beige-and-white decor. Rates for walk-ins can be cheaper than booking online.

Makassar Breeze Place Residence HOTEL $$
(☎0896 5007 3932; makassarbreeze@gmail.com; Jl Monginsidi 26E; r incl breakfast 295,000Rp; ❄📶) The bright, modern accommodation in this apartment-hotel complex offers fine value and comfort, and includes flat-screen TVs, kitchen facilities and attractive bathrooms. It has a high standard of cleanliness, and serves generous breakfasts in the block's communal dining room. The staff speak limited English, but do their best to help out travellers.

Asoka Homestay HOMESTAY $$
(☎0411-873-476; Jl Yosep Latumahina; r incl breakfast 250,000-300,000Rp; ❄📶) Just steps from the waterfront, this quiet homestay with its lacy, decorative frills may feel like your granny's house. Asoka offers spacious and airy, though slightly dated rooms, with private cold-water bathrooms and TVs, surrounding a little courtyard.

Hotel Yasmin HOTEL $$
(☎0411-362-8329; www.yasminmakassar.com; Jl Jampea 5; r incl breakfast from 368,000Rp; ❄@📶) Victorian-era patterned wallpaper and upholstered chairs add a little decadence to this bustling, decent-value hotel. Rooms are smallish but in good shape and the staff are professional. There's a cafe-restaurant and 24-hour room service.

Aston Makassar HOTEL $$$
(☎0411-362-3222; www.aston-international.com; Jl Sultan Hasanuddin 10; r incl breakfast from 800,000Rp; ❄@📶🏊) This towering city landmark enjoys a fine location within walking distance of the seafront and Fort Rotterdam.

Rooms are spacious and well appointed, and the buffet breakfast spread is a welcome sight for hungry bellies. On the top two floors you'll find a 30m indoor pool, a gym, a spa and a sky bar-restaurant.

Eating

For many visitors it's the food that makes Makassar a great destination. There's an abundance of seafood, Chinese dishes, a few international surprises and local specialities such as *coto Makassar* (a hearty, well-seasoned soup made from buffalo innards), *mie titi* (also called *mie kering* – crispy noodles with gravy, chicken and shrimp) and *pisang epe* (grilled flattened bananas covered with cane syrup and/or chocolate, found all around the city at night at small stalls).

Jl Timor, in the heart of the Chinese quarter, is where you'll find restaurants serving delicious *mie pangsit* (wonton soup).

★Lae Lae SEAFOOD $

(0411-334-326; Jl Datu Musseng 8; meals from 30,000Rp; noon-10pm) A famous seafood restaurant, Lae Lae is a crowded, unadulterated food frenzy: expect no-nonsense surrounds, discarded crab shells around your feet and great food. You enter via a smoking streetside barbecue area sizzling with grilled fish and seafood, and eat at long tables, where you'll rub shoulders with locals. Three accompanying sambal sauces are offered and there are tasty vegetable side dishes.

Rumah Makan Pate'ne INDONESIAN $

(Jl Sulawesi 48; mains 11,000-34,000Rp; 8am-9pm) Serving up delicious, inexpensive Javanese dishes and Indonesian classics, Pate'ne offers fine value and authentic flavours. Enjoy *soto ayam* (chicken soup) for just 11,000Rp, or feast on a filling *nasi campur* (rice with a choice of side dishes) for 27,500Rp. Fresh juices including melon, mango, apple and avocado are available.

Fish Warungs HAWKER $

(Jl Pasar Ikan; per fish around 25,000Rp; 5-10.30pm) A string of makeshift fish warungs set up every night on the foreshore opposite Fort Rotterdam and south along the waterfront, and serve some of the tastiest, cheapest seafood in town. Roaming buskers provide table-side entertainment.

Kampoeng Popsa INTERNATIONAL, INDONESIAN $

(Jl Pasar Ikan; meals from 25,000Rp; 8am-11pm) This large, open-sided food court facing the harbour has sea breezes, a young clientele, a gregarous vibe, space for kids to run around, and lots of choices, from *mei titi* to sushi, and noodle dishes to ice cream. Beers, including Heineken and Guinness, are served. There's often live music at night. Find it right across the street from Fort Rotterdam.

Sentosa INDONESIAN $

(0411-326-062; Jl Penghibur 26; soups 8000Rp; 8am-10pm) The Makassarese flock to this basic cafe with sea views for inexpensive grub, including tasty meatballs and delicious wonton soup.

Bistropolis INTERNATIONAL $$

(0411-363-6988; www.bistropolis.net; Jl Sultan Hasanuddin 18; meals 50,000-149,000Rp; 10am-11pm Mon-Fri, to 1am Sat, to midnight Sun;) A stylish, atmospheric bistro serving great international standards including pasta and pizza, (imported) steaks, ribs, fish and chips and a few Asian dishes. The ice cream (try the Bailey's flavour) is delectable and the espresso hits the spot. Subtle lighting, comfy seating and fine service make it a fine place for lingering over a meal.

RM Nelayan SEAFOOD $$

(0411-361-0523; Jl Alimalaka 25; meals 40,000-70,000Rp; 10am-10pm) It's tough to resist the aromas emanating from this highly popular restaurant's fish barbecue while strolling along Jl Alimalaka. Step inside and receive a selection of six condiments placed on your table. Fish and shrimp are offered in a variety of styles, including delicious *rica-rica* (a spicy stir-fry), and cold Bintangs are available.

Drinking & Nightlife

Many of the bars around the port area are little more than brothels disguised as karaoke bars and are best avoided by all but the proverbial drunken sailor.

Makassar does not have a big club scene; most venues are dotted along the harbourfront road. Entry costs from 35,000Rp to 60,000Rp, which usually includes a soft drink or a beer.

Kios Semarang BAR

(Jl Penghibur; noon-1am) Climb the stairs to the upper floors where you will be rewarded with a rowdy crowd downing beers and comfort grub (the spicy chicken wings are famous). It's a key expat hang-out, and the closest thing to a Makassar drinking institution.

Level BAR
(☎0411-831-400; www.thelevel.co.id; Jl Somba Opu 277C; ⏰10am-2am; 📶) A landmark white structure facing the floating mosque Masjid Amirul Mukminin, the Level attracts Makassar's young things and hipsters, and hosts DJ events and live bands. There are several zones including a lounge-cafe, the sunset bar, karaoke rooms and a bar-club. Dress sharp (no sandals or flip-flops). You can also drop by for a coffee or a meal during the day.

Zona Cafe CLUB
(www.zonacafe.info; Jl Pasar Ikan; admission 40,000-100,000Rp; ⏰8am-2am) This popular club draws a loyal young crowd with its DJs and bands from Jakarta and its regular drink promotions. Check its Twitter feed (@zonaholic) for upcoming events.

Ballairate Sunset Bar BAR
(Jl Pasar Ikan 10, Hotel Pantai Gapura; ⏰1-11pm) Built on stilts over the sea, this is the best-located bar in town. Walk right through Hotel Pantai Gapura to discover draft Bintang and a perfect view of the sunset from a large deck.

Kafe Kareba BEER GARDEN
(Jl Penghibur; ⏰5pm-midnight) This long-running outdoor beer garden on the seafront features live bands and is popular with locals and visitors alike. It also has a pretty extensive food menu.

☆ Entertainment

Studio 21 CINEMA
(www.21cineplex.com; Jl Sam Ratulangi) Shows current Western films in their original language (with Bahasa Indonesia subtitles). On the top floor of the Ratu Indah Mall complex.

Shopping

Shopping malls are dotted around the city and suburbs.

Jl Somba Opu has craft stores selling jewellery, 'antiques' and souvenirs. Look for Kendari filigree silver jewellery, Torajan handicrafts, Chinese pottery, Makassarese brass work and silk cloth from Sengkang.

Ratu Indah Mall MALL
(http://malratuindah.co.id; Jl Sam Ratulangi; 8am-10pm) The best central mall, with two (official) Apple retailers, a Body Shop, a Matahari department store, outdoor-adventure sports retailers, cafes and restaurants.

Makassar Mall MALL
(cnr Jl Kyai Kaji Ramli & Jl Agus Salim; ⏰7.30am-10pm) A sprawling mess and more like a market than a mall; come here to experience Makassar at its craziest.

ℹ Information

EMERGENCY

Police Station (☎110; Jl Ahmad Yani)

IMMIGRATION

Immigration Office (☎0411-584-559; Jl Perintis Kemerdekaan; ⏰7am-noon & 1-4pm Mon-Fri) Located 13km from the city centre, on the road to the airport.

INTERNET ACCESS

Internet centres are found across the city. Most charge 5000Rp per hour.

Expresso Cafe Net (cnr Jl Pasar Ikan & Jl Ahmad Yani; per hr 5000Rp; ⏰8am-midnight) Centrally located, clean private booths and fast connections.

MEDICAL SERVICES

RS Awal Bros Hospital (☎0411-452-725; http://makassar.awalbros.com; 43 Jl Jendral Urip Sumoharjo) The most convenient and well-equipped hospital. Some staff speak English here. It's out near the toll road.

MONEY

Banks and ATMs are dotted all over the centre of the city. You'll find several moneychangers and ATMs at the airport.

TELEPHONE

The most convenient option is to buy a local SIM card (from 5000Rp). Telkomsel is the carrier with the best coverage in Sulawesi.

TOURIST INFORMATION

Sulawesi Tourism Information Centre (☎0411-872-336; cnr Jl Sam Ratulangi & Jl Sungai Saddang; ⏰8am-4pm) There's little practical information available but the staff are helpful and friendly. Take any red *pete-pete* (a type of *mikrolet* or bemo) travelling south along Jl Jendral Sudirman to get here.

TRAVEL AGENCIES

Makassar has many travel agencies offering flight bookings and tours, including trips to Tana Toraja. Don't make a hefty payment up front; some travellers have reported making payments to seemingly professional 'tour organisers' whose tours never materialise.

He's not a conventional travel agent, but freelancer **Dodo Mursalim** (☎0812 412 9913; http://dodopenman.blogspot.com) helps hundreds of travellers each year with transport and tours, and has been doing so for decades. He's reliable, trustworthy and his rates are very reasonable.

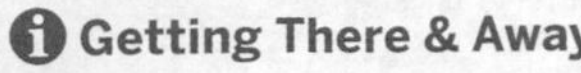

Getting There & Away

AIR

Makassar is well connected with other cities in Sulawesi and with Java, Kalimantan and Maluku. International flights include Air Asia to Kuala Lumpur and Silk Air to Singapore.

Note many airline's websites still use Makassar's former name, Ujung Pandang, for bookings.

Garuda (Garuda Indonesia; ☎0411-365-4747; Jl Slamet Riyadi 6) Flies directly to and from Manado, Denpasar, Jakarta, Jayapura, Surabaya and Yogyakarta among many other destinations.

Lion Air (☎0411-327-038; Jl Ahmad Yani 22) Flies daily to and from Manado, Kendari, Gorontalo, Palu, Yogyakarta, Surabaya, Balikpapan, Ternate and Sorong.

Sriwijaya Air (☎0411-424-800; Jl Lanto Daeng Pasewang) Flies to/from destinations including Ambon, Biak, Balikpapan, Gorontalo, Jayapura, Kendari, Manado, Palu, Surabaya and Ternate.

Wings Air (☎0411-327-038; Jl Ahmad Yani 22) Flies to/from Gorontalo, Kendari, Luwuk, Mamuju, Poso and Wakatobi.

BOAT

Around half the Pelni ferry fleet stops in Makassar, mostly on the way to Surabaya and Jakarta, East Kalimantan, Ambon and Papua. Useful services include the *Tidar* to Balikpapan, the *Sirimau* to Larantuka in Flores, and the *Tilongkabila* to Bau Bau and then up along the east coast to Kendari, Kolonedale, Luwuk, Gorontalo and Bitung.

The **Pelni office** (☎0411-331-401; Jl Jendral Sudirman 38; ⌚8am-2pm Mon-Sat) is efficient and computerised. Tickets are also available at agencies around town. Pelni boats use the chaotic **Pelabuhan Makassar** (off Jl Nusantara) port in the city centre.

BUS & KIJANG

Makassar has numerous terminals but three are most useful.

Terminal Daya Buses and Kijangs depart throughout the day to all points north, including Sengkang (55,000Rp to 78,000Rp, four hours) and Rantepao (110,000Rp to 220,000Rp, nine hours). There are some luxurious bus services to Rantapao, including night buses (most leave between 8.30pm and 10pm). To get to Terminal Daya, catch any *pete-pete* (5000Rp, 30 minutes) marked 'Daya' from Makassar Mall or from along Jl Bulusaraung. It's in the eastern suburbs on the road to the airport.

Terminal Mallengkeri Buses and Kijangs depart for destinations southeast of Makassar, including to Bulukumba (60,000Rp, four hours) and Pantai Bira (75,000Rp, five hours). For Pantai Bira, you may have to change in Bulukumba. Transport is most frequent in the morning, so it's good to get to the terminal early. It's about 8km southeast of the city centre; take a *pete-pete* marked 'S Minasa' from Makassar Mall or from along Jl Jendral Sudirman and ask to be dropped at Terminal Mallengkeri.

Terminal Sungguminasa Has regular *pete-pete* services to Malino (24,000Rp, 1½ hours). To get here take a *pete-pete* marked 'S Minasa' from Makassar Mall or from along Jl Jendral Sudirman.

Getting Around

TO/FROM THE AIRPORT

Hasanuddin Airport is 22km north of Makassar city centre. Using the toll road will save you considerable time.

Bus

Damri buses (27,000Rp) run every 20 to 30 minutes between 8am and 9pm daily from the basement level of the airport to Lapangan Karebosi in central Makassar.

Pete-Pete

These can be convenient (although time consuming) if you want to skip Makassar altogether. Free shuttles run from the basement level of the airport to the main road (about 500m from the terminal) about every 15 minutes; from there you can flag down a *pete-pete* to Terminal Daya. From Terminal Daya you can transfer to *pete-pete* going to the other bus terminals or get buses to points north, including Rantepao.

Taxi

Prepaid taxis are available in the arrivals area of the airport. Taxis between the airport and city cost from 105,000Rp to 125,000Rp.

PUBLIC TRANSPORT

Makassar is hot, so using a becak (bicycle rickshaw), *pete-pete* or taxi can be a relief.

Becak

Becak drivers like to kerb-crawl, hoping you'll succumb to their badgering and/or the heat. The going rate is from 7000Rp to 10,000Rp.

Pete-Pete

The main *pete-pete* terminal is at **Makassar Mall** (p645). The standard fare around town is 5000Rp.

Taxi

Air-conditioned taxis have meters and are worth using; a 2km ride costs about 14,000Rp. **Blue Bird** (☎ 0411-441-234) is reliable, comfortable and operates 24 hours.

Around Makassar

Pulau Samalona

A tiny speck just off Makassar, the white sands of Pulau Samalona are popular with day trippers, particularly on weekends. It takes a full two minutes to walk around the entire island. There are patches of (degraded) coral offshore, some reef fish, and you'll find snorkelling gear for hire. Compared to Makassar harbour, the water's pretty clear! Cold drinks (including beer) and fresh fish are available.

To get here you will have to charter a boat (400,000Rp to 500,000Rp return) from the special jetty in Makassar. Boats can take up to eight people.

Pulau Kayangan

This tiny tropical island (also spelt Khayangan) is a short ride (40,000Rp return in a public boat) from Makassar harbourfront. It's rammed with locals on Sundays and holidays but is pleasant enough to visit for a seafood meal the rest of the time; many of the island's restaurants are positioned over the water, and are perfect for sunsets.

Bantimurung

Air Terjun Bantimurung WATERFALL
(admission Indonesian/foreigner 25,000/255,000Rp)
These waterfalls 42km from Makassar are set amid lushly vegetated limestone cliffs. It's a highly scenic spot, but beware the absurdly overpriced entrance fee for foreigners.

Looking up, it's straight out of *Jurassic Park,* but then you scan the ground level and it's a classic *objek wisata* (tourist object), crowded with day trippers on weekends, and peppered with litter and creative concrete. Upstream from the main waterfall there's another smaller waterfall and a pretty, but treacherous, pool (take a torch to make it through the cave en route).

Bantimurung is also famous for its beautiful butterflies; however, numbers are plummeting, as locals trap them to sell to visitors.

Catch a Damri bus or *pete-pete* (10,000Rp, one hour) to Maros from Makassar Mall (p645) in Makassar, and a *pete-pete* to Bantimurung (7000Rp, 30 minutes).

Gua Leang Leang

The Gua Leang Leang **caves** (admission Indonesian/foreigner 5000/20,000Rp) are noted for their ancient paintings. The age of these is unknown, but relics from nearby caves have provided glimpses of life from 8000 to 30,000 years ago. There are 60 or so known caves in the Maros district; the limestone karsts here have more holes than a Swiss cheese.

Catch a *pete-pete* from Maros to the Taman Purbakala Leang-Leang turn-off on the road to Bantimurung, and walk the last couple of kilometres.

Alternatively, charter a *pete-pete* from Maros and combine it with a trip to Air Terjun Bantimurung waterfall.

Malino

☎ 0417

Malino is a hill resort, famous as the meeting place of Kalimantan and east Indonesian leaders who endorsed the Netherlands' ill-fated plans for a federation. More recently, peace agreements have been struck for Maluku and Poso here. There are many scenic walks, and **Air Terjun Takapala** (admission 3000Rp) is a spectacular waterfall set amid rice fields 4km east of town. Look for the 'Wisata Alam Lombasang Malino' sign as you come into town for the waterfall turn-off.

Grand Bukit Indah Resort (☎ 21277; hotel.bukitindah@yahoo.com; Jl Endang 2; r incl breakfast 250,000-375,000Rp) is not at all 'grand' but the spacious tiled rooms with private *mandis* (Indonesian-style bathrooms), flat-screen TVs and front porches are kept tidy. There are many warung in town.

Terminal Sungguminasa in Makassar has regular *pete-pete* services to Malino (16,000Rp, 2½ hours).

Pantai Bira

☎ 0413

Goats outnumber vehicles in the isolated coastal village and dive centre of Pantai Bira. The scruffy main village, home to most accommodation, is spread out and not particularly attractive; travellers are increasingly choosing to stay at the nearby beach of Bara,

Pantai Bira & Around

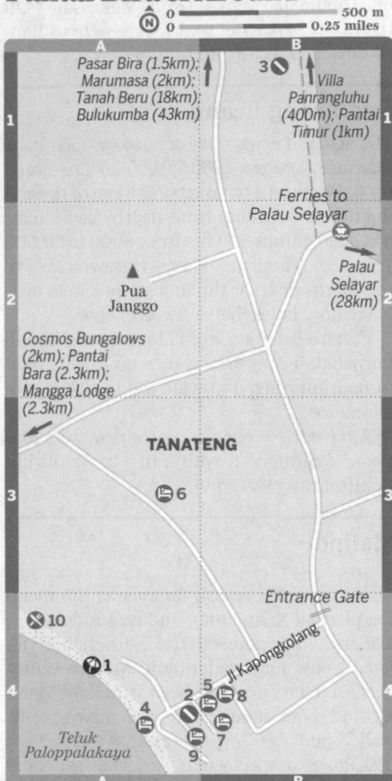

Pantai Bira & Around

where accommodation looks out over a sparkling stretch of powdery white sand.

Bira's beaches are very broad at low tide and there's decent snorkelling a short swim from the shore. There are several more remote bays, hiking trails and a few caves with freshwater pools to explore in the surrounding area. Unfortunately, rubbish is a big problem everywhere around Bira.

The diving here is dramatic, on a par with anywhere in Indonesia for 'big stuff': lots of sharks (including hammerheads), rays and pelagic fish. However, some sites are swept by strong currents and are only suitable for experienced divers.

Sights

Boat builders use age-old techniques to craft **traditional ships** at Marumasa, about half a kilometre east of Bira village, and at Tanah Beru on the road to Bulukumba. Wooden boats of various sizes can be seen at different stages of construction.

There is a small market, **Pasar Bira** (7am-5pm), held in the village every two days.

A short hike from the road near Pantai Timur takes you to the top of **Pua Janggo**, a small hill with great views.

Beaches

The Bira region is blessed with sweeping stretches of pale sand. Bear in mind that locals are fairly conservative. Wearing a bikini is fine (on beaches only) but you will get stared at and Makassar day trippers will probably ask to get their photo taken with you.

Pantai Bara BEACH

Around 3km northwest of Bira village, this is a fabulous crescent of white sand, fringed by low cliffs and palms. You can stroll here in 20 to 30 minutes from Bira along the coast with the sand between your toes (low tide only) and marvel at the turquoise water and tropical vegetation. At high tide use the shady dirt track behind the beach, which cuts through woodland that's home to monkeys and large monitor lizards.

Several excellent hotels have opened recently in Pantai Bara.

Pantai Barat BEACH

(West Beach) Pantai Barat is Bira's main beach, just west of the village centre. Its white sands are pleasant enough, though they get packed with day trippers on weekends, and there's some rubbish. The beachside warungs that sell grilled fish and banana-boat rides are very popular with locals.

Pantai Timur BEACH
(East Beach) Pantai Timur is a coconut-fringed affair near the boat dock in Bira village, but it's usually cursed with rubbish.

Activities

Bira is rightly renowned for its spectacular **scuba diving**. **Snorkelling** is also impressive. Full-day boat trips to Pulau Lihukan and Pulau Betang cost about 400,000Rp per day for a boat seating eight to 10 people. Snorkelling from both Bara and Barat is quite good, but due to the strong tides it's only possible for a few hours a day. Also, currents can be surprisingly strong and people have drowned. Equipment (mask and fins) can be rented for about 50,000Rp per day from several hotels, including Riswan Guest House (p650) and Bira Beach Hotel.

Sulawesi Dive Adventure DIVING
(0812 4137 6888; www.sulawesidiveadventure.com; Panrang Luhu; dives US$35) A recently opened, European-owned dive centre with new equipment, and excellent local dive instructors and guides who have decades of experience between them.

South Sulawesi Divers DIVING
(0812 4443 6626; www.south-sulawesi-diver.com; Jl Poros Bara; dives €35) A well-managed dive centre run by Elvis, a German dive instructor who has been leading dives around Bira for years. South Sulawesi Divers is reputable and well managed. Operates out of **Mangga Lodge** (p651).

Bira Divers DIVING
(0812 3720 0560; http://biradivers.com; Pantai Barat; dives €35, PADI Open Water Diver course €335) This dive school has good dive equipment and instructors. However, as they use small local fishing craft as dive boats, it's not possible to reach the offshore islands when the sea is choppy. We don't recommend staying at the affiliated beach hotel (the Bira Dive Camp), as thefts have occurred.

Sleeping

Budget accommodation is concentrated in Bira village; however, most places are ageing and not great value. Pantai Bara, 3km away, makes a lovely secluded place to stay.

BIRA'S TOP SCUBA-DIVING SITES

Famous as one of the 'sharkiest' spots in Indonesia, Bira offers truly spectacular scuba diving. The islands off Bira lie at the tip of southern Sulawesi where oceanic currents converge, bringing upswells of cool water from the depths and lots of pelagic life.

The seas can be rough off Pantai Bira and it's not always possible to reach islands such as Kambing, around 7km south, which has five dive sites. But there are more sheltered sites closer to shore, where you can spot macro life including nudibranchs, seahorses and prolific reef fish.

Swedish dive instructor Nick Lindberg, who worked in Bira for years, considers Kambing island to be the region's highlight. Lindberg's favourite sites include the following:

Great Wall of Goat Kambing means 'goat' in Indonesian, and the unpopulated island's eastern side has a remarkable vertical wall teeming with reef life. Sharks (including hammerheads and threshers) and rays (including mantas and devil rays) are typically encountered.

Cap Bira This impressive site off the extreme tip of the mainland has a lovely swim-through; white-tip sharks, shrimps and pipefish are common.

Shark Point This is an easier dive with a sloped profile on the eastern side of Liukang Loe island. Expect beautiful coral, turtles, sea snakes and, of course, lots of sharks, including 2m white-tips, black-tips and occasionally bull sharks.

Fish Market For experienced divers, this underwater sea mount teems with sea life, including huge groupers, jacks and Napoleon wrasse. It's a simply astonishing dive.

Mola-Mola Point On the western side of Kambing island, giant mola-mola are encountered at this site that's suitable for advanced divers. August and September are the best months.

SULAWESI SEAFARERS

The Bugis are Indonesia's best-known sailors, and carry and trade goods on their magnificent wooden schooners throughout Indonesia.

The Bugis' influence expanded rapidly after the fall of Makassar, which resulted in a diaspora from South Sulawesi in the 17th and 18th centuries. They established strategic trading posts at Kutai (Kalimantan), Johor (north of Singapore) and Selangor (near Kuala Lumpur), and traded freely throughout the region. Bugis and Makassarese *pinisi* (schooners) are still built along the south coasts of Sulawesi and Kalimantan, using centuries-old designs and techniques. You can see boats being built at Marumasa and Tanah Beru, both near Bira.

The Bajau, Bugis, Butonese and Makassarese seafarers of Sulawesi have a 500-year history of trading and cultural links with Indigenous Australians, and their ships are featured in pre-European Aboriginal cave art in northern Australia. British explorer Matthew Flinders encountered 60 Indonesian schooners at Melville Bay in 1803; today many more still make the risky (and illegal) journey to fish reefs in the cyclone belt off the northern coast of Australia.

Many Minahasans of North Sulawesi, relative newcomers to sailing folklore, work on international shipping lines across the world. As with their Filipino neighbours, the Minahasans' outward-looking culture, plus their language and sailing skills, make them the first choice of many captains.

Note prices are flexible at many places, with rates jacked up on holidays and discounts on offer during quiet times.

Bira Village Area

★Sunshine Guesthouse GUESTHOUSE $
(Nini's Place; ☎0821 9093 1175; http://ninibone.blogspot.co.uk; s/d 150,000/180,000Rp) Perched up on a hill, with village and bay views, British-and-Indonesian-run Sunshine has a wonderful terrace with sea breezes, a convivial atmosphere and is easily the best-tended place in the village. Comfy rooms in a big wooden house have spotless shared (hot-water) Western-style bathrooms.

Salassa Guest House GUESTHOUSE $
(☎0812 426 5672; salassaguesthouse@yahoo.com; s/d incl breakfast 120,000/150,000Rp) A fine family-run place, Salassa has six small rooms (separated by wooden walls) that share a *mandi* (Indonesian-style) bathroom. The owners are very helpful, speak English and can direct you to some great off-the-beaten-track locations around Bira. The downstairs restaurant is one of the best in town; the included breakfast is filling.

Riswan Guest House GUESTHOUSE $
(☎0812 426 5627, 0853 4166 4955; r with fan/air-con incl breakfast 150,000/300,000Rp; ❄@) All the tiled rooms at this guesthouse are kept very clean and tidy, and have private *mandi*; air-con options also have flat-screen TVs. Host Riswan is knowledgeable about the Bira region, speaks good English, and provides guests with tips and a map of the area for exploring.

Villa Panrangluhu BUNGALOW $$
(☎0812 4137 6888; www.villapanrangluhu.com; bungalows with fan/air-con incl breakfast from 300,000/500,000Rp; ❄) Opened in 2015, these four lovely, well-constructed wooden bungalows are operated by Sulawesi Dive Adventures. Each has a private bathroom, a front deck and enjoy a beachside location, but they are grouped quite close together.

Cici Guest House GUESTHOUSE $$
(☎0813 5592 2595; http://ciciguesthouse.blogspot.co.uk; r incl breakfast 260,000Rp; ❄) This new place is good value and has modern rooms with private bathrooms and TVs, all set in a cheery, banana-yellow-painted block. There's a restaurant on-site and it's about 150m inland from the beach.

Anda Bungalows BUNGALOW $$
(☎0413-82125; bungalows incl breakfast 475,000-750,000Rp; ❄) All the bungalows here have air-con and are set around a garden away from the sea. The newer cement bungalows are quite comfy; the cheaper wooden bungalows aren't as posh but are still OK value for Bira. The big restaurant here has lots of choices.

Amatoa Beach Resort RESORT $$$
(☎0812 4296 5500; www.amatoaresort.com; 6 Jl Pasir Putih; r incl breakfast 1,500,000-2,500,000Rp; ❄@📶🏊) Perched above the rocks and overlooking the ocean, this luxurious place has a Mediterranean feel to it. Think exposed stone work, driftwood and decking, cacti, neutral-toned drapes and cushioned daybeds. Service can be hit-and-miss, however, considering the rates charged.

Pantai Bara

The owners of Sunshine Guesthouse in Bira village had almost completed a new midrange place at Pantai Bara, **Nini's Beach Bungalows** (☎0821 9093 1175; www.facebook.com/ninisbeachbungalows; Pantai Bara; cottages incl breakfast 500,000-700,000Rp), at the time of research.

★**Cosmos Bungalows** BUNGALOW $$
(☎0822 9260 8820; http://cosmosbungalows.com; Pantai Bara; bungalows incl breakfast 250,000-500,000Rp) Run by young, well-travelled British owners who really look after their guests, Cosmos offers a handful of rustic-chic, beautifully built bungalows with shared Western-style bathrooms. The bungalows are located on a slim patch of land that stretches down to the coastal cliffs, where you'll find the lovely restaurant, high above Pantai Bara. Expect good vibes all round and great local information.

Bara Beach BUNGALOW $$
(☎0821 9413 1562; www.bara-beach.com; Jl Poros Bara; bungalow incl breakfast €50-70; ❄) Overlooking dreamy Pantai Bara, these tastefully presented, well-appointed bungalows are supersized with plush bathrooms and terraces; all are set in a lush, flowering garden. It's efficiently run by a German-Indonesian family and the seafront restaurant is perfect for a sundowner or an enjoyable meal.

Mangga Lodge HOTEL $$$
(☎0413-270-0756; www.mangga-lodge.com; Jl Poros Bara; r incl breakfast €60; ❄@) This is a German-run place where the comfortable, stylish rooms are perhaps a tad overpriced, but the location on Pantai Bara is divine. It's a good choice for divers (South Sulawesi Divers is based here) and there are lots of organised outings on offer to the surrounding area.

Eating & Drinking

Many guesthouses serve good local meals while the hotels have more expensive restaurants. On nearby Pantai Bara you'll only find hotel restaurants: both Cosmos Bungalows and Bara Beach have excellent waterfront locations and great food.

Salassa INDONESIAN $
(mains 30,000-45,000Rp; ⏲7am-10pm) This large purpose-built ground-floor restaurant within Salassa Guest House offers homestyle cooking (try the fish 'a la Salassa' with peppers and spices), chicken, rice and noodles dishes. It serves cold beer and fresh juices.

Warung Bamboo INDONESIAN $
(meals 20,000-40,000Rp; ⏲7am-10pm) A roadside place that hits the spot for tasty noodle dishes, seafood and delicious *ikan bakar* (grilled fish).

Warung INDONESIAN $
(meals from 15,000Rp; ⏲7am-10pm) For cheap grub, head to the beachfront warung for grilled fish and noodles dishes.

Information

Most services and amenities are located along a small section of Jl Kapongkolang, the road into Pantai Bira. Foreign tourists must pay 5000Rp per person at the toll booth when they first enter. There are BNI and BRI ATMs at the harbour entrance at Pantai Timur.

Amatoa Beach Resort is the only accommodation to offer wi-fi, but guesthouses and hotels offer (limited) internet access via data sticks and Telkomsel 3G.

Getting There & Away

BOAT

Note that departure times change frequently and ferries are regularly cancelled during high seas, sometimes for several days.

The harbour at Pantai Timur has twice-daily boats to Pulau Selayar (79,000Rp, two hours). There is also a direct boat to Labuanbajo in Flores (142,000Rp) on Sunday nights, but it's a slow ride, taking around 30 hours.

BUS, BEMO & KIJANG

From Makassar (Terminal Mallengkeri), a few Kijangs go directly to Pantai Bira (80,000Rp, five to six hours). Alternatively, catch a Kijang or bus to Bulukumba (60,000Rp), and another to Pantai Bira (20,000Rp; note that transport from Bulukumba to Pantai Bira stops at around 3pm).

Direct Kijangs returning from Pantai Bira to Makassar leave at 6am and 10am; book via your hotel the day before and you'll be picked up; alternatively, take a *pete-pete* from Pantai Bira to Bulukumba and then a Kijang or bus to Makassar from there.

Pulau Lihukan

This island, a short ride from Pantai Bira, is a popular destination for snorkelling trips. Weavers at **Ta'Buntuleng** make heavy, colourful cloth on hand looms under their houses. On the pretty beach west of the village there is an interesting old **graveyard**, and off the beach there are acres of sea grass and coral, but mind the currents.

Right on the white beach overlooking the mainland and in front of a good snorkelling spot, **Wisma & Restaurant Leukang Loe** (☎081 3425 78515; Pulau Lihukan; 250,000Rp per person incl 3 meals; ❄) has simple wood bungalows with private bathrooms and front porches for sea-gazing. The kind family owners cook up tasty fish and vegetable meals.

Boat charters to Lihukan and the nearby, uninhabited **Pulau Kambing** cost 500,000Rp per boat from Pantai Bira. Most Bira guesthouses and hotels will arrange trips.

Pulau Selayar

☎0414

This long, narrow island lies off the southwestern peninsula of Sulawesi and is inhabited by the Bugis, the Makassarese and the Konjo. Most reside along the infertile west coast and in **Benteng**, the main town. Selayar's long coastline is a repository of flotsam from nearby shipping lines, perhaps accounting for the presence of a 2000-year-old Vietnamese Dongson drum, kept in an annexe near the former **Benteng Bontobangun** (Bontobangun Fort), a few kilometres south of Benteng.

Selayar's main attractions are its sandy **beaches** and coral reefs. Snorkelling around Pulau Pasi, opposite Benteng, is good, but you will have to charter a boat.

Sleeping

Selayar Dive Resort RESORT $$$

(www.selayar-dive-resort.com; s/d with fan €85/135, with air-con €135/160; ⏲Oct-Apr; ❄) A well-run German-owned place with eight lovely thatched-roofed, sea-facing wooden bunaglows on a sandy beach. It's very much geared to divers, and there are experienced divemasters to guide you around the fringing reefs and wall dives close by. Rates include all meals; two dives cost €75.

Getting There & Away

Two daily ferries (75,000Rp, two hours) depart at 10am and 3pm from Pantai Timur harbour near Pantai Bira heading to/from Pamatata on Pulau Selayar. From Makassar, Wings Air operates flights twice-weekly (from 407,000Rp) and Aviastar once-weekly (368,000Rp) to Selayar airport.

Taka Bone Rate Islands

Southeast of Pulau Selayar and north of Pulau Bone Rate is the 2220-sq-km Taka Bone Rate, the world's third-largest coral atoll. The largest coral atoll, Kwajalein in the Marshall Islands, is just 20% bigger. Some of the islands and extensive reefs in the region are now part of **Taka Bone Rate Marine National Park** (Taman Laut Taka Bone Rate), a marine reserve with a rich variety of marine and bird life.

There is no official accommodation on the islands, but if you manage to get here you can stay with villagers if you ask the *kepala desa* (village head) at Bone Rate on Pulau Bone Rate. Boats leave irregularly from Selayar. Most visitors are divers on liveaboard trips.

Watampone

☎0481 / POP 85,600

Known more simply as Bone (bone-eh) by locals, Watampone is a small town with a good range of hotels. The only reason most foreigners come here is to go to/from Kolaka in Southeast Sulawesi from the nearby port of Bajoe or to break up a trip to Tana Toraja.

Sights

Museum Lapawawoi MUSEUM

(Jl Thamrin; ⏲7am-4pm) FREE While in town, visit Museum Lapawawoi, a former palace housing one of Indonesia's most interesting regional collections, including an odd array of court memorabilia.

Sleeping & Eating

Pantai Kering near the bus station has many warung and is the best place to eat.

Wisma Bulo Gading GUESTHOUSE $
(☎0418-24750; bulo_gading@yahoo.com; 38 Jl Ahmad Yani; r incl breakfast 200,000Rp; ❄📶) A good-value guesthouse where the rooms have en-suite bathrooms with hot water.

Getting There & Away

BOAT

Bajoe port, 8km east of Watampone has ferries to Kolaka (75,000/116,000Rp for deck/business class, eight hours), scheduled nightly at 8pm.

From Watampone, bemos go to Bajoe every few minutes from a stop behind the market. From the bus terminal at the end of the incredibly long causeway in Bajoe, buses head off to most places, including Makassar and Rantepao, just after the ferry arrives.

BUS & BEMO

The terminal is 2km west of town, so take an *ojek* (motorcycle that takes passengers) or bemo from Jl Sulawesi. Kijangs and buses travel to Bulukumba (60,000Rp, 3½ hours, hourly) for connections to Bira (20,000Rp, one hour), Rantepao (96,000Rp, seven hours) and Makassar (68,000Rp, four hours). Kijangs to Sengkang (38,000Rp, two hours) leave from Jl Mangga in the centre of Watampone. Bus agencies along Jl Besse Kajuara near the bus terminal sell bus-boat-bus tickets to Kendari (from 180,000Rp).

Sengkang

☎0485

Sengkang is a small yet traffic-clogged town with a nearby scenic lake and a traditional hand-woven silk industry. It's a convenient place to break the journey between Rantepao and Pantai Bira, and you'll find several decent hotels and guesthouses in town.

Sights & Activities

Danau Tempe LAKE
(entrance with guide 100,000Rp) This large, shallow lake is fringed by wetlands, with floating houses and magnificent birdlife. Hotels can help you charter a boat (160,000Rp for two hours), allowing you to speed along Sungai Walanae, visit Salotangah village in the middle of the lake, cross to Batu Batu village on the other side, and return within two hours. You could haggle for a cheaper rate at the longboat terminal opposite the sports field on Jl Sudirman.

Geologists believe the lake was once a gulf between southern Toraja and the rest of South Sulawesi. As the lands merged, the gulf disappeared, and geologists believe the lake will eventually disappear, too.

Silk Weaving Workshops SILK FARM
Sengkang is known for its *sutera* (silk) weaving industry. Silk-weaving workshops are found around 5km out of town, and the nearest silkworm farms are about 15km from Sengkang. Hotels can organise trips, or you can charter a *pete-pete* from the terminal.

Sleeping & Eating

★**Hotel BBC** HOTEL $$
(☎0485-21363; bbchotel_sgk@yahoo.com; Jl Palawaruka 17; r incl breakfast 375,000-475,000Rp; ❄📶) A modern, efficiently run hotel where the rooms are very inviting; all have impressive attention to detail, and pleasing colour schemes of muted greys and creams offset with purples and ruby-reds. There's 24-hour room service, a restaurant, and a coffee shop on the ground floor for all your espresso needs.

★**Lesehan Jetpur** INDONESIAN $
(Jl Tanjong; meals 10,000-20,000Rp; ⏲10am-9pm) A large, bustling place with alcove seating that's very popular with office workers, Lesehan Jetpur offers authentic, inexpensive local food, including spicy chicken such as *ayam tampa tulang mentega* (20,000Rp), plenty of fish and rice dishes, as well as fresh juices (from 10,000Rp). It's 1km south of the centre.

Getting There & Away

To get to/from Rantepao (six hours), take a bemo to Lawawoi (25,000Rp) and catch a bus from there (50,000Rp); alternatively you can go via Palopo. There are regular buses to/from Terminal Daya in Makassar (from 55,000Rp, six hours), but Kijangs (70,000Rp, four hours) take a shorter route. Bemos to local destinations leave from the bus terminal behind the market on Jl Kartini. Agencies for long-distance buses, Kijangs and Pelni boats are a few metres south of the terminal.

Pare Pare

☎0421 / POP 134,000

Pare Pare is a hilly city with plenty of greenery. It's sometimes used as a stopover between Tana Toraja and Makassar. It's home to the second-largest port in the region, and has many Pelni services and boats to Kalimantan.

Sleeping & Eating

Lotus Hotel HOTEL $

(☎0421-28799; Jl Zasilia 29; r from 175,000Rp; ❄📶) Around 250m southeast of the harbour this small hotel is very handy for those on a Pelni ferry mission. Accommodation is priced keenly; all options have private bathroom and reliable in-room wifi.

Restoran Asia CHINESE $$

(☎0421-21415; Jl Patompo 25; meals 35,000-60,000Rp) A well-run, clean, air-conditioned place with a particularly good seafood selection and great Chinese omelettes. Also offers cold Bintang beer.

Information

The town is stretched out along the waterfront. At night, the esplanade turns into a lively pedestrian mall with warungs. Most of what you might need can be found on the streets running parallel to the harbour, including many ATMs.

Getting There & Away

BOAT

Pare Pare has good boat connections to East Kalimantan. **Pelni** (☎0421-21017; Jl Andicammi) runs weekly connections to Balikpapan, and every one or two days passenger boats travel to Samarinda (22 hours) and Balikpapan (two nights), but these boats are far less safe than the Pelni ships. Schedules and bookings are available from agencies near the port and just north of **Restoran Asia** (p654).

BUS

Very regular buses and Kijangs go to Makassar (37,000Rp, 3½ hours) and Rantepao (64,000Rp, five hours). Most buses travel through Terminal Induk, several kilometres south of the city, but it's often easier to hail a bus as it flies through town.

Tana Toraja

With its vibrant tribal culture and stunning scenery the facinating region of Tana Toraja is rightly a mecca for travellers. Visually its allure is immediate, with villages of elaborately painted houses with boat-shaped roofs, and towering terraces of emerald green rice paddies, all of which is overseen by a protective necklace of jagged jungle-clad hills.

Culturally the Toraja, most of whom were animists until the early 20th century, are preoccupied with death. Though ancient ways are inevitably changing as this once-isolated region becomes better connected to the rest of the nation, profound (and very bloody) funeral ceremonies remain a vital part of Torajan tradition. Buffalo and pigs are sacrificed; there is a slew of traditional dances, and lashings of food and drink. High-class Toraja dead are entombed in cave graves or hanging graves in the steep cliffs, which are guarded over by *tau tau* (life-sized wooden effigies) carved in their image; you'll find these eerie yet beautiful cliff cemeteries scattered throughout the region.

The biggest funerals are usually held in the dry-season months of July and August, at which time tourism numbers soar, but there are funerals year-round. Famous for their hospitality, the Torajans are a hospitable bunch and visitors are usually more than welcome to attend these ceremonies; however, a guide is near-essential to make the most of the experience.

While most people consider attending a funeral as a highlight of their visit, Tana Toraja also offers some great do-it-yourself trekking, cycling and motorbiking through its evergreen landscape of spellbinding beauty.

Rantepao

☎0423 / POP 26,500

Something of an overgrown village, Rantepao is an easy-to-manage town that lies within striking distance of the region's major sites, and offers a good range of accommodation and restaurants. The centre is a tad scruffy, but traffic isn't too heavy and the streets quickly merge with farmers' fields on Rantepao's outskirts; you're never far from the crow of a rooster. Nights can be cool and there is rain throughout the year, even in the dry season.

Sights

Pasar Bolu MARKET

Rantepao's main market is held every six days; ask around in town for the exact day. It also operates daily in a reduced capacity. The main market is a very big, social occasion that draws crowds from all over Tana Toraja. There's a 10,000Rp charge to enter the livestock market, where the leading lights from the buffalo community are on parade; many of the animals cost more than a small car. Pasar Bolu is 2km northeast of town and easily accessible by bemo.

Rantepao

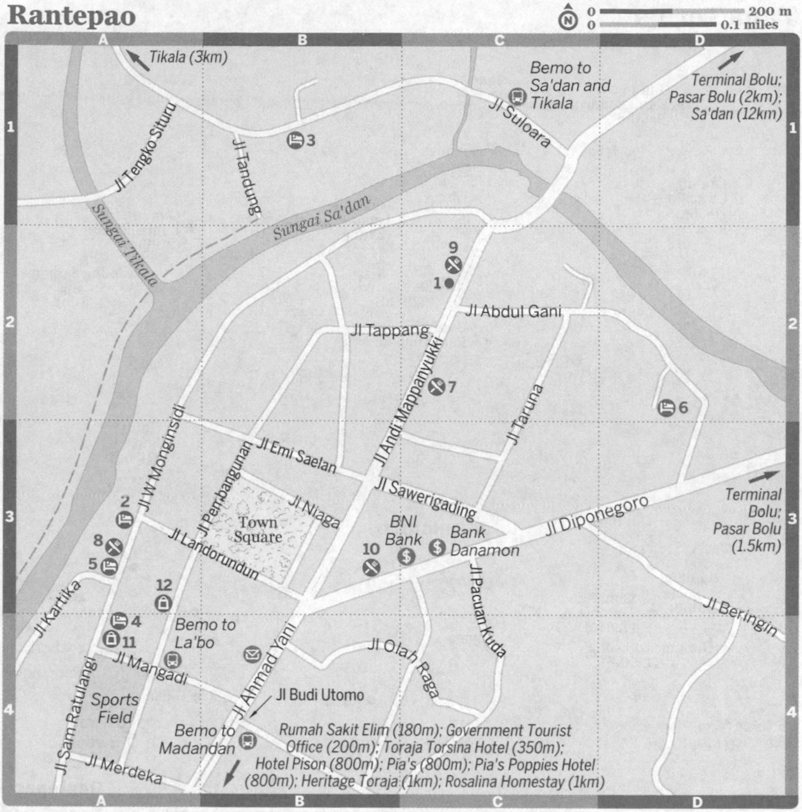

Rantepao

Activities, Courses & Tours

1 Indosella ... C2

Sleeping

2 Luta Resort Toraja ... A3
3 Madaranda ... B1
4 Wisma Maria I ... A4
5 Wisma Monika ... A3
6 Wisma Monton ... D2

Eating

7 Cafe Aras ... C2
8 Restoran Mambo ... A3
9 Rimiko Restoran ... C2
10 Rumah Makan Saruran ... B3

Shopping

11 Kaos Toraja ... A4
12 Todi ... A3

Activities

Most of the area's activities lie in the hills beyond Rantepao. Hotels that have swimming pools allow nonguests to swim for a fee (from 15,000Rp).

Tours

There are many independent guides based in Rantepao. Agencies can also arrange tours (including trekking and cultural tours), vehicles and guides.

Indosella HIKING, RAFTING
(☎0813 4250 5301, 0423-25210; www.sellatours.com; Jl Andi Mappanyukki 111) A reliable, experienced tour company that organises good hiking, white-water rafting and cultural excursions.

Tana Toraja

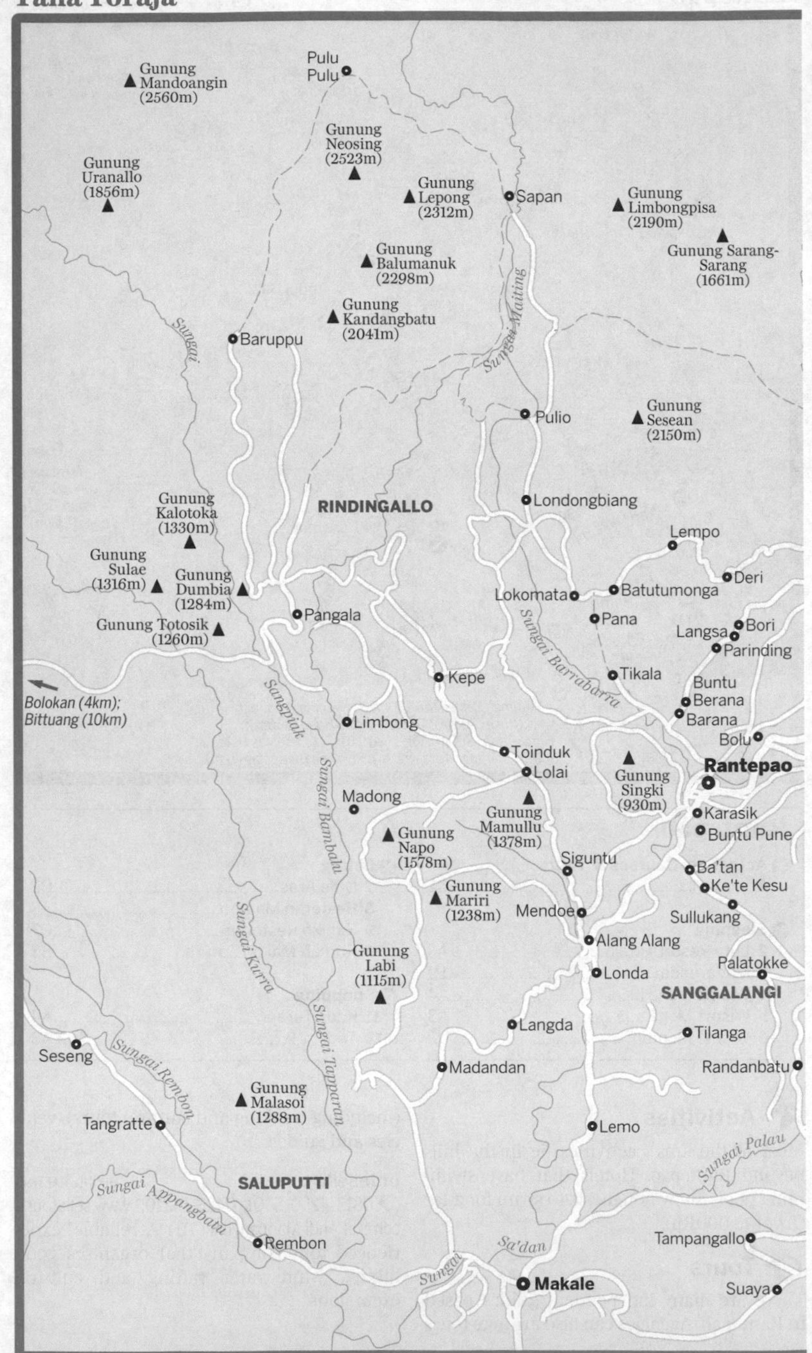
Pulu Pulu
Gunung Mandoangin (2560m)
Gunung Neosing (2523m)
Gunung Uranallo (1856m)
Gunung Lepong (2312m)
Sapan
Gunung Limbongpisa (2190m)
Gunung Sarang-Sarang (1661m)
Gunung Balumanuk (2298m)
Gunung Kandangbatu (2041m)
Sungai
Baruppu
Sungai Maiting
Pulio
Gunung Sesean (2150m)
Londongbiang
RINDINGALLO
Gunung Kalotoka (1330m)
Lempo
Gunung Sulae (1316m)
Gunung Dumbia (1284m)
Deri
Lokomata
Batutumonga
Pangala
Pana
Gunung Totosik (1260m)
Sungai Barrabarra
Langsa
Bori
Parinding
Tikala
Kepe
Buntu Berana
Barana
Bolokan (4km); Bittuang (10km)
Sangpiak
Limbong
Bolu
Toinduk
Lolai
Gunung Singki (930m)
Rantepao
Madong
Sungai Bambalu
Gunung Mamullu (1378m)
Karasik
Gunung Napo (1578m)
Buntu Pune
Siguntu
Ba'tan
Gunung Mariri (1238m)
Ke'te Kesu
Mendoe
Sullukang
Sungai Karra
Alang Alang
Gunung Labi (1115m)
Londa
Palatokke
SANGGALANGI
Sungai Tapparan
Langda
Tilanga
Seseng
Sungai Rembon
Madandan
Randanbatu
Gunung Malasoi (1288m)
Tangratte
Lemo
Sungai Palau
Sungai Appangbatu
SALUPUTTI
Rembon
Sa'dan
Tampangallo
Sungai
Makale
Suaya

Sleeping

Prices in Rantepao rise in the peak tourist season (June to August), when some private homes also accept guests. Air-conditioning is rare as nights are cool.

Location and views are often the selling points for midrange places along the roads to Makale or Palopo, which cater almost exclusively for tour groups.

★ Pia's Poppies Hotel GUESTHOUSE **$**
(☎0423-21121, 0813 4202 6768; poppiestoraja@yahoo.co.id; s/d 135,000/175,000Rp; 📶) Resembling an Alpine mountain lodge, this excellent place in a tranquil location 10-minutes' walk from the centre has very helpful staff and a welcoming ambience. Rooms face a verdant garden, have quirky details such as stone bathrooms and en-suites have hot water. Be sure to eat in the charming cafe which serves excellent local food. Breakfast not included.

Rosalina Homestay HOMESTAY **$**
(☎0423-25530; http://rosalinahomestayrantepao.blogspot.co.uk; Jl Pongitiku Karassik; d incl breakfast 200,000Rp; 📶) Opened in 2015, this fine place is owned by Enos, a highly experienced Torajan guide, and his family. They take really good care of their guests, including by preparing filling breakfasts. The spacious rooms are on the upper floor of the family's home, and overlook an ocean of ride paddies from a large shared balcony.

Wisma Maria I GUESTHOUSE **$**
(☎0423-21165; adespasaka1@yahoo.com; Jl Sam Ratulangi 23; s/d incl breakfast 115,000/137,000Rp, r with hot water bathroom from 170,000Rp; 📶) This cheap place has many plus points including the helpful owner, who can arrange guides and motorbikes, a garden and an attractive dining room decorated with tribal artefacts (where a very generous breakfast is served). However, the simple accommodation is very basic and varies a lot; look first before you commit to a room.

Hotel Pison HOTEL **$**
(☎0423-21344; s/d/tr from 135,000/150,000/350,000Rp; ❄📶) Tumbling down a hillside, the bland but fair-value Pison has 32 clean rooms in several price categories, with bathrooms and minibalconies or porches; all but the very cheapest have hot water. There's a good restaurant; breakfast not included.

Wisma Monton HOTEL $
(0423-21675; Jl Abdul Gani 14A; r incl breakfast 200,000-250,000Rp;) Hidden away down a side lane, this three-storey establishment has clean and comfortable rooms with hot water, and an attractive garden. The building is speckled with Toraja decoration and there's a rooftop restaurant with fine views.

Wisma Monika GUESTHOUSE $$
(0423-21216; 36 Jl Sam Ratulangi; r incl breakfast 250,000-400,000Rp;) A grandiose-looking cream villa in a central spot with a choice of plain but well-maintained and clean rooms, all with bedside reading lights. Staff prepare a good breakfast.

Madaranda HOTEL $$
(0423-23777; Jl Sadan 21; d incl breakfast 375,000Rp;) The huge Torajan-style house, compete with painted details and tribal carving, is the real draw here, and in low season you can easily bargain for better rates. Staff are friendly. It's located next to a busy road around a 10-minute walk from the centre.

Luta Resort Toraja HOTEL $$$
(0423-21060; www.torajalutaresort.com; 26 Jl Dr Ratulangi; r incl breakfast 675,000-1,100,000Rp;) This is the only luxury hotel in the centre and it's a stylish place to stay. Very comfortable accommodation is decorated with modern, muted colours, though bathrooms are small. Rooms either overlook the lush central garden or the river at the rear. Note the pool is tiny and wi-fi was limited to the lobby at the time of research.

Heritage Toraja RESORT $$$
(0423-21192; www.torajaheritage.com; r incl breakfast US$100-175;) The Heritage styles itself as a four-star resort, offering accommodation in huge *tongkonan*-style houses and a more conventional hotel block (which is fine, but not as atmospheric). Gardens are lush, the lagoon-like pool is great and there's a separate kids' pool. Overall, it's a solid choice, but the hotel would benefit from improving attention to detail. Located about 3km from town towards Ke'te Kesu.

Toraja Torsina Hotel HOTEL $$$
(0423-21293; www.hotel-torsina.com; s/d incl breakfast from US$48/62;) Set in the rice fields near the turn-off to Ke'te Kesu, the rooms here are clean and comfortable (if old-fashioned) and decent value. Service is good and the lovely L-shaped pool is a blissful place for all ages to chill.

Eating

Going to ceremonies or dining in local restaurants offer great opportunities to sample Torajan food. The best-known dish here is *pa'piong* (meat stuffed into bamboo tubes along with vegetables and coconut). If you want to try it in a restaurant, order several hours in advance because it takes time to cook.

Pia's INDONESIAN, INTERNATIONAL $
(0423-21121; meals 30,000-60,000Rp; 7-10am, 6-10pm;) The dining room at Pia's Poppies Hotel is a fine place to try local food including *pa'piong,* plus decent pizza. All food is cooked to order, so it's essential to order well ahead (at least two hours) or be prepared to wait. Bintangs cost just 30,000Rp. It's a ten-minute walk south of the centre. Note it's closed for lunch.

Rumah Makan Saruran INDONESIAN, CHINESE $
(Jl Diponegoro 19; mains from 15,000Rp; 8am-10pm;) Reliable, freshly prepared Indonesian-style Chinese food is served at this hopping restaurant that's popular with young Indonesians. It looks a bit scruffy from the street, but once you're past the kitchen's smoking woks you'll find the comfortable interior has plush banquette seating. There's a full bar and good juices for 12,000Rp.

Rimiko Restoran INDONESIAN $
(0423-23366; Jl Andi Mappanyukki 115; dishes 20,000-50,000Rp; 8am-10pm;) A long-running, very friendly place that serves authentic local food. It serves good Torajan specialities including buffalo, pork and eel in black sauce (50,000Rp), as well as Indo staples such as gado gado.

Restoran Mambo INTERNATIONAL $
(Jl Sam Ratulangi; dishes 25,000-60,000Rp; 10am-10pm Mon-Sat;) Geared towards tourists, this clean place has a long menu including everything from *sate* (satay) to steak (and an interesting interpretation of a burrito). No MSG is used.

Cafe Aras INDONESIAN, STEAK $$
(Jl Andi Mappanyukki; meals 35,000-100,000Rp; 7am-10pm;) This place is wildly popular with tour groups and travellers thanks to its tourist-friendly set-up (attractive seating, sensitive lighting and mellow music). The food is decent, and includes international dishes (such as steaks) and local options, but not exceptional; it's toned down a degree for Western palates.

BALOK

The markets held at Rantepao and Makale have whole sections devoted to the sale of the alcoholic drink *balok* (palm wine; also known as *tuak* and toddy). *Balok* is sold in huge jugs around town and comes in a variety of strengths, colours (from clear to dark red, achieved by adding bark) and flavours (from sweet to bitter).

 Shopping

Rantepao is a great place to find woodcarving, weaving and basketry, the main crafts of Tana Toraja. Look for specialities from the region's villages, such as Mamasan boxes (used to store magic, salt and betel nuts), huge horn necklaces and wooden figurines; and high-quality woodcarvings by Ke'te Kesu and Londa carvers, such as trays, panels and clocks, designed like the decorations on traditional houses.

Artefacts sold in souvenir shops, especially around the market building in town, also include small replicas of Torajan houses; weaving (that produced in Sa'dan is particularly good); and cloth from the Mamasa Valley. Necklaces made of seeds, chunky silver, and amber or wooden beads festoon the gift shops, but it's the orange-bead necklaces that are authentic Torajan.

Todi CRAFTS
(☎0423-27003; www.todi.co.id; Jl Pembangunan 70; ⏰8am-6pm Mon-Sat, to 2pm Sun) Sells high quality *ikat*, wood carvings and Torajan crafts. You can watch weavers in action on their looms here. Prices are quite high, but some bargaining is possible.

Kaos Toraja CLOTHING
(Jl Ratulangi 1; T-shirts 90,000Rp; ⏰10am-7.30pm) This store specialises in cool T-shirts (for both guys 'n' gals) made from quality cotton and nothing else. Check out its Toraja motifs and stylish designs.

If you're doing some serious hiking, pick up a copy of the detailed *Tana Toraja* (1:85,000) map, published by Periplus (best bought from home). Free wi-fi is standard in most hotels and guesthouses. Internet cafes are located all over town, and charge around 5000Rp per hour.

Bank Danamon (Jl Diponegoro) Has an ATM.

BNI Bank (Bank Negara Indonesia; Jl Diponegoro) Branch with an ATM.

Government Tourist Office (☎0423-21277; Jl Ahmad Yani 62A; ⏰9am-2pm Mon-Sat) The friendly staff here can provide accurate, independent information about local ceremonies and festivals, and recommend guides.

Post Office (Jl Ahmad Yani; ⏰8am-4pm Mon-Sat)

Rumah Sakit Elim (☎0423-21258; Jl Ahmad Yani; ⏰24hr) This is the main hospital in town; however, facilities are quite basic. Make for Makassar if you require international-standard medical care.

Getting There & Away

AIR

Aviastar was operating twice-weekly flights between Rantepao and Makassar at the time of research, but double-check the latest schedule as it's not a reliable connection. Planes are tiny and seats very limited; tickets can be booked via travel agents in town, not via Aviastar's website.

BUS & BEMO

Most long-distance buses leave from the bus company offices along Jl Andi Mappanyukki. Buses often run at night. Prices vary according to speed and the level of comfort and space.

Several bus companies offer comfortable buses to/from Makassar, including Charisma (which has wi-fi), Manggala Trans, Metro Permai and Bintang Prima. Litha buses are cheaper but pretty beat-up. Try to book your ticket a day or so in advance.

Various companies also have services to Mamuju via Polewali, from where there are connections to Mamasa. From Terminal Bolu, 2km north of Rantepao, there are regular vehicles to Palopo. From the corner of Jl Landorundun and Jl Andi Mapanyukki, Kijangs leave every few minutes to Makale (6000Rp, 20 minutes) and other places in Tana Toraja.

BUSES FROM RANTEPAO

DESTINATION	FARE (RP)	DURATION (HR)
Makassar (Terminal Daya)	110,000-220,000	8-9
Mamasa (via Makale)	135,000	12
Palu	180,000	20
Pare Pare	64,000	5
Pendelo	100,000	8
Poso	150,000	12
Tentena	130,000	10

THE TORAJA

The Toraja inhabit the vast, rugged landscape of the South Sulawesi highlands. Their name is derived from the Bugis word *toriaja*, which once had negative connotations similar to 'hillbilly' or 'bumpkin'.

For centuries Torajan life and culture survived the constant threat posed by the Bugis from the southwest. However, in 1905 the Dutch began a bloody campaign to bring Central Sulawesi under their control. Missionaries moved in on the heels of the troops, and by the time of WWII many of the great Torajan ceremonies (with the exception of funeral celebrations) were rapidly disappearing from Torajan culture.

Beliefs

Prior to the arrival of Christianity, the Toraja believed in many gods but worshipped Puang Matua as the special god of their family, clan or tribe. Christianity has undermined some traditional Torajan beliefs, but the ceremonies are still a vital part of life.

Torajan mythology suggests that their ancestors came by boat from the south, sailed up Sungai Sa'dan (Sa'dan River) and dwelt in the Enrekang region before being pushed into the mountains by the arrival of other groups.

Buffalo are a status symbol for the Toraja and are of paramount importance in various religious ceremonies. The buffalo has traditionally been a symbol of wealth and power; even land could be bought with buffalo. Sought-after albino buffalo can change hands for more than US$8000.

Despite the strength of traditional beliefs, Christianity in Toraja is a very active force. One of the first questions asked of you will be your religion, and Protestants are given immediate approval.

Traditional Houses

One of the most noticeable aspects about Tana Toraja is the size and grandeur of the *tongkonan* (traditional Torajan house). It is the place for family gatherings and may not be bought or sold.

The towering roof, which rears up at either end, is the most striking aspect of a *tongkonan*. Some believe the roof represents the horns of a buffalo; others suggest it represents the bow and stern of a boat. The more buffalo horns visible, the higher the household's status.

Getting Around

Rantepao is small and easy to walk around. A becak (bicycle rickshaw) should cost around 5000Rp in town. Motorbikes cost from 60,000Rp per day to hire; many guesthouses, including **Wisma Maria I** (p657), rent out bikes.

Makale

0423

Makale is the administrative capital of Tana Toraja but there's little reason to stick around, other than to switch buses or visit the market. Built around an artificial lake, the town is ringed by cloud-shrouded hills.

The market is a blur of noise and colour. Held every six days, you'll see pigs strapped down with bamboo strips for buyers' close inspection, buckets of live eels, piles of fresh and dried fish, and a corner of the market is reserved just for *balok* sales.

Getting There & Away

Kijangs connect Rantepao and Makale (6000Rp, 20 minutes) between dawn and dusk. Most of the bus companies based in Rantepao also have offices near the corner of Jl Merdeka and Jl Ihwan Rombe in Makale. The only direct bus connection between Tana Toraja and Mamasa is with Disco Indah, departing daily at around 8am (140,000Rp, 12 hours).

Around Tana Toraja

To really experience all that Tana Toraja has to offer, you'll need to spend a few days exploring the spectacular countryside. Stunning scenery, cascading rice fields, precipitous cliff graves, other-worldly *tau tau*, hanging

Funerals

Of all Torajan ceremonies, the most important is the *tomate* (funeral; literally 'deceased'). Without proper funeral rites the soul of the deceased will cause misfortune to its family.

The Toraja generally have two funeral ceremonies: one immediately after death and an elaborate second funeral after preparations have been made. The bigger funerals are usually scheduled during the dry months of July and August, but there are funerals year-round.

Until the time of the second funeral, the deceased remains in the family house. An invitation to visit the deceased is an honour. If you accept, remember to thank the deceased and ask permission of the deceased when you wish to leave – as you would of a living host.

The second funeral can be spread over several days and involve hundreds of guests. The Toraja believe that the souls of animals should follow their masters to the next life, hence the importance of animal sacrifices. Festivities often start with bullfights, where lots of lively betting takes place, and some famous fighting bulls may be imported for the event from the distant reaches of the country. Animal lovers are likely to find the bullfights disturbing and the sacrifices very traumatic; these two kinds of events are best avoided if you cringe at the sight of blood.

Visitors attending a funeral should wear black or dark-coloured clothing and bring gifts of sugar or cigarettes for the family of the deceased.

Graves & Tau Tau

The Toraja believe that you can take possessions with you into the afterlife, and the dead generally go well equipped to their graves. Since this historically led to grave plundering, the Toraja started to hide their dead in caves.

These caves are hollowed out by specialist cave builders. Coffins are taken deep inside the caves, and *tau tau* (life-sized carved wooden effigies of the dead) are placed on balconies in the rock face in front of the caves.

You can see *tau tau* carvers at work at Londa. There are many *tau tau* at Lemo and a few elsewhere, but it's becoming increasingly difficult to see them in Tana Toraja. So many have been stolen that the Toraja now keep them in their homes.

graves, soaring *tongkonan* and colourful ceremonies: this is the wild world of Tana Toraja.

There are many places that can be reached on day trips from Rantepao, and longer trips are possible by staying overnight in villages or camping out. The roads to major towns, such as Makale, Palopo, Sa'dan, Batutumonga, Madandan and Bittuang, are paved, but many other roads around Tana Toraja are constructed out of compacted boulders; vehicles won't get stuck, but your joints get rattled loose. Walking is often the only way to reach the remote villages.

A few areas such as Londa, Lemo, Tampangallo, Ke'te Kesu and, to a lesser extent, Palawa are pretty touristy, with stalls selling trinkets and offering a jaded welcome, but this is because these places are exceptionally beautiful. There are still plenty of lesser-visited gems to get to, especially if you take off on foot far from the tour-bus circuit.

Torajan funeral ceremonies are best visited with a guide, who will be able to explain cultural etiquette; for instance, you should always have a gift for the deceased family and it's customary to wear black or dark clothes.

If you're exploring the region on your own, note that signposts are few and far between, so take a map.

Activities

Trekking

Trekking is the best way to reach isolated areas and to really get a feel for Torajan countryside and the people. Always take good footwear; a water bottle and food; a torch (flashlight) for cave exploration; and an umbrella or waterproof gear – even in the dry season it's more likely than not to rain. It's highly advisable to take a good map, such as the detailed Tana Toraja (1:85,000) map, published by Periplus. If you're taking advantage of Torajan hospitality, be sure to pay your way.

Shorter hikes are available, but a few of the popular longer treks include the following routes:

Batutumonga–Lokomata–Pangala–Baruppu–Pulu Pulu–Sapan Three days of superb scenery. Batutumonga to Pangala is on a motorbike-accessible road, while the rest is more serious uphill-trail hiking.

Bittuang–Mamasa Three days.

Pangala–Bolokan–Bittuang Two days on a well-marked trail through pristine villages.

Sa'dan–Sapan–Pulu Pulu–Baruppu–Pangala Three days; tough and mountainous – a real mountain trek.

Rafting

The most professional and reliable rafting outfit is **Indosella** (☎0423-25210; www.sellatours.com; Jl Andi Mappanyukki 111, Rantepao), offering trips on Sungai Sa'dan's 20 rapids, including a few that are Class IV (read: pretty wild). Rafting trips, including transport to/from your hotel, equipment, guide, insurance and food, cost 800,000Rp per person (minimum two people) for one day on Class II to III rapids, or around US$300 per person for three days on Class III to IV rapids, with overnight stays in local rest huts. Trips get cheaper per person as the tour group gets bigger.

Getting Around

BEMO & KIJANG

Local public transport leaves from stops around central Rantepao, as well as from the scruffy and muddy Terminal Bolu north of Rantepao and the town of Makale; there are regular bemos and Kijangs to all main villages. Some of the more useful services head to the following destinations from Rantepao and Makale:

- **Bittuang** For treks to Mamasa; departs Makale only.
- **La'bo** Via Ke'te Kesu.
- **Lempo** Useful for hiking up to Batutumonga.
- **Pangala** Via Batutumonga.
- **Sa'dan** Usually via Tikala.
- **Sangalla** Departs Makale only.

MOTORBIKE & BICYCLE

Motorbikes (rental from 60,000Rp per day) and mountain bikes (from 40,000Rp) are available through hotels and agencies. Remember that roads out of Rantepao and Makale are good but often windy, steep and narrow, so they are more suitable for experienced motorcyclists. Bikes can be used along some walking routes, but the trails are often very muddy and rocky.

SITE ENTRANCE FEES

Most of the tourist sites around Tana Toraja have an entry fee of 20,000Rp. There is usually a ticket booth at each place, complete with the odd souvenir stall…or 10 or more in the case of Lemo and Londa.

Batutumonga

One of the easiest places to stay overnight in Tana Toraja, and also one of the most beautiful, Batutumonga occupies a dramatic ridge on the slopes of Gunung Sesean. From here you will have panoramic views of Rantepao and the Sa'dan Valley, and stunning sunrises. It's located about 20km north of Rantepao via Deri, so you could day-trip here for some hiking and a local lunch.

Sleeping & Eating

Mentirotiku GUESTHOUSE $
(☎0813 4257 9588; r 125,000-350,000Rp) With commanding views and landscaped grounds, this place has very authentic traditional *tongkonan* crash pads – thin mattresses squashed together in a tiny space – plus less interesting modern rooms with private bathrooms. The huge restaurant (geared for tour groups) serves decent, though not great, Indo-Toraja dishes for 30,000Rp to 50,000Rp. Mentirotiku is on the roadside before Batutumonga.

Mama Yos GUESTHOUSE $
(☎0812 4260 5043; per person incl breakfast & dinner 125,000Rp) Mama's simple wooden home has a row of small, clean rooms with mattresses on the floor and a basic *mandi* (Indonesian-style) shared bathroom. No English spoken. It's right on the roadside before Batutumonga.

Coffee Shop & Wisma Barande GUESTHOUSE $
(☎0812 4177 7417; r 150,000Rp) Extremely simple but clean concrete rooms (with balconies) below an attractive, orderly coffee shop and restaurant (good for snacks). It's very quiet here. Located in Tinimbayo village, 2km east of Batutumonga.

Getting There & Away

Bemo (12,000Rp, one hour) buzz up to Batutumonga from Terminal Bolu in Rantepao. Sometimes the bemo only goes as far as Lempo (a steep, but pleasant 2km walk away).

North of Rantepao

With dramatic bowls of cascading rice terraces, small villages of *tongkonan* and lots of harder-to-reach sights that don't make it on every tour-bus itinerary, the north is the most scenic region of Tana Toraja.

For good shopping, head to the weaving centre of **Sa'dan** (12km north of Rantepao; take a bemo from Terminal Bolu for 7000Rp), where local women set up a market to sell their woven cloth. It's all handmade on simple looms, though not all is produced in the village.

Activities

There are some good options for day walks in the area.

The walk from **Batutumonga** to **Tikala** is a very pleasant downhill hike (five hours on a paved road) through some of the finest scenery in Tana Toraja. From Batutumonga a beautiful walk west takes you to **Lokomata**, a village with cave graves hewn into a rocky outcrop, and outstanding scenery. Back-track and take a small, unmarked trail down the slopes to **Pana**, which has ancient hanging graves, and some baby graves in nearby trees. You can see tiny villages with towering *tongkonan*, women pounding rice, men scrubbing their buffalo and children splashing in pools. The path ends at Tikala and, from there, regular bemos return to Rantepao. Alternatively, back-track through Lempo to **Deri**, the site of rock graves; walk down to the Rantepao–Sa'dan road and catch a bemo back to Rantepao.

At 2150m above sea level **Gunung Sesean** isn't the highest peak in Sulawesi, but it's one of the most popular for hiking. The summit is accessible via a trail from Batutumonga. The return trip to the summit takes five hours. A guide is a good idea if you're inexperienced or speak little Bahasa Indonesia.

From **Pangala**, one of the biggest villages in the region, it's a lovely 10km hike to **Baruppu**. Pangala itself has a few streets, a little *ayam goreng* (fried chicken) stall, and is famous for being the hometown of Pongtiku, a fearless warrior who fought against the Dutch. Pangala is 35km from Rantepao (20,000Rp by bemo).

The traditional village of **Palawa**, east of Batutumonga, is similarly attractive and not often visited by tour groups; it has *tongkonan* houses and rice barns. It's possible to overnight in one of the traditional houses, but this can only be organised with a guide as part of a trek. In the dry season you can walk southwest, fording a river and walking through rice fields to **Pangli**, which has *tau tau* and house graves, and then to **Bori**, the site of an impressive *rante* (ceremonial ground) and some towering megaliths. About 1km south of Bori, **Parinding** also has *tongkonan* houses and rice barns. From here you can walk back to Rantepao or on to Tikala.

CHOOSING A GUIDE

Many guides in Tana Toraja hold a government-approved licence, obtained by undertaking a course in culture, language and etiquette, and being fluent in the local language. There are also competent guides with no certificate (and incompetent licensed guides). The best way to choose a guide is to sit down and talk through a trip before committing. If you feel you are being pressured (or hit on), this is probably a good sign to go and find a different guide.

Guides will approach you in guesthouses and cafes. Freelance guides charge 350,000Rp or so for an all-day circuit by motorbike, including a funeral if there's one on. You can also hire a guide with a car (for up to four people) for around 500,000Rp per day, but much of the Toraja region is only accessible on foot or by motorbike so this can be a limiting option. For trekking, guides charge about 500,000Rp per day. All these rates are slightly negotiable but the 100 or so guides in the area try to keep their rates equal and fixed. Larger tour agencies usually charge more than the rates quoted.

Hiring a guide can be useful to help you get your bearings, learn about the culture and cover a lot of ground quickly, but there's no reason why you can't explore the area without one if you have a decent map and a few relevant phrases of Bahasa Indonesia.

COFFEE IN TORAJA

Famous for its earthy, full-bodied taste (spicy, smokey and caramel notes, low acidity and a crisp finish), Toraja is one of Indonesia's most highly regarded regional coffees. Tana Toraja is one of the few areas where the Arabica bean (which is harder to cultivate and less disease resistant than other kinds) dominates, accounting for 96% of local cultivation. Due to the mountainous terrain, the crop is mostly grown on smallholdings, with low annual yields.

Coffee was introduced to Toraja in the mid-19th century by the Dutch, who controlled production. As its value increased exponentially, a 'coffee war' erupted between Bugis and Toraja over trade routes in 1890.

Today, most Torajan coffee is certified organic and produced by indigenous farmers: the volcanic soil, relatively cool climate and altitude (1400m to 1900m) is perfect for premium Arabica production. Coffee from the cooperative Petani Kopi Organik Toraja has fair-trade certification and is available in North America and Europe.

Torajan coffee is particularly sought after in Japan, where it's branded as Toarco Toraja. In the Toraja Utara district alone, 7000 small-scale farmers sell coffee beans to Toarco, accounting for an average of 50% of their income; this is way more than rice, for example.

You can tour the **Toarco coffee plantation** (0813 4380 0288; Bokin village; 1hr tours 10,000Rp; 7.30am-3pm Mon-Fri, to 12.30pm Sat), located near the village of Bokin, 14km southeast of Rantepao, and learn all about coffee production. Most of the beans are exported to Japan. You'll explore the grounds in company Jeeps. English-speaking guides are sometimes available; call and reserve a tour in advance.

West of Rantepao

About 2km west across the river from Rantepao, **Gunung Singki** (930m) is a steep hill with a slippery, overgrown hiking trail to the summit. From the top you'll get panoramic views across Rantepao and the surrounding countryside. Return to the road and head to **Siguntu** (7km from Rantepao), which offers more superb views of the valleys and Rantepao.

The 3km walk from Siguntu to the Rantepao–Makale road at **Alang Alang** is also pleasant. Stop on the way at the traditional village of **Mendoe**. From Alang Alang, where a covered bridge crosses the river, head a few hundred metres to **Londa**, back to Rantepao, or remain on the western side of the river and continue walking south to the villages of **Langda** and **Madandan**.

South of Rantepao

There are many popular cultural sights in this region and most are accessible by car. It's not a great region for walking, but it is suitable for a motorbike day tour.

Sights

Tour buses love this area for the easy access but also because the sights are simply stunning.

Karasik VILLAGE

On the outskirts of Rantepao, just off the road to Makale, Karasik has traditional-style houses arranged around a cluster of megaliths on a hill.

Buntu Pune VILLAGE

Buntu Pune village has two fine *tongkonan* houses and six rice barns. According to local legend, one of the two houses was built by a nobleman named Pong Marambaq at the beginning of the 20th century. During Dutch rule he was appointed head of the local district, but planned to rebel and was subsequently exiled to Ambon (Maluku), where he died. His body was returned to Tana Toraja and buried at the hill to the north of Buntu Pune.

Ke'te Kesu VILLAGE

About 5km south of Rantepao, Ke'te Kesu can get busy with tour groups in high season. The village is renowned for its woodcarving and traditional *tongkonan* and rice barns. On the cliff face behind the village there are some cave graves and very old hanging graves. Rotting coffins are suspended on wooden beams under an overhang. Others, full of bones and skulls, lie rotting in strategic piles.

Sullukang & Palatokke CAVE, GRAVE
From Ke'te Kesu you can walk on a paved road to Sullukang, which has a *rante* (ceremonial ground) marked by a number of large, rough-hewn megaliths, and on to Palatokke. In this beautiful area of lush rice paddies and traditional houses, there is an enormous cliff face containing several cave graves and hanging graves. Access to the caves is difficult (there's a steep path with rubble to scramble over), but the scenery makes it worthwhile. From Palatokke there are roads to La'bo and Randanbatu, where there are more graves, and on to Sangalla, Suaya and Makale.

Londa CAVE, GRAVE
(entry by guided tour 30,000Rp) At Londa, 6km south of Rantepao, you'll find an extensive (and very popular) burial cave below a massive cliff face; its entrance is guarded by a balcony of *tau tau*. Inside there's a collection of coffins, many of them rotted away, and bones lying either scattered or heaped in piles. A local myth says that the people buried here are the descendants of Tangdilinoq, chief of the Toraja. Mandatory English-speaking guides with oil lamps accompany all visitors through the cave.

If you're thin, and don't suffer from claustrophobia, squeeze through the tunnel that connects the two main caves, passing some interesting stalactites and stalagmites. Rantepao–Makale bemo will drop you off at the turn-off, about 2km from the cave. Visit in the morning for the best photos.

Tilanga SPRING
(admisssion 10,000Rp) Ten kilometres south of Rantepao, off the Rantepao–Makale road, Tilanga is a lovely, natural cool-water swimming pool. You can swim, but don't be surprised if some friendly eels come to say hello. It's best visited during the rainy season.

Lemo GRAVE
The best-known burial area in Tana Toraja is Lemo, 10km south of Rantepao. The sheer rock face has a whole series of balconies for *tau tau*. The biggest balcony has a dozen figures with white eyes and black pupils, and outstretched arms like spectators at a sports event. It's a good idea to go before 9am for the best photos. A Rantepao–Makale bemo drops you at the turn-off to the burial site, from where it's 15-minutes' walk to the *tau tau*.

According to local legend, these graves are for descendants of a Toraja chief who built his house on top of the cliff into which the graves are now cut.

East of Rantepao

This region is often visited on day tours heading between north and south Tana Toraja. It's flatter than the north and beautiful, with plenty of rice fields, sleepy traditional villages and grazing buffalo.

Sights

Marante VILLAGE
Marante is a fine traditional village, 5km from Rantepao, just north of the road to Palopo. Near Marante there are stone and hanging graves with several *tau tau*, skulls on the coffins and a cave with scattered bones. From Marante you can cross the river on the suspension bridge and walk to other pretty villages set in rice fields.

Nanggala VILLAGE
This village has a particularly grandiose traditional house and an impressive fleet of 14 rice barns. The rice barns have a bizarre array of motifs carved into them, including depictions of soldiers with guns, Western women and cars. Keep an eye out for a colony of huge black bats hanging from trees at the end of the village. It's about 16km southeast of Rantepao; take a bemo (6000Rp) from Terminal Bolu.

Activities

From Nanggala you can walk south to **Paniki**, a tough hike (about 7.5km, five hours) along a dirt track up and down the hills. The trail starts next to the rice barns, and along the way are coffee-plantation machines grinding away. From Paniki walk (two hours) to **Ledo** and **Buntao** (15km from Rantepao), which has some house graves and *tau tau*. Alternatively, catch a bemo from Paniki to Rantepao. About 2km from Buntao is **Tembamba**, which has more graves and is noted for its fine scenery. Regular bemos run from Paniki via Tembamba back to Rantepao.

East of Makale

This area is pretty far away from the tourist heartland, which means less crowds, and there are two very intriguing sights: the graves at Tampangallo and Kambira.

Sights

★Tampangallo GRAVE

Tampangallo's *tau tau* are some of the most impressive in Tana Toraja. Take a Kijang from Makale to Sangalla; get off about 1km after the turn-off to Suaya, and walk a short distance (less than 1km) through the rice fields to Tampangallo. The approach, following a small stream and rice paddies, is beautiful. You'll be greeted with a pile of skulls by the entrance.

The graves belong to the chiefs of Sangalla, descendants of the mythical divine being Tamborolangiq, who is believed to have introduced the caste system and death rituals into Torajan society.

Kambira Baby Graves GRAVE

Torajans traditionally bury babies in trees and this is one of the biggest of such graves in the region, holding around 20 deceased infants. By Torajan definition a baby is a child who hasn't yet grown teeth. The site is a shady, tranquil spot. The babies' bodies are buried upright and the belief is that they will continue to grow with the tree. Kambira is 1km south of Sangalla and served by Kijang from Makale.

WEST SULAWESI

Mamasa Valley

An area of outstanding natural beauty in Sulawesi, the Mamasa Valley offers wonderful highland scenery and deep tribal traditions. Unfortunately, it's notoriously tough to get to; the boulder-rich, mud-bound road links from nearby Tana Toraja deter most visitors.

Culturally there are both similarities and differences with neighbouring Toraja country. Torajan-style ceremonies survive in the Mamasa Valley; these are generally far less ostentatious affairs than Mamasan. Like Torajan traditional houses, Mamasan *tongkonan* have long extended roof overhangs and their exteriors are carved with animal and human motifs.

Mamasans have embraced Christianity with unfettered enthusiasm: choir groups regularly meet up and down the valley. *Sambu* weaving is a craft that still thrives: these long strips of heavy woven material are stitched together to make blankets, which provide ideal insulation against the cold mountain nights, and are sold by many villagers.

The best way to explore the valley is on foot. Trails tend to follow ridges, giving hikers stunning views of the mountainous countryside. There are few roads, and many paths to choose from, so you'll need to constantly ask directions or hire a guide.

GETTING TO THE TOGEAN ISLANDS FROM TANA TORAJA

Many visitors want to get from Tana Toraja to the Togean Islands (p677), and fast. Unfortunately, this is Sulawesi, and fast doesn't translate well along the winding, narrow mountain roads. Here are your options:

➡ **Cheapest but longest** Bus to Tentena; overnight or longer in Tentena; bus to Ampana; overnight in Ampana; ferry to Togean Islands. Total time: about three days.

➡ **Quicker but tough-going** Bus to Poso; minibus from Poso to Ampana; ferry to Togeans. Total time: two to 2½ days.

➡ **Most comfortable and quickest** Luxury overnight bus to Makassar; flight to Gorontalo; evening ferry to Togeans. Total time: 1½ days.

There are numerous other possibilities, including backtracking to Makassar and flying to Poso or Luwuk and then travelling overland to Ampana for the ferry.

The price for a private air-conditioned car to drive from Rantepao to Ampana, with an overnight break in Tentena, is about 2,200,000Rp. Sharing a car can be a great option, allowing you to stop as you wish for photographs and meals.

Any method is tiring, however, and will ultimately leave you happy to have a beach to lie on for a few days.

Mamasa

Mamasa is the only real town in the valley. The air is cool and clean; the folk are hospitable; and the rhythm of life has a languid pace. Market day is Monday, when hill people trade their produce and the streets are filled with colour and bustle.

Activities

The trek between Mamasa and **Bittuang** is a classic and there are a few ways to do it. The easiest route to follow is the Kijang road from Mamasa, stopping in Timbaan the first night (23km from Mamasa, about eight hours walking), continuing to Paku the next (20km, about six hours), then heading to Bittuang the following morning (16km, about three hours). Alternatively, you can take a quieter footpath though the jungle from Tandiallo, a few kilometres north of Mamasa, via Sóbok and Minanga to stay the first night in Kelama (about eight hours walking). The following night you can make it to Ponding, via Buka, Mawai and Tandung (eight hours) then continue on the main Kijang road to Bittuang the next day (about four hours). Both options take three days if you walk the whole way.

A third option takes in Salurea and Bulo Sandana, but takes four days to complete.

You can also trek between Mamasa and **Rantepao**, but be prepared to seriously rough it. The trek takes you through remote villages, coffee plantations and plenty of big mountain scenery. You'll start to see traditional Toraja boat-roofed architecture near Ponding, when you're officially on Tana Toraja land. Toilets along the way can be little more than a plank over a stream; a bed means a quilt on a hard floor; and you'll have absolutely no privacy (bring sarongs for showering). Half the village children will follow you with laughter and good-natured conversation. Losmen (budget accommodation; often unmarked so you'll have to ask around) along the way charge from 100,000Rp to 125,000Rp per person, which includes a simple breakfast and dinner. For lunch, ask around; someone will surely offer to make you a meal for around 25,000Rp. Bring plenty of water and/or a water filter (some boiled water is available at losmen) and warm clothes. The main route is straighforward to follow; a guide isn't necessary. You could consider shipping your gear to Rantepao by bus to lighten your load.

Sleeping & Eating

Wisma Tongkonan Mamasa GUESTHOUSE **$**
(☎0813 1919 5535, 0813 5543 6663; Jl Demmajannang; r 170,000-220,000Rp) One of best places in town, Wisma Tongkonan Mamasa's spacious rooms have en-suite bathrooms, and there's a family feel thanks to the china cups on the table waiting for tea. Serves excellent home-cooked food (meals cost from 20,000Rp to 30,000Rp).

Ramayana Inn GUESTHOUSE **$**
(☎0854 204 0478; just off Jl Buntu Budi, Kampung Baru Mamasa; r from 150,000Rp) This venerable place has been hosting travellers for years and remains a decent option, with two floors of spacious rooms in an attractive building decorated with Mamasa-style carvings. Also known as Mamasa Guest House.

Guest House Gereja Toraja GUESTHOUSE **$**
(Church Guesthouse; ☎0813 5581 9752; Jl Demmatande 182; r 100,000-130,000Rp) There are five basic rooms here in this simple wooden house surrounded by a wild garden. The more expensive ones have terraces. Little English is spoken.

Mantana Lodge 2 CABIN **$$**
(☎0852 4261 1875; Jl Poros Polowi; cabins incl breakfast 320,000Rp; wi-fi) On a little hill above the main road, these big double-occupancy polished pine cabins have hot-water bathrooms and pleasant terraces. They are clean and relatively comfy, but you may get local kids climbing on your roof in the morning to get a look at you. Breakfasts are very basic.

Dian Satria Restaurant INDONESIAN **$**
(Jl Poros Polowi; meals 20,000-30,000Rp; ⏲7am-9.30pm) A welcoming, atmospheric place serving generous portions of noodle and rice dishes, and cold beer. At night you may get serenaded by the local ladyboys who sing (very pro) karaoke.

Getting There & Away

BUS

Daily buses leave Rantepao for Mamasa at 8am (via Makale) and from Mamasa for Rantepao at the same time. The fare is 135,000Rp and it takes around 12 long, bumpy hours.

From Makassar, two daily buses leave Terminal Daya for Mamasa (130,000Rp, 12 hours) at 8am and 8.30am; four minibuses (115,000Rp) also depart in the morning between 6.30am and 9am. You can also travel via Polewali (65,000Rp,

Mamasa

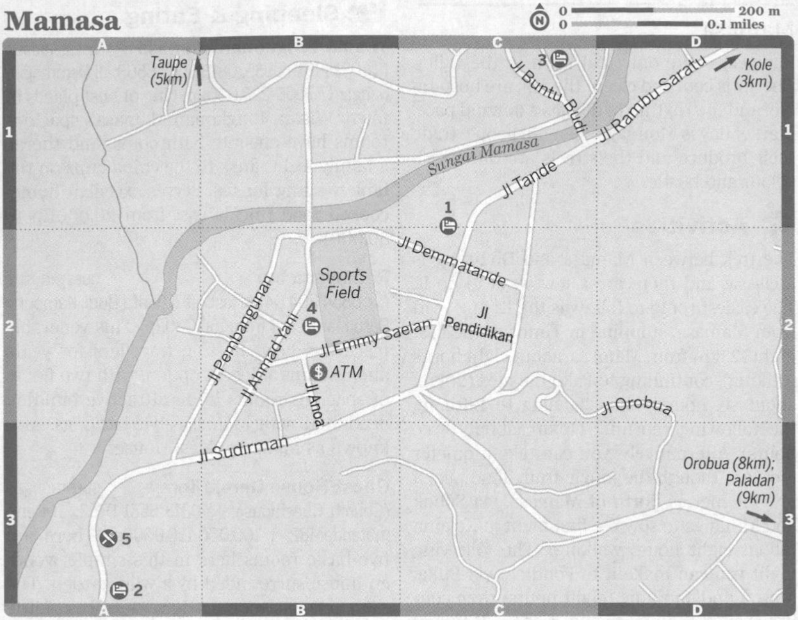

Mamasa

Sleeping

1 Guest House Gereja Toraja C1
2 Mantana Lodge 2 .... A3
3 Ramayana Inn C1
4 Wisma Tongkonan Mamasa B2

Eating

5 Dian Satria Restaurant A3

six hours) at other times, and connect by shared Kijang (70,000Rp, five hours) to Mamasa.

KIJANG

It's possible to take local transport between Mamasa and Rantepao via Bittuang – at least during the dry season – but it's rough going, requiring lots of transfers, and you'll probably have to stay overnight at least once along the way.

Kijangs leave Mamasa for Ponding daily at 10am (50,000Rp, three hours) and then head from Ponding to Bittuang the following day at 9am (50,000Rp, two to three hours). From Bittuang there are Kijangs to Makale (25,000Rp, one hour), where you can catch a bemo to Rantepao.

In the other direction, bemos head from Rantepao to Bittuang; Kijangs leave from Bittuang to Ponding daily at 9am and from Ponding to Mamasa the following day at 9am. Other vehicles, including motorbike drivers, also tackle this road and offer rides for the same price as the Kijang drivers.

Around Mamasa

The countryside surrounding Mamasa is strikingly beautiful. You can hire motorbikes around town for around 80,000Rp per day, or charter a bemo for about 250,000Rp. But note that footpaths and very slender suspension bridges offer the only access to most villages.

Many places are easy to reach from Mamasa, but take warm clothes and gifts for your hosts if you plan to stay overnight: condensed milk, chocolate, sugar, *kretek* (Indonesian clove cigarettes) and other goods from town are appreciated.

NORTH OF MAMASA

Rante Buda (4km from central Mamasa), has an impressive 25m-long *tongkonan* building known as Banua Layuk (High House), an old chief's place with colourful motifs. This *tongkonan* is one of the oldest and best preserved in the valley, built about 300 years ago for the chief of Rambusaratu, one of five local leaders. To visit, a donation of about 5000Rp is expected.

Kole (3km from Mamasa) has hot springs, tapped for the guests at its Mamasa Cottages. **Loko** (4km) is a traditional village with old houses, set in the jungle. The only way there is to hike via Kole or Tondok Bakaru. Hardy hikers can continue from Loko up the steep hill to **Mambulilin Sarambu** (Mambulilin Waterfall), and on to the peak of **Gunung Mambulilin** (9km). **Taupe** (5km) is a traditional village with jungle walks and panoramic views.

SOUTH OF MAMASA

Rante Sopang (12km from central Mamasa) is a busy centre for weaving and retailing crafts. The path up the hill from the roadside craft shop leads to a few workshops, where women weave long strips of heavy cloth for Mamasa's distinctive, colourful blankets.

Osango (3km from Mamasa) is the site of *tedong-tedong* (tiny structures over graves that look like houses), which are supposedly up to 200 years old. There are lots of paths and the village is *very* spread out, so you may find that you'll need to ask for directions along the way. **Mesa Kada** (2km) are hot springs that are suitable for a swim.

In **Tanete** (8km) you'll find mountain graves under a cave. Both Tanete and nearby **Taibassi** are also centres for traditional weaving and carving. **Rante Balla** (12km) has big, beautiful *tongkonan* and woven blankets and baskets.

Buntu Balla (15km from central Mamasa) has beautiful views, traditional weaving and *tedong-tedong* burial sites. Close to Buntu Balla there's a waterfall at **Allodio**, a traditional village at **Balla Peu**, megalithic remains at **Manta** and views along the whole valley from **Mussa**. Further south, **Malabo** (18km) has *tedong-tedong* burial sites.

Southeast of Mamasa, **Orobua** (9km) has a fine old *tongkonan;* it's one of the best in the area. There are more sweeping views to find from **Paladan** further south.

CENTRAL SULAWESI

Almost abandoned by tourism during and after a period of religious violence spanning eight years, Central Sulawesi is now back on the itinerary for travellers moving between the Togean Islands and Tana Toraja. Settlements on the vast lake of Danau Poso are an ideal place to break up a long bus ride, but there's much, much more to this province that's simply begging to be explored.

CENTRAL SULAWESI'S TROUBLED PAST

It's been pretty quiet in Central Sulawesi for the last decade, but the region was torn apart by Christian versus Muslim violence following the fall of President Suharto.

The big trouble began in 1998 when a drunken brawl between Christian and Muslim youths sparked clan fighting in Poso. By 2000 paramilitary groups called the Red Force (backing the Christians) and the Laskar Jihad (backing the Muslims) were engaged in full warfare against each other, armed with machetes and bows and arrows, as well as homemade bombs and artillery. Christians grouped in predominantly Christian Tentena, while Muslims stood their ground in Poso and Palu. The Indonesian government intervened in 2001 by organising the Malino Peace Treaty, signed in 2002 by both sides, which produced a decline in the violence but did not stop it. By the end of 2006, more than 1000 people had been killed, 60,000 had fled their homes, markets had been bombed and children beheaded. Tourists were never targets but the region was, for obvious reasons, best avoided.

It's still debated as to what caused these communities to start fighting each other after generations of living peacefully together. Some analysts believe this was just another arm in the fighting that had been going on between Muslim and Christian communities in the Maluku Islands. It's clear that an influx of Muslim immigrants from Java, under the transmigration program, abruptly shifted the balance of power in the region, creating tensions. But probably the biggest factors were the power vacuum resulting from Suharto's fall and the incendiary impact of extremist militias.

Today, locals chat easily about this dark time and about how happy they are it's over. As one Poso Muslim told us, 'Nowadays I go on vacation to Tentena but before I was afraid I'd get killed if I even went near there.'

DANAU POSO

Indonesia's third-largest lake, Danau Poso, covers an area of 32,300 hectares and reaches an average depth of 450m. The lake is 495m above sea level, so evenings here are pleasantly cool without being too cold. With mountains on all sides and mist hovering over the calm waters in the early morning, it's a captivating spot.

Tranquil Tentena is the easiest place to arrange treks into the Lore Lindu National Park, which is filled with mysterious megaliths and has a wildlife-rich jungle. Those with lots of time and a nose for anthropology should head to the adventurous Morowali Nature Reserve to seek out the Wana people. Divers and beach bums can laze around on the white sands of Tanjung Karang near Palu.

While some tensions remain in the region, and it's important to check the current situation, by late 2015 the region was largely calm, and things have been stable for some years. Indeed travellers are visiting Central Sulawesi in increasing numbers, with improved flight connections to all the airports of the region: Poso, Palu, Luwuk and Ampana.

History

Undated remains from a cave near Kolonedale indicate a long history of human settlement. The most spectacular prehistoric remains are the Bronze Age megaliths found throughout Central Sulawesi, but no one knows who was responsible for their creation. The highest concentration of these is along Sungai Lariang in the Bada Valley, and there are others throughout the region, down to Tana Toraja in South Sulawesi.

Between 1998 and 2006 this area was a hotbed for religious violence.

Pendolo

Pendolo is a dusty, sparse strip of a village right on the southern shore of Danau Poso. There's not much going on here beyond swimming at some of the area's surprisingly lovely white-sand beaches. It's this calm as well as the connection with the charming locals that draws in the few visitors that stop here.

There's a strip of decent and cheap *rumah makan* (restaurants or warungs) along the main road that cater to long-distance buses that stop here. Stay over at **Pendolo Cottages** (Jl Ahmad Yani 441; s/d bungalows 75,000/100,000Rp), right next to the boat landing about 1km east of the village centre; it's a rustic place that gets good traveller reviews on both service and ambience. **Mulia Poso Lake Hotel** (☎0813 4227 5454; Jl Pelabuhan Wisata 1; cottages 275,000-350,000Rp) is beautifully located on a sandy beach that has good swimming, but the bungalows are dated and service is patchy.

There are several daily buses to Tentena (24,000Rp, two hours), Poso (54,000Rp, four hours) and Rantepao (110,000Rp, eight hours) in daylight hours; locals know the exact schedule.

Tentena

☎0458

Tentena is a town of white picket fences and churches, cool breezes that come off the lake, and lots of wonderfully strange things to eat. Surrounded by clove-covered hills, it has an interesting market and some natural treasures to explore nearby. There are no beaches in the town itself, but it's easy to hire a motorbike or an *ojek* to get to some.

Sights & Activities

Most of the things to do and see are around Tentena itself. The best way to spend a day is either to rent a motorbike (70,000Rp per day; ask at your hotel) or hire an *ojek* (around 130,000Rp per day).

Air Terjun Salopa WATERFALL

(entrance 5000Rp) If you have wheels you can visit this impressive, powerful waterfall that drops in stages through rainforest, 15km south of Tentena. The falls are a spectacular place for a swim, and you can hike through the jungle and alongside a plunging river for a few kilometres – keep an eye out for monkeys and hornbills.

Beach BEACH

Around 20km south of Tentena the lovely golden beach by the Siuri Cottages has great swimming with a water temperature of around 26°C year-round. There's a restaurant for lunch and drinks.

Eel Traps AREA

Tentena's pretty covered 210m bridge marks where Danau Poso (Lake Poso) ends and Sungai Poso (Poso River) begins its journey to the coast. V-shaped eel traps north of the bridge snare the 2m monsters for which Tentena is famous. Live specimens are available for inspection and consumption in local warungs.

Chartering a boat to explore the lake can be surprisingly difficult; the asking rate is 120,000Rp for two hours.

Festivals & Events

Tentena is the host of the annual **Festival Danau Poso**, the undisputed highlight of Central Sulawesi's social calendar, in late August. Villagers from far afield gather for a colourful celebration of culture, with dancing, songs and traditional sports.

Sleeping

Tourism in Tentena suffered badly during the religious troubles (p669) between 1998 and 2006. Things are steadily improving, but many places have conseqently suffered from a lack of investment.

Hotel Victory GUESTHOUSE $

(0458-21392; victorytentena@yahoo.com; Jl Diponegoro 18; r incl breakfast 175,000-375,000Rp;) A very friendly family-run place with a wide choice of (ageing) rooms, from cell-like cheapies to spacious options with hot water. Most travellers happily end up here, thanks to the excellent info (maps are provided) and social areas. The owners can also sort out motorbikes, recommend good guides and do laundry. Prices drop by about 20% in the low season.

★**Dolidi Ndano Towale** BUNGALOW $$

(0812 4523 9357; www.dolidi-ndano-towale.com; s/d incl breakfast 300,000/400,000Rp;) This beautifully designed, newly opened Dutch-managed place has lovely lakeside cottages, a wonderful location on a sandy beach, and is a great spot for kids. There's a jetty for waterside drinks and a fine restaurant with sweeping views. Tours of the lake and national parks can be arranged. It's 7km south of Tentena, down a bumpy access road. Profits aid the orphanage next door. Book ahead.

Siuri Cottages COTTAGE $$

(0852 4105 8225; a.kalottong11@gmail.com; cottages incl breakfast 250,000-350,000Rp) Twenty kilometres from Tentena on the lakeside road to Pendolo, this isolated place is something of a time warp; its spacious, comfortable timber cottages are complete with original 1980s decor, and there's no wi-fi. However, its location on a lovely, unspoiled lakeside beach more than compensates for the lack of modernity. The staff are eager to please and there's western and local grub in the hotel's restaurant.

Call ahead and the owners will pick you up for free from Tentena; and if you stay a couple of nights, they'll drop you back there, too.

Eating

After dark don't miss trying the tasty *pisang molen* (banana fried in a sweet pastry), available at stalls in front of the eastern part of the bridge.

Ongga Bale SEAFOOD $

(10am-9.30pm;) A large, well-organised restaurant on the main strip with tables by thc lakcshore. Pick a fish from the pools, choose a sauce, order a beer, and you're set. A large *ikan bakar* (grilled fish) will set you back around 45,000Rp.

Rumah Makan Kawana INDONESIAN $

(meals 12,000-22,000Rp; 8am-8pm) For local specialities *sugili* (eel) and *ikan mas* (large goldfish), as well as spicy bat dishes, pull up a chair at one of the riverside *rumah makan* at the market near the bridge; the best is Rumah Makan Kawana.

Information

Guides in Tentena all organise treks to Lore Lindu National Park and Morowali Nature Reserve. Dolidi Ndano Towale and Hotel Victory provide good recommendations. There are a few internet cafes and two ATMs in town.

BUSES & BEMOS FROM TENTENA

DESTINATION	FARE (RP)	DURATION (HR)	FREQUENCY
Bomba (for Lore Lindu)	65,000	4	1 daily Mon-Sat
Palu	110,000	8	5 daily
Pendolo	32,000	2	frequent
Poso	38,000	2	every 2 hours
Rantepao	130,000	10	5 daily

Getting There & Away

BUS & BEMO

You'll need to catch an *ojek* (7000Rp) or organise a pick-up by your hotel to/from Tentena's bus and bemo terminal, which is 3km from the town centre. Note that there's a reduced service to Poso on Sundays.

JEEP

The availability and price of Jeeps to Gintu in Lore Lindu National Park depends on the condition of the road. Reckon on around 2,000,000Rp to charter one for a return day trip for up to four people. **Dolidi Ndano Towale** (p671) organises excellent three-day tours to Lore Lindu for 6,100,000Rp.

Poso

0452 / POP 49,300

Poso is the main town, port and terminal for road transport on the northern coast of Central Sulawesi. For years violence between Muslims and Christians (p669) made it a no-go zone but tensions have eased. However, there's still no reason to visit other than to catch a flight, change buses, or break up a trip to/from Ampana and the Togean Islands.

Sleeping & Eating

New Armada HOTEL $

(0452-23070; Jl Sumatera 117; r with shared bathroom 90,000Rp, private bathroom 165,000-200,000Rp) Right on the main drag, this hotel has a wide selection of bland but clean rooms, all of them good value. No English is spoken.

Hotel Natuna Poso HOTEL $$

(0813 5477 4446; Jl Natuna 1; r incl breakfast 200,000-350,000Rp, cottage incl breakfast 400,000Rp;) This fine new place on a quiet suburban lane has spotless rooms and cute cottages, all with air-conditioning, good facilities and modern bathrooms. It's about 500m from Jl Sumatera.

Rumah Makan Bunda INDONESIAN $

(Jl Tanjum Bulu; meals from 12,000Rp; 8am-9pm) This modern place by a roundabout 1km north of the centre does all the Indo classics well, such as a mean *nasi campur,* as well as juices and coffee.

Information

Most facilities, including ATMs, are on or near busy Jl Sumatera in the centre.

Getting There & Away

AIR

Poso's Kasiguncu airport, 15km west of town, is fast growing in popularity with travellers as flight connections multiply. Wings Air flies daily to Makassar (from 663,000Rp) and XpressAir connects Poso with Palu and Makassar.

BUS & MINIBUS

The bus terminal is about 5km out of town. There are plenty of *ojek* and bemo that will buzz you into central Poso for 5000Rp.

For Palu and Ampana, you can also catch the minibuses from offices along Jl Sumatera. Bemos to nearby villages and beaches leave from a terminal next to the market.

Around Poso

There are plenty of good places for swimming and snorkelling around Poso. **Pantai Madale** is a snorkelling spot 5km east; about 20km further east lies white-sand beach **Pantai Matako**; and **Pantai Toini**, 7km west of Poso, has a few *rumah makan* with great seafood.

Lembomawo village, 4km south of Poso, is renowned for its ebony wood carvers' workshops.

Destinations can be reached by bemo from Poso's market terminal.

BUSES FROM POSO

DESTINATION	FARE (RP)	DURATION (HR)	FREQUENCY
Ampana	75,000	5	5 daily
Kolonodale	120,000	8	8am daily
Manado	320,000	30	3 daily
Palu	80,000	6	7 daily
Tentena	38,000	2	every 2 hours

Lore Lindu National Park

As if having a lush jungle filled with impressive hornbills and shy tarsiers weren't enough, Lore Lindu is also famous for its megaliths (giant freestanding stones). Covering an area of 250,000 hectares, this remote national park, which is a Unesco Biosphere Reserve, has been barely touched by tourism. It's a perfect place to seek out an off-the-beaten-path adventure, but take note that it's rough-going. Trips are best organised from Palu or Tentena and it's highly recommended that you hire a guide.

Sights & Actvities

Attractions in the park include ancient megalithic relics, mostly in the **Bada**, **Besoa** and **Napu Valleys**; remote peaks, some more than 2500m high; and birdwatching, including the opportunity to spot hornbills, around **Danua Tambing**, the 3150-hectare lake **Danau Lindu**, the village of **Wuasa** and along the **Anaso Track** that leads to the top of 2300m-high **Gunung Rore Kitimbu**.

Hiking

Hikes (undertaken with a guide) include **Rachmat** to Danau Lindu (six hours one way) and **Sadaunta** to Danau Lindu (four hours one way).

The roads around Lore Lindu have improved in recent years and now many of the old hiking routes are used by motorbikes, although even these tracks can get muddy and impassable in the rainy season. One of the best places to get into the jungle, where it's free of motor noise but rich in wildlife, is the trail between **Doda** and **Gimpu** (a two-day walk); but note there aren't any megaliths on this route. Megalithic remains are found mostly along the motorbike road between **Tonusu** and Gimpu, via **Tuare** and **Moa**, or Doda and **Hangirah**. There are also megaliths to see along the road between Doda and Wuasa, which is accessible by car.

Bring mosquito repellent and sunblock lotion. You'll want warm clothes since it can get cold at night. Conversely, during the day it can get very hot, so you'll need to have plenty of water.

Guides

For long-distance trekking a guide is compulsory, and also necessary if you're intent on finding the megaliths. An organised one-day visit from Tentena with a guide and vehicle (for up to four people) costs about 2,200,000Rp, and prices go up from there. The guides from Tentena speak English.

If travelling independently, arrange a guide at Kulawi, Wuasa, Bomba, Badu or at the tourist office or national park office in Palu. Guides start at 400,000Rp per day, but few speak much English.

Sleeping

Losmen are spread around the fringes of the national park in several villages. Wuasa is the largest settlement and has several guesthouses. It makes a convenient base for those arriving from Palu, particularly for birdwatchers. There's electricity from 5pm to 10.30pm, mobile (cell) phone coverage and locals rent motorbikes for 100,000Rp per day.

Losmen Mona Lisa GUESTHOUSE **$**
(☎0853 4089 6417, 0821 9660 4295; Wuasa village; r incl all meals 180,000Rp) The owner of this simple, well-presented place speaks English, prepares excellent food and can arrange birdwatching guides and motorbike hire.

RM & Penginapan Sendy HOMESTAY **$**
(☎0852 4120 7372, 0813 4106 5109; Wuasa village; s/d 100,000/130,000Rp) This attractive homestay has seven tidy rooms with screen windows. It also has the added benefit of a good restaurant that serves filling meals (from 20,000Rp to 40,000Rp).

Information

You can buy national-park entry permits (150,000Rp) at the small field office (which has no accommodation) at Wuasa, and at the **Balai Taman Nasional Lore Lindu Office** (☎0451-457623; Jl Prof Mohammad Yamin SH) in Palu. Good information online can be found at the birdwatching website **Burung Nusantara** (www.burung-nusantara.org).

Getting There & Away

There are three main approaches to the park: one from Tentena and two from Palu. From Palu buses and Kijang run all the way to Wuasa (105km, four hours) and Doda (132km, five hours) three times a day from Terminal Petobu along a paved road (parts are potholed). From Tentena there is a daily bus to Bomba (66km, four hours); you can also charter Jeeps, but these run according to demand and road conditions. Motorbikes and *ojek* are readily available in Wuasa, Gimpu, Doda and Bomba.

Palu

☎0451 / POP 351,000

Palu, the capital of Central Sulawesi, is characterless but loaded with banks and supermarkets, and has a busy regional airport. It's a good place to do errands if you're heading to/from Kalimantan or Lore Lindu National Park. Nearby is the rarely visited yet wonderfully quaint village of Dongalla and the beach area of Tanjung Karang. Situated in a rain shadow for most of the year, Palu is one of the driest places in Indonesia.

The best part of town to wander around is the busy Jl Hasanuddin II area.

Sleeping & Eating

There are plenty of night warungs along the breezy seafront esplanade, Jl Raja Moili. If you like meat, Palu is famous for its *kaledo* (beef stew with bone marrow) restaurants; there are several on Jl Diponegoro.

Purnama Raya Hotel GUESTHOUSE $

(☎0451-423646; Jl Wahidin 4; s/d incl breakfast 75,000/100,000Rp; 📶) This family-run place in the heart of Palu has basic rooms with fans and en-suite *mandi* (Indonesian-style) bathrooms. The owners are friendly and can help with onward transport.

Hotel Santika Palu HOTEL $$

(www.santika.com/santika-palu; Jl Hatta 18; r incl breakfast from 488,000Rp; ❄@📶🏊) A smart, well-run modern hotel where the rooms have good-quality mattresses and linen, and there's fast wi-fi; rooms on the upper floors have mountain vistas. Staff are helpful and the tariffs are good value.

Hotel Sentral HOTEL $$

(☎0451-422789; http://hotel-sentral.indonesiahotel24.com; Jl Monginsidi 71-73; r incl breakfast 258,000-555,000Rp; ❄@📶) A dependable place where even the cheapest rooms have satellite TVs and air-con, though the decor is perhaps a little tired. There's a travel agent and an internet cafe here, and restaurants and a large supermarket are close by.

Rama Garden Hotel HOTEL $$

(☎0451-429500; www.hotelramagarden.com; Jl Monginsidi 81; r incl breakfast 260,000-600,000Rp; ❄📶🏊) This place is a garden of tranquillity inside, with winding paths, lots of plants and minilawn areas, plus a pool and a terrace dining area. Take a swim; order room service; and watch a movie.

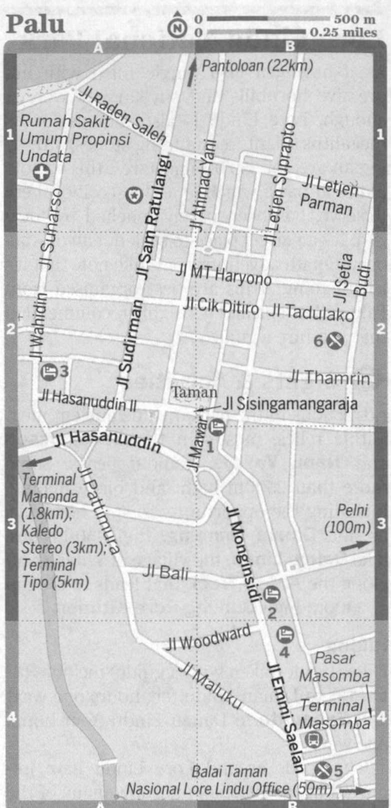

Palu

Sleeping

1 Hotel Santika Palu B3
2 Hotel Sentral B3
3 Purnama Raya Hotel A2
4 Rama Garden Hotel B4

Eating

5 Mall Tatura Palu B4
6 Restoran Marannu B2

Restoran Marannu CHINESE $

(Jl Setia Budi; mains 20,000-40,000Rp; ⏰8am-10pm) One of the smarter spots in town, the menu at Marannu includes good soups such as *coto Makassar* (beef soup with offal and ground peanuts), tasty seafood and Chinese cuisine.

Kaledo Stereo INDONESIAN $

(Jl Diponegoro; meals 25,000-50,000Rp; ⏲8am-9pm) This is perhaps the city's most famous *kaledo* restaurant, a bustling place where its beef stew is served in a bowl with a giant Fred Flintstone–style bone to chew on.

Mall Tatura Palu INDONESIAN, INTERNATIONAL $

(Jl Emmi Saelan; ⏲8am-9.30pm; 📶) Has a decent food court on the top level, as well as a few upmarket restaurants, cafes and a supermarket.

Information

Balai Taman Nasional Lore Lindu Office (☎0451-457623; www.lorelindu.info; Jl Prof Mohammad Yamin 53; ⏲7.30am-4pm Mon-Fri) Little English is spoken but staff does its best to help and can set you up with guides for hiking and trekking in Lore Lindu National Park.

Police Station (☎0451-421015; Jl Sam Ratulangi)

Rumah Sakit Umum Propinsi Undata (☎0451-421270; Jl Suharso; ⏲24hr) Large and reasonably well equipped hospital.

Tourist Office (☎0451-455260; Jl Dewi Sartika 91; ⏲8am-4pm Mon-Thu, to 3pm Fri) Inconveniently located and hard to find, about 5km west of the centre; has some information about Lore Lindu National Park.

Getting There & Away

AIR

Palu has a busy regional airport with flights to cities in Java, Kalimantan and other destinations in Sulawesi. Lion Air flies to Jakarta, Makassar, Balikpapan and Surabaya; Garuda flies to Jakarta and Makassar; XpressAir flies to Gorontalo, Luwuk, Manado and Poso; Sriwijaya Air flies to Balikpapan and Makassar; and Wings heads to Luwuk and Makassar.

BOAT

Few travellers use them these days but there are Pelni ferry connections to East Kalimantan and Sulawesi ports, including boats to Balikpapan and Bitung. Ferries dock at Pantoloan, 22km north of Palu, which is accessible by shared taxi from Terminal Manonda in Palu, or by metered taxi (75,000Rp). The **Pelni office** (☎0451-421696; Jl Kartini; ⏲7.30am-noon & 1-4pm Mon-Fri, 8am-noon Sat) in Palu is efficient; there's another one at Pantoloan.

BUS & KIJANG

Buses and minibuses to Poso (80,000Rp, six hours), Ampana (100,000Rp to 150,000Rp, 12 hours) and Rantepao (180,000Rp, 20 hours) leave from **Terminal Masomba**, and also from bus company offices that are inconveniently dotted around the suburbs of Palu. Kijangs to Donggala (22,000Rp; for Tanjung Karang) 36km away leave when full from Terminal Tipo, about 5km northwest of Palu, but it's easier to take an *ojek* (55,000Rp). There are three daily buses to Gimpu, Doda (132km, five hours) and Wuasa (105km, four hours) for Lore Lindu National Park, and shared Kijang (which leave when full) from Terminal Petobo, off Jl Prof Mohammed Yamin, about 6km southeast of Palu.

Getting Around

Palu's Mutiara airport is 6km southeast of town; it costs around 45,000Rp to/from the centre in a metered taxi. Damri airport buses are scheduled to operate between the airport and city centre from late 2015.

Transport around Palu is by bemo; routes are flexible, so just flag down one that looks like it's going your way.

Most taxis use meters.

Donggala & Tanjung Karang

☎0457

Donggala is a sleepy port full of colourful houses, flowering gardens and lots of interesting local characters. From here it's a short *ojek* ride to Tanjung Karang's slice of white sand, studded with rickety beach bungalows, roaming buffalo and a decent dive centre.

The town was once a Dutch administrative centre and briefly the most important port in Central Sulawesi. When the harbour silted up, ships used the harbours on the other side of the bay, and Palu became the regional capital.

Activities

The main attractions are sun, sand and water at Tanjung Karang (Coral Peninsula), about 5km north of Donggala. The reef off Prince John Dive Resort (p676) is good for **snorkelling** and beginner-level **diving**. Snorkelling gear costs €5 per day. Fun dives cost €29 (including equipment); PADI courses are also available here. The resort offers dolphin-watching tours.

Sleeping & Eating

There are lots of budget bungalows and warungs along Tanjung Karang.

Natural Cottages BUNGALOW $$

(☎0813 4147 1769; www.naturalcottages.com; bungalows 250,000Rp; 📶) This small resort has a selection of ageing blue-roofed bungalows that enjoy a fine beachfront location. It's more geared at local tourists and, though the staff does its best, very little English is spoken.

Prince John Dive Resort RESORT **$$$**
(☎0457-71710; www.prince-john-dive-resort.com; bungalows for 2 people incl 2 meals €70-110; ❄) This lovely resort is reason enough to come to Tanjung Karang. Three classes of rustic-chic wood-and-stone bungalows enjoy sea views. It's a well-managed German-run place and the only dive resort in the Palu area. The beach here has a few umbrellas for nonguests to rent. Wi-fi is confined to reception and lounge areas.

Getting There & Away

Kijangs to Donggala (22,000Rp) leave when full from Terminal Tipo, about 5km outside Palu. From Donggala you can catch an *ojek* the 5km to Tanjung Karang (8000Rp). A taxi/*ojek* from Palu costs around 120,000/55,000Rp.

Luwuk

☎0461 / POP 56,000

Set around a stunning natural harbour, Luwuk is the biggest town on Sulawesi's remote eastern peninsula. It's a possible stepping stone to the Togean Islands (and the remote Banggai Islands). Long isolated from the rest of Sulawesi, Luwuk now sees a trickle of travellers, thanks to improved air links.

Nearby attractions include **Air Terjun Hengahenga**, a 75m-high waterfall 3km west of Luwuk; and the **Bangkiriang Nature Reserve**, 80km southwest of Luwuk, which is home to Central Sulawesi's largest maleo-bird population.

Sleeping & Eating

Good budget places are hard to find in Luwuk. There are ample restaurants and warungs along the seafront strip.

Maleo Cottages GUESTHOUSE **$**
(☎0461-324068; www.maleo-cottages.com; Jl Lompobattang; s/d incl breakfast 180,000/200,000Rp) Owned by a French–Indonesian couple (a marine biologist and a lawyer), this fine coastal place has simple, atmospheric cottages and rooms. Great meals are available. It's a good place to arrange independent trips to the remote, beautiful Banggai Islands, liveaboards to the Togean Islands and rainforest treks. It's located 16km south of Luwuk, near the airport.

Estrella Hotel HOTEL **$$**
(☎0461-312-8080; http://estrellahotel.id; Jl Mandapar; r incl breakfast from 688,000Rp; ❄@🛜🏊) Overlooking Luwuk bay, around 2km south of the centre, this sleek business hotel has great facilities including a fine pool, fitness centre and good dining options. The modish rooms are stylish and spacious, and the staff are helpful.

Hotel Karaton HOTEL **$$**
(☎0461-21048, 0461-22618; http://hotelkaraton.com; Jl Dewi Sartika 123; r 280,000-330,000Rp, ste 440,000Rp; ❄🛜) A good midrange place on the south side of the town centre. Clean, whitewashed, air-conditioned accommodation with fresh linen and flat-screen TVs in four price categories.

Getting There & Around

Aviastar, XpressAir, Lion Air, Wings and Garuda all fly regularly to Luwuk airport, which is 12km south of the centre. There are several daily flights to Makassar and good links to Gorontalo and Palu. There's no bus service to/from the aiport; taxis charge around 55,000Rp.

The Pelni liner *Tilongkabila* links Luwuk weekly with Bau Bau and Bitung, and many stops in between; there's a **Pelni** (☎0461-23013; Jl Danau Limboto 74; ⏰8am-4pm Mon-Fri, to 1pm Sat) office in town.

One beat-up Honda Jaya bus leaves daily from Jl Santigiat at 7am for Ampana (68,000Rp, six hours); there are also more comfortable private minibuses (150,000Rp).

Ampana

☎0464

The main reason for travellers to come to Ampana is to catch a boat to/from the Togean Islands. It's a laid-back, pleasant coastal town with a vibrant market and makes a good stopover while you recover from, or prepare for, an assault on the Togeans.

Sleeping & Eating

A roster of excellent new accommodation options has opened in recent years. Warungs are plentiful along the seafront road Jl Yos Sudarso, just west of the main boat terminal.

Nebula Cottages BUNGALOW **$**
(☎0464-21743; http://nebulacottages.weebly.com; Jl Tanjung Api 5; bungalows incl breakfast with fan/air-con 150,000/250,000Rp; ❄🛜) A fine new place with tasteful, very spacious wooden bungalows that sit pretty in a coconut grove, close

to the sea. The staff are eager to help and can help with motorbike hire. Breakfast is excellent, with lots of fresh fruit and good tea and coffee. Located 2.5km east of the centre.

Oasis Hotel HOTEL $

(☎0464-21058; Jl Kartini; r incl breakfast with fan/air-con from 120,000/200,000Rp; ❄📶) Oasis benefits from a central location and has functional rooms, some with air-con; however, the proximity to the sounds of karaoke, cockerels and a mosque's call to prayer are serious drawbacks.

★**Marina Cottages** COTTAGES $$

(☎0464-21280; www.marina-cottages.com; Jl Tanjung Api 33; cottages incl breakfast 150,000-550,000Rp; ❄📶) Beautifully situated on a pebble beach 3km east of the centre, these 20 rustic, very well maintained cottages (in a wide choice of price bands) boast a lovely seafront setting. You couldn't wish for a nicer place for breakfast, beer or a meal (from 20,000Rp) than the idyllic restaurant, which makes the most of the views. Boats to Bomba leave from a jetty nearby.

Lawaka Hotel BOUTIQUE HOTEL $$

(☎0464-21690; http://lawakahotel.com; Jl Tanjung Lawaka 10; r 295,000-335,000Rp; ❄📶) A highly unexpected find in deeply provincial Ampana, Lawaka feels like a hip hostel with its zany decor, cool cafe and urban art-enriched rooms that face a central garden. There's bike hire available, too. It's about 1km east of the centre, just steps from the coast.

ℹ Information

Check http://infotogian.weebly.com for information about the town and the Togean Islands.

Ampana has plentiful banks and ATMs.

ℹ Getting There & Away

AIR

Access to Ampana will really take off when Garuda and Lion Air begin planned flights to Makassar. At the time of research the only connections were infrequent Aviastar flights to Palu, Luwuk and Gorontalo (on an 18-seater plane); check http://infotogian.weebly.com for the latest schedule. The airport is 7km east of the centre.

BUS & MINIBUS

Minibuses travel each day to Luwuk (150,000Rp, six hours, departing 8am), Poso (75,000Rp, five hours, departing 10am and 5pm) and Palu (150,000Rp, 12 hours, departing 10am and 5pm). There are also additional but much slower and less comfortable buses on these routes.

BOAT

Boats to Poso, Wakai (in the Togean Islands) and beyond leave from the main boat terminal at the end of Jl Yos Sudarso, in the centre of Ampana. Boats to Bomba in the Togeans leave from a jetty in Labuhan village, next to Marina Cottages.

WORTH A TRIP

TANJUNG API NATIONAL PARK

The 4246-hectare Tanjung Api (Cape Fire) National Park is home to *anoa* (pygmy buffaloes), *babi rusa* (wild deer-like pigs), crocodiles, snakes and maleo birds, but most people come to see the burning coral cliff fuelled by a leak of natural gas. To get here you need to charter a boat 24km east around the rocky peninsula from Ampana. A visit to the park is more interesting at dusk.

Togean Islands

Yes, it takes determination to get to the Togean Islands, but believe us, it takes much more determination to leave. Island-hop from one forested golden-beach beauty to the next, where hammocks are plentiful, the fish is fresh and the welcome is genuine. Most islands have only one or two family-run guesthouses, while popular Kadidiri has a small but lively beach scene with night-time bonfires and cold beers all around.

The rich diversity of marine life and astonishing coral formations in the Togeans are a magnet for divers and snorkellers; there are several professional scuba schools for training, courses and recreational dives. For truly spectacular diving, Una Una fits the bill perfectly.

When you decide to pull yourself out of the water, there's a surprising variety of wildlife to look for in the undisturbed and wild jungles, as well as other remote beaches to find. Seven or so ethnic groups share this region, but all are happy to see visitors and are exceptionally hospitable.

Most rooms are in wooden cottages and right on the beach. Bathroom facilities range from communal and rustic to private and porcelain. Prices are usually per person and rates include three local meals. It is a good idea to bring along some snacks and treats.

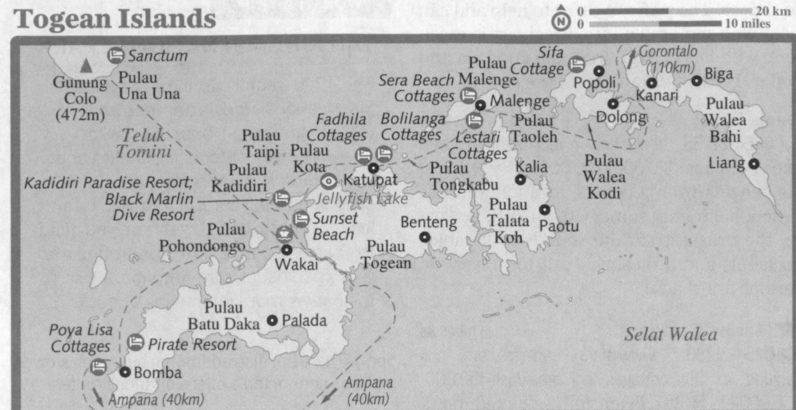

Beer, soft drinks and mineral water are all available from shops and homestays.

Bring plenty of cash as there are no banks on the islands. If your hotel or guesthouse has a faint mobile signal it is sometimes possible to pay by credit/debit card – but don't count on it.

Activities

The Togeans are the only place in Indonesia where you can find all three major reef environments – atoll, barrier and fringing reefs – in one location. Two atolls and their deep lagoons lie to the northwest of Pulau Batu Daka. Barrier reefs surround many islands at the 200m-depth contour (5km to 15km offshore), and fringing reefs surround all of the coasts, merging with sea grass and mangroves. There is also a well-preserved sunken WWII B-24 bomber plane (at a depth of between 14m and 22m).

The mix of coral and marine life is spectacular and unusually diverse. Dynamite and cyanide fishing has damaged some reefs in the past but recovery is well under way and many others remain untouched.

Highlights include spectacular open-water topography, with coral canyons, plunging drop-offs and some truly giant gorgonia corals. Reefs teem with hundreds of species of tropical fish, and macro life including seahorses, painted frogfishes and leaf scorpionfishes. Most sites in the Togeans rarely invite 'big stuff' but passing pelagics (including) hammerhead sharks are sometimes seen and schooling barracuda are regularly encountered. Colonies of dugong are also present.

Prices start from €25 per dive and PADI courses are available. Dive conditions (most of the year) are perfect for the inexperienced, with water temperatures of 28°C to 29°C, fine visibility and gentle currents. Pulau Kadidiri is the best place to organise activities.

Trips to a 'jellyfish lake', where you can swim with stinger-free jellyfish (one of only three places in the world where this is possible), cost from 50,000Rp per person. This trip can be organised from many places around the islands, as can treks around volcanic Pulau Una Una and to isolated beaches.

Getting There & Away

Yes, it's complicated. There are many ways to get to the Togeans, but all of them are time-consuming and none of them straightforward. Firstly the islands have no airport, so the only access is by boat. The two gateway cities are Ampana and Gorontalo. Consult the excellent www.infotogian.weebly.com for up-to-date information as schedules change regularly. It's also *essential* to factor in some wiggle room when travelling, as breakdowns and bad weather can affect ferry sailings, particularly in the rainy season (roughly from November to early April).

If you're travelling overland from South Sulawesi (including Tana Toraja), Ampana is the logical gateway. Six ferries run from there per week to the Togeans. Ampana also has a new airport, but was served by very limited flights at the time of research. Luwuk and Poso have more reliable air connections, but both towns are a six-hour overland trip from Ampana.

Gorontalo, in North Sulawesi, is the other main gateway. The city has excellent flight links to Makassar, very reliable air and bus links to

Manado and a twice-weekly overnight boat to the Togeans.

Representatives from many of the resorts and hotels meet ferries at arrival points in the Togeans, and often shuttle you to your accommodation free of charge.

FROM AMPANA

Ferries depart Ampana for the Togean Islands daily except Friday. The route is Ampana–Wakai–Katupat–Malenge–Dolong; the arrival time in Dolong is 8.30pm. Note on Monday and Thursday the ferry leaves at 9am and sails to Wakai only.

FERRY ROUTE	FARE (RP)	DEPARTURE TIME
Ampana–Wakai	52,000	10am
Wakai–Katupat	60,000	2.30pm
Katupat–Malenge	66,000	4.15pm
Malenge–Dolong	72,000	5.45pm

In the reverse direction the ferry leaves Dolong at 10pm on Sunday, Tuesday and Thursday, calling at all the stops. On Monday and Saturday it only operates from Wakai to Ampana.

To head directly to Bomba it's possible to take small local boats (34,000Rp, three hours) that leave on Monday, Thurday and Saturday from a jetty in Labuhan village, Ampana, next to **Marina Cottages** (p677).

FROM GORONTALO

From Gorontalo the KM *Tuna Tomini* sails directly to Wakai (economy class/air-con cabin for four 64,000Rp/500,000Rp, 13 hours) on Monday and Thursday and is the easiest option from this direction if you want to get to Katupat, Kadidiri or Bomba. On the way back, the boat departs Wakai on Thursday and Sunday at 5pm.

Alternatively, you could head to Bumbulan port (a three-hour taxi or four-hour bus ride from Gorontalo) and catch the KM *Cengkih Afo* to Dolong on Walea Kodi Island (economy class 56,000Rp, five hours) on Sunday and Thursday at 9am; it returns the same days at 4pm, arriving at the ungodly hour of 2am in Bumbulan.

Getting Around

Use the Ampana–Dolong ferries to island-hop or charter local boats. Public boats also connect Wakai with Una Una (32,000Rp, three per week, three hours).

> **GETTING IN TOUCH WITH THE TOGEANS**
>
> There's no internet in the Togean Islands and mobile phone reception is patchy at best. While many guesthouses have an email address and phone number, you may have to wait a few days or more before anyone writes back or returns your call. Except in high season (August) you won't need a reservation anyway and can just turn up.

Finding a charter is relatively easy in Wakai, Bomba and Kadidiri, but it's more difficult to arrange in smaller settlements. Rates are fairly standard among the cartel of local operators (around 450,000Rp from Wakai or Kadidiri to Bomba). Ask at your hotel.

Pulau Batu Daka

The largest and most accessible island in the Togeans is Pulau Batu Daka, which is home to the two main villages, Bomba and Wakai.

Bomba is a tiny outpost at the southwestern end of the island, which most travellers sail past on the way to and from Wakai. It's an appealing alternative to social Pulau Kadidiri, as it has some of the Togean's best beaches, good snorkelling and it's social in a very mellow way. It's a pleasant walk to the bat caves in the hills behind Bomba village, but you'll need a guide and a torch (flashlight).

The largest settlement in the Togeans, Wakai is a small port that's mainly used as the departure point for boats to Pulau Kadidiri, but there are several well-stocked general stores and a lively market. A small waterfall, a few kilometres inland from Wakai, is a pleasant hike; ask directions in the village.

Sleeping

Poya Lisa Cottages BUNGALOW $$

(Bomba; cottage per person incl all meals 150,000-200,000Rp) On its own (tiny) private island, this little paradise has two perfect beaches and a dozen or so big, simple wooden bungalows. The meals here are among the best in the Togeans and the family that runs the place is as sweet as can be, offering free snorkelling gear (and boat trips) for guests. Other excursions are offered, and diving can be arranged via a neighbouring resort.

CONSERVATION OF THE TOGEAN ISLANDS

Home to more than 500 types of coral, 600 reef-fish species and an estimated 500 mollusc, Teluk Tomini around the Togean Islands is one of the richest reef areas in all of Indonesia. In 2004 the Indonesian Ministry of Forestry signed a bill that turned 362,000 hectares of this fragile area into a national park; this was great news to conservation groups, but some local NGOs claim national-park status restricts local livelihoods and leaves the region open to other types of exploitation.

The Togeans' shaky ecological record really started when cyanide and dynamite fishing was introduced to the islands in the early 1990s. While this initially boosted the local catch, it also caused untold damage to fragile reef ecosystems. By the early 2000s locals (often with help from local NGOs and dive centres) began to understand the destructiveness of these practices and many returned to traditional fishing techniques. Some villages even began creating their own protected areas and helping to patrol reefs against illegal fishing. Today, islanders are hailing larger fishing yields closer to home and also the presence of healthy coral beds – proof that reef protection works.

Despite this, the Togeans are relatively poor islands and the fishing ain't what it used to be. The fishing of valuable Napoleon wrasse (for foreign Chinese restaurants) has all but wiped such fish out of these waters, and resulted in a catastrophic increase in the number of crown-of-thorns starfish, which destroy coral at an alarming rate.

Pulau Kadidiri–based Black Marlin Diving and other scuba schools are lobbying the Indonesian government to safeguard the islands' officially protected status with patrols against illegal fishing; they are also lobbying for the area to be declared a Unesco World Heritage Site.

Pitate Resort BUNGALOW **$$**
(☎0813 4107 7371; http://pitate-resort.weebly.com; r per person incl all meals 175,000Rp) This newly opened place on a slim sandy beach has simple, attractive wood-and-bamboo bungalows with decent bedding and private bathrooms. Snorkelling tours can be arranged.

Pulau Kadidiri

Beautiful, thickly wooded Kadidiri, a 30-minute boat trip from Wakai, is definitely the island to go to if you're feeling social. Its popular lodging options are all close together, so you can stroll along a fine strip of sand for a drink elsewhere if your place has run out of beer. It's a 15-minute walk from the hotels, through coconut groves, to a lovely sandy cove, **Barracuda Beach** (where you could camp).

Activities

Pulau Kadidiri is the easiest place to organise the range of activities available in the Togean Islands. There's good snorkelling and swimming only metres from the shore and superb diving beyond. In addition to diving equipment, snorkelling gear is available; in some places it's free for guests, in others you'll typically be charged 30,000Rp per day. Black Marlin Diving and Kadidiri Paradise Resort are the island's main dive centres.

Black Marlin Diving also has kayaks for hire, which you can use to explore the sheltered lagoon behind Kadidiri Paradise Resort or the offshore islets. You can also hike island trails.

Sleeping

Reserve rooms ahead in high season.

Kadidiri Paradise Resort RESORT **$$**
(☎0464-21058; www.kadidiriparadise.com; r per person incl all meals 200,000-325,000Rp) This resort enjoys a stunning location on a lovely beach and has extensive grounds that hug the coastline. Wooden bungalows are spacious and have generous front decks, though maintenance and attention to detail could be better. The dive centre is particularly well run.

Black Marlin Dive Resort BUNGALOW **$$**
(☎0435-831869; www.blackmarlindiving.com; bungalows per person incl all meals €18-30) A well-designed resort that has a good vibe thanks to its lounging areas and attractive restaurant, which are ideal for socialising. Bungalows are smallish but stylish, and all have sea views from their front terraces. The PADI dive school here is professional, environmentally conscious and well organised, and you'll find good packages available.

Pulau Una Una

Pulau Una Una, which consists mostly of active **Gunung Colo** (472m), was torn apart in 1983 when the volcano exploded. Ash covered 90% of the island, destroying all its houses and crops. Residents were safely evacuated, and many have now returned.

The offshore reefs here offer the best diving in the Togeans with schooling barracudas, Napoleon wrasse, packs of jacks and large rays. It's possible to climb the volcano in three hours, if conditions are favourable (it's highly active) and admire the awesome lava landscapes.

Pulau Una Una had only one place to stay when we visited, and it is a fine one: **Sanctum** (☎0812 8532 5669; www.unauna-sanctum.com; r nondiver/diver per person incl all meals 200,000/350,000Rp) has 11 lovely little rooms (all with porches, some with shared Western-style bathrooms) on a slim black-sand beach, with reasonable rates and world-class diving on tap. Expect great international and local food, served family-style. The scuba shop here has a good reputation, and snorkellers can rent gear for just 25,000Rp per day. Discounts available in the low season. Black Marlin Dive Resort, based on Pulau Kadidiri, is set to open a dive resort here too in 2016.

Togean & Katupat

Pulau Togean is large forested island, fringed by mangroves; Pulau Katupat is much smaller, and has a small village for supplies. Togean has just one place to stay (near Wakai); two other options are a five-minute boat ride from Katupat village.

Sleeping

Sunset Beach GUESTHOUSE **$$**
(☎0853 9838 1641, 0821 9919 4240; Pulau Togean; r per person incl all meals 200,000Rp) Under new ownership, Sunset Beach features a lovely dining area over a pretty beach, good food (including lots of choice for vegetarians) and a great location on a private island. The huts are very basic, however. Free boat transfers to Wakai.

Fadhila Cottages BUNGALOW **$$**
(☎0852 4100 3685; www.fadhilacottages.com; Pulau Katupat; bungalows per person incl all meals 250,000-350,000Rp) Clean wooden bungalows with terraces and hammocks line a palm-shaded beach facing either Katupat village or the ocean. There's a good PADI dive centre here and a breezy, classy restaurant area. Take a free canoe to find snorkelling spots around the island or enjoy one of Fadhila's excursions. Rates drop by 50,000Rp in the low season.

Bolilanga Cottages GUESTHOUSE **$$**
(☎0852 4100 3685; www.bolilangaresort.com; Pulau Katupat; bungalows per person incl all meals 225,000-525,000Rp) On a white-sand-beach-laden isle facing Katupat village, this family-run place is a slice of true tranquillity. Wooden bungalows (from basic to posh) with fresh-water bathrooms and mossie nets all face the turquoise sea.

Pulau Malenge

Malenge is remote and secluded, with wonderful snorkelling around the island; head to Reef 5 for the best coral and sealife.

Some locals, with the aid of NGOs, have established excellent walking trails around the mangroves and jungles to help spot the particularly diverse fauna, including macaques, tarsiers, hornbills, cuscuses and salamanders.

The main village of Malenge is also fascinating to explore; it's a traditional Bajau settlement of timber houses and has a famous kilometre-long rickety 'bridge' (actually more of a gangplank), which allows you to (almost) walk on water.

A new dive resort, **Bahia Tomini** (☎0881 238 802 777; http://bahiatomini.com), was under construction at the time of research.

Sleeping

Lestari Cottages GUESTHOUSE **$$**
(☎0852 4100 3685; www.lestari-cottages.com; bungalows per person incl all meals 150,000-200,000Rp) The setting here is spectacular, with jungle behind and a view in front of Malenge village, one of the prettiest stilt fishing villages in the archipelago. Lestari offers 10 sea-facing, rustic wooden bungalows, each with a veranda. When you're not snorkelling, you can try forest hikes and canoe excursions.

Sera Beach Cottages BUNGALOW **$$**
(☎0851 4590 6028; r per person incl all meals 175,000Rp) On the north side of Malenge, situated on a lovely white-sand beach, this newly opened place has well-built thatched bungalows and a warm vibe thanks to the chatty English-speaking manager. There are canoes for hire. A free shuttle service to Malenge is offered.

THE BAJAU SEA GYPSIES

Nomadic Bajau 'sea gypsies' still dive for trepang (sea cucumber), pearls and other commercially important marine produce, as they have done for hundreds, perhaps thousands, of years. The Bajau are hunter-gatherers who spend much of their lives on boats, travelling as families wherever they go.

There are several permanent Bajau settlements around the Togean Islands, and even some stilt villages on offshore reefs, but the itinerant character of Bajau culture survives. Newlyweds are put in a canoe and pushed out to sea to make their place in the world. When they have children, fathers dive with their three-day-old babies to introduce them to life on the sea.

Pulau Walea Kodi

Dolong is a busy fishing village, and the only settlement on the island. It's served by public boats from Malenge (12,000Rp, one hour). You'll find peace and paradise once you get to your resort.

Sifa Cottage (☎0821 9596 6721; www.waleakodi.com; cottage incl all meals 150,000-290,000Rp per person) is a remote but beautifully situated place with big, rustic wooden cottages gracing a flat, coconut-palm-covered white beach that extends to aqua blue. The house reef here is the best in the Togeans, so it's perfect for snorkellers. There's a dive centre here, too (fun dives €27). Rates drop in the low season.

Lia Beach (☎0821 9011 1340; www.pae-lia-beach.com; r incl all meals from 180,000Rp), built on eco-principles with a back-to-nature vibe, was set to open late 2015.

NORTH SULAWESI

North Sulawesi has lots to offer in a relatively condensed space. You can dive some of the world's best coral reefs at Bunaken one day, explore volcanic scenery near Tomohon the next, and visit the lowland Tangkoko-Batuangas Dua Saudara Nature Reserve and its wildlife the day after. The Bitung area's world-class muck diving (including very quirky macro life) is another huge draw.

Economic prosperity from tourism and agriculture (mostly cloves and coconuts) means that North Sulawesi is the most developed province on Sulawesi. The two largest distinct groups in the region are the Minahasans and the Sangirese, but there are many more subgroups. Dutch influence is stronger here than anywhere else in the country: the Dutch language is still spoken among the older generation, and well-to-do families often send their children to study in the Netherlands.

It's an easy region to access, with excellent flight connections from Manado to the rest of the archipeligo, and increasing air traffic to Gorontalo as well.

History

A group of independent states was established at a meeting of the linguistically diverse Minahasan peoples around AD 670 at a stone now known as Watu Pinabetengan (near Kawangkoan).

In 1677 the Dutch occupied Pulau Sangir (now Pulau Sangihe) and, two years later, a treaty with the Minahasan chiefs saw the start of Dutch domination for the next 300 years. Although relations with the Dutch were often less than cordial, and the region did not actually come under direct Dutch rule until 1870, the Dutch and Minahasans eventually became so close that the north was often referred to as the '12th province of the Netherlands'.

Christianity became a force in the early 1820s, and the wholesale conversion of the Minahasans was almost complete by 1860. Because the school curriculum was taught in Dutch, the Minahasans had an early advantage in the competition for government jobs and positions in the colonial army.

The Minahasan sense of identity became an issue for the Indonesian government after independence. The Minahasan leaders declared their own autonomous state of North Sulawesi in June 1957. The Indonesian government then bombed Manado in February 1958 and, by June, Indonesian troops had landed in North Sulawesi. Rebel leaders retreated into the mountains, and the rebellion was finally put down in mid-1961.

Gorontalo

☎0435 / POP 186,000

Gorontalo has the feel of an overgrown country town, where all the locals seem to know each other. The town features some of the best-preserved Dutch houses in Sulawesi and retains a languid colonial feel.

Gorontalo's local hero is Nani Wartabone, an anti-Dutch guerrilla, and there is a large statue of him in Lapangan Nani Wartabone, adjacent to the New Melati Hotel at Jl Wolter Monginsidi.

The city has steadily modernised in recent years, with the landmark **Gorontalo Mall** (Jl Sultan Botutihe; ⊙8am-9.30pm) dominating downtown, and several sleek new hotels opening close by.

Sights & Activities

Sights around Gorontalo are accessible by local transport. Diving is available with **Miguels Diving** (☎0852 4004 7027; www.miguelsdiving.com; Jl Yos Sudarso 218).

Lombongo Hot Springs HOT SPRING

(admission 8000Rp; ⊙8am-5pm) Seventeen kilometres east of Gorontalo, at the western edge of Bogani Nani Wartabone National Park, this large swimming pool is filled with hot-spring water. There's also a swimming hole at the foot of a 30m waterfall; it's a 3km walk past the springs.

Benteng Otanaha RUIN

FREE On the outskirts of Gorontalo this ruined Portuguese fort is on a hill overlooking Danau Limboto. The ruined remains include stone battlements and fortifications.

Sleeping

New Melati Hotel HOTEL $

(☎0435-822934; yfvelberg@yahoo.com; Jl Wolter Monginsidi 1; r incl breakfast 130,000-300,000Rp; ❄@🛜) This long-time backpacker favourite has English-speaking staff who are very well informed about transport connections. It's based around a lovely home, built in the early 1900s for the harbour master. There are three classes of rooms, from dated basic options (which could be cleaner) to very modern and inviting new choices in a two-storey block overlooking the rear garden.

Amaris Hotel HOTEL $$

(☎0435-830799; http://amarishotel.com; Jl Sultan Botutihe 37; r incl breakfast 421,000Rp; ❄🛜) This well-managed hotel offers 90 attractive, smallish rooms with clean lines and fast wi-fi that are (perhaps) short on character but big on cleanliness and comfort. It's a short walk from the Gorontalo Mall.

BOGANI NANI WARTABONE NATIONAL PARK

About 50km west of Kotamobagu, this rarely visited national park (287,115 hectares) has the highest conservation value in North Sulawesi, but it's pretty inaccessible. The park (formerly known as Dumoga-Bone) is at the headwaters of Sungai Dumoga (Dumoga River) and is a haven for rare flora and fauna. The maleo bird, a large megapode, is found in large numbers here (more than 3000 were released into the park in 2012). Other wildlife includes the *yaki* (black-crested macaque) and a species of giant fruit bat only discovered in the 1990s.

Visit the **Bogani Nani Wartabone National Park office** (☎0434-22548; Jl AKD Mongkonai; ⊙7.30am-noon & 1pm-4pm Mon-Fri), on the road to Doloduo, about 5km from central Kotamobagu, the nearest town. At this office you can buy park permits (30,000Rp per visit), pick up useful tips, look at decent trekking maps and ask lots of questions.

The area around the park entrance at Kosinggolan village has several trails, which take from one to nine hours to hike, and there are various options for overnight jaunts through the jungle if you have camping equipment. Take a regular *mikrolet* (small taxi) to Doloduo from the Serasi terminal in Kotamobagu. Then walk about 2km west (or ask the *mikrolet* driver to continue) to the ranger station at Kosinggolan, just inside the park, where you must register and pick up a compulsory guide for 100,000Rp per short hike (more for longer trips).

In Kotamobagu there are ATMs, a supermarket and several hotels. The **Hotel Ramayana** (☎0434-21188; Jl Adampe Dolot 50; s/d 70,000/110,000Rp) is recommended.

Eating & Drinking

The local delicacy is *milu siram,* a corn soup with grated coconut, fish, salt, chilli and lime. The night market has a vast number of warungs selling cheap and tasty food.

Rumah Makan Sabar INDONESIAN $
(Jl Sutoyo 31; meals from 15,000Rp; 7.30am-10pm) Boasts an attractive colonial-style terrace and is renowned for its delicious *nasi kuning* (yellow rice); its soups and sambals also hit the spot.

Getting There & Away

AIR

There are daily flights to Makassar divided between the carriers Garuda Indonesia, Batik Air, Lion Air and Sriwijaya. Wings Air flies daily to Manado and also has connections to Luwuk and Palu. Aviastar also has weekly flights to Ampana, Palu and Luwuk.

All airlines have offices at the airport; tickets can also be bought at agencies around town.

BOAT

Gorontalo has two harbours, both about 4km from the town centre: Talumolo port for the Togean Islands boats and Leato port for Pelni ferries. Both are easily accessible by *mikrolet* (small taxi) along Jl Tantu.

Every two weeks the Pelni liner *Tilongkabila* links Gorontalo with Bitung, and the *Sangiang* tackles the same route monthly. The **Pelni office** (0435-821089; cnr Jl 23 Januari & Jl Gajah Mada) is efficient and convenient.

BUS

The main bus terminal is 3km north of town and accessible by bemo, *bendi* (two person horse-drawn cart) or *ojek*. There are direct buses to Palu (160,000Rp, 18 hours) and Manado (regular/air-con 100,000/130,000Rp, nine hours), departing every hour. Most people make the Manado trip by minibus or Kijang (100,000Rp to 150,000Rp).

Getting Around

The airport is 32km west of Gorontalo. Airport buses (35,000Rp) meet flights, and shared taxis (70,000Rp) are also available; both will drop you anywhere in the city, or at either port. To get to the airport, book the same service through the airline, travel agency or your hotel.

Manado

0431 / POP 458,500

With an abundance of shopping malls and cavernous holes in the sidewalk, Manado doesn't usually register as one of North Sulawesi's highlights. It's a well serviced and friendly place, however, with more than its share of comfortable hotels and some good places to eat. Adventures lie nearby around the city at Bunaken, Tomohon, the Lembeh Strait and Tangkoko-Batuangas Dua Saudara Nature Reserve; to get to these places most travellers will have to spend a night or more in Manado.

History

In 1844 Manado was levelled by earthquakes, so the Dutch redesigned it from scratch. Fourteen years later the famous naturalist Alfred Wallace visited and described the city as 'one of the prettiest in the East'. Time hasn't been kind to the place.

Rice surpluses from Minahasa's volcanic hinterland made Manado a strategic port for European traders sailing to and from the 'Spice Islands' (Maluku). The Dutch helped unite the diverse Minahasan confederacy. By the mid-1800s, compulsory cultivation schemes were producing huge crops of cheap coffee for a Dutch-run monopoly. Many Minahasans suffered during this period, yet economic, religious and social ties with the colonists continued to intensify. Elsewhere, Minahasan mercenaries put down anti-Dutch rebellions in Java and beyond, earning them the name *anjing Belanda* (Dutch dogs).

The Japanese occupation of 1942–45 was a period of deprivation, and the Allies bombed Manado heavily in 1945. During the war of independence that followed, there was bitter division between the nationalists and those favouring Dutch-sponsored federalism, and the city was bombed (again), this time by the Indonesian military, in 1958.

Today, the development of Bitung's deep-sea port and Manado's good air links with Singapore and the rest of the nation have boosted the city's trade and tourism.

Sights & Activities

Most of the main sights lie beyond the city. The 'boulevard', Jl Piere Tendean, is a monstrous thoroughfare lined with shopping malls; it has limited coastal access.

Public Museum of North Sulawesi MUSEUM
(Museum Negeri Propinsi Sulawesi Utara; 0431-870308; Jl Supratman 72; admission 5000Rp; 8am-4pm Mon-Thu, to 11.30am Fri, 9am-2pm Sat) This museum features a large display of traditional costumes, and an exibit illustrating traditional pottery-making. There are captions in English.

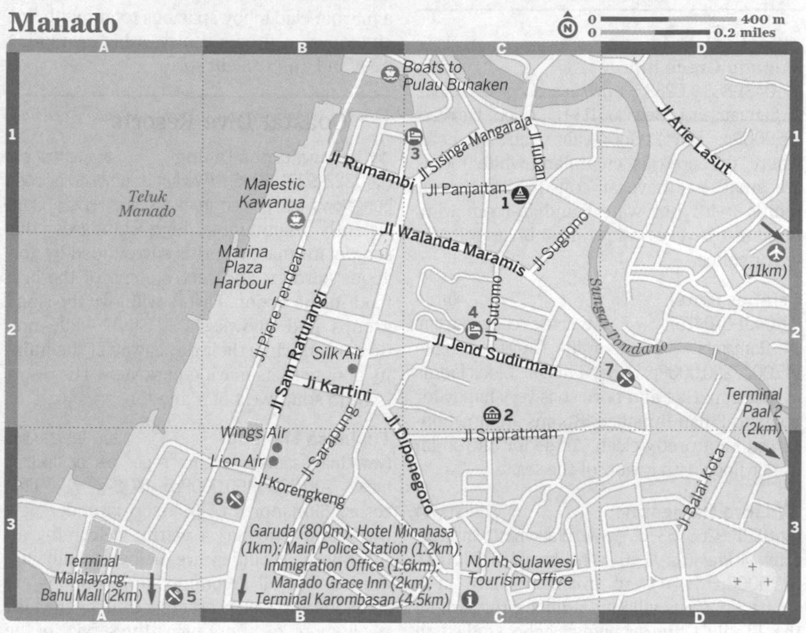

Manado

Sights

1 Kienteng Ban Hian Kong C1
2 Public Museum of North Sulawesi C2

Sleeping

3 Celebes Hotel C1
4 Sintesa Peninsula Hotel C2

Eating

5 Raja Sate A3
6 Rumah Makan Green Garden B3
7 Rumah Makan Raja Oci D2

Kienteng Ban Hian Kong BUDDHIST TEMPLE
(Jl Panjaitan) The 19th-century Kienteng Ban Hian Kong is the oldest Buddhist temple in eastern Indonesia and it has been beautifully restored. The temple hosts a spectacular festival in February (dates vary according to the lunar calendar).

Bunaken Tour Travel TOUR
(0898 443 5867; www.bunakentourtravel.com) A recommended tour company for trips around Minahasa. It works in partnership with tour guide Mikel Leitzinger, who runs Mountain View Resort in Tomohon.

Festivals & Events

Minahasans love an excuse to party. Watch out for festivals through the year.

Tai Pei Kong CULTURAL
(Feb) Chinese festival held at Kienteng Ban Hian Kong Buddhist temple.

Pengucapan Syukur CULTURAL
A harvest festival that can take place any time from June to August.

Traditional Horse & Bull Races CULTURAL
(Sep) Traditional races held in late September.

Sleeping

Most travellers choose to base themselves on Pulau Bunaken or in Tomohon, both less than an hour away; however, there are some excellent options in Manado, in all price bands.

Hotels near and on Jl Sam Ratulangi are an easy walk to food and shopping but can be noisy due to the traffic. Various dive lodges are about a 40-minute drive from town in peaceful settings.

The better budget places fill quickly, so reserve in advance.

In Town

Manado Grace Inn HOTEL $
(☎0431-888 0288; www.manadograceinn.com; Jl Samratulangi Manado 113-H; r incl breakfast 175,000Rp;) Good-value, newish hotel where the no-frills cream-and-white rooms are small but have air-con, private shower rooms (with hot water) and in-room wi-fi. Breakfast is very basic – just a bread roll and tea or coffee.

Celebes Hotel HOTEL $
(☎0431-870425; www.hotelcelebesmdo.com; Jl Rumambi 8A; r with fan/air-con from 145,000/250,000Rp;) This big block looms over the market and port, so is very handy for boats to Pulau Bunaken. Rooms are functional and kept pretty clean. Angle for one on an upper floor with a view of the sea.

★**Libra Homestay** HOMESTAY $$
(☎0821 9268 6320; www.librahomestaymanado.com; Jl Pramuka XI 16; r incl breakfast 300,000-325,000Rp;) An excellent place in a smart, spacious villa on a quiet street, where the kindly Chinese owner (who studied in London) looks after guests well. There are five rooms, all with air-con, cable TVs, desks and private bathrooms with hot water. It's in the south of the city, a five-minute walk from restaurants.

De Nearby HOTEL $$
(☎0431-833111; www.nearbyhotel.co.id; Blok C 16/17 1, Kompleks Bahu Mall, Jl Wolter Monginsidi; s/d incl breakfast 200,000/300,000Rp;) Steps from the seafront in the far south of town, this smart new boutique budget hotel offers excellent value, particularly for solo travellers. With a zany colour scheme and small but well-designed rooms it's a good choice. There are a few seafood restaurants close by.

Hotel Minahasa HOTEL $$
(☎0431-874871; www.hotelminahasa.com; Jl Sam Ratulangi 199; r with fan/air-con from 332,000/540,000Rp;) Flower-filled grounds stretch up to a hilltop villa, luxurious pool and fitness centre with city views. Fan rooms are basic so you may be tempted to upgrade to a much more elegant, superior room with a terrace and a view.

Sintesa Peninsula Hotel HOTEL $$$
(☎0431-855008; www.sintesapeninsulahotel.com; Jl Jend Sudirman; r from US$78;) A gleaming white fortress on a hill in the middle of town, the Sintesa has all bases covered: a marble-clad lobby, spacious rooms with fine city views, a fitness centre, a big swimming pool and an excellent spa.

Coastal Dive Resorts

★**Lumbalumba Diving** DIVE RESORT $$$
(☎0822 9291 9056; www.lumbalumbadiving.com; bungalows per person from €37.50;) Consistently maintaining high standards, this serene, intimate resort is surrounded by gorgeous gardens and serves some of the best food in the region. Divers will love the small groups and knowlegeable staff, while non divers can while their days away at the infinity pool with its marine-park view. The resort is 17km southwest of Manado.

Thalassa Manado DIVE RESORT $$$
(www.thalassamanado.com; r per person incl all meals 700,000-1,100,000Rp;) This resort 6km north of Manado is under new ownership and has a warm, welcoming atmosphere. Facilities are being steadily upgraded, but all accommodation options are spacious and well presented. Chill by the lush pool when you're not using the service of the professionally run PADI five-star dive centre. Consult its website for dive packages.

Bahowo Lodge GUESTHOUSE $$$
(☎0819 404 5261; www.bahowolodge.com; Bahowo Village; s/d incl breakfast & dinner from US$75/100;) Offering a personal touch, this British-owned place is a clean, modern lodge in Bahowo village on the coast 15km north of Manado. Stylish rooms have tiled floors, some have sea views and there's a lovely guest lounge. The lodge gets rave reviews for its home-cooked food, including lots of local specialities. Diving and snorkelling trips are organised with a neighbouring resort.

Eating

Adventurous Minahasan cuisine can be found around Manado. Get a taste for *rica-rica,* a spicy stir-fry made with *ayam* (chicken) or *babi* (pork). *Bubur tinotuan* (corn porridge) and fresh seafood are local specialities worth looking out for. You may also come across r.w. (pronounced 'air weh'; dog) on some menus. Note there are significant animal-welfare issues associated with the dog-meat trade.

Along Jl Sam Ratulangi, the main road running north–south, there are upmarket restaurants and supermarkets. Most of the city's malls have extensive food courts, including Bahu Mall.

Rumah Makan Green Garden CHINESE, INDONESIAN $
(Jl Sam Ratulangi 170; meals 20,000-50,000Rp; ⌚8am-midnight) Popular Indo-Chinese restaurant with excellent pork dishes (try it barbecued or go for the pork belly), as well as good seafood, fresh juices and Bintang beer.

Rumah Makan Raja Oci INDONESIAN $
(Jl Jend Sudirman 85; meals 25,000-40,000Rp; ⌚8am-10pm) This authentic *rumah makan* packs in the locals for its *ikan oci* (barbecued small fish), which are served with a spicy Minahasan sauce known as *dabu-dabu* (made of tomatoes, shallots and fresh chilli).

★ **Raja Sate** INTERNATIONAL, INDONESIAN $$
(☎0431-332-7380; www.rajasate.com; Jl Pierre Tendean 39; meals from 40,000Rp; ⌚11.30am-11pm Mon-Sat, 6-10.30pm Sun; ❄📶) Rightly renowned for its *sate* (you can't go wrong with a mixed plate that includes prawns, squid, chicken, beef and goat), but it also does great curries and even New Zealand steaks; everything is excellent. Air-con dining rooms are available if you book ahead.

Information

ATMs and banks are clustered along Jl Sam Ratulangi.

Immigration Office (☎0431-841688; Jl 17 Agustus; ⌚7am-noon & 1-4pm Mon-Fri) Visa extensions take around five days to process and typically involve three visits.

Main Police Station (☎emergencies 110, enquiries 0431-852162; Jl 17 Agustus) Main police station.

North Sulawesi Tourism Office (☎0431-852723; Jl Diponegoro 111; ⌚8am-2pm Mon-Sat) You can get a map and a few leaflets here.

Rumah Sakit Umum (☎0431-853191; Jl Monginsidi; ⌚24hr) The general hospital is about 4.5km from town and includes a decompression chamber.

Getting There & Away

AIR

Tickets for domestic flights often cost about the same at travel agencies as they do online.

A number of airlines have offices in town. **XpressAir** (www.expressair.biz) and **Batik Air** (www.batikair.com) also fly to Manado.

Garuda (☎0431-877737; Jl Sam Ratulangi 212; ⌚8.30am-6pm) Flies from Manado to Denpasar, Jakarta, Makassar, Sorong, Surabaya and Ternate.

Lion Air (☎0431-847000; Jl Sam Ratulangi; ⌚9am-6pm Mon-Sat) Flies from Manado to Balikpapan, Bandung, Denpasar, Jakarta, Makassar and Surabaya.

Silk Air (☎0431-863744; Jl Sarapung; ⌚9am-6pm Mon-Sat) Flies from Manado to Singapore.

Sriwijaya Air (☎0431-837688; Ruko Bahu Mall, Blok S/18, Jl Wolter Monginsidi; ⌚8am-6.30pm) Flies from Manado to Makassar and Ternate.

Wings Air (☎0431-847000; Jl Sam Ratulangi; ⌚9am-6pm Mon-Sat) Flies from Manado to Gorontolo, Sorong and Ternate.

BOAT

All Pelni boats use the deep-water port of Bitung, 55km from Manado. There's no Pelni office in Manado but you can get information and purchase tickets from numerous travel agents around the harbour.

Speed ferries operate daily to Siau (160,000Rp, four hours) and on to Tahuna (180,000Rp, 6½ hours) in the Sangihe-Talaud Islands. Tickets and information are available from **Majestic Kawanua** (p696).

There are also local boats to Maluku. Tickets are available from the stalls outside the port.

Boats to Bunaken Island leave from a harbour near Pasar Jengki fish market.

BUS

There are three reasonably orderly terminals for long-distance buses and the local *mikrolet*.

- **Terminal Karombasan** (5km south of the city) Connections to Tomohon (9000Rp) and other places south of Manado.
- **Terminal Malalayang** (far south of the city) Buses to Kotamobagu (55,000Rp) and Gorontalo (from 100,000Rp, nine hours).
- **Terminal Paal 2** (eastern end of Jl Martadinata) Varied public transport runs to Bitung (11,000Rp) and to the airport (5000Rp).

Getting Around

TO/FROM THE AIRPORT

Mikrolet from Sam Ratulangi International Airport go to Terminal Paal 2 (6000Rp), where you can change to a *mikrolet* for elsewhere. There are also four daily air-conditioned buses (30,000Rp) to/from Jl Piere Tendean. Fixed-price taxis cost around 75,000Rp from the airport to the city (13km).

PUBLIC TRANSPORT

Manado's *mikrolet* are everywhere; fares cost 3800Rp anywhere in town. Those with 'Wanea' on the window sign heading south on Jl Sam Ratulangi will go to Terminal Karombasan. Most *mikrolet* heading north go through Pasar 45 and past the Pasar Jengki fish market, but some go directly to Terminal Paal 2 along Jl Jend Sudirman. *Mikrolet* heading to Terminal Malalayang go down Jl Pierre Tendean.

For a taxi, call **Blue Bird** (☎0431-861234; ⏲24hr); cars all have meters. A 2km ride is about 15,000Rp.

Pulau Bunaken

☎0431

This tiny, coral-fringed isle is North Sulawesi's top tourist destination, yet it has managed to maintain a rootsy island soul. Tourist accommodation is spread out along two beaches. Other than that, the island belongs to the islanders; these friendly folk have a seemingly endless reserve of authentically warm smiles. There are no hassles here, just laid-back beachy bliss.

Most people come to Bunaken for the diving. The marine biodiversity is extraordinary, with more than 300 types of coral and 3000 species of fish, abundant corals and sponges and phenomenally colourful life on vertical walls. The 808-hectare island is part of the 75,265-hectare **Bunaken Manado Tua Marine National Park** (Taman Laut Bunaken Manado Tua), which includes Manado Tua (Old Manado), the dormant volcano that can be seen from Manado and climbed in about four hours; Nain and Mantehage islands; and Pulau Siladen, which also has accommodation options.

With the developing and expanding city of Manado right next door, Bunaken is becoming more and more accessible. Within two hours of arriving in Manado from Singapore or most parts of Indonesia, you can be in a bamboo beach shack on Bunaken watching the sunset. Unfortunately, this proximity also means that the huge amounts of garbage generated by the city can sweep onto Pantai Liang, turning the picturesque tropical beach into a refuse heap. The scarcity of fresh water has limited the island's development, and villagers must import their drinking water from Manado.

Prices (from accommodation to beer) are higher than in mainland Sulawesi and some resorts discriminate against nondivers, either by charging higher accommodation prices or by turning them away.

There's nothing that could be called a road on the whole island. A rough, rutted track of concrete paving, dirt and sand loops around the island; it can be (just about) tackled on a scooter.

Pulau Bunaken

0 — 500 m
0 — 0.25 miles

Tanjung Parigi
Pantai Liang
Pantai Pangalisang
Bunaken
SULAWESI SEA

Pulau Bunaken

Sleeping

1 Bunaken Island Resort A2
2 Cakalang Bunaken B2
3 Cha Cha B1
4 Daniel's Resort B3
5 Froggies A1
6 Happy Gecko A1
7 Living Colours B2
8 Lorenso's Beach Garden B2
9 Novita Homestay B3
10 Panorama Dive Resort A2
11 Two Fish B2
12 Village Bunaken B2

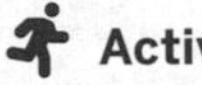

Activities

Most people go to Bunaken to dive or snorkel, but it's a lovely island to walk around too, and has very friendly villages and beautiful scenery.

If you're on the island during the second to third week of September, you'll be able to catch the **Bunaken Festival**, which features arts and cultural performances by all the ethnic groups around North Sulawesi.

DIVING & SNORKELLING AROUND PULAU BUNAKEN

Bunaken is uniquely surrounded by deep water with strong, nutrient-laden currents, while having a mangrove ecosystem that protects much of the beaches and corals from erosion; this makes it one of the best diving and snorkelling spots in the world. Beyond drop-offs you'll find caves and valleys full of brightly coloured sponges, thriving corals and biblical numbers of fish. It's very rare *not* to see several large hawksbill and green turtles on every dive, and you'll also encounter rays and sharks.

DIY snorkellers on the east coast will find the front of Lorenso's Beach Garden is an easy place to get in the water. Over on the west side, you'll find Likuan, a spectacular coral wall just off Pantai Liang.

Most guesthouses, resorts and dive centres have maps of all the sites around Bunaken; where you go will most likely depend on the current conditions. If you're staying somewhere without a dive centre, it's easy to shop around for outings with a nearby place.

Well-worn snorkelling equipment can be rented from most homestays for about 50,000Rp per day, but it is often worth paying a little more to rent some quality equipment from one of the dive centres.

Trips around Bunaken and nearby islands will cost around €35 per dive, with PADI Open Water courses about €375. Snorkellers can go along with the dive boats for around €5 per person.

At the time of research there were no dodgy dive schools operating in Bunaken. Still, you should always check the state of equipment and ask about the centre's safety procedures before you commit.

Dive Sites Around Bunaken

Pulau Bunaken's profile is incredible: it rises abruptly out of the big blue and its underwater topography is of vertical walls of coral. Neighbouring islands are no less impressive. Off the mainland there is muck diving and a wreck. Here are some dive-site highlights:

Likuan There are three dive sites on this remarkable coral wall, which plummets from the shallows into dark oblivion. Reef sharks and lots of turtles are typically encountered.

Fukui Point For sheer numbers of fish, this site is outstanding. It's something of a cleaning station for large fish and there are also garden eels and several giant clams.

Molas Wreck This is a huge Dutch cargo ship covered with soft corals and sponges. Because of its depth (24m to 40m), it's for advanced divers only.

Tanjung Kopi On the northern side of Manado Tua, with schools of barracudas, batfish and jacks; an advanced dive due to strong currents.

Celah Celah Great for macro life including ghost pipefish, nudibranchs and pygmy seahorses. Very popular with photographers.

Montehage Dramatic diving with barracuda, rays, Napoleon wrasse and schools of bumphead parrotfish. Hammerhead sharks are occasionally encountered, too.

Mandolin Huge gorgonians and a forest of whip corals; look out for Napoleon wrasse.

Sleeping & Eating

There are plenty of budget and midrange resorts on Bunaken, but no luxurious hideaways, so if you want serious comfort, stick with the mainland resorts or go to Pulau Siladen. Most rooms include at least a fan and a mosquito net and most places throw in transfers to and from the jetty in Bunaken village, or in some cases to the mainland.

Pantai Pangalisang

Forming the east coast, Pantai Pangalisang is a stretch of white sand tucked behind the mangroves, with some outrageous snorkelling just beyond. The beach all but disappears at high tide.

Lorenso's Beach Garden GUESTHOUSE $$
(0852 5697 3345; www.lorensobunaken.com; r per person incl all meals from €32;) Lorenso's

is an excellent choice for travellers; it has a good selection of accommodation on a pretty mangrove-lined bay, and there's world-class snorkelling offshore. The staff are helpful, there's a good communal vibe, and when the tin-can band rocks up, great live music. Walk-in rates (from 250,000Rp per person) are well below the offical prices quoted here.

Cakalang Bunaken GUESTHOUSE $$
(0811 431 0208; http://cakalang-bunaken.com; s/d incl all meals 425,000/650,000Rp;) Intimate new Dutch-owned place on a small cove with four attractive, spacious rooms and perhaps the fastest wi-fi on Bunaken. There's a good dive school and meals are excellent.

Novita Homestay GUESTHOUSE $$
(r per person incl all meals 150,000Rp) An authentic local experience right in Bunaken village (at the northern end of the island). Owned and operated by Vita, a terrific cook, who prepares filling, delicious local food.

Daniel's Resort GUESTHOUSE $$
(0823 4949 0270; r per person incl all meals from 230,000Rp;) Run by young party-minded locals, Daniel's is about as budget as it gets on Bunaken. Some of the creaky old wooden cottages are in need of renovation, but others are in decent shape and the garden setting is relaxing. Note that nondivers can be evicted during busy times.

★**Living Colours** DIVE RESORT $$$
(0812 430 6401; www.livingcoloursdiving.com; cottages per person incl all meals from €50;) This wonderful Finnish-owned place enjoys a lovely hillside setting. Its elegant wooden bungalows boast enormous terraces and spacious hot-water bathrooms. There's a little bar (the Safety Stop) by the shore, and meals are served in an open-sided restaurant above the bay. Living Colours' five-star PADI dive school is particularly well organised.

Village Bunaken RESORT $$$
(0813 4075 7268; www.bunakenvillage.com; cottages per person incl all meals from €50;) With beautiful shady grounds and Javanese-Balinese style, this is one of Bunaken's swankier options; well-maintained cottages have stylish features and there's a spa. Rates are good value given the tropical chic on offer, and its dive school gets good reports.

Two Fish DIVE RESORT $$$
(0811 432805; www.twofishdivers.com; r/cottages per person incl all meals from €25/45;) A well-run dive resort, with attractive cottages dotted around delightful grounds that include a pool. The professional, eco-aware dive centre is one of the best in North Sulawesi, with a maximum of four divers per guide, five boats and technical diving.

Cha Cha RESORT $$$
(0813 5600 3736; www.bunakenchacha.com; cottages/villas per person incl all meals from US$100/120;) In splendid isolation on the northeastern tip of the island, Cha Cha has an intimate atmosphere and impressive attention to detail. Accommodation (three-night minimum stay) has expanded in recent years to include luxurious villas, and the food gets rave reviews.

Pantai Liang

The beach at Pantai Liang has suffered from considerable erosion and rising sea levels, and has thus become a svelte though pleasant strip of white sand. Bungalows are close together, and there's some beachside action such as seaside food and trinket vendors. However, the beach is a sorry sight when rubbish washes in from Manado.

The beach just south of Pantai Liang is a protected turtle nesting ground, so keep off even though it looks inviting.

Happy Gecko BUNGALOW $$
(0852 9806 4906; www.happygeckoresort.com; s/d per person incl all meals €32/24;) Tumbling down a hillside at the northern end of Pantai Liang, these cute little cottages are a good deal for backpackers, with verandas, bamboo furniture and private bathrooms. Dives cost just €25 each.

Panorama Dive Resort BUNGALOW $$
(0813 4021 7027, 0813 4021 7306; www.bunakendiving.co; cottage per person incl all meals 250,000-350,000Rp;) A family-run place at the southern end of the beach, this large hillside complex has wooden bungalows with decks and commanding views. There's a good dive shop here too; fun dives cost 420,000Rp.

WORTH A TRIP

THE BANGKA ISLANDS: MINING VERSUS THE ENVIRONMENT

Strategically located off the northern tip of Sulawesi between Pulau Bunaken and the Lembeh Strait, the Bangka Islands are part of what makes this region a dive haven. This is where to go for pinnacle diving, and it's also a prime spot for big fauna: dolphins, manta rays and at least nine species of whale all migrate through these waters around March and April and again in August and September. At all times you're likely to see tuna, batfish, jacks and barracuda. There are often fairly strong currents but these make the plentiful soft corals bloom. Away from the pinnacles, you'll find pygmy seahorses, nudibranchs and leaf fish in the coral gardens.

But this pristine marine environment is threatened by the attentions of a Chinese company, Mikgro Metal Perdana, which commenced iron exploration on Pulau Bangka in 2012, and has subsequently constructed a concrete pier and roads. Locals believe this is the start of a massive mining operation and allege that about 70 Chinese workers are illegally working on Bangka, using heavy machinery.

Large-scale mining could damage not only the island's ecology but stir up underwater sediment and potentially threaten the coral life of the entire region. A legal case is ongoing. Locals believe Indonesian environmental laws should prohibit mining in Bangka, and they won a constitutional law court case in July 2015. You can keep up with developments via Twitter: @SaveBangka.

For now at least, it's still a phenomenal place to visit. Dive centres on Bunaken and Lembeh often dive the Bangka Islands, and you can also choose to stay at one of the increasing number of dive resorts on the islands. We recommend the following:

Mimpi Indah (☎0811 432264; www.mimpiindah.com; s/d per person incl all meals €49/64; 📶) An intimate place with a personal touch set in a former coconut plantation, Mimpi Inda has large thatched bungalows facing a pretty beach. There's an in-house dive school that employs good local guides.

Blue Bay Divers (www.blue-bay-divers.de; dive packages per day from €100) On the beautiful tiny island of Sahuang, across from Pulau Bangka, the German-owned Blue Bay Divers has beachfront bungalows and offers small-dive groups. Prices include three meals and two dives per day.

Froggies DIVE RESORT **$$**
(☎0812 430 1356; www.divefroggies.com; cottage per person incl all meals €27-42; ❄📶) One of the first dive centres and still going strong, with a fine beachfront location and 16 cottages (some with two bedrooms) all with terraces.

Bunaken Island Resort RESORT **$$$**
(☎0813 4021 7027; www.bunaken.nl; bungalows per person incl all meals €79; ❄📶) A hillside resort overlooking the sea; huge polished-wood bungalows sport hardwood furniture and rain showers in the bathrooms. The restaurant has fantastic views. High-season rates quoted here are indeed steep, but do drop.

Pulau Siladen

Three kilometres north of Pulau Bunaken and the smallest island of the archipelago, Siladen boasts wonderful white-sand beaches (though rubbish is an issue) and a wall of gorgeous corals.

Tante Martha Homestay GUESTHOUSE **$$**
(☎0852 4009 7488; bungalow per person incl all meals 270,000Rp) This ramshackle place offers very basic bungalows on a simply sublime beach, with great snorkelling steps away. Martha is a fine cook.

Bobocha Cottages Siladen COTTAGE **$$$**
(☎0853 4161 5044; www.bobochasiladen.com; cottage per person incl all meals €65; 📶) Beautifully designed cottages in a lovely beachside setting. The owner, Sarah, creates inventive home-cooked food. Located on the southwest side of the island, with sunset views.

Siladen Resort & Spa DIVE RESORT **$$$**
(☎0811 430 0641; www.siladen.com; r from €265; ❄📶🏊) Luxurious resort with 17 sumptuously furnished villas that boast all mod cons; the older villas are directly on the beach. Facilities include a (saltwater) lagoon pool, an indulgent spa and a PADI dive centre.

Tanta Moon BUNGALOW $$$

(☎0431-364-3859; www.tantamoon.ru; d incl all meals & transfers €65; ❄📶) Right on the water's edge these wood villas are packed closely together but are beautifully appointed. The hotel's chef is excellent. There's no dive centre.

ℹ Getting There & Away

Public boats leave for Bunaken village and Pulau Siladen from Manado (30,000Rp, one hour, Monday to Saturday) at about 3pm, from the harbour near Pasar Jengki fish market in Manado. They return between 7am and 8am from Monday to Saturday. There are also several unscheduled boats (which leave when full) at other times of the day, and you can charter a boat for 250,000Rp.

From the boat landing in Bunaken village you can walk or hire an *ojek* (around 10,000Rp to 25,000Rp) to your homestay. Local boats charge 60,000Rp (one-way) for the 20-minute trip between Bunaken and Siladen .

The more upmarket options on Bunaken offer on-demand boat shuttles to/from Manado for their clients. Otherwise, most guesthouses can help you charter a boat (often small and rickety) for around 250,000Rp.

When conditions are rough, the public boat stops running, but private boats will usually make the shorter, half-hour crossing between Bunaken and the mainland.

Tomohon

☎0431 / POP 96,500

Tomohon is the name for a number of small highland towns, surrounded by forests and volcanic peaks, that have merged together. A pleasant, cool respite from Manado, the area has a stunning setting. It's popular with city folk on weekends; for travellers, it's an excellent base to explore the **Minahasa region**, and for hiking, biking and birdwatching.

Sleeping

★**Mountain View Resort** COTTAGES $$

(☎0431-315-8666; www.mountainviewtomohon.com; Jl Kali-Kinilow; cottages incl breakfast 375,000-685,000Rp; @📶) Managed by a knowledgeable German who's spent decades guiding tours in Indonesia, this charming place has fine wooden cottages with attractive bathrooms, set around a pretty garden. The restaurant serves international and local food, and 'early bird' breakfasts for birdwatchers and hikers. There's a small spa and kids' play area. Follow the signs from 'Kinilow', 5km before Tomohon, on the road to Manado. It's on a side road off the highway.

Cekakak Hostel HOSTEL $$

(☎0431-315 8666; www.cekakak-hostel.blogspot.com; Jl Kali-Kinilow; dm/d incl breakfast 140,000/290,000Rp; @📶) This fine new hostel offers

MINAHASA ACTIVITIES

A temperate climate and spectacular volcanic landscapes means the Minahasa region is rapidly developing as an adrenaline centre. Tomohon makes a perfect base for exploring. Possible activities and prices (per person, mimimum two people required) include the following:

➡ **Gunung Lokon crater lake trek** (half day, 290,000Rp) Follow an old lava flow to the rim of the crater.

➡ **Gunung Soputan volcano trek** (full day, 900,000Rp) To the highest peak in North Sulawesi, which is an active volcano.

➡ **Gunung Klabat volcano trek** (two days, 1,500,000Rp) Around five hours to ascend, with wonderful views of Manado city.

➡ **White-water rafting, Nimanga River** (half day, 875,000Rp) Starts near Tomohon; 25 rapids and a good chance to spot wildlife.

➡ **Exploring Tekaan Telu waterfall** (half day; 290,000Rp) There are four seperate drops of up to 60m; abseiling and canyoning is possible, too.

➡ **Birdwatching Gunung Mahawu** (one day guided tour, from 600,000Rp) Follow in the footsteps of Alfred Russel Wallace and spot flycatchers, and perhaps a scaly kingfisher.

Mountain View Resort in Tomohon is a recommended tour operator, specialising in bespoke trips.

TOMOHON'S MACABRE MARKET

It's said that the Minahasan people will eat anything on four legs, apart from the table and chairs, and nowhere is this more evident than at Tomohon's daily market. Visiting the market (which is right next to the *mikrolet* terminal) is a slaughterhouse-like experience, with dead and alive dogs, pigs, rats and bats all on display. Sadly the market is known for displays of animal cruelty, and is likely to distress visitors with the slightest interest in animal welfare.

two good-quality dorms and a pleasant, tranquil setting in a lush valley. You'll find excellent tours and hiking information, and camping gear, mountain bikes and scooters are available for hire. Follow the signs from 'Kinilow', about 5km before Tomohon, on the road to Manado. It's on a side road, a few hundred metres from the highway.

Highland Resort RESORT **$$**
(☎0431-353333; www.highlandresort.info; Jl Kali-Kinilow; r incl breakfast €35-60; 📶) Located on a quiet lane off the Manado–Tomohon road, with a large collection of spacious, well-equipped wooden bungalows in lush grounds. The restaurant was closed at the time of research. Follow the signs from 'Kinilow', about 5km before Tomohon, on the road to Manado.

Onong's Palace B&B **$$**
(☎0431-315-7090; www.tomohon-onong.com; Jl Kali-Kinilow; r incl breakfast from 350,000Rp; @📶) More 'place' than 'palace', Onong's has large bungalows with big decks and ageing Bali-style design details, but enjoys an attractive, shady hillside location. It's very tranquil here (except for the call to prayer of the local mosque). Follow the signs from 'Kinilow', about 5km before Tomohon, on the road to Manado. It's on a side road, a few hundred metres from the highway.

Eating

Minahasan cuisine is served in a string of restaurants on a cliff overlooking Manado, just a few kilometres before Tomohon.

Rumah Makan MTV INDONESIAN **$**
(Jl Raya Tomohon; meals 7500-22,000Rp; ⏰7am-10pm; 📶) Half-way between Tomohon and Kinilow, this clean, busy dining hall has a long menu of local favourites including *bakso* (meatball soup) and noodles.

Food Market MARKET **$**
(⏰noon-7pm) In the town centre, Tomohon's daily food market has stalls offering lots of local specialities.

ℹ Getting There & Around

Mikrolet travel regularly to Tomohon (9000Rp, one hour) from Terminal Karombasan in Manado. From the terminal in Tomohon, *mikrolet* head to Manado, and *mikrolet* and buses go to Tondano and various other towns. A good way to see local sights in little time is to charter a *mikrolet* or a (more comfortable, but expensive) taxi.

Hotels rent motorbikes for 150,000Rp per day (including petrol).

Around Tomohon

Vulcanic **Gunung Lokon** (1580m) contains a simmering crater lake of varying hues. You can hike to it from Tomohon in about three hours, with another hour to reach the peak. However, it's *highly active,* and it's essential to check out its current status; ask at your hotel. You should also report to the **Vulcanology Centre** (Kantor Dinas Gunung Berapi; ☎0431-351076; Jl Kakashashen Tiga; ⏰7am-5pm), roughly 3km from the centre of Tomohon, which is worth a visit in person for its maps and photographs (but the staff do not speak English).

For more volcano thrills, you can drive almost all the way to the top of **Gunung Mahawu**, where you'll be rewarded with views over the whole region and into a 180m-wide, 140m-deep sulphuric crater lake, which you can walk around in less than an hour. There's no public transport to the volcano. This place gets swarmed by locals on the weekends.

There are numerous other places to explore from Tomohon, accessible by *mikrolet.* **Danau Linow**, a small, highly sulphurous lake that changes colours with the light, is home to extensive birdlife. Take a *mikrolet* to Sonder, get off at Lahendong and walk 1.5km to the lake.

Danau Tondano is a huge lake fringed with pretty villages, a small hot-spring-fed swimming pool, and some fish farms which you are welcome to visit.

WORTH A TRIP

TASIKOKI WILDLIFE RESCUE

About 9km southwest of Bitung, **Tasikoki Wildlife Rescue** (☎0857 5747 1090; www.tasikoki.org;) is an entirely volunteer-run organisation that rescues and cares for animals confiscated from smugglers. Goals are to rehabilitate the animals and release them back into the wild. You can make a day visit to the centre (donations appreciated); stay in the very comfortable ecolodge (per person including three vegetarian meals per day from US$70); or sign on longer as a volunteer. Note: if you turn up unannounced you will be curtly sent on your way.

There are more than 200 animals of 40 different species (including sun bears and sea eagles) at the centre, and during a visit you'll learn about the illegal animal trade and the animals themselves.

Bitung

☎0438 / POP 196,000

Bitung is the chief regional port in North Sulawesi and home to many factories. Despite its spectacular setting, the town is unattractive, so most travellers make for Manado or nearby Pulau Lembeh as soon as possible.

Regardless of what time you arrive by boat in Bitung, there will be buses going to Manado.

There's a selection of hotels in town and lots of *rumah makan* in the town centre and near the port. All the dive lodges are either on Pulau Lembeh or along the Lembeh Strait.

Getting There & Away

Buses and shared cars leave regularly from Terminal Paal 2 in Manado (11,000Rp, 1½ hours). Drivers stop at Terminal Mapalus, just outside Bitung, from where you can catch another *mikrolet* (10 minutes) into town or to the port.

The port is in the centre of Bitung, and home to a **Pelni** (☎0438-35818; ⏲7am-noon & 1-4pm Mon-Fri) office. Useful Pelni ferries include the *Tilongkabila*, which sails up and down the coast of Sulawesi to ports including Gorontalo, Luwuk, Kendari, Bau Bau and Makassar. The *Sangiang* sails to Ternate and ports in Malaku every two weeks.

Pulau Lembeh & the Lembeh Strait

The Lembeh Strait between Bitung and the large island of Pulau Lembeh is world famous for its muck diving and now has around a dozen scuba centres. There are also some reef dives, five wrecks for exploring, and fantastic night dives lit by phosphorescence.

Lembeh tends to attract hardcore divers from all over the world, including many photographers and geeky types intent on ticking off long lists of the bizarre sea critters that live here in profound numbers. Frankly, above land the physical environment isn't particularly attractive: the endless flow of container ships and close proximity to the ugly port of Bitung doesn't add up to a conventional holiday location. But if you've any interest in macro life it's well worth a dive or two here.

Two-tank dives cost around €70 and PADI Open Water Diver courses are usually about €375.

Sleeping & Eating

As Lembeh's fame grows, so does the number of dive resorts. All are set in their own secluded bays, but without your own boat it's near-impossible to travel between them and there's little to do besides dive.

NAD DIVE RESORT $$$

(☎0813 4026 2850; www.nad-lembeh.com; three-night packages per person incl five dives & all meals from US$395;) This easy-going place is moderately priced (for Lembeh). It is very well set up for anyone with an interest in dive photography, as one guide is assigned per two divers. House reef dives are free. Choose from stylish, attractive, recently renovated rooms or sea-view bungalows. There's a small dark-sand beach out front.

Black Sand Dive Retreat DIVE RESORT $$$

(☎0811 437736; www.blacksanddive.com; s/d per person incl all meals €125/100;) Enjoys a serene location on the mainland bay and is very well set up, including with a Nitrox facility and a dedicated camera room. It's a boutique operation; you'll get plenty of personalised attention and the owner is particularly passionate about local wildlife.

Lembeh Resort DIVE RESORT $$$

(☎0438-550-3139; www.lembehresort.com; cottages per person incl all meals from US$125;

DON'T MISS

WEIRD & WILD CRITTERS OF THE LEMBEH STRAIT

For the uninitiated, welcome to an alien world on our very own planet. The wonderful creatures that inhabit these murky depths are much admired by underwater photographers and have probably inspired more than a few movie monsters. Here's just a sample of what you may find:

- **Hairy frogfish** (*Antennarius striatus*) Camouflaged to look like a rock, covered in whispy-coral-like hairs and with a frown only the keenest diver could love, these guys are best known for the built-in appendage on their forehead, which they dangle like a worm to draw in prey. They don't swim like normal fish, but walk on their fins.
- **Mimic octopus** (*Thaumoctopus mimicus*) This recently discovered underwater thespian can convincingly imitate more than 15 other animals including sea snakes, crabs, stingrays and jellyfish. It does this by contorting its body into a new shape, changing colours then mimicking the behaviour of said species.
- **Pygmy seahorse** (*Hippocampus bargibanti*) Less than 2cm tall, these hard-to-spot cuties have the same texture and colour as the fan corals on which they live.

❄@📶🏊) This Balinese-style resort gets top marks for service, and has many returning customers. The pool area, strewn with day beds and loungers, is gorgeous, and you'll find a spa and plenty of nondive tours on offer.

Tangkoko-Batuangas Dua Saudara Nature Reserve

With 8800 hectares of forest bordered by a sandy coastline and offshore coral gardens, Tangkoko is one of the most impressive and accessible nature reserves in Indonesia. The park is home to black macaques, cuscuses and tarsiers, maleo birds and endemic red-knobbed hornbills, among other fauna, and rare types of rainforest flora. Tangkoko is also home to a plethora of midges, called *gonones*, which bite and leave victims scratching furiously for days afterwards. Always wear long trousers, tucked into thick socks, and covered shoes, and take plenty of insect repellent. Sadly, parts of the park are falling victim to encroachment by local communities, but money generated from visitors might help stave that off. Bring plenty of cash as there are no local ATMs.

Sights & Activities

Entrance to the park is 100,000Rp per person; guides (mandatory) cost 70,000Rp per half-day. Most people arrive at the park entrance at Batuputih in the afternoon, and take a guided afternoon/evening walk to see tarsiers (when sightings are nearly guaranteed). Morning walks are better for birdlife. Consider staying longer to enjoy the gorgeous beach setting at Batuputih and to take a variety of other tours available, including **dolphin-spotting and snorkelling tours** (full day up to 4 people 700,000Rp), and **birdwatching** (full day 350,000Rp) or **fishing tours** (5hr for up to 4 people 750,000Rp). All tours and walks can be arranged at your guesthouse, which will invariably be swarming with guides.

Sleeping & Eating

You'll find several guesthouses in and around Batuputih village, but there's nothing in the way of luxury.

★Tangkoko Hill GUESTHOUSE $$
(☎0813 4030 2444; www.tangkokohill.com; r incl all meals 400,000Rp; ❄) About 1km inland from the village, this lovely new place is the best option in the area, with hyper-clean rooms, quality mattresses, desks and TVs. The genial owner speaks good English and fine local food is served in the attractive dining room.

Dove Villas GUESTHOUSE $$
(☎0813 5624 5160; www.tangkokodovevillas.com; d incl breakfast 350,000Rp) At Dove Villas you get your own thatched, spacious villa with fan, mosquito net and cold-water bathroom. It's very friendly and serves good food. Located 8km south of the park entrance.

Tarsius Homestay GUESTHOUSE $$
(☎0813 5622 5545; Batuputih village; r per person incl all meals 150,000Rp; ❄📶) Clean, pleasant rooms, some with attached bathrooms and air-con. It's family run, superfriendly, and food portions are ample and tasty. Wi-fi is not great.

SANGIHE-TALAUD ISLANDS

Strewn across the sea between Indonesia and the southern Philippines are the volcanic island groups of Sangihe (also called Sangir) and Talaud. There are 77 islands, of which 56 are inhabited, with a total population of 224,000. Spice cultivation (vanilla, nutmeg and cloves) is a key industry. The two capitals are Tahuna, on Sangihe Besar, and Melonguane, in the Talaud group. Other major settlements are Lirung, on Pulau Salibabu, and Pulau Siau, which has a busy port.

The islands offer dozens of unspoilt sandy beaches, a few crumbling Portuguese forts, several volcanoes to climb, many caves and waterfalls to explore, and some superb diving and snorkelling (bring your own gear). Transport connections to the islands have improved a lot in recent years, and there are hotels, guesthouses and simple beach resorts, as well as ATMs and internet cafes in the main towns.

Speed ferries operate daily from Manado to Siau (160,000Rp, four hours) and on to Tahuna (180,000Rp, 6½ hours). Tickets and information are available from **Majestic Kawanua** (☎0851 0540 5499; majestickawanua@gmail.com; Komplek Marina Plaza, Jl Piere Tendean; ⏲8am-5pm) in Manado.

Wings Air flies from Manado to Tahuna (474,000Rp, 50 minutes, four weekly) and to Melonguane (595,000Rp, one hour, daily except Sunday). An airport is also under construction in Siau.

Nirwana Sangihe (☎0813 5434 2869; www.nirwanasangihe.com) is a good tour guide for both islands. Pak Nirwan speaks English and knows both of these archipelagos very well. Mikel from **Mountain View Resort** (p692) in Tomohon also leads tours.

Mama Roos GUESTHOUSE **$$**
(☎0813 4042 1454; mamaroos@ymail.com; r per person incl all meals 150,000Rp; wi-fi) The tiled rooms are pretty bare and could use a little TLC at this long-running guesthouse. Serves big but basic Indonesian meals. There's wi-fi in the evenings only.

ℹ Getting There & Away

To get to Batuputih from Manado, take a bus to Bitung (11,000Rp), get off at Girian (about 4km) and catch a *mikrolet* or pick-up truck (8000Rp) to Batuputih.

Tangkoko tours are possible from all over North Sulawesi, including Pulau Bunaken (a long, tiring day trip).

SOUTHEAST SULAWESI

Few visitors make it to Southeast Sulawesi, but if you're yearning to explore and have a passion for coral reefs and off-grid travel you'll be rewarded here.

The top attraction is Wakatobi Marine National Park, located in the remote Tukangbesi Islands off the southern tip, which offers some of Indonesia's best snorkelling and diving.

Transport links are surprisingly good, with daily flights from Makassar and boat connections from Pantai Bira.

History

Some of the earliest records of life in Southeast Sulawesi are depicted in prehistoric paintings on the walls of caves near Raha. The red ochre paintings include hunting scenes, boats and warriors on horseback.

The region's most powerful precolonial kingdom was Buton, based at Wolio, near Bau Bau. Its control and influence over other regional states was supported by the Dutch colonialists. Buton came under direct Dutch rule after the fall of Makassar in 1669, and was granted limited autonomy in 1906.

Other local trading centres maintained a low profile, probably for reasons of self-preservation. Kendari was one of the busiest.

The civil strife of the 1950s and 1960s was a time of extreme hardship for the people of the province. Farms and villages were plundered by rebel and government forces alike. Today, Southeast Sulawesi's economy is dominated by mining, fishing, agriculture and timber.

Kolaka

☎0405

The port of Kolaka is accessible by boats from Bajoe in South Sulawesi. The centre of town is grouped around the bus terminal, about 500m north of the ferry terminal. There are ATMs but not many other facilities.

All day and night, plenty of buses, bemos and Kijangs travel between Kolaka and Kendari (80,000Rp, six hours). A daily ferry travels overnight from Kolaka to Bajoe (75,000Rp, 10 hours). Up-to-date information is available at www.indonesiaferry.co.id.

Kendari

0401 / POP 319,000

The capital of Southeast Sulawesi province has long been the key port for trade between the inland Tolaki people and seafaring Bugis and Bajau traders. Kendari is a bustling city with little to recommend it except its range of decent accommodation.

Kendari begins in a tangle of lanes in the old *kota* (city) precinct adjacent to the original port in the east, and becomes progressively more modern in the suburbs to the west. One very, very long main road has most of the facilities, except the bus terminals.

Festival Teluk Kendari (Kenari Bay Festival; Apr) is the annual highlight of the social calendar, with dragon-boat races, traditional music and plenty of partying.

Sleeping & Eating

The night warungs lining the esplanade along Jl Bung Tomo are a popular hang-out in the evening.

Hotel Cendrawasih GUESTHOUSE $

(0401-312-1932; Jl Diponegoro 42; r with fan/air-con 120,000/170,000Rp;) A long-running cheapie, just off the main road, with friendly staff. The fan rooms are dated, but have balconies. The air-con rooms are in better shape.

Dragon Inn HOTEL $$

(0401-313-1889; http://dragoninnhotel.net; Jl Edi Sabara 8; r 250,000-440,000Rp;) Offering a slice of urban style, this zany-looking lime-green-and-orange hotel on the bay road has a good choice of small but well-presented rooms. There's a cafe-restaurant for meals.

Swiss-Belhotel Kendari BUSINESS HOTEL $$

(0401-312-8777; www.swiss-belhotel.com; Jl Edi Sabara 88; r/ste from 640,000/992,000Rp;) This is mainly a business hotel, but it has a fine pool and gym, and the staff are eager to please. Rooms and suites (in no less than six price categories) are in decent shape and spacious.

Getting There & Away

AIR

Kendari airport has a modern terminal. Flights connect to Makassar with Sriwijaya Air, Wings Air and Garuda; to Bau Bau with XpressAir; and to Jakarta with **Lion Air** (0401-329911; Jl Parman 84) and Garuda.

BOAT

Kendari has infrequent Pelni ferry connections; every fortnight the *Tilongkabila* heads to Kolonedale, Luwuk, Gorontalo and Bitung. In the other direction the same boat goes to Raha, Bau Bau and Makassar (22 hours). You'll find the **Pelni** (0401-321915; 8am-3pm Mon-Fri, 9am-noon Sat) office on top of a hill near the dock.

Two fast boats leave the Pelni dock: the Super-jet at 7.30am for Raha (137,000Rp, four hours) and Bau Bau (170,000Rp, six hours), and the *Sagori* at 1.30pm for Raha (120,000Rp, four hours). You can buy tickets by the dock.

Kendari

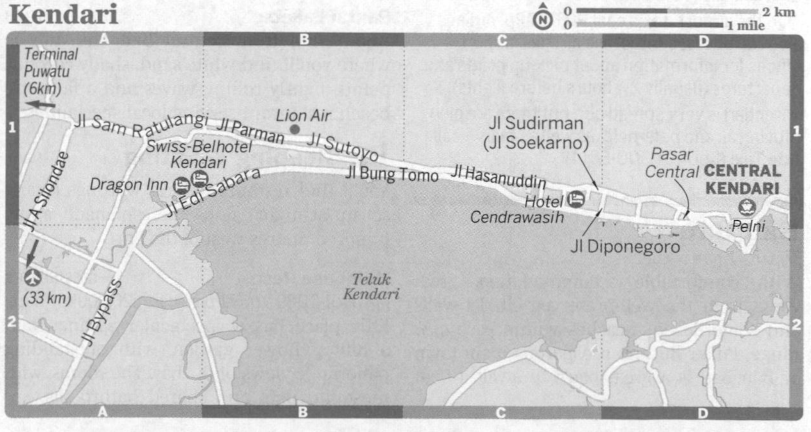

DON'T MISS

TARSIERS

If you're visiting Sulawesi's **Tangkoko-Batuangas Dua Saudara Nature Reserve** (p695) or **Lore Lindu National Park** (p673), keep your eyes peeled for something looking back at you: a tiny nocturnal primate known as a tarsier. These creatures are recognisable by their eyes, which are literally larger than their stomachs, so big in fact that they cannot rotate them within their sockets. Luckily, their heads can be rotated nearly 360 degrees, so their range of vision isn't compromised. Tarsiers also have huge, sensitive ears, which can be retracted and unfurled, and disproportionately long legs, which they use to jump distances 10 times their body length. They use their anatomical anomalies and impressive speed to catch small insects. Tarsiers live in groups of up to eight, and communicate with what sounds like high-pitched singing. They are found only in some rainforests of Indonesia and the Philippines.

BUS, BEMO & KIJANG

The main terminal is at Puwatu, about 10km west of town. From there, plenty of buses, Kijangs and bemos go to Kolaka (75,000Rp, six hours). It's more convenient to book a ticket (and board the bus) at one of the agencies in town along the main drag. Most buses leave Kendari at about 1pm to link with the 8pm ferry.

Getting Around

The airport is 28km southwest of Kendari. Shared taxis (35,000Rp) are available into town.

To the airport, taxis cost 90,000Rp. Airlines also run buses; contact the airlines' airport offices for information about pick-up points and departures (usually 2½ hours before flights).

Kendari is very spread out, but there are plentiful becak and *pete-pete*, as well as taxis – call **Ade Taxi** (☎0401-300-5014).

Bau Bau

☎0402 / POP 149,000

With comfortable accommodation, great views from the well-preserved citadel walls and some decent beaches within easy *ojek* range, Pulau Buton's prosperous main town of Bau Bau is a great place to await a boat connection to Maluku, North Sulawesi, or the diving paradise of Tukangbesi.

The terminal, main mosque and market are about 500m west of the main Pelni port, along Jl Kartini, which diverges from the seafront esplanade, Jl Yos Sudarso. Jl Kartini crosses a bridge then curves south past the post office towards the *kraton* (walled city palace).

Sights

The area around Bau Bau is blessed with beaches, waterfalls and caves.

Kraton PALACE

Banking steeply behind the town centre is the *kraton*, the Wolio royal citadel with impressively long and well-preserved 16th-century walls that offer great views over the town and its north-facing bay. Amid trees and flowers within the walls are evocative traditional homes and the old royal mosque.

Pusat Kebudayaan Wolio MUSEUM

(admission 7000Rp; ⏲8am-5pm) Some 500m beyond the citadel's south gate is Pusat Kebudayaan Wolio, a cultural centre and museum in a restored old mansion-palace, which is the focal point of Bau Bau's **Festival Kraton**, which features costumed parades, dances and displays of traditional fighting each September.

Pantai Nirwana BEACH

Eleven kilometres southwest of Bau Bau, the nearest white-sand beach is the attractively palm-lined Pantai Nirwana, though there is a certain amount of rubbish around.

Pantai Batuaga BEACH

The local's favourite beach, 21km southwest of Bau Bau, is ideal for swimming.

Pantai Lakeba BEACH

About 7km from central Bau Bau, this is where you'll find white sand, shady coconut palms, lightly rolling waves and a fantastic beach restaurant serving local specialities.

Sleeping & Eating

You'll find restaurants and warungs (many set up at night) along the esplanade, a few hundred metres west of the port.

Hillhouse Resort GUESTHOUSE $

(☎0401-21189; r incl breakfast 120,000Rp) This little place has a spectacular setting amid a hilltop flower garden, with outstanding panoramic views of the bay. The rooms, with mosquito nets and shared bathrooms, are simple. There's free tea and coffee for guests, and meals can usually be arranged by helpful owner Kasim if you give him notice. It's about half a click above Pusat Kebudayaan Wolio, the museum 500m beyond the citadel's south gate.

Hotel Calista Beach HOTEL $$
(☎0402-282-3088; Jl Yos Sudarso 25; r incl breakfast from 275,000Rp; ❄📶) This four-story scarlet-and-grey block has a fine seafront location by the harbour. Rooms are in good shape, many with bay views, and the staff are helpful.

ℹ Getting There & Away

AIR

Baubau airport is 3km southwest of town. Wings Air runs daily flights (45 minutes) between Makassar and Bau Bau; these continue to Wanci (20 minutes) in the Tukangbesi Islands. Garuda also has daily flights between Makassar and Bau Bau.

BOAT

To Raha & Kendari

The fast Super-jet takes 1½ hours to Raha (63,000Rp) and five hours to Kendari (170,000Rp).

To Tukangbesi Islands

An overnight boat from Bau Bau to Wanci Wanci (88,000Rp, nine to 11 hours) leaves at 8.30pm nightly. From Wanci, there are boats onward to Kaledupa (around two hours), from where you can catch a boat to Hoga (50,000Rp per boat). Another option is to take a smaller wooden ship that leaves a few times per week from Bau Bau to Buranga Harbour on Kaledupa Island (120,000Rp). Take an *ojek* (10,000Rp per person) from Buranga Harbour to Ambeua village, where there are boats to Hoga (60,000Rp per boat, 20 minutes).

To Elsewhere in Sulawesi

Every two weeks several Pelni liners link Bau Bau with Makassar; most also go to Ambon and/or Papua. Every two weeks the *Tilongkabila* heads along the east coast of Sulawesi, stopping off at Kendari and Bitung.

WORTH A TRIP

RAHA

The main settlement on Pulau Muna, Raha is a quiet backwater famous for its horse fighting, cave paintings and lagoons. Raha's main attraction is **Napabale**, a turquoise lagoon about 15km out of town. The lagoon is linked to the sea via a natural tunnel, so you can paddle through when the tide is low. It is a great area for hiking and swimming, and you can hire canoes (40,000Rp). An *ojek* here from Raha costs around 30,000Rp.

Super-jet boats between Kendari and Bau Bau stop in Raha. These boats are scheduled to leave for Kendari (137,000Rp, 3½ hours) at 8.30am and 1.30pm, and for Bau Bau (63,000Rp, 1½ hours) at about 1pm.

Tukangbesi Islands

Jacques Cousteau, when he surveyed the area in the 1980s, declared the Tukangbesi Islands to offer 'possibly the finest diving in the world'. Most of the islands are now part of **Wakatobi Marine National Park** (Taman Laut Wakatobi) and although the corals aren't in the same shape as when Cousteau visited, few divers leave disappointed. Positioned remotely off the far southeast coast of Sulawesi, the islands are difficult to reach, but they do offer superb snorkelling and diving, a blaze of corals and marine life, isolated beaches and stunning landscapes.

ℹ Getting There & Away

The easiest way to get to the Tukangbesi Islands is by taking a daily flight on Wings Air to Wanci, the islands' main settlement on Pulau Wangi Wangi, from Makassar. There's no public transport from Wanci airport; taxis charge a steep 100,000Rp; *ojek* ask for 40,000Rp.

From Wanci, public speedboats on to Pulau Hoga and Pulau Tomia leave from Pelabuhan Mola at around 9.30am. Public boats to Pulau Kaledupa (50,000Rp) leave Mola Utara (the 'northern jetty') about 1km north of the main harbour, daily at 9am.

Once every four weeks the Pelni liner *Kelimutu* travels from Makassar to Bau Bau then on to Ambon via Wanci.

Wanci (Pulau Wangi Wangi)

Wanci is the main wooden-boat-clogged settlement on Pulau Wangi Wangi. Cycling is a great way to get around this petite island, which is relatively flat and has good roads, with plenty of beaches and interesting caves to stop at. Central Wanci is a colourful place with a lively harbour and a night market with tasty goods.

Wanci has a surprising number of hotels and guesthouses, several of which are found along the busy road that leads south from the harbour to the market.

Patuno Resort Wakatobi (☎0811 400 2221; http://wakatobipatunoresort.co.id; bungalows incl breakfast from US$58; ❄📶) is a luxurious dive resort on a white beach close to the northern tip of the island, and offers free airport or harbour transfers.

Pulau Kaledupa

Much bigger than the main Tukangbesi island of Pulau Wangi Wangi and wilder, too, Pulau Kaledupa essentially has no tourist infrastructure on its beautiful, forested and beach-rich shores. The island is part of the Wakatobi Marine National Park, and its main village, Ambeua, is pleasant and lively. In general the island is just a stopover for many travellers, albeit a rather stunning one. If you want to stay overnight, homestays are easy to arrange.

Pulau Hoga & Pulau Tomia

For most travellers, the Tukangbesi Islands mean Pulau Hoga. This small desert island, 2km from the bigger Pulau Kaledupa, offers as close to a castaway existence as you could wish for. The water is turquoise; reefs are spectacular; and Bajau locals are superfriendly. Bring plenty of cash; there are no services at all besides the hotels. Fresh water is very scarce, so keep usage to a minimum.

Operation Wallacea, a British-based NGO, organises prebooked 'volunteer' programs in marine conservation, mainly between June and August. During these months the island is a little busier.

When not diving or snorkelling, you can walk around parts of the island (best at low tide; some areas are only accessible by boat) and visit the fishing village at the northern end.

Pulau Tomia is another small island, about 8km south of Pulau Kaledupa, and is known to the outside world mostly for its ultraexclusive Wakatobi Dive Resort.

Sleeping

All accommodation except Wakatobi Dive Resort are on Pulau Hoga. There's no backpacker place on Hoga, but it's often possible to stay in village homestays; speak to staff at Hoga Island Dive Resort.

Wisma Pondang HUT **$$**

(☎0821 4782 8544; Pulau Hoga; cabin per person incl all meals 250,000Rp) This is a simple cabin in the village with a decent mattress, mosquito net and *mandi* (Indonesian-style bathroom); more are planned. Owner Pondang speaks good English and can arrange tours.

★ **Hoga Island Dive Resort** DIVE RESORT **$$$**

(☎0852 4162 8287; www.hogaislanddiveresort.com; Pula Hoga; per person incl 2 dives & all meals 1,400,000Rp) Searching for that perfect barefoot vibe? Look no further: this lovely place enjoys an idyllic location, with big, wooden bungalows right on a white-sand beach. The ambience is warm thanks to the genial staff. Food is fresh, plentiful and very tasty, and the dive shop is well managed, with excellent guides.

The resort supports the community in various ways, such as by providing a boat for the local children to get to school on Pulau Kaledupa each day.

Wakatobi Dive Resort DIVE RESORT **$$$**

(www.wakatobi.com; Pulau Onemobaa; per person incl all meals from US$315; ❄@📶) On Pulau Onemobaa, just off Pulau Tomia, this ultra-exclusive hideaway offers beautiful bungalow accommodation and one of the most celebrated house reefs in Indonesia. Rates include a personal butler and full board; diving costs extra. It is also the base for the elegant liveaboard **Pelagian** (www.pelagian.wakatobi.com). Private charter flights direct to/from Bali are available.

Understand Indonesia

Indonesia Today

Nothing ever seems settled in Indonesia, whether it's the land, the sea or society itself. Yet there was justifiable cause for celebration after the 2014 national elections continued the almost entirely peaceful traditions set during the previous elections five years earlier. Not bad for a country with a violent political past, including a 1965 political genocide recalled by two widely praised documentaries. Still, economic and environmental challenges remain hugely significant as the nation feels its way to the future.

Best on Film

The Act of Killing (directed by Joshua Oppenheimer, 2012) A searing Oscar-nominated documentary about the 1965 slaughter of accused Communist sympathisers in Indonesia.

Look of Silence (directed by Joshua Oppenheimer, 2014) The follow-up to *The Act of Killing*.

Shackled (directed by Upi Avianto, 2012) A man driving in Jakarta finds a character in a rabbit suit and an abused woman in his car, with horrifying consequences.

Eat Pray Love (directed by Ryan Murphy, 2010) A flop at the box office and with critics, the film is Bali's glossiest appearance on screen.

Best in Print

A Brief History of Indonesia (2015) Indonesian expert Tim Hannigan's highly readable and entertaining narrative.

Indonesia Etc (2014) Elizabeth Pisani's brilliant travelogue and exploration of the nation.

This Earth of Mankind (1980) A canvas of Indonesia under Dutch rule by Pramoedya Ananta Toer (1925–2006), one of Indonesia's top writers.

Krakatoa – The Day the World Exploded (2003) Simon Winchester melds history, geology and politics, all centred on the 1883 eruption.

Jokowi

He was called the Indonesian Obama, and that exemplified the biggest hurdles that Joko Widodo faced after he won the landmark 2014 Indonesian election. The first democratically elected Indonesian president with no obvious ties to the old Suharto dictatorship or the military, Jokowi, as he's commonly known (or simply Joko), carried the dreams of every Indonesian who wants a brighter future for his or her country.

It's a huge load to carry and initially it seemed to overwhelm Jokowi. First came the wake-up call to wild expectations. Yes, he had humble roots and yes, he'd gained much praise as a reform-minded governor of Jakarta. But as the newly elected president, he gave no indication of being a radical ready to tear Indonesia away from the clutches of the powerful elite and military which have held control for decades. His vice president, Jusuf Kalla, has strong ties to the status quo (and in the landmark documentary *Act of Killing*, there's a clip of Kalla encouraging Suharto loyalists to commit violence). Jokowi took pains not to upset the establishment and in fact he showed an unexpected conservative streak.

He did nothing to stop the passage of religiously driven restrictions on the sale of alcohol and he tacitly allowed local governments in Aceh and elsewhere to become evermore fundamentalist. And Indonesia's relationship with Australia – always prone to drama – took a dive after Jokowi didn't stop the executions of two members of the so-called Bali Nine, Andrew Chan and Myuran Sukumaran in April, 2015. The pair had been convicted of drug offences in 2006 and had then languished in Bali's notorious Kerobokan prison during a long series of appeals and calls for clemency.

Many hoped that the perception of Jokowi as a man of the people would translate into compassion for prisoners but this was not the case. He not only rejected clemency for Chan and Sukumaran but stated that the 130 other people with Indonesian death sentences should expect similar treatment. Meanwhile, Indonesia's relations with Australia hit rock bottom as the plight of the Bali Nine became a *cause célèbre* and ill-fated Australian prime minister Tony Abbott ineffectually demanded they receive compassion. (It should be noted, however, that calls for Australians to boycott their favourite party spot, Bali, were largely unheeded.)

Jokowi's efforts to establish himself as President were hindered by his very own political party, the Indonesian Democratic Party of Struggle (PDI-P), especially after the party's chief, former Indonesian president Megawati Sukarnoputri, called him a mere functionary. His first cabinet was also filled with old party hacks who seemed more interested in quarrelling and jockeying for power than forcefully working to implement Jokowi's campaign promises of prosperity and economic fairness.

In August, 2015, Jokowi announced a major cabinet reshuffle, which saw technocrats named to replace party stalwarts as heads of powerful ministries. As he reached the end of his first year in office, Jokowi remained very much a work in progress as president, with many question marks around his ability to live up to his own lofty goals and those of the many people who had voted for him as a symbol of hope for a better Indonesia.

The Economy Sputters

For many years Indonesia has been one of Asia's top economic success stories. Its economy has grown by a robust 6% or more per year. But in 2015 this record ended as growth fizzled – the rate falling below 5% – which only added to the pressure on Jokowi.

Indonesia's rapidly expanding population requires a growth rate of at least 6% so that the economy can absorb all the people entering the workforce. And local expectations are high, especially after the boom years when fully half the population achieved middle class status as defined by the World Bank and a majority of workers no longer toiled in subsistence agriculture.

Meanwhile Indonesia's currency, the rupiah, all but collapsed against the US dollar. Although this is great for the relatively small number of US tourists who visit the archipelago, it's very bad news for Indonesia's small businesses which rely on goods and services with prices pegged to the dollar.

Economists says that Indonesia will have a hard time returning to rapid growth given that the prices of many of its exports like palm oil and coal have fallen. The nation's historic inefficiencies are also to blame. Protectionist laws and corruption benefit the old ruling class but do nothing to foster real competition. As an example, Indonesia's own anti-graft agency estimates that unlicensed forest clearing has cost the government billions in fees, money which could otherwise be used for vital projects to improve the nation's creaking – and often collapsing – infrastructure, itself a major drag on economic growth.

POPULATION: **255 MILLION**

AREA: **1,904,600 SQ KM**

GDP PER CAPITA: **US$3475**

NUMBER OF ISLANDS: **MORE THAN 17,000**

POPULATION DENSITY JAVA: **1130 PER SQ KM**

POPULATION DENSITY PAPUA: **11 PER SQ KM**

if Indonesia were 100 people

57 would be Javanese
20 would be Sumatran
2 would be Balinese
21 would be other

belief systems

(% of population)

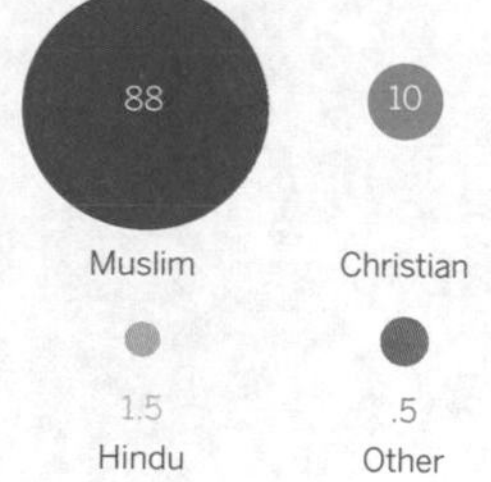

population per sq km

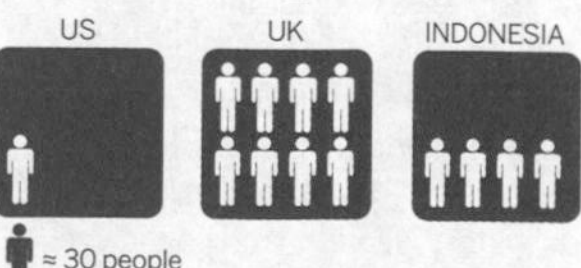

Etiquette

Places of worship Be respectful in sacred places. Remove shoes and dress modestly when visiting mosques; wear a sash and sarong at Bali temples.

Body language Use both hands when handing somebody something. Don't show displays of affection in public, or talk with your hands on your hips (it's seen as a sign of aggression).

Clothing Avoid showing a lot of skin, although many local men wear shorts. Don't go topless if you're a woman (even in Bali); you'll incite trouble in conservative areas and simply offend in others.

Photography Before taking photos of someone, ask – or mime – for approval.

Custom Respond to requests for donations and to fill in guestbooks in remote villages.

Unnatural Disasters

As the site of the modern world's greatest explosion (Gunung Tambora in 1815) and other cataclysms such as the tsunami in 2004, Indonesia has more than its fair share of natural disasters. In fact, volcanic eruptions are so frequent that when east Java's Gunung Raung and then Lombok's Gunung Rinjani sent out ash clouds which disrupted hundreds of flights to and from Bali in 2015, it was treated as routine by the local media.

But if nothing can be done about Indonesia's unsettled land and sea, it certainly seems like something could be done about the nation's propensity for manmade disasters. Over a two-year period starting in 2014, more than 350 people died in plane crashes, including 162 who died when an Indonesia AirAsia Airbus plunged into the ocean off Java just after Christmas 2014. The nation's dismal record for transport safety, which has been blamed on lax oversight and institutional malaise on the part of the airlines, seems intractable.

And if Indonesia's safety record is clouded, so too are its skies. Each year fires from (technically) illegal forest clearances on Sumatra and Kalimantan cause an acidic haze that blots out the sky over much of western Indonesia, as well as Singapore and parts of Malaysia (both countries drew harsh rebukes from Indonesia when they complained about the choking smoke).

In a break with past practice however, Jokowi personally asked for help from other nations in fighting the fires in 2015, which were the worst in two decades. It offered at least a hope that something might be done to tame the fires even as questions remained about whether any action would ever be taken against the palm oil producers, loggers and farmers responsible for the blazes and environmental destruction.

History

The story of how Indonesia became what it is today is a colourful dance of migrants and invaders, rebels and religions, kingdoms and empires, choreographed by Indonesia's island nature and its location on millennia-old Asian trade routes. It's a story full of heroes and villains, victors and victims, but the strangest part is how these 17,000-plus islands with over 300 spoken languages and diverse cultures ever came to be a nation at all.

The Trading Archipelago

Indonesians inhabit a diverse island world where a short sea voyage or journey inland can take a traveller into a whole new ecosystem providing a different set of useful commodities. Long ago, forest dwellers were collecting colourful bird feathers and tree resins and exchanging them for turtle shells or salt from people who lived by the sea. Some of these goods would find their way to nearby islands, from which they then reached more distant islands. By about 500 BC, routes sailed by Indonesian islanders began to overlap with those of sailors from mainland Asia. Thus, 2000 years ago, bird-of-paradise feathers from Papua could be depicted on beautiful bronze drums cast by the Dongson people of Vietnam, and some of the drums then ended up in Java, Sumatra and Bali.

Simple iron tools, such as axes and plough tips, arrived from China around 200 BC, spurring Indonesians to find their own metal deposits and make their own knives, arrowheads, urns and jewellery.

Indonesia's main western islands – Sumatra, Kalimantan and Java – lie in the middle of the sea routes linking Arabia, India, China and Japan. Indonesia was destined to become a crossroads of Asia, and trade has been its lifeblood for at least 2000 years. It has brought with it nearly all the biggest changes the archipelago has seen through the centuries – new people, new ideas, new crops, new technologies, new religions, new wars, new rulers.

Indian Influence & Sriwijaya

Contact between Indonesia and India goes back a long way. Pepper plants, originally from India, were spicing up western Indonesian food as early as 600 BC. Indonesian clothing got a lot smarter when boats from Indonesia reached India by the 2nd century BC and brought back cotton plants. In the early centuries AD, Hindu traders from southern India started to

TIMELINE

60,000–40,000 BC

Indonesia's western islands are still part of the Asian mainland. The first Homo sapiens arrive, probably ancestors of the Melanesians in today's population, who are now mainly in Papua.

About 8000 BC

Sea levels rise after the end of the last glacial period, separating Sumatra, Borneo, Java and Bali from the Asian mainland, and the island of New Guinea from Australia.

About 2000 BC

Austronesian people originating from Taiwan start to arrive in Indonesia, probably by sea routes. They absorb or displace Melanesians. The earliest evidence of settlement dates from the 6th century BC.

THE CHINESE IN INDONESIA

As Indonesian trading states grew richer and more complex they came increasingly to rely on their growing numbers of Chinese settlers to oil the wheels of their economies. Indonesia's first recorded Chinese settlement was located at Pasai, Sumatra in the 11th century. By the 17th century, Chinese were filling a whole spectrum of roles as middlemen, artisans, labourers, tax-collectors, businessmen, financiers, farmers and keepers of shops, brothels and opium dens. Today, ethnic-Chinese Indonesians own many of the country's biggest and most profitable businesses. For centuries they have also been the subject of jealousy and hatred, and the victims of repeated outbreaks of violence, including during the shocking 1998 Jakarta riots.

settle along the coast of mainland Southeast Asia. From there they found their way to early coastal trading settlements in Java, Sumatra and Kalimantan. The Indians brought jewellery, fine cloth, pottery, as well as Hindu and Buddhist culture.

From the 4th century AD, Chinese travellers too arrived in Indonesian ports, and in the 7th century Chinese reports started mentioning the port state of Sriwijaya. Buddhist Sriwijaya, in the Palembang-Jambi area of southeast Sumatra, may have been a grouping of ports or a single kingdom whose capital sometimes changed location. It was a powerful state, and its sailors were able to collect pepper, ivory, resins, feathers, turtle shells, mother of pearl and much more from Sumatra and ports around the Java Sea, and carry them to China, from which they brought back silk, ceramics and iron. An entrepôt for Indian, Indonesian, Arab, Southeast Asian and, eventually, Chinese traders, Sriwijaya remained important until the 14th century.

Traders from Arabia

The first Muslim traders from Arabia appeared in Indonesian ports within a few decades of the death of the Prophet Muhammad in AD 632. Arabian ships bound for China, carrying spices and rare woods or Indian cloth, would call in at Sumatra or other Indonesian islands to add local products such as aromatic woods, resins and camphor to their cargoes. By the 13th century, Arabs had established settlements in major Indonesian ports. Sulaiman bin Abdullah bin al-Basir, ruler of the small north Sumatran port of Lamreh in the early 13th century, was the first Indonesian ruler known to have adopted Islam and taken the title Sultan.

500–1 BC	5th century AD	6th century	7th century
Local trade routes mesh with mainland Asia's. Chinese iron tools, large Vietnamese bronze drums and Indian glass beads reach Indonesia. Local products such as spices reach India and China.	Under influence from India, some Indonesian trading ports turn from animism to Hinduism or Buddhism. Indonesia's earliest known inscriptions are carved in west Java and near Kutai, Kalimantan.	Muslim traders begin arriving in Indonesian ports bringing their religion as well as goods for trade. Over the next few centuries, thriving Muslim communities are established.	Farmers flourish by growing rice on lush islands across the archipelago. Terraces and complex irrigation systems are developed, allowing wealth to be accumulated.

Majapahit

The first Indonesian sultanates came into being while the greatest of Indonesia's Hindu-Buddhist states, Majapahit, was flourishing in eastern Java. Like the earlier Sriwijaya, Majapahit's success was trade-based. Its powerful fleets exacted tribute from ports spread from Sumatra to Papua (disobedient states were 'wiped out completely' by the Majapahit navies, according to court poet Prapanca), and enabled its traders to dominate the lucrative commerce between Sumatran ports and China. Prapanca reported that traders in Majapahit ports came from Cambodia, Vietnam and Thailand. He also claimed, less credibly, that Majapahit ruled a hundred foreign countries. Majapahit was eventually conquered by one of the newly Islamic north Java ports, Demak, in 1478.

The Majapahit kingdom reached its zenith during the reign of King Hayam Wuruk (r 1350–89) who was ably assisted by his prime minister and brilliant military commander Gajah Mada. Their names literally translate as Rotting Chicken and Rutting Elephant, respectively, but this had no ill-effect on the illustrious, expansive kingdom.

Spices & the Portuguese

As Islam continued to spread around the archipelago, another new breed of trader arrived – Europeans. With advanced ship design and navigation technology, European sailors could now cross oceans in search of wealth. Portuguese ships crossed the Indian Ocean from southern Africa to India and then pushed on eastward. In 1511 they conquered Melaka, key to the vital Strait of Melaka between Sumatra and Malaya, and set up bases strung across Indonesia. They also established settlements in mainland ports from India to China and Japan.

The prize that drew the Portuguese to Indonesia was three little plant products long prized in Europe, China, the Islamic world and Indonesia itself: cloves, nutmeg and mace. All three, in high demand because they made food taste more interesting, were native to Maluku, the Spice Islands of eastern Indonesia. Cloves (the sun-dried flower buds of a type of myrtle tree) were produced on a few small islands off the west coast of Halmahera. Nutmeg and mace, both from the nut of the nutmeg tree, came from the Banda Islands. The sultans of the small Maluku islands of Ternate and Tidore controlled most of the already valuable trade in these spices.

Portuguese traders joined western Indonesians in buying spices in Maluku. They brought exotic new things to the islands such as clocks, firearms, sweet potatoes and Christianity. Clove and nutmeg cultivation was stepped up to meet their demand. After they fell out with the Ternate sultan Babullah and were expelled in 1575, they set up on nearby Pulau Ambon instead.

The Portuguese also traded at Aceh (north Sumatra) and Banten (northwest Java) where the principal product was pepper, which had also been used for many centuries to liven up tastebuds in Europe, China and elsewhere.

The British, keen to profit from the spice trade, kept control of the Maluku island of Run until 1667. Then they swapped it for a Dutch-controlled island, Manhattan.

7th–13th centuries

Buddhist Sriwijaya in southeast Sumatra dominates in western Indonesia. It may have been a collection of ports or a single state; its trade routes reached China and India.

8th–9th centuries

The Buddhist Sailendra and Hindu Sanjaya (or Mataram) kingdoms flourish on Java's central plains, creating the huge Borobudur and Prambanan temple complexes, respectively.

1292

Marco Polo stops off in Sumatra on his way from China back to Persia, becoming the first of an all-star line-up of explorers to visit the islands.

1294–1478

The Hindu-Buddhist Majapahit kingdom, based in eastern Java, monopolises trade between Sumatra and China and exacts tribute from across Indonesia. The Majapahit court is imitated by many later Indonesian states.

In the 17th century the Portuguese were pushed out of the Indonesian condiment business by a more determined, better armed and better financed rival. The Dutch newcomers didn't just want to buy spices, they wanted to drive other Europeans out of Asian trade altogether.

From Animism to Islam

The earliest Indonesians were animists – they believed animate and inanimate objects had their own life force or spirit, and that events could be influenced by offerings, rituals or forms of magic. Indonesia's scattered prehistoric sites, and animist societies that have survived into modern times, provide evidence that there was often a belief in an afterlife and supernatural controlling powers, and that the spirits of the dead were believed to influence events. Megaliths, found from Pulau Nias to Sumba and Sulawesi's Lore Lindu National Park, are one manifestation of ancestor cults. Some megaliths may be 5000 years old, but in Sumba animist religion is still alive and well, and concrete versions of megalithic tombs are still being erected.

Hinduism & Buddhism

It was contact with the comparatively wealthy cultures of India in the first few centuries AD that first led Indonesians to adopt new belief systems. Indian traders who settled in Indonesia continued to practise Hinduism, or its offshoot Buddhism. Some built their own temples and brought in priests, monks, teachers or scribes. Impressed local Indonesian rulers started to use the Indian titles Raja or Maharaja or add the royal suffix *varman* to their names. It was a short step for them to cement their ties with the Indian world by adopting the Indians' religion or philosophy too. The earliest records of Indianised local rulers are 5th-century stone inscriptions in Sanskrit, found in west Java and near Kutai (now Tenggarong), Kalimantan. These record decrees and tales of the glorious deeds of the kings Purnavarman and Mulavarman, respectively.

Central Java's unmissable Borobudar and Prambanan complexes are the best ancient monuments in Indonesia, dating to the 8th century. The former is an iconic Buddhist monument built from two million stones while the latter has elaborate Hindu decoration.

The major Indonesian states from then until the 15th century were all Hindu or Buddhist. Sriwijaya, based in southern Sumatra, was predominantly Buddhist. In central Java in the 8th and 9th centuries, the Buddhist Sailendra kingdom and the predominantly Hindu Sanjaya (or Mataram) kingdom constructed the great temple complexes of Borobudur and Prambanan respectively. They sought to recreate Indian civilisation in a Javanese landscape, and Indian gods such as Shiva and Vishnu were believed to inhabit the Javanese heavens, though this did not obliterate traditional beliefs in magical forces or nature spirits. In the 10th century, wealth and power on Java shifted to the east of the island, where a series of Hindu-Buddhist kingdoms dominated till the late 15th century.

13th–15th centuries

Influenced by Arab merchants, two north Sumatran towns adopt Islam, followed by Melaka on the Malay peninsula, the eastern island of Ternate and northern Java ports including Demak, which conquers Majapahit.

1505

Portuguese ships reach Indonesian waters. Interested in spices, the Portuguese go on to establish trading settlements across the archipelago, joining Indians, Arabs, Chinese, Malays and islanders in the sea trade.

1520

Java's complete conversion to Islam means that Bali is isolated as a Hindu island. Religious and artistic refugees from Java greatly strengthen Bali's culture which flourishes.

16th–17th centuries

Islam continues to spread around Indonesian ports. The Islamic Mataram kingdom is founded (1581) in the lands of the old Hindu Sanjaya kingdom in central Java.

The greatest of these was Majapahit (1294–1478), based at Trowulan. Javanese-Indian culture also spread to Bali (which remains Hindu to this day) and parts of Sumatra.

Islam

Majapahit was eventually undone by the next major religion to reach Indonesia – Islam. Muslim Arab traders had appeared in Indonesia as early as the 7th century. By the 13th century Arabs had established settlements in major Indonesian ports, and it was then that the first local rulers, at Lamreh and Pasai in north Sumatra, adopted Islam. Gradually over the next two centuries, then more rapidly, other Indonesian ports with Muslim communities switched to Islam. Their rulers would become persuaded by Islamic teachings and, keen to join a successful international network, would usually take the title Sultan to proclaim their conversion. Melaka on the Malay Peninsula, controlling the strategic Strait of Melaka, switched to Islam in 1436 and became a model for other Muslim states to emulate.

In Java, Sumatra and Sulawesi, some Muslim states spread Islam by military conquest. The conversion of several north Java ports in the late 15th century meant that Hindu-Buddhist Majapahit was hemmed in by hostile states. One of these, Demak, conquered Majapahit in 1478.

Indonesian Islam has always had a 'folk religion' aspect in that legends of Islamic saints, holy men and feats of magic, and pilgrimages to sites associated with them, have played an important part in Muslim life. Tradition has it that Islam was brought to Java by nine *wali* (saints) who converted local populations through war or feats of magic.

The greatest of the Indonesian Muslim kingdoms, Mataram, was founded in 1581 in the area of Java where the Sailendra and Sanjaya kingdoms had flourished centuries earlier. Its second ruler, Senopati, was a descendant of Hindu princes and helped to incorporate some of the Hindu past, and older animist beliefs, into the new Muslim world.

In 1292, Marco Polo, on one of his forays east, visited Aceh and noted that local inhabitants had already converted to Islam.

Christianity

The last major religion to reach Indonesia was Christianity. The Catholic Portuguese made some conversions among Islamic communities in Maluku and Sulawesi in the 16th century, but most reverted to Islam. The Protestant Dutch, who gradually took control of the whole archipelago between the 17th and 20th centuries, made little effort to spread Christianity. Missionaries active in the 19th and 20th centuries were steered to regions where Islam was weak or nonexistent, such as the Minahasa and Toraja areas of Sulawesi, the Batak area of Sumatra, and Dutch New Guinea (now Papua).

1595

Four small Dutch ships reach the pepper port of Banten in northwest Java. Despite setbacks, the expedition returns home with enough spices to make a small profit.

1602

Holland merges competing merchant companies into the VOC (United East Indian Company). It aims to drive other European nations out of Asian trade, especially in spices.

1611–1700

From its headquarters at Batavia (now Jakarta), the VOC expands its control through deals, alliances and battles. A chain of Dutch-controlled ports leads to the Spice Islands.

1667

The Dutch gain complete control of the Banda Islands and in return give the British a little island in their North America colony named Manhattan.

Rajas & Sultans

The Hindu, Buddhist and Muslim states of Indonesia were not charitable organisations dedicated to their subjects' welfare. The great majority were absolute monarchies or sultanates, whose rulers claimed to be at least partly divine. Their subjects were there to produce food or goods which they could pay as tribute to the ruler, or to do business from which they could pay taxes, or to fight in armies or navies, or to fill roles in the royal entourage from astrologer to poet to tax collector to concubine. Land was generally considered to belong to the ruler, who permitted subjects to use it in exchange for taxes and tribute. Slaves were an integral part of the scene well into the 19th century.

Other states could pay tribute too and the largest kingdoms or sultanates, such as the Java-based Hindu-Buddhist Majapahit (1294–1478) and Muslim Mataram (1581–1755), built trading empires based on tribute from other peoples whom they kept in line through the threat of military force. Majapahit lived on in the memory of later Indonesian states for the fine manners, ceremony and arts of its court, and because some of its princes and princesses had married into the ruling families of Muslim sultanates. Many later rulers would assert their credentials by reference to family connections with the Majapahit kingdom.

The name Indonesia was coined in the 1850s by a Scot, James Logan (editor of the Singapore-published *Journal of the Indian Archipelago and Eastern Asia*) as a shorter equivalent for the term Indian Archipelago.

Shared religion was no bar to belligerence. Sultan Agung of Mataram had no qualms about conquering neighbouring Muslim states in the 1620s when he wanted to tighten control over the export routes for Mataram's rice, sugar and teak. Nor did past loyalty or even blood ties guarantee personal favour. In the first year of his reign, Agung's successor Amangkurat I massacred at least 6000 subjects, including his father's advisers and his own half-brothers and their families, to remove any possible challenges to his authority.

European Influence

The coming of Europeans in the 16th and 17th centuries introduced new ways for Indonesian states and contenders to get one over on their rivals. They could use the Europeans as trading partners or mercenaries or allies, and if the Europeans became too powerful or demanding, they expected they could get rid of them. In Maluku the Muslim sultanate of Ternate, a small but wealthy clove-growing island, drove out its former trading partners, the Portuguese, in 1575. It later awarded the Dutch a monopoly on the sale of its spices and used the revenue to build up its war fleet and extract tribute from other statelets. Ternate eventually controlled 72 tax-paying tributaries around Maluku and Sulawesi.

1670–1755

VOC exploits Mataram's internal turmoils to win control of the kingdom. In 1755 it splits Mataram into two kingdoms, with capitals at Yogyakarta and Surakarta (Solo) and now controls Java.

1795–1824

In the Napoleonic Wars, Britain seizes the possessions of the Dutch East Indies. An 1824 agreement divides the region between the Dutch and British; the borders are similar to modern Indonesia and Malaysia.

1800

The now overstretched, corrupt and bankrupt VOC is wound up. Its territories pass to the Netherlands crown, converting a trading empire into a colonial one, the Netherlands East Indies.

1815

In the biggest explosion in modern history, Gunung Tambora on Sumbawa erupts. Tens of thousands die on the island; the ash cloud results in 1816 being dubbed 'the year without summer' across the northern hemisphere.

Such agreements, and alliances and conquests, eventually gave the Dutch a hold over much Indonesian trade and territory. Their involvements in the endless internal feuds of the powerful Javanese Mataram kingdom won them such a stranglehold over the region that in 1749 the dying king Pakubuwono II willed them control over his kingdom. In 1755 the Dutch resolved yet another Mataram succession dispute by splitting it into two kingdoms, with capitals at Surakarta (Solo) and Yogyakarta. Both royal families later split again, so that by the early 19th century there were four rival royal houses in this tiny part of central Java.

So long as local rulers and aristocrats cooperated, the Dutch were content to leave them in place, and these traditional rulers eventually became the top rank of the 'Native' branch of the colonial civil service, continuing to run their kingdoms under the supervision of a sprinkling of Dutch administrators.

In the 1650s and 1660s Banten's Sultan Ageng Tirtajasa decreed that all men aged 16 or over must tend 500 pepper plants.

Dutch Domination

When the Dutch first arrived at Banten in 1595 and set up the United East India Company (Vereenigde Oost-Indische Compagnie; VOC) to conduct all their business in the East Indies in 1602, they did not plan to end up running the whole of what came to be Indonesia. They just wanted to drive other European powers out of the lucrative spice trade in Indonesia. Their strategy was to sign exclusive trade agreements with local rulers where possible, and to impose their will by military force where necessary. Their powerful fleets and effective soldiers made them a potent ally for local strongmen, and in return the Dutch could extract valuable trading rights.

Moving In

In the beginning the Dutch concentrated primarily on the spice trade. In 1605 they drove the Portuguese out of Ambon. They then set up their own chain of settlements in Muslim ports along the route to the Spice Islands, with their headquarters at Jayakarta, a small vassal port of Banten in northwest Java. When Banten, with English help, tried to expel them in 1619, the Dutch beat off the attack, rebuilt the town and renamed it Batavia. Today it's called Jakarta.

By varied means the Dutch took control of Banda in 1621, Melaka in 1641, Tidore in 1657, Makassar in 1669, and then several Javanese ports. In Banda they exterminated or expelled almost the whole population in the 1620s and replaced them with slave-worked nutmeg plantations.

The Javanese Mataram kingdom tried unsuccessfully to drive the Dutch out of Batavia in 1628 and again in 1629. In the 1640s, Mataram's

Nathaniel's Nutmeg by Giles Milton offers a fascinating account of the battle to control trade from the Spice Islands. Now known as the Banda Islands, they still have many colonial-era sites and are well worth visiting.

1825–30

Prince Diponegoro, supported by many Muslims, the poor and some fellow Javanese aristocrats, rebels against the Dutch and their vassals. Some 200,000 Javanese die, most from famine and disease.

1820s–1910

Holland takes control of nearly all the archipelago through economic expansion, agreements with local aristocrats and warfare. Many aristocrats become representatives of the Dutch administration.

1830–70

The Cultivation System: two million Javanese peasants have to grow and pay tax on export crops (coffee, tea, tobacco, indigo, sugar). Holland is saved from bankruptcy, but most peasants suffer.

1830

Slavery, which had flourished among various kingdoms and sultanates, goes into final decline when the Balinese royalty renounce the practice. Proceeds had been used to finance wars and palaces.

THE CULTIVATION SYSTEM

The seemingly intractable problems the Dutch had with their colony were made much worse by the devastating Diponegoro War in Java (1825–30). This conflict started when Prince Diponegoro got angry after the Dutch built a new road across land that contained his parents memorial. Hostilities began and the prince received widespread support by others in Java who had grievances with the Dutch. To quell the conflict, the Dutch eventually needed to bring in troops from Sulawesi, Holland and even Dutch African colonies at huge expense.

After the war, Holland desperately needed to make the East Indies profitable. Its answer was the new Cultivation (or Culture) System. Up to two million Javanese peasants were obliged to grow the export crops of coffee, tea, tobacco, indigo or sugar, and pay a proportion of their crop in tax, and sell the rest to the government at fixed prices. This saved Holland from bankruptcy, and while some villagers prospered, the cultivation system also resulted in famines, loss of rice-growing lands, poverty and corruption.

King Amangkurat I, facing a host of internal challenges, decided it was wiser to make peace with the VOC. He went further and gave it the sole licence to carry Mataram goods.

While Chinese, Arabs and Indians continued to trade in Indonesia in the 17th and 18th centuries, the VOC ended up with all the best business. Asian traders carried rice, fruit and coconuts from one part of the archipelago to another; Dutch ships carried spices, timber, textiles and metals to other Asian ports and Europe.

The Dutch introduced coffee to Indonesia in 1696. United East India Company (VOC) officials got west Java nobles to instruct their farmers to grow coffee bushes, paying with cash and textiles for the harvested beans.

The VOC's trading successes brought it an ever larger and costlier web of commitments around the archipelago. By 1800 it controlled most of Java and parts of Maluku, Sulawesi, Sumatra and Timor. It was overstretched, and corrupt – and bankrupt. The Dutch crown took over the company's possessions but then lost them (first to France, then to Britain) during the Napoleonic Wars. Control was restored to the Dutch in 1816 following the Anglo-Dutch Treaty of 1814.

Commerce Rules

As the 19th century progressed, European private enterprise was encouraged to take over export agriculture. Privately owned rubber and tobacco plantations, both of which featured brutal working conditions, helped to extend Dutch control into eastern Sumatra. The colonial administration concentrated on creating a favourable investment climate by the construction of railways, improving roads and shipping services, and quashing unrest. They also waged military campaigns to subjugate the last non-compliant local statelets.

1845–1900
Private (European) enterprise is encouraged, forced cultivation is slowly wound down. Transportation infrastructure is greatly improved. Notoriously brutal rubber and tobacco plantations develop on Sumatra.

1883
Mt Krakatau blows, almost completely destroying the namesake island in the Sumba Strait between Java and Sumatra. It's considered the loudest noise in recorded history.

1901
The Ethical Policy is introduced to raise Indonesian welfare through better irrigation, education and health but Europeans benefit most. The growth of cities spawns a new Indonesian middle class.

1912
Sarekat Islam (Islamic Union) emerges as a Javanese Muslim economic assistance group, with anti-Christian and anti-Chinese tendencies. It grows into a million-member anti colonial movement.

The Banjarmasin sultanate in Kalimantan came under direct Dutch rule in 1863 after a four-year war; resource-rich Aceh in northern Sumatra was finally subdued in 1903 after 30 years of vicious warfare; southwest Sulawesi was occupied from 1900 to 1910; and Bali was brought to heel, after several attempts, in 1906. Some Balinese aristocrats killed their families and retainers and committed suicide rather than submit to the Dutch. In the late 19th century Holland, Britain and Germany all agreed to divide up the unexplored island of New Guinea.

Clove-impregnated *kretek* cigarettes, popular throughout Indonesia today, were first marketed by Nitisemito, a man from Kudus, Java, in 1906. His Bal Tiga (Three Balls) brand grew into one of the biggest Indonesian-owned businesses in the Dutch East Indies.

The Ethical Policy

The end of the 19th century saw the rise of a new Dutch awareness of the problems and needs of the Indonesian people. The result was the Ethical Policy, launched in 1901, which aimed to raise Indonesians' welfare and purchasing power through better irrigation, education, health and credit, and with a decentralised government. The Ethical Policy's immediate effects were mixed, and its benefits often accrued to Europeans rather than Indonesians. An increase in private land ownership increased the number of locals without land. Local revolts and strikes were fairly frequent. But the colony's trade continued to grow. By the 1930s the Dutch East Indies was providing most of the world's quinine and pepper, over one-third of its rubber and almost one-fifth of its tea, sugar, coffee and oil.

Breaking Free

The longer-term effects of the Ethical Policy were truly revolutionary. Wider education spawned a new class of Indonesians aware of colonial injustices, international political developments and the value of their own cultures. These people were soon starting up diverse new political and religious groups and publications, some of which were expressly dedicated to ending Dutch colonial rule.

At the entrance to a neighbourhood or village you may see an arch with the words 'Dirgahayu RI' painted across it. This translates as 'Long live the Republic of Indonesia' and the arch has been built to celebrate Independence Day, 17 August.

The First Nationalists

Today, Indonesians look back to 1908 as the year their independence movement began. This was when Budi Utomo (Glorious Endeavour) was founded. Led by upper-class, Dutch-educated, Indonesian men, Budi Utomo wanted to revive monarchy and modernise Javanese culture for the 20th century. It was soon followed by more radical groups. Sarekat Islam (Islamic Union), which emerged in 1912, began as a Javanese Muslim economic mutual-help group, with a strong anti-Christian and anti-Chinese streak. Linking with other groups, it grew steadily into a million-member anticolonial movement trying to connect villagers throughout the colony with the educated elite.

1920

The Indonesian Communist Party (PKI) is founded. A pro-independence party with support from urbanites, it is sidelined when uprisings in Java (1926) and Sumatra (1927) are suppressed by the Dutch.

1927

The Indonesian National Party (PNI) emerges, led by a young engineer, Sukarno. It grows quickly into the most powerful pro-independence organisation. In 1930 its leaders are jailed.

1928

Nationalism is given a boost when the All Indonesia Youth Congress proclaims its historic Youth Pledge, establishing goals of one national identity and one language (Bahasa Indonesia).

1930s

The Dutch East Indies provides most of the quinine used in the world's tonic water, to the delight of gin lovers everywhere. Pepper, rubber and oil are also major exports.

PANCASILA – THE FIVE PRINCIPLES

In government buildings and TV broadcasts, on highway markers and school uniforms you'll see the *garuda,* Indonesia's mythical bird and national symbol. On its breast are the five symbols of the philosophical doctrine of Indonesia's unitary state, Pancasila (which means Five Principles in Sanskrit and Pali, the sacred languages of Hinduism and Buddhism). Pancasila was first expounded by Sukarno in 1945 as a synthesis of Western democracy, Islam, Marxism and indigenous village traditions. Enshrined in the 1945 constitution, it was raised to the level of a mantra by Suharto's New Order regime. Suharto's successor BJ Habibie annulled the requirement that Pancasila must form the basic principle of all organisations, but it remains an important national creed. The five symbols are:

- **Star** Represents faith in God, through Islam, Christianity, Buddhism, Hinduism or any other religion.
- **Chain** Represents humanitarianism within Indonesia and in relations with humankind as a whole.
- **Banyan Tree** Represents nationalism and unity between Indonesia's many ethnic groups.
- **Buffalo** Symbolises representative government.
- **Rice & Cotton** Represents social justice.

In 1920 the Indonesian Communist Party (PKI), which had operated within Sarekat Islam, split off on its own. A pro-independence party with support from urban workers, it launched uprisings in Java (1926) and Sumatra (1927) but was neutralised when these were quashed by the Dutch, who imprisoned and exiled thousands of communists.

A key moment in the growth of nationalist consciousness came in 1928 when the All Indonesia Youth Congress proclaimed its historic Youth Pledge, establishing goals of one national identity (Indonesian), one country (Indonesia) and one language (the version of Malay called Bahasa Indonesia). Meanwhile the Indonesian National Party (PNI), which emerged in 1927 from the Bandung Study Group led by a young engineer, Sukarno, was rapidly becoming the most powerful Indonesian nationalist organisation – with the result that in 1930 the Dutch jailed its leaders.

Nationalist sentiment remained high through the 1930s, but even when Germany invaded the Netherlands in 1940, the Dutch colonial government was determined to hold fast.

1936

Americans Robert and Louise Koke build simple bamboo bungalows on Bali's otherwise deserted Kuta Beach. They also introduce a sport called surfing they had learned in Hawaii.

1942

Japan invades Indonesia with little resistance. Europeans are sent to prison camps. Indonesians initially welcome the Japanese as liberators, but sentiment changes with the harshness of the occupation.

1942–45

The Japanese collaborate with nationalist leaders because of their anti-Dutch sentiments, and establish an Indonesian militia that later forms the backbone of the anti-Dutch resistance after WWII.

Aug 1945

Japan surrenders. Indonesian nationalist students kidnap Sukarno and Hatta and pressure them to declare independence, which they do on 17 August. Sukarno becomes president and Hatta vice-president.

WWII

Everything changed when Japan invaded the Dutch East Indies in 1942 and swept aside Dutch and Allied resistance. Almost 200,000 Dutch and Chinese civilians and Allied military were put into prison camps, in some of which 30% of the inmates would die. Many Indonesians at first welcomed the Japanese as liberators, but feelings changed as they were subjected to slave labour and starvation. The 3½-year Japanese occupation did however strengthen the Indonesian nationalist movement, as the Japanese used anti-Dutch nationalists to help them run things and allowed them limited political activity. Sukarno was permitted to travel around giving nationalist speeches. The Japanese also set up Indonesian home-defence militias, whose training proved useful in the Indonesians' later military struggle against the Dutch.

As defeat for Japan loomed in May 1945, the Investigating Agency for Preparation of Independence met in Jakarta. This Japanese-established committee of Indonesian nationalists proposed a constitution, philosophy (Pancasila) and extents (the whole Dutch East Indies) for a future Indonesian republic.

Anyone interested in the WWII campaigns in Indonesia, and the sites and relics that can be found there today, should check out the fascinating Pacific Wrecks (www.pacificwrecks.com).

The Revolution

When Japan announced its surrender on 15 August 1945, a group of *pemuda* (radical young nationalists) kidnapped Sukarno and his colleague Mohammed Hatta and pressured them to declare immediate Indonesian independence, which they did at Sukarno's Jakarta home on 17 August (you can see the text of their proclamation on the 100,000Rp banknote). A government was formed, with Sukarno president and Hatta the vice-president.

British and Australian forces arrived to disarm the Japanese and hold the Indonesian nationalists until the Dutch could send their own forces. But Indonesians wanted independence. Some, like Sukarno and Hatta, favoured a negotiated path to freedom; others wanted to fight to get it as fast as possible. The early months of the revolution were a particularly chaotic period with massacres of Chinese, Dutch and Eurasian civilians and Indonesian aristocrats; attempted communist revolutions in some areas; and clashes between Indonesian struggle groups and the British and Japanese. In the bloody Battle of Surabaya in November 1945, thousands died, not just from British bombing and in street fighting with the British, but also in nationalist atrocities against local civilians. In December the nationalists managed to pull diverse struggle groups together into a republican army.

Sep–Nov 1945

Allied troops suppress the nationalists. Sukarno wants independence through diplomacy, but other nationalists want to fight. The Battle of Surabaya between British and nationalist forces leaves thousands dead.

1946–49

Dutch troops arrive to regain control; the nationalists form a Republican Army. Despite Dutch offensives and rifts between Sukarno's government, Muslim movements and the Communists, resistance continues.

1949

Faced with an unwinnable war and hostile international opinion, the Netherlands transfers sovereignty over the Dutch East Indies (apart from Netherlands New Guinea) to the Indonesian republic.

1950–62

Armed movements challenge the republic. Darul Islam (House of Islam) wages guerrilla war in several islands, continuing until 1962 in western Java. Regionalist rebellions break out in Sumatra and Sulawesi.

By 1946, 55,000 Dutch troops had arrived. They soon re-captured major cities on Java and Sumatra. Ruthless tactics by Captain Raymond Westerling in southern Sulawesi saw at least 6000 Indonesians executed (40,000 by some accounts). The first of two big Dutch offensives – called 'police actions' – reduced republican territory to limited areas of Java and Sumatra in August 1947, with its capital at Yogyakarta.

Differences among the Indonesian forces erupted viciously. In Madiun, Java, the republican army and Muslim militias fought pro-communist forces in August 1948, leaving 8000 dead. The second Dutch 'police action' in December 1948 won the Dutch more territory, and they captured Sukarno, Hatta and their prime minister Sutan Syahrir. But the independence forces kept up a guerrilla struggle, and international (especially US) opinion turned against the Dutch. Realising that its cause was unwinnable, the Netherlands finally transferred sovereignty over the Dutch East Indies (apart from Dutch New Guinea) to the Indonesian republic on 27 December 1949. At least 70,000, possibly as many as 200,000, Indonesians had lost their lives in the revolution, along with 700 Dutch and British troops and some thousands of Japanese troops and European, Chinese and Eurasian civilians.

The Asia-Africa Conference staged at Bandung in 1955 launched the Non-Aligned Movement, comprising countries that wanted to align with neither the USA nor the USSR. It also gave birth to the term Third World, originally meaning countries that belonged to neither Cold War bloc.

'Bung' Karno

Independent Indonesia had a troubled infancy. Tensions between Muslims and communists persisted, with the secular nationalists like Sukarno and Hatta trying to hold everything together. The economy was in a sorry state after almost a decade of conflict, and a drop in commodity prices in the early 1950s made things worse.

Early Divisions

There were some who wanted Indonesia to be an Islamic republic, and there were some who didn't want their home territories to be part of Indonesia at all. The western-Java-based Darul Islam (House of Islam) wanted a society under Islamic law. It linked up with similar organisations in Kalimantan, Aceh and south Sulawesi to wage guerrilla war against the republic, which lasted until 1962 in western Java. In Maluku, Ambonese former soldiers of the Dutch colonial army declared an independent South Moluccas Republic in 1950. They were defeated within a few months.

Guided Democracy

Coalition governments drawn from diverse parties and factions never lasted long, and when the much-postponed parliamentary elections were finally held in 1955, no party won more than a quarter of the vote. Sukarno responded with 'Guided Democracy', effectively an uneasy coalition between the military, religious groups and communists, with increasing

1955

The PNI tops the polls in much-postponed parliamentary elections, but no clear winner emerges. Short-lived coalition governments continue. The economy struggles after commodity prices drop.

1957

Sukarno proclaims 'Guided Democracy', in the village tradition of achieving consensus through discussion. A military-Muslim-communist coalition replaces Western-style democracy.

1961–63

With the economy in the doldrums, Sukarno is aggressive towards Netherlands New Guinea. Indonesia takes control there in 1963. Subsequent opposition from the local Papuan people is brutally put down.

1963–66

Sukarno stages *konfrontasi* (confrontation) with the newly formed Malaysia. Fighting takes place along the Indonesia–Malaysia border in Borneo. The communist party (PKI) organises land seizures by hungry peasants.

power concentrated in the hands of the president (i.e. himself). In 1959 Sukarno also took on the job of prime minister for good measure. The elected legislature was dissolved in 1960, and of the political parties only the PKI continued to have any clout.

Sukarno's growing accumulation of power was one factor behind regional rebellions in Sumatra and Sulawesi in 1958, led by senior military and civilian figures. The rebels, who had backing from the CIA, were also opposed to the increasing influence of the communists, the corruption and inefficiency in central government, and the use of export earnings from the outer islands to import rice and consumer goods for Java. The rebellions were smashed within a few months and in response Sukarno forged a new alliance with Indonesia's army.

Monuments & Confrontations

Unable to lift the economy from the doldrums, Sukarno built a series of ostentatious nationalist monuments as substitutes for real development – such as Jakarta's National Monument (Monas, also dubbed 'Sukarno's last erection') and Mesjid Istiqlal. He diverted Indonesians' attention outward with a lot of bluster and aggression towards the supposedly threatening remnants of Western imperialism around Indonesia, Dutch New Guinea and Malaysia.

The New Guinea issue had already led Indonesia to seize all Dutch assets in the country and expel 50,000 Dutch people in 1957–58 after the UN rejected Indonesian claims to Dutch New Guinea. Bolstered by Soviet military backing, Indonesia finally took control of the territory in 1963 after a few military sorties and, more importantly, US pressure on the Netherlands to hand over. Subsequent opposition from the local Papuan population was brutally put down.

Coup & Anti-Communist Purge

Meanwhile back in the heartland, the PKI was encouraging peasants to seize land without waiting for official redistribution, leading to violent clashes in eastern Java and Bali. By 1965 the PKI claimed three million members, controlled the biggest trade union organisation and the biggest peasant grouping, and had penetrated the government apparatus extensively. Sukarno saw it as a potential counterweight to the army, whose increasing power now had him worried, and decided to arm the PKI by creating a new militia. This led to heightened tensions with the regular armed forces, and rumours started to circulate of a planned communist coup.

On 1 October 1965, military rebels shot dead six top generals in and near Jakarta. General Suharto, head of the army's Strategic Reserve, quickly mobilised forces against the rebels and by the next day it was clear the putsch had failed. Just who was behind it still remains a mystery, but there's no

Breaking the Silence (2012) is a collective memoir of 15 people who survived the anti-communist purges of 1965–66 when over 500,000 were killed. The acclaimed films *The Act of Killing* (2012) and *The Look of Silence* (2014) cover this same era, although censorship has prevented their showing in Indonesia.

1964–65

Worried by the military's power, Sukarno decides to arm the communist party by creating a new militia, heightening tensions with the regular forces. Rumours of a planned communist coup circulate.

1965

On 1 October, military rebels shoot dead six top generals in and near Jakarta. General Suharto mobilises forces against the rebels; the coup fails after only a day of fighting.

1965–1966

The armed forces and armed anti-communist civilians take the attempted coup as a cue to slaughter communists and supposed communists. More than 500,000 are killed, chiefly in Java, Bali and Sumatra.

1966–1968

When Suharto's troops surround his palace, Sukarno signs the 11 March Order (1966), permitting Suharto to act independently. After anti-Sukarno purges, the MPR names Suharto president (March 1968).

mystery about its consequences. The armed forces under Suharto, and armed anti-communist civilians, took it as a cue to ruthlessly target both communists and supposed communists. By March 1966, 500,000 or more people were killed, chiefly in Java, Bali and Sumatra. The anti-communist purge provided cover for settling all sorts of old scores.

The film and novel title *The Year of Living Dangerously* is that of a major 1964 speech by Sukarno, which was drawn from Italian leader Mussolini's slogan 'Live Dangerously', which itself was originally penned by 19th-century German philosopher Friedrich Nietzsche!

Sukarno Pushed Aside

Sukarno remained president but Suharto set about manoeuvring himself into supreme power. On 11 March 1966, Suharto's troops surrounded Sukarno's presidential palace, and Sukarno signed the 11 March Order, permitting Suharto to act on his own initiative to restore order. Sukarno loyalists in the forces and cabinet were soon arrested, and a new six-man inner cabinet including Suharto was established. After further anti-Sukarno purges and demonstrations, the People's Consultative Assembly (MPR) named Suharto acting president in March 1967. A year later, with Sukarno now under house arrest, the MPR appointed Suharto president.

Sukarno died of natural causes in 1970. An inspirational orator and charismatic leader, he is still held in great affection and esteem by many older Indonesians, who often refer to him as Bung Karno – *bung* meaning 'buddy' or 'brother'. He was a flamboyant, complicated and highly intelligent character with a Javanese father and Balinese mother, and was fluent in several languages. His influences, apart from Islam, included Marxism, Javanese and Balinese mysticism, a mainly Dutch education and the theosophy movement. He had at least eight wives (up to four at once) at a time when polygamy was no longer very common in Indonesia. Throughout his political career he strove to unite Indonesians and, more than anyone else, he was the architect and creator of Indonesia.

Peter Weir's gripping *The Year of Living Dangerously* (1982), based on the eponymous novel by Australian Christopher Koch (1978), stars Mel Gibson as a young Australian reporter caught up in Indonesia's 1965 upheavals. Mel's best movie?

'Pak' Harto

Once the dust had settled on the killing of communists and supposed communists, and a million or so political prisoners had been put behind bars, the 31 years of Suharto's rule were really one of the duller periods of Indonesian history. Such a tight lid was kept on opposition, protest and freedom of speech that there was almost no public debate. Under the New Order, as Suharto's regime was known, everybody just had to do what he and his generals told them to, if they weren't already dead or imprisoned.

Career Soldier

Whereas Sukarno had led with charisma, Suharto's speeches seemed designed to stifle discussion rather than inspire. 'Enigmatic' was one of the kinder epithets used in his obituaries when he died in 2008. The normally restrained *Economist* magazine called him a 'kleptocrat' and 'a cold-war

1967

Suharto's 'New Order', supported by the West, holds Indonesia together under military dictatorship for the next 30 years. The economy develops, dissent is crushed and corruption rages.

1971

The army party Golkar wins 236 of the 360 elective seats in the MPR, which now also includes 276 military and 207 Suharto appointees. Few believe this veneer of pseudo-democracy.

1973

Opposition parties are compulsorily merged – the Muslim parties into the Development Unity Party (PPP) and others into the Indonesian Democratic Party (PDI). Political activity in villages is banned.

1975

Indonesia invades and annexes former Portuguese colony East Timor, where left-wing party Fretilin has won a power struggle. A 20-year guerrilla war begins; over 125,000 die in fighting, famines and repression.

WHOSE COUP?

Some things about the 1965 attempted coup have never quite added up. Six of the country's top generals were killed by a group of officers who included members of Sukarno's palace guard and who said they were acting to save Sukarno's leadership – presumably from the threat of a plot. If that was really what they were doing, it was a very botched job.

These rebels appear to have made no effort to organise support elsewhere in the armed forces or the country. Both Sukarno and the communist leader DN Aidit visited the rebels at Halim air base near Jakarta but kept their distance from events – Sukarno leaving for the mountains in a helicopter and Aidit instructing his party to take no action and remain calm. If the officers expected the armed forces simply to fall into line under Sukarno's leadership, or the communists to rise up and take over, they miscalculated fatally.

The biggest question mark hangs over why they didn't also eliminate General Suharto, who was at least as senior as several of the generals they did kill. There is even a theory that Suharto himself might have been behind the attempted coup. Given his manipulatory talent and inscrutability, this can't be ruled out, though no evidence to confirm it has ever come to light.

monster', behind whose 'pudgily smooth, benign-looking face lay ruthless cruelty'. Suharto wielded a supreme talent for manipulating events in his own interests and outwitting opponents of all kinds.

Born in Java in 1921, he was always a soldier, from the day he joined the Dutch colonial army in his late teens. He rose quickly up the ranks of the Indonesian army in the 1950s, and was involved in putting down the South Moluccas and Darul Islam rebellions. He was transferred to a staff college after being implicated in opium and sugar smuggling in 1959, but in 1962 Sukarno appointed him to lead the military campaign against Dutch New Guinea.

The New Order

The New Order did give Indonesia stability of a sort, and a longish period of pretty steady economic development. Whereas Indonesians had thought of Sukarno as Bung Karno, Suharto was never more than the more formal Pak (father) Harto, but he liked to be thought of as Bapak Pembangunan – the Father of Development. Authoritarianism was considered the necessary price for economic progress.

Suharto and his generals believed Indonesia had to be kept together at all costs, which meant minimising political activity and squashing any potentially divisive movements – be they Islamic radicals, communists or the separatist rebels of Aceh, Papua (former Dutch New Guinea) and East Timor.

1979–84
The government's transmigration program reaches its peak with almost 2.5 million people moving to outer islands from overpopulated Java, Bali and Madura before the program ends in 2000.

1989
The Free Aceh Movement (GAM), founded in 1976, reemerges as a guerrilla force, fighting for independence for the conservatively Islamic Sumatran region. An estimated 15,000 people die through 2005.

1990s
NGOs, many of them started by middle-class Indonesians, emerge as a focus of dissent, campaigning on issues from peasant dispossessions to destructive logging and restrictions on Islamic organisations.

1997–1998
The Asian currency crisis savages Indonesia's economy. After troops kill four at a Jakarta demonstration in May 1998, rioting and looting cause an estimated 1200 deaths. Suharto quits on 21 May.

Suharto Inc

Near absolute power allowed the forces and Suharto's family and business associates to get away with almost anything. The army was not just a security force, it ran hundreds of businesses, legal and illegal, supposedly to supplement its inadequate funding from government. Corruption went hand-in-hand with secrecy and most notorious was the Suharto family itself. Suharto's wife Ibu Tien (nicknamed Madam Tien Per Cent) controlled the state monopoly on the import and milling of wheat; his daughter Tutut won the 1987 contract to build the Jakarta toll road; his son Tommy gained a monopoly on the cloves used in Indonesia's ultra-popular *kretek* cigarettes in 1989.

In 1995 Indonesia was ranked the most corrupt of all the 41 countries assessed in the first-ever Corruption Index published by Transparency International (TI). In 2004 TI placed Suharto at the top of its all-time world corruption table, with an alleged embezzlement figure of between US$15 billion and US$35 billion from his 32 years in power.

Of 18 people tried by an Indonesian human-rights court for abuses in East Timor in 1999, only militia leader Eurico Guterres was convicted. His conviction for a massacre of 12 people was quashed by the Indonesian Supreme Court in 2008.

Extending Indonesia

Suharto's regime saw to it that the former Dutch New Guinea stayed in Indonesia by staging a travesty of a confirmatory vote in 1969. Just over 1000 selected Papuan 'representatives' were pressured into voting unanimously for continued integration with Indonesia, in what was named the Act of Free Choice.

In 1975 the left-wing party Fretilin won a power struggle within the newly independent former Portuguese colony East Timor. The western part of Timor island, a former Dutch possession, was Indonesian. Horrified at the prospect of a left-wing government in a neighbouring state, Indonesia invaded and annexed East Timor. Fretilin kept up a guerrilla struggle and at least 125,000 Timorese died in fighting, famines and repression over the next 2½ decades.

The End of the New Order

The end of the New Order was finally precipitated by the Asian currency crisis of 1997, which savaged Indonesia's economy. Millions lost their jobs and rising prices sparked riots. Suharto faced unprecedented widespread calls for his resignation. Antigovernment rallies spread from universities to city streets, and when four students at Jakarta's Trisakti University were shot dead by troops in May 1998, the city erupted in rioting and looting, killing an estimated 1200. Even Suharto's own ministers called for his resignation, and he finally resigned shortly thereafter.

1998

Vice President BJ Habibie becomes president. He releases political prisoners and relaxes censorship, but the army kills at least 12 in a Jakarta student protest. Christian/Muslim violence erupts in Jakarta and Maluku.

1999

Some 78% vote for independence in East Timor. Militias backed by Indonesian military conduct a terror campaign before and after the vote. The region finally achieves independence in 2002.

Jun–Oct 1999

Following Indonesia's first free election since 1955, Abdurrahman Wahid of the country's largest Islamic organisation, Nahdlatul Ulama (Rise of the Scholars), becomes president as leader of a multi-party coalition.

1999–2001

Wahid tries to reform government, tackle corruption, reduce military power, bring Suharto to justice and address the grievances of Aceh and Papua. But his efforts are hamstrung by opponents.

EAST TIMOR TROUBLES

Indonesia, under President Habibie, agreed to a UN-organised independence referendum in East Timor, where human rights abuses, reported by Amnesty International among others, had blackened Indonesia's name internationally. In the 1999 vote, 78% of East Timorese chose independence. But the event was accompanied by a terror campaign by pro-Indonesia militia groups and Indonesian security forces, which according to Amnesty International killed an estimated 1300 people, and left much of East Timor's infrastructure ruined. The region finally gained full independence in 2002, and is now officially known as the Democratic Republic of Timor-Leste.

The Road to Democracy

Suharto's fall ushered in a period known as *reformasi* (reform), three tumultuous years in which elective democracy, free expression and human rights all advanced, and attempts were made to deal with the grievances of East Timor, Aceh and Papua. It was an era with many positives and some disasters and was ultimately a time when Indonesia's democracy emerged.

The Habibie Presidency

Suharto's vice-president BJ Habibie stepped up as president when Suharto resigned. Habibie released political prisoners, relaxed censorship and promised elections, but he still tried to ban demonstrations and reaffirmed the political role of the unpopular army. Tensions between Christians and Muslims in some parts of Indonesia also erupted into violence – especially Maluku, where thousands died in incidents between early 1999 and 2002.

The Wahid & Megawati Presidencies

Indonesia's first free parliamentary elections for 44 years took place in 1999. No party received a clear mandate, but the MPR elected Muslim preacher Abdurrahman Wahid president as leader of a coalition. The eccentric Wahid, from the country's largest Islamic organisation, Nahdlatul Ulama (Rise of the Scholars), was blind, had suffered two strokes and disliked formal dress and hierarchies. He embarked on an ambitious program to rein in the military, reform the legal and financial systems, promote religious tolerance, tackle corruption, and resolve the problems of Aceh and Papua. Unsurprisingly, all this upset everybody who was anybody, and in July 2001 the MPR dismissed Wahid over alleged incompetence and corruption.

2001

Violence erupts in Kalimantan between indigenous Dayaks and Madurese migrants. Over a million people are displaced by conflicts in Timor-Leste, Maluku, Kalimantan and elsewhere. Wahid is deposed.

2001–04

Vice-president Megawati Sukarnoputri, Sukarno's daughter, leading the PDI-P (Indonesian Democratic Party – Struggle) and supported by conservative elements, succeeds Wahid.

2002–05

Terrorist bombs in Kuta, Bali, in 2002 kill over 200, mainly foreign tourists. The Islamic militant group Jemaah Islamiah is blamed. Another series of bombs in Bali in 2005 kills 20.

2004

Anticorruption group Transparency International puts Suharto at the top of its all-time world corruption table, with an alleged embezzlement figure of between US$15 billion and US$35 billion from his 32 years in power.

UNREST AT THE EXTREMES

Two regions at opposite ends of Indonesia, Sumatra's Aceh and Papua resisted efforts to create a unified state over the last several decades, although Aceh now seems to have found a way to coexist.

Aceh

The conservatively Islamic, resource-rich region of Aceh was only brought under Dutch rule by a 35-year war ending in 1908. After the Dutch departed, Aceh wasn't happy about Indonesian rule either. The Free Aceh Movement (Gerakan Aceh Merdeka; GAM), founded in 1976, gathered steam after 1989, waging a guerrilla struggle for Acehnese independence. The 1990s saw Aceh under something close to military rule, with the population suffering from abuses by both sides. Peace talks collapsed in 2003 and Aceh was placed under martial law.

Everything changed with the tsunami on 26 December 2004, which wrought its biggest devastation on Aceh, killing some 170,000 people. The government was forced to allow foreign aid organisations into Aceh and to restart negotiations with GAM. A deal in 2005 formally ended three decades of armed struggle which had cost an estimated 15,000 lives. The peace has held since, even as the regional government becomes evermore fundamentalist while adhering to sharia law. In 2015 Christian churches were torn down and gay people were told they faced caning if they had sex.

Papua

Like Aceh, Papua wasn't brought into the Dutch East Indies until late in the colonial period. Papuan people are culturally distinct from other Indonesians, being of Melanesian heritage and having had very limited contact with the outside world until the 20th century. Today, most of them are Christian. Resistance to Indonesian rule has continued ever since Sukarno's takeover in 1963, in the form of sporadic guerrilla attacks by the Free Papua Organisation (Organisasi Papua Merdeka; OPM). The Indonesian army keeps a large number of troops in the province and there are sporadic skirmishes with rebels and regular reports of human rights abuses by international groups such as Human Rights Watch.

Papua is a resource-rich region seen by many Indonesians as ripe for exploitation. About half the population is Indonesian – primarily migrants – and this adds to Jakarta's reasons for keeping Papua close. That the economy and administration are dominated by non-Papuans fuels indigenous people's grievances and makes an Aceh-type autonomy solution impossible. Pro-independence sentiment among Papuans is high.

Vice President Megawati of the Indonesian Democratic Party – Struggle (PDI-P) took over as president in Wahid's place. Supported by many conservative, old-guard elements, Megawati – daughter of the legendary Sukarno – had none of her father's flair or vision and did little for reform in her three years in office.

Oct 2004	Dec 2004	2004–onwards	2006
In Indonesia's first direct presidential elections, Susilo Bambang Yudhoyono (SBY) of the new Democratic Party, a former general regarded as a liberal, wins a run-off vote against Megawati.	Over 200,000 Indonesians die in the 26 December tsunami that devastates large areas of Sumatra, especially Aceh. SBY restarts peace talks there, leading to a peace deal in 2005.	SBY and his successor see progress against B-list corruption. The army is edged away from politics and most of its business enterprises.	Bantul, near Yogyakarta, is hit by an earthquake on 27 May – 5800 die and 200,000 are left homeless across central Java. Another 700 die in a 17 July temblor.

The SBY Era

The year 2004 saw Indonesia's first-ever direct popular vote for president. Susilo Bambang Yudhoyono (SBY), leading the new Democratic Party (formed as his personal political vehicle), won in a run-off vote against Megawati. A popular and pragmatic politician, SBY quickly won favour by making sure foreign aid could get to tsunami-devastated Aceh and sealing a peace deal with Aceh's GAM rebels.

SBY's unspectacular but stable presidency saw the military forced to divest most of their business enterprises and edged away from politics (they lost their reserved seats in parliament in 2004). There was also progress against corruption. A former head of Indonesia's central bank, an MP, a governor of Aceh province and a mayor of Medan were all among those jailed thanks to the Corruption Eradication Commission, established in 2002, although no really big names were ensnared.

Fears of an upsurge in Islamic radicalism, especially after the Bali and Jakarta terrorist bombings of 2002 to 2005, proved largely unfounded. The great majority of Indonesian Muslims are moderate and while Islamic parties receive a sizeable share of the vote in elections, they can only do so by remaining in the political mainstream.

Indonesians clearly appreciated the stability and nonconfrontational style of SBY's presidency, and his successful handling of the economy, for they re-elected him in 2009 with over 60% of the vote. Interestingly neither religion nor ethnicity played a major part in determining how people voted, suggesting that many Indonesians valued democracy, peace and economic progress above sectarian or regional issues. Predictions that hardline Islamist parties would make huge gains proved false when they received only 8% of the vote.

Meanwhile, Indonesia's disasters – natural and otherwise – continued. In 2009, an earthquake killed over 1100 around Padang in West Sumatra. In 2010, an earthquake off the nearby coast killed 435 and spawned a tsunami that hit the Mentawai Islands. Over the same two-year period, there were eight fatal plane crashes (over 230 dead) and two ferry sinkings (over 275 dead). An SBY-ordered review of transport safety begun in 2007 made little difference.

Beginning in 2000, there were several terrorist attacks in Indonesia (including the Bali bombings in 2002 and 2005) blamed on Jemaah Islamiah, an Islamic terrorist group. Dozens were arrested and many were sentenced to jail, including three who were executed. Abu Bakar Bashir, a radical cleric who many thought was behind the explosions, eventually received a 15-year jail sentence in 2011.

Joko Ascends

Given that destructive colonialism, revolution, mass slaughter, ethnic warfare, dictatorship and more have been part of daily life in Indonesia in just the past 100 years, it's remarkable that recent elections have been so peaceful. The 2009 national elections were a watershed. More than a dozen parties waged high-energy campaigns. Rallies throughout the myriad islands were passionate and vibrant. Yet what happened in the end? The

2009

SBY is re-elected president with over 60% of the vote.

2012

Bali's ancient rice terraces and irrigation system *(subak)* gain Unesco World Heritage status, the first such designation in Indonesia since 2004 and only the eighth overall.

2014

Joko Widodo is elected president with 53% of the vote.

2014–15

Over 350 people are killed in a string of Indonesian aviation disasters including 162 in the crash of an Indonesian AirAsia flight off the coast of Java.

incumbent, SBY and his Democratic Party, won; Indonesians chose to go with the status quo.

Not bad given that it wasn't that long ago, at the Millennium, when there was blood in the streets from Lombok to the Malukus as religious and political factions settled scores and simply ran amok. Regional elections across the archipelago have also gone off without a hitch several times in recent years. All this set the stage in 2014 for Indonesia's most dramatic presidential election to date.

Representing Indonesia's old guard of wealth and the military was Prabowo Subianto, a former general who has long been dogged by allegations of human rights abuses during his time in East Timor and during the 1998 riots that led to the resignation of Suharto. Running against him was Joko Widodo, the populist mayor of Jakarta and a man possibly overburdened with platitudes such as 'humble', 'man of the people' and 'Obama-like'.

The word *sembako* refers to Indonesia's nine essential culinary ingredients: rice, sugar, eggs, meat, flour, corn, fuel, cooking oil and salt. When any of these become unavailable or more costly, repercussions can be felt right through to the presidency.

The election got was framed as old versus new and it attracted huge interest not only across Indonesia but across the world. This would be the greatest test yet of Indonesia's status as the world's third largest democracy (India is first followed by the US). Jokowi – as he's nearly universally known – captured the imagination of many voters fed up with the nation's endemic corruption and concentration of power among a tiny elite. There were even predictions of a Joko landslide; he won on July 9 with just over 53% of the vote to Prabowo's nearly 47%.

Despite rumblings from Prabowo's camp that they would challenge the results, the election was finally certified two weeks later. It seemed the old guard had been defeated in fair and peaceful elections, although this simple line doesn't necessarily hold up given that Joko's vice president is Jusuf Kalla, who held the same post under SBY from 2004 to 2009, and many other old guard stalwarts found their way into the administration. Interestingly, the coalition led by Prabowo won nearly 60% of the seats in the legislature, the People's Representative Council. At least at first they seemed content to work with Joko, although the long-term prospects of such cooperative spirit were by no means assured.

Culture

Across Indonesia's 17,000-odd islands you can hear over 300 different spoken languages and find a range of people from middle-class sophisticates of Jakarta, to subsistence communities speaking tribal dialects and following animist traditions deep in the mountains of West Timor. And then there are the cultural expressions, from the incredible richness of Bali to the buttoned-down conservatism of Aceh. Yet despite this diversity, almost everybody can speak one language: Bahasa Indonesia, a tongue that helps unify this sprawling, chaotic collection of peoples.

National Identity

Indonesia comprises a massively diverse range of societies and cultures; the differences between, say, the Sumbanese and Sundanese are as marked as those between the Swedes and Sicilians. Even so, a strong national Indonesian identity has emerged, originally through the struggle for independence and, following that, through education programs and the promotion of Bahasa Indonesia as the national language. This is despite the fact that Indonesia continues to be stretched by opposing forces: 'strict' Islam versus 'moderate' Islam, Islam versus Christianity versus Hinduism, outer islands versus Java, country versus city, modern versus traditional, rich versus poor, the modern world versus the past.

The popular annual Ubud Writers & Readers Festival (www.ubudwritersfestival.com) in Bali, held in October, showcases both local and international writers and has an annual theme.

One Culture or Many?

The differences within Indonesian culture may challenge social cohesion and have at times been used as an excuse to incite conflict, but the nation still prevails. And, with notable exceptions such as Papua, the bonds have grown stronger, with the notion of an Indonesian identity overlapping rather than supplanting the nation's many pre-existing regional cultures. The national slogan, *Bhinneka Tunggal Ika* (Unity in Diversity) – even though its words are old Javanese – has been adopted by Indonesians across widely varying ethnic and social standpoints.

Religion as Culture

A cultural element that bridges both the regional and the national is religion – the Pancasila principle of belief in a god holds firm. Though Indonesia is predominantly Islamic, in many places Islam is interwoven with traditional customs, giving it unique qualities and characteristics. Some areas are Christian or animist and, to leaven the mix, Bali has its own unique brand of Hinduism. Religion plays a role in the everyday: mosques and *musholla* (prayer rooms) are in constant use, and the vibrant Hindu ceremonies of Bali are a daily occurrence, to the delight of visitors.

Nationalism and Ethnic Conflict in Indonesia (2004) by Jacques Bertrand remains a solid primer on the reasons behind violence in areas such as Maluku and Kalimantan.

Trends & Traditions

Smart phones, huge malls, techno-driven nightclubs and other facets of international modernity are common in Indonesia. But while the main cities and tourist resorts can appear technologically rich, other areas remain untouched. And even where modernisation has taken hold, it's clear that Indonesians have a very traditionalist heart. As well as adhering to religious

SMALL TALK

One thing that takes many visitors by surprise in Indonesia is what may seem like over-inquisitiveness from complete strangers. Questions from them might include the following:

- *Dari mana?* (Where do you come from?)
- *Mau kemana?* (Where are you going?)
- *Tinggal dimana?* (Where are you staying?)
- *Jalan sendiri?* (Are you travelling alone?)
- *Sudah kawin?* (Are you married?)
- *Anak-anak ada?* (Do you have children?)

Visitors can find these questions intrusive or irritating, and in tourist areas they may just be a prelude to a sales pitch, but more often they are simply polite greetings and an expression of interest in a foreigner. A short answer or a Bahasa Indonesia greeting, with a smile, is a polite and adequate response. If you get into a slightly longer conversation, it's proper to ask some of the same questions in return. When you've had enough chatter, you can answer the question 'Where are you going?' even if it hasn't been asked. Try the following:

- *Jalan-jalan* (Walking around)
- *Saya pergi dulu* (literally 'I go first' nicely says that you can't pause for a pitch)

and ethnic traditions, Indonesians also maintain social customs. Politeness to strangers is a deeply ingrained habit throughout most of the archipelago. Elders are still accorded great respect. When visiting someone's home, elders are always greeted first, and often customary permission to depart is also offered. This can occur whether in a high-rise in Medan or a hut in the Baliem Valley.

Riri Riza's *Gie* (2005), the story of Soe Hok Gie, an ethnic Chinese antidictatorship activist, was submitted for consideration in the Best Foreign Film category of the Academy Awards. His *3 Hari Untuk Selamanya* (Three Days to Forever, 2007) is a classic road movie about a modern journey from Jakarta to Yogyakarta.

Lifestyle

Daily life for Indonesians has changed rapidly in the last decade or two. These days, many people live away from their home region and the role of women has extended well beyond domestic duties to include career and study.

Family Life

The importance of the family remains nevertheless high. This is evident during such festivals as Idul Fitri (Lebaran, the end of the Islamic fasting month), when highways become gridlocked, ferries get jammed and planes fill with those returning home to loved ones. Even at weekends, many travel for hours to spend a day with their relatives. In many ways, the notions of family and regional identity have become more pronounced: as people move away from small-scale communities and enter the milieu of the cities, the sense of belonging becomes more valued.

Village Life

Beyond family, the main social unit is the village, whether it is in the country or manifests in the form of a suburb or neighbourhood in an urban area. Less than half the population still lives in rural areas (it was 80% in 1975) where labour in the fields, the home or the market is the basis of daily life. So, for younger Indonesians, is school – though not for as many as might be hoped. Nine out of 10 children complete the five years of primary schooling, but barely over six out of 10 get through secondary school. Kids from poorer families have to start supplementing the family income at an early age.

The village spirit can be found on Jakarta's backstreets, which, for example, are home to tightknit neighbourhoods where kids run from house to house and everyone knows who owns which chicken. A sense of community may also evolve in a *kos* (apartment with shared facilities), where tenants, far from their families, come together for meals and companionship.

Cowboys in Paradise (2009), directed by Amit Virmani, has made headlines for its unflinching portrait of real-life gigolos in Bali. Fixtures of Kuta Beach, these men are popular with some female tourists.

Traditional Life

For the many Indonesians who still live in their home regions, customs and traditions remain a part of the everyday: the Toraja of Sulawesi continue to build traditional houses due to their social importance; the focus of a Sumbanese village remains the gravestones of their ancestors due to the influence they are believed to have in daily happenings. These aren't customs offered attention once a year – they are a part of life. And many Dayaks of Kalimantan still live in communal longhouses sheltering 20 families or more.

And even as modernity has found purchase across much of the nation, age-old traditions can still underpin life: Bali, for example, still scrupulously observes its annual day of silence, Nyepi (Balinese Lunar New Year), when literally all activity stops and everyone stays at home (or in their hotels) so that evil spirits will think the island uninhabited and leave it alone.

Gay Life

Contradictions also run through the status of gays in Indonesian society. Indonesians of both sexes are actively gay, and repression is mostly absent. However this isn't universally true, especially in Aceh where a 2015 incident received attention worldwide: two young women hugging were accused by Sharia police officers of being lesbians and taken in for questioning. A short time later, the Aceh government announced that gay people having sex would be punished with 100 strokes of the cane.

Positive recognition of gay identity or gay rights is largely missing. *Waria* (transgender or transvestite) performers and prostitutes have quite a high profile. Otherwise gay behaviour is, by and large, accepted without being particularly approved of. Bali, with its big international scene, and some Javanese cities have the most open gay life – although a gay wedding ceremony at a resort on Bali in 2015 drew an official rebuke.

Multiculturalism

Indonesia is a country of literally hundreds of cultures. Every one of its 700-plus languages denotes, at least to some extent, a different culture. They range from the matrilineal Minangkabau of Sumatra and the artistic Hindu Balinese, to the seafaring Bugis and buffalo-sacrificing Toraja of Sulawesi and Papua's penis-gourd-wearing Dani, to name but a few. Indonesia's island nature and rugged, mountainous terrain have meant

MIGRATION & HOMOGENISATION

Ethnic and cultural tensions in Indonesia have often been fuelled by *transmigrasi* (transmigration), the government-sponsored program of migration from more overcrowded islands (Java, Bali and Madura) to less crowded ones such as Kalimantan, Sumatra, Sulawesi and Papua. Over eight million people were relocated between 1950 and 2000. Local residents have often resented their marginalisation due to a sudden influx of people with little regard or use for local cultures and traditions. That the newcomers have the full sponsorship of the government adds to the resentment.

that groups of people have often developed in near isolation from each other, resulting in an extraordinary differentiation of culture and language across the archipelago. Even in densely populated Java there are distinct groups, such as the Badui, who withdrew to the western highlands as Islam spread through the island and have had little contact with outsiders.

One Nation, Many Cultures

The notion that all these peoples could form one nation is a relatively young one, originating in the later part of the Dutch colonial era. Indonesia's 20th-century founding fathers knew that if a country of such diverse culture and religion was to hold together, it needed special handling. They fostered Indonesian nationalism and a national language (Bahasa Indonesia, spoken today by almost all Indonesians but the mother tongue for only about 20% of them). They rejected ideas that Indonesia should be a federal republic (potentially centrifugal), or a state subject to the law of Islam, even though this is the religion of the great majority. Today, most Indonesian citizens (with the chief exceptions of many Papuans and some Acehnese) are firmly committed to the idea of Indonesia, even if there is a lingering feeling that in some ways the country is a 'Javanese empire'.

Rimbaud in Java: The Lost Voyage by Jamie James (2011) recreates poet Arthur Rimbaud's Java escape in 1876 when he first joined the Dutch army and then deserted, fleeing into the jungle.

Religion

Indonesia's constitution affirms that the state is based on a belief in 'the One and Only God'; yet it also, rather contradictorily, guarantees 'freedom of worship, each according to his/her own religion or belief'. In practice, this translates into a requirement to follow one of the officially accepted 'religions', of which there are now six: Islam, Catholicism, Protestantism, Hinduism, Buddhism and Confucianism.

Islam is the predominant religion, with followers making up about 88% of the population. In Java, pilgrims still visit hundreds of holy places where spiritual energy is believed to be concentrated. Christians make up about 10% of the population, in scattered areas spread across the archipelago. Bali's Hindus comprise about 1.5% of the population.

Nevertheless, old beliefs persist. The earliest Indonesians were animists who practised ancestor and spirit worship. When Hinduism and Buddhism and, later, Islam and Christianity spread into the archipelago, they were layered onto this spiritual base.

Islam

Islam arrived in Indonesia with Muslim traders from the Arabian Peninsula and India as early as the 7th century AD, within decades of the Prophet Muhammad receiving the word of Allah (God) in Mecca. The first Indonesian rulers to convert to Islam were in the small North Sumatran ports of Lamreh and Pasai in the 13th century. Gradually over the following two centuries, then more rapidly, other Indonesian states adopted Islam. The religion initially spread along sea-trade routes, and the conversion of Demak, Tuban, Gresik and Cirebon, on Java's north coast, in the late 15th century was an important step in its progress.

In the Shadow of Swords (2005) by Sally Neighbour investigates the rise of terrorism in Indonesia and beyond, from an Australian perspective.

The first Indonesian rulers to adopt Islam chose to do so from contact with foreign Muslim communities. Some other states were converted by conquest. Java's first Islamic leaders have long been venerated and mythologised as the nine *walis* (saints). Many legends are told about their feats of magic or war, and pilgrims visit their graves despite the official proscription of saint worship by Islam.

Customs

Today, Indonesia has the largest Muslim population of any country in the world and the role Islam should play in its national life is constantly debated. Mainstream Indonesian Islam is moderate. Muslim women are

RAMADAN

One of the most important months of the Muslim calendar is the fasting month of Ramadan. As a profession of faith and spiritual discipline, Muslims abstain from food, drink, cigarettes and other worldly desires (including sex) from sunrise to sunset. However, many of the casually devout will find loopholes in the strictures.

Ramadan is often preceded by a cleansing ceremony, Padusan, to prepare for the coming fast *(puasa)*. Traditionally, during Ramadan people get up at 3am or 4am to eat (this meal is called *sahur*) and then fast until sunset. Special prayers are said at mosques and at home.

The first day of the 10th month of the Muslim calendar is the end of Ramadan, called Idul Fitri or Lebaran. Mass prayers are held in the early morning, followed by two days of feasting. Extracts from the Koran are read and religious processions take place. During this time of mutual forgiveness, gifts are exchanged and pardon is asked for past wrongdoing.

During Ramadan, many restaurants and warungs are closed in Muslim regions of Indonesia. Those owned by non-Muslims will be open, but in deference to those fasting, they may have covered overhangs or will otherwise appear shut. In the big cities, many businesses are open and fasting is less strictly observed. Street stalls, mall food courts and warungs all come alive for the evening meal.

Though not all Muslims can keep to the privations of fasting, the overwhelming majority do and you should respect their values. Do not eat, drink or smoke in public unless you see others doing so.

Note that for a week before and a week after the official two-day Idul Fitri holiday, transport is chaotic; don't even consider travelling during this time as roads and buses are jammed, flights full and ferries bursting. You will be better off in non-Muslim areas – such as Bali, east Nusa Tenggara, Maluku or Papua – but even these areas have significant Muslim populations. Plan well ahead, find yourself an idyllic spot and stay put.

Ramadan and Idul Fitri move back 10 days or so every year, according to the Muslim calendar.

not segregated nor, in most of the country, do they have to wear the *jilbab* (head covering), although this has recently become more common. Muslim men are allowed to marry two women but must have the consent of their first wife. Even so, polygamy in Indonesia is very rare. Many pre-Islamic traditions and customs remain in place. The Minangkabau society of Sumatra, for example, is strongly Islamic but remains matrilineal according to tradition.

Islam requires that all boys be circumcised, and in Indonesia this is usually done between the ages of six and 11. Muslims observe the fasting month of Ramadan. Friday afternoons are officially set aside for believers to worship, and all government offices and many businesses are closed as a result. In accordance with Islamic teaching, millions of Indonesians have made the pilgrimage to Mecca.

In many Indonesian hotel rooms you'll notice a small arrow pointing in a seemingly random direction on the ceiling; it's actually indicating the direction of Mecca for Muslims who want to pray but can't get to a mosque.

Islamic Laws

An attempt by some Islamic parties to make sharia (Islamic religious law) a constitutional obligation for all Indonesian Muslims was rejected by the national parliament in 2002. Sharia was firmly outlawed under the Suharto dictatorship, but elements of it have since been introduced in some cities and regions. Aceh was permitted to introduce strict sharia under its 2005 peace deal with the government. In Aceh gambling, alcohol and public affection between the sexes are all now banned, some criminals receive corporal punishment, and the *jilbab* is compulsory for women. Public displays of intimacy, alcohol and 'prostitute-like appearance' are outlawed in the factory town of Tangerang on Jakarta's outskirts, and the *jilbab* is obligatory in Padang on Sumatra.

However the result of recent elections is that the great majority of Muslims are moderates and do not want an Islamic state. Neither of Indonesia's two biggest Muslim organisations (each has about 30 million members, but are not political parties) – the traditionalist Nahdlatul Ulama (Rise of the Scholars) and the modernist Muhammadiyah – now seek an Islamic state.

There are indications that a more conservative form of Islam is gaining some traction. While regions including Sumbawa, West Java and notably Aceh are quite conservative, changes are coming elsewhere. There are reports of mandatory Islamisation of young girls in some parts of West Papua and Sumatra.

Militant Islam

Militant Islamist groups that have made headlines with violent actions speak for only small minorities. Jemaah Islamiah was responsible for the 2002 Bali bombings and other acts of terror. The Indonesian government has captured or killed many of its principals, including cleric Abu Bakar Bashir who was jailed for 15 years in 2011.

Outside India, Hindus predominate only in Nepal and Bali. The Hinduism of Bali is literally far removed from that of India.

Christianity

The Portuguese introduced Roman Catholicism to Indonesia in the 16th century. Although they dabbled in religious conversion in Maluku and sent Dominican friars to Timor and Flores, their influence was never strong. The Dutch introduced Protestantism but made little effort to spread it. Missionary efforts came only after the Dutch set about establishing direct colonial rule throughout Indonesia in the 19th century. Animist areas were up for grabs and missionaries set about their work with zeal in parts of Nusa Tenggara, Maluku, Kalimantan, Papua, Sumatra and Sulawesi. A significant number of Chinese Indonesians converted to Christianity during the Suharto era.

Protestants (about 7% of the population) outnumber Catholics, largely because of the work of Dutch Calvinist and Lutheran missions and more recent Evangelical movements. The main Protestant populations are in the Batak area of Sumatra, the Minahasa and Toraja areas of Sulawesi, Timor and Sumba in Nusa Tenggara, Papua, parts of Maluku and Dayak areas of Kalimantan. Catholics comprise 3% of the population and are most numerous in Papua and Flores.

JAVA'S TOP FIVE CLASSICAL MOSQUES

Indonesia's most revered mosques tend to be those built in the 15th and 16th centuries in Javanese towns that were among the first to convert to Islam. The 'classical' architectural style of these mosques includes tiered roofs clearly influenced by the Hindu culture that Islam had then only recently supplanted. They are curiously reminiscent of the Hindu temples still seen on Bali today. During the Suharto era in the late 20th century, hundreds of standardised, prefabricated mosques were shipped and erected all around Indonesia in pale imitation of this classical Javanese style.

- **Mesjid Agung**, Demak (p151)
- **Mesjid Al-Manar**, Kudus (p152)
- **Mesjid Agung**, Solo (p134)
- **Mesjid Agung**, Banten (p74)
- **Masjid Kuno Bayan Beleq**, Lombok (p313)

BELIEFS OUTSIDE THE OFFICIAL BOX

Fascinating elements of animism, mostly concerned with the spirits of the dead or fertility rituals, survive alongside the major religions all over Indonesia today – especially among peoples in fairly remote places. These belief systems often involve elaborate rituals, which have become tourist attractions in their own right, and include the following:

- **Sumbanese**, Nusa Tenggara (p394)
- **Dayaks**, Kalimantan (p586)
- **Bataks**, Sumatra (p509)
- **Mentawaians**, Sumatra (p547)
- **Minangkabau**, Sumatra (p537)
- **Niassans**, Sumatra (p515)
- **Toraja**, Sulawesi (p660)
- **Dani**, Papua (p484)
- **Asmat**, Papua (p488)

Hinduism & Buddhism

These belief systems of Indian origin have a key place in Indonesian history but are now practised by relatively small numbers. Arriving with Indian traders by the 5th century AD, Hinduism and Buddhism came to be adopted by many kingdoms, especially in the western half of Indonesia. All of the most powerful states in the archipelago until the 15th century – such as Sriwijaya, based in southeast Sumatra, and Majapahit, in eastern Java – were Hindu, Buddhist or a combination of the two, usually in fusion with earlier animist beliefs. Indonesian Hinduism tended to emphasise worship of the god Shiva, the destroyer, perhaps because this was closer to existing fertility worship and the appeasement of malevolent spirits. Buddhism, more a philosophy than a religion, shunned the Hindu pantheon of gods in its goal of escaping from suffering by overcoming desire.

Though Islam later replaced them almost everywhere in Indonesia, Hinduism and Buddhism left a powerful imprint on local culture and spirituality. This is most obvious today in the continued use of stories from the Hindu Ramayana and Mahabharata epics in Javanese and Balinese dance and theatre – as well as in major monuments like the great Javanese temple complexes of Borobudur (Buddhist) and Prambanan (Hindu). Bali survived as a stronghold of Hinduism because nobles and intelligentsia of the Majapahit kingdom congregated there after the rest of their realm fell to Islam in the 15th century.

Most Buddhists in Indonesia today are Chinese. Their numbers have been estimated at more than two million, although this may come down at the next count following the reinstatement of Confucianism as an official religion in 2006. Confucianism, the creed of many Chinese Indonesians, was delisted in the Suharto era, forcing many Chinese to convert to Buddhism or Christianity.

> Author Djenar Maesa Ayu shook up Indonesia's literary scene with her candid portrayal of the injustices tackled by women. Her books include *Mereka Bilang, Saya Monyet* (They Say I'm a Monkey, 2001), *Nayla* (2005) and *1 Perempuan, 14 Laki-laki* (1 Woman, 14 Men, 2011).

Women in Indonesia

For Indonesian women, the challenges of balancing traditional roles and the opportunities and responsibilities of the modern era are most pronounced. Many are well educated and well employed; women are widely represented in the bureaucracy and business, although elections in 2009 and 2014 saw women win only about 18% of the seats, far below a goal of 30% professed by some of the parties. Two-income households are

'ANTIPORN' & OTHER RESTRICTIVE LAWS

One issue that continues to stir emotions in Indonesia is the 'antipornography' law finally passed by parliament and signed into law in 2008 after years of debate. Promoted by Islamic parties, the law has a very wide definition of pornography that can potentially be applied to every kind of visual, textual or sound communication or performance, and even conversations and gestures. Many traditional forms of behaviour across the archipelago are technically illegal – from wearing penis gourds on Papua, to the modest gyrations of traditional Javanese dancers (to say nothing of the brazenly topless on Bali's beaches).

Exactly what the antiporn law means is ill-defined. Behaviour not sanctioned in some areas continues in others. Although singled out by a quasi-governmental group for being 'immoral' in 2009, yoga on Bali is being taught and practised by more people than ever. And there have been assurances from the government that Balinese dance and other cultural forms of expression across the archipelago are safe from the law's ill-defined strictures. Opponents of the law include some secular political parties as well as women's, human-rights, regional, Christian, artists' and performers' groups and tourism industry interests.

Many internet providers block a wide range of sites deemed immoral and there has been a general chilling of freedom of expression. In 2011, the popular singer Ariel (aka Nazril Irham) was sentenced to more than three years in prison when a sex tape he made ended up on the internet, after his laptop was stolen. He was released in 2012 and has taken to performing with his band Noah overseas to escape the restrictions at home.

Recently there have been other efforts to curb behaviour seen as antithetical to more traditional Muslim beliefs:

- Restrictive alcohol sales laws (p745) passed and modified in 2015.
- Plans announced by Jakarta city counselors to require all nightclubs to close at midnight.

Of course, given the range of attitudes across the archipelago, the enforcement and interpretation of such dictates varies widely.

Bali: Island of Dogs, a film by Lawrence Blair and Dean Allan Tolhurst, shows the complicated lives of the island's misunderstood dogs. Many are being slaughtered in the ongoing – and misguided – effort to eradicate rabies.

increasingly common and often a necessity, however women typically still see roles such as housekeeping and child rearing as their domain.

As a predominantly Islamic society Indonesia remains male-oriented, though women are not cloistered or required to observe *purdah* (the practice of screening women from strangers by means of a curtain or all-enveloping clothes). The *jilbab* has become more common, but it does not necessarily mean that women who wear it have a subservient personality or even deep Islamic faith. It can also be a means of deflecting unwanted male attention.

It's also increasingly common to see women in Muslim areas wearing headscarves even as the popular media typically shows women without.

Tenuous Gains?

Despite the social liberation of women visible in urban areas, there are those who see the advances made by conservative Islam in the past decade as a threat to women. Pressure on women to dress and behave conservatively comes from elements of sharia law that have been introduced in areas such as Aceh.

An attempt to reform family law in 2005 and give greater rights to women never even got to be debated in parliament after Islamic fundamentalists threatened those who were drafting it. Women still cannot legally be heads of households, which presents particular problems for Indonesia's estimated six million single mothers.

Arts

Indonesians are very artistic people. This is most obvious in Bali, where the creation of beauty is part of the fabric of daily life, but it's apparent throughout the archipelago in music, dance, theatre, painting and in the handmade artisanry, of which every different island or area seems to have its own original form.

Theatre & Dance

Drama and dance in Indonesia are intimately connected in the hybrid form that is best known internationally – Balinese dancing. The colourful Balinese performances, at times supremely graceful, at others almost slapstick, are dances that tell stories, sometimes from the Indian Ramayana or Mahabharata epics. Balinese dance is performed both as entertainment and as a religious ritual, playing an important part in temple festivals.

Java's famed *wayang* (puppet) theatre also tells Ramayana and Mahabharata stories, through the use of shadow puppets, three-dimensional wooden puppets, or real people dancing the *wayang* roles. It too can still have ritual significance. Yogyakarta and Solo are centres of traditional Javanese culture where you can see a *wayang* performance.

The best bet for traditional dance? Ubud on Bali, where you can see several performances by talented troupes every night of the week.

Yogyakarta and Solo are also the centres of classical Javanese dance, a more refined, stylised manner of acting out the Hindu epics, performed most spectacularly in the Ramayana Ballet at Prambanan.

Many other colourful dance and drama traditions are alive and well around the archipelago. The Minangkabau people of West Sumatra have a strong tradition of Randai dance-drama at festivals and ceremonies, which incorporates *pencak silat* (a form of martial arts). The Batak Sigalegale puppet dance sees life-sized puppets dancing for weddings and funerals. Western Java's Jaipongan is a dynamic style that features swift movements to rhythms complicated enough to dumbfound an audience of musicologists. It was developed out of local dance and music traditions after Sukarno banned rock 'n' roll in 1961.

Central Kalimantan is home to the Manasai, a friendly dance in which tourists are welcome to participate. Kalimantan also has the Mandau, a dance performed with knives and shields. Papua is best known for its warrior dances, most easily seen at annual festivals at Danau Sentani and in the Baliem Valley and Asmat region.

Music

Traditional

Gamelan orchestras dominate traditional music in Java and Bali. Composed mainly of percussion instruments such as xylophones, gongs, drums and *angklung* (bamboo tubes shaken to produce a note), but also flutes, gamelan orchestras may have as many as 100 members. The sound produced by a gamelan can range from harmonious to eerie, with the tempo and intensity of sound undulating on a regular basis. Expect to hear powerful waves of music one minute and a single instrument holding court the next.

Jalanan, a 2013 documentary by Daniel Ziv, provides a compelling look at the lives of three Jakarta street musicians as they try to keep pace with rapid societal change.

Balinese gamelan is more dramatic and varied than the refined Javanese forms, but all gamelan music has a hypnotic and haunting effect. It always accompanies Balinese and Javanese dance, and can also be heard in dedicated gamelan concerts, particularly in Solo and Yogyakarta in Java. Similar types of ensembles are also found elsewhere, such as the *telempong* of West Sumatra.

Another ethereal traditional music is West Java's serene *kacapi suling*, which features the *kacapi* (a harplike instrument) and *suling* (a bamboo flute).

Contemporary

Indonesia has a massive contemporary music scene that spans all genres. The popular *dangdut* is a melange of traditional and modern, Indonesian and foreign musical styles that features instruments such as electric guitars and Indian tablas, and rhythms ranging from Middle Eastern pop to reggae or salsa. The result is sexy, love-drunk songs sung by heartbroken women or cheesy men, accompanied by straight-faced musicians in matching suits. The beats are gutsy, the emotion high, the singing evocative and the dancing often provocative.

Rock legend Iwan Fals has been around for decades but still packs stadiums. His anti-establishment bent has caused him to be arrested several times.

The writhings of *dangdut* star Inul Daratista (whose adopted stage name means 'the girl with breasts') were one reason behind the passage of Indonesia's controversial 'antipornography' legislation. She continues to sell out large venues around the archipelago.

No discussion of modern Indonesian music is complete without mention of the punk band Superman is Dead. From its start on Bali in 1995, the three-man group has gained fans across the country and the world. These days they're known for their environmental crusades.

Painting

Galleries in the wealthier neighbourhoods of Jakarta are the epicentre of Indonesia's contemporary art scene, which has flourished with a full panoply of installations, sculptures, performance art and more, and which can be either extremely original, eye-catching and thought-provoking, or the opposite. Jakarta (www.jakartabiennale.net) and Yogyakarta (www.biennalejogja.org) both hold big biennale art events.

Traditionally, painting was an art for decorating palaces and places of worship, typically with religious or legendary subject matter. Foreign artists in Bali in the 1930s inspired a revolution in painting: artists began to depict everyday scenes in new, more realistic, less crowded canvases. Others developed an attractive 'primitivist' style. Much Balinese art today is mass-produced tourist-market stuff, though there are also talented and original artists, especially in and around Ubud. Indonesia's most celebrated 20th-century painter was the Javanese expressionist Affandi (1907–90), who liked to paint by squeezing the paint straight out of the tube.

Architecture

Indonesia is home to a vast and spectacular variety of architecture, from religious and royal buildings to traditional styles of home-building, which can differ hugely from one part of the archipelago to another. Indian, Chinese, Arabic and European influences have all added their mark to locally developed styles.

Bali Style (1995), by Barbara Walker and Rio Helmi, is a lavishly photographed look at Balinese design, architecture and interior decoration. It captured a spare, tropical look that spawned oodles of copycat books and magazines and is today almost a cliché.

The great 8th- and 9th-century temples of Borobudur, Prambanan and the Dieng Plateau, in Central Java, all show the Indian influence that predominated in the Hindu-Buddhist period. Indian style, albeit with a distinctive local flavour, persists today in the Hindu temples of Bali, where the leaders of the Hindu-Buddhist Majapahit kingdom took refuge after being driven from Java in the 16th century.

Traditional Houses

For their own homes Indonesians developed a range of eye-catching structures whose grandeur depended on the family that built them. Timber construction, often with stilts, and elaborate thatched roofs of palm leaves or grass are common to many traditional housing forms around the archipelago. The use of stilts helps to reduce heat and humidity and avoid mud, floods and pests. Tana Toraja in Sulawesi, Pulau Nias off Sumatra, and the Batak and Minangkabau areas of Sumatra exhibit some of the most spectacular vernacular architecture, with high, curved roofs.

THE POWER OF SMILES

A smile goes a very long way in Indonesia. It's said Indonesians have a smile for every emotion, and keeping one on your face even in a difficult situation helps to avoid giving offence. Indonesians generally seek consensus rather than disagreement, so maintaining a sense of accord, however tenuous, is a good idea in all dealings. Anger or aggressive behaviour is considered poor form.

Royal Palaces

Royal palaces around Indonesia are often developments of basic local housing styles, even if far more elaborate as in the case of Javanese *kraton* (walled palaces). Yogyakarta's *kraton* is effectively a city within a city inhabited by over 25,000 people. On Bali, where royal families still exist – even if they often lack power – the 'palaces' are much more humble.

Colonial Buildings

The Dutch colonists initially built poorly ventilated houses in European style but eventually a hybrid Indo-European style emerged, using elements such as the Javanese *pendopo* (open-sided pavilion) and *joglo* (a high-pitched roof). International styles such as art deco started to arrive in the late 19th century as large numbers of factories, train stations, hotels, hospitals and other public buildings went up in the later colonial period. Bandung in Java has one of the world's largest collections of 1920s art deco buildings.

The Banda Islands in Maluku are a virtual theme park of Dutch colonial architecture with old forts and streets lined with old columned buildings sporting shady verandas.

The glossy monthly English-language magazine *Jakarta Java Kini* (http://emag.jjk.co.id) contains interesting articles on what's hot in the arts and entertainment, with a Jakarta focus. Another good source of Jakarta and Bali cultural news is *The Beat* (http://beatmag.com).

Modern Architecture

Early independent Indonesia had little money to spare for major building projects, though President Sukarno did find the funds for a few prestige projects such as Jakarta's huge and resplendent Mesjid Istiqlal. The economic progress of the Suharto years saw Indonesia's cities spawn their quota of standard international high-rise office blocks and uninspired government buildings, though tourism helped to foster original, even spectacular, hybrids of local and international styles in hotels and resorts. Bali in particular has some properties renowned for their architecture around the coast (especially on the Bukit Peninsula) and overlooking the river valleys near Ubud.

Balinese Architecture

The basic feature of Balinese architecture is the *bale* (pronounced 'ba-lay'), a rectangular, open-sided pavilion with a steeply pitched roof of palm thatch. A family compound will have a number of *bale* for eating, sleeping and working. The focus of a community is the *bale banjar,* a large pavilion for meeting, debate, gamelan practice and so on. Buildings such as restaurants and the lobby areas of hotels are often modelled on the *bale* – they are airy, spacious and handsomely proportioned.

Like the other arts, architecture has traditionally served the religious life of Bali. Balinese houses, although attractive, have never been lavished with the architectural attention that is given to temples. Even Balinese palaces are modest compared with the more important temples. Temples are designed to fixed rules and formulas, with sculpture serving as an adjunct, a finishing touch to these design guidelines.

Mosques

Mosque interiors are normally empty except for five main features: the *mihrab* (a wall niche marking the direction of Mecca); the *mimbar* (a raised pulpit, often canopied, with a staircase); a stand to hold the Koran; a screen to provide privacy for important worshippers; and a water source for ablutions. There are no seats and if there is any ornamentation at all, it will be verses from the Koran, although Indonesia's growing economy has fueled a construction boom of new and elaborately designed mosques.

All mosques are primarily places of prayer, but their specific functions vary: the *jami mesjid* is used for Friday prayer meetings; a *musalla* is used Sunday to Thursday; and the *mashad* is found in a tomb compound.

It's generally no problem for travellers to visit mosques, as long as appropriately modest clothing is worn – there is usually a place to leave shoes, and headscarves are often available for hire.

Crafts

History, religion, custom and modern styles are all reflected in Indonesia's vastly diverse range of crafts, which fills many an extra bag when visitors return home. Broadly speaking, there are three major influences: animism – traditions of animism and ancestor worship form the basis of many Indonesian crafts, particularly in Sumatra, Kalimantan, Sulawesi, Nusa Tenggara, Maluku and Papua; South Asian – the wave of Indian, and to a lesser extent Indo-Chinese, culture brought by extensive trading contacts created the Hindu-Buddhist techniques and styles reflected in Javanese and Balinese temple carvings, art forms, and crafts; and Islam – the third major influence only modified existing traditions. In fact, Islam actively employed arts and crafts for dissemination of the religion. The highly stylised floral motifs on Jepara woodcarvings, for example, reflect Islam's ban on human and animal representation.

Made in Indonesia: A Tribute to the Country's Craftspeople (2005), by Warwick Purser with photos by the ubiquitous Rio Helmi, provides beautiful images and background information on the crafts of the country.

Though the religious significance or practical function of many traditional objects is disappearing, the level of craftsmanship remains high. The sophistication and innovation of the craft industry is growing throughout the archipelago, driven by more discerning tourist tastes and by a booming export market. Javanese woodcarvers are turning out magnificent traditional panels and innovative furniture commissioned by large hotels, and Balinese jewellers influenced by Western designs are producing works of stunning quality.

Tourist centres are fostering an increasing cross-fertilisation of craft styles: the 'primitive' Kalimantan statues, so in vogue in Balinese art shops, may well have been carved behind the shop or – more likely – in the vast crafts factories of Java.

MASKS

Although carved masks exist throughout the archipelago, the most readily identifiable form of mask is the *topeng*, used in *wayang topeng*, the masked dance-dramas of Java and Bali. Dancers perform local tales or adaptations of Hindu epics such as the Mahabharata, with the masks used to represent different characters. Masks vary from the stylised but plain masks of Central and West Java to the heavily carved masks of East Java.

Balinese masks are less stylised and more naturalistic than in Java – the Balinese save their love of colour and detail for the masks of the Barong dance, starring a mythical lion-dog creature who fights tirelessly against evil. Look for masks in shops in and around Ubud, especially to the south in Mas.

EXQUISITE GIFTS

Amidst the endless piles of tourist tat, Indonesia has truly extraordinary items that make perfect gifts. The secret is finding them. Here are a few ideas:

- West Timor in Nusa Tenggara is home to fab textile markets. Look for shops selling local ikat, antique masks, statues, and carved beams, reliefs and doors from old Timorese homes.
- On South Sumatra, look for ceremonial *songket* sarongs that are used for marriages and other ceremonies near Palembang. They can take a month to make.
- Dayak rattan, *doyo* (bark beaten into cloth), carvings and other souvenirs from Kalimantan can be world-class.
- Street vendors in Bandaneira sell scrumptious kenari-nut brittle, a treat found only on the Banda Islands.
- On Bali, intricate and beautiful rattan items made in an ancient village are sold by Ashitaba, which has shops across the island full of exquisite and artful goods.
- Widely available in markets, look for *tikar* (woven palm leaf mats) that show careful workmanship and can be rolled up for travel.

Woodcarving

Though the forests are vanishing, woodcarving traditions are flourishing. Often woodcarving is practised in conjunction with more practical activities such as house building. All traditional Indonesian dwellings have some provision for repelling unwanted spirits. The horned lion heads of Batak houses, the water buffalo representations on Toraja houses and the serpent carvings on Dayak houses all serve to protect inhabitants from evil influences.

On the outer islands, woodcarvings and statues are crafted to represent the spirit world and the ancestors who live there. Woodcarving is an intrinsic part of the Toraja's famed funerals: the deceased is represented by a *tau tau* (a life-sized wooden statue), and the coffin is adorned with carved animal heads. In the Ngaju and Dusun Dayak villages in Kalimantan, *temadu* (giant carved ancestor totems) also depict the dead.

The most favoured and durable wood in Indonesia is *jati* (teak), though this is getting increasingly expensive. Sandalwood is occasionally seen in Balinese carvings, as is mahogany and ebony (imported from Sulawesi and Kalimantan). Jackfruit is a common, cheap wood, though it tends to warp and split. Generally, local carvers use woods at hand: heavy ironwood and *meranti* (a hard wood) in Kalimantan, and *belalu* (a light wood) in Bali.

Regional Carving

Perhaps Indonesia's most famous woodcarvers are the Asmat of southwestern Papua. Shields, canoes, spears and drums are carved, but the most distinctive Asmat woodcarvings are *mbis* (ancestor poles). These poles show the dead, one above the other, and the open carved 'wing' at the top of the pole is a phallic symbol representing fertility and power. The poles are also an expression of revenge, and were traditionally carved to accompany a feast following a head-hunting raid.

In many regions, everyday objects are intricately carved. These include baby carriers and stools from Kalimantan, lacquered bowls from South Sumatra, bamboo containers from Sulawesi, doors from West Timor and horse effigies from Sumba.

Balinese woodcarving is the most ornamental and elaborate in Indonesia. The gods and demons of Balinese cosmology populate statues, temple doors and relief panels throughout the island. Western influence and demand for art and souvenirs has encouraged Balinese woodcarvers to reinvent their craft, echoing the 1930s revolution in Balinese painting by producing simpler, elongated statues of purely ornamental design with a natural finish.

In Java the centre for woodcarving, especially carved furniture, is Jepara. The intricate crafts share Bali's Hindu-Buddhist tradition, adjusted to reflect Islam's prohibition on human representation. Another Javanese woodcarving centre is Kudus, where elaborate panels for traditional houses are produced.

Ikat

The Indonesian word 'ikat', meaning 'to tie' or 'to bind', signifies the intricately patterned cloth of threads that are painstakingly tie-dyed before being woven together. Ikat is produced in many regions, most notably in Nusa Tenggara.

Ikat garments come in an incredible diversity of colours and patterns: the spectacular ikat of Sumba and the elaborately patterned work of Flores (including *kapita*, used to wrap the dead) are the best known.

In Tenganan (Bali), a cloth called *gringsing* is woven using a rare method of double ikat in which both warp and weft threads are predyed.

Ikat Seasons

There are traditional times for the production of ikat. On Sumba the thread is spun between July and October, and the patterns bound between September and December. After the rains end in April, the dyeing is carried out. In August the weaving starts – more than a year after work on the thread began.

Making Ikat

Traditionally, ikat is made of hand-spun cotton. The whole process of ikat production – from planting the cotton to folding the finished product – is performed by women. Once the cotton is harvested, it is spun with a spindle. The thread is strengthened by immersing it in baths of crushed cassava, rice or maize, then threaded onto a winder.

CHOOSING IKAT

Unless you are looking for inexpensive machine-made ikat, shopping is best left to the experts. Even trekking out to an 'ikat village' may be in vain: the photogenic woman sitting at a wooden loom may be only for show. But if you insist, here are some tips on recognising the traditional product:

- **Thread** Hand-spun cotton has a less perfect 'twist' to it than factory cloth.
- **Weave** Hand-woven cloth, whether made from hand-spun or factory thread, feels rougher and, when new, stiffer than machine-woven cloth. It will probably have minor imperfections in the weave.
- **Dyes** Until you've seen enough ikat to get a feel for whether colours are natural or chemical, you often have to rely on your instincts as to whether they are 'earthy' enough. Some cloths contain both natural and artificial dyes.
- **Dyeing method** The patterns on cloths which have been individually tie-dyed using the traditional method are rarely perfectly defined, but they're unlikely to have the detached specks of colour that often appear on mass-dyed cloth.
- **Age** No matter what anybody tells you, there are very few antique cloths around. There are several processes to make cloth look old.

Traditional dyes are made from natural sources. The most complex processes result in a rusty colour known as *kombu* (produced from the bark and roots of the *kombu* tree). Blue dyes come from the indigo plant, and purple or brown can be produced by dyeing the cloth deep blue and then dyeing it again with *kombu*.

Any sections that are not coloured are bound together with dye-resistant fibre. Each colour requires a separate tying-and-dyeing process. The sequence of colouring takes into consideration the effect of each application of dye. This stage requires great skill, as the dyer has to work out – before the threads are woven – exactly which parts of the thread are to receive which colour in order to create the pattern of the final cloth. After the thread has been dyed, the cloth is woven on a simple hand loom.

Origins & Meaning of Ikat

Ikat technique was most likely introduced 2000 years ago by Dongson migrants from southern China and Vietnam.

Ikat styles vary according to the village and the gender of the wearer, and some styles are reserved for special purposes. In parts of Nusa Tenggara, high-quality ikat is part of a bride's dowry. Until recently on Sumba, only members of the highest clans could make and wear ikat textiles. Certain motifs were traditionally reserved for noble families (as on Sumba and Rote) or members of a specific tribe or clan (as on Sabu or among the Atoni of West Timor). The function of ikat as an indicator of social status has since declined.

Motifs & Patterns

Some experts believe that motifs found on Sumba, such as front views of people, animals and birds, stem from an artistic tradition even older than Dongson, whose influence was geometric motifs like diamond and key shapes (which often go together), meanders and spirals.

One strong influence was *patola* cloth from Gujarat in India. In the 16th and 17th centuries these became highly prized in Indonesia, and one characteristic motif – a hexagon framing a four-pronged star – was copied by local ikat weavers. On the best *patola* and geometric ikat, repeated small patterns combine to form larger patterns, like a mandala. Over the past century, European styles have influenced the motifs used in ikat.

Songket

Songket is silk cloth interwoven with gold or silver threads, although imitation silver or gold is often used in modern pieces. *Songket* is most commonly found in heavily Islamic regions, such as Aceh, and among the coastal Malays, but Bali also has a strong *songket* tradition.

Batik

The technique of applying wax or other dye-resistant substances (like rice paste) to cloth to produce a design is found in many parts of the world, but none is as famous as the batik of Java. Javanese batik dates from the 12th century, and opinion is divided as to whether batik is an indigenous craft or imported from India along with Hindu religious and cultural traditions.

The word 'batik' is an old Javanese word meaning 'to dot'. Javanese batik was a major weapon in the competition for social-status in the royal courts. The ability to devote extensive resources to the painstaking creation of fine batik demonstrated wealth and power. Certain designs indicated courtly rank, and a courtier risked public humiliation, or worse, by daring to wear the wrong sarong.

In 2009 Unesco added Indonesian batik to its Intangible Cultural Heritage list.

Batik painting, an odd blend of craft and art that all-too-often is neither, remains popular in Yogyakarta, where it was invented as a pastime for unemployed youth. Though most batik painting is tourist schlock, there are some talented artists working in the medium.

GIFTS FROM THE HEART

Looking to show close friends and relatives just how deep you plunged into Indonesian culture? Then give them a penis gourd.

Papua is the sweet spot for Indonesian penis gourds. Traditionally used by indigenous men in the province's highlands, they are attached to the testicles by a small loop of fibre. Sizes, shapes and colours vary across cultural groups but you can pick one up for around 5000Rp to 60,000Rp. A good place to check out the merchandise is Wamena. Remember: bargain hard as competition is stiff.

If you'd rather not give something as intimate as a penis gourd, then perhaps you should do just the opposite and give the prized possession of head-hunters everywhere: a *mandau* from Kalimantan. Once the Dayak weapon of choice, this indigenous machete is still slung from the hips of most men in the Kalimantan interior. A good place to shop is in the longhouse village of Tanjung Isuy.

Obviously, you'll need to check a bag to get a *mandau* home, but you can probably simply wear your new gourd. And if your visit doesn't take you near these places, you can always buy the top-selling souvenir on Bali: a bottle opener shaped like a penis.

Making Batik

The finest batik is *batik tulis* (hand-painted or literally 'written' batik). Designs are first traced out onto cloth, then patterns are drawn in hot wax with a *canting,* a pen-like instrument. The wax-covered areas resist colour change when immersed in a dye bath. The waxing and dyeing, with increasingly darker shades, continues until the final colours are achieved. Wax is added to protect previously dyed areas or scraped off to expose new areas to the dye. Finally, all the wax is scraped off and the cloth boiled to remove all traces of wax.

Basketwork & Beadwork

Some of the finest basketwork in Indonesia comes from Lombok. The spiral woven rattan work is very fine and large baskets are woven using this method; smaller receptacles topped with wooden carvings are also popular.

In Java, Tasikmalaya is a major cane-weaving centre, often adapting baskets and vessels to modern uses with the introduction of zips and plastic linings. The Minangkabau people, centred around Bukittinggi, also produce interesting palm-leaf bags and purses, while the *lontar* palm is used extensively in weaving on West Timor, Rote and other outer eastern islands. The Dayak of Kalimantan produce some superb woven baskets and string bags.

Some of the most colourful and attractive beadwork is made by the Toraja of Sulawesi. Beadwork can be found all over Nusa Tenggara and in the Dayak region of Kalimantan. Small, highly prized cowrie shells are used like beads and are found on Dayak and Lombok works, though the best application of these shells is as intricate beading in Sumbanese tapestries.

Kris

No ordinary knife, the wavy-bladed traditional dagger known as a kris is a mandatory possession of a Javanese gentleman; it's said to be endowed with supernatural powers and is to be treated with the utmost respect. A kris owner ritually bathes and polishes his weapon, stores it in an auspicious location, and pays close attention to every rattle and scrape emanating from the blade and sheath in the dead of the night.

Some think the Javanese kris (from *iris,* meaning 'to cut') is derived from the bronze daggers produced by the Dongson around the 1st century AD. Bas-reliefs of a kris appear in the 14th-century Panataran temple complex in East Java, and the carrying of the kris as a custom in Java was noted in 15th-century Chinese records. The kris remains an integral part of men's ceremonial dress.

Distinctive features, the number of curves in the blade and the damascene design on the blade are read to indicate good or bad fortune for its owner. The number of curves in the blade has symbolic meaning: five curves symbolise the five Pandava brothers of the Mahabharata epic; three represents fire, ardour and passion. Although the blade is the most important part of the kris, the hilt and scabbard are also beautifully decorated.

Although the kris is mostly associated with Java and Bali, larger and less ornate variations are found in Sumatra, Kalimantan and Sulawesi.

Puppets

The most famous puppets of Indonesia are the carved leather *wayang kulit* puppets. These intricate lace figures are cut from buffalo hide with a sharp, chisel-like stylus, and then painted. They are produced in Bali and Java, particularly in Central Java. The leaf-shaped *kayon* representing the 'tree' or 'mountain of life' is also made of leather and is used to end scenes during a performance.

Wayang golek are three-dimensional wooden puppets found in Central and West Java. The *wayang klitik* puppets are the rarer flat wooden puppets of East Java.

A carefully curated list of books about art, culture and Indonesian writers, dancers and musicians can be found at www.ganeshabooksbali.com, the website of the excellent Bali bookstore.

Jewellery

The ubiquitous *toko mas* (gold shop) found in every Indonesian city is mostly an investment house selling gold jewellery by weight – design and artisanship take a back seat. However, gold and silverwork does have a long history in Indonesia. Some of the best gold jewellery comes from Aceh, where fine filigree work is produced, while chunky bracelets and earrings are produced in the Batak region.

Balinese jewellery is nearly always handworked and rarely involves casting techniques. Balinese work is innovative, employing both traditional designs and those adapted from jewellery presented by Western buyers.

Kota Gede in Yogyakarta is famous for its fine filigree work. Silverware from here tends to be more traditional, but new designs are also being adapted. As well as jewellery, Kota Gede produces a wide range of silver tableware.

Sport

Soccer and badminton are the national sporting obsessions. Indonesian badminton players had a good record at the Olympics (three medals in 2008) until London in 2012 when two key players were booted off the team after they admitted to throwing matches in an effort to manipulate the quarter-final draw.

Although international success has eluded Indonesian soccer (football) teams, it is played with fervour on grassy verges across the archipelago.

Many regions, particularly those with a history of tribal warfare, stage traditional contests of various kinds to accompany weddings, harvest festivals and other ceremonial events. Mock battles are sometimes staged in Papua, *caci* whip fights are a speciality in Flores and men fight with sticks and shields in Lombok, but the most spectacular ceremonial fight is seen during Sumba's Pasola festival, where every February and March horse riders in traditional dress hurl spears at each other.

In Bali and other islands, the real sporting passion is reserved for cockfighting, which means the spectators (virtually all men) watch and bet while birds brawl. Although nominally illegal, many matches are held openly.

Food & Drink

When you eat in Indonesia you savour the essence of the country. The abundance of rice reflects Indonesia's fertile landscape, the spices are reminiscent of a time of trade and invasion, and the fiery chilli echoes the passion of the people. Indonesian cuisine is really one big food swap. Chinese, Portuguese, colonists and traders have all influenced the ingredients that appear at the Indonesian table, and the cuisine has been further shaped over time by the archipelago's diverse landscape, people and culture.

Regional Flavours

Indonesian cooking is not complex, and its ingredients maintain their distinct flavours. Coriander, cumin, chilli, lemon grass, coconut, soy sauce and palm sugar are all important elements; sambal is a crucial condiment and comes in myriad variations. Not surprisingly for an island nation, fish is a favourite.

Indonesians traditionally eat with their fingers, hence the stickiness of the rice. *Sate* (skewered meat), nasi goreng (fried rice) and gado gado (vegetables with peanut sauce) are some of Indonesia's most famous dishes. However, just like sambal, Indonesia's flavours come in many, many forms.

Java

The cuisine of the Betawi (original inhabitants of the Jakarta region) is known for its richness. Gado gado is a Betawi original, as is *ketoprak* (noodles, bean sprouts and tofu with soy and peanut sauce; named after a musical style, as it resembles the sound of ingredients being chopped). *Soto Betawi* (beef soup) is made creamy with coconut milk. There's also *nasi uduk* (rice cooked in coconut milk, served with meat, tofu and/or vegetables).

Java's Cianjur region is famous for its sweet, spicy cuisine. Dishes include *lontong* (sticky rice with tofu in a delicious, sweet coconut sauce); the best beef *sate* in Java, locally known as *marangi;* and *pandan wangi* rice, fragrantly flavoured rice that's often cooked with lemon grass and spices.

In West Java, the Sundanese love their greens. Their specialities include *karedok* (salad of long beans, bean sprouts and cucumber with spicy sauce), *soto Bandung* (beef-and-vegetable soup with lemon grass) and *ketupat tahu* (pressed rice, bean sprouts and tofu with soy and peanut sauce). Sundanese sweet specialities include *colenak* (roasted cassava with coconut sauce) and *ulen* (roasted sticky rice with peanut sauce); both best eaten warm. Bandung's cooler hills are the place for *bandrek* (ginger tea with coconut and pepper) and *bajigur* (spiced coffee with coconut milk).

Central Javan food is sweet, even the curries such as *gudeg* (jackfruit curry). Yogyakarta specialities include *ayam goreng* (fried chicken) and *kelepon* (green rice-flour balls with a palm-sugar filling). In Solo, specialties include *nasi liwet* (rice with coconut milk, unripe papaya, garlic and shallots, served with chicken or egg) and *serabi* (coconut-milk pancakes topped with chocolate, banana or jackfruit).

There's a lot of crossover between Central and East Javan cuisine. Fish is popular, especially *pecel lele* (deep-fried catfish served with rice and *pecel*). The best *pecel* (peanut sauce) comes from the town of Madiun.

Two very popular Madurese dishes are *soto Madura* (beef soup with lime, pepper, peanuts, chilli and ginger) and *sate Madura* (skewered meat with sweet soy sauce).

Bali

Balinese specialities are easy to find, as visitor-friendly warungs offer high-quality Balinese dishes, with several options of spiciness. Many restaurants offer the hugely popular Balinese dish, *babi guling* (spit-roast pig stuffed with chilli, turmeric, garlic and ginger) on a day's notice, although you're best off getting it from any of many warungs that specialise in it. Look for the pig's head drawn on the sign or a real one in a display case. Also popular is *bebek betutu* (duck stuffed with spices, wrapped in banana leaves and coconut husks, and cooked in embers).

The local *sate*, *sate lilit*, is made with minced, spiced meat pressed onto skewers. Look for spicy dishes like *lawar* (salad of chopped coconut, garlic and chilli with pork or chicken meat and blood).

Indonesia's food scene is better than ever. Bali has scores of world-class and renowned restaurants and you can find great eats in major cities including Jakarta and on Lombok, the Gilis and beyond. And now more remote areas once dismissed as culinary backwaters like Flores, West Timor and Sumba boast excellent restaurants, serving foods from Indonesia and beyond.

Nusa Tenggara

In dry east Nusa Tenggara you'll eat less rice (although much is imported) and more sago, corn, cassava and taro. Fish is popular and one local dish is Sumbawa's *sepat* (shredded fish in coconut and mango sauce).

The Sasak people of Lombok (and visitors!) like spicy *ayam Taliwang* (roasted chicken served with a peanut, tomato, chilli and lime dip) and *pelecing* sauce (made with chilli, shrimp paste and tomato). Also recommended is *sate pusut* (minced meat or fish satay, mixed with coconut, and grilled on sugar-cane skewers). Nonmeat dishes include *kelor* (soup with vegetables) and *timun urap* (cucumber with coconut, onion and garlic).

Maluku

A typical Maluku meal is tuna and *dabu-dabu* (raw vegetables with a chilli and fish-paste sauce). Sometimes fish is made into *kohu-kohu* (fish salad with citrus fruit and chilli). Sago pith is used to make porridge, bread and *mutiara* (small, jelly-like 'beans' that are added to desserts and sweet drinks). Boiled cassava *(kasbi)* is a staple in peoples' homes as it's cheaper than rice.

SURPRISING TASTES

Everyday eating in Indonesia can challenge your palate. Here are a few favourites:

- In Nusa Tenggara Timor (Alor and Flores in particular) there is a scintillating, spicy, oily, mildly astringent dish called *ikan kuah assam* (tamarind fish soup). It is absolutely sensational. It's basically a fish steak or half a fish (bones often included) steamed and swimming in spicy tamarind broth. It's simple, life affirming, bliss inducing and could easily be your favourite dish of the trip.
- The durian has a serious public-image problem. This fruit's spiky skin looks like a Spanish Inquisition torture tool; opening it releases the fruit's odorous power. Most people form a lifelong passion – or aversion – on their first taste of this sulphury, custardy fruit.
- Balinese specialities are readily available; look for warungs advertising *siobak* (minced pig's head, stomach, tongue and skin cooked with spices).
- For avocado juice, take an avocado, blend with ice and condensed milk (or chocolate syrup) and serve. Indonesians don't consider this strange, as the avocado is just another sweet fruit.

In the Banda Islands you'll find nutmeg jelly on bread and pancakes, which is fitting as these were the original Spice Islands, where nutmeg was first cultivated.

Indonesia's national dish is *nasi campur*, which is essentially the plate of the day. Served in stalls, warungs and restaurants, it is always a combination of many dishes and flavours. At warungs you often choose your own combination from dozens of tasty items on offer (15,000Rp to 40,000Rp).

Papua

Little rice is grown here: indigenous Papuans get their carbs from other sources and the rice eaten by migrants from elsewhere in Indonesia is mostly imported. In the highlands of Papua the sweet potato is king. The Dani people grow around 60 varieties, some of which can only be eaten by the elders.

In the lowlands the sago palm provides the starchy staple food: its pulped-up pith is turned into hard, moist sago cakes, to which water is added to make *papeda*, a kind of gluey paste usually eaten with fish in a yellow turmeric-and-lime sauce. You may find the fish tastier than the *papeda*. Some lowlanders also eat the sago beetle grubs found in rotting sago palms.

Sumatra

In West Sumatra, beef is used in *rendang* (beef coconut curry). The region is the home of Padang cuisine, and the market in Bukittinggi is a great place to sample *nasi Kapau* (cuisine from the village of Kapau). It's similar to Padang food but uses more vegetables. There's also *bubur kampiun* (mung-bean porridge with banana and rice yoghurt).

In North Sumatra, the Acehnese love their *kare* or *gulai* (curry). The Bataks have a taste for pig and, to a lesser extent, dog. Pork features in *babi panggang* (pork boiled in vinegar and pig blood, and then roasted).

The culinary capital of South Sumatra is Palembang, famous for *pempek* (deep-fried fish and sago dumpling; also called *empek-empek*). South Sumatra is also home to *pindang* (spicy fish soup with soy and tamarind) and *ikan brengkes* (fish in a spicy, durian-based sauce). Palembang's sweetie is *srikaya* (green custard made from sticky rice, sugar, coconut milk and egg).

MSG is widely used in Indonesia. In warungs, you can try asking the cook to hold off on the *ajinomoto*. If you get a look of blank incomprehension, well, the headache only lasts for a couple of hours.

Kalimantan

Dayak food varies, but you may sample *rembang*, a sour fruit that's made into *sayur asem rembang* (sour vegetable soup). In Banjarmasin, the Banjar make *pepes ikan* (spiced fish cooked in banana leaves with tamarind and lemon grass). Kandangan town is famous for *ketupat Kandangan* (fish and pressed rice with lime-infused coconut sauce). The regional soup, *soto Banjar*, is a chicken broth made creamy by mashing boiled eggs into the stock. Chicken also goes into *ayam masak habang*, cooked with large red chillies.

There is a large Chinese population and restaurants usually have specialities such as bird's nest soup and jellyfish on the menus.

THE REAL SAMBAL

Sambal, the spicy condiment, comes in myriad forms and can be the best part of a meal, but all too often, servers will assume you are a timid tourist who wants the tame ketchup-like stuff from a bottle. Insist on the real stuff (try saying '*sambal lokal?*' – 'local sambal?'), which will have been prepared fresh in the kitchen from some combination of ingredients that can include garlic, shallots, chilli peppers in many forms, fish sauce, tomatoes and more.

BALI COOKING COURSES

If you want to carry on enjoying the tastes of Indonesia after you go home, Bali has several cooking schools where you can learn everything from how to shop in the markets and the basics of Indonesian cuisine to advanced cooking techniques. Best of all though is that you get to eat what you make! The following are two of the best:

Bumbu Bali Cooking School (0361-774502; www.balifoods.com; Jl Pratama; course without/with market visit US$103/115; 6am-3pm Mon, Wed & Fri) Long-time resident and cookbook author Heinz von Holzen runs a cooking school from his excellent South Bali restaurant.

Casa Luna Cooking School (p254) Half-day courses cover cooking techniques, ingredients and the cultural background of the Balinese kitchen.

Sulawesi

South Sulawesi locals love seafood, especially *ikan bakar* (grilled fish). Another local dish is *coto Makassar* (soup of beef innards, pepper, cumin and lemon grass). For sugar cravers, there's *es pallubutun* (coconut custard and banana in coconut milk and syrup).

The Toraja people have their own distinct cuisine with a heavy emphasis on indigenous ingredients, many of them odd to Western palates. You can easily find *pa'piong,* which is meat or fish cooked in bamboo tubes with spices. Also look for *pamarasan,* a spicy black sauce used to cook meat.

If a North Sulawesi dish has the name *rica-rica,* it's prepared with a paste of chilli, shallots, ginger and lime. Fish and chicken are two versions (also look out for dog). Things get very fishy with *bakasang* (flavouring paste made with fermented fish), sometimes used in *bubur tinotuan* (porridge made with corn, cassava, rice, pumpkin, fish paste and chilli).

Drinks

Tea

Indonesia's most popular brew is black tea with sugar. If you don't want sugar ask for *teh pahit* (bitter tea), and if you want milk buy yourself a cow. Various forms of ginger tea are popular, including *bandrek* (ginger tea with coconut and pepper) and *wedang jahe* (ginger tea with peanuts and agar cubes slurped from a bowl).

A popular – and protein-filled – drink in Aceh is *kopi telor kocok,* one raw egg and sugar creamed together in a glass and topped up with coffee. Look for it in Takengon.

Coffee

Indonesian coffee, especially from Sulawesi, is of exceptional quality, though most of the best stuff is exported. Warungs serve a chewy concoction called *kopi tubruk* (ground coffee with sugar and boiling water). Most urban cafes and restaurants offer quality coffee; beans from Sumatra and Bali are especially prized.

Ice & Fruit Drinks

Indonesia's *es* (ice drinks) are not only refreshing, they are visually stimulating, made with syrups, fruit and jellies. There are plenty of places serving *es jus* (iced fruit juice) or cordial-spiked *kelapa muda* (young coconut juice). But beware of ice outside of urban areas (ice in cities is made with filtered water).

Alcoholic Drinks

Islam is the predominant religion in Indonesia and restrictions on alcohol sales are increasing. In early 2015 a law was enacted that banned the sale of alcoholic beverages – including beer – in minimarkets and shops across Indonesia. Given that these are the very places most people buy their beer, the law *could* have severely limited the availability of beer and other drinks across the archipelago. But this being Indonesia, enforcement and compliance was spotty at best. On Bali, some convenience stores covered up the windows of coolers. Elsewhere, beer continued to be openly sold or was kept off shelves but available for the asking.

After a few months of grumbling, the law was revised so that towns and regions could decide locally about beer sales as well as wine and some traditional drinks. With the exception of Aceh, parts of West Java, Sumbawa, Papua and some other very conservative areas, you can still buy a beer – although many warungs are dry.

Cradle of Flavor by James Oseland (the editor of *Saveur* magazine) is a beautiful tome covering the foods of Indonesia and its neighbours.

You will see traditional spirits for sale, including *tuak* (palm-sap wine), *arak* (rice or palm-sap wine) and Balinese *brem* (rice wine). Be careful when buying *arak*. In recent times there have been cases where it has been adulterated with chemicals that have proved deadly.

Of the domestic breweries, iconic Bintang, a clean, slightly sweet lager, is the preferred choice for many.

Note that rapacious duties are added to imported alcohol sold in stores and restaurants, which means that you will be hard-pressed to find affordable Australian wine or British gin on Bali. That bottle of Bombay Sapphire which is US$25 at duty-free shops before your flight is US$100 on Bali, so buy your allowed 1L. Elsewhere, it can be hard to find wine and spirits outside of top end resorts.

Celebrations

Whether a marriage, funeral or party with friends, food – and lots of it – is essential. Celebratory meals can include any combination of dishes, but for special occasions a *tumpeng* is the centrepiece: a pyramid of yellow rice, the tip of which is cut off and offered to the VIP.

Muslims

For Muslims, the largest celebrations are Ramadan and Idul Adha. Each day of Ramadan, Muslims rise before sunrise to eat the only meal before sunset. It might sound like a bad time to be in Indonesia – you may have

DINING WITH LOCALS

In Indonesia hospitality is highly regarded. If you're invited to someone's home for a meal, you'll be treated warmly and social hiccups will be ignored. Nevertheless, here are some tips to make the experience more enjoyable for everyone:

- When food or drink is presented, wait until your host invites you to eat.
- Indonesians rarely eat at the table, preferring to sit on a mat or around the lounge room.
- Don't be surprised if, when invited to a home, you're the only one eating. This is your host's way of showing you're special, and you should have choice pickings. But don't eat huge amounts, as these dishes will feed others later. Fill up on rice and take a spoonful from each dish served.
- While chopsticks are available at Chinese-Indonesian eateries, and a fork and spoon in restaurants, most Indonesians prefer to eat with their hands. In a warung, it is acceptable to rinse your fingers with drinking water, letting the drops fall to the ground. Use only your right hand. If left-handed, ask for a spoon.
- In Islamic areas, be sure not to eat and drink in public during Ramadan. Restaurants do stay open, though they usually cover the door so as not to cause offence.
- Though antismoking regulations are becoming common, smoking remains acceptable almost anywhere, anytime.

FRUITY DELIGHTS

It's worth making a trip to Indonesia just to sample the tropical fruits:

- *Belimbing* (star fruit) is cool and crisp; slice one to see how it gets its name.
- Durian is the spiky fruit people either love or hate.
- *Jambu air* (water apple) is a pink bell-shaped fruit with crisp and refreshing flesh.
- *Manggis* (mangosteen) is a small purple fruit with white fleshy segments and fantastic flavour.
- *Nangka* (jackfruit) is an enormous, spiky fruit that can weigh over 20kg. Inside are segments of yellow, moist, sweet flesh with a slightly rubbery texture. The flesh can be eaten fresh or cooked in a curry.
- *Rambutan* is a bright-red fruit covered in soft spines; the name means 'hairy'. Break it open to reveal a delicious white fruit similar to lychee.
- *Salak* is recognisable by its brown 'snakeskin' covering. Peel it off to reveal segments that resemble something between an apple and a walnut.
- *Sirsak* (soursop or zurzak) is a warty, green-skinned fruit with a white, pulpy interior that has a slightly lemonish taste.

to plan meals and go without lunch – but when sunset comes, the locals' appreciation of a good meal is contagious.

The first thing Indonesians eat after fasting is *kolak* (fruit in coconut milk) as a gentle way to reacquaint the body with food. Then, after prayers, the evening meal begins with aplomb. In some areas, such as in Bukittinggi, cooks set out food on the street. People gather to savour and enjoy their food as a community. Foreign guests are always made welcome.

After Ramadan, much of the nation seems to hit the road to go home to their families and celebrate Idul Fitri (Lebaran) with their families. During this time, *ketupat* (rice steamed in packets of woven coconut fronds) are hung everywhere, like seasonal ornaments.

At Banjarmasin's floating produce market in Kalimantan, you can sample exotic fruit to your heart's content. The range will include all manner of unfamiliar and unusual-looking treats such as the pungent, spiky durian.

Seventy days after Lebaran is Idul Adha, marked by the sight of goats tethered to posts on both city streets and rural pathways throughout the archipelago. Individuals or community groups buy these unfortunate animals to sacrifice in commemoration of Abraham's willingness to sacrifice his son at divine command. This is one of Indonesia's most anticipated festivals, as the sacrificial meat is distributed to the poor in each community.

Balinese

The Balinese calendar is peppered with festivals and such celebrations are always observed with a communal meal, sometimes eaten together from one massive banana leaf piled with dishes.

Festivals aside, every day in Bali you'll see food used to symbolise devotion: rice in woven banana-leaf pockets are placed in doorways, beside rice fields, at bus terminals – wherever a god or spirit may reside. Larger offerings studded with whole chickens and produce are made to mark special occasions such as *odalan* (anniversary of a temple). You'll see processions of women gracefully balancing offerings on their heads as they make their way to the temple.

Eating Out

Outside of larger cities and tourist areas, there are limited choices for dining out in Indonesia. Warungs are simple, open-air eateries that provide a small range of dishes. Often their success comes from cooking one dish better than anyone else. *Rumah makan* (eating house) or *restoran* refers to anything that is a step above a warung. Offerings may be as simple as those from a warung but usually include more choices of meat and vegetable dishes, and spicy accompaniments.

As Indonesia's middle class grows, the warung is also going upmarket. In urban areas, a restaurant by any other name advertises itself as a 'warung', and serves good local dishes to customers that become more demanding by the year.

Jajanan (snacks) are sold everywhere – there are thousands of varieties of sweet and savoury snacks made from almost anything and everything: peanuts, coconuts, bananas, sweet potato etc. They are cheap, so sample at will.

Indonesia's markets are wonderful examples of how food feeds both the soul and the stomach. There's no refrigeration, so freshness is dependent on quick turnover. You'll also find a huge range of sweet and savoury snacks. Supermarkets and convenience stores are common in cities and tourist areas.

Quick Eats

As many Indonesians can't afford fine service and surrounds, the most authentic food is found at street level. Even high rollers know this, so everyone dines at stalls or gets their noodle fix from roving vendors who carry their victuals in two bundles connected by a stick over their shoulders: a stove and wok on one side, and ready-to-fry ingredients on the other.

Then there's *kaki lima* (roving vendors) whose carts hold a work bench, stove and cabinet. '*Kaki lima*' means 'five legs': two for the wheels of the cart, one for the stand and two for the legs of the vendor. You'll find any and every type of dish, drink and snack sold from a *kaki lima*. Some have a permanent spot, others roam the streets, calling out what they are selling or making a signature sound, such as the 'tock' of a wooden *bakso* bell. In some places, *sate* sellers operate from a boat-shaped cart, with bells jingling to attract the hungry.

Vegetarian Fare

Vegetarians will be pleased to know that tempeh and *tahu* (tofu) are in abundance, sold as chunky slabs of *tempe penyet* (deep-fried tempeh), *tempe kering* (diced tempeh stir-fried with sweet soy sauce) and *tahu isi* (deep-fried stuffed tofu). Finding fresh vegies requires more effort. Look for Chinese establishments; they can whip up *cap cai* (mixed vegetables). Vegetarian fried rice or noodles can be found at many other eateries. And there's always the iconic gado gado.

A huge number of places, including Padang restaurants, offer what's essentially the national dish: *nasi campur* (rice with a variety of side dishes). Here you can skip meat options and go for things like tofu, tempeh, jackfruit dishes, egg dishes and leafy vegies.

And there's always fantastic fruit available at the local market.

Rice in the field is called *padi;* rice grain at the market is called *beras;* cooked rice on your plate is called *nasi.*

Eating with Kids

There's always the fear that a hidden chilli is going to make your child explode. But most Indonesian children dread chilli attacks, so a proprietor will often warn you if a dish is spicy. In any case, you can always ask '*Pedas tidak?*' ('Is it spicy?') or '*Makanan tidak pedas ada?*' ('Are there nonspicy dishes?').

Children may enjoy nasi goreng, *mie goreng* (fried noodles), *bakso* (meatball soup), *mie rebus* (noodle soup), *perkedel* (fritters), *pisang goreng* (banana fritters), *sate*, *bubur* (rice porridge), fruit and fruit drinks. Indonesia's sugar-rich iced drinks are useful secret weapons for when energy levels are low. All of these are available at street stalls and restaurants. Not available, however, are highchairs and kiddy menus. That's not to say children aren't welcome; in fact, they'll probably get more attention than they can handle.

In touristy areas and cities you'll find plenty of familiar fast food joints and convenience stores selling international snacks. A Magnum bar can quell the worst tantrum.

Food Glossary

acar	pickle; cucumber or other vegetables in a mixture of vinegar, salt, sugar and water
air	water
arak	spirits distilled from palm sap or rice
ayam	chicken
ayam goreng	fried chicken
babi	pork; since most Indonesians are Muslim, pork is generally only found in market stalls and restaurants run by the Chinese, and in areas where there are non-Muslim populations, such as Bali, Papua and Tana Toraja on Sulawesi
bakar	barbecued, roasted
bakso/ba'so	meatball soup
bandrek	ginger tea with coconut and pepper
brem	rice wine
bubur	rice porridge
cassava	known as tapioca in English; a long, thin, dark-brown root which looks something like a shrivelled turnip
colenak	roasted cassava with coconut sauce
daging kambing	goat
daging sapi	beef
es buah	combination of crushed ice, condensed milk, shaved coconut, syrup, jelly and fruit
gado gado	very popular dish of steamed bean sprouts and various vegetables, served with a spicy peanut sauce
gudeg	jackfruit curry
ikan	fish
jajanan	snacks
karedok	salad of long beans, bean sprouts and cucumber with spicy sauce
kelepon	green rice-flour balls with a palm-sugar filling
ketoprak	noodles, bean sprouts and tofu with soy and peanut sauce
ketupat tahu	pressed rice, bean sprouts and tofu with soy and peanut sauce
kopi	coffee
krupuk	shrimp with cassava flour, or fish flakes with rice dough, cut into slices and fried to a crisp
lombok	chilli
lontong	rice steamed in a banana leaf
martabak	a pancake-like dish stuffed with meat, egg and vegetables
mie goreng	fried wheat-flour noodles, served with vegetables or meat
nasi	rice
nasi campur	steamed rice topped with a little bit of everything (some vegetables, some meat, a bit of fish, a *krupuk* or two; usually a tasty and filling meal)
nasi goreng	fried rice
nasi liwet	rice with coconut milk, unripe papaya, garlic and shallots, served with chicken or egg
nasi uduk	rice cooked in coconut milk, served with meat, tofu and/or vegetables
nasi putih	white *(putih)* rice, usually steamed

pecel	peanut sauce
pecel lele	deep-fried catfish served with rice and *pecel*
pempek (empek-empek)	deep-fried/grilled fish and sago balls (from Palembang)
pisang goreng	fried banana fritters
rica-rica, rintek wuuk, RW	dog meat
roti	bread; nearly always white and sweet
sambal	a hot, spicy chilli sauce served as an accompaniment with most meals
sate	small pieces of various types of meat grilled on a skewer and served with peanut sauce
sayur	vegetables
serabi	coconut-milk pancakes topped with chocolate, banana or jackfruit
soto	meat and vegetable broth; soup
soto Bandung	beef-and-vegetable soup with lemon grass
soto Betawi	beef soup
soto Madura	beef soup with lime, pepper, peanuts, chilli and ginger
tahu	tofu or soybean curd
teh	tea
teh pahit	tea without sugar
telur	egg
tuak	palm-sap wine
udang	prawns or shrimps
ulen	roasted sticky rice with peanut sauce

Environment

It makes sense that Indonesians call their country Tanah Air Kita (literally, 'Our Land and Water'), as it is the world's most expansive archipelago. Of its 17,500-plus islands, about 6000 are inhabited. These diverse lands and surrounding waters have an impressive collection of plant and animal life. Yet this very bounty is its own worst enemy, as resource exploitation threatens virtually every corner of Indonesia.

The Land

Just as the mash-up of cultures that form the political entity of Indonesia happened not too long ago, the mash-up of land that Indonesians call home also occurred relatively recently – geologically speaking. If Sulawesi looks a bit like an island caught in a blender, that is because it is where three major chunks of Earth converged in a vortex of tectonic chaos. About 30 million years ago, the Australian plate (carrying Papua and the Mulukus) careened into the Sunda Shelf (carrying Sumatra, Java and Borneo) from the south, while the twirling Phillipine plate was pushed in from the east by the Pacific plate. The result: a landscape and ecology as diverse and dynamic as the people who live here.

British naturalist Alfred Russel Wallace was the first to notice Indonesia's duelling ecozones during eight years of exploration, which he describes with gentlemanly prose in *The Malay Archipelago*.

Volcanoes

Much of Indonesia is defined by its 150 volcanoes: spectacular peaks towering above the forests and people below. Some trekkers are drawn to their steaming summits, while others flock to their colourful lakes and bubbling mud pits. For the locals, nutrient-rich soils provide high crop yields, allowing for higher population density – a benefit that comes with significant risk.

Over five million Indonesians live within the 'danger zone' of active volcanoes. Large and small eruptions are a near constant occurrence, and some have literally made history. Ash from the cataclysmic 1815 eruption of Gunung Tambora in Sumbawa killed 71,000 people and caused crop failures in Europe. The 1883 eruption of Krakatau between Java and Sumatra generated tsunamis that killed tens of thousands. Super-volcano Toba on Sumatra, which may have halved the world's human population 75,000 years ago, quietly reawakened in 2015.

RING OF FIRE & FLOOD

Indonesia is stretched along part of the Pacific 'Ring of Fire'. Tectonic forces cause the Indo-Australian and Pacific plates to plunge under the Eurasian plate, where they melt 150km beneath the surface. Some of this molten rock works its way upward where it can erupt in violent and deadly explosions.

Even more pernicious, as these plates slide past each other, they can cause devastating earthquakes and tsunamis. The 2004 tsunami in Sumatra was caused by an offshore earthquake, the third-largest ever recorded, and generated waves up to 10m tall. The tsunami killed 167,799 Indonesians and displaced half a million more.

Understandably, volcanoes play a pivotal role in most Indonesian cultures. In Bali and Java, major places of worship grace the slopes of prominent volcanic cones, and eruptions are taken as demonstrations of divine disappointment or anger.

Wild Indonesia

From tiny tarsiers to enormous stinking flowers, Indonesia's natural diversity is astounding, and we still don't know the complete story. Scientists continually discover new species such as a fanged frog in Sulawasi in 2015, an owl in Lombok in 2013, and three walking sharks since 2007 in the Malukus. Meanwhile, the 'lost world' of Papua's Foja mountains is a constant source of firsts, including the world's smallest wallaby, recorded in 2010. Unfortunately, the pace of discovery lags far behind the rate of habitat destruction, meaning some of Indonesia's rich biological heritage will pass unrecorded into extinction.

In 2011, the International Rhino Foundation declared the Javan rhino extinct in Vietnam, leaving the estimated 60 living on Java's Ujung Kulon Peninsula the only examples left in the wild.

Animals

Great apes, tigers, elephants and monkeys – lots of monkeys – plus one mean lizard are just some of the more notable critters you may encounter in Indonesia. Here you can find an astonishing 12% of the world's mammal species, and 17% of its bird species.

The diversity is partly a result of evolution occurring in two distinct ecozones, the Australian and Asian, which were later brought together by tectonic migration. This is why you won't find marsupials on the western islands, or tigers in the east.

Orangutans

The world's largest arboreal mammal, Indonesia's orangutans are an iconic part of the nation's image. Although they once swung through the forest canopy throughout all of Southeast Asia, they are now found only in Sumatra and Borneo. The shaggy orange great apes rarely come down from the trees. They spend most of their day searching for and eating forest fruit before building their characteristic nests for the night. Some populations use tools to raid termite colonies (for a rare protein-rich delicacy), and researchers have observed individuals learning new behaviour from others, suggesting an intelligence rare in the animal kingdom.

Orangutans have long reproductive cycles, with mothers caring for their young for up to eight years. This makes them particularly susceptible to population decline, and less than 60,000 individuals remain in the wild. Researchers fear that the isolated populations will not survive the continued loss of habitat due to logging and agriculture.

BEST PLACES TO SEE ORANGUTANS

Some orangutan rehabilitation centres are open to visitors, but there is nothing like spotting these noble creatures in the wild.

➡ **Sumatra – Bukit Lawang** Home to around 5000 orangutans, this rehabilitation centre allows you to get up close and personal with Asia's great apes.

➡ **Kalimantan – Tanjung Puting National Park** Several stations feed free-roaming ex-captive orangutans reached by a romantic jungle river cruise.

➡ **Kalimantan – Palangka Raya** Circumnavigate Sungai Kahayan's Orangutan Island in high style.

➡ **Kalimantan – Kutai National Park** The most accessible place to see wild orangutans, and hear chainsaws.

Komodo Dragons

Tales of evil beasts with huge claws, menacing teeth and yellow forked tongues floated around the islands of Nusa Tenggara for centuries. This continued until around 100 years ago, when the first Westerners brought one out of its namesake island home near Flores.

As mean as these 3m-long 150kg lizards look, their disposition is worse. Scores of humans have perished after being attacked, and Komodos regularly stalk and eat small deer. One researcher compared the sound of a Komodo pounding across the ground in pursuit to that of a machine gun. They have also been known to follow bite victims for miles, waiting as the venom from glands located between their teeth slowly poisons and kills their prey within 24 hours.

One hawksbill turtle that visited Bali was tracked for the following year. Its destinations: Java, Kalimantan, Australia (Perth and much of Queensland) and then back to Bali.

Birds

Astrapias, sicklebills, rifle birds and manucodes are just a few of the 1600 species of exotic feathered creatures you'll see in the skies of Indonesia, 380 of which you'll only find here. On Papua alone, there isn't just one species called 'bird of paradise', but 30. For many a birder, watching a pair of these perform their spectacular mating dance is the dream of a lifetime.

Birdwatching is popular in many of the national parks. Guides are often fantastic at spotting birds, but may not know much more about them than you. The second edition of *A Photographic Guide to the Birds of Indonesia* is your most comprehensive resource. On Sulawesi, Tangkoko-Batuangas Dua Saudara Nature Reserve has regular birdwatching tours. In Bali, you can go on guided bird walks in and around Ubud.

Papua easily wins the birdwatching crown, however. Its range of birds includes migrating species from Australia and as far afield as Siberia.

Birds of Paradise

Papua's glamorous birds of paradise are a product of extreme sexual selection. In a place where food is abundant, and predators scarce, the main factor deciding who gets to reproduce is the female's choice of mate – and, it turns out, the ladies love a flamboyant fella.

While the female tends to look unremarkable, male birds of paradise may be adorned with fancy plumage, perform elaborate dances, or develop bizarre calls, all with the hopes of inspiring a lady to give him her number. The Wilson's bird of paradise, endemic to Indonesia, has both bright red and yellow feathers, as well as a curling tail like a handlebar moustache, while the Parotia dons a tutu and twirls for his potential mate.

For a stunning all-access look at the world's 39 birds of paradise, pick up the *National Geographic* coffee table book, *Birds of Paradise: Revealing the World's Most Extraordinary Birds*, by Tim Lamen and Edwin Scholes.

Life Underwater

Indonesia's incredible range of life on land is easily matched beneath the waves. The waters around Komodo, Sulawesi, the north coast of Papua, and even some spots in Java, Bali and Kalimantan are home to a kaleidoscope of corals, reef dwellers and pelagic marine life. In the Raja Ampat region of Papua there are at least 450 species of coral, six times more than found in the entire Caribbean. Thriving in that environment are over 1600 species of fish, with divers encountering up to 300 in a single dive. Manta rays are also found in abundance, along with 118 species of shark, including the endangered hammerhead and sawtooth.

Exit the oceans to head upriver, and the story continues: Irrawaddy dolphins and finless porpoises occupy many of Indonesia's bays; a single population of truly freshwater dolphins (called *pesut*) can be found in Kalimantan's Mahakam River; and the world's smallest fish (paedocypris progenetica, 7.9mm) occupies Sumatra's peat swamps.

BE THE SOLUTION

You will still see plenty of animal exploitation in Indonesia, including performing monkeys on street corners in big cities and endangered birds in markets. Taking photos or paying the handlers money only encourages this behaviour.

Shops sell turtle-shell products, rare seashells, snakeskin, stuffed birds and framed butterflies. Avoid these. Not only are they illegal, but importing them into most countries is banned and items will probably be confiscated by customs. See the Convention on International Trade in Endangered Species (CITES; www.cites.org) for more information.

Some animal exploitation is more subtle. Consider the life of a cute civet locked in a cage in a warehouse force fed coffee to 'naturally' process the beans, for example. It's a far cry from the happy story plantations sell to justify charging outrageous prices for *kopi luwak* (civet coffee).

Finally, rubbish is an obvious problem. And while packing out your biscuit wrapper from some already rubbish-strewn waterfall may feel futile, your guides and other trekkers will notice, and might even join you. It is a small, but important step in the right direction.

Plants

Indonesia's plant diversity rivals the Amazon, and its botanical riches have defined its history. Wars were fought over the archipelago's spices while high-value timber extraction has opened the forests for settlement and further exploitation.

Many species are showy bloomers, though these are usually rare outside of cultivated areas. Orchids are abundant (2500 different species at last count) and are best seen at Bali's excellent botanical gardens. You can expect a riot of fragrant frangipani, lotus and hibiscus blossoms as well as a festival of other blooms across the archipelago. Impossibly complex heliconias hang from vines in all their multifaceted crimson, orange and golden glory.

There are over 25,000 flowering plant species in Indonesia, and an estimated 40% exist nowhere else on earth.

Amid all of the flashy flora are many edible plants, including some of the world's most (in)famous fruits. Queen Victoria is reported to have been manic for the subtly sweet mangosteen from Maluku, while some strains of Kalimantan's durian are sought after by connoisseurs. Bananas are common in many varieties, all very different from the supermarket sameness back home.

Meanwhile, in forested areas, regal trees provide welcome shade from the equatorial sunshine. As you trek below, the plants in the canopy above are locked in a deadly battle for that very same sun. Towering dipterocarp rely on brute strength to push through the canopy, while vines and lianas sneak their way to the top on the shoulders of giants. Some fig species start life clinging to the upper branches of other trees before dropping a network of roots that surround, strangle, and occasionally kill their host.

Look for coffee plantations, especially in the hills of Bali near Munduk. On Maluku – the original Spice Island – you can still catch the scent of vanilla and cloves, the latter most often wafting off the glowing end of a sweet *kretek* cigarette.

But it wouldn't be Indonesia without some real characters. Consider *Rafflesia arnoldii*, the world's largest flower, and the *Amorphophallus titanum*, the world's tallest flower. Both can be found, usually by their smell, on Sumatra and parts of Kalimantan and Java.

In areas where the soils are poor, some plants have become carnivores. *Nepenthes* species, known as pitcher plants, lure ants and other insects into their slippery chambers full of digestive juices. When things get really tough, some turn to even more alternative sources of nitrogen: bat guano and shrew poop.

National Parks & Protected Areas

Despite a constant nipping at the edges by illegal loggers and farmers, Indonesia still has large tracts of protected forest and parks, and many new protected areas have been gazetted in recent years. National parks receive greater international recognition and funding than nature, wildlife and marine reserves, of which there are also many in Indonesia.

Most of Indonesia's national parks are isolated, but the extra effort required to get to them is more than rewarded by the country's magnificent wilderness. Visitor facilities are minimal at best, but at many of the parks you'll find locals who are enthusiastic about their land and are ready to guide you to its hidden gems.

Environmental Issues

Deforestation

Indonesia's islands continue to be deforested at an alarming rate through illegal logging, conversion to palm-oil plantations, and mining. Since the year 2000, over 16 million hectares of forest cover have been cleared in Indonesia, an area roughly the size of Greece. Six million hectares of that were old growth forest, with almost half of that occurring in theoretically protected areas. And this rate does not seem to be abating; indeed, in both 2009 and 2012 as much as two million hectares of forest was destroyed. Indonesia now destroys its forests almost twice as fast as Brazil.

Norway has placed $1 billion on the table to encourage Indonesia to get a handle on deforestation and climate change.

Feeling the heat of international pressure, Indonesia issued a sweeping moratorium on logging in 2011 that left loopholes large enough to drive a fleet of logging trucks through. Deforestation actually increased. Meanwhile, companies independently make grandiose green-washing pledges to end their deforestation, then turn around and hire local smallholders to clear and plant the land for them. The forestry department draws lines around swaths of newly protected land, while local ministers use different maps to carve it up and sell the logging rights. The government declares formal recognition of indigenous people's right to manage their forests, but their claims are then contested in long-running legal battles.

Mineral Extraction

Coal, oil, gold, nickel, tin, aluminium, copper, iron ore, diamonds…what lies beneath Indonesia's forest is just as tempting for exploitation as what grows above. Although mining can be done in an ecologically responsible manner, a lack of oversight and poor enforcement of regulations has resulted in a legacy of environmental disaster. Vast swaths of land have been dug open with little regard for environmental impact and almost no reclamation.

LOCAL ACTION

As the environmental situation becomes more dire, more Indonesians are taking notice. Although international groups like World Wildlife Fund and the Nature Conservancy have strong and effective presences in Indonesia, it is the burgeoning local environmental movements that will exact real and lasting change.

Profauna (www.profauna.net/en) operates throughout Indonesia to protect turtles and combat wildlife trade.

Walhi (Indonesian Friends of the Earth; www.walhi.or.id) works to protect the country's environment at many levels.

AMAN (Indigenous People's Alliance of the Archipelago; www.aman.or.id/en) helps secure indigenous rights to the natural forests necessary for their livelihood.

JATAM (Mining Advocacy Network; english.jatam.org) works toward environmental responsibility and human-rights protection in Indonesia's mining sector.

TOP 10 NATIONAL PARKS & RESERVES FOR TRAVELLERS

PARK	LOCATION	FEATURES	ACTIVITIES	BEST TIME TO VISIT	PAGE
Gunung Leuser	Sumatra	rivers, rainforest, mountains; tigers, rhinoceros, elephants, primates such as orangutans, white-breasted Thomas's leaf monkeys	orangutan viewing, wildlife spotting, birdwatching; trekking, rafting	Dec-Mar	p534
Tanjung Puting	Kalimantan	tropical rainforest, mangrove forest, wetlands; orangutans, macaques, proboscis monkeys, diverse wildlife	orangutan viewing, birdwatching	May-Sep	p600
Kelimutu	Nusa Tenggara	coloured lakes	vulcanology, short walks	Apr-Sep	p372
Gunung Rinjani	Nusa Tenggara	volcano	volcano hiking	Apr-Sep	p317
Ujung Kulon	Java	lowland rainforest, scrub, grassy plains, swamps, sandy beaches; one-horned rhinoceros, otters, squirrels, white-breasted Thomas's leaf monkeys, gibbons	jungle walks; wildlife spotting	Apr-Oct	p77
Gunung Bromo	Java	volcanic landscape	crater climbing	Apr-Oct	p183
Pulau Bunaken	Sulawesi	coral-fringed islands	snorkelling, diving, island lazing	Jun-Jan	p688
Kerinci Seblat	Sumatra	mountainous rainforest, one of Sumatra's highest peaks	trekking; wildlife spotting, birdwatching	Dec-Mar	p563
Komodo	Nusa Tenggara	Komodo dragon	snorkelling, diving; being chased by wildlife	Apr-Sep	p352
Bali Barat	Bali	low hills, grasslands, coral-fringed coasts	snorkelling, diving; wildlife spotting	year-round	p296

A ban on export of raw ore enacted in early 2015 will have serious implications for Indonesia as companies rush to build domestic smelters. These processing facilities will require extensive infrastructure investments, including power plants and roads, and will further tax natural resources. Environmental groups also worry that the historical lack of industry oversight in Indonesia will allow these new plants to cut corners and ignore safeguards.

Cascading Effects

The side effects of deforestation and resource extraction are felt across the nation and beyond: floods and landslides wash away valuable topsoil, rivers become sluggish and fetid, and haze from clearing fires blankets Malaysia and Singapore every dry season, increasing international tensions. The carbon released from deforestation and fires is a significant contributor to global climate change, which in a vicious cycle creates a longer dry season, allowing for more fires.

The problems flow right through to Indonesia's coastline and seas, where more than 80% of reef habitat is considered to be at risk. A long history of cyanide and bomb fishing has left much of Indonesia's coral lifeless or crumbled. Shark finning and manta hunting have taken their toll on populations, while overfishing threatens to disrupt the marine ecosystem.

Meanwhile, the burgeoning middle class is straining the nation's infrastructure. Private vehicles clog urban streets, creating choking air pollution; waste-removal services have difficulty coping with household and industrial refuse; and a lack of sewage disposal makes water from most sources undrinkable without boiling, putting further pressure on kerosene and firewood supplies.

Endangered Species

The Greater Sunda Islands, comprising Sumatra, Java, Kalimantan and Bali, were once connected to the Malaysian peninsula and Asian mainland. When the glaciers receded and ocean levels rose, the Sunda Shelf flooded, isolating the islands and the animal populations that migrated there. Some large Asian land animals still survive in this area, including tigers, rhinoceroses, leopards and sun bears – but their existence is tenuous at best.

Despite lingering claims of sightings, the Javan tiger was declared extinct in 2003. The Sumatran tiger is literally fighting for survival. There have been several incidents of tigers killing loggers trespassing in protected habitats, and of poachers killing tigers, also in protected habitats. Fewer than 500 individuals remain in the wild. Leopards (the black leopard, or panther, is more common in Southeast Asia) are rare but still live in Sumatra and in Java's Ujung Kulon National Park. This park is also home to the 60 remaining one-horned Javan rhinoceroses. Rhinos have not fared well in Indonesia and the two-horned variety, found in Sumatra and possibly Kalimantan, is also on the endangered list.

Perhaps the most famous endangered Indonesian animal is the orangutan, which is under constant threat from logging and conversion of habitat to palm-oil plantations. In one especially tragic case, an adult orangutan that wandered onto a palm-oil plantation died after locals set the tree it was sheltering in on fire to drive it off. Poachers regularly shoot mothers to sell their babies as pets. Also victims of the pet trade and habitat loss, all Indonesian gibbon species are endangered.

Fewer than 2000 Sumatran elephants remain in the wild, and are being driven into conflict with people since 70% of their habitat has been cleared for plantations and farming. The pygmy elephants in North Kalimantan have been reduced to fewer than 100.

TRADITIONAL MEDICINE?

Deforestation may have widespread implications, but an even more pernicious threat targets some of Indonesia's most imperilled species: the booming international trade in animals and animal parts. The growing demand is largely fuelled by the rise of China's wealthy class and their conspicuous consumption of exotic food and medicine. The use of animal parts is often loosely attributed to traditional Chinese medicine, though some products are relatively recent additions, and there is little to no scientific evidence that any have true medicinal value.

Regardless, tiger demand has increased as the newly rich seek out status-confirming products like tiger bone wine, which can sell for US$250 per bottle and is believed to cure arthritis. Shark fin soup, claimed to increase virility, drives a US$500-million-per-year 'finning' industry – a harvesting practice whereby poachers cut off fins and dump the sharks back in the water to bleed to death. In 2014, Indonesian authorities confiscated 55 porcupines, whose bezoar stones (sometimes found in their digestive tracts) are believed to cure cancer, and sun bear poaching is on the rise for their gall bladders.

The world's most trafficked animal, pangolin (or scaly anteater) are covered in scales which people dry and powder to treat everything from swelling and arthritis to 'women possessed by devils and ogres'. Their meat is also a highly prized delicacy throughout Asia, and in Vietnam, restaurants openly sell pangolin for US$250 a kilogram. A 2015 bust in Sumatra confiscated 96 live pangolins along with five tonnes more of frozen animals and 77kg of scales estimated to be worth US$1.8million.

Local Issues

There is much to be done to protect Indonesia's magnificence. While some steps are being made on the national scale to address the issues, a history of decentralisation and an ingrained culture of corruption means that many problems are rooted in the local and regional levels – which is where they must be addressed. Community organising is becoming more common as the local people grow increasingly frustrated with the situation, and less worried about the consequences of standing up for their land and their health.

Sumatra

Deforestation is a massive problem, threatening this island's rainforests and all its inhabitants, including the Sumatran tiger, Sumatran elephant, Sumatran rhinoceros, and Sumatran orangutan. National parks and other protected lands have consistently been sold off to logging companies and palm-oil plantations. Plans for hundreds of kilometres of new roads through the Leuser ecosystem threaten this critical habitat, while smoke from fires constantly chokes neighbouring Singapore and Malaysia during the dry season.

Rogue pilot Harrison Ford (yes, *that* one) lambasts Indonesia's forestry minister about Sumatra's deforestation in the documentary series, *Years of Living Dangerously*.

In a positive move, Indonesia finally ratified a 12-year-old transboundary haze agreement in 2014, becoming the last Southeast Asian nation to do so. Around the same time, anti-corruption officials arrested Riau's governor for allegedly accepting bribes from palm-oil companies. In late 2015, conservation groups backed by the Leonardo DiCaprio Foundation won the battle for a 60-year lease of 44,000 hectares of critical habitat.

Java

As Indonesia's most densely populated island, it's not surprising that rampant development causes widespread flooding in Jakarta, Semarang and other cities every rainy season. This results in mass social upheaval and chokes surviving coastal mangroves. Although Jakarta has begun purchasing heavy equipment to remove garbage from the city's rivers, unless something is done about the 70,000 tonnes of rubbish dumped into the waterways every year, it may be a losing battle.

Java's longest river, the Cirtarum, is also one of the world's most polluted from both rubbish and chemical dumping by a growing industrial sector. A 15-year US$500 million loan from the Asian Development Bank is supposed to go toward its clean-up and rehabilitation.

Kalimantan

Deforestation and resource extraction occur in Kalimantan on an unprecedented scale. Coal-mining permits for over half of the land around the city of Samarinda have been issued, resulting in widespread flooding that costs the government tens of millions of dollars in damages each year. Indonesian health officials have warned that residents along the Mahakam river are at high risk of illness and skin disease due to pollution.

During the dry seasons of 2014 and 2015, smog from hundreds of unstoppable fires shut down airports and caused widespread respiratory illness. For the first time, Indonesia's government began cracking down in 2015, fining multiple companies for intentionally starting fires. Meanwhile, several indigenous communities have secured official recognition of their rights to ancestral lands, and some are developing ecotourism initiatives to provide alternative income for their village.

Bali

This beautiful island is its own worst enemy: it can't help being popular. Walhi, the Indonesian Forum for Environment (www.walhi.or.id), estimates that the average hotel room uses 3000L of water. The typical golf course needs three million litres a day. Hence, a place fabled for its water is now running short. In addition, rice fields are being converted to commercial land at a rate of about 600 to 1000 hectares a year.

Meanwhile, a plan to create a golf course and shopping mall on top of 700 hectares of mangrove forest near Denpasar, euphemistically called the Benoa Bay Reclamation Project, continues to be a flashpoint for Bali's environmentalists. Feasibility studies predict the project will cause widespread flooding and destroy local fisheries.

Its proximity to the Philippines makes the port at Bitung on Sulawesi an unfortunate epicentre for wildlife smuggling. Tasikoki (www.tasikoki.org) is an entirely volunteer-run organisation that rescues and cares for animals confiscated from smugglers.

Sulawesi

Conflict over mining near the beautiful dive areas of Bangka Island took an ugly turn in 2014 when officers from the company harassed a group of foreign divers, forcing them to surface and hauling them to shore for questioning. The local government has granted a Chinese-owned company permits to mine for iron ore without performing an environmental impact assessment, and without approval from the Ministry of Forestry. Also threatening area reefs are organised networks of cyanide fishing bankrolled by foreign bosses.

Nusa Tenggara

On southern Lombok, unprecedented new development in the previously untouched and beautiful beach area of Kuta will have untold environmental consequences. On the other hand, in 2015, Lombok's governor did reject a plan to transport 23 million cubic metres of sand from his island to use as back-fill in the controversial Benoa Bay Reclamation Project on neighbouring Bali; and nearby, the Gili Eco Trust continues to make great strides toward greening the Gili islands.

Things are not looking good in West Sumbawa, however, where authorities struggle to get a handle on illegal gold mining where over 1000 small operations dump a steady stream of mercury into the island's waterways. Elsewhere, dynamite fishing and poaching by locals is an ongoing concern in Unesco-listed Komodo National Park.

Maluku

A timber-harvesting scheme threatens to destroy half of the forest of Aru, one of Indonesia's biodiversity hotspots. The land was slated for 500,000 hectares of sugar-cane plantations, but the plan was rejected in 2014 after international outcry. However, the plans resurfaced again in 2015.

Visit environmental news site mongabay.com for the latest information on Indonesia's conservation successes...and failures.

The Maluku islands are also prime poaching ground for the wild bird trade. Populations of endemic and rare species have plummeted in recent years, especially songbirds, which collectors buy to enter into lucrative singing contests.

Papua

At the time of research, President Jokowi was poised to recreate the environmental catastrophe of the failed Mega Rice Project, which destroyed millions of hectares of Kalimantan's peat forests and produced nothing. In a visit to Merauke in 2015 he announced plans to revitalise the controversial plan to clear 1.2 million hectares of forest over three years to make way for large-scale industrial agriculture. Ultimately the plan calls for 4.6 million hectares of new rice production in the area, despite the fact that the land is already home to some of Papau's long-marginalised indigenous groups.

Survival Guide

Responsible Travel

To visit Indonesia responsibly, try to tread lightly as you go, with respect for both the land and the diverse cultures of its people.

➡ **Watch your use of water** Water demand outstrips supply in much of Indonesia – even at seemingly green places like Bali. Take your hotel up on its offer to save water by not washing your sheets and towels every day. At the high end you can also forgo your own private plunge pool, or a pool altogether.

➡ **Don't hit the bottle** Those bottles of Aqua (a top local brand of bottled water, owned by Danone) are convenient but they add up. The zillions of such bottles tossed away each year are a serious blight. Since tap water is unsafe, ask your hotel if you can refill from their huge containers of drinking water. Some enlightened businesses already offer this service.

➡ **Support environmentally aware businesses** The number of businesses committed to good environmental practices is growing fast in Indonesia. Keep an eye out within this guide for the sustainable icon, which identifies environmentally savvy businesses.

➡ **Conserve power** Turn off lights and air-con when not using them.

➡ **Bag the bags** Refuse plastic bags, and say no to plastic straws, too.

➡ **Leave the animals be** Reconsider swimming with captive dolphins, riding captive elephants, and patronising attractions where wild animals are made to perform for crowds, interactions that have been identified by animal welfare experts as harmful to the animals. And don't try to pet, feed or otherwise interact with animals in the wild as it disrupts their natural behaviour and can make them sick.

Responsible Diving

The popularity of diving puts immense pressure on many sites. Consider the following tips when diving and help preserve the ecology and beauty of Indonesia's reefs:

➡ Avoid touching living marine organisms with your body or dragging equipment across the reef. Never stand on corals.

➡ Be conscious of your fins. The surge from heavy fin strokes near the reef can damage delicate organisms. When treading water in shallow reef areas, take care not to kick up clouds of sand. Settling sand can easily smother delicate reef organisms.

➡ Practise and maintain proper buoyancy control. Major damage can be done by divers descending too fast and colliding with the reef.

➡ Don't collect corals or shells.

➡ Ensure that you collect all your rubbish and any litter you find as well. Plastics in particular are a serious threat to marine life.

➡ Resist the temptation to feed fish.

➡ The best dive operators will require that you adhere to the points above.

Responsible Hiking & Trekking

To help preserve the ecology and beauty of Indonesia, consider the following tips when hiking and trekking (good guides will already be following these principles):

Rubbish

➡ Carry out *all* your rubbish. Don't overlook easily forgotten items, such as cigarette butts, and carry out rubbish left by others.

➡ Never bury your rubbish: it can take years to decompose and digging encourages erosion. Buried rubbish will likely be dug up by animals, which may be injured or poisoned by it.

- Minimise waste by taking minimal packaging and no more food than you will need. Take reusable containers or stuff sacks.
- Sanitary napkins, tampons, condoms and toilet paper should be carried out. They decompose poorly.

Human Waste Disposal

- Contamination of water sources by human faeces is a major problem. Where there are no toilets, dig a small hole 15cm (6in) deep and at least 100m (320ft) from any watercourse. Cover the waste with soil and a rock.

Washing

- Don't use detergents or toothpaste in or near watercourses, even if they are biodegradable.
- For personal washing, use biodegradable soap and a water container (or even a lightweight, portable basin) at least 50m (160ft) away from any watercourse.
- Wash cooking utensils 50m (160ft) from watercourses using a scourer instead of detergent.

Erosion

- Stick to existing tracks.
- If a track passes through a mud patch, walk through the patch so as not to increase its size.
- Avoid removing the plant life that keeps topsoils in place.

Fires & Low-Impact Cooking

- Don't depend on open fires for cooking. The cutting of wood for fires in popular trekking areas can cause rapid deforestation. Cook on a lightweight kerosene, alcohol or Shellite (white gas) stove and avoid those powered by disposable butane gas canisters.
- Fires may be acceptable below the tree line in areas that get very few visitors. If you light a fire, use an existing fireplace. Use only minimal, dead, fallen wood.
- Ensure that you fully extinguish a fire after use.

Wildlife Conservation

- Do not engage in or encourage hunting. Indonesia is full of endangered critters, which need all the help they can get to survive.
- Don't buy items made from endangered species.
- Discourage the presence of wildlife by not leaving food scraps behind you (or intentionally feeding wildlife).
- Do not encourage poaching/the illegal wildlife trade by posing for selfies with captive wildlife such as 'pet' monkeys.

Volunteering

There are excellent opportunities for aspiring volunteers in Indonesia, but Lonely Planet does not endorse any organisations that we do not work with directly, so it is essential that you do your own thorough research before agreeing to volunteer with or donate to any organisation. A three-month commitment is recommended for working with children.

For many groups fundraising and cash donations are the best way to help. Some also can use skilled volunteers to work as English teachers and provide professional services such as medical care. A few offer paid volunteering, whereby volunteers pay for room and board and perform often menial tasks.

A good resource to find NGOs and volunteer opportunities on Bali is www.balispirit.com/ngos.

Alam Sehat Lestari (www.alamsehatlestari.org/volunteer) Accepts skilled medical and conservation volunteers to help protect and restore Kalimantan's rainforest.

Borneo Orangutan Survival Foundation (www.orangutan.or.id) Accepts volunteers for its orangutan and sun bear rehabilitation and reforestation programs.

East Bali Poverty Project (☎0361-410 071; www.eastbalipovertyproject.org) Works to help children in the impoverished mountain villages of east Bali. Uses English teachers and has a solid child protection policy.

Friends of the National Parks Foundation (☎0361-977 978; www.fnpf.org) Has volunteer programs on Nusa Penida off Bali and Kalimantan.

IDEP (Indonesian Development of Education & Permaculture; ☎0361-294993; www.idepfoundation.org) Has projects across Indonesia; works on environmental projects, disaster planning and community improvement.

ProFauna (www.profauna.net) A large nonprofit animal-protection organisation operating across Indonesia; has been active in protecting sea turtles.

Project Hope Sumba (www.projecthopesumba.org) Works on Sumba to improve access to clean water, education, healthcare etc.

Sea Sanctuaries Trust (www.seasanctuaries.org) Diving-based marine conservation volunteering in Raja Ampat.

Smile Foundation of Bali (Yayasan Senyum; ☎0361-233758; www.senyumbali.org) Organises surgery to correct facial deformities.

Yayasan Bumi Sehat (☎0361-970002; www.bumisehatfoundation.org) Operates an internationally recognised clinic and gives reproductive services to disadvantaged women in Ubud; accepts donated time from medical professionals. The founder, Robin Lim, has had international recognition.

Yayasan Rama Sesana (☎0361-247363; www.yrsbali.org) Dedicated to improving reproductive health for women across Bali.

International Organisations

The following agencies may have information about long-term paid or volunteer work in Indonesia:

Australian Volunteers International (www.australianvolunteers.com) Organises all manner of programs, with many in Indonesia.

Global Volunteers (www.globalvolunteers.org) Arranges professional and paid volunteer work for US citizens.

Global Vision International (www.gviusa.com) Organises short-term volunteer opportunities; has offices in Australia, the UK and the US.

Go Abroad (www.goabroad.com) Lists mostly paid volunteer work.

Voluntary Service Overseas (www.vso.org.uk) British overseas volunteer program that accepts qualified volunteers from other countries.

Volunteer Service Abroad (www.vsa.org.nz) Organises professional contracts for New Zealanders.

Directory A–Z

Accommodation

Accommodation in Indonesia ranges from a basic box with a mattress to the finest five-star luxury resorts. Costs vary considerably across the archipelago, but in general Indonesia is one of the better bargains in Southeast Asia.

Travellers centres have plenty of reasonably priced food and accommodation. In Bali and other touristed areas like the Gilis, Labuanbajo on Flores, etc, you'll have a wide range of sleeping choices. Options diminish quickly as you get off the beaten track, although lavish resorts, surf camps and idyllic yet modest getaways can be found across the archipelago.

- Accommodation attracts a combined tax and service charge (called 'plus plus') of 21%. In budget places, this is generally included in the price, but check first. Many midrange and top-end places will add it on, which can add substantially to your bill.
- Rates quoted in this book include tax and are those that travellers are likely to pay during the high season. Nailing down rates is difficult, as some establishments publish the rates they actually plan to charge, while others publish rates that are pure fantasy, fully expecting to discount by 50%.
- Shop online and contact hotels directly to find the best rates. There's no one formula that works across Indonesia.

Hotels

Hotels in tourist areas can be excellent at any price range. But elsewhere in Indonesia, standards quickly fall: slack maintenance and uneven service are common, although staff are usually cheery.

BUDGET HOTELS

The cheapest accommodation is in small places that are simple but clean and comfortable. Names usually include the word 'losmen,' 'homestay,' 'inn' or '*pondok*.' Standards vary widely. Expect:

- Maybe air-con
- Maybe hot water
- Sometimes no window
- Private bathroom with shower and sometimes a Western-style toilet
- Often a pool (on Bali)
- Simple breakfast

MIDRANGE HOTELS

Many hotels have a range of rooms, from budget to midrange. The best may be called VIP or some other moniker. In addition to what you'll get at a budget hotel, expect:

- Balcony/porch/patio
- Satellite TV
- Small fridge
- Usually wi-fi

TOP-END HOTELS

Top-end hotels can range from international chains in Jakarta to beautiful resorts on Bali and lavish getaways elsewhere. Expect:

- Superb service
- Views – ocean, lush valleys and rice fields or private gardens
- Spa
- Maybe a private pool

Camping

Camping in national parks is popular among Indonesian youth, though formal camping grounds with power and other facilities are rare. Outside of the parks, camping is

BOOK YOUR STAY ONLINE

For more accommodation reviews by Lonely Planet authors, check out http://lonelyplanet.com/hotels/. You'll find independent reviews, as well as recommendations on the best places to stay. Best of all, you can book online.

SLEEPING PRICE RANGES

Accommodation rates are for high season (May to September and Christmas/New Year) and may drop during low season.

The following price ranges refer to a double room with bathroom. Unless otherwise stated relevant taxes are included in the price.

Bali & Lombok

$ less than 450,000Rp

$$ 450,000–1,400,000Rp

$$$ more than 1,400,000Rp

Rest of Indonesia

$ less than 250,000Rp

$$ 250,000–800,000Rp

$$$ more than 800,000Rp

unknown, and villagers will regard campers as a source of entertainment. Some Kalimantan and Papua treks may include camping, as will some mountain treks such as Gunung Rinjani on Lombok. Guides usually supply gear.

Hostels

Indonesia didn't used to have many hostels, mainly because there are so many inexpensive guesthouses. But now you can find hostels in Jakarta, Bali, the Gilis and beyond, including Flores.

Staying in Villages

In many places in Indonesia you'll often be welcome to stay in the villages. If the town has no hotel, ask for the *kepala desa* (village head), who is generally very hospitable and friendly, offering you not only a roof over your head in a homestay, but also meals. Consider the following:

- You may not get a room of your own, just a bed.
- Payment is usually expected: about the same price as a cheap losmen (50,000Rp to 100,000Rp) as a rule of thumb. The *kepala desa* may suggest an amount, but often it is *terserah* (up to you), and you should always offer to pay.
- While the village head's house sometimes acts as an unofficial hotel, you are a guest and often an honoured one. Elaborate meals may be prepared just for you. It's also a good idea to have a gift or two to offer – cigarettes, photographs or small souvenirs from your country are popular.
- Homestays and village stays are a great way to socialise with families and neighbours, contribute to the local economy and experience life at a much closer level.
- Villages on Baliem Valley trekking routes often have basic guesthouses for tourists.

Villas & Long-Term Accommodation

Luxury villas are popular accommodation on Bali, although they are not without their environmental costs in terms of water usage and placement amidst once pristine rice fields. Many come with pools, views, beaches and more. Often the houses are staffed and you have the services of a cook, driver etc.

Rates range from under US$200 per night for a modest villa to US$1200 per night and much more for your own tropical estate. There are often deals, especially in the low season, and several couples sharing can make something grand affordable.

Some things to keep in mind and ask about when renting a villa:

- How far is the villa from the beach and nightlife?
- Is a driver or car service included?
- If there is a cook, is food included?
- Is laundry included?

For longer stays, you can find deals easily for US$800 a month. Look in the *Bali Advertiser* (www.baliadvertiser.biz) or search Facebook. If your tastes are simple, you can find basic bungalows for US$300 a month.

Customs Regulations

Indonesia has the usual list of prohibited imports, including drugs, weapons, fresh fruit and anything remotely pornographic. Items allowed include the following:

- 200 cigarettes (or 50 cigars or 100g of tobacco)
- a 'reasonable amount' of perfume
- 1L of alcohol

Surfers with more than two or three boards may be charged a 'fee', and this could apply to other items if the officials suspect that you aim to sell them in Indonesia. If you have nothing to declare, customs clearance is usually quick.

Electricity

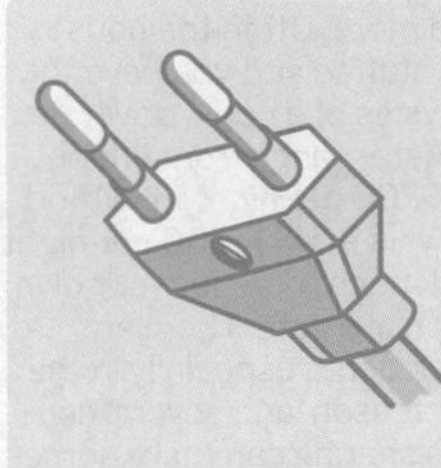

220V/230V/50Hz

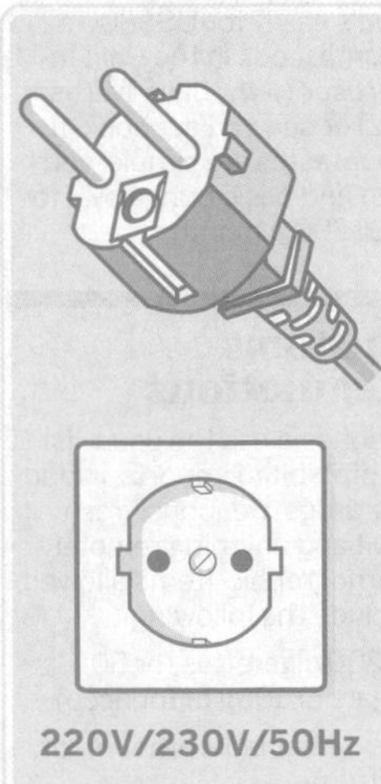

Embassies & Consulates

It's important to know what your own embassy can and can't do to help you if you get into trouble. Generally speaking, it won't be much help if whatever trouble you're in is remotely your own fault. Remember that you are bound by the laws of the country you are in. In genuine emergencies you might get some assistance, but only if other channels have been exhausted.

Foreign embassies are located in Jakarta; Bali and Medan have a few consulates. There are also some in towns close to foreign borders.

Bali

Australian Consulate (Map p240; ☎0361-241 118; www.bali.indonesia.embassy.gov.au; Jl Tantular 32, Denpasar; ⏰8am-4pm Mon-Fri) The Australian consulate has a consular sharing agreement with Canada.

US Consulate (☎0361-233 605; BaliConsularAgency@state.gov; Jl Hayam Wuruk 310, Renon, Denpasar; ⏰9am-noon & 1-3.30pm Mon-Fri)

Jakarta

Australian Embassy (Map p60; ☎021-2550 5555; www.indonesia.embassy.gov.au; Jln HR Rasuna Said Kav C 15-16, Jakarta Selatan)

Brunei Darussalam Embassy (Map p58; ☎021-3190 6080; www.mofat.gov.bn; Jln Teuku Umar No 51, Menteng)

Canadian Embassy (Map p60; ☎021-2550 7800; www.jakarta.gc.ca; 6th fl, World Trade Centre, Jln Jenderal Sudirman Kav 29-31)

Dutch Embassy (Map p60; ☎021-524 8200; http://indonesia.nlembassy.org; Jln HR Rasuna Said Kav S-3)

French Embassy (Map p58; ☎021-2355 7600; www.ambafrance-id.org; Jl MH Thamrin No 20)

German Embassy (Map p58; ☎021-3985 5000; www.jakarta.diplo.de; Jl MH Thamrin No 1)

Malaysian Embassy (Map p60; ☎021-522 4974; www.kln.gov.my/web/idn_jakarta/home; Jln HR Rasuna Said Kav X/6, No 1-3, Kuningan)

New Zealand Embassy (Map p60; ☎021-2995 5800; www.nzembassy.com; 10th fl, Sentral Senayan 2, Jl Asia Afrika No 8)

Papua New Guinea Embassy (Map p60; ☎021-725 1218; www.kundu-jakarta.com; 6th fl, Panin Bank Centre, Jl Jenderal Sudirman 1)

Singaporean Embassy (Map p60; ☎021-2995 0400; www.mfa.gov.sg/jkt; Block X/4 Kav 2, Jl HR Rasuna Said)

UK Embassy (Map p60; ☎021-2356 5200; ukinindonesia.fco.gov.uk; Jl Patra Kuningan Raya Blok L5-6)

US Embassy (Map p58; ☎021-3435 9000; jakarta.usembassy.gov; Jl Medan Merdeka Selatan, No 3-5)

Kupang

Timor-Leste Consulate (☎0813-3936 7558; Jl Eltari II; ⏰8am-4pm Mon-Thu, to 2pm Fri) The visa office for Timor-Leste.

Medan

Malaysian Consulate (Map p496; ☎061-453 1342; www.kln.gov.my/web/idn_medan; Jl Diponegoro 43)

Food

Indonesia has a vast array of culinary delights and regional specialities (p742).

Insurance

A travel-insurance policy to cover theft, loss and medical problems is essential. There is a wide variety of policies, most sold online; make certain your policy will cover speedy medical evacuation from anywhere in Indonesia.

Theft is a potential problem in Indonesia, so make sure that your policy covers expensive items adequately. Many policies have restrictions on laptops and expensive camera gear, and refunds

EATING PRICE RANGES

The following ranges represent the average cost of standard meals.

Bali & Lombok

$ less than 60,000Rp

$$ 60,000–250,000Rp

$$$ more than 250,000Rp

Rest of Indonesia

$ less than 50,000Rp

$$ 50,000–200,000Rp

$$$ more than 200,000Rp

are often for depreciated value, not replacement value.

Worldwide travel insurance is available at www.lonelyplanet.com/travel-insurance. You can buy, extend and claim online anytime – even if you're already on the road.

Internet Access

Indonesia is getting wired, though speed varies from fast to painfully slow.

- Wi-fi (pronounced 'wee-fee' in Indonesia) is commonly available in hotels except in rural areas. It is often free but watch out for hotels that may charge ridiculous rates by the hour or by data use.
- Data through your smartphone is often the fastest way to connect to the internet. 3G service is widespread.

Legal Matters

Drugs, gambling and pornography are illegal; the executions of two Australian nationals, among others, of the so-called Bali Nine in 2015 for drug offences serve as a grim reminder.

- It is an offence to engage in paid work without a formal working permit.
- Visa length of stay is strictly enforced; many a careless tourist has seen the inside of an immigration detention facility or paid large fines.
- Corruption remains a fact of life. If you are pulled over for a dubious traffic infringement, be polite and respectful as the officer lectures you and then suggests an alternative to a trip to the police station and a courthouse date. Generally, 50,000Rp is plenty, but 100,000Rp is more the norm on Bali.
- In the case of an accident involving serious injury or death, drive straight to the nearest police station as 'mob rule' can prevail, with blame falling on the foreigner.
- If you need to report a crime, head to a police station in respectable dress with an Indonesian friend or interpreter in tow but don't expect much.
- If you find yourself in serious trouble with the law, contact your embassy or consulate immediately. They will not be able to arrange bail but will be able to provide you with an interpreter and may be able to suggest legal counsel.

LGBT Travellers

Gay travellers in Indonesia should follow the same precautions as straight travellers: avoid public displays of affection. This is especially important in conservative areas such as Aceh, where two women hugging were sent for 'reeducation' by religious police in 2015.

- Gay men in Indonesia are referred to as *homo* or *gay;* lesbians are *lesbi*.
- Indonesia's community of transvestite/transsexual *waria* – from the words *wanita* (woman) and *pria* (man) – has always had a very public profile; also known by the less polite term *banci*.
- Islamic groups proscribe homosexuality, but queer-bashing is rare.
- Bali is especially LGBT-friendly, with a large community of expats and people from elsewhere in Indonesia. Although even

PRACTICALITIES

- **Media** English-language press includes the *Jakarta Post* and the *Jakarta Globe*. Both have good websites for news. Pirated DVDs are abundant and most can be played on all-region software, although you usually get what you pay for in terms of viewability. Legitimate copies are uncommon.
- **Water** Tap water is never safe to drink.
- **Weights & Measures** Indonesia uses the international metric system for weights and measures.
- **Smoking** Anti-smoking rules prohibit smoking in many public places but enforcement is uncommon.

RUPIAH REDENOMINATION

Indonesia has plans to redenominate the rupiah by removing three digits from the currency, although the timing of this has been debated for years. For example, the 20,000Rp note would become the 20Rp note. Changing the national currency is likely to be a very complex process, with many implications for travellers. These include:

- New notes will be introduced that are identical to the current ones, with the exception of the final three zeros missing. Long-term plans call for all-new designs.
- The government stresses that current banknotes will retain their value (eg the 100,000Rp note will be the same as the new 100Rp note), however, how this will play out is anyone's guess. In other nations, such as Russia, there has been widespread refusal to accept old notes, even after government guarantees of their value.
- It will likely take years for price lists and computer systems to be fully updated, so it will be up to customers to make certain that they are being charged – and paying – appropriately.
- Introduction of the new denominations is likely to occur with little notice to avoid financial upheavals.
- Old notes will remain good for at least six years after introduction, the Bank of Indonesia said in 2014.

here, there was controversy when a gay wedding was held at a resort in 2015.

Indonesian LGBT organisations include:

- **GAYa Nusantara** (www.gayanusantara.or.id) publishes the monthly magazine *GAYa Nusantara*.
- **Gaya Dewata** (YGD, www.gayadewata.com) is Bali's oldest and only community-run LGBT organisation.

Maps

Locally produced maps are often inaccurate. Periplus produces useful maps of most of the archipelago and the major cities, although the data for fast-changing areas such as Bali can be very out of date. Google maps is making quick progress around the nation.

Hikers will have little chance of finding accurate maps of remote areas. It's far more useful (and wise) to employ the services of a local guide, who will be able to navigate seemingly uncharted territory.

Money

The unit of currency used in Indonesia is the rupiah (Rp). Coins of 50Rp, 100Rp, 200Rp, 500Rp and 1000Rp are in circulation. Notes come in 2000Rp, 5000Rp, 10,000Rp, 20,000Rp, 50,000Rp and 100,000Rp denominations. For change in amounts below 50Rp, expect to receive a few sweets.

Try to carry a fair amount of money in bills 20,000Rp and under as getting change for larger bills is often a problem.

By government decree, all businesses are required to price goods and services in Rupiah. Many tourist outfits such as hotels and dive shops try to price in US dollars or euros to avoid currency fluctuations.

ATMs

- ATMs are common across Indonesia except in rural areas; most now accept cards affiliated with international networks. Bank BNI, with ATMs across the nation, is reliable.
- ATMs in Indonesia have a maximum limit for withdrawals; sometimes it is 2,000,000Rp, but it can be as low as 500,000Rp, which is not much in foreign-currency terms.
- Many ATMs have a sticker that specifies whether the machine dispenses 50,000Rp or 100,000Rp notes.
- Always carry a sizeable amount of rupiah when you are travelling outside of cities and tourist areas as ATM networks go down and/or you can be on an island where the only ATM is broken or non-existent.

Credit Cards

- In cities and touristed areas (eg Bali), credit cards will be accepted at midrange and better hotels and resorts. More expensive shops as well as travel agents will also accept them but often there will be a surcharge of around 3%.
- MasterCard and Visa are the most widely accepted credit cards. Cash advances are possible at many ATMs or banks.
- Before leaving home, inform your credit card issuer that you will be travelling in Indonesia, otherwise your account may be frozen for suspected fraud the first time you try to use it.

Moneychangers

- The US dollar is the most widely accepted foreign currency in Indonesia. Australian, British, euros and Japanese currencies are exchangeable only in the most touristed areas of Bali and Jakarta.

➡ Outside of cities and tourist areas, banks may only be willing to exchange crisp, new US$100 bills. In many rural areas banks won't offer any exchange.

➡ Moneychangers range from the honest to dishonest. Signs bearing the phrases such as 'official' and 'licensed' are meaningless. Follow these steps to avoid getting ripped off when exchanging money:

➡ Find out the going exchange rate online. Know that anyone offering a better rate will need to make a profit through other means.

➡ Stick to banks, exchange counters in airports or large and reputable storefront operations.

➡ Skip any place offering too-good exchange rates and claiming to charge no fees or commissions.

➡ Avoid exchange stalls down alleys or in otherwise dubious locations (that sounds obvious but scores of tourists are taken in daily).

➡ Common exchange scams include rigged calculators, sleight of hand schemes, 'mistakes' on the posted rates and demands that you hand over your money before *you* have counted the money on offer.

➡ Use an ATM to obtain rupiah. Check with your bank about fees; if they are not outrageous you'll avoid carrying large amounts of cash and get a decent exchange rate.

Tipping

Tipping a set percentage is not expected in Indonesia, but if the service is good, you can leave 5000Rp or 10% or more (this is expected on Bali).

➡ Most midrange hotels and restaurants and all top-end hotels and restaurants add 21% to the bill for tax and service (known as 'plus plus'). The service component is distributed among hotel staff (one hopes).

➡ Hand cash directly to individuals if you think they deserve recognition for their service.

➡ Tip good taxi drivers, porters, people giving you a massage or fetching you a beer on the beach etc; 5000Rp to 10,000Rp is generous.

THE ART OF BARGAINING

Many everyday purchases in Indonesia require bargaining. Accommodation has a set price, but this is usually negotiable in the low season, or if you are staying at the hotel for several days. Bargaining can be an enjoyable part of shopping, so maintain your sense of humour and keep things in perspective. Try following these steps:

➡ Have some idea what the item is worth.

➡ Establish a starting price – ask the seller for their price rather than making an initial offer.

➡ Your first price can be from one-third to two-thirds of the asking price – assuming that the asking price is not outrageous.

➡ With offers and counter-offers, move closer to an acceptable price.

➡ If you don't get to an acceptable price, you're entitled to walk – the vendor may call you back with a lower price.

➡ Note that when you name a price, you're committed – you must buy if your offer is accepted.

Opening Hours

The following are typical opening hours found across Indonesia.

Banks 8am to 2pm Monday to Thursday, 8am to noon Friday, 8am to 11am Saturday.

Government offices Generally 8am to 3pm Monday to Thursday, 8am to noon Friday.

Post offices 8am to 2pm Monday to Friday. (Note: in tourist centres, the main post offices are often open longer and/or on weekends.)

Private business offices 8am to 4pm or 9am to 5pm Monday to Friday. Many open until noon on Saturday.

Restaurants 8am to 10pm.

Shopping 9am or 10am to 5pm; larger shops and tourist areas to 8pm. Many closed Sunday.

Photography

Indonesia and Indonesians can be very photogenic, but whatever you do, photograph with discretion and manners. It's always polite to ask first, and if the person says no, don't take the photo. A gesture, a smile and a nod are all that is usually necessary.

Post

Sending postcards and normal-sized letters (ie under 20g) by airmail is cheap but not really fast. For anything over 20g, the charge is based on weight. You can send parcels up to 20kg and have them properly wrapped and sealed at any post office.

Every substantial town has a *kantor pos* (post office). In tourist centres, there are also postal agencies. They are often open long hours and provide postal services. Many will also wrap and pack parcels.

Public Holidays

Following are the national public holidays in Indonesia. Unless stated, they vary from year to year. Also, there are many regional holidays.

Tahun Baru Masehi (New Year's Day) 1 January.

Tahun Baru Imlek (Chinese New Year) Falls late January to early February.

Wafat Yesus Kristus (Good Friday) Late March or early April.

Nyepi (Balinese New Year) The island of Bali closes down for one day, usually in March, sometimes in April; it's a cultural marvel, albeit a quiet one.

Hari Buruh (Labour Day) 1 May.

Hari Waisak Marks the Buddha's birth, enlightenment and death. Falls in May.

Kenaikan Yesus Kristus (Ascension of Christ) May.

Hari Proklamasi Kemerdekaan (Independence Day) 17 August.

Hari Natal (Christmas Day) 25 December.

The following Islamic holidays have dates that change each year.

Muharram Islamic New Year.

Maulud Nabi Muhammad Birthday of the Prophet Muhammad.

Isra Miraj Nabi Muhammad Ascension of the Prophet Muhammad.

Idul Fitri Also known as Lebaran, this two-day national public holiday marks the end of Ramadan; avoid travel due to crowds.

Idul Adha Islamic feast of the sacrifice.

Safe Travel

It's important to note that, compared with many places in the world, Indonesia is fairly safe. There are some hassles from the avaricious, but most visitors face many more dangers at home. Petty theft occurs, but it is not prevalent.

Alcohol Poisoning

Outside of reputable bars and resorts, it's best to avoid buying *arak*, the locally produced fermented booze made from rice or palm. Deaths and injuries happen – especially on Bali and the Gilis – when unscrupulous vendors stretch stocks with poisonous chemicals.

Drugs

Indonesia has demonstrated its zero-tolerance policy towards drugs with a spate of high-profile arrests and convictions. The execution by firing squad in 2015 of two Australians, among others, convicted of drug offences as part of the 'Bali Nine' should serve as a stark warning.

➡ Random raids of nightclubs in Jakarta and Bali and mandatory urine tests for anyone found with drugs occur regularly (entrapment schemes are not unknown – that dealer may be a cop).

➡ Private parties on Bali have been raided, and hotel owners are required by law to report offenders.

➡ The law does not provide for differentiation of substance types or amounts, whether a full bag of heroin or a few specks of marijuana dust in your pocket.

Pollution

➡ Avoid beaches in built-up areas, especially after storms flush sewage out to the surf. This is especially true of many beaches in south Bali.

➡ Air quality can be terrible in heavily populated areas and across Sumatra during annual land clearances for palm oil plantations.

Safety

Security in touristed areas increased after the 2002 and

STOPPING CHILD SEX-TOURISM

Indonesia has become a destination for foreigners seeking to sexually exploit local children. A range of socio-economic factors render many children and young people vulnerable to such abuse and some individuals prey upon this vulnerability. The sexual abuse and exploitation of children has serious, life-long and even life-threatening consequences for the victims. Strong laws exist in Indonesia to prosecute offenders and many countries also have extraterritorial legislation which allows nationals to be prosecuted in their own country for these crimes.

Travellers can help stop child sex-tourism by reporting suspicious behaviour. Reports can be made to the Anti-Human Trafficking Unit (☎021 721 8098) of the Indonesian police. If you know the nationality of the individual, you can contact their embassy directly.

For more information, contact the following organisations:

➡ **ECPAT** (www.ecpat.net) A global network working on these issues, with over 70 affiliate organisations around the world. **Child Wise** (www.childwise.org.au) is the Australian member of ECPAT.

➡ **Humantrafficking.org** International group with numerous links to groups working to prevent human exploitation in Indonesia.

GOVERNMENT TRAVEL ADVICE

It is always worthwhile to check with official government sources before visiting Indonesia in order to check current travel conditions and the overall safety situation. But bear in mind that government sources generally take a conservative and over-cautious view. Follow news sources in order to get a more realistic picture.

Government travel advisories:

Australia www.smartraveller.gov.au

Canada travel.gc.ca

New Zealand www.safetravel.govt.nz

UK www.gov.uk/foreign-travel-advice

US www.travel.state.gov

2005 Bali bombings but has since been relaxed. The odds you will be caught up in such a tragedy are low. Large luxury hotels that are part of international chains tend to have the best security, though they also make the most tempting targets, as shown in Jakarta in 2003 and 2009.

Security issues in Indonesia are often exaggerated by the foreign media, who portray rambunctious protest rallies and minor incidents of civil unrest as nationwide pandemonium. Foreign governments add to the hype with heavy-handed, blanket travel warnings. While it's true that small sections of Indonesia experience flashes of conflict, overall the archipelago is safe.

Scams

As in most poor countries, plenty of people are out to relieve you of your money in one way or another. It's really hard to say when an 'accepted' practice like overcharging becomes an unacceptable rip-off, but plenty of instances of practised deceit occur.

- Con artists exist. Some are smooth-talking guides seeking to lead you to a shop or hotel where they receive commission.
- Bali is the home of many scams. And there are continuing reports of short-changing moneychangers.

As always, trust your common sense.

- Beggers (including children) are usually part of organised groups. Most Indonesians suffer in silence and would never ask for money; consider giving to aid programs if you want to help.
- Touts and hawkers are common in tourist areas. Completely ignore them.

Theft

Violent crime is uncommon, but bag-snatching from motorbikes, pickpocketing and theft from rooms and parked cars occurs. Take the same precautions you would in any urban area. Other common-sense tips:

- Secure money before leaving an ATM (and don't forget your card!).
- Don't leave valuables on a beach while swimming.
- Use front desk/in-room safes.

Telephone

Cheap SIM cards and internet calling make it easy to call from Indonesia at reasonable prices.

Internet Calling

Most hotel wi-fi will allow at least some form of internet calling such as Skype to work. Mobile carriers often have an access code so you can make international calls over the internet for about US$0.03 per minute. Ask when you buy your SIM card.

Mobile Phones

- SIM cards for mobile phones cost only 5000Rp. They come with cheap rates for calling other countries, starting at US$0.20 per minute.
- SIM cards are widely available and easily refilled with credit.
- Watch out for vendors who sell SIM cards to visitors for 50,000Rp or more. If they don't come with at least 45,000Rp in credit you are being ripped off.
- Reasonably fast 3G data networks are found across the nation.
- Data plans average about 200,000Rp for 3.5GB of data.
- Mobile numbers start with a four-digit prefix that begins with 08 and has a total of 10 to 12 digits.

Phone Codes

- Directory assistance: ☎108
- Indonesia country code: ☎62
- International call prefix: ☎001
- International operator: ☎102

Time

There are three time zones in Indonesia.

- Java, Sumatra, and West and Central Kalimantan are on Western Indonesian Time, which is seven hours ahead of GMT/UTC.
- Bali, Nusa Tenggara, South and East Kalimantan, and Sulawesi are on Central Indonesian Time, which is eight hours ahead of GMT/UTC.
- Papua and Maluku are on Eastern Indonesian Time, nine hours ahead of GMT/UTC.

In a country straddling the equator, there is of course no daylight-saving time.

Allowing for variations due to summer or daylight-saving time, when it is noon in Jakarta it is 9pm the previous day in San Francisco, midnight in New York, 5am in London, 1pm in Singapore, Bali and Makassar, 2pm in Jayapura and 3pm in Melbourne and Sydney.

Toilets

In most of Indonesia, the bathroom features a large water tank and a plastic scoop. *Kamar mandi* means bathroom and *mandi* means to bathe or wash.

➡ Don't go climbing into the water tank – it's your water supply and it's also the supply for every other guest that comes after you. Scoop water out of the tank and pour it over yourself.

➡ Most tourist hotels have showers, many have hot water.

➡ Indonesian toilets are basically holes in the ground with footrests on either side, although Western-style toilets are common in tourist areas. To flush the toilet, reach for the plastic scoop, take water from the tank and pour. Public toilets are rare; find a cafe and smile.

➡ Toilet paper is seldom supplied in public places, though you can easily buy it. Many Indonesians instead use their left hand and copious quantities of water – again, keep that scoop handy. Often there is a wastebasket next to the toilet where the toilet paper should go, as opposed to the easily clogged toilet.

➡ *Kamar kecil* is Bahasa Indonesia for toilet, but people usually understand 'way-say' (WC). *Wanita* means women and *pria* means men.

Tourist Information

Indonesia's Ministry of Tourism has a website (www.indonesia.travel) with decent, basic information.

Most tourist offices in Indonesia offer little of value. Notable exceptions are noted in the text, including tourist offices in Ubud, Bali; Yogyakarta, Java; and the Raja Ampat Tourism Management Office in Sorong, Papua.

Travellers with Disabilities

Indonesia has very little supportive legislation or special programs for people with disabilities, and it's a difficult destination for those with limited mobility.

Very few buildings have disabled access, and even international chain hotels often don't have proper facilities.

Pavements are riddled with potholes, loose manholes, parked motorcycles and all sorts of street life, and are very rarely level for long until the next set of steps. Even the able bodied walk on roads rather than negotiate the hassle of the pavement (sidewalk).

Public transport is difficult; cars with a driver can be hired readily at cheap rates. Guides are found readily in tourist areas and, though not usual, they could be hired as helpers if needed.

Bali, with its wide range of tourist services and facilities, is the most favourable destination for travellers with disabilities although this does not mean it is easy.

Visas

Visas are the biggest headache many travellers face in their Indonesian trip. They are not hard to obtain, but the most common – 30 days – is very short for such a big place. Many travellers find even the 60-day visa restrictive.

The visa situation is constantly in flux. It is essential that you confirm current formalities before you arrive. Failure to meet all the entrance requirements can see you on the first flight out or subject to heavy fines.

No matter what type of visa you are going to use, your passport must be valid for at least six months from the date of your arrival.

RENEWING YOUR VISA

You can renew a 30-day Visa on Arrival once (but not usually a Visa Free). The procedures are complex:

➡ At least seven days before your visa expires, go to an immigration office. These can usually be found in larger cities and regional capitals.

➡ Bring your passport, a photocopy of your passport and a copy of your ticket out of Indonesia (which should be for a date during the renewal period).

➡ Wear modest clothes, eg men may be required to wear long pants.

➡ Pay a fee of 250,000Rp. You may have to return to the office twice over a three- to five-day period.

One way to avoid the renewal hassle is to use a visa agent such as **ChannelOne** (Map p218; ☎0878 6204 3224; www.channel1.biz; Jl Sunset Road 100X, Kerobokan) on Bali who, for a fee, will do the bureaucratic work for you.

DON'T FORGET TO PACK...

- An emergency stash of cash for remote areas or when ATMs are down.
- Sunscreen and insect repellent; both are hard to find outside tourist areas.
- A set of earplugs for the rooster, mosque and traffic wake-up calls.
- A torch (flashlight).
- A sarong – which can be used for everything from a blanket to a beach mat, sheet, mattress cover, towel, sunshade, cover-up (for mosques) and, well, as an actual sarong.

At the time of research, the main visa options for visitors to Indonesia are:

- **Visa in Advance** Visitors can apply for a visa before they arrive in Indonesia. Typically this is a visitor's visa, which comes in two flavours: 30 or 60 days. Details vary by country; contact your nearest Indonesian embassy or consulate to determine processing fees and times. Note: this is the only way to obtain a 60-day visitor visa, even if you qualify for Visa on Arrival.
- **Visa on Arrival** Citizens of over 65 countries may apply for a 30-day visa when they arrive at major airports and harbours (but not most land borders). The cost is US$35; be sure to have the exact amount in US currency. Eligible countries include Australia, Canada, much – but not all – of the EU including France, Germany, Ireland, the Netherlands and the UK, plus New Zealand and the USA. VOA renewals for 30 days are possible. If you don't qualify for VOA, you must get a visa in advance.
- **Visa Free** Citizens of dozens of countries can receive a 30-day visa for free upon arrival. But note that this visa cannot be extended and you may be limited to which airports and ports you can use to exit the country, eg the Timor-Leste visa run may not work with this visa.

If you have obtained one of the coveted 60-day visas in advance, be sure the immigration official at the airport gives you a 60-day tourist card.

Fines for overstaying your visa expiration date are 300,000Rp per day and include additional hassles.

Study & Work Visas

You can arrange visas for study, short-term research, visiting family and similar purposes if you have a sponsor, such as an educational institution. These social/cultural *(sosial/budaya)* visas must be applied for at an Indonesian embassy or consulate overseas. Normally valid for three months on arrival, they can be extended every month after that for up to six months without leaving the country. Fees apply.

People wishing to study or work in Indonesia must apply directly to the Central Immigration Office in Jakarta for a Limited-Stay Visa (*Kartu Izin Tinggal Terbatas*, or *Kitas*). First, though, contact your nearest embassy for the most direct avenue and to find out what qualifies as 'study'. Those granted limited stay are issued a Kitas card, which is much-prized among travellers.

If you're planning to work in Indonesia your employer will need to organise your visa – it's a long and complicated process.

Travel Permits

Special permits are required for travel in Papua (p455).

Volunteering

Indonesia offers many opportunities for volunteering; Lonely Planet does not endorse any organisations that we do not work with directly, so it is essential that you do your own thorough research before agreeing to volunteer with/donate to any organisation (p764).

Women Travellers

Plenty of Western women travel in Indonesia either solo or in pairs, and most seem to travel through the country, especially on Bali, without major problems. However, women travelling solo or otherwise may receive unwanted attention. Some considerations:

- Dress modestly, especially in conservative Muslim areas. Even the tourist islands of the Gilis have signs asking women not to walk around off the beaches in bikinis. In Aceh, women are expected to wear head scarves and cover their arms, whether they are Muslim or not.
- Indonesian men are generally very courteous, however there is a macho element that indulges in puerile behaviour – horn honking, lewd comments etc. Ignore them totally, as Indonesian women do.
- If you're a solo female and you hire a car with driver for several days, it's not culturally appropriate for a male Muslim driver to be travelling alone with you. A third party will come along as a chaperone.

Transport

GETTING THERE & AWAY

There are many ways into Indonesia: by boat from Malaysia and Singapore, and overland to Kalimantan, Papua and West Timor. But most people will fly, landing at – or transiting through – Jakarta or Bali.

Flights, cars and tours can be booked online at lonelyplanet.com/bookings.

Entering the Country

Entering Indonesia by air is relatively simple and straightforward, once you navigate the complex visa options (p774). Numerous sea ports are similarly easy; if you're arriving by land, you'll have no problems as long as you have a valid visa in advance.

Passport

Your passport *must* be valid for six months after your date of arrival in Indonesia. Before passing through immigration you may fill out a disembarkation card, half of which you must keep to give to immigration when you leave the country.

Air

Indonesia is well connected to the rest of the world by numerous airlines. Many international flights, especially those to Bali, stop first in Singapore due to runway restrictions at Bali.

Airports & Airlines

The principal gateways for entry to Indonesia are Jakarta's **Soekarno-Hatta International Airport** (www.jakartaairportonline.com) and Bali's **Ngurah Rai International Airport** (DPS; http://bali-airport.com; Bali) (which is sometimes shown as Denpasar in schedules).

Both are in the midst of expansion and projects. Other airports with international links – albeit limited – include Balikpapan, Medan, Surabaya, Lombok and Manado.

Multiple international airlines service Indonesia:

Air New Zealand (www.airnewzealand.com) Serves Bali and Jakarta from Australia and New Zealand.

AirAsia (www.airasia.com) Serves a wide range of Indonesian destinations from Australia, Kuala Lumpur, Bangkok and Singapore.

Asiana (flyasiana.com) Serves Bali and Jakarta from Seoul.

Cathay Pacific Airways (www.cathaypacific.com) Serves Bali and Jakarta from Hong Kong.

China Airlines (www.china-airlines.com) Serves Bali and Jakarta from Taipei.

INDONESIAN AIRLINE SAFETY

There's no way around it: Indonesia's airlines do not have a good safety record. From 2014 to 2015 more than 350 people died in a string of aviation disasters. Flying conditions are often challenging (monsoons, volcanic eruptions etc), safety standards can be lax and the airlines themselves run in a less-than-professional manner especially as some expand very rapidly, outpacing efforts to instill a safety culture.

Many Indonesian airlines remain banned by the EU (www.ec.europa.eu/transport/air-ban/list_en.htm) from its airspace because of safety concerns. Notable exceptions are Garuda Indonesia and Indonesia AirAsia.

Should you be worried? The odds of a fatal flight in Indonesia are very small, even if they are higher than elsewhere. When possible, pick a major airline over a smaller one and in really remote locations, feel free to do your own inspection of the plane and crew before you fly.

DEPARTURE TAX

The departure tax at Indonesian airports is now almost always included in the price of the ticket.

Emirates (www.emirates.com) Serves Bali and Jakarta from Dubai.

Eva Air (www.evaair.com) Serves Bali and Jakarta from Taipei.

Firefly (www.fireflyz.com.my) Serves major cities on Sumatra from Kuala Lumpur and Penang in Malaysia.

Garuda Indonesia (www.garuda-indonesia.com) Indonesia's main national airline serves Bali and Jakarta from Australia, Asia and Amsterdam.

Japan Airlines (www.jal.co.jp) Serves Jakarta from Tokyo.

Jetstar/Qantas (www.qantas.com.au) Serves Bali and Jakarta from Australia.

KLM (www.klm.com) Serves Jakarta and Bali from Amsterdam via Singapore.

Korean Air (www.koreanair.com) Serves Bali and Jakarta from Seoul.

Lion Air (www.lionair.co.id) Rapidly expanding carrier with services across Indonesia and the region. Wings Air is its regional subsidiary.

Lufthansa (www.lufthansa.com) Serves Jakarta from Frankfurt.

Malaysia Airlines (www.mas.com.my) Serves Bali and Jakarta from Kuala Lumpur.

Qatar Airways (www.qatarairways.com) Serves Bali and Jakarta from Doha.

Silk Air (www.silkair.com) Serves numerous Indonesian destinations from Singapore including Bandung, Balikpapan, Lombok, Manado, Medan, Palembang, Pekanbaru, Surabaya and Yogyakarta.

Singapore Airlines (www.singaporeair.com) Numerous flights to Bali and Jakarta daily.

Sriwijaya Air (www.sriwijayaair.co.id) Expanding airline with routes to Malaysia, Singapore and Timor-Leste.

Thai Airways International (www.thaiair.com) Serves Bali and Jakarta from Bangkok.

Tiger Airways (www.tigerairways.com) Budget carrier serving Bali, Jakarta and Surabaya from Australia and Singapore.

Virgin Australia (www.virginaustralia.com) Serves Bali from several Australian cities.

Tickets

Check websites to get an idea of airfares to Indonesia. Don't limit yourself to major sites either; search for 'Indonesian airfares' and you may well find sites belonging to small travel agents who specialise in Indonesian travel. This can be particularly helpful when you are trying to book a complex itinerary to remote locations.

Asia Indonesia is closely linked to most of Asia. A plethora of airlines serves Bali and Jakarta.

Australia Australia is well served with numerous direct flights to Bali and Jakarta from all major cities on multiple carriers.

Canada From Canada you'll change planes at an Asian hub for Bali and Jakarta.

Continental Europe KLM and Lufthansa link Amsterdam and Frankfurt respectively with one-stop, same-plane service to Jakarta (and Bali for KLM). But a huge number of airlines such as Emirates, Qatar Airways and major Asian carriers, offer one-stop connections between major European cities and Jakarta, and often Bali as well.

New Zealand You can fly non-stop to Bali and Jakarta.

UK Options to fly to Jakarta and Bali from London (or Manchester) involve connecting through a major hub *somewhere* in the Middle East or Asia.

USA The best connections are through any of the major Asian hubs with nonstop service to Bali and Jakarta, although residents of the East Coast may find shorter routings via Europe or the Middle East. No US airline serves Indonesia.

Land

Border Crossings

There are four possible land crossings into Indonesia.

Regular buses between Pontianak (Kalimantan) and Kuching (Sarawak, eastern Malaysia) pass through the border post at Entikong. You can get a visa on arrival on this route. A crossing is possible between Lubok Antu, Sarawak and Badau, West Kalimantan provided you have a visa in advance.

The border crossing between West and East Timor (Timor-Leste) is open. Get a Timor-Leste visa in Kupang (p385); a visa is required when travelling from East to West Timor.

The road from Jayapura or Sentani in Indonesia to Vanimo in Papua New Guinea can be crossed, depending on the current political situation. A visa is required if travelling into Indonesia.

Sea

There is currently no sea travel between the Philippines, Papua New Guinea and Indonesia.

Australia

Major cruise lines often run cruise ships between Bali and Australia.

Timor-Leste

There are regular ferry services between Dili in Timor-Leste and Oecussi (including a new fast ferry), which borders West Timor. If crossing into Indonesia from here you will need to have organised your visa already in Dili.

Malaysia

Regular and comfortable high-speed ferries run the two-hour journey between Melaka (Malaysia) and Dumai (Sumatra). Similar ferries travel between Penang (Malaysia) and Belawan (Sumatra), taking about five hours.

From Johor Bahru in southern Malaysia, daily ferries run to Pulau Bintan in Sumatra's Riau Islands.

Ferries connect Tarakan and Nunukan in East Kalimantan with Tawau in Sabah. For these routes you'll need a visa in advance.

Singapore

From Batam speedboats travel to Tanjung Buton with minibus connections to Pekanbaru on the Sumatran mainland. Otherwise, Pelni ships pass through Batam to and from Belawan (the port for Medan) and Jakarta.

Boats also travel between Pulau Bintan and Singapore. Service includes **Bintan Resort Ferries** (www.brf.com.sg).

GETTING AROUND

Air

Airlines in Indonesia

Getting reliable information on Indonesian domestic flights is a challenge – many airlines don't show up on travel websites, although traveloka.com is fairly complete. You can also check with local airline offices and travel agents; local hotel and tour operators are often the best sources.

- The domestic flight network continues to grow; schedules and rates are in a constant state of flux.
- Small carriers servicing remote routes often operate cramped and dated aircraft.
- With tiny regional airlines, reconfirm your ticket and hang around the check-in desk if the flight is full. Sometimes reservations are 'lost' when another passenger with more clout shows up.

Almost a dozen major airlines fly domestically.

Citilink (www.citilink.co.id) Budget subsidiary to Garuda Indonesia which links major cities.

Garuda Indonesia (www.garuda-indonesia.com) Serves major destinations across the archipelago. Tickets are easily bought online.

Indonesia AirAsia (www.airasia.com) Fast-growing budget carrier that is a subsidiary of its Malaysian-based parent.

Kalstar (www.kalstaronline.com) Serves Kalimantan, with links to Jakarta.

Lion Air/Wings Air (www.lionair.co.id) Fast-growing Indonesian budget carrier (Wings Air operate prop planes to small destinations) with myriad flights. Has a premium-service subsidiary Batik Air.

Sriwijaya Air (www.sriwijayaair.co.id) Services across Indonesia.

Susi Air (fly.susiair.com) Routes across Indonesia.

Transnusa (www.transnusa.co.id) Good for flights within Nusa Tenggara and for flights from Denpasar to places like Labuanbajo.

Tickets

The larger Indonesian-based carriers have websites listing fares, however it may be hard, if not impossible, to purchase tickets over the internet using non-Indonesian credit cards. Consider these methods:

- **Travel Agents** A good way to buy domestic tickets once you're in Indonesia. This is often the best way to get the lowest fares.
- **Friends** Get an Indonesian friend or guesthouse owner to buy you a ticket using their credit card, then pay them back.

> **DOMESTIC DEPARTURE TAX**
>
> Most domestic departure tax fees are now included in ticket prices.

- **Airport** After airline employees were found selling bootleg tickets, sales by airline offices in airports were banned; however, some airlines will still sell you a ticket at the airport, although travel agents and airline city offices are more reliable.

ONLINE SALES

Large international booking websites such as expedia.com may only show Garuda Indonesia flights and then only offer very expensive airfares. Try the following to purchase tickets online:

Airline Websites Some carriers, notably Garuda Indonesia and Indonesia AirAsia, have websites that accept foreign credit cards. Lion Air is a notable exception.

skyscanner.com Accepts foreign cards but doesn't show all airlines.

tiket.com Not all foreign cards work but shows most domestic airlines.

traveloka.com Lists many domestic airlines although foreign cards don't always work. A good source for schedule info.

Bicycle

If reasonably fit, and with a bit of preparation and a ton of common sense, a cyclist will enjoy an incomparable travel experience almost anywhere in the archipelago. The well-maintained roads of Bali, Lombok, East Java and South Sulawesi are suitable for cyclists of all ability levels, while the adventuresome can head for the hills along the length of Sumatra or Nusa Tenggara.

Considerations include:

- Rest during the hottest hours of the day to avoid the tropical heat.
- Avoid most traffic problems by keeping to back roads or even jumping on a truck or bus to cover dangerous sections.
- Expect to be a constant focus of attention.
- You can rent bikes fairly easily in tourist centres – just ask at your accommodation. Rates range from 20,000Rp to 60,000Rp per day.
- Many tourist areas, particularly Bali, Lombok and Yogyakarta offer organised, vehicle-supported bicycle tours.
- At major sights you can usually find a parking attendant to keep an eye on your bicycle for 5000Rp. Bicycling is gaining popularity among Indonesians and bicycle clubs will be delighted to aid a foreign guest. **Bike to Work** (www.b2w-indonesia.or.id) has an extensive national network.

Boat

Sumatra, Java, Bali, Nusa Tenggara and Sulawesi are all connected by regular car ferries, and you can use them to island-hop all the way from Sumatra to West Timor. Local ferries run several times a week or daily (or even hourly on the busy Java–Bali–Lombok–Sumbawa routes). Check with shipping companies, the harbour office, travel agents or hotels for current schedules and fares.

Going to and between Kalimantan, Maluku and Papua, the main connections are provided by Pelni, the government-run passenger line.

Pelni

Pelni (www.pelni.co.id) has a fleet of large vessels linking all of Indonesia's major ports and the majority of the archipelago's outlying areas. Pelni's website is a good resource, showing arrivals and departures about a month in advance.

Its ships operate set routes around the islands, either on a fortnightly or monthly schedule. The ships usually stop for a few hours in each port, so there's time for a quick look around. Note that sailing times can be in flux until the last moment.

Fares can be quite cheap if you go for the economy classes but at higher levels of accommodation, budget airlines are competitive if not cheaper.

Pelni ships range from the modern, clean and well-run to less-modern, less-well-run and less-clean. Some considerations:

Booking Towns served by Pelni usually have a ticket office or agent. Book your ticket a few days in advance.

Classes Pelni ships have two to six classes. Economy class, which is the modern version of deck class, is a bare-bones experience. As you move up the price ladder, you exchange a seat on the deck for small accommodations until you reach a level that may give you your own private cabin with two beds (this is some variation of first class). Note that these are functional at best and far from lavish.

Security There are no locker facilities, so you have to keep an eye on your gear if you are in any kind of group class.

Crowding At busy times, such as Idul Fitri, boats seem to have passengers crammed into every available space including decks, passages and stairwells. Conditions can get grim.

Food Bring your own food and drink. Where there are food facilities, the conditions are basic and if the boat is crowded you may have a hard time stepping over other passengers to reach the restaurant.

Boarding Getting aboard a Pelni ship can leave you bruised as it is truly every man, woman and child for him or herself as people try to get to scarce space first.

Other Vessels

There's a whole range of boats you can use to hop between islands, down rivers and across lakes. Just about any sort of vessel can be rented in Indonesia. Some boat options:

Fast Ferries When available, these are a great alternative to the slow car ferries that link many islands.

Fishing boats Small boats can be chartered to take you to small offshore islands.

CLIMATE CHANGE & TRAVEL

Every form of transport that relies on carbon-based fuel generates CO_2, the main cause of human-induced climate change. Modern travel is dependent on aeroplanes, which might use less fuel per kilometre per person than most cars but travel much greater distances. The altitude at which aircraft emit gases (including CO_2) and particles also contributes to their climate change impact. Many websites offer 'carbon calculators' that allow people to estimate the carbon emissions generated by their journey and, for those who wish to do so, to offset the impact of the greenhouse gases emitted with contributions to portfolios of climate-friendly initiatives throughout the world. Lonely Planet offsets the carbon footprint of all staff and author travel.

TRAVELLING SAFELY BY BOAT

Boat safety is an important consideration across Indonesia, where boats that barely seem seaworthy may be your only option to travel between islands. In many cases these services are accidents waiting to happen, as safety regulation is lax at best.

This is especially true on the busy routes linking Bali, Nusa Lembongan, Lombok and the Gilis, where both the fast tourist boats and the public car ferries have had accidents. Given Indonesia's poor record, it is essential that you take responsibility for your own safety, as no one else will.

Consider the following points for any boat travel in Indonesia:

Bigger is better It may take you 30 minutes or more longer, but a larger boat will simply deal with the open ocean better than the over-powered small speedboats.

Check for safety equipment Make certain your boat has life preservers and that you know how to locate and use them. In an emergency, don't expect a panicked crew to hand them out. Also, check for life rafts.

Avoid over-crowding Travellers report boats leaving with more people than seats and with aisles jammed with stacked luggage.

Look for exits Cabins may only have one narrow entrance making them death traps in an accident.

Avoid fly-by-nighters Taking a fishing boat and jamming too many engines on the rear in order to cash in on booming tourism is a recipe for disaster.

Longboat The *longbot* is a long, narrow boat powered by a couple of outboard motors, with bench seats on either side of the hull for passengers to sit on. They are mainly used in Kalimantan where they are also called *klotok*.

Outrigger boats Used for some short inter-island hops, such as the trip out from Manado in North Sulawesi to the coral reefs surrounding nearby Pulau Bunaken. On Lombok they serve the Gilis, while Komodo National Park is served from Labuanbajo. On Bali they are called *jukung*.

River ferries Commonly found on Kalimantan, where the rivers *are* the roads. They're large, bulky vessels that carry passengers and cargo up and down the water network.

Tourist boats Often very fast speedboats outfitted to carry 40 or more passengers, most commonly used for quick trips between Bali, Nusa Lembongan, Lombok and the Gilis.

Bus

Buses are the mainstay of Indonesian transport (excepting Papua). At any time of the day, thousands of buses in all shapes and sizes move thousands of people throughout Indonesia. The 'leave-when-full' school of scheduling applies to almost every service, and 'full' sometimes means the aisles are occupied too. Consider the following:

- On major runs across Indonesia, air-con buses are at least somewhat tolerable.
- Crowded roads mean that buses are often stuck in traffic.
- On major routes, say the 24-hour run from Bali to Jakarta, budget airlines are competitive price-wise.
- Buses on non-major routes are usually not air-conditioned.
- Bring as little luggage as possible – there is rarely any room for storage. Large bags will ride on your lap.
- Take precautions with your personal belongings and keep your passport, money and any other valuables secure and concealed.

Classes

The main classes of bus:

- Economy-class *(ekonomi)* buses that run set routes between towns. They can be hot, slow and crowded, but they're also ridiculously cheap and provide a never-ending parade of Indonesian life.
- Express *(patas)* buses look much the same as the economy buses, but stop only at selected bus terminals en route and (officially) don't pick up from the side of the road. Air-con *patas* buses are more comfortable and seating is often guaranteed.
- Air-con buses (or 'executive' buses) come in a variety of price categories, depending on whether facilities include reclining seats, toilets, TV, karaoke (usually very bad) or snacks. These buses should be booked in advance; ticket agents often have pictures of the buses and seating plans; check to see what you are paying for when you choose your seat.

Tickets

Buses tickets are cheap. For long-distance buses, you can buy your ticket from a travel agent or you can visit the bus terminal where you may find several companies competing for your business. Book longer trips in advance, especially on air-con buses.

Often, hotels will act as agents or buy a ticket for you and will arrange for the bus to pick you up at the hotel – they sometimes charge a few thousand rupiah for this service but it's worth it.

Car & Motorcycle

Driving Licence

To drive in Indonesia, you officially need an International Driving Permit (IDP) from your local automobile association. This permit is rarely required as identification when hiring/driving a car in Indonesia, but police may ask to see it. Bring your home licence as well – it's supposed to be carried in conjunction with the IDP. If you also have a motorcycle licence at home, get your IDP endorsed for motorcycles, too.

Fuel

After decades of subsidies, fuel prices are now adjusted to reflect international oil prices. Only recently, premium petrol cost 9500Rp per litre (still cheap by Western standards). The opening of the domestic fuel market to foreign operators has spurred national oil company Pertamina to build full-service outlets *(pompa bensin)* throughout the archipelago.

Hire

CAR HIRE

Small self-drive 4WDs can be hired for as little as 100,000Rp to 300,000Rp a day with limited insurance in tourist areas.

It is very common for tourists to hire a car with a driver and this can usually be arranged for 400,000Rp to 1,400,000Rp per day (600,000Rp per day is average in popular places like Bali).

With a small group, a van and driver is not only economical but also allows maximum travel and touring freedom. Hotels can always arrange drivers.

Considering the relatively small cost of a driver in relation to the total rental, it makes little sense to take the wheel yourself. Driving requires enormous amounts of concentration and the legal implications of accidents can be a nightmare, as a foreigner – it's *your* fault.

MOTORCYCLE HIRE

Motorcycles and motorbikes are readily available for hire throughout Indonesia.

- Motorcycles and scooters can be hired for 30,000Rp to 100,000Rp per day.
- Wearing a helmet is required by law and essential given road conditions.
- In popular surfing areas, many motorbike rentals come with a surfboard rack.
- A licence is required by law, though you'll rarely need to show it unless stopped by the police, who may be looking for a 'tip'.
- Some travel insurance policies do not cover you if you are involved in an accident while on a motorcycle and/or don't have a licence. Check the small print.

Insurance

Rental agencies and owners usually insist that the vehicle itself is insured, and minimal insurance should be included in the basic rental deal – often with an excess of as much as US$100 for a motorcycle and US$500 for a car (ie the customer pays the first US$100/500 of any claim).

Your travel insurance may provide some additional protection, although liability for motor accidents is specifically excluded from many policies.

A private owner renting out a motorcycle may not offer any insurance at all. Ensure that your personal travel insurance covers injuries incurred while motorcycling.

Road Conditions

- Relentless traffic congestion across many parts of Indonesia makes driving an exhausting activity.
- Delays due to road works, poor conditions and congestion are common.
- Finding your way around can be a challenge, as roads are only sometimes signposted and maps are often out of date.
- In much of the country, count on averaging only 35km per hour.

Road Rules

Indonesians drive on the left side of the road (sometimes the right, sometimes the pavement), as in Australia, Japan, the UK and most of Southeast Asia.

Hitching

Hitching is not part of the culture but if you put out your thumb, someone may give you a lift. On the back roads where no public transport exists, hitching may be the only alternative to walking, and passing motorists or trucks are often willing to help.

Bear in mind, however, that hitching is never entirely safe in any country, so we do not recommend it. Travellers who decide to hitch should understand that they are taking a small but potentially serious risk.

Local Transport

Becak

These are three-wheeled carts either peddle- or motor-powered. The becak is now banned from the main streets of some large cities, but you'll still see them swarming the back streets, moving anyone and anything.

Negotiate your fare *before* you get in; and if there are two passengers, make sure that it covers both people, otherwise you'll be in for an argument when you get to your destination. Becak drivers are hard bargainers but they will usually settle on a reasonable fare, around 2000Rp to 5000Rp per kilometre.

Bus

Large buses aren't used much as a means of city transport except on Java (although there is a small system on Bali). There's an extensive system of buses in Jakarta and these are universally cheap; beware of pickpockets.

Dokar

A dokar is the jingling, horse-drawn, two-wheeled cart found throughout the archipelago including tourist areas. A typical *dokar* (or *cidomo* as it's known in some areas such as the Gilis) has bench seating on either side, which can comfortably fit three or four people.

Given that many horses and ponies are mistreated, we can't recommend *dokars*.

Minibus

Public minibuses are used for local transport around cities and towns, short intercity runs and the furthest reaches of the transport network.

Minibuses are known as *bemos* or *angkot*, although they are called *taksi* in many parts of Papua, Kalimantan and East Java. Other names include *opelet*, *mikrolet*, *angkudes* and *pete-pete*.

- Most minibuses operate a standard route, picking up and dropping off people and goods anywhere along the way.
- Minibus drivers may try to overcharge foreigners and ask you for triple the normal fare. It's best to ask somebody, such as your hotel staff, about the *harga biasa* (normal price); otherwise, see what the other passengers are paying and offer the correct fare.
- Drivers wait until their vehicles are crammed to capacity before moving, or they may go *keliling* – driving endlessly around town looking for a full complement of passengers.
- Conditions can be extremely cramped, especially if you have luggage.
- On Bali, motorbikes are nearly universal and the *bemo* system is in decline.

Ojek

Ojeks (or *ojegs*) are motorcycle riders who take pillion passengers for a bargainable price. They are found at bus terminals and markets, or just hanging around at crossroads. They will take you around town and go where no other public transport exists, or along roads that are impassable in any other vehicle. They are the preferred method for navigating Jakarta traffic. They can also be rented by the hour for sightseeing.

Go-jek (www.go-jek.com) is an Uber-style service where you can order an ojek using a smartphone app at a fair price. It operates in major cities.

Private Cars

Small air-con minivans carrying paying passengers (known in some areas as *Taksi Gelap*) are becoming common in some areas. Typically linking major towns on main highways, the cost can be only a bit more than a bus but offer greater comfort and speed. Hotels usually have info on these services and can arrange pick-ups.

However, these vehicles are unregulated and safety standards vary widely, if they exist at all.

Taxi

Metered taxis are readily available in major cities. If a taxi has a meter *(argo)*, make sure it is used. Where meters don't exist, you will have to bargain for the fare in advance. Offers of 'transport' are almost always more costly than using a metered taxi.

With services in major cities and tourist areas including south Bali, **Blue Bird Taxis** (www.bluebirdgroup.com) are a good choice as drivers use the meter, speak some English and are honest. The smartphone app makes ordering a taxi a breeze.

Uber (go.uber.com) is active in larger cities.

At airports, taxis usually operate on a prepaid system, payable at the relevant booth.

Tours

A wide range of trips can be booked from tour companies within Indonesia. Some of the best tours are with local guides, such as the ecotrips to Halimun National Park in Java with local guides in Bogor. We recommend dozens of local options.

There are also specialist tour companies that utilise their in-depth knowledge of local dialects, culture and experience to create experiences you'd have a hard time equalling independently.

Finally there are numerous operators that can transport you around the archipelago in high style, say in a classic sailing ship.

A few to consider:

Adventure Indonesia (www.adventureindonesia.com) Top Indonesian adventure-tourism firm.

Dewi Nusantara (www.dewi-nusantara.com) A 57m, three-masted traditional-style sailing ship that makes luxurious live-aboard diving journeys around the Malukus and Raja Ampat.

Laszlo Wagner (www.east-indonesia.info) An experienced Hungarian-born writer offers tailor-made trips around Maluku and Papua.

SeaTrek Sailing Adventures (www.seatrekbali.com) Runs itineraries on sailing ships from Bali to Flores, as well as Banda Islands and Papua trips.

Silolona Sojurns (www.silolona.com) This luxury yacht built in the style of classic Spice Islands trading vessels sails through Nusa Tenggara, Maluku and Papua.

Train

Train travel in Indonesia is restricted to Java and Sumatra.

In Java, trains are one of the most comfortable, fastest and easiest ways to travel. In the east, the railway service connects with the ferry to Bali, and in the west with the ferry to Sumatra. Sumatra's limited rail network runs in the south from Bandarlampung to Lubuklinggau, and in the north from Medan to Tanjung Balai and Rantau Prapat.

There are three classes; smoking is not allowed in any.

- Economy *(ekonomi)* – no air-con, crowded and unreserved.
- Business *(bisnis)* – no air-con but mandatory seat reservations.
- Executive *(eksecutif)* – air-con with mandatory reservations.

The railway's website (www.kereta-api.co.id) has information; use the drop-down menu 'Reservasi' and then '*Jadwal*' (schedule) for schedules.

Health

Treatment for minor injuries and common traveller's health problems is easily accessed in larger cities and on Bali but standards decline the more remote you get in Indonesia. For serious conditions, you will need to leave Indonesia.

Travellers tend to worry about contracting infectious diseases when in the tropics, but infections are a rare cause of serious illness or death in travellers. Pre-existing medical conditions, such as heart disease, and accidental injury (especially traffic accidents) account for most life-threatening problems.

It's important to note what precautions you should take in Indonesia. On Bali your major concerns are rabies, mosquito bites and the tropical sun. Elsewhere in the country there are numerous important considerations.

The advice we give is a general guide only and does not replace the advice of a doctor trained in travel medicine.

BEFORE YOU GO

Make sure all medications are packed in their original, clearly labelled containers. A signed and dated letter from your physician describing your medical conditions and medications (including generic names) is also a good idea. If you are carrying syringes or needles, be sure to have a physician's letter documenting their medical necessity.

If you happen to take any regular medication, bring double your needs in case of loss or theft. You can buy many medications over the counter without a doctor's prescription, but it can be difficult to find antidepressants, blood-pressure medications and contraceptive pills.

Insurance

Even if you are fit and healthy, don't travel without sufficient health insurance – accidents do happen. If you're uninsured, emergency evacuation is expensive – bills of more than US$100,000 are not uncommon.

Find out in advance if your insurance plan will make payments directly to providers or reimburse you later for overseas health expenditures.

Recommended Vaccinations

Specialised travel-medicine clinics are your best source of information; they stock all available vaccines and will be able to give specific recommendations for you and your trip.

Most vaccines don't produce immunity until at least two weeks after they're given. Ask your doctor for an International Certificate of Vaccination (otherwise known as the yellow booklet), which will list all the vaccinations you've received.

Vaccination recommendations for Southeast Asia include the following for all travellers:

- **Tetanus** Single booster recommended if none in the previous 10 years.
- **Hepatitis A** Provides almost 100% protection for up to a year; a booster after 12 months provides at least another 20 years' protection. Mild side effects such as headache and sore arm occur in 5% to 10% of people.
- **Typhoid** Recommended unless your trip is less than a week and only to developed cities. The vaccine offers around 70% protection, lasts for two to three years and comes as a single shot.
- **Rabies** Three injections in all. A booster after one year will then provide 10 years' protection. Side effects are rare – occasionally headache and sore arm. Essential for Bali, where there has been a rabies epidemic for years.

These vaccines are recommended if you are travelling beyond major cities, as well as Bali and Lombok:

HEALTH ADVISORIES & WEBSITES

It's usually a good idea to consult your government's travel-health website if one is available, before departure:

- **Australia:** www.smarttraveller.gov.au
- **UK:** www.gov.uk/foreign-travel-advice
- **USA:** www.travel.state.gov

There is a wealth of travel health advice on the internet.

World Health Organization (www.who.int/ith) Publishes a superb book called *International Travel & Health*, which is revised annually and is available online at no cost.

Centers for Disease Control & Prevention (www.cdc.gov) Good general information.

- **Hepatitis B** Now considered routine for most travellers. Given as three shots over six months. Lifetime protection occurs in 95% of people.
- **Cholera** An oral vaccine recommended for very remote travel.
- **Japanese B Encephalitis** Three injections in all. Booster recommended after two years. Sore arm and headache are the most common side effects.
- **Meningitis** Single injection. Recommended for long-term backpackers aged under 25.

Required Vaccinations

The only vaccine required by international regulations is yellow fever. Proof of vaccination will only be required if you have visited a country in the yellow-fever zone (primarily some parts of Africa and South America) within the six days prior to entering Southeast Asia.

Medical Checklist

Recommended items for a convenient personal medical kit (more specific items can be obtained in Indonesia if needed):

- antibacterial cream
- antihistamine – there are many options
- antiseptic (eg Betadine)
- contraceptives
- DEET-based insect repellent
- first-aid items such as scissors, bandages, thermometer (but not a mercury one) and tweezers
- ibuprofen or another anti-inflammatory
- steroid cream for allergic/itchy rashes (eg 1% to 2% hydrocortisone)
- sunscreen and hat
- throat lozenges
- thrush (vaginal yeast infection) treatment

IN INDONESIA

Availability & Cost of Health Care

It is difficult to find reliable medical care in rural areas, but most major cities now have clinics catering specifically to travellers and expats. These clinics are usually more expensive than local medical facilities, but are worth utilising, as they will offer a superior standard of care. Additionally, they understand the local system and are aware of the safest local hospitals and best specialists. They can also liaise with insurance companies should you require evacuation.

If you think you may have a serious disease, especially malaria, do not waste time – travel immediately to the nearest quality facility to receive attention.

Local medical care in general is not yet up to international standards. Foreign doctors are not allowed to work in Indonesia, but some clinics (such as those in Bali and Jakarta) catering to foreigners have 'international advisors'. Almost all Indonesian doctors work at government hospitals during the day and in private practices at night. This means that private hospitals often don't have their best staff available during the day. Serious cases are evacuated to Australia, Bangkok or Singapore.

Pharmacies

In Jakarta, other large cities and Bali, pharmacies *(apotik)* are usually reliable. The **Kimia Farma** chain (www.kimiafarma.co.id) is good and has many locations nationwide. Be careful at small, local pharmacies, as fake medications and poorly stored or out-of-date drugs are common.

Infectious Diseases

Bird Flu

Otherwise known as avian influenza, the H5N1 virus has claimed more than 100 victims in Indonesia. Most cases have been in Java. Treatment is difficult and every few years it reappears.

Dengue Fever

This mosquito-borne disease is a major problem and Indonesia has one of the world's highest infection rates. As there is no vaccine available it can only be prevented by avoiding mosquito bites. The mosquito that carries dengue bites day and night, so use insect avoidance measures at all times. Symptoms include high fever, severe headache and body ache. Some people develop a rash and experience diarrhoea. There is no specific treatment, just rest and paracetamol – do not take aspirin as it increases the likelihood of haemorrhaging. See a doctor to be diagnosed and monitored.

Hepatitis A

A problem throughout the region, this food- and water-borne virus infects the liver, causing jaundice (yellow skin and eyes), nausea and lethargy. There is no specific treatment; you just need to allow time for the liver to heal. All travellers to Southeast Asia should be vaccinated against hepatitis A.

Hepatitis B

The only sexually transmitted disease that can be prevented by vaccination, hepatitis B is spread by body fluids, including sexual contact. In some parts of Southeast Asia up to 20% of the population are carriers of hepatitis B.

HIV

HIV is a major problem in many Asian countries, and Bali has one of the highest rates of HIV infection in Indonesia. The main risk for most travellers is sexual contact with locals, prostitutes and other travellers.

The risk of sexual transmission of the HIV virus can be dramatically reduced by the use of a *kondom* (condom). These are available from supermarkets, street stalls and drugstores in tourist areas, and from the *apotik* in almost any town.

Japanese B Encephalitis

While this is a rare disease in travellers, many locals are infected each year. This viral disease is transmitted by mosquitoes. Most cases occur in rural areas and vaccination is recommended for travellers spending more than one month outside of cities. There is no treatment, and a third of infected people will die while another third will suffer permanent brain damage.

Malaria

The risk of contracting malaria is greatest in rural areas of Indonesia although only Java's main cities, Bali and the Gilis are considered malaria-free.

Two strategies should be combined to prevent malaria: mosquito avoidance and antimalarial medications.

Most people who contract malaria are taking inadequate or no antimalarial medication.

Travellers are advised to prevent mosquito bites by taking these steps:

- Use a DEET-containing insect repellent on exposed skin. Insect sprays and lotions such as Off are only reliably found in the areas with the least risk of malaria (eg Bali). Bring small containers of highly concentrated DEET repellent from your home country and follow the label directions carefully.
- Sleep under a mosquito net impregnated with permethrin.
- Choose accommodation with screens and fans (if not air-conditioned).
- Impregnate clothing with permethrin in high-risk areas.
- Wear long sleeves and trousers in light colours.
- Use mosquito coils.
- Spray your room with insect repellent before going out for your evening meal.

There are a variety of medications available (note that Artesunate and Chloroquine are ineffective):

- **Doxycycline** This daily tablet is a broad-spectrum antibiotic that has the added benefit of helping to prevent a variety of tropical diseases. Potential side effects include a tendency to sunburn, thrush in women, indigestion, heartburn, nausea and interference with contraceptive pills.
- **Lariam (Mefloquine)** Lariam has received much bad press, some of it justified, some not. This weekly tablet suits many people. Serious side effects are rare but include depression, anxiety, psychosis and having fits.
- **Malarone** A combination of Atovaquone and Proguanil. Side effects, most commonly nausea and headache, are uncommon and mild. It is the best tablet for scuba divers and for those on short trips to high-risk areas. It must be taken for one week after leaving the risk area.

Rabies

Rabies is a disease spread by the bite or lick of an infected animal, most commonly a dog or monkey. Once you are exposed, it is uniformly fatal if you don't get the vaccine very promptly. Bali has a major outbreak that dates to 2008. Cases have been reported across Indonesia.

To minimise your risk, consider getting the rabies vaccine, which consists of three injections in all. A booster after one year will then provide 10 years' protection. The vaccines are often unavailable on Bali, so get them before you go.

Also, be careful to avoid animal bites. Especially watch children closely.

Having the pre-travel vaccination means the post-bite treatment is greatly simplified. If you are bitten or scratched, gently wash the wound with soap and water, and apply an iodine-based antiseptic then consult a doctor.

Those not vaccinated will need to receive rabies immunoglobulin as soon as possible. Clean the wound immediately and do not delay seeking medical attention. Note that Indonesia regularly runs out of rabies immunoglobulin, so be prepared to go to Singapore immediately for medical treatment.

Typhoid

This serious bacterial infection is spread via food and water. Its symptoms are a high and slowly progressive fever, headache and possibly a dry cough and stomach pain. It is diagnosed by blood tests and treated with antibiotics.

Traveller's Diarrhoea

Traveller's diarrhoea (aka Bali belly) is by far the most common problem affecting travellers – between 30% and 50% of people will suffer from it within two weeks of starting their trip. In over 80% of cases, traveller's diarrhoea is caused by bacteria (there are numerous potential culprits), and therefore responds promptly to treatment with antibiotics.

Traveller's diarrhoea is defined as the passage of more than three watery bowel actions within 24 hours, plus at least one other symptom such as fever, cramps, nausea, vomiting or feeling generally unwell.

TREATMENT

Loperamide (aka Imodium) is just a 'stopper' and doesn't get to the cause of the problem. However, it can be helpful, for example, if you have to go on a long bus ride. Don't take Loperamide if you have a fever or blood in your stools. Seek medical attention quickly if you do not respond to an appropriate antibiotic. Otherwise:

- Stay well hydrated; rehydration solutions such as Gastrolyte are the best for this.
- Antibiotics such as Norfloxacin, Ciprofloxacin or Azithromycin will kill the bacteria quickly.

GIARDIASIS

Giardia lamblia is a parasite that is relatively common in travellers. Symptoms include nausea, bloating, excess gas, fatigue and intermittent diarrhoea. The parasite will eventually go away if left untreated but this can take months. The treatment of choice is Tinidazole, with Metronidazole being a second-line option.

Environmental Hazards

Air Pollution

Air pollution, particularly vehicle pollution, is a problem in cities. In addition, smog from fires used to clear land for palm oil plantations blankets Sumatra in the dry season. If you have severe respiratory problems, speak with your doctor before travelling. This pollution also causes minor respiratory problems such as sinusitis, dry throat and irritated eyes. Consider masks, which more and more Indonesians are wearing.

Diving

Divers and surfers should seek specialised advice before they travel to ensure their medical kit contains treatment for coral cuts and tropical ear infections, as well as the standard problems. Divers should ensure their insurance covers them for decompression illness.

Heat

Most parts of Indonesia are hot and humid throughout the year. For most people it takes at least two weeks to adapt to the hot climate. Swelling of the feet and ankles is common, as are muscle cramps caused by excessive sweating. Prevent these by avoiding dehydration and excessive activity in the heat. Be careful to avoid the following conditions:

- **Heat Exhaustion** Symptoms include feeling weak; headache; irritability; nausea or vomiting; sweaty skin; a fast, weak pulse; and a normal or slightly elevated body temperature. Treatment involves getting out of the heat and/or sun, fanning the victim and applying cool wet cloths to the skin, laying the victim flat with their legs raised, and rehydrating with water containing one-quarter of a teaspoon of salt per litre. Recovery is usually rapid.
- **Heatstroke** A serious medical emergency. Symptoms come on suddenly and include weakness, nausea, a hot dry body with a body temperature of over 41°C, dizziness, confusion, loss of coordination, fits and eventually collapse and loss of consciousness. Seek urgent medical help and commence cooling by getting the person out of the heat, removing their clothes, fanning them and applying cool wet cloths or ice to their body, especially to hot spots such as the groin and armpits.

ALCOHOL POISONING

There are ongoing reports of injuries and deaths among tourists and locals due to *arak* (the local spirits that should be distilled from palm or cane sugar) being adulterated with methanol, a poisonous form of alcohol. Although *arak* is a popular drink, it should be avoided outside established restaurants and cafes.

DRINKING WATER

- Never drink tap water in Indonesia.
- Widely available and cheap, bottled water is generally safe, however, check the seal is intact when purchasing. Look for places that allow you to refill containers, thus cutting down on landfill.
- Most ice in restaurants is fine if it is uniform in size and made at a central plant (standard for large cities and tourist areas). Avoid ice that is chipped off larger blocks (more common in rural areas).
- Fresh juices are a risk outside of tourist restaurants and cafes.

- **Prickly Heat** A common skin rash in the tropics, caused by sweat being trapped under the skin. The result is an itchy rash of tiny lumps. Treat by moving out of the heat into an air-conditioned area for a few hours and by having cool showers.

Bites & Stings

During your time in Indonesia, you may make some unwanted friends.

- **Bedbugs** These don't carry disease but their bites are very itchy. They live in the cracks of furniture and walls and then migrate to the bed at night to feed on you as you sleep. You can treat the itch with an antihistamine.
- **Jellyfish** Most are not dangerous, just irritating. Stings can be extremely painful but rarely fatal. First aid for jellyfish stings involves pouring vinegar onto the affected area to neutralise the poison. Anyone who feels ill in any way after being stung should seek medical advice.
- **Ticks** Contracted after walking in rural areas, ticks are commonly found behind the ears, on the belly and in armpits. If you have had a tick bite and experience symptoms such as a rash at the site of the bite or elsewhere, fever or muscle aches, you should see a doctor.

Skin Problems

- **Fungal Rashes** There are two common fungal rashes that affect travellers. The first occurs in moist areas that get less air such as the groin, armpits and between the toes. It starts as a red patch that slowly spreads and is usually itchy. Treatment involves keeping the skin dry, avoiding chafing and using an antifungal cream such as Clotrimazole or Lamisil.
- **Cuts & Scratches** Easily infected in tropical climates, take meticulous care of any cuts and scratches. Immediately wash all wounds in clean water and apply antiseptic. If you develop signs of infection see a doctor. Divers and surfers should be careful with coral cuts as they become easily infected.

Sunburn

Even on a cloudy day sunburn can occur rapidly, especially near the equator. Don't end up like the dopey tourists you see roasted pink on Bali's Kuta Beach. Instead:

- Use a strong sunscreen (at least factor 30).
- Reapply sunscreen after a swim.
- Wear a wide-brimmed hat and sunglasses.
- Avoid baking in the sun during the hottest part of the day (10am to 2pm).

Women's Health

In the tourist areas and large cities, sanitary products are easily found. This becomes more difficult the more rural you go. Tampons are especially hard to find.

Birth-control options may be limited, so bring adequate supplies of your own form of contraception.

Language

Indonesian, or Bahasa Indonesia as it is known to the locals, is the official language of Indonesia. It has approximately 220 million speakers, although it's the mother tongue for only about 20 million – most people also speak their own indigenous language. As a traveller you shouldn't worry too much about learning local languages, but it can be fun to learn a few words – we've included the basics for Balinese and Javanese in this chapter. For practical purposes, it probably makes better sense to concentrate your efforts on learning Bahasa Indonesia.

Indonesian pronunciation is easy to master. Each letter always represents the same sound and most letters are pronounced the same as their English counterparts. Just remember that c is pronounced as the 'ch' in 'chat' and sy as the 'sh' in 'ship'. Note also that kh is a throaty sound (like the 'ch' in the Scottish loch), and that the ng and ny combinations, which are also found in English at the end or in the middle of words such as 'ringing' and 'canyon' respectively, can also appear at the beginning of words in Indonesian. Syllables generally carry equal emphasis – the main exception is the unstressed e in words such as besar (big) – but the rule of thumb is to stress the second-last syllable.

In written Indonesian there are some inconsistent spellings of place names. Compound names are written as one word or two, eg Airsanih or Air Sanih, Padangbai or Padang Bai. Words starting with 'Ker' sometimes lose the e, eg Kerobokan/Krobokan. Some Dutch variant spellings also remain in use, with tj instead of the modern c (eg Tjampuhan/Campuan), and oe instead of u (eg Soekarno/Sukarno).

WANT MORE?

Pronouns, particularly 'you', are rarely used in Indonesian. Anda is the egalitarian form used to overcome the plethora of words for 'you'.

BASICS

Hello.	*Salam.*
Goodbye. (if leaving)	*Selamat tinggal.*
Goodbye. (if staying)	*Selamat jalan.*
How are you?	*Apa kabar?*
I'm fine, and you?	*Kabar baik, Anda bagaimana?*
Excuse me.	*Permisi.*
Sorry.	*Maaf.*
Please.	*Silahkan.*
Thank you.	*Terima kasih.*
You're welcome.	*Kembali.*
Yes.	*Ya.*
No.	*Tidak.*
Mr/Sir	*Bapak*
Ms/Mrs/Madam	*Ibu*
Miss	*Nona*
What's your name?	*Siapa nama Anda?*
My name is ...	*Nama saya ...*
Do you speak English?	*Bisa berbicara Bahasa Inggris?*
I don't understand.	*Saya tidak mengerti.*

ACCOMMODATION

Do you have any rooms available?	*Ada kamar kosong?*
How much is it per night/person?	*Berapa satu malam/orang?*
Is breakfast included?	*Apakah harganya termasuk makan pagi?*
I'd like to share a dorm.	*Saya mau satu tempat tidur di asrama.*
campsite	*tempat kemah*

guesthouse	*losmen*
hotel	*hotel*
youth hostel	*hostel untuk pemuda*

a ... room	*kamar ...*
single	*untuk satu orang*
double	*untuk dua orang*

air-conditioned	*dengan AC*
bathroom	*kamar mandi*
cot	*pondok*
window	*jendela*

DIRECTIONS

Where is ...?	*Di mana ...?*
What's the address?	*Alamatnya di mana?*
Could you write it down, please?	*Anda bisa tolong tuliskan?*
Can you show me (on the map)?	*Anda bisa tolong tunjukkan pada saya (di peta)?*

at the corner	*di sudut*
at the traffic lights	*di lampu merah*
behind	*di belakang*
in front of	*di depan*
far (from)	*jauh (dari)*
left	*kiri*
near (to)	*dekat (dengan)*
next to	*di samping*
opposite	*di seberang*
right	*kanan*
straight ahead	*lurus*

EATING & DRINKING

What would you recommend?	*Apa yang Anda rekomendasikan?*
What's in that dish?	*Hidangan itu isinya apa?*
That was delicious.	*Ini enak sekali.*
Cheers!	*Bersulang!*
Bring the bill/check, please.	*Tolong bawa kuitansi.*

I don't eat ...	*Saya tidak makan ...*
dairy products	*susu dan keju*
fish	*ikan*
(red) meat	*daging (merah)*
peanuts	*kacang tanah*
seafood	*makanan laut*
a table ...	*meja ...*

KEY PATTERNS

To get by in Indonesian, mix and match these simple patterns with words of your choice:

Where's (the station)?	*Di mana (stasiun)?*
When's (the next bus)?	*Jam berapa (bis yang berikutnya)?*
How much is it (per night)?	*Berapa (satu malam)?*
I'm looking for (a hotel).	*Saya cari (hotel).*
Do you have (a local map)?	*Ada (peta daerah)?*
Is there (a toilet)?	*Ada (kamar kecil)?*
Can I (enter)?	*Boleh saya (masuk)?*
Do I need (a visa)?	*Saya harus pakai (visa)?*
I have (a reservation).	*Saya (sudah punya booking).*
I need (assistance).	*Saya perlu (dibantu).*
I'd like (the menu).	*Saya minta (daftar makanan).*
I'd like to (hire a car).	*Saya mau (sewa mobil).*
Could you (help me)?	*Bisa Anda (bantu) saya?*

at (eight) o'clock	*pada jam (delapan)*
for (two) people	*untuk (dua) orang*

Key Words

baby food (formula)	*susu kaleng*
bar	*bar*
bottle	*botol*
bowl	*mangkuk*
breakfast	*sarapan*
cafe	*kafe*
children's menu	*menu untuk anak-anak*
cold	*dingin*
dinner	*makan malam*
dish	*piring*
drink list	*daftar minuman*
food	*makanan*
food stall	*warung*
fork	*garpu*
glass	*gelas*

QUESTION WORDS

How?	*Bagaimana?*
What?	*Apa?*
When?	*Kapan?*
Where?	*Di mana?*
Which	*Yang mana?*
Who?	*Siapa?*
Why?	*Kenapa?*

highchair	*kursi tinggi*
hot (warm)	*hangat*
knife	*pisau*
lunch	*makan siang*
menu	*daftar makanan*
market	*pasar*
napkin	*tisu*
plate	*piring*
restaurant	*rumah makan*
salad	*selada*
soup	*sop*
spicy	*pedas*
spoon	*sendok*
vegetarian food	*makanan tanpa daging*
with	*dengan*
without	*tanpa*

Meat & Fish

beef	*daging sapi*
carp	*ikan mas*
chicken	*ayam*
duck	*bebek*
fish	*ikan*
lamb	*daging anak domba*
mackerel	*tenggiri*
meat	*daging*
pork	*daging babi*
shrimp/prawn	*udang*
tuna	*cakalang*
turkey	*kalkun*

Fruit & Vegetables

apple	*apel*
banana	*pisang*
beans	*kacang*
cabbage	*kol*
carrot	*wortel*
cauliflower	*blumkol*
cucumber	*timun*
dates	*kurma*
eggplant	*terung*
fruit	*buah*
grapes	*buah anggur*
lemon	*jeruk asam*
orange	*jeruk manis*
pineapple	*nanas*
potato	*kentang*
raisins	*kismis*
spinach	*bayam*
vegetable	*sayur-mayur*
watermelon	*semangka*

Other

bread	*roti*
butter	*mentega*
cheese	*keju*
chilli	*cabai*
chilli sauce	*sambal*
egg	*telur*
honey	*madu*
jam	*selai*
noodles	*mie*
oil	*minyak*
pepper	*lada*
rice	*nasi*
salt	*garam*
soy sauce	*kecap*
sugar	*gula*
vinegar	*cuka*

Drinks

beer	*bir*
coconut milk	*santan*
coffee	*kopi*

SIGNS

Buka	Open
Dilarang	Prohibited
Kamar Kecil	Toilets
Keluar	Exit
Masuk	Entrance
Pria	Men
Tutup	Closed
Wanita	Women

juice	*jus*
milk	*susu*
palm sap wine	*tuak*
red wine	*anggur merah*
soft drink	*minuman ringan*
tea	*teh*
water	*air*
white wine	*anggur putih*
yogurt	*susu masam kental*

EMERGENCIES

Help!	*Tolong saya!*
I'm lost.	*Saya tersesat.*
Leave me alone!	*Jangan ganggu saya!*
Call a doctor!	*Panggil dokter!*
Call the police!	*Panggil polisi!*
I'm ill.	*Saya sakit.*
It hurts here.	*Sakitnya di sini.*
I'm allergic to (antibiotics).	*Saya alergi (antibiotik).*

SHOPPING & SERVICES

I'd like to buy ...	*Saya mau beli ...*
I'm just looking.	*Saya lihat-lihat saja.*
May I look at it?	*Boleh saya lihat?*
I don't like it.	*Saya tidak suka.*
How much is it?	*Berapa harganya?*
It's too expensive.	*Itu terlalu mahal.*
Can you lower the price?	*Boleh kurang?*
There's a mistake in the bill.	*Ada kesalahan dalam kuitansi ini.*

credit card	*kartu kredit*
foreign exchange office	*kantor penukaran mata uang asing*
internet cafe	*warnet*
mobile/cell phone	*henpon*
post office	*kantor pos*
signature	*tanda tangan*
tourist office	*kantor pariwisata*

NUMBERS

1	*satu*
2	*dua*
3	*tiga*
4	*empat*
5	*lima*
6	*enam*
7	*tujuh*
8	*delapan*
9	*sembilan*
10	*sepuluh*
20	*dua puluh*
30	*tiga puluh*
40	*empat puluh*
50	*lima puluh*
60	*enam puluh*
70	*tujuh puluh*
80	*delapan puluh*
90	*sembilan puluh*
100	*seratus*
1000	*seribu*

TIME & DATES

What time is it?	*Jam berapa sekarang?*
It's (10) o'clock.	*Jam (sepuluh).*
It's half to (seven; 6:30)	*Setengah (tujuh).*
in the morning	*pagi*
in the afternoon	*siang*
in the evening	*malam*
yesterday	*kemarin*
today	*hari ini*
tomorrow	*besok*

Monday	*hari Senin*
Tuesday	*hari Selasa*
Wednesday	*hari Rabu*
Thursday	*hari Kamis*
Friday	*hari Jumat*
Saturday	*hari Sabtu*
Sunday	*hari Minggu*

TRANSPORT

Public Transport

bicycle-rickshaw	*becak*
boat (general)	*kapal*
boat (local)	*perahu*
bus	*bis*
minibus	*bemo*
motorcycle-rickshaw	*bajaj*
motorcycle-taxi	*ojek*
plane	*pesawat*
taxi	*taksi*
train	*kereta api*
I want to go to ...	*Saya mau ke ...*

LOCAL LANGUAGES

Bahasa Indonesia is a second language for 90% of Indonesians. More than 700 *bahasa daerah* (local languages) rank Indonesia second only to Papua New Guinea in linguistic diversity. As a visitor, you'll never be expected to speak any local languages, but there's no doubt that locals will appreciate your extra effort.

Here are some useful basic phrases in Balinese (which has around four million speakers in Bali) and Javanese (spoken by about 80 million people in Java). Note that these languages don't have specific phrases for greetings like 'hello' or 'goodbye'. Also, there are three distinct language 'levels' – the differences are related to the social status of the speaker. We've provided the 'middle level' understood by all Balinese and Javanese speakers.

Balinese

How are you?	*Kenken kabare?*
Thank you.	*Matur suksma.*
What's your name?	*Sire wastene?*
My name is ...	*Adan tiange ...*
I don't understand.	*Tiang sing ngerti.*
How much is this?	*Ji kude niki?*
Do you speak Balinese?	*Bisa ngomong Bali sing?*
What do you call this in Balinese?	*Ne ape adane di Bali?*
Which is the way to (Ubud)?	*Kije jalan lakar kel (Ubud)?*

Javanese

How are you?	*Piye kabare?*
Thank you.	*Matur nuwun.*
What's your name?	*Nami panjenengan sinten?*
My name is ...	*Nami kula ...*
I don't understand.	*Kula mboten mangertos.*
How much is this?	*Pinten regine?*
Do you speak Javanese?	*Sampeyan saged basa Jawi?*
What do you call this in Javanese?	*Napa namine ing basa Jawi?*
Which is the way to (Kaliurang)?	*Menawi bade dateng (Kaliurang) langkung pundi, nggih?*

At what time does it leave?	*Jam berapa berangkat?*
At what time does it arrive at ...?	*Jam berapa sampai di ...?*
Does it stop at ...?	*Di ... berhenti?*
What's the next stop?	*Apa nama halte berikutnya?*
Please tell me when we get to ...	*Tolong, beritahu waktu kita sampai di ...*
Please stop here.	*Tolong, berhenti di sini.*

a ... ticket	*tiket ...*
1st-class	*kelas satu*
2nd-class	*kelas dua*
one-way	*sekali jalan*
return	*pulang pergi*

first/last	*pertama/terakhir*
platform	*peron*
ticket office	*loket tiket*
timetable	*jadwal*
train station	*stasiun kereta api*

Driving & Cycling

I'd like to hire a ...	*Saya mau sewa ...*
4WD	*gardan ganda*
bicycle	*sepeda*
car	*mobil*
motorcycle	*sepeda motor*

child seat	*kursi anak untuk di mobil*
helmet	*helem*
mechanic	*montir*
petrol	*bensin*
pump (bicycle)	*pompa sepeda*
service station	*pompa bensin*

Is this the road to ...?	*Apakah jalan ini ke ...?*
(How long) Can I park here?	*(Berapa lama) Saya boleh parkir di sini?*
The car/motocycle has broken down.	*Mobil/Motor mogok.*
I have a flat tyre.	*Ban saya kempes.*
I've run out of petrol.	*Saya kehabisan bensin.*

GLOSSARY

adat – traditional laws and regulations
air – water
air panas – hot water
air terjun – waterfall
AMA – Associated Mission Aviation; Catholic missionary air service operating in remote regions of Papua
anak – child
angklung – musical instrument made from different lengths and thicknesses of bamboo suspended in a frame
angkot – or *angkota;* short for *angkutan kota* (city transport); small minibuses covering city routes, like a *bemo*
angkudes – short for *angkutan pedesaan;* minibuses running to nearby villages from cities, or between villages
anjing – dog
arja – refined operatic form of Balinese theatre
Arjuna – hero of the *Mahabharata* epic and a popular temple gate guardian image

babi rusa – wild deer-like pig
bahasa – language; Bahasa Indonesia is the national language
bajaj – motorised three-wheeler taxi found in Jakarta
bak mandi – common Indonesian form of bath, consisting of a large water tank from which water is ladled over the body
bale – open-sided Balinese pavilion, house or shelter with steeply pitched roof; meeting place
balok– palm wine
bandar – harbour, port
bandara – airport
banjar – local division; a Balinese village consisting of married adult males
bapak – often shortened to *pak;* father; also a polite form of address to any older man
barat – west
Barong – mythical lion-dog creature
batik – cloth made by coating part of the fabric with wax, then dyeing it and melting the wax out
batik cap – stamped batik
batik tulis – hand-painted or literally 'written' batik
becak – bicycle-rickshaw
bemo – minibus
bendi – two-person horse-drawn cart; used in Sulawesi, Sumatra and Maluku
bensin – petrol
benteng – fort
bentor – motorised *becak*
Betawi – original name of Batavia (now Jakarta); ethnic group indigenous to Jakarta
bis – bus
bouraq – winged horselike creature with the head of a woman
Brahma – the creator; with Shiva and Vishnu part of the trinity of chief Hindu gods
bu – shortened form of *ibu*
bukit – hill
bule – common term for foreigner (Caucasian)
bupati – government official in charge of a *kabupaten*

caci – a ceremonial martial art in which participants duel with whips and shields
candi – shrine or temple; usually Hindu or Buddhist of ancient Javanese design
cenderawasih – bird of paradise
colt – minibus

dalang – puppeteer and storyteller of *wayang kulit*
danau – lake
dangdut – popular Indonesian music that is characterised by wailing vocals and a strong beat
desa – village
dinas pariwisata – tourist office
dokar – two-person, horse-drawn cart
dukun – faith healer and herbal doctor; mystic
Gajah Mada – famous Majapahit prime minister
gamelan – traditional Javanese and Balinese orchestra
gang – alley or footpath
Garuda – mythical man-bird, the vehicle of Vishnu and the modern symbol of Indonesia
gereja – church
gili – islet, atoll
Golkar – Golongan Karya (Functional Groupings) political party
gua – or *goa*; cave
gunung – mountain
gunung api – volcano; literally 'fire mountain'

harga touris – tourist price
hutan – forest, jungle

ibu – often shortened to *bu;* mother; also polite form of address to an older woman
ikat – cloth in which the pattern is produced by dyeing the individual threads before weaving

jadwal – schedule or timetable
jalan – abbreviated to Jl; street or road
jalan jalan – to go for a stroll
jalan pintas – short cut
jam karet – 'rubber time'; time is flexible
jamu – herbal medicine
jembatan – bridge
jilbab – Muslim head covering worn by women

kabupaten – regency
kain – cloth
kaki lima – mobile food carts; literally 'five feet' (the three feet of the cart and the two of the vendor)
kala – demonic face often seen over temple gateways
kamar kecil – toilet; literally 'small room'; also known as WC (pronounced way-say)
kampung – village, neighbourhood

kantor – office
Kantor Bupati – Governor's Office
karang – coral, coral reef, atoll
kav – lot, parcel of land
kepala desa – village head
kepulauan – archipelago
keraton – see kraton
ketoprak – popular Javanese folk theatre
Ketuktilu – traditional Sundanese (Java) dance in which professional female dancers perform for male spectators
kijang – a type of deer; also a popular Toyota 4WD vehicle, often used for public transport (Kijang)
kora-kora – canoe (Papua)
kramat – sacred
kraton – walled city palace
kretek – Indonesian clove cigarette
kris – wavy-bladed traditional dagger, often held to have spiritual or magical powers
krismon – monetary crisis
kulit – leather

lapangan – field, square
laut – sea, ocean
Legong – classic Balinese dance performed by young girls; Legong dancer
lontar – type of palm tree; traditional books were written on the dried leaves of the lontar palm
losmen – basic accommodation, usually cheaper than hotels and often family-run

MAF – Mission Aviation Fellowship; Protestant missionary air service that operates in remote regions
Mahabharata – venerated Hindu holy book, telling of the battle between the Pandavas and the Kauravas
Majapahit – last great Javanese Hindu dynasty, pushed out of Java into Bali by the rise of Islamic power
makam – grave
mandau – machete (Kalimantan)
marapu – term for all spiritual forces, including gods, spirits and ancestors
mata air panas – hot springs
menara – minaret, tower
meru – multiroofed shrines in Balinese temples; the same roof style also can be seen in ancient Javanese mosques
mesjid – *masjid* in Papua; mosque
mikrolet – small taxi; tiny *opelet*
moko – bronze drum from Pulau Alor (Nusa Tenggara)
muezzin – mosque official who calls the faithful to prayer five times a day

ngadhu – parasol-like thatched roof; ancestor totem of the Ngada people of Flores
nusa – island

Odalan – temple festival held every 210 days (duration of the Balinese year)
ojek – or *ojeg;* motorcycle taxi
oleh-oleh – souvenirs
opelet – small minibus, like a *bemo*
OPM – Organisasi Papua Merdeka; Free Papua Movement; main group that opposes Indonesian rule of Papua
orang kulit putih – white person, foreigner (Caucasian); *bule* is more commonly used

pak – shortened form of *bapak*
PAN – Partai Amanat Nasional; National Mandate Party
pantai – beach
pasar – market
pasar malam – night market
pasar terapung – floating market
pasir – sand
patas – express, express bus
patola – ikat motif of a hexagon framing a type of four-pronged star
PDI – Partai Demokrasi Indonesia; Indonesian Democratic Party
PDI-P – Partai Demokrasi Indonesia-Perjuangan; Indonesian Democratic Party for Struggle
pegunungan – mountain range
pelabuhan – harbour, port, dock
pelan pelan – slowly
pelawangan – gateway
Pelni – Pelayaran Nasional Indonesia; national shipping line with a fleet of passenger ships operating throughout the archipelago
pencak silat – form of martial arts originally from Sumatra, but now popular throughout Indonesia
pendopo – large, open-sided pavilion that serves as an audience hall; located in front of a Javanese palace
penginapan – simple lodging house
perahu – or *prahu;* boat or canoe
pesanggrahan – or *pasanggrahan;* lodge for government officials where travellers can usually stay
pete-pete – a type of *mikrolet* or *bemo* found in Sulawesi
PHKA – Perlindungan Hutan & Konservasi Alam; the Directorate General of Forest Protection & Nature Conservation; manages Indonesia's national parks; formerly PHPA
pinang – betel nut
pinisi – Makassar or Bugis schooner
PKB – Partai Kebangkitan Bangsa; National Awakening Party
pondok – or *pondok wisata;* guesthouse or lodge; hut
PPP – Partai Persatuan Pembangunan; Development Union Party
prahu – boat or canoe
prasada – shrine or temple; usually Hindu or Buddhist of ancient Javanese design
pulau – island
puputan – warrior's fight to the death; honourable, but suicidal, option when faced with an unbeatable enemy
pura – Balinese temple, shrine
pura dalem – Balinese temple of the dead
pura puseh – Balinese temple of origin
puri – palace
pusaka – sacred heirlooms of a royal family

puskesmas – short for *pusat kesehatan masyarakat;* community health centre

rafflesia – gigantic flower found in Sumatra and Kalimantan, with blooms spreading up to a metre

Ramadan – Muslim month of fasting, when devout Muslims refrain from eating, drinking and smoking during daylight hours

Ramayana – one of the great Hindu holy books; many Balinese and Javanese dances and tales are based on stories from the Ramayana

rangda – witch; evil black-magic spirit of Balinese tales and dances

rawa – swamp, marsh, wetlands

rebab – two-stringed bowed lute

reformasi – reform; refers to political reform after the repression of the Suharto years

RMS – Republik Maluku Selatan; South Maluku Republic; main group that opposed Indonesian rule of southern Maluku

rumah adat – traditional house

rumah makan – restaurant or *warung*

rumah sakit – hospital, literally 'sick house'

sarong – or *sarung;* all-purpose cloth, often sewn into a tube, and worn by women, men and children

Sasak – native of Lombok

sawah – an individual rice field; wet-rice method of cultivation

selat – strait

selatan – south

sembako – Indonesia's nine essential culinary ingredients: rice, sugar, eggs, meat, flour, corn, fuel, cooking oil and salt

semenanjung – peninsula

sirih pinang – betel nut, chewed as a mild narcotic

songket – silver- or gold-threaded cloth, hand woven using floating-weft technique

suling – bamboo flute

sungai – river

surat jalan – travel permit

taksi – common term for a public minibus; taxi

taman – ornamental garden, park, reserve

taman laut – marine park, marine reserve

taman nasional – national park

tanjung – peninsula, cape

tarling – musical style of the Cirebon (Java) area, featuring guitar, *suling* and voice

taxi – besides the Western definition which often applies, in some places this can be a small minibus like a *bemo*

taxi sungai – cargo-carrying river ferry with bunks on the upper level

telaga – lake

telepon kartu – telephone card

teluk – bay

timur – east

tirta – water (Bali)

TNI – Tentara Nasional Indonesia; Indonesian armed forces; formerly ABRI

toko mas – gold shop

tomate – Torajan funeral ceremony

tongkonan – traditional Torajan house with towering roof (Sulawesi)

topeng – wooden mask used in dance-dramas and funerary dances

tuak – homemade fermented coconut drink

uang – money

ular – snake

utara – north

wali songo – nine saints of Islam, who spread the religion throughout Java

Wallace Line – hypothetical line dividing Bali and Kalimantan from Lombok and Sulawesi; marks the end of Asian and the beginning of Australasian flora and fauna zones

waringin – banyan tree; large, shady tree with drooping branches that root and can produce new trees

warnet – short for *wartel internet;* internet stall or centre

warpostel – or *warpapostel;* wartel that also handles postal services

wartel – short for *warung telekomunikasi;* private telephone office

warung – simple eatery

wayang kulit – shadow-puppet play

wayang orang – or *wayang wong;* people theatre

wayang topeng – masked dance-drama

Wektu Telu – religion peculiar to Lombok that originated in Bayan and combines many tenets of Islam and aspects of other faiths

wisma – guesthouse or lodge

Behind the Scenes

SEND US YOUR FEEDBACK

We love to hear from travellers – your comments keep us on our toes and help make our books better. Our well-travelled team reads every word on what you loved or loathed about this book. Although we cannot reply individually to your submissions, we always guarantee that your feedback goes straight to the appropriate authors, in time for the next edition. Each person who sends us information is thanked in the next edition – the most useful submissions are rewarded with a selection of digital PDF chapters.

Visit **lonelyplanet.com/contact** to submit your updates and suggestions or to ask for help. Our award-winning website also features inspirational travel stories, news and discussions.

Note: We may edit, reproduce and incorporate your comments in Lonely Planet products such as guidebooks, websites and digital products, so let us know if you don't want your comments reproduced or your name acknowledged. For a copy of our privacy policy visit lonelyplanet.com/privacy.

OUR READERS

Many thanks to the travellers who used the last edition and wrote to us with helpful hints, useful advice and interesting anecdotes:

A Adloff Hortense, Alexander Echtermeyer, Alexander Pohlmann, Ana Zenic, Andrea Di Giovanni, Andy Counsell, Aniek van Gennip, Anja Hulzinga, Aron Vanoverberghe, Ash Enrici **B** Barbara Guthrie, Barbie Cole **C** Carolien Sala, Cees Nijland, Christian Faloppa, Clarissa Ferreira, Claudia Israilev **D** Danny Carney, David Cops, Dede Siliwangi, Delagloye Aurore, Deniz Çolak, Diego Sánchez, Don Turner, Doug Graeb **E** Eduardo Mariz, Elise Nabors, Elizabeth Dudley-Bestow, Elizabeth Goofers, Esther Groenendaal, Eugenia Casanova **F** Fabian Nydegger, Fergus Hadley, Flora Groothuizen, Francesca Piccini, Frank Kaiser, Frank Wagenaars, Franka Otten **G** Geoff Fox **H** Hilde Brontsema, Hugo Ideler **I** Ian Stuart, Igor De Ruitz **J** Jaap Timmer, Jacques Erard, Javier Guinea, Jeannette Schönau, Jesper Verhey, Jessica Coombes, John Canty, Julien Guilbert, Juras Vezelis **K** Katrien Laureyssens **L** Laura Flatau, Laura Sheed, Lena Willems, Lili Thiesen, Lorenzo Ambrosini, Lucas Hullegie, Lucy Periton **M** Mae Greenfield, Marc Gardner de Beville, Maria Peña, Mariette Huisjes, Mariza Attinger, Mark Snoeij, Marta Kaminska, Martijn van Graafeiland, Michele van Nes, Miguel Moreno, Mikael Kirkensgaard, Mike van Buul, Miriam van den Bent, Mojca Čebul **N** Natalia Nowinska, Nick Verberkmoes, Nicolas Combremont, Nienke Nieuwenhuis, Nigel Foster **P** Paul Bookallil, Paula Jones, Peter Mjos, Petra Glanzmann, Petra O'Neill, Phil Paille, Pierre Saraber, Poorna Beri **R** Rebecca Pierpont, Renata Grabowska, Richard Hill, Rob Falloon, Robyn Davis, Rotem Zur **S** Sabrina Haake, Sam Godding, Sara Molin, Sidsel Filipsen, Simon Morton, Simon Pridmore, Spencer Wood, Stefanus Prayogo, Stéphane Damour, Stephen Wilson, Stuart McBride **T** Tanja Nijhoff, Terence Pike, Teresa Wong, Tim Lovatt, Tim Mertens, Tobias Bloyd, Trent Paton **V** Vernesa Šaran, Vicky Sims **W** Walter Denzel **X** Xander Chong

AUTHOR THANKS

Loren Bell

Terima kasih banyak dua kali to every person I met while on the road – from local guides, to the villagers who kept refilling my glass with *tuak*, to the taxi driver who brought his extended family on our excursion. You are too numerous to name, but it's the people of Kalimantan that make this place amazing. And a special thank you to Kari – for your love, support, and patience, even when I might not have deserved it.

Stuart Butler

First and foremost I must, once again, thank my wife, Heather, and children, Jake and Grace, for their patience with this project. I know it's not easy for any of you. I would also like to thank Kosman Kogoya and porters for a great trek. The people of Obia village, Bony Kondahon, Charles Roring, Hans Mandacan, Andreas Ndruru and Bob Palege. Finally, I would like to thank Ben Wallis for being the world's oldest grom.

Trent Holden

First up a big thanks to Destination Editor Sarah Reid for giving me the opportunity to cover the Bali chapter; it was a dream gig. Thanks also to my fellow authors and the production team in Melbourne for putting this massive book together. Special thanks to all the Balinese people who I had the delight to deal with, whose good nature and humour made my job a joy. A shout out to Gusri Tri Putra, a highly recommended guide (look him up!), and to all the travellers I met on the trip who were full of useful tips and suggestions. Also to Eddie and Lynette, Cameron Munroe and Paul Jacobs for the beers and footy – a small world indeed! Finally, lots of love to my family and my girlfriend, Kate, who I have the great fortune to travel the world with.

Anna Kaminski

I would like to thank Sarah for entrusting me with the Sumatra chapter, Brett and Stuart for the contacts and advice, and all who helped me on the road. In particular: Luke in Sungai Penuh; Joshua and Wild Sumatra in Bengkulu; Sumatra Ecotravel in Bukit Lawang; Nachelle Homestay in Berastagi; Darmawan (and Rega) in Singkil and in the Banyaks; Josep and Doris in Ketambe; Annette in Tuk Tuk; Freddie on Pulau Weh; Alessandro, Ade and Harris on the Mentawais; Ulrich, Armando and Ling in Bukittinggi; Brigitte and Bruno in Padang; James and Murray in Krui; and all my drivers.

Hugh McNaughtan

All thanks are due to Tasmin and Sarah. And my little ladies, always.

Adam Skolnick

It's always a great pleasure to return to Indonesia again and again. Java is a manic mess, but it's always a blast and I cannot wait to return. Special thanks to Yudhi Suryana, Yuono and Novi Tartousodo, Eno Phadma, Fitri Ciptosari, Jason Wolcott, Brett Black, Made Dex Ati, Putri Indra, Eka, Yus and the whole Clear Café Family. Thanks also to Iain Stewart and the great RVB. Always a pleasure to work with you guys.

Iain Stewart

Thanks to Dodo for the warm welcome at Makassar airport, and his kindness and travel expertise. In Bira, Gavin and Nini helped me when my chips were down. Enos, thanks for your help in Toraja, as well as Adi in Palu and Reza in Luwuk. The Togeans would not have been the same without Fleuriette and the Kadidiri gang. While up in North Sulawesi, Mikel was the expert guide. Special thanks to Ady, dive instructor extraordinaire.

THIS BOOK

This 11th edition of Lonely Planet's *Indonesia* guidebook was researched and written by Loren Bell, Stuart Butler, Trent Holden, Anna Kaminski, Hugh McNaughtan, Adam Skolnick, Iain Stewart and Ryan Ver Berkmoes. The previous edition was researched and written by Ryan Ver Berkmoes, Brett Atkinson, Celeste Brash, Stuart Butler, John Noble, Adam Skolnick, Iain Stewart and Paul Stiles. This guidebook was produced by the following:

Destination Editor Sarah Reid

Product Editors Jenna Myers, Elizabeth Jones

Regional Senior Cartographer Julie Sheridan

Assisting Cartographers Julie Dodkins, Anthony Phelan

Book Designer Wendy Wright

Assisting Editors Andrew Bain, Carolyn Bain, Imogen Bannister, Paul Harding, Gabrielle Innes, Rosie Nicholson, Susan Paterson, Monique Perrin, Chris Pitts

Cover Researcher Naomi Parker

Thanks to Carolyn Boicos, Daniel Corbett, Grace Dobell, Jane Grisman, Victoria Harrison, Andi Jones, Anne Mason, Catherine Naghten, Karyn Noble, Kirsten Rawlings, Wibowo Rusli, Vicky Smith, Timothy Stewart-Page, Angela Tinson, Lauren Wellicome, Amanda Williamson

Ryan Ver Berkmoes

Many thanks to friends, like the extraordinary Amy Brenneman, Romy and Lola; the incomparable Hanafi; Patticakes, Ibu Cat, Stuart, Rucina and Kerry and Milt Turner. Off-Bali: Amber Clifton, Paul Landgraver, Ilham, Saripa, Philip, Edwin and many, many more were generous with time, ideas and expertise. And Alexis Averbuck, who I once met on Bali and who I married while writing this book.

ACKNOWLEDGMENTS

Climate map data adapted from Peel MC, Finlayson BL & McMahon TA (2007) 'Updated World Map of the Köppen-Geiger Climate Classification', *Hydrology and Earth System Sciences*, 11, 1633–44.

Cover photograph: Gunungs Penanjakan, Bromo, Batok, and Semeru in Java; Nigel Parvitt/AWL.

Index

Map Pages **000**
Photo Pages **000**

C

D

Map Pages **000**
Photo Pages **000**

Map Pages **000**
Photo Pages **000**

M

Map Pages **000**
Photo Pages **000**

N

R

Map Pages **000**
Photo Pages **000**

Y

Map Pages **000**
Photo Pages **000**

Map Legend

Sights

- Beach
- Bird Sanctuary
- Buddhist
- Castle/Palace
- Christian
- Confucian
- Hindu
- Islamic
- Jain
- Jewish
- Monument
- Museum/Gallery/Historic Building
- Ruin
- Shinto
- Sikh
- Taoist
- Winery/Vineyard
- Zoo/Wildlife Sanctuary
- Other Sight

Activities, Courses & Tours

- Bodysurfing
- Diving
- Canoeing/Kayaking
- Course/Tour
- Sento Hot Baths/Onsen
- Skiing
- Snorkelling
- Surfing
- Swimming/Pool
- Walking
- Windsurfing
- Other Activity

Sleeping

- Sleeping
- Camping

Eating

- Eating

Drinking & Nightlife

- Drinking & Nightlife
- Cafe

Entertainment

- Entertainment

Shopping

- Shopping

Information

- Bank
- Embassy/Consulate
- Hospital/Medical
- Internet
- Police
- Post Office
- Telephone
- Toilet
- Tourist Information
- Other Information

Geographic

- Beach
- Gate
- Hut/Shelter
- Lighthouse
- Lookout
- Mountain/Volcano
- Oasis
- Park
- Pass
- Picnic Area
- Waterfall

Population

- Capital (National)
- Capital (State/Province)
- City/Large Town
- Town/Village

Transport

- Airport
- Border crossing
- Bus
- Cable car/Funicular
- Cycling
- Ferry
- Metro/MRT/MTR station
- Monorail
- Parking
- Petrol station
- Skytrain/Subway station
- Taxi
- Train station/Railway
- Tram
- Underground station
- Other Transport

Note: Not all symbols displayed above appear on the maps in this book

Routes

- Tollway
- Freeway
- Primary
- Secondary
- Tertiary
- Lane
- Unsealed road
- Road under construction
- Plaza/Mall
- Steps
- Tunnel
- Pedestrian overpass
- Walking Tour
- Walking Tour detour
- Path/Walking Trail

Boundaries

- International
- State/Province
- Disputed
- Regional/Suburb
- Marine Park
- Cliff
- Wall

Hydrography

- River, Creek
- Intermittent River
- Canal
- Water
- Dry/Salt/Intermittent Lake
- Reef

Areas

- Airport/Runway
- Beach/Desert
- Cemetery (Christian)
- Cemetery (Other)
- Glacier
- Mudflat
- Park/Forest
- Sight (Building)
- Sportsground
- Swamp/Mangrove

Anna Kaminski

Sumatra Anna has been tramping through jungles around the world for over a decade, passing through both Sumatra and wilder Kalimantan during the course of her travels. On this occasion, she was delighted to re-explore Sumatra, particularly its remoter islands and its southern half. This yielded some wonderful surprises: the Kerinci Valley and the Bengkulu region. Though based in Europe, Anna returns to Southeast Asia (and Indonesia) as often as possible, drawn by the fiery cuisine and the constant travel challenges.

Hugh McNaughtan

Maluku A former English lecturer, Hugh decided visa applications beat grant applications, and turned his love of travel into a full-time thing. Having also done a bit of restaurant reviewing in his hometown (Melbourne), he's now eaten his way across Europe, Southeast Asia, the US and Sri Lanka (and can honestly say that nowhere is the fish as delicious as it is in Maluku). Never happier than when on the road with his two daughters (except perhaps on the cricket field), he's given his youth to the life peripatetic.

Adam Skolnick

Java Adam has written about travel, culture, health, sports, human rights and the environment for Lonely Planet, *The New York Times*, *Outside*, *Playboy*, *Men's Health*, *Travel & Leisure*, Salon.com, BBC.com and ESPN.com. He has authored or co-authored 25 Lonely Planet guidebooks, and is the author of *One Breath: Freediving, Death, and the Quest To Shatter Human Limits*, about the life and death of America's greatest freediver. You can read more of his work at www.adamskolnick.com. Find him on Twitter and Instagram (@adamskolnick).

Iain Stewart

Sulawesi Iain has visited Indonesia 10 times, and travelled from Pandang in West Sumatra to Kupang in Timor. He first went to Sulawesi back in 1994, when waiting for five days for a boat connection wasn't unusual. Travel is now somewhat easier but the island remains as enchanting as ever. Iain has contributed to numerous Lonely Planet guidebooks, including four editions of Indonesia – Sulawesi is his favourite island.

Read more about Iain at:
http://auth.lonelyplanet.com/profiles/stewpot

Ryan Ver Berkmoes

Nusa Tenggara, Plan, Understand, Survival Guide Ryan first visited Indonesia in 1993. On his visits since, he has criss-crossed the archipelago, trying to make a dent in those 17,000 islands. Recent thrills included the ancient villages of West Timor and finding his new favourite beach on Flores (it's near Paga). Off-island, Ryan travels the world writing and calls New York City home. Read more at ryanverberkmoes.com and at @ryanvb.

Read more about Ryan at:
http://auth.lonelyplanet.com/profiles/ryanvb

OUR STORY

A beat-up old car, a few dollars in the pocket and a sense of adventure. In 1972 that's all Tony and Maureen Wheeler needed for the trip of a lifetime – across Europe and Asia overland to Australia. It took several months, and at the end – broke but inspired – they sat at their kitchen table writing and stapling together their first travel guide, *Across Asia on the Cheap*. Within a week they'd sold 1500 copies. Lonely Planet was born.

Today, Lonely Planet has offices in Franklin, London, Melbourne, Oakland, Beijing and Delhi, with more than 600 staff and writers. We share Tony's belief that 'a great guidebook should do three things: inform, educate and amuse'.

OUR WRITERS

Loren Bell

Kalimantan, Environment Loren fell in love with Kalimantan during his three years managing a remote rainforest research station, and has returned every year since. For this book, he stoically slept in hotels (on real beds!) and ate in actual restaurants before darting back to the jungle in search of more remote Dayak villages and the forest *pondok* where he feels most at ease. He also writes about Indonesia's environment for Mongabay.com, and consults for NGOs working to protect Kalimantan's forests.

Stuart Butler

Papua Stuart first hit the shores of Indonesia many years ago at the end of a long trans-Asia surf trip. Not surprisingly, it was the highlight of his trip. Today, Stuart lives with his wife and two young children, Jake and Grace, on the beautiful beaches of southwest France. His love of hiking and interest in tribal cultures meant that covering Papua was a dream project for him. His travels have taken him across Indonesia and beyond, from Himalayan mountain trails to the savannahs of East Africa. His website is www.stuartbutlerjournalist.com.

Read more about Stuart at:
http://auth.lonelyplanet.com/profiles/stuartbutler

Trent Holden

Bali Trent first visited Bali as a young Aussie backpacker in 1997. Two decades later, without hesitation he jumped at the opportunity to cover it for Lonely Planet. A regular visitor to Indonesia, Trent believes Bali has lost none of its charms; if anything, it gets better by the year. He also rates the food among the tastiest in the world, and thrives upon his eternal quest to find the best Balinese *nasi campur*. Trent has covered around 25 titles for Lonely Planet, researching and writing about destinations from Sumatra and Phuket to India's Andaman Islands, Nepal and Uganda. Trent also wrote the Outdoor Adventures chapter for this title.

Published by Lonely Planet Publications Pty Ltd
ABN 36 005 607 983
11th edition – July 2016
ISBN 978 1 74321 028 4

10 9 8 7 6 5 4 3 2
Printed in China